The SAGE Handbook of
Organizational Institutionalism

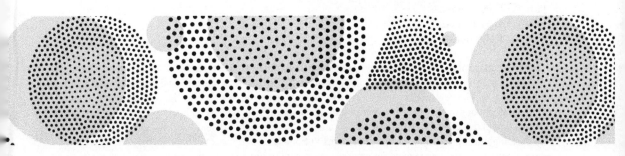

Institutional Theory is seen by many as *the* dominant theoretical perspective in organizational theory. *The SAGE Handbook of Organizational Institutionalism* brought together a wide coverage of aspects of Institutional Theory and an incredible array of top star academic contributors.

This new edition of the bestselling Handbook continues in the same rich vein. First edition chapters have been updated to maintain a mix of theory, how to conduct institutional organizational analysis, and contemporary empirical work. New chapters on Translation, Networks and Institutional Pluralism are included to reflect new directions in the field. The second edition has also been reorganized into six parts:

Part I: Beginnings (Foundations)
Part II: Organizations and their Contexts
Part III: Institutional Processes
Part IV: Conversations
Part V: Consequences
Part VI: Reflections

'The first edition of the *Sage Handbook of Organizational Institutionalism* in 2008 signaled a reenergizing of institutional scholarship, integrating notions of multiplicity, power, agency, and practices into institutional thought. The new edition builds on these developments, but also shows that the creative energy of the field continues unabated. Among important and exciting new themes addressed from an institutional perspective in this completely revised edition are emotions, materiality and visuality, categories, inequality, sustainability and race. As organizational institutionalism continues to expand its reach and relevance, this volume is clearly a must have for any serious student of organization theory.'
Ann Langley, Professor and Canada Research Chair, HEC Montreal, Canada

'Some argue that institutionalism has become the default theory in management and organisation studies. Such a status requires continuing refinement and challenge. Drawing on a wide range of disciplines, academic areas and nations the writing in this second edition of the Sage Handbook will outreach the success of its predecessor volume. The editors and authors deserve their success and the reader will take stimulation from this book for many years to come.'
Andrew Pettigrew OBE, FBA, Emeritus Professor of Strategy and Organisation, University of Oxford, UK

'The pluralism of organization theories is increasingly contained within the very broad category of institutional theory. There could be no better invitation to explore the richness and complexity of this now predominant approach than one finds in *The Sage Handbook of Organizational Intuitionalism*. The editors have assembled a stellar composition of chapters by the leading contributors. It will be appreciated wherever Doctoral candidates in the field gather.'
Stewart Clegg, Distinguished Professor, University of Technology Sydney, Australia

'There are several handbooks in management that are as comprehensive as this one, but absolutely none that I know of that approach the quality, rigour and insight of its scholarship. The authors and editors have my heartiest congratulations'
Danny Miller, Research Professor, HEC Montreal, Canada

'As the very impressive second edition of this Handbook makes evident, unlike its early emphases on stability and similarity, institutional theory keeps changing and taking on new areas of investigation, even acknowledging that other theoretical perspectives can inform it. The chapters in this volume consider previously unimaginable questions such as what might happen if the institutional environment isn't homogenous, and how institutional theory might learn from practice theory. This book is of great value both for institutional scholars and for other scholars who felt they have been cut off entirely from institutional approaches.'
Jean M. Bartunek, Robert A. & Evelyn J. Ferris Chair, Professor, Boston College, USA

'This new edition updates a classic reference for all things institutionalist. Alongside theory essays and reflections from many of the field's founders, it also includes fresh and fascinating chapters on how institutional forces shape inequality, organizational wrongdoing, and many other societal outcomes of consequence today. A valuable addition to your organizational-theory bookshelf!'
Forrest Briscoe, Associate Professor of Management and Sociology, PennState University, USA

'The first *SAGE Handbook of Organizational Institutionalism* – the 'green book' – has been an essential reference even for those of us whose main research interests were not (yet) in institutional theory. So many of its chapters have become landmarks in their lines of inquiry, or opened entirely new ones. The new edition is all of this again, and even more. A must read for scholars interested in institutional processes and those who are not (yet).'
Davide Ravasi, Professor of Strategic and Entrepreneurial Management, Cass Business School, UK

'Almost immediately after the first edition of the *Handbook* came out, it was colloquially dubbed the *Green Bible of Institutionalism* by many of its readers. Big news: the New Testament just came out. It is awesome! The first edition of the Handbook was an instant classic, a feat that is hard to top. But the editors and contributors to the second edition have done it again. This is without a doubt the book that will set the agenda for the fourth decade of organizational institutionalism.'
Pursey Heugens, Professor of Organization Theory, RSM Erasmus University, the Netherlands

'The second edition of this Handbook remains "must-reading" for any organization and management scholar. It provides a timely and comprehensive update of institutional theory and its relationships with other organization theories.'
Andrew H. Van de Ven, Vernon Heath Professor of Organizational Innovation and Change, Carlson School of Management, University of Minnesota

Sara Miller McCune founded SAGE Publishing in 1965 to support the dissemination of usable knowledge and educate a global community. SAGE publishes more than 1000 journals and over 800 new books each year, spanning a wide range of subject areas. Our growing selection of library products includes archives, data, case studies and video. SAGE remains majority owned by our founder and after her lifetime will become owned by a charitable trust that secures the company's continued independence.

Los Angeles | London | New Delhi | Singapore | Washington DC | Melbourne

The SAGE Handbook of
Organizational
Institutionalism

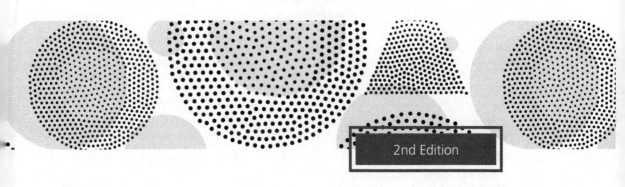

2nd Edition

Edited by
Royston Greenwood,
Christine Oliver,
Thomas B. Lawrence
and Renate E. Meyer

SSAGE reference

Los Angeles | London | New Delhi | Singapore | Washington DC | Melbourne

Los Angeles | London | New Delhi
Singapore | Washington DC | Melbourne

SAGE Publications Ltd
1 Oliver's Yard
55 City Road
London EC1Y 1SP

SAGE Publications Inc.
2455 Teller Road
Thousand Oaks, California 91320

SAGE Publications India Pvt Ltd
B 1/I 1 Mohan Cooperative Industrial Area
Mathura Road
New Delhi 110 044

SAGE Publications Asia-Pacific Pte Ltd
3 Church Street
#10-04 Samsung Hub
Singapore 049483

Editor: Delia Martinez-Alfonso
Editorial Assistant: Colette Wilson
Production Editor: Rudrani Mukherjee
Copyeditor: Elaine Leek
Proofreader: Jill Birch
Indexer: Avril Ehrlich
Marketing Manager: Alison Borg
Cover Design: Wendy Scott
Printed by
CPI Group (UK) Ltd, Croydon, CR0 4YY

At SAGE we take sustainability seriously. Most of our products are printed in the UK using FSC papers and boards. When we print overseas we ensure sustainable papers are used as measured by the PREPS grading system. We undertake an annual audit to monitor our sustainability.

Library of Congress Control Number: 2016953163

British Library Cataloguing in Publication data

A catalogue record for this book is available from the British Library

ISBN 978-1-4129-6196-7

Contents

List of Figures

List of Tables

Notes on the Editors
and Contributors

THE EDITORS

Royston Greenwood is the Telus Professor of Strategic Management in the School of Business, University of Alberta, Visiting Professorial Fellow at the University of Edinburgh, and Visiting Professor at the University of Cambridge. He is a Fellow of the Academy of Management and a former Chair of the Academy's Organization and Management Theory (OMT) Division. In 2013 the European Group for Organization Studies made him an Honorary Member and in 2014 he was the Distinguished Scholar of the Academy of Management OMT Division. His research focuses upon institutional and organizational change and a favoured empirical context is that of professional service firms. Recently he has turned to understanding the institutional foundations of corporate fraud. He serves or has recently served on the editorial and/or advisory boards of several leading journals, including the *Academy of Management Journal*, *Organization Science*, *Organization Studies*, the *Journal of Management Studies*, the *Academy of Management Discoveries* and the *Academy of Management Annals*, of which he is a former editor.

Christine Oliver is the Henry J. Knowles Chair of Organizational Strategy in the Schulich School of Business at York University, Toronto, Canada. Christine is interested in institutional processes and research questions that address the interface between strategy and poverty. Christine's work has appeared in *Administrative Science Quarterly*, *Academy of Management Review*, *Organization Studies*, *Academy of Management Journal*, *Journal of Management Studies*, *Strategic Management Journal*, *American Sociological Review* and other outlets. She won the award for Best Paper in *Academy of Management Review* in 1991 and in the *Canadian Journal of Administrative Science* in 1993. She is past Division Chair of the Academy's Organization and Management Theory Division and past Representative-At-Large on the Academy of Management Board of Governors. Christine is past Associate Editor (1993–1996) and Editor (1996–2003) of the *Administrative Science Quarterly*. She won the Organization and Management Theory Distinguished Scholar Award in 2009. In 2013 she was elected to the Fellows of the Academy of Management in Recognition of Distinguished and Scholarly Contributions to the Profession of Management.

Thomas B. Lawrence is a Professor of Strategy at the Saïd Business School, University of Oxford. He received his PhD in organizational analysis from the University of Alberta. His research focuses on the dynamics of agency, power and institutions in organizations and organizational fields. It has appeared in such journals as *Administrative Science Quarterly*, *Academy of Management Journal*, *Academy of Management Review*, *Harvard*

Business Review, Sloan Management Review, Organization Studies, Journal of Management Studies, Human Relations and the *Journal of Management.* He is a co-editor of *The SAGE Handbook of Organization Studies* (second edition) and *Institutional Work: Actors and Agency in Institutional Studies of Organizations* (Cambridge University Press, 2009).

Renate E. Meyer is the Chair of Organization Studies at WU Vienna University of Economics and Business. She is also a Permanent Visiting Professor at the Department of Organization, Copenhagen Business School and Co-Director of the Research Institute for Urban Management & Governance at WU. She works mainly from a phenomenological perspective on institutions. Her current research interests include novel management ideas and organizational and governance forms, framing and legitimation strategies, translation and role identities. She is Senior Editor for *Organization Studies* and has published in journals such as *Academy of Management Journal, Academy of Management Review, Academy of Management Annals, Organization Studies, Journal of Management Studies* and *Strategic Organization*, and has also (co-)authored several books and book chapters. Renate has been a member of the European Group for Organization Studies (EGOS) Executive Board since 2008 and acted as its chair between 2011 and 2014.

THE CONTRIBUTORS

Juan Almandoz is an Assistant Professor of managing people in organizations at IESE Business School. He received his PhD in Organizational Behaviour and Sociology from Harvard University. His research focuses on organizational theory, institutional logics, top management teams and the governance of organizations with economic and social missions. His work has been published in journals such as *Academy of Management Journal*, and *Administrative Science Quarterly*. He currently serves on the editorial board of *Administrative Science Quarterly.*

John Amis is Professor of Strategic Management and Organisation at the University of Edinburgh Business School. His research interests centre primarily on issues of organizational and institutional change. His work has been published in journals that include *Academy of Management Review, Academy of Management Journal, Organization Science, American Journal of Public Health, Human Relations* and *Organizational Research Methods.* He is co-editor of an upcoming Special Issue of *Organization Studies* titled 'Inequality, Institutions and Organizations'. John sits on a number of editorial boards, including *Academy of Management Review, Journal of Management Inquiry, Organization Studies, Strategic Organization* and *Journal of Change Management*, at which he is an Associate Editor.

Angela Aristidou is an independent researcher at the Saïd Business School, University of Oxford. This role is fully supported by a research grant from the UK National Institute for Health Research. Across her work, Angela builds on the foundations of practice theories to address puzzles that her empirical fieldwork uncovers and to examine and explain real-world, grand challenges in the dynamic service setting of health care. This approach has contributed to the literatures on role-based interactions and relationships, routines and service innovation. Angela received her PhD in Management Studies from the University of Cambridge in July 2015 and holds a research masters in Innovation and Technology from Harvard University, where she was a Fulbright scholar.

Stephen R. Barley is the Christian A. Felipe Professor of Technology Management at the College of Engineering at the University of California Santa Barbara. He holds an AB in English from the College of William and Mary, an MEd from the Ohio State University and a PhD in Organization Studies from the Massachusetts Institute of Technology. He is also the Richard Weiland Emeritus Professor of Management Science and Engineering. Barley co-founded and co-directed the Center for Work, Technology and Organization at Stanford's School of Engineering from 1994 to 2015. He was editor of the *Administrative Science Quarterly* from 1993 to 1997 and the founding editor of the *Stanford Social Innovation Review* from 2002 to 2004.

Julie Battilana is a Professor of Business Administration at Harvard Business School and the Alan L. Gleitsman Professor of Social Innovation at the Harvard Kennedy School. Her research examines hybrid organizations that pursue a social mission while engaging in commercial activities to sustain their operations. These hybrids diverge from the established organizational forms of both typical corporations and typical not-for-profits by combining aspects of both at their core. Her work aims to understand how these hybrids can sustainably pursue social and commercial goals and how they can achieve high levels of both social and commercial performance. Her work has been published in the *Academy of Management Annals*, *Academy of Management Journal*, *Journal of Business Ethics*, *Leadership Quarterly*, *Management Science*, *Organization*, *Organization Science*, *Organization Studies*, *Research in Organizational Behavior* and *Strategic Organization*.

Marya Besharov is an Associate Professor of Organizational Behavior at the ILR School at Cornell University. She received her PhD in Organizational Behavior and Sociology from Harvard University. Her research examines how organizations and their leaders navigate and sustain competing demands, with a particular focus on social-business hybrid organizations that combine social and commercial goals. Marya's work has been published in journals such as *Academy of Management Journal*, *Academy of Management Review*, *Business Ethics Quarterly*, *Academy of Management Learning and Education*, *Research in Organizational Behavior*, *Research in the Sociology of Organizations* and *Industrial and Corporate Change*. She currently serves on the editorial boards of *Academy of Management Journal*, *Academy of Management Review*, *Administrative Science Quarterly*, and *Organization Science*.

Emily S. Block is an Associate Professor of Strategic Management and Organization at the Alberta Business School. She received her PhD from the University of Illinois at Urbana-Champaign. Her research focuses on the generation (by organizations) and interpretation (by stakeholders) of formal and informal organization structures, language and practices. Just as non-verbal communication provides valuable information about individuals beyond their spoken words, symbols do the same for organizations. Symbols may be purposefully or unintendedly generated by organizations, and the ways that they are interpreted may have significant consequences. Her research, focusing on these consequences, can be found in *Academy of Management Journal* and *Strategic Management Journal*.

Romain Boulongne is a PhD student in strategic management at HEC Paris. His research interests examine how product and market categories affect social evaluation and performance of organizations, especially in the context of financial product categories. In his work, Romain has notably been looking experimentally at how variation in audiences' cognitive mechanisms ultimately impact the evaluation of ambiguity and novelty in markets. Romain is a member of the SnO Center at HEC Paris.

Eva Boxenbaum is Professor of Management at MINES ParisTech and affiliated also with Copenhagen Business School. She conducts research on how organizational actors shape the innovation, implementation and diffusion of new management practices and organizational forms. Her most recent work addresses cognitive, material and visual dimensions of these processes. Her research has been published in journals such as *Academy of Management Review*, *Academy of Management Annals*, *Organization Studies*, *California Management Review* and *Strategic Organization*.

Sean Buchanan is an Assistant Professor of Business Administration at the Asper School of Business at the University of Manitoba. He earned his PhD from the Schulich School of Business at York University. Sean's research broadly focuses on the relationships among actors, institutions, and society and specifically seeks to understand how the interactions between actors and institutions shape social and environmental outcomes. His research has been published in *Human Relations*, *Organization* and the *Academy of Management Proceedings*.

Jonathan Bundy is an Assistant Professor of Management in the W. P. Carey School of Business at Arizona State University, having previously served on faculty at Penn State University. He received his PhD from the University of Georgia. In his research, Professor Bundy takes a behavioral approach to strategic management and focuses on the social and cognitive forces that shape organizational behavior and outcomes. He is specifically interested in the topics of corporate reputation and social evaluations, crisis and impression management, stakeholder management, and corporate governance. His research has been published in *Academy of Management Review*, *Administrative Science Quarterly*, and *Journal of Management*.

Michael Cheely worked as a Research Assistant for Professor John Almandoz at IESE Business School and aided his research and case writing in organizational behavior, institutional logics, and community banks. He also contributed to research at IESE on industrial organization and the sharing economy. Michael now teaches World History at North Star Academy, a charter school in Newark, New Jersey, and, in the near future, he expects to obtain a doctorate degree in historical sociology or a related field.

W. E. Douglas Creed is Professor of Management at the University of Rhode Island. His work on the role of voice, social identity, emotions and agency in contested institutional change has appeared in the *Academy of Management Review*, *Academy of Management Journal*, *Organization Science*, *Journal of Management Inquiry*, *Journal of Applied Behavior Science*, and the *Journal of Management Studies*. Doug received his MBA and PhD from the Haas School of Business at the University of California, Berkeley. He received his MA in Religion from the Yale Divinity School and his BA (English) from Yale University.

Robert J. David is Professor of Strategy & Organization, Brodje Faculty Scholar, and Director of the Centre for Strategy Studies in Organizations at the Desautels Faculty of Management, McGill University. He holds a PhD in organization studies from Cornell University (2001). Professor David does research on the evolution of management practices, organizations, and markets. His current focus is on the reciprocal relationship between institutions and entrepreneurship in nascent markets, including projects on the emergence and growth of the Quebec wine industry and the development of the local food market category. Professor David's research has been published in the leading journals of his field, as well as in prestigious edited volumes. He is the co-editor of *Research in the Sociology of Work (Vol 21): Institutions and*

Entrepreneurship, serves on the editorial boards of a number of leading journals, and is co-editor of *Strategic Organization*.

Gerald F. (Jerry) Davis received his PhD from the Graduate School of Business at Stanford University and taught at Northwestern and Columbia before moving to the University of Michigan, where he is Wilbur K. Pierpont Collegiate Professor of Management and of Sociology. He has published widely in management, sociology and finance. Books include *Social Movements and Organization Theory* (Cambridge University Press, 2005); *Organizations and Organizing* (Pearson Prentice Hall, 2007); *Managed by the Markets: How Finance Reshaped America* (Oxford University Press, 2009); *Changing your Company from the Inside Out: A Guide for Social Intrapreneurs* (Harvard Business Review Press, 2015); and *The Vanishing American Corporation* (Berrett Koehler, 2016).

David L. Deephouse is the Foote Professor of International Business/Law in the Department of Strategic Management & Organization at the Alberta School of Business of the University of Alberta, as well as its Associate Dean for PhD Programs and for Research. He is also an International Research Fellow of the Oxford University Centre for Corporate Reputation and a founding member of the Business School Research Network. He earned his PhD at the University of Minnesota in 1994, his MBA from Georgia Tech in 1984, and his BA in Mathematics from Carleton College, Northfield, Minnesota, in 1982. His research focuses on social evaluations of organizations, especially legitimacy and reputation, and the causes and consequences of each. His theoretical interests include agenda-setting, institutional (in both organizational sociology and international business), media effects, stakeholder, strategic balance, and strategic choice theories.

Rich DeJordy is Assistant Professor of Management at California State University, Fresno. His research focuses on the lived (or 'inhabited') experiences of social embeddedness, and how that enables constrains and enables both individual and organizational action, particularly around social justice initiatives. Grounded in institutional theory, his research examines the interplay of identities and networks in the affective, behavioral, and cognitive mechanisms and outcomes of social embeddedness. His research has appeared in *Academy of Management Journal*, *Organization Studies*, *Research in the Sociology of Organizations*, and *Entrepreneurship Theory and Practice*, among other outlets.

Frank Dobbin is Professor of Sociology at Harvard. His *Inventing Equal Opportunity* (Princeton, 2009), which won the Distinguished Scholarly Book Award from the American Sociological Association, charts how corporations have sought to promote workforce diversity since the 1960s. With Alexandra Kalev, he is developing an evidence-based approach to promoting diversity that was featured in the summer 2016 issue of the *Harvard Business Review* ('Why Diversity Programs Fail'). With Kalev and Soohan Kim, he is studying the effects of diversity on corporate performance, and with Jiwook Jung and Ben Snyder he is analyzing the effects of board diversity on profits and share price.

Gili S. Drori is Associate Professor of sociology and anthropology at The Hebrew University of Jerusalem, Israel. She earned her academic education at Tel Aviv University (BA 1986; and MA 1989) and Stanford University (PhD, 1997, sociology). She served as Director of IR Honors Program and taught at Stanford University in 2000–2011 and also taught at the University of California Berkeley, the Technion (Israel), and University of Bergamo (Italy) and was a guest scholar at Uppsala University (Sweden). Gili's publications speak to her research interests in: globalization and glocalization; organizational change and rationalization; world society theory; science, innovation and higher education; technology divides; and, culture and policy regimes.

Rodolphe Durand is Professor at HEC Paris, founder and director of Society and Organizations Center. Rodolphe's primary research interests concern the sources of competitive advantage and the interplay between the strategic, social, and institutional determinants of performance. For his work on these questions that integrate research streams from sociology, philosophy, and management, Rodolphe received the American Sociological Association's R. Scott Award in 2005, the European Academy of Management/Imagination Lab Award for Innovative Scholarship in 2010, and was inducted Fellow of the Strategic Management Society in 2014. His last books, *The Pirate Organization* (with J.P. Vergne, HBR Press, 2012) and *Organizations, Strategy, and Society* (Routledge, 2014) put in perspective the evolution of capitalism and the legitimacy of management.

Mary Ann Glynn is the Joseph F. Cotter Professor of Management & Organization, Professor of Sociology (by courtesy), and Research Director of the Winston Center for Leadership and Ethics at Boston College. She earned her PhD at Columbia University and has served on the faculties of Yale, Emory, Michigan and the Copenhagen Business School. Her research interests combine micro-level cognitive processes (such as learning and creativity) and macro-level cultural influences (social norms and institutional arrangements), uses both qualitative and quantitative methods, and has been published in leading management journals, including *Administrative Science Quarterly, Academy of Management Journal, Academy of Management Review, Organizational Science, Strategic Management Journal*, as well as psychology and sociology journals. She is a Fellow of the Academy of Management and is the 2017–18 President of the Academy of Management.

Christian E. Hampel is a Research Associate (postdoc) at the Oxford University Centre for Corporate Reputation at Saïd Business School. He received his PhD from Judge Business School, University of Cambridge. His research explores how organizations manage reputational challenges with a particular focus on fighting stigmatization, reviving legitimacy and altering institutions.

Cynthia Hardy is a Laureate Professor in the Department of Management & Marketing at the University of Melbourne, Australia, and Professor at Cardiff Business School in the UK. Her research interests revolve around discourse, power, risk and organizational change. She has published more than 60 articles in refereed journals, including *Academy of Management Journal, Academy Management Review* and *Organization Studies*, as well as numerous book chapters and conference papers. She has published over 10 books, including two SAGE Handbooks: the *Handbook of Organization Studies*, which won the George R. Terry Book Award at the 1997 Academy of Management, and the *Handbook of Organizational Discourse*, which won the 2005 Outstanding Book at the Organizational Communication Division of the USA's National Communication Association. She is co-founder of the International Centre for Research in Organizational Discourse, Strategy and Change (ICRODSC), which links discourse researchers in Australia, the UK, Europe, North America and Japan.

C.R. (Bob) Hinings is a Professor Emeritus in the School of Business, University of Alberta and a Fellow of the Judge Business School, University of Cambridge. He has a long record of studying professionals in organizations and healthcare reorganization with an emphasis on organizational change. He is also involved in research into the organization of the Canadian wine industry. He received an Honorary Doctorate from the University of Montreal for his contributions to the discipline of organization theory. He received the Distinguished Scholar Award from the Organization and Management Theory Division of the US Academy of Management. He is a Fellow of the Royal Society of Canada and a Fellow of the US Academy of Management. He is an Honorary Member of the European Group for Organizational Studies and was JMI Scholar of the Western Academy of Management.

Andrew J. Hoffman is the Holcim (US) Professor of Sustainable Enterprise at the University of Michigan; a position that holds joint appointments at the Stephen M. Ross School of Business and the School of Natural Resources & Environment. Andy also serves as Education Director of the Graham Sustainability Institute. His research uses an organizational and strategic perspective to understand the cultural and institutional aspects of environmental issues for organizations. He has published more than 100 articles/book chapters as well as 14 books which have been translated into five languages. Among his list of honours, he has received the Aspen Institute Faculty Pioneer Award (2016), Strategic Organization Best Essay Award (2016), *O&E* Best Paper Award (2014), Maggie Award (2013), *JMI* Breaking the Frame Award (2012), Connecticut Book Award (2011), Aldo Leopold Fellowship (2011), Aspen Environmental Fellowship (2011 and 2009), Manos Page Prize (2009), and SSSS Rachel Carson Book Prize (2001). He earned his PhD in Management and Civil/Environmental Engineering from MIT.

Markus A. Höllerer is Professor in the Department of Management at WU Vienna University of Economics and Business; in addition, he is affiliated with the Research Institute for Urban Management and Governance, and also holds a position as Senior Scholar in Organization Theory at UNSW Australia Business School, Sydney. His work is broadly anchored in the phenomenological tradition of organizational institutionalism. Research interests include the dissemination and local adaptation of global organizational ideas – in particular heterogeneous theorizations and local variations in meaning – as well as the relationship between different bundles of managerial concepts and their underlying governance and business models in the public and private sectors. Recent projects focus on discursive framing and related research methodologies, the role of visuality and multimodality in processes of (de)institutionalization, intra-logic complexity, as well as novel forms of organizing and governance.

Dennis Jancsary is Assistant Professor at the Institute for Organization Studies at WU Vienna University of Economics and Business, Austria. His current research focuses on institutionalist approaches in organization theory, particularly the diffusion and theorization of management knowledge, as well as the role of verbal, visual, and multimodal forms of rhetoric, narrative, and symbolism in the construction and institutionalization of meaning. Empirically, his research engages with the interfaces between business, public administration, and civil society, as well as the embeddedness of public sector organizations in broader society. He has published his work in the *Academy of Management Annals* and *Research in the Sociology of Organizations*, and has also co-authored a book chapter on the critical analysis of visual and multimodal texts.

P. Devereaux (Dev) Jennings is the Thornton A. Graham Professor of Strategy and Organization and the Coordinator of the Canadian Center for Corporate Social Responsibility (CCCSR) at the Alberta School of Business. Dev's work as an organizations scholar has been in four areas: organizational structure and strategy, environmental management and regulation, innovation and tech start-ups, and gender and family business. Over the past twenty-five years, he has published with a diverse group of co-authors in a wide array of journals, including *Administrative Science Quarterly*, the *Academy of Management Journal*, the *Academy of Management Review*, the *Journal of Business Venturing*, and *Organization and Environment*. Dev has also served as action editor for the *Academy of Management Review*, co-founding editor of *Strategic Organization*, field editor of the *Journal of Business Venturing*, and associate editor at *Administrative Science Quarterly*. Dev received his PhD and MA from Stanford University and his AB from Dartmouth College.

Candace Jones is the Chair of Global Creative Enterprise at the University of Edinburgh Business School. Her research interests include creative industries and professional services from the lenses of networks, vocabularies, institutional logics, and materiality. She has published in *Academy of Management Review*, *Academy of Management Annals*, *Administrative Science Quarterly*, *Journal of Organizational Behavior*, *Organization Science*, *Organization Studies and Poetics*. She co-edited the *Oxford Handbook of Creative Industries* and is on the Editorial Review Boards of *Academy of Management Review*, *Journal of Professions and Organization*, *Organization Science and Organization Studies*. She was Division Chair for Organization and Management Theory Division, Academy of Management from 2011-2016. With Eva Boxenbaum, Renate Meyer and Silviya Svejenova, she was awarded a grant of $797,529 to study 'The Impact of Material Artifacts and Visual Representations on the Institutionalization of Innovations' by the Danish Council for Independent Research.

Stefan Jonsson is Professor of Organization at Uppsala University. He has worked on institutions and diffusion of practices, the diffusion of scandals, and the role of norms in shaping competitive interactions. Currently he is developing a research program on the organization of competition and what competition does to organizations. His research is published in *Administrative Science Quarterly*, *Sociological Theory*, *Organization Science*, *Strategic Management Journal* and *International Economic Review*.

Caroline Kaehr Serra is a postdoctoral researcher at the Desautels Faculty of Management of McGill University. She recently completed her PhD at the University of Geneva, Switzerland. Her research is situated at the intersection of entrepreneurship and organization theory, focusing on the growth and management of emerging organizations. She is interested in how individual actions are related to emergent, organizational and collective outcomes, and how the resulting cross-level dynamics shape organizational change.

Alexandra Kalev, a Princeton University PhD, is an Associate Professor of Sociology and Anthropology at the Tel Aviv University. With Frank Dobbin, Kalev examines the effects of organizational diversity programs on corporations and universities workforce diversity. Highlights from this research were featured in the July-August 2016 issue of the *Harvard Business Review* and received the HBR McKinsey Award for 2016. In research on Israel, Kalev studies the emergence and effectiveness of diversity management as well as Israeli-Palestinians integration in the Jewish economy. Kalev is a member of the Advisory Committee to the Israeli Equal Employment Opportunity Commission. She recently published a Diversity Index for the Israeli private-sector industries, which was presented to President Rivlin.

Matthew S. Kraatz is a Professor in the Department of Business Administration at the University of Illinois. His published research has examined a number of different organizational phenomena including change, learning, governance, legitimacy, reputation, identity and leadership. In recent years, his work has become more normatively oriented, focusing primarily on the role of values in institutional life. Matt has served on the editorial boards of several prominent journals and is a former Chair of the Academy of Management's Organization and Management Theory Division. He received his PhD from Northwestern University and his BA from Illinois College in Jacksonville, IL.

Jaco Lok is Associate Professor at UNSW Business School, University of New South Wales, Sydney, Australia, and Fellow of the Australian Graduate School of Management. His research aims to advance the microfoundations of organizational institutionalism through examining and theorizing the various ways people are constructed through, and engage with, institutions in lived, embodied practice. His research has appeared in *Academy of Management Journal*, *Academy of Management Review*, *Journal of Management Inquiry* and others. He serves on the editorial boards of *Academy of Management Review* and *Organization Studies*.

Danielle Logue is Senior Lecturer at UTS Business School, University of Technology Sydney, Australia, and Research Fellow at Skoll Centre for Social Entrepreneurship, University of Oxford, UK. Her research draws from a broad base of institutional theory, in exploring the diffusion and theorization of innovations within and across organizational fields and markets. She has published in *Academy of Management Annals*, *Human Relations*, *Journal of Management Inquiry*, *Organization Studies* and others. She also serves on the editorial board of *Journal of Management Inquiry*.

Michael Lounsbury is the Canada Research Chair in Entrepreneurship and Innovation at the University of Alberta School of Business. His research focuses on the relationship between organizational and institutional change, entrepreneurial dynamics and the emergence of new industries and practices. In addition to serving on a number of editorial boards, Professor Lounsbury is the series editor of *Research in the Sociology of Organizations*. He has previously served as Chair of the Organization and Management Theory Division of the Academy of Management, and Co-Editor of *Organization Studies* and *Journal of Management Inquiry*. His PhD is in Sociology and Organization Behavior from Northwestern University.

Steve Maguire is Professor of Strategy and Organization in the Desautels Faculty of Management at McGill University, where he is also Director of the Marcel Desautels Institute for Integrated Management and holds a Chair in Integrated Management. His research focuses on technological and institutional change driven by the emergence of new risks to health or the environment, with an emphasis on chemicals management. He has published more than 40 refereed journal articles, book chapters and edited volumes, including the 2011 *SAGE Handbook of Complexity and Management*. His scholarly activities have garnered significant funding and numerous awards, including the 2014 Page Prize for Integration of Sustainability Issues in Business Curricula, the 2010 Greif Research Impact Award and the Academy of Management's 'Organization and Natural Environment (ONE)' Best Doctoral Dissertation Award in 2001. From 2007 to 2011 he served on the Government of Canada Chemicals Management Plan's 'Challenge Advisory Panel' which advised Health Canada and Environment Canada on the screening of some 200 high priority substances. He is currently working with McGill's Department of Chemistry to expand 'green chemistry' into business schools.

Johanna Mair is a Professor of Organization, Strategy and Leadership at the Hertie School of Governance in Berlin. She is the PACS Distinguished Fellow at Stanford University and a

Senior Research Fellow at the Harvard Kennedy School. From 2001 to 2011 she served on the faculty at IESE Business School and has held a visiting position at the Harvard Business School and INSEAD. She earned her PhD in Management from INSEAD (France). Johanna's research focuses on how novel organizational forms and institutional arrangements create economic value and social impact and the role of innovation in this process. Her work has been published in leading academic journals, including the *Academy of Management Journal, Academy of Management Perspective, Journal of Management, Journal of Management Studies, Organization Studies* among others. Her recent book with Christian Seelos on *Innovation and Scaling – How Effective Social Entrepreneurs Create Impact* makes this research accessible to a broader audience.

Namrata Malhotra is an Associate Professor of Strategy in the Management Department at Imperial College Business School, Imperial College London. She received her PhD in Organizational Analysis from the University of Alberta. She is interested in understanding organizational change and institutional change processes, focusing especially on professional service organizations. She is currently involved in research examining micro-processes of institutional change unfolding in law firms with the emergence of innovative career models. She has also looked at how career pathing impacts on innovation capacity in professional services firms. In the past she has done research on internationalization strategies of engineering consulting firms. Her work is published in the *Journal of Management Studies, Journal of International Business Studies, Organization Studies, Academy of Management Perspectives* and *Research in the Sociology of Organizations* among others.

Christopher Marquis is the Samuel C. Johnson Professor in Sustainable Global Enterprise at the Johnson Graduate School of Management, Cornell University. He received his PhD from the University of Michigan. He studies the environmental sustainability and shared value strategies of global corporations, with a particular emphasis on firms in China. Theoretically, this research builds on his prior work that examined the mechanisms of how and why firm behaviour varies over time and across geographic communities in the contexts of community-based social networks and the evolution of the US banking industry.

John W. Meyer is Professor of Sociology, Emeritus, at Stanford. He has studied the rise of globally institutionalized models of society (*World Society: The Writings of John W. Meyer*, Oxford, 2009). A research focus has been on the worldwide expansion and effects of education and science (Drori et al., *Science in the Modern World Polity*, Stanford, 2003). Recent projects are on the organizational impact of globalization (Drori et al., *Globalization and Organization*, Oxford, 2006; Bromley and Meyer, *Hyper-Organization: Global Organizational Expansion*, Oxford, 2015). He studies curricular patterns in education, and the worldwide expansion of organization. He has honorary doctorates from the Stockholm School of Economics and the Universities of Bielefeld and Lucerne. He received the American Sociological Association's awards for lifetime contributions to the sociology of education, to the study of globalization and to the field generally. He received the Academy of Management's OMT award for lifetime contributions to organization theory.

Bjoern Mitzinneck is a PhD student in Management and Organizations at the Samuel Curtis Johnson Graduate School of Management at Cornell University. His research focuses on systemic change in the wake of social innovation and sustainability transitions. His current work examines the development of novel forms of organizing in the changing energy sector.

Kamal Munir is Reader in Strategy and Policy at the University of Cambridge where he has taught since 2001. Prior to that Kamal was finishing a PhD at McGill University, Canada. At Cambridge, Dr Munir is part of the Strategy and International Business Department within the University's Judge Business School. He has published several articles in journals including *Academy of Management Journal, Organisation Studies, Research Policy* and *Cambridge Journal of Economics*, among others. He is the founder of OTREG and has served as a Senior Editor for *Organisation Studies* and *Journal of Management Inquiry*. In addition to his academic work, he has published more accessible articles in newspapers including *The Financial Times, The Guardian, Dawn, Express Tribune, Herald* and *Economic and Political Weekly* (EPW). His work has been quoted and cited widely, including on BBC's *Hard Talk*, by *The Financial Times, Wall Street Journal*, CNN and *BusinessWeek*.

Achim Oberg is Assistant Professor at the Institute of Organization Studies at the Vienna University of Economics and Business, Austria, and senior researcher at the Institute for SME Research at the University of Mannheim, Germany. He has held positions at RWTH Aachen University and KIT Karlsruhe in Germany. His research focuses on organizational fields on the World Wide Web and on relational connections among management concepts. To capture and analyze these phenomena he applies social and semantic network analysis methods.

William Ocasio is the John L. and Helen Kellogg Professor of Management and Organizations at the Kellogg School of Management, Northwestern University. His research focuses on organizational and institutional change. In particular, he contributes to theory and research on institutional logics, the attention-based view of the firm, vocabularies and political dynamics. His PhD is in Organizational Behavior from Stanford University.

Donald Palmer is Professor of Management in the Graduate School of Management at the University of California, Davis. He received a BS in Molecular Biology from the University of Wisconsin, Madison and a PhD in Sociology from Stony Brook University. Palmer was Editor of *Administrative Science Quarterly* from 2003 to 2008. He is the author of *Normal Organizational Wrongdoing* (Oxford University Press), which won the 2013 Academy of Management (AOM) Social Issues in Management Division best book award and was a finalist for 2013 George R. Terry award. He is also co-editor (with Kristin Smith-Crowe and Royston Greenwood) of *Organizational Wrongdoing: Key Perspectives and New Directions* (Cambridge University Press).

Nelson Phillips is Abu Dhabi Chamber Professor of Strategy and Innovation at Imperial College London. His research interests include various aspects of organization theory, technology strategy, innovation, and entrepreneurship, often studied from an institutional theory perspective. He has published four books: *Discourse Analysis* with Cynthia Hardy published in 2002, *Power and Organizations* with Stewart Clegg and David Courpasson published in 2006, *Technology and Organization* with Graham Sewell and Dorothy Griffiths published in 2010, and the *Oxford Handbook of Innovation Management* with David Gann and Mark Dodgson published in 2014. He is also an Editor-in-Chief of the *Journal of Management Inquiry*, an Editor-in-Chief of *Innovation: Organization and Management*, and the Past Division Chair of the Organization and Management Theory Division of the Academy of Management.

Walter W. Powell is Professor of Education, Sociology, Organizational Behavior, and Management Science and Engineering at Stanford University. His most recent book, written with John F. Padgett is *The Emergence of Organizations and Markets*. His interests focus on the processes through which ideas are transferred across organizations, and the role of networks in facilitating or hindering innovation.

Claus Rerup is Professor of Management at the Frankfurt School of Finance and Management, Germany. From 2003 to 2017 he served on the faculty at the Ivey Business School, Canada. His research focuses on organizational sense-making, routine dynamics, and organizational learning with a particular interest in understanding how organizational and institutional change unfolds across time and boundaries. His publications have appeared in *Academy of Management Journal, Administrative Science Quarterly, Journal of Management, Journal of Management Studies*, and *Organization Science* among others. His PhD is in Organization Theory from the Aarhus School of Business, Denmark.

Fabio Rojas is Professor of Sociology at Indiana University, Bloomington. His research examines organizational behavior in educational, political, and health contexts. He is the author of *From Black Power to Black Studies: How a Radical Social Movement Became an Academic Discipline* (2007, The Johns Hopkins University Press) and *Theory for the Working Sociologist* (2017, Columbia University Press). He is co-author, with Michael T. Heaney, of *Party in the Street: The Antiwar Movement and the Democratic Party after 9/11* (2015, Cambridge University Press).

Kerstin Sahlin is Professor of Management at Uppsala University. Her research interests include transnational governance, public–private relations, governance of universities, and the expansion and circulation of management ideas. She is the editor of several books, including *Transnational Governance* (Cambridge University Press, 2006, with Marie-Laure Djelic), *The Expansion of Management Knowledge* (Stanford University Press, 2002, with Lars Engwall) and *The SAGE Handbook of Organizational Institutionalism* (Sage, 2008, with Royston Greenwood, Christine Oliver and Roy Suddaby). She is currently Secretary General for the Humanities and Social Sciences at the Swedish Research Council.

Marc Schneiberg is the John C. Pock Professor of Sociology at Reed College, in Portland Oregon. He is an economic and organizational sociologist whose research focuses on economic institutions, social movements, and the rise, contemporary fates, and economic consequences of alternatives to corporations in American capitalism. His work addresses the evolution of cooperative and other alternative enterprise systems in the US, including community banks, credit unions, electrical and agricultural cooperatives, insurance mutuals, and municipal utilities. It also addresses how organizational diversity via enterprise alternatives can help upgrade markets, subject corporations to countervailing forces, and foster more decentralized and local small stakeholder trajectories of capitalist development. This work has twice received National Science Foundation support. Schneiberg also studies association, regulation and self-regulation in American manufacturing and finance. His research appears in journals such as *Politics and Society, American Sociological Review, American Journal of Sociology, Organizational Studies, Socio-Economic Review, Seattle University Law Review*, and *Research in the Sociology of Organizations*. Schneiberg is Editor of *Socio-Economic Review*, and currently serves on the executive council of the Society for the Advancement of Socio-Economics.

W. Richard Scott is a Professor Emeritus of Sociology with courtesy appointments in the Graduate School of Business, Graduate School of Education, School of Engineering, and

Medical School, Stanford University. He is the author of two widely used texts on organization, *Institutions and Organizations and Organizations* and *Organizaing: Rational, Natural and Open Systems Perspectives* (with G. F. Davis). He is a long-term student of organizations, concentrating of the study of professional organizations, including educational, engineering, medical, research, social welfare, and nonprofit advocacy organizations. During the past three decades, he has concentrated his writing and research on the relation between organizations and their institutional environments. In addition to the two texts, he is the author or editor of over twenty books and more than 200 articles and book chapters.

Wesley D. Sine is a Professor of Management and Organizations at Cornell University. Professor Sine's research focuses on how the institutional context (the normative, regulative and cultural environment) shapes entrepreneurial behavior and new venture outcomes. His research context includes the United States, Latin America, and the Middle East. He has examined issues related to institutional change, industry and technology evolution and new venture structure and strategy. He has examined a diverse set of economic sectors ranging from the electric power industry to the emergence of the Internet. Sine has published in *Administrative Science Quarterly*, *Academy of Management Journal*, *Management Science*, *Organization Science*, *Strategic Management Journal*, and *Research Policy*. Sine is currently a senior editor at *Organization Science* and is the book review editor at *Administrative Science Quarterly*.

Michael Smets is an Associate Professor in Management and Organisation Studies at Saïd Business School, University of Oxford, where he also received his MSc and DPhil. Previously, he was a Lecturer at Aston Business School, Birmingham. Michael's research focuses on how competing institutional demands are encountered and managed in complex, 'hybrid' organizations – and especially in the everyday practice of individuals. As such, his work is mostly multi-level, connecting ethnographic understandings of everyday work to the institutional structures it is part of. He does so especially in the context of professional service organizations, such as in his *Academy of Management Journal* 'best paper' of 2012 or widely noted 'fly on the wall' study of Lloyd's of London, one of the UK's oldest financial institutions. Michael's research has appeared in leading management journals and practitioner publications. It has been covered by *The Financial Times*, *Forbes*, Bloomberg, CNN, CNBC, *The Guardian* and others.

Mark C. Suchman is a Professor of Sociology at Brown University. He holds a PhD in Sociology from Stanford University, a JD from Yale Law School, and an AB in Sociology from Harvard University. His research interests center on the relationship between law, innovation and entrepreneurship, particularly in the information technology, nanotechnology, and healthcare sectors. In addition to his work on organizational legitimacy, he has studied the role of law firms in the structuring of Silicon Valley, and the role of health information professionals in the governance of new clinical information technologies in American hospitals. He has also written on inter-organizational disputing practices, and on social science approaches to the study of contracts. He is currently Chair of the American Sociological Association's Section on Organizations, Occupations and Work, and a former Chair of the Section on Sociology of Law. He has also served as Special Research Advisor to the Board of Directors of the American Bar Foundation, and as Program Director for Social, Human and Organizational Factors and Resources in the National Science Foundation's Division of Advanced Cyberinfrastructure. Before moving to Brown in 2008, he held appointments as a Professor of Sociology and Law at the University of Wisconsin-Madison (1993–2008) and as a Visiting Professor of Law at

Cornell Law School (2006–2007). From 1999 to 2001, he was a Robert Wood Johnson Scholar in Health Policy Research at Yale, and in 2002–2003 he was a fellow at the Center for Advanced Study in the Behavioral Sciences at Stanford.

Patricia H. Thornton is Professor of Sociology and Entrepreneurship at Texas A&M University involved in the Grand Challenge Initiative for Entrepreneurship. She formerly held positions in Sociology and at the Fuqua School of Business, Duke University. Her research and teaching interests include organization and management theory, and innovation and entrepreneurship. She received her PhD in Sociology in 1993 from Stanford University.

Lee Plunkett Tost is an Assistant Professor of Management and Organization at the University of Southern California's Marshall School of Business. She studies the psychological and sociological dynamics of power and legitimacy in organizations. Her work on power focuses on how hierarchy affects team functioning, moral judgments, and ethical decision making. Her research on legitimacy is situated at the intersection of social psychology and institutional theory and explores the motivations underlying individuals' pursuits of social change. Her work has been published in a broad range of academic journals, including *Academy of Management Journal*, *Academy of Management Review*, *Psychological Science*, *Journal of Applied Psychology*, *Organizational Behavior and Human Decision Processes*, *Research in Organizational Behavior*, and *Personality and Social Psychology Review*. In addition, the implications of her research have been discussed in numerous media outlets, including the *New York Times*, *Washington Post*, *Financial Times*, *Forbes*, and *Harvard Business Review*.

Paul Tracey is Professor of Innovation and Organization and academic director of the Centre for Social Innovation at the Judge Business School, University of Cambridge. He received his PhD from the University of Stirling. His research interests include social innovation, regional innovation and institutional change.

Maxim Voronov (PhD, Columbia University) is Professor of Management at the Goodman School of Business, Brock University, Canada. His research is centrally concerned with dynamics of change and stability of social arrangements – at organizational, industry and societal levels. His research is informed by institutional theory, and he examines both human effort and its social embeddedness, as reflected in his work on emotion, power, entrepreneurship, and social judgements. Maxim's research has appeared or is forthcoming in *Academy of Management Review*, *Academy of Management Journal*, *Journal of Management Studies* and *Research in the Sociology of Organizations*, among other outlets.

Peter Walgenbach is Professor of Organization, Leadership, and Human Resource Management at Friedrich Schiller University Jena, Germany. He received his PhD and his Habilitation at the Business School of Mannheim University, Germany. Peter was a visiting scholar at Stanford University (USA) in 1999 and at Stockholm School of Economics (Sweden) in 2016. His research interests are organization and organization theory. In his empirical work, Peter focuses on comparative and/or historical analyses of institutions and organizations. His work builds on the phenomenological tradition of organizational institutionalism.

Linda Wedlin is Professor of Business Studies at Uppsala University. Her research interests include national and transnational regulatory reforms in higher education and research, the organizing of status and status competition in the public science system, and the role of classifications and monitoring mechanisms in forming organizational fields. She is the author and editor of several books, including *Ranking Business Schools* (Edward Elgar, 2006) and *Towards European Science* (Edward Elgar, 2015, together with Maria Nedeva). She is associated researcher at SCORE, the Stockholm Centre for Organizational Research.

Richard Whittington is Professor of Strategic Management at Saïd Business School and Millman Fellow at New College, University of Oxford. He has held visiting positions at Harvard Business School, HEC Paris and the University of Toulouse. He has authored or co-authored nine books, including the leading textbook *Exploring Strategy*, and published in a wide range of journals including the *Journal of Management Studies*, *Organization Science*, *Organization Studies* and the *Strategic Management Journal*. He is an Associate Editor of the *Strategic Management Journal*. His main current areas of research are Strategy as Practice and Open Strategy, and he is currently writing a book on the historical evolution of strategy as a professional field for Oxford University Press.

Melissa Wooten is an Associate Professor of Sociology at the University of Massachusetts, Amherst. She studies how the structure of race and racism influences institutions and the organizing process. Her book *In the Face of Inequality: How Black Colleges Adapt* (SUNY Press, 2015) empirically investigates how racism disadvantages organizational actors preventing them from gaining critical material and political resources. Her work appears in *Research in the Sociology of Organizations*, *Social Science History*, *Mobilization*, and *Education and Urban Society*.

Charlene Zietsma is Associate Professor and Ann Brown Chair of Organization Studies and Director of Entrepreneurship at the Schulich School of Business, York University in Toronto, Canada. Charlene uses institutional, social movement and entrepreneurship perspectives to focus on the multi-level, multi-actor processes leading to significant, large-scale change, usually in the context of sustainability. Charlene has published articles in *Administrative Science Quarterly*, *Academy of Management Journal*, *Academy of Management Journal*, *Academy of Management Annals*, *Organization Science*, *Journal of Business Venturing* and others. She, together with Tom Lawrence, was awarded the ASQ Scholarly Contribution award in 2016 for the article published in 2010 which most substantially shifted the field of organizational studies. Charlene is a Senior Editor for *Organization Studies* and serves on the editorial board for several other journals.

Tammar B. Zilber is Associate Professor of Organization Theory at Jerusalem School of Business, The Hebrew University, Israel. Her research focuses on the dynamics of meanings in institutional processes. She examines the translation of institutions over time, across social spheres and given field multiplicity; the role of discursive acts (like narrating) in constructing institutional realities; the institutional work involved in creating and maintaining field-level collective identity; and the role of the non-discursive (like emotions and spaces) in institutional processes. Professor Zilber is also interested in the institutional pressures and dynamics that ground knowledge production in academia, including the production and re-production of institutional theory itself.

Companion Website

The second edition of *The SAGE Handbook of Organizational Institutionalism* is supported by a companion website, which can be accessed at https://study.sagepub.com/orginstitutionalism2e

Visit the companion website to find fundamental chapters from the first edition and selected content from the second edition.

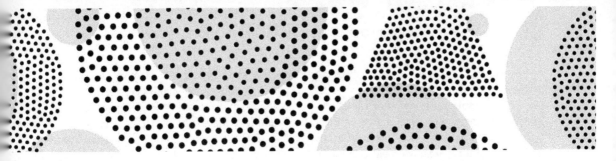

Introduction: Into the Fourth Decade

Royston Greenwood, Christine Oliver,
Thomas B. Lawrence and Renate E. Meyer

The first edition of this *Handbook* appeared in 2008.[1] Its contents and introductory chapter covered the evolution of institutional thinking from 1977 up to that date. In the introductory chapter of the second edition, we will not repeat nor reinterpret these three decades, but rather expand on what we see as important directions and developments in institutional theory since then and suggest what we regard as the most promising future research avenues.

Most of the themes identified in the first edition continued to be elaborated into the fourth decade, and the foundational concepts, notably legitimacy (see Deephouse, Bundy, Tost, & Suchman, Chapter 1) and organizational field (see Wooten & Hoffman, Chapter 2), remained core components of conceptual and empirical work. Both these chapters show the continuing elaboration and centrality of these concepts. However, in mapping the developments of this fourth decade, we find two overarching yet inter-related themes (which form Parts II and III)

to have become particularly central during the post-2008 era: first, a renewed interest in the complexity of relationships between organizations and their institutional context; and, second, a focus on processes and practices through which institutions are created, enacted, or altered, or through which they erode and are eventually deinstitutionalized. Running through both themes are conversations around the concepts of institutional logics and institutional work and related theorizing on the nature of agency within institutional theorizing. In addition, this fourth decade saw the emergence of several new conversations that elaborated and deepened institutional theorizing. Much is going on in the big 'institutional tent'!

However, if there is one area that distinguishes research over the last decade from earlier trends and that promises to redirect institutional scholarship, it is the attention being given to outcomes and consequences of institutions. Whereas earlier work directly or indirectly regarded the primary consequence of institutional processes rather abstractly as the accomplishment of legitimacy or the associated implications of field-level iso-morphism, today concrete and significant societal outcomes – such as racial discrimi-nation, inequality, organizational corruption, or environmental sustainability – are vying for centre stage.

ORGANIZATIONS AND THEIR CONTEXTS

In the last decade, scholarly interest in the relationship between organizations and their institutional context has taken three primary routes: one elaborates the nature of contex-tual features such as field-level governance structures, forms of community, and glo-balized contexts; a second gives emphasis to patterns of compliance – especially non-compliance – and the play of 'legitimacy management'; the third, and lesser devel-oped, focuses upon the world of legitimacy conveyors and upon how legitimacy judge-ments *per se* are socially constructed.

Field-Level Features and Governance

One way in which features of the context are addressed is through field-level infrastruc-tures and governance arrangement. Such aspects have figured to a greater or lesser degree throughout the development of insti-tutional theorizing (see Hinings, Logue & Zietsma, Chapter 6; Aldrich & Fiol, 1994), but it is only recently that they have received more explicit and systematic treatment. An important contribution is Lampel and Meyer's (2008) notion of 'field-configuring events' (FCEs). The term embraces events and actors such as trade shows, tournaments, festivals, ceremonies and rituals, accreditation exer-cises, rankings, and conferences, which collectively represent 'an important and understudied mechanism shaping the emer-gence and developmental trajectories of tech-nologies, markets, industries, and professions' (Lampel & Meyer, 2008: 1025). FCEs are not an entirely new idea – they are found in earlier studies – but Lampel and Meyer correctly suggest that giving more focus to FCEs should enhance our understanding of field dynamics because they are integral to 'the growth and evolution of institutional, organizational, and professional fields' (2008: 1025).

As Hinings et al. (Chapter 6) point out, the need to understand the nature and out-comes of FCEs for field structuration has, over the past few years, become more fully appreciated and various forms of FCEs have been studied (e.g., Garud, 2008; Hardy & Maguire, 2010; Moeran & Pedersen, 2011). They are recognized as important vehicles of field-level institutional governance that can profoundly shape how fields emerge, evolve, are displaced or sustained. They are also fundamental to how interests and privileges are asserted and concealed (Amis, Munir, & Mair, Chapter 27; Palmer, Chapter 28).

Nonetheless, questions remain. Schüssler, Rüling and Wittneben (2014), for example, argue that the role of FCEs in field structura-tion varies according to the relative maturity of the field. At the early moments of field evolution, these authors suggest, FCEs pro-vide the basis for trust and openness and hence can assist change. As fields mature, FCEs become less open because powerful actors enter the discourse – and thus FCEs *prevent* change. We also have much to learn about less obvious FCEs. Although they do not use the term, Vaccaro and Palazzo's (2015) study of resistance to the mafia high-lights a very different type of FCE. In their case it was not formal conferences but more clandestine meetings in places such as school buildings and activists' houses that provided the opportunity for normative changes that undermined deeply institutionalized arrange-ments. This study reminds us that not all FCEs are highly visible. We need to cast our net wider. Overall, however, whilst accepting that we have much yet to do in order to fully understand the range and roles of FCEs, Hinings et al. (Chapter 6) conclude that progress is promising and encouraging.

Emphasis upon FCEs illustrates how institutional theory has homed in on the organizational field as the level at which sociocultural pressures are particularly evident. The overwhelming majority of studies now take for granted that the organizational field or environment is the appropriate level of analysis (see Wooten & Hoffman, Chapter 2). The concept of field originally developed because of dissatisfaction with the term 'industry', which neglects the role of agencies such as professional and trade associations, regulators, the media and the state. Recognizing and empirically focusing upon the field was, and remains, a crucially important and distinctive feature of institutional theorizing. Nevertheless, the concept of organizational field may have been considered unduly narrowly, and although it has proved, and will continue to be, a useful level of analysis, it may have become too abstract and thus divorced from the sociopolitical community within which institutional and organizational processes occur. Other levels of analysis have been much less considered. As Greenwood, Diaz, Li and Lorente (2010: 15) put it:

> Analytical abstraction, intended to better capture contextual influences, has resulted in a relative blindness to how communities (regions) and their interaction with state logics affect organizations. The relationship between communities and organizations, informed through an ideology of the state, was integral to early institutional work (e.g., Selznick, 1949), but that focus has largely disappeared. A return to the traditional emphasis on community would be timely.

Encouragingly, however, studies have begun to acknowledge that organizations are also located within communities and that these communities may influence the particular expression of rationalized myths and institutional logics to which organizations have to respond (Almandoz, Marquis, & Cheely, Chapter 7; Marquis, 2003; Marquis, Glynn, &

Davis, 2007; Marquis & Lounsbury, 2007). Illustrations of the significance of community are provided by Baum-Snow and Pavan (2013), who show how geography affects income inequality, Allard and Small (2013), who connect community to social disadvantage, or Peredo and Chrisman (2006), who link community to the formation of social enterprises, Marquis (2003), who traces the connections between organizations and cultural associations within a bounded geographical setting, and Greenwood et al. (2010), who demonstrate how connections between organizations and local political elites influence decisions on the utilization of human resources.

Höllerer, Walgenbach and Drori (Chapter 8) employ yet another lens to explore the relationship of organizations and their contexts by asking how the increasingly globalized world (see also Meyer, Chapter 32; and Scott, Chapter 33) impacts organizations, their features, forms, practices, and the available building blocks for their management and governance. These authors argue that organizations display different degrees of global (versus local) orientation and that their responses and compliance mechanisms are shaped by the degree to which they are globally oriented. They then go further, suggesting that understanding the co-constitutive interplay between the local and the global is necessary to understand processes and dynamics in and across organizations, communities, fields, and the global world society; and that this interplay has important consequences for central institutional concepts such as legitimation, translation, or the question of how plurality unfolds and organizations respond. Scott (Chapter 33: 862) sees the institutional study of the transnational realm as 'arguably one of the most vibrant areas of institutional theorizing and research'.

Patterns of Compliance

Ever since Oliver (1991) introduced the idea of 'strategic responses' to institutional pressures there has been general acceptance that organizations are not 'passive receptors of legitimate ideas' (Gondo & Amis, 2013: 229). On the contrary, 'shades of rogueness' (Quirke, 2013: 1692) are accepted as part and parcel of all institutional contexts. In consequence, understanding why particular organizations engage in different patterns or forms of conformity, and how they do so, has become a rich focus for research. Moreover, recent accounts avoid the top-down imagery of earlier work, and the overly agentic bottom-up accounts that followed. Legitimacy management is very much seen as a complex process of reciprocal social construction (Boxenbaum & Jonsson, Chapter 3). Wedlin and Sahlin (Chapter 4: 103) carefully elaborate and remind us that the Scandinavian approach to diffusion always emphasized that ideas and practices 'do not remain unchanged as they flow but are subject to translation. [...] To imitate, then, is not just to copy but also to change and to innovate'. This approach is much more appreciated now than earlier and has spurred many studies on such 'translations'.

Various patterns of compliance or non-compliance continue to be elaborated. Boxenbaum and Jonsson (Chapter 3) indicate and review the continuing interest in decoupling – the strategy identified by Meyer and Rowan (1977) as a response to inconsistencies between technical and institutional demands. This distinction is much less assumed today, in that assumptions of technical prerequisites are more usually seen as institutional; but the idea of inconsistent institutional prescriptions remains of interest and has, in the fourth decade, triggered much research into institutional complexity (Greenwood, Raynard, Kodeih, Micelotta, & Lounsbury, 2011). In this volume, such complexity is particularly elaborated in the study of 'global' and 'local' dynamics (see Höllerer et al., Chapter 8) or 'hybrid' organizations (see Battilana, Besharov, & Mitzinneck, Chapter 5) – on which we say more later.

Before leaving decoupling, it is worth noting the disturbing study by Whitman and Cooper (2016), whose fieldwork revealed the connection between decoupling and systematic corporate social irresponsibility. These authors analysed how decoupling enabled an international firm 'to achieve certification for socially responsible corporate behavior alongside allegations of rape and irresponsible practices' (p. 116). As the acting editor for the paper commented, 'The paper [...] is not for the faint of heart' (p. 115). For us, it is an exemplar of the shift within institutional theory towards problems that matter.

In studying patterns of compliance, the focus has shifted away from identification of responses *per se* (in the Oliver tradition), in favour of identifying the attributes or circumstances that shape responses to particular institutional expectations (Deephouse et al., Chapter 1). An established example of this interest concerns new ventures. Because these organizations lack legitimacy their responses to institutional expectations are geared towards attaining legitimacy by closely following established practices, or by attaching themselves in some way to high status actors (e.g., see David, Sine, & Serra, Chapter 25). Another, complementary stream of research explores how organizations that have suffered loss of legitimacy that arose from an association with other organizations, might seek to *regain* legitimacy either for themselves (e.g., Jonsson, Greve, & Fujiwara-Greve, 2009) or their industry (e.g., Desai, 2011).

Other studies have probed the filtering attribute of status, suggesting that middle-status organizations are less likely to deviate from institutional prescriptions as compared to high- and low-status organizations, because high status protects from social penalties, and low status renders them less relevant (Phillips & Zuckerman, 2001). A rather different take is offered by Compagni, Mele and Ravasi (2015) who show that central and peripheral organizations within a field might have very different reasons for adopting an innovation: central players may see an innovation as a threat and adopt it in order to preserve their status, whereas peripheral players might see adoption as an opportunity by which to improve their status.

A very different attribute that defines an organization and shapes its responses, and that is attracting considerable scrutiny, is 'stigma'. 'Stigmatized' organizations violate broader social norms (Ashforth, Kreiner, Clark, & Fugate, 2007; Devers, Dewett, Mishina, & Belsito, 2009; Hudson, 2008) and not only lack legitimacy – they are positively *ill*egitimate and vilified. Yet, some are capable of 'seemingly cheating their fates' (Hampel & Tracey, 2016: 2). How these organizations are able to do so is capturing much interest. Answers put forward include 'opacity' (e.g., Briscoe & Murphy, 2012), various forms of 'concealment' (e.g., Hudson & Okhuysen, 2009; Vergne, 2012), 'substitution' (Okhmatovskiy & David, 2012), 'dilution' (Carberry & King, 2012; Sharkey, 2014), 'distraction' (Grougiou, Dedoulis, & Leventis, 2016), 'asset divestment' (Durand & Vergne, 2015), or, paradoxically, even the deliberate 'use' of that stigma (Helms & Patterson, 2014; Tracey & Phillips, 2016). Put more simply, organizations respond to being stigmatized in one of three ways – they use it, lose it, or conceal it.

The fact that stigmatized firms can survive underlines that legitimacy processes involve multiple audiences that confer or deny legitimacy and that these audiences (or 'sources' to use Deephouse et al.'s term, Chapter 1) often differ in their social evaluations. As such, and as emphasized by Hudson and Okhuysen (2009), recent studies – notably those focused upon 'hybrid organizations (see Battilana et al., Chapter 5) qualify and question the widely accepted definition of organizational legitimacy as a '*generalized* perception or assumption that the actions of an entity are desirable, proper, or appropriate' (Suchman, 1995: 574, emphasis added). Instead, legitimacy is a more complex interaction between organizations and their several audiences.

The Social Construction of Legitimacy Judgments

For the most part, studies of the legitimacy process assume the presence of social standards or criteria against which organizations and their behaviours can be assessed. In this portrayal, various legitimating agents – such as regulators, 'intermediaries' (e.g., analysts), field-level 'collective actors' (e.g., industry and professional associations, accreditation agencies), or the media – convey, monitor and enforce social expectations of appropriate conduct. As Deephouse et al. (Chapter 1) observe, much has been learned about the role of these actors in stabilizing institutional arrangements.

Two especially compelling recent contributions to understanding of these processes are the attention given to categories (Durand & Boulongne, Chapter 24), and, even more recently, the role of emotions in expressing and enforcing institutional judgments (Lok, Creed, DeJordy, & Voronov, Chapter 22). For us, these elaborations have reinvigorated interest in the legitimation process, the first by providing a language through which to better capture the process, and the latter by identifying a previously missing yet profound dimension (on which more below).

However, Bitektine and Haack (2015) turn the spotlight upon our relatively modest understanding of the networks and relationships that connect these 'legitimacy evaluators' and our lack of insight into the means by which legitimacy standards and judgments are themselves socially constructed and policed *within* the world of this community. In other words, although our appreciation of field-level governance mechanisms is growing both in scope and sophistication (Hinings et al., Chapter 6), and although the influence of these field-level actors and their often 'soft' governance for institutional stabilization and change is being recognized (Wedlin & Sahlin, Chapter 4), we need to probe much more inside their world in order to gain a better understanding of their working and consequences. Moreover, given – as we noted above – that the institutional context is not homogeneous, we suggest that understanding how the several worlds of social endorsement come together to socially construct institutional prescriptions and proscriptions, is an intriguing and important direction of future research.

INSTITUTIONAL PROCESSES

As we noted in the first edition, from the mid-1980s and through the 1990s there was considerable interest in showing patterns of diffusion, which were seen as indicators of institutional effects – especially of institutional isomorphism. That purpose – to 'prove' the institutional thesis by showing isomorphic tendencies under conditions of uncertainty – no longer holds, but interest in patterns of diffusion remains. So, too, does interest in a second process – institutional entrepreneurship – that was precipitated by DiMaggio's (1988) challenge for an explanation of institutional change.

Diffusion and Isomorphism

A core question of the institutional perspective concerns whether and to what extent organizations adopt similar structures and forms because they adapt 'to what they believe society expects of them'. The institutional explanation is that organizations become similar 'not through adaptation to an externally or technically demanding environment or through the "weeding out" of technical and social misfits, but through adaptation to a socially constructed environment' (Boxenbaum and Jonsson, Chapter 3: 81). Given its early centrality to institutional accounts, it is not surprising that this theme has attracted '[v]oluminous research' which Boxenbaum and Jonsson interrogate around five questions: In what respect are

organizations supposed to be similar? Does similarity result from mechanisms of diffusion? What is the relevant environment to which organizations are thought to become (or not to become) isomorphic? How does isomorphism occur where the institutional environment is not homogeneous? How can we account for dissimilarity?

What is notable from their review is that, although our understanding of these issues has significantly advanced, there are still many gaps and confusions. More recent research has begun to address what happens after adoption – to the practices that diffuse (e.g., Ansari, Fiss, & Zajac, 2010; Gehman, Trevino, & Garud, 2013) or the organizations (e.g., Weber, Davis, & Lounsbury, 2009), or how the adoption of practices influences future decisions depending on whether the practices enact the same or competing institutional logics (Meyer & Höllerer, 2016; Shipilov, Greve, & Rowley, 2010). There is, too, growing interest in how 'controversial or counter-normative' practices diffuse (or not). Nevertheless, Boxenbaum and Jonsson identify several additional areas that call for further work. But in doing so they raise a cautionary note, asking 'whether isomorphism still has a place as a distinct empirical concept'. They think that it does but point out that it requires much more careful theorizing in order to remove the current 'conceptual muddle' (Colyvas & Jonsson, 2011: 27). Time will tell!

Boxenbaum and Jonsson (2017: 93) make a more general and challenging point about the expansive nature of institutional theorizing. Noting that isomorphism and decoupling were initially put forward as related propositions, but have been treated as separate constructs, these authors criticize how theory develops by expansion and in doing so loses some rigour: 'Instead of focusing on how core concepts relate to each other, researchers tend to extend and enrich each separate line of inquiry'. Food for thought …

Wedlin and Sahlin (Chapter 4) present an overview of the Scandinavian variant of institutional theorizing. They highlight how that approach has always emphasized that ideas are translated and edited as they diffuse and are adopted. They also observe that studies of 'what' diffuses are now more likely to focus upon 'soft' regulations such as standards, evaluations and audits (we in the university world can certainly verify this shift in our world!), often spreading on a global level (Meyer, Chapter 32). But Wedlin and Sahlin suggest that in the last decade there has been more interest in *how* ideas are carried. Early studies pointed to the importance of direct linkages – e.g., interlocking directorates – as vehicles by which organizations 'learn' about circulating ideas. The implication is that organizations to which an organization is directly connected act as models to be followed. Other studies pointed to cultural linkages – i.e., to the category with which an organization identifies – implying that organizations within that category are the appropriate models. Wedlin and Sahlin (see also, Glynn, Chapter 9) suggest that it is 'identification' and identity that are often found to be a key mechanism of imitation: organizations imitate 'those one relates to and those with whom one identifies' (p. 107).

Similarly, there is renewed interest in the range of institutional 'carriers'. Wedlin and Sahlin (Chapter 4) and Höllerer, Walgenbach and Drori (Chapter 8) provide insights into the role of 'carriers' in the translation of globally spreading forms and practices. Bringing some order to the study of how ideas diffuse, Scott (2014: 58) identifies four types of carriers – symbolic, relational, routines, and artifacts – and suggests that each varies in the processes employed 'to transmit their messages' (Scott, 2014: 58). But for the Scandinavian approach it is not only the range of carriers that matters – also being sought is understanding of how and why different carriers affect how particular kinds of prescriptions and expectations are received and translated, the extent to which diffusing ideas generate contestation between carriers and promoters, and how those interpretive processes affect the subsequent deployment and practice usage.

Institutional Entrepreneurship and Change

Given the considerable effort devoted to understanding how and why institutional change occurs, it is not surprising that we are much more informed about from where and under what circumstances initiatives arise that prompt institutional disruption (Hardy & Maguire, Chapter 10). We have learned that it may follow from external 'jolts', the presence of endogenous contradictions, or through the incremental adjustments and improvisations that occur in the performance of day-to-day activities. We are also better informed about how new ideas are 'theorized', 'translated', or 'framed' so as to gain social endorsement and support. Insights from social movement theory continue to provide significant guidance (Schneiberg & Lounsbury, Chapter 11); more recently, so, too, has practice theory (Smets, Aristidou, & Whittington, Chapter 14) and identity theory (Glynn, Chapter 9).

Nevertheless, questions remain. Zietsma and Lawrence (2010: 190) conclude that studies that focus upon an organization's position within a field (e.g., whether 'central' or 'peripheral') as a predictor of the organization's openness to change 'have generated as many puzzles as answers'. Similarly, undue attention has been given to the discursive rather than the behavioral strategies deployed in the theorizing and mobilizing of change efforts (Phillips & Malhotra, Chapter 15). In comparison, the 'non-discursive dimension' of mobilization 'remains the subject of scant research' (Battilana, Leca, & Boxenbaum, 2009: 86).

A different and critical question raised by Hardy and Maguire (Chapter 10), is whether analyses of institutional change are too centred around the 'paradox of embedded agency' (Holm, 1995) – i.e., the conundrum of how actors embedded within an institutionalized setting are able to reflect upon existing arrangements and perceive alternatives (which implies that they are located in a peripheral position within the field), and yet have the ability to marshal resources to accomplish fundamental change (which implies the opposite). Hardy and Maguire observe 'two different narratives [...] one that is more actor-centric and focuses on the deliberate strategies of particular institutional entrepreneurs and another that is more process-centric and emphasizes the struggles associated with institutional entrepreneurship activities' (p. 273). Process studies, they note, have increased in recent years, and complement (some would say contradict) actor-centric accounts, which 'tend to be functionalist, painting a neat picture of relatively rational, linear, win–win problem solving activity' (p. 274).

A similar point has been pushed by other scholars (e.g., Hwang & Colyvas, 2011; Meyer, 2008; Powell & Colyvas, 2008). In his 'strategic action fields' approach, Fligstein (2013), for example, criticizes institutional accounts for their failure to properly acknowledge that even mature fields experience ongoing political struggles to sustain or alter patterns of interest and privilege (although see Scott, Chapter 33). A related but distinctive contribution to this debate is provided by Lawrence, Suddaby and Leca (2009), who, though giving less attention to political struggles, emphasize the importance of 'institutional work' as actors 'knowingly' seek to 'create, maintain, and disrupt the practices that are considered legitimate within a field (practice work) and the boundaries between sets of individuals and groups (boundary work), and the interplay of these two forms of institutional work' (Zietsma & Lawrence, 2010: 189). Despite the growing understanding of how change occurs, and of the roles of various actors and events, questions remain. Few studies analyse failed efforts to change institutions. We also have limited understanding of how fields

vary – the distinction between emerging and mature fields has been acknowledged, but there is little research, for example, on mature fields that lack a dominant logic. Nor do we have comparisons of different types of fields – such as highly professional fields with non-professional ones – or studies that compare fields that exhibit very different rhythms and sequences of change. Several years ago, Scott commented that 'although we have made headway in recent years [...] we have much yet to learn' (2010: 11). We still do.

The Microfoundations of Institutions

DiMaggio and Powell (1991) pointed out that we know very little about how institutional prescriptions affect and are affected by individuals. Powell and Colyvas (2008) re-emphasized the point, recommending that more effort be given to uncovering the microfoundations of institutional processes. Although there has always been some kind of microfoundation for institutional research, the nature of those foundations has too often been left implicit in our work. In this volume, Powell and Rerup (Chapter 12) revisit this theme and stress that 'institutions are sustained, altered and extinguished as they are enacted by collections of individuals in everyday situations' (p. 311) often 'born out of chance and naivete' (p. 332). This imagery contrasts with the more organized agency typically underpinning, for example, social movement accounts of institutional change. In their chapter, Powell and Rerup point to several literatures that speak to and inform analyses of micro-processes – including 'practice theory', the Carnegie school, sensemaking, and ethnography. All of these, Powell and Rerup show, have significant potential to uncover how individuals connect to broader, more macro, institutional processes, and to enrich our theorizing about stability and change.

At the core of institutional conceptions of social reality is the notion of meaning (see Zilber, Chapter 16). Although institutions have long been argued to represent particularly meaningful social structures and practices (Selznick, 1957), the degree to which meaning and meaningfulness have been a part of institutional studies of organizations has varied tremendously. As Zilber (Chapter 16) forcefully argues, attention to meaning has ebbed and flowed in institutional studies, playing a central role in early work, and then moving to the margins until it was picked up again in the 1990s and developed more explicitly as institutional scholars began to incorporate linguistic methods and theories. The role of language in conceptualizing and investigating institutions has flourished since the mid 2000s with scholars explicitly employing discursive, narrative, rhetorical and semiotic lenses (see Phillips and Malhotra, Chapter 15, and Jones, Meyer, Jancsary, & Höllerer, Chapter 23). Phillips and Malhotra tie this linguistic turn to recognition of the centrality of cognitive institutions, and argue, perhaps provocatively, for a separation of cognitive conceptions of institutions from what they suggest are less usefully understood as institutional normative and regulative pillars. Jones et al. (Chapter 23) challenge this exclusive linguistic focus with its cognitive preoccupation and argue for the inclusion of other semiotic modes of meaning construction.

'Practice theory' (Smets et al., Chapter 14) and the practice level of analysis have become particularly prominent in the study of microfoundations. The concept of a practice describes an 'embodied, materially mediated array[s] of human activity centrally organized around shared practical understanding' (Schatzki, 2001: 11). In their chapter, Smets et al. point to the shared heritage of institutional theory and practice theory, but conclude that although ideas from the latter have recently received 'more attention', they have done so 'often in a more colloquial and unreflexive way to

black box what people "do" without embracing the onto-epistomological assumptions underpinning practice theory' (p. 367). They elaborate how the practice approach could contribute more 'granularity' to current research themes, including questions of where and how change occurs, the nature of institutional work, the construction of institutional complexity, the role of practitioners as 'carriers' of ideas, and the play of emotions. The engagement of institutional and practice ideas holds much promise – maybe, at last, our declared interest in the microfoundations of institutional processes will resonate empirically and theoretically.

Wedlin and Sahlin (Chapter 4) recognize the similarity between Scandinavian institutionalism and recent 'practice' accounts of change and maintenance – especially the emphasis upon distributed improvisation and upon the 'mundane acts of translation performed by many' (p. 119). A difference between the two approaches is that practice theory does not foreground imitation as a driving mechanism – instead, improvisation arises from day-to-day, ongoing tasks. Both perspectives, however, spotlight the actual doing of work as the source of institutional adaptation and change.

Another lens by which to study micro-level institutional processes is provided by social network analysis. Powell and Oberg (Chapter 17) show how relational and institutional analyses can be brought together to offer deeper insights into how institutional patterns emerge, are maintained or changed. They start by reminding us that the classical notion of fields builds on inter-organizational networks and structural equivalence and highlight how differences in the relational positioning impact innovativeness, speed of adoption, environmental complexity and the legitimacy of an organization. An emerging and very promising area analyses how the meaning of ideas, concepts, constructs, etc. is constructed through their relationship to other ideas, concepts, and constructs. Such semantic network analyses may not only offer new and more fine-grained insights into diffusion and translation (see below), they make visible the relational core of institutions as a typification of actor and action (Berger & Luckmann, 1967) and offer a way to study how systems of categories are formed and constitute the building blocks of sedimented social knowledge. Finally, Powell and Oberg break new ground by illustrating how interlocked, multi-level networks are able to bring together relational ties among social entities and semantic meaning structures. Apart from a novel way of studying the structuration of organizational fields or the dynamics of issue fields, a multilevel network approach has the potential to study interactions among fields.

An issue that runs through all of these process-focused accounts of institutions, although it is often well below the surface, is the role of power. The relationship between power and institutions is, as Lawrence and Buchanan (Chapter 18) claim, 'an intimate one', but it is also a complex relationship. The intimacy of power and institutions is rooted in their mutual interdependence, with institutions existentially dependent on the degree to which they exert influence over the thoughts, feelings and behaviours of people and organizations; at the same time, recent writing on institutions as inhabited and the objects of institutional work demonstrate the ways in which institutions exist (are created, maintained and transformed) by courtesy of the politics of those same people and organizations. The importance of this relationship – between power and institutions – is, unfortunately, not very well reflected in our literature and there remains a striking ambivalence about incorporating power in institutional analyses. While studies of institutional entrepreneurship and institutional work have highlighted the politics of institutional change and stability, there has remained in our descriptions of institutions a metaphysical quality that seeks to detach them from the prosaic politics of organizations and communities. At the core of this ambivalence sits the contested

ontology of institutions: whether they exist strictly as taken-for-granted cognitive structures, as eloquently argued by Phillips and Malhotra (Chapter 15) and initially laid out by Meyer and Rowan (1977), or include non-cognitive mechanisms of social control, as suggested by Berger and Luckmann (1967) and Jepperson (1991) and implicit in much of the agency-focused writing on institutions (see also, Scott, Chapter 33). Both articulations represent important possibilities and so the challenge of squaring that particular institutional circle remains.

CONVERSATIONS

Institutional Logics and Hybrid Organizations

Precipitated in part by the overview and elaboration provided by Thornton, Ocasio and Lounsbury (2012), 'institutional logic' has become one of the key terms in the institutional vocabulary. Research using the term has 'exploded' in recent years (Ocasio, Thornton, & Lounsbury, Chapter 19). It provides a vehicle by which to define and explain institutional change and stability both at the level of the field and the organization. It connects to 'categories' (Durand & Boulongne, Chapter 24), which can be conceived as the cognitive building blocks of logics, and to both geographical and relational communities (Almandoz et al., Chapter 7), and, significantly, it defines institutional 'identity', which, for many theorists, has become an essential part of the institutional story (Glynn, Chapter 9). Further, it speaks to the macro–micro interface of institutional processes (Powell & Rerup, Chapter 12) and also raises the issue of how organizations cope when faced with 'institutional pluralism' (Kraatz & Block, Chapter 20). Today, such organizations are often referred to as 'hybrids' (Battilana et al., Chapter 5).

The idea that organizations might experience more than one set of institutional pressures is not new – D'Aunno, Sutton, & Price (1991), for example, referred to 'hybrid units' that face conflicting pressure 'from two sectors'. But interest in such arrangements languished until 'hybrids' were re-introduced by Battilana and Dorado (2010) and Pache and Santos (2010), who shared an interest in organizations that combine commercial with non-commercial goals (commonly referred to as 'social enterprises'). Today, understanding how organizations cope with multiple logics is a priority in institutional research because scholars acknowledge that such pluralism is rather the norm than the exception. Institutional theorists are not alone in recognizing that organizations are often challenged to cope with competing demands and expectations (a point emphasized by Battilana et al., Chapter 5; see also, Battilana & Lee, 2014). For us, however, studies of hybrid organizations represent a welcome return of attention within the institutional literature to the organization, thus countering the previous preoccupation with field-level processes.

According to Battilana et al. (Chapter 5) the focus of research has shifted in the last few years. One perspective (illustrated by Pache and Santos, 2013) essentially portrays individuals and groups within organizations as 'representatives' or 'carriers' of a particular logic and as committed to defending and promoting the practices associated with it. The imagery is of actors advancing 'their' logic. In this perspective, the use of discretion is relatively modest because actors find it difficult to overcome their existing preconceptions. An alternative perspective portrays actors as drawing upon different logics according to the situation at hand. Actors 'use logics strategically' (McPherson & Sauder, 2013: 182). In this perspective, the use of discretion is higher with logics used as 'cultural tool kits' (Swidler, 1986).

The distinction between actors as either 'representatives' or 'strategic users' of logics is probably better conceptualized as a continuum of embedded discretion; moreover, the position of one actor along that continuum is likely to vary across situations and over time. Many of the difficulties faced by 'nascent hybrids' in the early years of their founding, for example, may be very different from the challenges of sustaining an established hybrid organization. Introducing a new logic into a mature hybrid, or, removing one, are also very different settings and thus different mechanisms can be anticipated. Perhaps the most important question that should receive attention is whether multi-logic organizations *do* provide more innovative solutions to big and wicked problems. As Smets, Jarzabkowski, Burke and Spee (2015: 933) remind us: 'we know surprisingly little about how such benefits are reaped'. There is much yet to uncover.

Institutional Work

Around the time of the first edition of this *Handbook* a vibrant conversation within organizational institutionalism emerged that focused on the work of actors to shape the institutions around them. The concept of institutional work, introduced by Lawrence and Suddaby (2006) as an umbrella under which stood notions of institutional entrepreneurship, deinstitutionalization and institutional maintenance, has evolved into a distinct perspective in which the relationship between agency, experience and institutions sits at its core. Since then, the institutional work perspective has generated a significant body of research that explores how, why, and when actors work to shape sets of institutions, the factors that affect their ability to do so, and the experience of these efforts for those involved (Hampel, Lawrence, & Tracey, Chapter 21).

Along with a synthesis of research on the work done to create, transform and disrupt institutions, the institutional work perspective pointed to a lack of understanding of the role of agency in institutional persistence. Rather than assume that institutions were inherently enduring, as perhaps suggested by some definitions, Lawrence and Suddaby (2006) argued for the investigation of how actors might be working to maintain institutions. As Scott (2010: 10) observed, 'Many ideas, schema, and prescriptions are proposed, but only a relatively small subset survive [...] to become institutionalized. What are the forces that provide the coherence and stability – the glue – to some practices rather than others?' In response, there has been a stirring of interest in the work done to maintain institutions, sometimes in the face of active resistance.

Dacin, Munir and Tracey (2010), for example, show how seemingly incidental and repetitive practices – in their study, high table dining practices at a University of Cambridge college – can significantly contribute to the maintenance of a complex, societal institution, such as the British class system. Lok and DeRond (2013) and Heaphy (2013) go further, distinguishing various ways by which minor breakdowns – 'breaches' – at the practice level are redressed and in doing so repair and reproduce existing arrangements. Micelotta and Washington (2013) provide a more macro lens in their account of how Italian law firms maintained their institutionalized privileges in the face of disruption from international competition. Vaccaro and Palazzo (2015), in their analysis of change in societies dominated by organized crime, remind us that not all maintenance activities are quite so low-key.

Because a central concern of all institutional research is the persistence of social beliefs and arrangements, research on institutional maintenance may be one of the most important areas for further development. Institutional maintenance also possesses the potential to shed new light on taken-for-granted understandings that defy change by their social invisibility. Many of these understandings may also have their roots in deep structures of power that preconsciously reinforce the status quo.

The institutional work perspective did not develop in isolation of other, allied sets of concerns. It represents a part of a broader wave of interest in organizational institutionalism's 'people' problem, a wave that includes writing on 'inhabited institutions' (Hallett & Ventresca, 2006), microfoundations of institutions (Powell & Rerup, Chapter 12) and Barley's (Chapter 13) notion of 'coalface' institutionalism. Hallett and Ventresca's (2006: 213) important understanding of institutions as inhabited – 'populated with people whose social interactions suffuse institutions with local force and significance' – has provided institutional scholars with a powerful image of institutional life that has animated many thoughtful empirical investigations of how people in organizations cope with and manipulate their institutional contexts. This grounding of institutions in the cognitions and behaviours of people and collective actors has gained a fuller form in writing on the microfoundations of institutions.

The institutional work perspective is also closely tied to the practice theoretic writing and research that has flourished in social and organizational research, and more recently in organizational institutionalism (as noted by Smets et al., Chapter 14). Interesting connections between institutional work and practice theory have been developed (Jarzabkowski, Matthiesen, & Van de Ven, 2009; Smets & Jarzabkowski, 2013).

Perhaps the most pointed discussion of the people problem in organizational institutionalism has been Barley's (Chapter 13) argument for integrating the Chicago School of symbolic interactionism into institutional studies. Barley argues that institutional research took a wrong turn, from which it has never recovered, in ignoring the potential contributions of the Chicago School, with its emphasis on institutions as constituted in social interaction. A great strength of Chicagoan symbolic interactionism was its attendance to and systematic theorization of the everyday goings-on of specific social worlds. And, as Barley eloquently puts it, 'everyday life is institutional theory's coalface; it is where the rubber of theory hits the road of reality' (Chapter 13: 358).

Emerging Conversations

Throughout the central themes and the sub-themes within them that we have discussed, new ideas and questions continually arise and in doing so elaborate, nuance and at times stir up our understandings of institutional processes. Among these, three emerging and distinct conversations deserve particular notice: those to do with *emotions*, the *material and visual*, and *categories*.

Emotions

According to Lok et al. (Chapter 22), the cognitive emphasis within institutional theorizing 'has recently been challenged' because of the growing interest in uncovering the microfoundations of institutional processes. At one level, the possible significance of emotions is easily observable. Gabbioneta, Greenwood, Mazzola and Minoja (2013), for example, describe how analysts who raised questions about Parmalat (an Italian company that for over a decade successfully concealed its corrupted financial statements) were ridiculed into silence by other analysts and professional observers. Similarly, Senate Committees in the United States, and Parliamentary Committees of Inquiry in the UK, often display politicians angrily humiliating senior executives of accounting firms and investment bankers because of their failure to conform to social expectations of the role that their firms are supposed to perform as 'gatekeepers' of the market system. In a very real sense, these occasions are examples of actors 'swimming in a sea of shame' (Creed, Hudson, Okhuysen, & Smith-Crowe, 2014). Moreover, it has been shown that institutional stability and disruption are processes affected by the extent to which people 'feel emotionally and ideologically committed to them' (Pache & Santos, 2013: 10).

Yet, the play of emotions is 'conspicuously absent from institutional research' (Voronov & Vince, 2012: 59). Scott (Chapter 33: 860) says: 'there is little evidence that cognitive approaches have lost their grip'. Things, however, may be changing (Lok et al., Chapter 22). Importantly, the inclusion of emotions into institutional studies is not simply about the display of emotions. On the contrary, a key insight provided by Voronov and Weber (2016), is that 'emotions are central to the very constitution of people as competent institutional actors that hold a personal stake in an institution and are enabled to interpret and perform their own role within an institutional order'. By developing the idea of 'emotional competence', these authors show how individuals learn to express institutionally prescribed roles in a competent manner – a competence that includes not simply a cognitive understanding, but also understanding how and which emotions are legitimate and expected. As they put it: emotional competence is the 'capacity to belong in and inhabit an institutional order' (2016: 457). For the most part, Voronov and Weber discuss how individuals learn their institutional roles. But the same process, we would suggest, applies also to organizations and field-level actors. Professional associations, for example, learn appropriate emotional behaviours.

The significance of including emotions into institutional thinking is that it promises to open up strikingly new ways of understanding institutional stability and disruption (the emphasis of Lok et al., Chapter 22). Having learned and become committed to patterns of formative behaviour, individuals collectively monitor and enforce institutional arrangements. Further, the degree of desire for those arrangements influences the possibility of disruption. Toubiana and Zietsma (2016; see also Toubiana, Greenwood, & Zietsma, forthcoming) illustrate how the inclusion of emotions opens new insights into the current debate over the management of 'hybrids', i.e., organizations that encompass two or more logics. These authors point out that institutional logics contain 'emotional registers' – i.e., prescriptions about appropriate 'emotional content and expression' (2016: 4). Physicians in hospitals, for example, behave according to a different register than (for example) registers that apply to sports fans, or religious leaders etc. In effect, actors embody and deploy both a cognitive framework (in effect, a system of categories and concepts) by which they make sense of their social world) *and* an emotional register by which they socially construct and respond to situations. It follows that hybrid organizations composed of logics with different cognitive frameworks *and* emotional registers are likely to experience a particularly problematical version of institutional complexity. The extent to which different logics are compatible or incompatible may be a function not simply of their relative cognitive structures (the assumption of most current work in this area) but their respective emotional registers. It is thought-provoking to wonder whether cognitive or emotional incompatibility is the more challenging occurrence. It is also thought-provoking to speculate whether emotional incompatibility is more difficult to address than cognitive incompatibility.

The incorporation of emotions into institutional analysis is intriguing. Much can be anticipated as empirical work builds upon the theoretical groundwork provided by Creed et al. (2014), Massa, Helms, Voronov and Wang (2016), Toubiana and Zietsma (2016), Voronov and Vince (2012) and Voronov and Weber (2016). Indeed, while this area remains relatively nascent it has exciting possibilities for illuminating the micro- and group-level foundations of institutional expectations and behaviour. We have much to learn but the possibilities are exciting.

Materiality and visuality

Much as the role of emotions has been neglected within institutional scholarship, so too has the role of the material and the visual. And, as with emotions, the material and the visual bases of institutions are slowly becoming acknowledged. Jones et al. (Chapter 23) stress the significant role and influence of visual images and material artifacts for institutions and institutional processes and mechanisms. They argue that institutions are multimodal, i.e., sedimented in, and represented by, a variety of sign systems. However, currently too much of our existing knowledge on the workings of institutions relies on the study of verbal language. Material artifacts are durable and transferable (Jones, Boxenbaum, & Anthony, 2013); their characteristics and features contribute to 'relative permanence' and therefore influence what endures or decays. The visual has its own specific ways of organizing, transmitting, and storing meaning that distinguish it from verbal language. These characteristics include, for example, spatiality, immediacy of perception, the ability to evoke emotional responses, or (in contrast) the signaling of scientific detachment (as in the use of charts and graphs in presentations). The visual may become of even greater significance in the future because of the growth and increasing sophistication of communication technologies.

Jones et al. (Chapter 23) use core concepts such as legitimacy, institutional logics, or identity to outline the potential that embracing materiality and visuality has for institutional research. They discuss, for instance, how material and visual camouflage help legitimize innovations (e.g., electricity in the study by Hargadon & Douglas, 2001), or facilitate 'legitimacy spillovers' (e.g., Haack, Pfarrer, & Scherer, 2014) by connecting divergent elements in spatial arrangements. Indeed, they suggest that in addition to the various forms of legitimacy more usually captured (see Deephouse et al., Chapter 1), 'aesthetic legitimacy' also exists and needs to be studied. In addition, they encourage us to think of visual and/or material 'repertoires' that, similar to 'vocabularies' (e.g., Jones & Massa, 2013; Höllerer, Jancsary, Meyer, & Vettori, 2013), are characteristic for specific institutional logics, distinct communities, or are part of institutional infrastructures of particular fields. The ability to bridge between institutional domains (Höllerer et al., 2013) and to create boundary objects (e.g., Jones & Massa, 2013) increases the opportunities for organizations to comply with institutional pluralism or deal with complexity and may be an important resource for hybrid organizations or globally oriented organizations. Material artifacts and visual images are important 'tools' for the institutional work of actors. Translation, identity, categorization, and emotionality are further examples of core institutional concepts where materiality and visuality have a substantial impact and where further research into their workings may elicit new mechanisms or change our understandings of existing mechanisms and processes.

Categories

Initially, the study of categories emerged primarily in relation to ecological approaches and in particular the idea of a 'categorical imperative' (Zuckerman, 1999), which is tied tightly to notions of legitimacy. In general terms, categories represent socially constructed labels that differentiate 'objects, people, practices, and even time and space' (Lamont & Molnár, 2002: 168). Categories, from an ecological perspective, are constructed in terms of prototypes comprised of elements, such that possessing 'more (or fewer) of these features or elements [...] makes it possible to categorize an entity more (or less) securely in that category' (Durand & Paolella, 2013: 1101). Categories from this perspective are closely linked to cognitive institutions (see Phillips & Malhotra, Chapter 15), providing taken-for-granted boundaries within which actors, action and objects need to fit in order to gain legitimacy.

As Durand and Boulongne (Chapter 24) point out, a broader, more institutional understanding of categories would emphasize their embeddedness in and connections to social practice. From this perspective, a category's meaning is a function not only of cognitive constructions, but also of the social practices in which a category is embedded (Glynn &

Navis, 2013), practices that 'express and contribute to the social valuation of a category' (Delmestri & Greenwood, 2016; see also Glynn & Navis, 2013; Khaire & Wadhwani, 2010). As Glynn and Navis (2013: 1127) put it: 'categorizing is not purely cognitive, but socio-cultural as well because it is anchored in the context in which categorization occurs'. The social and evaluative nature of categories exposes them as potential objects of institutional work: one of the most famous examples of such work is 'the diamond invention', led by De Beers, which 'convert[ed] tiny crystals of carbon into universally recognized tokens of wealth, power, and romance', created an understanding of diamonds 'not as marketable precious stones but as an inseparable part of courtship and married life', and 'endow[ed] these stones with a sentiment that would inhibit the public from ever reselling them' (Epstein, 1982).

The theorization of categories within the institutional perspective is still unfolding, but recent studies indicate the rich insights that can be generated by doing so (see, for example, Cornelissen, Durand, Fiss, Lammers, & Vaara, 2015; Glynn & Navis, 2013; Kennedy & Fiss, 2013; Ocasio, Loewenstein, & Nigam, 2015; Wry, Lounsbury, & Glynn, 2011).

SOCIETAL CONSEQUENCES

Scott (Chapter 33: 853) compliments institutional theorists for a long-standing willingness 'to take on the tough fundamental questions'. Early studies in particular sought to understand important societal issues and the place of organizations within them. More recently, however, there has been disquiet regarding our distraction from broader issues of the societal consequences. Hardy and Maguire (Chapter 10), for example, conclude that most studies of institutional entrepreneurship ignore 'the power relations that pervade institutional fields', which means that we do not ask the fundamental question of 'Who benefits?'. Munir (2011: 114) rebukes the 'silence of institutional theorists' over the 2008 financial crisis. That silence, he says, implies that 'we have little or nothing to contribute'. Cooper, Ezzamel and Willmott (2008) even argue that institutional theory is unable to rigorously address issues of power, and by implication that it is an inappropriate lens for studying societal issues of this kind. For a response to this polemical assertion, see Lawrence and Buchanan (Chapter 18) and Hudson, Okhuysen and Creed (2015). Others have raised the need to focus upon problems such as climate change, corruption, exploitation, etc. (see Ferraro, Etzion, & Gehman, 2015 for a typical statement of this kind).

This unease within the institutional community is warranted and not restricted to institutional studies (see, for example, Pfeffer, 2016; Guthrie & Durand, 2008). It could be argued, moreover, that attention *has* been given to larger societal issues (see, for example, Schneiberg and Lounsbury's account of social movements, Chapter 11). Nevertheless, by and large, we are guilty as charged – or at least partly so. We have given insufficient attention to understanding some of the major societal consequences of institutional processes. But things are changing. Attention is turning from understanding institutional processes *per se*, to understanding their implications for major societal issues. The dependent variable has shifted from institutional processes towards institutional outcomes.

The rising conversation over the societal consequences of institutional processes is reflected in several new chapters in this volume. David, Sine and Serra (Chapter 25) connect those arrangements to economic development via entrepreneurial initiatives; two chapters (Davis, Chapter 26; and Amis et al., Chapter 27) look in very different ways at the institutional underpinnings of economic inequality; Palmer (Chapter 28) reviews the relationship between organizational wrongdoing (including corruption) and institutional arrangements; Jennings and Hoffman (Chapter 29) review the application of institutional theorizing to the natural environment; Rojas (Chapter 30) and Dobbin and Kalev (Chapter 31) analyse how institutional arrangements construct and differentially affect sociodemographic communities. Moreover, it would be inappropriate to conclude that these chapters are the only ones that speak to institutional consequences. The discussions contained in both in the 'new' and revised chapters reflect this shift in conversation towards societal consequences.

CONCLUSIONS

It is perhaps fitting that the concluding chapters of this edition are reflections by two of the most influential contributors to the institutional approach: John Meyer (Chapter 32) and Dick Scott (Chapter 33). John Meyer stresses the increasing rationalization in the modern stateless but globalized world and urges us not to forget that interested actors are institutionally constituted and not to overlook how 'models of organized actorhood expand, penetrate every social sector and country' (p. 848) – swallowing all other forms of coordinating activities and transforming them into formal organizations. Dick Scott, reviewing the development of the institutional approach to organizations, concludes that the theory is 'flourishing'. But, echoing our point above concerning consequences, he concludes by saying that: 'In a time when some of our most central institutional structures – political bodies, public agencies, financial institutions, corporations – are viewed by growing numbers as either corrupt, ineffective, or both, institutional theorists should be devoting more attention to examining what kinds of actions make them function better and what kinds undermine them (p. 866–867).'

And Where to Now?

Our first suggestion builds upon the above discussion of the need to better understand the consequences of institutions. Future scholars need to ask not about the degree of discretion institutional actors exhibit but how and when discretion is most formidable as a response to institutional constraints and how these variations in discretion wreak havoc or benevolence upon the organizations and societies that have previously taken these volitionally broken shared understandings as historical givens. We have established that institutionalized behaviours allow for discretion (the paradox of embedded agency, the witnessing of institutional work and entrepreneurship). The consequences of this discretion are especially crucial to future research. Such discretion is particularly profound for those on whom it is enacted because it represents the tearing down of practices, behaviours and structures that many may have felt were sacred, unshakeable or unworthy of abandonment. The fallout after discretion that has been successfully exercised is an important source of further study.

One might also go so far as to say that highly institutionalized organizations and contexts should only be interesting to organizational scholars to the extent that their maintenance or violation bring benefit or harm to organizations and societies. Whether highly institutionalized practices are relatively trivial versus consequential (e.g., the custom of a handshake versus the custom of racial segregation) should serve as one apt guidepost for future research in institutional theory. For future institutional analysis to be viewed as relevant, the responsibility will increasingly fall to the institutional scholar to convince us whether a handshake, for example, may carry deeper implications for organizations and the actors that reside within them and whether its discontinuity or withdrawal as an institutional practice should matter to organizational researchers. Institutions *per se* do not matter. It is the depth and profundity of their consequences, coupled with their ubiquity, that make them so indispensable to understanding organizations and organizational behaviour.

This suggested direction of future research is fortified by recent calls to place organizations squarely in the empirical investigation as the dependent variable of institutional studies. As Greenwood, Hinings and Whetten (2014: 1206) argue, 'institutional scholarship has become overly concerned with explaining institutions and institutional processes, notably at the level of the organization field, rather than with using them to explain and understand organizations'. We adhere strongly to this view, believing, as we noted at the outset, that our fundamental focus as organizational researchers surrounds organizing and organizations, their inhabitants and the surrounding communities affected by them. Scholars of institutional theory should, indeed, be more than proud of the strides that they have achieved in understanding the realms of what institutional pressures look like, what forms or categories they take (e.g., logics), how they exhibit predictable processes (e.g., institutional work), how the pillars of institutionalism (Scott, 2004) can be interpreted as a set of institutional typologies, and how institutional phenomena emerge and change over time. We see the need, however, for more studies in which institutional phenomena serve as the independent variable given that a review of the institutional literature indicates that the obverse has tended to characterize institutional theory's direction.

Equally important to the success of future institutional investigation is a scholarly loyalty among institutional theorists to the very roots of institutionalism – stasis and continuity – as influences upon organizations. Framed as a more generalized future recommendation, some scholars have simply asked us not to place an overemphasis on heterogeneity in studying institutionalization.

Although, admittedly, differences, change, or heterogeneity may seem more exciting compared to similarity, stability, resilience, or homogeneity, we want equally to emphasize that *institutional* organization theory ought to make sure not to lose sight of its central claim to study *institutions*. (Meyer & Höllerer, 2014: 1222, emphasis in original)

We believe that the study of stasis as a core characteristic of institutionalism raises the important dark side of institutional influence when it is manifested as latent compliance with harmful norms, unintended failures to recognize the potential evils of taken-for-granted beliefs that defy questioning or resistance, the looming danger of 'nonchoice behaviour' in which, for example, the inferiority of a race or gender is so taken-for-granted that granting votes or other citizen rights do not even occur to the members of the field. The stasis that characterizes some institutionalized behaviours begets cognitive lock-in that is disturbingly deterministic. As institutional theorists, we are only beginning to understand the deep structures of power that often attend stasis and continuity, but far more remains to be investigated. Responding to valid observations that institutional theory does not always rigorously encompass power in their explanations (Clegg, 2010; Meyer & Höllerer, 2014; Munir, 2011, 2015), we see fruitful lines of future inquiry into the deep structures of power (and often elitism) that perpetuate the status quo and its accompanying institutionalized behaviours to the disadvantage of organizations and marginalized participants due to taken-for-granted understandings that have their roots in longstanding historical inequalities that render the assumptions underlying them virtually invisible to those who are oppressed.

The failure to critique or in some cases even recognize unequal power is one of the most fascinating and haunting outcomes of the dark side of institutional theory because it excuses oppression or inequality as simply 'the way we have always done things around here' and is among the most highly validated evidence that something is institutionalized because it is no longer even questioned by even the most well-meaning (if ignorant) participant in the institutionalized process. This phenomenon is among the main reasons why we need to focus more on the 'ideational aspects' of institutionalism, as we note below.

Interestingly, the reverse possibility, that stasis and continuity may supply organizations with particular benefits has received almost no scholarly attention, even though these are the very characteristics that define institutionalization. This may be the point where we need to connect more deeply with the microfoundations of institutions and link stasis to those conditions under which the desires, interests, cognitions and motivations of individuals support either a well-reasoned or, alternatively, oppressive preference for continuity. One avenue is those scholars that advocate linking the literature on learning to the microfoundation of institutional theory to fully understand how and why organizations make the decisions they do to support or reject change (Chandler & Hwang, 2015). To date this area has received scant attention.

Our optimism for the significance of future institutional research rests partly on its catchment area as a topic that has preserved what can only be viewed as a preciously wide array of voices, methodologies, foci and underlying ontologies that a range of scholars continue to bring to the topic of institutionalism. Institutional conferences, colloquia, conversations and publications; cheek-by-jowl, sociologists, ecologists, critical theorists, strategy advocates, sociologists, international business scholars and die-hard positivists, all continue to spawn rich contributions and indictments of the theory. This form of inclusiveness, which is scintillating in its discourse and unsilencing in its depth of analysis, has given us the treasure of both intriguing theory extension and critical indignation at the types of agency, constraints and consequences that institutionalized behaviours create. Why the management field has been so fortunate as to attract such a hugely rich and potentially combative range of arguments and epistemologies in institutional theory is puzzling. We simply hope this rich form of inclusiveness will continue and we like to think it will because the theory is so relevant to so many aspects of organizations, including the important emerging conversations on topics like emotions, materiality and visuality, as well as societal consequences. To this end, we also share Suddaby's (2010: 15) request for more attention to 'the notion of meaning or what Scott (1994) terms the *ideational* aspects of organizations' [emphasis in original]. More emphasis on the subjective ways by which actors experience institutions is needed in order to redress the imbalance (pointed out quite correctly by Suddaby) that there is too often a preponderance of proxies for meaning.

Given our earlier premise in considering the dark side of institutionalism that 'actors themselves often do not understand their own motives for subordinating themselves to social pressure' (Suddaby, 2010: 16), there can be little doubt that institutional theory, in particular, should be taking its part in opening the black box of meanings, identifying those meanings (and their implications for power) rather than depending on proxies or researcher-attributed logics to teach us how meaning systems shape organizations so profoundly.

The elegance of institutional theory is that it holds to account both those agents who perpetuate the status quo (forces for coercive, isomorphic and normative isomorphism, for example) and those who assault the status quo to achieve significant change (institutional workers, institutional entrepreneurs). It is precisely at this nexus of stasis and change that we believe we may be able to learn the most about both institutional stability and change as fundamental source for good, for achieving effectiveness, and for combating harm to individuals and organizations. We feel that institutional theory's inclusiveness of such a wide range of perspectives and methodologies is a celebratory testament to the flexibility and intellectual vigor of those many scholars who investigate this theory's domain. We also hope that this scholarly range is indicative of the theory's true explanatory capacity and applicability to an unusually broad range of organizational phenomena.

Note

1   The first edition is available online.

REFERENCES

Aldrich, H. E., & Fiol, C. M. (1994). Fools rush in? The institutional context of industry creation. *Academy of Management Review, 19*(4), 645–670.

Allard, S. W., & Small, M. L. (2013). Reconsidering the urban disadvantaged: The role of systems, institutions, and organizations. *Annals of the American Academy of Political and Social Science, 647*(1), 6–20.

Ansari, S. M., Fiss, P. C., & Zajac, E. J. (2010). Made to fit: How practices vary as they diffuse. *Academy of Management Review, 35*(1), 67–92.

Ashforth, B. E., Kreiner, G. E., Clark, M. A., & Fugate, M. (2007). Normalizing dirty work: Managerial tactics for countering occupational taint. *Academy of Management Journal, 50*(1), 149–174.

Battilana, J., & Dorado, S. (2010). Building sustainable hybrid organizations: The case of commercial microfinance organizations. *Academy of Management Journal, 53*(6), 1419–1440.

Battilana, J., Leca, B., & Boxenbaum, E. (2009). How actors change institutions: Towards a theory of institutional entrepreneurship. *Academy of Management Annals, 3*(1), 65–107.

Battilana, J., & Lee, M. (2014). Advancing research on hybrid organizing – insights from the study of social enterprises. *Academy of Management Annals, 8*, 397–441.

Baum-Snow, N., & Pavan, R. (2013). Inequality and city size. *Review of Economics and Statistics, 95*(5), 1535–1548.

Berger, P. L., & Luckmann, T. (1967). *The social construction of reality*. London: Allen Lane.

Bitektine, A., & Haack, P. (2015). The 'macro' and the 'micro' of legitimacy: Toward a multilevel theory of the legitimacy process. *Academy of Management Review, 40*(1), 49–75.

Briscoe, F., & Murphy, C. (2012). Sleight of hand? Practice opacity, third-party responses, and the interorganizational diffusion of controversial practices. *Administrative Science Quarterly, 57*(4), 553–584.

Carberry, E. J., & King, B. G. (2012). Defensive practice adoption in the face of organizational stigma:

Impression management and the diffusion of stock option expensing. *Journal of Management Studies, 49*(7), 1137–1167.

Chandler, D., & Hwang, H. (2015). Learning from learning theory: A model of organizational adoption strategies at the micro-foundations of institutional theory. *Journal of Management, 41*(5), 1446–1476.

Clegg, S. (2010). The state, power, and agency: Missing in action in institutional theory?. *Journal of Management Inquiry, 19*(1), 4–13.

Colyvas, J. A., & Jonsson, S. (2011). Ubiquity and legitimacy: Disentangling diffusion and institutionalization. *Sociological Theory, 29*(1), 27–53.

Compagni, A., Mele, V., & Ravasi, D. (2015). How early implementations influence later adoptions of innovation: Social positioning and skill reproduction in the diffusion of robotic surgery. *Academy of Management Journal, 58*(1), 242–278.

Cooper, D. J., Ezzamel, M., & Willmott, H. (2008). Examining 'institutionalization': A critical theoretic perspective. In R. Greenwood, C. Oliver, R. Suddaby, & K. Sahlin-Andersson (Eds.), *The SAGE handbook of organizational institutionalism* (pp. 673–701). London: Sage.

Cornelissen, J. P., Durand, R., Fiss, P. C., Lammers, J. C., & Vaara, E. (2015). Putting communication front and center in institutional theory and analysis. *Academy of Management Review, 40*(1), 10–27.

Creed, W. D., Hudson, B. A., Okhuysen, G. A., & Smith-Crowe, K. (2014). Swimming in a sea of shame: Incorporating emotion into explanations of institutional reproduction and change. *Academy of Management Review, 39*(3), 275–301.

D'Aunno, T., Sutton, R. I., & Price, R. H. (1991). Isomorphism and external support in conflicting institutional environments: A study of drug abuse treatment units. *Academy of Management Journal, 34*, 636–661.

Dacin, M. T., Munir, K., & Tracey, P. (2010). Formal dining at Cambridge colleges: Linking ritual performance and institutional maintenance. *Academy of Management Journal, 53*(6), 1393–1418.

Delmestri, G., & Greenwood, R. (2016). How Cinderella became a queen: Theorizing radical status change. *Administrative Science Quarterly, 61*(4), 507–550.

Desai, V. M. (2011). Mass media and massive failures: Determining organizational efforts to defend field legitimacy following crises. *Academy of Management Journal, 54*(2), 263–278.

Devers, C. E., Dewett, T., Mishina, Y., & Belsito, C. A. (2009). A general theory of organizational stigma. *Organization Science, 20*(1), 154–171.

DiMaggio, P. J. (1988). Interest and agency in institutional theory. In L. G. Zucker (Ed.), *Institutional patterns and organizations* (pp. 3–22). Cambridge, MA: Ballinger.

DiMaggio, P. J., & Powell, W. W. (Eds.) (1991). *The new institutionalism in organizational analysis* (Vol. 17). Chicago, IL: University of Chicago Press.

Durand, R., & Paolella, L. (2013). Category stretching: Reorienting research on categories in strategy, entrepreneurship, and organization theory. *Journal of Management Studies, 50*(6), 1100–1123.

Durand, R., & Vergne, J. P. (2015). Asset divestment as a response to media attacks in stigmatized industries. *Strategic Management Journal, 36*(8), 1205–1223.

Epstein, E. J. (1982). Have you ever tried to sell a diamond? *Atlantic Monthly, 23*.

Ferraro, F., Etzion, D., & Gehman, J. (2015). Tackling grand challenges pragmatically: Robust action revisited. *Organization Studies, 36*, 363–390.

Fligstein, N. (2013). Understanding stability and change in fields. *Research in Organizational Behavior, 33*, 39–51.

Gabbioneta, C., Greenwood, R., Mazzola, P., & Minoja, M. (2013). The influence of the institutional context on corporate illegality. *Accounting, Organizations and Society, 38*(6), 484–504.

Garud, R. (2008). Conferences as venues for the configuration of emerging organizational fields: The case of cochlear implants. *Journal of Management Studies, 45*(6), 1061–1088.

Gehman, J., Trevino, L. K., & Garud, R. (2013). Values work: A process study of the emergence and performance of organizational values practices. *Academy of Management Journal, 56*(1), 84–112.

Glynn, M. A., & Navis, C. (2013). Categories, identities, and cultural classification: Moving beyond a model of categorical constraint. *Journal of Management Studies, 50*(6), 1124–1137.

Gondo, M. B., & Amis, J. M. (2013). Variations in practice adoption: The roles of conscious reflection and discourse. *Academy of Management Review, 38*(2), 229–247.

Greenwood, R., Díaz, A. M., Li, S. X., & Lorente, J. C. (2010). The multiplicity of institutional logics and the heterogeneity of organizational responses. *Organization Science, 21*(2), 521–539.

Greenwood, R., Hinings, C. R., & Whetten, D. (2014). Rethinking institutions and organizations. *Journal of Management Studies, 51*(7), 1206–1220.

Greenwood, R., Raynard, M., Kodeih, F., Micelotta, E. R., & Lounsbury, M. (2011). Institutional complexity and organizational responses. *The Academy of Management Annals, 5*(1), 317–371.

Grougiou, V., Dedoulis, E., & Leventis, S. (2016). Corporate social responsibility reporting and organizational stigma: The case of 'sin' industries. *Journal of Business Research, 69*(2), 905–914.

Guthrie, D., & Durand, R. (2008). Social issues in the study of management. *European Management Review, 5*(3), 137–149.

Haack, P., Pfarrer, M. D., & Scherer, A. G. (2014). Legitimacy-as-feeling: How affect leads to vertical legitimacy spillovers in transnational governance. *Journal of Management Studies, 51*(4), 634–666.

Hallett, T., & Ventresca, M. (2006). Inhabited institutions: Social interactions and organizational forms in Gouldner's patterns of industrial bureaucracy. *Theory and Society, 35*, 213–236.

Hampel, C. E., & Tracey, P. (2016). How organizations move from stigma to legitimacy: The case of Cook's travel agency in Victorian Britain. *Academy of Management Journal*, Advance online publication, doi: 10.5465/amj.2015.0365.

Hardy, C., & Maguire, S. (2010). Discourse, field-configuring events, and change in organizations and institutional fields: Narratives of DDT and the Stockholm Convention. *Academy of Management Journal, 53*(6), 1365–1392.

Hargadon, A. B., & Douglas, Y. (2001). When innovations meet institutions: Edison and the design of the electric light. *Administrative Science Quarterly, 46*(3), 476–501.

Heaphy, E. D. (2013). Repairing breaches with rules: Maintaining institutions in the face of everyday disruptions. *Organization Science, 24*(5), 1291–1315.

Helms, W. S., & Patterson, K. D. (2014). Eliciting acceptance for 'illicit' organizations: The positive implications of stigma for MMA organizations. *Academy of Management Journal, 57*(5), 1453–1484.

Höllerer, M., Jancsary, D., Meyer, R. E., & Vettori, O. (2013). Imageries of corporate social responsibility: Visual recontextualization and field-level meaning. *Research in the Sociology of Organizations, 39*(B), 139–174.

Holm, P. (1995). The dynamics of institutionalization: Transformation processes in Norwegian fisheries. *Administrative Science Quarterly, 40*(3), 398–422.

Hudson, B. A. (2008). Against all odds: A consideration of core-stigmatized organizations. *Academy of Management Review, 33*(1), 252–266.

Hudson, B. A., & Okhuysen, G. A. (2009). Not with a ten-foot pole: Core stigma, stigma transfer, and improbable persistence of men's bathhouses. *Organization Science, 20*(1), 134–153.

Hudson, B. A., Okhuysen, G. A., & Creed, W. D. (2015). Power and institutions: Stones in the road and some yellow bricks. *Journal of Management Inquiry, 24*(3), 233–238.

Hwang, H., & Colyvas, J. A. (2011). Problematizing actors and institutions in institutional work. *Journal of Management Inquiry, 20*(1), 62–66.

Jarzabkowski, P., Matthiesen, J., & Van De Ven, A. (2009). Doing which work? A practice approach to institutional pluralism. In T. B. Lawrence & R. Suddaby (Eds.), *Institutional work: Actors and agency in institutional studies of organizations* (pp. 284–316). Cambridge, UK: Cambridge University Press.

Jepperson, R. L. (1991). Institutions, institutional effects, and institutionalism. In P. J. DiMaggio & W. W. Powell (Eds.), *The new institutionalism in organizational analysis* (pp. 143–163). Chicago, IL: University of Chicago Press.

Jones, C., Boxenbaum, E., & Anthony, C. (2013). The immateriality of material practices in institutional logics. *Research in the Sociology of Organizations, 39*(A), 51–75.

Jones, C., & Massa, F. G. (2013). From novel practice to consecrated exemplar: Unity Temple as a case of institutional evangelizing. *Organization Studies, 34*(8), 1099–1136.

Jonsson, S., Greve, H. R., & Fujiwara-Greve, T. (2009). Undeserved loss: The spread of legitimacy loss to innocent organizations in response to reported corporate deviance. *Administrative Science Quarterly, 54*(2), 195–228.

Kennedy, M. T., & Fiss, P. C. (2013). An ontological turn in categories research: From standards of legitimacy to evidence of actuality. *Journal of Management Studies, 50*(6), 1138–1154.

Khaire, M., & Wadhwani, R. D. (2010). Changing landscapes: The construction of meaning and value in a new market category – modern Indian art. *Academy of Management Journal, 53*(6), 1281–1304.

Lamont, M., & Molnár, V. (2002). The study of boundaries in the social sciences. *Annual Review of Sociology*, 167–195.

Lampel, J., & Meyer, A. D. (2008). Guest editors' introduction: Field-configuring events as structuring mechanisms: How conferences, ceremonies, and trade shows constitute new technologies, industries, and markets. *Journal of Management Studies, 45*(6), 1025–1035.

Lawrence, T. B., & Suddaby, R. (2006). Institutions and institutional work. In S. Clegg (Ed.), *The SAGE handbook of organization studies* (pp. 215–254). Thousand Oaks, CA: Sage.

Lawrence, T. B., Suddaby, R., & Leca, B. (2009). *Institutional work: Actors and agency in institutional studies of organizations*. Cambridge, UK: Cambridge University Press.

Lok, J., & DeRond, M. (2013). On the plasticity of institutions: Containing and restoring practice breakdowns at the Cambridge University Boat Club. *Academy of Management Journal, 56*(1), 185–207.

Marquis, C. (2003). The pressure of the past: Network imprinting in intercorporate communities. *Administrative Science Quarterly, 48*(4), 655–689.

Marquis, C., Glynn, M. A., & Davis, G. F. (2007). Community isomorphism and corporate social action. *Academy of Management Review, 32*(3), 925–945.

Marquis, C., & Lounsbury, M. (2007). Vive la résistance: Competing logics and the consolidation of US community banking. *Academy of Management Journal*, *50*(4), 799–820.

Massa, F., Helms, W., Voronov, M., & Wang, L. (2016). Emotions uncorked: Inspiring evangelism for the emerging practice of cool climate winemaking in Ontario. *Academy of Management Journal*. Advance online publication. doi: 10.5465/amj.2014.0092

McPherson, C. M., & Sauder, M. (2013). Logics in action: managing institutional complexity in a drug court. *Administrative Science Quarterly*, *58*(2), 165–196.

Meyer, J. W. (2008). Reflections on institutional theories of organizations. In R. Greenwood, C. Oliver, R. Suddaby, & K. Sahlin-Andersson (Eds.), *The SAGE handbook of organizational institutionalism*. (pp. 790–811). London: Sage.

Meyer, J. W., & Rowan, B. (1977). Institutionalized organizations: Formal structure as myth and ceremony. *American Journal of Sociology*, *82*(2), 340–363.

Meyer, R. E., & Höllerer, M. A. (2014). Does institutional theory need redirecting? *Journal of Management Studies*, *51*(7), 1221–1223.

Meyer, R. E., & Höllerer, M. A. (2016). Laying a smoke screen: Ambiguity and neutralization as strategic responses to intra-institutional complexity. *Strategic Organization*, *14*(4), 373–406.

Micelotta, E. R., & Washington, M. (2013). Institutions and maintenance: The repair work of Italian professions. *Organization Studies*, *34*(8), 1137–1170.

Moeran, B., & Pedersen, J. S. (Eds.) (2011). *Negotiating values in the creative industries: Fairs, festivals and competitive events*. Cambridge: Cambridge University Press.

Munir, K. A. (2011). Financial crisis 2008–2009: What does the silence of institutional theorists tell us? *Journal of Management Inquiry*, *20*(2), 114–117.

Munir, K. A. (2015). A loss of power in institutional theory. *Journal of Management Inquiry*, *24*(1), 90–92.

Ocasio, W., Loewenstein, J., & Nigam, A. (2015). How streams of communication reproduce and change institutional logics: The role of categories. *Academy of Management Review*, *40*(1), 28–48.

Okhmatovskiy, I., & David, R. J. (2012). Setting your own standards: Internal corporate governance codes as a response to institutional pressure. *Organization Science*, *23*(1), 155–176.

Oliver, C. (1991). Strategic responses to institutional processes. *Academy of Management Review*, *16*(1), 145–179.

Pache, A. C., & Santos, F. (2010). When worlds collide: The internal dynamics of organizational responses to conflicting institutional demands. *Academy of Management Review*, *35*(3) 455–476.

Pache, A. C., & Santos, F. (2013). Inside the hybrid organization: Selective coupling as a response to competing institutional logics. *Academy of Management Journal*, *56*(4), 972–1001.

Peredo, A. M., & Chrisman, J. J. (2006). Toward a theory of community-based enterprise. *Academy of Management Review*, *31*(2), 309–328.

Pfeffer, J. (2016). Why the assholes are winning: Money trumps all. *Journal of Management Studies*, *54*(4), 663–669.

Phillips, D. J., & Zuckerman, E. W. (2001). Middle-status conformity: Theoretical restatement and empirical demonstration in two markets. *American Journal of Sociology*, *107*(2), 379–429.

Powell, W. W., & Colyvas, J. A. (2008). Microfoundations of institutional theory. In R. Greenwood, C. Oliver, R. Suddaby, & K. Sahlin-Andersson (Eds.), *The SAGE handbook of organizational institutionalism* (pp. 276–298). London: Sage.

Quirke, L. (2013). Rogue resistance: Sidestepping isomorphic pressures in a patchy institutional field. *Organization Studies*, *34*(11), 1675–1699.

Schatzki, T.R. (2011). Introduction: Practice theory. In T.R. Schatzki, K. Knorr-Cetina & E. Von Savigny (Eds.), *The practice turn in contemporary theory* (pp. 10–23). Hove: Psychology Press.

Schüssler, E., Rüling, C. C., & Wittneben, B. B. (2014). On melting summits: The limitations of field-configuring events as catalysts of change in transnational climate policy. *Academy of Management Journal*, *57*(1), 140–171.

Scott, W. R. (1994). Conceptualizing organizational fields: Linking organizations and societal systems. In H. U. Derlien, U. Gerhardt & F. W. Scharpf (Eds.), *Systemrationalitat und partialinteresse* (pp. 203–211). Baden Baden, Germany: Nomos Verlagsgesellschaft.

Scott, W. R. (2004). Institutional theory. *Encyclopedia of Social Theory*, *11*, 408–414.

Scott, W. R. (2010). Reflections: The past and future of research on institutions and institutional change. *Journal of Change Management*, *10*(1), 5–21.

Scott, W. R. (2014). *Institutions and organizations: Ideas, interests, and identities*. Los Angeles, CA: Sage.

Selznick, P. (1949). *TVA and the grass roots: A study of politics and organization* (Vol. 3). Berkeley, CA: University of California Press.

Selznick, P. (1957). *Leadership in administration: A sociological interpretation*. Berkeley, CA: University of California Press.

Sharkey, A. (2014). Categories and organizational status: The role of industry status in the response to organizational deviance. *American Journal of Sociology*, *119*(5), 1380–1433.

Shipilov, A. V., Greve, H. R., & Rowley, T. J. (2010). When do interlocks matter? Institutional logics and the diffusion of multiple corporate governance practices. *Academy of Management Journal*, *53*(4), 846–864.

Smets, M., & Jarzabkowski, P. (2013). Reconstructing institutional complexity in practice: A relational model of institutional work and complexity. *Human Relations*, *66*(10), 1279–1309.

Smets, M., Jarzabkowski, P., Burke, G., & Spee, P. (2015). Reinsurance trading in Lloyd's of London, UK: Balancing conflicting-yet-complementary logics in practice. *Academy of Management Journal*, *58*(3), 932–970.

Suchman, M. C. (1995). Managing legitimacy: Strategic and institutional approaches. *Academy of Management Review*, *20*(3), 571–610.

Suddaby, R. (2010). Challenges for institutional theory. *Journal of Management Inquiry*, *19*(1), 14–30.

Swidler, A. (1986). Culture in action: Symbols and strategies. *American Sociological Review*, *51*, 273–286.

Thornton, P. H., Ocasio, W., & Lounsbury, M. (2012). *The institutional logics perspective. A new approach to culture, structure and process*. Oxford: Oxford University Press.

Toubiana, M., Greenwood, R., & Zietsma, C. (forthcoming). Beyond ethos: Outlining an alternate trajectory for emotional competence and investment. *Academy of Management Review*.

Toubiana, M., & Zietsma, C. (2016). The message is on the wall? Emotions, social media and the dynamics of institutional complexity. *Academy of Management Journal*, Advanced online publication. doi: 10.5465/amj.2014.0208.

Tracey, P. and Phillips, N. (2016). Managing the consequences of organizational stigmatization:

Identity work in a social enterprise. *Academy of Management Journal*, *59*(3), 740–765.

Vaccaro, A., & Palazzo, G. (2015). Values against violence: Institutional change in societies dominated by organized crime. *Academy of Management Journal*, *58*(4), 1075–1101.

Vergne, J. P. (2012). Stigmatized categories and public disapproval of organizations: A mixed-methods study of the global arms industry, 1996–2007. *Academy of Management Journal*, *55*(5), 1027–1052.

Voronov, M., & Vince, R. (2012). Integrating emotions into the analysis of institutional work. *Academy of Management Review*, *37*(1), 58–81.

Voronov, M., & Weber, K. (2016). The heart of institutions: Emotional competence and institutional actorhood. *Academy of Management Review*, *41*(3), 456–478.

Weber, K., Davis, G. F., & Lounsbury, M. (2009). Policy as myth and ceremony? The global spread of stock exchanges, 1980–2005. *Academy of Management Journal*, *52*(6), 1319–1347.

Whitman, G., & Cooper, W.H. (2016). Decoupling rape. *Academy of Management Discoveries*, *2*(2), 115–154.

Wry, T., Lounsbury, M., & Glynn, M. A. (2011). Legitimating nascent collective identities: Coordinating cultural entrepreneurship. *Organization Science*, *22*(2), 449–463.

Zietsma, C., & Lawrence, T. B. (2010). Institutional work in the transformation of an organizational field: The interplay of boundary work and practice work. *Administrative Science Quarterly*, *55*(2), 189–221.

Zuckerman, E. W. (1999). The categorical imperative: Securities analysts and the illegitimacy discount. *American Journal of Sociology*, *104*(5), 1398–1438.

PART I

Beginnings (Foundations)

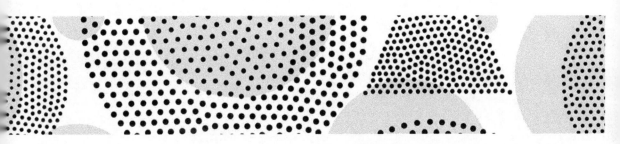

Organizational Legitimacy: Six Key Questions

David L. Deephouse, Jonathan Bundy,
Leigh Plunkett Tost and Mark C. Suchman

INTRODUCTION

Legitimacy is a fundamental concept of organizational institutionalism. It influences how organizations behave and has been shown to affect their performance and survival (Pollock & Rindova, 2003; Singh, Tucker, & House, 1986). As developed in organizational institutionalism the term has spread widely across the social sciences, and because of this, our current understandings of legitimacy and how it is managed are much more nuanced and elaborate than portrayed in early institutional accounts. In this chapter we seek to bring greater clarity and order to the growing and sometimes confusing literature, focusing on the conceptualization of legitimacy itself and how it changes over time.

This chapter builds from the previous edition (Deephouse & Suchman, 2008, available online at www.sage.org/organizational institutionalism/legitimacy). In updating that chapter we reviewed 1299 publications and conference papers that had the string 'legitim' in the title, abstract, or keywords. Reflecting the reach and power of legitimacy, these publications included books and a wide range of journals and across a wide range of disciplines (e.g., communication, political science, public administration, and sociology – not just management). Our goal was to identify broad trends in theory and research, highlight possible theoretical innovations, and suggest important applications for scholars in organizational institutionalism. From this review we identified six central questions around which this chapter is arranged: What is organizational legitimacy? Why does legitimacy matter? Who confers legitimacy, and how? What criteria are used (for making legitimacy evaluations)? and How does legitimacy change over time? These five questions are shown in Figure 1.1. Our final section asks the sixth question, Where do we go from here?, and offers suggestions for future research.

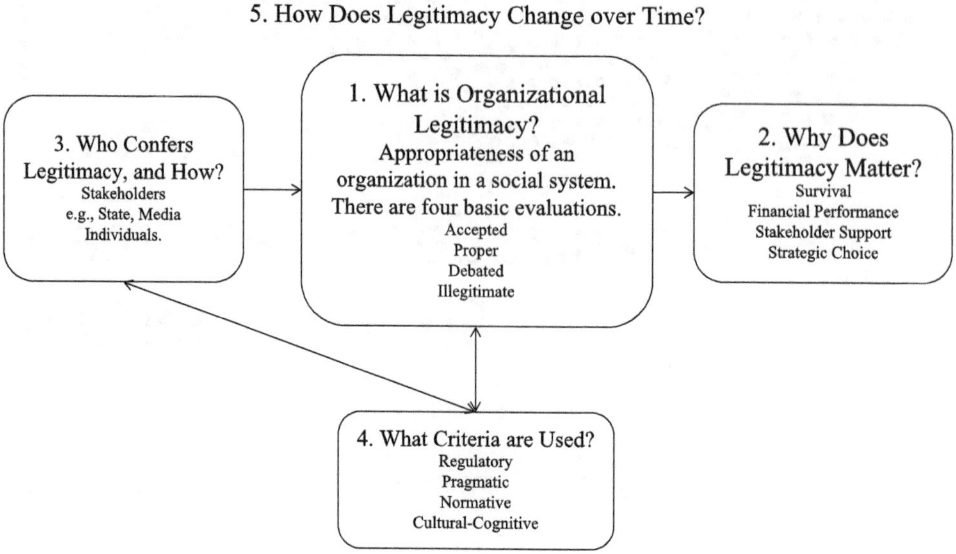

5. How Does Legitimacy Change over Time?

Figure 1.1   Overview of organizational legitimacy

We start with the question of 'What is legitimacy?' because we are concerned about the concept's ossification in recent years. Our review revealed that a large number of papers simply quote Suchman's (1995: 574) definition verbatim before moving on to discuss whatever particular type of legitimacy was studied in the paper. There has, however, been some noteworthy conceptual movement as well. Several authors have followed Deephouse and Suchman's (2008) recommendation that the term 'desirable' in Suchman's (1995) original definition be removed or bracketed to avoid potential confusion with status or reputation, especially if legitimacy is being examined alongside one or more of these other forms of social evaluation. More recently, there have been excellent recent elaborations of the definition of legitimacy (especially Bitektine, 2011 and Tost, 2011). Given these trends, the next section reviews and refines the definition of organizational legitimacy.

Having defined legitimacy, the obvious following question is 'Why does it matter?' We discuss why legitimacy matters, highlighting its many benefits to organizations. Having done so, we examine who confers legitimacy, and how. The short answer is that legitimacy can be granted by a variety of sources, each using a distinct routine. Whether through conscious deliberation or preconscious heuristics and taken-for-granted schemas, each source perceives and assesses legitimacy-relevant information, evaluates organizations using this information, and then endorses or challenges them based on those evaluations. Early treatments of legitimacy considered society as a whole as the relevant social system and viewed the nation-state as the primary source of legitimacy (Meyer & Scott, 1983; Parsons, 1956, 1960). Other early accounts viewed organizations in an organizational field as sources of legitimacy, and legitimacy was conferred by their endorsements, often in the form of formal inter-organizational relationships (Galaskiewicz, 1985; Singh et al., 1986). Subsequent treatments recognized that the media could be a source for society as a whole and for particular social systems within it (Deephouse, 1996; Dowling & Pfeffer, 1975; Lamin & Zaheer, 2012). More recent research has added to this list of legitimacy sources – which now includes individuals, investors, social movements, and other stake-holders (Schneiberg & Lounsbury, Chapter 11 this Volume; Tost, 2011). Researchers, in other words, are beginning to examine in greater depth which and how particular sources evaluate, both actively and passively, the legitimacy of organizations and how sources interact with each other and with subject organizations (Bitektine, 2011; Tost, 2011).

The fourth question that we address considers the criteria used by different sources as they evaluate the legitimacy of organizations and their actions. There are several types of criteria, and these can be useful for identifying different dimensions of legitimacy (e.g., regulatory, pragmatic, etc.). However, appreciation that legitimacy evaluations come from multiple sources highlights the possibility that legitimacy criteria may emerge interactively, in the interplay between the various sources evaluating a given organization and the organization itself. And, given the complexity and pluralism of the institutional environment it is possible that inconsistent prescriptions may arise and that debates may ensue among organizations and stakeholders, often in the public sphere. The variety of sources and their possibly conflicting evaluations inevitably bring to the foreground underlying debates at the micro- and meso-levels that influence macro-level legitimacy (Bitektine & Haack, 2015). Thus, we propose that the criteria used to assess legitimacy should be considered separately from the definition of legitimacy itself.

Our last question turns attention to how legitimacy changes over time. Fundamentally, organizations, sources, and criteria change over time, and organizations must retain legitimacy throughout these changes in order to benefit from it. New organizations gain legitimacy in order to become established (Aldrich & Fiol, 1994; Stinchcombe, 1965). An organization itself, moreover, changes over time as it moves through the organizational life cycle or changes its nature by diversification, intrapreneurship, or divestment. Corporate scandals, those still-too-common transgressions

in organizational action, can challenge legitimacy (Gabbioneta, Greenwood, Mazzola, & Minoja, 2013), sometimes leading to organizational death (e.g., Enron and Arthur Andersen) but mostly leading to lingering concerns about an organization (e.g., BP, ExxonMobil, Union Carbide). Similarly, in the longer term, changing social mores and regulations, often championed by social movements, alter the criteria by which legitimacy is evaluated, challenging those organizations that are slow to adapt (King & Soule, 2007). And at times, some organizations act as institutional entrepreneurs to alter legitimacy standards (Hardy & Maguire, Chapter 10 this Volume).

Thus, it is important when studying legitimacy to reject a static perspective and recognize that legitimacy is a continually unfolding process in which different scenarios can be identified at different points in time. Ashforth and Gibbs (1990) and Suchman (1995) offered tripartite categorizations of such scenarios, focusing on the processes of gaining and maintaining legitimacy, as well as the processes of responding to legitimacy challenges. We revisit and refine their categorizations, adding two additional dimensions to their frameworks that recognize major developments in recent research: *Challenged By* and *Institutionally Innovating*.

We conclude by summarizing the main points of our review and then highlighting some critical areas for future empirical research – thus answering the question Where do we go from here?

WHAT IS ORGANIZATIONAL LEGITIMACY?

Since the dawn of organizational institutionalism in 1977, the conceptualization of legitimacy has displayed substantial elasticity that engendered both productive conceptual evolution and unproductive conceptual stretching (Osigweh, 1989). As a result, the existing literature contains many partially overlapping definitions that have spawned alternate measures and a variety of theoretical propositions. However, this intellectual thicket received some pruning in the last ten years, encouraged by Deephouse and Suchman (2008). In this section, we review research on the definition of legitimacy and offer a refined formulation of the concept.

Legitimacy can be evaluated for a wide range of subjects (Deephouse & Suchman, 2008), including: organizational forms, structures, routines, practices, governance mechanisms, categories, company founders, top management teams, etc. (Bernstein & Cashore, 2007; Black, 2008; Cohen & Dean, 2005; Deeds, Mang, & Frandsen, 2004; Djelic & Sahlin-Andersson, 2006; Durand & Boulongne, Chapter 24 this Volume; Haack, Pfarrer, & Scherer, 2014; Higgins & Gulati, 2003, 2006; Johnson, 2004). We focus on *organizational legitimacy*. However, many of our refinements to the conceptualization of legitimacy of organizations may apply to the legitimacy of other subjects as well.

Most reviewers credit Weber with introducing legitimacy into sociological theory and thus into organization studies (Johnson, Dowd, & Ridgeway, 2006; Ruef & Scott, 1998; Suchman, 1995). He discussed the importance of social practice being oriented to 'maxims' or rules and suggested that legitimacy can result from conformity with both general social norms and formal laws (Weber, 1978). Parsons (1956, 1960) applied Weber's ideas and viewed legitimacy as congruence of an organization with social laws, norms and values.

New institutional theory emerged in 1977 with articles by Meyer and Rowan (1977) and Zucker (1977). Although Zucker only mentioned legitimacy once, Meyer and Rowan made it a central focus, invoking the term at least 43 times in some form. Their summary graphic (1977: 353, figure 2) placed 'legitimacy' and 'resources' together in the same box, and suggested that both of these

survival-enhancing phenomena may result not only from being efficient but also from conforming to institutionalized myths in the organizational environment. Although Meyer and Rowan (1977) did not offer an explicit definition of legitimacy, they presaged many of the dimensions explicated in the mid-1990s by stating that legitimacy can result from suppositions of 'rational effectiveness' (later termed pragmatic legitimacy), 'legal mandates' (regulatory or sociopolitical legitimacy), and 'collectively valued purposes, means, goals, etc.' (normative or moral legitimacy). They also highlighted how legitimacy insulates the organization from external pressures: 'The incorporation of institutionalized elements provides an account (Scott & Lyman, 1968) … that protects the organization from having its conduct questioned. The organization becomes, in a word, legitimate … And legitimacy as accepted subunits of society protects organizations from immediate sanctions for variations in technical performance' (Meyer & Rowan, 1977: 349, 351).

In 1983, Meyer and Scott discussed legitimacy in greater depth and provided this definition:

> We take the view that organizational legitimacy refers to the degree of cultural support for an organization – the extent to which the array of established cultural accounts provide explanations for its existence, functioning, and jurisdiction, and lack or deny alternatives … In such a[n] instance, legitimacy mainly refers to the *adequacy of an organization as theory*. A completely legitimate organization would be one about which no question could be raised. [Every goal, mean, resource, and control system is necessary, specified, complete, and without alternative.] Perfect legitimation is perfect theory, complete (i.e., without uncertainty) and confronted by no alternatives. (p. 201)

One noteworthy feature of this definition is its emphasis on legitimacy's 'cognitive' aspects – explanation, theorization and the incomprehensibility of alternatives.

Some theorizing expanded this formulation, embracing the basic proposition that legitimacy can be conceptualized as the presence or absence of questioning. Along these lines, Hirsch and Andrews (1984: 173–174) considered two types of legitimacy challenges:

> Performance challenges occur when organizations are perceived by relevant actors as having failed to execute the purpose for which they are chartered and claim support. The values they serve are not at issue, but rather their performance in 'delivering the goods' and meeting the goals of their mission are called into serious question ... Value challenges place the organization's mission and legitimacy for existence at issue, regardless of how well it has fulfilled its agreed-upon goals or function. ... [Both] entail fundamental challenges to the legitimacy of an organization's continued existence. Each places the target in an inherently more unstable situation than is addressed in comparative or longitudinal examinations of administrative efficiency.

Pfeffer and Salancik's (1978) foundational statement of resource-dependence theory adopted a similar 'negative definition' of legitimacy, asserting that 'Legitimacy is known more readily when it is absent than when it is present. When activities of an organization are illegitimate, comments and attacks will occur' (1978: 194). Knoke (1985: 222) restated this in the affirmative, defining legitimacy (in the context of political associations and interest groups) as 'the acceptance by the general public and by relevant elite organizations of an association's right to exist and to pursue its affairs in its chosen manner'.

The ability of an organization to pursue its own affairs (Knoke, 1985) resonates with Child's (1972) strategic choice perspective, which holds that legitimate organizations enjoy substantial latitude to choose their structures, products, markets, factors of production, etc. In other words, a legitimate organization has largely unquestioned freedom to pursue its activities (Brown, 1998; Deephouse, 1996).

The year 1995 could be viewed as a pivotal point in the development of legitimacy theory. Scott's book *Institutions and Organizations* (1995: 45) included the following definition:

> Legitimacy is not a commodity to be possessed or exchanged but a condition reflecting cultural alignment, normative support, or consonance with relevant rules or laws.

These three factors generated his cognitive, normative, and regulative bases of legitimacy.

Also in 1995, Suchman published his comprehensive paper 'Managing legitimacy: Strategic and institutional approaches' in the *Academy of Management Review*. He observed that legitimacy was 'an anchorpoint of a vastly expanded theoretical apparatus addressing the normative and cognitive forces that constrain, construct, and empower organizational actors', but he also cautioned that the existing literature provided 'surprisingly fragile conceptual moorings. Many researchers employ the term *legitimacy*, but few define it. Further, most treatments cover only a limited aspect ...' (1995: 571; emphasis in original). To remedy these weaknesses, Suchman (1995: 574) offered the following broad-based definition:

> Legitimacy is a generalized perception or assumption that the actions of an entity are desirable, proper, or appropriate within some socially constructed system of norms, values, beliefs, and definitions.

Within this scope, he delineated two basic perspectives: an institutional view emphasizing how constitutive societal beliefs become embedded in organizations, and a strategic view emphasizing how legitimacy can be managed to help achieve organizational goals.

These two publications raised the visibility of legitimacy, especially among management researchers studying for-profit organizations. Aldrich and Fiol (1994) had just highlighted the importance of legitimacy to entrepreneurs, and within a few years Kostova and Zaheer (1999) integrated legitimacy with multinational enterprises. Meanwhile, at a more theoretical level, Oliver (1997) drew heavily on arguments about legitimacy to integrate institutional theory with the resource-based view of the firm, and Deephouse (1999) developed strategic balance theory to address the tension between differentiating to attain profitability and conforming to attain legitimacy. This period also witnessed a sharp upsurge in references to legitimacy in the wider management literature. And this heightened attention led to a number of significant refinements in the field's understandings of the definition, dimensions, subjects and sources of legitimacy, as well as of the processes, antecedents and consequences of legitimation.

Overall, most research in the last two decades has, in some way, followed Suchman's (1995: 574) definition of legitimacy, evident by the many citations not only in management journals but in journals from other disciplines and languages.[1] Many papers simply repeated the definition verbatim (e.g., Demuijnck & Fasterling, 2016: 678; Fisher, Kotha, & Lahiri, 2016: 383, 386), while others used elements of this definition to build their own similar definitions. Some researchers followed Knoke (1985) and focused on the term 'acceptable' (Castelló, Etter, & Årup Nielsen, 2016; Deephouse & Carter, 2005; Scott, Ruef, Mendel, & Caronna, 2000: 237).

More recently, three works have moved beyond the seminal work of Suchman (1995) and reviewed extensively the definition. First, Deephouse and Suchman (2008) recommended that scholars cease using the term 'desirable' in the Suchman (1995) definition to avoid confusion with status and reputation. Perhaps as a result, this element has become less common as a standalone term in the last decade.

Second, following Wilson (1997), Bitektine (2011: 159) offered an enumerative definition of legitimacy:

The concept of organizational legitimacy covers perceptions of an organization or entire class of organizations, judgment/evaluation based on these perceptions, and behavioral response based on these judgments rendered by media, regulators, and other industry actors (advocacy groups, employees, etc.), who perceive an organization's processes, structures, and outcomes of its activity, its leaders, and its linkages with other social actors and judge the organization either by classifying it into a preexisting (positively evaluated) cognitive category/class or by subjecting it to a thorough sociopolitical evaluation, which is based on the assessment of the overall value of the organization to the individual evaluator (pragmatic legitimacy), his or her social group, or the whole society (moral legitimacy), and through the pattern of interactions with the organization and other social actors, the evaluating actor supports, remains neutral, or sanctions the organization depending on whether the organization provides the benefit(s) prescribed by the prevailing norms and regulations.

The enumerative definition is a helpful summary of legitimacy research that highlights the concept itself and salient antecedents and consequences (especially behavioral ones). It also reminds us that organizational legitimacy is a perception of organizations by stakeholders, and Bitektine (2011; Bitektine & Haack, 2015) expanded on the nature of these perceptions. However, its breadth and intricacy may challenge scholars attempting to operationalize the concept in a consistent and replicable fashion that as would be necessary to generate cumulative scholarly advances.

Third, and also consistent with the idea of legitimacy as perception, Tost (2011) developed a model of legitimacy that integrated institutional and social psychological perspectives. She focused more narrowly than Bitektine (2011), specifically examining legitimacy as perceived by an individual. As such, her definition (2011: 688–689) was concise; legitimacy is: 'the extent to which an entity is appropriate for its social context'.

The use of the word 'appropriate' as the singular adjective in this definition has the benefit of specificity and is also one of the three adjectives in Suchman's (1995) definition.

In sum, conceptual clarity is important in theorizing because it allows scholars to debate, replicate and refine theory (Dubin, 1976; Kaplan, 1964; Osigweh, 1989; Suddaby, 2010). Given our review, we offer the following, concise definition:

Organizational legitimacy is the perceived appropriateness of an organization to a social system in terms of rules, values, norms, and definitions.

Rules, values, norms and definitions reflect regulatory, pragmatic, moral and cultural-cognitive criteria or dimensions for evaluating legitimacy and are elaborated in section 4.

The conceptual range of legitimacy has generated much debate. Deephouse and Suchman (2008) argued that legitimacy is fundamentally dichotomous – an organization is either legitimate or illegitimate. Yet many researchers (ironically including Deephouse (1996)) have operationalized legitimacy using ordinal or continuous measures. We propose a refined view recognizing that there are four basic outcomes of legitimacy evaluations and hence four basic states of organizational legitimacy: accepted, proper, debated and illegitimate. *Accepted* should be used by scholars for more passive evaluations that reflect taken-for-grantedness, whereas *proper* should be used for judgments reached in a more deliberative fashion, as in evaluations of propriety (cf., Bitektine & Haack, 2015; Meyer & Rowan, 1977; Suchman, 1995; Tost, 2011). This distinction reflects that 'accepted' organizations are those that are not, or have not recently been, actively evaluated, whereas organization deemed 'proper' have been. For example, a long-standing food company may be taken-for-granted by consumers and thus accepted by this audience. However, it is also likely subject to regular formal inspections by the food inspection agency of the nation-state. From the perspective of the nation-state, therefore, the company's legitimacy as a purveyor of safe food is periodically monitored. Even if it receives a passing grade, and is thus labeled 'proper', its legitimacy is less secure than if it were more passively accepted.[2] Appropriate is a covering term for both acceptable and proper. The majority of organizations in a social system will be accepted by most stakeholders and viewed as proper by many others. Often, this acceptance will occur because propriety has been validated by another influential stakeholder, such as a state agency, in the recent past (Bitektine & Haack, 2015; Tost, 2011).

Debated reflects the presence of active disagreement within the social system, often among different stakeholders or between dissident stakeholders and the organization (we consider the various sources in the debate below.) Debate often includes questions or challenges by stakeholders about the organization's activities or its fundamental values (Hirsch & Andrews, 1984; Meyer & Scott, 1983). For instance, a food company that has a *Listeria* outbreak in its products may be challenged by stakeholders as to the appropriateness of its processes and perhaps even its values. Debate also occurs when an organization attempts to extend its domain into new areas or engage in institutional entrepreneurship. The example of genetically modified foods illustrates both cases. We view non-dichotomous measures of legitimacy as measuring these debates (e.g., Deephouse, 1996). Finally, *Illegitimate* reflects the assessment by the social system that the organization is inappropriate and that it should be radically reformed or cease to exist.

In addition to specifying these four states of legitimacy, we also conduct a *Gedankenexperiment* of how two stakeholders, an individual (Bitektine & Haack, 2015; Tost, 2011; see Deephouse (2014), for application to the closely related concept of reputation) and the nation-state where the individual resides (Kostova & Zaheer, 1999; Meyer, Boli, Thomas, & Ramirez, 1997; Wu & Salomon, 2016) evaluate the legitimacy of organizations within their boundary; this boundary is cognitive for the individual and geographic for the nation-state. The overwhelming majority of organizations for both stakeholders are legitimate. Most of the time, most stakeholders passively take most organizations for granted. As an individual, imagine the cognitive load if you made propriety legitimacy judgments for every organization you interacted with each day (Tost, 2011), such as the legitimacy of each item of food you buy. Similarly, the nation-state does not have the resources to actively and continually assess the propriety of each organization in its territory. Returning to our preferred terminology, most organizations are accepted, having been deemed proper and appropriate in the past and become taken-for-granted. The group of accepted organizations receives occasional validation by routine regulatory re-approval or unchallenging media mention; the level of scrutiny is so low that it merely reconfirms the inherent passivity of the evaluator. Another group of organizations may be deemed legitimate not because the organizations are passively accepted but because they have recently had their propriety assessed, and the resulting positive evaluations are salient to the evaluator. This could include organizations being actively audited by tax authorities or reassessed by concerned consumers. Smaller groups of organizations are being actively challenged and debated or are deemed illegitimate. We propose that there is a lower percentage of illegitimate organizations from the perspective of the nation-state compared to the individual, given the former's ability to close illegitimate organizations using its police power. Turning to relative numbers of debated organizations, we propose the individual has a lower percentage of organizations in this group because of the cognitive complexity and emotional effort of questioning.

Distinguishing these four states of legitimacy informs the measurement of organizational legitimacy at the level of a social system. We propose that legitimacy is fundamentally bounded. At one boundary, an organization is legitimate because it has demonstrated its appropriateness and goes unchallenged regarding societal rules, norms, values, or meaning systems (Hirsch & Andrews, 1984; Meyer & Scott, 1983; Suchman, 1995; Tost, 2011). Stakeholders within the social system may vary on their evaluations as to whether the organization is proper or accepted, but at the collective level of the social system the organization is appropriate. At the other boundary, illegitimate subjects are those that are so questioned that they are broadly viewed as lacking a right to exist. In between these bounds are subjects whose legitimacy is being questioned or challenged to varying degrees. Thus, as with the concept of 'satisficing' in bounded-rationality theory (Simon, 1976), legitimacy may not be fully dichotomous; however, strong cognitive pressures act to segregate most cases into the two ends of the spectrum and make the middle categories temporary and unstable.

WHY DOES LEGITIMACY MATTER?

Legitimacy matters because it has consequences for organizations. Primary among these consequences, particularly for organizational scholars, is that legitimacy has a clear effect on social and economic exchange: most stakeholders will only engage with legitimate organizations. In other words, no matter what the components of the marketing mix illegitimate organizations might offer, a large number of stakeholders will not transact with entities that are regarded as illegitimate (and indeed, many stakeholders may actively avoid debated organizations as well). Thus, legitimacy affects market access: 'An organization which can convince relevant publics that its competitors are not legitimate can eliminate some competition' (Brown, 1998; Deephouse & Carter, 2005; Pfeffer & Salancik, 1978: 194).

A few examples may be enlightening: One is gambling, divided into state-sanctioned and other forms. Many customers who would happily buy a state lottery ticket would never consider placing wagers with a bookie, even at substantially more favorable odds. Another example is petroleum marketing. Certain stakeholders who are concerned about the environment may refuse to patronize Exxon, Shell and BP in reaction to the *Exxon Valdez*, Brent Spar and Deepwater Horizon incidents, respectively. These concerned stakeholders may outrightly oppose the existence of these companies (and thus deem them illegitimate), or they may actively debate their legitimacy at a given point in time (for example, in reaction to the incidents listed). Regardless of their being deemed outright illegitimate or being debated, the concerned stakeholder will refuse to engage in commerce with the companies. A third example comes from the British Columbia forestry industry, where the province decided to grant timber access only to contractors who could demonstrate acceptable safety standards not only in their own operations but also in the operations of their subcontractors. In announcing the policy, the Provincial Forests Minister nicely captured the importance of legitimacy for market access: 'no one is going to get one of those tenders unless they have safety procedures applied through their operation ... they are a safe company and they meet our standards' (Kennedy, 2006: S3). A final, somewhat different example can be seen in the 1960s aphorism 'no one ever lost their job by buying IBM'. Here, the driving force was less pragmatic efficacy or normative approbation than cognitive taken-for-grantedness: IBM was the 'accepted' standard, and hence beyond reproach; the propriety of any other choice required explicit justification, and risked engendering explicit debate.

The effects of social and economic exchange have been assessed using a variety of outcome measures. Since Meyer and Rowan (1977: 353), institutionalists have argued that legitimacy enhances organizational survival. Supportive evidence abounds: Legitimacy measured by endorsements and inter-organizational relationships increased survival rates among Toronto non-profits (Baum & Oliver, 1991, 1992; Singh et al., 1986), and both managerial and technical legitimacy reduced exit rates for US hospitals (Ruef & Scott, 1998). Organizational ecology, too, has lent support to this claim, finding that legitimacy (measured by the density of firms in an industry) increases survival rates across a wide range of organizational populations, particularly in their early years (Hannan & Carroll, 1992). Some research

has considered how legitimacy could be used to facilitate survival. For instance, Walker, Schlosser and Deephouse (2014) found that solar energy producers leveraged four different dimensions of legitimacy to develop ingenuity strategies to adapt to and modify institutional constraints. One of these ingenuity strategies, forming inter-organizational collaborations, was a key antecedent of subsequent legitimacy. These collaborations were formed rapidly in this embryonic industry, contrary to Aldrich and Fiol's (1994) prediction for emergent industries and firms. These treatments of legitimacy are consistent with Scott's (1995: 45) view that: 'Legitimacy is not a commodity to be possessed or exchanged but a condition reflecting cultural alignment, normative support, or consonance with relevant rules or laws.'

As management scholars in business schools, especially in strategic management, developed an interest in legitimacy over the last 20 years, there have been more efforts to consider how legitimacy contributes directly to financial performance. This reflects the strategic view of legitimacy as a tool for achieving organizational goals and that '[l]egitimacy affects the competition for resources' (Pfeffer & Salancik, 1978: 201; Suchman, 1995). Researchers have developed and tested hypotheses predicting how legitimacy would affect a variety of performance measures, such as the value of initial public offerings (IPOs) (Cohen & Dean, 2005; Deeds et al., 2004; Pollock & Rindova, 2003), stock prices (Lamin & Zaheer, 2012), stock market risk (Bansal & Clelland, 2004), and stakeholder support (Choi & Shepherd, 2005). Legitimacy is also related to measures of financial performance through the legitimating and performance-enhancing impact of isomorphism (Deephouse, 1996; Heugens & Lander, 2009; Meyer & Rowan, 1977).

Early institutionalists proposed that a central benefit of legitimacy was avoiding questions or challenges from society (Hirsch & Andrews, 1984; Meyer & Rowan, 1977: 349, 351; Meyer & Scott, 1983). Legitimate organizations have largely unquestioned freedom to pursue their activities (Knoke, 1985). Consistent with this theme, Brown (1998: 35) stated: 'legitimate status is a *sine qua non* for easy access to resources, unrestricted access to markets, and long term survival'. In contrast, organizations whose legitimacy is debated have less freedom and are closely monitored. For instance, Deephouse (1996) highlighted that regulatory sanctions restricted the ability of banks to make certain types of loans. Thus, legitimacy matters because it enhances strategic choice, a key concern of strategists (Child, 1972).

WHO CONFERS LEGITIMACY, AND HOW?

Legitimacy is conferred by sources using routines. Sources are those internal and external stakeholders who observe organizations (and other legitimacy subjects) and make legitimacy evaluations, whether consciously or not, by comparing organizations to particular criteria or standards (Ruef & Scott, 1998: 880). We use the term 'source' to indicate an entity that makes either explicit or tacit legitimacy judgments about a focal organization. Other commonly used labels include 'audience' and 'evaluator'. The former, however, may connote too much passivity for some situations, while the latter may connote too much assertiveness. With 'source', we favor a more neutral middle ground. To be considered a source of legitimacy, the stakeholder must not only make an assessment about the legitimacy of the subject but that assessment must generalize into a broader view of the overall appropriateness of the organization in its social system. Commonly studied sources include: the state, its regulatory agencies, and its judiciary; the professions; licensing boards; public opinion; and the media (Bitektine & Haack, 2015; Knoke, 1985; Meyer & Scott, 1983; Ruef & Scott, 1998). Each of these sources

employs a distinct set of cognitive processes or routines (Bitektine, 2011; Nelson & Winter, 1982; Tost, 2011) for perceiving and processing legitimacy-relevant information, evaluating organizations using this information, and then communicating these evaluations to others in the social system.

Early legitimacy research focused on the importance of the state. For instance, Dowling and Pfeffer (1975) considered how the American Institute for Foreign Studies sought legitimacy from government officials. Others have recognized that most organizations are routinely evaluated by some agency of the state, such as banks by regulators and non-profits by taxation authorities (Deephouse, 1996; Singh et al., 1986). Even in an era of neo-liberal deregulation and 'private governance', such state actors remain important in conferring legitimacy (Reimann, Ehrgott, Kaufmann, & Carter, 2012).

Another long-studied source is public opinion as a reflection of social values. For example, Selznick (1949) showed that the Tennessee Valley Authority adapted its goals and methods to conform to public opinion. Public opinion can be measured by surveys and by studying public forms of communication (Dowling & Pfeffer, 1975). General-population surveys on the legitimacy of specific organizations are relatively rare, but surveys targeted on specific sectors or practices are more common (Finch, Deephouse, & Varella, 2015). The importance of public opinion and communication was reiterated in the special topic forum on communication, cognition and institutions of the *Academy of Management Review* (Bitektine & Haack, 2015; Cornelissen, Durand, Fiss, Lammers, & Vaara, 2015; Gray, Purdy, & Ansari, 2015).

The media have become a frequently studied source of legitimacy because of the link between media reports and public opinion (Abrahamson & Fairchild, 1999; Bansal & Clelland, 2004; Deeds et al., 2004; Lamertz & Baum, 1998; Lamin & Zaheer, 2012; Pollock & Rindova, 2003). Early work assumed that media reports reflected public opinion in the larger social system (Dowling & Pfeffer, 1975; Hybels, Ryan, & Barley, 1994; Schramm, 1949); however, later research recognized that media also influence public opinion (Deephouse, 1996; McCombs & Shaw, 1972). This duality is particularly noteworthy in the case of 'prestige media', such as *The New York Times* or *The Wall Street Journal*, as prestige media often set the agenda for less prestigious media outlets (Boyle, 2001; Gans, 1979). Prestige media have figured prominently in legitimacy studies (Bansal & Clelland, 2004; Lamin & Zaheer, 2012; Pollock & Rindova, 2003). Media reports are appealing to empirical researchers because many reports are readily available in electronic form. However, if scholars focus on prestige media alone, they may overlook underlying contestation because different types of media are connected to different stakeholders and their different interests (Carter & Deephouse, 1999; Vergne, 2011).

Today, the media world is rapidly changing as the cost of information and communication technologies has dropped. Mass communication is becoming less massive, and many traditional media empires are shrinking. Moreover, organizations, interest groups, social movements and individuals use digital technologies to inform and persuade others regarding the legitimacy of organizations and their practices. One intriguing consequence of this new dynamic is that the true meaning of media 'authority' can be questioned: prestige media can no longer set the tone without substantial input (and potentially pushback) from individuals across the social strata voicing their opinions and concerns on social media. Indeed, one Facebook post or one tweet on Twitter can lead to a legitimacy challenge for even the most well-established organization. Our hope is that future research will produce a better understanding of how the emergence of social media and the big data generated therein reflect and influence organizational legitimacy. For instance, Castelló

et al. (2016) examined how a multinational pharmaceutical corporation developed a networked legitimacy strategy to address institutional complexity by participating in open social media platforms and co-constructing agendas with pluralistic stakeholders.

Social movements and interest groups are also important influences on public opinion and government policy. They actively advocate for the legitimation of certain subjects and the de legitimation of others (Rao, Morrill, & Zald, 2000; Schneiberg & Lounsbury, Chapter 11 this Volume; Strang & Soule, 1998), often by focusing attention on particular criteria such as rights for GLBT people (Creed, Scully, & Austin, 2002; Elsbach & Sutton, 1992) and the natural environment (MacKay & Munro, 2012). Their arguments commonly appear in (social) media and are often adjudicated (albeit not always fully resolved) by regulators, courts, or legislators (Bitektine & Haack, 2015; Edelman & Suchman, 1997; Suddaby & Greenwood, 2005).

Although early experimental work by Zucker (1977) and Elsbach (1994) examined how individuals assessed legitimacy, most research has focused on legitimacy granted by influential sources at a collective level of analysis. Recently, however, two papers in *Academy of Management Review* have rekindled interest in how legitimacy is evaluated at the individual-level of analysis. Bitektine (2011) observed that research usually regarded evaluators as passive audiences; in contrast, he considered them as active information processors. Tost (2011) observed that evaluators are either individuals or comprised of individuals, when they are making decisions in organizations. She drew on the work of Dornbush and Scott (1975) to highlight a useful distinction between *propriety*, i.e., legitimacy assessed by individuals, and *validity*, i.e., legitimacy assessed by collectivities. Bitektine and Haack (2015) subsequently utilized this distinction in developing a multi-level process model linking micro and macro levels. This interest in the individual is consistent with research trying to bridge the micro–macro divide, both in institutional theory (e.g., Powell & Colyvas, 2008; Powell & Rerup, Chapter 12 this Volume; Scott, 1995) and in management more generally (Bamberger, 2008; Molloy, Ployhart, & Wright, 2011; Rousseau, 1985). For instance, Gray et al. (2015) considered the microprocesses and mechanisms that allow for bottom-up institutionalization of meanings and fields. Their theory focused on the role of framing to explain how micro-level interactions between stakeholders instantiate more macro structures of understanding.

Tost (2011) integrated arguments from social psychology and institutional theory to develop a model that focuses specifically on individuals as evaluators but also may inform evaluations of legitimacy by organizations. Her model consists of three stages: judgment formation, judgment use, and judgment reassessment. She argued that judgment formation can occur in one of two psychological 'modes': passive or evaluative. Most commonly, the judgments made by individuals are quick and effortless, characterized by passive acceptance of the legitimacy cues offered in the institutional environment. When legitimacy is contested, in contrast, individuals engage in a more active evaluative process of judging the subject along the various dimensions of legitimacy. Once a judgment is formed, it is used in a passive way until an event or exogenous shock triggers a reassessment of an organization. The judgment reassessment stage is theorized by Tost (2011) to always proceed in the 'evaluative' mode. The nature of the evaluative mode was elaborated in the process model developed by Bitektine and Haack (2015) that also made an important contribution in connecting individual-level and collective-level legitimacy dynamics. Consistent with this trend, empirical work in management has begun to investigate the role of the individual in legitimacy processes (Drori & Honig, 2013; Finch et al., 2015; Huy, Corley, & Kraatz, 2014; Westphal & Deephouse, 2011). Similarly, researchers

in other disciplines such as accounting (Milne & Patten, 2002; O'Dwyer, 2002) and criminology (Tyler, Fagan, & Geller, 2014) have also begun to apply legitimacy theory to the study of individual responses.

Much of the research on individual processes of legitimacy judgments focuses on cognitive efforts to make sense of organizations (cf. Bitektine, 2011; Bitektine & Haack, 2015; Tost, 2011). While this research recognizes the 'passive' processing of taken-for-granted legitimacy judgments (Tost, 2011: 692), including the role of cognitive biases, it has been largely silent on the role of emotions and affect. That is, while research has advanced our understanding of how individuals use reason and logic to make their legitimacy judgments, we know less about how individuals use their emotions and feelings to assess organizations. Parallel to emerging research on emotions and institutions (Lok, Creed, DeJordy, & Voronov, Chapter 22 this Volume; Voronov & Vince, 2012), research has only just begun incorporating emotions to the study of legitimacy. For example, Haack et al. (2014: 636) considered how the general public legitimates transnational governance schemes (such as the United Nations Global Compact) through an intuitive 'legitimacy spillover' process. These authors argued that the legitimation process is primarily 'affective', in that intuiters rely on their positive or negative feelings towards affiliate organizations to infer the legitimacy of transnational governance organizations. Similarly, Huy et al. (2014) show how positive emotional reactions to change initiatives can reduce stakeholders' resistance and enhance their evaluations of such initiatives (and how negative emotional reactions can increase resistance and lead to legitimacy challenges). Future research should build on this emergent stream to consider how cognitive and emotional systems interact to influence legitimacy judgments. However, we do not believe that legitimacy captures stakeholders' emotional evaluations exclusively because legitimacy is defined primarily by a sense of appropriateness, not by favorability or likeability, as in the case of reputation, nor by group membership and honor, as in the case of status (Bundy & Pfarrer, 2015; Deephouse & Suchman, 2008; Pollock, Lee, Jin, & Lashley, 2015).

We conclude our discussion of sources by recommending that researchers closely consider what specific sources of legitimacy *actually do* when evaluating organizations, that is: what routines they use to perceive and assess legitimacy-relevant information, make legitimacy evaluations, and communicate these evaluations. Recent attention to the cognitive processes of the individual has been excellent in this regard. We look for greater depth as scholars study the many influential sources that are themselves organizations – each with its own individual decision-makers, internal processes, and external environments. Such work should draw partly on other disciplines that focus on these sources, such as law, political science, and public administration. For instance, media stories do not appear out of a vacuum but instead are produced by people in organizations, as Hirsch (1977) reminded us forty years ago and has been elaborated by communication scholars (Shoemaker & Reese, 1991, 2014). Indeed, useful insights into the distinctions among prestige media, specialized media and social media might be gained by considering the different mix of field-level standards, organization-level routines and individual-level cognitions in these different contexts. The multi-level interplay of standards, routines and cognitions may be equally salient among non-media legitimacy sources as well. De-legitimation by fraudulent accounting stems from decisions made by accounting firms, as the cases of Enron and Parmalat should remind us (Gabbioneta et al., 2013). And of course, de-legitimation by government prosecution stems from the complex interplay of prescription and discretion within the criminal justice system.

Equally important, though, will be exchanges with other branches of organization theory. After all, many sources of legitimacy are organizations in their own right (Hirsch, 1977; Scott, 1987), and their actions need to be understood in organizational terms. A long-standing tenet of organizational theory from an open systems perspective is that each legitimacy-granting organization is connected to others, both within its sector and across sectors, and mimetic isomorphism often occurs. For instance, media monitor and report decisions by regulators (Deephouse, 1996). Similarly, Gabbioneta et al. (2013) showed that the various stakeholders influence each other – often unwittingly. Thus, the conferring of legitimacy by various sources is as amenable to organizational analysis as is the pursuit of legitimacy by a focal organization.

WHAT CRITERIA ARE USED?

Sources use four basic types of criteria for evaluating organizational legitimacy: regulatory, pragmatic, moral and cultural-cognitive. We acknowledge that these four types have been denoted as 'bases' (Scott, 2014) or 'dimensions' (Suchman, 1995) of legitimacy; we use the term *criteria* because it more clearly evokes the presence of implicit or explicit standards for evaluating organizations, consistent with our refined definition. We also acknowledge that we have positioned the types of criteria outside the box defining legitimacy in Figure 1.1. This choice reflects the fact that the specific criteria are not inherent to the definition of legitimacy, as dimensions would be. Instead, criteria emerge from negotiation and debate among organizations and stakeholders. Moreover, criteria vary depending on the specific source and particular organization under consideration. Nevertheless, we remain consistent with past research by recognizing that different types of legitimacy (e.g., moral legitimacy) result when certain criteria (moral values) are generally agreed upon within the social system.

Our selection of these four types is not surprising, given past research. Meyer and Rowan (1977) discussed the importance of rational effectiveness, legal mandates, and 'collectively valued purposes, means, goals, etc.' – approximately equivalent to our categories of pragmatic, regulatory, and moral criteria, respectively. Aldrich and Fiol (1994: 648) distinguished between cognitive and sociopolitical legitimacy, where 'cognitive legitimation refers to the spread of knowledge about a new venture ... Sociopolitical legitimation refers to the process by which key stakeholders, the general public, key opinion leaders, or government officials accept a venture as appropriate and right, given existing norms and laws' (cf., Bitektine, 2011; Deeds et al., 2004). Suchman (1995) proposed three general categories of 'pragmatic', 'moral' and 'cognitive' legitimacy and then elaborated this into a typology of twelve types. Scott (1995) proposed three bases of legitimacy linked to his three pillars of institutions: regulative, normative and cognitive. Subsequently (2014), he refined cognitive legitimacy to become cultural-cognitive legitimacy, reflecting both taken-for-grantedness and shared understandings. In contrast to Aldrich and Fiol (1994) and Scott (1995, 2014), Archibald (2004) equated sociopolitical legitimacy with regulative legitimacy and combined normative and cognitive legitimacy in a new category called cultural legitimacy. Cultural legitimacy accrues over time in professional and cultural contexts, whereas sociopolitical legitimacy is more directly managed within political contexts. Recently, Tost (2011) drew on conceptualizations of legitimacy from social psychology to introduce the relational category, reflecting the effect of an organization on an individual's identity and self-worth. This category may become more important, especially as institutionalists incorporate identity and identification into their work (Brown & Toyoki, 2013; Canivez, 2010; Drori, Honig, & Sheaffer, 2009); however, it is hard to say at present whether relational considerations will prove

to be a distinct fifth type of criteria or an overarching causal process through which any of the four core types can be applied.

More specific criteria related to particular types of organizations or contexts can be situated within these four general categories of criteria. For instance, Bansal and Clelland (2004) developed the concept of corporate environmental legitimacy, reflecting regulatory, moral and cultural-cognitive appropriateness in terms of a particular set of environmental practices and norms. Vergne (2011) focused on contextually and phenomenologically derived dimensions in developing his measure of legitimacy, including criteria focused on environmental and competitive norms.

Although we recognize that the categorizing of legitimacy criteria is important for theorizing and empirical research, we also recognize that such categories are analytic concepts, not fully separable empirical phenomena. Thus, we urge legitimacy researchers not to become fixated on defending the purity and independence of the different types. Early in the development of organizational institutionalism, Meyer and Scott (1983: 214) observed that 'the literature on legitimacy tends to distinguish sharply between its cognitive and normative aspects. This may overemphasize Western dualism.' This critique may become more relevant as globalization proceeds. Scott (1995: 143–144; cf., Tost, 2011) wrote that 'distinctions ... among [the three pillars of institutions] are analytical in the sense that concrete institutional arrangements will be found to combine regulative, normative, and cognitive processes together in varying amounts'. Thus, any act of legitimation may affect a number of criteria. For instance, certification contests in the early days of auto making provided both normative justification and cognitive validation for the young industry – as well as pragmatic promotion for those fortunate firms that could demonstrate superior capabilities (Rao, 1994). Many issues subject to regulation, such as food safety (Durant & Legge,

2006; Hemphill & Banerjee, 2015) and securities fraud (Gabbioneta et al., 2013), also have pragmatic, moral, cultural-cognitive and perhaps even relational implications.

HOW DOES LEGITIMACY CHANGE OVER TIME?

The preceding sections of this chapter have painted a general picture of legitimacy as a state of acceptance, propriety, debate or rejection at a particular point in time. We next turn to how legitimacy changes over time as organizations, sources, and criteria change over time.

Legitimation was defined in early research as the process by which an organization demonstrates its legitimacy to stakeholders (Maurer, 1971). Early work highlighted how organizations sought to enhance their legitimacy by donating to charities, forming director interlocks, and obtaining external endorsements (Dowling & Pfeffer, 1975; Galaskiewicz, 1985; Pfeffer & Salancik, 1978). This organization-centered view persisted in what Suchman (1995) labeled the 'strategic' approach to legitimacy research. However, an open-systems perspective recognizes that stakeholders are potentially agentic and legitimacy is often negotiated (Ashforth & Gibbs, 1990; Bitektine, 2011; Pfeffer & Salancik, 1978). Within this open-systems view, it is generally recognized that different legitimacy sources have different criteria that sometimes conflict (Fisher et al., 2016; Ruef & Scott, 1998). Thus, we extend our discussion to include stakeholders' actions to endorse or contest an organization's legitimacy as well as the organization's actions to defend itself. We begin this section by proposing five legitimation scenarios. We then highlight the symbolic and substantive tools used for managing legitimacy. Throughout, we observe that certain scenarios and tools differ systematically based on the type of organization or organizational form.

Managing legitimacy is important at all times, but different times call for different types of legitimation activities. Ashforth and Gibbs (1990: 182) proposed three 'purpose(s) of legitimation': Extending, Maintaining and Defending Legitimacy. Suchman (1995: 585) offered a similar framework of three 'challenges of legitimacy management': Gaining, Maintaining and Repairing Legitimacy. Rather than purposes or challenges, we propose the use of the term *Scenarios* because it better reflects evolving situations that can be viewed both from the organization's and from the stakeholders' perspective; also, scenarios are commonly used by planners as alternative future states (Cornelius, Van De Putte, & Romani, 2005; Hodgkinson & Healey, 2008; Schoemaker, 1993); nevertheless, we do follow prior work and take the perspective of the organization when selecting names for the scenarios. We add two categories of scenario to the earlier three-fold typologies: *Challenged By* and *Institutionally Innovating* (discussed below).

We prefer *Gaining* to Extending because before new organizations can extend legitimacy, they need to gain it in the first place – or risk falling victim to the liabilities of newness (Singh et al., 1986; Stinchcombe, 1965). Moreover, existing organizations can gain legitimacy for new activities in a variety of ways, not only by extending the umbrella of the organization's prior legitimacy to cover a new activity. Thus, gaining is more a comprehensive term. Gaining legitimacy occurs in a stable institutional environment, so that the organization must demonstrate its propriety and fit within pre-existing regulatory and pragmatic standards, moral values, and cultural-cognitive meaning systems. Based on the pioneering work of Aldrich and Fiol (1994), much research has examined how new entrepreneurial organizations gain legitimacy (Martens, Jennings, & Jennings, 2007; Zimmerman & Zeitz, 2002). As Bitektine (2011: 165) noted, entrepreneurs often accomplish this task by 'presenting their innovation broadly enough to encompass existing knowledge and to invoke familiar cognitive categories.' Importantly, we separate the scenario of gaining legitimacy, via displaying consistency with familiar norms, from the scenario of institutional innovating, which involves a more radical attempt to shift and challenge such norms. We detail this latter scenario shortly.

We continue with the term *Maintaining*. Maintaining involves routinized attention to reinforcing stakeholders' sense that the organization continues to adhere to standards of appropriateness and as reflected in various types of criteria. There is very little research on how organizations actively maintain legitimacy because stability does not create much theoretical drama or require much active managerial intervention (Locke & Golden-Biddle, 1997). However, organizations that maintain legitimacy are commonly used in quantitative studies of legitimacy over time (Deephouse, 1996). Research on ethics and compliance programs also often consider processes of maintaining legitimacy, often in the context of decoupling (Weaver, Trevino, & Cochran, 1999). Indeed, MacLean and Behnam (2010) considered the dangers of decoupling compliance, suggesting that decoupling can lead to organizational misconduct and challenges from stakeholders.

The first new scenario that we propose is called *Challenged By*. This scenario brings to the foreground the existence and point of view of multiple stakeholders (recognizing heterogeneous sources) who may question legitimacy on multiple grounds (recognizing heterogeneous criteria). Thus, we refine the more generic term 'challenges' to legitimacy (Hirsch & Andrews, 1984) by recognizing that such challenges may be heterogeneous. In doing so, we formally link performance challenges to regulatory and pragmatic legitimacy and value challenges to moral legitimacy. Further, we specify a new type of challenge, challenges to meanings, which undermine the cultural-cognitive legitimacy of a subject.

By separating the Challenged By scenario from the Responding scenario (detailed below), we seek to call attention to the fact that challenges based on norms or values may take distinctly different forms and involve unique processes compared to challenges based on performance or pragmatic utility. As Tost (2011) highlighted in her model of the legitimacy judgment process, instrumental evaluations and reassessments are distinct from relational or moral evaluations and reassessments. Similarly, challenges by different stakeholders also take unique forms (e.g., regulatory challenges from the state versus challenges from aggravated stakeholders). Others studying reputation and other social evaluations have also recognized these distinctions in terms of multiple stakeholders making multiple evaluations using multiple criteria (e.g., Bundy & Pfarrer, 2015; Mishina, Block, & Mannor, 2012). Thus, we seek to recognize the multiplicity inherent in legitimacy challenges by recognizing them as a unique part of the legitimation process, separate from the responses used to manage these challenges.

We also propose the term *Responding* rather than Defending or Repairing. We assume that challenges to legitimacy are a form of institutional pressure to which an organization can respond, and possible responses vary on the reactive/proactive dimension (Oliver, 1991). In contrast, Suchman (1995: 597) stated that repairing 'generally represents a reactive response to an unforeseen crisis', and Ashforth and Gibbs (1990: 182, Table 1) summarized defending legitimacy as reactive. Much research focuses on how organizations respond to challenges to their legitimacy. For instance, Pavlovich, Sinha and Rodrigues (2016) found that moral legitimacy was especially important for the Fonterra–Sanlu international joint venture in the scandal about its milk in China. Sinha, Daellenbach and Bednarek (2015) examined the responses of Air New Zealand to the demands of diverse stakeholders during its acquisition of Ansett Australia. Useful approaches for managing legitimacy in the face of inconsistent criteria have been identified, such as decoupling (Boxenbaum &

Jonsson, Chapter 3 this Volume) and hybridization (Battilana, Besharov, & Mitzinneck, Chapter 5 this Volume). Finally, Lamin and Zaheer (2012) considered different forms of impression management and the effect on legitimacy for different evaluators, including Wall Street and Main Street audiences. They found that these audiences responded differently to different impression management tactics, highlighting the need to consider the challenge and the response as separate scenarios.

Overall, effective responses may depend less on conforming to any single set of expectations than on determining which sources care about which criteria and constructing a viable bundle of reassurances that satisfy enough sources on enough criteria enough of the time. Performance challenges, for example, may require reassurances of organizational efficacy in order to sustain regulatory and pragmatic legitimacy, whereas value challenges require reassurances of good character and social responsibility in order to sustain moral legitimacy. Finally, challenges to meaning may require reassurances of comprehensibility, such as sense-making (Weick, 2001) or narrative emplotment (Downing, 2005), to sustain cultural-cognitive legitimacy.

We call our second new scenario *Institutionally Innovating*. This scenario focuses on the strategic creation of new institutions, frequently by institutional entrepreneurs (DiMaggio, 1988; Hardy & Maguire, Chapter 10 this Volume). We separate this from gaining legitimacy because the actions required to theorize and create new institutional rules, norms, and meaning systems in the institutional environment are qualitatively different from the actions required to demonstrate the appropriateness of a new instance of an already familiar form within a stable institutional regime (Aldrich & Fiol, 1994; Garud, Jain, & Kumaraswamy, 2002; Lounsbury & Glynn, 2001; Rao, 1994; Strang & Meyer, 1993). For example, Greenwood, Suddaby and Hinings (2002) provided an

early investigation of the process involved in institutional entrepreneurship. They induced a six-stage model of institutional change in highly professionalized fields. Moral and pragmatic legitimacies were theorized in stages four and five, and cognitive legitimacy occurred in stage six. Voronov, DeClerq and Hinings (2013) studied the wine industry in the Niagara peninsula for five years and found several different paths by which wineries de-legitimated prevailing wine-making practices that produced inexpensive wines and replaced them with new practices that adapted Old World techniques to the local context. Turcan and Fraser (2016) examined an international new venture in Moldova over an eleven-year period and developed a process model of new venture and new industry legitimacy in emerging markets.

Table 1.1 summarizes this discussion. It builds from Table 1 of Suchman (1995) using our revised definition of legitimacy, our types of criteria, and our expanded view of scenarios.

Given these scenarios, what types of tools do organizations typically use to manage legitimacy? Ashforth and Gibbs (1990) highlighted two basic types of legitimacy work and a total of ten categories of action. Symbolic management, with six actions, represents the efforts and changes that transform 'the *meaning* of acts' (1990: 180; emphasis in original) to make them appear consistent with social values and expectations. Substantive management, with four actions, represents the 'real, material changes in organizational goals, structures, and processes or socially institutionalized practices' (1990: 178). We consider both in turn.

Most legitimation research has examined how texts, generally construed, have been used in debates on legitimacy by both organizations and stakeholders. The examination of texts is often classified as symbolic management broadly, and one specific approach is impression management. In an early example, Elsbach (1994) found that verbal accounts acknowledging failings or referring

Table 1.1   Managing organizational legitimacy over time

Concept \ Scenario	Gaining	Maintaining	Challenged By	Responding	Institutionally Innovating
Legitimacy	Demonstrate propriety	Remain acceptable or taken-for-granted	Challenges of appropriateness	Demonstrate appropriateness	Create new definitions of propriety
Regulatory legitimacy	Apply and meet standards	Satisfy routine monitoring	Performance challenges	Verify performance *vis-à-vis* standards	Change regulations
Pragmatic legitimacy	Demonstrate adequate performance	Avoid poor performance	Performance challenges	Affirm adequate performance	Change performance criteria
Moral legitimacy	Show fit with social values	Don't violate social values	Value challenges	Affirm fit with social values	Change social values
Cultural-cognitive legitimacy	Conform to meaning systems	Don't violate meaning systems	Meaning challenges	Affirm fit with meaning systems	Change meaning systems

to the institutional environment are superior to accounts denying responsibility or referring to the technical environment. Lamin and Zaheer (2012) examined how organizations use text-based response strategies to defend themselves in the wake of negative events, specifically accusations of sweatshop labour. They found that highly defensive strategies hindered the recovery of legitimacy with the general public as measured by media reports. A recent impression management study by van Halderen, Bhatt, Berens, Brown, & van Riel (2016) examined the tactics used by BP and ExxonMobil to maintain corporate environmental legitimacy in the context of the grand challenge of climate change (Ferraro, Etzion, & Gehman, 2015; Whiteman, Hope, & Wadhams, 2013). Research in the field of public relations and communication has also considered the interplay of symbolic management and legitimacy (cf. Sellnow & Seeger, 2013).

Another approach to studying texts is discourse analysis, which includes individual speech acts ('little d' discourse) and hegemonic meaning systems ('Big D' discourse) (Alvesson & Karreman, 2000; Gee, 2011; Phillips, Lawrence, & Hardy, 2004). For instance, Suddaby and Greenwood (2005)

examined the discursive struggle between proponents and opponents of multidisciplinary partnerships in professional services. Vaara, Tienari and Laurila (2006) identified five 'discursive legitimation' strategies: normalization, authorization, rationalization, moralization and narrativization. Joutsenvirta (2012) identified five legitimation strategies regarding executive pay at a Finnish energy company using critical discourse analysis of media texts.

Overall, researchers have applied many different approaches to studying texts, including: rhetoric, both old and new (Erkama & Vaara, 2010; Green, 2004; Harmon, Green, & Goodnight, 2015; Sillince & Brown, 2009); narrative analysis (Brown, 1998; Golant & Sillince, 2007); discourse analysis, sometimes critical (Phillips et al., 2004; Vaara & Tienari, 2002); and framing (Benford & Snow, 2000; Cornelissen, Holt, & Zundel, 2011). These approaches and their methods typically remain in disciplinary silos with different assumptions of agency, level of analysis, etc., but empirically each typically connects a set of texts to legitimacy.

The prevalence of research on legitimation by words is hardly surprising, given the prevalence of textual data sources; however, legitimation by substantive actions, such as role performance and isomorphism, is arguably more important (Ashforth & Gibbs, 1990). One common form of substantive legitimacy management involves securing regulatory approvals, such as for new pharmaceuticals and restaurants. Rao (1994) demonstrated how the ability of early automobiles to complete and win endurance contests built legitimacy for the winning companies and the auto industry as a whole. These accomplishments demonstrate pragmatic legitimacy and are communicated to others in the social system. Deephouse (1996) showed that both isomorphism and financial performance increased normative and regulatory legitimacy within a population of competing commercial banks. Westphal, Gulati and Shortell (1997) found that conformity in TQM practices enhanced the legitimacy of hospitals. Similarly, corporate social responsibility (CSR) has been used as a tool to gain legitimacy (Beddewela & Fairbrass, 2016). Individuals and organizations have gained legitimacy using ingenious actions, often unconventional ones, in places like Silicon Valley and Southwestern Ontario (Kannan-Narasimhan, 2014; Walker et al., 2014). Divestment by companies from the global arms industry is another substantive example of how companies responded to legitimacy challenges (Durand & Vergne, 2015).

Finally, we recognize that managing legitimacy also depends on the type of organization in question. Early empirical work focused on schools and public sector organizations (Hannigan & Kueneman, 1977; Kamens, 1977; Meyer & Rowan, 1977; Rowan, 1982), but scholars later applied legitimacy to non-profits, businesses, hospitals, etc. (Carroll & Hannan, 1989; Deephouse, 1996; Ruef & Scott, 1998; Singh et al., 1986). There are marked differences between organizations in different societal sectors in terms of the sources who evaluate legitimacy, the criteria used, and the outcomes that result.

Within a societal sector, the specific organizational population is also important.

Following Hannan and Freeman (1977: 935–936), an organizational population consists of all organizations within a boundary sharing an organizational form; organizational form is 'a blueprint for organizational action', including formal structure, patterns of action, and the normative order recognized by organizational members and the relevant societal sector. Thus, within the financial sector, non-profit, member-owned credit unions and for-profit, investor-owned banks have different legitimacy processes involving different stakeholders (Barron, 1998; Haveman & Rao, 1997). And as implied above in our discussion of entrepreneurs gaining legitimacy, the stage of the organization in its life cycle is also important. Thus, there are distinct differences between new organizations and established organizations (Aldrich & Fiol, 1994; Fisher et al., 2016) and between established organizations and organizations encountering the liabilities of senescence (Barron, West, & Hannan, 1994).

CONCLUSION: WHERE DO WE GO FROM HERE?

Conceptual clarity has been a central concern of the social sciences for decades (Dubin, 1976; Kaplan, 1964; Osigweh, 1989; Suddaby, 2010). Our review has found considerable convergence in the last twenty years around the definition of legitimacy proposed by Suchman (1995). However, we wonder if such convergence is becoming formulaic and limiting the development of the legitimacy concept in the context of other social evaluations like status and reputation (Deephouse & Suchman, 2008) – concepts should evolve as they are used and juxtaposed with other concepts in the course of research (Kaplan, 1964; Wright, 1985). Thus, we applaud the many efforts to distinguish different social evaluations and the increased attention to sources of legitimacy at different levels and from different disciplines, ranging from individuals (Bitektine, 2011; Tost, 2011) in management to societal systems in sociology (Meyer & Rowan, 1977).

In this context, we have continued the work of Deephouse and Suchman (2008) in refining the legitimacy concept and making recommendations for future research. We first focused the definition on the concept of appropriateness and then offered four basic states of legitimacy: accepted, proper, debated, and illegitimate. We also advocated strongly for more in-depth research on the variety of sources and the variety of criteria in play for different types of organizations. We then refined the conceptualization of different legitimation scenarios (Ashforth & Gibbs, 1990; Suchman, 1995) by integrating them with challenges to legitimacy (Hirsch & Andrews, 1984) and by specifying institutional innovation as a separate scenario.

Before closing, we offer several recommendations for future research. First, in the prior section we listed many approaches to studying texts as part of symbolic legitimation (e.g., rhetoric, impression management, discourse analysis, etc.), and each of them has a large theoretical and methodological tradition. Perhaps our most ambitious recommendation is for future research to critically review these different approaches to verbal legitimation tactics with the goal of integrating and consolidating them in order to create cumulative knowledge rather than retaining theoretical autonomy and novelty (Barley, 2016). For instance, the same set of texts should be examined from multiple approaches (Van de Ven, 2007) – perhaps by a collaborative team representing several traditions, as demonstrated by the collaboration of Erez and Latham in goal-setting theory (Latham, Erez, & Locke, 1988). Organizational institutionalists could take inspiration from research in communication, where the *Journal of Communication* published a special issue comparing three theories of media effects: framing, agenda-setting and priming (Scheufele & Tewksbury, 2007). Bedeian (2004) observed that many

so-called novel theories overlook long histories of research both within and outside of management theory. The disciplines of communication, political science and public relations also have a long tradition of research on convincing by word, such as by Lippmann, Lasswell and others on propaganda, 'the management of collective attitudes by manipulation of significant symbols' (Lasswell, 1927: 627; Lasswell, Leites, & Associates, 1965; Lippmann, 1922), especially during the critical period of World War II. These fields have much to offer organizational scholars who wish to understand similar activities in other spheres.

Our second recommendation also considers integrating two research streams that have strong theoretical and methodological traditions: 'substantive management' and 'symbolic management' (Ashforth & Gibbs, 1990). While a small number of studies have combined the two (cf. Pfarrer Decelles, Smith, & Taylor, 2008; Zavyalova, Pfarrer, Reger & Shapiro, 2012), most studies focus only on one or the other. This has created a substantial gap in our knowledge, and we strongly encourage future scholars to consider how symbolic and substantive efforts interact with one another to influence legitimacy judgments. Indeed, many have criticized the symbolic approach, suggesting it acts as a form of deception or distraction from substantive issues of legitimacy (cf. Bundy & Pfarrer, 2015). However, we see value in both approaches, particularly when considered in combination. For example, symbolic management in the form of apologies is likely best received when combined with substantive efforts at repentance and restitution (Pfarrer et al., 2008). Moreover, we observe that some substantive actions also have symbolic impact, such as Johnson & Johnson's speedy recall of all Tylenol in 1982. However, and particularly within empirical research, we see only limited attempts to consider this combined management approach.

Third, there are several emerging empirical settings that should be fertile ground for growing research on legitimacy. Although the nation-state has historically been central to legitimacy, substitutes for state regulation have emerged, such as transnational governance (Djelic & Sahlin-Andersson, 2006; Haack et al., 2014; Höllerer, Walgenbach, & Drori, Chapter 8 this Volume; Scott, Chapter 33 this Volume) and private self-regulation (Bernstein & Cashore, 2007; Cashore, Auld, & Newsom, 2004; Prakash & Potoski, 2006). These new governance mechanisms are worthy of further study.

Future research could also examine how the major changes in digital technology affect legitimation. Many new organizations and practices have emerged, such as AirBnB, BitCoin, and Uber, and the legitimation efforts of these 'new economy' organizations have been hotly contested. These could be valuable settings to study; for example, Vergne has recently established a research center to study crypto-currencies (cf., Dodgson, Gann, Wladawsky-Berger, Sultan, & George, 2015). However, research should not forget the early work on ACT UP and Earth First! (Elsbach & Sutton, 1992) in showing how pragmatic legitimacy with certain legitimacy sources preceded the validation by the media, government regulators, and the judiciary during periods of institutional change when subjects are gaining legitimacy (Bitektine & Haack, 2015; Suchman, 1995). Digital technology is also giving sources new ways to influence legitimacy (Castelló et al., 2016). The importance of social media for legitimation is also clearly worthy of further work.

Two other empirical settings may also prove fertile for advancing legitimacy research. Much past research has used differences among the 50 United States to examine legitimacy and diffusion (Tolbert & Zucker, 1983). Currently under consideration are legalized marijuana sales and doctor-assisted suicide. These topics may be useful places to develop and replicate research on legitimacy. Finally, natural disasters, epidemics and wars generate large-scale crises that require multi-sectoral, transnational responses, and these may increase if anthropogenic global warming (AGW) continues as predicted by 97% of scientific reports in 1991–2011 taking a position on AGW (Cook et al., 2013; Cook et al., 2016). These responses will need to develop legitimacy in order to succeed (Christensen, Lægreid, & Rykkja, 2016).

Our review also has implications for the research methods used to study legitimacy. Given the bounded nature of legitimacy, limited dependent variable models may be more appropriate for statistical hypothesis testing. For example, Deephouse (1996) used censored regression (Tobit) to test a variable ranging from no challenging media reports to all challenging media reports and logistic regression to test categorical regulatory ratings. There is also renewed interest in experimental research. For example, in 2012 Bitektine and Haack started a series of workshops about using experimental methods in institutional theory, first at the Academy of Management annual meeting and then at the European Group for Organization Studies colloquium. Experimental studies of legitimacy have now appeared in many journals, such as Neto and Mullet's (2014) study of the legitimacy of executive pay among Portuguese citizens, and Weisburd, Hinkle, Famega and Ready's (2011) study of the legitimacy of policing. There is also much experimental research about ethical and moral judgments that are fundamental components of moral legitimacy (Cullen, Parboteeah, & Hoegl, 2004; Moore & Gino, 2013; Tyler, 2006). Such experimental studies improve our understanding of the microfoundations of legitimacy, and we expect and hope to see many more in the coming years.

From research methods we turn to research designs, and we recommend that researchers be more ambitious! More than two decades after Suchman's 1995 review of legitimacy, we still find, as he concluded then, that 'most treatments cover only a limited aspect' (1995: 571) of this complex but crucial subject. There are specific combinations of sources and criteria that apply to specific types of organizations under specific circumstances. Most empirical research, be it qualitative or quantitative, examines only one or at most two combinations (e.g., Wall Street and Main Street, in Lamin & Zaheer, 2012; Niagara wineries, in Voronov et al., 2013). There are some exemplary efforts to capture the complexity of legitimacy in the context of an evolving institutional field, such as Scott et al.'s (2000) examination of healthcare organizations and Wedlin's (2006) examination of European business schools. However, these works are books. The advancement of legitimacy research is being slowed by the norms of business schools in which many legitimacy researchers now work. Rewards at business schools clearly favor journal publications over longer works, leading to what Greenwood (2016) called 'salami slicing' research that impedes the development of comprehensive explanations for phenomena that are too complex to be explicated in the space of 30–40 pages. Hinings (2006) has advocated the pursuit of ambitious, large-scale research programs, to reach new heights in our understanding of complex organizational phenomena. Legitimacy is clearly one such complex phenomenon that would benefit from a large-scale collaborative research program involving the integrated efforts of many people over many years. Can such concerted endeavors become legitimate again?

Notes

1   As of June 15, 2016, this is the second most cited paper in *Academy of Management Review*.
2   We leave aside, for now, the question of how actively any given regulator actually assesses the propriety of any given target organization. In practice, it is certainly possible that some prominent and reputable organizations receive only pro forma regulatory scrutiny, making even the regulatory imprimatur more a matter of taken-for-granted acceptance than of carefully assessed propriety.

REFERENCES

Abrahamson, E., & Fairchild, G. (1999). Management fashion: Lifecycles, triggers, and collective learning processes. *Administrative Science Quarterly, 44*: 708–740.

Aldrich, H. E., & Fiol, C. M. (1994). Fools rush in? The institutional context of industry creation. *Academy of Management Review, 19*: 645–670.

Alvesson, M., & Karreman, D. (2000). Varieties of discourse: On the study of organizations through discourse analysis. *Human Relations, 53*: 1125–1149.

Archibald, M. E. (2004). Between isomorphism and market partitioning: How organizational competencies and resources foster cultural and sociopolitical legitimacy, and promote organizational survival. In C. Johnson (Ed.), *Research in the sociology of organizations*, Volume 22 (pp. 171–211). Amsterdam: Elsevier JAI.

Ashforth, B. E., & Gibbs, B. W. (1990). The double-edge of organizational legitimation. *Organization Science, 1*: 177–194.

Bamberger, P. (2008). Beyond contextualization: Using context theories to narrow the micro–macro gap in management research. *Academy of Management Journal, 51*: 839–846.

Bansal, P., & Clelland, I. (2004). Talking trash: Legitimacy, impression management, and unsystematic risk in the context of the natural environment. *Academy of Management Journal, 47*: 93–103.

Barley, S. R. (2016). 60th Anniversary Essay: Ruminations on how we became a mystery house and how we might get out. *Administrative Science Quarterly, 61*: 1–8.

Barron, D. M. (1998). Pathways to legitimacy among consumer loan providers in New York City, 1914–1934. *Organization Studies, 19*: 207–233.

Barron, D. N., West, E., & Hannan, M. T. (1994). A time to grow and a time to die: Growth and mortality of credit unions in New York. *American Journal of Sociology, 100*: 381–421.

Baum, J. A. C., & Oliver, C. (1991). Institutional linkages and organizational mortality. *Administrative Science Quarterly, 36*(6): 187–218.

Baum, J. A. C., & Oliver, C. (1992). Institutional embeddedness and the dynamics of organizational populations. *American Sociological Review, 57*(4): 540–559.

Beddewela, E., & Fairbrass, J. (2016). Seeking legitimacy through CSR: Institutional pressures and corporate responses of multinationals in Sri Lanka. *Journal of Business Ethics, 136*: 503–522.

Bedeian, A. G. (2004). The gift of professional maturity. *Academy of Management Learning & Education, 3*: 92–98.

Benford, R. D., & Snow, D. A. (2000). Framing processes and social movements: An overview and assessment. *Annual Review of Sociology*, *26*: 611–640.

Bernstein, S., & Cashore, B. (2007). Can non-state global governance be legitimate? An analytical framework. *Regulation & Governance*, *1*: 347–371.

Bitektine, A. (2011). Toward a theory of social judgment of organizations: The case of legitimacy, reputation, and status. *Academy of Management Review*, *36*: 151–179.

Bitektine, A., & Haack, P. (2015). The 'macro' and the 'micro' of legitimacy: Toward a multilevel theory of the legitimacy process. *Academy of Management Review*, *40*: 49–75.

Black, J. (2008). Constructing and contesting legitimacy and accountability in polycentric regulatory regimes. *Regulation & Governance*, *2*: 137–164.

Boyle, T. P. (2001). Intermedia agenda setting in the 1996 Presidential Election. *Journalism & Mass Communication Quarterly*, *78*: 26–44.

Brown, A. D. (1998). Narrative, politics and legitimacy in an IT implementation. *Journal of Management Studies*, *35*: 35–58.

Brown, A. D., & Toyoki, S. (2013). Identity work and legitimacy. *Organization Studies*, *34*: 875–896.

Bundy, J., & Pfarrer, M. D. (2015). A burden of responsibility: The role of social approval at the onset of a crisis. *Academy of Management Review*, *40*: 345–369.

Canivez, P. (2010). The search for a European identity: Values, policies and legitimacy of the European Union. *Philosophy & Social Criticism*, *36*: 857–870.

Carroll, G. R., & Hannan, M. T. (1989). Density dependence in the evolution of populations of newspaper organizations. *American Sociological Review*, *54*: 524–541.

Carter, S. M., & Deephouse, D. L. (1999). 'Tough talk' or 'soothing speech': Managing reputations for being tough and for being good. *Corporate Reputation Review*, *2*: 308–332.

Cashore, B., Auld, G., & Newsom, D. (2004). *Governing through markets: forest certification and the emergence of non-state authority*. New Haven, CT: Yale University Press.

Castelló, I., Etter, M., & Årup Nielsen, F. (2016). Strategies of legitimacy through social media: The networked strategy. *Journal of Management Studies*, *53*: 402–432.

Child, J. (1972). Organizational structure, environment and performance: The role of strategic choice. *Sociology*, *6*: 2–21.

Choi, Y. R., & Shepherd, D. A. (2005). Stakeholder perceptions of age and other dimensions of newness. *Journal of Management*, *31*: 573–596.

Christensen, T., Lægreid, P., & Rykkja, L. H. (2016). Organizing for crisis management: Building governance capacity and legitimacy. *Public Administration Review*, *76*(6): 887–897.

Cohen, B. D., & Dean, T. J. (2005). Information asymmetry and investor valuation of IPOs: Top management team legitimacy as a capital market signal. *Strategic Management Journal*, *26*: 683–690.

Cook, J., Nuccitelli, D., Green, S. A., Richardson, M., Winkler, B., Painting, R., Way, R., Jacobs, P., & Skuce, A. (2013). Quantifying the consensus on anthropogenic global warming in the scientific literature. *Environmental Research Letters*, *8*: 024024.

Cook, J., Oreskes, N., Doran, P. T., Anderegg, W. R. L., Verheggen, B., Maibach, E. W., … Rice, K. (2016). Consensus on consensus: A synthesis of consensus estimates on human-caused global warming. *Environmental Research Letters*, *11*: 048002.

Cornelissen, J. P., Durand, R., Fiss, P. C., Lammers, J. C., & Vaara, E. (2015). Putting communication front and center in institutional theory and analysis. *Academy of Management Review*, *40*: 10–27.

Cornelissen, J. P., Holt, R., & Zundel, M. (2011). The role of analogy and metaphor in the framing and legitimization of strategic change. *Organization Studies*, *32*: 1701–1716.

Cornelius, P., Van De Putte, A., & Romani, M. (2005). Three decades of scenario planning in Shell. *California Management Review*, *48*: 92.

Creed, W. E. D., Scully, M. A., & Austin, J. R. (2002). Clothes make the person? The tailoring of legitimating accounts and the social construction of identity. *Organization Science*, *13*: 475–496.

Cullen, J. B., Parboteeah, K. P., & Hoegl, M. (2004). Cross-national differences in managers' willingness to justify ethically suspect behaviors: A test of institutional anomie theory. *Academy of Management Journal*, *47*: 411–421.

Deeds, D. L., Mang, P. Y., & Frandsen, M. L. (2004). The influence of firms' and industries' legitimacy on the flow of capital into high-technology ventures. *Strategic Organization*, *2*: 9–34.

Deephouse, D. L. (1996). Does isomorphism legitimate? *Academy of Management Journal*, *39*: 1024–1039.

Deephouse, D. L. (1999). To be different, or to be the same? It's a question (and theory) of strategic balance. *Strategic Management Journal*, *20*: 147–166.

Deephouse, D. L. (2014). From the colours of the rainbow to monochromatic grey: An n=1+x analysis of Apple's corporate reputation, 1976–2013. *Socio-Economic Review*, *12*: 206–218.

Deephouse, D. L., & Carter, S. M. (2005). An examination of differences between organizational legitimacy and organizational reputation. *Journal of Management Studies*, *42*: 329–360.

Deephouse, D. L., & Suchman, M. C. (2008). Legitimacy in organizational institutionalism.

In R. Greenwood, C. Oliver, R. Suddaby, & K. Sahlin-Andersson (Eds.), *The SAGE handbook of organizational institutionalism* (pp. 49–77). London: Sage.

Demuijnck, G., & Fasterling, B. (2016). The social license to operate. *Journal of Business Ethics, 136*: 675–685.

DiMaggio, P. (1988). Interest and agency in institutional theory. In L. G. Zucker (Ed.), *Institutional patterns and organizations: Culture and environment* (pp. 3–21). Cambridge, MA: Ballinger.

Djelic, M.-L., & Sahlin-Andersson, K. (Eds.) (2006). *Transnational governance: Institutional dynamics of regulation.* New York: Cambridge University Press.

Dodgson, M., Gann, D., Wladawsky-Berger, I., Sultan, N., & George, G. (2015). Managing digital money. *Academy of Management Journal, 58*: 325–333.

Dornbush, S. M., & Scott, W. R. (1975). *Evaluation and the exercise of authority.* San Francisco, CA: Jossey–Bass.

Dowling, J., & Pfeffer, J. (1975). Organizational legitimacy: Social values and organizational behavior. *Pacific Sociological Review*, 18: 122–136.

Downing, S. (2005). The social construction of entrepreneurship: Narrative and dramatic processes in the coproduction of organizations and identities. *Entrepreneurship Theory and Practice, 29*: 185–204.

Drori, I., & Honig, B. (2013). A process model of internal and external legitimacy. *Organization Studies, 34*: 345–376.

Drori, I., Honig, B., & Sheaffer, Z. (2009). The life cycle of an internet firm: scripts, legitimacy, and identity. *Entrepreneurship: Theory & Practice, 33*: 715–738.

Dubin, R. (1976). Theory building in applied areas. In M. D. Dunnette (Ed.), *Handbook of industrial and organizational psychology* (pp. 17–40). Chicago, IL: Rand McNally.

Durand, R., & Vergne, J.-P. (2015). Asset divestment as a response to media attacks in stigmatized industries. *Strategic Management Journal, 36*: 1205–1223.

Durant, R. F., & Legge, J. S. (2006). 'Wicked problems,' public policy, and administrative theory: Lessons from the GM food regulatory arena. *Administration & Society, 38*: 309–334.

Edelman, L. B., & Suchman, M. C. (1997). The legal environments of organizations. *Annual Review of Sociology, 23*: 479–515.

Elsbach, K. D., & Sutton, R. I. (1992). Acquiring organizational legitimacy through illegitimate actions: A marriage of institutional and impression management theories. *Academy of Management Journal, 35*: 699–738.

Elsbach, K. D. (1994). Managing organizational legitimacy in the California cattle industry: The construction and effectiveness of verbal accounts. *Administrative Science Quarterly, 39*(1): 57–88.

Erkama, N., & Vaara, E. (2010). Struggles over legitimacy in global organizational restructuring: A rhetorical perspective on legitimation strategies and dynamics in a shutdown case. *Organization Studies, 31*: 813–839.

Ferraro, F., Etzion, D., & Gehman, J. (2015). Tackling grand challenges pragmatically: Robust action revisited. *Organization Studies, 36*: 363–390.

Finch, D., Deephouse, D. L., & Varella, P. (2015). Examining an individual's legitimacy judgment using the value–attitude system: The role of environmental and economic values and source credibility. *Journal of Business Ethics, 127*: 265–281.

Fisher, G., Kotha, S., & Lahiri, A. (2016). Changing with the times: An integrated view of identity, legitimacy, and new venture life cycles. *Academy of Management Review, 41*: 383–409.

Gabbioneta, C., Greenwood, R., Mazzola, P., & Minoja, M. (2013). The influence of the institutional context on corporate illegality. *Accounting, Organizations and Society, 38*: 484–504.

Galaskiewicz, J. (1985). Interorganizational relations. *Annual Review of Sociology, 11*: 281–304.

Gans, H. J. (1979). *Deciding what's news.* New York: Pantheon Books.

Garud, R., Jain, S., & Kumaraswamy, A. (2002). Institutional entrepreneurship in the sponsorship of common technological standards: The case of Sun Microsystems and Java. *Academy of Management Journal, 45*: 196–214.

Gee, J. P. (2011). *An introduction to discourse analysis: Theory and method* (3rd ed.). New York: Routledge.

Golant, B. D., & Sillince, J. A. A. (2007). The constitution of organizational legitimacy: A narrative perspective. *Organization Studies, 28*: 1149–1167.

Gray, B., Purdy, J. M., & Ansari, S. (2015). From interactions to institutions: microprocesses of framing and mechanisms for the structuring of institutional fields. *Academy of Management Review, 40*: 115–143.

Green, S. E. (2004). A rhetorical theory of diffusion. *Academy of Management Review, 29*: 653–669.

Greenwood, R. (2016). OMT, then and now. *Journal of Management Inquiry, 25*: 27–33.

Greenwood, R., Suddaby, R., & Hinings, C. R. (2002). Theorizing change: The role of professional associations in the transformation of institutionalized fields. *Academy of Management Journal, 45*: 58–80.

Haack, P., Pfarrer, M. D., & Scherer, A. G. (2014). Legitimacy-as-feeling: How affect leads to vertical legitimacy spillovers in transnational governance. *Journal of Management Studies, 51*: 634–666.

Hannan, M. T., & Carroll, G. R. (1992). *Dynamics of Organizational Populations: Density, Legitimation, and Competition*. New York: Oxford University Press.

Hannan, M. T., & Freeman, J. (1977). The population ecology of organizations. *American Journal of Sociology*, 82: 929–940, 946–949, 955–964.

Hannigan, J. A., & Kueneman, R. M. (1977). Legitimacy and public organizations: A case study. *Canadian Journal of Sociology/Cahiers canadiens de sociologie*, 2: 125–135.

Harmon, D. J., Green, S. E., & Goodnight, G. T. (2015). A model of rhetorical legitimation: The structure of communication and cognition underlying institutional maintenance and change. *Academy of Management Review, 40*: 76–95.

Haveman, H. A., & Rao, H. (1997). Structuring a theory of moral sentiments: Institutional and organizational coevolution in the early thrift industry. *American Journal of Sociology, 102*(6): 1606–1651.

Hemphill, T. A., & Banerjee, S. (2015). Genetically modified organisms and the U.S. retail food labeling controversy: Consumer perceptions, regulation, and public policy. *Business and Society Review*, 120: 435–464.

Heugens, P. P. M. A. R., & Lander, M. W. (2009). Structure! Agency! (and other quarrels): A meta-analysis of institutional theories of organization. *Academy of Management Journal, 52*: 61–85.

Higgins, M. C., & Gulati, R. (2003). Getting off to a good start: The effects of upper echelon affiliations on underwriter prestige. *Organization Science*, 14: 244–263.

Higgins, M. C., & Gulati, R. (2006). Stacking the deck: The effects of top management backgrounds on investor decisions. *Strategic Management Journal, 27*: 1–25.

Hinings, C. R. (2006). Keynote address – Reaching new heights. *Canadian Journal of Administrative Sciences*, 23: 175–182.

Hirsch, P. M. (1977). Occupational, organizational, and institutional models in mass media research: Towards an integrated framework. In P. M. Hirsch, P. V. Miller, & F. G. Kline (Eds.), *Strategies for communication research* (pp. 13–40). Beverly Hills, CA: Sage.

Hirsch, P. M., & Andrews, J. A. Y. (1984). Administrators' response to performance and value challenges: Stance, symbols, and behavior. In T. J. Sergiovanni & J. E. Corbally (Eds.), *Leadership and organizational culture* (pp. 170–185). Urbana, IL: University of Illinois Press.

Hodgkinson, G. P., & Healey, M. P. (2008). Toward a (pragmatic) science of strategic intervention: Design propositions for scenario planning. *Organization Studies*, 29: 435–457.

Huy, Q. N., Corley, K. G., & Kraatz, M. S. (2014). From support to mutiny: Shifting legitimacy judgments and emotional reactions impacting the implementation of radical change. *Academy of Management Journal, 57*: 1650–1680.

Hybels, R. C., Ryan, A. R., & Barley, S. R. (1994). *Alliances, legitimation, and founding rates in the U. S. biotechnology field, 1971–1989*. Paper presented at the annual meeting of the Academy of Management, Dallas.

Johnson, C. (2004). Introduction: Legitimacy processes in organizations. In C. Johnson (Ed.), *Research in the sociology of organizations*, Vol. 22 (pp. 1–24). Amsterdam: Elsevier JAI.

Johnson, C., Dowd, T. J., & Ridgeway, C. L. (2006). Legitimacy as a social process. *Annual Review of Sociology, 32*: 53–78.

Joutsenvirta, M. (2012). Executive pay and legitimacy: Changing discursive battles over the morality of excessive manager compensation. *Journal of Business Ethics*, 116: 459–477.

Kamens, D. H. (1977). Legitimating myths and educational organization: The relationship between organizational ideology and formal structure. *American Sociological Review*, 42: 208–219.

Kannan-Narasimhan, R. (2014). Organizational ingenuity in nascent innovations: Gaining resources and legitimacy through unconventional actions. *Organization Studies, 35*: 483–509.

Kaplan, A. (1964). *The conduct of inquiry*. New York: Chandler.

Kennedy, P. (2006). Forestry union denounces safety initiatives. *The Globe and Mail*, Jan. 19, 2006: S.3. Toronto.

King, B. G., & Soule, S. A. (2007). Social movements as extra-institutional entrepreneurs: The effect of protests on stock price returns. *Administrative Science Quarterly, 52*: 413–442.

Knoke, D. (1985). The political economies of associations. In R. G. Braungart & M. M. Braungart (Eds.), *Research in political sociology*, Vol. 1 (pp. 211–242). Greenwich, CT: JAI Press.

Kostova, T., & Zaheer, S. (1999). Organizational legitimacy under conditions of complexity: The case of the multinational enterprise. *Academy of Management Review, 24*: 64–81.

Kraatz, M. S., & Block, E. (2008). Organizational implications of institutional pluralism. In R. Greenwood, C. Oliver, R. Suddaby, & K. Sahlin-Andersson (Eds.), *The SAGE handbook of organizational institutionalism* (pp. 243–275). London: Sage.

Lamertz, K., & Baum, J. A. C. (1998). The legitimacy of organizational downsizing in Canada: An analysis of explanatory media accounts. *Canadian Journal of Administrative Sciences*, 15: 93–107.

Lamin, A., & Zaheer, S. (2012). Wall Street vs. Main Street: Firm strategies for defending legitimacy and their impact on different stakeholders. *Organization Science, 23*: 47–66.

Lange, D., Lee, P. M., & Dai, Y. (2011). Organizational reputation: A review. *Journal of Management, 37*: 153–184.

Lasswell, H. D. (1927). The theory of political propaganda. *American Political Science Review*, 21: 627–631.

Lasswell, H. D., Leites, N., & Associates. (1965). *Language of politics*. Cambridge, MA: MIT Press.

Latham, G. P., Erez, M., & Locke, E. A. (1988). Resolving scientific disputes by the joint design of crucial experiments by the antagonists: Application to the Erez-Latham dispute regarding participation in goal setting. *Journal of Applied Psychology, 73*: 753–772.

Lippmann, W. (1922). *Public opinion*. New York: Harcourt Brace.

Locke, K., & Golden-Biddle, K. (1997). Constructing opportunities for contribution: Structuring intertextual coherence and 'problematizing' in organizational studies. *Academy of Management Journal, 40*: 1023–1062.

Lounsbury, M., & Glynn, M. A. (2001). Cultural entrepreneurship: Stories, legitimacy and the acquisition of resources. *Strategic Management Journal*, 22: 545–564.

MacKay, B., & Munro, I. (2012). Information warfare and new organizational landscapes: An inquiry into the ExxonMobil–Greenpeace dispute over climate change. *Organization Studies, 33*: 1507–1536.

MacLean, T. L., & Behnam, M. (2010). The dangers of decoupling: The relationship between compliance programs, legitimacy perceptions, and institutionalized misconduct. *Academy of Management Journal, 53*: 1499–1520.

Martens, M. L., Jennings, J. E., & Jennings, P. D. (2007). Do the stories they tell them the money they need? The role of entrepreneurial narratives in resource acquisition. *Academy of Management Journal, 50*: 1107–1132.

Maurer, J. G. (Ed.). (1971). *Readings in organization theory: Open-system approaches*. New York: Random House.

McCombs, M. E., & Shaw, D. L. (1972). The agenda setting function of the mass media. *Public Opinion Quarterly, 36*: 176–187.

Meyer, J. W., Boli, J., Thomas, G. M., & Ramirez, F. O. (1997). World society and the nation-state. *American Journal of Sociology, 103*: 144–181.

Meyer, J. W., & Rowan, B. (1977). Institutionalized organizations: Formal structure as myth and ceremony. *American Journal of Sociology, 83*: 340–363.

Meyer, J. W., & Scott, W. R. (1983). Centralization and the legitimacy problems of local government. In J. W. Meyer & W. R. Scott (Eds.), *Organizational environments: Ritual and rationality* (pp. 199–215). Beverly Hills, CA: Sage.

Miller, G. A. (1959). The magical number seven, plus or minus two: Some limits on our capacity for processing information. *Psychological Review, 63*: 81–97.

Milne, M. J., & Patten, D. M. (2002). Securing organizational legitimacy: An experimental decision case examining the impact of environmental disclosures. *Accounting, Auditing and Accountability Journal*, 15: 372–405.

Mishina, Y., Block, E. S., & Mannor, M. J. (2012). The path dependence of organizational reputation: How social judgment influences assessments of capability and character. *Strategic Management Journal, 33*: 459–477.

Molloy, J. C., Ployhart, R. E., & Wright, P. M. (2011). The myth of 'the' micro–macro divide: Bridging system-level and disciplinary divides. *Journal of Management*, 37: 581–609.

Moore, C., & Gino, F. (2013). Ethically adrift: How others pull our moral compass from true North, and how we can fix it. *Research in Organizational Behavior, 33*: 53–77.

Nelson, R. R., & Winter, S. G. (1982). *An evolutionary theory of economic change*. Cambridge, MA: Harvard University Press.

Neto, J. M. S., & Mullet, E. (2014). Perceived legitimacy of executives' bonuses in time of global crisis: A mapping of Portuguese people's views. *Journal of Business Ethics, 133*: 421–429.

O'Dwyer, B. (2002). Managerial perceptions of corporate social disclosure: An Irish story. *Accounting, Auditing & Accountability Journal*, 15: 406;436.

Oliver, C. (1991). Strategic responses to institutional processes. *Academy of Management Review*, 16: 145–179.

Oliver, C. (1997). Sustainable competitive advantage: Combining institutional and resource-based views. *Strategic Management Journal, 18*: 697–713.

Osigweh, C. A. B. (1989). Concept fallibility in organizational science. *Academy of Management Review*, 14: 579–594.

Parsons, T. (1956). Suggestions for a sociological approach to the theory of organizations – I. *Administrative Science Quarterly*, 1: 63–85.

Parsons, T. (1960). *Structure and process in modern societies*. New York: Free Press.

Pavlovich, K., Sinha, P. N., & Rodrigues, M. (2016). A qualitative case study of MNE legitimacy: The Fonterra–Sanlu IJV corporate milk scandal in China. *International Journal of Emerging Markets*, 11: 42–56.

Pfarrer, M. D., Decelles, K. A., Smith, K. G., & Taylor, M. S. (2008). After the fall: Reintegrating the corrupt organization. *Academy of Management Review, 33*(3): 730–749.

Pfeffer, J., & Salancik, G. R. (1978). *The external control of organizations: A resource dependence perspective*. New York: Harper & Row.

Phillips, D. J., & Zuckerman, E. W. (2001). Middle-status conformity: Theoretical restatement and empirical demonstration in two markets. *American Journal of Sociology*, 107: 379–429.

Phillips, N., Lawrence, T. B., & Hardy, C. (2004). Discourse and institutions. *Academy of Management Review, 29*: 635–652.

Pollock, T. G., Lee, P. M., Jin, K., & Lashley, K. (2015). (Un)Tangled: Exploring the asymmetric coevolution of new venture capital firms' reputation and status. *Administrative Science Quarterly, 60*: 482–517.

Pollock, T. G., & Rindova, V. P. (2003). Media legitimation effects in the market for initial public offerings. *Academy of Management Journal, 46*: 631–642.

Powell, W. W., & Colyvas, J. A. (2008). Microfoundations of institutional theory. In R. Greenwood, C. Oliver, R. Suddaby, & K. Sahlin-Andersson (Eds.), *The SAGE handbook of organizational institutionalism* (pp. 276–298). London: Sage.

Prakash, A., & Potoski, M. (2006). *The voluntary environmentalists: Green clubs, ISO 14001, and voluntary regulations*. New York: Cambridge University Press.

Rao, H. (1994). The social construction of reputation: Certification contests, legitimation, and the survival of organizations in the American automobile industry: 1895–1912. *Strategic Management Journal, 15*: 29–44.

Rao, H., Morrill, C., & Zald, M. (2000). Power plays: How social movements and collective action create new organizational forms. In B. M. Staw & R. I. Sutton (Eds.), *Research in organizational behavior*, Vol. 22 (pp. 237–281). Greenwich, CT: JAI Press.

Reimann, F., Ehrgott, M., Kaufmann, L., & Carter, C. R. (2012). Local stakeholders and local legitimacy: MNEs' social strategies in emerging economies. *Journal of International Management, 18*: 1–17.

Rousseau, D. M. (1985). Issues of level in organizational research: Multi-level and cross-level perspectives. *Research in Organizational Behavior*, Vol. 7 (pp. 1–27). Greenwich, CT: JAI Press Inc.

Rowan, B. (1982). Organizational structure and the institutional environment: The case of public schools. *Administrative Science Quarterly, 27*: 259–279.

Ruef, M., & Scott, W. R. (1998). A multidimensional model of organizational legitimacy: Hospital survival in changing institutional environments. *Administrative Science Quarterly, 43*: 877–904.

Scheufele, D. A., & Tewksbury, D. (2007). Framing, agenda setting, and priming: The evolution of three media effects models. *Journal of Communication, 57*: 9–20.

Schoemaker, P. J. H. (1993). Multiple scenario development: Its conceptual and behavioral foundation. *Strategic Management Journal, 14*: 193–213.

Schramm, W. (1949). The nature of news. In W. Schramm (Ed.), *Mass communications* (pp. 288–303). Urbana, IL: University of Illinois Press.

Scott, M. B., & Lyman, S. M. (1968). Accounts. *American Sociological Review, 33*: 46–62.

Scott, W. R. (1987). *Organizations: Rational, natural, and open systems* (2nd ed.). Englewood Cliffs, NJ: Prentice-Hall.

Scott, W. R. (1995). *Institutions and organizations*. Thousand Oaks, CA: Sage.

Scott, W. R. (2014). *Institutions and organizations: Ideas, interests, and identities* (4th ed.). Thousand Oaks, CA: Sage.

Scott, W. R., Ruef, M., Mendel, P. J., & Caronna, C. A. (2000). *Institutional change and healthcare organizations: From professional dominance to managed care*. Chicago, IL: University of Chicago Press.

Sellnow, T. L., & Seeger, M. W. (2013). *Theorizing Crisis Communication*. Malden, MA: John Wiley & Sons.

Selznick, P. (1949). *TVA and the grass roots: A study in the sociology of formal organization*. Berkeley: University of California Press.

Shoemaker, P. J., & Reese, S. D. (1991). *Mediating the message: Theories of influences on mass media content*. White Plains, NY: Longman.

Shoemaker, P. J., & Reese, S. D. (2014). *Mediating the message in the 21st century: A media sociology perspective*. New York: Routledge/Taylor & Francis Group.

Sillince, J. A. A., & Brown, A. D. (2009). Multiple organizational identities and legitimacy: The rhetoric of police websites. *Human Relations, 62*: 1829–1856.

Simon, H. A. (1976). *Administrative behavior* (3rd ed.). New York: Free Press.

Singh, J. V., Tucker, D. J., & House, R. J. (1986). Organizational legitimacy and the liability of newness. *Administrative Science Quarterly, 31*: 171–193.

Sinha, P., Daellenbach, U., & Bednarek, R. (2015). Legitimacy defense during post-merger integration: Between coupling and compartmentalization. *Strategic Organization, 13*: 169–199.

Stinchcombe, A. L. (1965). Organizations and social structure. In J. G. March (Ed.), *Handbook of organizations* (pp. 142–193). Chicago, IL: Rand McNally.

Strang, D., & Meyer, J. W. (1993). Institutional conditions for diffusion. *Theory and Society, 22*: 487–511.

Strang, D., & Soule, S. A. (1998). Diffusion in organizations and social movements: From hybrid corn to poison pills. *Annual Review of Sociology, 24*: 265–290.

Suchman, M. C. (1995). Managing legitimacy: Strategic and institutional approaches. *Academy of Management Review, 20*: 571–610.

Suddaby, R. (2010). Editor's comments: Construct clarity in theories of management and organization. *Academy of Management Review, 35*: 346–357.

Suddaby, R., & Greenwood, R. (2005). Rhetorical strategies of legitimacy. *Administrative Science Quarterly, 50*: 35–67.

Tolbert, P. S., & Zucker, L. G. (1983). Institutional sources of change in the formal structure of organizations: The diffusion of civil service reforms 1880–1935. *Administrative Science Quarterly, 23*: 22–39.

Tost, L. P. (2011). An integrative model of legitimacy judgments. *Academy of Management Review, 36*: 686–710.

Turcan, R. V., & Fraser, N. M. (2016). An ethnographic study of new venture and new sector legitimation: Evidence from Moldova. *International Journal of Emerging Markets, 11*: 72–88.

Tyler, T. R. (2006). Psychological perspectives on legitimacy and legitimation. *Annual Review of Psychology, 57*: 375–400.

Tyler, T. R., Fagan, J., & Geller, A. (2014). Street stops and police legitimacy: Teachable moments in young urban men's legal socialization. *Journal of Empirical Legal Studies, 11*: 751–785.

Vaara, E., & Tienari, J. (2002). Justification, legitimization and naturalization of mergers and acquisitions: A critical discourse analysis of media texts. *Organization, 9*: 275–304.

Vaara, E., Tienari, J., & Laurila, J. (2006). Pulp and paper fiction: On the discursive legitimation of global industrial restructuring. *Organization Studies, 27*: 789–810.

Van de Ven, A. H. (2007). *Engaged scholarship: A guide for organizational and social research*. Oxford: Oxford University Press.

van Halderen, M. D., Bhatt, M., Berens, G. A. J. M., Brown, T. J., & van Riel, C. B. M. (2016). Managing impressions in the face of rising stakeholder pressures: examining oil companies' shifting stances in the climate change debate. *Journal of Business Ethics, 133*: 567–582.

Vergne, J.-P. (2011). Toward a new measure of organizational legitimacy: method, validation, and illustration. *Organizational Research Methods, 14*: 484–502.

Voronov, M., De Clercq, D., & Hinings, C. R. (2013). Conformity and distinctiveness in a global institutional framework: The legitimation of Ontario fine wine. *Journal of Management Studies, 50*: 607–645.

Voronov, M., & Vince, R. (2012). Integrating emotions into the analysis of institutional work. *Academy of Management Review, 37*: 58–81.

Walker, K., Schlosser, F., & Deephouse, D. L. (2014). Organizational ingenuity and the paradox of embedded agency: The case of the embryonic Ontario solar energy industry. *Organization Studies, 35*: 613–634.

Weaver, G. R., Trevino, L. K., & Cochran, P. L. (1999). Integrated and decoupled corporate social performance: Management commitments, external pressures, and corporate ethics practices. *Academy of Management Journal, 42*: 539–552.

Weber, M. (1978). *Economy and society: An outline of interpretive sociology*. Berkeley, CA: University of California Press.

Wedlin, L. (2006). *Ranking business schools: Forming fields, identities and boundaries in international management education*. Northampton, MA: Edward Elgar.

Weick, K. E. (2001). *Making sense of the organization*. Oxford, UK; Blackwell Publishers.

Weisburd, D., Hinkle, J. C., Famega, C., & Ready, J. (2011). The possible 'backfire' effects of hot spots policing: An experimental assessment of impacts on legitimacy, fear and collective efficacy. *Journal of Experimental Criminology, 7*: 297–320.

Westphal, J. D., & Deephouse, D. L. (2011). Avoiding bad press: Interpersonal influence in relations between CEOs and journalists and the consequences for press reporting about firms and their leadership. *Organization Science, 22*: 1061–1086.

Westphal, J. D., Gulati, R., & Shortell, S. M. (1997). Customization or conformity? An institutional and network perspective on the content and consequences of TQM adoption. *Administrative Science Quarterly, 42*: 366–394.

Whiteman, G., Hope, C., & Wadhams, P. (2013). Climate science: Vast costs of Arctic change. *Nature, 499*: 401–403.

Wilson, W. K. (1997). *The essentials of logic*. Piscataway, NJ: Research and Education Association.

Wright, E. O. (1985). Practical strategies for transforming concepts. In E. O. Wright (Ed.), *Classes* (pp. 292–302). London: Verso.

Wu, Z., & Salomon, R. (2016). Does imitation reduce the liability of foreignness? Linking distance, isomorphism, and performance. *Strategic Management Journal* [online] DOI: 10.1002/smj.2462.

Zavyalova, A., Pfarrer, M. D., Reger, R. K., & Shapiro, D. L. (2012). Managing the Message: The Effects of Firm Actions and Industry Spillovers on Media Coverage Following Wrongdoing. *Academy of Management Journal, 55*(5): 1079–1101.

Zimmerman, M. A., & Zeitz, G. J. (2002). Beyond survival: Achieving new venture growth by building legitimacy. *Academy of Management Review, 27*: 414–431.

Zucker, L. G. (1977). The role of institutionalization in cultural persistence. *American Sociological Review, 42*: 726–743.

Organizational Fields: Past, Present and Future

Melissa Wooten and Andrew J. Hoffman

INTRODUCTION

The term 'institutional theory' covers a broad body of literature that has grown in prominence and popularity over the past two decades. But, consistency in defining the bounds of this activity has not always been easy. The lament of DiMaggio and Powell in 1991 still holds true today: 'it is often easier to gain agreement about what it is *not* than about what it *is*' (1991: 1). There are a great number of issues that have and continue to remain divisive within this literature and among related literatures that apply institutional arguments (i.e., economics, political science, and history). What these literatures have in common, however, is an underlying skepticism towards atomistic accounts of social processes, relying instead on a conviction that institutional arrangements and social processes matter in the formulation of organizational action (DiMaggio and Powell, 1991).

At its core, the literature looks to the source of action as existing exogenous to the actor.

More than merely suggesting that action is a reaction to the pressures of the external environment, institutional theory asks questions about how social choices are shaped, mediated and channeled by the institutional environment. Organizational action becomes a reflection of the perspectives defined by the group of members that comprise the institutional environment; out of which emerge the regulative, normative, and cultural-cognitive systems that provide meaning for organizations (Scott, 1995, 2001). Action is not a choice among unlimited possibilities but rather among a narrowly defined set of legitimate options. As an organization becomes more profoundly aware of its dependence on this external environment, its very conception of itself changes, with consequences on many levels. As this happens, Selznick states, 'institutionalization has set in' (1957: 7). Hence, institutionalization represents both a process and an outcome (DiMaggio, 1988).

While not highly emphasized in early institutional analyses (i.e., Selznick, 1949, 1957), the central construct of neo-institutional theory has been the *organizational field* (Scott, 1991). Strictly speaking, the field is 'a community of organizations that partakes of a common meaning system and whose participants interact more frequently and fatefully with one another than with actors outside the field' (Scott, 1995: 56). It may include constituents such as the government, critical exchange partners, sources of funding, professional and trade associations, special interest groups, and the general public – any constituent that imposes a coercive, normative or mimetic influence on the organization (DiMaggio and Powell, 1991; Scott, 1991). But the concept of the organizational field encompasses much more than simply a discrete list of constituents; and the ways in which the institutional literature has sought to capture this complexity has evolved over the past decades, and continues to evolve. In this chapter, we present this evolution, discussing the past, present and future of this important construct. We illustrate its early conceptualization and present its progression in a way that invites scholars to both consider their work within this historical trajectory and contribute to its further development. In the first edition of the handbook we concluded the chapter with our thoughts on promising avenues for future research within the organizational field domain. We incorporate recent developments that fit within our calls for future research. Despite these advancements, the calls for future research remain as relevant now as they were then and we expand them. This provides an opportunity to consider the important ways in which the organizational fields literature has moved forward and the areas in which progress has yet to come.

ORGANIZATIONAL FIELDS: EARLY INCARNATIONS

For early neo-institutional theory, the central unit of analysis was variously referred to as the institutional sphere (Fligstein, 1990), institutional field (Meyer and Rowan, 1977; DiMaggio and Powell, 1991), societal sector (Scott and Meyer, 1992), and institutional environment (Orru et al., 1991; DiMaggio and Powell, 1991). But the term *organizational field* (Scott, 1991) has become the accepted term for the constellation of actors that comprise this central organizing unit. Like Bourdieu's field (1990, 1993), where an agent's actions within the political, economic, or cultural arena were structured by a network of social relations, institutional theorists conceptualized the organizational field as the domain where an organization's actions were structured by the network of relationships within which it was embedded (Warren, 1967). Warren used the example of community organizations such as banks, welfare organizations, churches, businesses, and boards of education, working in conjunction with one another to elucidate the importance of taking the 'inter-organizational' field as a unit of analysis. By focusing attention on this level of analysis, researchers could better understand the decision-making processes among distinct organizations that, while having dissimilar goals, felt it necessary and advantageous to interact with one another to accomplish a given task.

As studies of inter-organizational relations evolved, scholars broadened the field to include organizations that were not necessarily bound by geography or goals, but instead made up a recognized area of institutional life. These could include organizations that produced similar services or products, suppliers, resource and product consumers, regulatory agencies, and others (DiMaggio and Powell, 1983). What these organizations had in common was that they comprised a community of organizations that partook of a common meaning system and whose participants interacted more frequently and fatefully with one another than with other organizations (Scott, 1995). Such evolving definitions focused on the organizational field as a means to understand the impact of rationalization on organizations.

The behavior of organizations within fields was said to be guided by *institutions*: the cultural-cognitive, normative and regulative structures that provided stability and collective meaning to social behavior (Scott, 1995). These structures acted as 'social facts' that organizational actors took into account when determining appropriate action (Zucker, 1977; Meyer and Rowan, 1977). The transmission of social facts from one set of actors to another caused them to take on a rule-like and taken-for-granted status and thus become institutionalized (Zucker, 1977). Once a social fact had become institutionalized, it provided actors with templates for action which created unified or monolithic responses to uncertainty that led to *isomorphism* – a commonality in form and function (DiMaggio and Powell, 1983). The central notions of organizational field research focused on understanding the processes that guided the behavior of field members in unconscious ways.

Meyer and Rowan (1977) suggested that the incorporation of elements (i.e., structures, practices, procedures, etc.) from the institutional environment imbued an organization with *legitimacy*. Thus, for example, 'administrators and politicians champion programs that are established but not implemented; managers gather information assiduously, but fail to analyze it; experts are hired not for advice but to signal legitimacy' (DiMaggio and Powell, 1991: 3). An organization that appeared legitimate increased its prospects for survival because constituents would not question the organization's intent and purpose. As increasing numbers of organizations incorporated common institutional elements, most (if not all) organizations at the field level became homogeneous in structure, culture and output (DiMaggio and Powell, 1983). Much of the research using this notion of the organizational field centered on the premise that organizations sought survival and legitimacy as opposed to efficiency (Orru et al., 1991).

For example, Fligstein (1990) depicted the industry-wide transformation of executive leadership in America as resulting from shifting pressures from the government. DiMaggio and Powell (1991) cited the causes for the accepted form of art museums in American cities in the 1920s and 1930s as the result of efforts by museum workers to define a profession through conformity to demands from foundations, particularly the Carnegie Foundation. Leblebici et al. (1991) argued that the generation and acceptance of practices and technologies within the American radio broadcasting industry were the result of the actions of influential industrial actors. And Tolbert and Zucker (1983) looked to the spread of civil service reforms at the turn of the twentieth century as resulting from the pressure of legal requirements or the examples set by fellow cities.

Early field-level analyses allowed some degree of diversity in action, based on primacy in institutional adoption. For example, first adopters within a community of organizations tended to take action out of concerns for efficiency. But, later adoptions followed a different diffusion process with adoption of structures and practices designed to mimic the behavior of prior adopters. Tolbert and Zucker's (1983) study of the adoption of civil reforms by cities provides an exemplar of this phenomenon. Their study found that characteristics such as the percentage of foreign-born residents and the size of the city influenced the adoption of civil service reforms thought to improve city functioning in the early phases of the municipal reform movement. However, over time the city demographics no longer influenced the adoption of such reforms. The authors concluded that in the later periods, civil service reforms had taken on a legitimated status and, as such, became viewed as a necessary signal of a properly functioning municipal system.

Much work in the organizational field arena sought to identify institutionalization by contrasting the adoption of practices for rational or institutional motives, and by detecting how the quest for collective rationality led to homogeneity within field-level populations. Of particular interest was the *role of the state* and the influence of the legal/regulatory environment in leading organizations to collectively develop appropriate responses that ultimately led to uniformity in organizational form or structure.

For instance, Edelman (1992) studied organizations subject to affirmative action and equal employment opportunity legislation. This legislation required organizations to incorporate members from historically underrepresented groups into their hierarchy. Yet, the ambiguity of the legislation did not specify how an organization should demonstrate their compliance (i.e., how an organization could demonstrate that it had indeed incorporated women, racial/ethnic, and religious minorities into its operations). In response to this uncertainty, field-level actors pushed for the creation of Affirmative Action and Equal Employment Opportunity (AA/EEO) offices as a way to demonstrate their compliance with the new regulations. As other field members – namely the government – took the establishment of an AA/EEO office as evidence of compliance, the adoption of these offices became widespread. A similar process also led to the implementation of grievance systems (Sutton and Dobbin, 1996), internal job markets (Dobbin et al., 1993) and maternity leave policies (Kelly and Dobbin, 1999).

After focusing on the mimetic and regulative forces that led to adoption and isomorphism within an organizational field, institutional research took the so-called 'cognitive turn' (Meindl et al., 1994; Lindenberg, 1998). Work within the organizational field domain turned towards understanding the *cultural and cognitive processes* that guided field members' behavior. Researchers sought to uncover the material practices and symbolic constructions that served as organizing templates for field members (Friedland and Alford, 1991). These field-level 'logics' provided organizations with schemas to guide their behavior.

For example, Marquis (2003) highlighted the cultural-cognitive templates that guided

the construction of inter-corporate network ties. Firms located in communities that began before the era of auto and air travel had more locally based director connections than firms located in communities that began after auto and air travel became prevalent. Moreover, this logic of locally based network ties continued to guide the behavior of the firms in older communities long after auto and air travel became prevalent.

In other work, Thornton (2001) studied the evolution of logics within the higher education publishing industry and found that acquisition patterns varied according to which logic dominated the industry. When a market-logic dominated the industry, publishers that followed an imprint strategy and those with distribution contracts faced a greater risk of acquisition than other publishers. Yet, when an editorial-logic dominated the industry, imprint and distribution strategies had no significant effect on a publisher's likelihood of being acquired, suggesting that as the field-level logic changed, the acquisition behavior of the organizations within the field changed as well.

While the Marquis and Thornton studies highlighted the temporal dimension of cognitive processes, another study, by Davis and Greve (1997), highlighted the corresponding spatial dimensions by noting that cognitive perceptions regarding the legitimacy of a corporate practice varied based on the social and geographic distance among managers and board of director members. The implementation of the golden parachute, a practice that provided protection to top managers in the event of a hostile takeover, spread among firms within the same region, whereas the adoption of a poison pill, a practice that made hostile takeover prohibitively expensive, spread among firms that shared a board of director tie. Their investigation suggested that the proximity of actors affected the diffusion of firm behavior within a field.

Throughout this early stream of research, the overarching emphasis on similarity remained a constant. The organizational field was conceived as predominantly static in its configuration, unitary in its makeup and formed around common technologies, industries, or discrete network ties (DiMaggio, 1995; Greenwood and Hinings, 1996). Regulative, normative and cognitive influences bred homogeneity in the aggregate. But this emphasis within the literature soon became the subject of criticism.

ORGANIZATIONAL FIELDS: PRESENT CONFIGURATIONS

Beginning in the late 1990s, scholars argued that the institutional literature placed too much emphasis on the homogeneity of organizational populations and not the processes that created this outcome (Hirsch, 1997). This focus on isomorphism as the 'master hypothesis' (Hoffman and Ventresca, 2002) was seen by many as an unfortunate outcome of early theory development and the misrecognized empirical insights possible from institutional analyses. Critics contended that it facilitated a popular misconception of the theory as embodying stability and inertia as its defining characteristics. Homogeneity of form and practice was treated as evidence of institutional theories of organization (Kraatz and Zajac, 1996). DiMaggio, reflecting on 'what theory is not' (1995) suggested that core institutional claims in his oft-cited 1983 paper (DiMaggio and Powell, 1983) suffered asymmetric attention:

> Somewhat to my surprise papers cited our paper as support for the proposition that all organizations become like all others, regardless of field. Somehow the network argument that we authors regarded as so central had been deleted in the paper's reception. Within a few more years, the paper had turned into a kind of ritual citation, affirming the view that, well, organizations are kind of wacky, and (despite the presence of 'collective rationality' in the paper's subtitle) people are never rational. (DiMaggio, 1995: 395)

Scholars called for efforts to 'end the family quarrel' between old and new institutionalism (Hirsch and Lounsbury, 1997) and to bring agency, politics and change 'back' into the institutional literature (Perrow, 1986; DiMaggio, 1988; Brint and Karabel, 1991; DiMaggio, 1995; Greenwood and Hinings, 1996; Hirsch and Lounsbury, 1997), resurrecting it from the earlier traditions of macro-organizational literature (i.e. Selznick, 1949). In all, these criticisms were aimed at redressing the over-socialized view (Granovetter, 1985) that depicted recipients of field-level influence as a homogeneous collection of organizational actors, each behaving according to a social script designed by the social environment.

In response, emergent studies examined organizational 'field members' actions' in light of their institutional contexts (i.e., Holm, 1995; Kraatz and Zajac, 1996; Greenwood and Hinings, 1996). This new line of reasoning attended to several key aspects of field-level processes: moving beyond stability and inertia to introduce notions of change within the field; considering the role of organizational self-interests and agency within that context (Perrow, 1986; Covaleski and Dirsmith, 1988; DiMaggio, 1988) and advancing the view that some firms can respond strategically to institutional pressures (Oliver, 1991) to become what might be called institutional entrepreneurs (DiMaggio, 1988; Zucker, 1988; Fligstein, 1997; Lawrence, 1999).

The first target for reconfiguring conceptions of the field addressed the notion of *change*. As observers of the social world, scholars knew that change happened even within highly institutionalized contexts. Yet prevailing theory did not handle such occurrences adequately, in part because of the way in which scholars defined and operationalized organizational fields. Where previous definitions of the field centered around organizations with a common technology or market (i.e., SIC classification), the field began to be seen as forming around the issues that became important to the interests and objectives of a specific collective of organizations (Hoffman, 1999). Issues defined what the field was, drawing linkages that may not have been previously present.

Field-configuring events (Lampel and Meyer, 2008) provide stakeholders with venues to discuss, define and debate the issues at stake in a field's emergence and evolution. Though temporary in nature, field-configuring events offer participants the opportunity to recognize a shared interest and to cultivate the shared understandings essential to field formation and perpetuation. This literature also provides useful imagery and methodological tools for scholars. No longer an ephemeral space within our scholarly imagination, a field is a place where interested parties meet, such as at conferences or award ceremonies (Lampel and Meyer, 2008). By paying attention to such events, a researcher can easily witness a field in action.

These clarifications led to a conception of the organizational field that would bring together various field constituents with incongruent purposes, not common technologies or industries that assured some commonality of interests. For example, Bertels, Hoffman and DeJordy (2014) explore the heterogeneous nature of field-level membership, developing a method to identify configurations of social position, identity and work that result in a distinct set of challenger roles. Rather than locales of isomorphic dialogue, the field became *contested*; a 'field of struggles' (Bourdieu and Wacquant, 1992) where constituents engaged in 'a war or, if one prefers, a distribution of the specific capital which, accumulated in the course of previous wars, orients future strategies' (Calhoun, 1993: 86). Organizations engage in field-level conflict, out of which they gain skills and capital for future conflict.

Toward this end, Fligstein and McAdam (2012) urged scholars to conceptualize fields as spaces of *strategic action* wherein actors relate to one another out of shared, though not necessarily consensual, understandings about the field. According to these authors, incumbents and challengers constantly vie for advantage and membership shifts

depending on the issues at stake. In these settings, socially skilled actors seek to solidify their position by reproducing the status quo or acting as brokers between disjointed groups.

Thus, the organizational field became seen as *dynamic* and capable of moving towards something other than isomorphism; evolving both through the entry or exit of particular organizations or populations (Barnett and Carroll, 1993; Hoffman, 1999; Scott et al., 2000) and through an alteration of the interaction patterns and power balances among them (Brint and Karabel, 1991; Greenwood and Hinings, 1996). Others added that fields remained conflicted even when institutional norms were apparently 'settled' because powerful actors were continually working to maintain their legitimacy (Lounsbury and Glynn, 2001). With the field defined more in terms of contestation and debate, institutions were seen more as 'the products of human design, [and] the outcomes of purposive action by instrumentally oriented individuals' (DiMaggio and Powell, 1991: 8), such that we may expect to find more opportunity for deviance and *agency* among field members (Hirsch, 1997).

Several authors developed theoretical accounts of the sources of agency, change and variety within institutions and organizational fields. Oliver (1991) suggested that organizations crafted strategic responses and engaged in a multitude of tactics when confronted with the pressures presented by the institutional environment. She argued that an organization's willingness and ability to conform to institutional pressures depended on why these pressures were being exerted (cause), who was exerting them (constituents), what these pressures were (content), how or by what means they were exerted (control) and where they occurred (context). From this perspective, all organizations within a field did not march quietly down the path towards homogeneity.

Greenwood and Hinings (1996) pushed further to combine thoughts from both the old and new institutionalism literatures by developing a framework for understanding how the internal interests and conflicts of an organization's members influenced the organization's response to institutional pressures.

Seo and Creed (2002) highlighted an important interest that served as an impetus for change: field members' need to reconcile contradictory institutional arrangements. According to the authors, organizational fields were connected to and embedded within other and conflicting institutional systems. As field members tried to reconcile these differences by bringing the various institutional rules in line with their needs and interests, the fields inevitably changed.

Schneiberg (2007) has suggested that change and variation comes from within fields. If fields are indeed places where struggle and contestation take place, then inevitably these struggles leave behind organizational practices and forms that suffer defeat. These ideas may lay dormant for a time, but field members often resurrect these expired forms of organization and practice, which in turn leads to increased variation within the field.

Likewise, Quirke (2013) rooted the sources of variation within the field itself. Her investigation of private schools in Toronto, Canada highlighted the 'patchiness' of organizational fields. Not all organizations face the same pressure to conform. Fields that have weak oversight mechanisms, multiple logics, or constantly shifting constituent demands create a context in which organizations have more freedom. As a consequence, marginal or periphery field members can more easily sidestep isomorphic pressures and instead make alternate claims for legitimacy that rely on niche-status and uniqueness within the institutional landscape.

These theoretical accounts of change were used to develop new empirical insights. Emergent research looked not at homogeneity but at variation and change among organizations within a field as signs of institutional processes. For instance, by investigating the decline of the conglomerate organizational form among the 500 largest American industrial firms, Davis, Diekmann and Tinsley (1994) studied the abandonment of a well-institutionalized practice among organizations within a field rather than the adoption of such practices. Lounsbury (2001) provided an explanation of the institutional factors that influenced variation in the adoption of two recycling practices among US colleges and universities. The study highlighted the internal organizational dynamics of colleges that chose to incorporate recycling duties into current waste management policies in relation to those colleges that chose to create a new recycling administrator position.

This newfound emphasis on institutional change culminated with the publication of a special issue of the *Academy of Management Journal*, with each article in this volume seeking to interpret change and agency within an organizational field through the lens of institutional theory (Dacin et al., 2002).

But despite the insights that this new area of research brought to bear on organizational fields, early notions which implied that individual organizations can respond strategically to field pressures (Oliver, 1991) or may strategically influence the process of field change (Lawrence, 1999) treated the organization and the field as separate and distinct. The firm 'responded' to pressures by either adapting to or resisting those pressures. Critics argued that the interaction between firm and field was not unidirectional nor was it free from interpretation and *filtering processes*. This introduced concerns for sense-making, issue interpretation, selective attention and cognitive framing among field members (Dutton and Dukerich, 1991; Scott, 1994; Hoffman and Ocasio, 2001; Hoffman and Ventresca, 2002). The demands of the field were not uniformly understood by all members. Organization-level dynamics caused field members to filter and alter environmental demands. Further, members transmitted their interests back towards the field. The process of interaction became recursive as the social structure of the field became both the 'medium and outcome of the reproduction of practices. Structure enters simultaneously into the constitution of social practices, and "exists" in the generating moments of this constitution' (Giddens, 1979).

Scott (1994) claimed that the essence of the field perspective was its ability to analyze the ways in which organizations enact their environment and are simultaneously enacted upon by the same environment. The work of Bansal and Penner (2002) illustrated this process by investigating the interpretive processes among four newspaper publishers. The authors highlighted the importance of regional networks in influencing the frames and enactment processes developed to address the recycled newsprint issue. They found that the way in which feasibility, importance and organizational responsibility for recycling were interpreted within these networks helped account for variation in organizational response to this issue. By linking theory and argument from cognitive strategy theory on issue interpretation to institutional analysis, the authors provided an explanation of heterogeneity in field-level behavior.

Other work focused on the interconnectedness of organizations and the field by analyzing the role of *institutional entrepreneurs* (DiMaggio, 1988; Fligstein, 1997; Lawrence, 1999) in shaping the discourse, norms and the structures that guide organizational action (Maguire et al., 2004). As in all field-level debates, certain organizations have the ability to influence the rules of the game (Fligstein, 1990). Yet, even powerful actors cannot simply impose new logics and norms on a field. At some level, the norms must be accepted by other actors Beckert, 1999). The actors that lobby for the acceptance of these new logics, norms and practices illustrate the work that institutional entrepreneurs engage in to create and build legitimacy.

Suddaby and Greenwood's (2005) study of the creation of multidisciplinary practices provided insight into this process. The establishment of practices that included both accountants and lawyers threatened the previously agreed upon boundaries between the accounting and legal professions. Thus, creating a firm that included both lawyers and accountants within the same hierarchy required institutional entrepreneurs to provide a legitimating account for this organizational form. To build legitimacy entrepreneurs developed rhetorical strategies that served two purposes. First, they included institutional vocabularies that articulated the logic behind new organizational practices and forms. Second, these rhetorical strategies included language that accounted for the pace and necessity of change within the organizational field.

The attention to entrepreneurship and change within fields coalesced with the *institutional work* literature. First articulated by Lawrence and Suddaby (2006), studies of institutional work highlight the efforts of culturally competent actors as they attempt to create, maintain and disrupt institutions. Prior to the emergence of this literature, entrepreneurship was mostly investigated in connection with establishing or altering institutional rules and patterns. A key contribution of research in this area is its attention to the reality that entrepreneurial activities are required to maintain the social mechanisms that ensure compliance to institutional rules as well.

Others have taken the notion of the institutional entrepreneur further by acknowledging that institutional entrepreneurs do not act alone or in isolation. Individual agents form political networks and coalitions to act as 'important motors of institution-building, deinstitutionalization, and reinstitutionalization in organizational fields' (Rao et al., 2003: 796). This conception provided a bridge between institutional theory and *social movement* theory (Davis et al., 2005), focusing attention on the ability of social movements to give rise to new organizational fields and change the demography of existing organization fields (Rao et al., 2000).

Social movement scholars have long recognized the connection between their work and organizations (McCarthy and Zald, 1977; Strang and Soule, 1998; Campbell, 2005; Fligstein and McAdam, 2012). McCarthy and Zald (1977) incorporated concepts from organization theory to develop their resource mobilization perspective. According to this perspective, the availability and accumulation of resources served as an impetus for the formation of social movement organizations that bear a remarkable resemblance to other goal-directed, hierarchical organizations. Moreover, those social movement organizations with similar preferences for change constituted the social movement industry, a unit of analysis not unlike the organizational field. Organizational change agents became parts of these collective movements, using shared and accumulated resources and power to 'overcome historical inertia, undermine the entrenched power structures in the field or triumph over alternative projects of change' (Guillen, 2006: 43). These actions were often conducted in opposition to others in similarly configured collective movements (Zald and Useem, 1987; Meyer and Staggenborg, 1996).

Other work seeking to understand the bidirectional influence of organizations and fields built on the linkages between organizational fields, culture and societal institutions. In particular, researchers sought to explain how ideas and beliefs about organizational strategies and practice became standard and spread in highly structured fields of activity (Edelman, 1990; Guthrie and Roth, 1999; Washington and Ventresca, 2004). For example, Zilber's (2006) study highlighted the ways in which Israeli society, culture and fields are intertwined. High technology was mythologized as a tool enabling the creation of useful products, an area where gifted individuals excelled, and as a vehicle for national development and societal progress within the Israeli popular press. Each of these myths was found at the level of the organizational field as high technology companies incorporated elements of these myths in the job descriptions contained within employment advertisements. As a result, rationalizations of the benefits and purposes of high technology to Israeli society were incorporated within the employment activities of the high-technology organizational field.

In sum, the critiques of new institutional theory led to streams of field-level research that focused on change, variation and agency discussed above. But, while the past and present of organizational research differed from one another in terms of the outcome studied, they were connected by their conceptualization of fields as 'things' that produced outcomes. More recent critiques have suggested that the future of field research lies not in the further emphasis on outcomes but instead in conceptualizing fields as mechanisms (Hoffman and Ventresca, 2002; Davis and Marquis, 2005). This refocus allows for the specification of collective rationality and the possibility that fields serve as mechanisms for bringing about phenomena other than similarity (DiMaggio and Powell, 1983; Washington and Ventresca, 2004). We address these themes in the third section of this chapter.

ORGANIZATIONAL FIELDS: THE FUTURE

In the final section of this chapter we offer our thoughts on the future of organizational field research. We develop our arguments regarding future directions based on the critiques of past and present research as focusing on the outcomes of field membership as opposed to the processes that hold the members of a field together. Since the chapter's original publication, significant progress has been made. In particular, the literatures on field configuring events and institutional work speak directly to the concerns we raised regarding a lack of theorizing around the issues of field evolution and field-level activities.

While recognizing the strides made since this chapter's publication, we still need more scholarship to fully elaborate the utility of the *organizational field* as a conceptual and methodological construct. Given this, we center our concluding thoughts on the same themes as before. We continue to encourage those involved in organizational field research to focus on collective rationality within fields: how it is developed, which field members contribute to its development and maintenance, how it is transmitted to other actors, and how it changes over time. Furthermore, we take this as an opportunity to push scholars to use the organizational field perspective as a tool of analysis for meeting society's challenges in the twenty-first century.

Scott (2001) defined the field as a community of organizations that partake in a common meaning system and whose participants interact more frequently and fatefully with one another than with actors outside the field. DiMaggio and Powell (1983) defined the field as those organizations that in the aggregate represent a recognized area of institutional life. While both of these definitions treat the field as a collective of organizations, they also present an underlying notion that represents a future conception of the field; one where the field is a locale in which organizations relate to or involve themselves with one another. A definition that in some ways brings us back to the influence of Bourdieu – where a field is as much about the relationship between the actors as it is about the effect of the field on the actors.

To move away from the current focus on field outcomes and towards an understanding of why field-level interactions remain vital to organizations, fields must be seen, not as containers for the community of organizations, but instead as *relational spaces* that provide an organization with the opportunity to involve itself with other actors (Wooten, 2006; Emirbayer and Johnson, 2008). Fields are richly contextualized spaces where disparate organizations involve themselves with one another in an effort to develop collective understandings regarding matters that are consequential for organizational and field-level activities.

Moving beyond the notion of fields as being constructed around the physical proximity of actors (Warren, 1967) or issues (Hoffman, 1999), fields as relational spaces stresses the notion that organizations need to do nothing more than take note of one another to be considered part of the same field. This does not mean that actors formalize their relations via hierarchical arrangements or network ties (Djelic and Sahlin-Andersson, 2006). Instead, one actor takes note of another and through this process of referencing one another, actors bring a field into existence. Out of a relational notion of the field emerge several critical issues concerning formation, evolution, and boundaries.

- Why does one relational space with this set of actors form and not another? Why do disparate organizations and populations come together at the field level? How and why do fields form? What processes drive some organizations to interact more frequently and fatefully with one another than with other organizations, thus creating the boundaries of a field?

Research must highlight the organizational dynamics that lead actors to engage one another and start the field-level structuring or restructuring process. It is not evident, for example, why petrochemical companies would willingly engage environmental groups without understanding the dynamics of field-level engagement in field studies (i.e., Hoffman, 1999). Future research should investigate the dynamics that lead to field creation and the contextual factors that lead to one field form over another. For example, relations that form around a common technology, say coal production, are not likely to be similar to those relations that form around an issue such as environmental protection. Such differences will undoubtedly influence the character of the field (Stinchcombe, 1965) and the specification of collective rationality.

Entrance to or engagement within the field is often precipitated by disruptive events such as exogenous shocks that provide the impetus for organizations to make sense of a reconfigured environment. Disruptive events such as the threat of a hostile takeover (Davis, 1991), regulatory changes (Edelman, 1992), environmental catastrophes (Hoffman and Ocasio, 2001), rituals (Anand and Watson, 2004), or terrorism (Bail, 2012) create contradictions within the environment (Seo and Creed, 2002) and force organizations to (re)analyze their surroundings. Fields serve as the sites in which organizations come together to do this sense-making work. Future research will address what drives organizations to interact with one another and how those configurations are formed. It will also hold open the possibility that the field is not always in use. Instead, the field comes alive when organizations decide to interact with one another and this is the moment that researchers are encouraged to direct their attention towards as it provides tentative answers to the questions now being posed.

Indeed, the research on field-configuring events (Lampel and Meyer, 2008) posits just this. The temporary nature of these events suggests that field members need not assemble on a regular basis to recognize their common interests or to solidify their collective goals. For example, conferences offer a critical venue for field formation. In his study of cochlear implant technology, Garud (2008) found that this holds true even when the conference serves as a space of contestation. Participants were driven to a number of conferences to dispute single versus multiple electrode cochlear technologies. While short in duration, each conference signaled that a field existed, identified the key participants in the field, and the issues that would propel future interactions among these participants. Similarly, Schüssler, Rüling and Wittneben (2014) use United Nations climate change conferences to analyze how regular and high-stakes events in an event series interacted in producing and preventing institutional change in the transnational climate policy field. They found that growing field complexity and issue multiplication compromise the change potential of a field-configuring event series in favor of field maintenance.

- Once formed, how do fields evolve and change? What are the dynamics by which engagement takes place?

The essence of a field is its ability to serve as the meeting place where organizations have the opportunity to involve themselves with one another. Positioning fields in this manner brings scholarship back to the core concepts of the literature, refocusing on the development of 'collective rationality' (Scott, 2001), rather than the impact that collective rationality has on the field. But that field structure is not static. It evolves in makeup, interconnections and conceptual frames.

For example, Anand and various co-authors have articulated the role of award ceremonies as structuring events within the life of an organizational field. Be it the Booker Prize (Anand and Jones, 2008) or the Grammy Awards (Anand and Watson, 2004), these ceremonies represent public rituals that confer value and generate controversy all toward the ultimate goal of legitimating artistic works and the field itself.

Anand and Watson's (2004) study of the Grammy Awards illuminates this emerging conception of the organizational field. In addition to providing the music industry's members with an opportunity to meet annually and celebrate one another's accomplishments, the music industry as a field is engaged at this event. Artists fight for the creation of categories particular to their genre to legitimate their status as field members. The addition of new genres to the music industry causes the boundaries of the field to become contested. Thus, the Grammy Awards represent the site where conflicts among members are engaged and resolved. The petition for new categories represents a disruptive event and the current members engaging with the relational space of the field (i.e. the Grammy Awards) develop a new collective rationality about which artists belong within the field and which do not.

An actor's attempt to gain membership strains the existing order within an established field. Field members that once had limited interactions with one another may band together because of a common interest in locking a particular actor out of the field, thus changing the pre-existing coalitions. Under such circumstances, every aspect of a field's character is challenged. As new actors push for admittance, the inter-organizational structures and coalitions that once supported the field no longer make sense and the mutual awareness among the field members that they are involved in a common enterprise must be revisited.

This leads to an appreciation for contending logics as a force for institutional change (Seo and Creed, 2002; Suddaby and Greenwood, 2005). Reay and Hinings (2005), for example, develop a theoretical model to explain change in mature organizational fields by emphasizing the role of competing institutional logics as part of a radical change process. Rather than explaining the sources of change, they investigate how a field becomes re-established after the implementation of a radical structural change. Studying fields at these moments of restructuring increases our understanding of how collective rationality is developed.

- How can the activities within field-level populations be identified and defined? How do field members relate to one another?

While field constituents' actions may be initially conducted in opposition to one another (Zald and Useem, 1987; Meyer and Staggenborg, 1996; Davis et al., 2005), protracted institutional engagement can yield a gradual merging of interests with a concurrent alteration in the structure of the field itself. However, until that happens, the field is not a collective of isomorphic actors, but an intertwined constellation of actors who hold differing perspectives and competing logics with regard to their individual and collective purpose (McCarthy and Zald, 1977;

Fligstein and McAdam, 2012). As such, an appreciation for the diversity of activities and beliefs must be incorporated into field-level arguments, directing attention towards the development of a terminology for the differing roles that field members play.

Every social group has roles that members must adopt to perpetuate the group's existence. Moreover, these roles typically confer different responsibilities for the actors within them. For instance, the role of 'mother' has a different set of behavioral expectations than the role of 'brother'. Within field research, we have been neglectful of the differing roles that field members have. The exceptions may be our focus on entrepreneurs or change agents. Yet, even in this case, we label a member as an entrepreneur or not, a change agent or conversely a protector of the status quo. Conceptualizing the field as a relational space dictates that we take a closer look at the way in which actors relate to one another, especially the roles that certain members adopt to advance the field.

Lawrence and Suddaby's (2006) review of institutional theory provides a typology of the different types of activities that actors engage in to create, maintain and disrupt institutions. For example, during the creation stage actors advocate on behalf of an institution by mobilizing political and regulatory support. During the maintenance stage, advocacy becomes less important and actors instead aim to police the activities of others to ensure the institution's continuation. This suggests that at the level of the organizational field, different actors engage in various tasks. For example, during the creation stage of the field, it is highly unlikely that all members of an organizational field would need to advocate on the field's behalf. A more feasible scenario would involve a select number of field members devoting their time and energy towards this task while other field members focus their attention on other activities also vital to the field's emergence. With greater focus on the different types of work that actors perform comes a need for a language to articulate these distinct institutional roles. Labels for each member of the community of organizations become necessary according to the type of institutional activities performed. General terminology like buyer, supplier, or regulatory agency will no longer provide a sufficient explanation of the role organizations adopt or the work they perform within the field.

As the institutional work literature (Lawrence and Suddaby, 2006; Lawrence et al., 2009) has shown, labeling organizations in this manner provides deeper clarity on the collective understanding held by each field member regarding which actors perform what roles within the field. Just as organizational members can reduce uncertainty over work roles by developing agreement about the responsibilities that come with organizational roles, field members can also reduce the level of uncertainty they face by developing a corresponding understanding of what type of work each field member is responsible for given their role within the field.

Though we strongly encourage scholars to move away from the focus on outcomes within field research, we recognize that it may be difficult to wean ourselves off this line of inquiry. Therefore, we highlight several avenues of research based on the relational space perspective on fields.

- Beyond discerning appropriate behavior, what do the disparate organizations hope to gain from their involvement with one another?

As we move beyond the depiction of organizations as mere recipients of institutional pressures, it is also time to advance conceptions of what organizations take away from field membership. If we take the field as a relational space, we can envision other uses for the field beyond discerning appropriate behavior. Field-level interactions are best understood as mechanisms by which other organizational phenomena occur. For example, some have begun to investigate the field-level processes by which organizational

identities are formed. Within the organizational literature, identity is typically presented as an organizational-level property developed internally by the members of an organization. While research has suggested that organizational identity is influenced by outside parties (Dutton and Dukerich, 1991; Elsbach and Kramer, 1996), the general consensus holds that an organization's identity is what members see as central, distinctive and enduring about the organization (Albert and Whetten, 1985). Wedlin (2006) challenges this conception of organizational identity formation by positioning the organizational field as the site in which organizations develop their identity. In this view, identity formation is seen as an inherently social and inter-organizational process and the field is the place in which organizations take on this task.

Other work has sought to understand how field membership influences phenomena such as hiring (Williamson and Cable, 2003) and collaborative tie formation (Kenis and Knoke, 2002), both processes that had been thought to be reflective of dynamics internal to the organization. This is not to suggest that scholars recast every organizational process as being dependent upon field-level membership, as this would push the literature towards an over-socialized view once again. However, it does suggest that envisioning organizational fields as influential to the development of intra-organizational processes exposes a host of possibilities for research projects that shed light on the institutional factors that influence an organization's daily functioning.

- How is field-level interaction affected by mechanisms and structures internal to the individual organization, and how does this interaction change those mechanisms and structures?

Future organizational field research will focus on the processes of participating in a field and what this participation ultimately means for the inner workings of an organization (Hoffman, 2001). To date, field research has largely provided an explanation of macro to macro transitions; field-level interactions lead to changes in structure, culture and output at the aggregate field levels. Moving forward, field research will serve as a bridge between the macro and micro by providing detailed explanations of how field-level interactions influence internal organizational phenomena. This direction acknowledges that the field is made up of various actors that constitute a community of organizations (DiMaggio and Powell, 1983; Scott, 1995, 2001) while simultaneously acknowledging that organizational and field-level factors are interconnected in a reciprocal relationship.

Future research will continue to bridge the old and new institutionalisms in an effort to understand how field membership aids other intra-organizational processes. As discussed earlier, prior attempts to connect these literatures imported the concepts of agency and interests from the old-institutionalism to explain how organizational field members resisted isomorphic pressures. While this represents progress on one front, problems still remain with the way in which agency and interests are conceptualized in the institutional domain. Currently, both the old and new institutionalisms present the concepts of agency and interests in an atomistic fashion. Each holds that an organization's self-interests are developed internally and cause the organization to undertake some action such as cooptation or resistance (Oliver, 1991). Yet, Scott (1991) insisted that institutions define the ends and shape the means by which interests are determined and pursued. The formation and pursuit of interests must be seen as the product of field-level engagement. Just as research has recast organizational identity formation as a field-level process, so too will research reconceptualize organizational agency and self-interests by focusing on the possibility that field-level engagement enables an individual organization's pursuit of self-interests. This will redirect more attention to the way in which the field provides an organization with a context to enact agency.

• How do institutions spread or diffuse within field-level populations?

Just as institutional scholars (particularly within North America) emphasized mimetic or taken-for-granted forces as the primary mechanism by which organizational field members became homogeneous to one another (Mizruchi and Fein, 1999), we have also emphasized the diffusion model as an explanation for how institutional rules are adopted and spread throughout an organizational field. Theoretical and empirical works in the institutional literature imply that organizational practices spread through fields like wild-fires, with members succumbing to pressures to adopt these practices. Moreover, field members adopt these practices intact without adjusting or manipulating them to fit their specific needs or context. Yet, more recent research suggests that the uncritical adoption of practices encouraged by the diffusion process accounts for the failure of these practices to deliver the promised benefit to organizational functioning (Kitchener, 2002).

As we begin to view the field as a highly interactive relational space, relying so heavily upon the diffusion model will no longer suffice. Work within the European tradition provides an alternative understanding of how institutional norms and rules take hold at the field level. Instead of diffusing through a field, organizational practices are translated from the institutional level to the organizational level (Czarniawska and Joerges, 1996; Zilber, 2006). In the process of translation, the original meaning of an organizational practice changes as individual field members incorporate these items into their own organization. Much like literal translations from one language to another often have no meaning, incorporating a prevailing practice 'as-is' into an organization may not yield the intended consequences. Instead, field members must determine how to bend and shape a prevailing organizational practice such that it will hold meaning for their own organization and the field facilitates this translation process. As organizations relate to one another within the field, they can determine how other members incorporated the predominant practices and use this knowledge to determine how best to mold these practices for use within their own organization.

Another byproduct of the emphasis on the diffusion model has been that theoretical and empirical work using this model leaves the impression that the widespread adoption of a practice within an organizational field equals institutionalization. Zeitz, Mittal and McAulay (1999) caution us to reconsider. The authors suggest that just as organizations adopt a practice *en masse* they may also abandon the practice with the same vigor in a short amount of time. Instead of focusing on the presence of a practice at a finite moment in time, the authors implore researchers to focus on the micro-processes that allow a practice to take hold and become 'entrenched' within an organizational field (Zeitz et al., 1999). Future research will draw attention to the relational dynamics that facilitate not only the widespread adoption of certain practices over others, but also provide greater understanding of the intra-organizational processes (i.e., identity, interests, agency) that facilitate the entrenchment of certain practices over others.

- Why do fields matter?

Not only does a relational notion of the field encourage scholars to focus on issues of formation and evolution. It also encourages scholars to consider why fields matter not just for the organizations situated within them, but why fields matter for all that might feel the effects of the field itself. Fields are spaces that produce cultural and material products ranging from definitions of efficiency to organizational archetypes. Society must then wrestle with how to deal with the outcomes – how to become 'efficient' or how to reconfigure the organization into a newly favored form. Fields matter not only because

of their investigative power, but because actual people must deal with the consequences of their outcomes on a daily basis.

The advances taken in the years since this chapter's original publication have deepened our paradigmatic understanding of organizational fields. Yet, we have not learned as much as possible about how the processes that drive field development and evolution contribute to the production or erosion of societal ills (e.g., inequality, climate change, gender-based violence) with which we must contend. To some, this critique may bring to mind the problem versus paradigm approach to research articulated by Davis and Marquis (2005). Yet, instead of an either/or proposition, we instead encourage scholars to recognize the potential to adopt both approaches simultaneously. For instance, Wooten (2015) uses organizational fields as an analytical tool to investigate racial inequality among organizations – how it is produced and reified. In doing so the author adds to our theoretical understanding of fields as racially specific spaces while also addressing why this is problematic for the functioning of certain organizational actors. Organizations operating within racially stigmatized fields, such as black colleges, find it difficult to garner the political and financial resources necessary to survive (Wooten, 2015).

CONCLUSION

This chapter offers views on how the central concept of institutional theory – the organizational field – has changed over the past three decades. It presents a trajectory that began by focusing on the dynamics that led to conformity in behavior among organizations and evolved towards understanding the dynamics that allow for heterogeneity, variation and change. The chapter ends with thoughts on where the future of organizational field research lies, suggesting that scholars orient their research towards the processes that encourage field formation and collective rationality. The future of organizational field research is linked to the future of organization theory in general.

In speculating about the prospects for organization theory in the twenty-first century, Davis and Marquis (2005) suggest that research in this area has moved away from being paradigm-driven to being problem-driven. As such, field-level research is ready to make the transition from testing the core ideas of the new institutional theory paradigm to investigating fields as sites where problems of organizing are debated among disparate actors. The domain of organizational fields is now ready to move away from the simple outcomes of institutional processes, to instead explain why the field remains integral to understanding how organizations construct solutions to the problems of the twenty-first century. This moves beyond notions of institutions as barriers, as always taken-for-granted and as leading towards isomorphism, and instead refocuses on field-level dynamics, collective rationality within these fields and the behavior of individual organizations as integral parts of these processes. Researchers will return to a focus on the structuration processes with a particular interest in understanding how the structuring of fields contributes to intra- and inter-organizational processes. While not a complete agenda for future research, this represents a starting point for researchers wishing to understand the processes that lead organizations to relate to one another and to ultimately do so within the space we have come to know as an organizational field.

REFERENCES

Albert, Stuart and Whetten, David A. (1985) 'Organizational Identity.' In Robert Sutton and Barry Staw (eds), *Research in Organizational Behavior*. Greenwich, CT: JAI Press Inc. pp. 263–295.

Anand, N. and Jones, Brittany C. (2008) 'Tournaments Rituals, Category Dynamics, and Field Configuration: The Case of the Booker Prize.' *Journal of Management Studies* 45: 1036–1060.

Anand, N. and Watson, Mary R. (2004) 'Tournament Rituals in the Evolution of Fields: The Case of the Grammy Awards.' *Academy of Management Journal* 47: 59–80.

Bail, Christopher A. (2012) 'The Fringe Effect: Civil Society Organizations and the Evolution of Media Discourse about Islam since the September 11th Attacks.' *American Sociological Review* 77: 855–879.

Bansal, Pratima, and Penner, Wendy J. (2002) 'Interpretations of Institutions: The Case of Recycled Newsprint.' In Petter Holm and Marc Ventresca (eds), *Organizations, Policy, and the Natural Environment: Institutional and Strategic Perspectives*. Stanford, CA: Stanford University Press. pp. 311–326.

Barnett, Willam and Carroll, Glenn (1993) 'How Institutional Constraints Affected the Organization of Early US Telephony.' *Journal of Law, Economics and Organizations* 9: 98–126.

Beckert, Jens. (1999) 'Agency, Entrepreneurs, and Institutional Change: The Role of Strategic Choice and Institutionalized Practices in Organizations.' *Organization Studies* 20(5): 777–799.

Bertels, Stephanie, Hoffman, Andrew and DeJordy, Rich (2014) 'The Varied Work of Challenger Movements: Identifying Challenger Roles in the U.S. Environmental Movement.' *Organization Studies* 35: 1171–1210.

Bourdieu, Pierre (1990) *The Logic of Practice*. Stanford, CA: Stanford University Press.

Bourdieu, Pierre (1993) *The Field of Cultural Production: Essays on Art and Literature*. New York: Columbia University Press.

Bourdieu, Pierre and Wacquant, Loic (1992) *Invitation to Reflexive Sociology*. Chicago, IL: University of Chicago Press.

Brint, Steven, and Karabel, Jerome (1991) 'Institutional Origins and Transformations: The Case of American Community Colleges.' In Paul J. DiMaggio and Walter W. Powell (eds), *The New Institutionalism in Organizational Analysis*. Chicago, IL: The University of Chicago Press. pp. 337–360.

Calhoun, Craig (1993) 'Habitus, Field, and Capital: The Question of Historical Specificity.' In Craig Calhoun, Edward LiPuma and Moishe Postone (eds), *Bourdieu: Critical Perspectives*. Chicago, IL: University of Chicago Press. pp. 61–88.

Campbell, John L. (2005) 'Where Do We Stand? Common Mechanisms in Organizations and Social Movements Research.' In Gerald F. Davis, Doug McAdam, W. Richard Scott and Mayer N. Zald (eds), *Social Movements and Organization Theory*. New York: Cambridge University Press.

Covaleski, Mark A. and Dirsmith, Mark W. (1988) 'An Institutional Perspective on the Rise, Social

Transformation and Fall of a University Budget Category.' *Administrative Science Quarterly* 33: 562–587.

Czarniawska, Barbara and Joerges, Bernward (1996) 'Travels of Ideas.' In Barbara Czarniawska and Guje Sevon (eds), *Translating Organizational Change*. Berlin: Walter de Gruyter. pp. 13–48.

Dacin, M. Tina, Goodstein, Jerry and Scott, W. Richard (2002) 'Institutional Theory and Institutional Change: Introduction to the Special Research Forum.' *Academy of Management Journal* 45: 45–57.

Davis, Gerald F (1991) 'Agents Without Principles? The Spread of the Poison Pill Through the Intercorporate Network.' *Administrative Science Quarterly* 36: 583–613.

Davis, Gerald F., Diekmann, Kristina A. and Tinsley, Catherine H. (1994) 'The Decline and Fall of the Conglomerate Firm in the 1980s: The Deinstitutionalization of an Organizational Form.' *American Sociological Review* 59: 547–571.

Davis, Gerald F. and Greve, Henrich R. (1997) 'Corporate Elite Networks and Governance Changes in the 1980s.' *American Journal of Sociology* 103: 1–37.

Davis, Gerald F., McAdam, Doug W., Scott, Richard and Zald, Mayer N. (eds) (2005) *Social Movements and Organization Theory*. New York: Cambridge University Press.

Davis, Gerald F. and Marquis, Christopher (2005) 'Prospects for Organization Theory in the Early Twenty-First Century: Institutional Fields and Mechanisms.' *Organization Science* 16: 332–343.

DiMaggio, Paul J. (1988) 'Interest and Agency in Institutional Theory.' In Zucker, Lynne (ed.), *Institutional Patterns and Organizations*. Cambridge, MA: Ballinger. pp. 3–21.

DiMaggio, Paul J. (1995) 'Comments on "What Theory is Not".' *Administrative Science Quarterly* 40: 391–397.

DiMaggio, Paul J. and Powell, Walter W. (1983) 'The Iron Cage Revisited: Institutional Isomorphism and Collective Rationality in Organizational Fields.' *American Sociological Review* 48: 147–160.

DiMaggio, Paul J. and Powell, Walter W. (1991) 'Introduction.' In DiMaggio, Paul J. and Powell, Walter W. (eds), *The New Institutionalism in Organizational Analysis*. Chicago, IL: The University of Chicago Press. pp. 1–40.

Djelic, Marie-Laure and Sahlin-Andersson, Kerstin (2006) 'Introduction: A World of Governance: The Rise of Transnational Regulation.' In Marie-Laure Djelic and Kerstin Sahlin-Andersson (eds), *Transnational Governance: Institutional Dynamics of Regulation*. Cambridge: Cambridge University Press. pp. 1–28.

Dobbin, Frank, Sutton, John R., Meyer, John W. and Scott, W. Richard (1993) 'Equal Opportunity and the Construction of Internal Labor Markets.' *American Journal of Sociology* 99: 396–427.

Dutton, Jane E. and Dukerich, Janet M. (1991) 'Keeping an Eye on the Mirror: Image and Identity in Organizational Adaptation.' *Academy of Management Journal* 34: 517–554.

Edelman, Lauren (1990) 'Legal Environments and Organizational Governance: The Expansion of Due Process in the American Workplace.' *American Journal of Sociology* 95: 1401–1440.

Edelman, Lauren (1992) 'Legal Ambiguity and Symbolic Structures: Organizational Mediation of Civil Rights Law.' *American Journal of Sociology* 97: 1531–1576.

Elsbach, Kimberly D. and Kramer, Roderick M. (1996) 'Members' Responses to Organizational Identity Threats: Encountering the Countering the Business Week Rankings.' *Administrative Science Quarterly* 41: 442–476.

Emirbayer, Mustafa and Johnson, Victoria (2008) 'Bourdieu and Organizational Analysis.' *Theory and Society* 37: 1-44.

Fligstein, Neil (1990) *The Transformation of Corporate Control*. Cambridge, MA: Harvard University Press.

Fligstein, Neil (1997) 'Social Skill and Institutional Theory.' *American Behavioral Scientist* 40: 397–405.

Fligstein, Neil and McAdam, Doug (2012) *A Theory of Fields*. Oxford: Oxford University Press.

Friedland, Roger and Alford, Robert R. (1991) 'Bringing Society Back In: Symbols, Practices, and Institutional Contradictions.' In Paul J. DiMaggio and Walter W. Powell (eds), *The New Institutionalism in Organizational Analysis*. Chicago: The University of Chicago Press. pp. 232–266.

Garud, Raghu (2008) 'Conferences as Venues for the Configuration of Emerging Organizational Fields: The Case of Cochlear Implants.' *Journal of Management Studies* 45: 1061–1088.

Giddens, Anthony (1979) *Central Problems in Social Theory: Action, Structure, and Contradiction in Social Analysis*. Berkeley, CA: University of California Press.

Granovetter, Mark (1985) 'Economic Actions and Social Structure: The Problem of Embeddedness.' *American Journal of Sociology* 91: 481–510.

Greenwood, Royston and Hinings, C.R. (1996) 'Understanding Radical Organizational Change: Bringing Together the Old and the New Institutionalism.' *Academy of Management Review* 21: 1022–1054.

Guillen, Mauro (2006) *The Taylorized Beauty of the Mechanical: Scientific Management and the Rise of Modernist Architecture*. Princeton, NJ: Princeton University Press.

Guthrie, Doug and Roth, Louise (1999) 'The States, Courts, and Maternity Leave Policies in the US:

Specifying Institutional Mechanisms.' *American Sociological Review* 64: 41–63.

Hirsch, Paul (1997) 'Sociology without Social Structure: Neo-institutional Theory Meets a Brave New World.' *American Journal of Sociology* 102: 1702–1723.

Hirsch, Paul and Lounsbury, Michael (1997) 'Ending the Family Quarrel: Toward a Reconciliation of "Old" and "New" Institutionalisms.' *American Behavioral Scientist* 40: 406–418.

Hoffman, Andrew J. (1999) 'Institutional Evolution and Change: Environmentalism and the U.S. Chemical Industry.' *Academy of Management Journal* 42: 351–371.

Hoffman, Andrew (2001) 'Linking Organizational and Field-level Analyses: The Diffusion of Corporate Environmental Practice.' *Organization & Environment* 14: 133–156.

Hoffman, Andrew, and Ocasio, William (2001) 'Not All Events are Attended Equally: Toward a Middle-Range Theory of Industry Attention to External Events.' *Organization Science* 12: 414–434.

Hoffman, Andrew, and Ventresca, Marc (eds) (2002) *Organizations, Policy, and the Natural Environment: Institutional and Strategic Perspectives.* Stanford, CA: Stanford University Press.

Holm, Petter (1995) 'The Dynamics of Institutionalization: Transformation Process in Norwegian Fisheries.' *Administrative Science Quarterly* 40: 398–422.

Kelly, Erin and Dobbin, Frank (1999) 'Civil Rights Law at Work: Sex Discrimination and the Rise of Maternity Leave Policies.' *American Journal of Sociology* 105: 455–492.

Kenis, Patrick and Knoke, David (2002) 'How Organizational Field Networks Shape Interorganization Tie-Formation Rates.' *Academy of Management Review* 27: 275–293.

Kitchener, Martin (2002) 'Mobilizing the Logic of Managerialism in Professional Fields: The Case of Academic Health Centre Mergers.' *Organization Studies* 23: 391–420.

Kraatz, Matthew S. and Zajac, Edward J. (1996) 'Exploring the Limits of the New Institutionalism: The Causes and Consequences of Illegitimate Organizational Change.' *American Sociological Review* 61: 812–836.

Lampel, Joseph and Meyer, Alan D. (2008) 'Field-Configuring Events as Structuring Mechanisms: How Conferences, Ceremonies, and Trade Shows Constitute New Technologies, Industries, and Markets.' *Journal of Management Studies* 45:1025–1035.

Lawrence, Thomas B (1999) 'Institutional Strategy.' *Journal of Management* 25: 161–188.

Lawrence, Thomas B. and Suddaby, Roy (2006) 'Institutions and Institutional Work.' In Stewart Clegg, Cynthia Hardy, Thomas Lawrence and W.R. Nord (eds), *The SAGE Handbook of Organization Studies.* Thousand Oaks, CA: Sage. pp. 215–254.

Lawrence, Thomas B., Suddaby, Roy and Leca, Bernard (2009) 'Introduction: Theorizing and Studying Institutional Work.' In Thomas B. Lawrence, Roy Suddaby and Bernard Leca (eds), *Institutional Work: Actors and Agency in Institutional Studies of Organization.* Cambridge: Cambridge University Press. pp. 1–27.

Leblebici, Huseyin, Salancik, Gerald R., Copay, Anne, and King, Tom (1991) 'Institutional Change and the Transformation of Interorganizational Fields: An Organizational History of the U.S. Radio Broadcasting Industry.' *Administrative Science Quarterly* 36: 331–363.

Lindenberg, Siewart (1998) 'The Cognitive Turn in Institutional Analysis: Beyond NIE, and NIS?' *Journal of Institutional and Theoretical Economics* 154: 716–727.

Lounsbury, Michael (2001) 'Institutional Sources of Practice Variation: Staffing College and University Recycling Programs.' *Administrative Science Quarterly* 46: 29.

Lounsbury, Michael and Glynn, Mary Ann (2001) 'Cultural Entrepreneurship: Stories, Legitimacy, and the Acquisitions of Resources.' *Strategic Management Journal* 22: 545–564.

Maguire, Steve, Hardy, Cynthia, and Lawrence, Thomas B. (2004) 'Institutional Entrepreneurship in Emerging Fields: HIV/AIDS Treatment Advocacy in Canada.' *Academy of Management Journal* 47: 657–679.

Marquis, Christopher (2003) 'The Pressure of the Past: Network Imprinting in Intercorporate Communities.' *Administrative Science Quarterly* 48: 655–689.

McCarthy, John D. and Zald, Mayer N. (1977) 'Resource Mobilization and Social Movements: A Partial Theory.' *American Journal of Sociology* 82: 1212–1240.

Meindl, James, Stubbart, Charles and Porac, Joseph (1994) 'Cognition Within and Between Organizations – 5 Key Questions.' *Organization Science* 5: 289–293.

Meyer, John W. and Rowan, Brian (1977) 'Institutionalized Organizations: Formal Structure as Myth and Ceremony.' *American Journal of Sociology* 83: 41–62.

Meyer, David S., and Staggenborg, Suzanne (1996) 'Movements, Countermovements, and the Structure of Political Opportunity.' *American Journal of Sociology* 101: 1628–1660.

Mizruchi, Mark, and Fein, Lisa (1999) 'The Social Construction of Organizational Knowledge: A Study of the Uses of Coercive, Mimetic, and Normative Isomorphism.' *Administrative Science Quarterly* 43: 257–292.

Oliver, Christine (1991) 'Strategic Responses to Institutional Processes.' *Academy of Management Review* 16: 145–179.

Orru, Marco, Biggart, Nicole Woolsey and Hamilton, Gary C. (1991) 'Organizational Isomorphism in East Asia.' In Walter W. Powell and Paul J. DiMaggio (eds), *The New Institutionalism in Organizational Analysis*. Chicago, IL: University of Chicago Press. pp. 361–389.

Perrow, Charles (1986). *Complex Organizations: A Critical Essay*. New York: McGraw-Hill, Inc.

Quirke, Linda (2013) 'Rogue Resistance: Sidestepping Isomorphic Pressure in a Patchy Institutional Field.' *Organization Studies* 34: 1675–1699.

Rao, Hayagreeva, Monin, Phillipe and Durand, Rodolphe (2003) 'Institutional Change in Toque Ville: Nouvelle Cuisines an Identity Movement in French Gastronomy.' *American Journal of Sociology* 108: 795–843.

Rao, Hayagreeva, Morrill, Calvin and Zald, Mayer N. (2002) 'Power Plays: How Social Movements and Collective Action Create New Organizational Forms.' *Research in Organizational Behavior* 22: 239–282.

Reay, Trish and Hinings, C.R. (2005) 'The Recomposition of an Organizational Field: Health Care in Alberta.' *Organization Studies* 26: 351–384.

Schneiberg, Marc (2007) 'What's on Path? Path Dependence, Organizational Diversity and the Problem of Institutional Change in the US Economy, 1900–1950.' *Socio-Economic Review* 5: 47–80.

Schüssler, Elke, Rüling, Charles-Clemens and Wittneben, Bettina B.F. (2014) 'On Melting Summits: The Limitations of Field-Configuring Events as Catalysts of Change in Transnational Climate Policy.' *Academy of Management Journal* 57: 140-171.

Scott, W. Richard (1991) 'Unpacking Institutional Arguments.' In Paul J. DiMaggio and Walter W. Powell (eds), *The New Institutionalism in Organizational Analysis*. Chicago, IL: The University of Chicago Press. pp. 164–182.

Scott, W. Richard (1994) 'Conceptualizing Organizational Fields: Linking Organizations and Societal Systems.' In Hans-Ulrich Derlien, Uta Gerhardt and Fritz W. Scharpf (eds), *Systems Rationality and Partial Interests*. Baden-Baden, Germany: Nomos Verlagsgesselschaft. pp. 203–221.

Scott, W. Richard (1995. *Institutions and Organizations*. Thousand Oaks, CA: Sage.

Scott, W. Richard (2001) *Institutions and Organizations*. Thousand Oaks, CA: Sage.

Scott, W. Richard and Meyer, John W. (1992) 'The Organization of Societal Sectors.' In John W. Meyer and W. Richard Scott (eds), *Organizational Environments: Rituals and Rationality*. Newbury Park, CA: Sage. pp. 129–154.

Scott, W. Richard, Ruef, Martin, Mendel, Peter and Caronna, Carol (2000) *Institutional Change and Healthcare Organizations: From Professional Dominance to Managed Care*. Chicago, IL: University of Chicago Press.

Selznick, Philip (1949) *TVA and the Grass Roots*. Berkeley, CA: University of California Press.

Selznick, Philip (1957) *Leadership in Administration: A Sociological Interpretation*. Berkeley, CA: University of California Press.

Seo, Myeong-Gu and Douglas Creed, W.E. (2002) 'Institutional Contradictions, Praxis, and Institutional Change: A Dialectical Perspective.' *Academy of Management Review* 27: 222–247.

Stinchcombe, Arthur L. (1965) 'Social Structure and Organizations.' In James G. March (ed.), *Handbook of Organizations*. Chicago, IL: Rand McNally. pp. 142–193.

Strang, David, and Soule, Sarah A. (1998) 'Diffusion in Organizations and Social Movements: From Hybrid Corn to Poison Pills.' *Annual Review of Sociology* 24: 265–290.

Suddaby, Roy and Greenwood, Royston (2005) 'Rhetorical Strategies of Legitimacy.' *Administrative Science Quarterly* 50: 35–67.

Sutton, John R. and Dobbin, Frank (1996) 'The Two Faces of Governance: Responses to Legal Uncertainty in U.S. Firms, 1955 to 1985.' *American Journal of Sociology* 61: 794–811.

Thornton, Patricia H. (2001) 'Personal versus Market Logics of Control: A Historically Contingent Theory of the Risk of Acquisition.' *Organization Science* 12: 294–311.

Tolbert, Pamela S. and Zucker, Lynne G. (1983) 'Institutional Sources of Change in the Formal Structure of Organizations: The Diffusion of Civil Service Reform, 1880–1935.' *Administrative Science Quarterly* 28: 22–39.

Warren, Ronald L. (1967) 'The Interorganizational Field as a Focus for Investigation.' *Administrative Science Quarterly* 12: 396–419.

Washington, Marvin and Ventresca, Marc (2004) 'How Organizations Change: The Role of Institutional Support Mechanisms in the Incorporation of Higher Education Visibility Strategies, 1874–1995.' *Organization Science* 15: 82–97.

Wedlin, Linda (2006) *Ranking Business Schools: Forming Fields, Identities, and Boundaries in International Management Education*. Northampton, MA: Edward Elgar Publishing, Inc.

Williamson, Ian O. and Cable, Daniel M. (2003) 'Organizational Hiring Patterns, Interfirm Network Ties, and Interorganizational Imitation.' *Academy of Management Journal* 46: 349–358.

Wooten, Melissa E. (2006) 'The Evolution of the Black Higher Education Field, 1854–1996.' Unpublished Dissertation. Ann Arbor, MI: University of Michigan.

Wooten, Melissa E. (2015) *In the Face of Inequality: How Black Colleges Adapt.* Albany, NY: SUNY Press.

Zald, Mayer N. and Useem, Bert (1987) 'Movement and Countermovement Interaction: Mobilization, Tactics, and State Involvement.' In Mayer N. Zald and John D. McCarthy (eds), *Social Movements in an Organizational Society.* New Brunswick, NJ: Transaction Publishers.

Zeitz, Gerald, Mittal, Vikas and McAuly, Brian (1999) 'Distinguishing Adoption and Entrenchment of Management Practices: A Framework Analysis.' *Organization Studies* 20: 741–776.

Zilber, Tamar (2006) 'The Work of the Symbolic in Institutional Processes: Translation of Rational Myths in Israeli High Tech.' *Academy of Management Journal* 49: 281–303.

Zucker, Lynne G. (1977) 'The Role of Institutionalization in Cultural Persistence.' *American Sociological Review* 42: 726–743.

Zucker, Lynne (ed.) (1988) *Institutional Patterns and Organizations.* Cambridge, MA: Ballinger.

PART II

Organizations and Their Contexts

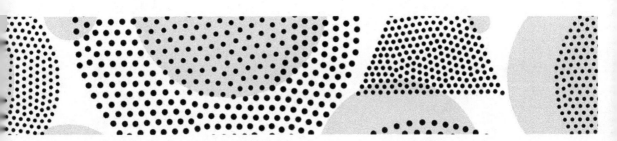

3

Isomorphism, Diffusion and Decoupling: Concept Evolution and Theoretical Challenges[1]

Eva Boxenbaum and Stefan Jonsson

INTRODUCTION

A longstanding question in organization research is what makes organizations more or less similar to each other. Early organization theorists pointed out that organizations that share the same environment tend to take on similar forms as efficiency-seeking organizations sought the optimal 'fit' with their environment. Institutional theories of organization have added two related claims to this literature. First, organizations adapt not only to technical pressures but also to what they believe society expects of them, which leads to *institutional isomorphism*. Organizations need a societal mandate, or legitimacy, to operate and this is gained by conforming to societal expectations. Second, when adaptations to institutional pressures contradict internal efficiency needs, organizations sometimes claim to adapt when in reality they do not; they decouple action from structure in order to preserve organizational efficiency. A large number of empirical studies have subsequently refined the related propositions of institutional isomorphism and decoupling, and also introduced new questions and dimensions to the original propositions. Our aim in this chapter is to bring clarity to this body of literature by first establishing the state of the art and then identifying important areas in need of further research.

A central idea of institutional isomorphism is that organizations conform to 'rationalized myths' in society about what constitutes a proper organization. These myths emerge as solutions to widely perceived problems of organizing and become rationalized when they are widely believed to constitute the proper solutions to these problems. As more organizations conform to these myths they become more deeply institutionalized, which subsequently leads to institutional isomorphism (Meyer and Rowan, 1977). Institutional isomorphism supposedly results from processes that stimulate the diffusion of ideas, practices and prescribed structures among organizations within an organizational field (DiMaggio and Powell, 1983). Although diffusion was introduced as a mechanism that led to isomorphism, many empirical researchers implicitly reversed this causal link and invoked isomorphism as a *cause* of diffusion. More recent work has corrected this misconception and now treats isomorphism as the potential *outcome* of diffusion, as originally intended.

The second claim about organizational similarity is that organizations *decouple* their formal structure from their production activities when institutional and task environments are in conflict, or when there are conflicting institutional pressures. Decoupling enables organizations to seek the legitimacy that adaptation to rationalized myths provides while they engage in technical 'business as usual'. Although decoupling is a core idea in institutional theory, it has received limited scholarly attention (see, e.g., Scott, 2001), a tendency that has recently begun to change. We review the empirical research that has refined and extended the notion of decoupling and the factors that have been found to predict or mediate this response to institutional pressure for conformity, as well as some of the possible organizational and field-level consequences of decoupling.

Despite the centrality of isomorphism and decoupling within institutional theory and their close theoretical ancestry, surprisingly little attention has been devoted to examine how they relate to each other. We review the few studies that address this shortcoming and suggest several interesting directions for future research. A fruitful empirical and theoretical research agenda is to clarify the relationship between isomorphism and decoupling under different field conditions.

We begin the chapter with an outline of the early theoretical formulations where we explicate the initial core theoretical statements of isomorphism and decoupling and proceed to trace how decades of empirical research have contributed to the refinement of these statements. This refinement has taken place against the backdrop of a wider shift within institutional theory toward a greater recognition of heterogeneity in the institutional environment and in organizational responses to institutional pressures (see Greenwood et al., 2011; Kraatz and Block, 2008). We discuss how this shift toward heterogeneity has impacted on our understanding of isomorphism and decoupling. The chapter ends with a discussion of what we identify as neglected areas of research as well as the relationship between institutional isomorphism and decoupling. It is our hope that this juxtaposition of empirical findings with our reflection on the interaction among isomorphism, diffusion and decoupling will catalyse new and exciting research questions that can propel institutional theory forward without abandoning its core characteristics.

EARLY THEORETICAL STATEMENTS

Isomorphism

Why are organizations so strikingly similar? DiMaggio and Powell (1983) proposed that institutionalized ideas pressure organizations to adopt similar structures and forms, and as a result they become increasingly similar. It was not a new idea in organization theory that organizations in the same environment over time also come to share their appearance. Already Weber argued that the 'iron cage of rationality' and competitive forces in society pressured organizations to similarity in structure and action. Rational adaptation theorists then claimed that organizational similarity results from efficiency-seeking organizational adaptation to a similar task environment (Scott, 1995). Playing down the aggregate effects of organization-level adaptation, population ecology theorists have subsequently argued that environmental competitive selection forces leave the surviving organizational population structurally similar.

Institutional isomorphism was distinct from these perspectives in its assertion that organizations became similar not through adaptation to an external or technically demanding environment or through the 'weeding out' of technical and social misfits, but through adaptation to a socially constructed environment. This statement about institutional isomorphism should be understood as a new take on a longstanding interest in the structure of organizations within organizational sociology, a heritage from open-systems theories of the 1960s, and the development of the population ecology school from 1977 and onwards (Scott, 2004).

DiMaggio and Powell outlined three pressures that lead organizations to become increasingly similar: *coercive*, *mimetic* and *normative* pressures. Coercive pressures result from power relationships and politics; prototypically these are demands of the state or other large actors to adopt specific structures or practices, or else face sanctions. Coercive pressures are not only by fiat but can also result from resource dependence, such as demands to adopt specific accounting practices to be eligible for state grants or requirements of ISO certification to become a supplier (see, for instance, work by Edelman, 1992; Guillen, 2001; Sutton et al., 1994). Mimetic pressures arise primarily from uncertainty. Under conditions of uncertainty, organizations often imitate peers that are perceived to be successful or influential (Haveman, 1993; Palmer et al., 1993). Normative pressures pertain to what is widely considered a proper course of action, or even a moral duty (Suchman, 1995), such as when there are signals from the organizational environment that the adoption of a particular practice or structure is a correct moral choice. Normative pressures are often associated with professions because the similar education and training instill similar professional values of what is considered appropriate for professionals to carry into organizations, a process that tends to favour the adoption of similar practices and structures across organizations (for instance, Galaskiewicz and Burt, 1991; Mezias, 1990).

These three pressures can also be thought of in terms of topographical directions from where institutional pressures emanate in an organizational field: regulative pressures normally come from vertically positioned actors (e.g., the state) whereas mimetic and normative pressures often stem from horizontally positioned peer organizations or groupings. For instance, Strang and Soule (1998) liken the three pressures to a mapping of diffusion channels in terms of (a) external pressure, such as the state, (b) peer pressure from other firms and (c) internal diffusion pressure from professional information networks.

DiMaggio and Powell proposed a dozen hypotheses relating to how organizations that are subject to institutional pressures respond to an increasingly institutionalized environment. These hypotheses range from predictions about the degree of isomorphism at the level of an organizational field to the rate by which different kinds of organizations are expected to morph to similarity with the field. The hypotheses relate to questions that were, at the time, topical in organization theory, most notably questions about organizational structure, implications of resource dependence across organizations, the effects of organizational and field goal ambiguity, and the level of professionalization of the workforce.

These theoretical statements and propositions were meant to further our understanding of how organizations became increasingly similar over time. They were intended to set the arena for much of the subsequent empirical work on isomorphism. However, empirical research fairly soon redirected our collective attention to further our understanding of the diffusion of practices and ideas (see Greenwood and Meyer, 2008 for a review of DiMaggio and Powell, 1983). As a result, some of the fundamental ideas of institutional isomorphism did not become subject to empirical investigation until much later, if at all. At the same time, some empirical findings have also prompted significant reformulation of some of the early theoretical statements (e.g., Bromley and Powell, 2012).

Decoupling

When organizations are pressured to adapt to societal rationalized myths about what organizations should look like and do, they face two problems: First, the rationalized myths may not comprise an efficient solution for the organization, and second, competing and mutually inconsistent rational myths can exist simultaneously. Meyer and Rowan (1977) proposed that organizations decouple their practices from their formal or espoused structure to solve these two problems of institutional pressures. In effect, decoupling means that organizations abide only superficially by institutional pressure and adopt new structures without necessarily implementing the related practices.

The idea of organizations decoupling structure and action reflected the perspective of organizations as loosely coupled systems that became popular in the mid-1970s. A group of organizational sociologists and social psychologists proposed loose coupling as a solution to problems of change and reform in US public schools (Hallet and Ventresca, 2006). In a challenge to the dominant system theory where organizations were seen as coherent units composed of densely linked and inter-dependent elements, they proposed instead that organizational elements are loosely coupled to one another. Drawing on this insight, they investigated different kinds of couplings and how these are created (e.g., Weick, 1979) also in relation to decision-making processes (Brunsson, 2002; March and Olsen, 1976). In reference to the general idea of organizations as loosely coupled systems, Meyer and Rowan (1977) introduced decoupling as a notion that refers specifically to a conscious disconnect between organizational practice and organizational structure. Inherent in decoupling in its initial formulation is the claim that practice is determined by perceived efficiency concerns, whereas organizational structure results from institutional pressure for conformity.

In its original statement, decoupling can be a rational response to demands for organizational adaptation that are inconsistent or harmful to the organization. When engaged in decoupling, organizations achieve legitimacy through their espoused structure but remain efficient or consistent through their actual action, which enhances their survival prospects. Gaining legitimacy without actually adapting relies critically on the 'logic of confidence and good faith', i.e., that people trust that the organization actually does what it says it will do (Meyer and Rowan, 1977: 357), which means that organizations that decouple must avoid close inspection or else they are exposed as frauds. A corollary to the decoupling proposition is therefore that when institutional pressures lead to decoupling, organizations will do their best to avoid scrutiny or at least to control the process of scrutiny.

EMPIRICAL EXAMINATION

Voluminous research has been conducted on institutional isomorphism and decoupling since the earliest theoretical formulations. Recognizing our inability to fairly represent the entire body of work, we structure the review of empirical work according to themes that emerged as salient after a systematic search of the most relevant literature. In the discussion section, we revisit the development of these themes in relation to the wider theoretical developments within institutional theory over the past four decades.

Isomorphism

The great majority of empirical studies on institutional isomorphism start from the theoretical premise that organizations in the same field do indeed become similar to one another over time. Only few studies have sought to empirically validate this core theoretical statement (e.g., Ashworth et al., 2009; Heugens and Lander, 2009; Tuttle and Dillard, 2007), a point to which we will return later.

Similar in what respect?

An important question about isomorphism is in what respect organizations are supposed to become similar. The early theoretical statement by DiMaggio and Powell is ambiguous on this topic, suggesting that isomorphism can be detected by 'the lessening in variance around some central dimension'. This ambiguity essentially left subsequent empirical researchers to their own devices (Oliver, 1988; Scott and Meyer, 1994). Early empirical studies that have investigated isomorphism as an outcome emphasize different dimensions and levels in their measurements of similarity. Meyer, Scott and Strang (1987) investigated isomorphism in the *structure* of US schools and found more evidence of isomorphism at higher than at lower levels of the administrative system, i.e., levels that were further removed from the local task environment of education. A decade later, Meyer, Boli, Thomas and Ramirez (1997) investigated the structure of national educational systems in a large-scale empirical study of world systems. In this study, they show that educational systems are becoming increasingly similar across the globe, especially so in countries that are more tightly integrated into the 'western cultural account'. Both studies point to the presence of isomorphism in organizational structures within the educational sector.

Other studies have focused more closely on isomorphism in organizational *output*. Levitt and Nass (1989) investigated isomorphism in the *content* of college text books. In their investigation of academic publishing, they found isomorphism to be more prevalent in the mature academic field of physics than in

sociology. Kraatz and Zajac (1996) showed that in a maturing field of US higher education, the homogeneity of college programmes decreased, rather than increased, suggesting that isomorphism did not occur, at least not in the programmes that colleges offered.

Ashworth et al. (2009) have subsequently argued that it is not only a question of *what* becomes isomorphic but also of *how we measure* isomorphism. They argue that there are different dimensions of isomorphism and distinguish between (1) behavioural compliance with institutional pressure and (2) organizational convergence to a common, widely accepted practice within a field (see also Greenwood et al., 2008). When using the former measure to investigate isomorphism among UK public organizations, they found a high degree of isomorphism, whereas the latter measure produced a much lower degree of isomorphism in the same population of organizations. They propose that empirical studies apply more comprehensive measures of isomorphism to better capture the complexities of this concept.

A common feature of these empirical studies is the ambiguity of the relevant dimension, measure and level of analysis where similarity should or should not occur in order to confirm the presence of institutional isomorphism. This ambiguity makes it difficult, even after three decades of research, to determine the degree of empirical support for the proposition of institutional isomorphism, including its limitations. More theoretical and methodological work clearly needs to be done in this area to render institutional isomorphism an empirically falsifiable theoretical proposition and to better understand how, and under which conditions, it is produced.

Similarity as resulting from diffusion?

Only a minority of empirical studies that invoke institutional isomorphism study isomorphism as an outcome variable. Rather than test isomorphism as an empirical outcome, studies have typically turned to the *mechanisms* through which isomorphism supposedly happens, notably the three institutional pressures outlined by DiMaggio and Powell. It was a typical early research strategy to test one (or more) of the institutional pressures against an efficiency or resource dependence perspective in order to explain the diffusion of certain practices and structures (for instance Kraatz and Zajac, 1996; Palmer et al., 1993). Yet, such studies do little to demonstrate that widespread diffusion indeed leads to isomorphism, let alone full institutionalization (Colyvas and Jonsson, 2011).

The various diffusion studies that invoke theories of institutional pressures can be organized according to the focal type of institutional pressure. Early studies found that *mimetic* pressures emanated most strongly from actors that are considered similar (Greve, 1998), successful and prestigious (Haveman, 1993). In addition, Haunschild (1993) found mimetic pressures to operate through networks of board members and the migration of executives (Jonsson, 2009; Kraatz and Moore, 2002). In recent work Still and Strang (2009) turn the analytical gaze around and investigate mimetic behaviour from the perspective of the imitator. Following the bench-marking efforts of an elite financial actor, they found that the bank chose to imitate practices of other firms from where they had recruited executives and from those firms that were highly prestigious.

Other studies found *normative* pressures to influence the manner in which large US firms adopted new accounting standards (Mezias, 1990) and the multidivisional form (Palmer et al., 1993). Empirical support was also found for the claim that legal measures provide *coercive* pressure. Edelman (1992) showed that coercive employment equity laws made organizations change their structure and subsequently their practice even if organizations were quite influential in interpreting what it meant to comply. Sanders and Tuschke (2007) show the importance of coercive pressures for the spread of stock option pay in Germany. Not much work has been done on the interaction effects among these three mechanisms (Greenwood and Meyer, 2008).

Among the three institutional pressures, mimesis has received the most attention (Mizruchi and Fein, 1999). One reason for this focus on mimetic pressures, as Mizruchi and Fein argue, is that power perspectives are out of vogue among North American social scientists, which is perhaps why coercive and normative pressures have received less attention. Another plausible explanation is that mimesis is easier to investigate using the quantitative methods that are popular among many institutionalist researchers, than are questions of normative influence or the exercise of coercion. A third possible explanation is that normative and coercive processes receive attention in other theoretical traditions or in specific institutional literatures, such as European institutional schools (cf. Mizruchi and Fein, 1999).

Recent work points to the relationship between diffusing entities as another determinant of spread. Shipilov, Greve and Rowley (2010) suggest that diffusion occurs through 'multiwave diffusion', meaning that an organization tends to adopt practices that are institutionally related to previously adopted practices. Extending this work, Meyer and Höllerer (2014) propose that diffusing entities travel in 'bundles', which determine their institutional fate (see also Fiss et al., 2012). They also show empirically that the diffusion and later loss in legitimacy of 'shareholder value' influenced the subsequent diffusion of 'corporate social responsibility' among Austrian companies (Meyer and Höllerer, 2016).

Empirical studies that invoke institutional isomorphism tend to elaborate on the mechanism by which practices spread, but rarely investigate the resulting level of isomorphism in the field. An exception is a meta-study by Heugens and Lander (2009) in which they test and find that organizational isomorphism results from coercive, normative and mimetic pressures. Another exception is a recent study on the early diffusion of robotic surgery in which Compagni, Mele and Ravasi (2015) show that early experiences with the implementation of robotic surgery contributed to a field-level outcome in the form of isomorphism (see also the earlier discussed study by Ashworth et al., 2009).

Similar to which institutional environment?

A central question with respect to isomorphism is what the relevant environment is to which organizations are thought to become (or not become) isomorphic? This is a question that is not often discussed, yet a dividing line can be drawn between empirical studies that conceptualize the institutional environment in terms of technical and goal-setting features, i.e., societal sectors (Scott and Meyer, 1983), and studies that consider the environment to be a socially constructed field (DiMaggio and Powell, 1983). The social sector approach differs from an organizational field perspective in the conceptualization of the institutional environment as external and exogenous to organizations. In social sector studies, it is the technical nature of the production task that determines the nature of the institutional environment, a factor that changes through technical development rather than through organizational action. Seeing the institutional environment as a field, in contrast, positions the institutional environment as a result of a structuration process that involves all field actors (Powell and DiMaggio, 1991; Zucker, 1987). A further difference is that the concept of institutional sectors is hierarchical in nature, with clear distinctions between horizontal and vertical ties (Scott and Meyer, 1983), whereas the field essentially represents a relational non-topographical space that stems from its ideational roots within network theory (Mohr, 2005). In this latter formulation, actors can occupy central or peripheral positions.

The perspective on the environment is important to our understanding of how institutional pressures can be thought to operate on organizations. An organizational sector approach, which broadly defines the relevant environment as input–output relations, makes technological shifts important drivers of changes in institutional pressures. If, in contrast, the arena for institutional pressures is thought of as socially constructed by organizations, then the source of institutional pressures is instead endogenous to the organizations. Importantly, this theoretical divide between two perspectives on the nature of the institutional environment is seldom reflected in empirical studies (see, however, Scott, 1987; Zucker, 1987). Instead we see empirical definitions of 'organizational fields' that are largely coterminous with the theoretical concept of societal sectors (for instance the typical 'industry' definition of a field), which are then matched with DiMaggio and Powell's theoretical apparatus of isomorphism in a socially constructed field. Few empirical studies of institutional isomorphism embrace DiMaggio and Powell's constructionist definition of the organizational field as socially constituted. This conflation of societal sectors with organizational fields may be unproblematic, we do not know, but it points to a need for further theoretical and empirical work on the nature of organizational fields and how we define them in empirical studies.

A recent development in this area is the introduction of the community as an intermediate unit of analysis, nested between organizations and fields (for more detail, see Almandoz, Marquis and Cheely, Chapter 7 this Volume). In their empirical study of corporate social action, Marquis, Glynn and Davis (2007) found that the nature and level of corporate social action aligned around communities rather than around sectors or fields.

Similarity in a heterogeneous environment

The very idea of institutional isomorphism presupposes an institutional environment with which the organization can morph. A crucial question is how institutional isomorphism can occur where the institutional environment is not homogenous. This question is all the more difficult to answer because of ambiguities in the original theoretical formulation of institutional isomorphism, in particular with respect to how the institutional environment (i.e., the organizational field) and its effects can be identified and delimited (cf. Mohr, 2005).

Early studies of isomorphism in organizational fields conceptualized the organizational field as unitary and examined how institutional pressures affected organizations, presumably in an equal manner (Scott, 2001). Tolbert and Zucker (1983), one of the earliest empirical studies of isomorphism, modified this proposal slightly by arguing that early adopters in a field are motivated by perceived efficiency gains whereas later adopters are driven primarily by the quest for legitimacy. Decades later, Kennedy and Fiss (2009) challenged their model in a study that showed both early adopters and late adopters to be motivated by anticipated gains in both efficiency and legitimacy. Common to these studies is a conceptualization of the organizational field as unitary at a given moment in time.

In more recent studies the field has increasingly become conceptualized as ambiguous and heterogeneous with multiple – often mutually incompatible – institutional pressures that result in conflicting pressures for conformity. Organizations may respond differently to this heterogeneity, which is often referred to as 'institutional complexity' (Greenwood et al., 2011). Initial studies in this research stream found that institutional pressures interact with competitive pressures and space (D'Aunno et al., 2000; Dacin, 1997) and vary over time (Dacin, 1997; Ruef and Scott, 1998). In a study of isomorphism in US higher education, Kraatz and Zajac (1996) show that the increasing maturity of the field does not lead to homogeneity (isomorphism) in educational programmes because of a simultaneous increase in competitive pressure to differentiate student programmes. Alvarez and colleagues (2005) came to a similar conclusion in their study of the heterogeneous field of European filmmaking, where creative directors pursued

optimal distinctiveness in response to contradictory institutional pressures. The directors sought to differentiate themselves from others while maintaining legitimacy. These studies testify to organizations deliberately mobilizing multiple, simultaneous pressures for conformity to position themselves strategically within a heterogeneous field.

Recent studies also address the question of how organizations in a heterogeneous field come to respond differently to similar institutional pressures. One proposal relates to the structure of networks through which the 'markers of similarity' travel, i.e., how entities diffuse. Greve (1996) studied the spread of new competitive strategies among radio stations and found that mimetic pressure led to practice polymorphism (islands of homogeneity) because imitation networks were geographically bounded in markets. Jonsson and Regnér (2009) also showed how diffusion could generate heterogeneity among firms in a competitive setting, but argued that it derived from differences in strength in professional collectives across firms. Similar findings are also reported in a number of empirical studies that investigate how initial practice variations developed into isomorphic patterns within bounded communities in the same heterogeneous field (Boxenbaum and Battilana, 2005; Marquis et al., 2007; Schneiberg, 2002). Practices may also provide an infrastructure for diffusion in the sense that previously adopted practices influence whether an organization adopts and implements a new diffusing practice (Meyer and Höllerer, 2014; Shipilov et al., 2010).

Another proposal relating to how heterogeneity forms is that organizations are active agents that respond strategically, within certain boundaries, to institutional pressure (Ingram and Clay, 2000). Oliver (1991) argued that organizations under certain circumstances have leeway to act strategically in the face of institutional pressures. She proposed five strategic responses that are available to organizations that face institutional pressure to conform. The first one, acquiescence (conformity), is essentially the response that leads to isomorphism while the second one, compromise, can manifest as decoupling (Scott, 2001). The third and fourth, avoidance and defiance, are two forms of resistance that organizations display when they disagree with the objectives of the constituents who put pressure on them to adopt a new organizational element. Manipulation, the fifth response, is akin to institutional entrepreneurship in the sense that it implies a deliberate attempt to change institutions in a certain direction.

Oliver's theoretical argumentation has triggered a number of empirical studies that relate strategic considerations to isomorphism (see for instance Goodrick and Salancik, 1996; Ingram and Simons, 1995). The most prominent streams of literature on organizational responses to field heterogeneity are arguably institutional complexity (Greenwood et al., 2011) and hybrid organizing (see Battilana and Lee, 2014 and Battilana, Besharov and Mitzinneck, Chapter 5 this Volume). Both literatures examine how organizations cope simultaneously with multiple institutional logics (see Almandoz, Marquis and Cheely on institutional logics, Chapter 7 this Volume). In a study of competing logics in the field of health care, Reay and Hinings (2009) identified four generic mechanisms through which actors respond to the same institutional pressures for conformity. Along similar lines, Scherer, Palazzo and Seidl (2013) found that organizations employ multiple responses simultaneously to enhance their legitimacy, the most effective orientation being a paradoxical strategy. Pache and Santos (2013) pointed to the selective coupling of competing institutional logics as a viable legitimation strategy. In an in-depth empirical study, Dalpiaz, Rindova and Ravasi (2016) identified processes through which organizations combine disparate institutional logics to generate new product and market opportunities at Alessi. Acknowledging that organizations in heterogeneous fields may respond simultaneously to disparate logics, and sometimes even combine them, Lepoutre and Valente (2012) found that organizations first need to distance themselves from any prevailing institutional logic that symbolically and/or materially prevents them from engaging with other logics.

A third account of heterogeneous responses to institutional pressures adopts a non-agentic perspective, in which institutions are conceptualized as 'social facts'. Heterogeneity results here from environmental contingencies, such as time, space and local competition, which introduce variation into organizational response even where the institutional pressures are similar and fully internalized (Beck and Walgenbach, 2005; D'Aunno et al., 2000; Dacin, 1997). Alternatively, organizations are simply not able to perfectly replicate an institutionally sanctioned structure or practice. That is the case even if institutional pressures have been internalized to such an extent that adoption of a structure or practice is perceived as self-evident and desirable. The implicit adaptation of a practice or structure to the local context has been broadly referred to as translation (see Wedlin and Sahlin on translation, Chapter 4 this Volume).

The institutional effects of these different processes have received limited attention so far. One institutional effect that is gaining scholarly attention is the surge of hybrid organizations in society (see Battilana and Lee, 2014). Another such effect is the simultaneous institutionalization of multiple organizational practices, each informed by a different logic, within a heterogeneous organizational field (Purdy and Gray, 2009). While these lines of research are very promising, more work is needed to identify field-level effects of organizational responses to field heterogeneity.

How can we account for dissimilarity at early stages of diffusion?

In contrast to the theoretical assumption that diffusion equals isomorphism, empirical findings have revealed many instances of organizational dissimilarity even in mature organizational fields. Dissimilarity manifests not only in heterogeneous responses to institutional pressures (discussed in the previous section), but also during the introduction of innovative practices in a field. Their introduction may result in organizations becoming *less* similar, particularly if the new practices and ideas run counter to institutionalized norms. Such novel practices are often called *contested* practices. While contested practices are initially illegitimate, they also carry the potential to evolve into new institutions.

Over the last two decades a number of studies have investigated the diffusion of controversial, or counter-normative, practices (Ansari et al., 2010). Of interest is that counter-normative practices do not follow the predictions of DiMaggio and Powell (1983). As carriers of norms, professional groups have been shown to facilitate the organizational practice that accords with prevailing norms (Mezias, 1990; Palmer et al., 1993). When the practice in question runs counter to institutional norms, these professional groups may instead resist and defer practice adoption. Jonsson (2009) shows how mutual fund firms with a strong financial analyst collective were much slower than firms with a less influential analyst collective to adopt controversial product innovations such as social responsible investment funds and index funds. Similarly, Schneiberg (2013) shows that the absence of the Grange (social) movement in a US state reduced the likelihood of the establishment of cooperatives, which was considered a counter-normative organizational form by incumbent firms. Furthermore, which earlier adopter becomes an important referent adopter may differ for a controversial practice and a non-controversial practice. Briscoe and Safford (2008) show that it is not the adoption by a 'leader' (cf. Haveman, 1993) that triggers diffusion of a contested practice but the adoption by an earlier staunch opponent of the practice in question, as this adopter signals that the practice is not very contested any longer.

Shipilov et al. (2010) show that adoption of a contested practice depends on earlier related practices, which testifies to the interrelatedness of diffusion trajectories. Sanders and Tuschke (2007) emphasize the participation of actors who have experience with contested practices and who are exposed to fields in which the innovation is legitimate. Raffaelli and Glynn (2014) demonstrate that relational networks also play an important role in facilitating the diffusion of contested practices (see also Fiss et al., 2012). Even though contested practices may diffuse widely, argue Green, Li and Nohria (2009), they must become uncontested, through rhetorical devices, in order to become institutionalized.

Over the past decade, empirical work on contested practices has increased, while studies on isomorphism as an outcome has decreased. This development may reflect a growing emphasis on the early stages of institutionalization, the role of actors in institutionalization processes, and/or increased interest in field heterogeneity. It would be interesting to follow up on this development in empirical work with a meta-study that relates the dynamics of contestation at an early stage of institutionalization to isomorphism as a potential outcome.

Decoupling

Does decoupling occur?

Several empirical studies have sought to confirm the existence of decoupling between the structure for action and the action of organizations. For instance, in a study of affirmative action policies in a small liberal arts college in the United States, Edelman, Abraham and Erlanger (1992) found that the affirmative action officer exercised significant flexibility in the hiring process although there were policies issued that reflected affirmative action legislation. By means of decoupling, organizational actors conferred legitimacy upon the college while simultaneously attending to divergent concerns related to its teaching staff. Similarly, Brunsson and Olsen (1993) found that a radical reform at Swedish Rail was formally implemented without significant impact on daily operations. Although management thought that the reform would result in near chaos, they discovered to their surprise that rail traffic and operational supervisors were virtually undisrupted by the reform. Decoupling made it easier for management to make decisions on reform since the operational departments collaborated more willingly as long as the reform did not affect their work in any significant way. Collectively, these studies provide empirical support for Meyer and Rowan's (1977) proposition that formal structure can be, and often is, decoupled from production activities. These findings leave unanswered questions, such as why and when decoupling occurs and what decoupling brings.

When do organizations decouple?

Just because organizations can decouple it does not mean that they always will do so. Institutional decoupling carries with it a risk of detection where it would no longer confer legitimacy, but probably shame, on the organization. So when do organizations decouple? Studies suggest that organizations decouple if they experience strong coercive pressure to implement a new practice (Seidman, 1983), and more so if they distrust the actor that asserts pressure on them (Kostova and Roth, 2002). Decoupling is also more frequent among organizations that do not fully believe in the efficacy of the practice in question. Investigating the introduction of long-term CEO compensation plans, Westphal and Zajac (1997) showed that late adopters of CEO compensation, i.e., those firms that adopted plans in response to institutional pressure rather than efficiency needs, were less likely than early adopters to actually implement these plans. This finding is corroborated by a study of how financial analysts initiate and abandon their coverage of firms (Rao et al., 2001). In an exemplary

case study, Turco (2012) shows how employees can refuse to engage in decoupling when it requires them to deviate too far from their professional role. Whereas belief in the efficacy of a practice may be a necessary condition for its implementation, it is apparently insufficient to prevent decoupling. An accepted practice may be unintentionally decoupled when the accompanying discourse is well established, hence increasing the likelihood that the practice will go unnoticed (Gondo and Amis, 2013: 242).

Even when subjected to similar institutional pressures, some organizations decouple while others do not. Investigating decoupling within and across subsidiary units of multinational corporations, Crilly, Zollo and Hansen (2012) show substantial variation in the likelihood of decoupling depending on the local environment as well as the internal environment of the multinational corporation. Internal power dynamics has been identified as an important variable that mediates the desire to decouple and the action of decoupling. In a longitudinal study of the response of large US corporations to pressure from external sources to adopt stock repurchase programs, Westphal and Zajac (2001) found that decoupling occurred more frequently when top executives had power over boards to resist external pressure for change. Similarly, a survey of 302 senior financial executives showed that they were less likely to decouple the company's ethics code from strategic decisions when they experienced strong pressure from market stakeholders like suppliers, customers or shareholders (Stevens et al., 2005). Marquis and Qian (2014) showed that companies are reluctant to decouple if they have a close relationship with the government and if that relationship implies that decoupling behaviours may be monitored. Similarly, firms are less likely to decouple standards for good corporate governance if they depend on constituents that value highly these governance practices (Okhmatovskiy and David, 2012).

Finally, networks and coalitions also mediate the decoupling response. Westphal and

Zajac (2001) found that top executives who had prior experience with decoupling or who had social ties to organizations that did, were more likely to engage in decoupling themselves. In contrast, Fiss and Zajac (2004) found that decoupling was least likely in companies where powerful and committed actors cared strongly about implementation and could influence the organizational response. Crilly et al. (2012) similarly found that external stakeholders mattered to the decoupling behaviour of MNC subsidiaries. Membership in social networks can also reduce decoupling, as shown by Lounsbury (2001) in a study of recycling. These findings confirm our point above that the field in which institutional processes take place is an important space to theorize. It is not only the institutional pressures that an organization experiences that are channelled through intra-field structures, but also the freedom of the organization to partly resist this pressure by decoupling.

Relating to the original prediction that organizations require external trust (i.e., a 'logic of good faith') to decouple, later work suggests that such faith can be actively sought by the decoupling organization. Brunsson (2002) argues that when an organization decouples action from structure, it can obfuscate this decoupling by 'talk' – i.e., saying one thing while doing another – what Brunsson calls 'organizational hypocrisy'. Instances of such hypocrisy have been identified in later studies (see, for example, Lim and Tsutsui, 2012). Similarly, a study by Fiss and Zajac (2006) concluded that it is those organizations that do not actually implement structural changes that most fervently proclaim their conformity to demands for strategic change. Briscoe and Murphy (2012) show that organizations that decouple their espoused action from their real action actively seek to conceal this behaviour.

Decoupling as a response to field heterogeneity

In their initial formulations, Meyer and Rowan suggested that decoupling was a response to two organization-level problems: contradictions between institutionalized pressures with internal organizational efficiency and contradictions among multiple institutionalized pressures. Early studies focused primarily on decoupling as a deliberate effort to safeguard organizational efficiency, whereas recent studies suggest that decoupling is a result of heterogeneous organizational fields that exert multiple and often contradictory pressures on the organization (cf. Heimer, 1999; Ruef and Scott, 1998). When faced with simultaneous contradictory pressures, organizations decouple to survive. Decoupling structure from practice can take multiple forms simultaneously. Brunsson (2002, see also George et al., 2006) suggests that organizations solve the dilemma of contradictory demands by meeting some demands by talk, others by decisions, and yet others by action. As an example, Aurini (2006) found that educational institutions routinely shed some of the most sacred schooling scripts, but flourished anyway because they responded to new pressures, such as consumer demands for individualized education programmes. They decoupled some institutions to be able to implement others, recognizing that there were several ways to obtain legitimacy in this heterogeneous field. A study of the Danish Red Cross came to a similar conclusion, showing that the organization became more robust when it decoupled ideology and structure from concrete programmes and activities (Christensen and Molin, 1995). Decoupling thus turned out to be a safeguarding mechanism in a heterogeneous field, i.e., an attempt to deal with conflicting demands in a way that minimizes risk.

Later research has further embraced field heterogeneity in empirical studies. Recent studies show that decoupling is not a standardized process but, as predicted by early theoretical work, potentially idiosyncratic to the organization (Binder, 2007; Tilcsik, 2010) as well as to the specific context (Crilly et al., 2012). Faced with a perceived need to decouple structure from action, organizations respond in many different ways, regardless of whether or not they decide to decouple.

The outcomes of decoupling

In many cases the idea to decouple structure from action can be a useful strategy for organizations. In one of the first quantitative studies of decoupling, Westphal and Zajac (1998) found that the market price of corporations increased when they adopted a legitimate practice, regardless of actual implementation. There are, however, other possible outcomes from decoupling – some of which are less positive for the decoupling organization.

First, decoupling is often understood as pretence, i.e., by formalizing a structure, an organization pretends to do something that it does not actually do. It is, however, not always possible for an organization to sustain such a purely ceremonial adoption; what starts out as decoupling can over time turn into coupling between structure and action. Edelman's (1992) study of organizations that initially decoupled the Employment Equity and Affirmative Action Legislation revealed that the formal organizational structure eventually was implemented anyway in organizational practice. Employees that were hired into the formal structure tried to fulfil their mandate even if it was meant to be entirely symbolic. They elaborated formal structures and created visible symbols of compliance in an effort to interpret what it meant to comply. Decoupling may thus lead to full implementation because most individuals refuse to see themselves as only ceremonial props (Scott, 2001).

The original formulation of decoupling pertained to internal organizational structures being decoupled from organizational practice. Yet institutional pressures can also manifest as demands for symbolic schemes that are supposed to shape organizational practice. Prime examples of such symbolic schemes are ratings, rankings and certifications of different sorts that suggest a scheme for valuing different aspects of organizational work as being more or less important. A university ranking system, for instance, will define whether peer-reviewed publications or staff diversity are most important for determining university 'quality' (Wedlin, 2007).

Even these structures can be difficult to decouple over time. Investigating the narratives of corporate responsibility initiatives, Haack, Schoeneborn and Wickert (2012) show how what is initially mainly talk becomes embedded in the organization. Sauder and Espeland (2009) draw on Foucault's work to explain how law school members internalize law school rankings by changing the way that the members think about the field in which they are engaged. Although rankings were initially understood as something that was acceptable to decouple, the internal acceptance of decoupling became less acceptable as the idea – or 'discipline' – of rankings was internalized so that, leading organizational members began to self-police its implementation.

Apart from the possibility that the decoupled structure and action can become coupled over time, organizations that decouple also set an internal precedence that may be harmful to its other operations. As MacLean and Behnam (2010) show, the decoupling of an internal compliance programme from actual sales practices created a 'legitimacy façade' that allowed unsound sales practices to flourish and consolidate within the organization. Since the compliance programme had been rendered ineffectual through decoupling, these practices were not checked, which brought on a loss of external legitimacy when they became too widespread to be contained within the confines of the organization. The study points to the larger issue of decoupling enabling corporate wrongdoings and internal tolerance for breaking norms and rules.

These findings pose new interesting questions about whether or not decoupling is sustainable over time, and what its ultimate institutional consequences may be. It seems that an organizational image that is persistently inconsistent with how organizational members see themselves will eventually provoke a corrective action, which is one of the known drivers of organizational change related to identity change (Dutton and Dukerich, 1991; Gioia et al., 2013). This dynamic points to a larger question, which is yet to be substantially addressed: where is decoupling really constituted? Is an organization engaged in decoupling if its members believe that they are implementing the action corresponding to the organizational structure, even if stakeholders do not agree? Conversely, is there decoupling if only the internal members believe it to be so?

An exciting new avenue of theorizing decoupling explores these kinds of questions; it suggests that the structure–action decoupling of Meyer and Rowan needs to be supplemented by a means–end decoupling (Bromley and Powell, 2012). Their point is that an organization can set up a structure and implement it fully, yet leave the essentials of its operations untouched by decoupling the means and the ends of the action. They use the example of universities, where there is institutional pressure for transparency with respect to the quality of education and research. A university can set up a structure to monitor 'quality' and implement this fully, so that there is no structure–action decoupling. If, however, the university is aware that this structure is a poor means to the end of measuring 'quality', the set-up arguably qualifies as a decoupled system. Bromley, Hwang and Powell (2013) show how this form of decoupling works in the non-profit sector. Extending the work of Bromley and colleagues, Wijen (2014) argues that means–end decoupling is likely to occur in highly opaque fields, even – and particularly so – when actors engage in substantial compliance. The reason for this paradoxical situation, he argues, is that the rigid rules associated with substantial compliance with the means block the flexibility that is required to achieve the intended outcomes (i.e., the end) in highly opaque fields.

DISCUSSION – CAUSAL RELATIONSHIPS

Our review of empirical studies on isomorphism and decoupling revealed that some aspects of the initial theory formulations have received empirical verification while others have been refined or qualified. The past decades of empirical research have consolidated and sharpened the sometimes initially vague formulations of institutional theory, but there are also important aspects that have escaped scrutiny altogether. Most striking is the limited research attention that has gone into confirming some of the core causal relationships of institutional theory. A number of empirical studies have in a piecemeal manner investigated theoretical concepts and mechanisms without questioning or verifying whether they generate the theorized outcomes. One case in point is that empirical examinations of institutional isomorphism and decoupling have largely developed along separate lines of inquiry, even though these concepts are tightly coupled theoretically. Somewhat simplistically, inquiries associated with institutional isomorphism have explored the external consequences of institutional pressures, i.e., organizational similarity, whereas decoupling research has investigated how organizations deal internally with institutional pressure for conformity. An exception to this pattern is a study by Åberg (2013), which found that organizations sometimes engage in decoupling in order to respond strategically to conflicting pressures for conformity in a heterogeneous field. In another study, Oh and Jackson (2011) found that isomorphism and decoupling co-existed in relation to the South Korean practice of eating dog meat, a co-existence they call 'tactful resistance'. A third study argues that isomorphism is more likely to occur in relatively uniform fields, whereas decoupling increases in heterogeneous fields (Rodrigues and Craig, 2007). These empirical advancements are promising, but much remains to be studied in the interaction dynamics between decoupling and isomorphism, including the conditions under which they occur and the institutional effects they produce.

The relative neglect of how decoupling and isomorphism relate to each other weakens the theory and should be addressed. This poorly developed causal relationship may well contribute to widening the scope of institutional theory. Instead of focusing on how core concepts relate to each other, researchers tend to extend and enrich each separate line of inquiry. This widening only accelerates when empirical studies investigate a single one level of analysis at a time. The organizational level of analysis is most common in decoupling studies whereas isomorphism and diffusion studies are more likely to use the field as the only level of analysis. Naturally, the relationship between isomorphism and decoupling would be easier to study if more empirical studies used a multi-level approach (cf. Schneiberg and Soule, 2005). Perhaps the first step is to theoretically formulate how isomorphism and decoupling relate to one another in light of the initial theory formulations and the past decades of empirical research. The variables that predict decoupling in empirical studies may inform this research agenda, just as can recent insight into how organizations respond to institutional pressures in heterogeneous fields.

The causal relationship between decoupling and isomorphism is not the only one in need of development. There are other ambiguous causal relationships *within* each line of inquiry that also merit careful attention in the future, a topic to which we now turn.

Isomorphism

Although institutional isomorphism has attracted much research attention, a number of causal relationships have not received the careful empirical attention that they deserve. First, there is the relationship between isomorphism and diffusion. There is a natural empirical affinity between isomorphism and diffusion, but this empirical affinity can be theoretically treacherous (Colyvas and Jonsson, 2011). As mentioned earlier, the majority of the studies that invoke the concept of institutional isomorphism have treated the diffusion of a particular practice or structure as the outcome variable of interest, under the implicit assumption that diffusion leads to isomorphism. A research strategy that substitutes the process of diffusion for the outcome of isomorphism provides at best a limited test of institutional isomorphism. Moreover, as others have pointed out, the outcome of similarity may also be explained by competing theoretical frameworks, particularly resource dependence theory (Scott, 1987; Zucker, 1987). It is important to the theoretical development of institutional theory that the relationship between diffusion and isomorphism be sharpened significantly, both theoretically and empirically.

A closely related point is that the causal relationship between isomorphism and legitimacy also needs better articulation. Organizations are supposedly driven by a quest for legitimacy when they acquiesce to institutional pressures for conformity. Citing Meyer and Rowan (1977), DiMaggio and Powell (1983: 148) explained: 'As an innovation spreads, a threshold is reached beyond which adoption provides legitimacy rather than improves performance'. Institutional isomorphism presupposes that legitimacy is the driving force behind the organizational adoption of an extensively diffused innovation (cf. Meyer and Rowan, 1977; Tolbert & Zucker, 1983). In support of this claim, Freitas and Guimarães (2007) found in their study of operational auditing a mutually reinforcing mechanism involving cognitive legitimacy and isomorphism. Yet the diffusion of innovations may also occur without any legitimacy-seeking behaviour (Rossman, 2014). For instance, organizations may replace an existing structure with another one if they receive a substantial state subsidy to do so. They are not forced, uncertain, or under any moral obligation to do so, they simply see an opportunity to control costs, and it leads to isomorphism. Although many organizations may adopt this structure, it is far-fetched to argue that their adoption is an example of institutional isomorphism when it is not driven by legitimacy concerns. Essentially, not everything that diffuses enhances organizational legitimacy. Nor does the widespread diffusion of an innovation necessarily lead to its institutionalization (Colyvas and Jonsson, 2011).

Relatedly, the causal relationship between diffusion and institutionalization could benefit from more clarification. In the widely popular 'two-stage model' suggested by Tolbert and Zucker (1983), diffusion is assumed to *lead to* institutionalization (see Greenwood and Meyer, 2008: 262 for a similar point relating to common interpretations of DiMaggio and Powell, 1983). This finding subsequently became established within institutional theory as the 'two-stage model' of institutionalization, which suggests that a practice is introduced as the result of an efficiency search, and then, as it is adopted by others over time, it becomes institutionalized and adoption efficiency ceases to predict further spread (see, for instance, Westphal et al., 1997). However, as pointed out by Scott (1995), a sharp increase in the rate by which an innovation is adopted need not reflect more institutionalization. Only if the innovation is adopted for legitimacy reasons and begins to be taken for granted within the field does it make sense to talk about diffusion leading to institutionalization (Fiss et al., 2012). Without this crucial element, the two-stage model of institutionalization closely resembles the standard two-stage diffusion model from the 1950s (Katz et al., 1963), the main difference being that the contagion phase is renamed institutionalization phase. An important point is that there are plausible alternative explanations to the second stage in the diffusion phase, such as social-level learning (Levitt and March, 1988) or other

general 'bandwagon' processes (Abrahamson and Rosenkopf, 1993). To convincingly demonstrate that a practice that diffuses quickly is becoming institutionalized would require empirical research to use other indicators of institutionalization than a simple increase in the number of adopters (Schneiberg and Clemens, 2006; Fiss et al., 2012). Such indicators can be methodologically challenging to identify. It should be shown that adoption is associated with changing norms, collective beliefs or laws, and studies should identify the conditions under which diffusion is causally related to institutionalization.

Future research should also address the relationship between isomorphism and field heterogeneity. The growing recognition of heterogeneity in the institutional environment calls for reflection on how isomorphism fits with the core claims of institutional theory. If organizations become isomorphic with the total complexity of their institutional environment as some studies suggest (Goodrick and Salancik, 1996; Heimer, 1999), then the notion of isomorphism resonates with predictions of 'requisite variety' in early population ecology and systems-oriented theories (Scott, 2004). This possibility prompts the provocative (and evocative) question of whether institutional isomorphism still has a place as a distinct theoretical and empirical concept (cf. Kraatz and Zajac, 1996) under conditions of field heterogeneity. We think it does, but institutionalists need to sharpen core concepts and core causal relationships to avoid that institutional theory becomes an ambiguous umbrella-term for assorted organization theory. There is currently a tendency for institutional theory to expand into dimensions of organizational life that have traditionally been associated with other theories. While such expansion has enriched institutional theory by making it more comprehensive, it also draws attention away from clarifying core causal relationships, such as those among isomorphism, diffusion, legitimacy, and institutionalization, all of which need to be strengthened significantly. Herein lies an important challenge for future theoretical and empirical research, one that we think should take precedence over expansion of the scope of institutional theory.

Decoupling

Although there is less empirical research on decoupling than there is on institutional isomorphism, institutional pressures, and diffusion, we have seen a surge in attention to decoupling in recent years. There is reason to believe that this trend will continue as institutionalists pay increasing attention to organizational and individual factors in the processes of institutionalization and deinstitutionalization. Decoupling research may reveal the seeds of an endogenous model of institutional change, but first the notion of decoupling needs clarification and better articulation with isomorphism.

Meyer and Rowan (1977) defined decoupling as a deliberate disconnection between organizational structures that enhance legitimacy and organizational practices that are believed within the organization to be technically efficient. Some empirical studies have interpreted structure to include organizational elements such as programmes, policies, images and decisions. In so doing they came very close to confounding decoupling with the more general notion of 'loose coupling' (cf. Weick, 1979). The theoretical idea of organizations as loosely coupled systems is more comprehensive in scope than the idea of decoupling in institutional theory. Studies that examine weak links between changing organizational practice and organizational decision-making (e.g., Child, 1972) are thus better characterized as studies of loose coupling than of institutional decoupling. Studies of decoupling need to be distinguishable from studies of loosely coupled organizations in a similar manner to the need for empirical studies of institutional isomorphism to be distinguishable from diffusion studies.

The causal relationship on decoupling that has received most attention so far is the variables that predict or mediate the act of decoupling. As our review revealed, some organizational variables have already been identified; they include perceived advantages of decoupling, internal power dynamics, concerns about the organizational image and unintentional effects of discursively legitimizing a practice. In addition, empirical research has identified inter-organizational variables such as external network formations and the power of external stakeholders. We think more attention should be devoted to investigating the interaction among the already-identified variables that seem to predict or mediate institutional decoupling, though it may also prove fruitful to consider other organizational or inter-organizational variables. The unintended effects of decoupling, such as whether it affects morale and fosters cynicism within the organization, certainly merit attention as well. Furthermore, if organizations actively decouple to avoid being evaluated, entire groups of (isomorphic) organizations collectively embrace opaqueness in structure and actions. Such a broad prediction would be interesting to verify empirically, perhaps also to contrast with recent movements toward greater transparency and accountability, not least in public management. As there has been virtually no scholarly attention paid to the field-level consequences of decoupling, this is an area of research that should be particularly fruitful.

Some field-level variables also seem to influence the likelihood of decoupling, though the pattern is still obscure. Late adopters seem more likely to engage in decoupling than do early adopters, but why is this the case? Perhaps organizational or individual variables explain this pattern, perhaps power relations within a field influence the likelihood of decoupling. Is there a 'middle-status conformity' situation (Philips and Zuckerman, 2001) or does a central position in the field make it more illegitimate for an organization to engage in decoupling? Or is decoupling directly correlated with isomorphism in such a way that decoupling becomes more common once isomorphism gains in prevalence? As mentioned previously, attention to the causal relationship between isomorphism and decoupling has been almost entirely neglected so far and should be given priority in future research.

Methodological Considerations

In calling for more empirical studies of core causal relationships, we advocate more attention to the role of the observer. Isomorphism could be seen as an illusory effect of particular research strategies that create distance between the observer and the phenomenon. For instance, when researchers use archival data to study institutional change over a period of several decades, they are more likely to see something that looks like isomorphism than if they had collected observational data in a contemporary organization. In other words, the further distanced the observer is, in terms of abstracting or simplifying the object under study, the more isomorphism there will seem to be (Forssell and Jansson, 2000). This stance would explain the observation that the clearest evidence of isomorphism is found within the world systems literature, where the unit of analysis is highly aggregated. In contrast, case-based research provides excellent evidence for the variation in organizational response to institutional pressures (see Djelic and Quack, 2003; Sahlin-Andersson and Engwall, 2003). For instance, a historical analysis of Copenhagen Business School showed that the organization gradually absorbed elements of different myths from its institutional environment, which resulted in an organization that embodies five different models that are loosely coupled to one another (Borum and Westenholz, 1995). What appears as decoupling may simply be a multi-faceted organization that has conformed to changing institutional pressures over a long period of time while not fully discarding the old institutional elements. The role of time in how organizations cope with institutional pressures is an interesting topic that is beginning to gain traction.

The role of the observer is also reflected in the interpretive approach to institutionalist inquiry. According to interpretivism, practice is always mediated by an interpreter – whether the interpreter is the object of study or the researcher conducting the study. As for the former, Alvarez and colleagues (2005) showed that maverick film directors relied on their own strategic interpretations when they decided to differentiate themselves from other film directors in the organizational field of film-making. Similarly, key players in the organizational field of Danish hospitals strategically reinterpreted the same institutionalized belief to fit their own political preferences (Borum, 2004). In yet another study, actors interpreted the imported practice of diversity management in a way that deliberately reflected local institutions and established organizational practices (Boxenbaum, 2006). This interpretivist orientation is reflected in the notion of institutional entrepreneurship (Battilana et al., 2009) and in the institutional effects of different modes of communication (see Jones, Meyer, Jancsary and Höllerer on the material and visual basis of institutions, Chapter 23 this Volume).

The act of interpretation is not always conscious and strategic, but is often implicitly governed by institutionalized beliefs and norms. A study on school teachers in California showed, for instance, that teachers' pre-existing beliefs and practices implicitly mediated the nature of the message that they delivered in the classroom (Coburn, 2004). A less strategic approach to interpretation is evident in the literature on translation, which posits that ideas and practices undergo change every time they are applied in a new organizational context (Czarniawska and Joerges, 1996; Sahlin-Andersson, 1996). These interpretive studies suggest that decoupling is an act of interpretation that is shaped by contextual and institutionalized factors. This line of inquiry has expanded in recent years in response to increased interest in how organizations and individuals respond to institutional pressures.

CONCLUSION

This chapter presented the theoretical formulations of isomorphism and decoupling and carefully reviewed the empirical research that has been conducted on these two central theoretical concepts in institutional theory. These are central concepts because they set institutional theory apart from other organization theories. Isomorphism plays an important role in organization theory as an alternative to efficiency-based explanations of organizational change (Scott, 1987; Zucker, 1987), and decoupling provides an explanation for why organizations seem to be constantly reforming (Brunsson and Olsen, 1993). In a more general sense, these two concepts have also moved structuralist and cultural-symbolical understandings of organization closer to one another (Lounsbury and Ventresca, 2003; Scott, 2001).

The first contribution of this chapter was to delineate how empirical studies have carved out the initial formulations of isomorphism and decoupling respectively. A related contribution was to highlight some ambiguous causal relationships that pertain to theories of isomorphism and decoupling and that merit careful attention in future research. Disproportionate attention has been devoted to studying the relationship between institutional pressure and diffusion, to the neglect of the associated outcomes of decoupling and/or isomorphism. Consequently, some of the causal relationships that define institutional theory have largely escaped empirical inquiry. This limitation weakens institutional theory and restricts its extension into other levels of analysis that carry with them new independent and intervening variables. The

greatest risk, as we see it, is that institutionalism becomes a catch-all phrase for various organization theories. Institutionalists put the explanatory power of institutional theory at risk if they do not prioritize to validate and substantiate the core claims of institutional theory before adding new layers of complexity to its core claims.

An interesting discovery was that surprisingly little attention has been devoted to examining how isomorphism and decoupling interact with each other. Organizations supposedly adopt new organizational structures to enhance their legitimacy, and then decouple these same structures from their practices to maintain technical efficiency in a competitive quest for survival. We see real potential in combining and juxtaposing what we know about isomorphism and decoupling to develop a stronger and more dynamic theory of institutions. As we noted in our review, many interesting questions have never been asked. For instance, does decoupling become more frequent when a field becomes more isomorphic or mature? Perhaps the possibility of decoupling is crucial for obtaining a high level of isomorphism in an organization field. It is certainly possible that such insights could provide answers to the vexing question of how best to measure isomorphism. It may also open an intriguing avenue for studying endogenous institutional change processes without resorting to methodological individualism.

Another finding of this review of empirical studies is the conflation between institutional studies and diffusion studies. We noted that there is a close but complicated relation between diffusion (i.e., the spread of things) and isomorphism. In many cases diffusion is a prerequisite for isomorphism, but diffusion need not always lead to isomorphism; conversely all that looks similar need not be the result of diffusion (cf. Zucker, 1987). Isomorphism and diffusion have often been conflated in empirical studies where the spread of something is treated as an outcome synonymous with isomorphism. It is commonplace to contrast mimetic institutional pressure with efficiency and/or resource dependence theory as an explanation for the spread of a particular form or practice (see, for instance, the well-cited studies of Fligstein, 1985; Haveman, 1993; Palmer et al., 1993). The conflation of institutionalism and diffusion is unfortunate because diffusion studies include a larger set of phenomena where practices are not necessarily adopted for legitimacy gains and do not necessarily lead to institutionalization. In contrast, legitimacy is central to the kind of diffusion that pertains to institutionalism, whether the outcome is isomorphism or decoupling. We thus argue that the relationship between institutionalism and diffusion needs more careful empirical and theoretical parsing.

A final topic that is worth noting is the growing recognition that institutional environments are heterogeneous, just as are organizational responses to institutional pressure. This trend makes for a lot of heterogeneity, possibly more than the theory can sustain. While there are a number of good studies that argue for the importance of heterogeneity in institutional analysis, we find little work that steps back from this argument and considers the theoretical implications of acknowledging heterogeneity at various levels. One question that arises is what will happen to studies of organizational fields as the analytical lens expands simultaneously 'down' to individuals and 'up' to institutional logics. Will the organizational field level become depopulated, or will other research communities migrate to this area of inquiry and take on the challenging task of clarifying the link between different levels of analysis?

A related fundamental question is whether isomorphism is a useful and distinct theoretical concept if we believe in a world of fragmented institutional environments. For instance, is institutional isomorphism a more useful concept than that of 'requisite variety' that was proposed in the 1960s? If this question is answered in the negative, then we need to reflect upon how important the theoretical concept of isomorphism is to institutional

theory. Conversely, would the notion of legitimacy still have meaning and be sufficiently distinct without the assumption of some form of homogeneity in the organizational field?

Note

1   We are grateful for Lisa Östling's qualified assistance and for financial support received from The Danish Council for Independent Research (grant DFF – 1327-00030), The French National Research Agency (grant ANR-14-CE29-0008-01), and The Swedish Research Council (grant 421-2014-1721).

REFERENCES

Åberg, P. (2013) 'Managing expectations, demands and myths: Swedish study associations caught between civil society, the state and the market.' *Voluntas: International Journal of Voluntary and Nonprofit Organizations* 24(3): 537–558.

Abrahamson, E. and Rosenkopf, L. (1993) 'Institutional and competitive bandwagons: Using mathematical modeling as a tool to explore innovation diffusion.' *Academy of Management Review* 18: 487–517.

Alvarez, J. L., Mazza, C., Strandgaard Pedersen, J. and Svejenova, S. (2005) 'Shielding idiosyncrasy from isomorphic pressures: Towards optimal distinctiveness in European filmmaking.' *Organization* 12: 863–888.

Ansari, S. M., Fiss, P. C. and Zajac, E. J. (2010) 'Made to fit: How practices vary as they diffuse.' *Academy of Management Review* 35(1): 67–92.

Ashworth, R., Boyne, G. and Delbridge, R. (2009) 'Escape from the iron cage? Organizational change and isomorphic pressures in the public sector.' *Journal of Public Administration Research and Theory* 19(1): 165–187.

Aurini, J. (2006) 'Crafting legitimation projects: An institutional analysis of private education businesses.' *Sociological Forum* 21: 83–111.

Battilana, J., Leca, B. and Boxenbaum, E. (2009) 'How actors change institutions: Toward a theory of institutional entrepreneurship'. *Academy of Management Annals* 3(1): 65–107.

Battilana, J. and Lee, M. (2014) 'Advancing research on hybrid organizing: Insights from the study of social enterprises.' *Academy of Management Annals* 8(1): 397–441.

Beck, N. and Walgenbach, P. (2005) 'Technical efficiency or adaptation to institutionalized expectations? The adoption of ISO 9000 standards in the German mechanical engineering industry.' *Organization Studies* 26: 841–866.

Binder, A. (2007) 'For love and money: Organizations' creative responses to multiple environmental logics.' *Theory and Society* 36(6): 547–571.

Borum, F. (2004) 'Means–end frames and the politics and myths of organizational fields.' *Organization Studies* 25: 897–922.

Borum, F. and Westenholz, A. (1995) 'The incorporation of multiple institutional models: Organizations field multiplicity and the role of actors'. In W.R. Scott and S. Christensen (ed.), *The Institutional Construction of Organizations: International and Longitudinal Studies*. Thousand Oaks, CA: Sage. pp. 113–131.

Boxenbaum, E. (2006) 'Lost in translation? The making of Danish diversity management.' *American Behavioral Scientist* 49(7): 939–948.

Boxenbaum, E. and Battilana, J. (2005) 'Importation as innovation: transposing managerial practices across fields.' *Strategic Organization* 3: 355–383.

Briscoe, F. and Murphy, C. (2012) 'Sleight of hand? Practice opacity, third-party responses, and the interorganizational diffusion of controversial practices.' *Administrative Science Quarterly* 57(4): 553–584.

Briscoe, F. and Safford, S. (2008) 'The Nixon-in-China effect: Activism, imitation, and the institutionalization of contentious practices.' *Administrative Science Quarterly* 53: 460–491.

Bromley, P., Hwang, H. and Powell, W.W. (2013) 'Decoupling revisited: Common pressures, divergent strategies in the US nonprofit sector.' *M@n@gement* 15(5): 469–501.

Bromley, P. and Powell, W. W. (2012) 'From smoke and mirrors to walking the talk: Decoupling in the contemporary world.' *Academy of Management Annals* 6(1): 483–530.

Brunsson, N. (2002) *The Organization of Hypocrisy*. Oslo: Abstract Liber.

Brunsson, N. and Olsen, J. P. (1993) *The Reforming Organization*. London and New York: Routledge.

Child, J. (1972) 'Organization structure and strategies of control: A replication of the Aston study.' *Administrative Science Quarterly* 17(2): 163–178.

Christensen, S. and Molin, J. (1995) 'Origin and transformation of organizations.' In R. W. Scott and S. Christensen (eds), *The Institutional Construction of Organizations: International and Longitudinal Studies*. Thousand Oaks: Sage. pp. 67–90.

Coburn, C. E. (2004) 'Beyond decoupling: Rethinking the relationship between the institutional environment and the classroom.' *Sociology of Education* 77: 211–244.

Colyvas, J. A. and Jonsson, S. (2011) 'Ubiquity and legitimacy: Disentangling diffusion and institutionalization.' *Sociological Theory* 29(1): 27–53.

Compagni, A., Mele, V. and Ravasi, D. (2015) 'How early implementations influence later adoptions of innovation: Social positioning and skill reproduction in the diffusion of robotic surgery.' *Academy of Management Journal* 58(1): 242–278.

Crilly, D., Zollo, M. and Hansen, M.T. (2012) 'Faking it or muddling through? Understanding decoupling in response to stakeholder pressures.' *Academy of Management Journal* 55(6): 1429–1448.

Czarniawska, B. and Joerges, B. (1996) 'Travels of ideas.' In B. Czarniawska and G. Sevón (eds), *Translating Organizational Change*. Berlin: Walter de Gruyter. pp. 13–47.

D'Aunno, T., Succi, M. and Alexander, J. A. (2000) 'The role of institutional and market forces in divergent organizational change.' *Administrative Science Quarterly* 45: 679–703.

Dacin, T. (1997) 'Isomorphism in context: the power and prescription of institutional norms.' *Academy of Management Journal* 40: 46–81.

Dalpiaz, E., Rindova, V. and Ravasi, D. (2016) 'Combining logics to transform organizational agency: Blending industry and art at Alessi.' *Administrative Science Quarterly*. Published online February 26, 2016, doi:10.1177/0001839216636103.

DiMaggio, P. J. and Powell, W. W. (1983) 'The iron cage revisited: Institutional isomorphism and collective rationality in organizational fields.' *American Sociological Review* 48: 147–160.

Djelic, M.-L. and Quack, S. (2003. *Globalization and institutions: Redefining the rules of the economic game*. Cheltenham, UK: Edward Elgar.

Dutton, J. and Dukerich, J. (1991) 'Keeping an eye on the mirror: Image and identity in organizational adaptation.' *Academy of Management Journal* 34(3): 517–554.

Edelman, L. B. (1992) 'Legal ambiguity and symbolic structures: Organizational mediation of civil rights law.' *American Journal of Sociology* 6: 1531–1576.

Edelman, L. B., Abraham, S. E. and Erlanger, H. S. (1992) 'Professional construction of law: The inflated threat of wrongful discharge.' *Law and Society Review* 26: 47–94.

Fiss, P. and Zajac, E. J. (2004) 'The diffusion of ideas over contested terrain: The (non)adoption of a shareholder value orientation among German firms.' *Administrative Science Quarterly* 49: 501–534.

Fiss, P. and Zajac, E. J. (2006) 'The symbolic management of strategic change: Sensegiving via framing and decoupling.' *Academy of Management Journal* 49(6): 1173–1193.

Fiss, P. C., Kennedy, M. T. and Davis, G. F. (2012) 'How golden parachutes unfolded: Diffusion and variation of a controversial practice.' *Organization Science* 23(4): 1077–1099.

Fligstein, N. (1985) 'The spread of the multidivisional form among large firms 1919–1979.' *American Sociological Review* 50: 377–391.

Forssell, A. and Jansson, D. (2000. *Idéer som fängslar. Recept för en offentlig reformation.* (trans.: Ideas that imprison: a recipe for reform of public management.) Malmö: Liber.

Freitas, C. A. S. D. and Guimarães, T. D. A. (2007) 'Isomorphism, institutionalization and legitimacy: Operational auditing at the court of auditors.' *Revista de Administração Contemporânea* 11(SPE1): 153–175.

Galaskiewicz, J. and Burt, R. S. (1991) 'Interorganizational contagion in corporate philantropy.' *Administrative Science Quarterly* 36: 88–105.

George, E., Chattopadhyay, P. and Sitkin, S. B. (2006) 'Cognitive underpinnings of institutional persistence and change: A framing perspective.' *Academy of Management Review* 31: 347–365.

Gioia, D.A., Patvardhan, S.D., Hamilton, A.L. and Corley, K.G. (2013) 'Organizational identity formation and change.' *Academy of Management Annals* 7(1): 123–193.

Gondo, M. B. and Amis, J. (2013) 'Variations in practice adoption: The roles of conscious reflection and discourse.' *Academy of Management Review* 38(2): 229–247.

Goodrick, E. and Salancik, G. R. (1996) 'Organizational discretion in responding to institutional practices: Hospitals and cesarean births.' *Administrative Science Quarterly* 40: 1–28.

Green, S. E., Li, Y. and Nohria, N. (2009) 'Suspended in self-spun webs of significance: A rhetorical model of institutionalization and institutionally embedded agency.' *Academy of Management Journal* 52(1): 11–36.

Greenwood, R. and Meyer, R. E. (2008) 'Influencing ideas: A celebration of DiMaggio and Powell (1983).' *Journal of Management Inquiry* 17(4): 258–264.

Greenwood, R., Oliver, C., Sahlin, K. and Suddaby, R. (2008) 'Introduction.' In R. Greenwood, C. Oliver, R. Suddaby and K. Sahlin-Andersson (eds), *The SAGE Handbook of Organizational Institutionalism*. London: Sage. pp. 1–46.

Greenwood, R., Raynard, M., Kodeih, F., Micelotta, E. R. and Lounsbury, M. (2011) 'Institutional complexity and organizational responses.' *Academy of Management Annals* 5(1): 317–371.

Greve, H. R. (1996) 'Patterns of competition: the diffusion of a market position in radio broadcasting.' *Administrative Science Quarterly* 41: 29–60.

Greve, H. R. (1998) 'Managerial cognition and the mimetic adoption of market positions: What you

see is what you do.' *Strategic Management Journal* 19: 967–988.

Guillen, M. F. (2001) 'Is globalization civilizing, destructive or feeble? A critique of five key debates in the social science literature.' *Annual Review of Sociology* 27: 235–260.

Haack, P., Schoeneborn, D. and Wickert, C. (2012) 'Talking the talk, moral entrapment, creeping commitment? Exploring narrative dynamics in corporate responsibility standardization.' *Organization Studies* 33(5–6): 815–845.

Hallet, T. and Ventresca, M. (2006) 'How institutions form: Loose coupling as mechanism in Gouldner's patterns of industrial bureaucracy.' *American Behavioral Scientist* 49: 908–924.

Haunschild, P. R. (1993) 'Interorganizational imitation: The impact of interlocks on corporate acquisition activity.' *Administrative Science Quarterly* 38: 564–592.

Haveman, H. A. (1993) 'Follow the leader: Mimetic isomorphism and entry into new markets.' *Administrative Science Quarterly* 38: 593–627.

Heimer, C. A. (1999) 'Competing institutions: Law, medicine, and family in neonatal intensive care.' *Law and Society Review* 33: 17–66.

Heugens, P. P. and Lander, M. W. (2009) 'Structure! Agency! (and other quarrels): A meta-analysis of institutional theories of organization.' *Academy of Management Journal* 52(1): 61–85.

Ingram, P. and Clay, K. (2000) 'The choice-within-constraints new institutionalism and implications for sociology.' *Annual Review of Sociology* 26: 525–546.

Ingram, P. and Simons, T. (1995) 'Institutional and resource dependence determinants of responsiveness to work-family issues.' *Academy of Management Journal* 38: 1466–1482.

Jonsson, S. (2009) 'Refraining from imitation: Professional resistance and limited diffusion in a financial market.' *Organization Science* 20(1): 172–186.

Jonsson, S. and Regnér, P. (2009) 'Normative barriers to imitation: social complexity of core competences in a mutual fund industry.' *Strategic Management Journal* 30(5): 517–536.

Katz, E., Levin, M. L. and Hamilton, H. (1963) 'Traditions of research in the diffusion of innovation.' *American Sociological Review* 28: 237–252.

Kennedy, M. T. and Fiss, P. C. (2009) 'Institutionalization, framing, and diffusion: The logic of TQM adoption and implementation decisions among US hospitals.' *Academy of Management Journal* 52(5): 897–918.

Kostova, T. and Roth, K. (2002) 'Adoption of an organizational practice by subsidiaries of multinational corporations: Institutional and relational effects.' *Academy of Management Journal* 45(1): 215–233.

Kraatz, M. S. and Block, E. S. (2008) 'Organizational implications of institutional pluralism.' In R. Greenwood, C. Oliver, R. Suddaby and K. Sahlin-Andersson (eds), *The SAGE Handbook of Organizational Institutionalism*. London: Sage. pp. 243–275.

Kraatz, M. S. and Moore, J. H. (2002) 'Executive migration and institutional change.' *Academy of Management journal* 45(1): 120–143.

Kraatz, M. S. and Zajac, E. J. (1996) 'Exploring the limits of the new institutionalism: The causes and consequences of illegitimate organizational change.' *American Sociological Review* 61: 812–836.

Lepoutre, J. M. W. N. and Valente, M. (2012) 'Fools breaking out: The role of symbolic and material immunity in explaining institutional nonconformity.' *Academy of Management Journal* 55(2): 285–313.

Levitt, B. and March, J. G. (1988) 'Organizational learning.' *Annual Review of Sociology* 14: 319–340.

Levitt, B. and Nass, C. (1989) 'The lid on the garbage can: Institutional constraints on decision making in the technical core of college-text publishers.' *Administrative Science Quarterly* 34: 190–207.

Lim, A. and Tsutsui, K. (2012) 'Globalization and commitment in corporate social responsibility: Cross-national analyses of institutional and political-economy effects.' *American Sociological Review* 77: 69–98.

Lounsbury, M. (2001) 'Institutional sources of practice variation: Staffing college and university recycling programs.' *Administrative Science Quarterly* 46: 29–56.

Lounsbury, M. and Ventresca, M. (2003) 'The new structuralism in organizational theory.' *Organization* 10: 457–480.

MacLean, T. L. and Behnam, M. (2010) 'The dangers of decoupling: The relationship between compliance programs, legitimacy perceptions, and institutionalized misconduct.' *Academy of Management Journal* 53(6): 1499–1520.

March, J. G. and Olsen, J. P. (1976) *Ambiguity and Choice in Organizations*. Bergen: Universitetsforlaget.

Marquis, C., Glynn, M.A. and Davis, G.F. (2007) 'Community isomorphism and corporate social action.' *Academy of Management Review* 32(3): 925–945.

Marquis, C. and Qian, C. (2014) 'Corporate social responsibility reporting in China: Symbol or substance?' *Organization Science* 25(1):127–148.

Meyer, J. W., Boli, J., Thomas, G. and Ramirez, F. (1997) 'World society and the nation state.' *American Journal of Sociology* 103: 144–181.

Meyer, J. W. and Rowan, B. (1977) 'Institutionalized organizations: Formal structure as myth and ceremony.' *American Journal of Sociology* 83: 340–363.

Meyer, J. W., Scott, R. W. and Strang, D. (1987) 'Centralization, fragmentation, and school district complexity.' *Administrative Science Quarterly* 32(2): 186–202.

Meyer, R. E. and Höllerer, M. A. (2014) 'Does institutional theory need redirecting?' *Journal of Management Studies* 51: 1221–1233.

Meyer, R. E. and Höllerer, M. A. (2016) 'Laying a smoke screen: Ambiguity and neutralization as strategic responses to intra-institutional complexity.' *Strategic Organization*, pp. 1–34. doi: 10.1177/1476127016633335.

Mezias, S. J. (1990) 'An Institutional model of organizational practice: financial reporting at the Fortune 200.' *Administrative Science Quarterly* 35: 431–457.

Mizruchi, M. and Fein, L. C. (1999) 'The social construction of organizational knowledge: A study of the uses of coercive, mimetic and normative isomorphism.' *Administrative Science Quarterly* 44: 653–683.

Mohr, J. W. (2005) 'Implicit terrains: Meaning, measurement, and spatial metaphors in organizational theory.' Unpublished manuscript. Available at http://www.soc.ucsb.edu/ ct / pages / JWM / Aboutme.html

Oh, M. and Jackson, J. (2011) 'Animal rights vs. cultural rights: Exploring the dog meat debate in South Korea from a world polity perspective.' *Journal of Intercultural Studies* 32(1): 31–56.

Okhmatovskiy, I. and David, R. J. (2012) 'Setting your own standards: Internal corporate governance codes as a response to institutional pressure.' *Organization Science* 23(1):155–176.

Oliver, C. (1988) 'The collective strategy framework: An application to competing predictions of isomorphism.' *Administrative Science Quarterly* 33: 543–561.

Oliver, C. (1991) 'Strategic responses to institutional processes.' *Academy of Management Review* 16: 145–179.

Pache, A.-C. and Santos, F. (2013) 'Inside the hybrid organization: Selective coupling as a response to competing institutional logics.' *Academy of Management Journal* 56(4): 972–1001.

Palmer, D., Jennings, D. and Zhou, X. (1993) 'Late adoption of the multidivisional form by large U.S. corporations: Institutional, political and economic accounts.' *Administrative Science Quarterly* 38: 100–131.

Philips, D. J. and Zuckerman, E. W. (2001) 'Middle-status conformity: Theoretical restatement and empirical demonstration in two markets.' *American Journal of Sociology* 107: 379–429.

Powell, W. W. and DiMaggio, P. J. (1991) 'Introduction.' In P. J. DiMaggio and W.W. Powell (eds), *The New Institutionalism in Organizational Analysis*. Chicago: University of Chicago Press. pp. 1–38

Purdy, J. M. and Gray, B. (2009) 'Conflicting logics, mechanisms of diffusion, and multilevel dynamics in emerging institutional fields.' *Academy of Management Journal* 52(2): 355–380.

Raffaelli, R. and Glynn, M.A. (2014) 'Turnkey or tailored? Relational pluralism, institutional complexity, and the organizational adoption of more or less customized practices.' *Academy of Management Journal* 57(2): 541–562.

Rao, H., Greve, H. R. and Davis, G. F. (2001) 'Fool's gold: Social proof in the initiation and abandonment of coverage by wall street analysts.' *Administrative Science Quarterly* 46: 502–526.

Reay, T. and Hinings, C. R. (2009) 'Managing the rivalry of competing institutional logics.' *Organization Studies* 30(6): 629–652.

Rodrigues, L. L. and Craig, R. (2007) 'Assessing international accounting harmonization using Hegelian dialectic, isomorphism and Foucault.' *Critical Perspectives on Accounting* 18(6): 739–757.

Rossman, G. (2014) 'The diffusion of the legitimate and the diffusion of legitimacy.' *Sociological Science* 1: 49–69.

Ruef, M. and Scott, R. W. (1998) 'A multidimensional model of organizational legitimacy: Hospital survival in changing institutional environments.' *Administrative Science Quarterly* 43: 877–904.

Sahlin-Andersson, K. (1996) 'Imitating by editing success: The construction of organizational fields and identities.' In B. Czarniawska and G. Sevón (eds), *Translating Organizational Change*. Berlin: De Gruyter. pp. 69–92.

Sahlin-Andersson, K. and Engwall, L. (2003) *Expansion of Management Knowledge: Carriers, Flows and Sources*. Stanford, CA: Stanford University Press.

Sanders, W. G. and Tuschke, A. C. (2007) 'The adoption of institutionally contested organizational practices: The emergence of stock option pay in Germany.' *Academy of Management Journal* 50(1): 33–56.

Sauder, M. and Espeland, W. N. (2009) 'The discipline of rankings: Tight coupling and organizational change.' *American Sociological Review* 74(1): 63–82.

Scherer, A. G., Palazzo, G. and Seidl, D. (2013) 'Managing legitimacy in complex and heterogeneous environments: Sustainable development in a globalized world.' *Journal of Management Studies* 50(2): 259–284.

Schneiberg, M. (2002) 'Organizational heterogeneity and the production of new forms: Politics, social movements and mutual companies in American fire insurance, 1900–1930.' In M. Lounsbury and M. Ventresca (eds), *Research in the Sociology of Organizations*. Greenwich, CT: JAI Press. pp. 39–89.

Schneiberg, M. (2013) 'Movements as political conditions for diffusion: Anti-corporate movements and the spread of cooperative forms in American capitalism.' *Organization Studies* 34: 653–82.

Schneiberg, M. and Clemens, E. S. (2006) 'The typical tools for the job: Research strategies in institutional analysis.' *Sociological Theory* 3: 195–227.

Schneiberg, M. and Soule, S. A. (2005) 'Institutionalization as a contested, multi-level process: The case of rate regulation in American fire insurance.' In J. Davis, D. McAdam, R. W. Scott and M. N. Zald (eds), *Social Movements and Organization Theory: Building Bridges*. Cambridge: Cambridge University Press. pp. 122–160.

Scott, W. R. (1987) 'The adolescence of institutional theory.' *Administrative Science Quarterly* 32: 493–511.

Scott, W. R. (1995) *Institutions and Organizations*. London: Sage.

Scott, W. R. (2001) *Institutions and Organizations*. Newbury Park, CA: Sage.

Scott, W. R. (2004) 'Reflections on a half-century of organizational sociology.' *Annual Review of Sociology* 30: 1–21.

Scott, W. R. and Meyer, J. W. (1983) 'The organization of societal sectors.' In J. W. Meyer and W. R. Scott (eds), *Organizational Environments: Ritual and Rationality*. Beverly Hills, CA: Sage. pp. 1–16.

Scott, W. R. and Meyer, J. W. (1994) 'Environmental linkages and organizational complexity: public and private schools.' In W. R. Scott and J. W Meyer (eds), *Institutional Environments and Organizations: Structural Complexity and Individualism*. London: Sage. pp. 137–159.

Seidman, W. H. (1983) 'Goal ambiguity and organizational decoupling: The failure of "rational systems" program implementation.' *Educational Evaluation and Policy Analysis* 5: 399–413.

Shipilov, A. V., Greve, H. R. and Rowley, T. J. (2010) 'When do interlocks matter? Institutional logics and the diffusion of multiple corporate governance practices.' *Academy of Management Journal* 53(4): 846–864.

Stevens, J. M., Steensma, H. K., Harrison D. A. and Cochran, P. L. (2005) 'Symbolic or substantive document? The influence of ethics codes on financial executives' decisions.' *Strategic Management Journal* 26: 181–195.

Still, M. C. and Strang, D. (2009) 'Who does an elite organization emulate?' *Administrative Science Quarterly* 54(1): 58–89.

Strang, D. and Soule, S. A. (1998) 'Diffusion in organizations and social movements: From hybrid corn to poison pills.' *Annual Review of Sociology* 24: 265–290.

Suchman, M. C. (1995) 'Managing legitimacy: Strategic and institutional approaches.' *Academy of Management Review* 20: 571–610.

Sutton, J. R., Dobbin, F., Meyer, J. and Scott, R. W. (1994) 'The legalization of the workplace.' *American Journal of Sociology* 99: 944–971.

Tilcsik, A. (2010) 'From ritual to reality: Demography, ideology, and decoupling in a post-communist government agency.' *Academy of Management Journal* 53(6): 1474–1498.

Tolbert, P. S. and Zucker, L. G. (1983) 'Institutional sources of change in the formal structure of organizations: the diffusion of civil service reform.' *Administrative Science Quarterly* 28: 22–39.

Turco, C. (2012) 'Difficult decoupling: Employee resistance to the commercialization of personal settings.' *American Journal of Sociology* 118(2): 380–419.

Tuttle, B. and Dillard, J. (2007) 'Beyond competition: Institutional isomorphism in US accounting research.' *Accounting Horizons*, 21(4): 387–409.

Wedlin, L. (2007) 'The role of rankings in codifying a business school template: Classifications, diffusion and mediated isomorphism in organizational fields.' *European Management Review* 4(1): 24–39.

Weick, K. (1979) *The Social Psychology of Organizing*. New York: McGraw-Hill.

Westphal, J. D., Gulati, R. and Shortell, S. M. (1997) 'Customization or conformity? An institutional and network perspective on the content and consequences of TQM adoption.' *Administrative Science Quarterly* 42: 366–394.

Westphal, J. D. and Zajac, E. J. (1997) 'Defections from the inner circle: Social exchange, reciprocity and the diffusion of board independence in U.S. corporations.' *Administrative Science Quarterly* 42: 161–183.

Westphal, J. D. and Zajac, E. J. (1998) 'The symbolic management of stockholders: Corporate governance reforms and shareholder reactions.' *Administrative Science Quarterly* 43: 127–153.

Westphal, J. D. and Zajac, E. J. (2001) 'Decoupling policy from practice: The case of stock repurchase programs.' *Administrative Science Quarterly* 46(2): 202–228.

Wijen, F. (2014) 'Means versus ends in opaque institutional fields: Trading off compliance and achievement in sustainability standard adoption.' *Academy of Management Review* 39(3): 302–323.

Zucker, L. G. (1987) 'Institutional theories of organization.' *Annual Review of Sociology* 13: 443–464.

4

The Imitation and Translation of Management Ideas[1]

Linda Wedlin and Kerstin Sahlin

Organizational institutionalism grew from observations of a widespread expansion, rationalization and homogenization of organizations across sectors and continents. Empirical foundations of this research combine large-scale empirical studies of diffused world society blue prints and homogenized organizational patterns worldwide, with qualitative studies of the circulation of ideas and of the interplay of ideas and organizations. This latter research tradition is the main focus for this chapter, even if clear connections with a broader field of organizational institutionalism are also spelled out. The ambition of the chapter is to highlight and elaborate on the key contributions of this literature to our understanding of the circulating ideas and of processes of imitation, translation and editing.

Elaborated formal organizational structures, Meyer and Rowan (1977) convincingly showed, cannot primarily be understood as devices for enhanced coordination and control, but reflect societal institutions, or rational myths. They also showed how new and elaborated formal organizational structures are built of widely circulated ideas or organizational building blocks, with organizational homogeneity becoming the visible outcome of such circulation. However, as they diffuse, those building blocks also become 'considered proper, adequate, rational, and necessary' for organizations in various contexts and settings (Meyer and Rowan, 1977: 345), thus forming the context for further adoption and diffusion. At a certain point, organizations merely have to adopt those organizational elements in order to appear modern and to be considered legitimate. In this process, ideas are not only picked up by individual organizations but also by other actors forming the regulatory and normative context for organizations in general, thus becoming embedded in processes and mechanisms aimed at assessing and evaluating organizational activities and actions. As ideas circulate they become the currency through which organizations are formed, perceived and assessed.

As is well known, Meyer and Rowan's seminal article inspired several generations of studies of the rationalization, elaboration and homogenization of organizational structures, and of translation of widely circulated ideas. In this chapter, we identify a particular stream of this research, focusing on the circulation and translation of management ideas. We note three distinct areas of interest in this research, reflecting largely also the evolution of this research field over time. Initially, the focus of this research was on individual organizations, and how their formal structures became at the same time increasingly complex and increasingly similar as they incorporated institutional elements from their environments. Subsequently, the research interest of many scholars turned to wondering about how such institutional elements came to be 'littered around the social landscape' (Meyer and Rowan, 1977: 345). Thus, they began to study the 'supply side' of myths: how institutional elements came to be produced and diffused. Following that, several studies have moved further and developed our knowledge of how such myths become 'considered proper, adequate, rational, and necessary' – thus how it becomes essential that organizations incorporate them in order to avoid being considered 'illegitimate'.

Guided by the overarching questions of why and how organizations adopt ideas that circulate, studies have particularly theorized and elaborated on the central mechanisms whereby ideas circulate: imitation, identification and fashion. A common message of these studies is that ideas do not remain unchanged as they flow but are subject to translation. While many qualitative studies have concentrated on the adoption of circulated ideas by certain sets of organizations (e.g., Brunsson and Olson, 1993; Wedlin, 2006) or on the circulation of certain types of ideas (Sahlin-Andersson and Engwall, 2002; Djelic and Sahlin-Andersson, 2006a) a key point is that individual ideas do not diffuse in a vacuum

but are actively transferred and translated in a context of other ideas, actors, traditions and institutions. To imitate, then, is not just to copy, but also to change and to innovate. As diffused ideas get translated throughout their circulation, and as they evolve differently in different settings, they do not only lead to homogenization but also to variation and stratification (Drori et al., 2014).

As a key insight here, we note that not only are ideas subject to translation as they are being circulated, but these ideas also impact on other ideas and on those organizations involved in the diffusion and adoption of ideas. Hence, the translation of ideas and their embeddedness in organizational practices and actions should be understood as sets of dynamic and mutually influencing processes. Another way to phrase this is that several processes of translation interplay in what we here term ecologies of translation. We suggest that such a conceptualization can further help to explain the many complex interactions and relations, actions and actors involved in continuous translation processes both within and outside the organizational context. When using the notion of ecologies of translation we also want to emphasize that these developments evolve in dynamic processes including a multitude of activities, actors and interests, but as a whole, they are not controlled or planned.

Even if many studies of circulating ideas have paid attention to how ideas flow and how they are edited as they circulate, emphasis in earlier research was on the travel routes and means rather than on the content of the ideas as such (Meyer, 1996: 250). In later works, more emphasis is placed on the content and form of the ideas that were spread, and on their formalization into regulatory and normative systems guiding organizations. Studies find that many ideas form the foundation of and inspiration for new regulations – in the form of standards, guidelines, assessing criteria and templates. This has triggered a stream of research addressing issues on how soft regulation and governance – of the kinds just mentioned – emerges, and with what consequences (e.g., Mörth, 2004; Djelic and Sahlin-Andersson, 2006a). This denotes a shift that we characterize as one from prototypes to templates, highlighting the content and form of ideas and how they spread, and its implication for local translation processes. This shift has also been accompanied by an increased interest in the consequences that circulated ideas bring, such as changes in individual organizations' identities, in field transformations and in more general institutional change (Wedlin, 2006). This focus on the continuous translation further highlights the complex relations and processes that make up the ecology of translation.

An overview of the research tradition is structured in three sections below, largely following the chronology of how this research stream has developed over the years, as described above. We first elaborate on the circulation and adoption of ideas. We then put focus especially on the role of actors, interests and activities in translation. A third section is devoted to what kinds of ideas circulate, and looks at how the nature of ideas changes, both as ideas circulate and as the institutional settings in which ideas spread change. Rather than end this chapter with a clear summary of these findings, we will conclude with a translation story: the story of how central institutional theoretical concepts have developed into a distinct Scandinavian approach, and how it compares to the current organizational institutionalism agenda.

THE CIRCULATION AND ADOPTION OF MANAGEMENT IDEAS

Many scholars of organizations noticed in the 1980 and 1990s that organizations were picking up popular ideas and seeking to incorporate them into their formal structures. Mainly, diffused ideas appeared to be fashionable management ideas. These were techniques and models for better management,

often introduced by consultants or other proponents of improved management, some of them specifically labeled with acronyms that quickly become part of management vocabulary. These waves included total quality management (TQM), business process reengineering (BPR), management by objectives (MBO), supply chain management (SPC), service management, new public management (NPM), project management, integrated management control, intercultural management, knowledge management and others. In the early 2000s popular waves of ideas have included various forms of evaluations, assessments and rankings, certifications and accreditation procedures and evidence-based guidelines. Together with those models, organizations came to incorporate a new – and what was seen to be more modern – terminology.

Much, but far from all, of the early work in this tradition was performed in Scandinavia, largely in studies of public sector organizational reforms (see, e.g., Brunsson, 1989; Brunsson and Olsen, 1993; Czarniawska and Sevón, 1996a). Many of these were case studies of individual organizational reforms and thus the focus was on how individual organizations picked up, adopted and incorporated new ideas or organizational elements. The introduction of new management principles was particularly evident in this sector as references to private sector management were becoming increasingly common, but the imported ideas at the time still stood out as very different from the administrative tradition of the public sector. Striking examples were the introduction of the service and customer concepts in the public sector (see, e.g., Forssell and Jansson, 1996; Sahlin-Andersson, 1996). The new terminology and the new techniques were introduced into the public sector organizations together with a widespread questioning of the previous ways of working. Furthermore, the new techniques did not always work as planned and were in many cases found to be decoupled from the daily operations (Brunsson, 1989, 2006;

Brunsson and Olsen, 1993). In later works, this focus on processes of translation of individual ideas and on individual organizations has been further developed (see, e.g., Røvik, 2007, 2011, 2016; Wæraas and Sataøen, 2014).

These observations were clearly in line with those proposed by both Meyer and Rowan, and DiMaggio and Powell. Even if not in opposition to the assumptions of core institutional writings by, for example, Meyer and Rowan (1977) and DiMaggio and Powell (1983), two kinds of observations from these Scandinavian studies called for an extended framework and additional conceptual tools. These were elaborated in the edited volume *Translating Organizational Change* (Czarniawska and Sevón, 1996a). First, even if instances of decoupling repeatedly occurred, in many instances the introduced language and models did have clear consequences in terms of how the organizations and practices came to be identified, assessed and presented. Diffused ideas could add to or result in changes to organizational identities and to what appeared as normal, desirable and possible – thus circulated ideas appeared to trigger organizational as well as institutional change (Forssell and Jansson, 1996; Sahlin-Andersson, 1996; Brunsson and Sahlin-Andersson, 2000; Blomgren, 2003).

The second, and more detailed, set of observations point out that the framework developed around the concept of diffusion appeared too static and mechanical in relation to the observations made. The concept of diffusion was easily associated with a physical process, as though what was spreading was a physical entity originating from one source and (while gaining its power to spread from this source) then becoming more diffuse and diffused. This view has led researchers and practitioners to seek best practices to identify 'the original' source of an idea. The perspective is an instrumental one – assuming that good and powerful ideas spread more widely than less effective ones. This reasoning may lead to a call for more historical studies to

satisfy the need to go back to search for the original source. Once we start analyzing and comparing ideas, however, it is difficult to distinguish any intrinsic success criteria for ideas that will 'make it'. Hence, it is often pointless – if not downright impossible – to find an origin (Bourdieu, 1977). So it appears to be not so much a case of ideas flowing widely because they are powerful, but rather, of ideas becoming powerful as they circulate. For example, some ideas seem to become popular not primarily because of their properties, but because of who transports and supports them and how they are packaged, formulated and timed (Czarniawska and Joerges, 1996; Røvik, 1998). Ideas become legitimate, popular and even taken-for-granted as being effective and indispensable as a result of having been adopted by certain actors in the field (Tolbert and Zucker, 1983; Westphal et al., 1997). In this way, managerial fads and fashions evolve, some ideas becoming popular for a time then disappearing again or becoming institutionalized (Abrahamsson, 1991, 1996; Collins, 2000). Again, historical and contextual studies are called for, but not solely with the aim of looking for the original source of diffused ideas; close studies of the circulation of ideas do, in fact, show why some turn out to be so attractive and powerful. Particularly, the observations suggested that such circulating processes need to be understood in social rather than physical terms. What was spreading were not ready-made and unchangeable particles or goods, but ideas subject to repetitive translation (see further Czarniawska and Sevón, 1996b, 2005; Czarniawska and Joerges, 1996; Czarniawska, 2008).

In empirical terms, these observations were not novel. As suggested by DiMaggio and Powell (1983), models were not imported whole cloth, and Westney's (1987) work on the imitation and innovation that formed the modern Japanese society clearly pointed to the way in which imitated models were transformed as they were transferred from one setting to another. Her analysis was clearly one of institutional change, as the imitated models were not just ceremonially adopted, but formed the basis for building the modern Japanese society.

In theoretical terms, however, the Scandinavian institutionalism, as Czarniawska and Sevón (1996b: 3) called it, formed a conceptual framework that put these dynamics at the center and thus formed a more constructivist foundation than the one rooted in the diffusion concept, mainly developed in the United States. In addition, the European studies were more micro and qualitative than the mainstream US ones. This approach recognized that while ideas are translated when introduced in a new context, also the perception and identity of that same context is changed (Sahlin-Andersson, 1996; Brunsson and Sahlin-Andersson, 2000; Wedlin, 2007). Furthermore, and in line with our proposed conceptualization of this as ecologies of translation, this suggests that it is not isolated ideas that are translated, but that circulated ideas are translated in relation to other ideas as well as in relation to ideals and contexts that are themselves translated and transformed.

Appropriateness and Fashion

Meyer and Rowan, and DiMaggio and Powell emphasized that the main motive for incorporating rationalized myths and for mapping those organizations that were seen as central and successful was to gain or maintain legitimacy. The Scandinavian scholars combined this insight with a more micro perspective, as they studied the processes of adoption and sought to make sense of how individuals and organizations acted in relation to the introduced models. They acted according to a logic of appropriateness, as proposed by March (1981). When initiating changes and when attending to and adopting new ideas, they reasoned as follows: 'Who am I?', What situation is this?' and 'What does a person such as I, or an organization such as this, do in a situation such as this?' Thus individuals

and organizations were depicted as clearly embedded in an environment that provided them with expectations, identities and rules for action.

In an epilogue to the 1996 volume edited by Czarniawska and Sevón, Meyer commented upon what distinguished this 'European flavored' research from the main US tradition. He used the term 'soft actor' to clarify how these European writers saw actors as clearly embedded in cultural material. A soft actor, thus, is an actor with interests, resources, identities and abilities, but at the same time the analysis acknowledges that these interests, resources, identities and abilities are neither stable nor intrinsic to individuals or organizations. Individuals and organizations develop their interests, identities, resources and abilities in their social context, and partly from the ideas they pick up and in relation to those they imitate. Thus actorhood as such needs to be understood as a process of social construction (Brunsson and Sahlin-Andersson, 2000).

Those individuals and organizations that pick up ideas have been depicted not only as acting according to a logic of appropriateness but more specifically as fashion followers. The word 'fashion' here points to the temporal and social logics of processes of adoption. In several early studies fashion was sometimes coupled with fads; both of these were associated with the idea that certain desires and models came in waves. Abrahamsson (1996) illustrated the bell-shaped curve of the spread of popular ideas such as quality circles, stressing the wave-like movement through which ideas flow among organizations and between contexts. He suggests that organizations adopt managerial practices and models, such as TQM, to conform to general norms of rationality and progress.

Czarniawska and Sevón (2005) portrayed fashion as the 'steering wheel' of translation and the flow of ideas. Fashion guides imitation and the attention of actors to specific ideas, models and practices, and fashion identifies but also creates what is appropriate and desirable at a given time and place. This leads organizations to adopt, but also to translate, these ideas, thus changing both what is translated and those who translate.

Authors of management fashions stress the inherently contradictory nature of fashion-following; the adoption of fashionable practices and ideas is driven by both the need for differentiation and the need for conformity with expectations and the practices of others. This dynamic between differentiation and imitation provides the dynamic and the driving force for idea diffusion (Røvik, 1996). Fashion followers act differently in order to act in the same way. While building on the recognition of Blumer (1969) that fashion is a competition mechanism, the institutional writers suggest that fashion-following is simultaneously an act of conformism and creativity (Czarniawska and Joerges, 1996: 34–35) and that following fashion means both working within, thus reproducing, and altering the existing institutional order. Thus, fashion incorporates both change and tradition (Røvik, 1996; Czarniawska, 2005). The concepts of appropriateness and fashion both point to the social processes of idea circulation. Ideas are circulated as individuals are exposed to each other and as they compare themselves with and view themselves in relation to others. Imitation is a basic mechanism, then, through which ideas circulate.

Imitation and Identification

Imitation is a basic social mechanism tying people together (Tarde, 1969 [1902]). Actors tend to imitate those they want to resemble (Sevón, 1996). As certain models, actors or practices become widely known, they shape the wishes, ideals and desires of others and thus provide the impetus for further imitation. Thus, perceived identity shapes imitation: one imitates those one relates to and those with whom one identifies. The process of imitation involves both self-identification and recognition of what one

would like to become (Sahlin-Andersson, 1996; Sevón, 1996). The opposite is also true, however, in that imitation shapes identity. Imitation constructs new relationships, references, and identifications and opens new avenues for comparison and for creating new identities. In this way fashions and trends largely form through processes of imitation.

When one views the circulation of ideas as processes of imitation, and as involving dynamics of identity formation, it becomes clear that some organizations tend to be more prone to imitate – and more receptive to widely circulated ideas – than others. Moreover, some organizations and ideas are imitated more than others. While DiMaggio and Powell (1983) associated the mechanism of mimesis to uncertainty, the close studies of individual organizational reforms – and imitation – suggest identification rather than uncertainty to be the main explanatory concept. Brunsson and Sahlin-Andersson (2000) saw a common pattern in those management ideas that were triggering organizational reforms in the public sector. They suggested, first, that the organizational elements that were adopted by public sector units tended to come in packages or strings rather than individually. They suggested further that those ideas were based on a common identity programme – together they reconstructed adopting units to become more clearly identified with those associated primarily with the adopted new ideas. This again paved the way for further imitation and for further identity transformation.

A main motivation for imitation is to become similar to others, and, even more, to become similar to the most prestigious, leading organizations. Several studies have argued that successful, prestigious and influential organizations are the most likely to be imitated (see, for instance, Haveman, 1993; Palmer et al., 1993). Imitation may also, however, be motivated by a desire to distinguish oneself from others, to be different. As explained by Czarniawska (2005), building on Tarde (1962 [1890]), the processes of identity formation and of imitation both involve a process of alterity construction – the formation of perceptions of being different. As important as the question 'Who am I like?' is the question 'How am I different?' Both these motives are grounded in identity. In order to understand and explain, then, who is imitating whom and why, we should also study who and what organizations identify with. The identity of a subject – a person or an organization – is defined in relation to others; it is derived from its reference to and relationship with others.

The concept of organizational fields has been used to explore how organizations identify themselves and thus what they seek to imitate. Groups of organizations whose activities are defined in similar ways have been conceived of as shaping organizational fields. This notion has of course been a core concept in organizational institutionalism. There are many variants of such field models, building on various theories and taking inspiration from a range of disciplines. Most commonly references are made to DiMaggio and Powell (1983). Elsewhere, we have argued for the importance of looking beyond this concept to trace the many frameworks and theoretical traditions that the field concept refers to and builds on (Djelic and Sahlin-Andersson, 2006b; Hedmo et al., 2005).

When using the field concept to understand motivations for and processes of imitation, we especially build on Bourdieu's notion of fields. Bourdieu (1977, 1984) argued that fields were formed and held together by the common belief in and upholding of the importance of certain activities. In this sense, fields form reference systems, shaping the participants' attention structures and identities – what they view as important issues (cf. March and Olsen, 1995). The field may also be described as a system of relations – relations that have evolved between the actors who define their activities as being concerned with similar issues. In the field, a structure of central and peripheral positions evolves. Dominating organizations form reference points and models for the rest of the organizations in the same field. Coherent patterns of action and meaning thus develop, even without any single actor or group of actors intentionally striving for coherence or conformity. Moreover, peripheral actors challenge dominant understandings, which they try to modify and/or displace. Central actors have a tendency to protect and defend the status quo. They may envision bending and adapting dominant understandings somewhat, if only to anchor and stabilize them further. This dynamic is behind active processes of imitation.

Translation and Editing

Imitation is an active process, and can be distinguished from diffusion insofar as the latter is defined as a phenomenon whereby a certain model, idea or practice, once created, spreads next to a number of *passive* recipients or trend followers. In contrast, imitation has been conceptualized as a *performative* process (Sevón, 1996; Sahlin-Andersson and Sevón, 2003). This points to the importance of understanding how ideas are translated, shaped and changed through processes of imitation. The Scandinavian scholars emphasized the social aspects of idea circulation and thus found that the predominant conceptual framework with physical connotations tended to lead researchers' attention in unwanted directions. Czarniawska and Sevón wrote:

Diffusion suggests a physical process, subject to laws of physics, and thus the explanation of phenomena denoted by this term provokes a further train of physical metaphors, like 'saturation' or 'resistance.' Latour (1986) proposes to replace it with *translation* calling attention to the richness of meanings associated with this term, of which only some are evoked in everyday life ... It is this richness of meaning, evoking associations with both movement and transformation, embracing both linguistic and material objects, that induced Latour and Callon, and the contributors of this volume after them, to borrow the notion of translation from a contemporary French philosopher, Michel Serres. (Czarniawska and Sevón, 1996b: 6–7)

It should be noted that 'translation' is not used in a linguistic sense, but is used to point to the simultaneous processes of movement and transformation; things change as they are moved. With this conceptual framework at hand, these authors could follow where and how management ideas traveled, and with what result. As management ideas were circulating they were translated into objects such as books, models and presentations (see Czarniawska and Joerges, 1996; Czarniawska and Sevón, 2005) and these translations were done in the various contexts and by the many actors involved in circulating ideas. What is being transferred from one setting to another is not an idea or a practice as such, but rather accounts and materializations of a certain idea or practice. Such accounts undergo translation as they spread, resulting in local versions of models and ideas in different local contexts (Czarniawska and Joerges, 1996). Both those seeking to be imitated and those imitating translate ideas and practices to fit their own wishes and the specific circumstances in which they operate.

In search of a concept that could be used to analyze in more detail how ideas were being transferred, transposed and transformed as they circulated, one of the authors of this chapter chose to analyze such translations as an editing process (Sahlin-Andersson, 1996). Based in studies of the circulation of the customer concept into public sector organizations and studies of a particular fashion at the time – that of building research parks – the editing concept showed how models and prototypes seen as 'successes' were formulated and reformulated as they circulated. Similarities between contexts and conditions for adoption were emphasized, while differences that might hinder the prototype to be adopted were downplayed. In such processes of translation, new meanings were created and ascribed to activities and experiences, and in each new setting a history of earlier experiences was reformulated in light of the present circumstances and visions. The circulation was a continuous editing process performed by a number of involved editors. Thus, those circulating management ideas were co-constructing these same ideas (Czarniawska and Joerges, 1996, 2005; Sahlin-Andersson, 2001; Sahlin-Andersson and Engwall, 2002).

The editing concept highlights the continuous reformulation and recontextualization of models and prototypes as they are moved between contexts and settings. This recontextualization may change the formulation as well as the meaning and content of experiences and models. At first glance, such editing processes might seem to be creative and open-ended. However, the processes of translation observed in these studies were rather characterized by social control, conformism and traditionalism – thus following rule-like patterns. Thus editing rules restrict and direct the translation – or editing – in each phase of circulation. The term 'rule' did not imply that there were written or explicit instructions for the telling and retelling of stories and ideas; neither did it imply that these translations followed clear intentions and established techniques among the editors. Although there are no explicit rules to follow, edited stories reveal how these translations were formed by the institutional setting in which they were performed. Thus they reveal rules that have been followed.

Such editing rules may be more specific or more general, and by following the routes of circulation one can see how different contexts provide different editing rules. However, our studies revealed three kinds of rules that appear to work more generally as ideas are widely circulating (see Sahlin-Andersson, 1996). A first set of rules concerns the context. When models are applied in a setting that is different from that of the prototype, time- and space-bounded features tend to be excluded. Specific local prerequisites are de-emphasized or omitted. In such a way widely circulated ideas tend to be formulated in general and abstract terms, and ideas and experiences are made available for others to imitate or adopt (Røvik, 1998; Greenwood et al., 2002). A second set of rules concerns logic. As initiatives and effects are presented, the logic of the story is often reconstructed. Developments may acquire a more rational-istic flavor. Effects are presented as resulting from identifiable activities, and processes are often described as following a problem-solving logic. Attention may be paid to a certain aspect of a development, while other aspects are omitted or erased. Plans tend to circulate more easily than effects (Sahlin-Andersson, 2001; Hwang, 2003), and mod-els that are perceived to be plannable and rational circulate more easily than others. As experiences in one place are edited into a model they tend to be rationalized, scientized and theorized (cf. Strang and Meyer, 1993).

A third set of editing rules concerns for-mulation. As circulating ideas and their effects are presented and represented, they acquire labels and may also be dramatized as they are told in a certain kind of language. These accounts acquire certain formats or, stated differently, they are formed into narra-tives of certain genres (Czarniawska, 1997). Concepts, categories, prototypical examples, counter-examples, references and ideological frameworks are used to structure, narrate and make sense of a certain procedure or to draw others' attention to a certain development. In the editing process various techniques may be packaged under a common heading, or they may be repackaged under a different heading than they had before (cf. Frenkel, 2005; Solli et al., 2005).

Through editing, an idea or an account of a practice may be formulated more clearly and made more explicit; however, the editing process may also change not only the form of the idea or account but also its focus, con-tent and meaning. Even small reformulations of an idea, which may accrue as the idea is transferred from one context to another, may fundamentally change its meaning or focus. Thus, it is only after the fact that one can dis-tinguish revolutionary or fundamental shifts from less substantial 'semantic'-type changes arising from editing. Furthermore, while some aspects of an idea may remain stable as the idea circulates, other aspects may become transformed. Though labels often remain the same as they diffuse easily between settings, this does not necessarily mean that the atten-dant technologies and meanings remain the same as the idea spreads from one context to another (see, e.g., Solli et al., 2005). It may also be the case the technologies are simi-lar, but that they come with different or dis-tinct ideological, or programmatic, content (Bäckström, 1999; Sahlin-Andersson, 2001). Vrangbæck (1999), for instance, analyzed the introduction of a system of customers' choice in the Danish healthcare system, calling it a 'Trojan horse'. This system was conceived and argued for in technical terms but when it was implemented, it changed the logic of the whole operation. New comparisons, frames of reference, assumptions, and overall objec-tives were invoked by the newly introduced techniques (see also Blomgren, 1999). In this way, circulating and edited ideas also triggers identity change.

ACTORS, INTERESTS AND ACTIVITIES IN TRANSLATION

The theoretical framework that was pre-sented in the previous section clearly paints a broad pattern of idea circulation. Most empirical studies referred to above primarily focused on those organizations that incorpo-rated institutional elements from their environment, and on how individual ideas or sets of ideas were attended to, translated and edited in the local settings. The strong Scandinavian tradition of case studies of individual organizations, decision processes and reforms kept many researchers' attention primarily on those organizations that adopted new ideas. In subsequent studies, though, interest more clearly turned to understanding where those ideas came from and how they were produced and circulated – or, to connect again to Meyer and Rowan (1977: 345), how ideas came to be 'littered around the social landscape'.

The metaphor of travel has been used to describe the circulation of ideas to emphasize that management ideas do not flow automatically, but follow certain often highly structured and well-worn routes (Czarniawska and Sevón, 1996b). Unlike other suggested metaphors, such as that of viruses (Rövik, 2011), the concept of travel indicates an active process: there are means of transportation that carry the ideas from one place to another. The travel metaphor is helpful in the sense that it directs our attention to those travel routes and means of travel. Connections between actors in the field may explain the likely routes through which ideas travel and the rate and speed of diffusion (Rogers, 1983). The formation of networks and other contacts thus enables ideas to flow. With intensified interactions among carriers, channels have opened for the transfer of ideas. However, as is the case with many metaphors in organization theory, this one should be used with some caution. If taken too literally, it may give the impression that ideas flow via direct interaction. The concept of imitation has sometimes led to a similarly limited view; imitation still seems to be understood primarily in terms of individual relationships, in which a single actor imitates one or several models. Many studies suggest, however, that greater emphasis should be placed on the complex webs of imitation processes, on how several imitation and translation processes may be interconnected, and on how one process of imitation may lead to another. And just as the term 'circulate' indicates, the processes involve not only the transport, flow or movement through established channels – like blood circulating through the arteries and veins of the body – but also the distribution, spreading, transmission or broadcasting of messages to wider groups.

To make this point, we have in previous writing, based on our studies of the proliferation of management education (Hedmo et al., 2005), distinguished between three modes of imitation. A first mode of imitation is one in which a central model inspires imitation. This can be called the *broadcasting mode* (March, 1999: 137). In this mode, imitation is based on a specific model or core set of ideas, which is picked up by actors in various settings and incorporated into local practices. Such imitation will likely lead to the homogenization of practices and to further emphasis on a single central model that becomes a prototype to be imitated. Even if the dynamics of this mode resemble those of diffusion, in which a strong central idea or model drives imitation, imitation in the broadcasting mode is driven by the active participation, initiatives, and motives of those doing the imitating. Both those imitated and those imitating are active shapers of the process (Sevón, 1996).

March (1999: 199) distinguished between this broadcasting mode and a *chain mode of imitation*. While broadcasting, by definition, originates in one place and spreads all around, in chain imitation an idea is imitated, and then this imitation is in turn imitated, and so on. This is, in fact, the main mode of imitation as described by Tarde (1962 [1890]). The one who is imitating may in fact have no knowledge of the 'origin' of the model; thus we can sometimes discern only after the fact that the imitation is part of a larger trend or development. This process is akin to the one identified in relation to fashions: fashions may have no clear initiator, driver or direction (Czarniawska, 2005; Löfgren, 2005). The trend or fashion is created through chains of imitation and the ensuing translations.

The third mode of imitation is one in which the relationships between those being imitated and those imitating are *mediated by other organizations and actors*. Imitation does not always proceed from those imitated to those imitating. Many persons and organizations act as carriers and/or mediators (Sahlin-Andersson and Engwall, 2002). For example, researchers, media, expert committees, and international organizations report on actions and events occurring elsewhere, but also take action or pursuing interests in such events that significantly influences how models, ideas and practices are portrayed and understood (see, for instance, Finnemore, 1996; Barnett and Finnemore, 1999; Sahlin, 2014).

Those who circulate ideas have been analyzed as *carriers*. For some, this concept may have a somewhat passive association: someone or something carrying a package, a passenger, or even a disease. The way the concept has been used in studies of the circulation of ideas, however, has been to convey a mix of passivity and activity, of supporting, transporting and transforming. Jepperson (1991) used the carrier concept to point to the importance of activities to institutional development; institutions do not just exist independently but are enacted in a host of supporting and reproducing practices. In this view, both the reproduction and the alteration of institutions involve activity: this ongoing activity is directed and limited by institutions while the activity reproduces as well as alters institutions (Scott, 1995; see also Giddens, 1979, 1984).

Along a similar line of conceptualization, but using a different terminology, John Meyer (1994, 1996) has used the term 'others' (inspired by G.H. Mead in 1934) to capture such carriers with their specific features and activities, thereby distinguishing them from 'actors', who are assumed to pursue their own interests and policies and are held responsible for their actions. Even though 'others' may present themselves as neutral mediators, they engage in activities that are crucial for the circulation and translation of ideas. Such 'other' organizations not only mediate ideas, they also influence and shape the activities that take place under their auspices, as they 'discuss, interpret, advise, suggest, codify, and sometimes pronounce and legislate [and] develop, promulgate, and certify some ideas as proper reforms, and ignore or stigmatize other ideas' (Meyer, 1996: 244). As editors (Sahlin-Andersson, 1996,

2000) they also formulate and reformulate and thus frame and reshape ideas, models and practices in the process. Moreover, they teach (Finnemore, 1996) – more or less directly – other organizations how to act in order to be acknowledged as legitimate.

Sahlin-Andersson and Engwall (2002) explicitly used the carrier concept when analyzing those who are professing, providing and circulating management ideas. With the expansion of carriers such as consultants, business schools and the media the supply of management ideas has expanded. Thus, Sahlin-Andersson and Engwall (2002) claimed, the intensified circulation and adoption of management ideas among organizations is largely supply driven. Abrahamsson (1996) also stressed the role of such carrying organizations, or 'others', in forming fashions, naming them a 'fashion-setting community' that continuously identifies ideas, fashions a discourse that presents these ideas as rational and progressive, and markets these back to the management community. This way, the fashion-setting community redefines conceptions of what constitutes rational progress in managerial practice and produces waves of managerial fashions (Abrahamsson, 1996).

We should be careful of letting this seemingly actor- and action-focused terminology lead us to see only the interactions and actors. Strang and Meyer (1993) suggest that relational models of diffusion are not enough to explain the wide distribution of models and practices in contemporary society. They stress that linkages can also be cultural – the cultural understanding that social entities belong to a common category constructs a tie between them. Such cultural linkages form identities and identification that shapes and directs processes of imitation and change, as expectations and norms diffuse among actors within the category or group. Empirical studies of the translation of accounting reforms (Hyndman et al., 2014), shareholder value ideals (Meyer and Höllerer, 2010) and risk regulation practices (Czarniawska, 2011) in different countries show how such cultural categories, guided also by political and social linkages and embeddedness, provides the context for distinct translations and developments of these ideas in different contexts.

Such diffusion within cultural categories is enhanced by theorization, or the development of abstract categories and generalized, complex models and patterned relationships (Strang and Meyer, 1993). Mediating organizations, again, play important roles in such processes as they theorize practices and models for change driving organizational as well as institutional change and development (Greenwood et al., 2002; Rao et al., 2003). However, such theorizing can also lead to less distinctiveness and a cultural embeddedness that stretches beyond the national, towards the global. In the volume by Drori, Höllerer and Walgenbach (2014), several examples are given of the significant role of mediators, or what Meyer terms the 'highly schooled mediating actors' (Meyer, 2014: 419), in the local translation of global models for management and organizations. Be they managers, civil servants, academic leaders, consultants, media professionals or interpreters, all are 'themselves deeply infused with standardizing global rational ideology' (Meyer, 2014: 419), making their translations and contributions to the translation process highly structured. Here, local distinctiveness and local translations tend to take form in highly rationalized global processes, creating local variation but in a rather restricted and 'glocalized' form (Drori et al., 2014: 12–13).

Ecologies of Translation

Many of the above-cited studies have focused on one idea and followed its circulation. However, as emphasized above, studies of translation have also shown the many actors, activities and settings involved in processes of translation, and also the multitude of interplaying ideas. In the introduction to this chapter we suggested that the concept of ecologies of translation captures this interplay. The concept of ecology points to the importance of bringing into the analysis the dynamic interaction among circulating ideas and the interaction of those ideas with their environments. Such complex interactions have been analyzed through multilayered analysis (e,g., Buhr, 2008; Frenkel, 2014) and through combined diacrone and syncrone analyses and through the combination of close-up studies of individual ideas and organizations with broader historical studies and network (e.g., Grafström, 2006, Djelic, 2014).

This increased interest in the interplay of ideas is in line with a more general development of organizational institutionalism with developed analysis of institutional pluralism and institutional complexity (e.g., Kraatz and Block, 2008; Greenwood et al., 2011). With an increased interest in institutional complexity, studies have developed on the interplay of those institutions. The most common way of analyzing ways in which organizations respond to institutional complexity has been through decoupling (for an overview see Bromley and Powell, 2012). Such analyses resonate with an understanding of organizational change in terms of shifting and parallel ideal types. While decoupling still appears as one important mechanism in organizational practices in the context of institutional complexity, translation studies also show that institutions as well as circulated ideas mix in more profound ways (e.g., Djelic, 2014; Sahlin, 2012, 2014).

The above findings lead to the conclusion that idea circulation is process-driven rather than interest-driven – not in the sense that interests are lacking, but in that interests largely form endogenously in the processes. The studies and analyses referred to have repeatedly pointed to the open-ended and ambiguous nature of translation processes. Sahlin (2014) pointed to three dynamics of ambiguity following on processes of idea translation and emergent global themes. First, each individual idea or theme tends to be characterized by ambiguity as it is being translated and edited across contexts. As described above, studies have portrayed widely disseminated management knowledge as being packaged with clear labels and stories and simultaneously highly plastic, varied and ambiguous. This feature of assessments and models – combining ambiguity and precision – means that they seem capable of being applied in many settings, and is one explanation for their success as global management models (Sahlin-Andersson and Engwall, 2002: 285; also see Czarniawska and Sevón, 2005). However, for the individual organization, leader, or employee this also means ambiguity when it comes to how to deal with the new ideas and their accompanied directives, assessments etc.

Second, ambiguity follows from the interplay of ideas. Ideas can become intertwined with other ideas as they are translated and adopted, and may both build on and reinforce each other. And third, as circulated ideas are institutionally framed and translated, they can reflect and reinforce different institutional frames. At the same time, when they emerge, diffuse and impact organizations, they may lead to ceremonial adoption but also to changed practices and institutions. Hence, idea circulation often includes and shapes more fundamental institutional ambiguity.

Ambiguity was an important topic of organization research in the 1970s (e.g., March and Olsen, 1976). Observations in studies of idea circulation can be further illuminated through this earlier work. Seen in the framework of Cohen et al. (1972), idea circulation resembles the main characteristic of organized anarchies; they are highly organized, but with problematic preferences, unclear technology and fluid participation. 'Garbage-can-inspired' analysis of these processes can add to the understanding of those processes, with the same ambition that Cohen et al. expressed at the end of their seminal article: 'The great advantage of trying to see garbage can phenomena together as a process is the possibility that that process

can be understood, that organizational design and decision making can take account of its existence and that, to some extent, it can be managed' (Cohen et al., 1972: 17).

FROM PROTOTYPES TO TEMPLATES

The focus of research has in later years turned from studies of how and why ideas circulate to studies of what kinds of ideas circulate, and on how the nature of ideas changes, both as ideas circulate and as the institutional settings in which ideas spread change. We can describe this change as a shift in focus from ideas as prototypes to ideas as templates.

Prototypes are exemplars, models to be imitated and put into practice. Such prototypes are typically picked up and edited by those organizations that want to become, or be perceived as, successful in accordance with the exemplary models. So, for instance, when a number of municipalities developed their civil services, this became known as a successful model – or a prototype – to be imitated and other municipalities followed suit (Tolbert and Zucker, 1983). Models for total quality management were associated with success and thus were picked up by organizations that wanted to become or appear successful (Westphal et al., 1997) and, with reference to Silicon Valley, research parks became associated with successful regional development and thus developed among regional planners into a prototype for how to enable development and growth (e.g., Hall and Marcusen, 1985; Saxenian, 1988; Sahlin-Andersson, 1996). We have shown above that these processes of imitation are largely mediated with consultancies, media organizations, international organizations and the like carrying those models from one setting to another and at the same time editing them into success models. From this follows the great number of studies focusing on particular, often global, models of management and organization and their local translations, including those of TQM (Özen and Berkman, 2007; Erçek and Say, 2008; Özen, 2014; Strang, 2014), lean (Morris and Lancaster, 2006; Andersen and Røvik, 2015), balanced scorecard (Ax & Bjørnenak, 2005; Madsen, 2014), diversity management (Boxenbaum, 2006; Klarsfeld, 2009; Barbosa and Cabral-Cardoso, 2014; Frenkel, 2014), and reputation management (Wæraas and Sataøen, 2014).

More than models and prototypes for specific imitation, however, templates for assessing and evaluating practices are also circulating among organizations and between contexts. These templates are frames or targets that actors use to compare or benchmark their activities, and they prescribe how success should be assessed. Templates serve as the currency, the medium of abstraction used to assess, monitor and present practices. These can be evaluation criteria, rankings, standards, or just widespread notions of what constitutes success that individuals, groups and organizations aspire to or compare themselves with. The formulation and diffusion of templates shapes identities and identification with a category or group of organizations, and guide the search for models and organizations to imitate (Wedlin, 2007).

Soft Regulation and Governance

This change in research focus from prototypes to templates was primarily triggered by empirical observations. The most fashionable and popular organizational ideas during the 1980s and 1990s largely concerned and strengthened management and leaders. Slightly different ideas have come to be most commonly circulating during the new century. Classification systems (Bowker and Star, 1999), standards (Brunsson and Jacobsson, 2000) and rules (March et al., 2000) have increased in number and have been developed and applied across organizations and around the world (Djelic and Sahlin-Andersson, 2006b). Evaluations and

audits (Power, 1997), accounting systems (Meyer, 1994; Olson et al., 1998), assessments and accreditation (Hedmo, 2004) and comparisons and rankings (Miller, 1996; Wedlin, 2006) have all expanded and become widespread.

Thus, focus has shifted from management to regulation, from an intra-organizational to inter-organizational focus, and from talk of efficiency to talk of transparency. In general, this shift is clearly following the logic of an audit society, the early signs of which Michael Power (1997) pointed out. With an 'audit explosion' the logic of the financial audit has been replicated to new societal arenas and issues, and it is seen as constituting a new system of governance that inculcates 'new norms and values by which external regulatory mechanisms transform the conduct of organizations and individuals in their capacity as "self-actualizing individuals"' (Shore and Wright, 2000: 61). Thus, this 'audit society' is a society where audits expand into almost all aspects of social life, and operations and organizations are increasingly structured in ways that make them 'auditable' (see also Strathern, 2000; Shore and Wright, 2000).

'Transparency' along with 'governance', 'flexibility', 'quality', and 'performance' are concepts that have spread almost universally. In parallel with this emerging transparency regime (Kjaer and Sahlin, 2007) are techniques and models for how to respond to such monitoring. These techniques are ways of auditing and making auditable – they have been characterized as transparency technologies (Blomgren and Sahlin, 2007) or, more commonly, as soft modes of governing and regulating. Soft regulations are nonhierarchical rules that are not legally binding (Mörth, 2004, 2006). Furthermore, such rules are largely informal and flexible in the sense that they are open to interpretation and adjustment by those being regulated (cf. Kirton and Trebilcock, 2004). The domain and applicability of soft rules and the conditions for compliance are defined together with the rules themselves. Rather than predefined, authority must be built into each governing relationship.

Despite much general talk about deregulation, empirical observations point to the increasing scope and breadth of regulatory and governance activities of all kinds. The intensity of the latter, in fact, is such that it would probably be more accurate to talk of regulatory 'activism'. Regulatory activism can take the form of a re-regulation of certain spheres that had already been regulated, but generally at the national level. This is the case, for example, with education (Engwall and Morgan, 1999), health, labor markets (Jacobsson, 2004) and accounting and financial reporting (Tamm Hallström, 2004; Botzem and Quack, 2006). All of those spheres are increasingly subject to regulatory activities and initiatives with a transnational scope.

Regulatory activism can also take the form of an expansion into virgin territories – towards spheres of social life that were not regulated before. This is the case, for example, with environmental and pollution issues (Frank et al., 2000; McNichol and Bensedrine, 2003; Power, 2003); ethical, social and environmental aspects of corporate activities (e.g., Cutler et al., 1999; Kirton and Trebilcock, 2004); the life and rights of animals (Forbes and Jermier, 2002); administrative procedures (Brunsson and Jacobsson, 2000; Beck and Walgenbach, 2002) or the structuring of love and intimate relationships (Franck and McEneaney, 1999). The present world, indeed, is a 'golden era of regulation' (Levi-Faur and Jordana, 2005) marked by a profound transformation of regulatory patterns (see also Braithwaite and Drahos, 2000). We witness both the decline of state-centered control and the rise of an 'age of legalism' (Schmidt, 2004). New regulatory modes – such as contractual arrangements, standards, rankings and monitoring frames – are taking over and are increasingly being used by states, too (Hood et al., 1999). New organizations, alliances and networks emerge

everywhere. Particularly salient is the almost exponential growth of international organizations (e.g., Boli and Thomas, 1999). An important task for many of these organizations is to issue rules, but they may also be involved in elaborating and activating processes to monitor adoption and implementation of those rules.

Hence, we find that just as fashionable management ideas circulated more or less worldwide during the previous decades, the early 2000s has seen the circulation of various kinds of regulatory and governing activities. These bring templates for organizing and for evaluating, assessing and judging practices and procedures. We can point to organizational as well as institutional consequences of the new emerging trends. Before turning to these, however, we need to say a few more words on the dynamics of the circulation of templates.

Circulation of Templates

The circulation of templates follows some of the same dynamics as the circulation of prototypes – the management ideas – discussed above. They display patterns of fads and fashion, they are picked up and displayed as organizations seek to appear modern and rational, they are supplied and circulated by many carrying organizations that look for ways of attracting resources and attention, and they are perceived as ways for all these many organizations to seek more central and dominating positions in their respective fields. Some consequences of their circulation appear familiar, too: they add to the elaboration and increased complexity of organizational structure, structures that are more or less decoupled from the daily operations of those organizations, and they lead to isomorphism, at least as long as we look at the formal organizational structures.

The circulation of templates seems to have one additional consequence for organizations, in that it puts increasing focus on aspects such as image, reputation and identity-formation of organizational actors (see, for instance, Wedlin, 2006). We can particularly note how organizations become increasingly occupied with presenting themselves, in ways that clearly remind us of those ways of 'the presentation of self' that were highlighted by Goffman (1959; see also, e.g., Ramirez, 2006). Also this presentation of self is aided by intermediate, or carrying, organizations, such as the media (Pallas and Wedlin, 2014).

Empirical studies of fields such as health care and management education have emphasized the importance of monitoring organizations, such as accreditation bodies and media, in creating and circulating templates within fields (Erlingsdottir and Lindberg, 2005; Hedmo et al., 2006). These have provided categories and measures on the basis of which activities and organizations are compared, monitored and assessed (Hedmo et al., 2005). It was particularly noted that the entrance of these mediating bodies was followed not only by more imitation among organizations but also by an enhanced emphasis on self-presentation. The rules set by the monitoring bodies regulate what is considered to be good and appropriate self-presentation, and they also frame and structure how the audience views the self-presentations. Organizations engage in producing and editing presentations of themselves and their performance in light of such standard criteria for evaluation and description (Corvellec, 1997; Pallas, 2007). With this increased attention to self-presentation follows changes in organizational structure.

Studies of corporate branding (Schultz et al., 2005), of corporate expressiveness (Hatch and Schultz, 1997) and of corporate reputation (Fombrun, 1996; Deephouse, 2000; Pollock and Rindova, 2003), as well as daily reports on the way corporations are traded and valued on the stock markets worldwide all seem to reveal the central importance of the way corporations are presented and conceptualized. In fact, many would claim that brands and presentations *are* the core of many modern corporations. The way in which corporations are presented and monitored by the media may thus have a direct effect on their finances, their development and even their survival (cf., e.g., Jonsson, 2005). Mediatization is thus a powerful institutional idea increasingly forming organizational realities (Pallas, 2007; Pallas et al., 2016).

We have suggested the term 'edited corporation' to emphasize this (Engwall and Sahlin, 2007). The activities of organizations are increasingly geared, as described above, to the *editing* of texts picked up by the organization from the environment – management ideas, market information, news of competitors, and so on – or texts about the company intended for its stakeholders or for other uses. Further, the term 'editing' suggests the presence of reciprocal processes in which several individuals and units inside and outside the corporation interact with one another. Moreover, such texts are shaped – in fact, *edited* – according to those circulating templates that we discussed above.

The edited corporation, then, is a corporation that is clearly embedded in and dependent upon circulated templates; it is a corporation in which a great many activities are devoted to editing work, and to managing and organizing for this embeddedness. The edited presentation of an organization and its activities is not directed at an external audience only. The templates also function as mirrors of organizational activities, whereby the edited organization appears in an auto-communicative process in which activities are presented in external assessments, rankings, media, audits, etc., which in turn informs people in the organization about their own situation and operations.

As organizations, groups and individuals categorize, give accounts of their activities, and benchmark themselves in relation to templates, forming themselves according to the templates, these efforts can drive institutional change. Rather than serving as direct blueprints or models to be imitated or adopted, however, these templates shape identities and identifications of organizations and groups that can lead to 'identity-movements' that significantly alters institutional logics or practices (cf. Rao et al., 2003). The result of such change, however, is not necessarily or exclusively an increasing homogenization of organizational structures or activities. Rather, studies have noted both compliance and resistance to isomorphic pressures introduced by new evaluation and assessment systems (Townley, 2002), and have shown how templates provided by monitoring activities leave substantial room for diverse interpretations and local identity formation processes, thus mediating isomorphic pressures (Wedlin, 2007). We can thus expect, and have observed, both similarity and difference to follow from the circulation and formulation of templates. This is in line with contemporary writings on institutional change, showing differential responses to new evaluation mechanisms, performance measures and professional standards that produce both stability and change in organizational practices and routines (Casile and Davis-Blake, 2002; Greenwood et al. 2002; Townley, 2002).

In this section we have described and discussed a shift from prototypes to templates. This, however, should not be understood as meaning that prototypes are no longer circulating. However, the prevalence of monitoring and scrutinizing activities of the kind described above opens spaces for the circulation of prototypical models for how those scrutinized organizations can be improved relative to the template measures. Thus with this shift we find a more densely populated institutional and organizational landscape. Again, studies have most clearly pointed to the emergence of new and increasingly complex institutional structures and procedures. A critical remark that has been made about much of organizational institutionalism can be repeated relative to the present studies: what are the limits of the processes described? Which forces drive in the opposite

direction? Obviously there needs to be some counter-forces working against intensified circulation, deinstitutionalization and homogenization but these are only rarely discussed in studies of institutionalization processes. Even if the Scandinavian studies reviewed in this chapter have sought to address these issues by looking more closely at the dynamics of institutionalization and circulation, and to account for variation, many intriguing and difficult questions about limits to institutionalization, deinstitutionalization and deregulation remain.

SCANDINAVIAN INSTITUTIONALISM – A TRANSLATION STORY

This chapter has directed focus onto a distinct framework for understanding institutional change and development. With an explicit focus on the concept of translation, and the process whereby institutional ideas, models and practices travel across contexts and setting, what we have here termed Scandinavian institutionalism is a modified version of mainstream institutional theory – a translation. Thus, the story of this research tradition is itself a story of a translation process; showing how the translation of theoretical models and ideas become embedded and transformed in local contexts and settings, resulting in similarity but also variation in concepts, arguments and practice. The result of such translation is not to be read as just a variation on current themes in institutional theory, however. It is a distinct interpretative framework for understanding institutional processes and outcomes. In an attempt to set out more clearly how the translation perspective differs from other institutional theoretical accounts, we will here briefly try to set out the distinctiveness of this approach in relation to some of the contemporary themes in mainstream institutional theory. Just to be clear, we do not argue that there is a mainstream institutional account and that the

Scandinavian institutionalism is different. Instead, the way we read the landscape of organizational institutionalism is that several variants of this theme have evolved over the years, through processes of translation. Hence, Scandinavian institutionalism is one among many possible translations (see also O'Mahoney, 2016; Wæraas and Agger Nielsen, 2016). Furthermore, just as is the case with all subthemes under the umbrella of organizational institutionalism, what is here called Scandinavian institutionalism has its own variants and nuances and develops, as shown in this chapter, through continued processes of translation.

The first distinctive feature of the Scandinavian institutional theory framework is the understanding of change. With translation as the framework, change is understood as constant and continuous: while ideas travel and get translated, they continuously change and transform, get revised and modified, to such an extent that it is not often possible – or even desirable – to clearly establish what is 'original', what is new and what is a modification (Sahlin-Andersson, 1996, 2001; Czarniawska and Sevón, 2005). There is also not always a clear source of translation attempts, and the object of translation may itself change in the process (Nicolini, 2010). As has been shown in the account of Scandinavian research, the inspiration came from several sources; sociological accounts of institutional processes, studies of decision-making in public sector organizations, European studies of science and technology, and sociological studies of translation, among others. These were variously drawn on and combined, modified and adapted to develop into a distinct theoretical tradition in Scandinavian management studies.

With this notion of change follows a different understanding of actors and actorhood, which is the second distinctive feature of Scandinavian institutionalism. As noted above, Meyer (1996) termed this actorhood 'soft', stressing the cultural embeddedness of actors. With such a perspective, actors

become translators, themselves shaped by local contexts and situations, and their interests and motives in translation processes are considered both contextually and culturally shaped and dependent. While most translation studies to date have focused on the embeddedness of actors in national and local contexts (see, for instance, Saka, 2004; Boxenbaum, 2006; Zilber, 2006; Morris and Lancaster, 2006; Meyer and Höllerer, 2010; Kirkpatrick et al., 2013; Hyndman et al., 2014), recent works of Scandinavian scholars have also pointed to the importance of professional values and assumptions in shaping motives and interests of actors in translation processes (Waldorff and Greenwood, 2011; Lindberg, 2014; Blomgren and Waks, 2015; Pallas et al., 2016).

Focusing here on an embedded rather than a 'strategizing' notion of actors in translation (cf. Kirkpatrick et al., 2013), we note how a translation perspective offers an alternative understanding of the role of actors in institutional change. Rather than attempting to pinpoint the role and driving force of individual actors, sometimes referred to as institutional entrepreneurs (for overviews see Garud et al., 2007; Hardy and Maguire, Chapter 10 this volume), translation focuses on the rather mundane acts of translation performed by many. Using the metaphor of anthills to depict institutions, Czarniawska describes it as 'not a building erected according to a plan; it is a practice of long standing, taken-for-granted by the ants' (2009: 438). As such, it is built over time, dependent on the local construction and elaboration of many ants, and it is delimited to a particular place at a particular time. It takes many ants to build the anthill, and 'as individuals they are indispensable but not irreplaceable' (2009: 438).

To the extent that the rather mundane, continuous work of actors is stressed, the notion of translation seems closer to the concept of institutional work. Institutional work is used to describe and explain 'the purposive action of individuals and organizations aimed at creating, maintaining and disrupting institutions' (Lawrence and Suddaby, 2006: 215). Particularly linking the activities and interests of various actors to the development and promotion of management fashions, Perkmann and Spicer (2008) have used the concept of institutional work to explain the institutionalization of management ideas. They identify three forms of institutional work discussed in work on management fashions and ideas (see Table 1 in Perkmann and Spicer, 2008 for an overview): political work, technical work and cultural work. Political work includes activities such as advocating for new rules and engaging other actors and interests to promote new practices (cf. Lawrence and Suddaby, 2006); technical work includes theorizing and crafting categorizations others can use; and cultural work includes framing and anchoring the new idea/practice in a wider normative framework (Perkmann and Spicer, 2008: 817). This perspective highlights some of the central features also of a translation perspective: institutional work can take many forms, it is performed by many actors and it is continuous.

Also the story of Scandinavian institutionalism has been told as a story of institutional work (Boxenbaum and Strandgaard Pedersen, 2009), stressing the active work of a few 'leading figures' in building institutions and networks important for the continued travel of institutional theory inspiration to the Scandinavian context. While not denying the importance of these efforts for the spread and translation of this research tradition, it is unlikely that the efforts at that time were completely 'purposive' of creating a Scandinavian institutionalism tradition. Returning to the metaphor of the anthill, we can recognize that while the ants themselves are clearly involved in, and constitutive of, the practices that make up the anthill, they may be unaware of both the justifications for the anthill and the rationalities that delimit its existence. These would be, however, clear to a biologist seeing the building of the anthill as part of the larger ecosystem (Czarniawska,

2009: 438). Thus, while making up a significant part of the narrative of how a particular institution is constructed (Czarniawska, 2009: 439), rationalities, 'purpose' and intentions may only become clearly visible in retrospect. It may also come as unintentional, or unexpected, effects of other actions, such as increasing transatlantic research collaborations (Boxenbaum and Strandgaard Pedersen, 2009: 179).

An elaborated translation perspective on the development of Scandinavian institutionalism would put increasing focus on the continuous efforts, of these and many other actors, to translate elements of institutional theory into other contexts and settings. This would mean emphasizing efforts following the initial, 'entrepreneurial', ones, studying – in the case of the Scandinavian institutionalism tradition – how ideas get enacted into educational programs, tutorials and doctoral training courses, for instance, eventually making its way into doctoral thesis and other scholarly work (Eriksson-Zetterqvist, 2009). Following the continued processes of translation in various contexts and settings in this way, detailed, qualitative and close-up studies of organizational change processes and reform initiatives and how these take shape locally have been instrumental, often including extensive interview studies, observation or shadowing techniques (see. for instance, Waldorff, 2013; Lindberg, 2014; Pallas et al., 2016).

This raises another, our third, salient point for the translation perspective, namely its close relation to the study of practice. While not alone to stress the practice dimension of institutional processes (see Lounsbury, 2007; Lounsbury and Crumley, 2007; Smets, Aristidou and Whittington, Chapter 14 this volume), the translation perspective highlights the role of actors in shaping and interpreting local practice and their relations to larger institutional frames and elements. Highlighting the active and micro-level work of actors in transforming ideas into everyday work, scholars have noted the active work of managers and workers in aiding habitualization of new practices and meanings in local organizational settings (Reay et al., 2013). Stressing also the importance of local maintenance work to avoid disruptions of practice, Lok and de Rond (2013) argue that institutions also offers a certain 'plasticity', making it possible for local actors to translate and for practices to change without necessarily challenging the institutionalized order. Such explicit focus on practices and practice work thus provides grounds for understanding both change and stability in institutionalized practices.

As was highlighted also in the definition of the anthill – as a practice of long standing – the Scandinavian perspective clearly frames institutions and institutional processes as closely aligned with, and dependent on, local action and existing practices. It highlights how institutional ideas travel, but stresses that in order to travel such ideas must first be removed from local practice, or theorized (Strang and Meyer, 1993): made into stories, words and accounts that can be told and narrated (Czarniawska, 1997). In the continued translation process, actors become carriers as they narrate and move institutional elements and ideas between contexts, but also link them to practice. Institutional elements thus become embedded in local practice as they materialize and are 'enacted', thus giving materiality and object a more central role in institutional processes (Czarniawska, 2008; Tryggestad and Georg, 2011). This is related, again, to the notion of change. Stressing the role of actors as local interpreters and translators of institutional models and ideas, translation necessarily becomes a local, and pragmatic, activity that actors perform continuously to adapt, adopt and adjust these institutional elements to fit local practices, assumptions and values. This changes both that which is being translated, and the organization in which translation occurs (Pipan and Czarniawska, 2010).

Using this view of institutionalization processes, Scandinavian institutionalists have provided additional understanding to the spread and shape of institutional logics, and, most significantly, on how logics get embedded in and enacted through local practices and organizational day-to-day activities (Waldorff, 2013; Lindberg, 2014; Pallas et al., 2016). Providing a largely field-level perspective on institutional change, institutional logics literature has primarily focused on the processes whereby logics govern actions, thus positioning logics to precede action and provide the frames through which organizations – and other actors – have to (strategically) respond (Thornton et al., 2012). In contrast, these Scandinavian scholars have suggested that logics become embedded into organizational practices, routines and principles through continuous efforts of translation, shaping not only the organizational practices but also the shape and meaning of various elements of institutional logics (Pallas et al., 2016; see also Hinings, 2011). In this sense, logics do not necessarily exist 'out there', but must be 'performed into being' in particular organizational contexts and situations (Lindberg, 2014: 485). This adds theoretically to questions of how institutional logics are accessed, activated and altered locally (Delbridge and Edwards, 2013; Reay and Hinings, 2009; Thornton et al., 2012), how they guide and shape translation processes (Waldorff and Greenwood, 2011), and how they come to constitute organizational realities (Currie and Spyridonidis, 2015).

As our fourth, and final, point, we would like to point to one of the distinctive results of translation processes: variation. Scandinavian institutionalists find similarities but also differences: in practices, in interpretations, in meanings (Meyer and Höllerer, 2010), and in concepts, for instance, and it takes effort to understand local variations across contexts and settings (Hyndman et al., 2014). This goes also for the translation of institutional theory in its Scandinavian form. Thus, also the idea of institutional theory changes as it travels, and is translated along the way. The outcome, as we have intended to show in this chapter, is variation: many translations seem possible, and each is embedded in a temporal, structural and cultural context, framed by the actors involved in translation and the process whereby the translation occurs.

Note

1 This chapter is a revised version of Sahlin, Kerstin and Wedlin, Linda (2008) Circulating ideas: Imitation, translation and editing. In R. Greenwood, C. Oliver, R. Suddaby and K. Sahlin-Andersson (eds), *The SAGE Handbook of Organizational Institutionalism*. London: Sage. pp. 218–242.

REFERENCES

Abrahamsson, Eric (1991) 'Managerial fads and fashion: The diffusion and rejection of innovations', *Academy of Management Review*, 16: 586–612.

Abrahamsson, Eric (1996) 'Technical and aesthetic fashion', in Barbara Czarniawska and Guje Sevón (eds), *Translating Organizational Change*. Berlin: Walter de Gruyter. pp. 117–138.

Andersen, Hege and Røvik, Kjell-Arne (2015) 'Lost in translation: a case-study of the travel of lean thinking in a hospital', *BMC Health Services Research*, 15: 401.

Ax, Christian and Bjørnenak, Trond (2005) 'Bundling and diffusion of management accounting innovations – the case of the balanced scorecard in Sweden', *Management Accounting Research*, 16(1): 1–20.

Bäckström, Henrik (1999) 'Den krattade manegen. Svensk arbetsorganisations utveckling under tre decennier', Unpublished doctoral thesis, no. 79, Department of Business Studies, Uppsala University.

Barbosa, Iris and Cabral-Cardoso, Carlos (2014) 'Words fly quicker than actions: the globalization of the diversity discourse', in G. Drori, M. Höllerer and P. Walgenbach (eds), *Global Themes and Local Variations in Organization and Management*. New York and London: Routledge. pp. 146–160.

Barnett, Michael N. and Finnemore, Martha (1999) 'The politics, power and pathologies of international organizations', *International Organization*, 53(4): 699–732.

Beck, Nikolaus and Walgenbach, Peter (2002) 'The institutionalisation of the Quality Management Approach in Germany', in Kerstin Sahlin-Andersson and Lars Engwall (eds), *The Expansion of Management Knowledge: Carriers, Flows and Sources*. Stanford, CA: Stanford University Press. pp. 145–174.

Blomgren, Maria (1999) 'Pengarna eller livet? Sjukvårdande professioner och yrkesgrupper i mötet med en ny ekonomistyrning'. Unpublished doctoral thesis, no. 78, Department of Business Studies, Uppsala University.

Blomgren, Maria (2003) 'Ordering a profession: Swedish nurses encounter new public management reforms', *Financial Accountability and Management*, 19(1): 45–71.

Blomgren, Maria and Sahlin, Kerstin (2007) 'Quests for transparency signs of a new institutional era in the health care field', in Tom Christensen and Per Laegreid (eds), *Transcending New Public Management. The Transformation of Public Sector Reform*. Aldershot: Ashgate.

Blomgren, Maria and Waks, Caroline (2015) 'Coping with contradictions: Hybrid professionals managing institutional complexity', *Journal of Professions and Organization*, 2: 78–102.

Blumer, Herbert G. (1969) 'Fashion: From class differentiation to collective selection', *Sociological Quarterly*, 10: 275–291.

Boli, John and Thomas, G. M. (eds) (1999) *Constructing World Culture*. Stanford, CA: Stanford University Press.

Botzem, Sebastian and Quack, Sigrid (2006) 'Contested rules and shifting boundaries: International standard-setting in accounting', in Marie-Laure Djelic and Kerstin Sahlin-Andersson (eds), *Transnational Governance: Institutional Dynamics of Regulation*. Cambridge: Cambridge University Press. pp. 266–286.

Bourdieu, Pierre (1977) 'The production of belief. Contribution to an economy of symbolic goods', *Media, Culture and Society*, 2(3) 261–293.

Bourdieu, Pierre (1984) *Distinction. A Social Critique of the Judgement of Taste*. Cambridge, MA: Harvard University Press.

Bowker, Geoffrey C. and Star, Susan Leigh (1999) *Sorting Things Out: Classification and Its Consequences*. Cambridge, MA: MIT Press.

Boxenbaum, Eva (2006) 'Lost in translation? The making of Danish diversity management', *American Behavioral Scientist*, 49: 939–948.

Boxenbaum, Eva and Strandgaard Pedersen, Jesper (2009) 'Scandinavian institutionalism – a case of institutional work', in Tom Lawrence, Roy Suddaby and Bernard Leca (eds), *Institutional Work: Actors and Agency in Institutional Studies of Organization*. Cambridge: Cambridge University Press. pp. 178–204.

Braithwaite, John and Drahos, Peter (2000) *Global Business Regulation*. Cambridge: Cambridge University Press.

Bromley, P. and Powell, W. W. (2012) 'From smoke and mirrors to walking the talk: Decoupling in the contemporary world', *The Academy of Management Annals*, 6(1): 483–530.

Brunsson, Nils (1989) *The Organization of Hypocrisy: Talk, Decisions and Actions in Organizations*. Chichester: Wiley.

Brunsson, Nils (2006). *Mechanisms of Hope. Maintaining the Dream of Rationality in Organizations.* Malmö: Copenhagen Business School Press, Liber, Universitetsforlaget.

Brunsson, Nils and Jacobsson, Bengt (eds) (2000) *A World of Standards.* Oxford: Oxford University Press.

Brunsson, Nils and Olsen, Johan P. (eds) (1993) *The Reforming Organization.* London: Routledge.

Brunsson, Nils and Sahlin-Andersson, Kerstin (2000) 'Constructing organizations: the example of public sector reform', *Organization Studies*, 21(4): 721–746.

Buhr, Helena (2008) 'Multi stakeholder Partnerships and the Dynamics of Fields: GAVI's Attempts to Create a Healthy Vaccine Market', Unpublished Licentiate thesis, Department of Business Studies, Uppsala University.

Casile, Maureen and Davis-Blake, Alison (2002) 'When accreditation standards change: factors affecting differential responsiveness of public and private organizations', *Academy of Management Journal*, 45(1): 180–195.

Cohen, M. D., March, J. G. and Olsen, J. P. (1972) 'A garbage can model of organizational choice', *Administrative Science Quarterly*, 17: 1–25.

Collins, David (2000) *Management Fads and Buzzwords.* London: Routledge.

Corvellec, Hervé (1997) *Stories of Achievements – Narrative Features of Organizational Performance.* New Brunswick, NJ: Transaction Publishers.

Currie, Graeme and Spyridonidis, Dimitrios (2015) 'Interpretation of multiple institutional logics on the ground: Actors' position, their agency and situational constraints in professionalized contexts', *Organization Studies*, 37(1): 77–97.

Cutler, Claire A., Haufler, Virginia and Porters, Tony (eds) (1999) *Private Authority and International Affairs.* New York: State University of New York Press.

Czarniawska, Barbara (1997) *Narrating the Organisation: Dramas of Institutional Identity.* Chicago, IL: University of Chicago Press.

Czarniawska, Barbara (2005) 'Fashion in organizing', in Barbara Czarniawska and Guje Sevón (eds), *Global Ideas. How Ideas, Objects and Practices Travel in the Global Economy.* Malmö: Liber and Copenhagen Business School Press. pp. 129–146.

Czarniawska, Barbara (2008) 'How to misuse institutions and get away with it: some reflections on institutional theory(ies)', in R. Greenwood, C. Oliver, R. Suddaby and K. Sahlin-Andersson (eds), *The SAGE Handbook of Organizational Institutionalism.* Thousand Oaks, CA: Sage. pp. 769–782.

Czarniawska, Barbara (2009) 'Emerging institutions: Pyramids or anthills?' *Organization Studies*, 30(4): 422–441.

Czarniawska, Barbara and Joerges, Bernward (1996) 'Travels of ideas', in Barbara Czarniawska and Guje Sevón (eds), *Translating Organizational Change.* Berlin: Walter de Gruyter. pp.13–47.

Czarniawska, Barbara and Sevón, Guje (eds) (1996a) *Translating Organizational Change,* Berlin: Walter de Gruyter.

Czarniawska, Barbara and Sevón, Guje (1996b) 'Introduction', in Barbara Czarniawska and Guje Sevón (eds), *Translating Organizational Change.* Berlin: Walter de Gruyter. pp. 1–12.

Czarniawska, Barbara and Sevón, Guje (eds) (2005) *Global Ideas. How Ideas, Objects and Practices Travel in the Global Economy.* Malmö: Liber and Copenhagen Business School Press.

Deephouse, David (2000) 'Media reputation as a strategic resource: An integration of mass communication and resource-based theories', *Journal of Management*, 26(6): 1091–1112.

Delbridge, Rick, and Edwards, Tim (2013) 'Inhabiting institutions: Critical realist refinements to understanding institutional complexity and change', *Organization Studies*, 34: 927–947.

DiMaggio, Paul and Powell, Walter (1983) 'The iron cage revisited: Institutional isomorphism and collective rationality in organizational fields', *American Sociological Review*, 48: 147–160.

Djelic, Marie-Laure (2014) 'Competition regulation in Africa between global and local: a banyan tree story', in G. Drori, M. Höllerer and P. Walgenbach (eds) *Global Themes and Local Variations in Organization and Management.* New York and London: Routledge. pp. 90–104.

Djelic, Marie-Laure and Sahlin-Andersson, Kerstin (2006a) *Transnational Governance: Institutional Dynamics of Regulation.* Cambridge: Cambridge University Press.

Djelic, Marie-Laure and Sahlin-Andersson, Kerstin (2006b) 'Introduction: A world of Governance. The rise of transnational regulation', in Marie-Laure Djelic and Kerstin Sahlin-Andersson (eds). *Transnational Governance: Institutional Dynamics of Regulation.* Cambridge: Cambridge University Press. pp. 1–28.

Drori, Gili, Höllerer, Markus and Walgenbach, Peter (2014) *Global Themes and Local Variations in Organization and Management.* New York and London: Routledge.

Engwall, Lars and Morgan, Glenn (1999) 'Regulatory regimes' in Morgan, Glenn and Lars Engwall (eds), *Regulations and Organisations.* London and New York: Routledge. pp. 82–105.

Engwall, Lars and Sahlin, Kerstin (2007) 'Corporate governance and the media. From agency theory to Edited corporation', in Peter Kjaer and Tore Slatta (eds), *The Rise of the Nordic Business Press.* Copenhagen: Copenhagen Business School Press.

Erçek, Mehmet and Say, Arzu İşeri (2008) 'Discursive ambiguity, professional networks and peripheral contexts: the translation of total quality management in Turkey, 1991–2002', *International Studies of Management and Organization*, 38(4): 78–99.

Eriksson-Zetterqvist, Ulla (2009) *Institutionell teori: ideer, moden, förändring.* Malmö: Liber.

Erlingsdóttir, Gudbjörg and Lindberg, Kajsa (2005) 'Isomorphism, isopraxism and isonymism: Complementary or competing processes?', in Barbara Czarniawska and Guje Sevón (eds), *Global Ideas: How Ideas, Objects and Practices Travel in the Global Economy*. Malmö: Liber and Copenhagen Business School Press. pp. 47–70.

Finnemore, Martha (1996) *National Interests in International Society*. Ithaca, NY: Cornell University Press.

Fombrun, Charles (1996) *Reputation: Realizing Value from the Corporate Image*. Boston, MA: Harvard Business School Press.

Forbes, Linda and Jermier, John M (2002) 'The institutionalization of bird protection: Mabel Osgood Wright and the early Audobon Movement', *Organization and Environment*, 15: 458–474.

Forssell, Anders and Jansson, David (1996) 'The logic of organizational transformation: On the conversion of non-business organizations', in Barbara Czarniawska and Guje Sevón (eds), *Translating Organizational Change*. Berlin: Walter de Gruyter. pp. 93–115.

Frank, David, Hironaka, Ann and Schofer, Evan (2000) 'The nation state and the natural environment over the twentieth century', *American Sociological Review*, 65: 96–116.

Frank, David and McEneaney, Elizabeth H. (1999) 'The individualization of society and the liberalization of State policies on same-sex sexual relations, 1984–1995', *Social Forces*, 77 (March): 911–944.

Frenkel, Michal (2005) 'Something new, something old, something borrowed: The cross-national translation of the "family-friendly organization" in Israel', in Barbara Czarniawska and Guje Sevón (eds), *Global Ideas: How Ideas, Objects and Practices Travel in the Global Economy*. Malmö: Liber and Copenhagen Business School Press. pp. 147–166.

Frenkel, Michal (2014) 'Toward a multi-layered glocalization approach: states, multinational corporations and the transformation of gender contracts', in G. Drori, M. Höllerer, and P. Walgenbach (eds), *Global Themes and Local Variations in Organization and Management*. New York and London: Routledge. pp. 133–145.

Garud, Raghu, Hardy, Cynthia, and Maguire, Steve (2007) 'Institutional entrepreneurship as embedded agency: An introduction to the Special Issue', *Organization Studies*, 28(7): 957–969.

Giddens, Anthony (1979) *Central Problems in Social Theory: Action, Structure and Contradiction in Social Analysis*. Berkeley, CA: University of California Press.

Giddens, Anthony (1984) *The Constitution of Society*. Berkeley, CA: University of California Press.

Goffman, Erving (1959) *The Presentation of Self in Everyday Life*. New York: Doubleday.

Grafström, Maria (2006) The Development of Swedish Business Journalism: Historical Roots of an Organisational Field. Dissertation, Uppsala University.

Greenwood, R., Raynard, M., Kodeih, F., Micelotta, E. R., and Lounsbury, M. (2011) 'Institutional complexity and organizational responses', *Academy of Management Annals*, 5(1) 317–371.

Greenwood, R., Suddaby, R. and Hinings, C. R. (2002) 'Theorizing change: The role of professional associations in the transformation of institutionalised fields', *Academy of Management Journal*, 45(1): 58–80.

Hall, Peter, and Marcusen, Ann (1985) *Silicon Landscapes*. Boston, MA: Allen and Unwin.

Hatch, Mary-Jo and Schultz, Majken (1997) 'Relations between organizational culture, identity and image', *European Journal of Marketing*, 31(5/6): 356–366.

Haveman, Heather A. (1993) 'Follow the leader: Mimetic isomorphism and entry into new markets', *Administrative Science Quarterly*, 38: 593–627.

Hedmo, Tina (2004) Rulemaking in the Transnational Space: The Development of European Accreditation of Management Education. Unpublished doctoral thesis 109, Department of Business Studies, Uppsala University.

Hedmo, Tina, Sahlin-Andersson, Kerstin and Wedlin, Linda (2005) 'Fields of imitation: The global expansion of management education', in Barbara Czarniawska and Guje Sevón (eds), *Global Ideas: How Ideas, Objects and Practices Travel in the Global Economy*. Malmö: Liber and Copenhagen Business School Press. pp. 190–212.

Hedmo, Tina, Sahlin-Andersson, Kerstin and Wedlin, Linda (2006) 'The emergence of a European regulatory field of management education,' in Marie-Laure Djelic and Kerstin Sahlin-Andersson (eds), *Transnational Governance: Institutional Dynamics of Regulation*. Cambridge: Cambridge University Press. pp. 308–328.

Hinings, Bob (2011) 'Connections between institutional logics and organizational culture', *Journal of Management Inquiry*, 21: 98–101.

Hood, Christopher, Scott, Colin, James, Oliver, Jones, George and Travers, Tony (1999) *Regulation Inside Government*. Oxford: Oxford University Press.

Hyndman, Noel, Liguori, Mariannunziata, Meyer, Renate, Polzer, Tobias, Rota, Silvia and Seiwald, Johann (2014) 'The translation and sedimentation of accounting reforms: A comparison of the UK, Austrian and Italian experiences', *Critical Perspectives on Accounting*, 25: 388–408.

Hwang, Hokyu (2003) 'Planning development'. Unpublished PhD Dissertation, Stanford University.

Jacobsson, Kerstin (2004) 'Between deliberation and discipline: Soft governance in EU employment policy', in Ulrika Mörth (ed.), *Soft Law in Governance and Regulation*. Cheltenham: Edward Elgar. pp. 81–102.

Jepperson, Ronald L. (1991) 'Institutions, institutional effects and institutionalism', in Walter W. Powell and

Paul DiMaggio (eds), *The New Institutionalism in Organizational Analysis*. Chicago, IL: University of Chicago Press.

Jonsson, Stefan (2005) 'Naming me and shaming you: Inaccuracies in mechanisms for loss of legitimacy'. Paper presented at the GEMS workshop at Oxford University, August 2005.

Kirkpatrick, Ian, Bullinger, Bernadette, Lega, Federico and Dent, Mike (2013) 'The translation of hospital management models in European health systems: A framework for comparison', *British Journal of Management*, 24(3): 48–61.

Kirton, John J. and Trebilcock, Michael J, (2004) *Hard Choices, Soft Law*. Aldershot: Ashgate.

Kjaer, Peter and Sahlin, Kerstin (2007) 'Media Transparency as an Institutional Practice' in Kjaer, Peter and Tore Slaatta (eds), *Mediating Business: The expansion of business journalism*. Copenhagen, Denmark: Copenhagen Business School Press. pp. 285–315.

Klarsfeld, Alain (2009) 'The diffusion of diversity management: the case of France', *Scandinavian Journal of Management*, 25(4): 363–373.

Kraatz, M. S., and Block, E. S. (2008) 'Organizational implications of institutional pluralism', in R. Greenwood, C. Oliver, R. Suddaby and K. Sahlin-Andersson (eds), *The SAGE Handbook of Organizational Institutionalism*. Thousand Oaks, CA/London: Sage.

Latour, Bruno (1986) 'The powers of association', in John Law (ed.), *Power, Action and Belief*. London: Routledge and Kegan Paul. pp. 264–280.

Lawrence, T. B. and Suddaby, R. (2006) 'Institutions and institutional work', in S. Clegg (ed.), *The SAGE Handbook of Organization Studies*. Thousand Oaks, CA: Sage. pp. 215–254.

Levi-Faur, David and Jordana, Jacinta (2005) 'The rise of regulatory capitalism', *Annals of APSA*, vol. 598.

Lindberg, Kajsa (2014) 'Performing multiple logics in practice', *Scandinavian Journal of Management*, 30: 485–497.

Lounsbury, Michael (2007) 'A tale of two cities: Competing logics and practice variation in the professionalizing of mutual funds', *Academy of Management Journal*, 50: 289–307.

Lounsbury, Michael and Crumley, E (2007) 'New practice creation: An institutional perspective on innovation', *Organization Studies*, 28: 993–1012.

Löfgren, Orvar (2005) 'Cultural alchemy: Translating the experience economy into Scandinavia', in Barbara Czarniawska and Guje Sevón (eds), *Global Ideas. How Ideas, Objects and Practices Travel in the Global Economy*. Malmö: Liber and Copenhagen Business School Press. pp. 15–29.

Lok, Jaco and de Rond, Mark (2013) 'On the plasticity of institutions: Containing and restoring practice breakdowns at the Cambridge University Boat Club', *Academy of Management Journal*, 56(1): 185–207.

Madsen, Dag Ø (2014) 'Interpretation and use of the Balanced Scorecard in Denmark: evidence from suppliers and users of the concept', *Danish Journal of Management and Business*, 3: 13–25.

March, James G. (1981) 'Decisions in organizations and theories of choice', in Andrew Van de Ven and William F. Joyce (eds), *Perspectives of Organizational Design and Behavior*. New York: Wiley. pp. 205–244.

March, James G. (1999) 'A learning perspective on the network dynamics of institutional integration', in M. Egeberg and P. Laegreid (eds), *Organizing Political Institutions*. Oslo: Scandinavian University Press. pp. 129–155.

March, James G., and Olsen, Johan P. (1995) *Democratic Governance*. New York: The Free Press.

March, J. G., and Olsen, J. P. (1976) *Ambiguity and Choice in Organizations*. Oslo: Universitetsforlaget.

March, James G., Schultz, Majken, and Zhou, X (2000) *The Dynamics of Rules*. Stanford, CA: Stanford University Press.

McNichol, J. and Bensedrine, J. (2003) 'Multilateral rule-making: transatlantic struggles around genetically modified food', in Marie-Laure Djelic and Sigrid Quack (eds), *Globalization and Institutions*. Cheltenham, UK: Edward Elgar. pp. 220–244.

Meyer, John (2014) 'Empowered actors, local settings, and global rationalization', in G. Drori, M. Höllerer and P. Walgenbach (eds), *Global Themes and Local Variations in Organization and Management*. New York and London: Routledge. pp. 413–424.

Meyer, John W. (1994) 'Rationalized environments', in W. R. Scott and John W. Meyer (eds), *Institutional Environments and Organizations: Structural Complexity and Individualism*. London: Sage. pp. 28–54.

Meyer, John W. (1996) 'Otherhood: The promulgation and transmission of ideas in the modern organizational environment', in Barbara Czarniawska and Guje Sevón (eds), *Translating Organizational Change*. Berlin: Walter de Gruyter. pp. 241–252.

Meyer, John W. and Rowan, Brian (1977) 'Institutionalized organizations: Formal structure as myth and ceremony', *American Journal of Sociology*, 2: 340–363.

Meyer, Renate and Höllerer, Markus (2010) 'Meaning structures in a contested issues field: a topographic map of shareholder value in Austria', *Academy of Management Journal*, 53(6): 1241–1262.

Miller, Peter (1996) 'Dilemmas of accountability: The limits of accounting', in Paul Hirst and Sunil Kihlnani (eds), *Reinventing Democracy*. Oxford: Blackwell. pp. 57–69.

Morris, Timothy and Lancaster, Zoe (2006) 'Translating management ideas', *Organization Studies*, 27(2): 207–233.

Mörth, Ulrika (2004) *Soft Law in Governance and Regulation*. Cheltenham: Edward Elgar.

Mörth, Ulrika (2006) 'Soft regulation and global democracy', in Marie-Laure Djelic and Kerstin

Sahlin-Andersson (eds), *Transnational Governance: Institutional Dynamics of Regulation.* Cambridge: Cambridge University Press. pp.119–135.

Nicolini, Davide (2010) 'Medical innovation as a process of translation: a case from the field of telemedicine', *British Journal of Management*, 21: 1011–1026.

Olson, Olov, Guthrie, James and Humphrey, Christopher (eds) (1998) *Global Warning: Debating International Developments in New Public Financial Management.* Oslo: Cappelen Akademisk Forlag.

O'Mahoney, Joe (2016) 'Archetypes of translation: recommendations for a dialogue', *International Journal of Management Reviews*, 18(3): 333–350.

Özen, Şükrü (2014) 'Rhetorical variations in the cross-national diffusion of management practices: a comparison of Turkey and the US', in G. Drori, M. Höllerer, and P. Walgenbach (eds), *Global Themes and Local Variations in Organization and Management.* New York and London: Routledge. pp. 119–132.

Özen, Şükrü and Berkman, Ümit (2007) 'Cross-national reconstruction of managerial practices: TQM in Turkey', *Organization Studies*, 28(6): 825–851.

Pallas, Josef (2007) 'Talking organizations.' Dissertation manuscript. Department of Business Studies. Uppsala University.

Pallas, Josef, Fredriksson, Magnus and Wedlin, Linda (2016) 'Translating institutional logic – when the media logic meets professions', *Organization Studies*, 37(11): 1661–1684.

Pallas, Josef and Wedlin, Linda (2014) 'Governance of science in mediatized society: media rankings and the translation of global governance models', in G. Drori, M. Höllerer, and P. Walgenbach (eds), *Global Themes and Local Variations in Organization and Management.* New York and London: Routledge. pp. 295–307.

Palmer, Donald, Jennings, Devereaux and Zhou, Xueguang (1993) 'Late adoption of the multidivisional form by large U.S. corporations: institutional, political and economic accounts', *Administrative Science Quarterly*, 38:100–131.

Perkmann, Marcus and Spicer, André (2008) 'How are management fashions institutionalized? The role of institutional work', *Human Relations*, 61(6): 811–844.

Pipan, Tatiana and Czarniawska, Barbara (2010) 'How to construct an actor-network: Management accounting from idea to practice', *Critical Perspectives on Accounting*, 21(3): 243–251.

Pollock, Timothy G. and Rindova, Violina P. (2003) 'Media legitimation effects in the market for initial public offerings', *Academy of Management Journal*, 46(5): 631–642.

Power, Mike (1997) *The Audit Society: Rituals of Verification.* Oxford: Oxford University Press.

Power, Mike (2003) 'Evaluating the audit explosion', *Law and Policy*, 25(3): 115–202.

Ramirez, Francisco (2006) 'The rationalization of universities', in Marie-Laure Djelic and Kerstin

Sahlin-Andersson (eds), *Transnational Governance: Institutional Dynamics of Regulation.* Cambridge: Cambridge University Press. pp. 225–244.

Rao, Hayagreeva, Philippe Monin and Rodolphe Durand (2003) 'Institutional change in Toque Ville: Nouvelle cuisine as an identity movement in French gastronomy', *American Journal of Sociology*, 108(4): 795–843.

Reay, Trish, Chreim, Samia, Golden-Biddle, Karen, Goodrick, Elizabeth, Williams, Bernie, Casebeer, Ann, Pabli, Amy and Hinins, Bob (2013) 'Transforming new ideas into practice: An activity based perspective on the institutionalization of practices', *Journal of Management Studies*, 50(6): 963–990.

Reay, Trish and Hinings, C. R. (2009) 'Managing the rivalry of competing institutional logics', *Organization Studies*, 30: 629–652.

Rogers, Everett M. (1983) *Diffusion of Innovations.* New York: Free Press.

Røvik, Kjell-Arne (1996) 'Deinstitutionalization and the logic of fashion', in Barbara Czarniawska and Guje Sevón (eds), *Translating Organizational Change.* Berlin, New York: Walter de Gruyter. pp.139–171.

Røvik, Kjell-Arne (1998) *Moderne Organisasjoner. Trender i organisasjonstenkninger ved tusenårsskiftet.* Norge: Fagbokforlaget.

Røvik, Kjell-Arne (2007) *Trender och translationer.* Oslo: Universitetsforlaget.

Røvik, Kjell-Arne (2011) 'From fashion to virus: an alternative theory of organization's handling of management ideas', *Organization Studies*, 32(5): 631–654.

Røvik, Kjell-Arne (2016) 'Knowledge transfer as translation: review and elements of an instrumental theory', *International Journal of Management Reviews*, 18(3): 290–310.

Sahlin, K. (2012) 'The interplay of organizing models in higher education: What room is there for collegiality in universities characterized by bounded autonomy?', in B. Stensaker, J. Välimaa and C. Sarrico (eds), *Managing Reforms in Universities: The Dynamics of Culture, Identity and Organizational Change.* London: Routledge.

Sahlin, K. (2014) 'Global themes and institutional ambiguity in the university field: Rankings and management models on the move', in G. S. Drori, M. Höllerer and P. Walgenbach (eds), *Organization and Management Ideas: Global Themes and Local Variations.* London: Routledge.

Sahlin-Andersson, Kerstin (1996) 'Imitating by editing success: The construction of organizational fields', in Barbara Czarniawska and Guje Sevón (eds), *Translating Organizational Change.* Berlin, NewYork: Walter de Gruyter. pp. 69–92.

Sahlin-Andersson, Kerstin (2000) 'Arenas as Standardizers', in Nils Brunsson and Bengt Jacobsson (eds), *A World of Standards.* Oxford: Oxford University Press. pp. 100–113.

Sahlin-Andersson, Kerstin (2001) 'National, international and transnational constructions of New Public

Management', in Tom Christensen and Per Laegreid (eds), *New Public Management: The Transformation of Ideas and Practice*. Aldershot: Ashgate. pp. 43–72.

Sahlin-Andersson, Kerstin and Engwall, Lars (2002) *The Expansion of Management Knowledge: Carriers, Flows and Sources*. Stanford, CA: Stanford University Press.

Sahlin-Andersson, Kerstin and Sevón, Guje (2003) 'Imitation and identification as performatives', in Barbara Czarniawska and Guje Sevón (eds), *The Northern Lights: Organization Theory in Scandinavia*. Malmö: Liber. pp. 249–265.

Saka, Ayse (2004) 'The cross-national diffusion of work systems: Translation of Japanese operations in the UK', *Organization Studies*, 25(2): 209–228.

Saxenian, Annalee (1988) 'The Cheshire cat's grin: Innovation and regional development in England', *Technology Review*, 91(2): 67–75.

Schmidt, P. (2004) 'Law in the age of governance: Regulation, networks and lawyers', in Jordana, Jacint and David Levi-Faur (eds), *The Politics of Regulation*. Cheltenham: Edward Elgar. pp. 273–295.

Schultz, Majken, Antorini, Yun Mi and Csaba, Fabian (eds) (2005) *Corporate Branding: Towards the Second Wave of Corporate Branding*. Copenhagen: Copenhagen Business School Press.

Scott, Richard (1995) *Institutions and Organizations*. Thousand Oaks, CA: Sage.

Sevón, Guje (1996) 'Organizational imitation in identity transformation', in Barbara Czarniawska and Guje Sevón (eds), *Translating Organizational Change*. Berlin/New York: Walter de Gruyter. pp. 49–67.

Shore, Cris and Wright, Susan (2000) 'Coercive accountability: The rise of audit culture in higher education', in Marilyn Strathern (ed.), *Audit Cultures: Anthropological Studies in Accountability, Ethics and the Academy*. London: Routledge. pp. 57–89.

Solli, Rolf, Demediuk, Peter and Sims, Robert (2005) 'The Namesake: On best value and other reform-marks', in Barbara Czarniawska and Guje Sevón (eds), *Global Ideas: How Ideas, Objects and Practices Travel in the Global Economy*. Malmö: Liber and Copenhagen Business School Press. pp. 30–46.

Strang, David (2014) 'Boomerang Diffusion at a Global Bank: Total Quality Management and National Culture' in G. Drori, M. Höllerer, and P. Walgenbach (eds), *Global Themes and Local Variations in Organization and Management*. New York and London: Routledge. pp. 107–118.

Strang, David and Meyer, John W. (1993) 'Institutional conditions for diffusion', *Theory and Society*, 22: 487–511.

Strathern, Marilyn (2000) *Audit Cultures: Anthropological Studies in Accountability, Ethics and the Academy*. London: Routledge.

Tamm Hallström, Kristina (2004) *Organizing International Standardization*. Cheltenham: Edward Elgar.

Tarde, Gabriel (1962 [1890]) *The Laws of Imitation*. New York: Henry Holt.

Tarde, Gabriel (1969 [1902]) 'Invention', in Terry N. Clark (ed.), *Gabriel Tarde on Communication and Social Influence*. Chicago, IL: University of Chicago Press. pp. 149–164.

Thornton, Patricia, Ocasio, William and Lounsbury, Michael (2012) *The Institutional Logics Perspective: A New Approach to Culture, Structure and Process*. Oxford: Oxford University Press.

Tolbert, P. S. and Zucker, Lynne G. (1983) 'Institutional sources of change in the formal structure of organizations: The diffusion of civil service reform', *Administrative Science Quarterly*, 28: 22–39.

Townley, Barbara (2002) 'The role of competing rationalities in institutional change', *Academy of Management Journal*, 45(1): 163–179.

Tryggestad, Kjell and Georg, Susse (2011) 'How objects shape logics in construction', *Culture and Organization*, 17(3): 181–197.

Vrangbæck, K. (1999) *Marknedsorientering i syghussektoren*. Dissertation, Institute of Political Science, University of Copenhagen.

Waldorff, Susanne (2013) 'Accounting for organizational innovations: Mobilizing institutional logics in translation', *Scandinavian Journal of Management*, 29: 219–234.

Waldorff, Susanne and Greenwood, Royston (2011) 'The dynamics of community translation: Danish healthcare centres', *Research in the Sociology of Organizations*, 33: 113–142.

Wæraas, Arild and Agger Nielsen, Jeppe (2016) 'Translation theory "translated": Three perspectives on translation in organizational research', *International Journal of Management Reviews*, 8(3): 236–270.

Wæraas, Arild and Sataøen, Hogne L. (2014) 'Trapped in conformity? Translating reputation management into practice', *Scandinavian Journal of Management*, 30(2): 242–253.

Wedlin, Linda (2006) *Ranking Business Schools: Forming Fields, Identities and Boundaries in International Management Education*. Cheltenham: Edward Elgar.

Wedlin, Linda (2007) 'The role of rankings in codifying a business school template: Classifications, diffusion and mediated isomorphism in organizational fields', *European Management Review*, 4: 24–39.

Westney, Elenore D. (1987) *Imitation and Innovation: The Transfer of Western Organizational Patterns to Meiji Japan*. Cambridge, MA: Harvard University Press.

Westphal, James D., Gulati, Ranjay and Shortell, Stephen M. (1997) 'Customization or conformity? An institutional and network perspective on the content and consequences of TQM adoption', *Administrative Science Quarterly*, 42: 366–394.

Zilber, Tammar (2006) 'The work of the symbolic in institutional processes: Translations of rational myths in Israeli high tech', *Academy of Management Journal*, 49: 281–303.

5

On Hybrids and Hybrid Organizing: A Review and Roadmap for Future Research

Julie Battilana, Marya Besharov
and Bjoern Mitzinneck[1]

Hybrid organizations present a puzzle for institutional theory. Because they combine distinct institutional logics (Battilana & Dorado, 2010; Pache & Santos, 2013b), identities (Albert & Whetten, 1985; Glynn, 2000) and/or organizational forms (Ruef & Patterson, 2009; Tracey, Phillips, & Jarvis, 2011), hybrids seem to run counter to the core proposition of neo-institutionalism – that organizations must conform to institutionalized templates in order to be regarded as legitimate (DiMaggio & Powell, 1983; Greenwood & Hinings, 1993; Haveman & Rao, 2006). Yet organizational theorists, including institutionalists, have long recognized that organizations frequently combine seemingly incompatible elements (Albert & Whetten, 1985; Friedland & Alford, 1991; Meyer & Rowan, 1977). Particularly in the health and education sectors, hybrids have existed for centuries, and they continue to emerge, survive and even thrive in the contemporary organizational landscape (Battilana, Lee, Walker, & Dorsey, 2012;

Hoffman, Badiane, & Haigh, 2012). For example, biotechnology companies borrow elements from both the academic and commercial sectors (Powell & Sandholtz, 2012), public–private partnerships bring together elements from state bureaucracies and the business or non-profit sectors (Jay, 2013), and commercial microfinance organizations combine elements from the development and banking sectors (Battilana & Dorado, 2010).

Despite recognition of the prevalence of hybridity in organizations (Besharov & Smith, 2014; Kraatz & Block, 2008) and research on its antecedents, processes and outcomes (Battilana & Lee, 2014), the study of hybrids remains fragmented. Different studies tend to adopt disparate theoretical lenses, examining hybridity either as the combination of multiple organizational identities, multiple organizational forms, or multiple societal rationales, with limited cross-fertilization between these three approaches (for exceptions, see Pache & Santos, 2013b; Tracey et al., 2011). The purpose of this chapter is to advance research on hybrids by bringing together work from these multiple perspectives; identifying common themes in the antecedents, challenges, opportunities and management strategies associated with hybridity; and highlighting critical directions for future research.

To do so, we first conducted a systematic review of uses of the term 'hybrid' in the organizational studies literature. This review surfaced eight distinct perspectives on hybrids, which respectively focus on organizational identity, transaction cost economics, network forms, categories, organizational archetypes, institutional logics, culture and transitioning economic regimes. These perspectives cluster into three broad approaches, one emphasizing hybrid organizational identities, a second focusing on hybrids as distinct forms, and a third conceptualizing hybrids as the combination of multiple societal-level rationales or logics. While the eight perspectives differ in how they define hybrids and in their underlying ontological stance, there are also important but currently underdeveloped points of connection between them. To demonstrate and strengthen these connections, we synthesize across the eight perspectives to define hybridity as the mixing of core organizational elements that would not conventionally go together. Drawing on studies across multiple perspectives, we then explain how hybrids, as well as the challenges and opportunities they confront, emerge due to a combination of external and internal factors. We further explain how hybrids manage challenges and opportunities through strategies that tend to either integrate or differentiate their multiple identities, forms, or rationales. Building on these ideas, we argue that future research should further explore the linkages between different perspectives, as well as account for the complexity of hybrids that may combine more than two identities, forms, or rationales. We also suggest that instead of focusing exclusively on hybrid organizations as a distinct type, future studies should treat hybridity as a matter of degree and examine how and to what extent organizations engage in various forms

of hybrid organizing. This line of research is particularly important and promising given that organizations increasingly transcend boundaries between the for-profit, not-for-profit and public sectors, thereby developing different forms and degrees of hybridity.

HYBRIDS AND HYBRIDITY IN ORGANIZATIONAL THEORY

To comprehensively account for research on hybrids and hybridity in the organizational studies literature, we conducted a systematic review using a keyword search. We included all words derived from the root 'hybrid', such as hybridity, hybridization and hybridize, as well as any composite words, such as hybrid organization, hybrid arrangement, hybrid governance and hybrid enterprise. We used these search terms in the three most comprehensive management and organization studies databases: Web of Science, ABI Informs and Business Source Complete. We focused our search on forty-three journals publishing organizational research. We included peer-reviewed journals from management and organization studies, sociology, public administration, voluntary and non-profit sector research, as well as political science and business history (see Appendix for a complete list of journals). In this first step, we generated a raw set of 658 articles referencing at least one variant of the term 'hybrid'. As a second step, we excluded articles in which 'hybrid' terms were not used to refer to organizational phenomena (e.g., 'hybrid algorithms' to denote combinations of mathematical algorithms in management science, 'hybrid research method' to describe mixed-method studies). In cases where the exclusion decision was not straightforward, multiple members of the research team independently assessed each article. Whenever their assessments diverged (which happened for less than 3% of the articles reviewed), we resolved disagreements through discussion. This process yielded a final set of 254 articles. We then systematically coded each of these articles to identify different uses of the hybrid concept in the extant literature.

Eight distinct perspectives on hybrid organizations emerged from this first phase of our coding process. These perspectives respectively focus on organizational identity, transaction cost economics, network forms, categories, organizational archetypes, institutional logics, culture and transitioning economic regimes. Figure 5.1a depicts the prevalence of each perspective over time, for articles explicitly using any variant of the term 'hybrid'. As we explain in more detail below, these perspectives differ in their conceptualization of hybridity and in their underlying ontological assumptions, falling on a spectrum from primarily positivist to primarily interpretivist. These ontological differences reflect a broader split in the social sciences between positivist and interpretivist approaches (Astley & Van de Ven, 1983; Berger & Luckmann, 1967; Burrell & Morgan, 1979; Czarniawska, 2009; Lincoln & Guba, 1985). Perspectives leaning toward positivism focus on readily observable signs of hybridity such as governance structure or category systems. They also tend more towards quantitative research methods and large-scale comparative studies. In contrast, the more interpretivist perspectives focus on social actors' perceptions and intangible signs of hybridity such as the articulation of different logics or identity claims. Studies adopting an interpretivist stance tend to be qualitative, and many are based on in-depth case studies.

In a second phase of coding, we grouped the eight perspectives into three broader approaches, each corresponding to a different level of analysis. The first approach, which includes studies in the organizational identity perspective and operates at the intra-organizational level, treats hybridity as a matter of multiple identities, or shared views among members about 'who we are' and 'what we do' as an organization. The second approach encompasses the transaction cost economics, network forms, categories and organizational archetypes perspectives and focuses on the organizational level, conceptualizing hybridity as a combination of organizational forms. The third approach includes the institutional logics, culture and transitioning economic regimes perspectives and operates mostly at the extra-organizational level, defining hybridity as the combination of broader societal-level rationales. Figure 5.1b shows the prevalence of these three broad approaches over time.

Despite conceptual and ontological differences across the eight perspectives that we identified, we believe there is considerable untapped potential for cross-fertilization. To highlight these opportunities, we organize our discussion below around the three broad conceptual approaches of hybrid identities, forms and rationales. Our discussion builds not only on the studies we identified in our systematic literature search, but also on pertinent work that does not necessarily use the hybrid terminology, yet is central to the various perspectives that we review. Table 5.1 provides a summary of the conceptualization of hybridity for each perspective.

Hybrid Identities

Organizational identity refers to the central, enduring and distinctive features that define 'who we are' and 'what we do' as an organization (Albert & Whetten, 1985; Gioia, Patvardhan, Hamilton, & Corley, 2013). From an *identity perspective*, hybrids possess multiple identities that 'would not normally be expected to go together' (Albert & Whetten, 1985: 271). Whether such multiplicity is permanent or more transitory, however, is a subject of debate. Some research conceptualizes identity as arising from an organization's claims to membership in externally defined organizational types (e.g., a bank, a school) and treats hybrid identities as relatively fixed and enduring (Whetten, 2006; Whetten & Mackey, 2002). Studies adopting this view of identity emphasize that

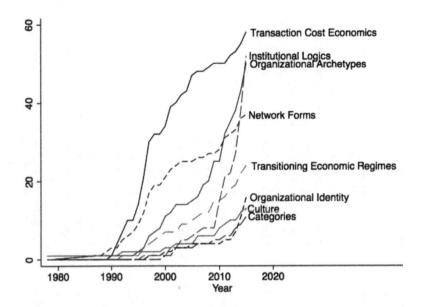

Figure 5.1a   Prevalence of distinct perspectives on hybrids in organizational research (cumulative article count)

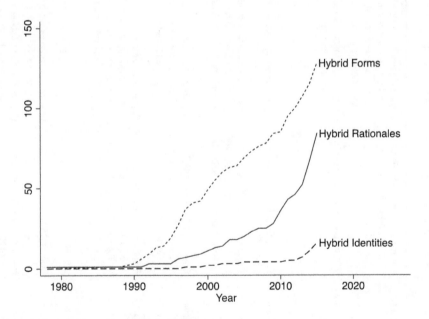

Figure 5.1b   Prevalence of identity, forms and rationales approaches to hybrids in organizational research (cumulative article count)

1. Figures only include articles explicitly using at least one variant of the term 'hybrid'. Articles that address the concept of hybrids or hybridity without explicitly using the hybrid terminology are covered in the text but not included in the figures.
2. Figures are based on counts of articles in each of the eight perspectives. Because some articles draw on multiple perspectives, cross-classification is possible. In these instances, we include articles in the count for each perspective on which they draw.
3. Forty-six articles identified in our systematic literature search did not draw on any one of the eight primary perspectives identified in our coding process and are therefore excluded from Figures 5.1a and 5.1b.

Table 5.1 Theoretical perspectives on hybrids

	Theoretical perspective	Illustrative studies	Definition of hybrid	Key assumptions
(I) Hybrid Identities	1. Organizational Identity	Albert & Whetten (1985); Glynn (2000); Ashforth & Reingen (2014)	Organization with multiple identities which would not be expected together, where identity refers to an organization's central, distinct, and enduring characteristics	• Identity elements are internally defined by organizational members • Some studies assume identities are relatively stable, while others treat them as more dynamic
(II) Hybrid Forms	2. Transaction Cost Economics	Williamson (1985, 1991, 1996)	Intermediary form of governance that falls in between hierarchical and market forms	• Transaction is the core unit of analysis • Hybrids exist due to market failure or infeasibility of integrated hierarchical structures • Hybrid forms are relatively stable
	3. Network Forms	Powell (1990); Podolny & Page (1998)	Form of governance based on network ties and trust	• Hybrid forms are relatively stable
	4. Categories	Zuckerman (1999); Pólos, Hannan, & Carroll (2002); Wry, Lounsbury, & Jennings (2014)	Organization that spans multiple established social categories, combining features from the organizational forms associated with each one	• Audiences define categories and category membership, as well as the organizational identity and specific features associated with each category • Hybrid forms may be transitional
	5. Organizational Archetypes	Greenwood & Hinings (1993); Tracey, Phillips, & Jarvis (2011); Battilana & Lee (2014)	Organization combining elements from multiple distinct and socially legitimate configurations of structures and practices	• Hybrid forms may be transitional
(III) Hybrid Rationales	6. Institutional Logics	Friedland & Alford (1991); Battilana & Dorado (2010); Thornton, Ocasio, & Lounsbury (2012)	Organization adhering to multiple, often conflicting institutional logics, where logics refer to societal-level patterns of values and practices that shape cognition and guide action	• Organizations and their members are influenced by culturally entrenched rationales for appropriate action • Organizational fields tend to be characterized by distinct institutional logics or sets of logics • Logics are relatively stable and change only over long periods of time
	7. Culture	Bhabha (1994); Waring (2015)	Organization characterized by ongoing blending of distinct cultures	• Hybridization is a process, not a state • Hybridity is relatively enduring • Hybrids are transitional
	8. Transitioning Economic Regimes	Nee (1992); Nee & Matthews (1996)	Organization that combines institutional arrangements from state socialism and free market economies	

organizations often belong to multiple types, leading to multiple, conflicting identities that endure over time. For example, research universities (Albert & Whetten, 1985), symphony orchestras (Glynn, 2000), cooperatives (Ashforth & Reingen, 2014; Foreman & Whetten, 2002), healthcare organizations (Pratt & Rafaeli, 1997) and social enterprises (Moss, Short, Payne, & Lumpkin, 2011; Smith & Besharov, 2016) all combine normative identities that emphasize cultural or ideological principles with utilitarian identities stressing economic principles. In other words, these organizations all have hybrid identities.

In their foundational work on organizational identity, Albert and Whetten (1985) delineate two types of hybrid identity organizations. In 'ideographic' organizations, distinct subgroups and/or separate units hold each identity. In 'holographic' organizations, all members and units hold multiple identities, rather than just a single one. Most empirical research on hybrid identity organizations focuses on the ideographic type (for exceptions, see Besharov, 2014; Golden-Biddle & Rao, 1997; Smith & Besharov, 2016), and emphasizes hybrid identities as sources of conflict and contestation between distinct subgroups (e.g., Anteby & Wrzesniewski, 2014; Ashforth & Reingen, 2014; Pratt & Rafaeli, 1997; Voss, Cable, & Voss, 2006). For example, Glynn (2000) describes conflict between musicians and administrators in the Atlanta Symphony Orchestra, with the former viewing the organization as an artistic entity and the latter treating it as an economic entity. Even when conflict is not overt, hybrid identities can be a source of ambivalence, which may be costly for both organizations and their members (Pratt & Foreman, 2000; Pratt & Corley, 2007). For example, Pratt and Rafaeli (1997) show how rehabilitation and acute care identities in a hospital nursing unit created ambivalence among staff, manifest in conflicts about the unit's dress code.

In contrast, other identity studies conceptualize identity not as relatively fixed and enduring, but rather as dynamically constructed and negotiated by members through sense-making and sense-giving processes (Dutton & Dukerich, 1991; Fiol, 1991; Gioia & Thomas, 1996; Gioia, Schultz, & Corley, 2000; Ravasi & Schultz, 2006). Studies adopting this conceptualization of identity tend to depict multiple identities as temporary and transitional. For example, Clark, Gioia, Ketchen and Thomas (2010) describe multiple identities during the initial phases of a merger between two previously independent healthcare organizations. Over time, multiple interpretations of organizational identity led to a transitional identity which coalesced into a single, unified identity reflecting members' shared understanding of the integrated entity. Corley and Gioia (2004) find multiple identity interpretations creating ambiguity and ultimately leading to a new identity in the context of an organizational spin-off.

Ontologically, even studies that conceptualize hybrid identities as deriving from an organization's membership in externally defined types tend to adopt an interpretivist stance in that an organization's identities are determined based on members' perceptions and claims about who the organization is and what it does. Indeed, a key feature of the identity perspective is a focus on hybridity as defined from within, by organizational members themselves. To understand hybridity, studies often consider the link between organizational members' own identity/ies and the identity/ies of their organization (Besharov, 2014; Elsbach, 2001; Pratt & Rafaeli, 1997). However, organizational identity research in general recognizes that identity is influenced by outsiders' expectations, not just insiders' interpretations (Gioia et al., 2000). Drawing on the concept of 'external image' – defined as outsiders' perceptions of who the organization is and who it should be (Barich & Kotler, 1991; Dukerich, Golden, & Shortell, 2002; Gioia & Thomas, 1996) – identity researchers have examined how identity and image interact to occasion identity change (Dutton & Dukerich, 1991; Gioia et al., 2000; Hatch

& Schultz, 2002). While organizational identity research has not explicitly examined the possibility of hybrid images, a related idea is developed in work within the categories perspective, described below, which considers outsiders' views of who the organization is in terms of its belonging to one or more social categories (e.g., Hsu, Hannan, & Koçak, 2009; Wry, Lounsbury, & Jennings, 2014).

Hybrid Forms

The term 'hybrid' has been used not only to refer to a combination of organizational identities but also to refer to combinations of different forms of organizing. Form-based perspectives on hybrids are evident in a variety of social science disciplines. There is variation across these perspectives, however, in underlying ontological assumptions and in whether hybrids are viewed as transitory or relatively permanent. In *transaction cost economics*, scholars have long conceptualized hybrids as an intermediate form of economic organization combining market and hierarchical forms of governance (Williamson, 1985, 1991, 1996). In markets, transactions are governed by the price mechanism. In hierarchical firms, lines of command and control exist that lower transaction costs relative to markets under certain conditions (Coase, 1937). For example, hierarchies reduce transaction costs when the same transaction occurs frequently, is of uncertain volume or involves uncertain technologies and behaviors of different parties or requires investment in very specific assets (Williamson, 1985, 1991). Hybrid forms, such as franchises, combine price mechanisms and hierarchical authority structures. In this way, they are intermediate forms (e.g., Shane, 1996). This perspective tends to treat hybrid forms as relatively stable, in the sense that as long as enabling conditions are met, hybrid forms are likely to emerge and survive. Moreover, the underlying ontological stance is positivist, as scholars assume hybridity can be determined based on observable characteristics of exchange arrangements.

Some organizational theorists also conceptualize hybridity in terms of particular governance, ownership and control relations (Denis, Ferlie, & Van Gestel, 2015). Unlike transaction cost economists, however, these scholars treat the hybrid form as distinct, rather than as an intermediary between markets and hierarchies (Podolny & Page, 1998; Powell, 1990). In this perspective, hybridity entails governance, ownership and control through *network forms*, as in alliances and other inter-organizational relationships (Gereffi, Humphrey, & Sturgeon, 2005). Scholars argue that unlike adversarial relations in markets and the chain of command in hierarchies, network ties generate trust, creating a distinct basis for exchange (Podolny & Page, 1998; Uzzi, 1997). Compared to the transaction cost perspective, the network forms perspective is more interpretivist in that the distinctive nature and benefits of the hybrid form are in part determined through participants' experiences and interpretations (i.e., the development of trust), rather than being solely based on externally observable features of exchange relations.

Two other form-based perspectives on hybrids are evident within organizational theory – categories and organizational archetypes – and both tend toward a more interpretivist stance. Instead of defining hybridity as the combination of distinct forms of governance, ownership and control, these perspectives understand hybrid organizations as those that combine elements from two or more socially constructed categories or archetypes. The emphasis here is on the social legitimacy of different forms of organization, as viewed by a particular audience, in contrast to the transaction cost and network perspectives that focus more on the efficiency or social structure of hybrid forms.

The *categories perspective* on hybrids, which is rooted in population ecology, conceptualizes hybrids as organizations that combine features associated with multiple social categories of organizational forms (Hannan, Pólos, & Carroll, 2007; Minkoff, 2002; Ruef, 2000; Ruef & Patterson, 2009). For ecologists, a particular organizational form can be viewed as a social category that specifies a cluster of features that define the organization's identity in the eyes of audiences (Ruef, 2000). The features delineating a category are 'socially coded' in that they are both 'a set of signals, as in genetic code, and a set of rules of conduct, as in the penal code' (Pólos, Hannan, & Carroll, 2002: 89). Categories of organizational forms thus describe both what an organization is and what it ought to be or do. Audiences categorize organizations based on these features and thus also come to expect certain behaviors and characteristics of organizations (Hannan et al., 2007).

Empirically, this literature stream has focused mostly on quantitative population-level investigations of hybrid forms in contexts as diverse as healthcare (Ruef, 2000), movie production (Hsu, Negro, & Perretti, 2012), voluntary associations (Minkoff, 2002) and carbon technology start-ups (Wry et al., 2014). For example, nanotechnology start-ups integrate features of two distinct categories: science and technology (Wry et al., 2014). Audiences expect science start-ups to focus on basic research, have executives with scientific backgrounds, and maintain ties to the scientific community. In contrast, the category of technology start-ups is associated with expectations surrounding applied research, executives with expertise in technology commercialization, and commercially oriented collaborations. Hybrids defy such expectations by mixing features from both categories, having for example a scientific top management team but working on applied research.

Because hybrids span categories and violate the expected codes held by audiences, they risk being socially sanctioned (Hsu et al., 2009) and discounted by audiences (Hsu et al., 2012; Zuckerman, 1999). However, as

a particular combination of features from distinct categories becomes more prevalent and gains legitimacy with audiences, it may eventually become a new form in its own right. Thus, implicit in this perspective is the idea that the perception of hybridity need not be permanent.

The categories perspective conceptually connects to the identity perspective, in that both define hybridity in terms of the combination of multiple conceptions of what an organization is and what it does or should do. However, as noted above, the identity perspective treats identity as constructed by organizational members. For ecologists, in contrast, membership in a specific category is not freely chosen by an organization but is ascribed, primarily by external audiences, and is associated with certain membership standards that these audiences expect organizations to meet (Hsu & Hannan, 2005). In this respect category membership is more akin to the concept of organizational image in the organizational identity literature (Gioia et al., 2013).

Finally, the *organizational archetypes perspective*, which is rooted in neo-institutional theory, defines hybrids as organizations that combine two or more archetypal configurations of organizational structures and practices that are 'given coherence by underlying values regarded as appropriate within an institutional context' (Greenwood & Hinings, 1988, 1993; Greenwood & Suddaby, 2006: 36; Tolbert, David, & Sine, 2011). Some studies focus on factors such as organizational strategy, management, marketing, human resource management, and knowledge management (Greenwood & Suddaby, 2006) as key elements of an organizational form, while others highlight organizational goals, authority relations, technology and target markets (Perkmann & Spicer, 2007). Regardless of their focus, studies adopting this perspective tend to examine observable organizational features. Whether those features constitute a hybrid or pure form, however, is based on how those features are understood and interpreted by participants in the organization's field, not just on the features themselves. In this respect, similar to the categories perspective, archetype-based conceptions of hybridity adopt a somewhat more interpretivist stance than the transaction cost economics and network forms perspectives described previously. Unlike the categories perspective, however, the organizational archetypes perspective focuses less on whether audiences view an organization as conforming to a particular category and more on whether particular configurations of organizational features come to be institutionalized such that they are treated as a 'social fact' (Rao, Morrill, & Zald, 2000: 241) and imbued with legitimacy by actors within the field.

Empirically, research that adopts this perspective often focuses on novel types of organizations arising at the boundaries of different institutional spheres, including social enterprises that blend for-profit and non-profit archetypes (Coates & Saloner, 2009; Cooney, 2006; Hockerts, 2015; Lee & Jay, 2015; Mair, Battilana, & Cardenas, 2012; Sud, Vansandt, & Baugous, 2009; Tracey et al., 2011); state agencies that adopt 'new public management' approaches and thereby blend public and private organizational forms (e.g., Gulbrandsen, Thune, Borlaug, & Hanson, 2015; Lindqvist, 2013); biotechnology firms blending archetypes associated with research institutions and business firms (Oliver & Montgomery, 2000; Powell & Sandholtz, 2012); and networked business incubators combining different incubator models (Bollingtoft & Ulhoi, 2005). New legal designations such as the Low-Profit Limited Liability Company and the Benefit Corporation in the United States, as well as the Community Interest Company in the United Kingdom (Haigh, Kennedy, & Walker, 2015; Page & Katz, 2012; Sabeti, 2011), may also be understood as hybrid forms in that they blend for-profit and non-profit archetypes. As these examples imply, studies in this perspective allow for hybridity

to be transitory: particular hybrid combinations may become seen as legitimate, institutionalized archetypes in themselves over time.

Hybrid Rationales

A third broad approach conceptualizes hybrids as organizations that combine multiple societal rationales. By rationales, we mean patterns of cultural and political values, beliefs and practices. Two of the three perspectives that define hybrids based on the combination of societal rationales, the institutional logics and culture perspectives, tend to be primarily interpretivist in nature, in that the elements being combined involve beliefs and values, not just externally observable organizational features. In contrast, the third perspective within the rationales approach, which conceptualizes hybrids in terms of the combination of multiple economic regimes, is somewhat more positivist in its ontological stance and treats hybrids as relatively temporary and transitional.

The *institutional logics perspective* on hybrids has become a dominant stream of research in institutional theory. Institutional logics are 'socially constructed, historical patterns of material practices, assumptions, values, beliefs and rules by which individuals produce and reproduce their material subsistence, organize time and space, and provide meaning to their social reality' (Thornton & Ocasio, 1999: 804; see also Friedland & Alford, 1991; Thornton, Ocasio, & Lounsbury, 2012). Each institutional logic provides a 'set of assumptions and values, usually implicit, about how to interpret organizational reality, what constitutes appropriate behavior, and how to succeed' (Thornton & Ocasio, 1999: 804). Logics thereby provide societal rationales that guide individuals and organizations.

In their seminal work on logics, Friedland and Alford (1991) emphasize that while society consists of distinct domains, each one governed by a distinct institutional logic (e.g., the family, the state, the church, the market, the corporation, the professions), these domains often overlap such that individuals and organizations confront multiple institutional logics. Early research tended to focus on multiplicity at the field level, studying fields in transition from one dominant logic to another (e.g., Haveman & Rao, 1997; Thornton, 2002), as well as the enduring presence of multiple logics within a single field (e.g., Dunn & Jones 2010; Lounsbury, 2007; Reay & Hinings, 2005, 2009). Building on the recognition that multiple logics often persist within a field over time, scholars have more recently sought to understand the organizational implications of such multiplicity (Besharov & Smith, 2014; Kraatz & Block, 2008; Greenwood, Raynard, Kodeih, Micelotta, & Lounsbury, 2011), and research on this issue is expanding rapidly (see Figure 5.1a).

From an institutional logics perspective, hybrids are organizations that instantiate the values and practices associated with multiple distinct field- or societal-level logics (e.g., Battilana & Dorado, 2010; Jay, 2013; Fossestol, Breit, Andreassen, & Klemsdal, 2015; Pache & Santos, 2013b; Smets, Jarzabkowski, Burke, & Spee, 2015). Empirically, this perspective has been used to investigate many different hybrid organizations, including community banks (Almandoz, 2012, 2014), social enterprises (Battilana & Dorado, 2010; Mair, Mayer, & Lutz, 2015; Pache & Santos, 2013b; Santos, Pache, & Birkholz, 2015; Ramus, Vaccaro, & Brusoni, 2016) and educational organizations (Schiersmann, 2014; Teelken, 2015). Because it locates specific logics not only at the societal level (Friedland & Alford, 1991) but also at the level of organizational fields or sectors (Thornton & Ocasio, 1999, 2008), this perspective also lends itself to the study of public–private partnerships and other sector-spanning organizations (Bruton, Peng,

Ahlstrom, Stan, & Xu, 2015; Jay, 2013; Pestoff, 2014).

The institutional logics perspective has some important similarities with the culture perspective, which comes from research on cultural hybridization within anthropology and sociology (Ackermann, 2012; Bhabha, 1994; Pieterse, 2001), and the transitioning economic regimes perspective, which is based on research at the intersection of political science, economic sociology and organizational studies (Brownlee, 2009; Lee, 2005; Nee, 1992). The *culture perspective* conceptualizes hybridization as a process in which individuals combine and blend elements from different cultures (Waring, 2015). Some organizational research has begun to embrace these ideas to study how managers in multinational corporations hybridize a global corporate culture with local cultures (Shimoni & Bergmann, 2006), how local culture shapes organizational modernization based on Western management practices (Yousfi, 2014) and how professionals migrating from public to private sector organizations hybridize the cultural practices of the two sectors (Waring, 2015). This perspective offers the potential to span levels of analysis in research on hybrids and hybridity, as individual interpretive efforts and actions form the basis for the blending of cultural elements to occur at the organizational level (Shimoni & Bergmann, 2006), which may in turn link to the development of hybrid logics at the institutional field level (Nigam & Ocasio, 2010; Tan & Wang, 2011).

On the other hand, the *transitioning economic regimes perspective* conceptualizes hybrids as organizations that span different regimes, particularly market economies and socialist planned economies (Nee, 1992; Nee & Matthews, 1996). Studies in this stream of research have focused in particular on the emergence of hybrids during economic regime shifts in China and countries of the former Soviet Bloc (Chow & Luo, 2007; Keister, 1998; Suhomlinova, 1999;

Xin & Pearce, 1996; Zhou, 2000). In China, for example, hybrids have emerged as state-owned enterprises, which have begun to adopt market practices in a national economy increasingly opening to the world market (Guthrie, 1999). Through hybridization, state-owned enterprises have thus gradually transitioned into an increasingly privatized market economy in which 'government officials themselves have become market oriented actors' (Walder, 1995: 295). At the same time, the need for legitimacy has drawn private entrepreneurs to mimic the legal form of state-owned enterprises while maintaining market-based practices typically associated with private firms (Nee & Opper, 2012). Hybrids thereby have functioned as an important organizational form in the rapid expansion of China's transitioning economy.

State-owned enterprises and other organizations that span different political and economic regimes could be described as combining market and state logics (Thornton et al., 2012). However, the transitioning economic regimes perspective tends to treat hybrids as facilitating transitions between regimes and thus as temporary in nature (Cheung, 2006; Garcia-Zamor & Noll, 2009; Nee, 1992; Xu, Lu, & Gu, 2014). In contrast, scholars within the institutional logics perspective see hybrids as relatively persistent over time (Reay & Hinings, 2009; Smets et al., 2015).

Overall, our review of the literature reveals that approaches emphasizing organizational identity, organizational forms and societal rationales have been used extensively to make sense of and examine hybrids and hybridity in organizations. Although the eight perspectives we presented above have tended to evolve on relatively separate tracks, they have important commonalities in their understanding of hybridity. Bringing together these perspectives, we define hybridity as the mixing of core organizational elements that would conventionally not go together. The concept of core

elements has a long tradition in organizational research (Hannan & Freeman, 1984; Parsons, 1960). We use the term to refer to aspects such as identities, forms and rationales that contribute to defining organizational goals and shaping forms of authority. In specifying core elements that 'would conventionally not go together' we mean combinations that violate institutionalized rules about what is appropriate or compatible. For example, hybrids may combine different types of identities that draw from separate value systems (Albert & Whetten, 1985). They may also span categories that audiences treat as distinct (Hsu et al., 2009) or blend organizational archetypes whose combination is not considered legitimate (Tracey et al., 2011). Finally, they may mix multiple societal rationales that convey distinct and often competing messages about the appropriate way to organize (Jay, 2013). In this way, whether studies focus on identities, forms, or rationales as a basis for hybridity, they tend to concur that hybrids are prone to inherent tensions.

Moreover, while the three broad approaches focus on different aspects of the phenomenon, the concepts of hybrid identities, forms and rationales are related to each other, which creates many opportunities for bridging the various perspectives on hybrids. For example, organizational archetypes are often embedded in specific institutional logics, thus offering potential to interlink these two perspectives (e.g., Pache & Santos, 2013b; Tracey et al., 2011). The institutional logics perspective is also tied to the transaction cost perspective in that the economic institution of the market is governed by a societal-level market logic, while hierarchies are associated with a corporate logic (cf. Thornton et al., 2012). In turn, institutional logics are related to organizational identities, as logics provide the 'cultural materials that organizational members assemble' to articulate 'essential identity elements' (Glynn, 2008: 426; see also Besharov & Brickson, 2016). In the

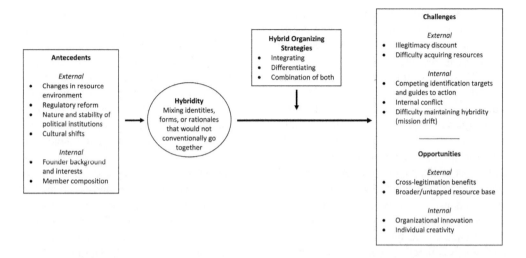

Figure 5.2   Antecedents, challenges, opportunities and strategies for managing hybridity

spirit of harnessing complementarities, we draw from these multiple perspectives in the next section to highlight key insights that relate to the emergence, development and sustainability of hybrids. In keeping with the focus of this volume, we concentrate on those perspectives closest to institutional theory.

ANTECEDENTS, CHALLENGES, OPPORTUNITIES AND STRATEGIES FOR MANAGING HYBRIDITY

Taken together, the various perspectives reviewed above allow for considerable insight into the antecedents, challenges and opportunities of hybridity. They can also be used to derive strategies through which hybrids can be managed to address the associated challenges and exploit opportunities. Below, we systematically account for the external and internal conditions that are more or less conducive to the emergence and subsequent development of hybrid organizations, and we describe how organizations engage in integrating and/or differentiating strategies to navigate the challenges and

opportunities of hybridity. Figure 5.2 offers an overarching framework.

Antecedents of Hybridity

Given that isomorphic pressures towards the reproduction of institutionalized organizational forms tend to work against hybridization (DiMaggio & Powell, 1983; Tolbert et al., 2011), how and under what conditions do hybrids emerge? Two broad types of explanations are evident in the extant literature, one emphasizing forces external to an organization, the other emphasizing the agency of internal organizational actors.

Externally, characteristics of the institutional environment may be more or less conducive to the founding of hybrid organizations. For example, accounting for national differences, Anheier and Krlev (2014) propose that national economic and welfare system characteristics are likely to influence the emergence of hybrid organizations in the social services sector. Beyond national differences, local community differences may also play an important role. For example, Seelos, Mair, Battilana and Dacin (2011) propose that community-level characteristics, such as political stability and network closure, as well as the existence of a local entrepreneurial tradition, may influence the emergence of hybrid organizations.

While some characteristics of the institutional environment are stable, others may change over time. In particular, shifts in institutional logics within a field can create pressures and opportunities for organizations to develop hybrid forms and identities that reflect multiple logics rather than just one. Such shifts may occur due to broader regulatory, political, or cultural changes and can be amplified by concomitant shifts in the resource environment. First, regulatory changes can be conducive to hybridity by compelling organizations that historically conformed to a single organizational form and associated identity to adopt elements associated with another form and identity. For example, new public management reforms have required many public sector organizations to integrate corporate and market-based structures and practices with their existing practices (Christensen & Lægreid, 2011; Fossestol et al., 2015; Schiersmann, 2014). Other regulatory shifts have been less coercive in pressuring organizations to hybridize but opened opportunities for those wanting to do so. For example, recent regulatory developments towards more flexible legal statuses such as the Benefit Corporation and Low-Profit Limited Liability Company in the United States and the Community Interest Company in the United Kingdom, mentioned above, offer new possibilities to blend for-profit and charitable organizational characteristics (Rawhouser, Cummings, & Crane, 2015; Sabeti, 2011).

Second, shifts in political institutions also influence which logics are considered appropriate guides to organizational action, and in doing so may facilitate the emergence of hybrids. In countries transitioning from state-controlled to market economies, for example, organizations that combine state and private ownership are better positioned to address uncertainty about which set of political rules will dominate (Nee & Matthews, 1996). Such collaboratively owned enterprises 'hedge their bets' by trying to appeal to both the state and the private market (Nee, 1992).

Finally, broader cultural shifts can also influence which logics are considered appropriate within a given field. Such shifts may result from the coordinated activity of social movements (Haveman, Rao, & Paruchuri, 2007) or from more emergent phenomena such as globalization (Pieterse, 1995). These cultural shifts create pressure for organizations to develop structures and practices that combine elements of multiple societal rationales, rather than just one. For example, the market logic has entered many domains of Western society (Davis & Marquis, 2005), including fields that were historically dominated by a professional logic, such as publishing (Thornton, 2002), medicine (Reay & Hinings, 2005, 2009; Scott, Ruef, Mendel, & Caronna, 2000), education (Teelken, 2015) and charity (Hwang & Powell, 2009). In many of these fields, the rise of the market logic has been accompanied by changes in the resource environment. Non-profits, for example, find themselves increasingly faced with less public funding and growing pressure to hybridize into commercial activities to generate alternative revenue streams (Dees, 1998; Galaskiewicz, Bielefeld, & Dowell, 2006). At the same time, in fields historically dominated by the market and corporate logics, a social welfare logic now exerts some influence, as evident in demands that corporations be socially and environmentally responsible (Hoffman, 2015; Lee & Jay, 2015; Margolis & Walsh, 2003). Finally, globalization and the rise of large multinationals also occasion more national culture hybridization in the workplace as rationales and logics from different societies exert their influence on organizations (Delmestri, 2006). For example, employees in multinational enterprises that combine different national institutional infrastructures frequently confront complex demands and must develop working compromises (Kostova, Roth, & Dacin, 2008; Kostova & Zaheer, 1999).

In addition to external forces, intra-organizational factors also influence the emergence of hybrids. While the literature has described various internal factors, most center on the role of individuals, either founders or broader groups of organizational members, who adhere to particular identities, forms or societal rationales. Proactive action by founders figures particularly prominently in accounts of hybridity that explore intra-organizational dynamics. For example, Tracey and coauthors (2011) describe how the founders of the British social enterprise Aspire deliberately set out to create an organization that provided social support to the long-term unemployed through a financially sustainable business. Smith and Besharov (2016) show how a commitment to helping people move out of poverty, by running a commercial data entry business, motivated the founders of the social enterprise Digital Divide Data. Other research suggests that individuals differ in terms of their likelihood of founding a hybrid and in their capacity to manage hybrids. For example, among social venture founders, men seem to be more likely than women to create hybrid organizations that combine aspects of business and charity (Dimitriadis, Lee, Ramarajan, & Battilana, Forthcoming). Moreover, social venture founders who were exposed to the business sector either vicariously through their parents' professional experience or directly through their own professional experience are more likely to create a hybrid that combines aspects of business and charity (Lee & Battilana, 2016). Still other work argues that founder identity influences hybrid venture creation, showing how role and personal identities shape how entrepreneurs combine social welfare and commercial logics (Wry & York, 2016).

Beyond founders, other studies suggest organizational members at large are an important influence on hybridity due to the combination of logics and identities they carry (Almandoz, 2014; Besharov, 2014; Besharov & Smith, 2014; Foreman & Whetten, 2002; Glynn, 2000; Pache & Santos, 2013a). For example, Zilber (2002) shows how a rape crisis center, which initially adhered to a feminist rationale reflected in the values and identities of its members, became hybridized as volunteers associated with a therapeutic rationale joined the organization. Similarly, Waring (2015) shows how professionals moving between organizations in different sectors can hybridize their new host organization. Such hybridization may frequently be accompanied by internal power struggles between different organizational factions. Kim, Shin and Jeong (2016), for instance, find that hybridity in Korean universities resulted from intra-organizational competition amongst subgroups of members. Guided by different institutional logics, powerful incumbents advocated an appointment system for presidential selection while challengers favored direct voting. Universities in which neither group was dominant settled these political struggles by adopting hybrid systems.

Challenges and Opportunities of Hybridity

Whether hybridity emerges from external or internal forces, or some combination of the two, it tends to create tensions due to the mixing of elements not conventionally associated. Much extant research has consequently focused on the challenges that hybrids face compared to other organizations. Yet, studies also argue that hybrids enjoy unique opportunities and advantages compared to organizations that primarily reflect just one identity, form or rationale. We view challenges and opportunities as two sides of the same coin, both arising from the tensions inherent in the hybrid character of an organization. Below, we explain how these challenges and opportunities manifest externally in how hybrids relate to external constituencies and internally in how organizational members interact with and relate to their organization.

External challenges and opportunities

All organizations depend on external resource inflows and productive relations with target audiences. For this purpose they need to be deemed acceptable and legitimate by their external constituencies (Bitektine, 2011; Suchman, 1995). Because hybrids span established social categories, they run the risk of confusing audiences and not effectively catering to their needs, thus suffering a legitimacy discount (Hsu, 2006; Hsu et al., 2009; Zuckerman, 1999). For example, production companies in Hollywood that hybridized by developing genre-spanning films had a significantly higher failure rate than 'purist' companies that produced films within genres (Hsu et al., 2012). Similarly, restaurants that straddled haute and nouvelle cuisine were down-rated by the *Guide Michelin* (Rao, Monin, & Durand, 2005). By appealing to diverse constituencies, hybrids also tend to face more dissimilar and even incommensurate external expectations. As a jack of all trades they risk being a master of none (Hsu, 2006). Work integration organizations, for example, which operate under both a commercial and a social welfare logic, need to meet divergent expectations of business and non-profit stakeholders to be seen as legitimate by these audiences (Pache & Santos, 2013b; Smith & Besharov, 2016). While the former value managerial expertise and financial performance as a basis for legitimacy, the latter emphasize social mission and impact. It is therefore difficult to satisfy both groups at the same time. Acquiring legitimacy in the eyes of important external constituents thus presents a considerable challenge to hybrid organizations, making it hard to obtain vital resources.

While these legitimation and resource acquisition challenges for hybrids are well established and documented, accumulating research suggests possible moderating factors.

Although hybrids suffer from violating established categories, high-status hybrids may be granted more room to deviate from audience expectations without sanction (Zuckerman, Kim, Ukanwa, & von Rittmann, 2003). The discount hybrids experience may also be attenuated when the category system itself is in flux (Ruef & Patterson, 2009), when category combinations are seen as meaningful (Phillips, Turco, & Zuckerman, 2013), or when categories are losing their distinctiveness due to increasing numbers of violators (Rao et al., 2005). In sectors that are themselves undergoing considerable reform and change, such as energy (Liu & Wezel, 2015) and healthcare (Cappellaro & Dacin, 2015; Reay & Hinings, 2009), social sanctions of hybridity may therefore be considerably reduced. Similarly, increasing numbers of social enterprises may progressively face fewer legitimation challenges, as new legal forms such as the United States Benefit Corporation or the United Kingdom Community Interest Company help to institutionalize hybrid categories in themselves (Rawhouser et al., 2015).

Despite the distinct challenges they face as a result of spanning categories, if hybrids do acquire legitimacy in the eyes of relevant external audiences, they have the opportunity to benefit from a broader or previously untapped resource base than organizations that primarily reflect a single institutional logic or organizational form (Pache & Santos, 2013b). Wry and coauthors (2014) find that nanotechnology start-ups that conform to an acceptable hybridization pattern can increase their resource base by acquiring additional venture capital financing, as long as they foreground technology commercialization aims in their hybridization of science and technology categories. Similarly, collaboratively owned hybrid transition organizations can draw on both state resources and private capital in the changing economic regime in China, if they effectively manage relations with both constituent groups (Peng & Heath, 1996; Xin & Pearce, 1996). Other hybrids may broaden their potential resource base by including minority logics to appeal to new constituent groups untapped by existing organizations (Durand & Jourdan, 2012). They may also utilize underappreciated assets, such as recruiting disabled staff to compete in the commercial marketplace (Hockerts, 2015). Hybrids may also have a special appeal for audiences with complex demands, such as clients who need different types of legal services typically offered by separate organizations. These audiences value inclusive category spanners that are better positioned to handle complex situations (Paolella & Durand, 2016).

A related opportunity arises due to the cross-legitimation benefits that hybrids gain by being associated with well-established parental organizational forms. Both Minkoff (2002) and Xu and coauthors (2014) find that the failure rate for new hybrid forms adapted from established parental forms decreases as the density of the parental forms increases (up to a point). These results suggest that the cognitive legitimacy of parental organizational forms, which increases when their density is higher, is transferred to hybrid forms.

Internal challenges and opportunities

At the intra-organizational level, hybrids face challenges in terms of member identification, internal conflict and, ultimately, organizational stability. First, the convention-defying and complex nature of a hybrid may render it challenging for members to identify with their organization and their role therein (Croft, Currie, & Lockett, 2015; McGivern, Currie, Ferlie, Fitzgerald, & Waring, 2015). Members may be torn between the different sides of their organization. In cooperatives, for example, members may identify with both the pragmatic and idealistic elements of their organization but experience cognitive tensions due to their uneasy coexistence (Ashforth & Reingen, 2014; Foreman & Whetten, 2002). This may lead to considerable stress on individuals. Similarly, if organizations espouse multiple institutional logics, their members

may struggle to determine the appropriate action in any particular situation (Pache & Santos, 2013a; Voronov, De Clercq, & Hinings, 2013). Members of hybrids thus experience institutional complexity on a personal level as they go about their work (Smets et al., 2015). Many professionals in public healthcare systems, for example, are continuously confronted with both a medical care and a managerial logic, which can place considerable strain on them (Currie & Spyridonidis, 2015; Reay & Hinings, 2009). Conflicting national cultural rationales can have similar effects on members of multinational enterprises. For instance, research suggests that managers of subsidiaries in host countries that are more institutionally distant from the parent company's home country are more likely to experience role conflicts (Vora & Kostova, 2007).

Second, because hybrids combine identities, forms, or rationales that conventionally do not go together, they are more likely than other organizations to give rise to a plurality of interpretations of organizational reality. Members may therefore disagree on organizational issues, and this can escalate to open and increasingly intractable conflict (Ashforth & Reingen, 2014; Besharov & Smith, 2014). This is particularly likely when natural fault lines exist between subgroups due to structural separation or the presence of multiple professional groups (e.g., Almandoz, 2014; Battilana & Dorado, 2010; Glynn, 2000). For example, in Glynn's (2000) study of a symphony orchestra, conflict developed between musicians and administrators, with the former prioritizing artistic excellence and the latter emphasizing economic performance. Conflict is also likely to be greater when both elements of the hybrid are core to the organization with no clear dominance ordering between them (Besharov & Smith, 2014).

A third internal challenge concerns the maintenance of hybridity. Intra-organizational power struggles or shifts in the influence and resources of external constituencies can result in the dominance of one identity, form, or rationale at the expense of others. Studies of organizations that combine social and commercial elements tend to refer to this phenomenon as 'mission drift' and generally focus on the risk that commercial elements will dominate at the expense of the social (Ebrahim, Battilana, & Mair, 2014; Pestoff, 2014; Santos et al., 2015). For example, a study of more than 20,000 third sector organizations in the United Kingdom finds that commercial income is negatively associated with the attainment of non-monetary objectives (Thompson & Williams, 2014). In the field of microfinance, evidence from more than 2,500 organizations indicates mission drift when these hybrids transition from a non-profit to for-profit organizational form: the size of their gross loan portfolio and the number of active borrowers increases, but their average loan size and focus on impoverished clients decreases, suggesting they shift away from their mission of helping the poor and focus more on improving financial performance (Zhao & Grimes, 2016).

While the inherent heterogeneity in hybrid organizations may thus present considerable challenges, it also offers opportunities, particularly in terms of creativity and innovation. Indeed, some organizations deliberately integrate additional rationales in order to spur innovation and disrupt established structures. Dalpiaz, Rindova and Ravasi (2016) illustrate how household goods producer Alessi purposely incorporated additional logics to change production and product development. Alessi's products can now not only be found on coffee tables in households around the world but also on exhibition in many design museums. In a different sector, Jay (2013) illustrates how tensions between different institutional logics of the Cambridge Energy Alliance, a public–private partnership, have triggered not only phases of organizational stasis but also phases of innovation in which novel solutions to problems were developed. Such innovation may eventually be rewarded by external audiences. Hsu and coauthors (2012) find that while genre-spanning movie production firms had a higher failure rate than 'purists', these firms also produced the rare innovative block-busters that successfully defied traditional categories and broke box office records.

Last but not least, hybridty can also enhance individual creativtiy. Being exposed to multiple logics can enable organizational members to generate new ideas to perform their work more effectively or in novel ways (Jarzabkowski, Smets, Bednarek, Burke, & Spee, 2013). For example, McPherson and Sauder (2013) find that professionals working in a drug court drew on a variety of different logics quite skillfully to resolve complex client cases. These benefits of hybridity, at both the individual and organizational levels, are consistent with research on organizational paradox that emphasizes contradictory yet interrelated tensions in organizations. Studies in this stream of research argue that engaging both the inconsistencies and synergies of multiple oppositional demands can spark virtuous cycles (Smith & Lewis, 2011), enabling learning and creativity (Miron-Spektor, Gino, & Argote, 2011; Rothenberg, 1979) as well as flexibility and adaptability (Farjoun, 2002; Weick & Quinn, 1999).

Managing Hybridity

Considering the evidence on the challenges and opportunities hybrids confront, a key question is whether, and if so how, managers of hybrids may be able to buffer their organizations from challenges and position them to benefit from the opportunities. Extant research on this issue distinguishes between management approaches that integrate versus differentiate a hybrid's distinct identities, forms or rationales (Battilana & Lee, 2014; Greenwood et al., 2011; Kraatz & Block, 2008; Pratt & Foreman, 2000). Through integration, hybrids amalgamate the different components they bring together, creating a unified blend. In contrast, through differentiation hybrids keep their constituent elements separate, forming an organization with multiple, distinct parts. While most studies of hybrids emphasize either integrating or differentiating the components of hybrids, some recent work describes management strategies that appear to combine integration and differentiation. Each of these approaches is evident in how hybrids deal with both the external and internal challenges and opportunities they confront.

Integration strategies

Integration approaches can involve an organization's formal structures and practices as well as its people. Focusing on structural integration, Ebrahim and coauthors (2014) describe how the social enterprise VisionSpring integrates commercial and social welfare logics within a single organizational unit in order to pursue its mission of hiring and training poor women to sell affordable eyewear to people in developing countries. In the organizational identity literature, this approach has been described as 'holographic' (Albert & Whetten, 1985), meaning that a hybrid's multiple identities are shared across all organizational units, rather than each identity being held by a separate subunit.

Integration can also involve organizational practices. For example, Pache and Santos (2013b) describe how some French work integration social enterprises selectively coupled practices associated with the social welfare logic held by state actors and practices linked to the commercial logic held by private investors, thus appeasing both constituencies at once. Mair and coauthors (2015) find a similar pattern in a comparative study of the governance practices of 70 social enterprises: many social enterprises tried to meet the minimum requirements of the social welfare and commercial logics by selectively adhering to elements of both. Such integration strategies may be more successful in relatively novel fields where categorical boundaries are not as rigid or when hybrid identities involve ambiguous components (Ruef & Patterson, 2009).

A third common way of achieving integration is through organizational members. Battilana and Dorado (2010) describe such an approach in the Los Andes microfinance organization, which combined banking and development logics. Los Andes hired relatively inexperienced employees and then socialized them into both the development and banking logics simultaneously. As a result of this approach, organizational members developed a hybrid profile, being equally versed in all elements of the hybrid. Using people to enable and subsequently maintain integration may have the advantage of minimizing internal conflict potential. If everyone can relate to all aspects of the hybrid organization, disagreements are less likely to escalate into paralyzing internal conflict and fault lines between different subgroups can be avoided (Brewer, Ho, Lee, & Miller, 1987; Gaertner, Dovidio, Anastasio, Bachman, & Rust, 1993).

Integration is often described as having the potential to yield novel organizational forms and innovative products and services through the synthesis of seemingly incompatible elements (Seo & Creed, 2002; Thornton et al., 2012). Indeed, integration approaches may lead to the development of a new, blended organizational identity, form, or rationale which melds elements that were previously distinct (e.g., Clark et al., 2010; Nigam & Ocasio, 2010; Powell & Sandholtz, 2012; Tan & Wang, 2011), providing organizational members with a unified and consistent framework for cognition and action. The hybrid that achieves such blending may become an institution in its own right, achieving relative autonomy and power vis-à-vis its environment, even as it is deeply embedded in that environment (Selznick, 1957). Achieving such integration is challenging, however, because members often retain strong ties to professional associations and other powerful external referents associated with distinct institutional logics (Greenwood et al., 2011), making it hard for them to give up their adherence to the constituent elements of a hybrid.

Externally, integrated hybrids that transcend conventional category boundaries may also be able to negotiate stable relationships with constituent audiences over time (Kraatz & Block, 2008). Indeed, Lee (2015) finds that among hybrid organizations that combine aspects of business and charity, those that are characterized by better integration of the commercial and social activities in which they engage are more effective when it comes to raising funds from external parties. These positive effects of integration may also depend in part on organizational status, as high status can enable organizations to avoid social sanctions, including those associated with hybridity (Podolny, 2005; Rao et al., 2005). Generally, however, integration approaches pose a risk of misalignment with external audiences and resource providers in that the hybrid organization conforms to none of the established categories deemed legitimate by audiences.

Moreover, integration approaches may place considerable psychological strain on individuals, due to the challenges of combining seemingly contradictory identities and rationales for action (Ashforth & Reingen, 2014; Croft et al., 2015). Individuals seem to vary in their ability to cope with such strain. In a study of how European academics in public research institutions responded to the accountability demands of an incipient managerial logic, for example, Teelken (2015) identifies four general coping mechanisms that differed in how much they accommodated (versus resisted) the new logic: 'formal instrumentality' and 'rational resignation', both of which lead organizational members to accommodate the new dual demands, albeit with varying degrees of choice; and 'professional pragmatism' and 'symbolic compliance', which entail prolonged resistance to change. McGivern and coauthors (2015) find a similar pattern in medical organizations: physicians varied in their ability to embrace a new managerial logic in addition to their medical professional logic, depending on whether they were able to craft

new nested identities that combined multiple roles associated with the different sides of the hybrid. In such identity work, the ability to assign different saliency to the various identity aspects seems to be an important moderator (Spyridonidis, Hendy, & Barlow, 2015), and it is more easily accomplished when new aspects are seen as offering the potential for enrichment (Waring, 2015). A risk of this coping mechanism, however, is that if different individuals prioritize different identities or rationales, intrapersonal strain may be transformed into interpersonal conflict. For example, Ashforth and Reingen (2014) find that members of a natural foods cooperative identified with both idealist and pragmatist organizational identities and experienced internal tensions between them. They responded by gravitating toward just one identity, creating two subgroups of members, each one emphasizing a competing identity. In this manner, the strain arising from attempts to integrate conflicting elements may paradoxically lead to approaches that emphasize differentiation, which we discuss in the next section.

Differentiation strategies

A second broad approach to managing hybridity involves differentiating one element of the hybrid from the other. As with integration, this approach is evident in how hybrids address competing external expectations and in how they navigate competing internal demands. Also analogous to integration approaches, differentiation may be accomplished through an organization's formal structures and practices as well as through its people.

Structural separation, which involves enacting different logics or identities in separate subunits of the organization, can enable each unit to better align with the external audience most relevant to its operation. In the organizational identity literature, this approach is referred to as 'ideographic', as explained above (Albert & Whetten, 1985). A comparable approach is evident in studies of hybrids adopting the institutional logics perspective.

In her study of a transitional housing organization, for example, Binder (2007) finds that while the housing department followed a bureaucratic state logic aligned with its public resource providers, the family support department focused more on a social support logic targeted to its main client base. Organizations and their members may also develop work practices that differentiate the components of a hybrid. For example, Voronov and coauthors (2013) find that employees in Ontario's fine wine industry use different scripts to engage with wineries' aesthetic logic ('farmer' and 'artist' scripts) and their market logic ('business professional' script), which enable them to keep the logics separate yet engage both in their daily work.

Other studies describe differentiation strategies involving people. In particular, organizations may rely on 'specialists' who represent one or the other of a hybrid's identities or logics. Reay and Hinings (2009), for example, illustrate how managers in Canadian regional health authorities represent the organization's 'business-like' logic while physicians represent the 'medical professional' logic. Evidence from microfinance suggests such a mix of specialists may be quite effective. Canales (2014) finds that microfinance branches performed best when they had a mix of loan officers who were 'bureaucratic' specialists emphasizing standardization and 'relational' specialists emphasizing flexibility.

In addition to possible internal performance benefits, differentiation approaches may have legitimacy benefits. Because such approaches involve having distinct units, practices, or people representing each component of the hybrid, external stakeholders associated with each part can readily detect conformity. This approach may therefore help hybrids garner legitimacy from critical constituencies, both in the moral sense of 'a positive normative evaluation of the organization and its activities' and in the cognitive sense of comprehensibility and taken-for-grantedness (Suchman, 1995: 579). This is especially true when the hybrid combination is novel or seemingly socially taboo, as in the case of religious and market logics in religious mutual funds (Peifer, 2014).

At the same time, differentiation approaches may exacerbate the risk of internal conflict. In Canales' (2014) microfinance study, for example, the branches with a mix of bureaucratic and relational specialists performed best but also had the longest and most contentious credit committee meetings. Because differentiation relies on the continuous resolution of institutional complexity by individuals on the ground, it creates many opportunities for disagreements to arise. It also renders fault lines between different employee groups more apparent and thus provides fertile ground for conflict to escalate, as each distinct subunit or subgroup tries to uphold its component of the hybrid. This is particularly likely when differences are based on professional affiliations (Abbott, 1988; Dunn & Jones, 2010) or overlap with demographic distinctions (DiBenigno & Kellogg, 2014).

Recognizing these challenges, research has started to identify approaches for mitigating the tensions that arise in differentiated hybrids. In their study of work integration social enterprises, Battilana, Sengul, Pache and Model (2015) find that structurally differentiated organizations, in which social and commercial activities are assigned to distinct groups, can avoid paralyzing conflicts between these groups by creating spaces of negotiation – arenas of interaction that allow staff members throughout the organization to discuss and come to an agreement on how to handle the daily trade-offs they face between the demands of their social and commercial activities. These spaces of negotiation are created through a combination of mandatory meetings and formal processes, such as work plan scheduling and beneficiary performance appraisals, which foster coordination between social and commercial activities. Spaces of negotiation ensure the maintenance of a productive tension between staff members in charge of each of these activities.

Although they may be costly to create and maintain, such spaces can enable hybrids to achieve high levels of performance along both dimensions of the hybrid (i.e., social and commercial in the case of work integration social enterprises).

Governance mechanisms offer another means of mitigating the potential for conflict that arises in differentiated hybrids. For example, Pache, Battilana and Santos (2015) show how governance mechanisms can prevent conflict from erupting between founders of work integration social enterprises who come from different institutional spheres. Other studies suggest that inter-group tensions arising from differentiated approaches can be managed through boundary objects (Bechky, 2003). For example, Christiansen and Lounsbury (2013) describe how employees at the global brewery Carlsberg created a Responsible Drinking Guidebook that brought together the social responsibility and market logics represented by separate departments, offering guidance for how members could resolve conflicts between the two logics.

Combining integration and differentiation

While many studies describe approaches to managing hybridity that emphasize either integration or differentiation of a hybrid's constituent elements, some recent work depicts combinations of these two approaches. In part, this recent focus may be motivated by the observation that integration or differentiation alone can create additional problems even as they mitigate others, whereas in combination they are more beneficial (Smith, Besharov, Wessels, & Chertok, 2012). Similarly, related work on organizational paradoxes, particularly paradoxes involving exploration and exploitation, points to the value of both integrating and differentiating to benefit from competing demands (Andriopoulos & Lewis, 2009; Smith, 2014; Smith & Lewis, 2011).

As noted above, differentiation on its own can cause tensions between subunits and increase the salience of fault lines along which conflicts can emerge. Creating some integrating mechanisms can enable hybrids that emphasize differentiation to mitigate conflict and exploit productive tension between their constituent elements. Writing about inter-group conflict more generally, Fiol, Pratt and O'Connor (2009) propose a staged model of first differentiating in order to strengthen each subgroup's identity and reduce feelings of threat, then integrating to enable subgroups to find common ground and avoid intractable conflict. Besharov's (2014) study of the socially responsible grocery chain 'Natural Foods' shows how people and practices can provide such integrating mechanisms. Frontline employees at Natural Foods were specialists. One group, the 'idealists', identified with the company's social mission of promoting organic food, environmental sustainability and community involvement. A second group, the 'capitalists', valued the company's business mission of generating profits and growth for shareholders. To mitigate conflict between members of the two groups, the organization hired store managers who identified with both the social and business missions. These generalists brought a measure of integration to an otherwise differentiated workforce through management practices that appealed to both groups. For example, they promoted products that were financially profitable and also consistent with the social mission, and they developed work practices that enabled both idealists and capitalists to feel welcome in the workplace. In a similar fashion, ambidexterity studies show how organizations with separate subunits for exploiting an existing business and exploring a new innovation can address tensions between subunits by developing integrative senior leadership practices (O'Reilly & Tushman, 2008; Tushman, Smith, Wood, Westerman, & O'Reilly, 2010). Such practices are facilitated when leaders adopt a paradoxical frame (Miron-Spektor et al., 2011; Smith & Tushman, 2005) or use integratively complex thinking (Suedfeld, Tetlock, & Streufert, 1992).

Full integration also creates tensions, albeit intrapersonally instead of interpersonally, as contradictions and inconsistencies between multiple identities or rationales provoke anxiety (see Lewis, 2000). In response, adopting some differentiating practices can reduce the intrapersonal strain that would otherwise develop in integrated hybrids. Smets and coauthors (2015) illustrate this combination of integrating and differentiating practices in their study of brokers working at Lloyds of London's internal reinsurance market. The brokers adhered to both the market and community institutional logics that infused the organization. In their daily work practices, however, brokers did not always integrate the two logics. Rather, they developed a combination of differentiating and integrating practices to manage tensions between logics. In 'segmenting', for example, brokers conducted different activities in different physical spaces in order to keep the competing demands of the market and community logics separate. Similarly, in 'demarcating', they worked to maintain the boundaries of each logic. In contrast, 'bridging' involved enacting practices associated with one logic in the physical space dominated by the other, for example enacting the community logic on the trading floor where the market logic usually dominated. In sum, these recent studies suggest a combination of integration and differentiation may be key to benefitting from hybridity.

IMPLICATIONS AND DIRECTIONS FOR FUTURE RESEARCH

Our review surfaced several general patterns in the literature on hybrids that merit attention in future research. These concern both the nature of hybrids as well as the reasons for and consequences of hybridity. We see considerable potential in studying hybrid organizations in their full complexity, both by expanding our attention beyond combinations of only two distinct identities, forms or

societal rationales and by better integrating across theoretical perspectives. In addition, we believe that a focus on hybridity as a matter of degree rather than type will enable scholars to extrapolate important lessons from the study of hybridity for organizational research more generally. Specifically, by focusing on hybridity as a matter of degree, future studies will be positioned to move beyond an exclusive focus on hybrid organizations to a broader focus on organizations that engage in hybrid organizing to various extents. Finally, there are opportunities for future research to delve further into the antecedents and performance implications of hybrid organizing.

Embracing the Complexity: Multiplicity in Elements, Perspectives and Methods

Our systematic literature review revealed an encouraging plurality of theoretical approaches to hybrid organizations, each one highlighting important aspects of the phenomenon. Their varied nature is an impressive testament to the underlying complexity of hybrids. Yet within each approach, hybrids have mostly been conceptualized as combinations of but two distinct identities, forms or rationales that conventionally do not go together. Similarly, integration between the eight different theoretical perspectives we identified in our literature review remains limited (see Table 5.1). In future research, we need to work towards more multiplicity both in constituent elements of hybrids and in approaches to understanding this organizational phenomenon.

Accounting for multiple elements

Despite previous calls to study more than two distinct identities (Ramarajan, 2014) or institutional logics (Besharov & Smith, 2014; Greenwood et al., 2011), much extant work has focused on the combination or blending of two elements in hybrids. While this approach has yielded important insights, many questions remain. For example, how do organizations and their members relate three or more identities or logics to one another and what tensions spring from such increased complexity (see, e.g., Greenwood, Diaz, Li, & Lorente, 2010; Goodrick & Reay, 2011)? Two identities or logics can either be blended or not. They can be kept in balance or one can dominate the other. With three or more, some combinations may be blended while others may be kept separate. One logic may be allowed to dominate while all others are kept on par at a subordinate level. There is thus a considerably larger set of possible relations that the constituent elements of a hybrid may have to one another, and we know very little about the effects this may have on the inherent tensions so characteristic of hybrids.

In organizational and individual identity research, configurational approaches have been suggested as a promising means of understanding more complex combinations of identities (Pratt & Foreman, 2000; Ramarajan, 2014). In institutional theory, the concept of institutional complexity, which arises 'whenever [organizations] confront incompatible prescriptions from multiple institutional logics' (Greenwood et al., 2011: 318), accounts for the fact that actors, be they organizations or individuals, may be subject to more than two institutional logics at once. These theoretical approaches provide a starting point for future hybrids research that examines the combination of more than two elements, but there is a need for empirical studies exploring how hybrids and their organizational members deal with such complexity.

Bridging across perspectives

Beyond considering hybridity involving more than two components, more bridging across the eight perspectives we discussed above is also needed. The extant hybrids literature appears to resemble the parable of the Blind Men and the Elephant. Each of the men, setting out to learn what an elephant may be, grabs hold of a different part of the animal. They thus draw very different conclusions about the nature of the elephant – each one correct in their view, yet not seeing the full picture. Certainly, there are differences in ontological stance and underlying assumptions that may at least partially explain the limited cross-fertilization among different approaches to studying hybrids. By continuing on separate paths, however, organizational scholars forego an opportunity for synergies and novel contributions.

In the preceding sections, we collected and synthesized insights gained across different literature streams. We hope that our attempt at building bridges across these literatures will open the way for more cross-level and cross-perspective research. Such an approach is needed in order to develop a more comprehensive understanding of hybrid organizations and hybrid organizing. Combining perspectives will need to be done with care, however, given their different ontological assumptions. Writing about research that integrates multiple theoretical perspectives, Okhuysen and Bonardi (2011) recommend checking the compatibility of underlying assumptions and working out potential differences to avoid incompatibilities between theories. This may entail placing perspectives on an unequal footing and only selectively drawing compatible aspects into integrative theorizing. Such efforts promise considerable theoretical leverage in areas in which a focal perspective is comparatively weak and may be enriched with elements of another. The combination of perspectives may in this way offer greater explanatory potential than each perspective on its own. To illustrate, we describe below a few combinations that we believe may be especially valuable for future research on hybrids.

First, while the transaction cost economics and institutional logics perspectives may have some of the most distinct foundational assumptions amongst the eight perspectives we identified, there are also important points of connection that could allow for dialogue in future studies. Market governance mechanisms are arguably embedded in the institutional logic of the market, while hierarchical governance mechanisms are embedded in a corporate or state bureaucratic institutional logic (Thornton et al., 2012). Alliances and other hybrid organizational arrangements that combine governance forms thereby bring together different underlying rationales of action, creating the potential for internal tensions. In studying hybridization decisions and their consequences, it may therefore be important to consider not only transaction cost efficiencies but also costs associated with managing intra-organizational conflict. Particularly when studying the increasing numbers of public–private partnerships and cross-sectoral collaborations, a dialogue between the transaction cost economics and institutional logics perspectives may thus yield greater insight into hybrid organizations. For example, alliance partners' distinct institutional logics may help explain particularly high coordination costs due to increased inter-partner diversity (White & Siu-Yun, 2005). At the same time, transaction cost efficiencies can help explain the impetus for such hybrid organizational configurations. Together, the two perspectives may capture more aspects of the hybrid organization under study.

Second and relatedly, connections between the network forms and institutional logics perspectives also hold promise, particularly as public–private partnerships and cross-sector alliances become more prevalent (Reast, Lindgreen, Vanhamme, & Maon, 2010; Utting & Zammit, 2009). These organizational arrangements are hybrids both in the sense of being network forms and in the sense of being organizations that combine multiple logics, and studying them from both these perspectives may enable researchers to better understand the challenges and opportunities they face, as well as how those can be managed.

A third promising combination involves the organizational identity and organizational archetypes perspectives. Identity theory may enrich research on how hybrid archetypes are created by offering insight into internal tensions that arise when organizations blend practices and structures from distinct parental blueprints. Practices and structures vary in how central, enduring and distinctive they are to organizational members (Gioia, Price, Hamilton, & Thomas, 2010). Those that are perceived as less important to the organization's identity may spur less internal unrest when replaced by other institutional 'building blocks' (Meyer & Rowan, 1977). In this way, an identity perspective may help explain why some combinations of organizational archetypes are less contentious and more easily adopted than others.

A fourth opportunity for combining perspectives involves organizational identity and institutional logics. As we noted previously, institutional logics imply distinct organizational identities. At the same time, organizational identities serve as a filter influencing how institutional logics are interpreted and enacted internally by members (Besharov & Brickson, 2016; Glynn, 2008). For example, organizations with strong and coherent identities may be less responsive to external pressures (Besharov & Brickson, 2016), helping to explain why, in fields characterized by multiple competing logics, some organizations are less likely than others to develop hybridity. In contrast, organizations with weak or fractured identities may be more susceptible to external pressures toward hybridization.

Leveraging multiple methods

Finally, within each of the hybrid perspectives we identified, future research may benefit from employing a wider range of research methods. Quantitatively oriented perspectives, such as categories research, tend to conduct comparative studies at the industry or field level (e.g., Minkoff, 2002; Ruef, 2000; Xu et al., 2014). While this research has contributed important insights into hybrids, particularly around the negative consequences of category spanning (Hsu, 2006; Zuckerman, 1999) and factors that moderate these effects (Ruef & Patterson, 2009; Wry et al., 2014), it might be considerably enriched by in-depth qualitative case studies at the organizational and intra-organizational levels (see, e.g., Phillips et al., 2013). Such work could illuminate the strategies organizations use to avoid confusing audiences despite spanning categories, as well as the ways in which organizations influence which category codes are salient to relevant audiences. How hybrid organizing is actually accomplished in hybrids that span categories also warrants further attention.

In a parallel fashion, perspectives that have to date focused primarily on in-depth, qualitative case studies would benefit from larger-scale, comparative, quantitative research. Qualitative studies within the organizational archetypes, organizational identity and institutional logics perspectives have identified concrete strategies for hybrid organizing and offered rich insights into specific challenges and opportunities facing hybrids. Qualitative studies of social entrepreneurs, for example, explain how social enterprises can overcome the challenges of combining aspects of business and charity at their core (e.g., Battilana & Dorado, 2010; Pache & Santos, 2013b; Smith & Besharov, 2016; Tracey et al., 2011). Indeed, a recent in-depth review of the literature on social enterprises published in academic journals over the last fifteen years revealed that the vast majority of studies are qualitative and focus on building theory through a single case or small number of cases (Lee, Battilana, & Wang, 2014). Despite numerous calls for complementing these rich case studies with quantitative research, such studies are still rare. In research on social enterprises and hybrids more generally, larger N, quantitative studies can address critical questions about the prevalence of differentiating and integrating strategies and the effectiveness of different hybridity management strategies. In sum,

research using a wider set of methods and analytical tools stands to advance our understanding of hybrids within each of the perspectives considered.

Hybridity: A Matter of Type versus Degree?

Much of the extant literature either implicitly or explicitly conceptualizes hybrids as a distinct type of organization, qualitatively different from non-hybrid organizations and consequently facing different challenges, opportunities and organizing demands. For example, research on hybrids emerging at the intersection of category boundaries has produced valuable insights on the potential perils of category spanning (e.g., Hsu, 2006; Zuckerman, 1999), suggesting that hybrids deal with unique challenges not applicable to other organizations. However, hybrids may also be understood as falling on the extreme end of a spectrum of organizations combining conventionally unassociated elements. The emphasis here is on hybridity as a matter of degree rather than type. For example, within the institutional logics perspective, Besharov and Smith (2014) theorize how logics differ in their compatibility and in their centrality to organizational functioning. As a result, organizations vary in the extent to which they confront multiple logics that are equally important in guiding organizational decisions and in the extent to which those logics imply contradictory courses of action. Similarly, writing from an identity perspective, Pratt and Foreman (2000) describe multiple identity organizations as varying in the number of identities they combine and in the extent to which these identities are synergistic.

Conceptualizing hybridity as a matter of degree rather than as a distinct type not only better reflects the empirical reality of many organizations; it also provides an opportunity for research on hybridity to offer insight into challenges, opportunities and management strategies that are relevant for a broader set of organizations. In social enterprises, for example, the challenges arising from combining multiple institutional logics are readily observable, because social welfare and commercial logics tend to be equally central to the organization's functioning, yet they offer incompatible prescriptions for action (Battilana & Dorado, 2010; Pache & Santos, 2013b; Smith & Besharov, 2016). However, commercial corporations faced with corporate social responsibility expectations may find themselves confronting similar challenges, albeit to a lesser degree (see Besharov & Smith, 2014). More generally, treating hybridity as a matter of degree allows for insights to be developed in contexts in which the dynamics of hybridity are most visible and then transferred to other contexts in which they exist in more muted form. Future studies would thus benefit from examining the extent to which various kinds of organizations exhibit hybridity and how they handle it, rather than treating hybrid organizations as a unique and qualitatively different type. In doing so, research will need to shift from focusing on hybrid entities (the noun) to hybrid organizing (the verb).

Such an approach is particularly important as growing numbers of organizations across sectors exhibit some degree of hybridity. Non-profits face pressure to commercialize (Dees, 1998; Galaskiewicz et al., 2006), state-owned enterprises and government agencies undergo marketization (Considine & Lewis, 2003; Fotaki, 2011; Hayllar & Wettenhall, 2013; Nee & Matthews, 1996), corporations increasingly adopt social responsibility and sustainability practices (Margolis & Walsh, 2003), and organizations of all types confront more institutionally complex environments in a global, networked world (Ferreira, 2014; Marano & Kostova, 2016; Schemeil, 2013). The epitome of these trends is the increase in organizations positioned at the intersection of the commercial and social sectors. Often referred to as social enterprises, these organizations primarily pursue a social mission

while engaging in commercial activities to sustain their operations (Battilana & Lee, 2014; Smith, Gonin, & Besharov, 2013). Our stance toward this hybrid organizing movement is not normative. Rather, we believe that institutional theory, and organizational theories more generally, can help explain the nature of organizations that participate in this movement and their role in society. The study of these convention-defying organizations may in turn help scholars refine theories of institutions and organizations more broadly.

Antecedents and Performance Implications of Hybrid Organizing

In studying various approaches to hybrid organizing across sectors, it is important that future research examine antecedents as well as performance implications. As we highlighted above, research has already identified a number of conditions that are more or less conducive to the emergence of hybrids. However, we need to know whether these conditions differ across configurations of hybrid organizing and, if so, how. This will help us understand why certain organizations engage in hybrid organizing to a greater extent than others.

While research on the antecedents of hybrid organizing will be extending previous research efforts, studies examining the performance implications of hybrid organizing will open up a new path of research. Research to date has primarily focused on whether and how organizations can sustain their hybrid nature over time but has not systematically accounted for the performance implications of hybrid organizing. Examining performance implications is challenging because it requires assessing organizational performance on multiple dimensions instead of just one. In the case of social enterprises, for example, this would entail more systematically measuring their economic *and* social performance.

Understanding hybrid performance will also require attention to the interaction of distinct challenges, opportunities and management strategies. To date, research from each perspective has emphasized different factors. The categories perspective, for example, provides strong evidence of external legitimacy challenges, while the identity perspective highlights internal challenges of conflict between subgroups and multiple, competing identity targets. Interaction effects between different challenges, opportunities and management strategies remain largely underexplored. For example, how does structural compartmentalization in an ideographic hybrid (Kraatz & Block, 2008) affect the potential for individual creativity of organizational members (McPherson & Sauder, 2013)? What extent of hybrid organizing is optimal to harness its benefits? How and why does it vary across contexts and organizations? Hybrid management strategies adopted as a remedy for one challenge may well cause another, and strategies to exploit hybrid opportunities may have unintended consequences. These potential side-effects of different approaches to managing hybridity need to be explored more fully if we are to understand the performance implications of hybrid organizing. Doing so is particularly important in order to generate knowledge that is not just theoretically rigorous but also practically relevant (George, Howard-Grenville, Joshi, & Tihanyi, 2016; Mair, Wolf, & Seelos, 2016).

In closing, we hope that this chapter will provide useful foundations for future research not only on hybrid organizations but also, and more broadly, on hybridity and hybrid organizing. Such research is especially needed at a time when the boundaries between sectors are increasingly blurred. While the divides between the for-profit, non-profit, and public sectors have structured our economic and social life over the last century, hybrid organizing is transforming it through the creation of a more organizationally diverse form of capitalism (Schneiberg, 2011), one in which organizations increasingly diverge from existing institutionalized templates by combining various identities, forms and/or

societal rationales. If organizational scholars want to study and understand this evolution, they will need to break the silos that separate research on corporations, non-profits and public organizations, and account for hybrid organizing dynamics.

Note

1   The authors' names are listed alphabetically. All were equal contributors.

ACKNOWLEDGMENTS

We thank Royston Greenwood for his feedback and guidance on this chapter. We also appreciate comments and advice received from Victor Nee, Ben Rissing and Wendy Smith. We are indebted to Marissa Kimsey for her research assistance.

REFERENCES

Abbott, A. D. (1988). *The system of professions: An essay on the division of expert labor*. Chicago, IL: University of Chicago Press.

Ackermann, A. (2012). Cultural hybridity: Between metaphor and empiricism. In P. Stockhammer (Ed.), *Conceptualizing cultural hybridization* (pp. 5–25). Berlin: Springer.

Albert, S., & Whetten, D. A. (1985). Organizational identity. *Research in Organizational Behavior, 7*: 263–295.

Almandoz, J. (2012). Arriving at the starting line: The impact of community and financial logics on new banking ventures. *Academy of Management Journal, 55*(6): 1381–1406.

Almandoz, J. (2014). Founding teams as carriers of competing logics: When institutional forces predict banks' risk exposure. *Administrative Science Quarterly, 59*(3): 442–473.

Andriopoulos, C., & Lewis, M. W. (2009). Exploitation–exploration tensions and organizational ambidexterity: Managing paradoxes of innovation. *Organization Science, 20*(4): 696–717.

Anheier, H. K., & Krlev, G. (2014). Welfare regimes, policy reforms, and hybridity. *American Behavioral Scientist, 58*(11): 1395–1411.

Anteby, M., & Wrzesniewski, A. (2014). In search of the self at work: Young adults' experiences of a dual identity organization. In H. Greve & M.-D. Seidel (Eds.), *Adolescent experiences and adult work outcomes: Connections and causes: Research in the sociology of work*, vol. 25 (pp. 13–50). Bingley: Emerald Group Publishing.

Ashforth, B. E., & Reingen, P. H. (2014). Functions of dysfunction: Managing the dynamics of an organizational duality in a natural food cooperative. *Administrative Science Quarterly*, 59(3): 474–516.

Astley, W. G., & Van de Ven, A. H. (1983). Central perspectives and debates in organization theory. *Administrative Science Quarterly*, 28(2): 245–173.

Barich, H., & Kotler, P. (1991). A framework for marketing image management. *Sloan Management Review*, 32(2): 94–104.

Battilana, J., & Dorado, S. (2010). Building sustainable hybrid organizations: The case of commercial microfinance organizations. *Academy of Management Journal*, 53(6): 1419–1440.

Battilana, J., & Lee, M. (2014). Advancing research on hybrid organizing: Insights from the study of social enterprises. *Academy of Management Annals*, 8(1): 397–441.

Battilana, J., Lee, M., Walker, J., & Dorsey, C. (2012). In search of the hybrid ideal. *Stanford Social Innovation Review*, 10(3): 51–55.

Battilana, J., Sengul, M., Pache, A.-C., & Model, J. (2015). Harnessing productive tensions in hybrid organizations: The case of work integration social enterprises. *Academy of Management Journal*, 58(6): 1658–1685.

Bechky, B. (2003). Object lessons: Workplace artifacts as representations of occupational jurisdiction. *American Journal of Sociology*, 109(3): 720–752.

Berger, P. L., & Luckmann, T. (1967). *The social construction of reality: A treatise in the sociology of knowledge*. Garden City, NY: Anchor Books.

Besharov, M. L. (2014). The relational ecology of identification: How organizational identification emerges when individuals hold divergent values. *Academy of Management Journal*, 57(5): 1485–1512.

Besharov, M. L., & Brickson, S. L. (2016). Organizational identity and institutional forces: Toward an integrative framework. In M. Pratt, M. Schultz, B. Ashforth, & D. Ravasi (Eds.), *Oxford handbook of organizational identity* (pp. 396–414). New York: Oxford University Press.

Besharov, M. L., & Smith, W. K. (2014). Multiple institutional logics in organizations: Explaining their varied nature and implications. *Academy of Management Review*, 39(3): 364–381.

Bhabha, H. K. (1994). *The location of culture*. New York: Routledge.

Binder, A. (2007). For love and money: Organizations' creative responses to multiple environmental logics. *Theory and Society*, 36(6): 547–571.

Bitektine, A. (2011). Toward a theory of social judgments of organizations: The case of legitimacy, reputation, and status. *Academy of Management Review*, 36(1): 151–179.

Bollingtoft, A., & Ulhoi, J. P. (2005). The networked business incubator: Leveraging entrepreneurial agency? *Journal of Business Venturing*, 20(2): 265–290.

Brewer, M., Ho, H.-K., Lee, J.-Y., & Miller, N. (1987). Social identity and social distance among Hong Kong schoolchildren. *Personality and Social Psychology Bulletin*, 13(2): 156–165.

Brownlee, J. (2009). Portents of pluralism. How hybrid regimes affect democratic transitions. *American Journal of Political Science*, 53(3): 515–532.

Bruton, G., Peng, M., Ahlstrom, D., Stan, C., & Xu, K. (2015). State-owned enterprises around the world as hybrid organizations. *Academy of Management Perspectives*, 29(1): 92–114.

Burrell, G., & Morgan, G. (1979). *Sociological paradigms and organisational analysis: Elements of the sociology of corporate life*. London: Heinemann.

Canales, R. (2014). Weaving straw into gold: Managing organizational tensions between standardization and flexibility in microfinance. *Organization Science*, 25(1): 1–28.

Cappellaro, G., & Dacin, M. T. (2015). Institutionalizing hybrids in Italian health care: The case of public–private organizations. Working paper.

Cheung, A. B. L. (2006). How autonomous are public corporations in Hong Kong? The case of the airport authority. *Public Organization Review*, 6(3): 221–236.

Chow, K. W., & Luo, L. Q. (2007). Contending approaches and models for rationalizing Chinese public organizations: The case of western China. *Public Organization Review*, 7(1): 69–91.

Christensen, T., & Lægreid, P. (2011). Complexity and hybrid public administration: Theoretical and empirical challenges. *Public Organization Review*, 11(4): 407–423.

Christiansen, L., & Lounsbury, M. (2013). Strange brew: Bridging logics via institutional bricolage and the reconstitution of organizational identity. In M. Lounsbury & E. Boxenbaum (Eds.), *Institutional logics in action: Research in the sociology of organizations*, vol. 39B (pp. 199–232). Bingley: Emerald Publishing Group.

Clark, S. M., Gioia, D. A., Ketchen, D. J., & Thomas, J. B. (2010). Transitional identity as a facilitator of organizational identity change during a merger. *Administrative Science Quarterly*, 55(3): 397–438.

Coase, R. H. (1937). The nature of the firm. *Economica*, 4(16): 386–405.

Coates, B., & Saloner, G. (2009). The profit in nonprofit. *Stanford Social Innovation Review*, 7(3): 68–71.

Considine, M., & Lewis, J. M. (2003). Bureaucracy, network, or enterprise? Comparing models of governance in Australia, Britain, the Netherlands, and New Zealand. *Public Administration Review*, 63(2): 131–140.

Cooney, K. (2006). The institutional and technical structuring of nonprofit ventures: Case study of a U.S. hybrid organization caught between two fields. *Voluntas*, 17(2): 137–155.

Corley, K., & Gioia, D. A. (2004). Identity ambiguity and change in the wake of a corporate spin-off. *Administrative Science Quarterly*, 49(2): 173–208.

Croft, C., Currie, G., & Lockett, A. (2015). Broken 'two-way windows'? An exploration of professional hybrids. *Public Administration*, 93(2): 380–394.

Currie, G., & Spyridonidis, D. (2015). Interpretation of multiple institutional logics on the ground: Actors' position, their agency and situational constraints in professionalized contexts. *Organization Studies*, 29(5): 855–865.

Czarniawska, B. (2009). Distant readings: Anthropology of organizations through novels. *Journal of Organizational Change Management*, 22(4): 357–372.

Dalpiaz, E., Rindova, V., & Ravasi, D. (2016). Combining logics to transform organizational agency: Blending industry and art at Alessi. *Administrative Science Quarterly*, 61(3): 347–392.

Davis, G. F., & Marquis, C. (2005). Prospects for organization theory in the early twenty-first century: Institutional fields and mechanisms. *Organization Science*, 16(4): 332–343.

Dees, J. G. (1998). Enterprising nonprofits. *Harvard Business Review*, 76(2): 55–67.

Delmestri, G. (2006). Streams of inconsistent institutional influences: Middle managers as carriers of multiple identities. *Human Relations*, 59(11): 1515–1541.

Denis, J.-L., Ferlie, E., & Van Gestel, N. (2015). Understanding hybridity in public organizations. *Public Administration*, 93(2): 273–289.

DiBenigno, J., & Kellogg, K. C. (2014). Beyond occupational differences. *Administrative Science Quarterly*, 59(3): 375–408.

DiMaggio, P., & Powell, W. (1983). The iron cage revisited: Institutional isomorphism and collective rationality in organizational fields. *American Sociological Review*, 48(2): 147–160.

Dimitriadis, S., Lee, M., Ramarajan, L. & Battilana, J. (Forthcoming). Blurring the boundaries between the social and commercial sectors: The interplay of gender and social context in the commercialization of social ventures. *Organization Science*, In Press.

Dukerich, J. M., Golden, B. R., & Shortell, S. M. (2002). Beauty is in the eye of the beholder: The impact of organizational identification, identity, and image on the cooperative behaviors of physicians. *Administrative Science Quarterly*, 47(3): 507–533.

Dunn, M. B., & Jones, C. (2010). Institutional logics and institutional pluralism: The contestation of care and science logics in medical education, 1967–2005. *Administrative Science Quarterly*, 55(1): 114–149.

Durand, R., & Jourdan, J. (2012). Jules or Jim: Alternative conformity to minority logics. *Academy of Management Journal*, 55(6): 1295–1315.

Dutton, J. E., & Dukerich, J. M. (1991). Keeping an eye on the mirror: Image and identity in organizational adaptation. *Academy of Management Journal*, 34(3): 517–554.

Ebrahim, A., Battilana, J., & Mair, J. (2014). The governance of social enterprises: Mission drift and accountability challenges in hybrid organizations. *Research in Organizational Behavior*, 34: 81–100.

Elsbach, K. (2001). Coping with hybrid organizational identities: Evidence from California legislative staff. In J. Wagner (Ed.), *Advances in qualitative organizational research*, vol. 3 (pp. 59–90). Oxford: Elsevier Science.

Farjoun, M. (2002). The dialectics of institutional development in emerging and turbulent fields: The history of pricing conventions in the on-line database industry. *Academy of Management Journal*, 45(5): 848–874.

Ferreira, S. (2014). Sociological observations of the third sector through systems theory: An analytical proposal. *Voluntas*, 25(6): 1671–1693.

Fiol, C. M. (1991). Managing culture as a competitive resource: An identity-based view of sustainable competitive advantage. *Journal of Management*, 17(1): 191–211.

Fiol, C. M., Pratt, M. G., & O'Connor, E. J. (2009). Managing intractable identity conflict. *Academy of Management Review*, 34(1): 32–55.

Foreman, P., & Whetten, D. A. (2002). Members' identification with multiple-identity organizations. *Organization Science*, 13(6): 618–635.

Fossestol, K., Breit, E., Andreassen, T. A., & Klemsdal, L. (2015). Managing institutional complexity in public sector reform: Hybridization in front-line service organizations. *Public Administration*, 93(2): 290–306.

Fotaki, M. (2011). Towards developing new partnerships in public services: Users as consumers, citizens and/or co-producers in health and social care in England and Sweden. *Public Administration*, 89(3): 933–955.

Friedland, R., & Alford, R. R. (1991). Bringing society back in: Symbols, practices, and institutional contradictions. In W. W. Powell & P. J. DiMaggio (Eds.), *The new institutionalism in organizational analysis* (pp. 232–266). Chicago: University of Chicago Press.

Gaertner, S. L., Dovidio, J. F., Anastasio, P. A., Bachman, B. A., & Rust, M. C. (1993). The common ingroup identity model: Recategorization and the reduction of intergroup bias. In W. Stroebe & M. Hewstone (Eds.), *European review of social psychology*, vol. 4 (pp. 1–26). New York: John Wiley.

Galaskiewicz, J., Bielefeld, W., & Dowell, M. (2006). Networks and organizational growth: A study of community based nonprofits. *Administrative Science Quarterly, 51*(3): 337–380.

Garcia-Zamor, J.-C., & Noll, S. (2009). Privatization of public services in Leipzig: A balancing act between efficiency and legitimacy. *Public Organization Review, 9*(1): 83–99.

George, G., Howard-Grenville, J., Joshi, A., & Tihanyi, L. (2016). Understanding and tackling societal grand challenges through management research. *Academy of Management Journal, 59*(6): 1880–1895.

Geretti, G., Humphrey, J., & Sturgeon, T. (2005). The governance of global value chains. *Review of International Political Economy, 12*(1): 78–104.

Gioia, D. A., & Thomas, J. B. (1996). Identity, image, and issue interpretation: Sensemaking during strategic change in academia. *Administrative Science Quarterly, 41*(3): 370–403.

Gioia, D. A., Patvardhan, S. D., Hamilton, A. L., & Corley, K. G. (2013). Organizational identity formation and change. *Academy of Management Annals, 7*(1): 123–193.

Gioia, D. A., Price, K. N., Hamilton, A. L., & Thomas, J. B. (2010). Forging an identity: An insider–outsider study of processes involved in the formation of organizational identity. *Administrative Science Quarterly, 55*(1): 1–46.

Gioia, D. A., Schultz, M., & Corley, K. G. (2000). Organizational identity, image, and adaptive instability. *Academy of Management Review, 25*(1): 63–81.

Glynn, M. A. (2000). When cymbals become symbols: Conflict over organizational identity within a symphony orchestra. *Organization Science, 11*(3): 285–298.

Glynn, M. A. (2008). Beyond constraint: How institutions enable organizational identities. In R. Greenwood, C. Oliver, R. Suddaby, & K. Sahlin-Andersson (Eds.), *The SAGE handbook of organizational institutionalism* (pp. 413–430). London: Sage.

Golden-Biddle, K., & Rao, H. (1997). Breaches in the boardroom: Organizational identity and conflicts of commitment in a nonprofit organization. *Organization Science, 8*(6): 593–611.

Goodrick, E., & Reay, T. (2011). Constellations of institutional logics: Changes in the professional work of pharmacists. *Work and Occupations, 38*(3): 372–416.

Greenwood, R., & Hinings, C. R. (1988). Organizational design types, tracks and the dynamics of strategic change. *Organization Studies, 9*(3): 293–316.

Greenwood, R., Diaz, A. M., Li, S. X., & Lorente, J. C. (2010). The multiplicity of institutional logics and the heterogeneity of organizational responses. *Organization Science, 21*(2): 521–539.

Greenwood, R., & Hinings, C. R. (1993). Understanding strategic change: The contribution of archetypes. *Academy of Management Journal, 36*(5): 1052–1081.

Greenwood, R., Raynard, M., Kodeih, F., Micelotta, E. R., & Lounsbury, M. (2011). Institutional complexity and organizational responses. *Academy of Management Annals, 5*(1): 317–371.

Greenwood, R., & Suddaby, R. (2006). Institutional entrepreneurship in mature fields: The big five accounting firms. *Academy of Management Journal, 49*(1): 27–48.

Gulbrandsen, M., Thune, T., Borlaug, S. B., & Hanson, J. (2015). Emerging hybrid practices in public–private research centres. *Public Administration, 93*(2): 363–379.

Guthrie, D. (1999). *Dragon in a three-piece suit: The emergence of capitalism in China.* Princeton, NJ: Princeton University Press.

Haigh, N., Kennedy, E. D., & Walker, J. (2015). Hybrid organizations as shape-shifters: Altering legal structure for strategic gain. *California Management Review, 57*(3): 59–82.

Hannan, M. T., & Freeman, J. (1984). Structural inertia and organizational change. *American Sociological Review, 49*(2): 149–164.

Hannan, M. T., Pólos, L., & Carroll, G. (2007). *Logics of organization theory: Audiences, codes, and ecologies.* Princeton, NJ: Princeton University Press.

Hatch, M., & Schultz, M. (2002). The dynamics of organizational identity. *Human Relations, 55*(8): 989–1018.

Haveman, H. A., & Rao, H. (1997). Structuring a theory of moral sentiments: Institutional and organizational coevolution in the early thrift industry. *American Journal of Sociology, 102*(6): 1606–1651.

Haveman, H. A., & Rao, H. (2006). Hybrid forms and the evolution of thrifts. *American Behavioral Scientist, 49*(7): 974–986.

Haveman, H. A., Rao, H., & Paruchuri, S. (2007). The winds of change: The progressive movement and the bureaucratization of thrift. *American Sociological Review, 72*(1): 117–142.

Hayllar, M. R., & Wettenhall, R. (2013). As public goes private, social emerges: The rise of social enterprise. *Public Organization Review, 13*(2): 207–217.

Hockerts, K. (2015). How hybrid organizations turn antagonistic assets into complementarities. *California Management Review, 57*(3): 83–106.

Hoffman, A. J. (2015). *How culture shapes the climate change debate.* Stanford, CA: Stanford University Press.

Hoffman, A. J., Badiane, K. K., & Haigh, N. (2012). Hybrid organizations as agents of positive social change: Bridging the for-profit and non-profit divide. In K. Golden-Biddle & J. E. Dutton (Eds.), *Using a positive lens to explore social change and organizations* (pp. 131–153). Hoboken, NJ: Taylor & Francis.

Hsu, G. (2006). Jacks of all trades and masters of none: Audiences' reactions to spanning genres in feature film production. *Administrative Science Quarterly*, *51*(3): 420–450.

Hsu, G., & Hannan, M. T. (2005). Identities, genres, and organizational forms. *Organization Science*, *16*(5): 474–490.

Hsu, G., Hannan, M. T., & Koçak, Ö. (2009). Multiple category memberships in markets: An integrative theory and two empirical tests. *American Sociological Review*, *74*(1): 150–169.

Hsu, G., Negro, G., & Perretti, F. (2012). Hybrids in Hollywood: A study of the production and performance of genre-spanning films. *Industrial and Corporate Change*, *21*(6): 1427–1450.

Hwang, H., & Powell, W. W. (2009). The rationalization of charity: The influences of professionalism in the nonprofit sector. *Administrative Science Quarterly*, *54*(2): 268–298.

Jarzabkowski, P., Smets, M., Bednarek, R., Burke, G., & Spee, P. (2013). Institutional ambidexterity: Leveraging institutional complexity in practice. In M. Lounsbury & E. Boxenbaum (Eds.), *Institutional logics in action: Research in the sociology of organizations,* vol. 39B (pp. 37–61). Bingley: Emerald Group Publishing.

Jay, J. (2013). Navigating paradox as a mechanism of change and innovation in hybrid organizations. *Academy of Management Journal*, *56*(1): 137–159.

Keister, L. A. (1998). Engineering growth: Business group structure and firm performance in China's transition economy. *American Journal of Sociology*, *104*(2): 404–440.

Kim, T.-Y., Shin, D., & Jeong, Y.-C. (2016). Inside the 'hybrid' iron cage: Political origins of hybridization. *Organization Science*, *27*(2): 428–445.

Kostova, T., Roth, K., & Dacin, M. T. (2008). Institutional theory in the study of multinational corporations: A critique and new directions. *Academy of Management Review*, *33*(4): 994–1006.

Kostova, T., & Zaheer, S. (1999). Organizational legitimacy under conditions of complexity: The case of multinational enterprises. *Academy of Management Review*, *24*(1): 64–81.

Kraatz, M., & Block, E. (2008). Organizational implications of institutional pluralism. In R. Greenwood, C. Oliver, R. Suddaby, & K. Sahlin-Andersson (Eds.), *The SAGE handbook of organizational institutionalism* (pp. 243–276). London: Sage.

Lee, E. W. Y. (2005). Nonprofit development in Hong Kong: The case of a statist-corporatist regime. *Voluntas*, *16*(1): 51–68.

Lee, M. (2015). Mission and markets? The organizational viablity of hybrid social ventures. Working paper.

Lee, M., & Battilana, J. (2016). Experience matters: Vicarious and experiential imprinting and the founding of hybrid social ventures. Working paper.

Lee, M., Battilana, J., & Wang, T. (2014). Building an infrastructure for empirical research methods: Challenges and opportunities. In J. C. Short, D. J. Ketchen, & D. D. Bergh (Eds.), *Social entrepreneurship and research methods*, vol. 9 (pp. 241–264). Bingley: Emerald Group Publishing.

Lee, M., & Jay, J. (2015). Strategic responses to hybrid social ventures. *California Management Review*, *57*(3): 126–148.

Lewis, M. W. (2000). Exploring paradox: Toward a more comprehensive guide. *Academy of Management Review*, *25*(4): 760–776.

Lincoln, Y. S., & Guba, E. G. (1985). *Naturalistic inquiry*. Beverly Hills, CA: Sage.

Lindqvist, K. (2013). Hybrid governance: The case of household solid waste management in Sweden. *Public Organization Review*, *13*(2): 143–154.

Liu, M., & Wezel, F. C. (2015). Davids against Goliath? Collective identities and the market success of peripheral organizations during resource partitioning. *Organization Science*, *26*(1): 293–309.

Lounsbury, M. (2007). A tale of two cities: Competing logics and practice variation in the professionalizing of mutual funds. *Academy of Management Journal*, *50*(2): 289–307.

Mair, J., Battilana, J., & Cardenas, J. (2012). Organizing for society: A typology of social entrepreneuring models. *Journal of Business Ethics*, *111*(3): 353–373.

Mair, J., Mayer, J., & Lutz, E. (2015). Navigating institutional plurality: Organizational governance in hybrid organizations. *Organization Studies*, *36*(6): 713–739.

Mair, J., Wolf, M., & Seelos, C. (2016). Scaffolding: A process of transforming patterns of inequality in small-scale societies. *Academy of Management Journal*, *59*(6): 2021–2044.

Marano, V., & Kostova, T. (2016). Unpacking the institutional complexity in the adoption of CSR practices in multinational enterprises. *Journal of Management Studies*, *53*(1): 28–54.

Margolis, J. D., & Walsh, J. P. (2003). Misery loves companies: Rethinking social initiatives by business. *Administrative Science Quarterly*, *48*(2): 268–305.

McGivern, G., Currie, G., Ferlie, E., Fitzgerald, L., & Waring, J. (2015). Hybrid manager-professionals' identity work: The maintenance and hybridization of medical professionalism in managerial contexts. *Public Administration*, *93*(2): 412–432.

McPherson, C. M., & Sauder, M. (2013). Logics in action: Managing institutional complexity in a drug court. *Administrative Science Quarterly*, *58*(2): 165–196.

Meyer, J., & Rowan, B. (1977). Institutionalized organizations: Formal structure as myth and ceremony. *American Journal of Sociology*, *83*(1): 340–363.

Minkoff, D. C. (2002). The emergence of hybrid organizational forms: Combining identity-based service provision and political action. *Nonprofit and Voluntary Sector Quarterly, 31*(3): 377–401.

Miron-Spektor, E., Gino, F., & Argote, L. (2011). Paradoxical frames and creative sparks: Enhancing individual creativity through conflict and integration. *Organizational Behavior and Human Decision Processes, 116*(2): 229–240.

Moss, T. W., Short, J. C., Payne, G. T., & Lumpkin, G. T. (2011). Dual identities in social ventures: An exploratory study. *Entrepreneurship Theory and Practice, 35*(4): 805–830.

Nee, V. (1992). Organizational dynamics of market transition: Hybrid forms, property rights, and mixed economy in China. *Administrative Science Quarterly, 37*(1): 1–27.

Nee, V., & Matthews, R. (1996). Market transition and societal transformation in reforming state socialism. *Annual Review of Sociology,* 22: 401–435.

Nee, V., & Opper, S. (2012). *Capitalism from below: Markets and institutional change in China.* Cambridge, MA: Harvard University Press.

Nigam, A., & Ocasio, W. (2010). Event attention, environmental sensemaking, and change in institutional logics: An inductive analysis of the effects of public attention to Clinton's health care reform initiative. *Organization Science, 21*(4): 823–841.

Okhuysen, G., & Bonardi, J. P. (2011). Editors' comments: The challenges of building theory by combining lenses. *Academy of Management Review, 36*(1): 6–11.

Oliver, A. L., & Montgomery, K. (2000). Creating a hybrid organizational form from parental blueprints: The emergence and evolution of knowledge firms. *Human Relations, 53*(1): 33–56.

O'Reilly, C., & Tushman, M. (2008). Ambidexterity as a dynamic capability: Resolving the innovator's dilemma. *Research in Organizational Behavior,* 28: 185–206.

Pache, A.-C., Battilana, J., & Santos, F. (2015). Governance in hybrid organizations: How can boards contribute to the joint pursuit of social and commercial goals? Working paper.

Pache, A.-C., & Santos, F. (2013a). Embedded in hybrid contexts: How individuals in organizations respond to competing institutional logics. In M. Lounsbury & E. Boxenbaum (Eds.), *Institutional logics in action: Research in the sociology of organizations,* vol. 39B (pp. 3–35). Bingley: Emerald Group Publishing.

Pache, A.-C., & Santos, F. (2013b). Inside the hybrid organization: Selective coupling as a response to competing institutional logics. *Academy of Management Journal, 56*(4): 972–1001.

Page, A., & Katz, R. A. (2012). The truth about Ben & Jerry's. *Stanford Social Innovation Review, 10*(4): 39–43.

Paolella, L., & Durand, R. (2016). Category spanning, evaluation, and performance: Revised theory and test on the corporate law market. *Academy of Management Journal, 59*(1): 330–351.

Parsons, T. (1960). *Structure and process in modern society.* Glencoe, IL: Free Press.

Peifer, J. L. (2014). The institutional complexity of religious mutual funds: Appreciating the uniqueness of societal logics. In P. Tracey, N. Phillips, & M. Lounsbury (Eds.), *Religion and organization theory: Research in the sociology of organizations,* vol. 41 (pp. 339–368). Bingley: Emerald Group Publishing.

Peng, M. W., & Heath, P. S. (1996). The growth of the firm in planned economies in transition: Institutions, organizations, and strategic choice. *Academy of Management Review, 21*(2): 492–528.

Perkmann, M., & Spicer, A. (2007). 'Healing the scars of history': Projects, skills and field strategy in institutional entrepreneurship. *Organization Studies, 28*(7): 1101–1122.

Pestoff, V. (2014). Hybridity, coproduction, and third sector social services in Europe. *American Behavioral Scientist, 58*(11): 1412–1424.

Phillips, D. J., Turco, C. J., & Zuckerman, E. W. (2013). Betrayal as market barrier: Identity-based limits to diversification among high-status corporate law firms. *American Journal of Sociology, 118*(4): 1023–1054.

Pieterse, J. N. (1995). Globalization as hybridization. In M. Featherstone, L. Scott, & R. Robertson (Eds.), *Global modernities* (pp. 45–68). London: Sage.

Pieterse, J. N. (2001). Hybridity, so what? The anti-hybridity backlash and the riddles of recognition. *Theory, Culture & Society,* 18(2–3): 219–245.

Podolny, J. M. (2005). *Status signals: A sociological study of market competition.* Princeton, NJ: Princeton University Press.

Podolny, J. M., & Page, K. L. (1998). Network forms of organization. *Annual Review of Sociology,* 24: 57–76.

Pólos, L., Hannan, M. T., & Carroll, G. R. (2002). Foundations of a theory of social forms. *Industrial and Corporate Change, 11*(1): 85–115.

Powell, W. W. (1990). Neither market nor hierarchy: Network forms of organization. *Research in Organizational Behavior,* 12: 295–336.

Powell, W. W., & Sandholtz, K. W. (2012). Amphibious entrepreneurs and the emergence of organizational forms. *Strategic Entrepreneurship Journal, 6*(2): 94–115.

Pratt, M. G., & Corley, K. (2007). Managing multiple organizational identities: On identity ambiguity, identity conflict, and members' reactions. In C. A. Bartel, S. Blader, & A. Wrzesniewski (Eds.), *Identity and the modern organization* (pp. 99–118). Mahwah, NJ: Lawrence Erlbaum Associates.

Pratt, M. G., & Foreman, P. O. (2000). Classifying managerial responses to multiple organizational identities. *Academy of Management Review*, *25*(1): 18–42.

Pratt, M. G., & Rafaeli, A. (1997). Organizational dress as a symbol of multilayered social identities. *Academy of Management Journal*, *40*(4): 862–898.

Ramarajan, L. (2014.) Past, present and future research on multiple identities: Toward an intrapersonal network approach. *Academy of Management Annals*, *8*(1): 589–659.

Ramus, T. A., Vaccaro, A., & Brusoni, S. (2016). Institutional complexity in turbulent times: Formalization, collaboration, and the emergence of blended logics. *Academy of Management Journal*, In Press.

Rao, H., Monin, P., & Durand, R. (2005). Border crossing: Bricolage and the erosion of categorical boundaries in French gastronomy. *American Sociological Review*, *70*(6): 968–991.

Rao, H., Morrill, C., & Zald, M. N. (2000). Power plays: How social movements and collective action create new organizational forms. *Research in Organizational Behavior*, 22: 237–281.

Ravasi, D., & Schultz, M. (2006). Responding to organizational identity threats: Exploring the role of organizational culture. *Academy of Management Journal*, *49*(3): 433–458.

Rawhouser, H., Cummings, M., & Crane, A. (2015). Benefit corporation legislation and the emergence of a social hybrid category. *California Management Review*, *57*(3): 13–35.

Reast, J., Lindgreen, A., Vanhamme, J., & Maon, F. (2010). The Manchester super casino: Experience and learning in a cross-sector social partnership. *Journal of Business Ethics*, *94*(1): 197–218.

Reay, T., & Hinings, C. R. (2005). The recomposition of an organizational field: Health care in Alberta. *Organization Studies*, *26*(3): 351–384.

Reay, T., & Hinings, C. R. (2009). Managing the rivalry of competing institutional logics. *Organization Studies*, *30*(6): 629–652.

Rothenberg, A. (1979). *The emerging goddess*. Chicago, IL: University of Chicago Press.

Ruef, M. (2000). The emergence of organizational forms: A community ecology approach. *American Journal of Sociology*, *106*(3): 658–714.

Ruef, M., & Patterson, K. (2009). Credit and classification: The impact of industry boundaries in nineteenth-century America. *Administrative Science Quarterly*, *54*(3): 486–520.

Sabeti, H. (2011). The for-benefit enterprise. *Harvard Business Review*, *89*(11): 98–104.

Santos, F., Pache, A.-C., & Birkholz, C. (2015). Making hybrids work: Aligning business models and organizational design for social enterprises. *California Management Review*, *57*(3): 36–58.

Schemeil, Y. (2013). Bringing international organization in: Global institutions as adaptive hybrids. *Organization Studies*, *34*(2): 219–252.

Schiersmann, C. (2014). Hybridity and governance changes in continuing education. *American Behavioral Scientist*, *58*(11): 1464–1474.

Schneiberg, M. (2011). Toward an organizationally diverse American capitalism? Cooperative, mutual, and local, state-owned enterprise. *Seattle University Law Review*, *34*(4): 1409–1434.

Scott, W. R., Ruef, M., Mendel, P. J., & Caronna, C. A. (2000). *Institutional change and healthcare organizations: From professional dominance to managed care*. Chicago, IL: University of Chicago Press.

Seelos, C., Mair, J., Battilana, J., & Dacin, T. (2011). The embeddedness of social entrepreneurship: Understanding variation across geographic communities. In C. Marquis, M. Lounsbury, & R. Greenwood (Eds.), *Communities and organizations: Research in the sociology of organizations*, vol. 33 (pp. 333–363). Bingley: Emerald Group Publishing.

Selznick, P. (1957). *Leadership in administration: A sociological interpretation*. New York: Harper & Row.

Seo, M.-G., & Creed, W. (2002). Institutional contradictions, praxis, and institutional change: A dialectical perspective. *Academy of Management Review*, *27*(2): 222–247.

Shane, S. (1996). Hybrid organizational arrangements and their implications for firm growth and survival: A study of new franchisors. *Academy of Management Journal*, *39*(1): 216–234.

Shimoni, B., & Bergmann, H. (2006). Managing in a changing world: From multiculturalism to hybridization: The production of hybrid management cultures in Israel, Thailand, and Mexico. *Academy of Management Perspectives*, *20*(3): 76–89.

Smets, M., Jarzabkowski, P., Burke, G. T., & Spee, P. (2015). Reinsurance trading in Lloyd's of London: Balancing conflicting-yet-complementary logics in practice. *Academy of Management Journal*, *58*(3): 932–970.

Smith, W. K. (2014). Dynamic decision making: A model of senior leaders managing strategic paradoxes. *Academy of Management Journal*, *57*(6): 1592–1623.

Smith, W. K., & Besharov, M. L. (2016). Bowing before dual gods: How structured flexibility sustains organizational hybridity. Cornell University working paper, Ithaca NY.

Smith, W. K., Besharov, M. L., Wessels, A. K., & Chertok, M. (2012). A paradoxical leadership model for social entrepreneurs: Challenges, leadership skills, and pedagogical tools for managing social and commercial demands. *Academy of Management Learning and Education*, *11*(3): 463–478.

Smith, W. K., Gonin, M., & Besharov, M. L. (2013). Managing social-business tensions: A review and research agenda for social enterprise. *Business Ethics Quarterly*, *23*(3): 407–442.

Smith, W. K., & Lewis, M. W. (2011). Toward a theory of paradox: A dynamic equilibrium model of organizing. *Academy of Management Review*, *36*(2): 381–403

Smith, W. K., & Tushman, M. (2005). Managing strategic contradictions: A top management team model for managing innovation streams. *Organization Science*, *16*(5): 522–536.

Spyridonidis, D., Hendy, J., & Barlow, J. (2015). Understanding hybrid roles: The role of identity processes amongst physicians. *Public Administration*, *93*(2): 395–411.

Suchman, M. C. (1995). Managing legitimacy: Strategic and institutional approaches. *Academy of Management Review*, *20*(3): 571–610.

Sud, M., Vansandt, C. V., & Baugous, A. M. (2009). Social entrepreneurship: The role of institutions. *Journal of Business Ethics*, *85*(1): 201–216.

Suedfeld, P., Tetlock, P., & Streufert, S. (1992). Conceptual/integrative complexity. In C. Smith, J. Atkinson, D. McClelland, & J. Verof (Eds.), *Motivation and personality: Handbook of thematic content analysis* (pp. 393–400). Cambridge: Cambridge University Press.

Suhomlinova, O. O. (1999). Constructive destruction: Transformation of Russian state-owned construction enterprises during market transition. *Organization Studies*, *20*(3): 451–484.

Tan, J., & Wang, L. (2011). MNC strategic responses to ethical pressure: An institutional logic perspective. *Journal of Business Ethics*, *98*(3): 373–390.

Teelken, C. (2015). Hybridity, coping mechanisms, and academic performance management: Comparing three countries. *Public Administration*, *93*(2): 307–323.

Thompson, P., & Williams, R. (2014). Taking your eyes off the objective: The relationship between income sources and satisfaction with achieving objectives in the UK third sector. *Voluntas*, *25*(1): 109–137.

Thornton, P. H. (2002). The rise of the corporation in a craft industry: Conflict and conformity in institutional logics. *Academy of Management Journal*, *45*(1): 81–101.

Thornton, P. H., & Ocasio, W. (1999). Institutional logics and the historical contingency of power in organizations: Executive succession in the higher education publishing industry, 1958–1990. *American Journal of Sociology*, *105*(3): 801–843.

Thornton, P. H., & Ocasio, W. (2008). Institutional logics. In R. Greenwood, C. Oliver, R. Suddaby, & K. Sahlin-Andersson (Eds.), *The SAGE handbook of organizational institutionalism* (pp. 1–46). London: Sage.

Thornton, P. H., Ocasio, W., & Lounsbury, M. (2012). *The institutional logics perspective: A new approach to culture, structure and process*. Oxford: Oxford University Press.

Tolbert, P. S., David, R. J., & Sine, W. D. (2011). Studying choice and change: The intersection of institutional theory and entrepreneurship research. *Organization Science*, *22*(5): 1332–1344.

Tracey, P., Phillips, N., & Jarvis, O. (2011). Bridging institutional entrepreneurship and the creation of new organizational forms: A multilevel model. *Organization Science*, *22*(1): 60–80.

Tushman, M. L., Smith, W. K., Wood, R., Westerman, G., & O'Reilly, C. A. (2010). Organizational design and innovation streams. *Industrial and Corporate Change*, *19*(5): 1331–1366.

Utting, P., & Zammit, A. (2009). United Nations-business partnerships: Good intentions and contradictory agendas. *Journal of Business Ethics*, *90*(1): 39–56.

Uzzi, B. (1997). Social structure and competition in interfirm networks: The paradox of embeddedness. *Administrative Science Quarterly*, *42*(1): 35–67.

Vora, D., & Kostova, T. (2007). A model of dual organizational identification in the context of multinational enterprise. *Journal of Organizational Behavior*, *28*(3): 327–350.

Voronov, M., De Clercq, D., & Hinings, C. R. (2013). Institutional complexity and logic engagement: An investigation of Ontario fine wine. *Human Relations*, *66*(12): 1563–1596.

Voss, Z. G., Cable, D. M., & Voss, G. B. (2006). Organizational identity and firm performance: What happens when leaders disagree about 'who we are'? *Organization Science*, *17*(6): 741–755.

Walder, A. G. (1995). Local governments as industrial firms: An organizational analysis of China's transitional economy. *American Journal of Sociology*, *101*(2): 263–301.

Waring, J. (2015). Mapping the public sector diaspora: Towards a model of inter-sectoral cultural hybridity using evidence from the English healthcare reforms. *Public Administration*, *93*(2): 345–362.

Weick, K. E., & Quinn, R. E. (1999). Organizational change and development. *Annual Review of Psychology*, 50: 361–386.

Whetten, D. (2006). Albert and Whetten revisited: Strengthening the concept of organizational identity. *Journal of Management Inquiry*, *15*(3): 219–234.

Whetten, D., & Mackey, A. (2002). A social actor conception of organizational identity and its implications for the study of organizational reputation. *Business and Society*, *41*(4): 393–414.

White, S., & Siu-Yun, L. S. (2005). Distinguishing costs of cooperation and control in alliances. *Strategic Management Journal*, *26*(10): 913–932.

Williamson, O. E. (1985). *The economic institutions of capitalism: Firms, markets, relational contracting*. New York; London: Free Press; Collier Macmillan.

Williamson, O. E. (1991). Comparative economic organization: The analysis of discrete structural alternatives. *Administrative Science Quarterly*, *36*(2): 269–296.

Williamson, O. E. (1996). Economic organization: The case for candor. *Academy of Management Review, 21*(1): 48–57.

Wry, T., Lounsbury, M., & Jennings, P. D. (2014). Hybrid vigor: Securing venture capital by spanning categories in nanotechnology. *Academy of Management Journal, 57*(5): 1309–1333.

Wry, T., & York, J. G. (2016). An identity-based approach to social enterprise. *Academy of Management Review*, In Press.

Xin, K. R., & Pearce, J. L. (1996). Guanxi: Connections as substitutes for formal institutional support. *Academy of Management Journal, 39*(6): 1641–1658.

Xu, D., Lu, J. W., & Gu, Q. (2014). Organizational forms and multi-population dynamics. *Administrative Science Quarterly, 59*(3): 517–547.

Yousfi, H. (2014). Rethinking hybridity in postcolonial contexts: What changes and what persists? The Tunisian case of Poulina's managers. *Organization Studies, 35*(3): 393–421.

Zhao, E. Y., & Grimes, M. (2016). Commercial pressures, organizational identity commitments, and mission drift among social enterprises. *Academy of Management Best Paper Proceedings*.

Zhou, X. G. (2000). Economic transformation and income inequality in urban China: Evidence from panel data. *American Journal of Sociology, 105*(4): 1135–1174.

Zilber, T. (2002). Institutionalization as an interplay between actions, meanings, and actors: The case of a rape crisis center in Israel. *Academy of Management Journal, 45*(1): 234–254.

Zuckerman, E. W. (1999). The categorical imperative: Securities analysts and the illegitimacy discount. *American Journal of Sociology, 104*(5): 1398–1438.

Zuckerman, E. W., Kim, T.-Y., Ukanwa, K., & von Rittmann, J. (2003). Robust identities or nonentities? Typecasting in the feature film labor market. *American Journal of Sociology, 108*(5): 1018–1073.

APPENDIX: JOURNALS INCLUDED IN STRUCTURED LITERATURE SEARCH

Academy of Management Annals; Academy of Management Journal; Academy of Management Perspectives; Academy of Management Review; Administrative Science Quarterly; American Behavioral Scientist; American Journal of Political Science; American Journal of Sociology; American Review of Public Administration; American Sociological Review; Annual Review of Sociology; Business Ethics Quarterly; Business History; Business History Review; California Management Review; Development; Enterprise and Society; Entrepreneurship Theory and Practice; Episteme; Ethics; Global Governance; Harvard Business Review; Human Relations; International Studies Quarterly; Journal of Applied Ethics; Journal of Business Ethics; Journal of Business Venturing; Journal of Public Administration Research and Theory; Journal of Social Entrepreneurship; Management Science; MIT Sloan Management Review; Nonprofit and Voluntary Sector Quarterly; Organization Science; Organization Studies; Philosophy and Public Affairs; Public Administration; Public Organization Review; Social Forces; Stanford Social Innovation Review; Strategic Entrepreneurship Journal; Strategic Management Journal; Voluntas; World Development

6

Fields, Institutional Infrastructure and Governance

C.R. (Bob) Hinings, Danielle Logue and
Charlene Zietsma

INTRODUCTION

In their seminal article, Greenwood, Raynard, Kodeih, Micelotta and Lounsbury (2011) introduce the idea of institutional infrastructure while discussing institutional complexity. They drew attention to institutional infrastructure as the features that bind a field together and govern field interactions. They also suggested that the lack of a developed conceptual framework for comparing fields could be dealt with, at least partially, by an analysis of institutional infrastructure. One of our aims in this chapter is to draw together these two ideas of institutional infrastructure and field comparison to review whether and how the former differs across fields.

We argue that a field's institutional infrastructure can be usefully delineated for the purpose of better understanding different states or conditions of fields and how they affect processes of field maintenance and change. However, there is relatively little work on institutional infrastructure. As such,

we will first explore the definitions of organizational fields, as the bounded area within which infrastructure exists as a way of elaborating that concept beyond the descriptors used by Greenwood et al. (2011). Following on from that we explore the use of the concept institutional infrastructure across several scholarly fields, and develop our definition and elaborate the field elements involved. We argue that clarifying differences in field infrastructure would allow us to develop a better understanding of organizational field dynamics, enabling field comparisons and improved theorizing.

The idea of institutional infrastructure is related to that of governance of organizational fields. In developing our arguments, we consider governance as the formal mechanisms that maintain the 'rules of the game' within a field. Institutional infrastructure thus includes field governance arrangements, but also other cultural, structural and relational elements that generate the normative, cognitive and regulative forces that reinforce field governance, and render field logics material and field governance performable. However, as with institutional infrastructure, there is very little written on the governance of organizational fields *per se*. As Kraatz and Block (2008) point out, there has been work on the role of the state, professions and field-level actors in general, that examine influence and control. But this has not been developed as *governance*, yet we know that questions of control are central to understanding fields. So we explore how the concept has been used, develop a definition and examine the relationship between institutional infrastructure and governance.

To examine these relationships more closely, we analyze three different fields (professional services, forestry and impact investing) describing their institutional infrastructure, its degree of elaboration and associated governance mechanisms. From the comparison of the infrastructure of those fields, we then describe different configurations and states of institutional infrastructure and discuss their implications for the maintenance and change of organizational fields and their associated governance. We close with a number of provocations for further study of institutional infrastructure, field governance and field-level institutional dynamics.

ORGANIZATIONAL FIELDS

The concept of an organizational field is one of the cornerstones of institutional theory (Wooten & Hoffman, 2008; Scott, 2014), an 'increasingly useful level of analysis' (Reay & Hinings, 2005: 351), and the concept that is 'vitally connected to the agenda of understanding institutional processes and organizations' (Scott, 2014: 219; Wooten and Hoffman, 2017; Hardy and Maguire, 2017; Kraatz and Block, 2017). Yet, definitions of organizational fields vary in their scope and emphasis, and we have no clear classification of different types or conditions of

fields (Greenwood et al., 2011; Zietsma, Groenewegen, Logue, & Hinings, 2017). Various studies have described fields as being in different states or conditions, such as emerging (Maguire, Hardy, & Lawrence, 2004), mature (Greenwood, Suddaby, & Hinings, 2002; Greenwood & Suddaby, 2006), fragmented (Meyer, Scott, & Strang, 1987), or turbulent (Farjoun, 2002).

The terms 'organizational fields' and 'institutional fields' (Wooten and Hoffman, 2008; Scott, 2014) are often used interchangeably (Meyer, 2008). Other related terms include 'strategic action fields' (Fligstein & McAdam, 2012) and simply fields (Bourdieu, 1986). Most scholars in the institutional theory of organizations use DiMaggio and Powell's definition, which states that fields comprise 'a recognized area of institutional life: key suppliers, resource and product consumers, regulatory agencies and other organizations that produce similar services or products' (1983: 148). This definition appears to privilege relationships among actors, or networks, and yet the structuration arguments on which it is based also emphasize shared understandings of power, knowledge, identities and boundaries among actors, as fields are formed by

> an increase in the extent of interaction among organizations in the field; the emergence of sharply defined inter-organizational structures of domination and patterns of coalition; an increase in the information load with which organizations in a field must contend; and the development of a mutual awareness among participants in a set of organizations that they are involved in a common enterprise. (DiMaggio & Powell, 1983: 148)

Scott's definition of organizational fields, 'a collection of diverse, interdependent organizations that participate in a common meaning system' (Scott, 2014: 106), emphasizes these shared understandings, as do definitions like Greenwood and Suddaby's (2006: 28), defining the organizational field as 'clusters of organizations and occupations whose boundaries, identities and interactions are defined and stabilized by shared institutional logics'.

Yet other definitions of fields emphasize conflict, rather than sharedness. Bourdieu, for example, viewed the field as 'networks of social relations, structured systems of social positions within which struggles or maneuvers take place over resources, stakes and access' (Oakes, Townley, & Cooper, 1998: 260). While this definition doesn't necessarily indicate differences in meaning systems (simply competition over the pie), Hoffman (1999: 351) laid the foundation for differences in meaning systems by arguing that an organizational field

> forms around a central issue – such as the protection of the natural environment – rather than a central technology or market … fields become centers of debates in which competing interests negotiate over issue interpretation. As a result, competing institutions may lie within individual populations (or classes of constituencies) that inhabit a field.

Recent work extends this view that fields may be contested by focusing upon multiple, often competing, institutional logics (Reay & Hinings, 2005, 2009; Greenwood et al., 2011). A major thrust of this body of work has been on the movement from one logic to another within a field or, more recently, managing the existence of multiple logics in a field (Reay & Hinings, 2009; Scott, 2014). Indeed, the emphasis in discussing fields over the past decade has been primarily focused on the element of meaning, under the rubric of institutional logics (Thornton, Ocasio, & Lounsbury, 2012), though the idea of a plurality of actors being related to a plurality of logics brings networks and logics together to some extent (Hoffman, 1999; Lounsbury, 2002; Dunn & Jones, 2010; Voronov, DeClerq, & Hinings, 2013).

It is because of the emphasis on institutional logics in organizational fields that Greenwood et al. (2011) introduced the idea of institutional infrastructure. It is a recognition that fields are more than logics and directs attentions to the structural elements underpinning field activity. For example,

the positions of actors, their networks and relations, how they are governed, are key components of organizational fields. Power relations and subject positions, defined as 'the socially "constructed" and legitimated identities available in a field' (Maguire et al., 2004: 658), are central to both Bourdieu's (1984) conceptualization of fields and also to Fligstein and McAdams' (2012) idea of strategic action field. DiMaggio and Powell (1983) list suppliers, resource and product consumers, regulators and others. And they together with Wooten and Hoffman (2008) and Scott (2014) emphasize that these actors are in networks of relationships. Indeed, DiMaggio (1995) regretted that the network aspect of their argument had been lost. Padgett and Powell (2012: 2), from their work on fields, say 'in the short run, actors create relations; in the long run, relations create actors'.

Such relations are made performable and reinforced by governance and field coordinating structures, practices and organizational structures that regulate and regularize day-to-day interactions in fields. Together, these elements are the 'interlaced material, discursive, and organizational dimensions of field structure', which align to create field stability (Levy & Scully, 2007: 971). It means that changing any one element may not be sustainable, if other elements overlap and reinforce old patterns, maintaining the field much as it was. Thus it is important to understand the *set* of institutions, or the institutional infrastructure and its elaboration and coherency in a field, in order to understand governance as well as field dynamics and change.

INSTITUTIONAL INFRASTRUCTURE

The idea of infrastructure is of the basic physical and organizational structures and facilities that are needed for the operation of a society or enterprise. 'Infra' itself refers to 'below, underneath, beneath' (*Oxford English Dictionary*). So, in examining *institutional* infrastructure we are looking, first, for the elements that provide for its elaboration and coherency in a field; second, how such elements are organized as to overlap with and underpin the formal governance of a field.

Conceptual Roots

The origins of the concept of 'institutional infrastructure' are in comparative political economy (Hamilton & Biggart, 1988; Soskice, 1991; Ostrom, Schroeder, & Wynne, 1993; Piatkowski, 2002), though the term has been used across multiple scholarly fields. The political economy work has compared the formal (e.g., legal and regulatory systems of a nation) and informal institutions (e.g., cultural norms and values of doing business) in national innovation and business systems, finding both influential for economic outcomes. For example, institutional infrastructure elements of democracy (Rodrick, 1997), income inequality, sociopolitical stability, and other measures of institutional quality (Alesina & Perotti, 1996) have been studied in relation to economic growth (Gimenez & Sanau, 2007), and corruption, the rule of law, bureaucracy, repudiation of contracts and risk of expropriation have been studied in relation to economic performance. Institutional infrastructure is seen as the set of political, legal and cultural institutions (Boettke, 1994), that form the backdrop for economic activity and governance, enabling (or constraining) its smooth operation. These elements overlap, reinforce one another, and may sometimes substitute for one another. Marquis and Raynard (2015), for example, describe how informal institutional infrastructural elements, such as networks and business groups, intermediary organizations, and business processes, may substitute for missing formal institutional infrastructure in emerging markets.

Work on transnationalization (Djelic & Quack, 2008), and globalization and world society theory (Drori, 2008) has also examined the development of institutional infrastructure in the form of institutions across national boundaries that enable/constrain and govern trade (Djelic & Quack, 2008). There has been an increase in these international organizations, such as the World Trade Organization, NAFTA, GATS, and associated regulatory networks such as the International Competition Network, the SEC, that have become institutionalized. 'Many non-governmental organizations have been established that engage in standard setting, accreditation and other forms of soft regulation' (Djelic & Quack, 2008: 311). Drori (2008) recognizes this development of an institutional infrastructure at the transnational level, through the lens of world society theory, emphasizing 'the diffuse state of authority of the global system, on the role of institutional mechanisms in the cross-national diffusion of ideas and practices, and on the rationalizing and standardizing impact of international organizations, the professions, and the universalized models they carry' (p. 449).

Institutional infrastructure has also been used to study smaller social groups. Within neighborhoods, institutional infrastructure has been used to describe 'the level and quality of formal organizations in the neighborhood', measured by the existence of neighborhood organizations and their ability to influence policy makers on behalf of the neighborhood (Temkin & Rohe, 1998: 70). In education, the institutional infrastructure for coordinating children's services was noted to include five aspects: '(a) convening and goal-structuring processes, (b) institutional interests and reward systems, (c) relations to external environments through institutional activity, (d) communication linkages, and (e) institutional conventions' (Smylie & Crowson, 1996: 3). Again, both formal and informal institutions are included, though it must be acknowledged that institutional infrastructure at the level of smaller or more local groups is affected by the societal infrastructure within which the group is embedded.

Elements of Institutional Infrastructure in Organizational Theory

In organization theory *per se*, the idea of institutional infrastructure reflects understandings of the embeddedness of organizations within fields and the structuration of fields that occurs through interactions and institutional activity amongst actors (DiMaggio & Powell, 1983; Dacin, Ventresca, & Beal, 1999). For example, Waddock (2008) sees infrastructure being developed through activities such as certifying, assuring and reporting against principles, codes and standards; by forming new associations and networks of relations among organizations. Compagni, Mele and Ravasi (2015) emphasize the importance of constructing institutional infrastructure through professional associations and conferences to structure social relationships, develop field narratives of quality and contribute to the diffusion of new practices. The emphasis is on a set of institutions whose coherency and degree of elaboration underpin field activity, and interact with formal governance systems.

Greenwood et al. (2011) specifically use the term institutional infrastructure in developing their arguments about institutional complexity. They mention: collective actors (especially professional associations, and the state); social control agents; infomediaries; tournament rituals; theorization; mechanisms of enforcement; and state regulation. They have no definition of institutional infrastructure *per se,* but their descriptors are primarily a set of actors or structures which have the role of judging, governing or organizing other actors in the field. Collectively, they provide the structures by which status in the field is determined, by which interests and values are made collective and enacted, and by which the behavior of rank-and-file field members

is guided or enforced. These authors see institutional infrastructure as important in producing a framework for comparing fields. In particular, they draw attention to and stress the role of collective actors such as professional associations, international, national and local governments. They also point to the processes that bind a field together as part of institutional infrastructure, such as mechanisms of enforcement and various kinds of regulation or field governance. These ideas are taken up by Raaijmakers et al. (2015) who particularly mention professional associations, health and safety inspection agencies and media as part of institutional infrastructure that underpins the governance of the field. Bell, Filatotchev and Aguilera (2014) similarly draw attention to the importance of regulatory institutions, governmental organizations, legislation and court decisions as 'primary regulative agents'. Other authors refer to status conferring events or structures such as awards (Anand & Watson, 2004) or quality ratings, accreditation or standards bodies (Sauder, 2008), conferences and professional associations (Lampel & Meyer, 2008; Compagni et al., 2015), fairs and film festivals (Moeran & Strandgaard Pedersen, 2011), and coordinating mechanisms or collective interest organizations such as industry collaborative R&D, lobbying or trade bodies (Gurses & Ozcan, 2015), market information providers (Marquis & Raynard, 2015), and legitimized structures such as organizational templates (Greenwood et al., 2002; Suddaby & Greenwood, 2005), as components of a field's institutional infrastructure.

Thus, the concept of institutional infrastructure is defined as the set of institutions that prevail in a field. This structural approach to understanding field dynamics provides two benefits: (1) redirecting attention to understandings of field dynamics as beyond logics and meaning, and (2) offering opportunity to compare across fields by having a means by which to define and typologize field conditions. While the definition of institutional infrastructure is seemingly all encompassing, what matters for understanding field dynamics and comparing conditions across fields is considering its degree of elaboration and its coherency (Zietsma et al., 2017). Thus, based on these conceptual roots, suggestive theorizing by Greenwood et al. (2011) and our review of the concept and its (limited) use we consider main elements of institutional infrastructure to include collective interest organizations, regulators, informal governance bodies, field-configuring events, status differentiators, organizational templates, categories or labels, and norms.

INSTITUTIONAL INFRASTRUCTURE AND GOVERNANCE

Governance has been identified as a key aspect of fields (Fiss, 2007; Kraatz & Block, 2008; Scott, 2014). Studying field-level governance is about control, authority, influence and legitimacy. While these are ongoing themes in institutional theory (cf. Scott, 2014), they have not been set with the overall notion of governance. This is surprising given the emphasis that Fiss (2007), Kraatz and Block (2008), Fligstein and McAdam (2012) and Scott (2014) give to it, and also the extensive work that has been carried out on comparative organizational governance (Aguilera & Jackson, 2010). Scott (2014) states that governance is an important subset of relational systems within a field. Kraatz and Block (2008) point out that governance has not been treated as something that varies across fields, or examined in situations of pluralism or institutional complexity (unlike work on organizational governance). Scott (2014: 231) states that 'each organization field is characterized by a somewhat distinctive governance system' thus pointing the way to a comparative analysis of governance.

Thus, governance is a critical part of organizational fields; there has been work on governance actors without locating them within a theory of field governance; and there is a need for a comparative lens. But in order to do this, it is necessary to understand the difference between, and the relationship of governance with, institutional infrastructure.

As per our definition, we consider institutional infrastructure as being more than field governance, yet necessarily overlapping. We define field governance as the formal mechanisms that enable or constrain field activity and dynamics. For example, some of the elements of institutional infrastructure cited by Greenwood et al. (2011), Bell et al. (2014) and Raaijmakers et al. (2015) clearly relate to field governance. Defined as 'combinations of public and private, formal and informal systems that exercise control within a field' (Scott, 2014: 244), or units and processes that ensure compliance with rules and facilitate 'the overall smooth functioning and reproduction of the system' (Fligstein & McAdam, 2012: 14), governance most tangibly includes regulations, standards, reward systems and social control agents that monitor and enforce those regulations, standards and reward systems. Yet underpinning these formal governance systems are cultural norms, taken-for-granted assumptions, scripts and practices, incentives and interest structures, roles, relationships and organizational and field structures, all of which are part of the broader institutional infrastructure of a field. Rather than subsuming each of these elements into governance, we refer to formal governance roles and structures as governance, and include the informal norms, meanings, status differentiators, etc. as part of the institutional infrastructure, which supports the functioning of governance mechanisms.

Governance, then, is a subset of institutional infrastructure, and both are field-level constructs. Institutional infrastructure covers the set of institutions that prevail in a field, including a wide range of subject positions, relationships, practices, events and structures, some of which are to do with governance and some of which are not. Many collective actors such as regulators, professional associations and governments are part of the governance

Table 6.1   Dimensions of institutional infrastructure and governance

Institutional infrastructure element	Examples in literature
Collective interest organizations	Unions, professional associations (Greenwood, Suddaby, & Hinings, 2002; Lounsbury, 2002; Purdy & Gray, 2009; Washington, 2004), industry associations (Porac et al., 1989; van Wijk et al., 2013)
Regulators	National (Dobbin & Dowd, 1997), provincial (Greve, Palmer, & Pozner, 2010), industry, transnational (Djelic & Quack, 2003), geographic (Marquis, Lounsbury, & Greenwood, 2011)
Informal governance bodies	Certification or standards bodies (Reinecke, Manning, & Von Hagen, 2012), infomediaries (Deephouse & Heugens, 2009; King, 2008; Hoffman & Ocasio, 2001); boundary organizations (O'Mahoney & Bechky, 2008); accreditation organizations (Quinn Trank & Washington, 2009; Zuckerman, 1999); voluntary governance organizations (Washington, 2004)
Field configuring events	Events, conferences (Lampel & Meyer, 2008), exogenous shocks (Zilber, 2009), trade shows (Garud, 2008), Olympics (Glynn, 2008), fairs and festivals (Moeren & Strandgaard Pedersen, 2011)
Status differentiators	Labels, measures, signals, rankings, resources, education, historical position, award ceremonies (Anand & Watson, 2004; Rao, 1994; Wedlin, 2005); infomediaries (Anand & Peterson, 2000; Sauder, 2008)
Organizational models or templates	Professional partnerships (Greenwood, Hinings & Brown, 1990), managed professional businesses (Cooper, Greenwood, Hinings & Brown, 1996), hybrid organizations (Battilana & Lee, 2014)
Categories/Labels	Genres (Hsu, 2006), technology classes (Wry & Lounsbury, 2013), mutual funds into high and low risk (Lounsbury & Rao, 2004), listed corporations into industries (Zuckerman, 1999), partitioning of markets (Pachucki & Breiger, 2010;)
Norms	Education and professional training (Greenwood, Suddaby, & Hinings, 2002)
Relational channels	Normative networks (Lawrence & Suddaby, 2006; van Wijk et al., 2013; Garud, Jain & Kumaraswamy, 2002)

of a field. Greenwood et al. (2011) also see events such as trade shows and award shows as part of institutional infrastructure but, for us, these are not part of governance, which is about the formalized systems that ensure control and compliance within a field. Table 6.1 summarizes the dimensions of institutional infrastructure and governance that we have developed.

INSTITUTIONAL INFRASTRUCTURE AND ORGANIZATIONAL FIELD CONDITIONS

Institutional infrastructure has significant implications for the conditions of organizational fields, depending on the extent of its elaboration and its relative coherency (see also Zietsma et al., 2017). Where institutional infrastructure is highly elaborated and there is a unitary dominant logic within the field, we describe the field as *established* and relatively stable – the institutional infrastructure is highly coherent. Formal governance and informal infrastructure elements are plentiful in such a field and are likely to reinforce one another significantly, leading to a coherent sense of what is legitimate or not within the organizational field. Many studies of field change begin with the field in an established state (e.g., Greenwood et al., 2002; Zietsma & Lawrence, 2010). In fields where there are competing logics (low coherency) and highly elaborated institutional infrastructure, we would again see multiple formal governance and institutional infrastructure elements, but these may conflict with one another or compete for dominance (Reay & Hinings, 2005; Rao, Morrill, & Zald, 2000). We would describe the field as *contested*. Where there are compartmentalized or prioritized logics within organizational fields, and highly elaborated institutional infrastructure and governance,

Table 6.2 Institutional infrastructure and organizational fields

Relative coherency/Elaboration of institutional infrastructure	Unitary (high coherency)	Competing (low coherency)	Compartmentalized/Prioritized (coherency within subfields, ordering of subfields)
High elaboration	Established	Contested	Subfields
Low elaboration	Aligned/emerging	Fragmented	Emerging subfields/fragmented

we would describe the field as arrayed in subfields, with coherency within subfields, and incoherency between them, but which coexist without substantial competition. Consider Weber, Heinze and DeSoucey's (2008) description of the grass-fed beef sector, wherein grass-fed beef producers had cultural codes, markets, supply chains, etc., which were both separate from and different than those of mainstream beef producers. Similarly, studies of medical fields often include compartmentalized physician, nursing and administrative institutional infrastructures. Table 6.2 outlines these different fields.

When infrastructure has a low degree of elaboration, we would describe fields with unitary logics (high coherency) as emerging or *aligning*. The satellite radio field, for example, began with an aligned sense of what the field was about (Navis & Glynn, 2010), as did the information schools described by Patvardhan, Gioia and Hamilton (2015). Fields with low coherency and limited elaboration of institutional infrastructure are described as *fragmented*, with competing conceptions of what is legitimate. Fields with compartmentalized coherency and low elaboration are described as having *emerging subfields*.

INSTITUTIONAL INFRASTRUCTURE AND GOVERNANCE IN THREE FIELDS

To further develop our arguments, we turn now to an examination of three specific organizational fields with differences in their institutional infrastructure, their governance

and their states of development and change processes: those of professional service firms (Empson, Muzio, Broschak, & Hinings, 2015), forestry in British Columbia, Canada (Zietsma & Lawrence, 2010) and impact investing in Australia (Logue, 2014). We summarize our discussion in Table 6.3. The most effective way to illustrate how institutional infrastructure and governance interact is by examining field level change, and thus we discuss changes in these fields over time.

The Professional Services Field

Historically, the *professional services field* was stable, tightly controlled and a highly normative space of interaction, with a unitary logic. Firms, professional associations, educational providers and regulators, were part of a highly elaborated and coherent institutional infrastructure that linked them, often at a provincial or national level. Collective interest organizations worked together with formal regulators; consequently, processes of structuration were strong. As trustees of the rule of law, with a close compact with the state, this normative basis of power was reproduced and maintained as part of a well-understood, elaborated, governance structure. Mandatory membership with routines of licensing, training and professional development and the monitoring and disciplining of behavior were (and remain) critical cognitive and regulative mechanisms of both governance and institutional infrastructure. Governance was centrally organized around professional associations and regulators with high levels of coordination and well-defined processes of field entry. In addition, institutional infrastructure included large firms,

Table 6.3 Institutional infrastructure and governance in three fields

	Professional service firms	Forestry	Impact investing
Logics	Initially unitary yet increasingly complex and challenged	Initially unitary, then contested then environmental elements were embedded in the forestry field's logic	Emerging, unitary around market logic
Relative elaboration of institutional infrastructure	Highly elaborated institutional infrastructure	High – from highly elaborated yet unitary, to highly elaborated with subfields	Low yet aligned/emerging
Governance	Formal mechanisms highly elaborated and powerful via licensing, accreditation	Formal, via legislation and government oversight; official stakeholder consultation structures were instituted in response to contestation; lobbying and voluntary agreements eventually changed formal regulations	Formal governance mechanisms absent, drawing upon rules of market
Collective interest organizations, e.g. unions, associations, trade and lobbying organizations	Deeply institutionalized and established and providing relational channels across field; involved in formal (maintaining accreditation, professional development) and informal governance arrangements (codes of conduct)	Trade associations coordinated lobbying, joint R&D, international trade, etc.; union and supplier organizations; astroturf group; environmental groups coordinated informally. Later, key environmental groups and forest companies formed the Coast Forest Conservation Initiative	Absent, yet to form, some collective interest organizations in form of associations of charity and non profit organizations yet little voice of market
Regulators	Highly regulated at local, state, national levels. International regulators exist yet have less coercive power; proliferation of standards	Highly regulated at provincial level (primary). National level and internationally through trade agreements	Working out the rules of this new space, existing regulators form other fields, often a barrier
Informal governance bodies	Transnational nature of practices activity leads to more interaction with civil society groups and use soft power	Lobbying, environmental movement via norms and collaborations, sustainability certifications via national and international voluntary governance bodies	Absent
Field configuring events	Not important as field is highly established (difficult to disrupt via FCE?); some international FCEs may generate new subfields of expertise, e.g. climate change law etc ? Indirect affect of FCEs?	Stakeholder consultation tables	Important in gathering together diverse stakeholders in a new space, negotiating and working out who is in/out of field
Status differentiators	Based at organizational level (firm age, size, success), based on field of expertise/practice (law, accounting, consulting) – more normative than formal rankings/ratings	Not strong, status based on resources, market share and ability to mobilize or direct/redirect field attention; some differentiation made possible through the introduction of sustainability certifications	Not strong, status based on resources in this emergent stage, thus supply side/investors leading development of space
Organizational models or templates	Highly institutionalized although move over recent decades from Professional Partnership to Managed Professional Business (MPB) without significant change in institutional infrastructure or governance, mainly to address client needs	Harvesting model was highly institutionalized for forestry firms; new harvesting practices changed the model, but were integrated into existing organizational templates	Being borrowed from other fields, leading to hybrid forms (e.g., social enterprises)
Categories/Labels	Not important part of institutional infrastructure or governance	Sustainability certifications – using labeling to challenge status and direct attention	Labels for new organizational forms and activities important for understanding the boundaries of the emerging field (identity; who is in/out)
Norms	Trustees of the rule of law, normative basis of power	Profitability and control norms adjusted by embedding new norms on environment and sustainability into the market logic	Increasingly draw from logic of the market (underpinning analogy)

which, while not formally part of governance, were important actors with high status in establishing legitimated organizational forms and centers of training, along with universities (Greenwood et al., 1990; Malhotra, Morris, & Hinings, 2006; Leblebici & Sherer, 2015). Central to the field has been a well-developed organizational model or template, the Professional Partnership or P^2 form (Greenwood et al., 1990; Greenwood, Hinings, & Prakash, 2017), reflective of norms of self-governance and arguably social hierarchy. Because of this stability in both governance and institutional infrastructure there are no significant field-configuring events, nor the use of categories or labels.

While the PSF field remains basically unitary, it has become increasingly complex with challenges to existing governance. This institutional change of recent decades has been a subject of much scholarly examination focusing on both field and organizational levels (for a summary see Empson et al., 2015). This change was partly driven by actors already within this unitary field – clients – whose demand for services and increasingly transnational business activities, led to changing institutional infrastructure and governance, especially as a consequence of a stronger presence of a market logic into the field. Thus, as jurisdictional boundaries and demand for services have become transnational, there has been a shift from a highly normatively structured professional field to a globally competitive field governed by the market and increased regulations, standards, and trade agreements. PSFs have become an international one-stop-shop for various and increasingly dispersed clients.

As a result of these changes both institutional infrastructure has become even more elaborated and governance has become more complex. More actors have entered the field, especially new kinds of collective interest organizations such as business and civil society groups; clients have been increasing their role and strengthening their relationships with service providers. Indeed, the power and

status of clients has increased. Regulation has become more complex with oversight boards at both the national, transnational and international levels being added to existing regulatory structures. More networks that cross national boundaries have developed and this has produced informal governance bodies with 'soft regulation' (Djelic & Quack, 2008). All of this has involved the proliferation of rules, standards, classification schemes, evaluation procedures, and attempted standardization and formalization of public reporting across policy fields with international trade agreements. There are more implicit rules, templates and schemas. Thus, within this the institutional infrastructure has become both more complex and more fragmented as it extends over multiple jurisdictions. Power has also shifted somewhat to large transnational firms.

The P^2 organizational form is now contested and some have suggested that there has been some transformation to a Managed Professional Business (Cooper, Hinings, Greenwood, & Brown, 1996; Malhotra et al., 2006). This reflects the stretching of field boundaries (Morgan & Quack, 2006; Djelic & Quack, 2008; Bousseba & Morgan, 2015) and the presence of a stronger market logic.

There are many more actors involved in field governance. While professional associations remain important in establishing credentials and controlling the flow of labor, there are now competition authorities, stock market regulators and public oversight boards and, with the field becoming transnational, actors such as the World Trade Organization and transnational regulatory bodies are active. Both regulators and collective interest organizations have increased in number.

All of this represents a change in normative structure due to the breakdown of the compact between the professions and the state. These new kinds of regulators and collective interest organizations are introduced as guardians of the public interest, an acknowledgement that the professional associations have not been concerned with this as a primary function. They are supported by new actors such as NGOs, who are also involved in standard setting and developing new categorizations, often drawing power from international agreements as they monitor activity within the field. However, the national, singular professional field system still exists and provides barriers to entry for labor. This historical structuration for the continued operation of the field has been preserved.

Thus, the governance of the field is both voluntary (through certifications, marketing agreements, trade associations, lobbying, etc.) and mandatory by the state (local, provincial, national). It is normative (professional associations, education), and negotiated (as transnational, many stakeholders), as well as having elements of coercion (through pressures from stakeholders) and traditional disciplinary measures relating to practice. The shift from national, singular professional service fields to transnational, multi-service professional service fields is seemingly the blending of structurally equivalent fields. While field boundaries and practices have expanded, and pressures of globalization have loosened national controls, professional service firms have maintained normative power (and in a sense, the closure of the field) through the preservation of institutional infrastructure that enables the reproduction of ideals of self-governance and societal positioning, and so continued operation of the field.

While the change that we are describing in this field may appear radical in both institutional infrastructure and governance, it has occurred over a lengthy period of time and was, in part, endogenous. What we actually see is both continuity and change (Malhotra & Hinings, 2015). Table 6.3 summarizes the professional service firm field's institutional infrastructure and governance.

The Forestry Field

In their study of the field of *forestry in British Columbia (BC)*, Zietsma and Lawrence (2010) explored the institutional work of actors as the field underwent considerable change over a 20-year period. At the beginning of their study period (1985), a small number of long-established forestry firms and the provincial government together (and in close relationship) dominated the field, which was highly regulated, had a highly elaborated institutional infrastructure and featured a unitary, highly coherent industrial forestry logic that emphasized gaining maximum economic value (profitability and jobs) from forest resources, and replanting them for future use. A number of collective interest organizations existed, including industry associations (again, dominated by the elite forestry firms) and organizing bodies for shared research and development, international trade and marketing. A strong union organized forest workers, and engaged in sector-wide bargaining. Independent suppliers of transportation were organized into a Truck Loggers Association. The professional association of foresters worked with the faculties of forestry at BC universities to develop the normative framework for forest practices, to materialize the norms into practices and train and socialize professional foresters into these normative/practice frameworks. This centralized and mutually reinforcing set of institutional infrastructure elements served to produce stable governance institutions and thus maintain consistent action within the field, determining which actors had influence on field decision-making. Indeed, institutional infrastructure elements almost completely reinforced one another.

From the 1960s onward, however, there has been an increase in societal concern for the environment. The environmental field is a social movement field (Zietsma et al., 2017) with its own institutional infrastructure. Various environmental non-governmental organizations (ENGOS) play different roles (Bertels, Hoffman, & de Jordy, 2014): educational institutions teach principles and practices of environmental science and management, and consultants, business organizations and government agencies are dedicated to environmental improvements and management. The field's institutional infrastructure is decentralized with many actors, informal networks and little to no formal governance. Key normative principles exist, however. They involve the valuing of the natural environment for its own sake, preventing or mitigating climate change impacts, halting environmental degradation and loss of habitat and biodiversity, promoting sustainable natural resource use, reducing risks and problems of waste/emissions and disposal, air and water quality, etc.[1] The environmental field seeks to add environmental issues to multiple other fields' governance arrangements and infrastructure, focusing on fields in which environmental degradation is occurring. Environmental field members often seek to have new governance arrangements applied to other fields such as increased environmental regulations, monitoring and enforcement, along with multi-stakeholder consultation processes and sustainability certifications. Forestry has been an early focus for the field. ENGO campaigners that focused on forestry developed a set of practices, principles, relationships and mechanisms, which they used to gain access to and influence within the BC forestry field: in effect, they formed an issue field with two subfields, with divergent infrastructure, to challenge the BC forestry field. Their relational channels included other ENGOs, First Nations peoples,[2] the media, the public (through campaign events), regulators related to forestry and the environment in BC, and eventually, other businesses that used or sold wood or paper products. Initially, they were not part of the normal relational channels of forestry firms or the government, since at the beginning, they lacked the attention of both the voters and the customers of the forest companies, and there was no role in the forestry field for actors of their type. They thus were excluded from the power structure of the field, and had no impact on field governance. The forestry field's infrastructure provided multiple, overlapping barriers for their influence.

Over time, however, the ENGOs were able to gain the normative support of many voters, and thus had some impact on government action. In response, forestry firms activated the employees and forest-dependent community members into an 'astroturf' (or pseudo-grass roots) group, to countervail the green voters, and lobbied their government network, curtailing government action. All of this points to an increasingly complex infrastructure and an existing governance system that was under pressure but not yet replaced by a new, legitimated one.

ENGOs then pursued a market-based strategy, convincing international customers of the forestry firms to demand more sustainable practices. Once these demands came from the field's usual relational channels (customers), thus becoming consistent with the market logic, the forestry firms very quickly began to assimilate infrastructural elements desired by ENGOs into their own field infrastructure. Clear-cutting was abandoned by the lead firm overnight (in 1998), and others followed soon after. Sustainability certifications were adopted. Lead forestry firms and environmental groups together formed a collective interest organization called the Coast Forest Conservation Initiative, which conducted joint research and participated influentially in multi-stakeholder consultation structures. These structures were field-configuring processes to negotiate new eco-system based management forest practices to protect ancient forests, wildlife corridors and First Nations' rights (Zietsma & McKnight, 2009). Together, members of the stakeholder consultation structure lobbied the government to change forest regulations to mandate these ecosystem-based practices, ensuring stakeholder interests were permanently embedded in forestry field governance arrangements, and over time into the forestry field's logic, through continued elaboration of infrastructure (certification practices and reports, environmental reports, changes in harvesting models embedded in the organizational template, etc.). Thus, out of that changing institutional infrastructure, a new governance system was instituted that included the interests of a wider range of actors, new networks and changed power relations. New infrastructure came into play when new actors demanded influence – initially they were unable to influence formal governance mechanisms, yet eventually, through relationships and changes to institutional infrastructure elements that the environmentalists could gain access to, there were new regulations governing the field. Stakeholder concerns also became embedded (and performative) within firms, and within the institutional infrastructure of the forestry field.

From this case example, we saw that logic (meaning and practice), relational channels, power and governance elements that ENGOs sought to bring into the BC forestry field were blocked for many years by elements of the forestry field's infrastructure for which they were inconsistent. These changes would reduce the power of firms and their regulators, contradict their established field logic and violate field governance arrangements, and they came from new actors outside of field relational channels. Each of these mutually reinforcing infrastructural elements had to be unlocked before sustainable forest practices could be instituted. When the change came, however, it happened quite rapidly across each of the elements of institutional infrastructure, producing a new governance structure. Table 6.3 summarizes the forestry field's institutional infrastructure and governance.

The Impact Investing Field

In contrast to the established and historical fields of professional services and forestry, *impact investing* is a nascent field with lower elaboration of institutional infrastructure, yet rather unitary in its emergence, making it an aligned/emerging field. Its emerging governance, both formal and informal is grounded in the idea, and so the rules, of a market. The practice of impact investing involves investing in companies, organizations and funds with the intention of generating measurable social and environmental impacts as well as financial returns. This market-building social movement gained speed after the Global Financial Crisis, with philanthropists, global institutions, banks and consulting firms supporting the notion (with varying motivations) that profit-seeking investment can generate social and environmental good, and could go towards addressing the complex, multidisciplinary, intractable and 'wicked' problems (Rittel & Weber, 1973) facing nations and the world in general.

As a new field, impact investing is emerging at the intersection of other fields – philanthropy, investment and finance, corporate social responsibility and social entrepreneurship. The institutional infrastructure is emerging in an interstitial space; this is interesting for institutional scholars as interstitial spaces (between fields) and field-to-field relations (Evans & Kay, 2008; Furnari, 2014; Pache & Santos, 2010; Van Wijk, Stam, Elfring, Zietsma, & den Hond, 2013) are neglected yet theoretically generative areas (Zietsma, et al., 2017). In impact investing, the desired governance and institutional infrastructure of the field seems rather coherent, despite a diversity of stakeholders being involved in market-building efforts, drawn from the idea of a self-governing market. While the field itself may be emerging from the intersection of several fields, the dominant logic is that of the market, which is present to a greater or lesser degree in each of the surrounding fields. The idea of the all-knowing efficient market, and the well-institutionalized scripts that come with it, is translated and transferred from other sectors (Wall Street but also education, health); the consequent materials required for this impact investing market are drawn from taken-for-granted assumptions and ideas about what a market needs to function – supply, demand, rankings, ratings and those to do the ratings (Logue, 2014). The market thus becomes the central, naturalizing analogy for organizing and building institutional infrastructure for this field, providing a powerful cognitive force (Logue, Clegg, & Gray, 2016).

If we look at the emergence of this field in Australia, this recent market-building activity was led by the government (Logue, 2014), which set about structuring the relations between diverse and disparate actors through a Senate Inquiry, an early *field-configuring event*. Some existing *collective interest groups*, such as associations of charities and non-profit groups, participated, although they were few when compared to the diverse range and large number of other organizations – banks, religious organizations, investors, superannuation funds, social enterprises, corporate foundations, etc.

Emanating from this field-configuring event was a dominant discourse that the supply side of the market was under developed. So to support early market-building activity, the government provided matching funding to catalyze the establishment of three impact investing firms (supply side). The actions and practices of these firms are increasingly seen as the appropriate way to perform impact investing, particularly the measuring and public reporting on such investments. *Formal regulation* is lagging, with little formal structuring and actors needing to operate within existing frameworks from their fields of origin. For example, non-profit structures and restrictions on equity financing, public reporting on charitable donations, corporate financial structures (such as superannuation firms and trusts) requiring pursuit of maximum financial return (referred to as the 'sole purpose test' in the Superannuation Industry Act) and not allowing pursuit of lesser financial return for social return. The institutional infrastructure was being built up, with the government taking a leading role in identifying actors, but without any real specification of relationships. Thus, pre-existing networks came into play and power rested with established market actors.

Informal governance of the field is emerging through certifying social impact through new global organizations such as BLab, which awards companies a BCorporation certification if they are achieving financial, social and environmental returns. This certification can be withdrawn if a company fails to maintain this triple bottom line performance. This certification is increasingly used as a short-cut for impact investors needing due diligence on possible investment opportunities, as evidenced by some social stock exchanges only listing BCorporation certified companies. Globally, the market also seems to be converging on another measurement system of impact investments, Global Impact Investment Ratings System (GIIRS) that measures impact of companies, investments, funds and fund managers. Control partly rests with rating agencies. Beyond certification, other *status differentiators* are not strong, and field positions in this early stage are mainly based on resources such as capital.

Even at this early stage, the field is seemingly converging around common *organizational templates and models*. Although there is yet to be an agreed-upon archetypal organizational template (Greenwood & Hinings, 1993) for such hybrid organizations (Battilana & Lee, 2014), the discourse frequently focuses on for-profit models suitable for generating impact investing, providing debt and equity options for such investors. For example, debate continues as to whether Australia needs a new legal corporate form such as the UK's Community Interest Corporations, or the US Benefit Corporation to address such investor needs. In this way, the charity or non-profit models becomes just one organizational form in the new social economy (Logue & Zappala, 2014). Field configuring debates increasingly *categorize and label* organizations as 'social enterprises', these labels determining who is considered eligible (or legitimate even) to participate in this new field, particularly on the demand side (social enterprises, social businesses, non-profits, charities). This labeling begins to set the boundaries of the field and elaborate institutional infrastructure.

All of this market-building activity further supports the emergence of educational actors offering programs to get social enterprises 'investor ready', by both private intermediaries and consulting programs offering accelerators programs, to universities offering Masters programs (within Business Schools) specializing in social entrepreneurship. Not only does this educate incoming actors into this market, it establishes the dominant cognitive framework from business (as opposed to say, social justice). Having formally recognized postgraduate courses also goes towards aligning and legitimizing the activities of this nascent field by other fields and contributes to establishing a *normative framework* for field activity. Thus, governance at this nascent stage is more normative, based on influence and attempts to educate actors, rather than structural or based on formal regulation or rights.

What is also interesting in the emergence of this market, is the frequent cry in Australia and many other national markets, that there is a lack of 'investor ready enterprises', or that investors also need to be educated. So, while there is both a visible demand side to this market, and a willing supply side, the market itself fails to emerge without the necessary institutional infrastructure in place. There is yet to emerge a common language or meaning system through which these different groups of actors can readily communicate and interact. A body of literature across the social sciences has demonstrated how markets are socially constructed rather than being entities 'out there', and has highlighted the crucial role of culture and politics involved in the organization of markets and in creating the governing 'rules of the game' (e.g., North, 1990; Fligstein, 2001; Fligstein & McAdam, 2012; Padgett & Powell, 2012). These categories, labels, certifications, practices, events and educational programs begin to provide the necessary infrastructure for these actors to frequently and fatefully meet, connect and transact. This infrastructure enables and supports the development of relationships,

norms and beliefs amongst actors, and so the necessary governance and social structure of the market to form (McKague, Zietsma, & Oliver, 2015).

As a nascent, emerging field, we see an initially fragmented, unstructured and decentralized institutional infrastructure with such governance as there is being imported from intersecting fields. Power in the field rests both with governments as they attempt to organize the field and also through the acceptance of market-based approaches. The elements of governance begin to emerge in certification, educational programs and field-configuring events but there is still not a definitive governance system. Table 6.3 summarizes the impact of investing's institutional infrastructure and governance.

Cross-field Comparison

Overall, our three examples show both major contrasts and some similarities. In terms of an overall field description we categorize the institutional infrastructure of professional services as established to begin with but becoming more complex and with challenges to existing infrastructure and governance. Forestry is also initially established but becomes contested and then compartmentalized into distinct subfields. These two fields began with a period of stasis, with a set of mutually reinforcing, highly elaborated, institutional infrastructure elements that maintained and governed the field. In both fields, there was a strong relationship between the state and the professions (PSF) and firms (forestry), which enabled significant self-governance (especially among professions), or which gave considerable input by firms and professions into field regulations. Thus, collective interest organizations represented firms and the profession with key roles for the professional associations (PSF) and the industry associations (forestry), both of which were dominated by members from the top firms in the field.

Status differentiation in these fields was based in the large firms. In both cases, education and professional associations reinforced field norms, practices and regulations. In both fields, what one 'must do' to be legitimate was relatively clear, prescriptive and policed through self-regulation and well-established categorization. Organizational models were highly institutionalized.

While the starting point for these two fields was similar, the nature of the changes in both institutional infrastructure and governance were different. In the PSF field, we saw endogenous and incremental processes of change, largely unimpeded by infrastructural barriers and existing governance. In contrast, in the forest industry, the field's institutional infrastructure acted as a significant barrier to change, and little change happened until a radical shift appeared which seemed quite sudden. What accounts for these differences? In both cases, new logics arose in society that were brought into the field – globalization and market logics for the PSF field, and environmental and social justice logics for the forestry field – yet they had dramatically different effects as they interacted with the institutional infrastructure and governance of the respective fields.

In the PSF field, the new logics had some complementarity with existing logics, which already included norms for client service and profitability, but they also emerged from 'normal' (cognitively and morally legitimate) sources, both collective actors and high status field members. PSF firms were asked by their customers to expand their practices both internationally and by discipline (Greenwood et al., 2002), which fit with PSF firms' norms of client service and profitability. Governments, for their part, were also experiencing strong pressures for globalization and market logics from many other sources at the same time, including other states and state agencies, lobbyists, voters and other influencers. These logics were seen as modern and fully consistent with a government's focus on the economic prosperity of their state.

These logics, and the organizational structures and practices that materialized them, also did not disrupt existing power structures and professional norms to a great extent. PSFs remained largely self-governing although new organizational models were available. While states saw their power falling because of the increasingly transnational nature of the business, new regulators were added to take part in governance and new regulations and reporting requirements were introduced to protect their citizens' interests. At the transnational level, new collective actors and regulators came into being; NGOs worked to counterbalance rising PSF power (and the rising market logic) by pushing for voluntary governance arrangements in order to preserve professional standards. While there were frictions with each change, the changes were largely consistent with, and preservative of, existing institutional infrastructure, and thus they proceeded relatively smoothly. No new categories or labels were introduced.

In the BC forestry case where two fields came together, the environmental field's institutional infrastructure was inconsistent with that of the forestry field in multiple ways: based in different norms, and advocating different practices. It also emerged from illegitimate relational channels, threatening the traditional power structure of the forestry field and expressly violating existing governance arrangements. The path of change took much longer and shifted more radically than incrementally when change occurred. New collective actors were introduced and this led to more status differentiation. Forestry firms used their relationships with regulators to block changes, and activated their employees and forest-dependent communities to provide a normative counter-argument to those of ENGOs based on economic prosperity. Thus, the various collective actors were in conflict. Furthermore, they normatively supported and policed each other to maintain solidarity against these divergent pressures. When the pressures for change finally came from legitimate channels (voters for the government, and customers for the forestry firms), and when they became more consistent with the forestry field's market-based logic because of customer demands, forest companies changed their practices and began in earnest to negotiate new governance arrangements that eventually became inscribed in law and organizational structures. Governance became more inclusive and institutional infrastructure more supportive of a range of actors and regulators together with new norms.

The difference between the PSF case and the forestry case is the relative consistency or inconsistency with existing infrastructure that determined the path of change (and the consequent resistance to the changes faced in fields). In two highly institutionalized fields, with mutually supporting infrastructural elements, we can expect changes that are inconsistent with institutional infrastructure to take longer and appear more dramatic, as the multiple, mutually reinforcing infrastructural elements act as supports for each other. Opening the door to change was difficult because the door had multiple locks. By contrast, when changes were more consistent with institutional infrastructure, the door was at least partially open, and the changes that did occur took place relatively uneventfully over time.

Even challenges that appear inconsistent with the field's infrastructure may lead to incremental change, however, if field elites recognize a potential threat that they feel they can control, maintaining existing power structures. In the mainstream tourism field in the Netherlands, for example, incumbents faced demands from a sustainable tourism field in a fragmented state (limited institutional infrastructure and competing logics) (van Wijk et al., 2013). The mainstream tourism field's institutional infrastructure, by contrast, was much more elaborated and internally consistent. Incumbents from the trade association and top firms tried to co-opt the weakly structured sustainable tourism field, creating a governance framework

that left existing power structures intact, and incrementally assimilated the sustainable tourism field's interests into the tourism industry's field infrastructure.

When we examine the impact investing field, we see a different story again. As an emerging field, its institutional infrastructure is largely undeveloped. As a result there is considerable experimentation with various governance forms, negotiating different arrangements, and seeing what sticks. There is very little resistance to that experimentation, as there is a very limited institutional infrastructure to block it. Collective actors are absent; regulation is ambiguous; there is little status differentiation; there are no taken-for-granted organizational templates; and norms diverge, especially around market and social practices.

Constraints instead come from surrounding fields in which members of the impact investing field hold legitimate subject positions, as such subject positions have yet to be clearly defined and legitimated in the impact investing field itself. These constraints identify what members must not do, but do not prescribe with much certainty what should be done. Until infrastructure elements become developed (and mutually reinforcing), however, there is considerably more freedom for experimentation, but a corresponding lack of certainty around what is legitimate within the field.

IMPLICATIONS

A major aim was to draw together the ideas of institutional infrastructure, a subset of which is field governance, and use them as a basis for comparison across fields. In dealing with the rather limited literature within institutional theory for each concept we developed a definition of governance as the formal mechanisms of roles, structures, rules and standards that maintain the 'rules of the game' within a field. Institutional infrastructure we defined as including, but wider than governance. The main elements of institutional infrastructure include collective interest organizations, regulators, informal governance bodies, field configuring events, status differentiators, organizational templates, categories or labels, and norms. We have further suggested that the institutional infrastructure of a field can be described in terms of degrees of elaboration (high, low) and coherency (unitary, competing, compartmentalized).

We then illustrated the nature of institutional infrastructure and governance, and their interrelationship through the analysis of three fields, professional service firms, forestry and impact investing. From the comparison of the governance and infrastructure of those fields, we were able to describe different configurations of institutional infrastructure and governance, focusing on their relative coherency and elaboration to identify six field conditions. In doing so, we have argued that these field conditions, based on the field's institutional infrastructure and governance, are important for understanding field dynamics, since infrastructural states affect processes of field creation, maintenance and change. Our analysis and comparison of the three fields of professional services, forestry and impact investing is a first step in showing what these differences are and the effects that they have. What becomes important are the implications of this analysis for a more general understanding of field differences and institutional change, field emergence and institutional work.

Implications for Theorizing Field Differences and Institutional Change

Some of the primary topics of the past decade, i.e., institutional entrepreneurship, institutional work and institutional logics, have often directly or indirectly centered on change at the field level. It is surprising then that the issue of what exactly has been

changing within a field and how change takes place has been relatively under-theorized. As Greenwood et al. (2011) point out, there is a lack of frameworks for understanding fields. We have discussed elements of institutional infrastructure as formal governance, collective interest organizations, informal governance, field-configuring events, status differentiators, organizational models or templates, categories and labels, and norms, which reinforce each other in established fields, but may conflict or be compartmentalized in other fields. Such elements form the basis for a classification of fields with the idea that they come together in a circumscribed set of ways. However, as institutional theory has developed a very strong emphasis on changes in, and contestation over, institutional logics (Dunn & Jones, 2010; Lounsbury, 2007; Marquis & Lounsbury, 2007; Reay & Hinings, 2009; Thornton, Jones, & Kury, 2005) as a central concern over the past decade (Thornton & Ocasio, 2008; Thornton et al., 2012), these other infrastructural elements of fields – that may enable or constrain change – have been neglected.

Our focus on institutional infrastructure in the case studies shows that logics alone cannot account for institutional dynamics. Logics are not disconnected influences which change fields automatically when they arise. They are attached to particular groups of actors, and come with their own relational channels, bases for legitimacy, and power and governance structures, and are materialized in various elements of institutional infrastructure. Our examination of the different cases suggests that logics which travel through the field's institutionalized relational channels appear to stimulate change while those that do not are more likely to be ignored or resisted. When they disrupt existing power structures or violate existing governance arrangements, they are likely to be resisted even more fiercely (Furnari, 2016). We argue that the infrastructural elements operate in concert, and thus must be considered together. When infrastructural elements overlap and reinforce one another, they each function as separate locks on a door that acts as a barrier to institutional change. Each of the locks must be unlocked before the door can be opened and institutional change can occur.

On the other hand, the lack of reinforcing institutional infrastructure in an emerging field, while it creates considerable room for experimentation and change, limits field members' ability to define and acquire legitimacy, and thus contributes to ambiguity, and potentially, the need to draw on ill-suited infrastructure from adjacent fields. Weak infrastructure may leave a field open to colonization or cooptation (van Wijk et al., 2013), and change may be frequent, but difficult to institutionalize.

When fields feature institutional complexity, with diverging meanings, practices and prescriptions for action, institutional infrastructure may be organized in competing subfields within a field, such as the BC forestry field containing the sustainable forestry field (Zietsma & Lawrence, 2010), which is consistent with the issue fields that Hoffman (1999) identified. In these cases, different sets of institutional infrastructure exist in the field among different groups of actors and each subfield's proponents may compete vigorously for dominance in the field, as we saw, for example, with alternative dispute resolution (Rao et al., 2000). On the other hand, subfields may co-exist in fields if their jurisdictions are bounded and they themselves preserve a hierarchical ordering and governance that manages the relations among them (O'Mahoney & Bechky, 2008; Raynard, 2016).

While not comprehensive, our illustrations reveal that considering institutional infrastructure as a whole is central to the understanding of institutional dynamics, and different configurations of institutional infrastructure are associated with different patterns of institutional change in response to challenges. *This insight is critical.* While DiMaggio and Powell's (1983) idea of

structuration suggests that fields 'settle down' into established sets of actors with formal, legitimated relationships, that view is not supported by work of the past decade which suggests, at least in part, that there is less field stability than initially theorized (Heugens & Lander, 2009; Greenwood et al., 2011). All fields are subject to change, and that change is in the elements of institutional infrastructure. The characteristics of the infrastructural elements, we argue, impact the pace and scope of change (Amis, Slack, & Hinings, 2002). By developing a better understanding of the mutually reinforcing nature of institutions that prevail in fields, we can better understand when they are likely to change and when change is more likely to be symbolic, temporary resisted or blocked altogether.

While we have come some way in identifying the effects of infrastructure configurations on institutional dynamics, we are primarily laying down a framework and posing a number of issues that require further attention; there is significant work to do. A central research issue is to identify a typology of infrastructural configurations and their effects on pathways of institutional change under different conditions.

Implications in Understanding Field Emergence

Our example of impact investing, a setting of field emergence, directs attention to a broader gap in organizational institutional literature on processes of field emergence and construction (Padgett & Powell, 2012), and how this occurs in contemporary settings. Indeed, the issue of processes of *emergence* of not only markets but organizational forms, fields and practices more broadly is of broader concern in organizational studies (Padgett & Powell, 2012; see Maguire et al., 2004; Munir & Phillips, 2005; Khaire & Wadhwani, 2010; Navis & Glynn, 2010). Our example shows that the characteristics of emerging fields makes them an important area of study due to the uncertainty in the institutional order (providing scope for institutional entrepreneurs) and also how they develop given there are fewer isomorphic pressures (with the absence of shared values, established norms, or leaders to mimic) (Maguire et al., 2004). There are two main insights for institutional infrastructure. First, some existing work (Weber et al., 2008; Navis & Glynn, 2010) implicitly refers to institutional infrastructure through a consideration of categories, labels and cultural codes. This work could be extended to explicitly consider how these categories (so central to the process of emergence) are then mutually reinforced in the development of the institutional infrastructure of the field, shaping governance and field dynamics. Several studies (Weber et al., 2008; Khaire & Wadhwani, 2010; Navis & Glynn, 2010; Wry, Lounsbury, & Glynn, 2011; Gurses & Ozcan, 2015; Patvardhan et al., 2015) have focused on the development of claims and meaning around collective identities, these often being manifested in categories and cultural codes that discursively get 'filled out' and locked into place by associated evaluation criteria, and reinforced by audience recognition and repeated application via audience decision making. Furthermore, the performance of these categories and codes create new relational channels, and new practices and governance arrangements. Categories thus become part of the institutional infrastructure of a field, through a process of stakeholders debating, contesting, performing and sense-making, eventually becoming taken-for-granted (Durand & Paolella, 2013; Grodal, Gotsopoulos, & Suarez, 2015; Gurses & Ozcan, 2015; Patvardhan et al., 2015). These categories and their enactment contribute to the institutional infrastructure. This fosters field-level identity, cohesion and also differentiation from adjacent fields (Khaire & Wadhwani, 2010; Navis & Glynn, 2010; Weber et al., 2008).

Second, fields are emerging often at the intersection of other fields, so institutional infrastructure from other fields may be borrowed or cobbled together (in a process of bricolage), and may be inadvertently constraining or competing. Fields often emerge from disparate, heterogeneous actors using varying resources and materials (Lounsbury & Crumley, 2007) to forge innovation via new relations and networks of activities. As we note in our example of impact investing, fields often emerge in spaces between fields, or from field-to-field relations (Evans & Kay, 2008; Pache & Santos, 2010; Van Wijk et al., 2013; Furnari, 2014). What we may observe by focusing on institutional infrastructure is the power bases and resources that are drawn upon (for example from other nearby or related fields) in developing or transforming structures for interaction and eventual governance (see, for example, Furnari, 2016). It directs our attention to the sets of institutions that will enable fields to coalesce and cohere, enabling their operation. We note that the institutional infrastructure does not have to be developed collectively, but efforts and activities need to at least be aligned towards achieving a common agenda and mutually reinforcing for a field to emerge. Emerging at the intersection of these fields, we may see infrastructure borrowed, transposed, and translated from nearby fields. How it becomes mutually reinforcing amongst such diversity and possible contestation is an interesting line of inquiry in understanding field dynamics (Furnari, 2014, 2016).

Implications for Institutional Work

We recognize that the institutional infrastructure of a field is created, maintained and disrupted by organizational actors (Lawrence & Suddaby, 2006; Lawrence, Suddaby, & Leca, 2011); their lived experience is both structuring and structured by that same institutional infrastructure – the paradox of embedded agency. Recently Lawrence et al. (2011) described how institutional work involves the 'physical or mental effort aimed at affecting an institutions or set of institutions' (2011: 53), a set of institutions being how we conceptualize the institutional infrastructure of a field.

As such, we are cautious not to privilege infrastructure over agency in our theorizing, specifically issues of intentionality, effort and power of actors (Lawrence et al., 2011) and the 'need to consider the permanent recursive and dialectical interaction' that we observe between actors and institutional infrastructure (Lawrence et al., 2011: 55). This is highlighted in our forestry field example where the interrelation between institutional work (practice work and boundary work) and periods of either stability or change provide a more nuanced account of field dynamics.

The capacity to generate change may be related to individual subject positions occupied in a field (Battilana, 2006), and we argue that those positions may be reinforced by the prevailing institutional infrastructure. The various elements of institutional infrastructure may be defended or challenged by existing or new actors. There may be actors who intentionally maintain certain pieces of infrastructure, such as certification and rating systems, or professional licensing. This may be done at a local level, yet have broader field level effects in mutually reinforcing other elements of the field. This effort may be focused or distributed, coordinated or uncoordinated, complementary or contradictory, as actors work within the field to maintain various parts of infrastructure, or when faced with external challenges. For example, related to our example of Professional Services Firms, Quack (2007) shows how in transnational law-making, legal professionals perform institutional work via practice and politicking, with each form of institutional work supporting the other.

We may also see the interaction between institutional work and institutional infrastructure in the struggle to transform, elaborate or expand infrastructure as individuals navigate the pressures of 'must do', 'must not do' and 'may do', or similarly the struggles and contestation observed in settings

of field emergence. This also connects to power bases of the institutional infrastructure and perhaps particular groups of actors who control elements of infrastructure – for example, lawyers maintaining control of professional licensing and so somewhat preserving the self-governance of the field, even with new organizational forms such as MPB. Institutional infrastructure may produce systematic bias (for example, application processes for prestigious universities), it may privilege one group over others in the production and reinforcement of field positions, and in doing so silence some groups or create barriers for others. Importantly, this consideration of institutional work, or rather agency and action, reveals how institutional infrastructure of fields is metaphorically 'alive'. It may be taken-for-granted and solidified, but it is so because of the ongoing institutional work being performed.

Our point is that institutional infrastructure is an integral part of institutional work. When creating, maintaining or transforming a field, the kinds of institutional work being done are critically about institutional infrastructure, the institutions of governance, power, legitimacy and control. While the concept of institutional work introduces an important element of agency into institutional theory it is important to go beyond the classification of types of work (Lawrence & Suddaby, 2006) to analyzing what is being worked on, i.e., institutional infrastructure.

CONCLUSION

We have observed that the institutional infrastructure of fields, its elaboration, and the way it coheres or diverges, has substantial implications for institutional change dynamics, field emergence and agency within fields. Importantly, given the dominance of institutional logics as an approach in recent years, it also provides another important lens into field change that includes actors and relations, power structures and also the materiality of fields as embedded in governance and inter-organizational and organizational structures. We argue that taking the approach of analyzing the institutional infrastructure of fields provides a way to compare across fields, and impacts opportunities and pathways for institutional change that can sharpen our theorizing. We also argue that in comparing across fields that we are likely to find configurations of institutional infrastructural elements.

A further important area is the emergence and intersection of fields, including field overlaps and interstitial spaces between fields. Once we go beyond the movement of logics from one field to another and pay attention to the infrastructure that both underpins those logics and also has a degree of independence from them, then we have a better handle on the emergence of fields. Our argument is that the emergence and subsequent institutionalization of a field is as much about the development and establishment of the infrastructural elements as it is about logics *per se*. And in those processes of developing, establishing and legitimizing new institutional infrastructure there is a very important area of research in examining the ways in which fields intersect to allow the transporting and translating of infrastructural elements between fields.

Importantly, we have also suggested that the elements that make up institutional infrastructure give us a valuable starting point for comparing fields and establishing whether there are a limited number of configurations of these elements. But we believe that the real utility of such an approach is to theorize field differences and, as a result, understand better their role in the institutional dynamics of change. We have argued that different paths of field level change occur as a result of interactions, of logics in particular, with institutional infrastructure. Essentially there are different field level conditions, best apprehended through ideas of institutional infrastructure, that effect field-level change. An important research agenda is to systematically examine this proposition and identify

a typology of infrastructural configurations and their effects on pathways of institutional change under different conditions.

Notes

1   Summarized from various sources including: http://www.findlaw.com.au/articles/407/principles-of-environmental-management.aspx; https://en.wikipedia.org/wiki/Ceres_(organization); http://www.climateinstitute.org.au/verve/_resources/Climate_roundtable_joint_principles_290615.pdf; http://www.greenpeace.org/international/en/about/our-core-values/.

2   First Nations, or Canada's aboriginal peoples, became allies with ENGOs because they were attempting to gain decision-making power and resource rights over the land they claimed as their traditional territories.

REFERENCES

Aguilera, R. V., & Jackson, G. (2010). Comparative and international corporate governance. *The Academy of Management Annals*, 4(1), 485–556.

Alesina, A., & Perotti, R. (1996). Income distribution, political instability, and investment. *European Economic Review*, 40(6), 1203–1228.

Amis, J., Slack, T., & Hinings, C. R. (2002). Values and organizational change. *Journal of Applied Behavioral Science*, 38(4), 436–465.

Anand, N., & Peterson, R. A. (2000). When market information constitutes fields: Sensemaking of markets in the commercial music industry. *Organization Science*, 11(3), 270–284.

Anand, N., & Watson, M. R. (2004). Tournament rituals in the evolution of fields: The case of the Grammy Awards. *Academy of Management Journal*, 47(1), 59–80.

Battilana, J. (2006). Agency and institutions: The enabling role of individuals' social position. *Organization*, 13(5), 653–676.

Battilana, J., & Lee, M. (2014). Advancing research on hybrid organizing: Insights from the study of social enterprises. *Academy of Management Annals*, 8(1), 397–441.

Bell, R. G., Filatotchev, I., & Aguilera, R. V. (2014). Corporate governance and investors' perceptions of foreign IPO value: An institutional perspective. *Academy of Management Journal*, 57(1), 301–320.

Bertels, S., Hoffman, A. J., & DeJordy, R. (2014). The varied work of challenger movements: Identifying challenger roles in the US environmental movement. *Organization Studies*, 35(8), 1171–1210.

Boettke, P. J. (1994). Privatization, public ownership and regulation of natural monopoly. *Journal of Economic Literature*, *32*(4), 1916–1918.

Bourdieu, P. (1984). *Distinction: A social critique of taste*. Trans. Richard Nice. Cambridge, MA: Harvard University Press.

Bourdieu P (1986). The forms of capital. In J. G. Richardson (Ed.), *Handbook for theory and research in the sociology of education* (pp. 241–258). New York: Greenwood Press.

Boussebaa, M., & Morgan, G. (2015). Internationalization of professional service firms: Drivers, forms and outcomes. In J. Broschak & L. Empson (Eds.), *The Oxford handbook of professional service firms* (pp. 71–91). Oxford: Oxford University Press.

Compagni, A., Mele, V., & Ravasi, D. (2015). how early implementations influence later adoptions of innovation: social positioning and skill reproduction in the diffusion of robotic surgery. *Academy of Management Journal*, *58*(1), 242–278.

Cooper, D. J., Hinings, B., Greenwood, R., & Brown, J. L. (1996). Sedimentation and transformation in organizational change: The case of Canadian law firms. *Organization Studies*, *17*(4), 623–647.

Dacin, M. T., Ventresca, M. J., & Beal, B. D. (1999). The embeddedness of organizations: Dialogue and directions. *Journal of Management*, *25*(3), 317–356.

Deephouse, D. L., & Heugens, P. P. (2009). Linking social issues to organizational impact: The role of infomediaries and the infomediary process. *Journal of Business Ethics*, *86*(4), 541–553.

DiMaggio, P. J. (1995). Comments on 'What theory is not'. *Administrative Science Quarterly*, 391–397.

DiMaggio, P. J., & Powell, W. W. (1983). The Iron Cage revisited: Institutional isomorphism and collective rationality in organizational fields. *American Sociological Review*, 48, 147–160.

Djelic, M. L., & Quack, S. (2003). Conclusion: Globalization as a double process of institutional change and institution building. In *Globalization and institutions. Redefining the rules of the economic game* (pp. 302–333). Cheltenham: Edward Elgar.

Djelic, M. L., & Quack, S. (2008). Institutions and transnationalization. In R. Greenwood, C. Oliver, R. Suddaby, & K. Sahlin-Andersson (Eds.),*The SAGE handbook of organizational institutionalism* (pp. 299–323). London: Sage.

Dobbin, F., & Dowd, T. J. (1997). How policy shapes competition: Early railroad foundings in Massachusetts. *Administrative Science Quarterly*, 501–529.

Drori, G. S. (2008). Institutionalism and globalization studies. In R. Greenwood, C. Oliver, R. Suddaby, & K. Sahlin-Andersson (Eds.), *The SAGE handbook of organizational institutionalism* (pp. 449–472). London: Sage.

Dunn, M. B., & Jones, C. (2010). Institutional logics and institutional pluralism: The contestation of care and science logics in medical education, 1967–2005. *Administrative Science Quarterly*, *55*(1), 114–149.

Durand, R., & Paolella, L. (2013). Category stretching: Reorienting research on categories in strategy, entrepreneurship, and organization theory. *Journal of Management Studies*, *50*(6), 1100–1123.

Empson, L., Muzio, D., Broschak, J., & Hinings, B. (2015). Researching professional service firms: An introduction and overview. In J. Broschak & L. Empson (Eds.), *The Oxford handbook of professional service firms* (pp. 1–22). Oxford: Oxford University Press.

Evans, R., & Kay, T. (2008). How environmentalists 'greened' trade policy: Strategic action and the architecture of field overlap. *American Sociological Review*, *73*(6), 970–991.

Farjoun, M. (2002). The dialectics of institutional development in emerging and turbulent fields: The history of pricing conventions in the on-line database industry. *Academy of Management Journal*, *45*(5), 848–874.

Fligstein, N. (2001). *The architecture of markets: An economic sociology of twenty-first-century capitalist societies*. Princeton, NJ: Princeton University Press.

Fligstein, N., & McAdam, D. (2012). Toward a general theory of strategic action fields. *Sociological Theory*, *29*, 1–26.

Fiss, P. C. (2007). A set-theoretic approach to organizational configurations. *Academy of Management Review*, 32, 1180–1198.

Furnari, S. (2014). Interstitial spaces: microinteraction settings and the genesis of new practices between institutional fields. *Academy of Management Review*, *39*(4), 439–462.

Furnari, S. (2016). Institutional fields as linked arenas: Inter-field resource dependence, institutional work and institutional change. *Human Relations*, *69*(3): 551–580.

Garud, R. (2008). Conferences as venues for the configuration of emerging organizational fields: The case of cochlear implants. *Journal of Management Studies*, *45*(6), 1061–1088.

Garud, R., Jain, S., & Kumaraswamy, A. (2002). Institutional entrepreneurship in the sponsorship of common technological standards: The case of Sun Microsystems and Java. *Academy of Management Journal*, *45*(1), 196–214.

Gimenez, G., & Sanau, J. (2007). Interrelationship among institutional infrastructure, technological innovation and growth: an empirical evidence. *Applied Economics*, *39*(10), 1267–1282.

Glynn, M. A. (2008). Configuring the field of play: How hosting the Olympic Games impacts civic community. *Journal of Management Studies*, *45*(6), 1117–1146.

Greenwood, R., & Hinings, C. R. (1993). Understanding strategic change: The contribution of archetypes. *Academy of Management Journal*, *36*(5), 1052–1081.

Greenwood, R., Hinings, C. R., & Brown, J. (1990). 'P2-form' strategic management: corporate practices in professional partnerships. *Academy of Management Journal*, *33*(4), 725–755.

Greenwood, R., Hinings, C.R., & Prakash, R. (2017). From P2 to P3? *Journal of Professions and Organizations*.

Greenwood, R., Raynard, M., Kodeih, F., Micelotta, E., & Lounsbury, M. (2011). Institutional complexity and organizational responses. *Academy of Management Annals*, *5*(1), 317–371.

Greenwood, R., & Suddaby, R. (2006). Institutional entrepreneurship in mature fields: The big five accounting firms. *Academy of Management Journal*, *49*, 27–48.

Greenwood, R., Suddaby, R., & Hinings, C. R. (2002). Theorizing change: The role of professional associations in the transformation of institutionalized fields. *Academy of Management Journal*, *45*(1), 58–80.

Greve, H. R., Palmer, D., & Pozner, J. E. (2010). Organizations gone wild: The causes, processes, and consequences of organizational misconduct. *Academy of Management Annals*, *4*(1), 53–107.

Grodal, S., Gotsopoulos, A., & Suarez, F. F. (2015). The coevolution of technologies and categories during industry emergence. *Academy of Management Review*, *40*(3), 423–445.

Gurses, K., & Ozcan, P. (2015). Entrepreneurship in regulated markets: framing contests and collective action to introduce Pay TV in the US. *Academy of Management Journal*, *58*(6), 1709–1739.

Hamilton, G. G., & Biggart, N. W. (1988). Market, culture, and authority: A comparative analysis of management and organization in the Far East. *American Journal of Sociology*, S52–S94.

Hardy, C., & Maguire, S. (2017). Institutional Entrepreneurship and Change in Fields. In R. Greenwood, C. Oliver, T. Lawrence & R. Meyer (Eds.), *The SAGE Handbook of Organizational Institutionalism*. Thousand Oaks, CA/London: Sage. 2nd edition.

Heugens, P. P., & Lander, M. W. (2009). Structure! Agency! (and other quarrels): A meta-analysis of institutional theories of organization. *Academy of Management Journal*, *52*(1), 61–85.

Hoffman, A. (1999). Institutional evolution and change: Environmentalism and the U.S. chemical industry. *Academy of Management Journal*, *42*, 351–371.

Hoffman, A. J., & Ocasio, W. (2001). Not all events are attended equally: Toward a middle-range theory of industry attention to external events. *Organization Science*, *12*(4), 414–434.

Hsu, G. (2006). Jacks of all trades and masters of none: Audiences' reactions to spanning genres in feature film production. *Administrative Science Quarterly*, *51*(3), 420–450.

Khaire, M., & Wadhwani, R. D. (2010). Changing landscapes: The construction of meaning and value in a new market category – Modern Indian art. *Academy of Management Journal*, *53*(6), 1281–1304.

King, B. G. (2008). A political mediation model of corporate response to social movement activism. *Administrative Science Quarterly*, *53*(3), 395–421.

Kraatz, M. S., & Block, E. (2008). Organizational implications of institutional pluralism. In R. Greenwood, C. Oliver, R. Suddaby, & K. Sahlin-Andersson (Eds.), *The SAGE Handbook of Organizational Institutionalism* (pp. 243–275). Thousand Oaks, CA/London: Sage.

Kraatz, M. & Block, E. (2017) Institutional Pluralism Revisited. In R. Greenwood, C. Oliver, T. Lawrence & R. Meyer (Eds.), *The SAGE handbook of organizational institutionalism*. Thousand Oaks, CA/London: Sage. 2nd edition.

Lampel, J., & Meyer, A. D. (2008). Guest editors' introduction: Field-configuring events as structuring mechanisms: How conferences, ceremonies, and trade shows constitute new technologies, industries, and markets. *Journal of Management Studies*, *45*(6), 1025–1035.

Lawrence, T. B., & Suddaby, R. (2006). 1.6 institutions and institutional work. In S. R. Clegg, C. Hardy and W. R. Nord (eds.), *The SAGE Handbook of Organization Studies* (p. 215). London: Sage.

Lawrence, T., Suddaby, R., & Leca, B. (2011). Institutional work: Refocusing institutional studies of organization. *Journal of Management Inquiry*, *20*(1), 52–58.

Leblebici, H., & Sherer, P. (2015). Governance in professional services firms: from structural and cultural to legal normative views. In J. Broschak & L. Empson (Eds.), *The Oxford handbook of professional service firms* (pp. 189–212). Oxford: Oxford University Press.

Levy, D., & Scully, M. (2007). The institutional entrepreneur as modern prince: The strategic face of power in contested fields. *Organization Studies*, *28*(7), 971–991.

Logue, D. (2014). The 'stuff' of markets: An institutional analysis of impact investing. In *Academy of Management Proceedings* (Vol. 2014, No. 1, p. 10480). Academy of Management.

Logue, D., Clegg, S., & Gray, J. (2016). Social organization, classificatory analogies and logics: Institutional theory revisits Mary Douglas. *Human Relations*, *69*(7): 1587–1609.

Logue, D., & Zappala, G. (2014). The emergence of the 'social economy': The Australian not-for-profit sector in transition. https://opus.lib.uts.edu.au/bitstream/10453/29350/1/Logue%20and%20Zappala_The%20

Emergence%20of%20the%20Social%20Economy_ August%202014.pdf.

Lounsbury, M. (2002). Institutional transformation and status mobility: The professionalization of the field of finance. *Academy of Management Journal*, *45*(1), 255–266.

Lounsbury, M. (2007). A tale of two cities: Competing logics and practice variation in the professionalizing of mutual funds. *Academy of Management Journal*, *50*(2), 289–307.

Lounsbury, M., & Crumley, E. T. (2007). New practice creation: An institutional perspective on innovation. *Organization Studies*, 28, 993–1012.

Lounsbury, M., & Rao, H. (2004). Sources of durability and change in market classifications: A study of the reconstitution of product categories in the American mutual fund industry, 1944–1985. *Social Forces*, *82*(3), 969–999.

Maguire, S., Hardy, C., & Lawrence, T. B. (2004). Institutional entrepreneurship in emerging fields: HIV/AIDA treatment advocacy in Canada. *Academy of Management Journal*, *47*, 657–679.

McKague, K., Zietsma, C., & Oliver, C. (2015), 'Building the social structure of a market', *Organization Studies*, *36*(8), 1063–1093.

Malhotra, N., & Hinings, C. B. (2015). Unpacking continuity and change as a process of organizational transformation. *Long Range Planning*, *48*(1), 1–22.

Malhotra, N., Morris, T., & Hinings, C. R. (2006). Variation in organizational form among professional service organizations. *Research in the Sociology of Organizations*, *24*(6), 171–202.

Marquis, C., & Lounsbury, M. (2007). Vive la résistance: Competing logics and the consolidation of US community banking. *Academy of Management Journal*, *50*(4), 799–820.

Marquis, C., Lounsbury, M., & Greenwood, R. (2011). Introduction: Community as an institutional order and a type of organizing. *Research in the Sociology of Organizations*, 33.

Marquis, C., & Raynard, M. (2015). Institutional strategies in emerging markets. *Academy of Management Annals*, *9*(1), 291–335.

Meyer, J., Scott, W. R., & Strang, D. (1987). Centralization, fragmentation, and school district complexity. *Administrative Science Quarterly*, 186–201.

Meyer, R. E. (2008). New sociology of knowledge: Historical legacy and contributions to current debates in institutional research. In R. Greenwood, C. Oliver, R. Suddaby, & K. Sahlin-Andersson (Eds.), *The SAGE Handbook of Organizational Institutionalism* (pp. 517–536). London: Sage.

Moeran, B., & Strandgaard Pedersen, J. (Eds.) (2011). *Negotiating Values in the creative industries: Fairs, festivals and competitive events*. Cambridge: Cambridge University Press.

Morgan, G., & Quack, S. (2006). The internationalisation of professional service firms: global convergence, national path-dependency or cross-border hybridisation? In R. Greenwood & R. Suddaby (Eds.), *Professional service firms* (pp. 403–431). Bingley, UK: Emerald Group Publishing.

Munir, K. A., & Phillips, N. (2005). The birth of the 'Kodak Moment': Institutional entrepreneurship and the adoption of new technologies. *Organization Studies*, *26*(11), 1665–1687.

Navis, C., & Glynn, M. A. (2010). How new market categories emerge: Temporal dynamics of legitimacy, identity, and entrepreneurship in satellite radio, 1990–2005. *Administrative Science Quarterly*, *55*(3), 439–471.

North, D. C. (1990). *Institutions, institutional change and economic performance*. Cambridge: Cambridge University Press.

Oakes, L. S., Townley, B., & Cooper, D. J. (1998). Business planning as pedagogy: Language and control in a changing institutional field. *Administrative Science Quarterly*, 43, 257–292.

O'Mahoney, S., & Bechky, B. (2008). Boundary organizations: Enabling collaboration among unexpected allies. *Administrative Science Quarterly*, *53*(3), 422–459.

Ostrom, E., Schroeder, L., & Wynne, S. (1993). Analyzing the performance of alternative institutional arrangements for sustaining rural infrastructure in developing countries. *Journal of Public Administration Research and Theory*, *3*(1), 11–45.

Pache, A. C., & Santos, F. (2010). When worlds collide: The internal dynamics of organizational responses to conflicting institutional demands. *Academy of Management Review*, *35*(3), 455–476.

Pachucki, M. A., & Breiger, R. L. (2010). Cultural holes: Beyond relationality in social networks and culture. *Annual Review of Sociology*, *36*, 205–224.

Padgett, J., & Powell, W. (2012). *The Emergence of Organizations and Markets*. Princeton, NJ: Princeton University Press.

Patvardhan, S. D., Gioia, D. A., & Hamilton, A. L. (2015). Weathering a meta-level identity crisis: Forging a coherent collective identity for an emerging field. *Academy of Management Journal*, *58*(2), 405–435.

Piatkowski, M. (2002). *The new economy and economic growth in transition economies: The relevance of institutional infrastructure* (No. 2002/62). WIDER Discussion Papers//World Institute for Development Economics (UNU-WIDER).

Porac, J. F., Thomas, H., & Baden-Fuller, C. (1989). Competitive groups as cognitive communities: The case of Scottish knitwear manufacturers. *Journal of Management Studies*, *26*(4), 397–416.

Purdy, J. M., & Gray, B. (2009). Conflicting logics, mechanisms of diffusion, and multilevel dynamics in emerging institutional fields. *Academy of Management Journal, 52*(2), 355–380.

Quack, S. (2007). Legal professionals and transnational law-making: A case of distributed agency. *Organization, 14*(5), 643–666.

Quinn Trank, C., & Washington, M. (2009). Maintaining an institution in a contested organizational field: the work of AACSB and its constituents. In T. B. Lawrence, R. Suddaby, & B. Leca (Eds.), *Institutional work: Actors and agency in institutional studies of organizations* (pp. 236–261). Cambridge: Cambridge University Press.

Raaijmakers, A. G., Vermeulen, P. A., Meeus, M. T., & Zietsma, C. (2015). I need time! Exploring pathways to compliance under institutional complexity. *Academy of Management Journal, 58*(1), 85–110.

Rao, H. (1994). The social construction of reputation: Certification contests, legitimation, and the survival of organizations in the American automobile industry: 1895–1912. *Strategic Management Journal, 15*(S1), 29–44.

Rao, H., Morrill, C., & Zald, M. N. (2000). Power plays: How social movements and collective action create new organizational forms. *Research in Organizational Behavior, 22*, 237–281.

Raynard, M. (2016). Deconstructing complexity: Configurations of institutional complexity and structural hybridity. *Strategic Organization, 14* (4): 310–335.

Reay, T., & Hinings, C. R. (2005). The recomposition of an organizational field: Health care in Alberta. *Organization Studies, 26,* 351–384.

Reay, T., & Hinings, C. R. (2009). Managing the rivalry of competing institutional logics. *Organization Studies, 30,* 629–652.

Reinecke, J., Manning, S., & Von Hagen, O. (2012). The emergence of a standards market: Multiplicity of sustainability standards in the global coffee industry. *Organization Studies, 33*(5-6), 791–814.

Rittel, H. W. J., & Webber, M. (1973). Dilemmas in a general theory of planning. *Policy Sciences, 4*(2), 155–169.

Rodrick, D. (1997). *Trade policy and economic performance in Sub-Saharan Africa.* Cambridge, MA: Harvard University Press.

Sauder, M. (2008). Interlopers and field change: The entry of US news into the field of legal education. *Administrative Science Quarterly, 53*(2), 209–234.

Scott, W.R. (2014). *Institutions and Organizations,* 4th ed. Thousand Oaks, CA: Sage.

Smylie, M. A., & Crowson, R. L. (1996). Working within the scripts: Building institutional infrastructure for children's service coordination in schools. *Educational Policy, 10*(1), 3–21.

Soskice, D. (1991). The institutional infrastructure for international competitiveness: a comparative analysis of the UK and Germany. *The Economics of the New Europe,* 45–66.

Suddaby, R., & Greenwood, R. (2005). Rhetorical strategies of legitimacy. *Administrative Science Quarterly, 50*(1), 35–67.

Temkin, K., & Rohe, W. M. (1998). Social capital and neighborhood stability: An empirical investigation. *Housing Policy Debate, 9*(1), 61–88.

Thornton, P. H., Jones, C., & Kury, K. (2005). Institutional logics and institutional change in organizations: Transformation in accounting, architecture and publishing. *Research in the Sociology of Organizations,* 23, 127–172

Thornton, P. H., & Ocasio, W. (2008). Institutional logics. In R. Greenwood, C. Oliver, R. Suddaby, & K. Sahlin-Andersson (Eds.), *The SAGE handbook of organizational institutionalism* (pp. 99–128). Thousand Oaks, CA/London: Sage.

Thornton, P. H., Ocasio, W., & Lounsbury, M. (2012). *The institutional logics perspective.* Oxford: Oxford University Press.

Van Wijk, J., Stam, W., Elfring, T., & Zietsma, C., den Hond, F. (2013). Activists and incumbents structuring cange: The interplay of agency, culture and networks in field evolution. *Academy of Management Journal,* 56: 358–386

Voronov, M., De Clercq, D., & Hinings, C. R. (2013). Conformity and distinctiveness in a global institutional framework: The legitimation of Ontario fine wine. *Journal of Management Studies, 50*(4), 607–645.

Waddock, S. (2008). Building a new institutional infrastructure for corporate responsibility. *The Academy of Management Perspectives, 22*(3), 87–108.

Washington, M. (2004). Field approaches to institutional change: The evolution of the National Collegiate Athletic Association 1906–1995. *Organization Studies, 25*(3), 393–414.

Weber, K., Heinze, K. L., & DeSoucey, M. (2008). Forage for thought: Mobilizing codes in the movement for grass-fed meat and dairy products. *Administrative Science Quarterly, 53*(3), 529–567.

Wedlin, L. (2011). Going global: Rankings as rhetorical devices to construct an international field of management education. *Management Learning, 42*(2): 165–181.

Wooten, M., & Hoffman, A. J. (2008). Organizational fields: Past, present and future. In R. Greenwood, C. Oliver, R. Suddaby, & K. Sahlin-Andersson (Eds.), *The SAGE handbook of organizational institutionalism* (pp.130–147). Thousand Oaks, CA/London: Sage.

Wooten, M., & Hoffman, A. J. (2017). Organizational fields: Past, present and future. In R. Greenwood, C. Oliver, T. Lawrence & R. Meyer (Eds.), *The SAGE handbook of organizational institutionalism.* Thousand Oaks, CA/London: Sage. 2nd edition.

Wry, T., & Lounsbury, M. (2013). Contextualizing the categorical imperative: Category linkages, technology focus, and resource acquisition in nanotechnology entrepreneurship. *Journal of Business Venturing, 28*(1), 117–133.

Wry, T., Lounsbury, M., & Glynn, M. A. (2011). Legitimating nascent collective identities: Coordinating cultural entrepreneurship. *Organization Science, 22*(2), 449–463.

Zietsma, C., Groenewegen, P., Logue, D., & Hinings, C. R. (2017). Field or fields? Building the scaffolding for cumulation of research on organizational fields: An important and critical issue in a field of research. *Academy of Management Annals.*

Zietsma, C., & Lawrence, T. B. (2010). Institutional work in the transformation of an organizational field: The interplay of boundary work and practice work. *Administrative Science Quarterly, 55,* 189–221.

Zietsma, C., & McKnight, B. (2009). Building the iron cage: co-creation work in the context of competing proto-institutions. In T. B. Lawrence, R. Suddaby, & B. Leca (Eds.), *Institutional work: Actors and agency in institutional studies of organizations* (p. 143). Cambridge: Cambridge University Press.

Zilber, T. B. (2009). Institutional maintenance as narrative acts. In T. B. Lawrence, R. Suddaby, & B. Leca (Eds.). *Institutional work: Actors and agency in institutional studies of organizations* (pp. 205–235). Cambridge: Cambridge University Press.

Zuckerman, E. (1999). The categorical imperative: securities analysts and the illegitimacy discount. *American Journal of Sociology, 104*: 1398–1438.

7

Drivers of Community Strength: An Institutional Logics Perspective on Geographical and Affiliation-Based Communities

Juan Almandoz, Christopher Marquis and Michael Cheely

Recent research on communities and organizations has engaged in two broad and disconnected conversations. On the one hand, sociologists and organizational scholars have explored the enduring influence of embeddedness in geographical communities on organizations (see Marquis & Battilana, 2009 for a review). For example, Almandoz (2012) showed that one important factor affecting the success of local bank founding teams was the teams' local embeddedness and presence of community logics. This research shows that despite global trends, local phenomena are still important because different locations comprise distinct historical, cultural and normative environments that determine appropriate personal and organizational practices (Lounsbury, 2007; Marquis, 2003; Marquis, Davis, & Glynn, 2013).

On the other hand, several scholars have also explored the impact and governance of new types of affiliation-based communities that are often enabled by technology and do not depend on physical proximity (Jeppesen & Frederiksen, 2006; Mok, Wellman, & Carrasco, 2010; O'Mahony & Ferraro, 2007; Preece, 2000, 2001; Preece & Maloney-Krichmar, 2005). New, free and widespread communication technology has transformed the popular meaning of community to encompass not only close-knit groups in a shared space but also location-independent networks of individuals bounded by strong, meaningful and supportive relationships (Wellman, 2001; Wellman & Gulia, 1999). This second stream of research has explored for instance how virtual communities govern themselves to collaborate more effectively in the production of collective goods (O'Mahony & Ferraro, 2007), and how organizations can create and harness those types of communities to reach higher levels of organizational performance and achieve innovation (Autio, Dahlander, & Frederiksen, 2013).

The existence of those two streams of research on classical (geographical) and modern (affiliation-based) forms of community were foreshadowed by the early work of Wellman on the 'community question'. Wellman and colleagues demonstrated that modern communication and mobility – modern technology enabling multiple social networks – did not eliminate but rather made possible meaningful community ties spreading onto wider geographical spaces. Intimate social relations still existed but they were no longer confined to cohesive and insulated neighborhoods or geographical communities (Wellman, 1979). Comparing and contrasting these two research streams on geographical and affiliation-based communities invites an exploration of the two topics addressed by this chapter: first, the similarities and differences in notions of community underlying research on geographical and affiliation-based communities; and second, the mechanisms by which a community logic can produce cultural and material resources for organizations (Marquis, Lounsbury, & Greenwood, 2011; Thornton, 2004). Addressing those questions is important to understand more fully the nature of communities, and to understand also the mechanisms affecting when and how communities influence organizations.

Our analysis takes an institutional logics perspective (Thornton, Ocasio, & Lounsbury, 2012), a theoretical framework that views society as composed of a number of different fields or contexts, known as institutional orders, each having a pattern of beliefs, practices, values, assumptions and rules that determine what is meaningful and legitimate in that context (Friedland & Alford, 1991; Thornton & Ocasio, 1999). Under an institutional logics perspective, a community logic can influence individual and organizational behavior by providing a framework of action, evoking norms, competing with other institutional orders (Greenwood, Raynard, Kodeih, Micelotta, & Lounsbury, 2011; Nigam & Ocasio, 2010) and, as a result, it can facilitate resources to those who appeal to community motivations (DiMaggio, 1988; Luo, Chung, & Sobczak, 2009). An institutional logics perspective is useful for understanding the two types of communities we examine

for two reasons. First, this perspective provides a structured framework that serves as a basis of comparison between geographical and affiliation-based communities. For example, there are meaningful distinctions in the root metaphor (Thornton et al., 2012) that determine how knowledge is structured and action organized in those two forms of community; or there may be differences in the sources of legitimacy, authority and norms, identity and other factors. Second, since it is a society-level perspective, the institutional logic approach can further help unpack how different logics – for example, political, economic and religious – interact in multiple geographical and virtual settings, showing how the impact of a community logic may depend on the relative strength (or weakness) of competing logics in society.

A new engagement with community research under an institutional logic perspective is important because new forms of community have emerged with the help of Internet technology that have shown tremendous impact on social, economic and political events, and have forced us to reconsider the nature and impact of communities. Open communities in some settings have become powerful agents achieving impressive performance results even for standards of hierarchical organizations. A new engagement with community research is greatly facilitated by the institutional logics lens, a powerful tool to analyze multiple forms of communities in society, one that only recently has focused on the community logic.

This paper makes several theoretical contributions. First, it develops and deepens the concept of a community institutional logic, which was recently introduced as such in the literature (Marquis et al., 2011; Thornton et al., 2012); second, it develops the distinction between geographical (traditional) and affiliation-based (modern) communities and explores drivers of community strength in how those types of communities impact organizations (thus conceptualizing community orientation as a variable); and third, it brings a new and especially powerful lens, the institutional logics perspective, into the traditional question of how modern life has influenced the relevance of communities in society.

COMMUNITY AS AN INSTITUTION

In line with Marquis, Lounsbury and Greenwood (2011), we define communities as 'collections of actors whose membership in the collective provides social and cultural resources that shape their action. Membership can result from a number of factors including propinquity, interest in a common goal or common identity' (p. xvi). In this definition, two critical components include the potential to draw resources from the community and the motives of interaction (Weber, 1921) which lead to a sense of belonging, shared identity, and goodwill towards other community members. Even if the community was formed to achieve shared interests, central to this definition of community is that relationships among members transcend self-interest – even though they may also include it. Ideal-type examples of communities would be a cohesive village in a rural area, a religious group that meets regularly, or an active fan group of a famous musician that shares a platform where members exchange songs, news and stories about their idol.

Another key component of community is also captured by Brint (2001), who said that members in communities are 'bound together *principally* by relations of affect, loyalty, common values, and/or personal … interest in the personalities and life events of one another' (p. 8). In this definition, the word *principally* distinguishes communities from other organizations or associations that have primarily another purpose but may have adopted, primarily for instrumental reasons, a community culture. To qualify as a community, community members must value the community for its own sake or for the

positive impact it has on common values, and not only for its instrumental benefits. Closely connected with the definition of community, but not strictly necessary to it, are its small size, the presence of dense social ties, joint involvement and collaboration, democratic relationships, perceptions of similarity, and intrinsic motivation. Concepts antithetical to community include rational-legal authority, hierarchy, and interested and instrumental purposes.

The definition suggests that there may be degrees of community. A small rural village may be more of a community than another with lower degrees of affect, loyalty, and common values. Interestingly, much of the literature on geographical communities has revealed that these are often riddled with power, interest, and division, often concealing a structure of privilege – i.e., they are not really communities (Coleman, 1961; Hunter, 1953). Harley Davidson, a profit-seeking business organization with a large community of fans, may not itself be a community because of its primary instrumental purpose. It could perhaps be better described as a business organization that has adopted a community institutional logic for instrumental reasons. But the collective of fans of Harley Davidson´s products may be a community to the extent that members value the group not for company objectives but for its own sake. A food cooperative that has an instrumental purpose – say, to make money for its members – may be more likely to develop into a community than a corporation because of its democratic and egalitarian ethos, which is more compatible with meaningful relationships among members than the legal-rational-hierarchical relationships among members of corporations.

Our definition of community as a group of people bound together by meaningful relationships from which members can extract cultural and material resources is broad enough to exist within or outside a formal organization – as long as those relationships are not merely instrumental. It could be a partial organization, like international standard organizations or human rights groups, existing outside and between formal organizations (Ahrne & Brunsson, 2008), or a professional association, or a crowd-funding network – if their members are bound together by meaningful relationships. A community may also emerge over time, for example as neighbors start developing deeper and more meaningful relationships. Religious groups are likely to form particularly strong communities because the religious logic has a 'vertical' dimension and many other components connected with belief, worship, ceremony and other religious practices that create meaningful bonds among members – but there may be different degrees in the extent to which religious groups form communities. For some scholars, like Durkheim (1965[1915]), religion is a product of society and thus he reduces the religious logic to a special case of a community logic. However, the institutional logics perspective clearly differentiates those two logics. In sum, the strength of a community derives in part from the extent to which it has value in itself, above other instrumental benefits that members derive from it.

Our definition of geographical community is different from that of *field*, a central concept in institutional theory. The concept of field developed originally to provide a wider context for organizations than the term 'industry' by including other critical actors and resource providers, such as agencies, professional and trade associations, regulators, the media and the state (Wooten & Hoffman, 2008). Geographical community, as we define it, is also different from local relational networks (Meyer, 1977; Meyer & Scott, 1983) or more broadly the local context, which provides variable cues about normative and institutional appropriateness and legitimacy to organizations (Marquis & Battilana, 2009). While it is true that geographic communities include people nested in a great variety of institutions and organizations that define a local field – or local context of organizations – critical to our definition of

community is the meaningful nature of the relationships among community members. According to our definition, one local context may be a geographical community and not another. The institutional logics perspective explains how it is there can be a high degree of variation in how present a community institutional logic is in a given context. The reasons may include historical factors, available categories, mechanisms directing attention, presence of institutional entrepreneurs, etc. (Thornton et al., 2012).

The concept of affiliation-based community, as we define it, may be more closely associated in some instances with social movements that energize and mobilize people and provide resources to create, transform or resist institutional arrangements (McCarthy & Zald, 1977; Schneiberg & Lounsbury, 2008) because collective action for a common cause often engenders a sense of community, where group members share common beliefs and are bound together principally by relations of affect, loyalty and common values. If participants in the social movement value each other for their common values more than the instrumental benefits they may obtain from the collective action, then such a movement may be seen as a community.

GEOGRAPHICAL AND AFFILIATION-BASED COMMUNITIES

While more fine-grained categories of communities could be created, as noted, we subdivide all communities into two basic types. We define *geographical communities* as those communities that are in some way based upon the shared geography of its members, including neighborhoods, towns and cities (see Marquis & Battilana, 2009). At the empirical level, researchers have focused on the city, the neighborhood and even the county as the units of analysis. The government census establishes geographical demarcations based on commuting distance, which is a helpful way of capturing the possibility of face-to-face interactions among residents. Another way of measuring communities may be in terms of relational networks, i.e., what geographical boundary would place any two individuals with a high probability at two degrees of separation of a face-to-face relationship among community members. We define *affiliation-based communities* as broad networks of individuals expanding beyond a geographical location and bounded by strong, meaningful and supportive relationships built on voluntary membership and shared interests, identities and values (Wellman, 2001; Wellman & Gulia, 1999). While Internet platforms have enabled or changed significantly many affiliation-based communities, we do not consider that use of such platforms imply a new category of community beyond our two basic types.

Both types of communities are generally motivated by community members' need to belong (Baumeister & Leary, 1995; Bruhn, 2011). The main distinction between the two types is that, while affiliation-based communities are generally designed and constructed to achieve a particular goal, geographical communities emerge incidentally from the relationships between people living in close proximity to one another. The process of living and working together becomes, under certain circumstances, a source of identification and meaning for those living in a given place (Cuba & Hummon, 1993), and renders their relationships with one another more meaningful and supportive. Based on that distinction, we would consider regions and nations with a strong degree of shared identification (what Anderson (1983) called 'imagined communities') as affiliation-based and not geographical communities. In larger geographical settings, the common boundary shared by members is usually too wide to ensure face-to-face relationships. Based on our definition perhaps Andorra and Liechtenstein could be considered a geographical community but not the United States or Spain.

We consider those categories – geographical and affiliation-based communities – to be all-encompassing, i.e., covering the full spectrum of communities. This categorization is similar to that of Brint (2001), who divided communities into geographic and choice-based categories. However, our categories are obviously not mutually exclusive. There are certainly communities with a clear goal driving the affiliations of their members that also share a clear geographical boundary. Examples may be a local charity or a community foundation. Those hybrid communities that are both geographical and affiliation-based would exhibit characteristics of both types of community.

Scholars have traditionally argued that the changes associated with modernity, such as globalization, social mobility and improvements in communication technology, will result in the decline over time of the influence of communities on individuals and organizations (DiMaggio & Powell, 1983; Meyer, Boli, Thomas, & Ramirez, 1997; Tönnies, 1887). But this conventional argument presumes a geographically bounded understanding of community. The institutional logics perspective, however, includes within the scope of communities other types of communities that are not necessarily geographically constrained (Marquis et al., 2011). Examples of these other communities include academic communities (Crane, 1969; Knorr-Cetina, 1999), collaborative communities (Adler, 2001; Heckscher & Adler, 2006), occupational communities (Bechky, 2003; Orr, 1996), online communities (Butler, 2001; Fayard, DeSanctis, & Roach, 2004), open source communities (Dahlander & O'Mahony, 2011), brand and consumer communities (Kruckeberg & Starck, 2004; McAlexander, Schouten, & Koenig, 2002; Muniz Jr & O'Guinn, 2001), and user communities (Morrison, Roberts, & Von Hippel, 2000; Von Hippel, 2005; see O'Mahony & Lakhani, 2011, for a review).

These affiliation-based types of communities are more prevalent than ever, even if the members of the communities interact physically with less frequency and share fewer affective and normative ties (Gläser, 2001). Interestingly, some of the modern processes that have contributed to the decline of geographical communities may have enabled the creation of affiliation-based communities (O'Mahony & Ferraro, 2007). Virtual communities of open source programmers, for instance, could likely not exist without such modern trends as the improvements in communication technology and networks (Von Krogh & Von Hippel, 2006). Similarly, globalization, which disseminated various norms, values and practices all over the world, contributed to the development of various dispersed communities based on affiliation, bringing people together in collaborative projects as complex as Wikipedia (Piskorski & Gorbatai, 2013).

While both forms of community fit into the framework of a community institutional logic, there are also meaningful differences that could be relevant in determining the factors driving the strength of each form of community. The mechanisms by which both types of communities operate and influence organizations can be usefully expressed in terms of the constitutive elements of community logics elaborated by Thornton et al. (2012), such as root metaphor, sources of legitimacy, sources of authority and norms, sources of identity, and bases of attention and strategy. Using this structured set of categories can shed light on mechanisms by which cultural and material resources made available by the community logic can become community capital – defined here as the capacity and motivation of a community to produce resources that can be used by organizations in community-oriented endeavors.

The following categories used by Thornton, Ocasio and Lounsbury (2012) to make sense of differences among institutional logics (p. 73) could be useful to conceptualize differences among geographical and affiliation-based communities: root metaphor, sources of legitimacy, sources of authority and norms, sources of identity, and basis of attention and strategy.

Root Metaphor

In geographical communities, the root metaphor, which determines the manner in which knowledge is structured and action organized, is a common boundary (Thornton et al., 2012). This boundary separates those who are members and those who are not. It could be any kind of geographical, political, cultural, commercial, or symbolic dividing line, including rivers, road intersections, markets areas, political jurisdictions that could have an impact on the actors and organizations enclosed within it (Carroll & Swaminathan, 2000; Dobbin, 1994; Guthrie, 2003; Wade, Swaminathan, & Saxon, 1998). Inclusion within a common boundary is associated with other homogeneity-producing factors such as the presence of layers of institutional and cultural infrastructures that can perpetuate institutional legacies, create a common frame of reference and shape future behavior (Marquis, 2003; Marquis & Lounsbury, 2007; Raynard, Lounsbury, & Greenwood, 2012; see Marquis & Battilana, 2009 for a review). Such inclusion can often be accompanied by multiple layers of shared identity among community members in religion, class, culture, language, accent, provenance and ethnicity. Irish immigrant neighborhoods in New York, like Woodlawn in the Bronx, or West Brighton in Staten Island, were communities that reflected distinctions in all those relevant dimensions (Alba, Logan, & Crowder, 1997; Kantrowitz, 1969). Additionally, as shown by network research, the physical proximity of community members structures and facilitates social relationships and frequent interaction (Galaskiewicz, 1997; Podolny, 2001; Turk, 1977). These multiple contexts for interaction generate thick local networks in which everybody knows everybody else. These 'overlapping' and 'redundant' ties among members and the multiple layers of shared identity are likely to make the boundary thicker and the community stronger (Burt, 2000; Coleman, 1988; Granovetter, 1985; Portes & Sensenbrenner, 1993).

In affiliation-based communities, the root metaphor is the community members' conscious affiliation and belief in a particular value, product, interest, goal, etc. (Brint, 2001; Marquis et al., 2011; Storper, 2005). This shared affiliation can be the basis of a rich collaboration among members in a common cause or project (Adler, 2015). Members of affiliation-based communities, however, are not as likely as members of geographical communities to share deep relational networks as these tend to be place-bound (Becattini, 1990; Putnam, 1993), nor are they as likely to interact with other community members in a variety of different contexts. Finally, the commonalities of members of affiliation-based communities are likely to be more limited than what is found in geographical communities (Brint, 2001). Members of a professional community of accountants, for instance, may share a profession, but they are no more likely to share race, religious views, political affiliations, or hobbies, than any other two people (see Thornton, Jones, & Kury, 2005). Ordinarily, we would expect this narrow scope of identification to weaken the strength of the affiliation-based community, at least compared to geographical communities where the bonds between members are wider in scope. This can be counteracted, however, if the shared affiliation of the members is central to their core identity (McCall & Simmons, 1978; Stryker, 2000; Watson, 2008).

Sources of Legitimacy

In geographical communities, the community members' belief in trust and reciprocity is the source of legitimacy (i.e., the means by which power or influence is institutionalized and given a moral grounding) (Coleman, 1988; Thornton et al., 2012). When one community member (individual or organization)

enjoys relationships based on trust and reciprocity with the community and is perceived as trustworthy by other community members, the others will accept this member's influence. The belief in trust and reciprocity in geographical communities stems from, among other things, the presence of redundant and overlapping ties connecting community members (Uzzi, 1996, 1999). The community ties ensure that news about a community member's untrustworthy behavior are disseminated rapidly, thus deterring such behavior.

The source of legitimacy in affiliation-based communities is primarily the unity of will of the members (Raymond, 1999; Thornton et al., 2012). Members who share the same affiliation are more likely to accept the power and influence of one another, but only in matters directly related to the goals of the community (Algesheimer, Dholakia, & Herrmann, 2005). Affiliation-based communities are not, like geographical communities, necessarily legitimized by belief in trust and reciprocity, because members of affiliation-based communities rarely have redundant and overlapping ties or points of contact. However, building trust is an important component in the success of those affiliation-based communities (Boyd, 2002, 2003). Because trust and reciprocity may be taken for granted and therefore potentially abused, affiliation-based communities may require mechanisms such as reputation systems to punish the deviant behavior of community abusers (Jøsang, Ismail, & Boyd, 2007).

Sources of Authority and Norms

In both geographical and affiliation-based communities, the source of authority, or reason why a particular authority is obeyed, is the community members' commitment to the community and to the values or ideology of the community (Almandoz, 2012; Thornton et al., 2012), not hierarchical control (Blau, 1968). Members are embedded in their community, and from it they receive a certain sense of belonging which they share with the other members of the community. This shared sense of belonging is connected to a desire to fit in, socialize with, and care about the concerns of the others in the community. These shared priorities contribute to a real commitment of the community members to the values of the community as a whole. In geographical communities, the source of authority may be rooted in the community itself more than the content of shared values and identities of community members. By contrast, in affiliation communities, the source of authority may be centered in the values or identities of the communities more than in the community itself (Rao, Monin, & Durand, 2003). This commitment to those community values or identities can be the source of an effective collaboration among community members that may not need hierarchical coordination and control (Adler, 2015).

The basis of norms that leads both geographical and affiliation-based community members to accept normative restrictions is group membership in a valued community that imposes local standards for organizational practices (Lazaric & Lorenz, 1998; Owen-Smith & Powell, 2004; Storper, 1997) and shapes local norms (Litwak & Hylton, 1962; see Marquis et al., 2011 for a review). Members accept subjection to the norms of the community because they hold the community and/or its values in high regard. There may be different degrees of compliance with community norms depending on how much the community or its values are important to the members. In geographical communities where membership may be more accidental – resulting from convenience or happenstance rather than affective involvement or joint sense of identity – more variation is expected in member's subjection to community norms. In affiliation-based communities where at least in some cases a common purpose has been embraced by all members, community norms are likely to have a higher degree of acceptance, although

some degree of free-riding is unavoidable (Walsh & Warland, 1983).

Sources of Identity

The sources of identity in geographical communities are the emotional connections that members share and the value that they obtain from reputation in the community (Almandoz, 2012; Thornton et al., 2012). These factors are fostered by the community members' multiple levels of shared identity, which, due to homophily, lead similar individuals to like and relate to one another (McPherson, Smith-Lovin, & Cook, 2001). A community identity in a geographic setting is 'cobbled together from existing elements or bits of meaning, symbols or values' that are provided by distinctive elements of the community that are shared by its members (Glynn, 2008). The greater or more encompassing the similarity, the more that we expect community members to like and relate to one another. These multiple levels of shared identity can also foster greater emotional connection through the accentuation of an us-versus-them mentality (Ashforth & Mael, 1989). When the distinction between community insiders and outsiders embraces multiple dimensions, the identities of the two groups may be separated by fault lines (Lau & Murnighan, 1998), leading to an even higher degree of contrast between the two groups. This multi-layered contrast between community insiders and outsiders accentuates us-versus-them behaviors and attitudes and reinforces the community's sense of identity.

The source of identity for affiliation-based communities, on the other hand, is reputation and ego-boosting in the context of a purposeful association, as well as the intrinsic value or interest that brings members together into the community, more than multi-layered connections among members (Lerner & Tirole, 2004; Osterloh & Frey, 2000; Raymond, 1999; Thornton et al., 2012). As mentioned earlier, identification in affiliation-based communities is generally narrower in scope than the identification in a geographical community and it leaves many dimensions of a person's identity unaddressed. Members of affiliation-based communities generally have fewer interactions with one another and – to the extent that the relations between members are sustained through long-distance, cold and impersonal communication technology – those interactions are expected to generate weaker community ties than those expected in geographical communities – of course, unless the shared values that constitute the reason for the community are deeply meaningful to the core identity of the members (McCall & Simmons, 1978; Stryker, 2000). On the other hand, since those narrow affiliation-based community identities constitute the whole reason for interactions among community members it is likely that agreement and consensus may be more easily attained than in geographical communities where conflicting identities may be at play.

As other research has noted, the expansion of membership and the creation of coherent stories play a crucial role in legitimating the collective identity of groups (Wry, Lounsbury, & Glynn, 2011) in both geographical and affiliation-based communities.

Basis of Attention and Strategy

In a geographical community, the basis of attention, or that which attracts and focuses attention of members, is the community member's investment in the group, while the basis of strategy, or what motivates a member's behavior, is the desire to increase honor and status in the community (Podolny, 1993; Raymond, 1999; Thornton & Ocasio, 1999). The investment of a geographical community member includes deeply personal matters such as a home, social network, and attachment to the local culture and environment, and therefore it understandably commands a considerable measure of attention. In affiliation-based communities, on the other hand, the main basis of attention is likely to be the personal investment in the shared values and interests that led to the creation of the group in the first place (Algesheimer et al., 2005). The influence of an affiliation-based community (unlike that of a geographical community) will therefore only be activated in contexts that immediately relate to the purpose of the community (Ridings & Gefen, 2004).

All those meaningful differences between geographical and affiliation-based communities (see Table 7.1) are likely to have important

Table 7.1   Constitutive elements of community logics: contrasting geographical and affiliation-based communities

	Geographical community	Affiliation-based community
Root metaphor	A common geographical boundary	Conscious affiliation and belief in a particular cause
Sources of legitimacy	Belief in trust and reciprocity	Unity of will of the members in community goals
Sources of authority and norms	Commitment to membership in a valued community	Commitment to community values and identities
Sources of identity	Community reputation and emotional connection with other members (wide scope of shared identity)	Reputation in a purposeful community and intrinsic value of the community's goals (narrow scope of shared identity)
Basis of attention and strategy	Investment in and honor and status within the community, relevant in multiple settings and contexts	Investment in and honor and status within the community, relevant in limited contexts connected with the purpose of the community

consequences in the degree to which a community is stronger or weaker and the degree to which its strength is affected by the factors examined below.

FACTORS DRIVING COMMUNITY STRENGTH

After describing the attributes and constitutive categories of geographical and affiliation-based communities, we can consider factors driving community strength, explore how these factors relate to the geographical and affiliation-based community forms, and illustrate how those factors increase the community´s capacity to provide resources to community-oriented organizations. We focus on five such drivers that seem especially relevant and have been previously discussed in the literature: identification with the community (which often includes resistance to an opposing institutional logic), effective community organization or structure, pivotal events, enforceability of trust, and the presence of strong community leaders.

Identification with the Community

When community members identify closely with their community, they are more likely to be influenced by the community and its particular norms, values and practices, and as a result more likely to provide support to causes aligned with the community. At the geographical level, the community member's identification with the community can be reinforced by a variety of factors, such as the cohesiveness of local networks that contribute to cooperation and build trust (Fleming, King, & Juda, 2007; Fleming & Marx, 2006; Greenwood, Díaz, Li, & Lorente, 2010), and pride in local surroundings, history and iconic landmarks (Nowell, Berkowitz, & Foster-Fishman, 2006). Brown and Humphreys (2006), in their field study of

employees and managers at a British college, found that unattractive physical surroundings made employees less likely to view their work place as a community. The presence of beautiful, unique, historical or otherwise meaningful landmarks – whether natural or man-made – increase people's sense of identification and thus the strength of the community (Cuba & Hummon, 1993). Other factors may also increase 'place attachment' (Brown, Perkins, & Brown, 2003), such as the degree of home ownership in the area (Taylor, 1996) which is correlated with knowing more neighbors (Fischer, 1982), and participation in community groups (Rossi & Weber, 1996).

Community identity at the geographical level can also be reinforced by the incursion of outside groups or opposing logics that may challenge the community. Individuals may view the entrance of global corporations and standards as a threat to the uniqueness of their community (Marquis & Lounsbury, 2007; Robertson, 1995) and may choose to demarcate their boundaries more clearly (Scott & Storper, 2003; Sorge, 2005). The entrance of carriers of an opposing logic can serve as a clarion call that galvanizes resistance to that logic, increasing community members' identification with their community, and strengthening the community as a whole. In the context of banking, the community logic was a source of resistance to the advance of the logic of market efficiency embodied by large, centralized banks acquiring small local banks that thus lost their community orientation (Marquis & Lounsbury, 2007). The disappearance of those small community banks, which were often seen as a symbol of the community, drove community members to organize founding groups to attempt to establish new banks.

In the context of Dutch bars, a community logic became the cultural framework to organize opposition led by local bar owners to government's anti-smoking regulations that could jeopardize (profitable) community building in those bars (Simons, Vermeulen,

& Knoben, 2016). Finally, community opposition to fire insurance by the Amish was similarly a case of a conflict between market and community logics. The Amish saw their close-knit, traditional, community lifestyle threatened by the influence of the commercial logic of the market represented by fire insurance contracts. The Amish, acting upon the logic of the community, forbade fire insurance contracts because of the potentially negative effect such contracts would have on reciprocity and community-building – compared to calling on each other for help (Marglin, 2008). In short, community identification can be reinforced through opposition to another, more general logic that is becoming progressively more dominant and can be seen as a threat.

Communities with a strong sense of identification can be fruitful avenues to obtain organizational resources for actors who can position their organization, product, or service as a representative of the community logic, while casting their competitors as representatives of an opposing logic. A new group of bank founders, for instance, may appeal to community motivations by appointing community leaders to the bank board, serving primarily local borrowers and local depositors, and donating to local charities, while casting larger banks as indifferent or possibly even harmful to the community (Almandoz, 2012, 2014). Dutch bar owners, by appealing to the community motivations, managed to draw support from local residents, who were increasingly loyal to their bars (Simons et al., 2016). Similarly, members of an Amish community that has rejected fire insurance because of its incompatibility with their community values are more likely to show up and provide support when a neighbor's barn needs to be rebuilt (Marglin, 2008).

In affiliation-based communities the degree of identification of members is also an important source of community strength that can result in abundant resources of community capital, especially when those communities are rooted in core identities of its

members. Religious communities, for example, can more easily provide resources to causes linked to those particular communities (Park & Smith, 2000). The ongoing competition from an opposing logic can also present a uniquely important means to strengthen the affiliation-based community and gather support from community members. Open source computer programmers thrive as a community in part thanks to Microsoft's dominant and closed proprietary server software and also thanks to their presumed monopolistic practices (Kogut & Metiu, 2001). International green activists reacting to an oil industry oblivious to the environment (Gelbspan, 2005) and animal rights groups responding to the cruelty of dog and cock fights (Beers, 2006) are other examples of affiliation-based communities driven by opposing logics that strengthen the identification of members to the community and make that community more likely to provide resources to related causes. The main difference between affiliation-based and geographical communities is that the latter are likely to provide resources only to narrowly targeted purposes related to the goals of the community.

Effective Community Governance

The effective governance of a community is another driver that can strengthen a community and thereby increase its capacity to provide community capital. Communities that are well governed and establish clear procedures for communication and coordination can more easily transcend personal interests and guide collective action, more effectively unlock resources, and deal with harmful elements, and more successfully compete with opposing logics.

The effective governance of geographical communities can be provided by local elite groups, unions, fraternal organizations, booster clubs, universities, cultural, educational, and corporation boards, parish groups, philanthropic organizations of various kinds, economic development and government organizations and more – when well run and when sufficient significant time investment is devoted to them – are likely to facilitate the provision of community capital (Davis & Greve, 1997; Piore & Sabel, 1984; Useem, 1984; Wry, Greenwood, Jennings, & Lounsbury, 2010). Che and Qian (1998) highlight how local community governments in rural China served essentially as the board of directors and management of the township-village enterprises (TVEs) and showed how their effective governance of the TVEs helped to ignite great economic and employment growth in those communities. Similarly, the effective governance of Chicago's South Shore neighborhood allowed it to benefit from the community development bank Shorebank's housing rehabilitation projects and credit provision services while other communities that lacked this underlying organizational structure were not as able to benefit from bank services (Taub, 1994). The South Shore neighborhood was organized by committed citizens with steady jobs who were actively engaged in and intensely interested in the well-being of their community and were willing and able to band together to remove destabilizing elements from their community. Similarly, the effective governance of worker cooperatives[1] – by means of wide, meaningful membership, participation in committees, contractual agreements, and promises of support that endowed members with a good deal of trust – allowed them to compete successfully with other forms of governance from markets and hierarchies, support its members in times of economic loss, and contribute to the development of immigrant and religious groups that could survive and flourish in an era of corporations. In tough times, community members were able to appeal to others in the cooperatives and managed to attain the resources that they needed to carry on (Schneiberg, 2002; Schneiberg, King, & Smith, 2008).

Effective community governance is also an important factor driving the strength of affiliation-based communities. As affiliation-based communities are geographically dispersed, they are far more reliant on effective communication and structure to maintain an effective community. But given that such communities have relatively simple and targeted purposes and tend to be connected through technology, an upfront investment in setting up a system greatly facilitates – with little ongoing maintenance – the governance of the community. Efficient communication methods, via websites, chain text messages, and general wireless Internet use was especially important in igniting the region-wide chain of protests that came to be known as the Arab Spring (Eltantawy & Wiest, 2011; Khondker, 2011). The rapid communication between protest organizers and followers in a wide region helped to keep the flame of the rebellion burning and worked to strengthen the community and gather support to its cause. Similarly, a new wireless infrastructure, location-sensing wireless mechanisms, and community supercomputers enable collective action, with minimum additional governance, in communities devoted to a myriad of purposes: political change, celebrity-stalking, efficient transportation in crowded cities, etc. (Rheingold, 2007). Good design of a community website with an orderly structure, comprehensible processes, and clear disclosure of benefits and responsibilities for community members are good governance practices that can facilitate the success of an affiliation-based community (see Shneiderman, 2000).

Pivotal Events

Pivotal events, which comprise mega-events like the Super Bowl or major political conventions, natural disasters like earthquakes and hurricanes, and economic and environmental shocks, have been shown to prompt shifts in institutional logics in local environments (Glynn & Lounsbury, 2005; Tilcsik & Marquis, 2013), strengthening communities and increasing their capacity to provide community capital. Researchers have shown how different kinds of pivotal events can create a sense of unity in a community, enhance local corporate actors' sense of citizenship, increase the levels of solidarity and altruism in communities, or serve as a powerful impetus to community fervor as community members join together in the wake of a crisis or opportunity (Hiller, 2000; Truno, 1995; Waitt, 2001). All of these factors strengthen geographical communities.

Community actors can take advantage of these pivotal events to appeal to community motivations and attain resources needed for their ends. How successful they are in taking advantage of the opportunity afforded by those pivotal events may depend on the degree of identification of members with the community and the presence of efficient community governance. Local non-profits and community leaders, for example, can take advantage of the natural disasters and mega-events by appealing to local corporations for donations (Schwartz, 1997). Because the events are likely to make community development goals more salient (Burbank, Andranovich, & Heying, 2001), the local non-profits will be more likely to attain resources from the local corporations. Tilcsik and Marquis (2013) have noted the increase in corporate giving in the wake of mega-events and natural disasters, an effect that declines over time.

Pivotal events also have the potential to strengthen affiliation-based communities and unlock related community capital. For example, as recent news have demonstrated, public insults against the Prophet Muhammad from Western media provoke united, angry and strong reactions from wide segments of the worldwide Muslim community who consider such impious utterances as blasphemous. Those insults have spontaneously mobilized Muslim organizations and individuals to protest, launch legal complaints, lobby, and those protests have resulted in violence, including the attack producing the death of 11 people in the French satirical weekly newspaper *Charlie Hebdo* in Paris (Eko & Berkowitz, 2009). Similarly, community banks were indirectly able to take advantage of the Financial Crisis of 2008 (a pivotal event) to attain community capital in the form of increased deposits. As many blamed Wall Street banks for the crisis, community bankers spurred a social movement/community called 'Move your Money Project' which encouraged depositors to abandon Wall Street banks to turn to Main Street Banks (see Brescia & Steinway, 2013).

The difference between the effect of pivotal events on affiliation-based communities compared to that on geographical communities is that, unless affiliation-based communities are based on core dimensions of member identities, the impact of pivotal events may be short-lived. Unless community members are frequently connected as they would be in geographical communities the effect of a pivotal event in focusing attention on a community need may quickly dissipate. Not surprisingly, in spite of the initial outrage against Wall Street banks, the Move Your Money Project quickly lost momentum and did not cause a significant change in the behavior of bank customers. As they went on with the business of their ordinary lives, the bank customers quickly forgot about their concerns about Walls Street banks. By contrast, the community support generated in the aftermath of the 9-11 attack in New York City or of Hurricane Katrina in New Orleans (Beller, 2015; Berry, 2013; Gotham, 2008; Tierney, 2003) were more enduring not only because the impact of such events was comparatively more devastating for community members but also because they were constantly facing those events on a daily basis in their frequent relationships with other community members.

Enforceability of Trust

Another driver that strengthens communities and facilitates the provision of community capital is the enforceability of trust (Dacin, Ventresca, & Beal, 1999; Podolny & Page, 1998; Portes & Sensenbrenner, 1993). When trust is enforceable, or when the community can collectively and effectively penalize those who act in an untrustworthy manner, the community is more likely to retain high levels of trust, which in turn makes the community stronger. The enforceability of trust in geographical communities stems from, among other things, the presence of redundant and overlapping ties, as well as the visibility of actions. In short, overlapping and redundant ties ensure that information about deviant actions is spread rapidly. These factors serve as an informal control mechanism that deter untrustworthy behavior, and ultimately lead to higher levels of trust as community members have confidence that others will act in a trustworthy manner. Uzzi (1996) highlights how the trust between individuals who share long term, close commercial ties can reduce transaction costs and create new opportunities for the exchange of goods, resources and useful information. These resources can be crucial for the success of an enterprise.

Trust, however, is not equally enforceable in geographical and affiliation-based communities. In affiliation-based communities, trust can be more difficult to enforce, which in ordinary circumstances could lead to a weakening of community strength. As already mentioned, because relational systems are generally place-bound (Becattini, 1990; Putnam, 1993), affiliation-based community members are generally not in frequent contact with one another unless it is for the purpose that brings them together in the community. For this reason, information about one community member's untrustworthy behavior may not be as widely disseminated, nor will community members be as upset when their relationship with another community member is damaged – it is possible to have never even met the other person. These factors remove many of the possible deterrents to untrustworthy behavior that are

present in geographical communities and thereby decrease the level of trust in the community thus weakening communities as a whole.

Some affiliation-based communities, however, use a variety of means to make trust enforceable, making up for what is ordinarily lacking in affiliation-based communities. They may require community members to generate a profile that includes their real name, an authentic photograph, and other personal information, or they may erect barriers to exiting and rejoining the community, and may prominently display references from other community members and third party certifications of each community member's conduct. These measures, which serve to connect the members' identity in the affiliation-based community with their identity in the real world, help to generate real consequences for untrustworthy behavior. Other measures to promote enforceable trust include providing guarantees with compensation if one of the community members is dissatisfied with a given exchange and facilitating dispute resolution services (see Shneiderman, 2000). These measures facilitate the creation of community capital by increasing levels of trust.

The ridesharing service Uber, lodging rental service AirBnB, and the e-commerce website eBay, each use a number of the above-mentioned trust enforcing mechanisms to great effect and, consequently, have been able to attain community capital in the form of valuable user reviews, free publicity and new customers (Boyd, 2002; Marquis & Yang, 2014). At first glance, these three institutions, as businesses and carriers of the institutional logic of the market, may seem to be poor examples of communities and, therefore, may appear to be irrelevant to our current conversation. After all, they provide goods and services and seek to maximize profits. Yet a key success factor of these organizations – whether they can be considered communities or not based on our conceptualization – has been their ability to transcend the definition of a business into an affiliation-based community where strong and meaningful relationships are expected (Wellman, 2001; Wellman & Gulia, 1999). The philosophy that underlies these organizations – that people are good and can generally be trusted to deal equitably with one another if the necessary safeguards are in place – could be considered a manifestation of the community logic. Further, these organizations give their members the freedom to connect with one another and to provide services person to person without necessarily dictating prices or making excessive use of intermediaries. Over time, individuals' participation in the communities, whether by provision or consumption of their services or by the contribution of reviews or other valuable information, can become a source of trust and identification (Bagozzi & Dholakia, 2006; Hertel, Niedner, & Herrmann, 2003; Jones & George, 1998 reach a similar conclusion in the context of open-source Linux User Groups).

The ability of these organizations to rise to the status of communities, or at least to incorporate the community logic into their model, while still maintaining the market logic, has unlocked crucial resources that allowed them to succeed phenomenally by the standards of the community logic – drawing numerous members and developing a strong sense of identification – and ironically by the standards of the market logic, especially in promoting innovation and collaboration (Adler, 2015) – expanding the sizes of their companies and generating impressive profits. These institutions provide an interesting example of how, in certain situations, various institutional logics can mutually sustain and strengthen one another rather than merely compete (Greenwood et al., 2010).

Community Leaders

The presence of community leaders is another factor that can strengthen communities and drive the creation of community capital. Community leaders can strengthen communities by promoting identification, unity, and trust, for example by developing a distinctive community culture, or by making the impact of community activities visible, so that community approaches are legitimate and preferred over alternative approaches (Podolny, Khurana, & Hill-Popper, 2004; Suddaby & Greenwood, 2005). This style of leadership is quite different from the command-and-control hierarchical and bureaucratic approach prevalent in organizations. Effective community leaders, in addition to building identification and trust, can boost two other drivers of community strength by reinforcing mechanisms of community governance and taking advantage of pivotal events.

Bill Bowerman, the track coach of the University of Oregon and Co-founder of Nike, Inc., strengthened his local community of Eugene, Oregon by developing a unique, attractive community culture that the locals could be proud of (Howard-Grenville, Metzger, & Meyer, 2013). Bowerman engaged the inhabitants of the town in the training, supporting and fundraising of the University's track program and runners and went even further by organizing jogging clubs in order to encourage the inhabitants of Eugene to participate in the sport itself. By the end of Bowerman's tenure as head coach, the town was so famous for the skill of its runners and devotion of its fans that it had won the moniker 'Track Town, USA'. When a community is energized by a leader, it is more capable of providing community capital, often to causes and projects led by the community leaders themselves. Bill Bowerman was able to draw all-star track athletes from across the country to his program at the University of Oregon, fundraise for the enormous Hayward Field running track, and develop an early support group and customer base for his fledgling shoe company, later known as Nike, Inc.

The motivations of local community leaders may be purely altruistic or mixed with self-interest tied to the economic or social development of the community. Bill Bowerman's community-building experience was instrumental to his success with Nike. Similarly, the success of many political candidates has often been built on careers of public and community service (Light, 1999). Almandoz (2012) also found a mix of altruism and self-interest in the composition of founding boards of community banks. These often include restaurant owners, non-profit managers, people with real estate backgrounds, and others who have a personal stake in the development of the community.

Leaders also play a crucial role in strengthening communities in affiliation-based communities that need not share a common local geography. Charismatic religious and political leaders at the national level often play an important role in energizing and providing unity and direction to purposeful communities and social movements at a national or international level (Conger & Kanungo, 1988; Davis, McAdam, Scott, & Zald, 2005). Nelson Mandela, the first black president of South Africa, managed to unite a country deeply divided by the structure and legacy of apartheid and succeeded in drawing support and moving forward a number of important social and economic development goals. His influence before and after becoming President was built on dialogue, collective empowerment and connective leadership (Kirk & Shutte, 2004). Martin Luther King attracted a wide base of support from people unified by deeply felt values – including religious beliefs, nonviolence philosophy, democratic theory and pragmatism (McAdam 1996; Platt & Lilley 1994) – thus succeeding in creating a collective identity among his followers (Morris & Staggenborg, 2004) and energizing a well-organized social movement that was called into action by particular pivotal events (Carson, 1987).

The above drivers of community strength are summarized in Table 7.2.

Table 7.2 Drivers of community strength

	Geographical	Affiliation-based	Both
Identification with the community	Place attachment. Pride in local surroundings, history and iconic landmarks	Stronger if the community is related to the core identity of community members (i.e., religious community)	Stronger when cohesive networks and when community is threatened
Effective community governance	Local elite groups, trade organizations, cooperatives, etc., which may require significant and ongoing time investment	Stronger if enabled by clear and efficient technology and a targeted purpose. Upfront investment needed but limited ongoing investment	Clear procedures for communication and coordination support collective action in pursuit of a collective good
Pivotal events	Extraordinary events affecting a local area attract attention and support from local organizations	Extraordinary events affecting a cause attract sustained attention to the degree that community-members are deeply affected in their core identity or interests	Other drivers such as members' identification with the community and effective governance may moderate the impact of pivotal events
Enforceability of trust	Information about deviant actions spreads rapidly because of redundant and overlapping ties	Guarantees, dispute resolution mechanisms, and third party references can generate trust	Visibility of actions and frequency of positive interactions facilitates trust
Community leaders	Motivated by altruism and self-interest linked to community development	Charisma often plays an important part in meaning-making and shaping a community culture	Promoting identification and unity by developing a distinctive community culture, or by making the impact of the community visible

CONCLUSION

This study has taken a societal level perspective in the original spirit of Friedland and Alford (1991) and has examined the influence of different types of communities on organizations. Rather than entering the old debate on whether communities are still relevant for organizations, we have considered the factors that drive or reduce the impact of two different types of communities on organizations. In the service of this goal, we conceptualized community strength as a variable for both geographical and affiliation-based communities. While this simple categorization hides an enormous amount of diversity, it still serves the purposes both of highlighting the variability of the concept and the need to better understand how those differences affect community strength.

This study suggests multiple directions for future research, especially avenues considering community as an independent variable. First, in line with a society-level analytical perspective (Friedland & Alford, 1991) researchers could explore further, in different settings, how the overarching logics of family, government, or religion support or contradict the community institutional logic. This line of research should perhaps focus on moderators of community influence in organizational responses to multiple and complex institutional logics (Greenwood et al., 2010). For example, are community-oriented strategies more or less welcome in sectors with a strong presence of family and religion institutional logics? Under what conditions do those logics reinforce one another or compete for attention (Ocasio, 1997)? A systematic analysis of the interaction of other institutional logics with the community logic in different sectors (healthcare, government, the arts, etc.) would enrich our society-level understanding of the community institutional logic.

Second, at the field level, a question that deserves more attention is under what conditions community logics are especially powerful in environments dominated by contradictory logics. Adler (2015) observed that in individualistic and competitive contexts (i.e., 'capitalist' societies) community may assume greater 'ideological prominence' precisely to compensate for its absence as 'society's material foundation'. Under what conditions can a community logic become a source of differentiation for organizations that, despite legitimacy concerns, can provide community capital to those organizations? This question could perhaps be fruitfully explored in the context of the impact of community-related corporate social responsibility activities in various sectors (law, banking, real estate ...). The mechanisms and drivers of community strength theorized in this chapter – identification with the values of the community, pivotal events, etc. – could be empirically tested in those future studies.

Third, at the field/organizational level, many researchers have issued calls to integrate perspectives involving interest-driven and purposive behavior in institutional work (DiMaggio, 1988; Greenwood, Oliver, Suddaby, & Sahlin-Andersson, 2008). Given how institutional environments shape organizations, one critical dimension of agent behavior would be how an organization may shape a community for its own ends. Certainly, marketing approaches to develop a sense of community seem to have worked well for Harley Davidson, Macintosh and BMW. Could those strategies be replicated successfully by other business organization in other sectors? In what contexts would creating a community or fostering a community orientation among stakeholders be most helpful? Would the answer vary depending on what performance outcomes are pursued? Online communities have been successful, for example, in producing high levels of collaboration and innovation. What mechanisms are most effective to achieve those outcomes?

Fourth, also at the field/organizational level, more research can be focused on communities as agents that help translate demands from the external environment to the local. Community organizations – those that coordinate and energize a geographical community – have recently been shown to be important in the translation of institutional prescriptions from the external environment to the local level (Binder, 2007; Boxenbaum & Johnsson, 2008; Sahlin & Wedlin, 2008; Zilber, 2006). More research on translation could help explain how community processes edit institutional models, by making them generalizable and plannable (Sahlin & Wedlin, 2008) and then fill in specific and selective elements aligned with community identities, interests and needs (Lok, 2010; Zilber, 2006).

Fifth, at the organizational/individual level, other studies have explored how the community identities of key decision-makers within organizations influence the extent to which a community logic affects organizational strategies and values (Almandoz, 2012, 2014; Pache & Santos, 2010). More research could explore how community identities are affected by career backgrounds in different sectors and how identities and career backgrounds may be especially helpful as channels to draw community capital. For example, what professional fields are most helpful and for what types of community resources (including money, time and social legitimacy)? What mechanisms are used by professionals in different fields to link the organization with those key resources? While we may expect that professionals in different careers are connected to different sorts of resource networks, which may be more or less conducive to community support, an important question to continue exploring is to what extent community capital is contingent on access to community networks or on other motivational factors instead, including identification, commitment and trust of those key decision makers (see Almandoz, 2012).

Communities could also be explored as the dependent variable at the field or societal level. This study has briefly considered how modern social trends, including the impact of technology, may have had a negative impact on geographical communities and a positive

impact on affiliation-based communities – as they have greatly facilitated the latter. Most studies rooted on an institutional logics perspective have developed a uniform characterization of community logics. To the degree that researchers have studied heterogeneity in institutional logics, such heterogeneity has been based on the difference between the community logic and other such institutional logics as the financial or market logic. Perhaps it is time to explore further heterogeneity, or what others have called intra-logic heterogeneity (Meyer & Höllerer, 2014) within each of the overarching institutional logics, including the community logic, as a result of variations in space and time, or as a result of other such factors as improvements in communication technology. If individuals in society satisfy their need for belonging in technology-enabled 'minimalist' communities with limited face-to-face interactions, and weaker affective and normative ties (Gläser, 2001), will the total social and community capital in society become richer or poorer? Will there be more or less collaboration and attention to civic affairs?

Second, while we have conceptually separated geographical and affiliation-based communities as a tool to help us understand the variegated nature of communities, we may also ask to what extent and under what conditions do affiliation-based communities depend also on local communities to connect more deeply with community members and draw community support. Our study suggests differences in both kinds of community, especially in how they generate trust, which could greatly influence the impact of those communities. Certainly, technology has greatly facilitated the creation and governance of affiliation-based communities in ways that do not require much face-to-face interactions. But can those purposive communities replace the old-fashioned local communities in how they produce a sense of belonging that may later have positive consequences for community endeavors? Are those two types of community complementary or are they substitutes for each other so that investments in one undermine the effectiveness of investments in the other?

Note

1   We consider worker cooperatives as communities in this case because of the more meaningful relationships involved among members.

REFERENCES

Adler, P. S. (2001). Market, hierarchy, and trust: The knowledge economy and the future of capitalism. *Organization Science*, *12*, 215–234.

Adler, P. S. (2015). Community and innovation: From Tönnies to Marx. *Organization Studies*, *36*(4), 445–471.

Ahrne, G., & Brunsson, N. (2008). *Meta-organizations*. Cheltenham: Edward Elgar.

Alba, R. D., Logan, J. R., & Crowder, K. (1997). White ethnic neighborhoods and assimilation: The greater New York region, 1980–1990. *Social Forces*, *75*(3), 883–912.

Algesheimer, R., Dholakia, U. M., & Herrmann, A. (2005). The social influence of brand community: Evidence from European car clubs. *Journal of Marketing*, *69*(3), 19–34.

Almandoz, J. (2012). Arriving at the starting line: The impact of community and financial logics on new banking ventures. *Academy of Management Journal*, *55*(6), 1381–1406.

Almandoz, J. (2014). Founding teams as carriers of competing logics: When institutional forces predict banks' risk exposure. *Administrative Science Quarterly*, *59*(3), 442–473.

Anderson, B. (1983). *Imagined Communities*. London, UK: Verso.

Ashforth, B. E., & Mael, F. (1989). Social identity theory and the organization. *Academy of Management Review*, *14*(1), 20–39.

Autio, E., Dahlander, L., & Frederiksen, L. (2013). Information exposure, opportunity evaluation, and entrepreneurial action: An investigation of an online user community. *Academy of Management Journal*, *56*(5), 1348–1371.

Bagozzi, R. P., & Dholakia, U. M. (2006). Open source software user communities: A study of participation in Linux user groups. *Management Science*, *52*(7), 1099–1115.

Baumeister, R. F., & Leary, M. R. (1995). The need to belong: Desire for interpersonal attachments as a fundamental human motivation. *Psychological Bulletin*, *117*(3), 497–529.

Becattini, G. (1990). The Marshallian industrial district as a socioeconomic notion. In F. S. Pyke, G. Becattini, & W. Sengenberger (eds.), *Industrial districts and inter-firm co-operation in Italy* (pp. 37–51). Geneva: International Institute for Labour Studies.

Bechky, B. A. (2003). Sharing meaning across occupational communities: The transformation of understanding on a production floor. *Organization Science*, *14*, 312–330.

Beers, D. L. (2006). *For the prevention of cruelty: The history and legacy of animal rights in the United States*. Athens, OH: Ohio University Press.

Beller, T. (2015). Don't call it Katrina. Retrieved from www.newyorker.com/culture/cultural-comment/dont-call-it-katrina. Accessed on 8 July 2015.

Berry, J. (2013). Eight years after Hurricane Katrina, New Orleans has been resurrected. Retrieved from www.thedailybeast.com/articles/2013/08/29/eight-years-after-hurricane-katrina-new-orleans-has-resurrected.html. Accessed on 8 July 2015.

Binder, A. (2007). For love and money: Organizations' creative responses to multiple environmental logics. *Theory and Society*, *36*(6), 547–571.

Blau, P. M. (1968). The hierarchy of authority in organizations. *American Journal of Sociology*, *73*(4), 453–467.

Boxenbaum, E., and S. Jonsson. (2008). Isomorphism, diffusion and decoupling. In R. Greenwood, C. Oliver, R. Suddaby, & K. Sahlin-Andersson (eds.), *The SAGE Handbook of Organizational Institutionalism* (pp. 78–98). London: Sage.

Boyd, J. (2002). In community we trust: Online security communication at eBay. *Journal of Computer-Mediated Communication*, *7*(3).

Boyd, J. (2003). The rhetorical construction of trust online. *Communication Studies*, *54*(3), 249–264.

Brescia, R. H., & Steinway, S. (2013). Scoring the banks: Building a behaviorally informed community impact report card for financial institutions. *Fordham Journal of Corporate and Financial Law*, *18*, 339–378.

Brint, S. (2001). Gemeinschaft revisited: A critique and reconstruction of the community concept. *Sociological Theory*, *19*(1), 1–23.

Brown, A. D., & Humphreys, M. (2006). Organizational identity and place: A discursive exploration of hegemony and resistance. *Journal of Management Studies*, *43*(2), 231–257.

Brown, B., Perkins, D. D., & Brown, G. (2003). Place attachment in a revitalizing neighborhood: Individual and block levels of analysis. *Journal of Environmental Psychology*, *23*(3), 259–271.

Bruhn, J. G. (2011). *The sociology of community connections*. New York: Springer Science & Business Media.

Burbank, M. J., Andranovich, G. D., & Heying, C. H. (2001). *Olympic dreams: The impact of mega-events on local politics*. Boulder, CO: Lynne Rienner.

Burt, R. S. (2000). The network structure of social capital. *Research in Organizational Behavior, 22,* 345–423.

Butler, B. S. (2001). Membership size, communication activity, and sustainability: The internal dynamics of networked social structures. *Information Systems Research, 12*(4), 346–362.

Carroll, G. R., & Swaminathan, A. (2000). Why the microbrewery movement? Organizational dynamics of resource partitioning in the U. S. brewery industry. *American Journal of Sociology, 106*(3), 715–762.

Carson, C. (1987). Martin Luther King, Jr: Charismatic leadership in a mass struggle. *Journal of American History, 74*(2), 448–454.

Che, J., & Qian, Y. (1998). Institutional environment, community government, and corporate governance: Understanding China's Township-Village Enterprises. *Journal of Law, Economics, & Organization, 14*(1), 1–23.

Coleman, J. S. (1961). *The adolescent society.* New York: Free Press.

Coleman, J. S. (1988). Social capital in the creation of human capital. *American Journal of Sociology, 94,* S95–S120.

Conger, J. A., & Kanungo, R. N. (1988). *Charismatic leadership: The elusive factor in organizational effectiveness.* San Francisco, CA: Jossey–Bass.

Crane, D. (1969). Social structure in a group of scientists: A test of the 'invisible college' hypothesis. *American Sociological Review, 34,* 335–352.

Cuba, L., & Hummon, D. M. (1993). A place to call home: Identification with dwelling, community, and region. *Sociological Quarterly,* 111–131.

Dacin, M. T., Ventresca, M. J., & Beal, B. D. (1999). The embeddedness of organizations: Dialogue and directions. *Journal of Management, 25*(3), 317–356.

Dahlander, L., & O'Mahony, S. (2011). Progressing to the center: Coordinating knowledge work. *Organization Science, 22*(4), 961–979.

Davis, G. F., & Greve, H. R. (1997). Corporate elite networks and governance changes in the 1980s. *American Journal of Sociology, 103*(1), 1–37.

Davis, G. F., McAdam, D., Scott, W. R., & Zald, M. N. (2005). *Social movements and organization theory.* New York, NY: Cambridge University Press.

DiMaggio, P. (1988). Interest and agency in institutional theory. In L. G. Zucker (Ed.), *Institutional patterns and culture* (pp. 3–21). Cambridge, MA: Ballinger.

DiMaggio, P. J., & Powell, W. W. (1983). The iron cage revisited: Institutional isomorphism and collective rationality in organizational fields. *American Sociological Review, 48,* 147–160.

Dobbin, F. (1994). *Forging industrial policy: The United States, Britain, and France in the railway age.* New York: Cambridge University Press.

Durkheim, Emile (1965 [1915]). *The elementary forms of the religious life.* New York: Free Press.

Eko, L., & Berkowitz, D. (2009). Le Monde, French secular republicanism and the Mohammed cartoons affair: Journalistic re-presentation of the sacred right to offend. *International Communication Gazette, 71*(3), 181–202.

Eltantawy, N., & Wiest, J. B. (2011). The Arab Spring. Social media in the Egyptian revolution: Reconsidering resource mobilization theory. *International Journal of Communication, 5*(18).

Fayard, A., DeSanctis, G., & Roach, M. (2004). The language games of online forums. Proceedings of the Sixty-third Annual Meeting of the Academy of Management (CD), ISSN 1543-8643. Retrieved from http://oz.stern.nyu.edu/seminar/1118.pdf.

Fischer, C. S. (1982). *To dwell among friends.* Chicago, IL: University of Chicago Press.

Fleming, L., King, C., & Juda, A. (2007). Small worlds and regional innovation. *Organization Science, 18,* 938–954.

Fleming, L., & Marx, M. (2006). Managing creativity in small worlds. *California Management Review, 48*(4), 6–27.

Friedland, R., & Alford, R. R. (1991). Bringing society back in: Symbols, practices and institutional contradictions. In W. W. Powell & P. J. DiMaggio (eds.), *The new institutionalism in organizational analysis* (pp. 232–262). Chicago, IL: The University of Chicago Press.

Galaskiewicz, J. (1997). An urban grants economy revisited: Corporate charitable contributions in the twin cities, 1979–81, 1987–89. *Administrative Science Quarterly, 42,* 445–471.

Gelbspan, R. (2005). *Boiling point: How politicians, big oil and coal, journalists and activists are fueling the climate crisis – and what we can do to avert disaster.* New York, NY: Basic Books.

Gläser, J. (2001). 'Producing communities' as a theoretical challenge. *Proceedings of the Australian Sociological Association,* 1–11.

Glynn, M. A. (2008). Beyond constraint: How institutions enable identities. In R. Greenwood, C. Oliver, R. Suddaby, & K. Sahlin-Andersson (eds.), *The SAGE Handbook of Organizational Institutionalism* (pp. 413–430). London: Sage.

Glynn, M. A., & Lounsbury, M. (2005). From the critics' corner: Logic blending, discursive change and authenticity in a cultural production system. *Journal of Management Studies, 42*(5), 1031–1055.

Gotham, K. F. (2008). From 9/11 to 8/29: Post-disaster recovery and rebuilding in New York and New Orleans. *Social Forces, 87*(2), 1039–1062.

Granovetter, M. (1985). Economic action and social structure: The problem of embeddedness. *American Journal of Sociology, 91*(3), 481–510.

Greenwood, R., Díaz, M. A., Li, S. X., & Lorente, J. C. (2010). The multiplicity of institutional logics and the heterogeneity of organizational responses. *Organization Science, 21*(2), 521–539.

Greenwood, R., Oliver, C., Suddaby, R., & Sahlin-Andersson, K. (2008). *The SAGE handbook of organizational institutionalism*. London: Sage.

Greenwood, R., Raynard, M., Kodeih, F., Micelotta, E. R., & Lounsbury, M. (2011). Institutional complexity and organizational responses. *Academy of Management Annals, 5*(1), 317–371.

Guthrie, D. (2003). *Survey on corporate–community relations*. New York: Social Sciences Research Council.

Heckscher, C., & Adler, P. S. (2006). *The firm as a collaborative community: The reconstruction of trust in the knowledge economy*. New York, NY: Oxford University Press.

Hertel, G., Niedner, S., & Herrmann, S. (2003). Motivation of software developers in Open Source projects: an Internet-based survey of contributors to the Linux kernel. *Research Policy, 32*(7), 1159–1177.

Hiller, H. H. (2000). Mega-events, urban boosterism and growth strategies: An analysis of the objectives and legitimations of the Cape Town 2004 Olympic bid. *International Journal of Urban and Regional Research, 24*, 439–458.

Howard-Grenville, J., Metzger, M. L., & Meyer, A. D. (2013). Rekindling the flame: Processes of identity resurrection. *Academy of Management Journal, 56*(1), 113–136.

Hunter, F. (1953). *Community power structure: A study of decision makers*. Chapel Hill, NC: University of North Carolina Press.

Jeppesen, L. B., & Frederiksen, L. (2006). Why do users contribute to firm-hosted user communities? The case of computer-controlled music instruments. *Organization Science,17*(1), 45–63.

Jones, G. F., & George, J. M. (1998). The experience and evolution of trust: Implications for cooperation and teamwork. *Academy of Management Review, 23*(3), 531–546.

Jøsang, A., Ismail, R., & Boyd, C. (2007). A survey of trust and reputation systems for online service provision. *Decision Support Systems, 43*(2), 618–644.

Kantrowitz, N. (1969). Ethnic and racial segregation in the New York metropolis, 1960. *American Journal of Sociology, 74*(6), 685–695.

Khondker, H. H. (2011). Role of the new media in the Arab Spring. *Globalizations, 8*(5), 675–679.

Kirk, P., & Shutte, A. M. (2004). Community leadership development. *Community Development Journal, 39*(3), 234–251.

Knorr-Cetina, K. (1999). *Epistemic cultures: How sciences make knowledge*. Cambridge, MA: Harvard University Press.

Kogut, B., & Metiu, A. (2001). Open-source software development and distributed innovation. *Oxford Review of Economic Policy, 17*(2), 248–264.

Kruckeberg, D., & Starck, K. (2004). The role of ethic of community building for consumer products and services. In M. L. Gallician (Ed.), *Handbook of product placement in mass media: New strategies in marketing theory, practice, trends and ethics* (pp. 133–146). New York, NY: Best Business Books.

Lau, D. C., & Murnighan, J. K. (1998). Demographic diversity and faultlines: The compositional dynamics of organizational groups. *Academy of Management Review, 23*(2), 325–340.

Lazaric, N., & Lorenz, E. (1998). Trust and organizational learning during inter-firm cooperation. In N. Lazaric & E. Lorenz (eds.), *Trust and economic learning* (pp. 207–225). Cheltenham: Edward Elgar.

Lerner, J., & Tirole, J. (2004). Efficient patent pools. *American Economic Review, 94*(3), 691–711.

Light, P. C. (1999). *The new public service*. Washington, D.C.: Brookings Institution Press.

Litwak, E., & Hylton, L. F. (1962). Interorganizational analysis: A hypothesis on co-ordinating agencies. *Administrative Science Quarterly, 6*(4), 395.

Lok, J. (2010). Institutional logics as identity projects. *Academy of Management Journal, 53*(6), 1305–1335.

Lounsbury, M. (2007). A tale of two cities: Competing logics and practice variation in the professionalizing of mutual funds. *Academy of Management Journal, 50*(2), 289–307.

Luo, X., Chung, C., & Sobczak, M. (2009). How do corporate governance model differences affect foreign direct investment in emerging economies? *Journal of International Business Studies, 40*(3), 444–467.

Marglin, S. A. (2008). *The dismal science: How thinking like an economist undermines community*. Cambridge, MA: Harvard University Press.

Marquis, C. (2003). The pressure of the past: Network imprinting in intercorporate communities. *Administrative Science Quarterly, 48*, 655–689.

Marquis, C., & Battilana, J. (2009). Acting globally but thinking locally? The enduring influence of local communities on organizations. *Research in Organizational Behavior, 29*, 283–302.

Marquis, C., Davis, G. F., & Glynn, M. A. (2013). Golfing alone? Corporations, elites and nonprofit growth in 100 American communities. *Organization Science, 24*(1), 39–57.

Marquis, C., & Lounsbury, M. (2007). Vive la résistance: Competing logics and the consolidation of U.S. banking. *Academy of Management Journal, 50*(4), 799–820.

Marquis, C., Lounsbury, M., & Greenwood, R. (2011). Introduction: Community as an institutional order and a type of organizing. In C. Marquis, M. Lounsbury, & R. Greenwood (eds.), *Research in the sociology of organizations*, Vol. 33 (pp. ix–xxvii). Greenwich, CT: JAI Press.

Marquis, C., & Yang, Z. (2014). The sharing economy in China: toward a unique local model. *China Policy Review*, (9), 109–111.

McAdam, D. (1996). The framing function of movement tactics: Strategic dramaturgy in the American civil rights movement. In D. McAdam, J. D. McCarthy, & M. N. Zald (eds.), *Comparative perspectives on social movements* (pp. 338–356). New York, NY: Cambridge University Press.

McAlexander, J. H., Schouten, J. W., & Koenig, H. F. (2002). Building brand community. *Journal of Marketing*, 66, 38–54.

McCall, G. J., & Simmons, J. L. (1978). *Identities and interactions*. New York: Free Press.

McCarthy, J. D., & Zald, M. N. (1977). Resource mobilization and social movements: A partial theory. *American Journal of Sociology*, 1212–1241.

McPherson, M., Smith-Lovin, L., Cook, J. M. (2001). Birds of a feather: Homophily in social networks. *Annual Review of Sociology*, 27, 415–444.

Meyer, J. W. (1977). The effects of education as an institution. *American Journal of Sociology*, 83(1), 55–77.

Meyer, J. W., Boli, J., Thomas, G. M., & Ramirez, F. O. (1997). World society and the nation-state. *American Journal of Sociology*, 103(1), 144–181.

Meyer, R. E., & Höllerer, M.A. (2014). Does institutional theory need redirecting? *Journal of Management Studies*, 51(7):1221–1233.

Meyer, J. W., & Scott, W. R. (1983). *Organizational environments: ritual and rationality*. Beverly Hills, CA: Sage.

Mok, D., Wellman, B., & Carrasco, J. (2010). Does distance matter in the age of the Internet? *Urban Studies*, 47(13), 2747–2783.

Morris, A., & Staggenborg, S. (2004). Leadership in social movements. In D. A. Snow, S. A. Soule, & H. Kriesi (eds.), *The Blackwell companion to social movements* (pp. 171–196). Oxford: Blackwell.

Morrison, P. D., Roberts, J. H., & von Hippel, E., (2000). Determinants of user innovation and innovation sharing in a local market. *Management Science*, 46(12), 1513–1527.

Muniz Jr, A. M., & O'Guinn, T. C. (2001). Brand community. *Journal of Consumer Research*, 27(4), 412–432.

Nigam, A., & Ocasio, W. (2010). Event attention, environmental sensemaking, and change in institutional logics: An inductive analysis of the effects of public attention to Clinton's health care reform initiative. *Organization Science*, 21(4), 823–841.

Nowell, B. L., Berkowitz, Z. D., & Foster-Fishman, P. (2006). Revealing the cues within community places: Stories of identity, history, and possibility. *American Journal of Community Psychology*, 37(1–2), 29–46.

Ocasio, W. (1997). Towards an attention-based view of the firm. *Strategic Management Journal*, 18(S1), 187–206.

O'Mahony, S., & Ferraro, F. (2007). The emergence of governance in an open source community. *Academy of Management Journal*, 50(5), 1079–1106.

O'Mahony, S., & Lakhani, K. R. (2011). Organizations in the shadow of communities. In C. Marquis, M. Lounsbury, & R. Greenwood (eds.), *Research in the sociology of organizations*, Vol. 33 (pp. 3–36). Greenwich, CT: JAI Press.

Orr, J. E. (1996). *Talking about machines: An ethnography of a modern job*. Ithaca, NY: ILR Press.

Osterloh, M., & Frey, B. S. (2000). Motivation, knowledge transfer, and organizational forms. *Organization Science*, 11(5), 538–550.

Owen-Smith, J., & Powell, W. W. (2004). Knowledge networks as channels and conduits: The effects of spillovers in the Boston biotechnology community. *Organization Science*, 15(1), 5–21.

Pache, A., & Santos, F. (2010). When worlds collide: The internal dynamics of organizational responses to conflicting institutional demands. *Academy of Management Review*, 35(3), 455–476.

Park, J. Z., & Smith, C. (2000). 'To whom much has been given ...': Religious capital and community voluntarism among churchgoing protestants. *Journal for the Scientific Study of Religion*, 39(3), 272–286.

Piore, M. H., & Sabel, C. F. (1984). *The second industrial divide: Possibilities for prosperity*. New York: Basic Books.

Piskorski, M. J., & Gorbatai, A. D. (2013). Testing Coleman's social-norm enforcement mechanism: Evidence from Wikipedia. Harvard Business School Strategy Unit Working Paper (11–055).

Platt, G. M., & Lilley, S. J. (1994). Multiple images of a charismatic: Constructing Martin Luther King Jr's leadership. In G. Platt & C. Gordon (eds.), *Self, collective behavior and society: Essays honoring the contributions of Ralph H. Turner* (pp. 55–74). Greenwich, CT: JAI Press.

Podolny, J. M. (1993). A status-based model of market competition. *American Journal of Sociology*, 98(4), 829–872.

Podolny, J. M. (2001). Networks as the pipes and prisms of the market. *American Journal of Sociology*, 107(1), 33–60.

Podolny, J. M., Khurana, R., & Hill-Popper, M. (2004). Revisiting the meaning of leadership. *Research in Organizational Behavior*, 26, 1–36.

Podolny, J. M., & Page, K. L. (1998). Network forms of organization. *Annual Review of Sociology*, 24, 57–76.

Portes, A., & Sensenbrenner, J. (1993). Embeddedness and immigration: Notes on the social determinants of economic action. *American Journal of Sociology*, 98(6), 1320–1350.

Preece, J. (2000). *Online communities: Designing usability and supporting sociability*. New York, NY: John Wiley & Sons, Inc.

Preece, J. (2001). Sociability and usability in online communities: Determining and measuring success. *Behavior & Information Technology*, 20(5), 347–356.

Preece, J., & Maloney-Krichmar, D. (2005). Online communities: Design, theory, and practice. *Journal of Computer-Mediated Communication*, *10*(4), DOI: 10.1111/j.1083-6101.2005.tb00264.x.

Putnam, R. D. (1993). *Making democracy work: Civic traditions in modern Italy.* Princeton, NJ: Princeton University Press.

Rao, H., Monin, P., & Durand, R. (2003). Institutional change in Toque Ville: Nouvelle cuisine as an identity movement in French gastronomy. *American Journal of Sociology*, *108*(4), 795–843.

Raymond, E. S. (1999). *The cathedral and the bazaar: Musings on Linux and open source by an accidental revolutionary.* Cambridge, MA: O'Reilly.

Raynard, M., Lounsbury, M., & Greenwood, R. (2012). Legacies of logics: Sources of community variation in CSR implementation in China. In M. Lounsbury & E. Boxenbaum (eds.), *Research in the sociology of organizations*, Vol. 39 (pp. 243–276). Greenwich, CT: JAI Press.

Rheingold, H. (2007). *Smart mobs: The next social revolution.* New York, NY: Basic Books.

Ridings, C. M., & Gefen, D. (2004). Virtual community attraction: Why people hang out online. *Journal of Computer-Mediated Communication*, *10*(1), DOI: 10.1111/j.1083-6101.2004.tb00229.x.

Robertson, R. (1995). Glocalization: Time-space and homogeneity–heterogeneity. In M. Featherstone, S. Lash, & R. Robertson (eds.), *Global modernities* (pp. 25–44). Thousand Oaks, CA: Sage.

Rossi, P. H., & Weber, E. (1996). The social benefits of homeownership: Empirical evidence from national surveys. *Housing Policy Debate*, 7, 1–35.

Sahlin, K., & Wedlin, L. (2008). Circulating ideas: Imitation, translation and editing. In R. Greenwood, C. Oliver, R. Suddaby, & K. Sahlin-Andersson (eds.), *The SAGE handbook of organizational institutionalism* (pp. 218–242). London: Sage.

Schneiberg, M. (2002). Organizational heterogeneity and the production of new forms: Politics, social movements and mutual companies in American fire insurance, 1900–1930. In M. Lounsbury & M. Ventresca (eds.), *Research in the sociology of organizations*, Vol. 19 (pp. 39–89). Greenwich, CT: JAI Press.

Schneiberg, M., King, M., & Smith, T. (2008). Social movements and organizational form: Cooperative alternatives to corporations in the American insurance, dairy, and grain industries. *American Sociological Review*, *73*, 635–667.

Schneiberg, M., & Lounsbury, M. (2008). Social movements and institutional analysis. In R. Greenwood, C. Oliver, R. Suddaby, & K. Sahlin-Andersson (eds.), *The SAGE handbook of organizational institutionalism* (pp. 648–670). London: Sage.

Schwartz, D. (1997). *Contesting the Super Bowl.* New York: Routledge.

Scott, A. J., & Storper, M. (2003). Regions, globalization, development. *Regional Studies*, *37*, 549–579.

Shneiderman, B. (2000). Designing trust into online experiences. *Communications of the ACM*, *43*(12), 57–59.

Simons, T., Vermeulen, P., & Knoben, J. (2016) There is no beer without a smoke: Community cohesion and neighboring communities' effects on organizational resistance to anti-smoking regulations in the Dutch hospitality industry. *Academy of Management Journal*, *59*(2), 545–578.

Sorge, A. (2005). *The global and the local: Understanding the dialectics of business systems.* Oxford: Oxford University Press.

Storper, M. (1997). *The regional world: Territorial development in a global economy.* New York, NY: Guilford Press.

Storper, M. (2005). Society, community, and economic development. *Comparative International Development*, *39*(4), 30–57.

Stryker, S. (2000). Identity competition: Key to differential social movement involvement. In S. Stryker, T. Owens, & R. White (eds.), *Identity, self, and social movements* (pp. 21–40). Minneapolis, MN: University of Minnesota Press.

Suddaby, R., & Greenwood, R. (2005). Rhetorical strategies of legitimacy. *Administrative Science Quarterly*, *50*(1), 35–67.

Taub, R. P. (1994). *Community capitalism: The South Shore Bank's strategy for neighborhood revitalization.* Boston, MA: Harvard Business School Press.

Taylor, R. B. (1996). Neighborhood responses to disorder and local attachments: The systemic model of attachment, social disorganization, and neighborhood use value. *Sociological Forum*, *11*, 41–74.

Thornton, P. H. (2004). *Markets from culture: Institutional logics and organizational decisions in higher education publishing.* Stanford, CA: Stanford University Press.

Thornton, P. H., Jones, C., & Kury, K. (2005). Institutional logics and institutional change in organizations: Transformation in accounting, architecture, and publishing. In C. Jones & P. H. Thornton (eds.), *Research in the sociology of organizations*, Vol. 23 (pp. 125–170). Bingley, UK: Emerald Group.

Thornton, P. H., & Ocasio, W. (1999). Institutional logics and the historical contingency of power in organizations: Executive succession in the higher education publishing industry, 1958–1990. *American Journal of Sociology*, *105*(3), 801–843.

Thornton, P. H., Ocasio, W., & Lounsbury, M. (2012). *The institutional logics perspective: A new approach to culture, structure and process.* Oxford: Oxford University Press.

Tierney, K. J. (2003). *Conceptualizing and measuring organizational and community resilience: Lessons from the emergency response following the September 11, 2001 attack on the World Trade Center.* Newark, DE: University of Delaware Disaster Research Center.

Tilcsik, A., & Marquis, C. (2013). Punctuated generosity: How mega-events and natural disasters affect corporate philanthropy in U.S. communities. *Administrative Science Quarterly, 58*(1), 111–148.

Tönnies, F. (1887). *Gemeinschaft und Gesellschaft: Abhandlung des Communismus und des Socialismus als empirischer Culturformen*. Leipzig: Fues.

Truno, E. (1995). Barcelona: City of sport. In M. De Moragas & M. Botella (eds.), *The keys to success: The social, sporting, economic and communications impact of Barcelona '92* (pp. 43–56). Barcelona: Centre d'Estudis Olimpics I de l'Esport, Universitat Autonoma de Barcelona.

Turk, H. (1977). *Organizations in modern life*. San Francisco, CA: Jossey–Bass.

Useem, M. (1984). *The inner circle: Large corporations and the rise of business politics in the U.S. and U.K.* New York, NY: Oxford University Press.

Uzzi, B. (1996). The sources and consequences of embeddedness for the economic performance of organizations: The network effect. *American Sociological Review, 61*, 674–698.

Uzzi, B. (1999). Embeddedness in the making of financial capital: How social relations and networks benefit firms seeking financing. *American Sociological Review, 64*, 481–505.

von Hippel, E. (2005). *Democratizing innovation*. Cambridge, MA: MIT Press.

von Krogh, G., & von Hippel, E. (2006). The promise of research on open source software. *Management Science, 52*(7), 975–983.

Wade, J. B., Swaminathan, A., & Saxon, M. S. (1998). Normative and resource flow consequences of local regulations in the American brewing industry, 1845–1918. *Administrative Science Quarterly, 43*, 905–935.

Waitt, G. (2001). The Olympic spirit and civic boosterism: The Sydney 2000 Olympics. *Tourism Geographies, 3*, 249–278.

Walsh, E. J., & Warland, R. H. (1983). Social movement involvement in the wake of a nuclear accident: Activists and free riders in the TMI area. *American Sociological Review, 48*(6), 764–780.

Watson, J. (2008). *Nursing: The philosophy and science of caring*. Boulder, CO: University Press of Colorado.

Weber, M. (1978 [1921]). *Economy and society*. Berkeley, CA: University of California Press.

Wellman, B. (1979). The community question: The intimate networks of East Yorkers. *American Journal of Sociology, 84*(5), 1201–1231.

Wellman, B. (2001). Physical place and cyberplace: The rise of personalized networking. *International Journal of Urban and Regional Research, 25*(2), 227–252.

Wellman, B., & Gulia, M. (1999). Virtual communities as communities: Net surfers don't ride alone. In P. Kollock & M. A, Smith (eds.), *Communities in cyberspace* (pp. 167–194). London: Routledge.

Wooten, M., & Hoffman, A. J. (2008). Organizational fields: Past, present and future. In R. Greenwood, C. Oliver, R. Suddaby, & K. Sahlin-Andersson (eds.), *The SAGE handbook of organizational institutionalism* (pp. 130–147). London: Sage.

Wry, T., Greenwood, R., Jennings, P. D., & Lounsbury, M. (2010). Institutional sources of technological knowledge: A community perspective on nanotechnology emergence. In N. Phillips, G. Sewell, & D. Griffiths (eds.), *Research in the sociology of organizations*, Vol. 29 (pp. 149–176). Bingley, UK: Emerald Group Publishing.

Wry, T., Lounsbury, M., & Glynn, M. A. (2011). Legitimating nascent collective identities: Coordinating cultural entrepreneurship. *Organization Science, 22*(2), 449–463.

Zilber, T. B. (2006). The work of the symbolic in institutional processes: Translations of rational myths in Israeli high tech. *Academy of Management Journal, 49*(2), 281–303.

8

The Consequences of Globalization for Institutions and Organizations

Markus A. Höllerer, Peter Walgenbach and
Gili S. Drori

INTRODUCTION

Globalization is the principal, and inevitable, feature of the institutional environment of organizations. In abstract terms, the notion of 'globalization' refers to the spatial-temporal processes of change that underpin a transformation in human affairs by expanding, linking and intensifying social relations across distant localities (Giddens, 1991; Held et al., 1999). And, as much as globalization is characterized by the increasing global integration that arises from the interchange of worldviews, values, capital, goods, technology, or ideas (e.g., Albrow and King, 1990), it has also resulted in the constitution of a global social realm (Meyer et al., 1997). With that, globalization steers and imprints institutions and organizations both by affording the sphere for exchange, transference and transformation, and by constituting a globalized 'menu' of organizational templates and managerial scripts that are increasingly influential for the workings of modern organizations.

With the emergence of sociological neo-institutional theory in the late 1970s and early 1980s (e.g., Meyer and Rowan, 1977; DiMaggio and Powell, 1983), a transnational variant of such line of scholarly inquiry soon began taking shape. Initially, comparative neo-institutionalism turned its attention to three primary features of globalization and organization (see Meyer et al., 1975; Meyer and Hannan, 1979). First, this literature highlighted the striking similarity across organizational entities worldwide, pointing to globalization as the source for such isomorphism. Second, it claimed that globalization affects all kinds of organizations, even those that we consider to be the most local ones, or those that seemed immune. And third, it stressed that in addition to carrying economic, political and material consequences for organizations, globalization is a forceful and influential cultural phenomenon. Shortly thereafter, the 'world society' approach (see Finnemore, 1996; Drori and Krücken, 2009; Buhari-Gulmez, 2010) advocated a focus on the impact of global polity and global culture, as well as on the entities embedded in world society. It highlights, in particular, the top-down consequences of globalization and the role of organizations operating across cultural boundaries as premier carriers of global models of organization and management (Drori et al., 2006). More recently, influenced by the notion of 'glocalization' (e.g., Tomlinson, 1993; Robertson, 1995; Ritzer, 2003; Roudometof, 2015), new venues of neo-institutionalism opened to expand the range of consequences and to consider the co-constitutive influences of 'the global' and 'the local'. The new themes in this tradition pertain to global orientation and to co-constitution, rather than unidirectional influence (Drori et al., 2014a, 2014b). 'Globally-oriented organizations' – be they for-profit firms, philanthropic foundations, universities, NGOs, or governmental agencies – are regularly exposed to a variety of different cultural environments (e.g., Drori et al., 2006; Bromley and Meyer, 2016), which together reflect the complexity of global organization and impose 'appropriate' organization and management performance (Walgenbach et al., 2017). On the whole, and following several decades of development, the comparative and global line of neo-institutional research furthered discussions on core institutional notions. It was instrumental to debates on, for instance, structuration (e.g., Meyer, 2002; Beckfield, 2010), theorization and rationalization (e.g., Strang and Meyer, 1993; Drori et al., 2006), diffusion (e.g., Strang and Meyer, 1993; Dobbin et al., 2007; Boxenbaum and Jonsson, Chapter 3 this volume), carriers of diffusing ideas (e.g., Finnemore, 1993; Sahlin-Andersson and Engwall, 2002), and translation (e.g., Czarniawska and Joerges, 1996; Sahlin-Andersson, 1996) – and with this, to the process of institutionalization itself (e.g., Meyer et al., 1997).

This handbook chapter sets out to explore the consequences of globalization for institutions, its far-reaching effects on organization and organizations, and its relevance for studies of organization and management through an institutional theory prism. We proceed in several steps. First, we commence by examining the scholarly development of neo-institutional approaches that engage with the *cultural dimensions of globalization* and the *institutional environment of organizations* (section 2). This includes a succinct review of the literatures of both *globalization* and *glocalization* that we regard as relevant for the phenomenological study of issues of organization and management. We then address the *relationship between global dynamics and organizations* more explicitly, and suggest that a better understanding of modern organizations can be achieved by taking their *degree of global orientation* into account (section 3). In a next step, we probe deeper into *organizational consequences of glocalization* by systematically highlighting the effects of a globalized – or, more precisely, glocalized – institutional environment on globally-oriented organizations; in particular, we explore the *formal, practice and meaning dimensions of organization* (section 4). Finally, we expand on the far-reaching implications such understanding of organization has for *expanding central concepts within organizational institutionalism* (section 5), before closing with some *concluding remarks* (section 6).

GLOBALIZATION OF THE INSTITUTIONAL ENVIRONMENT

The 1990s' fascination with globalization swept organizational scholars along, also reviving some old interests in comparative aspects of organization, organizations and organizing. While organization studies have long included comparative (e.g., Blau and Scott, 1962) and cross-national analyses (e.g., Hickson et al., 1974; Meyer and Hannan, 1979), the era of globalization made obvious the particular contribution of neo-institutional theory to globalization studies and to the study of organizations. Applied to global macro issues, institutionalist scholarship stipulated that world-level phenomena resemble highly relevant institutional contexts that organizations need to maneuver, and that a broad variety of organizations are embedded within such a global environment (Meyer et al., 1997).

From its initial steps (Meyer et al., 1975; Meyer and Hannan, 1979) through its more mature statements (Meyer et al., 1987; Boli and Thomas, 1997; Meyer et al., 1997), the Stanford School of Sociological Institutionalism championed a global cultural approach and contributed to a new understanding of globalization while, at the same time, adding to the richness of institutional thinking and analysis. In discussions of globalization and its impact on organizations, it challenged the then-reigning perspectives in comparative research – dependency and modernization theories – by adding institutionalist and cultural tones to the highly instrumentalist discourse of the times. The emergent 'world society' theory also highlighted the constitution of the global as an additional – or alternative – level to the international and transnational. In this way, it also disputed the common vision of nation-states as premier autonomous entities (e.g., Whitley, 1999) by drawing attention to the consolidating supra-level social sphere and to the top-down diffusion of ideas and practices from such a global social core. Furthermore, it added macro-level discussions to institutional thinking by situating organizations within a broader institutional environment, elaborated the phenomenological tradition within institutional theory, and enhanced the empirical grounding of institutional research with quantitative work.

Building upon these groundbreaking claims regarding globalization, we observe an expansion of institutionalist approaches to comparative, international and global studies of organization and organizations. More

recent scholarly work focuses, in particular, on the carriers (e.g., Finnemore, 1993; Sahlin-Andersson and Engwall, 2002) and adopters (e.g., Gooderham et al., 1999; Guler et al., 2002) of globalized ideas and templates of organization and management. It illustrates the key mechanisms underlying the processes of diffusion and institutionalization, such as abstraction (e.g., Strang and Meyer, 1993) and re-contextualization (e.g., Czarniawska and Joerges, 1996; R.E. Meyer, 2014; Wedlin and Sahlin, Chapter 4 this volume). Finally, it highlights the relationship of the global and the local in the conceptual notion of glocalization (e.g., Drori et al., 2014a, 2014b).

Debating Globalization from an Institutional Perspective

Globalization emerged as a new concept in the early to mid-1990s, flourishing as a social science phrase (e.g., Guillén, 2001; Fiss and Hirsch, 2005), in spite of the long history of comparative work in sociology and the other social sciences. Yet it is these theoretical roots in various traditions of comparative studies that shape the current scholarly debates regarding globalization (see Drori, 2008, for more details). Notably, the world-views of dependency and modernization theorists, who fiercely debated the nature of world affairs and international processes during most of the twentieth century, rose again with a new energy in the globalization debates between world-system (e.g., Wallerstein, 1974, 2000) and neoliberal theoreticians (e.g., Przeworski et al., 2000; Acemoglu and Robinson, 2005), respectively. These theoretical traditions differ on almost every aspect of globalization – from the nature of the global system, to the principal agents of globalization, to the dynamic forces and trajectory of globalization. For instance, while both theoretical camps recognize the dramatic acceleration of cross-national flows of capital and migration and the ensuing growth of inter-dependencies, neoliberal theorists consider 'growth through integration' to be both a development strategy and a description of globalization to date, whereas world-system theorists note the exploitative nature of global production and trade and highlight the resulting expansion of inequalities between classes of nations and regions. Likewise, whereas modernization theorists see a system of transaction relations among competing, yet cooperating, nation-states and international organizations, world-system theorists see a system of exploitative and manipulative dominance of global elites led by multinational corporations.

By the 1970s, and up until well into the 1990s, these two views had reached, and remained in, a theoretical impasse: Although the (neoliberal) modernization and world-system theories shared a structural and global perspective on social processes, the debates between them were stagnating. They repeatedly argued over the nature of global processes (i.e., progress or accumulation), the motivation for global change (i.e., benevolent or malicious), and the projections for future prospects (i.e., closing gaps versus widening divides). The main approach of both theories was, and still is, a realist perspective: in their understanding of the world system, both theoretical traditions highlight a mechanistic image of the relations among global players and assume that the players are rational and bounded actors. At their root, both theories are functionalist and thus share an ontological belief in rationality. Contemporary neo-institutional insights responded to these debates with a reorientation of discussions towards the cultural and constructivist aspects of global dynamics.

The point of departure of institutional thinking centers on the dual matters of culture and rationalization (see also Scott, 2014). First, institutionalists highlighted the power of culture and norms: 'Culture involves far more than *general values* and knowledge that influence tastes and decisions; it defines the *ontological value* of actors and action' (Meyer et al., 1987: 22; emphasis in original). Second, rationalization, which is defined as 'the structuring of everyday life

within standardized impersonal rules that constitute social organization as a means to collective purpose' (Meyer et al., 1987: 24), is fundamental to describing the influence of culture on behavior and structure. Such institutionalist emphasis on rationalization turns the discourse of rationality on its head: it regards action and its formal justifications (in policy and other statements) as scripts of purposive and instrumentalized intention that carry symbolic, ritualized, and ceremonial importance. Emerging from insights on the constituted nature of collective units, institutionalists challenged the realist view of the units of the international system (such as nation-states or organizations) as bounded and rational, and that societies are simply aggregates of individual interests, capacities, and actions. Rather, they understand actors as socially constructed entities, even if reified, and study actorhood and agency as a Western cultural model (e.g., Frank and Meyer, 2002; Bromley and Meyer, 2015). Second, drawing on the notion of institutional isomorphism (DiMaggio and Powell, 1983; Zucker, 1987), institutionalists challenge the realist expectation that intrinsic needs and unique histories result in distinctive trajectories and features. Rather, they demonstrate that organizations worldwide share many dominant features and argue that the source of such similarity and convergence toward it is due to the enveloping world society (e.g., Drori et al., 2006; Beck et al., 2012). Third, based on institutional understandings of loose coupling (Weick, 1976; March and Olsen, 1976), institutionalists challenge functionalists to explain the recurring disconnection between policy and action by noting the ceremonial role of policy as inherently separate from its implementation (e.g., Bromley and Powell, 2012). And fourth, whereas functionalists explain failures as problems of effective coordination of social relations (due to either incompetence or manipulation), institutionalists draw on the notion of ceremonial and ritualized conformity (Meyer and Rowan, 1977) to demonstrate the power of legitimacy and other symbolic resources (e.g., Drori and Meyer, 2006). Overall, institutionalists added a constructivist, phenomenological dimension to the study of organizations under conditions of globalization, noting the co-constitutive relations between actors and their social context.

Comparative institutionalism's critique of realist approaches has, without doubt, matured over time, drawing on elaborations from institutional theory more broadly and on the consolidation of globalization as a formal field of study. The institutional point about the embeddedness of actors in their wider environment – which is often called the open system model – was something of a moot issue in international and comparative studies: all theoretical perspectives addressed the international system and considered societies, states and organizations within the context of that wider environment. Yet institutional theory pushed this point further by analyzing the global itself: the global was not only the context for the practices of nation-states and other organizations, but it became an analytic unit. In this way, institutionalists came to redefine globalization as an ontological interpretive grid, which constituted the world as a social horizon.

In institutional terms, globalization is a dual process: global institutionalization of world society and diffusion of global models, templates and scripts across entities embedded in world society (Drori et al., 2006; Bromley and Meyer, 2015). Globalization is therefore neither a mere adjustment of national institutions to global conditions, nor is it adaptation of organizations to these now global pressures. Rather, it is also about 'institution building in the transnational arena' (Djelic and Quack, 2003: 3). Therefore, whereas globalization is commonly defined as interaction and integration on a global scale, with a particular focus on economic and political flows, institutionalists accentuate the impact of cultural dynamics on global structuration. From this perspective, globalization is defined as the intensifying of worldwide exchanges and flows, which are driven by isomorphic pressures emanating from a shared cultural core, as well as the consolidation of the world into an 'imagined community' (see also Anderson, 1983). Examples of these two complementary dimensions of globalization are abundant: ISO standards, for instance, drive the cross-national and cross-sectoral diffusion of managerial, accounting and business ethics practices, while the accumulation of many such instances consolidates the global field of management and organization, highlighting these organization principles as globally shared practices and beliefs.

Such an institutionalist definition of globalization has been a clear departure from realist definitions. Globalization goes beyond the worldwide and intensifying transactions and interdependencies (e.g., Keohane and Nye, 2000; Kearney, 2007), or transference and transformation (Bartelson, 2000), into an ontology that transcends the boundaries of globally embedded entities. Moreover, globalization is highly dynamic, dialectically containing both institutional change and institutional work. It is therefore described as a process of 'building [...] and stabilization' (Djelic and Quack, 2003: 6), a world of rules and order infused with reinvention and reordering (Djelic and Sahlin-Andersson, 2006), and a process that combines theorization and abstraction with translation and re-contextualization (Drori et al., 2014b). In these ways, the era of globalization reflects not only a remarkable intensification of global exchanges and flows, and a dramatic thickening of international and transnational webs of relations, but also a change in the organizing logic from the particularistic to the universalized.

Implications of Globalization: Global Polity and Culture in World Society

Along with the recognition of a global economy, an international political system, a global ecology and worldwide interdependencies in terms of, for instance, health issues or migration, comes an awareness of a distinct world society. This awareness of the global is evident in the increasing availability of world-level information: Hwang (2006) demonstrates that information about the category of the 'world' (rather than 'nation' or 'region') is increasingly available across many social issues. Such statistical aggregation at the world level, which also assists in tackling global social problems and 'grand challenges' (e.g., Ritzer, 2004), confirms the vision of the world as the relevant social unit and imagined community.

The economy is the social category that seems mostly affected in terms of aggregation to the global level. Indeed, the world economy is the first issue on everyone's mind when considering globalization, and most information compiled at the global level concerns global trade, production and finance. Nevertheless, along with the rise of the world society, many other social issues are now considered global features. Among them, the dominant issues are those where systemic interdependence – now worldwide – can be argued, such as ecology, or human rights. Even beyond these spheres, issues from social responsibility to citizenship that were once confined to the boundary of the nation or the state are now extended to worldwide relevance and enjoy heightened attention in policy-making and social action. The common thread of these themes is their universal appeal: Their description is composed in the language of interdependency and trans-locality. Such a universalized vision of society has had an important impact on global governance: Contemporary world polity is a reflection of worldwide cultural trends as much as it is a codification of such trends into formal structures of action and policy-making.

The world as the primary social horizon has worked to energize international and global organizing. Today's world polity constitutes a complex configuration of relations among nation-states, governmental agencies, civil society organizations, for-profit firms and social movements (Drori et al., 2003;

Beckfield, 2010). This array is further multiplied by the expansive, and ever-changing, substantive scope of global organization, which covers many issues, and by the international reaches of local organizations and social movements (see Boli and Thomas, 1997). As a result, world polity is experiencing both intense structuration and high heterogeneity.

Most importantly, in the absence of an authoritative global state (Meyer, 2000), world polity is characterized by associational relations and diffuse authority. Even the dominant international governmental organization, the United Nations, carries its global missions in partnership with many non-governmental, for-profit and benevolent partners. The diffuse nature of authority is reflected in the looseness of conformity mechanisms, combining coercive and 'soft law' strategies to encourage compliance with international laws and global norms alike, where authority is derived from the legitimacy of culture models that are carried by global civil society and its network of organizations (e.g., Djelic and Quack, 2003, 2011; Barnett and Finnemore, 2004). Global normative pressure, more than functional requirement, drives the institutionalization of shared modes of governance, such as models of transparency, accountability and 'governance by numbers' (e.g., Jang et al., 2014). World culture encodes the models and templates that are made sacred. Although culture is an illusive concept, the recognition of the global moral order comes in celebrations (i.e., announcements and titles) and certifications (i.e., awards and licenses), which vary by degrees of formality and rationalization (Drori, 2005; Boli, 2006). Yet in spite of the variety of specific substantive issues exalted worldwide, from environmentalism through rights and equality to security, the primary cultural themes remain guided by progress and justice (Meyer et al., 1997; also Drori, 2005). These twin pillars of Western, now global, culture (Meyer et al., 1987) mark the sanctified themes of the still-evolving global normative consensus.

Coupled with the focus on the twin substantive pillars of progress and justice, much of this global normative 'sacred canopy' conveys two general logics: rationalization and actorhood (Meyer et al., 2006). Rationalization, or the systematization and standardization of social life (Jepperson, 2002) with scientization as its pronounced axis (Drori and Meyer, 2006), establishes organizational sites and nodes. It calls for coordination, supervision, planning and study, all of which build on the mythology of universality, thus undercutting mythologies of national or local culture and further enhancing the spirit of a world society. Intertwined with the notion of an ordered world is the idea of the world being manageable, expressed in the theme of actorhood, or the sense of empowered agency attributed to social actors (i.e., individuals and organizations alike; Meyer and Jepperson, 2000). The two cultural features of rationalization and actorhood imprint organizations, behaviors and practices, resulting in a hyperactive world society that is increasingly proactive through organizations and guided by world culture.

Most importantly, world society serves as a powerful context for embedded organization. Globalization has not merely posed an exogenous shock to the operations, behavior and structure of organizations, but rather globalization is also constituted by, and embodied in, the global scope of organization, organizations and organizing. Indeed, globalization is *the* most powerful engine for formal organization (Drori et al., 2006; Bromley and Meyer, 2015), imprinting embedded entities with the Western, now global, model and culture of organization. Modern organization, which means, at its core, rationalized, professionalized and agentic forms of formal organization, has intensified in several different ways: Alongside the expansion of rule-making, more social sectors and activities, even those once weakly organized, are infused with organization principles and become formally organized. Indeed, non-profit

organizations (Hwang and Powell, 2009), family firms (Miller et al., 2013), religious organizations (Putnam and Campbell, 2010), and educational institutions such as schools and universities (Krücken and Meier, 2006), have become elaborate modern organizations, while 'passive state bureaucracies are pressed by the "New Public Management" and "reinventing government" movements to become accountable, purposive, decision-making organizations' (Meyer and Bromley, 2013: 367). Such structuration clarifies that the meaning of organization has drastically changed:

> 'Formal organization' no longer means bureaucratic, in the Weberian sense of hierarchically-organized, well-defined roles, and explicit regulations. Rather, it adds to these Weberian prerequisites of explicit and predictable structures, rules, and roles a whole set of new standards of appropriateness. These new standards of appropriateness are built around professionalized or scientific knowledge, the expanded human rights and capacities of participants, and expanded principles of rationality. (Drori and Meyer, 2006: 34)

In many ways, world society puts clear demands on embedded entities. For example, North-American hegemony drives nation-states and organizations to adopt American-style governance principles (Djelic, 1998) and inter-governmental organizations are able to impose various standards onto national bureaucracies (e.g., McNeely, 1995; Jang et al., 2014). And still, the complexity and heterogeneity of global polity (see Djelic and Sahlin-Andersson, 2006) position globally-oriented organizations within a juncture of often-conflicting administrative and normative global contexts. Such a multiplicity of contexts – local and global, and of various sectors – results in what is described as the 'glocalization' of organization, namely processes of translation and amalgamation on the global–local scale and the resulting hybridized forms that combine elements from what have been thought of as contradictory models, or dichotomies (Drori et al., 2014b).

Glocalization: The Co-Constitution of Global and Local

The 'local' and the 'global' are, first and foremost, analytical categories; neither the local nor the global exist in their pure form. Organizational reality is more 'messy' and characterized by a constant interplay between local and global forces. In the two decades since the coining of the term, glocalization therefore has come to stand for more than what the word literally encompasses: It refers not only to the synergy between global and local elements, but rather it spearheads the challenge on the numerous dichotomies that have dominated previous discussions of globalization (Drori et al., 2014b). Moreover, the two poles condition each other: In fact, it is impossible to conceptualize one without the other as a point of reference (Drori, 2016). On the one hand, local practices are instantiations of global templates; on the other hand, 'the global' is illusive, exciting beyond aggregation of locals and beyond Western hegemony. Contrary to perspectives that tend to reify the global, we argue that what we call global is an abstraction and aggregate of various local instantiations of the very same abstract idea, floating in the global sphere and being repeatedly enacted in local contexts.

The term 'glocalization' – as an extension of earlier conceptualizations of globalization – captures the very processes linked to de-contextualization, diffusion and re-contextualization of ideas; it also includes 'bottom-up' and 'rebound' effects, as well as an amalgamation across categories and entities; it also highlights the hybridized result that combines elements from what have been assumed to be dichotomies. Drori et al. (2014a) argue that with this, consequently, it transcends the simple, yet naïve, distinction of global versus local.

Elaborating on the 1990s' notion of glocalization, which privileges a solely global–local co-constitution (Tomlinson, 1993; Robertson, 1995; Ritzer, 2003; Roudometof, 2015), Drori et al. (2014a, 2014b) delineate three distinct axes, or dimensions, of glocalization. These are: (a) a 'vertical' axis that stands for the difference among hierarchically ordered, or nested, categories and entities, namely the global and local (in the narrow sense of the word); (b) a 'horizontal' axis that stands for the difference between equivalent entities, such as sectors, fields, or other institutional domains in society; and, finally, (c) a 'temporal' axis that marks differences in era or stage of process. Taken together, these three dimensions create scales for variation – and/ or similarity – across related entities; they define glocalization by specifying time and space, the direction of impact and the dimensions along which sameness and variation are constructed and observed. Drori et al. (2014b: 91) note that 'until recently, discussions of space conflated horizontal and vertical relations; there was not much distinction between the travel of ideas, structures, and practices among nested entities or among equivalent entities'. They propose that such distinction is crucial, also because it allows for the parsing of matters of power and/or enactment. Further, the role of time as the bridging of then and now, and vice versa, has not yet been fully considered. Therefore, the inclusion of the temporal dimension affords the understanding of the vitalization and revitalization of the global and the local. The three axes come into play in creating a process model for the de-contextualization, diffusion and re-contextualization of ideas, spanning and linking across various levels of analysis (i.e., the micro, meso and macro level) and allowing for a sequenced process of glocalization to unfold.

Most importantly, by highlighting the co-constitution of the so-called global and local, glocalization refers to the duality of sameness and variation, and, in fact, to the universalism of particularism. In this way, 'glocalization' is inherently a catchphrase for – in fact, institutional – plurality, multidimensionality and complexity. Such an insight begs to revisit other core concepts within organizational institutionalism. However, before we do so, we intend to focus more closely on the organizational level, exploring the features of the globally-oriented organization as well as the consequences that come with glocalization.

THE GLOBALLY-ORIENTED ORGANIZATION

Conditions of globalization are the 'air that organizations breathe', resulting in globally-oriented organizations that have glocalization's co-constitutive and presumably contradictory tendencies as integral features. Such organizations are locally situated and yet draw on a globalized 'menu' of organizational templates and managerial scripts. The globally-oriented organization is characterized by rationalization, professionalization and prescribed agency alongside particular operational and cultural nuances drawn from the diverse local settings it is engaged with. Therefore, whereas institutional studies of globalization and organization have focused primarily on the diffusion of organizational and managerial ideas and analyzed how these are locally interpreted, translated and modified, adopted and enacted, or decoupled, discussions of glocalization demand a language of global orientation. The complexity of globalization challenges the overly simplified descriptors of internationality or multi-nationality of organizations; it also identifies glocality as all-inclusive and thus evasive. Therefore, under conditions of glocalization, organizations are marked by their global (and local) orientation.

Global Models of Organization and Management

Contemporary organizations share a large number of features, both in terms of formal structure and practices of organizing (Powell, 2001), regardless of their respective area of operation, industry, sector, or national context. It has been argued that global 'templates' (e.g., Wedlin and Sahlin, Chapter 4 this volume) specify how certain 'archetypes' of organization should look (see also Greenwood et al., 2014; Meyer and Höllerer, 2014), and thereby guide organizational actors in their quest for legitimacy. For instance, corporations throughout the world resemble each other in terms of structural design or corporate governance procedures to a stunning degree, with the idea of the 'private limited company', among others, as a globally institutionalized social category (Djelic and Quack, 2011; Djelic, 2013). In a similar vein, such organizations promote and practice similar, globally available management concepts: shareholder value orientation in corporate control, corporate social responsibility to manage the interface with society, diversity management as an integral part of human resource management that aligns the corporation to the principles of social and human rights, total quality management, corporate branding and many more.

At the same time, it is recognized that all organizations necessarily are rooted in – sometimes multiple – local contexts, and organizational action is consistently executed in specific local institutional settings (Tempel and Walgenbach, 2007). For instance, and as described in great detail by the 'varieties of capitalism' and 'business systems' literatures (e.g., Hollingsworth and Boyer, 1997; Whitley, 1999; Hall and Soskice, 2001), the individual components of organizational design or corporate governance procedures are influenced by the broader governance configurations in place within a local institutional field (see also Djelic and Quack, 2003; Gourevitch and Shinn, 2007). Or, as Meyer and Höllerer (2010, 2016) demonstrate, certain organizational/managerial ideas and practices may become imbued with a rather different meaning, depending on the cultural setting they are applied to. Such a perspective highlights that global ideas and templates are constantly brought to life through their local enactments; the global and the local are, therefore, mutually constitutive. Diagnosing 'glocalization' as global 'similarity cum variation', Walgenbach et al. (2017) suggest conceptualizing the contemporary organization as a 'globally-oriented organization': global in its orientation while, at the same time, exposed to local material and ideational demands.

Rationalized and Globally-Oriented Organization

Mainstream international business research holds that organizations adopt structural designs and practices of organizing to adapt to specific local 'host' contexts in response to institutional demands (Westney, 1993; Boisot and Child, 1999; Davis et al., 2000; Kostova and Roth, 2002; Dacin et al., 2007). Yet pronouncements of agency, strategic choice and interests often ignore the rampant isomorphism that is driven by universalistic prescriptions of organizational rationality. The ubiquity of a limited set of managerial strategies across organizations worldwide, as well as their expansive nature, suggest that these strategies are divorced from, or often only loosely related to, functionality. Indeed, the very justification of similarity among organizations as a rational choice to adopt 'best practice', and of difference among organizations as a natural adjustment to varying conditions, is in itself a rationalized account. Overall, operationally, numerous managerial initiatives, organizational structures and behaviors have but little impact on efficiency, effectiveness and/or profitability. From a conceptual standpoint, the presupposition regarding the rationality of organizational action tends to overlook the global institutional context as well as the rationalized and ritualized nature of a broad range of such action. As Walgenbach et al. (2017) argue in more detail, contemporary global organization is rife with a new form of authority, rooted in professionalized

and scientized legitimacy, and set in a rather diffuse manner (Drori et al., 2006; Drori and Krücken, 2009; Meyer and Bromley, 2013). Organizations embedded in world society are, therefore, attuned to their many constituents and manage this cacophony of complex demands through loosely coupled operations and practices.

Organizational institutionalism emphasizes the important global cultural dimension of organization, and highlights that modern organizations are not only pervasive, but are also globally gripped with rationalization, professionalization and actorhood (Drori et al., 2006, 2009; Bromley and Meyer, 2015). Therefore, globally, organizations do indeed involve formalization, taking on the form of incorporation, registration, quantification and the like. Yet, still, 'much current organizational expansion is an exception to both liberal norms of self-interested private profit and the illiberal expansion of state power' (Meyer and Bromley, 2013: 367). This points us in the direction of cultural and institutional drivers to global organization: The cultural origins of global organization produce entities that are structured less according to functional needs or interdependencies, and more around the constitution of such organizations as modern, rational, purposive social actors. And it is the self-identification, or enactment, of the role of a rational (economic) entity that spurs, for instance, corporations into adopting and adapting rationalized scripts of agency and rationality, as these are propagated by management experts worldwide (Sahlin-Andersson and Engwall, 2002). However, the pathways for the adoption and adaptation of prescribed practices are complex. Beyond the recognition of strategic adaptation to multiple social contexts, the modern organization is primarily shaped by the diffusion, adoption and adaptation of organizational and managerial ideas along the vertical, horizontal and temporal axes of glocalization (Drori et al., 2014a, 2014b).

Walgenbach et al.'s (2017) notion of the globally-oriented organization contests the widely accepted idea within international business studies that certain kinds of organizations – specifically transnationally operating entities or business organizations such as multinational corporations (MNCs) – are decisively different from, for instance, domestic firms or any other form of organization (Kostova et al., 2008). Walgenbach et al. (2017) also contest the common description of global and local as oppositional and of globalization as a strictly top-down process (e.g., Cooper et al., 1998; Ailon-Souday and Kunda, 2003). Rather, all organizations are simultaneously exposed to both global *and* local institutional demands. And like all other organizations, transnationally operating entities or business organizations can be assessed, in terms of their operations and, most importantly, their identity, along a continuum of their global vs. local orientation. Both poles, again, represent 'ideal types' and remain analytical categories. With the omnipresent features of global polity and world society, one might be hard pressed to find concrete examples of organizations that are exclusively entrenched in a local setting and fully shielded from global developments, or organizations that are exclusively global. Even organizations that seem to be most likely local in their orientation, such as the corner grocery store, are part of a global value chain, and confess their global orientation when they explicitly label some products they offer as 'regional', or emphasize products' compliance with global fair trade standards.

The acknowledgment of world-level processes involves a redefinition of globalization as a process that goes beyond transference and transformation, thus defining globalization as primarily a process of 'transcendence of those distinctions that together condition unit, system and dimension identity', 'defying the standard ontologization of the world into units and system, and [...] disputing its compartmentalization into sectors or dimensions' (Bartelson, 2000: 189). Such a nuanced definition of the global context also requires a change in terminology to accurately describe

an organizational entity that is situated, or embedded, within a world of diffuse authority and strong modernist culture (Drori et al., 2006, 2009; Meyer and Bromley, 2013). From this perspective, it is the degree of orientation towards the world – or away from it – that characterizes the organization. In this way, the *degree of global orientation* becomes an important contingency for organizations, for their field and community membership, for their exposure to institutional demands and logics, or their way of maneuvering institutional complexity and handling organizational hybridity.

'Global orientation' is, by no means, just a fanciful way of describing functional or operational globality. Rather, it accounts for the multidimensionality of contemporary cultural global environments where global and local are not opposites but co-constitutive and intertwined in glocal forms (Drori et al., 2014a, 2014b). Moreover, global orientation highlights the enactment of globality as a way of supplementing and driving operational matters. The core argument here is that identity is constructed around the idea of globality, and therefore by enacting the role of a globally-oriented organization. Such an identity construction has direct operational dimensions; for example, a globally-oriented corporate identity is exhibited in global hiring or in compliance with global standards, even if both are neither required, nor technically meaningful. Such an enactment also involves intense identity work, where the corporation signals that its social horizon is the world. To be a globally-oriented organization is, therefore, to have a 'state of mind', or credo, more than a 'state of operations'. Unlike the international or multinational organizational form (such as the MNC [multinational corporation]), for which criteria are functional or operational in nature, the globally-oriented organization revolves around self-identification and enactment that is also manifested in the many daily operations and various structural elements. The self-identification becomes visible, for instance, in the composition of management teams: Management teams in the modern, globally-oriented organization are no longer diverse just because of operational or technical requirements, but because such organizations conform to diversity as a global norm that is defined by a standardized set of criteria that mirror what is considered to be diversity. Likewise, it becomes visible in the decision of organizations from non-English speaking countries to make English the language of board meetings, even if all board members speak the language of the corporation's 'home country' fluently (see, for a similar argument, Piekkari and Westney, 2017).

Global orientation also entails that there is no necessary contradiction between attending, at the same time, to global and local demands. In fact, all kinds of organizations are inherently glocal, and their glocality is an echo of their constituents. For instance, many Israeli start-ups are highly global in orientation, even when their operations are still limited to a specific local setting. Such start-ups look towards cutting-edge consumer engineering, and their business strategy regularly aims at being noticed and subsequently acquired by global firms. And yet others, such as the Israeli food and beverage group Strauss, are pronouncedly identified by their national origin, even if their operations are worldwide. Strauss, while firmly describing itself as an Israeli firm and being exclusively traded on the Tel Aviv Stock Exchange, grew through purchasing food and beverage companies from Brazil to Australia, with some of its member companies having stores from Singapore to New York, and it becoming, for instance, the largest coffee company in Eastern Europe.

Organizations display their glocality in many ways, primarily along dimensions of *self-assigned identity* as the formal and lived orientedness, and, related to operations and stakeholder expectations, the *identity perceived* by an organization's constituents. Consequently, organizations may vary by their degree of global orientation. It is, after all, the enactment of a role that defines the globally-oriented organization. In this respect, even local, regional and national organizational entities are likely to be globally-oriented, because their (self-)categorization as such is made in reference to, or along the dimensions of, the global model, role and template.

Defining organizations by degree of orientation, rather than in binary terms, affirms the complexity of the contemporary global environment in which organizations operate. Global governance is increasingly heterogeneous, global inter-organizational relations are increasingly webbed, and global authority increasingly diffused. The globally-oriented organization is embedded in a dense and yet loosely coupled array of relations. In fact, it is itself organized as a network, rather than as a unitary entity and actor. This relational perspective thus regards the organization's 'internal' operations and 'external' relations as webbed and diverse and organizational boundaries as rather porous.

GLOCALIZATION – AND THE CONSEQUENCES FOR ORGANIZATION

Formal organization is globally conceptualized, firmly scripted and heavily rationalized (e.g., Drori and Meyer, 2006; Bromley and Meyer, 2016). Organizations are, then, modeled according to these global templates of rational organization and management. That is, organization is enacted following abstract prescriptions: All contemporary, globally-oriented organizations more or less aim to adhere to the conceptualizations of rationalized organization – despite the fact that this global template sometimes deviates from, or occasionally even contradicts, vital local conditions.

To describe the range of consequences derived from glocalization, we set an analytic framework that distinguished among three dimensions of organization and organizations: formal, practice and meaning.

This analytic framework echoes Lefebvre's (1991), albeit its focus is specific to matters of space and power, which distinguishes among the *conceived*, *lived* and *perceived* dimensions. Much like Crang's (1999) re-reading of globalization research with Lefebvrian registers, we employ this three-dimensional scheme, and yet we adapt it to dissect the impact of glocalization on organization. Therefore, somewhat departing from Lefebvre's scheme in order to be commensurate with neo-institutional insights, we define these analytic dimensions as follows. The *formal dimension* echoes Lefebvre's conceived dimension, highlighting the formal impact that glocalization has on organization through the drafting of rules and regulations, plans and other formal requirements. The *practice dimension* traces the lived, highlighting the performed impact of glocalization on organization through the behavior and action of organizations and people in and around them. And, the *meaning dimension* follows the perceived dimension, highlighting the beliefs, opinions, interpretations and understandings of the impact that glocalization bears on organization. Of course, the distinction among the three dimensions is conceptual in essence; and still, this perspective goes beyond recent approaches in institutional theory on global organization, which primarily highlight how formal organization is globally conceived (Bromley and Meyer, 2015), thus tending to neglect the practice and meaning dimensions, or otherwise tending to conflate all three. How organization is conceived is, indeed, highly consequential; equally important are the added activated and interpreted dimensions of a globally-oriented organization. Importantly, glocalization affects organizations along these dimensions both directly and indirectly. Specifically, glocalization drives the formalization of organization, while also doing so through the formal means of rules and regulations. For the practice dimension, glocalization activates organization, infusing it with a sense of agency, while also doing so through agents

of glocalization. For the meaning dimension, glocalization alters the understandings of organization, primarily positioning it as the taken-for-granted and legitimate form.

Glocalization and the Formal Dimension of Organization

Organization is conceptualized, theorized, prescribed and advocated by knowledge entrepreneurs of various sorts. Academics (for instance, in the area of business management, engineering, political science, or law) and professionals (for instance, consultants and professional service firms), as well as practitioners of organizational design, develop modeled descriptions of what globalization and organization are or ought to be, based on their 'research imagination' (Appadurai, 2000). The attention given by knowledge professionals to organization, management and governance has increased exponentially over the past several decades (e.g., Meyer et al., 2006), accounting for the centrality of rationalization and formalization of both organization and social processes such as glocalization. This discussion of, and about, formal organization and glocalization is held in professional fora and public media alike, disseminating – verbally, visually, or in multimodal ways (Meyer et al., 2013) – the very ideas that resemble the constitutive elements and practices of organization and organizing, and accounting for the trend of worldwide structuration and isomorphism.

With such professional encouragement, organizations worldwide express the formal dimension by means such as accreditation and certification of their structural elements and procedural practices, or by designing organization charts, internal rules, standards, and manuals. They not only take the prescribed form, but also take on a particular set of features: from the mandatory HR Department to mission statements to TQM or the M-Form, to name just a few. In these many ways, organization and management professionals advocate the importance of formal organization, even in writings on post-bureaucratic organizations that de-emphasize the relevance of formal organization (see Oberg and Walgenbach, 2008). It is in this respect that conceptions of organization, captured in a system of semantic signs and signifiers, are transmitted to all domains of society, serve as general blueprints for more or less standardized organizational designs, which – seemingly a paradox – form what is called 'organizational identity'.

At the same time, it is the abstract conceptualizations of organization that afford organizations to be conceived as rational, effective and efficient. For a long time, the Weberian ideal-type description of the characteristics of modern bureaucracy (Weber, 1978) has been seen in non-German-speaking countries as a *normative* conception of effective and efficient organization. This misunderstanding of Weber's writings was – not in the least – due to his emphasis on officialdom, including its functions and functionalities. The same holds – but now intentionally – for the bulk of the general and popular management literature, which explicitly aims at identifying effective and efficient organizational designs (Abrahamson, 1996; Kieser, 1997). Such organizational designs appear as being effective and efficient only because the descriptions of the designs are able to abstract – or simplify by means of generalization – from the technical and institutional peculiarities that real-world organizations are confronted with.

The glocalization of the modeled organization – which includes conceptualization and theorization of what an organization is, what it should look like, and which ends it serves – combines both the global and universal as well as local and context-specific 'imaginations'. The result is manifold conceptualizations, often complex and contradictory, that hybridize or come into conflict with each other. For instance, globally diffusing management ideas may not fit local conceptions, or may even, in their theorization, provide organizational 'solutions' for organizational 'problems' that do not exist at all in a specific setting, as shown by Meyer (2004; Meyer and Höllerer, 2010) for the case of shareholder value diffusion into Austria. Therefore, glocal forms may reflect the imbalance of power, which may not always be in favor of the global and universal conception. Yet, globally-oriented organizations, which might pay attention to the global only because some of their local institutional environments (for instance the media, state regulators, or the capital market) are globally-oriented, have to adopt and live up to the different locally and globally rationalized and theorized conceptions of organization at the same time.

Glocalization and the Practice Dimension of Organization

Glocalization also induces the practice dimension of organization, by abstracting, adapting, re-contextualizing and translating (through interpretation and sense-making), and adopting models for how organization can be enacted and practiced, and how people in and around organizations ought to behave. Organizations worldwide are imbued with agency, thus enacting the conceptualizations of rational organization by, for instance, legal incorporation, the articulation of a mission in their constitutive documents, the explication and displaying of strategies and business plans, or the creation of corresponding formal units due to their alignment to the idea of global sourcing. They also activate and enact their role as organizations through, for instance, means such as – however ritualized – board meetings and other decision-making acts, or through merging with (or acquiring) other organizations and related reorganization acts. Likewise, people in organizations enact and practice the impact of glocalization: they participate in activities, initiate encounters and, literally, dress their part in the globally-oriented organization. In these ways, this second dimension is reflected in the everyday activities, practices, behaviors and routines – namely the *praxis* – of daily life of, and within, organizations.

Through the enactment of conceptions of rational organization, organizations corroborate the ideas of effectiveness and efficiency of formal organization. What an organization is, what it intends to be and how it wishes to be perceived becomes observable in its actions and behavior, namely the embodied and activated elements in organization. The formal dimension becomes lived in the adoption, implementation, usage (or non-usage in form of decoupling) of formal organization. Sometimes the lived reflects upon the formal dimension, for example through acts of evaluation and assessment of the impact that plans, strategies and structural elements as well as management tools have on organizational performance; in this respect, organization is also lived in the practice of (self-)evaluation, or the use of metrics and indicators.

While we argue that the formal dimension of organization generally tends to be more global, abstract, universalized and standardized, we consider the practice dimension to be more locally rooted and particularized. The practice dimension is set in a specific locale and era. For example, the ISO 9000 standard is a global management standard that aims at structuring the quality management system of organizations through structuring the documentation of their quality management system. The ISO 9000 standard has been adopted by all kinds of organizations around the globe (e.g., Guler et al., 2002). However, as Walgenbach has shown (2001), the implementation of the standard differs substantially across organizations. The variation in the implementation can be due to technical reasons, such as size or industry of the organization, or due to other institutional reasons, such as the existence of deviating and often more demanding local quality management system standards. Subsequently, different parts of certified

quality management systems are decoupled by the adopting organizations, while others are used intensely. As organizations are aware of variations in the implementation of the ISO 9000 standard, that is differences in the degree of coupling of formal documents with actual practices, they locally call the reliability of certified quality management systems of other organizations into question, however, they nevertheless accept the global standard. In this way, worldwide variations among organizations, or the glocalization of organization, are explained as the gap between the formal and the practice dimensions, otherwise noted as the gap between policy and its implementation (see, for example, Schofer and Hironaka [2005] regarding implementation of international policies by governments; Stensaker and Falkenberg [2007] regarding implementation of a corporate agenda in an international firm). This often loosely coupled relationship between the formal and the practice dimensions is an inherent feature of glocal organization, and may result from the interjection of the meaning dimension of glocal organization.

Glocalization and the Meaning Dimension of Organization

Eventually, glocalization also affects the more cognitive dimension of organization, which describes the perceptions of, and interpretations by, the various constituents of organizations. Obviously, some such perceptions are formalized in the organization's mission statement and planning, while other perceptions are embodied in action and behavior, and thus refer to the practice dimension. And still the cognitive dimension carries the distinction of describing and referring to the ideas and opinions that are not necessarily made formally explicit or acted upon. It also refers to the image of the organization, as perceived by stakeholders from inside and outside the organization. The meaning dimension of the globally-oriented organization thus describes both the process of sense-making in the organization prior to the adoption of a global template and the considerations of different audiences after the adoption. Overall, the meaning dimension of globally-oriented organization echoes the cognitive pillar of institutions (e.g., Scott, 2014).

Glocalization evokes cognitive, as well as emotional, reactions that render the globally-oriented organization legitimate – or not (see Deephouse et al., Chapter 1 this volume). Such reactions range from accommodation to resistance, taking the form of pride in, or contestation of, the adoption and adaptation of global models of organization (e.g., Vaara et al., 2006; Fiss et al., 2012). Such reactions also come from various audiences: among them are organizational members, customers and suppliers, investors, state regulators, civil society, or the media. Note that much of the cognitive response to glocal institutional change may be a non-reaction, manifested in taken-for-granted beliefs and values that subsequently set a platform for formal organization and practice.

To summarize, the globally-oriented organization impacts on organization, organizations and organizing on the dimensions, or spheres, of formality, practice and meaning. The analytic clarity that comes from this distinction among the Lefebvrian dimensions does not negate the importance of their interlacing. The impact of glocalization on organization is indeed irreducible to one dimension or a pair of dimensions, but rather benefits from their interrelations and the multiplicative effect of three-dimensional integration. Therefore, much like the three pillars of institutions, the three dimensions of glocal impact are related but distinguishable bases for legitimacy (Scott, 2014). The globally-oriented organization appears to be legitimate if the materializations and actions are perceived to be in line with the conceptualizations that have been rationalized in its relevant global and local environments. It is when the materializations (i.e., the formal organization) are in line with

global and local ideas of rational organization and management that an organization is considered to be a unitary, bounded and rational actor exercising control and acting as an agent. Such is the case with, for example, a global or local market player, or non-profit organization, with a coherent identity, which acts on behalf of its own interests, and the interests of other actors, non-actors and legitimate principles (Meyer and Jepperson, 2000).

IMPLICATIONS: EXPANDING CORE CONCEPTS OF ORGANIZATIONAL INSTITUTIONALISM

The process of diffusion, with theorization as its central 'prerequisite' (Strang and Meyer, 1993), undergirds the dynamics of institutionalization. The duality of the global and local, however, requires a rethinking of these conceptual mechanisms. First, insights from our discussion of glocalization demand the inclusion of multiple levels of translations, in addition to noting bottom-up effects, and with that the *process* of constitution and diffusion of structures, practices and ideas. Second, seeing that the global orientation of organizations is constituted upon 'ideal-types' of organizations, which score either high or low on this orientation scale, glocalization carries implications for discussions of the institutional *context* and thus also for core concepts of organizational institutionalism, such as legitimacy, fields and community, or logics, plurality and (responses to) complexity.

Implications for Institutionalization and Diffusion: Two-Step Translation and Bottom-Up Effects

With the omnipresent features of world society, a global 'menu' of organizational templates and managerial scripts that potential adopters draw from has come into existence. In fact, one of the most important consequences of globalization is the global availability of an extensive range of ready-made solutions to tackle allegedly existing organizational and/or managerial problems. With this, the very processes that allow organizational ideas to gain relevance in a broad variety of cultural settings around the globe become even more a key focus of institutional analysis (e.g., Drori et al., 2006; Bromley and Meyer, 2015). The global 'travel of ideas' (Czarniawska and Joerges, 1996; Czarniawska and Sevón, 2005) is facilitated by three key mechanisms: *de-contextualization* (i.e., abstraction and theorization), *construction of equivalency* and *re-contextualization* (i.e., translation and adaptation). It is further influenced by what we suggest conceptualizing as *bottom-up and rebound effects*. As a note of clarification: Our discussion on such matters revolves specifically around ideas, and yet our arguments equally address structures, practices and behaviors because – for the purposes of the following discussions – we regard all these as expressions of organization, organizations and organizing.

De-contextualization as abstraction and theorization: The emergence of global templates

A mainstream line of research in organizational institutionalism has dealt with processes of diffusion of organizational forms and/or managerial practices. Institutional and social movement scholars have highlighted the relevance of emergent legitimacy for the meaning of practices as a prerequisite for their spread (e.g., Sahlin-Andersson, 1996; Benford and Snow, 2000; Meyer, 2004). In order to diffuse on a larger scale, practices must be given broader cultural significance, such as a set of meanings about what they are good for, and where they might be appropriate (Clemens, 1997). In this process, practices are abstracted and de-contextualized (Strang and Meyer, 1993); they are compacted into their core underlying ideas and

principles. It is in such a way that Strang and Soule (1998; see also Sahlin-Andersson, 1996) argue that, rather than practices, specific 'framings' of practices are referenced, imitated and therefore disseminated; or, as Strang and Meyer (1993: 499) note, 'what flows is not a copy of some practice existing elsewhere [...], it is the theoretical model that is likely to flow'. In this process of 'sense-giving', a substantial amount of theorization takes place. Theorizations are increasingly provided by the 'high priests' of world society, that is by 'legitimated theorizers' (Strang and Meyer, 1993), such as professionals, scientists, or think tanks, who have interpretative sovereignty.

Successful theorization has to fulfill two requirements in order for a practice to achieve legitimacy. First, a generic definition of an organizational problem or organizational failing must be created – which requires abstraction. Second, it must be made apparent as to how a particular, yet abstract, solution will remedy the previously specified problem (e.g., Greenwood et al., 2002); such an explication of cause and effect also implies theorization (Strang and Meyer, 1993). Moreover, successful theorization of global templates of organizational and managerial practice regularly entails ready-made 'accounts' (Scott and Lyman, 1968) as justifications provided for unanticipated activities. Actors may use them to explicate reasons for their conduct (Strang and Meyer, 1993) and to substantiate their adoption motivation (Kennedy and Fiss, 2009). The routinization of accounts is essentially part of the theorization of a practice, and goes hand in hand with the institutionalization of ideas (e.g., Berger and Luckmann, 1967; Tolbert and Zucker, 1996; Strang and Soule, 1998).

Construction of equivalency

Any diffusion of organizational forms and/or managerial practices requires the construction of equivalency across social entities, which is enabled by the typification of potential adopters and/or areas of application.

It implies the extraction of common features and the confirmation of comparability on the basis of such commonality; in this way, theorization and abstraction, on the one hand, and comparability and equivalency, on the other, are complementary processes (Strang and Meyer, 1993; Drori, 2016). The construction of equivalency may happen across all axes of glocalization, but it is especially relevant on the horizontal one (Drori et al., 2014a; see also above). In constructing comparability, firms, for instance, benchmark themselves (or are being benchmarked) against other firms, governmental agencies review policy guidelines that were drafted by other governments and deemed to be best practice, and even the professionalization of non-profit organizations that is inspired by management routines of the for-profit sector draws upon the definition of both organizational types as standard forms of organization. Notions of equivalency enable the emulation and diffusion of ideas, structures and practices from entities that are assumed to be 'comparable'.

Against the backdrop of constructing equivalency, any theorization of a practice – defined as the 'self-conscious development and specification of abstract categories and the formulation of patterned relationships such as chains of cause and effect' (Strang and Meyer, 1993: 492) – contains these abstract typifications of adopters, actions involved and suggested effects, the latter being reflected in the adoption motivation of organizations. Hence, the theorization of a practice implies the construction of cultural categories of actors – as either the subject or the object of the theorized practice – as well as of actions that directly or indirectly link these categories. Theorization, however, is not only significant by means of social construction of actors and actions involved in a specific practice: As a discursive process, theorization in itself is an essential part of the diffusion mechanism; the higher the degree of abstraction and theorization, the clearer the construction of equivalency, the more

rapid the diffusion and the less dependent it is on relational networks.

Several scholars have therefore emphasized the 'structural and cultural bases of diffusion' (Strang and Soule, 1998: 266) as well as the assignment of cultural meaning to diffusing practices. Meaning – the term refers to interpretations, understandings and shared beliefs that are produced and processed through social action (Zilber, 2002, 2008) – does not reside somewhere 'out there' but is instead socially constructed (Berger and Luckmann, 1967). Consequently, objects imbued with cultural meaning cannot spread 'wholesale' but must be interpreted, adapted and related to local contexts – a process that is referred to as translation (see below). This is where 'carriers' of globally spreading organizational forms and/or managerial practices play an important role in constructing equivalency: the 'legitimated theorizers' who have interpretative sovereignty (Strang and Meyer, 1993); media championing, opposing, or transforming novel ideas and practices and the theorizations that accompany them (e.g., Meyer, 2004; Pallas and Wedlin, 2014); and, finally, the globally-oriented organizations themselves in adopting or referencing globally rationalized management practices and organizational forms, and their assigned meaning. As Strang and Meyer (1993: 498–499) conclude, when 'potential adopters internally reproduce and act on the basis of the theoretical model, we might describe theorization itself as the diffusion mechanism'.

Re-contextualization: Two-step translation and adaptation

Global templates remain abstract. During the diffusion of organizational and managerial practices – or, more precisely, their theorizations – they are constantly adapted to fit local contexts and opportunity structures; global templates are regularly subject to interpretation and modification. Several authors stress that diffusing ideas and practices need to be (re-)interpreted, adapted and related to locally existing legitimating accounts (e.g., Benford and Snow, 2000; Lounsbury and Glynn, 2001; Creed et al., 2002). Meyer and Höllerer (2010), for instance, show that even if ideas are globally available, regarded as modern, and have been theorized to a high degree (i.e., come with a lot of credibility), they nonetheless need to pass through a powerful filter of local structural and cultural constraints in order to become legitimate in new contexts. With this, the successful diffusion of a global template equally depends on its theorization and the construction of equivalency, as it does on adopter-level sense-giving and categorization, and thus on an active interpretation and construction of meaning, in local contexts (e.g., Hardy and Maguire, 2008). The Scandinavian School of Institutionalism coined the notions of 'translation' (Czarniawska and Joerges, 1996, borrowing from Latour, 1986) and 'editing' (Sahlin-Andersson, 1996) to refer to such adaptations (see also Wedlin and Sahlin, Chapter 4 this volume). In more recent work, the richness of the cultural dimensions of these processes as well as the nature of global flows has been captured by the terminology of re-contextualization, 're-localization' (e.g., R.E. Meyer, 2014), and 'domestication' (Alasuutari, 2014). It is important to note that, when examining the diffusion of a global template into various local contexts, the 'local' becomes apparent in two different instances: as the local *field* level (such as, for instance, the continental European governance context, or the Israeli high-tech sector, or even more local 'communities'), and the local *organizational* level (such as the individual corporation, or subunits thereof). Translation, thus, proceeds in at least two steps: A translation of the fully theorized, globally available template from the macro to the meso level (i.e., field, regional, sectoral, or similar) and, in a second step, from the meso to the micro level (i.e., organizational actors as adopters).

Much in line with these arguments, a considerable number of publications (e.g., Kraatz and Moore, 2002; Maguire et al.,

2004; Marquis et al., 2007; Marquis and Lounsbury, 2007) has pointed to a new direction of institutional research that focuses less on isomorphic diffusion in one organizational field and more on practice variation and on the 'heterogeneity of actors and activities that underlie apparent conformity' (Lounsbury, 2007: 289). This implies the need to conceptualize institutional environments as more fragmented, contested and influenced by multiple and competing logics (e.g., Schneiberg and Soule, 2005; Lounsbury, 2007; Reay and Hinings, 2009; Greenwood et al., 2011), consequently redirecting the study of institutional diffusion toward the translation of symbolic systems of meaning (e.g., Czarniawska and Sevón, 1996; Wedlin and Sahlin, Chapter 4 this volume; Zilber, Chapter 16 this volume).

Bottom-up and rebound effects

Building on the two-step translation and diffusion process, which is usually modeled in a top-down way, we witness reverse 'bottom-up' and 'rebound' effects: Established local-level practices influence the way global templates look. Global solutions to organizational problems rarely originate from the drawing board, but are often heavily influenced by, and developed out of, best practice on the local field or organizational level. For instance, several quality control practices in the Japanese or German automotive industry shaped the global standard of quality management that subsequently diffused into other countries – and also into different sectors constructed as 'equivalent'. At the same time, field-level practices are themselves often molded by a limited number of actors that apply them (i.e., by specific enactments). Depending on whether such practices are novel and emerging, or adaptations of already established global templates, we suggest discussing these as 'bottom-up' or 'rebound' effects.

Despite their crucial influence, such effects that describe how more local instantiations influence, alter and further develop global templates, have not received much attention within the scholarly literature (for exceptions, see, for instance, Djelic and Quack, 2003; Strang 2014). In their seminal article, Strang and Meyer (1993: 493) refer to '"bottom-up" theorizing' in passing; more recent organizational institutionalism research, however, has largely neglected the implications of local, post-diffusion theorization (i.e., especially of the 'echo' of local variants and of practice variation caused by fairly active adopters modifying the models they enact) on the global 'master' theorization. Finally, little attention has been paid to the fact that theorization might take place simultaneously at various levels or local settings that are not isolated from each other, but that are in a constant state of mutual influence. We argue that taking 'glocalization' seriously will account for this complex and mutually influential relationship between the global and the local.

Implications for Global Orientation of Organizations: Fields and Communities, Plurality and Complexity, and Legitimacy

The formal, practice and meaning dimensions (see above) result in varying degrees of global orientation of individual organizations. While the first two dimensions encapsulate the conceived and lived – and therefore essentially self-assigned – identity of an organization in terms of global orientedness, the latter engages with the perception of an organization's constituents. Taken as an aggregate, two 'ideal types' of global orientation emerge at the extreme ends of this scale: they are, namely, organizations that score high on global orientation, and those that score low. Either way, organizations formalize, practice and assign meanings in reference to global templates. 'Global players', differentiated as they may be on the scale of global orientation, reveal their global orientation in their conceived formal structures, they

live these organizational templates and managerial scripts in daily practices, and they perceive and are perceived as globally-oriented. This is also true of organizations that score fairly low on the formal, practice, and meaning dimensions (such as the typical corner grocery store), as they too reveal their orientation, albeit a local one, thus distancing themselves from the global in formal structures, in practices and in meanings assigned by their various constituents.

These three types of expression of orientation – in formal, practice and meanings – offer validation for the organization, in reference to global templates. And, these global templates, while being a principal institutional condition, are merely a part of a broader set of features of the institutional context of globally-oriented organizations. In the following section, we outline the implications of focusing on globally-oriented organizations for discussions of the institutional *context*, and thus also for core concepts of organizational institutionalism, such as fields and communities, complexity, plurality and nesting, and logics.

Fields and communities

The organizational field is – both as a primary unit and level of analysis – a central and, at the same time, hotly debated construct for research anchored in organizational institutionalism (Wooten and Hoffman, Chapter 2 this volume). Following Scott (1994: 207–208), the 'notion of field connotes the existence of a community of organizations that partakes of a common meaning system and whose participants interact more frequently and fatefully with one another than with actors outside of the field'. Such an understanding corresponds with DiMaggio and Powell's (1983: 148) original definition of the organizational field as a social space that encompasses 'those organizations that, in aggregate, constitute a recognized area of institutional life', delimited by a particular distribution of institutionalized rules, positions, and resources (Phillips et al., 2000). Another, more recent approach conceptualizes organizational fields that have not formed around markets or technologies but have emerged around central disputes and 'issues that bring together various field constituents with disparate purposes' (Hoffman, 1999: 352). Organizational fields are, thus, 'centers of debates in which competing interests negotiate over issue interpretation' (Hoffman, 1999: 351). In a parallel vein, Meyer (2004; see also Meyer and Höllerer, 2010) defines the 'totality of relevant actors' (DiMaggio and Powell, 1983: 148) of an 'issue field' as those actors that engage in the 'politics of signification' (Benford and Snow, 2000: 625). She also reveals the striking interface with social movement research as she conceptualizes fields as the social space in which actors have to mobilize support and legitimacy. Organizations, especially those that score highly on global orientation, are commonly anchored in multiple organizational fields (e.g., Hoffman, 2001). Consequently, they have to attend to a multiplicity of social relations, institutionalized rules, distributions of resources and power, and configurations of discourse around key issues. As we will argue in more detail below, this has consequences for issues of legitimacy and organizational responses to institutional complexity.

At the meso level, organizations and organizational fields alike are embedded in, and influenced by, the dynamics on a more macro level: the world society. Global polity and culture (see above) are the key institutional frame of reference. They crucially influence the distribution of material and discursive resources, actor positions, institutionalized rules and issues on the agenda within a field. Towards the micro level, organizations and organizational fields as 'communities of organizations' (Scott, 2014) are equally anchored: they rely on 'moorings' (Walgenbach et al., 2017) in local communities as permanent structures that secure organizations (e.g., Marquis and Battilana, 2009) and that comprise distinct historical, cultural and normative environments

that determine appropriate organizational behavior. The argument of how and why local phenomena 'continue to matter for organizations in a global age' (Marquis and Battilana, 2009: 283) very much supports the conceptual shift from globalization to glocalization that we have championed in this chapter, and the need to re-focus on understanding the effects of local factors and influences. Marquis and Battilana (2009: 283) argue 'that with globalization, not only has the local remained important, but in many ways local particularities have become more visible and salient'. They suggest that 'because organizations are simultaneously embedded in geographic communities and organizational fields, by accounting for both of these areas, researchers will better understand isomorphism and change dynamics' (Marquis and Battilana, 2009: 283). Hüther and Krücken (2016), for example, describe the complex array of nested and still not overlapping fields in which European universities are embedded and the ensuing homogenization and differentiation among these universities. Almandoz et al. (Chapter 7 this volume) add affiliation-based communities as another, more modern form of community that influences organizations, which are often enabled by technology and do not depend on physical proximity (such as open-source software communities). Despite being dispersed, such communities nonetheless resemble similar characteristics of particularity, and thus, the local. Organizations that score high on global orientation are simultaneously exposed to several levels of institutional settings: global-level world society, meso-level organizational fields, and local-level communities. In general, globally-oriented organizations are necessarily facing a plurality of institutional logics and prescriptions – and chances of being confronted with institutional complexity rise dramatically.

Plurality and complexity

Organizations are regularly exposed to a number of institutional demands, usually discussed under the 'institutional logics perspective' (Thornton et al., 2012). Developed by Alford and Friedland (1985; see also Friedland and Alford, 1991) to describe the belief systems of modern societies, the notion of institutional logics is one of the most opalescent and widely used in organizational institutionalism. As Friedland (2009: 61) stresses, an institutional logic is the organizing principle of an institutional order, 'a bundle of practices organized around a particular substance'. It provides social actors with vocabularies of motive and, thus, a sense of self. More recent empirical studies have emphasized the competition between alternative institutional logics within or across fields (for an overview, see Ocasio et al., Chapter 19 this volume). Social actors are routinely exposed to multiple institutional demands that shape their preferences as well as the repertoires of behaviors by which they may attain them. For most organizations, and especially for those high on global orientation, being exposed to various logics at the same time – institutional pluralism (e.g., Kraatz and Block, Chapter 20 this volume) – is the norm. As Friedland and Alford (1991) point out, organizations transform the institutional relations of society by skillfully maneuvering these constellations of logics.

Plurality, however, turns into complexity when institutional demands become incompatible and/or contradictory (Greenwood et al., 2011; Meyer and Höllerer, 2016). Such complexity, especially in nested or multilayered fields, translates to unclear or porous boundaries among subfields, whose actors, logics or governance structures messily overlap (Scott, 2014). This has ample implications for organizations that score high on global orientation, as they need to handle such complexity at different levels simultaneously, and because they have to develop and apply multiple, orchestrated response strategies in order to maintain their legitimacy. Beyond discussions of commensurability among institutional

logics, such institutional complexity has, for globally-oriented organizations, formal, practice and meaning dimensions. Formally, embeddedness in a pluralistic context means that organizations are subject to the regulatory and 'soft law' constrains of each of the nested fields. Practice-wise, such field-level complexity means that organizations draw from multiple global templates, thus straining the coherence of, and coupling among, elements. And meaning-wise, in spite of the immense efforts to categorize dominant logics and, with that, to put order into the conversation about multiple worlds of meaning, the reality of many globally-oriented organizations is particularly messy. Organizations embedded in such a complex global context, especially those strongly oriented towards the global array of fields and communities, are often overwhelmed by the plurality of referentials – which constitute a rich global 'menu' of templates – and thus struggle to gain footing and acquire legitimacy.

Legitimacy

Organizations do not only require material resources and technical information if they are to survive and thrive in their social environments; they also need social acceptability and credibility (Scott et al., 2000). Legitimacy is therefore an 'anchor-point of a vastly expanded theoretical apparatus addressing the normative and cognitive forces that constrain, construct, and empower organizational actors' (Suchman, 1995: 571; Deephouse et al., Chapter 1 this volume). It is conferred when 'stakeholders – that is, internal and external audiences affected by organizational outcomes – endorse and support an organization's goals and activities' (Elsbach and Sutton, 1992: 700). Hence, an organization is regarded as legitimate if its objectives and activities appear 'appropriate' within a specific institutional framework.

Despite the fact that, conceptually, legitimacy has always been thought of in the plural – as organizations are embedded in many environments, or fields – most empirical research has focused on legitimacy within a single institutional setting. Applying the concept of glocalization it becomes, however, obvious that legitimacy is a more complex challenge for organizations – and even more so for those that score high on global orientation. As 'global players', one might argue that they might get away when deviating slightly from local cultural norms. On the other hand, due to their entanglement with various different institutional settings, they are highly vulnerable and always at risk of struggling with contradicting institutional demands and prescriptions, from very local to global ones. Consequently, legitimacy must not only be understood as a multifacetted and multidimensional concept; glocalization implies that different institutional levels impact on organizational legitimacy, and need to be adequately addressed due to potential spillover effects.

Highly globally-oriented organizations address this multilevel problem of legitimacy by creating and exposing distinct global and local identities at the same time. Where needed, they cultivate the image of a unitary global actor, although they are constituted by a number of often only loosely coupled units (for instance, national, regional, or local subsidiaries) that are able to address the more local demands and institutional requirements of fields and communities. Due to this, they manage to develop not only a global identity, but also a variety of local identities, firmly embedded in local contexts, to which local legitimacy is conferred. The German-based engineering firm Siemens is a shining example for excelling in such a legitimation strategy: While Siemens is, without doubt, perceived as a 'global player' and certainly acts as such, it equally exposes its national heritage by stating, for instance, that Siemens and Germany are inextricably linked with each other, and also engages strongly in stakeholder relationships at the regional and community level – incrementally nurturing identities on all these levels.

CONCLUDING REMARKS

Recognizing that globalization drives intense structuration and propels interdependencies among entities, we have argued in the chapter at hand for a phenomenology-informed institutional perspective to analyze the impact of globalization on institutions and organization(s). From such a perspective, organizations worldwide are distinguished not so much by their formal categorization, strategic choices, or historic contingencies, but rather by their embeddedness within world society – namely within the web of organizations that constitutes the global polity and sets global normative order. Seeing that one feature of the model of global organization is formalization, indeed globalization begets further rationalized formal organizations and recasts more traditional forms of authority into this scheme. And yet, as highlighted in this chapter, the result of such embeddedness is not uniformity; rather, globalization is characterized by stylized organizational forms that are constituted around scripts of empowered agency and of distinctive identity. In this fashion, 'both conformity and variation are shaped by a rapidly expanding global system' (J.W. Meyer, 2014: 414) – and glocal forms of organization and organizing dominate.

The notion of glocalization and its manifold consequences for institutions and organizations requires a new paradigmatic approach. Rather than considering contextual complexity as an exogenous constraint upon global organization and its management, we here set out an approach that describes the relations between the global and the local, between the globally-oriented organizations and their global as well as local environments, as co-constitutive. And, rather than focusing on instrumental exchanges among interdependent entities, we highlight the mechanisms and the multidimensionality of global and local impacts on organizations and globally available ideas of organization and management. In this regard, we re-emphasize the role of culture and of institutional dynamics in constituting both institutions and organizations. We therefore suggest returning to the phenomenological tradition of organizational institutionalism that acknowledges isomorphic pressures alongside an array of variation, and with that explores the paradox of universalism of particularism, of glocal enactment and identity. Acknowledging the complex array of organizational fields, we also propose a relational perspective that traces webbed forms of embeddedness. These two features – variable isomorphism and webbed relations – set several researchable propositions for a comparative, global institutionalist analysis of organization.

In closing, we are reminded of Scott (2008: 209), who points out what we would miss in organizational analysis if we lost sight of institutions: 'Although it would appear that a field-level focus would detract attention from our attempt to understand the behavior of individual organizations, I believe that this is far from being true. Just as the attributes and actions of a character in a play are not fully comprehensible apart from knowledge of the wider drama being enacted – including the nature and interest of the other players, their relationships, and the logics that guide their actions – so we can better fathom an organization's behavior by seeing it in the context of the larger action and meaning system in which it participates.' We fully concur. And we firmly add that the same argument holds true for the two other levels that imprint organizations: world society, on the one hand, and local communities and other forms of local-level collective organizing, on the other. Only taken together, through multilevel analysis, can we hope to truly understand modern organizations.

REFERENCES

Abrahamson, E. (1996). Management fashion. *Academy of Management Review*, 21 (1): 254–285.

Acemoglu, D. and Robinson, J.A. (2005). *Economic Origins of Dictatorship and Democracy*. Cambridge: Cambridge University Press.

Ailon-Souday, G. and Kunda, G. (2003). The local selves of global workers: The social construction of national identity in the face of organizational globalization. *Organization Studies*, 24 (7): 1073–1096.

Alasuutari, P. (2014). Cosmopolitanism and banal localism: The domestication of global trends in Finnish cities. In G.S. Drori, M.A. Höllerer and P. Walgenbach (eds), *Global Themes and Local Variations in Organization and Management: Perspectives on Glocalization*. New York, NY: Routledge. pp. 396–411.

Albrow, M. and King, E. (eds) (1990). *Globalization, Knowledge, and Society: Readings from International Sociology*. London: Sage.

Alford, R.R. and Friedland, R. (1985). *Powers of Theory: Capitalism, the State and Democracy*. Cambridge: Cambridge University Press.

Anderson, B.R.O. (1983). *Imagined Communities: Reflections on the Origin and Spread of Nationalism*. London: Verso.

Appadurai, A. (2000). Grassroots globalization and the research imagination. *Public Culture*, 12 (1): 1–19.

Barnett, M. and Finnemore, M. (2004). *Rules for the World: International Organizations in Global Politics*. Ithaca, NY: Cornell University Press.

Bartelson, J. (2000). Three concepts of globalization. *International Sociology*, 15 (2): 180–196.

Beck, C.J., Drori, G.S. and Meyer, J.W. (2012). World influences on human rights language in constitutions: A cross-national study. *International Sociology*, 27 (4): 483–501.

Beckfield, J. (2010). The social structure of the world polity. *American Journal of Sociology*, 115 (4): 1018–1068.

Benford, R.D. and Snow, D.A. (2000). Framing processes and social movements: An overview and assessment. *Annual Review of Sociology*, 26 (1): 611–639.

Berger, P.L. and Luckmann, T. (1967). *The Social Construction of Reality: A Treatise in the Sociology of Knowledge*. New York, NY: Anchor Books.

Blau, P.M. and Scott, W.R. (1962). *Formal Organizations: A Comparative Approach*. Stanford, CA: Stanford University Press.

Boisot, M. and Child, J. (1999). Organizations as adaptive systems in complex environments: The case of China. *Organization Science*, 10 (3): 237–252.

Boli, J. (2006). The rationalization of virtue and virtuosity in world society. In M.-L. Djelic and K. Sahlin-Andersson (eds), *Transnational Governance: Institutional Dynamics of Regulation*. Cambridge: Cambridge University Press. pp. 95–118.

Boli, J. and Thomas, G.M. (1997). World culture in the world polity: A century of international non-governmental organization. *American Sociological Review*, 62 (2): 171–190.

Bromley, P. and Meyer, J.W. (2015). *Hyper-Organization: Global Organizational Expansion.* Oxford: Oxford University Press.

Bromley, P. and Meyer, J.W. (2016). 'They are all organizations': The cultural roots of blurring between nonprofit, government and business sectors. *Administration and Society.* Advance online publication. doi: 0.1177/0095399714548268.

Bromley, P. and Powell, W.W. (2012). From smoke and mirrors to walking the walk: The causes and consequences of decoupling in the contemporary world. *Academy of Management Annals*, 6 (1): 483–530.

Buhari-Gulmez, D. (2010). Stanford school on sociological institutionalism: A global cultural approach. *International Political Sociology*, 4 (3): 253–270.

Clemens, E.S. (1997). *The People's Lobby: Organizational Innovation and the Rise of Interest Group Politics in the United States, 1890–1925.* Chicago, IL: University of Chicago Press.

Cooper, D.J., Greenwood, R., Hinings, B. and Brown, J. L. (1998). Globalization and nationalism in a multinational accounting firm: The case of opening new markets in Eastern Europe. *Accounting, Organizations and Society*, 23 (5): 531–548.

Crang, M. (1999). Globalization as conceived, perceived and lived spaces. *Theory, Culture and Society*, 16 (1): 167–177.

Creed, W.E.D., Scully, M.A. and Austin, J.R. (2002). Clothes make the person? The tailoring of legitimating accounts and the social construction of identity. *Organization Science*, 13 (5): 475–496.

Czarniawska, B. and Joerges, B. (1996). Travel of ideas. In B. Czarniawska and G. Sevón (eds), *Translating Organizational Change.* Berlin: de Gruyter. pp. 13–48.

Czarniawska, B. and Sevón, G. (1996). *Translating Organizational Change.* Berlin: de Gruyter.

Czarniawska, B. and Sevón, G. (eds) (2005). *Global Ideas: How Ideas, Objects and Practices Travel in the Global Economy.* Frederiksberg, Denmark: Liber and Copenhagen Business School Press.

Dacin, M.T., Oliver, C. and Roy, J.-P. (2007). The legitimacy of strategic alliances: An institutional perspective. *Strategic Management Journal*, 28 (2): 169–187.

Davis, P.S., Desai, A.B. and Francis, J.D. (2000). Mode of international entry: An isomorphism perspective. *Journal of International Business Studies*, 31 (2): 239–258.

DiMaggio, P.J. and Powell, W.W. (1983). The iron cage revisited: Institutional isomorphism and collective rationality in organizational fields. *American Sociological Review*, 48 (2): 147–160.

Djelic, M.-L. (1998). *Exporting the American Model: The Postwar Transformation of European Business.* Oxford: Oxford University Press.

Djelic, M.-L. (2013). When limited liability was (still) an issue: Mobilization and politics of signification in 19th-century England. *Organization Studies*, 34 (5–6): 595–621.

Djelic, M.-L. and Quack, S. (2003). Introduction. In M.-L. Djelic and S. Quack (eds), *Globalization and Institutions: Redefining the Rules of the Economic Game.* New York: Edward Elgar Publishing. pp. 1–14.

Djelic, M.-L. and Quack S. (2011). The power of 'limited liability': Transnational communities and cross-border governance. *Research in the Sociology of Organizations*, 33: 79–109.

Djelic, M.-L. and Sahlin-Andersson, K. (2006). A world of governance: The rise of transnational regulation. In M.-L. Djelic and K. Sahlin-Andersson (eds), *Transnational Governance: Institutional Dynamics of Regulation.* Cambridge: Cambridge University Press. pp. 1–28.

Dobbin, F., Simmons, B. and Garrett, G. (2007). The global diffusion of public policies: Social construction, coercion, competition, or learning? *Annual Review of Sociology*, 33 (1): 449–472.

Drori, G.S. (2005). United Nations' dedications: A world culture in the making? *International Sociology*, 20 (2): 177–201.

Drori, G.S. (2008). Institutionalism and globalization studies. In R. Greenwood, C. Oliver, R. Suddaby and K. Sahlin-Andersson (eds), *The SAGE Handbook of Organizational Institutionalism.* Thousand Oaks, CA: Sage. pp. 798–842.

Drori, G.S. (2016). Global and comparative studies of organization and management: Moving from 'sameness and difference' to 'glocalization and orientation'. In B. Czarniawska (ed.), *A Research Agenda for Management and Organization Studies.* Cheltenham, UK: Edward Elgar. pp. 96–106.

Drori, G.S., Höllerer, M.A. and Walgenbach, P. (2014a). The glocalization of organization and management: Issues, dimensions and themes. In G.S. Drori, M.A. Höllerer and P. Walgenbach (eds), *Global Themes and Local Variations in Organization and Management: Perspectives on Glocalization.* New York, NY: Routledge. pp. 3–23.

Drori, G.S., Höllerer, M.A. and Walgenbach, P. (2014b). Unpacking the glocalization of organization: From term, to theory, to analysis. *European Journal of Cultural and Political Sociology*, 1 (1): 85–99.

Drori, G.S., Jang, Y.S. and Meyer, J.W. (2006). Sources of rationalized governance: Cross-national longitudinal analyses, 1985–2002. *Administrative Science Quarterly*, 51 (2): 205–229.

Drori, G.S. and Krücken, G. (2009). World society: A theory and a research program in context. In G. Krücken and G.S. Drori (eds), *World Society: The Writings of John W. Meyer.* Oxford: Oxford University Press. pp. 3–35.

Drori, G.S. and Meyer, J.W. (2006). Scientization: Making a world safe for organizing. In M.-L. Djelic and K. Sahlin-Andersson (eds), *Transnational Governance: Institutional Dynamics of Regulation.* Cambridge: Cambridge University Press. pp. 32–52.

Drori, G.S., Meyer, J.W. and Hwang, H. (2009). Global organization: Rationalization and actor-hood as dominant scripts. *Research in the Sociology of Organizations*, 27: 17–43.

Drori, G.S., Meyer, J.W., Ramirez, F.O. and Schofer, E. (2003). *Science in the Modern World Polity: Institutionalization and Globalization.* Stanford, CA: Stanford University Press.

Elsbach, K.D. and Sutton, R.I. (1992). Acquiring organizational legitimacy through illegitimate actions: A marriage of institutional and impression management theories. *Academy of Management Journal*, 35 (4): 699–738.

Finnemore, M. (1993). International organizations as teachers of norms: The United Nations educational, scientific, and cultural organization and science policy. *International Organization*, 47 (4): 565–597.

Finnemore, M. (1996). Norms, culture, and world politics: Insights form sociology's institutionalism. *Institutional Organization*, 50 (2): 325–347.

Fiss, P.C. and Hirsch, P.M. (2005). The discourse of globalization: Framing and sensemaking of an emerging concept. *American Sociological Review*, 70 (1): 29–52.

Fiss, P.C., Kennedy, M.T. and Davis, G.F. (2012). How golden parachutes unfolded: Diffusion and variation of a controversial practice. *Organization Science*, 23 (4): 1077–1099.

Frank, D.J. and Meyer, J.W. (2002). The contemporary identity explosion: Individualizing society in the post-war period. *Sociological Theory*, 20 (1): 86–105.

Friedland, R. (2009). Institution, practice, and ontology: Toward a religious sociology. *Research in the Sociology of Organizations*, 27: 45–83.

Friedland, R. and Alford, R.R. (1991. Bringing society back in: Symbols, practices, and institutional contradictions. In W.W. Powell and P.J. DiMaggio (eds), *The New Institutionalism in Organizational Analysis.* Chicago, IL: University of Chicago Press. pp. 232–263.

Giddens, A. (1991). *The Consequences of Modernity.* Cambridge: Polity Press.

Gooderham, P.N., Nordhaug, O. and Ringdal, K. (1999). Institutional and rational determinants of organizational practices: Human resource management in European firms. *Administrative Science Quarterly*, 44 (3): 507–531.

Gourevitch, P.A. and Shinn, J. (2007). *Political Power and Corporate Control: The New Global Politics of Corporate Governance.* Princeton, NJ: Princeton University Press.

Greenwood, R., Hinings, C.R. and Whetten, D. (2014). Rethinking institutions and organizations. *Journal of Management Studies*, 51 (7): 1206–1220.

Greenwood, R., Raynard, M., Kodcih, F., Micelotta, E.R. and Lounsbury, M. (2011). Institutional complexity and organizational responses. *Academy of Management Annals*, 5 (1): 317–371.

Greenwood, R., Suddaby, R. and Hinings, C.R. (2002). Theorizing change: The role of professional associations in the transformation of institutionalized fields. *Academy of Management Journal*, 45 (1): 58–80.

Guillén, M.F. (2001). Is globalization civilizing, destructive or feeble? A critique of five key debates in the social science literature. *Annual Review of Sociology*, 27: 235–260.

Guler, I., Guillén, M.F. and Macpherson, J.M. (2002). Global competition, institutions, and the diffusion of organizational practices: The international spread of ISO 9000 quality certificates. *Administrative Science Quarterly*, 47 (2): 207–232.

Hall, P.A. and Soskice, D. (2001). *Varieties of Capitalism: The Institutional Foundations of Comparative Advantage.* Oxford: Oxford University Press.

Hardy, C. and Maguire, S. (2008). Institutional entrepreneurship. In R. Greenwood, C. Oliver, R. Suddaby and K. Sahlin-Andersson (eds), *The SAGE Handbook of Organizational Institutionalism.* London: Sage. pp. 198–217.

Held, D., McGrew, A., Goldblatt, D. and Perraton, J. (1999). *Global Transformations: Politics, Economics and Culture.* Stanford, CA: Stanford University Press.

Hickson, D.J., Hinings, C.R., McMillan, C.J. and Schwitter, J.P. (1974). The culture-free context of organization structure: A tri-national comparison. *Sociology*, 8 (1): 59–80.

Hoffman, A.J. (1999). Institutional evolution and change: Environmentalism and the US Chemical Industry. *Academy of Management Journal*, 42 (4): 351–371.

Hoffman, A.J. (2001). *From Heresy to Dogma: An Institutional History of Corporate Environmentalism.* Stanford, CA: Stanford University Press.

Hollingsworth, J.R. and Boyer, R. (eds) (1997). *Contemporary Capitalism: The Embeddedness of Institutions.* Cambridge: Cambridge University Press

Hüther, O. and Krücken, G. (2016). Nested organizational fields: Isomorphism and differentiation among European universities. *Research in the Sociology of Organizations*, 46: 53–83.

Hwang, H. (2006). Planning development: Globalization and the shifting locus on planning. In G.S. Drori, J.W. Meyer and H. Hwang (eds), *Globalization and Organization: World Society and Organizational Change*. Oxford: Oxford University Press. pp. 69–90.

Hwang, H. and Powell, W.W. (2009). The rationalization of charity: The influences of professionalism in the nonprofit sector. *Administrative Science Quarterly*, 54 (2): 268–298.

Jang, Y.S., Cho, M. and Drori, G.S. (2014). National transparency: Global trends and national variations. *International Journal of Comparative Sociology*, 55 (2): 1–24.

Jepperson, R.L. (2002). Policial modernities: Disentangling two underlying dimensions of institutional differentiation. *Sociological Theory*, 20 (1): 61–85.

Kearney, A.T. (2007). Measuring globalization: The global top-20. *Foreign Policy*, November/December: 74–81.

Kennedy, M.T. and Fiss, P.C. (2009). Institutionalization, framing, and diffusion: The logic of TQM adoption and implementation decisions among US hospitals. *Academy of Management Journal*, 52 (5): 897–918.

Keohane, R.O. and Nye, J.S. Jr (2000). Globalization: What's new? What's not? (And so what?). *Foreign Policy*, 118: 104–119.

Kieser, A. (1997). Rhetoric and myth in management fashion. *Organization*, 4 (1): 49–74.

Kostova, T. and Roth, K. (2002). Adoption of an organizational practice by subsidiaries of multinational corporations: Institutional and relational effects. *Academy of Management Journal*, 45 (1): 213–233.

Kostova, T., Roth, K. and Dacin, M.T. (2008). Institutional theory in the study of multinational corporations: A critique and new directions. *Academy of Management Review*, 33 (4): 994–1006.

Kraatz, M.S. and Moore, J.H. (2002). Executive migration and institutional change. *Academy of Management Journal*, 45 (1): 120–143.

Krücken, G. and Meier, F. (2006). Turning the university into an organizational actor. In G.S. Drori, J.W. Meyer and H. Hwang (eds), *Globalization and Organization: World Society and Organizational Change*. Oxford: Oxford University Press. pp. 241–257.

Latour, B. (1986). Visualization and cognition: Thinking with eyes and hands. In H. Kuklick (ed.), *Knowledge and Society: Studies in the Sociology of Culture Past and Present*, Vol. 6. Greenwich, CT: JAI Press. pp. 1–40.

Lefebvre, H. (1991). *The Production of Space*. Oxford: Blackwell.

Lounsbury, M. (2007). A tale of two cities: Competing logics and practice variation in the professionalizing of mutual funds. *Academy of Management Journal*, 50 (2): 289–307.

Lounsbury, M. and Glynn, M.A. (2001). Cultural entrepreneurship: Stories, legitimacy, and the acquisition of resources. *Strategic Management Journal*, 22 (6–7): 545–564.

Maguire, S., Hardy, C. and Lawrence, T.B. (2004). Institutional entrepreneurship in emerging fields: HIV/AIDS treatment advocacy in Canada. *Academy of Management Journal*, 47 (5): 657–679.

March, J.G. and Olsen, J.P. (1976). *Ambiguity and Choice in Organizations*. Oslo, Norway: Universitetsforlaget.

Marquis, C. and Battilana, J. (2009). Acting globally but thinking locally? The enduring influence of local communities on organizations. *Research in Organizational Behavior*, 29: 283–302.

Marquis, C., Glynn, M.A. and Davis, G.F. (2007). Community isomorphism and corporate social action. *Academy of Management Review*, 32 (3): 925–945.

Marquis, C. and Lounsbury, M. (2007). Vive la résistance: Competing logics in the consolidation of US community banking. *Academy of Management Journal*, 50 (4): 799–820.

McNeely, C. (1995). *Constructing the Nation-State: International Organization and Prescriptive Action*. Westport, CT: Greenwood Press.

Meyer, J.W. (2000). Globalization: Sources and effects on national states and societies. *International Sociology*, 15 (2): 233–248.

Meyer, J.W. (2002). Globalization and the expansion and standardization of management. In K. Sahlin-Andersson and L. Engwall (eds), *The Expansion of Management Knowledge*. Stanford, CA: Stanford University Press. pp. 33–44.

Meyer, J.W. (2014). Empowered actors, local settings, and global rationalization. In G.S. Drori, M.A. Höllerer and P. Walgenbach (eds), *Global Themes and Local Variations in Organization and Management: Perspectives on Glocalization*. New York, NY: Routledge.

Meyer, J.W., Boli, J. and Thomas, G.M. (1987). Ontology and rationalization in the western cultural account. In G.M. Thomas, J.W. Meyer, F.O. Ramirez and J. Boli (eds), *Institutional Structure: Constituting State, Society, and the Individual*. Newbury Park, CA: Sage. pp. 12–40.

Meyer, J.W., Boli-Bennet, J. and Chase-Dunn, C. (1975). Convergence and divergence in development. *Annual Review of Sociology*, 1 (1): 223–246.

Meyer, J.W. and Bromley, P. (2013). The worldwide expansion of 'organization'. *Sociological Theory*, 31 (4): 366–389.

Meyer, J.W., Drori, G.S. and Hwang, H. (2006). Globalization and organization: World society and the organizational actor. In G.S. Drori, J.W. Meyer and H. Hwang (eds), *Globalization and Organization: World Society and Organizational Change*. Oxford: Oxford University Press. pp. 25–49.

Meyer, J.W., Frank, D., Hironaka, A., Schofer, E. and Tuma, N. (1997). The structuring of a world environmental regime, 1870–1990. *International Organization*, 51 (4): 623–651.

Meyer, J.W. and Hannan, M.T. (eds) (1979). *National Development and the World System: Educational, Economic, and Political Change, 1950–1970*. Chicago, IL: University of Chicago Press.

Meyer, J.W. and Jepperson, R.L. (2000). The 'actors' of modern society: The cultural construction of social agency. *Sociological Theory*, 18 (1): 100–120.

Meyer, J.W. and Rowan, B. (1977). Institutionalized organizations: Formal structure as myth and ceremony. *American Journal of Sociology*, 83 (2): 340–363.

Meyer, R.E. (2004). *Globale Managementkonzepte und lokaler Kontext: Organisationale Wertorientierung im österreichischen öffentlichen Diskurs*. Vienna: WUV Universitätsverlag.

Meyer, R.E. (2014). 'Re-localization' as micro-mobilization of consent and legitimacy. In G.S. Drori, M.A. Höllerer and P. Walgenbach (eds), *Global Themes and Local Variations in Organization and Management: Perspectives on Glocalization*. New York, NY: Routledge. pp. 79–89.

Meyer, R.E. and Höllerer, M.A. (2010). Meaning structures in a contested issue field: A topographic map of shareholder value in Austria. *Academy of Management Journal*, 53 (6): 1241–1262.

Meyer, R.E. and Höllerer, M.A. (2014). Does institutional theory need redirecting? *Journal of Management Studies*, 51 (7): 1221–1233.

Meyer, R.E. and Höllerer, M.A. (2016). Laying a smoke screen: Ambiguity and neutralization as strategic responses to intra-institutional complexity. *Strategic Organization*. Advance online publication. doi: 10.1177/1476127016633335.

Meyer, R.E., Höllerer, M.A., Jancsary, D. and Van Leeuwen, T. (2013). The visual dimension in organizing, organization, and organization research: Core ideas, current developments, and promising avenues. *Academy of Management Annals*, 7 (1): 487–553.

Miller, D., Le Breton-Miller, I. and Lester, R.H. (2013). Family firm governance, strategic conformity, and performance: Institutional vs. strategic perspectives. *Organization Science*, 24 (1): 189–209.

Oberg, A. and Walgenbach, P. (2008). Hierarchical structures of communication in a network organization. *Scandinavian Journal of Management*, 24 (3): 183–198.

Pallas, J. and Wedlin, L. (2014). Governance of science in mediatized society: Media rankings and the translation of global governance models for universities. In G.S. Dori, M.A. Höllerer and P. Walgenbach (eds), *Global Themes and Local Variations in Organization and Management: Perspectives on Glocalization*. New York, NY: Routledge. pp. 295–308.

Phillips, N., Lawrence, T.B. and Hardy, C. (2000). Inter-organizational collaboration and the dynamics of institutional fields. *Journal of Management Studies*, 37 (1): 23–44.

Piekkari, R. and Westney, D.E. (2017). Language as meeting ground for research on the MNC and organization theory. *Research in the Sociology of Organizations*, 49: 192–232.

Powell, W.W. (2001). The capitalist firm in the 21st century: Emerging patterns. In P.J. DiMaggio (ed.), *The Twenty-First Century Firm: Changing Economic Organization in International Perspective*. Princeton, NJ: Princeton University Press. pp. 33–69.

Przeworski, A., Alvarez, M.E., Cheibub, J. A. and Limongi, F. (2000). *Democracy and Development: Political Institutions and Well-Being in the World, 1950–1990*, Vol. 3. Cambridge: Cambridge University Press.

Putnam, R.D. and Campbell, D.E. (2010). *American Grace: How Religion Divides and Unites Us*. New York: Simon and Schuster.

Reay, T. and Hinings, C.R. (2009). Managing the rivalry of competing institutional logics. *Organization Studies*, 30 (6): 629–652.

Ritzer, G. (2003). Rethinking globalization: Glocalization/grobalization and something/nothing. *Sociological Theory*, 21 (3): 193–209.

Ritzer, G. (ed.) 2004. *The Handbook of Social Problems: A Comparative International Perspective*. Thousand Oaks, CA: Sage.

Robertson, R. (1995). Glocalizaton: time–space and homogeneity–heterogeneity. In M. Featherstone, S. Lash and R. Robertson (eds), *Global Modernities*. London: Sage. pp. 25–44.

Roudometof, V. (2015). Mapping the glocal turn: Literature streams, scholarship clusters and debates. *Glocalism: Journal of Culture, Politics, and Innovation*, 3: 1–21.

Sahlin-Andersson, K. (1996). Imitating by editing success: The construction of organizational fields. In B. Czarniawska and G. Sevón (eds), *Translating Organizational Change*. Berlin: de Gruyter. pp. 69–92.

Sahlin-Andersson, K. and Engwall, L. (eds) (2002). *The Expansion of Management Knowledge: Carriers, Flows, and Sources*. Stanford, CA: Stanford University Press.

Schneiberg, M. and Soule, S. (2005). Institutionalization as a contested, multilevel process: The case of rate regulation in American fire insurance. In G. Davis, D. McAdam, W.R. Scott and M. Zald (eds),

Social Movements and Organizations. Cambridge: Cambridge University Press. pp. 122–160.

Schofer, E. and Hironaka, A. (2005). The effects of world society on environmental protection outcomes. *Social Forces,* 84 (1): 25–47.

Scott, M.B. and Lyman, S.M. (1968). Accounts. *American Sociological Review,* 33 (1): 46–62.

Scott, W.R. (1994). Conceptualizing organizational fields: Linking organizations and societal systems. In H. Derlien, U. Gerhardt and F.W. Scharpf (eds), *Systemrationalität und Partialinteresse.* Baden-Baden: Nomos Verlagsgesellschaft. pp. 203–221.

Scott, W.R. (2008). *Institutions and Organizations,* 3rd edn. Thousand Oaks, CA: Sage.

Scott, W.R. (2014). *Institutions and Organizations: Ideas, Interests, and Identities,* 4th edn. Los Angeles, CA: Sage.

Scott, W.R., Ruef, M., Mendel, P.J. and Caronna, C.A. (2000). *Institutional Change and Healthcare Organizations.* Chicago, IL: University of Chicago Press.

Stensaker, I. and Falkenberg, J. (2007). Making sense of different responses to corporate change. *Human Relations,* 60 (1): 137–177.

Strang, D. (2014). Boomerang diffusion at a global bank: Total quality management and national culture. In G.S. Drori, M.A. Höllerer and P. Walgenbach (eds), *Global Themes and Local Variations in Organization and Management: Perspectives on Glocalization.* New York, NY: Routledge. pp. 107–118.

Strang, D. and Meyer, J.W. (1993). Institutional conditions for diffusion. *Theory and Society,* 22 (4): 487–511.

Strang, D. and Soule, S.A. (1998). Diffusion in organizations and social movements: From hybrid corn to poison pills. *Annual Review of Sociology,* 24 (1): 265–290.

Suchman, M.C. (1995). Managing legitimacy: Strategic and institutional approaches. *Academy of Management Review,* 20 (3): 571–610.

Tempel, A. and Walgenbach, P. (2007). Global standardization of organizational forms and management practices? What new institutionalism and the business-systems approach can learn from each other. *Journal of Management Studies,* 44 (1): 1–24.

Thornton, P.H., Ocasio, W. and Lounsbury, M. (2012). *The Institutional Logics Perspective: A New Approach to Culture, Structure and Process.* Cambridge: Oxford University Press.

Tolbert, P.S. and Zucker, L.G. (1996). The institutionalization of institutional theory. In S.R. Clegg,

C. Hardy and W.R. Nord (eds), *The SAGE Handbook of Organization Studies.* London: Sage. pp. 175–190.

Tomlinson, J. (1993). *Globalization and Culture.* Chicago, IL: University of Chicago Press.

Vaara, E., Tienari, J. and Laurila, J. (2006). Pulp and paper fiction: On the discursive legitimation of global industrial restructuring. *Organization Studies,* 27 (6): 789–813.

Walgenbach, P. (2001). The production of distrust by means of producing trust. *Organization Studies,* 22 (4): 693–714.

Walgenbach, P., Drori, G.S. and Höllerer, M.A. (2017). Between local mooring and global orientation: A neo-institutional theory perspective on the contemporary multinational corporation. *Research in the Sociology of Organizations,* 49: 99–125.

Wallerstein, I. (1974). *The Modern World-System I: Capitalist Agriculture and the Origins of the European World-Economy in the Sixteenth Century,* Vol 1. New York: Academic.

Wallerstein, I. (2000). Globalization or the age of transition? A long-term view of the trajectory of the world-system. *International Sociology,* 15 (2): 249–265.

Weber, M. (1978). *Economy and Society: An Outline of Interpretive Sociology,* Vols 1–2. Berkeley, CA: University of California Press.

Weick, K.E. (1976). Educational organizations as loosely coupled systems. *Administrative Science Quarterly,* 21 (1): 1–19.

Westney, D.E. (1993). Institutionalization theory and the multinational corporation. In S. Ghoshal and D.E. Westney (eds), *Organizational Theory and the Multinational Corporation.* New York: St. Martin's Press. pp. 53–75.

Whitley, R.D. (1999). *Divergent Capitalisms: The Social Structuring and Change of Business Systems.* Oxford: Oxford University Press.

Zilber, T.B. (2002). Institutionalization as an interplay between actions, meaning, and actors: The case of a rape crisis center in Israel. *Academy of Management Journal,* 45 (1): 234–254.

Zilber, T.B. (2008). The work of meanings in institutional processes and thinking. In R. Greenwood, C. Oliver, R. Suddaby and K. Sahlin-Andersson (eds), *The SAGE Handbook of Organizational Institutionalism.* London: Sage. pp. 151–169.

Zucker, L.G. (1987). Institutional theories of organization. *Annual Review of Sociology,* 13: 443–464.

9

Theorizing the Identity–Institution Relationship: Considering Identity as Antecedent to, Consequence of, and Mechanism for, Processes of Institutional Change

Mary Ann Glynn[1]

The construct of identity has long been central to the study of institutions and institutionalization, although the relationship between the two constructs has been modeled in a wide variety of ways. In early institutional accounts (e.g., Selznick, 1957; Berger & Luckmann, 1966; DiMaggio & Powell, 1983), the production of identity was conceptualized as an outcome of institutional processes, particularly in mature or changing fields. More recently, however, scholars focusing on the emergence of entrepreneurial activity, especially in new fields and new market categories (e.g., Navis & Glynn, 2010, 2011; Rao, Monin, & Durand, 2003; Santos & Eisenhardt, 2009), have shown how identity formation may be a forerunner to institutionalization. And, beyond these causal roles – as outcome or antecedent – identity has also been theorized as an integral mechanism in the process by which institutions are established, maintained and transformed over time (e.g., Glynn & Abzug, 2002; Lawrence, Suddaby, & Leca, 2009). Taken together, this stream of work suggests that the relationship between identity and institutionalization is a rich, complex and varied one; in its essence, it is a theoretical challenge to untangle, a challenge I take up in this chapter.

In the management literature, the research streams on organizational identity and institutionalism had different points of origin, different theoretical foundations and different paths of development, with few points of intersection along the way (see Glynn, 2008 for a discussion). And yet, there is much promise in their intersection, as suggested by several recent studies (e.g., Creed, DeJordy, & Lok; 2010; Lok, 2010). Moreover, the cultural turn currently sweeping the social sciences (Weber & Dacin, 2011) has raised the prospect of discovering new potential for conceptual affinities between the two constructs. Cultural approaches have become prominent in both neo-institutionalism (e.g., DiMaggio & Powell, 1983, 1991; Scott, 2008) and in organizational identity (e.g., Albert &

Whetten, 1985; Whetten & Godfrey, 1998), suggesting that there are new and promising theoretical opportunities for exploring the identity–institutionalism linkage. Forging such a link is important because, in spite of early acknowledgments of their intersection (e.g., Selznick, 1957), attempts to integrate identity and institutional perspectives remain sparse to date (Glynn, 2008).

Theories of organizational identity and institutionalism have likely diverged in management studies because of significant differences in the focal levels of analysis, the key outcomes of interest and the ways in which the processes of their emergence, maturation and change are modeled. Differences are evident in their early theorization. Broadly speaking, institutions can be conceptualized as the 'reciprocal typification of habitualized action by types of actors' (Berger & Luckmann, 1966: 54) that are comprised of 'regulative, normative and cognitive-cultural elements that, together with associated activities and resources, provide stability and meaning to social life' (Scott, 2008: 48). More generally, institutions consist of those shared beliefs and social structures that are made meaningful 'with value beyond the technical requirements of the task at hand' (Selznick, 1957). Traditionally, neo-institutional scholars have tended to focus on how macro forces at the level of the organizational field or industry have homogenizing effects, leading to similarity and stability among actors within a field (see Dacin et al., 2002); thus, the emphasis has been on the constraints imposed by isomorphic pressures for conformity as actors sought to legitimate their endeavors. In recent work, some of these assumptions have been relaxed, as greater allowance has been afforded to individual agency in interpretation and action (e.g., Weber & Glynn, 2006) and cultural entrepreneurship (e.g., Lounsbury & Glynn, 2001).

In contrast to institutionalists, organizational identity researchers have generally focused on lower levels of analyses (i.e., organizations or their individual members)

and on the individuation (or distinctiveness) of firms. Work on organizational identity highlights the micro-processes at play within firms, showing how polymorphous action is guided by an organization's unique, central and enduring attributes (e.g., Albert & Whetten, 1985; Dutton & Dukerich, 1991). Here, organizational identity refers not only to the values or ideology claimed by an organization, but also to the meaningful alignment of an organization's defining attributes or character ('who we are') with its core practices and behaviors ('what we do') (e.g., Navis & Glynn, 2010; Wry, Lounsbury & Glynn, 2011). The organization's identity functions to categorize the organization, to its internal members and external audiences, in a classification system defined by fields, markets or industries (Lounsbury & Glynn, 2001; Wry et al., 2011). Moreover, although identity can arise from an organization's claims to a set of characteristics (Albert & Whetten, 1985), it can also be catalogued by external audiences who apply 'identity codes' to different types of organizations (Hsu & Hannan, 2005; Hannan, 2010) which, in turn, create audience expectations of organizational behavior; meeting those expectations can also serve to legitimate the organization.

In this chapter, I seek to advance theoretical synthesis between the organizational identity and institutional perspectives. To do this, I leverage Karl Weick's (1979, 1989) wisdom in suggesting that theory is usefully developed through the conduct of heterogeneous, independent thought trials of possible conceptual linkages. It is a process used effectively by other researchers in processes of theorization (e.g., Astley & Van de Ven, 1983, cited in Weick, 1989: 522; Tunarosa & Glynn, 2016). As Weick (1989: 522) explains it: 'In general, a theorizing process characterized by a greater number of diverse conjectures produces better theory than a process characterized by a smaller number of homogeneous conjectures. The key property is heterogeneity among thought trials.' Weick (1989: 522) continues in this line of thought to suggest that: 'Independence among thought trials can be achieved by other means than strong classification systems. Any device that short circuits memory, foresight, or preference in the generation of thought trials increases the independence of these trials.' A technique that Weick advances to cultivate heterogeneous thought trials is by the generation of multiple relational algorithms, using various 'connector words', such as and, or, against, in, etc., to illuminate possible connections between two concepts (Crovitz, 1970).

Using this technique of relational algorithms alerts us to the fact that perhaps one connector word – 'and' – has been the default in considering the link between identity and institutions. To move theory forward, I advance three additional and different connections between identity and institutionalism: Identity as *antecedent to* processes of institutionalization; identity as a *consequence of* processes of institutionalization; and identity as a *mechanism in* processes of institutionalization. I discuss and then contextualize these three approaches to theorizing the identity–institutionalism linkage within the dynamics of their focal organizational fields, in processes of field emergence, maturation and change. To do this, I build on some of my earlier work (Glynn, 2008) and on other empirical studies in order to elaborate how identity can function in processes of institutionalization by creating meaning for organizations and fostering legitimacy in fields.

I attempt to use the relational algorithm technique to link identity and institutionalism in expansive ways. By identity, I refer to those specific claims made by an organization to describe its central, distinctive or enduring characteristics (e.g., Albert & Whetten, 1985; Glynn, 2000) or to position the organization in a market space, categorizing it as one type of organization and not another (e.g., Glynn & Abzug, 2002). By institutionalization, I refer to the process described by Tolbert and Zucker (1996), who highlight how Berger and Luckman's (1966) 'habitual typifications'

become habitualized, objectified, sedimented and having exteriority or 'possessing a reality of their own' (Berger & Luckmann, 1966: 58), functioning as taken-for-granted 'social givens'.

The chapter unfolds as follows. I begin with an overview of the use of the technique of relational algorithms in the service of theory development. Using this technique with three connector words (to; of; for), I explore three variations in relating identity and institutionalism: two are causal, framing identity as either an independent variable (antecedent to) or dependent variable (consequence of) institutionalization, and the third, processual, framing identity as a key mechanism for institutionalization. I illustrate these by drawing on published empirical studies and drawing out implications for future research on the theorization of the relationships between identity and institutionalism.

FORGING THORETICAL LINKAGES BETWEEN IDENTITY AND INSTITUTIONS

Theory develops when scholars use novelty in their attempts to understand focal phenomena, a set of problems or long-held assumptions. This novelty may spring from looking at what has been overlooked in previous work, associating concepts that have been previously unassociated, or questioning assumptions that may be taken-for-granted or uncontested. And, although thinking-outside-the-box creativity is an integral part of theory development, such imagination needs to be both generative and disciplined (Weick, 1989) if it is to be effective. As March (2003) reminds us, passion – the powerful and enthusiastic pursuit of our imaginative dreams – must be balanced with discipline.

Discipline in theorizing can arise in several different ways. One mode of discipline in developing 'strong' theory (Sutton & Staw, 1995: 378) is to explicitly invoke a set of selection criteria that is used to guide the choice of those 'conjectures generated during theory construction ... based on judgments of their plausibility, which can be assessed by a variety of selection criteria' (Weick, 1989: 525). Weick (1979: 253) enumerates several possible criteria for judging plausibility, leveraging Davis' (1971) notion of 'That's Interesting,' and adding 'That's Connected'. The latter criterion – 'That's Connected' – affords a way of exploring novel relationships between 'pairs of things,' a strategy particularly relevant to theorizing the identity–institutionalism link. Weick (1989: 526–527) explains one way of using the criterion of connectedness, i.e., by asking:

> Is this event connected to that event? Theorists often assume that events are unrelated and reactions of interest often result when unexpected connections are discovered (Davis, 1971). To discover an unexpected connection is to discover a new set of implications ... The assumption that events are unrelated is disconfirmed when people discover they are connected and the reaction that's interesting serves as a clue to retain the conjecture.

Weick (1989: 526–527) proposes the use of a cognitive technique that can activate the selection criterion of connections and enable heterogeneous thought trials: relational algorithms. He describes the method:

> Crovitz (1970) developed the relational algorithm as a device to generate novel solutions to sticky problems. He extracted all 42 relational words that were used in the 850-word language system called Basic English and proposed that meaning essentially is established when one item is placed in one of these 42 relations to another item. Thus, in a situation with a speaker and an audience, the event is very different if we have a situation in which a person speaks down to an audience, up to an audience, about an audience, behind an audience, without an audience, among an audience, beneath an audience, or over an audience. When faced with a theoretical problem, a theorist can generate thought trials by selecting pairs of domain words from the problem ... and then put them together with all possible relational words to generate conjectures about why the problem occurs. (Weick, 1989: 526–527)

Ungson, Braunstein and Hall (1981: 123), in theorizing causal modeling, make a similar argument for relational algorithms: 'In the process of causal modeling, conceptual heuristic operations are used to combine cues in some cause–effect relationship. Crovitz (1967) described this process as a relational algorithm based on the notion that an idea was a statement of one thing (cue) taken in relation to some other thing (cue)'. These authors cite the application of relational algorithms in research on problem-solving and preference choices by Newell and Simon (1972) and Bouwman (1978). Ironically, however, in spite of its utility, researchers have infrequently adopted Weick's suggested application of the relational algorithm (Anderson, 2006).

Using Relational Algorithms to Connect Identity and Institutions

Relational algorithms offer a myriad of possibilities for connecting different conceptual domains because they use a variety of 'connector words' to be inserted into a sentence of the form: 'Take one thing [... relate it to ...] another thing' (Weick, 1979: 253). The 'relate it to' phrase can use any of 42 connector words originally proposed by Crovitz (1970: 42), replicated by Weick (1979: 253), and subsequently expanded by VanGundy (1988) to include 19 prepositions. The original 42 relational words are the following: about; across; after; against; among; and; as; at; because; before; between; but; by; down; for; from; if; in; near; not; now; of; off; on; opposite; or; out; over; round; still; so; then; though; through; till; to; under; up; when; where; while; with. To use the relational algorithm technique, consider the different theorizations suggested by the insertion of different connector words between our two focal concepts of identity and institutions.

To begin, 'and' is, perhaps, the most prevalent (and perhaps overused) connector word for our key concepts, i.e., identity *and* institutions. At best, however, it offers only minimal theoretical traction. For instance, the relational algorithm employed by 'and' offers very little detail about how distinctiveness and polymorphism (associated with identity) might relate to sameness and isomorphism (associated with institutions) in field-level dynamics; it simply puts the constructs in the same theoretical space without a consideration of their causal, processual or other linkages. Other relational algorithms, however, can reveal more about novel and underexplored relationships between identity and institutions. For instance, identity *through* institutions suggests that identity can result inadvertently from, or perhaps penetrate through, institutional processes over time. Identity *as* institutions suggests that identity can function much like institutions, perhaps as an institutional logic that disciplines which actions are appropriate for a particular group of actors in a particular type of organization or event. And identity *opposite* institutions evokes situations in which identity may contest or contradict institutional beliefs, as when an actor holds values that are contrary to those embedded in an institution.

I focus on using three of Crovitz's (1970) proposed 'connector words' – to; of; for – to advance theory on connections (or relationships) describing the identity–institution relationship. I chose these three because they describe basic ways in which concepts may be related and because they capture both causal and processual ways of relating, that can be both predictive and explanatory in theorization. Using these three 'connector words', I outline three different, independent, and heterogeneous thought trials that can enable theorization: Identity as *antecedent to* institutionalization; Identity as *consequent of* institutionalization; Identity as *mechanism for* institutionalization. For each of these three, I first describe the nature of the proposed linkage, articulate the core identity question implied by this perspective, and offer empirical examples to illustrate the theorized linkage.

Identity as Antecedent to Institutionalization

Perhaps identity is nowhere more evident in processes of institutionalization than when it is part of the initiating conditions, serving as a touchstone or imprint for the subsequent institutionalization that unfolds. This is evident in cases where identities are key in the emergence of new fields or market categories, particularly when 'entrepreneurs become skilled users of cultural tool kits rather than cultural dopes' (Rao, 1994: 41). When actors function as cultural entrepreneurs, they engage in symbolic action, such as storytelling 'that mediates between extant stocks of entrepreneurial resources and subsequent capital acquisition and wealth creation' (Lounsbury & Glynn, 2001: 545). In doing so, the entrepreneurial identity (Navis & Glynn, 2011) often becomes a cornerstone, shaping and directing the progression of institutionalization.

Wry and colleagues (2011: 450) describe how the emergence of a collective identity is integral to cultural entrepreneurship processes and shaping a nascent field:

> efforts to gain the attention of, and be validated by, external audiences require a form of active and strategic cultural entrepreneurship (Lounsbury & Glynn 2001) – that is, the production of rationalizing accounts or stories that astutely deploy vocabulary (Nigam & Ocasio, 2010) and rhetoric (Suddaby & Greenwood, 2005) to shape the attention (Ocasio, 1997) and perceptions of various audiences, justifying the group's legitimacy and helping to coordinate its expansion. ... the meaning and labels associated with a collective identity are narrative constructions that are bound to the stories communicated by members.

Empirical work on entrepreneurship supports the validity of this approach (e.g., Martens, Jennings, & Jennings, 2007; Zott & Huy, 2007).

Cultural entrepreneurship is itself an exercise in claiming an identity by using cultural resources to develop and communicate a sense of the entrepreneurial self and associating repertoires for appropriate action; indeed, Swidler (1986) describes her model of culture as a toolkit as an 'identity model of culture'. To be causally antecedent in the process of institutionalization, identities need to be visible, potent and evidence cultural resonance such that they align with 'a specific issue and more enduring cultural themes' (Gamson, 1988: 243) that seem to be 'natural and familiar' (Gamson, 1992: 135). In its essence, understanding identity as antecedent to institutionalization is the case where identity often *becomes* the institution. The imprint of identity in institutionalization can produce novel institutions that are culturally distinctive, stylized, normalized, and/or legitimized via cultural entrepreneurship. The identity question that is implied is this: What kind of institution is this? And, the identity answer: A distinctive institution.

We can see how identity can be antecedent to institutionalization in the case of Martha Stewart and the establishment of her namesake organization, Martha Stewart Living Omnimedia (MSLO). Stewart's company is not unique in being eponymous; adopting the name of founders (or partners) is fairly widespread; such naming is a strong marker of the imprint of identity. Consider, for instance, that the following companies were named for people: Abercrombie & Fitch, Air Jordon, Bell Telephone Company, Calvin Klein, Dell, Dow Jones, Gucci, Guinness, Hilton Hotels, Kellogg, McDonald's, Pfizer, Reuters, Sherwin-Williams, and TAG Heuer (https://en.wikipedia.org/wiki/List_of_companies_named_after_people).

Stewart's identity became the MSLO institution over time, not only in name but also in its focal offerings in the market and the particular cultural tone it set. Stewart's firm, MSLO, pioneered and successfully sold a cultural product, that of lifestyle, i.e., a bundle of attitudes and behaviors that pertains to social relations, patterns of consumption and entertainment, traditions of marking occasions, as well as one's dress and home décor, specific to a given time and place. The cultural framing of one's business changed consumers' orientation to products, from one that focused on its functional attributions to one that reflected their lifestyle. Stewart rationalized lifestyle and the array of forms in which her firm packaged and sold it, i.e., in television and radio shows; magazines; products for the home and garden; books on cooking, entertaining, housekeeping, landscaping, and weddings, among others, in ways that appealed to her audience. Lifestyle had cultural resonance for Stewart's followers because it, 'like other forms of high culture, combines concrete practices with a compelling story linking those practices to transcendent meanings and identities' (DiMaggio, 2006: 932). This resonance arose in part, not only from the kinds of offerings that MSLO marketed, that effectively 'solved' the problems of living, but also in the rhetoric that enrobed the products and practices that she marketed. Lockwood and Glynn (2016: 5) describe MSLO's offerings as follows:

> Through her multi-media programming and other products, Stewart traffics in traditions, offering them as solutions to modern concerns of 'living,' and imbuing them with meaning and values that transcend their functionality. For instance, in one magazine column, the Thanksgiving turkey is portrayed as 'our most conservative holiday meal, with an unchallengeable body of myth built up around the roasted bird that makes it as sacrosanct as the flag' ('Turkey 101,' November 1995, MSL magazine). Similarly, an article on vacuuming asserts that 'the invention of the vacuum cleaner is a rags-to-riches story as American as the door-to-door salesman' ('Vacuuming 101,' December 1995/January 1996, MSL).

Stewart herself was a key part of this rhetoric; it was her own identity narrative that was called forth in the organization's storytelling, e.g.

> Martha's story begins the way millions of American stories have begun with a voyage of courage a century ago. Martha's Polish grandparents sailed by the Statue of Liberty into New York Harbor in 1905. The new immigrants set up home first in Newark, later, Edward Kostyra, Martha's father, would move to Nutley, New Jersey, just 20 minutes

from Manhattan. (Larry King Live, airing 05/04/02, http://transcripts.cnn.com/TRANSCRIPTS/0205/04/ pitn.00.html, accessed 08/30/08)

In general, Stewart's cultural entrepreneurship, with its development of the lifestyle perspective, and associated products and practices, aided the founding and success of her business (MSLO), as well as her own institutionalization as a symbolic icon. To wit:

[Stewart] had become ubiquitous, the face of the age. She had become so famous that, as the New York Times rightly pointed out, she no longer needed a last name. She had become simply 'Martha' ... In fact, she'd become more than that—not simply a one-word name, but a human adjective ... just decorate a holiday centerpiece with gold-leaf pinecones and every woman at the table could be counted on to gaze admiringly on the display and declare, 'Very Martha.' (Byron, 2002: 195)

Stewart's case illustrates how identity can be *antecedent to* institutionalization. Stewart leveraged her own personhood to rationalize her firm's offerings and to give coherence to the 'multimedia' sets of activities and products in which the firm engaged. Using the relational algorithm technique, with the connector word 'to,' exposes how institutions can be agentically created, founded and emergent from distinctive and resonant identities; in other words, novel or unfamiliar identities through the processes of institutionalization can eventually become familiar, legitimate and even taken-for-granted.

To date, there has been limited work in this vein, but research is emerging that is clearly relevant (e.g., Navis & Glynn, 2010, 2011). For instance, Rao et al. (2003), in their study of changes in French gastronomy over time, demonstrated that identities – and especially, identity-discrepant cues – helped to shift the institutionalized meaning systems associated with traditional French cuisine to launch nouvelle cuisine. Moreover, the view of identity as antecedent to institutionalization highlights the agentic role of actors, even individual actors (such as Martha Stewart) in ways that are consistent with recent interest

in 'inhabited institutions' (Creed et al., 2010; Hallett & Ventresca, 2006; Scott, 2008).

Next, I use a relational algorithm to move along the causal chain of possibilities for linking identity and institutionalization, from considering identity as an antecedent to institutionalization to considering identity as a consequence. For this, we use the connector word 'of' in the relational algorithm device.

Identity *as* Consequence of Institutionalization

Treating identity *as a consequence of* institutionalization is a hallmark of the 'old' institutionalism, perhaps best exemplified by Selznick. Selznick (1957: 40) postulated that institutionalization – the infusion of value in organizations – 'produces a distinct identity for the organization.' More recently, Podolny, Khurana and Hill-Popper (2004: 8) echo the same theorization: 'Turn an organization into an institution, by infusing the organization with values and creating a distinct organizational identity and sense of purpose that is in fact internalized by organizational members as meaningful.' In these accounts, processes of institutionalization are focused at the organizational level, with identity occurring during maturation or in later stages of institutionalization. The underlying mechanism creating identity is that of value infusion (Selznick, 1957) or the sedimentation of organizational meaning, purpose and valuations of worth. The result is that the firm becomes something more than an efficient, functional operation; rather, it takes on a distinct character or identity that is transcendent.

Identity can also result from institutionalization processes at the level of the field. Here, the mechanisms driving identity formation are isomorphic forces – coercive, mimetic or normative pressures for conformity – that elicit organizational sameness in an attempt to secure credibility or legitimation. Institutionalization involves the diffusion of novel practices throughout a field and, 'As an innovation spreads, a threshold is reached beyond which adoption provides legitimacy rather than improves performance' (DiMaggio & Powell, 1983: 148).

Thus, the relational algorithm 'of' highlights how, at both the organizational and field levels, identity is the outgrowth *of* institutionalization, reflecting something of significance that goes beyond mere functionality, operational concerns or efficiency. Instead, identity captures claims to the organization's values or its legitimacy, i.e., the 'generalized perception or assumption that the actions of an entity are desirable, proper, or appropriate within some socially constructed system of norms, values, beliefs, and definitions' (Suchman, 1995: 574).

Key markers of organizational identities, firm names, have demonstrated these effects, revealing how identity can be the product of institutionalization processes. The observed homogeneity of organizational names within an industry has been shown to be the outcome of the process of symbolic isomorphism, i.e. 'the resemblance of an organization's symbolic attributes to those of other organizations within its institutional field' (Glynn & Abzug, 2002: 267).

In a series of empirical studies, Glynn and her collaborators (Glynn & Abzug, 1998, 2002; Glynn & Marquis, 2004, 2005) have demonstrated the power of symbolic isomorphism in the choices of organizational names (for organizations changing their names) as well as the identity categories that they claim. For instance,

> In contrast to the rich, descriptive and lengthy names of the 1800s (The Peninsular and Oriental Steam Navigation Company), the names of more recent vintage are brief and concise (GE, Philco). ... Names trended from being more descriptive in the 19th century, to more abstract in the mid 20th century, and back to invoking more familiar products, brands, and identifiers at the close of the 20th century (Ambstar to Domino Sugar). At the turn of the millennium, naming tendencies reflected a new driver – corporate ventures into cyberspace – and we observe a role in popularity

> of the form *www.name.com*. Over time, organizational names have changed, but they have done so with patterned regularity; isomorphism may drive identity symbols. (Glynn & Abzug, 2002: 268)

And, even organizational identities that positioned themselves in the ether of cyberspace changed when that source of institutional legitimacy changed. Glynn and Marquis (2004: 148), in empirical studies of 'dot-com' names, found that 'Many of the same companies, which had expediently appended "dot-com" to their names, just as quickly divorced themselves in name from an Internet gone bust. ... [and that] organizations quickly conformed to a new institutional order.'

Overall, this body of work shows that organizational name choices are neither entirely random nor purely idiosyncratic to the organization; rather, they align in form and content with the prevailing standards of the institutional fields in which they are embedded. As a result, institutionalization produces identities that are not entirely organization-centric but stylized, normalized and legitimized, i.e., institutionalized via isomorphic pressures. Organizations conform because such alignment can confer legitimacy; organizational names that closely resemble the institutionalized template tend to be more comprehensible and viewed as more credible (Glynn & Abzug, 1998, 2002).

When identity is modeled as consequent to institutionalization, the identity question becomes: What kind of identity characterizes this entity? And, the answer is largely categorical: Identity classifies this entity as one kind of thing and not another (e.g., Glynn & Navis, 2013) and, in doing so, such categorization enables more easy and clear recognition by audiences. Zuckerman (1999) has shown how an illegitimacy discount accrues to non-conforming organizations, when identities tend to defy categorization in well-established systems of valuation or fields of meaning. For instance, Glynn and Marquis (2005) have shown that names such as First National Bank and Tony's Pizza conform to institutional expectations and thus tend to be valued and legitimated by audiences; by contrast, names like First National Pizza or Tony's Bank, in spite of their legality, tend to be perceived as less legitimate.

Thus, identities are not simply bundles of particularistic attributes (e.g., Albert & Whetten, 1985) but are also claims to membership in categories that define institutionalized fields. And, although institutional forces can narrow possibilities for (appropriate) identity symbols through ritualized conformity, thereby decreasing the probability of some names (e.g., First National Pizza), they can also enable identities, by supplying the raw materials and processes needed for 'identity-work' (Glynn, 2008). Institutions encode meanings and values that organizations can appropriate as building blocks in identity formation. Organizations, as social actors, can creatively bricolage such materials through the process of cultural entrepreneurship (Lounsbury & Glynn, 2001) and symbolic management (Navis & Glynn, 2011). Actors can appropriate publicly available symbolic forms through which they themselves experience meaning and express values or preferences (Swidler, 1986: 273); more generally, 'People can be artful in their mobilization of different institutional logics to serve their purpose' (Westenholz, 2006: 1019). Thus, even as consequences of institutionalization processes, identities need not be fully determined or constrained (Glynn, 2008). Moreover, fields change over time and with them, institutional standards that serve as touchstones for identity and legitimation. Institutional periodicity over time patterns the choices organizations make in changing their names and organizations adapt to conform (Glynn & Abzug, 2002); external changes in institutional environments change legitimacy dynamics and, in turn, affect organizational identity and survival (Glynn & Marquis, 2004).

As the preceding discussion illustrates, identities can be *consequences of* processes of institutionalization. In many ways, this model of the identity–institutionalization linkage draws on a long line of work that extends back to early articulations of institutional theory (e.g., Selznick, 1957) as well as the importance of the symbolic and representational (Meyer & Rowan, 1977). Many of the key mechanisms – diffusion, isomorphism, periodicity and legitimation – have been well documented; however, these have tended to focus more on the adoption of new practices and less on the possibilities for identity formation and change. And yet, understanding identity in institutional dynamics seems like a fertile area of inquiry, given the demonstrated 'complexity of identity dynamics and how they are predicated upon micro-level organizational processes and macro-level field dynamics' (Glynn & Abzug, 2002: 267).

Thus far, I have discussed the application of two connector words – (antecedent) *to* and (consequent) *of* – that point to possible causal relationships in the identity–institutions linkage. Next, I take up a third and non-causal option, that of how identities and institutions may be intertwined processes such that identity is a motor, or mechanism, *for* institutionalization.

Identity as Mechanism for Institutionalization

Theorizing identity as a mechanism for processes of institutionalization invites us to explore how the constructs are inter-related, particularly at multiple levels of analysis, i.e., at the level of the individual organization and at the level of the institutional field. In the previous section, I highlighted how organizational identities in institutional fields changed in response to changes in those focal institutional fields or industries; here, I focus on how changes in the identity of the field are interwoven with changes in the identities of those organizations that populate the field. Such a perspective is especially salient in processes of establishing, maintaining or transforming institutions, especially in early or formative stages. For instance, new or emerging market categories that originate as 'unstable, incomplete and disjointed conceptual systems held by market actors ... become coherent as a result of consumers and producers making sense of each other's behaviors' (Rosa et al., 1999: 64), largely through the construction of meanings and identities that make the category understandable, viable and 'real' (Kennedy, 2008).

In contrast to understanding identity in institutionalization as a causal input (antecedent to) or output (consequent of), the positioning of identity in the process of institutionalization is less demarcated; identity is intertwined with institutionalization dynamically, as meanings are created and established in the creation, constitution and ongoing practices of actors in fields. Identity is intimated in institutional dynamics. For instance, identity can function as a kind of institutional logic (Friedland & Alford, 1991), serving as a set of 'shared rules and typifications that identify categories of social actors and their appropriate activities or relationships' (Barley & Tolbert, 1997: 96). Lok (2010: 1305) explains:

> The concept of identity is of central importance to understanding shifts in institutional logics, which comprise organizing principles for broad, suprarational orders, because identity is thought to form an important link between institutional logics and the behavior of individuals and organizations.

Because identities and institutionalization are co-evolving as fields emerge, change and mature over time, the key identity question becomes: When and how, in the process of institutionalization, does identity matter? And the answer is found by teasing apart the identities in institutionalization via time, events, levels of analysis or actors' agency.

As an illustration of levels of analysis, consider the emergence and early growth of the new market category of satellite radio (Navis & Glynn, 2010) and how, in the process, both organizational and collective categorical identities emerged.

Market category emergence is a complex but dynamic process, involving the social construction of meaning by market actors, such as producers, consumers, and relevant audiences, so as to legitimate the nascent category as an outcome of institutionalization. Initially, creating the meaning of the market category involves defining a collective identity in which all the member organizations share. In the case of satellite radio, collective identity formation focused on describing the identity element of 'what we do' as satellite radio organizations. In the early stages of category formation, it was an identity that blanketed the two satellite radio firms, XM and Sirius, as undifferentiated actors within the new market category. However, as the new category became understood, legitimate and 'real' (Kennedy, 2008), the identity dynamics shifted: As the category was institutionalized, organizational identities increasingly focused on 'who we are' as satellite radio organizations. The result was to frame the satellite radio organizations (XM and Sirius) as differentiated actors within a new market category and as distinct strategic competitors.

Thus, in the earliest period of new market category emergence, organizational identities were claimed as similar in order to enable the formation of collective meaning about the category. Identity development thus became the initial means or mechanism by which the institutionalization of the category occurred. With category legitimation, firms shifted their identity claims to emphasize their distinctiveness from each other. The process of identity formation was intimately bound up with the process of institutionalization; not only did one fuel the other, but shifts in one enabled shifts in the other. Navis and Glynn (2010: 466) concluded that 'the evolution of fields, like that of markets, will exhibit a significant contextual shift, from market-building to firm-building, and that this will be indicated by a legitimacy threshold.' Overall, then, there was a contextualization of organizational identities within the emergence, development and institutionalization of a new field.

In the case of identity as a mechanism for institutionalization, identity functions as the means by which a group rationalizes the institutionalization of practices, professions or logics, or the means by which it protects its institutionalized status or the process by which it creates the stability for institutionalization to occur. All these dynamics are evident in Rao et al.'s (2003) study of the emergence and institutionalization of nouvelle cuisine in France. The authors demonstrated that an identity movement – whereby French chefs redefined 'who' they were and 'what they do' – claimed a new collective identity which they claimed as a group; it was this identity that motored the adoption and institutionalization of the new type of cuisine ('nouvelle') and the abandonment of the old type of cuisine ('classic'). This new identity of the chef was that of 'innovator, creator, and owner' (Rao et al., 2003: 807), a sharp contrast to the dominant identity that was institutionalized as classic cuisine where 'The chef was an employee of the restaurant owner and was in the background' (p. 801). The new identity was not simply a claim but a mandate to action; the nouvelle cuisine chefs created new types of dishes, re-did menus and tried to create new taste preferences. Moreover, as one might expect in processes of institutionalization (DiMaggio & Powell, 1983), 'In the case of nouvelle cuisine, culinary journalists sympathetic to nouvelle cuisine played an important role in creating a shared symbolic environment for chefs and the public to appreciate the new logic and identity' (Rao et al., 2003: 816). Thus, the new professional identity as French chefs was a critical mechanism in the institutionalization of the new cuisine.

To summarize, our consideration of how identities are mechanisms for processes of institutionalization highlighted the dynamic and interactive play between the two over time. Rather than identity being entirely antecedent to or a consequence of institutionalization, this processual approach reveals how identities – and organizations' claims to those identities – are predicated upon the shifting context of field emergence, growth and maturation. When identities and institutionalization processes are in flux, each shifts to adapt to the other, punctuated by key developments in the field.

DISCUSSION AND CONCLUSIONS

In this chapter, I set out to explore the potential for relating identity *and* institutions. I sought to move beyond the simple conjunction 'and' and describe broader and more diverse ways of thinking about the connection between the two constructs. To do this, I used the technique of relational algorithms, which is predicated upon the use of 'connector words' to think about how one construct may relate to another. By using three specific connector words – to; of; for – I examined three modes for understanding identity in processes of institutionalization: as antecedent to, consequence of, and mechanism for.

First, I focused on identity as a causal *antecedent to* processes of institutionalization, especially noticeable during the emergence of new fields or market categories. To illustrate this type of relationship, I used the case of Martha Stewart (e.g., Glynn, 2011; Glynn & Dowd, 2008; Lockwood & Glynn, 2016) who, as a cultural entrepreneur, imprinted her personal identity in a durable and meaningful way on the firm she founded and led, Martha Stewart Living Omnimedia. Drawn from her own personal experience, Stewart injected her new venture with her sense of the aesthetic and style that made her offerings of products and services distinctive in the market. As a result, Stewart's case is instructive on how institutions may be agentically created, founded and emergent from the distinctive and valued identities of an entrepreneur in a way that is causally antecedent.

Second, I focused on identity as a causal *consequence of* processes of institutionalization, especially in maturing or changing fields. To illustrate this relationship, I used examples taken from empirical studies of organizational name changes (Glynn & Abzug, 1998, 2002; Glynn & Marquis, 2004, 2005). These revealed how identities are shaped by, and conform to, isomorphic forces in the institutional field that push organizations toward conformity. Moreover, this conformity was ongoing: As fields changed with periodicity over time, so too did the names that marked organizational identities as they sought to align isomorphically. As a consequence of institutionalization, identities are not simply bundles of particularistic or individuated attributes but, instead, stylized claims to institutionalized categories that can endow the firms with legitimacy and audience endorsement.

Third, I focused on identity as a *mechanism for* processes of institutionalization, as part of establishing, maintaining or transforming institutions. For this processual relationship, I offered illustrations from the study of the emergence of the market category of satellite radio (Navis & Glynn, 2010), which demonstrated the mutuality of change in processes of identity development and institutionalization. Rather than delineating identity as either cause or consequence, a mechanisms-based view (Davis & Marquis, 2005) revealed the complexity of interactions between the two constructs.

I found the use of relational algorithms to be generative in yielding the kinds of heterogeneous thought trials that enabled theory development. The three relationships on which I focused, two causal and one processual, afforded a different view of identities and institutionalization, as well as their interrelationship. However, this is but an initial foray; there is more to do in explicating the relationship between identity and institutions. Following, I offer some possible extensions that might be pursued in future research. To do so, I encourage interested researchers to conduct three additional thought experiments: (1) invoke, complicate and deepen the use of relational algorithms as a technique of

theory development; (2) explore the potential connections between institutional work and identity work; and (3) consider the possibility of how identity logics might function as a companion to institutional logics. Next, I discuss each in turn.

Relating Identities and Institutions via Extended Use of Relational Algorithms

In this chapter, I explored only five connector words – and; in; to; of; for – from Crovitz's (1970) set of 42 and not any of the 19 additional connector words proposed by VanGundy (1988). Clearly, there is a vast frontier of relational possibilities awaiting researchers. One possibility worth pursuing might be suggested by connector words like 'opposite' or 'not', which instead of finding commonalities, would emphasize differences, or perhaps even conflict or contestation, between identities and institutions. This might be the case, for instance, when institutions oppose certain kinds of identities.

In recent years, we have seen the contestation over the institution of marriage and the legal, religious, or legitimate rights of non-heterosexual couples to wed; in an earlier century, such thinking might have also extended to those Americans of different races. Creed and colleagues (2010) examine another institutional contradiction, that between the role of Protestant ministers and the marginalized identities of gay, lesbian, bisexual and transgender (GLBT) individuals. Their interviews with GLBT ministers revealed how it was identity work, at the individual level by the minister, which resolved the institutional contradiction. Other connector words might reveal nuances in the relationship between identities and institutions that can surface both positive and negative relationships or instances of contradiction or conflict, thus expanding theorization.

Beyond my focus on discerning the relationship between identity and institutionalization, this work also suggests the utility of the technique of relational algorithms in theory development, a technique that has been under-used by organizational scholars (Anderson, 2006). More generally, then, relational algorithms can be a tool in the arsenal for advancing theoretical explorations on a wide variety of topics.

The Interplay between Institutional Work and Identity Work

There is an interesting assumption in the literature that is made about both institutions and identities, i.e., that both require 'work' of some sort to maintain their integrity and durability over time and in the face of challenges. Lawrence and colleagues (2009: 215) define institutional work as 'the purposive action of individuals and organizations aimed at creating, maintaining and disrupting institutions'. More generally, this description '[h]ighlights the intentional actions taken in relation to institutions, some highly visible and dramatic ... but much of it nearly invisible and often mundane, as in the day-to-day adjustments, adaptation, and compromises of actors attempting to maintain institutional arrangements' (Lawrence, 2009: 1).

Identity work, according to Snow and Anderson (1987: 1348) consists of the 'range of activities that individuals engage in to create, present, and sustain personal identities that are congruent with and supportive of the self-concept'. Kreiner, Hollensbe and Sheep (2006: 1032) state that identity work involves

'people being engaged in forming, repairing, maintaining, strengthening or revising the constructions that are productive of a sense of coherence and distinctiveness (Sveningsson & Alvesson, 2003: 1165). Social group members engage in identity work in order to negotiate and optimize the boundaries between personal and social identity.'

In their study of religious ministers, Kreiner and colleagues demonstrate how identity work is aimed at resolving the tension experienced between integration and differentiation, or conformity and deviation.

The notion of active, engaged 'work' seems almost counterintuitive in that both constructs, in their essence, are about durability (e.g., Rao et al., 2003). And yet, each is tasked with maintaining constancy in the face of change, discrepancies or threats. It would be interesting to examine how this 'work' is conducted, and to what effect, in stabilizing identities and institutions. Lok (2010), for instance, notes their intersection in recognizing that identity work is 'an important form of institutional work that is central to the creation of new institutions by institutional entrepreneurs'. Beyond their surface resemblance, one might speculate on whether their underlying dynamics or mechanisms are similar. Or, if identities that are antecedent to, consequent of, or mechanisms for institutionalization vary in their functionality or effectiveness over time in making institutions more (or less) durable.

Identity Logics as a Companion to Institutional Logics

Institutional logics have gained recent currency in the organizational literature (Glynn, 2013); however, less attention has been given to the notion of identity logics. Future researchers might look to ways of bringing institutional and identity logics into conversation together, an inquiry foreshadowed by Rao and colleagues (2003: 795) in their statement that 'logics constitute the identities of actors'.

Institutional logics are cultural accounts (Meyer, Boli & Thomas, 1987) that can endow spheres of activity or organizational fields with meaning and legitimacy. Thornton, Ocasio and Lounsbury (2012) draw out how actions are associated with logics; they define an institutional logic as 'the socially constructed, historical pattern of material practices, assumptions, values, beliefs, and rules by which individuals produce and reproduce their material subsistence, organize time and space, and provide meaning to their social reality'.

The logic of identity is a theorization advanced by March (2003), who uses it as a contrast to the logic of consequence. If the logic of consequence is about the outcomes or the end results of behavior, the logic of identity is about the appropriateness of that behavior, governed by the questions: 'Who am I? What situation am I in? What does a person like me do in a situation like this?' The notion of appropriateness underlying the logic of identity seems to bear a close resemblance to that of legitimation, associated with the logic of institutions.

Management scholars have recognized the duality between the logics of institutions and identities: as much as institutions can construct identities through typifications (Weber & Glynn, 2006), identities can construct institutions, both in terms of their entrepreneurial foundings as well as their ongoing accomplishment through activity. Lok (2010: 1331) notes their intersection:

> the particular ways in which actors understand themselves can influence the ways in which they reproduce and translate new institutional logics. This suggests that both researchers' understanding of institutionalization in the form of the adoption of uniform practices, as well as methods for determining the degree of institutionalization, may need to be revised to allow for subtle local adaptations and transformations of institutionalized practices, as well as of the meanings and identities attached to them.

To conclude, this chapter offered a foray into exploring variations in the identities–institutional linkage by the use of relational algorithms. It is rich territory, as evidenced by the myriad of ways that the two constructs can be connected. Herein, I sought to offer some initial possibilities in the hope of spurring future research into investigating this fertile terrain.

Note

1   An earlier version was presented at the EGOS conference, Athens, Greece in July 2015; I gratefully acknowledge the helpful feedback from participants in developing the chapter, as well as the superb editorial guidance of Christine Oliver.

REFERENCES

Albert, S., & Whetten, D. (1985). Organizational identity. In L.L. Cummings & B.M. Staw (Eds.), *Research in organizational behavior*, Vol. 7 (pp. 263–295). Greenwich, CT: JAI Press.

Anderson, M.H. (2006). How can we know what we think until we see what we said?: A citation and citation context analysis of Karl Weick's The Social Psychology of Organizing. *Organization Studies*, 27, 1675–1692.

Barley, S.R., & Tolbert, P.S. (1997). Institutionalization and structuration: Studying the links between action and institution. *Organization Studies*, 18, 93–117.

Berger, P.L., & Luckmann, T. (1966). *The social construction of reality: A treatise in the sociology of knowledge.* Garden City, NY: Anchor Books.

Bouwman, M.J. (1978). An information processing model of financial diagnosis. Unpublished manuscript, Graduate School of Industrial Administration, Carnegie Mellon University.

Byron, C. (2002). *Martha Inc: The incredible story of Martha Stewart Living Omnimedia.* New York: Wiley.

Creed, W.E.D., DeJordy, R., & Lok, J. (2010). Being the change: Resolving institutional contradiction through identity work. *Academy of Management Journal*, 53, 1336–1364.

Crovitz, H.F. (1967). The form of logical Solutions. *American Journal of Psychology*, 461-462

Crovitz, H.F. (1970). *Galton's walk: Methods for the analysis of thinking, intelligence and creativity.* New York: Harper & Row.

Dacin, M.T., Goodstein, J., & Scott, W.R. (2002). Institutional theory and institutional change: Introduction to the special research forum. *Academy of Management Journal*, 45, 45–56.

Davis, G. F., & Marquis, C. (2005). Prospects for organization theory in the early twenty-first century: Institutional fields and mechanisms. *Organization Science*, 16(4), 332–343.

Davis, M.S. (1971). That's interesting: Towards a phenomenology of sociology and a sociology of phenomenology. *Philosophy of the Social Sciences*, 1, 309–344.

DiMaggio, P. (2006). Book Review of 'Accounting for taste: The triumph of French cuisine', *American Journal of Sociology*, 112 (3), 932–934.

DiMaggio, P.J., & Powell, W.W. (1983). The iron cage revisited: Institutional isomorphism and collective rationality in organizational field. *American Sociological Review*, 48 (2), 147–160.

DiMaggio, P., & Powell, W. (1991). *The new institutionalism in organizational analysis.* Chicago, IL: University of Chicago Press.

Dutton, J., & Dukerich, J. (1991). Keeping an eye on the mirror: Image and identity in organizational adaptation. *Academy of Management Journal, 34*, 517–554.

Friedland, R., & Alford, R.R. (1991). Bringing society back in: Symbols, practices and institutional contradictions. In W.W. Powell & P.J. DiMaggio (Eds.), *The new institutionalism in organizational analysis* (pp. 232–263). Chicago, IL: University of Chicago Press.

Gamson, W.A. (1988). Political discourse and collective action. *International Social Movement Research, 1*(2), 219–244.

Gamson, W.A. (1992). *Talking politics*. New York, NY: Cambridge University Press.

Glynn, M.A. (2000). When cymbals become symbols: Conflict over organizational identity within a symphony orchestra. *Organization Science, 11*, 285–298.

Glynn, M.A. (2008). Beyond constraint: How institutions enable identity. In R. Greenwood, C. Oliver, R. Suddaby, & K. Sahlin-Andersson (Eds.), *The SAGE handbook of organizational institutionalism* (pp. 414–430). London: Sage.

Glynn, M.A. (2011). The 'Martha' Moment: Wading into Others' Worlds. In A. Carlsen, & J. Dutton (Eds.), *Research Alive: Generative Moments for Doing Qualitative Research* (pp. 63–66). Copenhagen: Copenhagen Business School Press.

Glynn, M.A. (2013). Book Review: 'The institutional logics perspective: A new approach to culture, structure, and process' (by Thornton, Ocasio & Lounsbury). *Administrative Science Quarterly, 58*(3), 493–495.

Glynn, M.A., & Abzug, R.A. (1998). Isomorphism and competitive differentiation in the organizational name game. In J.A.C. Baum (Ed.), *Advances in strategic management*, Vol. 15 (pp. 105–128). Greenwich, CT: JAI Press.

Glynn, M.A., & Abzug, R. (2002). Institutionalizing identity: Symbolic isomorphism and organizational names. *Academy of Management Journal, 45*, 267–280.

Glynn, M.A. & Dowd, T. (2008). Charisma (Un) Bound: Emotive Leadership in Martha Stewart Living Magazine, 1990–2004. *Journal of Applied Behavioral Science, 44*: 71–93.

Glynn, M.A., & Marquis, C. (2004). When good names go bad: Symbolic illegitimacy in organizations. In C. Johnson (Ed.), *Research in the sociology of organizations: Legitimacy processes in organizations*, Vol. 22 (pp. 147–170). New York: JAI/Elsevier Science.

Glynn, M.A., & Marquis, C. (2005). Fred's Bank: How institutional norms and individual preferences legitimate organizational names. In A. Rafaeli & M. Pratt (Eds.), *Artifacts and organizations* (pp. 223–239). Mahwah, NJ: Erlbaum.

Glynn, M.A., & Navis, C. (2013). Categories, identities, and cultural classification: moving beyond a model of categorical constraint. *Journal of Management Studies, 50*, 1124–1137.

Hallett, T., & Ventresca, M.J. (2006). Inhabited institutions: Social interactions and organizational forms in Gouldner's patterns of industrial bureaucracy. *Theoretical Sociology, 35*, 213–236.

Hannan, M.T. (2010). Partiality of memberships in categories and audiences. *Annual Review of Sociology, 36*, 159–181.

Hsu, G., & Hannan, M.T. (2005). Identities, genres, and organizational forms. *Organization Science, 16*, 474–490.

Kennedy, M.T. (2008). Getting counted: Markets, media, and reality. *American Sociological Review, 73*(2), 270–295.

Kreiner, G.E., Hollensbe, E.C., & Sheep, M.L. (2006). Where is the 'me' among the 'we'? Identity work and the search for optimal balance. *Academy of Management Journal, 49*, 1031–1057.

Lawrence, T.B., Suddaby, R., & Leca, B. (2009). *Institutional work: Actors and agency in institutional studies of organizations*. Cambridge: Cambridge University Press.

Lockwood, C., & Glynn, M.A. (2016). The micro-foundations of mattering: Domestic traditions as institutionalized practices in everyday living. In J. Gehman, M. Lounsbury, & R. Greenwood (Eds.), *Research in the sociology of organizations*. Beverly Hills, CA: Sage.

Lok, J. (2010). Institutional logics as identity projects. *Academy of Management Journal, 53*, 1305–1335.

Lounsbury, M., & Glynn, M.A. (2001). Cultural entrepreneurship: stories, legitimacy, and the acquisition of resources. *Strategic Management Journal, 22*, 545–564.

March, J.G. (2003). Passion and discipline: Don Quixote's lessons for leadership. Stanford University film, at www.gsb.stanford.edu/insights/don-quixotes-lessons-leadership

Martens, M.L., Jennings, J.E., & Jennings, P.D. (2007). Do the stories they tell get them the money they need? The role of entrepreneurial narratives in resource acquisition at IPO. *Academy of Management Journal, 50*, 1107–1132.

Meyer, J.W., Boli, J., & Thomas, G. M. (1987). Ontology and rationalization in the western cultural account. *Institutional Structure: Constituting State, Society, and the Individual*, 12–37.

Meyer, J.W., & Rowan, B. (1977). Institutionalized Organizations: Formal Structure as Myth and Ceremony. *American Journal of Sociology, 83*(2), 340–363.

Navis, C., & Glynn, M.A. (2010). How new market categories emerge: Temporal dynamics of legitimacy, identity, and entrepreneurship in satellite radio, 1990–2005. *Administrative Science Quarterly, 55*, 439–471.

Navis, C., & Glynn, M.A. (2011). Legitimate distinctiveness and the entrepreneurial identity: Influence on investor judgments of new venture plausibility. *Academy of Management Review*, 36, 479–499.

Newell, A., & Simon, H.A. (1972). *Human problem solving*. Englewood Cliffs, NJ: Prentice Hall.

Nigam, A., & Ocasio, W. (2010). Event attention, environmental sensemaking, and changes in institutional logics: an inductive analysis of the effects of public attention to Clinton's health care reform initiative. *Organization Science*, *21*(4), 823–841.

Ocasio, W. (1997). Towards an attention-based view of the firm. *Strategic Management Journal*, 18, 187–206.

Podolny, J.M., Khurana, R., & Hill-Popper, M. (2004). Revisiting the meaning of leadership. *Research in Organizational Behavior*, 26, 1–36.

Rao, H. (1994). The social construction of reputation: Certification contests, legitimation, and the survival of organizations in the American automobile industry, 1895–1912. *Strategic Management Journal*, 15, 29–44.

Rao, H., Monin, P., & Durand, R. (2003). Institutional change in Toque Ville: Nouvelle cuisine as an identity movement in French gastronomy. *American Journal of Sociology*, 108, 795–843.

Rosa, J.A., Porac, J.F., Runser-Spanjol, J., & Saxon, M.S. (1999). Sociocognitive dynamics in a product market. *Journal of Marketing*, 63, 64–77.

Santos, F.M., & Eisenhardt, K.M. (2009). Constructing markets and shaping boundaries: Entrepreneurial power in nascent fields. *Academy of Management Journal*, 52, 643–671.

Scott, W.R. (2008). *Institutions and organizations*, 3rd edn. Thousand Oaks, CA: Sage.

Selznick, P. (1957). *Leadership in administration*. Berkeley, CA: University of California Press.

Snow, David A., & Anderson, Leon A. (1987). Identity Work among the Homeless: The Verbal Construction and Avowal of Personal Identities. *American Journal of Sociology*. JSTOR, 1336–1371.

Suchman, M.C. (1995). Managing legitimacy: Strategic and institutional approaches. *Academy of Management Review*, 20, 571–610.

Suddaby, R., & Greenwood, R. (2005). Rhetorical strategies of legitimacy. *Administrative Science Quarterly*, 50, 35–67.

Sutton, R.I., & Staw, B.M. (1995). What Theory is Not. *Administrative Science Quarterly*, 40(3), 371–384.

Sveningsson, S., & Alvesson, M. (2003). Managing managerial identities: Organizational fragmentation, discourse and identity struggle. *Human Relations*, 56, 1163–1193.

Swidler, A. (1986). Culture in action: Symbols and strategies. *American Sociological Review*, 51, 273–286.

Thornton, P.H., Ocasio, W., & Lounsbury, M. (2012). *The institutional logics perspective: A new approach to culture, structure and process*. Oxford: Oxford University Press.

Tolbert, P.S., & Zucker, L.G. (1996). The institutionalization of institutional theory. [Electronic version]. In S. Clegg, C. Hardy, & W. Nord (Eds.), *Handbook of organization studies* (pp. 175–190). London: Sage.

Tunarosa, A., & Glynn, M. A. (2016). Strategies of Integration in Mixed Methods Research Insights Using Relational Algorithms. *Organizational Research Methods*, 1094428116637197.

Ungson, G.R., Braunstein, D.N., & Hall, P.D. (1981). Managerial information processing: A research review. *Administrative Science Quarterly*, 26, 16–134.

VanGundy, A.B. (1988). *Techniques of structured problem solving*, 2nd edn. New York: Van Nostrand Reinhold.

Weber, K., & Dacin, M.T. (2011). The cultural construction of organizational life: Introduction to the special issue. *Organization Science*, 22, 287–298.

Weber, K., & Glynn, M.A. (2006). Making sense with institutions: Context, thought and action in Karl Weick's theory. *Organization Studies*, 27, 1639–1660.

Weick, K.E. (1979). *The social psychology of organizing*, 2nd edn. New York: McGraw-Hill.

Weick, K. (1989). Theory construction as disciplined imagination. *Academy of Management Review*, 14, 516–531.

Westenholz, A. (2006). Beyond actor/structure and micro/macro distinctions in an empirical analysis of IT workers. *American Behavioral Scientist*, 49, 1015–1029.

Whetten, D., & Godfrey, P. (Eds.) (1998). *Identity in organizations*. Thousand Oaks, CA: Sage.

Wry, T., Lounsbury, M., & Glynn, M.A. (2011). Legitimating nascent collective identities: coordinating cultural entrepreneurship. *Organization Science*, 22, 449–463.

Zott, C., & Huy, Q.N. (2007). How entrepreneurs use symbolic management to acquire resources. *Administrative Science Quarterly*, 52, 70–105.

Zuckerman, E.W. (1999). The categorical imperative: Securities analysts and the illegitimacy discount. *American Journal of Sociology*, 104(5), 1398–1438.

PART III

Institutional Processes

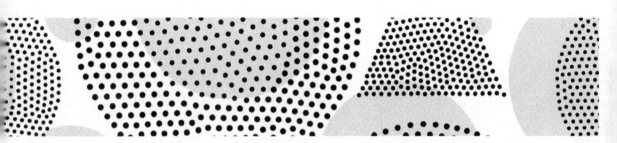

10

Institutional Entrepreneurship and Change in Fields[1]

Cynthia Hardy and Steve Maguire

INTRODUCTION

The term 'institutional entrepreneurship' refers to the 'activities of actors who have an interest in particular institutional arrangements and who leverage resources to create new institutions or to transform existing ones' (Maguire, Hardy, & Lawrence, 2004: 657); while institutional entrepreneurs are those actors to whom the responsibility for new or changed institutions is attributed. These concepts are most closely associated with DiMaggio's (1988: 14) work in which he argued that 'new institutions arise when organized actors with sufficient resources (institutional entrepreneurs) see in them an opportunity to realize interests that they value highly'. Institutional entrepreneurs are therefore typically associated with change in fields in the form of new institutions or radical changes in existing ones, although institutional entrepreneurs can also work to maintain or to disrupt and dismantle institutions (Lawrence

& Suddaby, 2006). Some studies indicate that individual institutional entrepreneurs play highly influential, if not determining, roles in bringing about institutional change. Other writers, however, are more cautious of attributing too much agency to specific actors and have, instead, emphasized the collective, incremental and multilevel effects of institutional entrepreneurship on institutional fields, including its unintended consequences.

Underpinning much of the interest in institutional entrepreneurship is the paradox of embedded agency (DiMaggio & Powell, 1991; Seo & Creed, 2002).

The theoretical puzzle is as follows: if actors are embedded in an institutional field ... how are they able to envision new practices and then subsequently get others to adopt them? Dominant actors in a given field may have the power to force change but often lack the motivation; while peripheral players may have the incentive to create and champion new practices, but often lack the power to change institutions. (Garud, Hardy, & Maguire, 2007: 961)

The concept of embedded agency raises an interesting question for institutional theorists: how do actors envision and champion institutional change if they are embedded in an institutional field and subject to its regulative, normative and cognitive pressures? As Maguire (2007: 674) points out, 'actors who are truly embedded' are not supposed to imagine, desire or realize alternative ways of doing things 'because institutionalized arrangements and practices structure cognitions, define interests and, in the limit, produce actors' identities'. So, dominant actors seem less likely to come up with particularly novel ideas or to be motivated by the idea of change – they often fail to see beyond 'prevailing "recipes"', they are 'exposed to normative processes', and their interests are 'aligned with current practices' (Greenwood & Suddaby, 2006: 29). Conversely, peripheral actors in a field, who are less embedded, are less privileged by existing institutional arrangements, and therefore have more to gain from change. Less constrained by dominant practices, they may also be more innovative and have more ideas as to what change might look like (e.g., Leblebici, Salancik, Copay, & King, 1991). However, these actors are unlikely to have the power and resources necessary to realize change, especially if it means convincing or coercing other members in the field – including dominant players – to alter their practices (Maguire, 2007). So, dominant central actors have the means to drive institutional change, but lack the motivation and the vision to be institutional entrepreneurs; while peripheral actors have both motivation and vision, but lack the resources and networks to bring about field-level change.

Work on institutional entrepreneurship has developed as scholars have explored this paradox, seeking to understand how actors in a field bring about institutional change. In this chapter, we review this body of research.[2] We start by examining the types of actor that are most likely to take on the role of institutional entrepreneur, by reviewing research that explores the attributes of institutional

entrepreneurs, as well as the place they occupy in the field they are trying to change. The second section describes the field conditions that help to initiate institutional entrepreneurship – how particular aspects of an institutional field provide a context in which ideas for change are more likely to emerge and take hold. In the third section we consider the role of interpretive struggles and examine how contests over meaning are associated with processes of institutional entrepreneurship. In the fourth section, we discuss intervention strategies – patterned action by institutional entrepreneurs as they seek to change a field. In reviewing this literature, we reflect on the actor-centric and process-centric accounts of institutional entrepreneurship noted in our chapter in the first edition of this Handbook (Hardy & Maguire, 2008). We argue that, in many respects, much of the more recent work has taken the institutional entrepreneurship process seriously. Nonetheless, and somewhat ironically, this has led to the continuation of portrayals of 'heroic' actors. We suggest that future research might provide greater insight from a more reflexive, critical orientation of institutional entrepreneurship.

INSTITUTIONAL ENTREPRENEURS

Who can become an institutional entrepreneur? Who are the actors who 'break away from scripted patterns of behaviour' (Dorado, 2005: 388) and strive 'to develop strategies and shape institutions' (Leca & Naccache, 2006: 627). At a basic level, researchers have examined different types of actors that initiate institutional change and act as institutional entrepreneurs, including individuals (Fligstein, 2001b; Lawrence & Phillips 2004; Maguire et al., 2004; Dew, 2006; Tracey, Phillips, & Jarvis, 2011; Wright & Zammuto, 2013a), organizations (e.g., Garud, Jain, & Kumaraswamy, 2002; Hensman, 2003; David, Sine, & Haveman, 2013), various levels of government and their agencies

(Montiel & Husted, 2009; Nasra & Dacin, 2010; Stål, 2011; Buhr, 2012; Covaleski, Dirsmith, & Weiss, 2013), and other forms of social groups and communities, including networks, associations, and social movements (Rao, Morrill, & Zald, 2000; Lounsbury, Ventresca, & Hirsch, 2003; Demil & Bensédrine, 2005; Dorado, 2005, 2014).

Researchers have, however, explored more complex questions than whether individuals, organizations or collectives can act as institutional entrepreneurs. Accordingly, we examine work that has linked institutional entrepreneurship to properties associated with particular types of actor, as well as to the specific positions that actors occupy in a given field.

Properties

One approach to understanding who initiates institutional change focuses explicitly on the properties – special characteristics, qualities and abilities – that distinguish institutional entrepreneurs from others in the field and which allow them to envision and promote alternative arrangements (e.g., Henfridsson & Yoo, 2014). Lepoutre and Valente (2012) argue that 'institutional nonconformity' is only possible when organizations possess cognitive/symbolic and material immunity to dominant institutional logics. Such work sees the institutional entrepreneur as an 'analytically distinguished social type who has the capability to take a reflective position towards institutionalized practices and can *envision* alternative modes of getting things done' (Beckert, 1999: 786, emphasis in original). At the level of the individual, the notion of an institutional entrepreneur thus opens up avenues of research informed by cognitive psychology and 'the development of systematic tools for predicting how individual cognition is translated into actions in the institutional environment' (George, Chattopadhyay, Sitkin, & Barden, 2006: 348). Avenues of research informed by psychodynamic

approaches are also opened up. For example, Kisfalvi and Maguire (2011) identify the psychosocial influences on one institutional entrepreneur – Rachel Carson – and argue that events in her life influenced her cognitive and emotional make up, which in turn shaped the meanings she attached to institutionalized practices and, hence, her entrepreneurial activities.

Other work has examined the characteristics of institutional entrepreneurs using a critical realist perspective (Leca & Naccache, 2006; Mutch, Delbridge, & Ventresca, 2006). For example, Mutch (2007) uses Archer's (2003) work to study Sir Andrew Barclay Walker, who pioneered the practice of directly managed public houses in England. Mutch (2007) suggests that Walker was able to act as an institutional entrepreneur because of his reflexivity. Specifically, he was an 'autonomous reflexive' – an actor who reflected in relative isolation from the concerns of others, as a result of which he was more likely to experience conflict with the structures that surrounded him and, therefore, to seek opportunities for change. Leca & Naccache (2006) use critical realism to explore the activities of an organization, rather than an individual – ARESE, the first company to act as a social rating agency in France. These authors show how, despite being embedded, reflexivity allowed this organization to contribute to the institutionalization of socially responsible investment in that country.

Work in the critical realist tradition, while focusing on the institutional entrepreneur, also places considerable emphasis on the institutional context, reminding us that actors are products of the institutional fields in which they operate. Actors and their interests, goals and strategies are institutionally, culturally and historically shaped (Clemens & Cook, 1999; Meyer, 2006). Which actors have 'the right to have interests, what interests are regarded as reasonable or appropriate, and what means can be used to pursue them are all products of socially constructed rules', such that 'who has the right to take self-determined and self-interested actions – is expected to vary over time and place' (Scott, 1995: 140). In order to recognize this mutually constitutive nature of actors and fields, some research has focused more directly on the actor's position in the field as we discuss in the next section.

Positions

To emphasize that the institutional entrepreneur is as much a product of the field as an architect of it, researchers have investigated the way in which fields create a limited number of subject positions (Maguire, Phillips, & Hardy, 2001) or social positions (Battilana, 2006), i.e., those legitimated identities available in a field from which actors can take action (Bourdieu, 1990). Institutional fields are 'structured systems of social positions within which struggles or maneuvers take place over resources, stakes and access' (Oakes, Townley, & Cooper, 1998: 260). Power relations – including the capital or resources available to different actors, as well as a sense of the social 'game' being played, or what Bourdieu calls 'habitus' (see Everett, 2002) – are thus embedded in the field rather than 'owned' or 'possessed' by individual actors. The actor's position in the field provides the individuals or organizations located in that position with institutionally defined interests and opportunities (Bourdieu & Wacquant, 1992) and, in some cases, the opportunity to exert power over the field at a particular point in time (Bourdieu, 1986). According to this view, institutional entrepreneurs do not 'have' power; instead, they occupy (or fail to occupy) subject positions that allow them to exercise power in – and on – a particular field. For example, Maguire et al. (2004), in their study of the emerging field of HIV/AIDS advocacy in Canada, found that institutional entrepreneurs were actors who occupied subject positions that provided them with legitimacy with respect to diverse stakeholders, enabling

them to bridge stakeholders in ways that facilitated access to dispersed resources.

Empirical studies have found that, despite the paradox of embedded agency, powerful actors located in dominant positions in mature fields do sometimes initiate institutional change. For example, the provincial government in Alberta, Canada, imposed business-planning practices on government departments by fiat (Townley, 2002). Similarly, it was the largest accounting firms that promoted the adoption of the multidivisional form in the Canadian accounting field (Greenwood, Suddaby, & Hinings, 2002; Greenwood & Suddaby, 2006). In the field of French cuisine, change in the form of nouvelle cuisine came from chefs 'in the centre of the French culinary world who had received honors from the French state and had garnered plaudits from the Guide Michelin' (Rao, Monin, & Durand, 2003: 804).

Such research has shown that central actors may not be as embedded in a single field as strong institutionalist views would suggest. Those who act as institutional entrepreneurs may have access to alternative practices in other fields through a variety of mechanisms. For example, many leading French chefs visited Japan and obtained new ideas from a completely different culinary field to develop nouvelle cuisine (Rao et al., 2003). Large Danish organizations introduced American practices of diversity management as a result of employees and consultants who had experience of other fields, including overseas work and involvement in the feminist movement (Boxenbaum & Battilana, 2005). Research has also shown that the large, elite accounting firms that introduced the multidivisional form into the field of Canadian accounting were not as embedded as might have been thought, given their central location in a highly institutionalized mature field. Greenwood and Suddaby (2006: 40) found that these firms bridged a number of organizational fields, including those of their global clients. This 'boundary bridging' exposed actors to alternative practices, while their scope and size insulated them from regulatory pressures and their reliance on in-house training reduced their exposure to normative influences, both of which might have prevented change (although, ultimately, the change was unsuccessful).

Research has also shown how less dominant, peripheral actors can initiate institutional change. These actors are attracting increasing research attention, as a result of both a backlash against the obsession with individual 'heroic' institutional entrepreneurs (e.g., Levy & Scully, 2007), as well as the growing interest in practice-driven institutional change (Smets, Morris, & Greenwood, 2012). For example, despite the fierce defense of traditional distribution networks in the American music industry, 'disruptive challengers' like Napster were able to undermine 'status quo incumbents' and open up space for new practices (Hensman, 2003). Fringe players initiated change in the US broadcasting industry by introducing new practices that were adopted by dominant players and became conventions in the field (Leblebici et al., 1991). Activist organizations, such as environmental NGOs, have played an important role in the institutionalization of recycling practices (Lounsbury et al., 2003). Consumers have catalyzed institutional change in the form of text messaging (Ansari & Phillips, 2011). Institutional entrepreneurship can also be initiated from outside the field as in the case of Rachel Carson, whose work led to changes in institutionalized practices of pesticide use (Maguire & Hardy, 2009; Kisfalvi & Maguire, 2011). Similarly, David and colleagues (2013) show how actors located outside of the field were able to leverage non-traditional resources to establish the nascent field of management consulting. New actors in a field can also initiate change (Sauder, 2008).

Peripheral and external actors are expected to find it easier to develop ideas for change because they are less embedded in the field – less aware of institutional norms and prescriptions and more likely to be exposed to alternative ideas outside the field (Greenwood & Suddaby, 2006; Maguire, 2007). They are also likely to be motivated to bring about change since they are often disadvantaged by prevailing arrangements (Leblebici et al., 1991). The paradox in this situation is less about how such actors come up with ideas for institutional change but, rather, how they get other field members to adopt them, as we discuss in more detail in the section on intervention strategies below.

In sum, individuals and various types of organizations can act as institutional entrepreneurs. Some research emphasizes institutional entrepreneurs' unique abilities and features that, in effect, make them a privileged 'species' of actor – one 'increasingly endorsed with specific qualities "normal" actors do not possess' (Meyer, 2006: 732). Other studies seek to explain who becomes an institutional entrepreneur with reference to the position they occupy in a field. The latter approach, which seeks to establish an institutional grounding of the institutional entrepreneur, appears to be more robust insofar as it recognizes that the 'exceptional' ability of institutional entrepreneurs to see or create 'a window of opportunity' needs to be considered in relation to the way in which the field produces their interests, skills and stocks of knowledge (Meyer, 2006), as we explore in the next section.

INITIATING FIELD CONDITIONS

Another line of enquiry concerned with resolving the paradox of embedded agency has tried to identify particular field conditions that create opportunities for institutional entrepreneurship. We begin this section by summarizing work that explores how particular stimuli may trigger institutional entrepreneurship. We then discuss how the state of a particular field can also facilitate institutional entrepreneurship.

Stimuli

Some research, especially work that adopts an economic approach to institution building and views actors as rational, argues that uncertainty in a field prompts institutional change as actors seek to reduce it. Generally speaking, uncertainty is 'the degree to which future states of the world cannot be anticipated and accurately predicted' (Pfeffer & Salancik, 1978: 67). In economics, it refers to situations where actors cannot define rational strategies because they cannot calculate probabilities for decision outcomes (Beckert, 1999). According to this view, institutions, because they structure and make predictable actors' behaviour, are solutions to the problems faced by cognitively limited actors whose interdependence with other actors creates the possibility of opportunistic behaviour and increased transaction costs (Coase, 1937; North, 1990). Working in this tradition, Dew (2006: 16) elaborates the concept of Coasian-style institutional entrepreneurship as 'the activity of initiating, creating and leading organizations that specialize in developing institutional frameworks that lower transaction costs' for other actors in the field. He offers the example of a grocery executive who pioneered the now widespread and institutionalized technology standards and associated practices for using bar codes and universal product codes, to facilitate exchange relationships.

In this way, institutional entrepreneurship is associated with identifying and solving problems in a field. For example, adverse performance of the major accounting firms in Canada called into question the efficiency of the traditional organizational form in the field, prompting some to adopt a new multidivisional form (Greenwood & Suddaby, 2006). Similarly, the inflexibility of the Association to Advance Collegiate Schools of Business (AACSB) model of business education in light of increasingly diverse student demands and business school mandates created 'ambiguity, scarcity in legitimizing resources ... [and] selection pressures' which, in turn, led to moves to expand the field to include European business schools (Durand & McGuire, 2005: 184). The rise of socially responsible investing in France created the problem of how to measure corporate social performance, as a result of which institutional entrepreneurs sought to institutionalize standardized measures (Déjean, Gond, & Leca, 2004). The problem of heart disease in Finland has led to new institutions aimed at changing grass-roots understandings of the relationship between food, other lifestyle factors, and heart health (Ritvala & Granqvist, 2009). Once some actors in the field adopt new practices, evidence of their effectiveness such as positive market feedback or improved social welfare outcomes, increases their legitimacy among other actors and encourages their wider diffusion and adoption (e.g., Lee & Pennings, 2002).

According to such work, institutional entrepreneurs bring about change as they try to solve problems and reduce uncertainty. One would therefore expect to see acts of institutional entrepreneurship correlated with field-level problems or a high degree of field-level uncertainty. Interestingly, Beckert (1999: 783) argues the opposite: 'strategic agency that violates existing institutional rules can be expected in situations characterized by relatively high degrees of certainty within an institutional field.' He argues that this is because actors, if rational, need to be able to assign probabilities to the possible consequences of their choices and to work out whether change is going to be profitable or beneficial *before* taking action. Consequently, he suggests that uncertainty *follows* the 'creative destruction' of the institutional order associated with institutional entrepreneurship, rather than precedes it. The exact nature of the relationship between uncertainty and institutional entrepreneurship is, therefore, not entirely clear, and further research is warranted.

Another body of work has focused on the tensions and contradictions that are present in fields, even mature ones. A range of writers have noted that, despite work that sees institutional fields as totalizing and shared phenomena, they are in fact riven with inconsistencies and conflict (Seo & Creed, 2002; Zilber, 2002; Rao et al., 2003; Dorado, 2005; Creed, DeJordy, & Lok, 2010). So, although institutional processes may appear to be stable because differences among actors are 'temporarily resolved by socially negotiated consensus', this appearance of stability is 'misleading' (Greenwood et al., 2002: 59). Institutions are not homogenous or complete. Nor do they precisely determine behaviour. Instead, multiple institutions may exist in a given field and conflict with each other, new members with different histories and experiences may join a field, and existing members may have access to more than one field and therefore exposure to a range of practices (Clemens & Cook, 1999). Institutional change thus results as human praxis is brought to bear on these tensions and contradictions. Individuals use them to reflect on and critique the limits of present institutional arrangements and to inspire ideas for new ones, leading them to mobilize and engage other actors in collective action intended to reconstruct the field (Seo & Creed, 2002).

States

Another body of work has focused on how the particular state of the field is associated with greater likelihood of institutional entrepreneurship (e.g., Dorado & Ventresca, 2013). Consistent with the work on contradictions, which allow actors to reflect on existing institutional arrangements, and the work on uncertainty or problems, which provide actors with a motivation for institutional change, it has been argued that fields in a state of crisis may be particularly conducive to institutional entrepreneurship. A crisis can surface contradictions and tensions in even highly structured, mature fields and give rise to problems that require solutions (Fligstein

& Mara-Drita, 1996). Accordingly, 'disruptive events' (Hoffman, 1999), 'shocks' (Fligstein, 1991), 'triggering events' (Rao et al., 2003) and 'jolts' (Meyer, 1982) – which can take the form of social upheaval, technological disruptions, regulatory change, or the publication of books, reports, and media stories (e.g., Davis, Diekmann, & Tinsley, 1994; Garud et al., 2002; Lounsbury, 2002; Maguire & Hardy, 2009) – in generating some form of crisis are conducive to institutional entrepreneurship.

Fligstein (2001a) shows how a crisis in the European Union enabled the European Commission to act as an institutional entrepreneur and develop the Single Market Program. Disruptive events are capable of 'ending what has become locked in by institutional inertia' through the way they create 'disruptive uncertainty for individual organizations, forcing the initiation of unorthodox experiments that diverge from established practice' and 'throwing entire industries into the throes of quantum change' (Hoffman, 1999: 353). Such events may precipitate the entry of new players into an organizational field, facilitate the ascendance of existing actors, or change the intellectual climate of ideas, making it easier to disrupt existing practices and raise awareness of possible new ones (Greenwood et al., 2002; Greenwood & Suddaby, 2006).

It has also been argued that emerging fields offer considerable scope for institutional entrepreneurship (Maguire et al., 2004; also see Purdy & Gray, 2009). Child, Lu and Tsai (2007) show how the state took advantage of the emergent nature of China's environmental protection field to act as an institutional entrepreneur, drawing on developments in other fields related to international environmental concerns and domestic economic reform. Nasra and Dacin (2010), in examining the role of the state as institutional entrepreneur in the Middle East, show how the emergence of Dubai's unique institutional environment and political economy from the beginning of the nineteenth century until the present day provided opportunities for Dubai's rulers to act as institutional entrepreneurs. Avetisyan and Ferrary (2013) focus on the role of rating agencies as institutional entrepreneurs in the emerging field of corporate social responsibility, noting differences between France and the United States. What these studies collectively indicate is that the constraints in emerging fields are fewer compared to mature fields since there are fewer established patterns to mimic and power is more diffuse. This lack of institutionalized practices and clearly identifiable norms, combined with fluid relationships and conflicting values, makes it easier for actors to bring about institutional change, as well as affording them considerable advantage as they shape the field.

A new development concerning the state of the field and institutional entrepreneurship is the work on 'field-configuring events', which are 'temporary social organizations … in which people from diverse organizations and with diverse purposes assemble periodically, or on a one-time basis' (Lampel & Meyer, 2008: 1026). This work focuses on particular events that bring members of the field together at certain points, changing the state of the field temporarily, i.e., for a delimited period of time. Field-configuring events generate new, interconnected 'discursive spaces' that are not normally available to members of the field, and in which the normal understandings and rules in the field regarding appropriate forms of text production, distribution and consumption are suspended or modified. In addition, the co-location of actors means that texts flow more readily between discursive spaces than they normally do (Hardy & Maguire, 2010). In this way, field-configuring events provide a temporary setting in which there is more scope for institutional entrepreneurship and change, although Schüssler, Rüling and Wittneben's (2014) examination of discursive spaces in the United Nations' climate change negotiations shows that field-level maintenance, rather than change, can also be the outcome.

In sum, certain stimuli – uncertainty, problems, tensions and contradictions in a field – can establish favorable initiating conditions for institutional entrepreneurship by motivating and furnishing ideas for change. Additionally, fields in particular states, especially mature fields in crisis following a disruptive event, emerging fields and fields in which field-configuring events are staged, appear more likely to present opportunities for institutional entrepreneurship. Much of this work tends to conceptualize the state of the field as a set of objective conditions that triggers (or fails to trigger) institutional entrepreneurship. Munir (2005), however, reminds us that the way in which events and contexts are interpreted and given meaning is an important part of institutional entrepreneurship. In other words, for an event to be deemed disruptive – creating a situation of uncertainty, contradiction or tension, causing a crisis, or representing a temporary hiatus in institutionalized rules – requires that actors *interpret* it as such. The role of interpretation in institutional entrepreneurship is discussed in more detail in the following section.

INTERPRETIVE STRUGGLES

The paradox of embedded agency recognizes that some form of struggle is likely between field members when some want change and others do not. As a result, researchers have delved into the complex, ongoing interpretive struggles over meaning that accompany institutional entrepreneurship activities, the outcomes of which are not necessarily predictable or controllable (Covaleski et al., 2013). Emphasizing translation at the micro level (Zilber, 2002) and discourse at the macro level (Phillips, Lawrence, & Hardy, 2004; Schmidt, 2008, 2010), this work builds on the idea that institutions are formed as meanings come to be shared and taken for granted. In contrast to the diffusion metaphor that has dominated much of institutional theory, and which 'connotes a transmission of a given entity', the translation metaphor 'connotes an interaction that involves negotiation between various parties, and the reshaping of what is finally being transmitted' (Zilber, 2006: 283). Field members are not carriers of predetermined institutional meanings, diffusing them intact and unchanged throughout a field; rather, they are active narrators and interpreters of accounts of practices whose meanings are negotiated in ongoing, complex processes (Sahlin & Wedlin, 2008; Maguire & Hardy, 2009; Hardy & Maguire, 2010).

Individuals' interpretations can thus be seen 'as part of institutional agency – the social actions that create, reproduce, and change institutions' (Zilber, 2002: 236). Institutional entrepreneurs are also 'institutional interpreters, that translate and communicate institutional pressures' (Rothenberg & Levy, 2012: 34) by drawing on different discourses and finding new ways to frame and theorize change. From this perspective, institutional entrepreneurship is seen to emerge from novel interpretations and struggles over meaning, such as the struggle between neoliberalist entreaties on the part of the Governor of Wisconsin in trying to transform the state's welfare system and the appeals to fairness and poverty-reduction on the part of opponents (Covaleski et al., 2013). Meaning thus takes on multiple roles in an institutional field. First, it is the outcome for which actors struggle. Different actors have stakes in particular meanings and attempt to assert their preferred ones (Grant & Hardy, 2004). Second, meanings are the medium through and within which power struggles take place as actors try to influence institutional change (Zilber, 2006). In this regard, meanings are a resource (Zilber, 2002) – actors draw on them to support their positions and to undermine those of opponents. Third, meanings are a constraint, since field- and societal-level logics (Thornton & Ocasio, 2008), myths (Zilber, 2006) and discourses (Phillips et al., 2004) are not infinitely pliable.

Drawing on these ideas, a growing body of work has explored the processes of discursive struggle through which institutional entrepreneurship succeeds or fails. Zilber (2002: 251) shows how struggle over the meaning of institutionalized practices at a rape crisis centre – whether they were 'feminist' or 'therapeutic' – affected power relations inside the organization and, as a result, the services that it provided, although not in predictable, predetermined or clearly managed ways. Maguire and Hardy (2006) examine the creation of the Stockholm Convention on Persistent Organic Pollutants, which is a new global regulatory institution that, consistent with the discourse of 'precaution', bans toxic chemicals based on uncertain scientific knowledge of the risks they pose. The new institution was the outcome of discursive struggle among actors over the meaning of precaution: some actors promoted the new discourse of precaution, while others countered with the legacy regulatory discourse of 'sound science'. As a result, actors on both sides were forced to engage with and reconcile competing discourses. It was out of this struggle that the particular institution emerged.

In another study, Zilber (2007) shows how institutional entrepreneurship in the high-tech industry in Israel following the 2000 dot.com crash involved the construction of a shared story of the crisis that reinforced the established institutional order. Yet, at the same time, actors were also telling separate 'counter-stories' that called for changes in the institutional order. Actors used stories both to protect vested interests in the current institutional order, as well as to agitate for change – all at the same time. Maguire and Hardy (2009) show how complex processes of producing, distributing and consuming texts led to the deinstitutionalization of practices of using the pesticide DDT in the United States between 1962 and 1972. In this case, institutional entrepreneur Rachel Carson (1962) problematized the use of chemical pesticides including DDT with her book *Silent Spring*. However, the eventual outcome emerged from a struggle involving countless scientific, legal, regulatory, government and public texts – and counter-texts – during which meanings were translated, and even subverted, in ways never intended by Carson.

As these examples illustrate, this body of work emphasizes the complex and contradictory processes through which meaning is negotiated and stabilized. It highlights not only the potential 'messiness' of institutional entrepreneurship processes as discursive maneuvers are met with counter-moves, but also the potential for outcomes that are not necessarily those originally intended by the actors involved. It stands in contrast to the bulk of work on institutional entrepreneurship, which seeks to explain the effectiveness or success of institutional entrepreneurs in bringing about *intended* institutional change, usually with reference to specific strategies for intervening in a field, as we discuss in the next section.

INTERVENTION STRATEGIES

Institutional entrepreneurship requires actors to dislodge existing practices (in the case of mature fields), introduce new ones and then ensure that they become widely adopted and taken for granted by other actors in the field. How do institutional entrepreneurs, whether they are central or peripheral players, succeed in their struggles to change institutional fields? This question occupies a large portion of the literature, which focuses on identifying and explicating the strategic interventions made by institutional entrepreneurs to bring about change. We synthesize this diverse work in terms of three broad themes: the mobilization of resources, the construction of rationales for institutional change, and the forging of new inter-actor relations to bring about collective action. Collectively, this work suggests that if institutional entrepreneurs are to bring about institutional change, they must mobilize and recombine materials, symbols and people in novel and

even artful ways (see Misangyi, Weaver, & Elms, 2008; Aldrich, 2012).

Resources

Resource mobilization has been central to the notion of institutional entrepreneurship since DiMaggio's (1988: 14) definition highlighted the necessity of 'sufficient resources' to create or change institutions. Despite this centrality, research is often vague as to what is meant by the term 'resources' as well as what is done with them. Certainly, a wide range of resources have been mentioned in the literature, including political, financial and organizational resources (Beckert, 1999; Greenwood & Suddaby, 2006), material resources (Lawrence & Suddaby, 2006; Monteiro & Nicolini, 2015), cultural resources (Creed, Scully, & Austin, 2002; David et al., 2013), affiliations and networks (Montiel & Husted, 2009; Ritvala & Granqvist, 2009; Raffaelli & Glynn, 2014), and discursive resources (Hardy & Phillips, 1999; Hensman, 2003; Lawrence & Phillips, 2004; Maguire & Hardy, 2006), including scientific knowledge (Ritvala & Granqvist, 2009) and history (McGaughey, 2013). In this section, we focus on material resources,[3] which, research suggests, are mobilized by institutional entrepreneurs as a lever against other actors – subsidiary actors, allies and external constituencies – to negotiate support for the change project in question (DiMaggio, 1988). In some instances, powerful actors may control sufficient resources to impose change on an institutional field by themselves (Dorado, 2005), but it appears that, most of the time, institutional entrepreneurship involves a degree of dependency on other actors and their resources to make bargaining and negotiating inevitable. This view is consistent with Colomy's (1998) claim that institutional entrepreneurs employ strategies that operate through exchange mechanisms: support for a project is contingent on the perception that tangible and/or intangible benefits are forthcoming to other actors. Some entrepreneurial strategies are premised on positive inducements offered to prospective allies in exchange for their support. Others are premised on negative inducements in the form of threats to establish a bargaining relationship in which the coerced party's 'best hope is that it will be no worse off than it would have been had the coercive relationship never commenced' (Turner & Killian, 1987: 298–299; quoted in Colomy, 1998: 280). In this way, institutional entrepreneurship involves materially rewarding supporters and punishing opponents.

If institutional entrepreneurs do not control rewards and punishments, they can recruit allies that do. Several studies draw attention to how institutional change in a given field depends upon other extant institutions, especially legal and professional ones in which institutions to be changed are nested (cf. Holm, 1995). In other words, the formal authority of other actors such as the state and professional associations can be harnessed as a resource to support change. For example, in his study of the early stages of the emergence of the automobile industry, Rao (2002) demonstrates how one mechanism for generating constitutive legitimacy for innovative products around which new industries emerge is the enactment of laws that make the product legal and specify how it can be made, sold, used, etc., thus authorizing and codifying understandings of the new artifact and practices of using it. Similarly, Garud et al. (2002) note how the legal system can be drawn upon to create new rules or to enforce old ones, both of which can be used to advance institutionalization projects. Of course, opponents of institutionalization projects can also seek to enroll higher authorities, and different authorities may clash. So, while Greenwood et al. (2002) show how professional associations lent their authority to the elite accounting firms' adoption of a new multidivisional organizational form, they also note the ultimately determining role played by the state in legislating an end to experimentation with this form.

Rationales

Institutional entrepreneurship also involves interventions in the discursive or ideational realm as actors construct and communicate rationales or reasons to other actors concerning why they should support or, at a minimum not resist, the institutionalization project in question. Institutional entrepreneurs therefore construct entrepreneurial (Colomy, 1998) or legitimating accounts (Creed et al., 2002) of their projects. In so doing, they may 'theorize' institutional change by specifying problems associated with existing practices and justifying new ones as a solution (Greenwood et al., 2002; Monteiro & Nicolini, 2015); tell stories or narratives (Zilber, 2007; Hardy & Maguire, 2010); and deploy rhetoric strategically (Harmon, Green, & Goodnight, 2015) – although sometimes unsuccessfully (Suddaby & Greenwood, 2005; McGaughey, 2013). An array of arguments may be developed for different constituencies, providing each with a different rationale for participating in the institutional project (Maguire et al., 2004); and it is through the production, distribution and consumption of texts (Phillips et al., 2004) that ideas and arguments are shared (Boxenbaum & Battilana, 2005).

Institutional entrepreneurs thus frame desired changes in ways that will generate collective action (Garud et al., 2002; Lounsbury et al., 2003). A collective action frame is a coherent interpretive structure that accomplishes three tasks: punctuation, which identifies a problem and defines it as important; elaboration, which includes a diagnosis of the problem describing who or what is responsible for it, as well as a prognosis describing what is required to correct it; and motivation, which encourages actors to participate in change (Creed et al., 2002; Misangyi et al., 2008). By using particular frames, institutional entrepreneurs can increase the chances of successful institutional change as collective interpretations evolve and amplify to become institutionalized and shape subsequent interpretations (Gray, Purkey, & Ansari, 2015). In framing and offering rationales for their projects, the validity of claims 'is rarely demonstrated in an unequivocal way, however, and rests chiefly on the project's perceived conformity to institutional myths' (Colomy, 1998: 289). As a result, institutional entrepreneurs often draw on existing field-level logics (Seo & Creed, 2002) and dominant discourses (Hardy & Phillips, 1999; Lawrence & Phillips, 2004) to position their projects in terms of existing categories and schema (Hargadon & Douglas, 2001) in order to make change comprehensible and meaningful to other actors. For example, Tracey and colleagues (2011) show how institutional entrepreneurs reframed solutions to the problem of homelessness by combining two different institutional logics (for-profit and non-profit) that had previously appeared contradictory. Appealing to investors (by emphasizing the for-profit nature of initiative) and potential clients (by emphasizing the social benefits), they were able to develop a new hybrid organizational form that dealt with the homeless in new, innovative ways.

Relations

Institutional entrepreneurship often involves establishing new inter-actor relations to bring about change, primarily – as much of the work discussed above indicates – through collective action (Garud et al., 2002; Lawrence, Hardy, & Phillips, 2002; Wijen & Ansari, 2007). Given that institutional entrepreneurship involves altering deeply embedded norms, values and practices, it is not surprising that it depends upon more than a single individual or organization. As a result, both the mobilization of material resources and the construction and communication of rationales for change serve to develop new relations among actors, such as collaborations, coalitions and alliances (e.g., Buhr, 2012).

Institutional entrepreneurship is, then, associated with various forms of collaborative relations – partnerships, coalitions, etc. – that require the cooperation of other actors. It requires 'the assent or, minimally, the acquiescence of various groups as well as the capacity to prevail over opposition' (Colomy, 1998: 278). For this reason it has been suggested that institutional entrepreneurs' unique political and social skills (Perkmann & Spicer, 2007; Maguire et al., 2004) provide them with 'the ability to induce cooperation among others' (Fligstein, 2001a: 112). We can, then, see a link between intervention strategies that mobilize material resources, those that communicate rationales, and the subsequent leveraging of inter-actor relations to get actors to participate in collective action (as well as the properties of 'exceptional' individuals). In this way, institutional entrepreneurship is connected to the exercise of power (Fligstein, 2001b): the overt mobilization of material resources, such as offering financial incentives, imposing penalties, or invoking formal authority, can help to coerce other field members into supporting change; while more unobtrusive harnessing of symbolic resources, in the form of discursive interventions to construct and communicate convincing rationales that legitimize new practices, can help to engender voluntary support for change. In this way, institutional entrepreneurs leverage dependencies and formal authority to change behaviors (Nasra & Dacin, 2010), use stories and narrative accounts to induce cooperation (Fligstein, 2001b; Zilber, 2007; Hardy & Maguire, 2010), and rely on framing to enroll allies and to build coalitions (Rao et al., 2000).

Institutional entrepreneurship can be therefore seen as the realignment – and stabilization – of material, discursive and relational arrangements in an institutional field (Levy & Scully, 2007), with significant overlap among the three categories of intervention strategy discussed here. However, because of a bias towards studying successful instances of institutional entrepreneurship and the interest in the 'heroic' entrepreneur; other actors, especially non-cooperative actors, are frequently ignored. As a result, field members that resist these intervention strategies do not figure as prominently in analyses as one might expect. We will expand upon this observation in the next section.

INSIGHTS

Most studies have found that, despite the paradox of embedded agency, institutional entrepreneurs are highly influential in shaping and changing their institutional fields; and research on 'institutional entrepreneurship' is now an established body of work within institutional theory – one that seeks to understand change in fields. Battilana, Leca and Boxenbaum (2009: 67) argue the 'concept of institutional entrepreneurship should be central to future developments of institutional theory because it enables us to explore actors' degrees of agency, however institutionally embedded'.

Empirical work shows that institutional entrepreneurship has resulted in new formal regulatory institutions at national, international and global levels of analysis, including national regulations governing industrial wastes (Demil & Bensédrine, 2005), the reconstitution of the European Union (Fligstein, 2001a), the Stockholm Convention on Persistent Organic Pollutants (Maguire & Hardy, 2006), and the inclusion of aviation in the EU Emissions Trading Scheme (Buhr, 2012). Institutional entrepreneurs have also helped to create new industries (Aldrich & Fiol, 1994), such as socially responsible investment (Déjean et al., 2004), whale-watching (Lawrence & Phillips, 2004), management consulting (David et al., 2013), recycling (Lounsbury et al., 2003) and power production (Hargadon & Douglas, 2001; Russo 2001). New organizational forms, such as the multidivisional organizational form in publishing (Thornton, 2002) and social enterprise hybrids (Tracey et al., 2011) have also emerged as a result

of institutional entrepreneurship activities. Institutional entrepreneurs have also been responsible for the adoption of new practices, ranging from the introduction of business plans in museums (Oakes et al., 1998), new forms of diversity management (Boxenbaum & Battilana, 2005), new ways of dealing with heart disease (Ritvala & Granqvist, 2009), new exchange media in radio broadcasting (Leblebici et al., 1991), changes in welfare provision (Covaleski et al., 2013), and new technological standards (Garud et al., 2002). In the empirical literature, there are some, but far fewer, cases of failure to change institutions or of institutional maintenance through institutional entrepreneurship (e.g., Greenwood et al., 2002; Greenwood & Suddaby, 2006; McGaughey, 2013; Schüssler et al., 2014), although some researchers have examined institutional maintenance (e.g., Heaphy, 2013; Micelotta & Washington, 2013).

In reviewing this literature, we can see evidence of two different narratives of institutional entrepreneurship – one that is more actor-centric and focuses on the deliberate strategies of particular institutional entrepreneurs and another that is more process-centric and emphasizes the struggles associated with institutional entrepreneurship activities. Research that focuses on the properties of particular actors that distinguish them as institutional entrepreneurs appears more likely to produce actor-centric accounts because of its cognitive, individualistic orientation. So, too, does the work exploring how individuals and organizations occupying central, dominant positions bring about institutional change. Even the work on peripheral institutional entrepreneurs often glorifies them as a result of the focus on success under conditions of adversity. Research on institutional entrepreneurship as a form of problem-solving or uncertainty reduction project, also tends to promote the view of a (rational) independent, omnipotent actor. The work on contradictions and tensions – even though socially constructionist – can also be actor-centric through the way it attributes the ability to make sense of contradictions to specific actors, as well as the way it often treats the state of the field and contradictions themselves as objective and unproblematic.

Such actor-centric accounts tend to be functionalist, painting a neat picture of relatively rational, linear, win–win problem-solving activity. The (usually successful) institutional entrepreneur possesses a degree of reflexivity or insight that allows them to identify opportunities for change as a result of some stimuli, such as uncertainty or contradictions, or to address a recognized problem in the field. Then, using their superior political and social skills, the institutional entrepreneur intervenes strategically to realize institutional change by combining and mobilizing resources, rationales and relations in creative ways. Other actors play minor, supporting – and usually cooperative – roles if they figure at all, while conflict and struggle is pushed to the background.

Process-centric accounts focus on institutional entrepreneurship as an emergent outcome of activities of diverse, spatially dispersed actors, who face considerable difficulty in achieving effective collective action, and where gains for one group may imply significant losses for others. Process-centred accounts appear more likely to pay attention to other members of the field who may engage in some form of counter-framing, produce counter-narratives, or make discursive counter-moves. The outcomes that follow from institutional entrepreneurship tend to be more varied, including failure and inertia – perhaps because the struggle is self-defeating or because the prevailing discourses are too constraining. For example, Schüssler and colleagues' (2014) study of two decades of United Nations' climate change negotiations shows that what was hoped to be a catalyst of institutional change morphed into a mechanism of field maintenance.

Whether the focus is on the actor or the process, it is important to note that both types of account are constructions of the *researcher*.

The way in which a researcher conducts his or her research has significant implications for the nature of their 'findings' – empirical design and theoretical conceptualization are never 'neutral'. For example, Wright and Zammuto (2013a, 2013b) produce both actor-centric and process-centric accounts of changes in the sport of English county cricket between 1943 and 1962. In one paper (2013a: 51), they examine how actors 'use their field positions to create opportunities for institutional entrepreneurship'. They focus on one particular individual – Colonel Rait-Kerr, who is named more than fifty times in the paper – and his role in several key governance committees. Although the Colonel died before the change was finally implemented, we are left in no doubt as to his role as an institutional entrepreneur who brought about a new format for playing cricket.

> The success of [the change] ... after several decades of field opposition to its introduction ... suggests that actors were sufficiently mobilized after Colonel Rait-Kerr's death to collaboratively complete his institutional entrepreneurship project. (p. 62)

In another paper, Wright & Zammuto (2013b) provide a more process-centric account of institutional entrepreneurship. The period featured in the earlier paper is extended both backwards and forwards to provide a longer time frame. The Colonel is not mentioned at all. Instead, the authors focus on organizational actors, which are classified as 'central elites', 'peripheral elites' and 'marginal players' and among whom there was considerable struggle. Rather than rest on the actions of an individual, this process-centric account argues that institutional change depended upon more complex alignments across societal, field and organizational levels.

There is then a choice as to whether researchers wish to focus on the actor or the process. Early research appeared to emphasize the former (Hardy & Maguire, 2008). More recently, as more qualitative research has been brought to bear on institutional entrepreneurship, the number of process-centric accounts has increased. They contain rich descriptions of complexity and struggle, which some actors have been able to navigate. Somewhat ironically, the richness of this research, while providing greater insight into the processual complexities of institutional entrepreneurship and change, has indirectly focused even more attention on particular individuals and organizations that have been 'successful' in escaping the way in which their 'intentions, actions, and rationality are conditioned by the institutions they wish to change' (Clegg, 2010: 10).

In doing so, much of the research on institutional entrepreneurship ignores the power relations that pervade institutional fields (Munir, 2015; Willmott 2015); and fails to reflect critically on the outcomes of institutional entrepreneurship, with resulting changes to the field assumed to be an improvement on the earlier situation. The notion of 'better' institutional arrangements is rarely problematized and the question of who benefits from – and who is disadvantaged by – institutional entrepreneurship is seldom addressed in these accounts (for exceptions see Khan, Munir, & Willmott, 2007; Levy & Scully, 2007; Martí & Fernández, 2013). Studies rarely focus on how changes to the field can serve the interests of dominant actors who may adopt new practices but nonetheless typically retain their dominance. In fact, regardless of whether they or other actors initiate institutional change, the reason why they change their practices is often to ensure that they *remain* dominant (e.g., Kodeih & Greenwood, 2014). Institutional change projects are therefore much more likely to be 'elaborative' than 'reconstructive' (Colomy, 1998). Even when other actors engage in institutional entrepreneurship, new institutional arrangements typically emerge from 'hegemonic accommodation', with dominant actors willing to cede only limited ground (Levy & Scully, 2007).

There is, then, scope for a far more critical appreciation of institutional entrepreneurship. For example, Suddaby (2015: 93)

suggests that researchers should 'resist the temptation of adopting the viewpoint of managerial or shareholder elites'. A second approach would be to assess critically the outcomes of institutional entrepreneurship. Another complementary approach might be to take the viewpoints of actors other than institutional entrepreneurs more seriously. In many cases, members of the field other than the champions of the institutional change project are simply ignored. Even when they are not ignored, they tend to be positioned at the passive end of a unilateral relationship where the institutional entrepreneur persuades them (Dew, 2006; Garud et al., 2002), reorganizes their preferences (Fligstein, 2001a), and aligns (Demil & Benésdrine, 2005) or aggregates (Fligstein, 1997) their interests in relation to the institutionalization project. Focusing on those who occupy different positions in the field and are disadvantaged by current and future practices and who resist change (or fail to do so) offers a way to look at institutional entrepreneurship from a different vantage point.

Such approaches may go some way to putting power relations on the research agenda but, even so, the 'conception of competent agency' remains paramount, privileging and naturalizing 'the exercise of conscious, sovereign calculation to achieve desired ends with appropriate means' (Cooper, Ezzamel, & Willmott, 2008: 675). To redress this problem, Willmott (2011: 67) calls for a more radical solution – a 'critically reflexive appreciation of the "individual" as an institution' by revising our understanding of human agency and power. One way to do this is through the incorporation of Foucauldian conceptions of power (Clegg, 2010). While Foucault's work (e.g., Foucault, 1979; 1980) has greatly enhanced other areas of organization and management theory, institutional theory remains largely immune to it. Very few studies use a Foucauldian framework to explore institutional entrepreneurship and change (for exceptions see Maguire & Hardy, 2009; Creed et al., 2014). This is, perhaps, surprising since, two decades ago, Clegg and Hardy (1996) pointed to clear parallels between Foucault's understanding of power and the constraining, inescapable effects of institutionalization; while, more recently, others have noted the relevance of discipline and governmentality to institutional theory (Sauder & Espeland, 2009; Creed et al., 2014; Vallentin, 2015). Given rising inequality and continuing environmental degradation associated with contemporary capitalism, future research on institutional entrepreneurship that is willing to interrogate concepts of agency and power could yield insights that are theoretically, socially and practically relevant.

We conclude this chapter by acknowledging that, while the interest in institutional entrepreneurship is a response to a desire to put agency back into institutional analyses of organizations, there remains a risk of the pendulum swinging too far in the other direction – 'celebrating heroic "entrepreneurs" and great "leaders" who bring about change intentionally, strategically and creatively' – and reifying fields, actors and the process of change itself (Hardy & Maguire, 2008: 213). In 2008, we called for more process-centric accounts to mitigate this threat, arguing that we needed 'research that interrogates critically and in more depth the phenomena that interest us, and we believe the way to do so is to keep matters of power and process open when studying institutional change'. It appears that researchers have delivered on process but, less so, on power.

Notes

1   The authors gratefully acknowledge the financial support of the Social Sciences and Humanities Research Council of Canada (435-2014-0256) and the Australian Research Council (Discovery funding scheme, project number DP110101764).
2   In order to focus on this body of work, we have had to omit discussion of related topics such as institutional logics. We refer readers to the dedicated chapter on logics in this Handbook (Chapter 19).
3   As can be seen from this heterogeneous list, the notion of resource mobilization can include material, symbolic and human/organizational resources. However, because of important differences among them, particularly how they relate to power, we address them separately in terms of three themes – resources, rationales and relations. Broadly speaking, these themes correspond to the three interlaced dimensions of field structure – material, discursive and organizational – proposed by Levy and Scully (2007). At the same time, we acknowledge the overlap. For example, as David and colleagues (2013) show in the case of the emerging field of management consulting, resources can take the form of cultural capital and become intertwined with the creation of rationales (also see Misangyi et al., 2008).

REFERENCES

Aldrich, H. E. (2012). The emergence of entrepreneurship as an academic field: A personal essay on institutional entrepreneurship. *Research Policy*, *41*(7), 1240–1248.

Aldrich, H. E., & Fiol, M. (1994). Fools rush in? The institutional context of industry creation. *Academy of Management Review*, *19*(4), 645–670.

Ansari, S., & Phillips, N. (2011). Text me! New consumer practices and change in organizational fields. *Organization Science*, *22*(6), 1579–1599.

Archer, M. (2003). *Structure, agency and the internal conversation*. Cambridge: Cambridge University Press.

Avetisyan, E., & Ferrary, M. (2013). Dynamics of stakeholders' implications in the institutionalization of the CSR field in France and in the United States. *Journal of Business Ethics*, *115*(1), 115–133.

Battilana, J. (2006). Agency and institutions: The enabling role of individuals' social position. *Organization*, *13*(5), 653–676.

Battilana, J., Leca, B., & Boxenbaum, E. (2009). How actors change institutions: towards a theory of institutional entrepreneurship. *Academy of Management Annals*, *3*(1), 65–107.

Beckert, J. (1999). Agency, entrepreneurs, and institutional change: The roles of strategic choice and institutionalized practices in organizations. *Organization Studies*, *20*(5), 777–799.

Bourdieu, P. (1986). The forms of capital. In J. G. Richardson (Ed.), *Handbook of theory and research for the sociology of education* (pp. 241–258). New York: Greenwood Press.

Bourdieu, P. (1990). *The logic of practice* (R. Nice, Trans.). Cambridge: Polity Press.

Bourdieu, P., & Wacquant, L. J. D. (1992). *An invitation to reflexive sociology.* Chicago, IL: University of Chicago Press.

Boxenbaum, E., & Battilana, J. (2005). Importation as innovation: transposing managerial practices across fields. *Strategic Organization, 3*(4), 355–383.

Buhr, K. (2012). The inclusion of aviation in the EU emissions trading scheme: Temporal conditions for institutional entrepreneurship. *Organization Studies, 33*(11), 1565–1587.

Carson, R. (1962). *Silent spring.* New York, NY: Houghton Mifflin.

Child, J., Lu, Y., & Tsai, T. (2007). Institutional entrepreneurship in building an environmental protection system for the People's Republic of China. *Organization Studies, 28*(7), 1013–1014.

Clegg, S. (2010). The state, power, and agency: missing in action in institutional theory? *Journal of Management Inquiry, 19*(1), 4–13.

Clegg, S. R., & Hardy, C. (1996). Representations. In S. R. Clegg, C. Hardy, & W. R. Nord (Eds.), *Handbook of organization studies* (pp. 676–708). London: Sage.

Clemens, E. S., & Cook, J. M. (1999). Politics and institutionalism: Explaining durability and change. *Annual Review of Sociology, 25*(1), 441.

Coase, R. (1937). The nature of the firm. *Economica, 16*(4), 386–405.

Colomy, P. (1998). Neofunctionalism and neoinstitutionalism: Human agency and interest in institutional change. *Sociological Forum, 13*(2), 265–300.

Cooper, D. J., Ezzamel, M., & Willmott, H. (2008). Examining 'institutionalization': A critical theoretic perspective. In R. Greenwood, C. Oliver, R. Suddaby, & K. Sahlin-Andersson (Eds.) *The SAGE handbook of organizational institutionalism* (pp. 673–701). London: Sage.

Covaleski, M. A., Dirsmith, M. W., & Weiss, J. M. (2013). The social construction, challenge and transformation of a budgetary regime: The endogenization of welfare regulation by institutional entrepreneurs. *Accounting, Organizations and Society, 38*(5), 333–364.

Creed, W. D., DeJordy, R., & Lok, J. (2010). Being the change: Resolving institutional contradiction through identity work. *Academy of Management Journal, 53*(6), 1336–1364.

Creed, W. D., Hudson, B. A., Okhuysen, G. A., & Smith-Crowe, K. (2014). Swimming in a sea of shame: incorporating emotion into explanations of institutional reproduction and change. *Academy of Management Review, 39*(3), 275–301.

Creed, W. D., Scully, M. A., & Austin, J. A. (2002). Clothes make the person? The tailoring of legitimating accounts and the social construction of identity. *Organization Science, 13*(5), 475–496.

David, R. J., Sine, W. D., & Haveman, H. A. (2013). Seizing opportunity in emerging fields: How institutional entrepreneurs legitimated the professional form of management consulting. *Organization Science, 24*(2), 356–377.

Davis, G. F., Diekmann, K. A., & Tinsley, C. H. (1994). The decline and fall of the conglomerate firm in the 1980s: The deinstitutionalization of an organizational form. *American Sociological Review, 59*(4), 547–570.

Déjean, F., Gond, J.P., & Leca, B. (2004). Measuring the unmeasured: An institutional entrepreneur strategy in an emerging industry. *Human Relations, 57*(6), 741–764.

Demil, B., & Bensédrine, J. (2005). Processes of legitimization and pressure toward regulation. *International Studies of Management and Organization, 35*(2), 56–77.

Dew, N. (2006). Institutional entrepreneurship: A Coasian perspective. *International Journal of Entrepreneurship and Innovation, 7*(1), 13–22.

DiMaggio, P. (1988). Interest and agency in institutional theory. In L. Zucker (Ed.), *Institutional patterns and culture* (pp. 3–22). Cambridge, MA: Ballinger Publishing.

DiMaggio, P. J., & Powell, W. W. (Eds.) (1991). *The new institutionalism in organizational analysis,* Vol. 17. Chicago, IL: University of Chicago Press.

Dorado, S. (2005). Institutional entrepreneurship, partaking, and convening. *Organization Studies, 26*(3), 385–414.

Dorado, S. (2014). Microfinance re-imagined: personal banking for the poor. In T. Baker & F. Welter (Eds.), *The Routledge companion to entrepreneurship.* London: Routledge.

Dorado, S., & Ventresca, M. J. (2013). Crescive entrepreneurship in complex social problems: Institutional conditions for entrepreneurial engagement. *Journal of Business Venturing, 28*(1), 69–82.

Durand, R., & McGuire, J. (2005). Legitimating agencies in the face of selection: The case of AACSB. *Organization Studies, 26*(2), 165–196.

Everett, J. (2002). Organizational research and the praxeology of Pierre Bourdieau. *Organizational Research Methods, 5*(1), 56–80.

Fligstein, N. (1991). The structural transformation of American industry: An institutional account of the causes of diversification in the largest firms, 1919–1979. In W. W. Powell & P. DiMaggio (Eds.), *The new institutionalism in organizational analysis* (pp. 311–336). Chicago, IL and London: University of Chicago Press.

Fligstein, N. (1997). Social skill and institutional theory. *American Behavioral Scientist, 40*(4), 397–405.

Fligstein, N. (2001a). Institutional entrepreneurs and cultural frames – the case of the European Union's single market program. *European Societies, 3*(3), 261–287.

Fligstein, N. (2001b). Social skill and the theory of fields. *Sociological Theory, 19*(2), 105–125.

Fligstein, N., & Mara-Drita, I. (1996). How to make a market: reflections on the attempt to create a single market in the European Union. *American Journal of Sociology, 102*(1), 1–33.

Foucault, M. (1979). *Discipline and punish: The birth of the prison.* Harmondsworth: Penguin.

Foucault, M. (1980). *Power/Knowledge: Selected interviews and other writings 1972–1977* (C. Gordon, ed.). Brighton: Harvester Press.

Garud, R., Hardy, C., & Maguire, S. (2007). Institutional entrepreneurship as embedded agency: An introduction to the special issue. *Organization Studies, 28*(7), 957–969.

Garud, R., Jain, S., & Kumaraswamy, A. (2002). Institutional entrepreneurship in the sponsorship of common technological standards: The case of Sun Microsystems and Java. *Academy of Management Journal, 45*(1), 196–214.

George, E., Chattopadhyay, P., Sitkin, S. B., & Barden, J. (2006). Cognitive underpinning of institutional persistence and change: A framing perspective. *Academy of Management Review, 31*(2), 347–385.

Grant, D., & Hardy, C. (2004). Struggles with organizational discourse. *Organization Studies, 25*(1), 5–14.

Gray, B., Purkey, J. M., & Ansari, S. (2015). From interactions to institutions: Microprocesses of framing and mechanisms for the structuring of institutional fields. *Academy of Management Review, 40*(1), 115–143.

Greenwood, R., & Suddaby, R. (2006). Institutional entrepreneurship in mature fields: The big five accounting firms. *Academy of Management Journal, 49*(1), 27–48.

Greenwood, R., Suddaby, R., & Hinings, C.R. (2002). Theorizing change: The role of professional associations in the transformations of institutionalized fields. *Academy of Management Journal, 45*(1), 58–80.

Hardy, C., & Maguire, S. (2008). Institutional entrepreneurship. In R. Greenwood, C. Oliver, R. Suddaby, & K. Sahlin-Andersson (Eds.), *The SAGE handbook of organizational institutionalism* (pp. 198–217). London: Sage.

Hardy, C., & Maguire, S. (2010). Discourse, field-configuring events, and change in organizations and institutional fields: Narratives of DDT and the Stockholm Convention. *Academy of Management Journal, 53*(6), 1365–1392.

Hardy, C., & Phillips, N. (1999). No joking matter: Discursive struggle in the Canadian refugee system. *Organization Studies, 20*(1), 1–24.

Hargadon, A., & Douglas, Y. (2001). When innovations meet institutions: Edison and the design of the electric light. *Administrative Science Quarterly, 46*(3), 476–501.

Harmon, D. J., Green, S. E., & Goodnight, G. T. (2015). A model of rhetorical legitimation: The structure of communication and cognition underlying institutional maintenance and change. *Academy of Management Review, 40*(1), 76–95.

Heaphy, E. D. (2013) Repairing breaches with rules: Maintaining institutions in the face of everyday disruptions. *Organization Science, 24*(5), 1291–1315.

Henfridsson, O., & Yoo, Y. (2014). The liminality of trajectory shifts in institutional entrepreneurship. *Organization Science, 25*(3), 932–950.

Hensman, M. (2003). Social movement organizations: A metaphor for strategic actors in institutional field. *Organization Studies, 24*(3), 355–381.

Hoffman, A.J. (1999). Institutional evolution and change: Environmentalism and the U.S. chemical industry. *Academy of Management Journal, 42*(4), 351–371.

Holm, P. (1995). The dynamics of institutionalisation: Transformation processes in Norwegian fisheries. *Administrative Science Quarterly, 40*(3), 398–422.

Khan, F., Munir, K., & Willmott, H. (2007). A dark side of institutional entrepreneurship: Soccer balls, child labor and postcolonial impoverishment. *Organization Studies, 28*(7), 1055–1077.

Kisfalvi, V., & Maguire, S. (2011). On the nature of institutional entrepreneurs: Insights from the life of Rachel Carson. *Journal of Management Inquiry, 20*(2), 152–177.

Kodeih, F., & Greenwood, R. (2014). Responding to institutional complexity: The role of identity. *Organization Studies, 35*(1), 7–39.

Lampel, J., & Meyer, A. D. (2008). Guest editors' introduction: Field-configuring events as structuring mechanisms: How conferences, ceremonies, and trade shows constitute new technologies, industries, and markets. *Journal of Management Studies, 45*(6), 1025–1035.

Lawrence, T., Hardy, C., & Phillips, N. (2002). Institutional effects of interorganizational collaboration: The emergence of proto-institutions. *Academy of Management Journal, 45*(1), 281–290.

Lawrence, T., & Phillips, N. (2004). From Moby Dick to Free Willy: macro-cultural discourse and institutional entrepreneurship in emerging institutional fields. *Organization, 11*(5), 689–711.

Lawrence, T., & Suddaby, R. (2006). Institutions and institutional work. In S. R. Clegg, C. Hardy, T. B. Lawrence, & W. R. Nord (Eds.), *Handbook of organization studies* (pp. 215–254). London: Sage.

Leblebici, H., Salancik, G., Copay, A., & King, T. (1991). Institutional change and the transformation of interorganizational fields: An organizational history of the U.S. radio broadcasting industry. *Administrative Science Quarterly, 36*(3), 333–363.

Leca, B., & Naccache, P. (2006). A critical realist approach to institutional entrepreneurship. *Organization*, *13*(5), 627–651.

Lee, K., & Pennings, J. M. (2002). Mimicry and the market: Adoption of a new organizational form. *Academy of Management Journal*, *45*(1), 144–162.

Lepoutre, J. M., & Valente, M. (2012). Fools breaking out: The role of symbolic and material immunity in explaining institutional nonconformity. *Academy of Management Journal*, *55*(2), 285–313.

Levy, D., & Scully, M. (2007). The institutional entrepreneur as modern prince: The strategic face of power in contested fields. *Organization Studies*, *28*(7), 971–991.

Lounsbury, M. (2002). Institutional transformation and status mobility: the professionalization of the field of finance. *Academy of Management Journal*, *45*(1), 255–266.

Lounsbury, M., Ventresca, M., & Hirsch, P.M. (2003). Social movements, field frames and industry emergence: a cultural–political perspective on US recycling. *Social Economic Review*, *1*(1), 71–104.

Maguire, S. (2007). Institutional entrepreneurship. In S. Clegg and J. R. Bailey (Eds.), *International encyclopedia of organization studies* (pp. 674–678). London: Sage.

Maguire, S., & Hardy, C. (2006). The emergence of new global institutions: A discursive perspective. *Organization Studies*, *27*(1), 7–29.

Maguire, S., & Hardy, C. (2009). Discourse and deinstitutionalization: The decline of DDT. *Academy of Management Journal*, *52*(1), 148–178.

Maguire, S., Hardy, C., & Lawrence, T. (2004). Institutional entrepreneurship in emerging fields: HIV/AIDS treatment advocacy in Canada. *Academy of Management Journal*, *47*(5), 657–679.

Maguire, S., Phillips, N., & Hardy, C. (2001). When 'Silence = Death', keep talking: Trust, control and the discursive construction of identity in the Canadian HIV/AIDS treatment domain. *Organization Studies*, *22*(2), 285–312.

Martí, I., & Fernández, P. (2013). The institutional work of oppression and resistance: Learning from the Holocaust. *Organization Studies*, *34*(8), 1195–1223.

McGaughey, S. L. (2013). Institutional entrepreneurship in North American lightning protection standards: Rhetorical history and unintended consequences of failure. *Business History*, *55*(1), 73–97.

Meyer, A. D. (1982). Adapting to environmental jolts. *Administrative Science Quarterly*, *27*(4), 515–537.

Meyer, R. E. (2006). Visiting relatives: Current developments in the new sociology of knowledge. *Organization*, *13*(5), 725–738.

Micelotta, E., & Washington, M. (2013). Institutions and maintenance: the repair work of Italian professions. *Organization Studies*, *34*(8), 1137–1170.

Misangyi, V. F., Weaver, G. R., & Elms, H. (2008). Ending corruption: The interplay among institutional logics, resources, and institutional entrepreneurs. *Academy of Management Review*, *33*(3), 750–770.

Monteiro, P., & Nicolini, D. (2015). Recovering materiality in institutional work prizes as an assemblage of human and material entities. *Journal of Management Inquiry*, *24*(1), 61–81.

Montiel, I., & Husted, B. W. (2009). The adoption of voluntary environmental management programs in Mexico: First movers as institutional entrepreneurs. *Journal of Business Ethics*, *88*(2), 349–363.

Munir, K. A. (2005). The social construction of events: A study of institutional change in the photographic field. *Organization Studies*, *26*(1), 93–112.

Munir, K. A. (2015). A loss of power in institutional theory. *Journal of Management Inquiry*, *24*(1), 90–92.

Mutch, A. (2007). Reflexivity and the institutional entrepreneur: a historical exploration. *Organization Studies*, *28*(7), 1123–1140.

Mutch, A., Delbridge, R., & Ventresca, M. (2006). Situating organizational action: The relational sociology of organizations. *Organization*, *13*(5), 607–625.

Nasra, R., & Dacin, M. T. (2010). Institutional arrangements and international entrepreneurship: the state as institutional entrepreneur. *Entrepreneurship Theory and Practice*, *34*(3), 583–609.

North, D. C. (1990). *Institutions, institutional change and economic performance*. Cambridge: Cambridge University Press.

Oakes, L. S., Townley, B., & Cooper, D. J. (1998). Business planning as pedagogy: Language and control in a changing institutional field. *Administrative Science Quarterly*, *43*(2), 257–292.

Perkmann, M., & Spicer, A. (2007). Healing the scars of history: Projects, skills and field strategies in institutional entrepreneurship. *Organization Studies*, *28*(7), 1101–1122.

Pfeffer, J., & Salancik, G. (1978). *The external control of organizations*. New York: Harper and Row.

Phillips, N., Lawrence, T., & Hardy, C. (2004). Discourse and institutions. *Academy of Management Review*, *29*(4), 1–18.

Purdy, J. M., & Gray, B. (2009). Conflicting logics, mechanisms of diffusion, and multilevel dynamics in emerging institutional fields. *Academy of Management Journal*, *52*(2), 355–380.

Raffaelli, R., & Glynn, M. A. (2014). Turnkey or tailored? Relational pluralism, institutional complexity, and the organizational adoption of more or less customized practices. *Academy of Management Journal*, *57*(2), 541–562.

Rao, H. (2002). Tests tell: Institutional activists, constitutive legitimacy and consumer acceptance in the American automobile industry, 1895–1912.

Advances in Strategic Management the New Institutionalism in Strategic Management, 19, 307–335.

Rao, H., Monin, P., & Durand, R. (2003). Institutional change in Toque Ville: Nouvelle cuisine as an identity movement in French gastronomy. *American Journal of Sociology, 108*(4), 795–843.

Rao, H., Morrill, C., & Zald, M. (2000). Power plays: How social movements and collective action create new organizational forms. *Research in Organizational Behavior, 22,* 237–281.

Ritvala, T., & Granqvist, N. (2009). Institutional entrepreneurs and local embedding of global scientific ideas: The case of preventing heart disease in Finland. *Scandinavian Journal of Management, 25*(2), 133–145.

Rothenberg, S., & Levy, D. L. (2012). Corporate perceptions of climate science: The role of corporate environmental scientists. *Business & Society, 51*(1), 31–61.

Russo, M. V. (2001). Institutions, exchange relations, and the emergence of new fields: Regulatory policies and independent power production in America, 1978–1992. *Administrative Science Quarterly, 46*(1), 57–86.

Sahlin, K., & Wedlin, L. (2008). Circulating ideas: Imitation, translation and editing. In R. Greenwood, C. Oliver, R. Suddaby, & K. Sahlin-Andersson (Eds.), *The SAGE handbook of organizational institutionalism* (pp. 218–242). London: Sage.

Sauder, M. (2008). Interlopers and field change: the entry of US News into the Field of Legal education. *Administrative Science Quarterly, 53*(2), 209–234.

Sauder, M., & Espeland, W. N. (2009). The discipline of rankings: Tight coupling and organizational change. *American Sociological Review, 74*(1), 63–82.

Schmidt, V. A. (2008). Discursive institutionalism: The explanatory power of ideas and discourse. *Annual Review of Political Science, 11,* 303–326.

Schmidt, V. A. (2010). Taking ideas and discourse seriously: explaining change through discursive institutionalism as the fourth 'new institutionalism'. *European Political Science Review, 2*(1), 1–25.

Schüssler, E., Rüling, C. C., & Wittneben, B. B. (2014). On melting summits: The limitations of field-configuring events as catalysts of change in transnational climate policy. *Academy of Management Journal, 57*(1), 140–171.

Scott, R. (1995). *Institutions and organizations.* Thousand Oaks, CA: Sage.

Seo, M., & Creed, D. (2002). Institutional contradictions, praxis and institutional change: A dialectic perspective. *Academy of Management Review, 27*(2), 222–248.

Smets, M., Morris, T. I. M., & Greenwood, R. (2012). From practice to field: A multilevel model of practice-driven institutional change. *Academy of Management Journal, 55*(4), 877–904.

Stål, H. (2011). Examining the relationship between emerging and prevailing institutional logics in an early stage of institutional entrepreneurship. *Journal of Change Management, 11*(4), 421–443.

Suddaby, R. (2015). Can institutional theory be critical? *Journal of Management Inquiry, 24*(1) 93–95.

Suddaby, R., & Greenwood, R. (2005). Rhetorical strategies of legitimacy. *Administrative Science Quarterly, 50*(1), 35–68.

Thornton, P. H. (2002). The rise of the corporation in a craft industry: Conflict and conformity in institutional logics. *Academy of Management Journal, 45*(1), 81–101.

Thornton, P. H., & Ocasio, W. (2008). Institutional logics. In R. Greenwood, C. Oliver, R. Suddaby, & K. Sahlin-Andersson (Eds.), *The SAGE handbook of organizational institutionalism* (pp. 99–128). London: Sage.

Townley, B. (2002). The role of competing rationalities in institutional change. *Academy of Management Journal, 45*(1), 163–179.

Tracey, P., Phillips, N., & Jarvis, O. (2011). Bridging institutional entrepreneurship and the creation of new organizational forms: A multilevel model. *Organization Science, 22*(1), 60–80.

Turner, R., & Killian, L. (1987). *Collective behaviour.* Englewood Cliffs, NJ: Prentice Hall.

Vallentin, S. (2015). Governmentalities of CSR: Danish government policy as a reflection of political difference. *Journal of Business Ethics, 127*(1), 33–47.

Wijen, F., & Ansari, S. (2007). Overcoming inaction through collective institutional entrepreneurship: Insights from regime theory. *Organization Studies, 28*(7), 1079–1100.

Willmott, H. (2011). Institutional work: for what? Problems and prospects of institutional theory. *Journal of Management Inquiry, 20*(1), 67–72.

Willmott, H. (2015). Why institutional theory cannot be critical. *Journal of Management Inquiry, 24*(1), 105–111.

Wright, A. L., & Zammuto, R. F. (2013a). Creating opportunities for institutional entrepreneurship: The colonel and the cup in English county cricket. *Journal of Business Venturing, 28*(1), 51–68.

Wright, A. L., & Zammuto, R. F. (2013b). Wielding the willow: Processes of institutional change in English county cricket. *Academy of Management Journal, 56*(1), 308–330.

Zilber, T. B. (2002). Institutionalization as an interplay between actions, meanings and actors: The case of a rape crisis center in Israel. *Academy of Management Journal, 45*(1), 234–254.

Zilber, T. B. (2006). The work of the symbolic in institutional processes: Translations of rational myths in Israeli hi-tech. *Academy Management Journal, 49*(2), 281–303.

Zilber, T. B. (2007). Stories and the discursive dynamics of institutional entrepreneurship: The case of Israeli high-tech after the bubble. *Organization Studies, 28*(7), 1035–1054.

11

Social Movements and the Dynamics of Institutions and Organizations

Marc Schneiberg and Michael Lounsbury

Calls for reintroducing agency, politics and contestation into institutional analysis are now legion, spanning more than two decades since DiMaggio's (1988) classic piece, and gaining new urgency as scholars struggle to explain institutional emergence and change. Institutionalists face persistent difficulties in these tasks. Working from arguments about isomorphism, diffusion, or path dependence, they often invoke ad hoc explanations like exogenous shocks in order to reconcile change and path creation with theories that stress the contextual sources of stability, continuity and conformity (Greenwood and Hinings 1996; Clemens and Cook 1999; Campbell 2004; Schneiberg 2005; Streeck and Thelen 2005). To address these difficulties, institutionalists have begun to revise both their conceptions of fields and their views of action. From a more structural approach to agency, some scholars increasingly view fields as comprised of multiple logics, or by indeterminacy, ambiguities or contradictions, opening theoretical spaces for action (Stryker

2000; Seo and Creed 2002; Lounsbury 2007; Schneiberg 2007; Fligstein and McAdam 2012; Padgett and Powell 2012; Thornton et al. 2012; Ocasio, Thornton and Lounsbury, Chapter 19 this volume;). Focusing more on interests, other scholars have brought new attention to actors and what they do, producing studies of 'institutional entrepreneurs' (Beckert 1999; Hwang and Powell 2005; Hardy and McGuire 2008) and institutional work (Lawrence et al. 2013). Within this milieu, scholars have also sought to overcome 'excessive institutional determinism' by turning to social movement theory and the study of collective mobilization.

Spanning sociology and political science, social movement theory has produced a wealth of concepts and research on change, including studies of students organizing to register black voters in the 1960s (McAdam 1988), the mobilization of farmers, workers and women to make claims on the state (Clemens 1997), shareholder activism to contest managerial control over corporations

(Davis and Thompson 1994), the growth of identity movements pursuing peace, gay/lesbian rights and environmentalism (e.g., Laraña et al. 1994), and the rise of transnational pressure groups (Keck and Sikkink 1998). What these studies share is an interest in contestation and collective mobilization processes – how groups coalesce to make claims for or against certain practices or actors in order to create or resist new institutional arrangements or transform existing ones. They also share an interest in tracing how contestation and collective action rest on the capacity of groups to mobilize resources and recruit members, their ability to engage in cultural entrepreneurship or frame issues to increase acceptance of their claims (Lounsbury and Glynn 2001; Werner and Conelissen 2014), and the political opportunity structures that constrain or enable mobilization (McAdam et al. 1996). This chapter focuses on how engaging collective mobilization and social movement theory has inspired new work in institutional analysis.

The integration of movements into institutional analysis revised imageries of institutional *processes*, *actors* and the *structure of fields*, generating new leverage for explaining change and path creation. Regarding processes, it has added contestation, collective action, framing and deliberate mobilization for alternatives to conceptual repertoires of legitimation, diffusion, isomorphism and self-reproducing taken-for-granted practices (Jepperson 1991; Colyvas and Powell 2006). Regarding actors, it counterposes challengers and champions of alternatives to accounts of states, professions and other incumbents as key players. Regarding structure, it moves from images of isomorphic worlds of diffusion, path dependence and conformity toward conceptions of fields as sites of contestation, organized around multiple and competing logics and forms.

As will be clear, work that integrates movements into neo-institutionalism parallels work on institutional entrepreneurship in key respects (Hardy and McGuire 2008).

Both emphasize agency, deliberate or strategic action, and self-conscious mobilization around alternatives. Both wrestle with problems or paradoxes of how actors embedded within institutions can change those systems, how institutions limit or support change, and how actors draw on the elements or contradictions of existing institutions to forge new ones. Both identify some of the same processes as critical for change, including framing, theorization, transposition and the recombination of logics. Yet where institutional entrepreneurship research often attributes substantial casual efficacy to individuals, studies linking movements and institutionalism are more deeply rooted in contextually situated approaches to agency. They thus place greater emphasis on politics and collective mobilization as motors of change, and more systematically address the relations between activity, collective organization and existing institutional contexts.

Our central claim is that analyzing movements within neo-institutional theory is essential for understanding when and how: (1) paths or fields become constituted around multiple, competing logics; and (2) multiple logics, contradictions and ambiguities fuel field-level change and new path creation. In making this claim, we accept, rather than dismiss, contextual arguments about durability, path dependence and stability that give institutionalism its analytical edge in explaining continuity, differences or 'higher order' effects on organizations (Schneiberg and Clemens 2006). Institutions exhibit increasing returns and positive feedbacks (Pierson 2000). Actors empowered by existing institutions use their advantages to elaborate institutions to preserve their power and preclude alternatives. Diffusion, adoption and the resulting communities of practice create isomorphic pressures that make conformity a condition for legitimacy, fueling further diffusion. Institutionalized theories of order render alternatives unthinkable or inappropriate, ensuring that even opposition occurs in those terms, deepening the paths it contests.

In short, rather than simply assert an actor-centered institutionalism, we begin with the structural insight that limits on alternatives and pressures for continuity or convergence often exercise considerable force. Reflexive action, the capacity to articulate alternatives, the salience of multiple logics, or their translation into change, cannot be assumed. To the contrary, these are often fragile achievements that ultimately rest on the emergence and efficacy of social movements.

Using existing and ongoing research, this chapter outlines analytical strategies for addressing the rise and effects of movements on institutional fields and organizations. We pay particular attention to how those strategies revise existing institutional accounts of change and path creation. In sections 1 and 2 we consider movements as agents and infrastructures of change, outlining two approaches to what movements do and how they affect fields. One treats movements as forces *against* institutions, as forces operating outside established channels to assert new visions and disrupt or directly contest existing arrangements, evoking legitimacy crises, sense-making and other institutional processes within fields. This approach revises two canons in institutional theory – the two-stage model of institutionalization and histories of change as punctuated equilibrium. It also provides insights into how fields become constituted around multiple logics.

A second approach considers the rise and impact of movements *within* fields, examining movements as institutional forces or infrastructures for institutional processes including theorization, recombination and diffusion. This approach reveals how diffusion, translation and adoption are political processes that often depend on collective action. It also begins to shed light on how movements emerge from and exploit contradictions or multiple logics within fields to mobilize support, forge new paths or produce change. While our discussion analytically segregates outside, challenger movements

from insider movements, we note that these distinctions are often blurred in reality. In fact, some of the most exciting recent work emphasizes the processes by which outsider movements catalyze movements and changes inside fields and organizations, how movements can combine outsider and insider efforts, and how challengers and incumbents inside and outside of fields interact and influence each other, collectively producing change.

In section 3 we turn from movements as agents of change to analyses of how institutions serve as contexts that shape contestation and collective action. Institutionalists have recognized that institutions constrain and enable mobilization, create openings for challengers, and shape their capacities to produce change. This has led them to the movements literature on political opportunity structure and institutional mediation (e.g., Amenta et al. 1992; Davis and Thompson 1994; McAdam 1999), prompting new insights about opportunity structures, a reinvigoration of multilevel approaches, and new strategies for analyzing movements, existing institutions and change. Taking a decidedly cultural cast, these strategies reformulate arguments about political opportunity structures as institutional opportunity structures, highlighting how movements and change are endogenously shaped by institutions.

Based on these discussions, we turn in section 4 to suggest new directions for research on how movements and institutional dynamics combine to produce change. One key direction is methodological: to develop clearer, more direct measures of movements and to exploit the analytical leverage of multivariate approaches. This will help assess and systematize claims from qualitative and historical work about movement effects and the relations between movements, institutional contexts and outcomes. Three other directions involve substantively rethinking the relationships between movements, institutional dynamics and context in fueling path creation and change. One direction for future research flips the imagery in opportunity structure arguments of institutions as contexts for movements, and analyzes *movements as contexts and political conditions for diffusion* and other institutional processes. Insofar as alternatives are contested or suppressed by vested interests, their diffusion will depend on collective action and the mobilization of power by champions of new practices and forms. In cases like these, movements can moderate institutional processes, supporting diffusion or translation in three ways: by serving as field-wide mechanisms for mobilizing power, by working as political forces within organizations to increase their receptivity to alternatives, or by working between organizations to increase innovators' influence as exemplars. Taking this approach to how movements operate in fields can help explain the diffusion of alternatives and more diverse outcomes related to practice variation.

A second direction for future work retains the imagery of institutions as contexts or conditions for mobilization, but analyzes those contexts as *opportunity structures characterized by institutional heterogeneity, multiple institutions, or architectures of multiple, adjacent or overlapping fields* (Evans and Kay 2008; Greenwood et al. 2011; Mora 2014). Such contexts contain substantial potentials for transposing forms and frames within or across settings, using changes, processes or disruptions in nearby fields to alter dynamics within a field, or leveraging and repurposing institutions in one domain for path creation and change in another. Pursuing this approach broadens our conception of opportunity structures, highlighting how institutional contexts can provide activists with opportunities for using dissonance, cross-field pressures, or inter-institutional effects to more effectively translate numbers, organization and action into change.

In a third direction for future research, we consider the *origins of movements and institutions*, taking an historical approach and considering the relationship between institutions and movements as an ongoing process in which combinations or sequences of movements cumulatively produce change. Movements might figure in the production of unintended and incremental *trajectories* of change. That is, even when they are defeated or their time has passed, movements may leave legacies, elements of institutional orders, and bits and pieces of paths not taken, producing diffuse but important effects, and creating possibilities for subsequent movements, institution-building and transformation (Schneiberg 2007). Focusing on these possibilities sheds further light on how movements and their effects are endogenously produced, helping researchers avoid the trap of invoking movements, like exogenous shocks, as a *deus ex machina*.

MOVEMENTS *FROM OUTSIDE* INSTITUTIONS: CHALLENGER/ DOMINANCE APPROACHES

One way to integrate movements into institutional research preserves the analytical distinction between movements, contestation and deliberate mobilization, on the one hand, and institutional processes like the reproduction of taken-for-granted practices, on the other, taking movements as an 'extra-institutional' force that impacts change or new path creation. This approach hardly exhausts possible relations between movements and institutions. But it captures the wide class of cases where movements arise outside of or on the peripheries of established fields, acting as outsiders/challengers to assert new visions of order, disrupt existing systems, or secure representation or policies from established authorities (Fligstein and McAdam 2012). Thinking in these terms also extends the institutional framework to highlight processes left exogenous by existing accounts of emergence and change, opening up a blackbox of 'pre-institutional' dynamics, and adding new imageries and mechanisms to our conceptual repertoire.

Consider two canonical formulations in neo-institutional analysis. In the two-stage model of institutionalization, the emergence of fields is a 'bottom-up' phenomenon: (1) organizations or states adopt structures or policies in response to local problems, politics or characteristics, which then spark (2) processes of mimesis, theorization and diffusion, eventually crystallizing a broader community of practice around a core set of principles or models (Tolbert and Zucker 1983; Baron et al. 1986; Galaskiewicz and Wasserman 1989; Strang and Chang 1993; Schofer and Meyer 2005). As solutions diffuse, they become taken-for-granted as an accepted norm, serving as baselines to which organizations must subsequently conform as a condition for legitimacy. In punctuated equilibrium models, change occurs as a sequence of shock, disruption, deinstitutionalization and reinstitutionalization (Edelman 1990, 2006; Fligstein 1990, 2001; Sutton et al. 1994; Sutton and Dobbin 1996). Shocks like new laws or court rulings subvert existing routines, vested interests and established understandings, evoking uncertainty, sensemaking and a succession of players and models as new groups emerge to define the situation and establish their solutions as new bases of order.

Both models shed light on key institutional processes: (1) mutual monitoring, mimesis and the diffusion or transposition of practices across organizations; (2) theorization, codification or the endorsement of best practices by professional associations; and (3) interventions by states to ratify, redraw or reject field boundaries and emerging solutions (e.g., Strang and Meyer 1993). Yet both tend to neglect the origins of new ideas and practices as well as the sources of disruption, leaving key players and processes unanalyzed. However, in many canonical cases featuring isomorphism, the instigating shocks or motivations for adoption were the direct and deliberate results of social movements – municipal reformers and progressives fighting corruption in city government, civil rights

activists demanding state intervention to end discrimination and agrarian populists contesting corporate consolidation.

Schneiberg and Soule's (2005) study of rate regulation in insurance develops one model of the role of movements in the institutionalization process, revising canonical accounts. It conceptualizes institutions as political settlements. Moreover, it analyzes path creation as a contested process grounded in sequences of mobilization, disruption and conventional institutional dynamics, tracing how mobilization outside established channels catalyzes path creation and change. Specifically, their study shows how rate regulation by American states in the early twentieth century was sparked neither by exogenous shocks, nor by scattered and unconnected politics or problem-solving behavior, but rather by anti-corporate movements who worked to contest corporate consolidation and assert alternative forms of economic order. Mobilizing in response to 'trusts' and 'combines', the Grange, Farmers Alliance and other groups directly opposed 'corporate liberal' models of order based on for-profit corporations, national markets and unregulated industry. Instead, they pursued 'producer republican' logics that envisioned American capitalism as a regionally decentralized and cooperatively organized economy of independent producers, farmers and self-governing towns. And in targeting insurance, Grangers and other groups secured anti-trust laws to break up the 'insurance trust', organized consumer-owned mutual firms, and otherwise disrupted insurance markets, fueling legitimacy crises, public hearings and new interventions within key states.

These disruptions and interventions, in turn, sparked politics and conventional institutional processes within the insurance field. They evoked inter-state diffusion in which key players monitored other states, theorized rate regulation as a solution to the 'insurance problem', recombined elements to forge those solutions and adopted laws passed by other states. They also evoked supra-state or field-wide process in which courts and the professions endorsed regulation, promulgated model laws, and built field-wide administrative organs. Taken together, these institutional processes shifted the balance of power *within* states, crystallizing insurance around economic models and regulatory solutions that settled political struggles over industry governance (see also Schneiberg 1999, 2002; Schneiberg and Bartley 2001).

Rao, Clemens, Hoffman and recent work on contemporary anti-corporate mobilization also go beyond canonical accounts by foregrounding movements, understanding paths as political settlements, or analyzing path creation as sequences of movements, mobilization and institutional processes. Rao (1998) shows how the consumer watchdog agencies and product rating schemes that are now taken-for-granted were the product of consumer mobilization and contestation over whether scientific testing and the power of informed consumers should be blended with the role of labor, unionization and concerns about production. At first, consumer groups fought for two different logics of reform, one that blended consumer advocacy with unionism and one that focused more narrowly on the consumer. But broader political dynamics eliminated the more comprehensive radical change frame from the path, segregating 'consumer' and 'worker', and ensuring the dominance of a consumer-only impartial testing logic (see Carruthers and Babb 1996 for a similar analysis of monetary systems).

Clemens and Hoffman more directly address how change flows from combinations of movements and institutional processes. For Clemens (1993, 1997), interest group politics became a core feature of the American polity through successive waves of mobilization and transposition by three outsider/challenger groups. Acting collectively to contest parties and patronage, first unions, then farmers and then women's groups built on previous efforts to disrupt existing arrangements (strikes, boycotts, protests) by transposing fraternals, cooperatives, clubs

and other kinds of apolitical associations into mainstream politics. These sequences of actions fundamentally altered the terms of political representation and influence, creating access and clout for previously disenfranchised groups and institutionalizing lobbying, legislative monitoring, and other now taken-for-granted modes of American politics. For Hoffman (1999), movements and institutional dynamics play pivotal roles in field creation and change in contemporary environmentalism. Conflicts over competing institutions and successive rounds of environmental mobilization, scandal and legislative activity provoked new forms of discourse, theorization and new patterns of interactions among firms, non-profits and governments. These dynamics, in turn, helped produce an increasingly structured environmental field.

Work on contemporary anti-corporate politics has likewise located change in sequences or combination of mobilization and institutional processes, paying growing attention to movement disruption of firms and how corporations engage in non-market strategies to appease activists, fueling diffusion of reforms and new practices (Bartley 2007; Briscoe and Safford 2008; Soule 2009; King and Pearce 2011; Vasi and King 2012; De Bakker et al. 2013; McDonnell and King 2013; McDonnell et al. 2015; Vasi et al. 2015; Hiatt et al. 2015). King and Soule (2007) importantly show how protestors are effective in driving down a firm's stock price when they target issues dealing with critical stakeholder groups such as workers and consumers. In response to these and other threats to their reputations and bottom lines, firms have borrowed, transposed and embraced corporate social responsibility practices, domestic partner benefits and the like (Briscoe and Safford 2008; Soule 2009). They have also collaborated with non-profit groups in organizing and diffusing private governance systems and now ubiquitous rating and ranking schemes (Bartley 2007), while becoming more sophisticated in counter-mobilization efforts including astroturfing strategies by corporations to create impressions of grass-roots support for a policy or product (Walker 2014; Walker and Rea 2014). This has stimulated important research on elite mobilization (Soule 2009; Ingram et al. 2010; Zald and Lounsbury 2010; Rao et al. 2011; Yue 2015).

As a group, these studies substantially revise canonical accounts of path creation and change. First, they support a view of institutions as settlements of political struggles over the character of fields fueled by the mobilization of challengers around competing projects and logics (Davis and Thompson 1994; Fligstein 1996; Armstrong 2005; McAdam and Scott 2005). Emphasizing contestation and collective action, this view departs from 'cooler' imageries of paths as based in diffusion, taken-for-granted practice, theorization and normative endorsement by professions or states. Thus, insurance rate regulation represented a political solution of struggles between insurers, who pursued economic logics of corporations, markets and unregulated industry associations, and challenger groups, who sought anti-trust laws, regulation and mutual alternatives to promote more decentralized and cooperatively organized economies. Conflicts over these visions yielded structural innovations, but were not resolved until field members crafted packages that combined regulation with private association, and mutuals with for-profit corporations. The consumer advocacy field likewise reflected a settlement of struggles and mobilization around competing logics, albeit one that involved a clear-cut victory of one logic of consumerism over another.

Second, these studies suggest an image of the *process* of institutionalization as a sequence or combination between contestation and mobilization around alternative visions of order, on the one hand, and more conventional institutional dynamics, on the other. In insurance, challengers mobilized outside the system to contest the 'insurance combine' and impose alternative forms and anti-trust policies on the industry. Regulators and reformers within the field responded, in turn, by theorizing, endorsing and diffusing regulatory policies that recombined multiple forms into new packages. Similarly, farmers, unions and women's groups reconstructed the American state via successive waves of mobilization, contestation and translation, much like contemporary anti-corporate activists did for neoliberal governance, with successive mobilizations sparking the theorization and diffusion of corporate social responsibility and private governance.

Third, these studies provide a more varied understanding of how movements fuel path creation and change by mobilizing outside established channels to contest extant systems. At a minimum, by introducing multiple logics and promoting awareness of problems, challenger movements subvert the taken-for-grantedness of existing arrangements, fueling legitimacy crises and institutional politics (Stryker 2000), and providing insiders with cultural resources for criticism, reflexive action or 'mindful deviation' (Garud and Karnoe 2001). Thus, as anti-corporate forces, consumers and women's groups took action and asserted new logics, they not only evoked media attention and public debate, creating openings for challengers and reformers to delegitimate dominant institutional systems. They also supplied experts, reformers and other groups with models and cultural resources for criticizing and revising extant paths such as by combining or layering them with new forms and elements.

Challenger movements can likewise introduce new organizational forms into fields, working outside established channels to build parallel, alternative systems of organization, including craft breweries (Carroll and Swaminathan 2000), nouvelle cuisine (Rao et al. 2003), mutual and cooperative enterprises (Schneiberg 2002) and community-based, non-profit recycling centers (Lounsbury et al. 2003; see also Clemens 1997; Rao et al. 2000). These efforts may not be disruptive in intent. Yet promoting alternative forms can foster new competitive dynamics and populate fields with instances of new logics, with quite disruptive effects. By translating apolitical forms of association into state, agrarians, unions and women's groups altered both the terms of competition in American politics and prevailing conceptions of appropriate political action. By promulgating mutual insurance, Grangers and other groups instantiated cooperativism and transformed the terms of competition in a key sector, forcing insurance corporations to engage in new forms of rivalry based on prevention, re-reengineering and loss reduction. By introducing the science based, not-for-profit product testing agency, the consumer movement transformed the terms of trade throughout the economy, as in an odd twist did contemporary anti-corporate activists, whose efforts helped fuel the spread of rating and ranking, corporate self-regulation, and other forms of private governance, laying key foundations for a neoliberal order.

Finally, challenger movements can spark path creation and change by quite directly and deliberately disrupting existing arrangements (e.g., den Hond and de Bakker 2007; van Wijk et al. 2013; Bertels et al. 2014). They can mobilize masses, networks and political support to pressure states and other power centers for new agencies, laws and policies that ban or mandate practices, producing uncertainties or prohibitions associated with new laws, agencies and mandates that profoundly destabilize existing systems, fueling sustained institutional dynamics (Fligstein 1990; Edelman 1992; Dobbin and Dowd 1997; Hoffman 1999). And like ACT UP and Earth First!, challenges from without can and do use protests, boycotts and direct actions to dramatize problems and directly disrupt daily operations and routines (Elsbach and Sutton 1992; Hoffman 1999; King and Soule 2007; King 2008). Challenger movements can scale up their efforts and impact by constructing and participating in field-configuring events (Maguire et al. 2004; Hardy and Maguire 2008; Lampel and Meyer 2008). In all of these ways, movements and counter-movements can fuel path creation

and change as political-cultural forces for contestation, confrontation and disruption. Instantiating new logics, they can evoke controversy and debate within fields, conflicts and policy responses within organizations, inter-organizational diffusion and field-wide association, while supplying insiders and reformers with templates, political support and cultural resources for theorization, transposition, recombination and the assembly of new institutions.

Simple in its essentials, a conception that emphasizes sequences of outsider movements, mobilization and institutional processes has supported increasingly sophisticated analyses of path creation and change. As we show in section 3, a 'movements from outside institutions' conception lends itself readily to multilevel analyses of fields, and to consideration of how existing institutions or political opportunity structures shape challengers' capacities to mobilize and effect change. Yet this conception does not exhaust the ways that movements figure as agents of path creation and change.

MOVEMENTS *WITHIN* INSTITUTIONS: COLLECTIVE MOBILIZATION AS INSTITUTIONAL PROCESS

Groups seeking change often mobilize collectively outside established institutions to assert new logics and disrupt taken-for-granted arrangements. Yet institutionalists have recognized movements also arise *within* institutions or fields, mobilizing insiders and well as outsiders, using established networks and resources to diffuse alternative practices, and drawing effectively on existing institutional elements and models to craft new systems (see Fligstein 1996, 2001). Indeed, while movements can drive change by directly opposing existing schemes, generating legitimacy crises or otherwise disrupting institutions, they sometimes promote path creation and change incrementally by engaging in institutional processes (or becoming institutional forces). That is, movements can emerge and operate within established channels and power structures, drawing on existing institutions and taken-for-granted understandings to theorize, articulate and combine new projects or practices with prevailing models and arrangements. In so doing, movements may themselves become vehicles or established channels for diffusion, theorization, recombination and other institutional processes within fields.

This broader conception of movements risks a loss of analytical specificity and a diminished focus on contesting power structures, especially where movements become synonymous with collective or quasi-collective action geared toward any type of change (Scully and Segal 2002; Scully and Creed 2005). Yet as suggested above, analyzing movements as intra-institutional forces productively blurs distinctions between 'extra-institutional' and 'institutional', 'mobilization' and 'self-reproducing' process, or 'contentious' versus 'conventional' politics. It has led to new insights about parallels between institutional phenomena and collective action processes studied by movement scholars (Wade et al. 1998; Campbell 2005; Davis and Zald 2005; Strang and Jung 2005). It has led to new understandings of the relations between movements, institutions and organizations, including how institutional reproduction and diffusion depend on mobilization, political resources and contestation (Thelen 2004; Weber et al. 2008; Sine and Lee 2009). It supports research that goes beyond analyzing movements as 'extra-institutional' producers of multiple logics to consider also how movements and contestation are products of – and mobilize – contradictions and multiple logics or models within fields (Strkyer 2000; Seo and Creed 2002; Morrill 2006). Indeed, it has let institutionalists interested in movements supplement images of change as disruption, conflict and settlement with analyses of how movements also work in an incremental and embedded

fashion, producing trajectories of path creation or change as reconfiguration, recombination or layering (Clemens and Cook 1999; Streeck and Thelen 2005; Schneiberg 2007). It also opens up possibilities for understanding trajectories of outsider challengers moving inside fields and organizations, and the emergence of *tempered radicals* working from within to refashion organizational policies via more conventional means (Meyerson and Scully 1995).

Lounsbury and colleagues' studies of recycling address how movements can enter into and operate within fields and organizations as institutional forces, emphasizing their role as agents of *theorization, classification, and the diffusion of codified arguments, frames or theoretical resources* (Lounsbury 2001, 2005: Lounsbury et al. 2003). Initially, eco-activists pursued recycling outside established channels, working independently against the waste industry to organize thousands of local non-profit, drop-off recycling centers. These were part of a broader project to restructure capitalism. They were articulated within a holistic frame that theorized recycling as a way to rebuild community, create local closed-loop production and consumption, and reduce community dependence on conglomerates and capitalist commodity systems. Yet the commitment of industry and state agencies to a resource recovery logic that emphasized landfill, waste-to-energy programs and large-scale incineration left the recycling movement isolated and its centers without outlets for materials.

In fact, a viable infrastructure for recycling did not emerge until activists, working through the National Recycling Coalition, entered mainstream policy negotiations, forged ties with solid waste handlers, and retheorized recycling as a for-profit service that built on curb-side programs and complemented landfills and incineration. Coupled with grass-roots mobilization against new incinerators, and negotiations with state agencies to buy recycled materials, theorizing recyclables as commodities transformed cultural beliefs and discourse about waste in the industry, creating institutional conditions for diffusing recycling practices (see also Strang and Meyer 1993; King et al. 2005).

In addition, environmental movements served as institutional forces by operating inside organizations (see Zald and Berger 1978 for an early statement). The Student Environmental Action Coalition promoted recycling within universities by codifying arguments, building inter-collegiate networks and disseminating standardized arguments and facts about similar programs elsewhere. And the College and University Recycling Coordinators provided universities and colleges with standards and classification schemes for measuring the progress, costs and benefits of programs, which helped deepen discourse and theorization of recycling as a rational economic activity. Thus, as Greenwood, Suddaby and Hinings (2002) document for professional associations, social movements can create cultural and theoretical foundations for new activities, forms and fields. They can operate within existing power structures as agents of theorization, classification and diffusion, and can themselves become infrastructures for those processes within fields. Indeed, as recycling became institutionalized, the movement itself blurred into professional association-alism. Activists became recycling employees; employees used the National Recycling Coalition to form a professional association; and the association forged new identities, statuses and procedures for recycling managers within the new field.

Research by Morrill, Creed, Scully and colleagues, and Moore on the institutionalization of alternative dispute resolution, domestic partner benefits and public science likewise document how movements operate as forces within mainstream institutions, de-emphasizing confrontational tactics in favor of their role as mobilizers of multiple logics and as agents or vehicles for *recombination, assembly, translation and diffusion.* In Morrill's (2006) study of alternative dispute

resolution (ADR), mobilization for alternatives and contestation themselves rested fundamentally on the presence and recombination of multiple logics of practice in the socio-legal field. In this case, institutional processes of bricolage, hybridization and innovation preceded broader mobilization. Lawyers, social workers, community activists and judges working at the interstices or overlaps between fields during the 1960s drew in an ad hoc fashion on therapeutic techniques, community mediation and other forms of non-adversarial negotiating and group discussion to help process minor disputes in small claims, family and other courts. As the 'litigation crisis' deepened, these early efforts supported the mobilization of two competing critical masses of ADR activists – one around a 'community mediation' model, the other around the 'multi-door courthouse'.

Both groups devoted considerable energy into theorizing and disseminating their approach, holding conferences, publishing manifestos in prominent law journals and seeking support from foundation or other established centers. Both also worked hard to articulate and recombine their models with prevailing models and institutions, including the 'Great Society' vision of federally funded community social programs and the increasingly ascendant new federalism. Moreover, once advocates could articulate ADR with the divorce revolution and no-fault divorce as a non-adversarial solution to custody and interpersonal problems, they gained a lever for professionalizing mediation and diffusing its practices. They used conferences, new organizations, instructional videos, newsletters and the like to further codify and disseminate ADR, effectively layering ADR into the legal system as an increasingly taken-for-granted complement to conventional legal arrangements.

Creed, Scully and colleagues' studies of gay rights/LGBT activists shed additional light on how movements working within existing institutions can help establish new practices by exploiting contradiction and multiple logics, importing or redeploying logics across settings, and articulating or recombining new elements with prevailing models, myths or concerns (Creed and Scully 2000; Creed et al. 2002; Scully and Segal 2002; Scully and Creed 2005; see also Raeburn 2004). Decisive here were activists' use of contradiction and recombination to disturb taken-for-granted assumptions, highlight injustice, and legitimate claims for reform. For example, activists strategically deployed identity in face-to-face encounters with co-workers and supervisors. They used casual mentions of partners' gendered names when sharing experiences of mundane activities and enacted non-stereotypical behavior to challenge stigma. They also employed narratives of discrimination or inequality to highlight hypocrisies, evoking understandings that everyday routines produce injustice, and activating listeners' identities as non-prejudiced persons.

In addition, activists used their knowledge and status as insiders and loyal corporate citizens to couch reforms like domestic partner benefits as good business practice or expressions of firms' espoused commitments to diversity. Furthermore, like those fighting for the federal Employment Non-Discrimination Act, activists within firms imported higher order logics or frames, articulating domestic partner benefits and other gay friendly policies with broader civil rights frames, values of fairness and equality, corporate social responsibility, and concerns with competitiveness in an increasingly diverse world. In a sense, LGBT movements worked for change by simultaneously coming out and fitting in; that is, by carefully articulating and combining difference, assertions of LGBT identity and new practices with 'normal' everyday life, insider identities as dutiful corporate citizens, and ongoing organizational concerns. Here too, diffusion of new practices like domestic partner benefits was a political process, resting on mobilization, contestation, framing and the recombination of prevailing models and cultural elements in and across firms.

As Moore shows, the institutionalization of public science organizations in American politics also rested critically on multiple logics, mobilization by insiders and the role of movements as bricoleuer-agents of recombination and redeployment (Moore 1996, 2013; Moore and Hala 2002). During the 1960s and 1970s, university scientists faced increasingly severe contradictions between the logic of public service or social utility, on the one hand, and the logics of objectivity, non-partisanship and detachment as scientists, on the other. In fact, extant ways of joining science and politics – serving the public interest by serving the state – had become distinct liabilities. University scientists not only faced attacks by anti-war and environmental groups for their connections to the military and chemical industry, they also began to criticize themselves and their peers for these connections.

At first, activists tried to link science and politics and mobilize for change within established science associations. But mixing partisanship and 'pure science' produced public discord within the scientific community and directly challenged its legitimacy as an impartial, objective producer of facts. This led scientist-activists to create a hybrid form – the public science organization – that resolved this tension by recombining science and politics in novel ways. Through dedicated organizations like the Union for Concerned Scientists and Scientists' Institute for Public Information, scientists could provide nuclear safety information, challenge non-scientists' uses of science and address the public interest without risking their credibility as scientists by acting in openly partisan ways. Moreover, hybrid organizations separate from professional and political associations provided activists with a vehicle for public science that directed attention away from the inner workings of the scientific community, letting scientists mobilize politically without calling their legitimacy as scientists into question or sparking conflict within professional communities.

All of these studies highlight rich opportunities for exploring the role of movements within existing institutions and organizations. In general, social life is rife with collective mobilization, and whether these efforts are made by challengers working as outsiders to redefine existing arrangements, insiders seeking change from within, or elites striving to keep existing structures intact (Fligstein 1990, 1996), a focus on movements expands our understanding of institutional dynamics. Moreover, mobilization can occur at the level of the field as with anti-corporate forces or ecological activists promoting communitarian alternatives to corporate capitalism and with scientists forging new associations to link expertise to politics. Or it can occur within and between organizations as recycling advocates pressed for more substantive forms of recycling or as gay and lesbian groups pushed for recognition and benefits. A focus on movements, therefore, sheds new light on path creation and change, particularly when it attends to the multilevel character of the institutional context.

To be sure, the distinction between movements operating outside and inside fields raises questions for future work about their different enabling conditions, trajectories or effects. Insiders will likely pursue different tactics and forms of contestation than outsider groups. They will likely mobilize collectively in different ways, frame problems and solutions differently, and differentially negotiate or exploit structures, networks and institutional frames provided by established fields. They may also be more likely to err on the conservative side. Conversely, outsiders pursuing disruptive activities face legitimacy dilemmas that may pressure them to mobilize as insiders, articulate their projects with existing institutional logics, or form separate, decoupled organizations for disruptive and conventional action (Elsbach and Sutton 1992). As we suggest in section 4, we can also profitably consider how outsider and insider movements occur in waves or sequences, producing historical trajectories of change.

Fortunately, future work on both kinds of movements can exploit existing research on how institutional contexts more generally shape mobilization and movement efficacy.

INSTITUTIONAL FIELDS AS CONTEXTS FOR MOVEMENTS

While the work just described provides rich depictions of movements as agents of institutional creation and change, analysts of 'outsider' and 'insider' movements have also paid careful attention to the institutional context of social movements. They have not only begun to theorize how multiple logics within fields can motivate contestation and collective action (Stryker 2000; Seo and Creed 2002; Morrill 2006; Marquis and Lounsbury 2007), but have also considered how existing institutional contexts shape mobilization and movements' capacities for producing change. Addressing relations between movements, institutional contexts and outcomes lays the foundation for more sophisticated analyses of power and agency. It lets scholars go beyond simple power elite or interest group arguments about agency and change to consider how extant institutions block access, provide challengers with levers and openings, and otherwise condition actors' ability to translate numbers, resources or organization into change. Moreover, in exploring relations between movements, contexts and outcomes, institutionalists have made good use of research on political opportunity structure (McAdam 1982, 1999; Tarrow 1998) and related arguments about institutional mediation (Amenta and Zylan 1991; Amenta et al. 1992) and institutional contingency (Thornton and Occasio 1999; Bartley and Schneiberg 2002; Lounsbury 2007), supporting a deepening integration of movements research and neo-institutional analysis.

Work at this interface has identified various features of institutional and political fields that condition movement dynamics or success. These include the legacies of prior policies, divisions among elites and the receptivity of institutional authorities toward challengers' claims, the concentration of resources within a field, and the prevalence of certain cultural models. Work on contexts has also shown how the multilevel character of fields provides openings for challengers, and how movements evoke counter-movements within fields.

Davis and colleagues' studies of shareholder movements nicely document how success can hinge on the institutional context (Davis and Thompson 1994; Davis and Greve 1997; Vogus and Davis 2005). During the 1980s, shareholder activists mobilized to promote new conceptions of the corporation, transform markets for corporate control and break managers' hold over large US firms. They formed new organizations, launched takeover actions and used existing governance machinery to oust entrenched managers, relying on their considerable material resources and connections. Yet activists' ability to translate resources into change was institutionally mediated. The concentration of assets held by institutional investors provided shareholder activists with critical leverage in firm-level conflicts with management over the control of corporations. Review by the US Securities and Exchange Commission (SEC) of proxy rules weakened managers' control over votes and signaled a favorable regulatory stance toward shareholders and reform. State governments dependent on franchise fees for incorporation were reluctant to alienate shareholder groups by passing anti-takeover statutes that would deprive them of a key weapon.

Soule and her colleagues likewise trace how the ability of the women's movement to secure equal rights amendments from American states rested on political and institutional opportunity structures (Soule and Olzak 2004; Soule and King 2006). Mobilization for equal rights amendments was more likely to result in ratification in states with a high level of electoral competitiveness, histories of civil rights legislation and favorable (Democratic) allies in power. It was also more effective in public opinion climates where new conceptions of women's roles in private and public spheres prevailed.

Particularly noteworthy here are findings that public opinion climates enhance prospects for movements, which point beyond traditional realist formulations about political opportunity structure to consider how culture shapes mobilization and change. As research on environmentalism has highlighted, institutionalized models or logics can be potent cultural resources for mobilization, framing and change. Shifts in the recycling field from a radical, holistic logic to a technocratic logic facilitated the creation of recycling advocacy groups in urban regions to contest waste management through incineration (Lounsbury 2005). More broadly, the diffusion of environmentalism as a global blueprint for the nation-state has enhanced the capacity of domestic environmental activists to organize and slow environmental degradation (Frank et al. 2000; Hironaka and Schofer 2002; Schofer and Hironaka 2005). Formal mechanisms (e.g., impact assessments) and the prevalence globally of environmentalism as a valued cultural model have legitimated environmental movements, fueling organization, while creating rhetorical and procedural opportunities for activists to point out failures and pursue legal actions.

Studies of movements and institutional contexts have also documented how the multilevel and segmented character of institutions can create opportunities for movements. The multilevel nature of fields is central to institutionalist imageries of context (Scott 1994, 2001; Scott et al. 2000; Schneiberg and Clemens 2006), and bears directly on movements' capacities to produce change in organizations, states and nation-states. As Davis and colleagues' analyses of shareholder activism show, challengers sometimes have to mobilize simultaneously at multiple levels to assert new models and effect change (Davis and Greve 1997; Davis and Thompson 1994; Vogus and Davis 2005). Shareholder groups were mainly interested in promoting new conceptions of the corporation and contesting entrenched management at the firm ('lower order') level. But they quickly found that they also had to take the fight to the state and federal level. Influencing these 'higher order' units was essential for challengers' ability to make change, since state and federal laws set the terms for mobilization and access at the firm-level, defining rules for proxy systems, takeovers and whether shareholders could act collectively. By blocking anti-takeover legislation, securing new proxy rules and so on, shareholder activism at state and federal levels created critical opportunities for mobilization against and within corporations.

Multilevel institutions similarly created opportunities for anti-corporate groups to regulate insurance rates in the American states in the early twentieth century (Schneiberg 1999; Schneiberg and Bartley 2001; Schneiberg and Soule 2005). Challengers seeking to contest insurance corporations were largely closed out of policy making and had little leverage for their regulatory ambitions in New York, Connecticut and other centers of the 'insurance trust'. But, agrarian states proved more open to populist pressures, which let challengers shift venues sideways and enact statist regulatory measures in Texas and Kansas, disrupting the insurance field. Insurers tried to close off access entirely by mobilizing sideways and up, suing in state and federal courts to void states' rights to regulate insurance prices. Yet, that strategy backfired when advocates of regulation found an unexpected ally in the US Supreme Court, which ruled that insurance was 'affected with a public interest' and thus subject to the states' authority, providing activists with venues with leverage to win rate regulation laws in a range of states.

Indeed, the multilevel character of institutions can also create possibilities for movements for coupling field-level and intra-organizational mobilization with the characteristics of organizations serving as opportunity structures that shape the capacities of movements *within organizations* to produce change. Ecological activists were better able to gain footholds for securing full-blown recycling programs at larger colleges and universities with more resources, selective colleges with histories of activism and universities with environmental majors that could serve as local allies or institutional conduits for field-level pressures (Lounsbury 2001; see also King 2008).

Multilevel contexts can even create possibilities for coupling national organizing with mobilizing up, *transnationally*, and down, with transnational structures containing opportunity structures for pressuring states and corporation for change. Developing hand in hand with neoliberalism and 'the decline of the state' has been considerable organizing at the transnational level, including the proliferation of rights discourses, new models of order, associations, governance schemes, standard-setting organizations, conferences and advocacy networks (Meyer et al. 1997; Boli and Thomas 1999; Djelic and Quack 2003; Djelic and Sahlin-Andersson 2006; Bartley 2007; Smith 2008). Such structures and cultural models can serve as platforms for mobilization, providing environmental, anti-sweatshop and civil rights activists with leverage in the form of globally accepted prescriptions, environmental impact statements, transnational certification schemes, international exposure and the like to place new pressures on firms and nations-states (e.g., Skretny 2002; Bartley 2007; Hironaka 2014). They can also serve as platforms for sustaining movements when access and mobilization within nations are blocked, providing activists venues outside nation-states to organize, develop networks, arguments and allies, and with opportunities to mobilize attention, criticism and allies transnationally to exert pressures downward on intransigent targets (Keck and Sikkink 1998; Alfinito Vierira and Quack 2016).

Finally, researchers attending to context have also found that outcomes are shaped by whether or not initial movements catalyze counter-movements within fields. Vogus and Davis' (2005) study of anti-takeover legislation takes one step in this direction by analyzing how managerial and local elites counter-organized in response to shareholder activism to obtain legislation that protected corporate managers from raiders and hostile takeovers. Soule and colleagues' analyses go one step further. In analyzing states' adoption of the Equal Rights Amendment (ERA), they simultaneously include variables for the presence or strength of women's movement groups (NOW and AAUW) *and* anti-ERA organizations (Soule and Olzak 2004; Soule and King 2006; see also Soule 2004 on anti-hate crime laws). Ingram and Rao (2004) also address movements and counter-movements, but elaborate a different research strategy, analyzing the passage and repeal of legislation banning chain stores to get at populist mobilization and chain store counter-mobilization over the rise of new market forms. In this way also the capacities of movements to promote change or new path creation rests not just on size, resources or movement strength, but also on the structures – and dynamics – of the political and institutional context.

SOCIAL MOVEMENTS AND NEO-INSTITUTIONAL THEORY: FUTURE DIRECTIONS

We conclude our review by discussing new frontiers for analyzing combinations, interactions and sequences of institutional process and social movements as sources of path creation and change. Future work, we suggest, can and should attend more carefully to key methodological issues of measurement and modeling. It can also fruitfully consider three substantive issues: how movements produce change as political conditions for diffusion; how opportunity structures characterized by institutional heterogeneity, multiple institutions or overlapping fields shape

movements' abilities to translate resources into change; and how movements and institutions co-evolve historically, shaping one another over time. Thinking historically and contextually foregrounds how movements are endogenously produced and always institutionally conditioned. Such an approach captures the substantial benefits of introducing contestation and collective action into institutional analysis. But it does so while avoiding the traps of either invoking movements as extra-institutional forces or simply using movements to assert agency and abandon institutional context entirely. Such an approach, in other words, engages, rather than avoids, the paradoxes of embeddedness and analytical impasses involved in explaining path creation and change (Seo and Creed 2002; Schneiberg 2007). We begin with a discussion of methodological issues, and then emphasize three major substantive categories for future research – *the outcomes of movements, heterogeneity and field overlap* and *the origins of institutions and movements.*

Measuring and Modeling Movements

Much work on movements from a neo-institutional perspective has relied on qualitative and historical methods, playing to those methods' strengths in theory construction and producing a rich body of theory and thick description. Supplementing qualitative work with multivariate quantitative research can not only help systematize theory construction in important ways, it can also help clarify causal relations, isolate effects and strengthen inferences about movement emergence and outcomes.

There are substantial methodological challenges involved in documenting movement effects on path creation and change, challenges that literally multiply as researchers address the moderating influence of existing institutional contexts. At a minimum, documenting effects depends on credibly measuring movement development, strength and activity. Existing research linking movements, organizations and institutions has made real progress here, using the presence of movement organizations or chapters, counts of movement organizations and the number of movement members and chapters to document movement emergence and strength (e.g., Lounsbury 2001; Schneiberg 2002; Soule and King 2006; Schneiberg et al. 2008; Lee and Lounsbury 2015). Future work can also tap such effects by measuring protests and other movement activity, or by using newspaper coverage, public hearings or other measures of controversy to assess whether movements have been able to force issues or new conceptions on the public agenda or call existing arrangements into question (e.g., King and Soule 2007).

Documenting movement effects also rests critically on using multivariate approaches to isolate the effects of movement strength or activity, mobilizing structures, framing and institutional or political opportunity structures (e.g., Vogus and Davis 2005). Absent multivariate designs or careful comparative analysis, inferences about movement effects on change remain vulnerable to counter-claims about spurious relations. Attending explicitly to multiple factors is also particularly important for addressing how existing institutions and opportunity structures enhance or undermine movements' capacities for influence, disruption and new path creation. Research on institutions or opportunity structures sometimes analyzes those factors additively. But whether made by movement scholars or neo-institutionalists, arguments about political opportunity and institutional mediation are fundamentally arguments about interaction effects (Thornton and Occasio 1999; Bartley and Schneiberg 2002; Schneiberg and Clemens 2006). They are arguments that political or institutional configurations amplify or blunt the effects of movement numbers, resources or activities on policies, paths and change. And they can

be implemented empirically in straightforward ways (Amenta and Zylan 1991; Amenta et al. 1992; Schneiberg 2002; Soule 2004; Soule and Olzak 2004).

Mobilization Outcomes: Movements, Politics and Diffusion

A second, more substantive direction for future research revisits the relationship between collective mobilization and diffusion, and reconsiders how movements operate as political forces in promoting the spread of alternatives. Institutionalists have addressed numerous cases of diffusion. Yet the spread of innovations and new forms via conventional institutional dynamics of diffusion, emulation and theorization can spark resistance and counter-mobilization by those unfamiliar with new practices and by powerful vested interests threatened by novel practices (Djelic 1998; Fiss and Zajac 2004; Schneiberg and Soule 2005; Sanders and Tuschke 2007). Such counter-attacks can be covert or openly political, involving the use of state power, and can hinder, halt or even reverse the diffusion of new forms. Under these conditions, diffusion is a contested political process, and the unfolding of canonical diffusion processes may depend on whether or not innovators or advocates can muster political support to place and keep alternatives on the agenda (Schneiberg 2013; also King et al. 2005; Soule and King 2006). Under these conditions, dynamics of diffusion, exposure and emulation depend on supporters' abilities to mobilize sufficient power and resources to secure authorizing legislation, defend alternatives politically, and so on. Under these conditions, diffusing practices are vulnerable to substantial modification and editing as they travel (Czarniawksa and Joerges 1996; Campbell 2004; Sahlin and Wedlin 2008).

Djelic's analysis of the diffusion of American mass production across Europe after World War II, and Schneiberg's study of the diffusion of cooperatives across states and industries in the United States take two steps toward documenting these relations between diffusion and mobilization. As Djelic (1998) shows, key conditions and conduits for the diffusion of American corporate organization were fully in place after 1945, including crisis and the discrediting of European models, the undisputed triumph and legitimation of American models of economic organization, developed networks between the United States and European policy makers, and extensive theorization of the efficiencies of the vertically integrated firm. Yet with efforts via the Marshall Plan to transpose the American model into Europe sometimes blocked by counter-mobilization by unions and business, conventional diffusion dynamics only unfolded in countries where modernizing elites were able to avoid or overcome resistance. Schneiberg (2013) builds on this notion, documenting first that conventional diffusion dynamics of prevalence, exposure and emulation did fuel the spread of cooperative forms across states and industries. Exposure, proximity and prevalence effects mattered, with cooperatives spreading more extensively in states as they became increasingly common in surrounding states, and in industries as they increasingly populated related industries. Yet with corporations organizing in markets and politics to prevent contagion and break links between senders and receivers, prevalence effects and the diffusion of cooperatives across states and industries depended ultimately on effective mobilization by Grangers and anti-corporate forces to defend these forms. Here, movements matter not just as a promoter, theorizer or assembler of frames and new forms, but also as an accumulator of political power – as a bridge or amplifier for diffusion, theorization and the like – and thus an essential *political condition for diffusion* (see also Briscoe et al. 2015).

Considering movements as political conditions for diffusion revises conventional views of the relationship between movements,

institutions and outcomes. Political opportunity structure arguments emphasize how existing institutional structures condition the effects of movements and mobilization on policies and change. Here, *politics and power* are *institutionally* contingent (Amenta et al. 1992; Thornton and Occasio 1999; Schneiberg and Bartley 2001). As institutional systems become more open to challengers or provide them with elite allies, movements' abilities to translate conventional resources into desired outcomes will increase. Favorable institutional contexts amplify the effect of movement numbers, organizations or resources on change outcomes.

Conceptualizing movements as political forces for diffusion inverts this logic, suggesting that *institutional dynamics* of diffusion are *politically* contingent. Whether or not actors can adopt, borrow or translate novel forms depends on the capacities of movements to amass political resources, defend novel forms against counter-attacks, and make or break favorable political contexts for the spread of alternatives. Here, canonical institutional effects depend on movement power. Generally speaking, the likelihood of an organization adopting a new practice increases as professional communities endorse the practice and the number of prior adopters increase. Professional endorsement and increased prevalence of practices increase exposure, familiarity and legitimacy. But, where novel forms are subject to contestation, diffusion will require the mobilization of numbers, resources or organization to defend and protect these alternatives. Absent mobilization, endorsement or prior adoption may have little or no effect on subsequent adoption. Yet as champions of alternatives mobilize and shift the balance of power, endorsement and prior adoptions can have increasingly powerful effects on subsequent adoption, translation or other institutional processes.

While, our knowledge of how movements create favorable political contexts for the diffusion and translation of alternatives is relatively undeveloped, future research can draw on both a multilevel perspective and existing strategies for modeling diffusion. In principle, movements can condition diffusion as a political force at either the field level or within organizations. They can raise (or lower) the infectiousness of innovators and the overall receptivity of organizations to new practices by amassing numbers and resources to contest (or support) field-wide authorities, report (or discredit) success stories in media, enhance (or diminish) the visibility of new practices, or demonstrate (or disprove) the possibility of disruption and change. As movements mobilize effectively at this level, they create political space for alternatives and multiple logics across entire fields, increasing the risk of adoption of novel practices in the aggregate. Alternatively, movements can enhance receptivity by mobilizing 'locally' as political forces within individual organizations, making particular organizations or subsets of organizations more or less susceptible to alternatives that are endorsed or adopted by peers, and fueling differential flows of novel practices across organizations.

Furthermore, as movements become more powerful, they can fuel variation in the practices that diffuse within fields. In the recycling case, activist groups on campuses pushed colleges and universities to go beyond minimal approaches to recycling staffed by part-time custodial staff to adopt programs with full-time ecologically committed coordinators (Lounsbury 2001). In the insurance case, increasing the political strength of anti-corporate forces drove some states beyond limited, anti-discrimination forms of price regulation to fuller control measures that gave regulators authority to evaluate and order changes in rate levels (Schneiberg and Bartley 2001). More generally, mobilization, growing movement strength and counter-mobilization can yield substantial editing and refashioning of practices as they travel across organizations, fields or nations and as efforts to fit or reject

them to local, receiving contexts unfold (Czarniawska and Joerges 1996; Djelic 1998; Sahlin and Wedlin 2008).

Fortunately, well-developed quantitative tools are available for analyzing movements as political conditions for diffusion, provided measures of movement strength or presence are available. To analyze how movements create possibilities for diffusion by shifting the balance of power in fields, models of adoption could employ interaction effects to examine whether the overall political strength of movements moderates the effects on organizational adoption of prior adoption by peers or endorsement by expert-professionals. An interaction effects strategy could be employed at the organizational level, provided measures of the presence, strength or efficacy of movements within organizations are available. Alternatively, one could use heterogeneous diffusion models (Davis and Greve 1997; Strang and Soule 1998; Briscoe 2015) to see whether increasing movement strength within organizations renders them more susceptible to the influence of peers or professions. As Soule's (2006) study of university divestment shows, student protests on campuses against investing in South Africa did not directly promote divestment. But by increasing awareness among administrators of university and surrounding communities, demonstrations were a nagging reminder that rendered colleges and universities more vulnerable to legitimacy pressures, making them more likely to divest as their peers jumped on the bandwagon.

Finally, future research could use existing analytical strategies like competing hazards models to begin to analyze quantitatively how growing movement strength might promote the diffusion of increasingly varied, edited or enhanced alternatives (Lounsbury 2001; Schneiberg and Bartley 2001). In this way, too, institutionalists could address how movements as political forces shape not just the overall flow of practices across fields, but also the differential flow of alternatives and practice variants within them.

Opportunity Structures Revised: Institutional Heterogeneity and Overlapping Fields

Alternatively, future work could retain the conventional imagery of institutions and opportunity structures as contexts for movement effects, enhancing or diminishing the effects of numbers, organization and activity on change, but analyze more systematically how opportunity structures are sometimes constituted by overlapping fields, multiple institutions or institutional complexity. This work could exploit a renewed emphasis in institutional and sociological research on heterogeneity, field structure, inter-institutional systems and the role of linking processes across fields in fueling emergence and change (Greenwood et al. 2011; Fligstein and McAdam 2012; Padgett and Powell 2012; Thornton et al. 2012). It would also substantially develop the central insight of this chapter and work by Morrill and others on interstitial emergence that multiple logics, fields or institutions represent platforms for mobilizing collective action and for disturbing, delegitimating or challenging existing arrangements. Specifically, future work could revise imageries of opportunity structure by analyzing (1) configurations of adjacent or overlapping fields, (2) multiple institutions in a setting, or (3) institutional heterogeneity within fields, and how they condition or moderate movement effects on change.

While there is relatively little of this work to date, scholars studying movements have explored the first possibility. In an important early effort, Evans and Kay (2008) analyze how opportunity structures as 'architectures of field overlap' enabled environmental activists to exploit linkages at the intersection of fields to overcome political weakness, gain a place at the NAFTA negotiating table, and secure side agreements for transnational standards and enforcement. Environmentalists had been closed out of the US trade policy and transnational trade negotiating fields. Yet they were able to piggyback on labor allies and the concordance between environmental critiques of liberalism and a 'fair trade' frame already existing in the US trade policy field, to couple environmental and labor issues within a 'labor–environmental standards' frame. Exploiting concordance between field frames, activists linked and adapted environmentalism with frames ascendant in the US trade policy field to recast political discourse there, getting environmental arguments on the trade agenda, while recasting opposition to NAFTA as concerns with environmental degradation and standards in the transnational trade negotiation field. This let challengers defend themselves against the protectionist label in a context where neoliberal frames prevailed.

At key steps in the negotiations, activists were also able to mobilize rule-making linkages, resource dependencies and networks between non-state fields (environmental and community organizations) and legislative fields (Congress), and between legislative and the US and transnational trade policy fields. During deliberations over authorizations, activists used those links to help opponents develop claims in Congress about US plants moving to Mexico to avoid labor and environmental enforcement, which threw fast track authorization into doubt and prompted the US Trade Representative (USTR) to concede a role for environmental organizations on the USTR advisory committees to the NAFTA talks. During substantive and supplemental negotiations, activists used grassroots mobilization to shift public opinion against free trade, generating pressure in Congress to vote NAFTA down, and activating rule-making linkages between Congress, the US trade field and ultimately the transnational trade field to force Mexican officials to negotiate side agreements for international standards and enforcement mechanisms.

Mora (2014)'s study of the emergence of the Hispanic ethnic category also shows how overlapping fields provide activists with opportunities to exploit cross-field or co-constitutive effects in which changes or dynamics in one field enable, spark and amplify transformations in another. Struggles over ethnic classification in the state field, and deepening boundary-spanning advisory board connections among the Census Bureau's data experts, and organizations like National Council of La Raza and Univision in the civil society, media and marketing fields produced a new ethnic category, Hispanic. The rise of this category not only transformed the Bureau's data gathering and reporting operations, but also generated an important resource that was rapidly appropriated and transposed from the state into civil society and media fields, producing important changes there. In civil society, the new classification prompted the NCLR to redefine its identity as a Hispanic, rather than Chicano, organization, providing it with categories and data for securing foundation grants to support community projects and enabling it to recruit Mexican Americans, Cuban Americans and Puerto Ricans as a pan-ethnic community. In the media field, this category and data enabled Univision to shed its relatively marginalized status as a regional player by reframing itself – and the market – as pan-ethnic, and to work with marketing organizations to develop information on this market, attracting corporate advertisers needed to fund its expansion.

In a similar vein, Gastón (2013) traces how links between fields enabled unions in Southern California to provoke and use crises in the fields of municipal and community organization to reorder the dynamics of contention in the hospitality field. Unions held a weak bargaining position in workplace centered-conflicts with Los Angeles area hotels that were part of global chains and owned by firms that contracted out operations. But they could gain some leverage by allying with local churches, and with community and immigrant rights groups in 'living wage' campaigns and protests over local development projects, targeting hotels that were most vulnerable to disruptions in these proximate domains.

In ongoing work, Mair, Schneiberg and Wagner (2017) pursue the second possibility for revising opportunity structure arguments, tracing how the presence of multiple institutions in a setting enabled activists in rural India to leverage cross- or inter-institutional effects to transform established sanitary practices of open defecation and public bathing. As is increasingly common in such efforts, the organization spearheading this work relied on local, grassroots mobilization of women in villages. It helped women develop advocacy skills and organize themselves via committees to mobilize resources and commitment for constructing private bathing and flush toilet facilities from and for every household in their village. This effort and the transformation of sanitary practices it sought involved a substantial enhancement of the status, dignity and power of women within villages, potentially eroding some pillars of traditional patriarchy.

Yet the project also re-purposed and leveraged the traditional marriage institution of exchanging brides between villages to put added pressures on households via a 'no toilet, no bride' campaign. Participating villages agreed to take or receive brides from other villages that signed up to the program. In effect, activists linked marriage and sanitation and re-purposed marriage institutions to alter institutionalized sanitary practices, a strategy that substantially increased the numbers of new flush toilets constructed and used. This strategy proved particularly effective in villages where women were poor in conventional power resources, suggesting that inter-institutional effect might help challengers overcome political weakness.

Developing these insights quantitatively would be an important step forward, supporting more direct analyses of whether and how the prospects for movement success and the effects of numbers, organizations and protests on outcomes increase (or decrease) in the presence of heterogeneity, multiple institutions or overlapping fields. These analyses could deploy well-developed research designs, reviewed above, that use multivariate approaches and interaction effects to assess whether opportunity structures as overlapping or multiple institutions, logics or fields moderate the effects of mobilization and movements' strengths on outcomes. But charting this new terrain requires developing plausible measures of overlap, heterogeneity and the structural potentials they create for cross-field effects, inter-institutional leverage or destabilizing dissonance within fields.

One possibility suggested by prior work (Evans and Kay 2008; Gastón 2013; Mora 2014) involves measuring opportunity structures as field overlap using networks between fields or the dependence of actors or organizations in one field on resources held by organizations in another. Trade flows, ownership ties, foreign investments, supplier relationships, shared personnel or membership in other organizations all seem potentially useful measures of overlaps, cross-field effects and exposure (e.g., Fiss and Zajac 2004; Sanders and Tuschke 2007), as would the extent to which such flows or ties were concentrated or not across multiple fields. These measures could be developed at the organizational level to assess, for example, whether anti-corporate activists might have better success in making numbers and protests count when a target corporation depends heavily on other organizations in one or a small number of proximate fields for resources, status or personnel. Or they could be developed at the field level to assess potential vulnerabilities created by the aggregate set of ties or dependencies of organizations in one field to those in proximate fields and by the concentration of those ties within one or a small number of fields, a strategy that might even adapt measures of structural autonomy (Burt 1992). One could also envision parallel strategies for tapping variability in associational or rule-making linkages between fields, including the number of regulatory bodies or associations with jurisdiction across fields, the extent to which associations draw members from multiple fields, or whether rule-making structures that span

fields contain veto points for actors to exert cross field influence. It might even be possible to use semantic or discourse analyses to track the rise or salience of frames in one field that might resonate with those in another or to detect parallels or shared terms, arguments or rhetoric between field frames ascendant in proximate domains in order to detect concordances that contain opportunities to transpose or link frames across domains.

Greenwood and colleagues (2011) provide a framework for doing parallel work on opportunity structures as institutional heterogeneity within fields, that is, for analyzing how multiple logics and field structures that refract those logics might expand opportunities for activists to translate numbers, resources and organization into success. One possible starting point would use conventional prevalence measures of forms or discursive terms to tap the salience or spread of logics within fields (see also Schneiberg and Clemens 2006). In contexts historically characterized by a dominant logic, tracking the rising counts or proportions over time of organizations adopting new forms or practices or of the use of discursive frames that instantiate new logics could provide a crude, but direct measure of increasing heterogeneity. In cases less settled or when multiple logics are in play, researchers could instead track the prevalence or proportions of forms or terms tapping each logic, and then combine them in conventional diversity indexes over time. In either case, the measures produced could be used to assess whether increasing heterogeneity amplifies the effects of movements on outcomes, providing activists with increasingly diverse symbolic resources and material practices for subjecting organizations to new evaluative standards, fostering dissonance, calling the legitimacy of existing institutions into question, or forcing them to negotiate new norms or organizing principles. As Greenwood et al. (2011) suggest, activists' ability to subject organizations or key institutions to focused normative pressures via insurgent logics could vary considerably with the structure of fields, including whether different logics are segregated within contained field segments, whether field wide associations prevail and the extent to which decision making authority is dispersed or concentrated within a field. But these in principle could be coded, measured and incorporated into analyses of opportunity structures as institutionally complex.

Less developed are strategies for measuring how multiple institutions in a setting provide leverage for re-purposing or mobilizing inter-institutional effects, highlighting the continued need to build such measures from deep reconstructions of case and context. Mair, Schneiberg and Wagner (2017) provide one example of building a measure of leverage potential in their study of how activists used marriage institutions of inter-village bride exchanges to transform sanitary practices, tracking for each village the number of surrounding villages that embraced new sanitary practices and signed on to the 'no toilet, no bride' campaign. As more villages signed on, the circle of options for non-participating villages narrowed, which enhanced the leverage for change traditional marriage practices provided, and accelerated changes in sanitary practices. Deeply rooted in the idiosyncratic characteristics of the case, this measure of opportunity structure as inter-institutional leverage suggests that future work could fruitfully consider the extent to which activists capture or achieve closure around unrelated but pivotal institutions (or targets' level of dependence on those institutions). Such measures could then permit analyses of whether inter-institutional leverage amplifies the effects of numbers, organization or activity on outcomes, or compensates for weakness in those regards.

Origins of Institutions: History, Sequence and Layering

Centrally important questions in neo-institutionalism are *where do institutions such as fields, practices or paths come from*

and how are they forged or elaborated over time? As sociologists have emphasized, there is never a clean slate; rather, most new kinds of arenas in social life are constructed from the rubble, or flotsam and jetsam, of previous institutions or paths not taken (Stark 1996; Schneiberg 2007) or from variations produced within extant fields (Lounsbury and Crumley 2007). After all, as Meyer and Rowan (1977: 345) observe in their classic piece, 'the building blocks for organizations come to be littered around the social landscape; it takes only a little entrepreneurial energy to assemble them into a structure'. Moreover, new systems are rarely created in one fell swoop, through one wave of diffusion or comprehensive settlements. Rather, paths emerge through multiple waves, over time, via sequences or successive stages of translation, layering, theorization and assembly that elaborate and innovate on previous, partial accomplishments (Streeck and Thelen 2005). And at the core of all field and path creation is some sort of collective mobilization or movement, not just a single burst of organization, but also waves or cycles of mobilization.

The parallels between institutionalist imageries of path creation as waves of layering, on the one hand, and movement research on cycles of mobilization and protest, on the other, suggest that linking these two conceptions can provide new insights for future research on path creation and change, adding an important historical dimension to neo-institutional scholarship. Movement scholars have highlighted the sequencing of social movements and cycles of protest (e.g., Tarrow 1998), tracing, among other things, how contentious politics that involve tactics such as protest are transformed into more conventional forms of political action such as lobbying (Meyer and Tarrow 1998; also Kriesi et al. 1995). Minkoff (1993, 1997) extends the analysis of sequences, adding an organizational dimension, and showing how the proliferation of radical organizations created a favorable context, legitimacy and political opportunities for subsequent organization by advocacy and practitioner groups, institutionalizing civil rights more deeply in American politics. Such sequences can even involve shifts in scale and loci, including shifts of movements from outside to inside institutions as tempered radicals (Meyerson and Scully 1995) emerge to leverage external pressures or accomplishments to refashion the workings of organizations from within (Zald and Berger 1978; Kellogg 2009; Soule 2009), and vice versa, as when activists working inside institutions or organizations find their efforts blocked, and opt instead to mobilize outside existing organizations (Schneiberg 2002, 2017).

Institutionalists have just begun to think in these terms, but efforts to analyze path and field creation in terms of waves or sequences of mobilization, institutional development and layering, with outcomes of earlier mobilizations producing inputs for later efforts. Lounsbury, Ventresca and Hirsh (2003) took one step in this direction, showing how efforts by 'outsider' environmental movements in the 1960s and 1970s to restructure capitalism via not-for-profit, community based recycling centers unintentionally laid foundations for subsequent mobilization by insider groups in the 1980s to create a for-profit recycling industry. Most non-profit recycling centers proved economically non-viable, but they nonetheless trained a generation of Americans in the habits of saving, cleaning and sorting their trash, a critical cultural infrastructure for the creation of markets based on curb-side pick up.

Schneiberg (2007, 2013, 2017) likewise moves in this direction in analyzing efforts by populist and radical anti-corporations to restructure American corporate capitalism in the late nineteenth and early twentieth centuries. For the most part, these movements faced decisive defeats in their efforts to contest corporate capitalism and collapsed. But even though defeated, they nevertheless left behind a variety of organizational, cultural and institutional legacies – bits and pieces

of the alternative orders they had pursued, including theories of order, regulatory fragments, local movement chapters, systems of mutual, cooperative and publicly owned enterprise in key industries. These legacies of previous mobilization, in turn, served as resources, platforms and infrastructures for subsequent mobilization in the same or related industries, first, in the Progressive era, and then in the early New Deal. Indeed, successive waves of reformers and anti-corporate forces built or transposed alternatives out from insurance and other sites of mutual organization into dairy and grain, electrical utilities and banking, elaborating a secondary path of industrial order in the US economy.

Nor are these processes confined to economic industries or organizations. As Armstrong (2002, 2005) illustrates, the legacy of initial movements may also include the establishment of new identities, cultural tools such as frames and logics, and 'creative contexts' that enable subsequent groups to continue struggles, mobilize and realize new gains in their efforts. The rise of the New Left in the 1960s enabled the creation of new kinds of lesbian/gay organizational identities in San Francisco in the early 1970s. The development of gay identity politics, in turn, proved crucial both in the proliferation of lesbian/gay organizations and in enabling change within mainstream organizations such as the establishment of domestic partner benefits (Creed and Scully 2000; Scully and Creed 2005). And as Alfinito Vieira and Quack (2016) show in their study of indigenous movements in Brazil, sequences of mobilization and institutional development can unfold across levels, supporting changes virtually impossible under initial conditions. Through the late 1960s, indigenous peoples in Brazil were fully disenfranchised under a 'tutorship regime' and military dictatorship that denied claims to land, sought to eradicate indigenous identities and drove indigenous communities off traditional domains into reservations. These policies also forced into exile the anthropologists who might publicize this state of affairs, inadvertently fueling the formation of a transnational network of critical anthropologists, deepening ties and institutional cross-referencing between this network, liberation theology missionaries and international journalists, and a series of key institutional developments. These included the Barbados Declaration, which articulated a critique of indigenism in Latin America, the organization of the Indigenous Missionary Council by progressive Jesuits to help communities advance land claims, and the formation of indigenous support organizations. They also included reports by international journalists, NGOs and even the state's own bureaucracy that embarrassed the regime, subjected it to growing legitimacy pressures, and prompted defensive reforms, most notably the Indigenous Statute, in an effort to demonstrate the regime's alignment with indigenous rights. That statute had little immediate relevance for indigenous communities. But along with the support organizations and National Assemblies, it created opportunity structures in Brazil that enabled the indigenous movement to advance and secure measures during democratization and the National Constitutional Assembly that institutionalized indigenous identities and claims to land in the new constitution.

CONCLUSION

Overall, the approach to movements and institutions that we advocate celebrates the heterogeneity of actors, multiple logics and practice variation. A focus on such multiplicity revises the isomorphic imagery of the canonical two-stage diffusion and punctuated equilibrium models. Such a perspective concentrates less on the contagion of unitary practices or a singular rationality, but rather on multiple forms of rationality that inform the decision making of actors in fields (Bourdieu 1984), and provide foundations for

ongoing struggle and contestation. This conceptualization of institutionalization and fields as multiple, fragmented and contested and is a crucial ontological starting point for a new wave and generation of institutional scholars. And when combined with a renewed attention to movements, it directs analytical attention to how historical legacies of prior social action become embedded in existing fields, providing bases for sequences of mobilization, and the construction of new paths from the elements or ruins of old or forgotten orders. Early work in this direction has proven fruitful and promises to propel institutional analysis for many years to come.

REFERENCES

Alfinito Vieira, A. and Quack, S. 2016). Trajectories of transnational mobilization for indigenous rights in Brazil: Rediscovering the role of forgotten political actors. *Revista de Administração de Empresas*, 56, 380–394.

Amenta, E., Carruthers, B. and Zylan, Y. (1992). A hero for the aged? The Townsend movement, the political mediation model, and the U.S. old-age policy, 1934–1950. *American Journal of Sociology*, 98, 308–339.

Amenta, E. and Zylan, Y. (1991). It happened here: Political opportunity, the new institutionalism and the Townsend movement. *American Sociological Review*, 56, 250–265.

Armstrong, E.A. (2002). Crisis, collective creativity, and the generation of new organizational forms: The transformation of lesbian/gay organizations in San Francisco. *Research in the Sociology of Organizations*, 19, 369–406.

Armstrong, E.A. (2005). From struggle to settlement: The crystallization of a field of lesbian/gay organizations in San Francisco, 1969–1973. In G.F. Davis, D. McAdam, W.R. Scott and M.N. Zald (eds), *Social Movements and Organization Theory*. Cambridge: Cambridge University Press. pp. 161–188.

Baron, J.P., Dobbin, F. and Jennings, P.D. (1986). War and peace: The evolution of modern personnel administration in U.S. industry. *American Journal of Sociology*, 92, 250–283.

Bartley, T. (2007). Institutional emergence in an era of globalization: The rise of transnational private regulation of labor and environmental conditions. *American Journal of Sociology*, 113, 297–351.

Bartley, T. and Schneiberg, M. (2002). Rationality and institutional contingency: The varying politics of economic regulation in the fire insurance industry. *Sociological Perspectives*, 45(1), 47–79.

Beckert, J. (1999). Agency, entrepreneurs, and institutional change. The role of strategic choice and institutionalized practices in organizations. *Organization Studies*, 20, 777–799.

Bertels, S., Hoffman, A.J, and DeJordy, R. (2014). The varied work of challenger movements: Identifying challenger roles in the US environmental movement. *Organization Studies*, 35, 1171–1210.

Boli, J. and Thomas, G. (eds) (1999). *Constructive World Culture: International Nongovernmental Organizations Since 1875*. Stanford, CA: Stanford University Press.

Bourdieu, P. (1984). *Distinction: A Social Critique of the Judgement of Taste*. Cambridge, MA: Harvard University Press.

Briscoe, F. (2015). STATA heterogeneous diffusion routine.[online]. Available at: www.personal.psu.edu/fsb10/index/STATA-hdiff.html [accessed 6 November 2015].

Briscoe, F., Gupta, A. and Anner, M. (2015). Social activism and practice diffusion: How activist tactics affect non-targeted organizations. *Administrative Science Quarterly*, 60: 300–332.

Briscoe, F. and Safford, S. (2008). The Nixon-in-China effect: Activism, imitation, and the institutionalization of contentious practices. *Administrative Science Quarterly*, 53, 460–491.

Burt, R.S. (1992). *Structural Holes: The Social Structure of Competition*. Cambridge, MA: Harvard University Press.

Campbell, J. (2004). *Institutional Change and Globalization*. Princeton, PJ: Princeton University Press.

Campbell, J. (2005). Where do we stand? Common mechanisms in organizations and social movements research. In G.F. Davis, D. McAdam, W.R. Scott and M.N. Zald (eds), *Social Movements and Organization Theory*. Cambridge: Cambridge University Press. pp. 41–68.

Carroll, G.R. and Swaminathan, A. (2000). Why the microbrewery movement? Organizational dynamics of resource partitioning in the U.S. brewing industry. *American Journal of Sociology*, 106, 715–762.

Carruthers, B.G. and Babb, S. (1996). The color of money and the nature of value: Greenbacks and gold in Postbellum America. *American Journal of Sociology*, 101, 1556–1591.

Clemens, E.S. (1993). Organizational repertoires and institutional change: Womens' groups and the transformation of U.S. politics, 1890–1920. *American Journal of Sociology*, 98, 755–798.

Clemens, E.S. (1997). *The People's Lobby: Organizational Innovation and the Rise of Interest Group Politics in the United States, 1890–1925*. Chicago, IL: University of Chicago Press.

Clemens, E.S. and Cook, J. (1999). Politics and institutionalism: Explaining durability and change. *Annual Review of Sociology*, 25, 441–466.

Colyvas, J. and Powell, W. (2006). Roads to institutionalization. *Research in Organizational Behavior*, 27, 305–353.

Creed, W.E.D. and Scully, M.A. (2000). Songs of ourselves: Employees' deployment of social identity in workplace encounters. *Journal of Management Inquiry*, 9, 391–412.

Creed, W.E.D., Scully, M.A. and Austin, J.R. (2002). Clothes make the person: The tailoring of legitimating accounts and the social construction of identity. *Organization Science*, 13, 475–496.

Czarniawska, B. and Joerges, B. (1996). Travels of ideas. In B. Czarniawska and G. Sevón (eds), *Translating Organizational Change*. New York: Walter de Gruyter. pp 13–47.

Davis, G.F. and Greve, H.R. (1997). Corporate elite networks and governance changes in the 1980s. *American Journal of Sociology*, 103, 1–37.

Davis, G.F. and Thompson, T. (1994). A social movement perspective on corporate control. *Administrative Science Quarterly*, 39, 141–173.

Davis, G.F. and Zald, M.N. (2005). Social change, social theory, and the convergence of movements and organizations. In G.F. Davis, D. McAdam, W.R. Scott and M.N. Zald (eds), *Social Movements and Organization Theory*. Cambridge: Cambridge University Press. pp. 335–350.

De Bakker, F., Hond, R., King, B. and Weber, K. (2013). Social movements, civil society and corporations. *Organization Studies*, 34(5–6), 573–593.

den Hond, F. and de Bakker, F.G.A. (2007). Ideologically motivated activism: How activist groups influence corporate social change activities. *Academy of Management Review*, 32, 901–924.

DiMaggio, P.J. (1988). Interest and agency in institutional theory. In Lynne Zucker (ed.), *Institutional Patterns and Organizations*. Cambridge, MA: Ballinger. pp. 3–22.

Djelic, M. (1998). *Exporting the American Model: Postwar Transformations of European Business*. Oxford: Oxford University Press.

Djelic, M. and Quack, S. (eds) (2003). *Globalization and Institutions. Redefining the Rules of the Economic Game*. Cheltenham: Edward Elgar.

Djelic, M. and Sahlin-Andersson, K. (eds) (2006). *Transnational Governance: Institutional Dynamics of Regulation*. Cambridge: Cambridge University Press.

Dobbin, F. and Dowd, T. (1997). How policy shapes competition: Early railroad foundings in Massachusetts. *Administrative Science Quarterly*, 42, 501–529.

Edelman, L.B. (1990). Legal environments and organizational governance: The expansion of due process in the American workplace. *American Journal of Sociology*, 95, 1401–1440.

Edelman, L.B. (1992). Legal ambiguity and symbolic structures: Organizational mediation of civil rights law. *American Journal of Sociology*, 97, 1531–1576.

Edelman, L.B. (2006). Constructed legalities: The endogeneity of law. In W. Powell and D. Jones (eds), *How Institutions Change*. Chicago, IL: University of Chicago Press.

Elsbach, K. and Sutton, R. (1992). Acquiring organizational legitimacy through illegitimate actions: A marriage of institutional and impression management theories. *Academy of Management Journal*, 4, 699–738.

Evans, R. and Kay, T. (2008). How environmentalists 'greened' trade policy: strategic action and the architecture of field overlap. *American Sociological Review* 73, 970–91.

Fiss, P.C. and Zajac, E.J. (2004). The diffusion of ideas over contested terrain: The (non)adoption of a shareholder value orientation among German firms. *Administrative Science Quarterly*, 49 pp. 501–534.

Fligstein, N. (1990). *The Transformation of Corporate Control*. Cambridge, MA: Harvard University Press.

Fligstein, N. (1996). A political-cultural approach to market institutions. *American Sociological Review*, 61, 656–673.

Fligstein, N. (2001). *The Architecture of Markets: An Economic Sociology of Twenty-First-Century Capitalist Societies*. Princeton, NJ: Princeton University Press.

Fligstein, N. and McAdam, D. (2012). *A Theory of Fields*. Oxford: Oxford University Press.

Frank, D.B., Hironaka, A. and Schofer, E. (2000). Environmentalism as a global institution. *American Sociological Review*, 65, 122–127.

Galaskiewicz, J. and Wasserman, S. (1989). Mimetic processes within an interorganizational field: An empirical test. *Administrative Science Quarterly*, 34, 454–479.

Garud, R. and Karnoe, P. (eds) (2001). *Path Dependence and Creation*. Mahwah, NJ: Lawrence Erlbaum.

Gastón, P. (2013). Community and union: Politicizing workplace conflict in the finance era. *Social Science History Association*, Chicago, November 2013.

Greenwood, R. and Hinings, C.R. (1996). Understanding radical organizational change: Bringing together the old and the new institutionalism. *Academy of Management Review*, 21, 1022–1054.

Greenwood R., Raynard, M., Kodeih, F., Micelotta, E.R. and Lounsbury, M. (2011). Institutional complexity and organizational responses. *Academy of Management Annals*, 5, 317–371.

Greenwood, R., Suddaby, R. and Hinings, C.R. (2002). Theorizing change: The role of professional associations in the transformation of institutional fields. *Academy of Management Journal*, 45, 58–80.

Hardy, C. and Maguire, S. (2008). Discourse, field-configuring events, and change in organizations and institutional fields: Narratives of DDT and the Stockholm Convention. *Academy of Management Journal*, 53, 1365–1392.

Hiatt, S., Grandy, J. and Lee B. (2015). Organizational responses to public and private politics: An analysis of climate change activists and U.S. oil and gas firms. *Organization Science*, 26, 1769–1786.

Hironaka, A. (2014). *Greening the Globe: World Society and Environmental Change*. Cambridge: Cambridge University Press.

Hironaka, A. and Schofer, E. (2002). Decoupling in the environmental arena: The case of environmental impact assessments. In A. Hoffman and M. Ventresca (eds), *Organizations, Policy and the Natural Environment*. Stanford, CA: Stanford University Press.

Hoffman, A. (1999). Institutional evolution and change: Environmentalism and the US Chemical Industry. *Academy of Management Journal*, 42, 351–71.

Hwang, H. and Powell, W.W. (2005). Institutions and entrepreneurship. In S.A. Alvarez, R. Agarwal and O. Sorenson (eds), *Handbook of Entrepreneurship Research*. Dordrecht: Kluwer. pp. 179–210.

Ingram, P. and Rao, H. (2004) Store wars: The enactment and repeal of anti-chain store legislation in America. *American Journal of Sociology*, 110, 446–487.

Ingram, P., Yue, L.Q. and Rao, H. (2010). Trouble in store: Probes, protests and store openings by Wal-Mart: 1998–2005. *American Journal of Sociology*, 116, 53–92.

Jepperson, R. (1991). Institutions, institutional effects, and institutionalism. In W.W. Powell and P.J. DiMaggio (eds), *The New Institutionalism in Organizational Analysis*. Chicago, IL: University of Chicago Press. pp, 143–163.

Keck, M.E. and Sikkink, K. (1998). *Activists Beyond Borders: Advocacy Networks in International Politics*. Ithaca, NY: Cornell University Press.

Kellogg, K.C. (2009). Operating room: relational spaces and microinstitutional change in surgery. *American Journal of Sociology*, 115, 657–711.

King, B.G. (2008). A political mediation model of corporate response to social movement activism. *Administrative Science Quarterly*, 53, 395–421.

King, B.G., Cornwall, M. and Dahlin, E.C. (2005). Winning woman suffrage one step at a time: Social movements and the logic of the legislative process. *Social Forces*, 83, 1211–1234.

King B.G. and Pearce, N.A. (2011). The contentiousness of markets: Politics, social movements, and institutional change in markets. *Annual Review of Sociology*, 36, 249–267.

King, B.G. and Soule, S.A. (2007). Social movements as extra-institutional entrepreneurs: The effect of protests on stock price returns. *Administrative Science Quarterly*, 52, 413–442.

Kriesi, H., Koopmans, R., Duyvendak, J.W. and Giugni, M.G. (1995). *The Politics of New Social Movements in Western Europe: A Comparative Analysis*. Minneapolis, MN: University of Minnesota Press.

Lampel, J. and Meyer, A.D. (2008). Field-configuring events as structuring mechanisms: How conferences, ceremonies, and trade shows constitute new technologies. *Journal of Management Studies*, 45, 1025–1035.

Laraña, E., Johnston, H. and Gusfield, J.R. (eds) (1994). *New Social Movements: From Ideology to Identity*. Philadelphia, PA: Temple University Press.

Lawrence, T.B., Leca, B. and Zilber, T.B. (2013). Institutional work: Current research, new directions and overlooked issues. *Organization Studies*, 34, 1023–1033.

Lee, M.D. and Lounsbury, M. (2015). Filtering institutional logics: Community logic variation and differential responses to the institutional complexity of toxic waste. *Organization Science*, 26, 847–866.

Lounsbury, M. (2001). Institutional sources of practice variation: Staffing college and university recycling programs. *Administrative Science Quarterly*, 46, 29–56.

Lounsbury, M. (2005). Institutional variation in the evolution of social movements: Competing logics and the spread of recycling advocacy groups. In G.F. Davis, D. McAdam, W.R. Scott and M.N. Zald (eds), *Social Movements and Organization Theory*. Cambridge: Cambridge University Press. pp. 73–95.

Lounsbury, M. (2007). A tale of two cities: Competing logics and practice variation in the professionalizing of mutual funds. *Academy of Management Journal*, 50(2): 289–307.

Lounsbury, M. and Crumley, E.T. (2007). New practice creation: An institutional approach to innovation. *Organization Studies*, 28, 993–1012.

Lounsbury, M. and Glynn, M.A. (2001). Cultural entrepreneurship: Stories, legitimacy and the acquisition of resources. *Strategic Management Journal*, 22, 545–564.

Lounsbury, M., Ventresca, M.J. and Hirsch, P.M. (2003). Social movements, field frames and industry emergence: A cultural-political perspective of U.S. recycling. *Socio Economic Review*, 1, 71–104.

Maguire, S., Hardy, C. and Lawrence, T.B. (2004). Institutional entrepreneurship in emerging fields: HIV/AIDS treatment advocacy in Canada. *Academy of Management Journal*, 47(5), 657–679.

Mair, J., Schneiberg, M. and Wagner, S. (2017). No toilet, no bride: Gender power, inter-institutional leverage and sanitary practices in rural India. Unpublished ms.

Marquis, C. and Lounsbury, M. (2007). Vive la résistance: Competing logics and the consolidation of U.S. community banking. *Academy of Management Journal*, 50, 799–820.

McAdam, D. (1982). *Political Process and the Development of Black Insurgency, 1930–1970*. Chicago, IL: University of Chicago Press.

McAdam, D. (1988). *Freedom Summer*. Oxford: Oxford University Press.

McAdam, D. (1999). *Political Process and the Development of Black Insurgency, 1930–1970*, revised edn. Chicago, IL: University of Chicago Press.

McAdam, D., McCarthy, J.D. and Zald, M.D. (1996). *Comparative Perspectives on Social Movements*. NY: Cambridge University Press.

McAdam, D. and Scott, W.R. (2005). Organizations and movements. In G.F. Davis, D. McAdam, W.R. Scott and M.N. Zald (eds), *Social Movements and Organization Theory*. Cambridge: Cambridge University Press. pp. 4–40.

McDonnell, M.H. and King, B. (2013). Keeping up appearances: Reputation threat and prosocial responses to social movement boycotts. *Administrative Science Quarterly*, 58, 387–419.

McDonnell, M.H., King, B.G. and Soule, S.A. (2015). A dynamic process model of contentious politics: Activist targeting and corporate receptivity to social challenges. *American Sociological Review*, 80, 654–678.

Meyer, D.S. and Tarrow, S. (eds) (1998). *The Social Movement Society*. Lanham, MD: Rowman and Littlefield.

Meyer, J.W., Boli, J., Thomas, G. and Ramirez, F. (1997). World society and the nation-state. *American Journal of Sociology*, 103, 144–181.

Meyer, J.W. and Rowan, B. (1977). Institutionalized organizations: Formal structure as myth and ceremony. *American Sociological Review*, 83, 340–363.

Meyerson, D.E, and Scully, M.A. (1995). Tempered radicalism and the politics of ambivalence and change. *Organization Science*, 6 (5), 585–600.

Minkoff, D.C. (1993). The organization of survival: Women's and racial-ethnic voluntarist and activist organizations, 1955–1985. *Social Forces*, 71, 887–908.

Minkoff, D.C. (1997). The sequencing of social movements. *American Sociological Review*, 62, 779–799.

Moore, K. (1996). Organizing integrity: American science and the creation of public interest organizations, 1955–1975. *American Journal of Sociology*, 101, 1592–1627.

Moore, K. (2013). *Disrupting Science: Social Movements, American Scientists, and the Politics of the Military, 1945–1975*. Princeton, NJ: Princeton University Press.

Moore, K. and Hala, N. (2002). Organizing identity: The creation of science for the people. *Research in the Sociology of Organizations*, 19, 311–343.

Mora, G.C. (2014). Cross-field effects and ethnic classification: The institutionalization of Hispanic panethnicity, 1965 to 1990. *American Sociological Review*, 79, 183–210.

Morrill, C. (2006). Institutional change and interstitial emergence: The growth of alternative dispute resolution in American law, 1965–1995. In W. Powell and D. Jones (eds), *How Institutions Change*. Chicago, IL: University of Chicago Press.

Meyerson, D and Scully, M. (1995). Tempered Radicalism and the Politics of Ambivalence and Change. *Organization Science*, 6: 585–600.

Padgett, J.F. and Powell, W.W. (2012). *The Emergence of Organizations and Markets*. Princeton, NJ: Princeton University Press.

Pierson, P. (2000). Increasing returns, path dependence, and the study of politics. *American Political Science Review*, 94, 251–267.

Raeburn, N. (2004). *Inside Out: The Struggle for Lesbian, Gay and Bisexual Rights in the Workplace*. Minneapolis, MN: University of Minnesota Press.

Rao, H. (1998). Caveat emptor: The construction of nonprofit consumer watchdog organizations. *American Journal of Sociology*, 103, 912–961.

Rao, H., Monin, P. and Durand, R. (2003). Institutional change in Toque Ville: Nouvelle cuisine as an identity movement in French gastronomy. *American Journal of Sociology*, 4, 795–843.

Rao, H., Morrill, C. and Zald, M.N. (2000). Power plays: Social movements, collective action and new organizational forms. *Research in Organizational Behavior*, 22, 237–282.

Rao, H., Yue, L.Q. and Ingram, P. (2011). Laws of attraction: Regulatory arbitrage in the face of activism in right-to-work states. *American Sociological Review*, 76, 365–385.

Sahlin, K. and Wedlin, L. (2008). Circulating ideas: Imitation, translation and editing. In R. Greenwood, C. Oliver, R. Suddaby and K. Sahlin-Andersson (eds), *The SAGE Handbook of Organizational Institutionalism*. London: Sage. pp. 220–242.

Sanders, G. and Tuschke, A. (2007). The adoption of institutionally contested practices: The emergence of stock option pay in Germany. *Academy of Management Journal*, 50, 33–56.

Schneiberg, M. (1999). Political and institutional conditions for governance by association: Private order and price controls in American fire insurance. *Politics and Society*, 27, 67–103.

Schneiberg, M. (2002). Organizational heterogeneity and the production of new forms: Politics, social movements and mutual companies in American fire insurance, 1900–1930. *Research in the Sociology of Organizations*, 19, 39–89.

Schneiberg, M. (2005). Combining new institutionalisms: Explaining institutional change in American property insurance. *Sociological Forum*, 1, 93–137.

Schneiberg, M. (2007). What's on the path? Path dependence, organizational diversity and the problem of institutional change in the US economy, 1900–1950. *Socio-Economic Review*, 5, 47–80.

Schneiberg, M. (2013). Movements as political conditions for diffusion: Anti-corporate movements and the spread of cooperative forms in American capitalism. *Organization Studies*, 34, 653–82.

Schneiberg, M. (forthcoming 2017). Resisting and regulating corporations through ecologies of alternative enterprise: Insurance and electricity in the US case. In A. Spicer and G. Baars (eds), *The Corporation: A Critical, Interdisciplinary Handbook*. Cambridge: Cambridge University Press.

Schneiberg, M. and Bartley, T. (2001). Regulating American industries: Markets, politics, and the institutional determinants of fire insurance regulation. *American Journal of Sociology*, 107, 101–146.

Schneiberg, M. and Soule, S.A. (2005). Institutionalization as a contested, multilevel process: The case of rate regulation in American fire insurance. In G.F. Davis, D. McAdam, W.R. Scott and M.N. Zald (eds), *Social Movements and Organization Theory* Cambridge: Cambridge University Press. pp. 122–160.

Schneiberg, M. and Clemens, E.S. (2006). The typical tools for the job: Research strategies in institutional analysis. *Sociological Theory*, 3, 195–227.

Schneiberg, M., King, M. and Smith, T. (2008). Social movements and organizational form: Cooperative alternatives to corporations in the American insurance, dairy and grain industries. *American Sociological Review*, 73: 635–667.

Schofer, E. and Hironaka, A. (2005). The effects of world society on environmental protection outcomes. *Social Forces*, 84, 25–47.

Schofer, E. and Meyer. J. (2005). The worldwide expansion of higher education in the twentieth century. *American Sociological Review*, 70, 898–920.

Scott, W.R. (1994). Conceptulizing organizational fields: Linking organizations and societal systems. In Hans-Ulrich Derlien, Uta Gerhardt and Fritz W. Scharpf (eds), *Systemrationalitat und Partial Interesse*. Baden-Baden, Germany: Nomos Verlagsgellschaft. pp. 203–221.

Scott, W.R. (2001). *Institutions and Organizations*, 2nd edn. Newbury Park, CA: Sage.

Scott, W.R., Ruef, M., Mendel, P. and Caronna, C. (2000). *Institutional Change and Organizations:*

Transformation of a Healthcare Field. Chicago, IL: University of Chicago Press.

Scully, M. and Creed, W.E.D. (2005) Subverting our stories of subversion. In G. Davis, D. McAdam, W.R. Scott and M. Zald (eds), *Social Movements and Organizational Theory*. New York: Cambridge University Press. pp. 310–332.

Scully, M. and Segal, A. (2002). Passion with an umbrella: Grassroots activists in the workplace. *Research in the Sociology of Organizations*, 19, 127–170.

Seo, M. and Creed, W.E.D. (2002). Institutional contradictions, praxis, and institutional change: A dialectical perspective. *Academy of Management Review*, 27, 222–247.

Sine, W.D. and Lee, B.H. (2009). Tilting at windmills? The environmental movement and the emergence of the U.S. wind energy sector. *Administrative Science Quarterly*, 54, 123–155.

Skretny, J. (2002). *The Minority Rights Revolution*. Cambridge, MA: Harvard University Press.

Smith, J. (2008). *Social Movements for Global Democracy*. Baltimore, MD: Johns Hopkins Press.

Soule, S. (2004). Going to the chapel? Same-sex marriage bans in the United States, 1973–2000. *Social Problems*, 4, 453–477.

Soule, S. (2006). Divestment by colleges and universities in the United States: institutional pressures toward isomorphism. In W. Powell and D. Jones (eds), *How Institutions Change*. Chicago, IL: University of Chicago Press.

Soule, S.A. (2009). *Contention and Corporate Social Responsibility*. New York, NY: Cambridge University Press.

Soule, S. and Olzak, S. (2004). When do movements matter? The politics of contingency and the Equal Rights Amendment. *American Sociological Review*, 69, 473–97.

Soule, S. and King, B. (2006). The stage of the policy process and the Equal Rights Amendment, 1972–1982. *American Journal of Sociology*, 6, 1871–1909.

Strang, D. and Chang, M.Y. (1993). The International Labor Organization and the welfare state: Institutional effects on national welfare spending, 1960–1980. *International Organization*, 47, 235–262.

Strang, D. and Meyer, J.W. (1993). Institutional conditions for diffusion. *Theory and Society*, 22, 487–512.

Strang, D. and Jung, D. (2005). Organizational change as an orchestrated social movement: Recruitment to a corporate quality initiative. In G.F. Davis, D. McAdam, W.R. Scott and M.N. Zald (eds), *Social Movements and Organization Theory*. Cambridge: Cambridge University Press. pp. 280–309.

Strang, D. and Soule, S.A. (1998). Diffusion in organizations and social movements: From hybrid corn to poison pills. *Annual Review of Sociology*, 24, 265–290.

Stark, D. (1996). Recombinant property in East European capitalism. *American Journal of Sociology*, 101, 993–1027.

Streeck, W. and Thelen, K. (2005). *Beyond Continuity: Institutional Change in Advanced Political Economies*. Oxford: Oxford University Press.

Stryker, R. (2000). Legitimacy processes as institutional politics: Implications for theory and research in the sociology of organizations. *Research in the Sociology of Organizations*, 17, 179–223.

Sutton, J.R. and Dobbin, F. (1996). Responses to legal uncertainty in U.S. firms, 1955 to 1985. *American Sociological Review*, 61, 794–811.

Sutton, R., Dobbin, F., Meyer, J.W. and Richard Scott, W. (1994). The legalization of the workplace. *American Journal of Sociology*, 99, 944–971.

Tarrow, S. (1998). *Power in Movement: Social Movements and Contentious Politics*, 2nd edn. New York: Cambridge University Press.

Thelen, K. (2004). *How Institutions Evolve: The Political Economy of Skills in Germany, Britain, the United States and Japan*. New York, Cambridge University Press.

Thornton, P.H. and Ocasio, W. (1999). Institutional logics and the historical contingency of power in organizations: Executive succession in the higher education publishing industry, 1958–1990. *American Journal of Sociology*, 105, 801–843.

Thornton, P.H., Ocasio, W. and Lounsbury, M. (2012). *The Institutional Logics Perspective: A New Approach to Culture, Structure and Process*. Oxford: Oxford University Press.

Tolbert, P.S. and Zucker, L.G. (1983). Institutional sources of change in the formal structure of organizations: The diffusion of civil service reform, 1880–1935. *Administrative Science Quarterly*, 28, 22–39.

van Wijk, J., Stam, W., Elfring, T., Zietsma, C. and den Hond, F. (2013). Activists and incumbents structuring change: The interplay of agency, culture, and networks in field evolution. *Academy of Management Journal*, 56, 358–386.

Vasi, I.B. and King, B. (2012). Social movements, risk perceptions, and economic outcomes. *American Sociological Review*, 77, 573–596.

Vasi, I.B., Walker, E.T., Johnson, J.S. and Tan, H.F. (2015). No fracking way! Documentary film, discursive opportunity, and local opposition against hydraulic fracturing in the United States, 2010 to 2013. *American Sociological Review*, 80, 934–959.

Vogus, T.J. and Davis, G.F. (2005). Elite mobilizations for antitakeover legislation, 1982–1990. In G.F. Davis, D. McAdam, W.R. Scott and M.N. Zald (eds), *Social Movements and Organization Theory*. Cambridge: Cambridge University Press. pp. 96–121.

Wade, J.B., Swaminathan, A. and Saxon, M.S. (1998). Normative and resource flow consequences of local regulations in the American brewing industry,

1845–1918. *Administrative Science Quarterly*, 43, 905–935.

Walker, E.T. (2014). *Grassroots for Hire: Public Affairs Consultants in American Democracy*. Cambridge: Cambridge University Press.

Walker, E.T. and Rea, C.M. (2014). The political mobilization of firms and industries. *Annual Review of Sociology*, 40, 281–304.

Weber, K., Heinze, K.L. and deSoucey, M. (2008). Forage for thought: Mobilizing codes in the movement for grass-fed meat and dairy products. *Administrative Science Quarterly*, 53, 529–567.

Werner, M.D. and Cornelissen, J.P. (2014). Framing the change: Switching and blending frames and their role in instigating institutional change. *Organization Studies*, 35, 1449–1472.

Yue, L.Q. (2015). Community constraints on the efficacy of elite mobilization: The issuance of currency substitutes during the Panic of 1907. *American Journal of Sociology*, 120, 1–46.

Zald, M.N. and Berger, M.A. (1978). Social movements in organizations: Coup d'état, insurgency, and mass movements. *American Journal of Sociology*, 83, 823–861.

Zald, M.N. and Lounsbury, M. (2010). The Wizards of Oz: Towards an institutional approach to elites, expertise and command posts. *Organization Studies*, 31, 963–996.

Opening the Black Box: The Microfoundations of Institutions

Walter W. Powell and Claus Rerup

INTRODUCTION

In the first edition of this handbook, Powell and Colyvas (2008) argued that much could be gained by making the microfoundations of institutional theory more explicit. That chapter concluded that the standard macro accounts associated with institutional theory needed an accompanying argument at the micro level. Our new essay represents such a journey, with stops along the way at several ports of call. We wend our way through such themes as enactment, interpretation, sense-making and transposition. The central message of this voyage is that institutions are sustained, altered and extinguished as they are enacted by collections of individuals in everyday situations. We expand on the earlier chapter by building on Pierre Bourdieu's (1984) argument that to understand important aspects of French society, investigators need to look into daily affairs and the people who conduct them. In this respect, we embrace Jim March's (2008) observation that

'history is not produced by the dramatic actions and postures of leaders, but by complex combinations of large numbers of small actions by unimportant people'.

From a micro perspective, institutions are reproduced through the routine activities of ensembles of individuals. Members of organizations go about their daily practices, discover puzzles or anomalies in their work, problematize these questions, posit theories and develop answers to them, drawing on their existing stock of knowledge. In turn, participants ascribe meaning to their solutions. In so doing, they develop rules of thumb, or more abstractly theories, and reproduce new understandings that become taken-for-granted. When the established routines for conducting everyday life prove limiting, people begin to search and perhaps even experiment with new lines of activity.

Seen in this light, institutional transformation is often rather subtle, not particularly abrupt and apparent only after a considerable period of time. Rather than embrace perspectives that highlight either blind replication or heroic change agents, we stress that most micro activities are fairly mundane, aimed at sense-making, alignment and muddling through. As groups of people engage in such actions and resist others' attempts as well, they may well transform practices and theories and alter personal identities.

Institutional analysis can benefit from more attention to everyday processes and actions, as opposed to exogenous events and shocks. In the same vein, more focus on the less powerful members of organizations instead of only leaders or champions would be welcome, as would more emphasis on the cultural and cognitive aspects of organizational life (Howard-Grenville et al., 2011). Institutional influences shape both organizational and individual interests and desires, often framing the possibilities for action and influencing whether behaviors result in persistence or change. Institutional forces are instantiated in individuals and carried by them through their actions, tools and technologies (Orlikowski and Scott, 2008). Some actions reinforce existing practices, while others will reframe or alter them. Ideas can be picked up in one setting and transposed to another. Tools can be multipurpose, and some settings are rife with multiple interpretations and points of view. Such situations afford latitude for human agency.

The various members of an organization often view situations quite differently and thus push competing points of view and divergent responses. Rather than thinking of such diverse opinions as merely noise, or regard the everyday affairs of organizations as simple routines, we stress that habit and routine often involve mindful reflection, effort and maneuvering to accomplish ordinary work. Amplifying this observation, we underscore a distinction between effortful and emergent accomplishments (Feldman and Orlikowski, 2011: 1245). The first form emphasizes agency that continues an already established pattern, deepening the ruts in the road, so to speak, whereas the second highlights agency

that initiates a new or altered pattern of activity, turning onto a new road (Feldman, 2016). Emirbayer and Mische (1998: 980) make the point nicely:

> While repertoires are limited by individual and collective histories and may be more or less extensive and flexible, they do require a certain degree of maneuverability in order to assure the appropriateness of the response to the situation at hand. ... In unproblematic situations, this maneuvering is semiconscious or taken for granted, the result of an incorporation of schemas of action into one's embodied practical activity. On the other hand, the application of such repertoires remains intentional insofar as it allows one to get things done through habitual interactions or negotiation. ... There may be much ingenuity and resourcefulness to the selection of responses from practical repertoires, even when this contributes to the reproduction of a given structure.

A decade ago, our survey of the literature on microfoundations was admittedly eclectic and sparse. Today, there has been a good deal of progress in both sociology (Jepperson and Meyer, 2011) and management (Felin et al., 2015) in developing theoretical arguments about how micro-level explanations provide depth and texture to accounts of macro-level events and relationships. At the same time, we need to understand how macro forces are interpreted at the local level. We continue to believe that it is a mistake to equate change solely with the micro level and persistence with the macro. People frequently 'pull down' larger, societally approved justifications for their actions, just as on-the-ground practices can 'build up' into broader institutional patterns. Our goal is to develop multilevel explanations that account for these recursive influences.

Our overview of the current literature is wide ranging but by no means exhaustive. We used two principles to select the building blocks. First, we wanted to bring several literatures together that previously developed separately. Second, we seek to create cross-pollination between classic and more recent theory. We begin with recent work under the umbrella of practice theory, as it highlights our arguments about the micro and the mundane. We then revisit the central contributions of the Carnegie School, with its focus on cognition and routines, and update the Carnegie approach by reference to more recent scholarship. We turn next to another valuable older literature, ethnomethodology, which is often overlooked in mainstream research. We then engage with research on sense-making, pioneered by Karl Weick and now pursued by many scholars. To illustrate the relationship between everyday activities and organizational transformation, we offer four short cases from different settings as empirical examples that depict how micro-actions are linked to long-term institutional change. We conclude with a discussion of the implications of our arguments for future research.

PRACTICE THEORY

Practice theory subscribes to the idea that social and organization life is enacted through everyday activities or practices (Feldman and Orlikowski, 2011; Feldman and Worline, 2016; Nicolini and Monteiro, 2017). With its focus on performances, processes and dynamics, practice theory is oriented towards unpacking social reality, which entails reducing the grain size of analysis from abstract social structures to concrete actions performed by specific people. For Theodore Schatzki (2012: 13), practices are 'an organized constellation of different people's activities'. To Michel de Certeau (1998: xi), a practice is the 'microbe-like operations proliferating within technocratic structure and deflecting their functioning by means of a multitude of "tactics" articulated in the details of everyday life'. Clearly, practice theorists foreground human agency but some also put action on the same footing as structure. Giddens (1984), for example, says that practices are the everyday situational actions that recursively generate and regenerate the structures that restrict and facilitate human endeavors.

Three elements are central to the current practice turn in the social sciences: the 'what', 'who' and 'how' (Jarzabkowski et al., 2016). The 'what' element captures the particular practices that organizations adopt and start to use to accomplish work. But practice and practitioners are entangled. As a result, it is important to also focus on 'who' is enacting the specific practices within an organization, including the concrete roles and positions of individuals. In addition, practices are not performed in the same way in every context. An espoused practice may vary substantially from an enacted practice, so it is important also to focus on 'how' a practice is performed. Practice theory has been used as a lens to study a wide range of phenomena, including communities of practice (Lave and Wenger, 1991), technology use (Orlikowski, 2000), business strategy (Whittington, 1992), institutions (Barley and Tolbert, 1997), and routines (Feldman and Pentland, 2003). Seen in this light, ideas, routines, technologies and institutions do not take on meaning as a result of their innate features but through the relationality of mutual constitution (Emirbayer, 1997).

Over the past 15 years, empirical studies of organizational routines have used a practice lens to unpack their internal dynamics (Howard-Grenville and Rerup, 2017). To facilitate this push, scholars engaged in several conceptual and empirical moves. Conceptually, Feldman and Pentland (2003) made a distinction between the performative and the ostensive aspects of organizational routines. The former term refers to the (specific) performances of a routine in specific times and places, whereas the latter refers to the abstract patterning of a routine that emerges though repeated performances of it. The ostensive aspect is never a homogeneous, singular 'thing', because multiple participants always have different points of view. By following the recursive relationship between ostensive and performative aspects, it is possible to trace stability and change in routines as an accomplishment that takes effort (Pentland and Reuter, 1994).

Rerup and Feldman (2011) used this distinction to analyze the hiring routines in a new public venture, Learning Lab Denmark (LLD). They unpacked the internal dynamics of hiring, showing how both performative and ostensive aspects were linked to higher-level structures such as LLD's interpretive schema and the public university context in which LLD was housed. Initially, the founders of LLD espoused an image of it as an entrepreneurial, non-bureaucratic organization that operated on a private sector model. In line with this schema, LLD started to hire people, offering private sector salaries. This choice created an ostensive patterning of the hiring routine, because private sector hiring was thought to require high salaries and swift offers. Because the salaries for equivalent jobs were 30–40% higher in LLD than in the Danish Pedagogical University (DPU) where LLD was housed, DPU's HR department began to reject the job contracts that were forwarded by LLD. The Lab took several creative actions to side-step DPU and continue hiring people at high salaries. Eventually, both LLD's schema and the ostensive aspects of the hiring routine became better aligned with the public sector context in which it operated. The process of solving seemingly mundane problems with the hiring routine contributed to questioning the schema and, ultimately, to the emergence of a new, more complex schema. These shifts happened over several years through actions carried out by a number of people across LLD. By documenting how an ecology of observable actions morphed over a three-year period, Rerup and Feldman showed how the mundane tasks of hiring gradually changed, altering the ostensive aspects of the employment process and the schema.

Orlikowski (2000) used a practice lens to study how Notes software technology was enacted by consultants and technologists in Alpha, a large multinational consulting company with offices around the world. In the late 1980s, the chief information officer (CIO) believed that Notes could help Alpha share knowledge quickly across its offices, and thereby prevent consultants working on similar projects from reinventing the wheel. He ordered the 40 technologists working in his department to buy and install thousands of copies of Notes to build a network for sharing knowledge. Notes was also installed on the technologists' computers. They used the software to send emails and frequently contributed to building data bases to create shared solutions to recurrent technical problems. The consultants, however, used the technology in a different way: they rarely used it to send email, and they almost never contributed any knowledge to the shared database.

Why did the use of Notes differ so sharply in the two communities of professionals? The work culture for the technologists was collaborative. Norms of knowledge sharing and helping behaviors motivated them to use Notes to further their collective performance. In contrast, the work culture for the consultants was competitive and strongly influenced by an 'up or out' career structure. The individual consultants were reluctant to share knowledge, because it might give colleagues a competitive edge. 'Who' uses a technology and 'how' matters a great deal.

In a study of strategy-making by top managers at three British universities, Jarzabkowski (2008) demonstrated how senior managers did not have comparable influences on practice. The same practice ('what') may have different performance implications in disparate organizations because the executives implementing strategy have varying social skills and operate in different contexts. The social skills ('how') of senior managers ('who') matter because universities have diffuse power relationships and an empowered workforce. As a result, academic leaders cannot simply implement new programs; they must actively persuade knowledge workers to use new technologies or practices.

Practice theory has also been incorporated into institutional theory (Barley and Tolbert, 1997), and several recent studies stress how the mundane activities of specific practitioners struggling to accomplish their work can instigate field-level institutional change (Reay et al., 2013; Mair and Hehenberger, 2014; Smets et al., 2015). In a study of a global law firm, Smets, Morris and Greenwood (2012), for instance, traced how practice-driven institutional change unfolds through recursive processes that connect practice, organization and field. Essentially, small, situated improvisations in response to problems with accomplishing work on the front line can *trickle up* and initiate change at the organizational and field levels. Despite these theoretical developments, institutional research has largely focused on how the creation of organizational fields *trickles down* and shapes individual action and cognition.

Powell and Colyvas (2008: 277) lamented that the individuals who frequently populate institutional analysis are portrayed as either 'cultural dopes' (Garfinkel, 1967: 68–75) or heroic 'change agents' (Strang and Sine, 2002: 503–507). Surely, heroic actors and cultural dopes are a poor representation of the gamut of human behavior. Practice theory offers students of institutional analysis a perspective of the social world as a web of actions knitted together by ordinary people 'in such a way that the result of one performance becomes the resource for another' (Nicolini, 2012: 2). It provides a basis for addressing how 'institutions and actors meet in the throes of everyday life' (Barley, 2008: 510).

THE CARNEGIE SCHOOL

The Carnegie School is identified with a series of path-breaking books and papers written by Herbert Simon, James G. March and Richard Cyert. The debt of institutional theory to Carnegie work is large, although not fully appreciated (for discussion, see DiMaggio and Powell, 1991: 18–20). In the 1950s and early 1960s, a group of interdisciplinary social scientists at the newly founded Graduate School of Industrial Administration at Carnegie Mellon University set about trying to develop a behavioral approach to understand how individuals and organizations act and make decisions in the real world. They developed a menu of insights that students of organizations now take as foundational ingredients. Concepts such as bounded rationality, satisficing, premises, aspiration levels and standard operating procedures were developed to describe individuals and organizations acting in the face of the 'uncertainties and ambiguities of life' (March and Simon, 1958: 2). The Carnegie School developed a rich, process-oriented understanding of how decision-making takes place in organizations, drawing on ideas from cognitive science, economics, psychology and sociology.

This line of work emphasizes how uncertainty is managed through the creation of organizational routines; therefore, the allocation of attention is central to how decisions are made. Most decisions are made under conditions of ambiguity about preferences; consequently the decision-making process is often a political one involving multiple groups and coalitions with inconsistent preferences (Cyert and March, 1963). The behavioral project of Simon, March and Cyert was oriented toward capturing how individuals and organizations behave in a diverse set of tasks, from pricing, budgeting and accounting to information gathering and purchasing. They found that neoclassical economics paid little attention to the institutional and cognitive constraints on organizational behavior, and thus allowed scant room for individual human mistakes, foolishness and divided attention.

And even though the Carnegie work focused primarily on the limits of human knowledge and computation, its implications for how organizations operate were profound. For example, Simon's (1945: 88–90) early work on habit recognized that habitual behavior is not passive, but rather a means by which attention is directed to selected aspects of a situation, so that one might rule out competing aspects. His rich discussion of the role of premises captures how perceptions in organizations are selectively shaped by those in charge and by the execution of routines (Simon, 1945). Indeed, March and Simon (1958) and Cyert and March (1963) emphasized that organizational behavior involves rule-following more than the calculation of consequences. Simon's view of bounded rationality as both an input to, and learned outcome of, decision processes has stood the test of time: it earned him a Nobel prize in economics, the discipline that he so enjoyed criticizing for its unrealistic assumptions (Simon, 1978).

The Carnegie perspective highlights that decision-makers are often confronted by the need to balance several, sometimes incompatible goals, and that instead of assuming a fixed set of choices, decision-makers often search for alternatives, following implicit rules about aspiration levels. This type of search is guided by variations in organizational resources, referred to as slack. Organizations and the individuals within them typically rely on routines or rules of thumb learned from experience or based on the premises set by others, rather than attempt to calculate the consequences of their alternatives. Organizational learning consists of adapting to feedback; positive feedback, however, can lead to myopia and superstition, whereas negative feedback can lead to endless search. Learning, in the Carnegie sense, can be a double-edged sword (March, 2010).

The Carnegie program has perhaps had its deepest influence on evolutionary economics (Nelson and Winter, 1982), but it has also shaped behavioral economics, work in strategy on capabilities, and the study of organizational learning. We do not go into these rich veins of work here; instead we focus on how a set of ideas about routines can be valuable for institutional analysis. Although the Carnegie School opened the door to daily life inside organizations, the theories treated the workplace as if it were largely inhabited by top managers. To be sure, most management

research has an executive bias, and some current work under the neo-Carnegie rubric continues this selective focus. For example, Gavetti et al. (2012: 15) state: 'A key determinant of organizational attention is the power of key players, particularly the CEO and the senior executives.' The language conveys a telling message: top managers control the keys, and the troops have little voice or agency. Most executives wish that life were so simple!

To make the Carnegie School more useful as a microfoundation for institutional analysis, the routines need to be inhabited; too often they are presented as people-less 'black-boxes' or else the dictates of senior managers (Feldman, 2000; Feldman and Pentland, 2003). Organizational routines are not algorithms that run the same way with every enactment. Moreover, a good deal of skill and effort is involved in performing a routine the same way. This is a point that Michael Cohen (2007, 2012) emphasized in his work on replication, and one also underscored by ethnomethodologists (see below). Agency is often more critical in execution than in the orders or programs executed.

The question of where routines reside – in the organization's rules and memory or in the individuals who carrying them out – is crucial (for overviews see Parmigiani and Howard-Grenville, 2011; Salvato and Rerup, 2011). Cohen (2007) and Winter (2013) both draw on Dewey's (1922) ideas to emphasize that the enactment of routines is based in part on deliberation. Winter (2013: 131) offers especially rich imagery here; invoking Dewey he suggests that ordinary decision-making is like a 'kaleidoscope offering innumerable complex and different patterns, featuring the three primary colors of habit, impulse, and deliberation. If you ask why such a complex picture is not simply confusing, … it is largely because habit steadies both the real picture and the hand that holds the kaleidoscope, and sometimes the external environment also cooperates in sustaining the picture that is that steadied.'

In work underway at the time of his unfortunate demise, Cohen was studying the critical role of routines in health care. Within medical organizations, mundane social processes – such as socialization into roles and the routines of problem-solving – allow for the coordination of complex and difficult tasks. Consider the delicate interplay among surgical teams or in hospital emergency rooms: all their coordinated efforts are made possible because the routine participants are *socialized* into performing particular patterns of the routines. Nevertheless, fumbles during 'simple' performances of patient handoffs between medical shifts are, sadly, a leading cause of death in hospitals, and they indicate deficient enactments of routines by the participants involved (Cohen and Hilligoss, 2010; Vogus and Hilligoss, 2016; LeBaron et al., 2016). This work on highly professional medical staff underscores that routines, in order to be successful and save lives, must be effortful accomplishments rather than mere replication (Levinthal and Rerup, 2006).

A second step needed in bridging the Carnegie work and institutional analysis is greater recognition of the ways that premises, routines and standard operating procedures are 'pulled down' from the larger environment. Routines have often been described as unitary 'things' that float around in time and space. When an organization finds out that its performance of a task falls short of its aspiration level, it usually selects a routine from the 'environment' to solve the problem. If the routine is not working, a new routine is selected and tried out until the problem has been solved (Cyert and March, 1963). Theories that conceptualize routines as uninhabited 'things' provide few details on how such replacement and selection happens. These missing details create an 'important challenge for micro research' (Greve, 2008: 199).

The heightened attention to benchmarking, metrics or evaluations, and rankings in many contexts provides a context for exemplifying why more micro research is needed. The current contention over the lack of diversity at largely male Silicon Valley tech firms vividly illustrates how a wider societal concern becomes instantiated in local hiring criteria. The process by which universities, especially professional schools of law and business, became slaves to external rankings, is another all-too-familiar example (Espeland and Sauder, 2007; Sauder and Espeland, 2009). It is remarkable that a profession that is supposed to comprise the best minds in the country allowed its admission routines to be shaped by magazine and newspaper rankings based on thin data. Such 'pulling down' or selection of wider fashions and dictates can alter how organizations conduct their daily affairs as well as how they represent themselves to their publics.

Responses to external debates are not, however, mere window dressing. Institutionalized expectations in the wider environment may constrain organizational behavior by becoming incarnate in both individuals and organizational culture. An apt example is Hallett's (2010) ethnographic study of teachers' compliance with purported accountability reforms at a public elementary school. Hallett (2010: 53) observes a dynamic that he calls recoupling, 'creating tight couplings where loose couplings were once in place.' In Hallett's case, the hiring of a determined, reform-minded school principal transformed a previously ceremonial commitment to accountability into a new classroom reality. The disruption of teachers' autonomy and teaching routines led to uncertainty, turmoil and even political mobilization. By focusing on the local, micro-level dynamics of wider movements for reform in schools, Hallett showed that recoupling of institutionalized myths created resistance and ultimately altered the legitimacy of reform endeavors. What began as reform momentum ended up in a morass of ambiguity and frustration. Pulling down higher-order reforms is not done seamlessly.

ETHNOMETHODOLOGY

In the 1960s, Harold Garfinkel at UCLA, along with his students and colleagues, developed a distinctive line of inquiry that stressed how interactive skills emerge from everyday encounters, and in turn generate sociability and reproduce the social order. His ethnomethodological approach, with its focus on practice as '[c]ontingent on ongoing accomplishments' (Garfinkel, 1967: 11), provided tantalizing insights for institutional theory. These can be seen most clearly in Zucker's (1977) work, where she argues that many taken-for-granted understandings are 'built up' from the ground level by participants in interactions, and in DiMaggio and Powell's (1991: 22–27) outline of a theory of practical action.

Ethnomethodology never developed into an expansive subfield, and given both its cult-like approach and the controversies it provoked, perhaps it never had the chance.[1] Nevertheless, Garfinkel's focus on practical reasoning and the role of 'accounts' in normalizing and legitimating the social order offers considerable insight into the implicit and contested assumptions that make organizational life possible. Rather than find social order in cultural norms or social roles, ethnomethodologists examine the methods that people use to demonstrate the appropriateness of their behaviors. Simply put, ethnomethodology asks what kind of knowledge it takes to get by in the world.

There are several compelling reasons to revisit this line of work (see also LeBaron et al., 2016). Contemporary scholars are largely unaware of just how much of this research focused on work and organizations. Garfinkel and colleagues understand that 'everyday reasoning' requires that individuals negotiate organizational rules and procedures reflexively to assure themselves and others around them that their behavior is sensible. Meticulous studies of record-keeping procedures in juvenile justice facilities (Cicourel, 1968), high mortality wards

in hospitals (Sudnow, 1967), and psychiatric clinics (Garfinkel and Bittner, 1967) reveal that counting, reporting and legal requirements are often highly improvised, as veteran staff draw on deep, tacit knowledge of how reports ought to be assembled. Other work examined case files, folders and dockets to ascertain the classification schemes used in psychiatry or a public welfare agency, where documents could be treated either as 'plain facts' or the opportunity to construct an account that provides grounds for accepting the testimony of the document against the testimony of the welfare applicant (Zimmerman, 1969).

Bittner's (1967) studies of policing on skid row illuminate how officers performed complicated and demanding work with relative ease, without any real personal or peer recognition of their skills. Given that the destitute and mentally ill were often the objects of police work among the down-and-out, perhaps the lack of high regard is to be expected. But Bittner showed how strongly a powerful sense of craftsmanship among the police was rendered routine, even as it went unacknowledged. Similarly, Sudnow (1965) analyzed how the penal code was used by public defenders with great facility. Lawyers took into account a welter of 'facts' – the ecological characteristics of a community, the biographies of criminals and victims, and past records of criminal activity. They transformed a criminal action into a shorthand representation that was intelligible to attorneys and judges. Sudnow's brilliant analysis revealed how delicate teamwork between the offices of public defender and public prosecutor in the face of a demanding organizational calendar jointly facilitated the construction of 'normal crimes', a proverbial characterization that certain kinds of illegal actions were typically committed by particular types of people. Once such categorizations were made, plea bargaining ensued, based on unstated recipes for reducing original charges to lesser defenses to avoid the costs of trial.

West and Zimmerman (1987), in a highly cited article on 'doing gender', argued that gender is performed in interactions, and that behaviors are assessed based on socially accepted conceptions of gender. They focused on the interactional level where gender is both invoked and reinforced. Doing gender is based on the degree to which an actor is masculine or feminine, in light of societal expectations about what is appropriate for one's sex category. In this view, gendered behaviors are methods that individuals use for making their actions socially acceptable. Suchman (1987), in her work on human–machine interaction, introduced the idea of situated action to also highlight the interrelationship between an action and the context of its performance. In studies of the early development of artificial intelligence, she captured the common sense procedures that individuals invoke to engage with 'expert' systems.

In ethnomethodological studies, categories and classifications become interpretive schemas that members of organizations draw on. Over time, these schemas become a repository of organizational knowledge. Particular schemas become routinized through repeated application and use: they become habitual, taken-for-granted. As Berger and Luckman (1967) emphasized, once joint activities are habitualized and reciprocally interpreted, patterns both harden and deepen as they are transmitted to others, particularly newcomers. When schemas become perceived as objective, exteriorized facts, their contingent origins are obscured. Organizations do have rich and varied repertoires, however, and multiple schemas are available. The possibility of mixing or combining practices in alternative or novel ways to produce different patterns is ever present.

Throughout this rich vein of research, ethnomethodologists demonstrate that classifications and categorizations are invoked on the fly by skilled actors to keep peace on the streets, in the courts, in hospital wards and in welfare agencies. Contrast this view with the conception of organization found in many other lines of organization theory. Rather than struggling with or coping with uncertainty, the practical reasoning view emphasizes how situations are rendered comprehensible, and it sees such efforts as an on-going, contingent accomplishment. In contrast, ever since Weber, most students of organizations regard formal structures and procedures as 'ideally possible, but practically unattainable' (Bittner, 1965). Selznick (1949), for example, attributed these limitations to the recalcitrance of the tools of action, whereas Weber conceived of the typical bureaucracy more as a target or an idealization. For the ethnomethodologists, however, bureaucracy is neither a rarefied nor a lofty goal, but is deeply embedded in common-sense routines of everyday life. Organization is a formula to which all sorts of problems can be brought for solution (Bittner, 1965).

This focus on practical reasoning as a routine accomplishment emphasizes how people in organizations both make and find a reasonable world. Garfinkel (1968) described this accomplishment aptly: 'how jurors know what they are doing when they do the work of jurors.' Organizational life entails constant doing and achieving. Social order is created on the ground floor, through situated local practices. As practices are reproduced over time and across settings, macro categories emerge from these interactions and negotiations.

SENSE-MAKING

Sense-making is a social process that is activated when cues interrupt ongoing activities. It is a fundamentally social process by which people 'interpret their environment in and through interactions with each other' to retrospectively elaborate plausible meanings that rationalize what they should be doing (Maitlis, 2005: 21). People convert situated circumstances into action through the reciprocal interpretation of who they are and how they understand their environment (Weick, 1995; Reinecke and Ansari, 2015). In situations where existing mental frames no longer provide guidance, people ask 'What's the story?' and 'Now what?' (Weick et al., 2005). People ask these questions because they are 'attending to and bracketing cues in the environment, creating intersubjective meaning through cycles of interpretation and action, and thereby enacting a more ordered environment from which further cues can be drawn' (Maitlis and Christianson, 2014: 13).

Sense-making scholars draw on many strands of micro-sociology, including Garfinkel's (1967) insight that rationality is constructed through commonplace interactions and Goffman's (1974) use of frames as providing a structure to social context. As pointed out in reviews by Maitlis and Christianson (2014) and Sandberg and Tsoukas (2015), sense-making is not a homogeneous or monolithic block of ideas. It is a lens made up of various theoretical orientations, including cognitive psychology, phenomenology and discursive orientations. These various orientations conceptualize sense-making quite differently. We will not go into these details here, as we mainly draw on Karl Weick's thinking due to the outsize influence of his work in organization studies and management, and the lively conversation it has instigated.

Sense-making analyses share with ethnomethodology a methodological stance privileging cases that reveal rather than represent. But there are notable distinctions as well. Whereas ethnomethodologists highlight the cognitive work of individuals in creating social order, the Weickian approach to sense-making focuses on the contextualized way in which this work occurs by highlighting how norms and roles influence the process (Weick and Roberts, 1993). From the sense-making perspective, conceptions of identity and logics of action are relational, constructed not only through projections of self and others' perceptions, but also through expectations and scripted interactions in relation to what

others are 'supposed to do'. Individuals are enmeshed in a structure of relationships, taking cues from both situations and other people, and these guideposts provide substance for them to enact their environments. For instance, in an ethnographic study conducted at a local US television station, Patriotta and Gruber (2015) explored how workers in the news department plan their stories on a daily basis and adjust their plans when new stories break. They found that the making of news is molded by frameworks such as norms and role structures that set expectations about what is going to happen during the day, and typifications that make it possible for the newsmakers to classify emerging stories on the basis of their importance. In the world of newsmaking, expectancy frameworks and typifications are crucial sense-making resources that allow news workers to respond to the flow of unexpected events.

In his analysis of the 1948 Mann Gulch fire disaster in Montana, Weick (1993) demonstrates how a breakdown in sense-making unfolded in a trained smokejumping crew. The inability of the crew to comprehend 'What's the story?' and 'Now what?' in the face of unexpected conditions impeded the firefighters' ability to draw on their stock of experiences to generate a novel means of survival or to comply with their leader, who did survive. Weick attributes the tragic deaths of these skilled men to three features: a breakdown in role structure among members of the team; stalwart adherence to a less critical categorization of the fire; and practical challenges to their identities as firefighters. All these features are reflected in the difficulties that the firefighters faced to make sense of who they were, the situation they encountered and the repertoire of actions they should take. Because the stock of knowledge of the firefighters did not match their less critical categorization of the fire when they arrived on the scene, the situation was rendered meaningless, as 'less and less of what they saw made sense' (Weick 1993: 635). Cues from other firefighters (e.g., stopping for dinner and taking pictures) reinforced a spurious categorization of the fire, and impeded the firemen's ability to activate a different course of action. When the leader of the crew, confronted with looming disaster, lit a fire in the only escape route, lay down in its ashes, and called on his crew to drop their tools and join him, the team disintegrated. The firefighters' identities hindered their ability to comprehend an order to drop the very materials that defined who they were and comprehend the practicality of a solution that could have saved their lives. Weick's (1993: 633) analysis demonstrates that teams can falter when 'the sense of what is occurring and the means to rebuild that sense collapse together'.

Because sense-making is triggered by interruptions of expectations, most studies capture sense-making in crisis or unexpected, non-routine situations (Maitlis and Sonenshein, 2010). But studying crises alone can lead to oversimplified models (Weick, 2010). From a sense-making view, many features of organizational life are uncertain, which creates ignorance or the inability to estimate future consequences of present actions. Organization life is generally wrought with ambiguity, which reflects the inability to attribute clear, mutually exclusive categories, codes or specifications. These distinctions are important because although information can provide a remedy for uncertainty, it can also increase ambiguity, as we saw in the Mann Gulch fire, when new information did not fit preconceived categories. Weick also draws on Garfinkel to emphasize that equivocality is present when numerous or disputed interpretations exist. As with Garfinkel's jurors, people may justify multiple incompatible accounts, often with the same evidence. Weick argues that uncertainty, ambiguity and equivocality may occasion different triggers to, and remedies for, sense-making.

The majority of sense-making studies have been inspired by Weick's (1995) influential attention to how events disrupt ongoing cognition and practice and trigger efforts at sense-making. This focus, however, is somewhat puzzling, because Weick has also argued that most organizations experience a multitude of mundane disturbances of their ongoing routine activities, rather than major breakdowns of day-to-day practice. In fact, Weick (2009: 225) has pondered, 'Why does the extensive literature on organizational change focus on how to create change rather than how to cease change?' A similar question could be redirected at the sense-making research: Why does the literature attend to episodes that create sense-making rather than to sense-making as a continuous process? Some have called for considering more routine situations because the predominant focus on disruptive episodes at the expense of more mundane and continuous forms implicated in routine activities might lead to oversimplified models (Sandberg and Tsoukas, 2015). Weick has, to some degree, already started to redress this imbalance in his work on mindful organizing in so-called 'high-reliability organizations' (HROs), such as aircraft carrier flight decks and nuclear power control rooms, which experience nearly error-free performance despite operating under trying circumstances (Schulman, 1993; Weick and Roberts, 1993; Barton et al., 2015). HROs sustain reliable performance through frontline processes of mindful organizing, a type of collective sense-making focused on detecting and correcting the unexpected (Weick and Sutcliffe, 2007). Mindful organizing is oriented toward ongoing revisions of day-to-day activities because high-reliability is not a constant, but an effortful accomplishment that must be continually renewed by the everyday work of ordinary people (Vogus et al., 2014; Vogus and Colville, 2017).

Most sense-making studies have been conducted at the team or organizational level. Because sense-making is largely a theory of local practice, it has not been studied at the macro level, although many have called for pursuing such work (Weick et al., 2005; Maitlis and Christianson, 2014; Sandberg and Tsoukas, 2015). Specifically, Weber and Glynn (2006) argued that Weick 'overlooks the role of larger social, historical or institutional contexts in explaining cognition' and 'appears to neglect, or at least lack an explicit account of, the embeddedness of sense-making in social space and time'. Most research has focused on how sense-making unfolds *within* a boundary (e.g., a team or organization) and has not examined how it also might unfold *across* boundaries (Strike and Rerup, 2016).

Today, scholars assume that larger social systems edit and constrain local sense-making, but we also need to consider how institutions facilitate and enable as well. For example, how do new or updated bottom-up accounts of what is going on become shared and eventually institutionalized? Sense-making is an issue of talk and communication, and individual accounts become collective accounts when doubts are turned into belief. Social movements take hold when individuals doubt a settled aspect of the world that is taken for granted. 'Doubts ... aris[e] when ... continuance is interrupted, represent[ing] a potential inadequacy in [our] habitual ways of understanding and acting' (Locke et al., 2008: 908). Doubt might rupture the frames that currently provide the foundation for interpretation and reality construction. As they act, both doubters and believers can shape the enactment of a new account by nudging 'the sense-making and meaning construction of others toward a preferred redefinition of ... reality' (Gioia and Chittipeddi, 1991: 442).

In sum, research has yet to explore how sense-making scales up, despite its criticality to the institutionalization and deinstitutionalization of various phenomena (Gray et al., 2015). This topic strikes us as the next research frontier. As one illustration, Kaplan (2008) explored the way in which people turn individual frames into collective frames. She traced how individuals from different functional groups within an organization attempted to sway each other to adopt competing frames. In Kaplan's model, framing contests end when the coalition supporting one frame dominates the people who support alternatives. Studying how dominant frames and interpretations are successfully imbricated in organizations and public life is an important area for future research. We take up that challenge in the next section.

INSTITUTIONAL CHANGE VIEWED THROUGH A MICRO LENS

We turn now to a discussion of several cases involving important organizational transformations that have typically been analyzed by reference to broader social and political transformations. In such accounts, external forces are given primacy in explaining organizational change. Indeed, when discussion of these changes is directed at the organizational level, most reports emphasize the agency of risk-taking entrepreneurs. In contrast, we aim to demonstrate how much explanatory purchase can be gained by examining the micro-level processes that underpinned these important changes. We emphasize that the purported entrepreneurs did not even consider that they were taking risks, but instead were responding to everyday, unanticipated situations.

Universities and Academic Entrepreneurship

Today it is widely assumed that universities function as engines of economic development, generating valuable intellectual property in the form of patents and marketable discoveries for local and national economies. The third mission of universities, the transfer of knowledge, is now firmly established alongside teaching and research. Indeed, some worry that an entrepreneurial focus monopolizes more faculty and administrative time than does teaching.

It was not always this way; indeed, the initial steps in this direction, taken back in the 1970s, were met with considerable resistance and surprise. At that time, scientific break-throughs in molecular biology and genetics were transforming the biological sciences. As Ron Cape, a cofounder of the first bioengineering company, Cetus, noted in regard to the pent-up feelings of the era: 'It was like maybe a dam waiting to burst or an egg waiting to hatch, but the fact is there were a lot of Nobel Prizes but no practical applications' (Cape, 2006). Science journalist Stephen Hall (1987: 21) captured the tumult that recombinant DNA research brought to biology in the 1970s with a memorable line: 'It was like the microscope had been reinvented. Everything had to be reexamined, and the molecular biologists roared like Huns through the other scientists' turf.' Hall noted that the young molecular biologists 'had the reputation of being opportunistic, of trespassing onto other scientists' intellectual turf in search of answers'.

But when the first director of the new Office of Technology Licensing at Stanford University, Nils Reimers, approached the faculty in the early 1970s about commercializing breakthroughs in DNA technology, he was met with surprise and shock. Professor Stanley Cohen, a co-author of a foundational DNA paper, initially responded, 'Gee, this can't be patented. This is basic research. How can you patent basic research? And besides, it's dependent on all these findings that have occurred for the past fifteen to twenty years' (Chemical Heritage Foundation, 1997: 133). Professor Paul Berg, who subsequently was co-winner of the Nobel Prize for his work on recombinant DNA, had an even stronger adverse reaction to the idea of patenting: 'Hey wait a minute! I mean, where does Stanford and the University of California get the entitlement to this whole thing?' (Chemical Heritage Foundation, 1997: 129).

The company most associated with the transformation of basic research ideas into new biomedical products was Genentech, a South San Francisco firm legally formed in 1976. It forged a recombination of scientific and commercial cultures, leading to the creation of new organizational practices

and forms of discovery. Genentech broke the mold. It encouraged publishing, transposing an academic invisible college model into a new business model (Powell and Sandholtz, 2012). As co-founder Bob Swanson (2001: 56–57), commented: 'It was always clear that we were going to publish our results. Everybody wanted to publish in *Nature* and *Science*, and so what we did had to be of a quality that it would be published. So we said, let's publish the results; let's make sure we get the patents and we'll make the patent attorneys work overtime to get them filed before you actually get the papers out.' Genentech's philosophy spread to other companies and rebounded back into universities. Now it is commonplace for faculty members to think of publishing and commercial application simultaneously. As but one illustration, the esteemed scientist Marc Tessier-Lavigne, who headed research and development at Genentech from 2003 to 2011, overseeing 1,400 scientists, was recently named the 11th president of Stanford University.

In looking back, many think of the origins of these new organizational models as profoundly creative and entrepreneurial. The story of this era has been chronicled by both science journalists and academics (Kenney, 1986; Orsenigo, 1989; Teitelman, 1989; Gambardella, 1995; Hughes, 2001; Colyvas and Powell, 2006; Vettel, 2006; Colyvas, 2007; Berman, 2012). But viewed up close, with a careful historical lens on the time, such actions were hardly inventive; they were profoundly mundane. Today there is enormous attention to the new CRISPR technology, and journalists ask if we can now engineer the human race. The US scientific community is responding to the excitement and furor with meetings on the ethics and use of gene editing, amid speculation that science is moving too fast. Back in 1975, at a meeting at the Asilomar Conference Grounds in Pacific Grove, California, biologists gathered to discuss the hazards of their research as the age of modern genetics dawned (Fredrickson, 2001). At Asilomar, which itself has become a storied place for such meetings, participants decided to pause gene splicing with mammalian cells and to focus on mice, which were seen as much less controversial subjects than humans.

Out of that meeting came the rather unusual origins of the company Genentech. A young struggling investor, named Bob Swanson, acquired the list of names of attendees at the meeting. He started cold-calling them to ask if the scientists thought there was a possibility of commercializing the research. Swanson, then only 28 years old, was unemployed. He was an MIT graduate, who had worked at Citibank's venture investment group and briefly at the new venture capital firm Kleiner Perkins Caufield and Byers. He was living on a $410 monthly unemployment check. But he had been reading scientific journals and was intrigued by the burgeoning research on recombinant DNA, and he had vague ideas of forming a bioscience venture. As he recalls: 'So what triggered this idea of starting a company was I needed to get a job. I probably had three job interviews a day for three or four months. This was a pretty scary period' (Swanson, 2001: 10). Swanson took the list of names associated with the Asilomar meeting and went through it alphabetically. The first scientist who actually talked with him at any length was Herbert Boyer at the University of California, San Francisco. Boyer was coauthor with Stanford's Stanley Cohen on the 1973 papers that specified the methods for making recombinant DNA. He was an associate professor, and the NIH had recently turned down a grant proposal for his work to produce a human protein in *E. coli* bacteria because reviewers thought it would take too long to do so.

Boyer asked Swanson how he had gotten his name. Swanson replied that he took a list of names associated with Asilomar and went through it alphabetically. Boyer said that Stanford's Paul Berg must have turned Swanson down: 'I suppose I am next on the list.' Swanson wanted to talk with Boyer, and Boyer told the young man to

come by his lab on a Friday afternoon at a quarter to five. Powell has used this story in lectures around the world, to flesh out the ideas on transposition and recombination in the Padgett and Powell volume (2012). The wide array of responses to the question he puts to the audience – What does a quarter to five mean? – suggests that the moment was pregnant with possibilities. Some audience members say it is a clear sign that the meeting wasn't important and Boyer was going to give Swanson very little time. Others wonder whether Boyer did not want his colleagues to see Swanson, and so had him come at the end of the day. Still others say a quarter to five shows the primacy of academic science; thinking about commercial applications is something done only at day's end. Others wonder if it is a test of Swanson's 'moxie', to see if he has the energy and initiative to find parking and actually get to the building at the very end of the work week. Some see an opportunity to go for drinks if the discussion goes well. All of these thoughts were probably running through Boyer's mind, and there was no preconceived plan. As it turned out, Swanson 'introduced himself, talked about what he wanted to do, did I think the technology was ready to be commercialized? He said he had access to some money, and I thought it would be a good way to fund some postdocs and some work in my laboratory, because we needed money to do that. We spent a good deal of time that evening talking about it' (Boyer, 2001: 71). Out of that Friday evening discussion, Genentech was born, even though for its first two years the startup 'existed' at UC San Francisco and City of Hope Hospital in Los Angeles (see discussion of its history in Padgett and Powell, 2012: 418–420). The rest, as they say, was history.

Commercial Engagement by Non Profit Organizations

In the non-profit world, discussions of commercialization are often heated. Some portray the clash between mission and finance as a debate between 'love and money' (Binder, 2007). Many more non profits are pursuing a wide array of commercial activities to secure funding, and some have turned to earned-income activities to enhance their budgets (Weisbrod, 1998). Not only are the fiscal challenges faced by non profits considerable, but many external funding sources support and even require entrepreneurial efforts. Indeed, a growing array of courses, programs and elite entrepreneurs proselytize about the benefits of importing business-minded entrepreneurship into the non profit sector. And some in the sector prefer to deliver goods and services in a fashion that does not create dependency, as they view heavy reliance on donors as a sign of vulnerability. For these social sector leaders, entrepreneurial activities can generate autonomy and build capabilities (Dees, 1998).

Most of the literature on commercial activities follows two themes. One argument stresses the need to augment the social sector with practices from the business world. It focuses attention on the individuals and organizations involved in the transfer and circulation of ideas across sectors (Letts et al., 1997). To these analysts, entrepreneurial ventures have become the hallmark of a successful non profit. A chorus of scholars and practitioners make the contrary argument; they worry that earned income strategies are particularly difficult for non profit organizations and fraught with challenges (Foster and Bradach, 2005). Some fear that too much attention to earned income draws organizations away from their core missions. In general, these debates are healthy, as they not only highlight the tension between making profits and staying true to mission, but also emphasize that basing decisions solely on mission can threaten financial survival, whereas putting business concerns ahead of mission can have negative long-term consequences (Minkoff and Powell, 2006).

The rival pulls of mission and business can lead to internal strife within non profit organizations. These tensions are often manifest in art museums, between curators, who are the traditional guardians of art, and museum directors, who are responsible for the financial viability of the organization. But debates over the benefits or disadvantages of earned income activities do not typically examine how these challenges play out in day-to-day operations. Close analysis of the rather rare successful cases of revenue generation reveal that local action has often emerged as a necessity in response to unexpected conditions. Pragmatic responses triggered steps that eventually led to significant organizational changes, which subsequently became linked to larger debates and discussions, but were not prompted by them. We find, instead, maneuverability on the part of flexible managers who found that mixing practices could prompt surprise and even novelty.

A notable case of successful nonprofit entrepreneurship is Minnesota Public Radio (MPR), one of the nation's largest and richest public radio stations. MPR is known for its award-winning documentaries and innovative programs, and today, its extraordinary success at income generation. Between 1986 and 2000, MPR's for-profit ventures generated 175 million dollars in earned income for the radio station, including a 90 million dollar contribution to an endowment (Phills and Chang, 2005). The origins of this success illuminate how innovative organizational behavior is often constructed on the fly, and the extent to which surprise and necessity can drive entrepreneurship.[2]

In the late 1970s and early 1980s, MPR developed a satirical show called *A Prairie Home Companion*. They offered it to National Public Radio, but NPR declined, saying it would not have nationwide appeal. It is possible that MPR was peeved by National Public Radio's decision to decline the show, and that rejection fueled their desire to make the show successful. By the early 1980s, *A Prairie Home Companion* had generated a healthy audience. In 1981, Garrison Keillor, the show's highly popular host, offered listeners a free poster of his mythical sponsor, Powdermilk Biscuits. The fictitious sponsor was part of a regular ongoing gag on the show. To everyone's surprise, more than 50,000 listeners requested a copy of the poster. MPR faced a $60,000.00 printing bill. In such circumstances of surprise, sense-making efforts often spring into action. And so MPR continued the tradition of the fictitious sponsor by turning it into a real commercial product. To avert financial calamity, MPR President William King recalled, 'We decided to print on the back of a poster an offer for other products you could buy, like a Powdermilk Biscuit t-shirt. The idea worked. I think we netted off that poster, which was really our first catalog, fifteen or twenty thousand dollars.' (William Kling, quoted in Phills and Chang, 2005: 65). 'It instantly became clear that there were things like that you could do' (Kling, quoted in Khan, 1995).

To tap the popularity of *A Prairie Home Companion*, MPR created the Rivertown Trading Company, a mail order business that sold coffee mugs, t-shirts, novelties and kitschy Nordic-themed products related to Keillor's radio show. The new entity grew rapidly, to everyone's surprise. By 1986, it was reorganized as a separate, for-profit subsidiary of MPR in order to remove any legitimacy questions, as well as tax issues related to a non profit organization's ownership of a highly profitable business. By 1994, Rivertown Trading's capabilities with catalogs led it to distribute five different catalogs, including *Wireless*, *Signals*, *Seasons*, *Circa* and *Classica*. And it also ran the US Golf Association's catalog. The product selection extended well beyond the original focus on gifts associated with *A Prairie Home Companion*. MPR subsequently exited the catalog business, selling it for a hefty sum, only a few years before the Internet disrupted the mail-order business. MPR's timing was fortunate.

In December 1995, MPR asked a handful of employees to assist Rivertown Trading on a voluntary basis to fulfill numerous back-logged holiday orders. MPR employees were told that Rivertown would make donations to their favorite charities or contribute to a holiday party for those who volunteered. Nine employees pitched in, working two to three hours apiece, earning $350.00 each for their favorite charities. The expectation at MPR was that employees at the non-profit radio station and the for-profit catalog company should come from common backgrounds. Indeed, Kling, the general counsel, and other key staff were executives at both companies. 'We didn't want to hire people who work for Lands' End or Williams Sonoma', William Kling commented. 'We wanted people who held the values of the nonprofit.' This decision, however, led to a firestorm of protest and controversy.

Politicians in Minnesota, newspaper reporters and other public broadcasting officials were highly critical that employees of the non-profit radio station also worked with the for-profit Rivertown Trading and received considerably higher wages to boot. Instead of seeing standard routines and organizational continuity, critics saw a pattern of insider dealing, conflict of interest and public funding for an entrepreneurial effort. They raised concerns about unfair compensation and a lack of transparency. It is not our task here to assess the merits of these criticisms. We note instead that Kling and his colleagues' response was to stress that the interests of the radio station and the catalog company were compatible. Kling emphasized that the $4 million in annual support given by Rivertown to MPR over two decades exceeded the budgets of the great majority of public radio stations, and the $90 million endowment that the sale of Rivertown produced secured MPR's future. 'We could have done a lot of things with MPR, but suffice to say the $170 million contribution made it possible to do things we could not have been able to otherwise. It allowed us to paint on a larger canvas.' Rather than debate with critics or assume the role of entrepreneurial champion, Kling focused on the everyday needs of a radio broadcaster: more reporters, better signal coverage, more investigative journalism and the ability to acquire struggling public radio stations in other parts of the country.

MPR is not the only non profit that has generated earned income through new or alternative means in recent years. In recent years we have seen all manner of activities pursued by organizations as diverse as the Girl Scouts, choral groups, zoos and aquaria, and art museums. As government support has declined or stagnated, non profits have increasingly turned to revenue generation. But their efforts are most likely to be successful – financially, organizationally and politically – when they flow from existing operations. In the MPR context, success at the catalog business built on Garrison Keillor's performances. Although critics opined that 'if Garrison Keillor ever gets laryngitis, Bill Kling is out of business!',[3] Kling commented, 'My fear is that there are too many nonprofits seeking the holy grail … if it doesn't come naturally to you, you shouldn't do it.'[4]

In response to public criticisms in the late 1990s of the large sums generated by the for-profit operation and the financial rewards that Kling and his colleagues reaped from the sale of the catalog business, Kling invoked a political account of the activity: that entre-preneurial efforts with Riverside Trading were enhanced by the 'imprimatur from the Reagan administration; that it is OK to go out and think that way, indeed we encourage you to think this way.'[5] Interestingly, none of the dozens of reports, newspaper columns and magazine articles written in the 1980s or early 1990s employed a political mandate as a rationale. More than a decade after the fact, the signature of the Reagan era was 'pulled down' to justify the entrepreneurial effort.

The story of MPR is notable for both accomplishment and controversy. Few other non profits have been so successful at revenue generation or as agile in securing a siz-able endowment to guarantee a sustainable future. But rather than linking their efforts to broader trends in social entrepreneur-ship, MPR's leadership responded modestly to critics, emphasizing that earned income activities were initially a response to an unex-pected emergency. One might say that MPR learned to perform as entrepreneurs, rather than 'strategize' about this performance. Moreover, actions that critics interpreted as inherently conflictual and questionable stemmed from an organizational routine: executives should oversee the actions of both the station and the company in order to ensure continuity between them. This choice clearly reflected a managerial desire to routinize the efforts of both branches of the organization and to engage in sense-making around for-profit activities in service of non-profit goals.

Mediated Sense-Making in Family Firms

Family firms balance the dual goals of busi-ness and family and make up 80–90% of firms worldwide, but in the academic litera-ture, scholars typically study widely held firms. Family firms are seen as outliers (Salvato and Aldrich, 2012; Peterson-Withorn, 2015). This focus is perhaps puz-zling, given that in the United States 35% of S&P 500 companies and 60% of all publicly held firms are family controlled (Astrachan and Shanker, 2003). Family firms represent an untapped context for studying how non-family members influence the sense-making process of members of the family, and even-tually the direction of the firm (Strike, 2012, 2013). Family firms also represent an ideal setting for tracing how sense-making unfolds across boundaries, and demonstrating the subtle effects of the broader social context on local sense-making.

In many contexts, people are vulnerable to overvaluing past experience as a guide to new situations. The smokejumpers in Weick's (1993) study of the Mann Gulch disaster were entrapped by the belief that they would be able to put out any fire by 10 o'clock the next morning. Similarly, workers at the Bhopal methyl isocyanate plant had concluded that 'nothing serious could happen in a factory when all the installations were turned off' (Lapierre and Moro, 2002: 279–280). This frame turned out to be false: on December 2–3, 1984, the factory leaked deadly gas that killed thousands of people.

Adaptive sense-making occurs when one or more individuals begin to doubt the sense that has already been made (Christianson, 2009). When people engage in such questioning they incorporate more cues and available data; they edit and update their story of what is going on and what is expected to happen. In more technical language, adaptive sense-making refers to puncturing an entrapped frame (Cornelissen et al., 2014). In previous studies, updating largely took place within a bounded context, such as the cockpit (Weick, 1990), plant control room (Weick, 2010), or emergency room (Christianson, 2009).

In a longitudinal study of six family firms and their Most Trusted Advisors (MTA), Strike and Rerup (2016) explored whether 'outsiders' to the family potentially could influence the adaptive sense-making process among core family members. They found that in entrepreneurial family firms, the Family Business Entrepreneur (FBE) moves quickly, often without considering input from other family members. FBEs can move fast because they often have sole or majority ownership, and do not need approval from a board or major shareholders (Strike, 2013). Like many entrepreneurs, FBEs are driven. They believe that fast action is needed to pursue new opportunities; consensus building and listening to other family members can interfere with the pace of the entrepreneurial process. But such urgency runs the risk of binding themselves in early commitments. To counter this risk and slow them down, Strike and Rerup found that FBEs often employ a Most Trusted Advisor (MTA), who plants seeds of doubt to invite the entrepreneur to consider an issue or opportunity from a different point of view, and thereby engage in

a broader and ongoing process of adaptive sense-making.

As Strike (2012, 2013) pointed out, MTAs are well-rounded people who counsel wealthy families that own and operate a business. A popular image of the MTA is the consigliere to the mob boss in the 1972 motion picture *The Godfather*. In the movie, the consigliere, played marvelously by Robert Duvall, was a close and trusted confidant, but he was neither family nor Sicilian. The consigliere has rare access to the boss's ear, and is one of the few people who can challenge him. Another image of the MTA is the statesman, a person who has deep knowledge of how to be just and who looks after the best interests of the citizens. Strike and Rerup found that the MTAs in the firms they studied occupied dual roles. Formally, they were members of the board of the family holding company. Informally, they operated across boundaries that most other people could not cross. For instance, they were trusted by family members who often did not trust one another. They were equally liked and respected by different generations of the family because they were able to see an issue from multiple points of view. Consequently, although the MTAs were not ordinarily part of the biological family, their relationships with members ran deep. Some of them had been with the family for more than 30 years. In sum, 'As mediators, the MTAs inhabit intersecting social worlds and can thus create circumstances that are rich with potential, in which cues in one world are made available to be coupled with entrapped frames in another world' (Strike and Rerup, 2016: 881).

Mediated sense-making is the process through which a mediator brings forward cues and points of view to generate pause, doubt and inquiry among people who operate within prescribed boundaries. The MTA in family firms sets the pace in a series of steps. First, because the FBE often has bracketed off certain cues, the MTA induces pause into the FBE's sense-making to create an opportunity to attend more carefully to cues in the wider environment. Slowing down the FBE often requires multiple conversations or subtle nudges. Second, the MTA introduces doubt into the process by asking questions or raising red flags. Slowly, questions about the viability of projects, decisions, or ideas lower the FBE's commitment to a particular frame. Third, once the FBE is less committed to a particular line of action, the MTA mediates different voices and perspectives to expose the FBE to more complex information and expand his/her frame. For instance, ideas from family members that the FBE would otherwise have ignored are introduced. Often, these voices lead the FBE to raise his own questions, which further lower commitment to a particular frame. On other occasions, the MTA motivates other people – board members, family members, other advisors – to voice their opinions. Multiple voices rather than a lone voice are more likely to cause the FBE to consider alternatives and engage in an expanded process of sense-making.

The subtle influence of the MTA on the FBE's sense-making is easy to miss because it is difficult to gain access to what occurs behind the scene (Goffman, 1974). Further, social scientists are often advised to focus on phenomena that are 'transparently observable' (Eisenhardt, 1989: 537). Nevertheless, to capture the microfoundation of institutions it is necessary to attend to phenomena that are spread out over time and space and thus less available for instantaneous observation. For example, to understand why and how change is either occurring or not, it might be valuable to zoom in and focus on individuals within a narrow context, but it might also be necessary to zoom out and consider how individuals on the fringes influence the center. Thus mediated sense-making incorporates micro and macro contextual features, demonstrating subtle effects of the broader social context on local sense-making. Strike and Rerup (2016) remind us that people within the boundary of an institution may be greatly influenced by those who are able to straddle multiple positions.

Balancing Conflicting Organizational Goals in Innovation

Work is accomplished through organizational routines, but the role of routines in balancing conflicting organizational goals has largely been overlooked. The reasons are twofold. First, most theories focus on how a single routine is performed by participants to accomplish one organizational goal (March and Simon, 1958; Cyert and March, 1963; Feldman and Pentland, 2003). Second, early research conceptualized routines as inert entities that respond poorly to competing goals. More recent work on routines dynamics has started to trace how routine participants perform patterns of action to balance conflicting organizational goals (Rerup and Feldman, 2011; Turner and Rindova, 2012; D'Adderio, 2014). This work reveals that people may engage in different types of action to direct routine enactments towards conflicting goals. Despite this growing body of research, much still remains to be learned about how routines can be a potential source for managing conflicting organizational goals.

March and Simon's (1958) classic account of organizations portrays a routine as a 'performance program' – a stable action pattern performed predictably to accomplish a single, specific organizational goal. When organizations are viewed as coalitions representing various interests, routines are one means to manage conflict resolution because accomplishing even a single organizational goal can evoke conflict among participants and the vested interests they support (Cyert and March, 1963: 164). Further, in situations where participants need to accomplish conflicting organizational goals, the Carnegie School suggests that conflicts can be resolved in one of two ways. First, managers can create a new routine that incorporates and resolves a conflict. Second, managers can sequentially separate the performance of conflicting goals in space or time. Although resolving conflict through these managerial steps can be valuable, this perspective does not consider how the frontline of an organization responds to the simultaneous pursuit of conflicting organizational goals.

Building on the Carnegie School, Nelson and Winter (1982) proposed that conflicts are rarely completely transparent between conflicting participants, in part because routines represent implicit organizational 'truces' that effectively ease conflicts for a specified period of time. When the participants enact a routine as a truce, they take a step back and agree to perform their part without requesting that solid changes be made to the enactment of the routine. The truce does not entirely subdue the conflicting interests and orientations between members. Rather, they become latent and unobservable: 'where once upon a time there was overt conflict … in most cases it is largely over when the observer comes to the scene' (Cohen et al., 1996: 662). The routine-as-truce view underlines how organizations reduce conflict between organizational goals by keeping 'areas of behavioral discretion' within the routine, in which participants perform a specific routine with some flexibility (Nelson and Winter, 1982: 109). These areas of discretion keep minor disagreements in check. In a study of a pricing routine in a manufacturing company, Zbaracki and Bergen (2010) found that for small changes the truce would keep the peace between the sales and marketing departments. With larger changes, however, the truce would break down, and senior management had to step in to keep the organization running. The routine-as-truce argument reveals how stability is maintained, but it offers limited insight into the dynamics and flexibility of truces.

Over the past 15 years, researchers have investigated organizational routines as flexible, living processes that require constant enactment. Scholars are exploring how multiple goals can be accomplished through the performance of organizational routines (Birnholtz et al., 2007; Turner and Rindova, 2012; D'Adderio, 2014). An emerging theme is that by performing various types of mundane actions, participants are able to flexibly enact different patterns of the same routine to accommodate replication and change, as well as multiple organizational goals. Despite this progress, the current literature has not fully articulated the types of actions that allow the same group of individuals to balance conflicting routine goals repeatedly over time.

To fill this gap, Salvato and Rerup (2017) conducted a longitudinal inductive study (1970–2006) of how members of a storied Italian design company, Alessi, simultaneously achieved the conflicting goals of new product development (NPD) and affordable commercial acceptance. Alessi was founded in 1921, and in 1970 it started to create design products. From 1970 to 1990, Alessi produced expensive design objects in stainless steel on a small scale. From 1991, it also manufactured less expensive and mass-produced toy-like products in plastic. Members of Alessi referred to products in the more expensive line as 'The Dream Factory' whereas products in the mass-produced line were known as 'The Efficient Factory'. The empirical puzzle is that throughout Alessi's history it has used only a single NPD routine to accomplish the conflicting goals of design and efficiency.

Salvato and Rerup (2017) identified different types of observable micro-actions that allowed routine participants distributed across the rank and file to enact conflicting goals flexibly. They noted the importance of breaking the category 'action' into types of action because only by doing so is it possible to capture the details of how stability or change is performed into specific routines. And it is by capturing these details that observers are able to understand how an organization balances conflicting goals by performing routines. First, various *mundane actions* accomplished the myriad tasks involved in product development. Second, *trials* – experimental actions through which the participants responded to relational conflicts or 'problems' – emerged as they were trying to enact the two conflicting routine goals. Gradually, the problems turned into relational contention over how to perform the NPD routine that prompted people to experiment with actions. The trials were initiated by routine participants at different positions and levels in the organizational hierarchy. They aimed to create opportunities – junctures – for the various team members supporting the Dream Factory and the Efficient Factory to collaborate and recreate a truce for performing the competing goals (Quick and Feldman, 2014). Third, *regulatory actions* emerged through trials. These routine actions that allowed participants to flexibly enact conflicting organizational goals by creating junctures between the participants, and provided them with opportunities to experience the conflict between different ways of enacting the contrasting organizational goals. Three types of regulatory actions were performed: (a) *Alternative splicing* recombined activities and participants; (b) *Activating* switched on particular actions to deal with NPD projects that were particularly complex and controversial; and (c) *Repressing* switched off particular actions in the NPD routine to reduce complexity.

This ecology of actions accomplished the two conflicting goals, and created a more dynamic truce. Specifically, from 1995 to 2006, members of Alessi were not enacting a stable and predictable pattern of the NPD routine that accomplished a single goal. Instead, they flexibly enacted the NPD routine as a dynamic, living system that allowed them to pursue both the Dream Factory and the Efficient Factory goals. But the NPD routine as truce disintegrated during the years from 1991 to 1995. A new, more flexible truce was created as participants engaged in trials that later turned into regulatory actions. In previous research, a truce was stitched together through zones of discretion in which one or more participants had some autonomy to perform the routine and other groups mutually agreed not to interfere (Nelson and Winter, 1982: 108). Zones of discretion create islands of stability that keep a truce intact

and unchanging. The truce that emerged at Alessi in the period between 1995 and 2006 was stitched together through an ecology of actions, most notably regulatory ones.

Routine regulation and the idea that truces are actively constructed and maintained through experimental trials and other forms of fairly mundane actions distributed across the rank and file suggest that it is important to link the performances of routines more closely to the microfoundations of institutions. Specifically, the findings from Alessi ask whether the same mechanisms and processes might operate at different levels of analysis. Regulatory routine actions at the level of the organization create and maintain a flexible truce in which participants balance conflicting organizational goals through a single routine.

Could regulatory actions also create flexible and dynamic institutions? Are regulatory actions taken to accomplish routines at the organizational level linked to higher-level institutions? Evidence suggests that we might be able to understand stability and change in higher-level structures by tracing lower-level micro-actions taken to accomplish routines. In a study of a greenfield organization, Rerup and Feldman (2011) traced the connection between organizational routines and firm-level organizational interpretive schemas, defined as sets of shared assumptions and values that give meaning to everyday activities and guide the actions of organizational members. The actions taken to enact organizational routines connected the organizational routines and the schemas. By extension, we propose that regulatory actions and other actions taken to accomplish organizational routines as flexible truces might be connected to the stability or flexibility of higher-level structures such as institutions.

IMPLICATIONS AND CONCLUSION

These four cases show that activities take form through micro-processes of organizational development, and that mundane routine actions can have much larger consequences and become more broadly institutionalized. Drawing on simple scripts, such as going down a list of names alphabetically or deciding to respond to unanticipated audience demand, had unanticipated, outsized consequences. These instances of practical reasoning were subsequently ascribed larger meaning and purpose as they crystallized into organizational practices and models that became widely scrutinized and emulated. In the case of family firms, the mediator role balances the dual interests of family and fortune and subtly influences the sense-making of family members, crossing boundaries that individuals rooted in one world find difficult. At the noted Italian design firm Alessi, regulatory routine actions partitioned conflicting interests, allowing participants to toggle between the challenges of innovative product design and affordable consumer products.

A common mechanism in the cases was transposition, that is, using the typical coin of the realm in one domain in a different one, to fresh effects (Padgett and Powell, 2012: 12–15, 438–440). Such moves can overcome the 'inherent lethargy of social life' and open up possibilities by creating traffic across social worlds (White, 2008: 279–283). In order to effect transpositions, individuals often violate institutional boundaries, repurposing old tools or recombining past practices in an unusual manner. Such people have been termed 'moral entrepreneurs' or 'rule creators' by the sociologist Howard Becker (1963). In these cases, participants create new social spaces and synthesize existing cultural practices in unfamiliar circumstances, sometimes resulting in marked departures from the past. In the case of Genentech, the transposition was born out of chance and naïveté. It was neither deliberative nor visionary; instead pragmatic agency brought two strangers with common interests together. In the case of family business advisors, trust looms large in importance but again the social skill to move between the worlds of family and

business is what gives the consiglieres their influence.

Our cases also illustrate the challenges involved in distinguishing emergent from intentional actions. Rather than assign simplistic labels, such as saying the founding of Genentech was emergent whereas Minnesota Public Radio's success was calculative, we emphasize that both reveal reflexivity (Garfinkel, 1967; Giddens, 1984). Similarly, it would oversimplify the skill involved in the role switching that characterizes the trusted family advisor to label such toggling intentional. When enacted successfully, switching roles or routines, as in the Alessi case, appears seamless. Thus, in our view, it matters less whether the actions were planned or opportunities simply seized, instead it is the awareness of how to overcome constraints or challenge the lethargy of social life that characterizes moments of transformation.

Our four cases are admittedly unusual in several respects. Several involve organizations that eventually became highly successful at activities that were initially regarded as novel, even questionable. As the new practices and identities became institutionalized, the organizations were held up for attention and debate, and then veneration and emulation (Colyvas and Powell, 2006). The Italian design firm Alessi has become internationally recognized for its combination of style and affordability. One advantage of studying such hallmark cases is the rich documentary trail that can be analyzed. But it is also possible to analyze sense-making as it occurs, provided one uses a sufficiently wide lens and has deep engagement with practitioners over a period of time. Reinecke and Ansari (2015) studied price-setting for coffee, tea and cotton products at Fairtrade International, observing how organizational members engaged with the complex idea of what a fair price is. Rather than focus on how accounts were settled after the fact or routines were explained and made sensible to others, research done in the here and now reveals how participants make practical judgments in response to the ongoing demands of organizational life.

In sum, a focus on the who, the what and the how points researchers toward the creation of the everyday knowledge needed for organizations to function. Such efforts are always influenced by institutionalized expectations, as participants extract cues and scripts from the larger environment. But it is also the case that arguments, practices and routines emerge from daily interactions among ensembles of people. These solutions to mundane exigencies may have larger consequences, reverberating across social worlds and becoming more general abstract packages of solutions.

Notes

1   See the review symposium on Garfinkel's *Studies in Ethnomethodology* in the January 1968 *American Sociological Review*, notably Coleman's (1968) critique. Lewis Coser (1975) used his presidential address at the ASA meetings to argue that ethnomethodology was a 'method in search of a theory'.

2   The Center for Social Innovation at the Stanford Graduate School of Business and National Arts Strategies, a non-profit consultancy for the arts, jointly developed a case on Minnesota Public Radio for classroom use. The case has been taught numerous times in MBA classes and with arts administrators. James Phills and Ed Martenson were the primary contributors to the case's development. We draw on the case, the article in the *Stanford Social Innovation Review*, and a video interview with William Kling by Martenson for this extended example.

3   Ron Russell, 'Public Radio's Darth Vader invades L.A. by gobbling up a sleepy Pasadena college station.' *New Times Los Angeles*, June 29, 2000.

4   Interview with William Kling by Ed Martenson.

5   Interview with William Kling by Ed Martenson.

ACKNOWLEDGMENT

We are grateful to Shaz Ansari, Tany Fernandez, Martha Feldman, Royston Greenwood, Yanfei Hu, Kathleen Much, Vanessa Strike and Tim Vogus for their very helpful comments on an earlier draft of the manuscript. Research support for Rerup was provided by the Ivey Business School at Western University.

REFERENCES

Astrachan, J. H. and Shanker, M. C. (2003). Family businesses' contribution to the U.S. economy: A closer look. *Family Business Review*, 16: 211–219.

Barley, S. R. (2008). Coalface institutionalism. In R. Greenwood, G. Oliver, R. Suddaby and K. Sahlin-Andersson (eds), *The SAGE Handbook of Organizational Institutionalism*. London: Sage. pp. 490–515.

Barley, S. R. and Tolbert, P. S. (1997). Institutionalization and structuration: Studying the links between action and institution. *Organization Studies*, 18 (1): 93–117.

Barton, M. A., Sutcliffe, K. M., Vogus, T. J. and DeWitt, T. (2015). Performing under uncertainty: Contextualized engagement in wildland firefighting. *Journal of Contingencies and Crisis Management*, 23 (2): 74–83.

Becker, H. S. (1963). *Outsiders: Studies in the Sociology of Deviance*. Glencoe, IL: The Free Press.

Berger, P. L. and Luckman, T. (1967). *The Social Construction of Reality*. Garden City, NJ: Doubleday.

Berman, E. P. (2012). *Creating the Market University: Science, the State, and the Economy, 1965–1985*. Princeton, NJ: Princeton University Press.

Binder, A. (2007). For love and money: Organizations' creative responses to multiple environmental logics. *Theory and Society*, 36 (6): 547–571.

Bittner, E. (1965). The concept of organization. *Social Research*, 32: 239–255.

Bittner, E. (1967). The police on skid row: A study in peacekeeping. *American Sociological Review*, 32 (5): 699–715.

Birnholtz, J. P., Cohen, M. D. and Hoch S. V. (2007). Organizational character: On the regeneration of Camp Poplar Grove. *Organization Science*, 18: 315–332.

Bourdieu, P. (1984). *Distinction: A Social Critique of the Judgment of Taste*. Cambridge, MA: Harvard University Press.

Boyer, H. W. (2001). Recombinant DNA research at UCSF and commercial application at Genentech. Oral history conducted in 1994 by Sally Smith Hughes, Regional Oral History Office, The Bancroft Library, University of California–Berkeley.

Cape, R. (2006). Ronald Cape: biotech pioneer and cofounder of CETUS. Oral history conducted in

2003 by Sally Smith Hughes, Regional Oral History Office, The Bancroft Library, University of California, Berkeley.

Chemical Heritage Foundation. (1997). The emergence of biotechnology: DNA to Genentech. Transcript of June 13 conference.

Christianson, M. K. (2009). Updating as part of everyday work: An interactional perspective. Unpublished doctoral dissertation, University of Michigan.

Cicourel, A. (1968). *The Social Organization of Juvenile Justice*. New York: John Wiley.

Cohen, Michael D. (2007). Reading Dewey: Reflections on the nature of routine. *Organization Studies*, 28 (5): 773–786.

Cohen, M. D. (2012). Perceiving and remembering routine action: Fundamental micro-level origins. *Journal of Management Studies*, 49 (8): 1383–1388.

Cohen, M., Burkhart, R., Dosi, G., Egidi, M., Marengo, L., Warglien, M. and Winter, S. G. (1996). Contemporary issues in research on routines and other recurring action patterns of organizations. *Industrial and Corporate Change*, 5: 653–698.

Cohen, M. D. and Hilligoss, P. B. (2010). The published literature on handoffs in hospitals: Deficiencies identified in an extensive review. *BMJ Quality and Safety*, 19 (6): 493–497.

Coleman, J. S. (1968). Review of studies in ethnomethodology. *American Sociological Review*, 33 (1): 126–130.

Colyvas, J. (2007). From divergent meanings to common practices: The early institutionalization of technology transfer at Stanford University. *Research Policy*, 36 (4): 456–476.

Colyvas, J. and Powell, W. W. (2006). Roads to institutionalization. *Research in Organizational Behavior*, 21: 305–353.

Cornelissen, J. P., Mantere, S. and Vaara, E. (2014). The contraction of meaning: The combined effect of communication, emotions, and materiality on sensemaking in the Stockwell shooting. *Journal of Management Studies*, 51: 699–736.

Coser, L. A. (1975). Two methods in search of a substance. *American Sociological Review*, 40 (6): 691–700.

Cyert, R. and March, J. G. (1963). *A Behavioral Theory of the Firm*, 2nd edn (1992). Oxford: Blackwell.

D'Adderio, L. (2014). The replication dilemma unravelled: How organizations enact multiple goals in routine transfer. *Organization Science*, 25: 1325–1350.

De Certeau, M. (1998). *The Practice of Everyday Life*. Minneapolis, MN: University of Minnesota Press.

Dees, J. G. (1998). Enterprising nonprofits. *Harvard Business Review*, 76 (1): 54–67.

Dewey, J. (1922). *Human Nature and Conduct*, 2nd edn (2002). Mineola, NY: Dover.

DiMaggio, P. J. and Powell, W. W. (1991). Introduction. In W. W. Powell and P. J. DiMaggio (eds), *The New Institutionalism in Organization Analysis*. Chicago, IL: University of Chicago Press. pp. 1–38.

Eisenhardt, K. M. (1989). Building theories from case study research. *Academy of Management Review*, 4: 532–549.

Emirbayer, M. (1997). Manifesto for a relational sociology. *American Journal of Sociology*, 103 (2): 281–317.

Emirbayer, M. and Mische, A. (1998). What is agency? *American Journal of Sociology*, 103: 962–1023.

Espeland, W. N. and Sauder, M. (2007). Rankings and reactivity: How public measures recreate social worlds. *American Journal of Sociology*, 113 (1): 1–40.

Feldman, M. S. (2000). Organizational routines as a source of continuous change. *Organization Science*, 11: 611–629.

Feldman, M. S. (2016). Routines as process: Past, present, and future. In J. H. Howard-Grenville, C. Rerup, A. Langley and H. Tsoukas (eds), *Organizational Routines: A Process Perspective. Perspectives on Process Organization Studies*, Volume 6. Oxford: Oxford University Press. pp. 23–46.

Feldman, M. S. and Orlikowski, W. J. (2011). Theorizing practice and practicing theory. *Organization Science*, 22 (5): 1240–1253.

Feldman, M. S. and Pentland, B. T. (2003). Reconceptualizing organizational routines as a source of flexibility and change. *Administrative Science Quarterly*, 48 (1): 94–118.

Feldman, M. S. and Worline, M. (2016). The practicality of practice theory. *Academy of Management Learning and Education*, 15 (2): 304–324.

Felin, T., Foss, N. and Ployhart, R. (2015). Microfoundations movement in strategy and organization theory. *Academy of Management Annals*, 9: 575–632.

Foster, W. and Bradach, J. (2005). Should nonprofits seek profits? *Harvard Business Review*, 83 (2): 92–100.

Fredrickson, D. N. (2001). *The Recombinant DNA Controversy: A Memoir*. Washington, DC: ASM Press.

Gambardella, A. (1995). *Science and Innovation: The U.S. Pharmaceutical Industry during the 1980s*. New York: Cambridge University Press.

Garfinkel, H. (1967). *Studies in Ethnomethodology*. Englewood Cliffs, NJ: Prentice Hall.

Garfinkel, H. (1968). The origins of the term 'ethnomethodology'. In R. Turner (ed.), *Ethnomethodology*. Harmondsworth: Penguin Books, 1974. pp. 15–18.

Garfinkel, H. and Bittner, E. (1967) Good organizational reasons for bad clinic records. In H. Garfinkel (ed.), *Studies in Ethnomethodology*. Englewood Cliffs, NJ: Prentice-Hall. pp. 186–207.

Gavetti, G., Greve, H. R., Levinthal, D. A. and Ocasio, W. (2012). A Neo-Carnegie perspective on strategy and organizations. *Academy of Management Annals*, 6 (1): 1–40.

Giddens, A. (1984). *The Constitution of Society: Outline of the Theory of Structuration*. Cambridge: Polity Press.

Gioia, D. A. and Chittipeddi, K. (1991). Sensemaking and sensegiving in strategic change initiation. *Strategic Management Journal*, 12: 433–448.

Goffman, E. (1974). *Frame Analysis*. Cambridge: Harvard University Press.

Gray, B., Purdy, J. M. and Ansari, S. (2015). From interactions to institutions: Microprocesses of framing and mechanisms for the structuring of institutional fields. *Academy of Management Review*, 40 (1): 115–143.

Greve, H. R. (2008). Organizational routines and performance feedback. In M. Becker (ed.), *Handbook of Organizational Routines*. Northampton, MA: Elgar. pp. 187–204.

Hall, S. S. (1987). *Invisible Frontiers: Race to Synthesize a Human Gene*. New York: Atlantic Monthly Press.

Hallett, T. (2010). The myth incarnate recoupling processes, turmoil, and inhabited institutions in an urban elementary school. *American Sociological Review,* 75 (1): 52–74.

Howard-Grenville, J., Golden-Biddle, K., Irwin, J. and Mao, J. (2011). Liminality as cultural process for cultural change. *Organization Science*, 22 (2): 522–539.

Howard-Grenville, J. and Rerup, C. (2017). A process perspective on organizational routines. In A. Langley and H. Tsoukas (eds), *Handbook of Process Organizational Studies*. London: Sage. pp. 323–339.

Hughes, S. S. (2001). Making dollars out of DNA: The first major patent in biotechnology and the commercialization of molecular biology, 1974–1980. *Isis* 92 (3): 541–75.

Jarzabkowski, P. (2008). Shaping strategy as a structuration process. *Academy of Management Journal*, 51 (4): 621–650.

Jarzabkowski, P., Kaplan, S., Seidl, D. and Whittington, R. (2016). On the risk of studying practices in isolation: Linking what, who, and how in strategy research. *Strategic Organization*, 14 (3): 270–274.

Jepperson, R. and Meyer, J. (2011). Multiple levels of analysis and the limitations of methodological individualisms. *Sociological Theory*, 29: 54–73.

Kaplan, S. (2008). Framing contests: Strategy making under uncertainty. *Organization Science*, 19 (5): 729–752.

Kenney, M. (1986). *Biotechnology: The University-Industrial Complex*. New Haven, CT: Yale University Press.

Khan, A. (1995). MPR successful raising money: Its for-profit sister is even better. *St. Paul Pioneer Press*, February 26, 1995.

Lapierre, D. and Moro, J. (2002). *Five Past Midnight in Bhopal*. New York: Warner.

Lave, J. and Wenger, E. (1991). *Situated Learning: Legitimate Peripheral Participation*. New York: Cambridge University Press.

LeBaron, C., Christianson, M., Garrett, L. and Ilan, R. (2016). Coordinating flexible performance during everyday work: An ethnomethodological study of handoff routines. *Organization Science*, 27 (3): 514–534.

Letts, C., William, R. and Grossman, A. (1997). Virtuous capital: What foundations can learn from venture capital. *Harvard Business Review*, March–April: 36–44.

Levinthal, D. A. and Rerup, C. (2006). Crossing an apparent chasm: Bridging mindful and less mindful perspectives on organizational learning. *Organization Science*, 17: 502–513.

Locke, K., Golden-Biddle, K. and Feldman, M. (2008). Making doubt generative: Rethinking the role of doubt in the research process. *Organization Science*, 19: 907–918.

Mair, J. and Hehenberger, L. (2014). Front-stage and backstage convening: The transition from opposition to mutualistic coexistence in organizational philanthropy. *Academy of Management Journal*, 57(4): 1174–1200.

Maitlis, S. (2005). The social processes of organizational sensemaking. *Academy of Management Journal*, 48: 21–49.

Maitlis, S. and Christianson, M. (2014). Sensemaking in organizations: Taking stock and moving forward. *Academy of Management Annals*, 8: 57–125.

Maitlis, S. and Sonenshein, S. (2010). Sensemaking in crisis and change: Inspiration and insights from Weick (1988). *Journal of Management Studies*, 47: 551–580.

March, J. G. (2008). *Heroes and History: Lessons for Leadership from Tolstoy's War and Peace*, film written and narrated by James March, and produced and directed by Steven Schecter, Graduate School of Business, Stanford University.

March. J. G. (2010). *The Ambiguities of Experience*. Ithaca, NY: Cornell University Press.

March, J. G. and Simon, H. A. (1958). *Organizations*. New York: Wiley.

Minkoff, D. and Powell, W. W. (2006). Nonprofit mission: Constancy, responsiveness, or deflection? In W. W. Powell and R. Steinberg (eds), *The Nonprofit Sector: A Research Handbook*, 2nd edn. New Haven, CT: Yale University Press. pp. 591–611.

Nelson, R. R. and Winter, S. J. (1982). *An Evolutionary Theory of Economic Change*. Cambridge, MA: Harvard University Press.

Nicolini, D. (2012). *Practice Theory, Work, and Organization: An Introduction*. Oxford: Oxford University Press.

Nicolini, D. and Monteiro, P. (2017). The practice approach: For a praxeology of organisational and management studies. In H. Tsoukas and A. Langley (eds), *The Sage Handbook of Process Organization Studies*. London: Sage. pp. 110–126.

Orlikowski, W. J. (2000). Using technology and constituting structures. *Organization Science*, 11 (4): 404–428.

Orlikowski, W. J. and Scott, S. V. (2008). Sociomateriality: Challenging the separation of technology, work and organization. *Academy of Management Annals*, 2 (1): 433–474.

Orsenigo, L. (1989). *The Emergence of Biotechnology: Institutions and Markets in Industrial Innovation*. London: Pinter.

Padgett, J. F. and Powell, W. W. (2012). *The Emergence of Organizations and Markets*. Princeton, NJ: Princeton University Press.

Parmigiani, A. and Howard-Grenville, J. (2011). Routines revisited: Exploring the capabilities and practice perspectives. *Academy of Management Annals*, 5: 413–453.

Patriotta, G. and Gruber, D. (2015). Newsmaking and sensemaking: Navigating temporal transitions between planned and unexpected events. *Organization Science*, 26 (6): 1574–1592.

Pentland, B. T. and Reuter, H. H. (1994). Organizational routines as grammars of action. *Administrative Science Quarterly*, 39: 484–510.

Peterson-Withorn, C. (2015). New report reveals the 500 largest family-owned companies in the world. *Forbes*, April 20, 2015.

Phills, J. and Chang, V. (2005). The price of commercial success. *Stanford Social Innovation Review*, Spring: 65–72.

Powell, W. W. and Colyvas, J. A. (2008). The microfoundations of institutions. In R. Greenwood, C. Oliver, R. Suddaby and K. Sahlin-Andersson (eds), *The SAGE Handbook of Organizational Institutionalism*. London: Sage. pp. 276–298.

Powell, W. W. and Sandholtz, K. (2012). Amphibious entrepreneurs and the emergence of organizational forms. *Strategic Entrepreneurship Journal*, 6 (2): 94–115.

Quick, K. S. and Feldman, M.S. (2014). Boundaries as junctures: Collaborative boundary work for building efficient resilience. *Public Administration Research and Theory*, 24: 673–695.

Reay, T., Chreim, S., Golden-Biddle, K., Goodrick, E., Williams, B. E., Casebeer, A., Pablo, A. and Hinings, C. R. (2013). Transforming new ideas into practice: An activity based perspective on the institutionalization of practices. *Journal of Management Studies*, 50 (6): 963–990.

Reinecke, J. and Ansari, S. (2015). What is a 'fair' price? Ethics as sensemaking. *Organization Science*, 26 (3): 867–888.

Rerup, C. and Feldman, M. (2011). Routines as a source of change in organizational schemata: The role of trial-and-error learning. *Academy of Management Journal*, 54 (3): 577–610.

Salvato, C. and Aldrich, H. (2012). That's interesting! *Family Business Review*, 25: 125–135.

Salvato, C. and Rerup, C. (2011). Beyond collective entities: Multi-level research on organizational routines and capabilities. *Journal of Management*, 37: 468–490.

Salvato, C. and Rerup, C. (2017). Routine regulation: Balancing conflicting goals in organizational routines. *Administrative Science Quarterly*, Forthcoming

Sandberg, J. and Tsoukas, H. (2015). Making sense of the sensemaking perspective: Its constituents, limitations, and opportunities for further development. *Journal of Organizational Behavior*, 36 (1): S6–S32.

Sauder, M. and Espeland, W. N. (2009). The discipline of rankings: Tight coupling and organizational change. *American Sociological Review*, 74 (1): 63–82.

Schatzki, T. R. (2012). A primer on practices. In J. Higgs, R. Barnett, S. Billett, M. Hutchings and F. Trede (eds), *Practice-Based Education: Perspectives and Strategies*. Rotterdam: Sense. pp. 13–26.

Schulman, P. R. (1993). The negotiated order of organizational reliability. *Administration and Society*, 25(3): 353–372.

Selznick, P. (1949). *TVA and the Grass Roots*. Berkeley, CA: University of California Press.

Simon, H. A. (1945). *Administrative Behavior*, 4th edn (1997). New York: Simon and Schuster.

Simon, H. A. (1978). Rationality as process and product of thought. *American Economic Review*, 68: 1–16.

Smets, M., Jarzabkowski, P., Burke, G. T. and Spee, P. (2015). Reinsurance trading in Lloyd's of London: Balancing conflicting-yet-complementary logics in practice. *Academy of Management Journal*, 58 (3): 932–970.

Smets, M., Morris, T. and Greenwood, R. (2012). From practice to field: A multilevel model of practice-driven institutional change. *Academy of Management Journal*, 55 (4): 877–904.

Strang, D. and Sine, W. (2002). Interorganizational institutions. In J. A. C. Baum (ed.), *Companion to Organizations*. Malden, MA: Blackwell. pp. 497–519.

Strike, V. (2012). Advising the family firm: Reviewing the past to build the future. *Family Business Review*, 25: 156–177.

Strike, V. (2013). The most trusted advisor and the subtle advice process in family firms. *Family Business Review*, 26: 293–313.

Strike, V. and Rerup, C. (2016). Mediated sensemaking. *Academy of Management Journal*, 59 (2): 880–905.

Suchman, L. (1987). *Plans and Situated Actions: The Problem of Human–Machine Communication*. Cambridge: Cambridge University Press.

Sudnow, D. (1965). Normal crimes: Sociological features of the penal code in a public defender's office. *Social Problems*, 12 (3): 255–276.

Sudnow, D. (1967). *Passing On: The Social Organization of Dying*. Englewood Cliffs, NJ: Prentice-Hall.

Swanson, R. A. (2001). Robert A. Swanson: Co-founder, CEO, and Chairman of Genentech, Inc., 1976–1996. Oral history conducted in 1996 and 1997 by Sally Smith Hughes, Regional Oral History Office, The Bancroft Library, University of California–Berkeley.

Teitelman, R. (1989). *Gene Dreams: Wall Street, Academia, and the Rise of Biotechnology*. New York: Basic Books.

Turner, S. F. and Rindova, V. (2012). A balancing act: How organizations pursue consistency in routine functioning in the face of ongoing change. *Organization Science*, 23: 24–46.

Vettel, E. J. (2006). *Biotech: The Countercultural Origins of an Industry*. Philadelphia, PA: University of Pennsylvania Press.

Vogus, T. and Colville, I. 2017. Sensemaking, simplexity, and mindfulness. In A. Langley., and H. Tsoukas (eds.), *The SAGE Handbook of Process Organizational Studies*. London: Sage. pp. 340–355.

Vogus, T. J. and Hilligoss, B. (2016). The underappreciated role of habit in highly reliable healthcare. *BMJ Quality and Safety*, 25 (3): 141–146.

Vogus, T. J., Rothman, N. B., Sutcliffe, K. M. and Weick, K. E. (2014). The affective foundations of high reliability organizing. *Journal of Organizational Behavior*, 35 (4): 592–596.

Weber, K. and Glynn, M. A. (2006). Making sense with institutions: Context, thought, and action in Karl Weick's theory. *Organization Studies*, 27 (11): 1639–1660.

Weick, K. E. (1990). The vulnerable system: An analysis of the Tenerife air disaster. *Journal of Management*, 16: 571–593.

Weick, K. E. (1993). The collapse of sensemaking in organizations: The Mann Gulch disaster. *Administrative Science Quarterly*, 38 (4): 628–652.

Weick, K. E. (1995). *Sensemaking in Organizations*. Thousand Oaks, CA: Sage.

Weick, K. E. (2009). Emergent change as a universal in organizations. In *Making Sense of the Organization Volume 2. The Impermanent Organization*. Chichester: Wiley. pp. 225–227.

Weick, K. E. (2010). Reflections on enacted sensemaking in the Bhopal disaster. *Journal of Management Studies*, 47: 537–550.

Weick, K. E. and Roberts, K. H. (1993). Collective mind in organizations: Heedful interrelating on flight decks. *Administrative Science Quarterly*, 38: 357–381.

Weick, K. E. and Sutcliffe, K. M. (2007). *Managing the Unexpected: Resilient Performance in an Age of Uncertainty*, 2nd edn. San Francisco, CA: Jossey–Bass.

Weick, K. E., Sutcliffe, K. M. and Obstfeld, D. (2005). Organizing and the process of sensemaking. *Organization Science*, 16 (4): 409–421.

Weisbrod, B. (ed.) (1998). *To Profit or Not: The Commercial Transformation of the Nonprofit Sector*. New York: Cambridge University Press.

West, C. and Zimmerman, D. (1987). Doing gender. *Gender and Society*, 1 (2): 125–151.

White, Harrison C. (2008). *Identity and Control*, 2nd edn. Princeton, NJ: Princeton University Press.

Whittington, R. (1992). Putting Giddens into action: Social systems and managerial agency. *Journal of Management Studies*, 29 (6): 693–712.

Winter, S. G. (2013). Habit, deliberation, and action: Strengthening the microfoundations of routines and capabilities. *Academy of Management Perspectives*, 27 (2): 120–137.

Zbaracki, M. J. and Bergen, M. (2010). When truces collapse: A longitudinal study of price adjustment routines. *Organization Science*, 21: 955–972.

Zimmerman, D. H. (1969). Record-keeping and the intake process in a public welfare agency. In S. Wheeler (ed.), *On Record: Files and Dossiers in American Life*. New York: Russell Sage. pp. 319–354.

Zucker, L. G. (1977). The role of institutionalization in cultural persistence. *American Journal of Sociology*, 42: 726–743.

Coalface Institutionalism

Stephen R. Barley

> Famous personages and also periods in the history ... may be reassessed, some being demoted and others raised up or even rediscovered ... Some are found worthless, stale; others provide stimulating ideas and even technology which can be built on ... their ideas and work are more 'relevant' – not merely more useful or suggestive – than that of many contemporaries ... No matter that the ancestors might be turning uncomfortably in their graves if they knew how their lives and works were reinterpreted and selectively used. (Strauss 1982: 179)

INSTITUTIONALISM, SOCIAL CONSTRUCTION AND ETHNOMETHODOLOGY

Neo-institutionalism appeared in the late 1970s with the goal of challenging rational theories of organizing that had ruled organization studies since the 1960s (Meyer and Rowan 1977; Zucker 1977; DiMaggio and Powell 1983). It also arrived just in time to counterbalance newly emerging transaction cost and ecological theories of organizational form (Williamson 1975; Hannan and Freeman 1977). Whereas transaction cost theory breathed new life into rational views of organizing by building on the calculus of a make or buy decision, the ecologists professed that human agency of any kind was largely irrelevant, if not illusory. This left the neo-institutionalists to reinforce the sociological line in organization studies. In what are widely acknowledged as seminal papers that staked out neo-institutionalism's stance, Zucker (1977), Meyer and Rowan (1977) and DiMaggio and Powell (1983) argued that organizations not only act, but that they often do so for cultural, interpretative and symbolic reasons, and that these actions matter for an organization's fate. For ethnographers of work and organizations, many of whom still worked in the spirit of industrial sociology, the neo-institutionalists seemed like kin. Here, finally, were bona fide organizational theorists who dared to stake their macro theories on a micro sociology.[1]

The institutionalists' micro-sociologies of choice were phenomenological constructivism and ethnomethodology. Zucker made the most use of both (Zucker 1977, 1987; Tolbert and Zucker 1996). She combined Berger and Luckmann's (1967) concepts of typification, reification, and objectivation with Garfinkel's (1967) notion of accounts to argue that institutions are best treated as taken-for-granted understandings:[2]

> Institutionalized acts then, must be perceived as both *objective* and *exterior*. Acts are *objective* when they are potentially repeatable by other actors without changing the common understanding of the act, while acts are *exterior* when the subjective understanding of acts is reconstructed as intersubjective ... so that the acts are seen as part of the external world (see Berger and Luckmann, 1967 on 'reification' and 'objectivation') ... When acts have ready-made accounts they are institutionalized; that is both objective and exterior. (Zucker 1977: 728; emphasis in original)

Although less expansively, Meyer and Rowan (1977) made nearly identical use of the same micro-sociologies. Crediting Berger and Luckmann, they wrote: 'Institutionalized rules are classifications built into society as reciprocated typifications or interpretations' (1977: 341). Later, citing Scott and Lyman (1968), they connected institutions to the ethnomethodological notion of accounts: 'The incorporation of institutionalized elements provides an account of its activities that protects the organization from having its context questioned' (1977: 349).

Published six years later, DiMaggio and Powell's (1983) canonical article contained no mention of either constructivism or ethnomethodology, except for passing reference to a paper by Aaron Cicourel (1970). But in the introduction to their influential book *The New Institutionalism in Organizational Analysis*, DiMaggio and Powell (1991: 19–22) highlighted both micro-sociologies. They concluded: 'Ethnomethodology and phenomenology together provide the new institutionalism with a micro-sociology of considerable power' (1991: 21). Since these original manifestos, however, institutionalists have devoted little attention to ethnomethodology, to social construction, or for that matter, to micro-sociology of any kind. As institutionalism spread, its micro-social concerns disappeared into the background.

In retrospect, the disappearance is unsurprising. Ethnomethodology was from the start an odd choice for linking organizations to situated action and cognition. With a few notable exceptions (Bittner 1965; Silverman 1971; Cicourel 1967), ethnomethodologists had little to say about organizations.[3] They certainly spoke of institutions, but their institutions were of a different order than those that preoccupied institutionalists. Ethnomethodologists have usually focused on taken-for-granted understandings that are widely shared by members of a culture or subculture: for example, how to do gender (Garfinkel 1967), how to do power (Grimshaw 1981), how to do being a doctor (Emerson 1970) or how to take turns in a conversation (Sachs et al. 1974). In fact, for ethnomethodologists, interpretive procedures were the ultimate institutions. By interpretive procedures ethnomethodologists meant deep, taken-for-granted rules necessary for engaging in everyday interaction in precisely the same way that grammars are the deep rules for everyday speech (Cicourel 1970, 1972, 1981). Among the interpretive procedures that interested ethnomethodologists were: a *reciprocity of perspectives* (the assumption that others see the same world I see), *indexicality* (the assumption that to make sense of what is being said or done I need to take the immediate context into account) and a *retrospective–prospective sense of occurrence* (the assumption that others will eventually do or say something that will clarify what they have done or said so far). Clearly, these taken-for-granteds are of a different order than civil service reform (Tolbert and Zucker 1983), internal labor markets (Dobbin et al. 1993), or changing forms of corporate control (Fligstein 1993). The latter are components of social or political systems that operate at a much higher level of analysis than the phenomena typically of concern to ethnomethodologists.

Furthermore, ethnomethodology is primarily a cognitive rather than a behavioral or political sociology (Cicourel 1974). In ethnomethodology, as in institutional theory, sense-making trumps vested action. Ethnomethodology's cognitive perspective, as well as Berger and Luckmann's notions of reification, objectivation and sedimentation, make it easier to view institutions as stable constraints rather than as shifting resources. In fact, as Heritage notes (1993), ethnomethodologists have written more about the replication of social order than about its change. Paul DiMaggio (1988: 10) acknowledged a similar proclivity in institutional theory nearly three decades ago:

> If the focus of institutional theory on norms, taken-for-granted assumptions, and cognitive and coordinative limitations represent substantive reasons for the neglect (relative to other theoretical traditions) of interests, part of this neglect is implicit not in the logic of institutional arguments but in the rhetoric that institutional theorists have used to advance them. The 'iron cage' is one such phrase, with its implicit portrayal of humans as powerless .... Similar are assertions that institutionalized organizations 'take on a life of their own' ... Presumably if an organization 'takes on a life of its own' one need not attend to individual or group motives to understand behavior ... The most widespread rhetorical, as opposed to analytic, dismissals of agency ... occur in the chronic use of passive constructions and, where nouns are used as the subjects of active verbs, in the selection of subjects so broad of reference as to be substantively empty ... [T]he locutions ... [that institutionalists use] systematically de-emphasize human agency. Institutional myths 'are highly institutionalized,' and some structural elements are ... 'societally legitimated.' Another approach ... would be to ask, 'Who has institutionalized the myths (and why)?' and 'Who has the power to "legitimate" a structural element?'

Ironically, institutionalism might have avoided these issues and others to which they have subsequently been forced to attend had they looked to a different micro-sociology for inspiration: Chicago School sociology as practiced by Everett C. Hughes and his students.[4]

INTERACTIONISM: THE ROAD NOT TAKEN

Chicago School sociologists, especially Hughes, saw their agenda as the study of institutions and institutionalized behavior.[5] George Herbert Mead, whose work strongly influenced Chicago sociology, had defined society as a 'body of institutions' (Athens 2005: 305). Hughes, in turn, equated sociology with the study of institutions. 'Sociology is that one of the social sciences,' he wrote, 'which is especially and peculiarly, by intent and not by accident, a science of social institutions' (1942: 15). Zucker (1977: 726) recognized Hughes' relevance for the neo-institutionalists' agenda and opened her influential paper by citing one of Hughes' quip-like definitions: 'The only idea common to all usages of the term "institution" is that of some sort of establishment of relative permanence of a distinctly social sort' (Hughes 1936: 180). But, she subsequently made little use of the Chicagoans. Meyer and Rowan (1977) made even less: their paper contains no mention of Hughes and only passing references to Dalton (1950) and Goffman (1967), who studied with Hughes at Chicago. DiMaggio and Powell (1983) referenced no Chicago School sociologists at all.

Substantial acknowledgement of Hughes' contribution to the study of institutions awaited the publication of Richard Scott's (1995) *Institutions and Organizations*. Early in his treatise, Scott (1995: 8) credited Hughes with being an early institutionalist, noted that Hughes was particularly interested in the relationship between individuals and institutions and credited the Chicagoans for carrying institutionalism 'forward in an uninterrupted fashion' in occupational sociology (1995: 9). Scott scolded organizational sociologists for not having done the same, but then said nothing more about the Chicagoans' contributions. In fact, later in the book, when mapping levels of analysis to bodies of theory and research on institutions Scott (1995: 59), presented ethnomethodology as the only institutional sociology that operates at the level of the organization and below.

Scott may have skipped the Chicago sociologists, not only because they studied occupations, but also because he classified them as symbolic interactionists who saw meaning as 'internalized and subjective' rather than as objective and exterior (1995: 42).[6] If by symbolic interactionists Scott had Herbert Blumer (1962) and his students in mind, then his charge of subjectivism is warranted. As Athens (2005: 307–208) points out, Blumer downplayed Mead's notion of institutionalized (exterior) meaning (what Mead called, 'common maxims'), because he apparently believed that the notion of an institution was less relevant for 'modern, mass societies' than it had been in traditional societies.[7] However, the charge of subjectivism cannot be so easily levelled against Hughes, Anselm Strauss (1968, 1978a; Strauss et al. 1964), Howard Becker (1952, 1953, 1963, 1982) and others who collaborated or studied with Hughes. Hughes and Blumer were both students of Robert Park and Ernest Burgess (1921), both were influenced by Mead (1934) and were later colleagues on the faculty at Chicago, but Hughes' work differed significantly from Blumer's precisely because institutions were front and center in Hughes' image of society.[8] Hughes wrote about real estate boards, professional associations, medical schools and hospitals among other settings. Perhaps most importantly, he studied the processes by which occupations become professions: Processes which, for Hughes, entailed the construction of precisely the sort of institutions that neo-institutionalists study.

Perhaps it is because the institutionalists overlooked the Chicagoans that they have generally turned to social psychology when they need to link meaning to social structure and explain how institutional rules are interpreted and negotiated (rather than imposed or coerced):

> By contrast [to institutionalists], social psychologists are more likely to emphasize the interactive and negotiated nature of those choices. Constitutive rules need not simply be externally imposed on actors. Weick (1979), for example, emphasizes that understandings and scripts emerge out of actions as well as guide them and that collective symbols are as likely to be used to justify past behaviors as to guide current ones. These newer versions of role and identity theory emphasize that individuals play an active part, using existing rules and social resources to construct a social identity with some consistency across varying situations ... A cognitive conception of institutions stresses the central role played by the socially mediated construction of a common framework of meaning. (Scott 1995: 45)

Hughes and his students spent half a century developing and refining an understanding of how actors negotiate understandings, rules, roles and meaning, albeit from a decidedly sociological and institutional perspective.

I suspect, however, that institutionalists overlooked the Chicagoans for the same reason that other sociologists have done so: Hughes and his students are widely thought to have developed no theory. The perception of the Chicagoans as theory-less arises, in part, because Hughes and his students eschewed top-down theory in favor of amassing data to generate what Glaser and Strauss (1967) would eventually call 'grounded theory'. Fine (1991: 165) makes precisely this point when discussing how interactionists have dealt with institutional constraints. 'Any approach to social order', Fine wrote, must recognize that although actors themselves affect how they define their world, others – corporate, collective, imaginary, or metaphoric – considerably influence their choices. Our ethnographies, grounded in institutional realities and individual recognitions of these realities, demonstrate this, but our theory lags behind.' In other words, institutions served Hughes and his students as an ever-present backdrop for their field studies. The concept of institutions is tightly woven into their writings. However, they had little need for an explicit theory of institutions because they did not have institutionalism's agenda of developing an alternative to rationalism.[9]

Nevertheless, to say that Chicago School sociologists built no explicit theory is not to say that they had no perspective at all. As Rock (1979: 83) noted, the theoretical looseness that scholars find troubling about the Chicagoans was less a matter of muddled minds than a practiced guard against premature generalization. Hughes and his students aimed their investigations at bounded 'social worlds' (Shibutani 1955; Strauss 1978b). Their guiding notion was that valid theoretical concepts could only emerge by comparing the particulars of a variety of settings (Glaser and Strauss 1967). If a construct was to be relevant for a range of cases, its reach had to be demonstrated empirically. As a consequence, the picture of how the Chicagoans understood institutions is scattered across forty years of research.

In recent years, scholars have begun to acknowledge the relevance of interactionist sociology for institutionalism (Basu et al. 1999; Fligstein 2001; Lounsbury and Kaghan 2001; Hallett and Ventresca 2006).[10] My goal is to go further and explain in detail how Hughes and his students understood institutions and institutionalization. As we shall see, their ideas are not only consistent with neo-institutionalism, but their perspective offers a micro-sociology that treats institutions as constraints while emphasizing the role that human agency and vested interests play in creating, maintaining and changing institutions. I begin by documenting how the Chicagoans defined institutions and then explicate Anselm Strauss' notions of negotiated orders and social worlds, concepts that capture, respectively, the institutionalists' image of institutions as social processes and structures. The discussion subsequently turns to two issues that currently concern institutionalists and about which the interactionists had much to say: legitimation and the nature of institutional complexes. My agenda

is to suggest how researchers might proceed if they assume, as did the Chicagoans, that action always occurs within the constraints of an institutional matrix that humans wittingly or unwittingly create, maintain and alter.

INSTITUTION IN THE CHICAGO TRADITION

'Institution' and its various semantic derivatives peppered the writings of the Chicagoans, but other than Hughes, few said directly what they meant by the term. The same is true of the entire constellation of concepts (career, role, identity, etc.) with which the interactionists routinely worked (Barley 1989). Scholars must, therefore, infer what the Chicagoans had in mind by examining the context in which the terms appear. In general, Hughes and his students used 'institution' in three ways. The first was to denote types or classes of organizations: hospitals, schools, labor unions, firms and so on. The second was closer to how Mead (1934) and Merton (1957) employed the term: broad sectors or domains of society such as the family, science, religion and economy. The third usage, which is more frequent and more interesting, is harder to specify, although it underwrites the other two. To grasp this more diffuse notion of institution, it is useful to turn to passages drawn from a number of texts.

Hughes begins 'The Study of Institutions' by inventorying, in his down-home, discursive way, concrete examples of institutions of different 'orders':

A large portion of the people in our society live together in *families* ... Likewise, people go to work in *factories*; they study, teach and play in *schools* ... If they are residents of Latin American villages, they will engage once a year in a great *fiesta*: if they live in the rural Middle West, they might possibly be annually mobilized by a *county fair*. In all these instances people are mobilized to *take their places* – important or minor, casual or regular, voluntary or involuntary – in a *collective enterprise carried on in a somewhat established and expected way*. The things

I have named – and many others as well – have been called institutions. Some of the other things which have been called by the same name are of quite different orders. It is not my purpose to explore the limits of a concept. (1942: 307; emphasis added)

Hughes then goes on to say that students of institutions should concern themselves with two phenomena: action and social forms, the first of which occurs 'within' the latter. Given this, he cautions that trying to decide whether something is or is not an institution is a waste of time:

I rest the case by saying that I conceive of the study of institutions to be part of *the study of society in action*. The center of the field lies where *the action takes place within forms which are somewhat firmly established*. The student of institutions will, however, be interested also in seeing how *social forms* become established, how they bend and yield under pressure, how they give place to new, and what functions they perform. He will, if his interest is in the structure and functioning of society, be only incidentally concerned to answer categorically the question whether the newspaper, the beer parlor, the Republican Party or property is an institution at a given moment. (1942: 307; emphasis added)

These passages contain four ideas key to the interactionists' concept of an institution. First, institutions were 'social forms', a term drawn directly from Simmel (1964).[11] For Simmel, as for Hughes, a social form was a pattern both of and for social action. It was exterior to those who participated in it and independent of the particulars of their behavior. Form is a structural concept in the sense that genre, script, role, template and grammar are structures. For Simmel, forms were the building blocks of society. Thus, it is fair to say that like Berger and Luckmann, Hughes saw institutions as constructions that had become objectified and exteriorized, although perhaps less reified.

Second, when Hughes spoke of institutions of different 'orders', he implied that institutions vary in their scope or range of application. Some institutions cover the actions of large portions of society (a form of family or notions of property), while others

are relatively local (a fiesta or a county fair). Third, institutions are 'collective enterprises', in the sense that they are jointly produced through ongoing action and interaction. Finally, institutionalized actions and interactions are to some degree scripted; people 'take their places' in the sense that they play roles in a 'somewhat established or expected way'. Without such consistency, institutions could not exist.

In a paper written twenty years later, Hughes (1971 [1962]) was more explicit about what constituted a social form. Much like Mead, who claimed that behavior was institutionalized when people behaved according to 'common maxims', Hughes pointed to conventions.

Since a common feature of definitions of institutions is that they are *clusters of conventions*, the obvious things to put into a list are those phenomena that are beyond dispute conventional, the things that have a place in the more established public *statements of how we do things* (strongly tinged with the notion that these are *the right way to do things*). But if we close our lists there, we miss the main and more fascinating part of the sociologist's work, which is to understand how social values and *collective arrangements are made and unmade*: how things arise and how they change. To make progress with our job, we need to give full and comparative attention to the not-yets, the didn't-quite-make-its, the not-quite-respectable, the unremarked and the openly 'anti' goings-on in our society. (1971 [1962]: 52; emphasis added).

This passage points to three additional attributes of Hughes' notion of an institution. First, like the ethnomethodologists, Hughes viewed institutions as taken-for-granted cultural understandings and practices. But, unlike the ethnomethodologists, he implied that taken-for-granteds could be articulated as 'how we do things' and that they had moral force. In other words, institutions carry some notion of 'ought'. As a result, Hughes attributed behavioral status to institutions without denying that they also had a cognitive element. For interactionists the social, cognitive and behavioral were inseparable. Second, Hughes claimed that conventions 'cluster', they occur in complexes. That institutions co-occur or intersect to form a social fabric is an important and recurring image in interactionist sociology. Finally, as did most Chicagoans, Hughes thought it important to study institutions in process. For the interactionists, institutions were not fixed: They morphed as people created, attempted to change and sometimes eliminated them.

By combining these various attributes, we can synthesize an approximate definition of what Hughes meant by an institution. Institutions are social forms or templates composed of clusters of conventions that script behavior to varying degrees in given contexts. Institutions are socially constructed and are subsequently maintained or changed by people who act and interact with each other. For the Chicagoans, then, an institution was an abstract and flexible heuristic applicable at a variety of levels of analysis. Thus, for example, Goffman (1983) could, in a single paper, employ the term to talk about the social meaning of acquaintanceship as well as the form of a service encounter (practices that address customers' expectations that they be treated equitably, equally and with courtesy):

> Take for example (in our own society) acquaintanceship, or, better still, 'knowership.' This is a critical institution from the perspective of how we deal with individuals in our immediate, or in our telephonic, presence, a key factor in the organization of social contacts. What is involved is the right and obligation mutually to accept and openly to acknowledge individual identification on all initial occasions of incidentally produced proximity (p. 13) ... I have suggested in schematic terms elements of the structure of service transactions that can be taken as institutionalized and official, such that ordinarily when they are seen to apply in a particular service setting, those present feel that nothing marked or unacceptable or out of the ordinary has occurred by way of substance or ceremony. (1983: 15)

Although Goffman's renderings resembled an ethnomethodologist's take on institutions

(see especially Goffman 1981), other Chicagoans spoke of institutions at levels of analysis that have preoccupied the neo-institutionalists. Consider, for example, Strauss and Schatzman's comments on forms of psychiatric hospitals:

> Socio-cultural changes in American life account both for much of what is claimed that the mentally ill need and for the kinds of institutions and practices being fashioned for them. Institutions, like people, have historical and social loci .... For example, Americans may be developing certain forms of institutional practice, not so much because they are designed for better psychiatric treatment but because they ... meet the requirements of some special public ... Design for psychiatric treatment may be a *rationalization of ideological sentiment* ... for behind mental institutions *are social and philosophical trends*, which give rise to *ideas about appropriate institutional forms*. ... During the latter half of the nineteenth century, the United States developed the state mental hospital. We are all familiar with this form of hospital ... Today they are widely regarded as medieval, cruel, or totally unsuitable for the treatment of the mentally ill. Yet they were once regarded as suitable ... [they] siphoned off many of the poor, the indigent, and the unassimilated immigrants, and effectively hid them from public view and concern. They relieved the cities and states of special welfare and protection problems and saved whole families from the threat of downward mobility. All this they did with a minimum of cost ... We would say that this *institutional form* was *appropriate* simply *because at that time it reflected the needs, ideas, and character of American life*. Sociologically, it fit. Today it no longer fits. Now we are developing new institutional forms and practices appropriate to the needs, ideas, and character of American life today – and not necessarily appropriate to the needs of the mentally ill. (Schatzman and Strauss 1966: 12; emphasis added)

This passage points to two additional attributes of institutions, as Chicagoans understood them. First, institutions are historically situated and sociologists would do well to approach them with a long view. Second, institutions are tied to ideologies championed by specific segments of society that lend the institution legitimacy. As ideologies change, legitimacy will change and, hence, so will the institution.

In short, the Chicagoan's image of institutions encompasses much of neo-institutionalism's more cognitive view. Like institutionalists, the Chicagoans argued that institutions were typifications – taken-for-granted ways of acting, doing, seeing and thinking. As Fine put it:

Learning to act appropriately requires understanding the 'type' of situation faced and knowing what behaviors fit ... Further, [situations] are perceived as being controlled by and constitutive of organizations, groups, institutions, and societies ... Our reading of situations involves creating typifications of macro-structures that serve as the basis for addressing future interactions. (1991: 165)

Like institutionalists, Hughes and his students also understood that perceptions of legitimacy were crucial to the emergence and maintenance of institutions and that legitimation was integrally tied to ideologies whose rhetorics offered justificatory accounts. Finally, although 'social form' connotes a broader concept of social structure than that which most institutionalists employ, it easily encompasses the institutionalists' concern with types of organizations and organizational structures. Indeed, interactionists routinely used 'institution' to refer to organizational forms (Strauss et al. 1964; Schatzman and Strauss 1966; Bucher and Stelling 1977; McCallion and Maines 2002).

At the same time, the Chicagoans' view of institutions differed from the institutionalists' in theoretically and empirically important ways. First, they saw institutions as processes. Institutions not only constrained human action, human action, in turn, created, maintained and changed institutions. Said differently, institutions were both a product of and resources for interaction and negotiation in everyday life. Second, institutions occurred in clusters and these clusters defined the context for action in the social worlds they covered. Institutions were, therefore, integral to the segmentation of society. To see how these ideas might benefit contemporary institutionalists requires turning from Hughes to Anselm Strauss' work on negotiated order (Strauss 1978a) and social worlds (Strauss 1978b, 1982, 1984).[12] The former amounts to an action-oriented take on institutions and institutionalization, while the latter provides a way of conceptualizing, investigating and analyzing institutional clusters.

NEGOTIATED ORDERS

Despite Berger and Luckmann's interest in human agency and Garfinkel's preoccupation with practice, the institutionalists who invoked them paid little attention to agency and practice. Sometimes, this seemed purposeful. For instance, Meyer and Rowan (1977) apparently separated structure from action as part of a gambit for challenging the idea that organizational structures direct work intentionally and rationally:

There is need for an explanation of [the rise of formal organizations] that is partially free from the assumption that, in practice, formal structures actually coordinate and control work. Such an explanation should account for the elaboration of purposes, positions, policies, and procedural rules that characterizes formal organizations, but *must do so without supposing that these structural features are implemented in routine work activity.* (1977: 343; emphasis added)

Meyer and Rowan's agenda was to undercut the assumption that plans and structures cause action, a myth that Bittner (1965) and Silverman (1971) had already debunked from an ethnomethodological stance. However, to say that action is not rationally linked to structures, purposes, positions and policies, is not equivalent to saying there is no relationship at all.

Early on, DiMaggio warned that dismissing agency was neo-institutionalism's Achilles' heel. Noting that the 'role of interest and agency in institutional theory remains somewhat obscure', DiMaggio (1988: 3–5) took institutionalists to task for emphasizing 'factors that make actors unlikely to recognize or to act on their interests' and 'circumstances that cause actors who do recognize and try to act on their interests to be unable to do so effectively'. He went on to call attention to what he called the paradox of institutionalization:

> Institutionalization as an outcome places organizational structures and practices beyond the reach of interest and politics. By contrast, institutionalization as a process is profoundly political and reflects the relative power of organized interests and the actors who mobilize around them. (DiMaggio 1988: 13)

DiMaggio argued that most institutional research had emphasized outcomes over process. In response, he called for studies of institutional entrepreneurs – men and women who intentionally or unintentionally create institutions as a way of achieving their own interests or the interests of groups they represent.

Taking DiMaggio's call seriously, a number of institutionalists have recently begun to investigate how individuals, organizations or professions wittingly or unwittingly created institutions by pursuing lines of action (Fligstein 2001; Seo and Creed 2002; Venkatesh and Shin 2005; Greenwood and Suddaby 2006; Battilana 2006; Leca 2006). Young scholars have also paid more attention than earlier institutionalists to how people cast meaning (Lawrence and Phillips 2004; Munir and Phillips 2005; Grodal 2007). Nevertheless, because the idea of an entrepreneur encourages studies of 'foundings', tales of entrepreneurial agency usually end once an institution has been established. Although the actions of entrepreneurs are surely a crucial part of the story of institutionalization, focusing on entrepreneurs skirts the idea that agency and action are also important for maintaining and modifying institutions.[13]

Some scholars, realizing that agency is implicated at all phases of an institution's lifespan, have attempted to reformulate institutionalization in light of Giddens' (1984) concept of structuration (Barley and Tolbert

1997; Lounsbury and Kaghan 2001; Sandfort 2003; Battilana 2006).[14] Structuration theory portrays institutions simultaneously as constraints on and products of social action. Giddens (1984) called this reciprocal causality the 'duality of structure'. Furthermore, structuration implies that researchers can only document how individual and collective action creates, preserves or changes institutions by taking a longitudinal view. Having made these points, however, Giddens says little about how to identify much less study structure's duality. The need to forge empirical tools led Barley (1986) to blend structuration theory with Strauss's more pragmatic notion of negotiated order and to study 'structuring' by observing how scripted interactions evolved over time.[15]

The notion of structuring was long latent in interactionist scholarship. For instance, Blumer (1962: 189–190) argued that a reciprocal relationship between actions and institutions lay at the core of symbolic interactionism's view of society:

> concerns with organization on one hand and with acting units on the other hand set the essential difference between conventional views of human society and the view of it implied in symbolic interaction ... The difference is along two major lines. First, from the standpoint of symbolic interaction the organization of a human society is the framework inside of which social action takes place and is not the determinant of that action. Second, such organization and changes in it are the product of the activity of acting units and not of 'forces' which leave such acting units out of account ... Social organization enters into action only and to the extent to which it shapes situations in which people act, and the extent to which it supplies fixed sets of symbols which people use in interpreting their situations. (1962: 189–190)

Structural duality was also implicit in how interactionists understood the core constructs around which they organized their research: roles, rules, careers, status, identity and so on. For Hughes and his students, these Janus-faced concepts oriented attention simultaneously in two directions (Barley 1989). On one hand, they pointed to patterned forms of action and participation characteristic of life in some social domain. In the case of a role, for instance, the relevant patterns were the recurrent behaviors and types of interactions that were more or less common to and expected of all who fill a role. To be a policeman entails wearing a specific kind of uniform, carrying a gun, stopping speeding motorists, handing out parking tickets, keeping a watchful eye on public events, making court appearances, persuading loiterers to move along, directing traffic, issuing orders to people from various walks of life, and having those orders obeyed, however grudgingly (see Van Maanen 1973, 1975). Similarly, having a career also denotes a structured and recognized form of participation in a social world: A stream of identifiable positions, offices, statuses and situations that serve as landmarks for gauging a person's movement through an organization, occupation, family, avocation or subculture (Hughes 1937: 403; Goffman 1961: 127; Becker 1963: 24; Faulkner 1974: 132; Braude 1975: 141). In Hughes' terminology, this constitutes the 'objective' (Berger and Luckman would say, 'objectivated') aspect of a role or a career – its institutional or public face which requires some kind of overt behavior.

On the other hand, for Chicagoans, role and career also pointed to the incumbent's subjective experience. By subjective experience interactionists meant the meanings that individuals attribute to their role or career. The subjective side of a role entails accounts or definitions of both self and others that enable individuals to orient to situations.[16] In the case of policing, for instance, Van Maanen (1978) described how interpretations of self and others are crucial to how police classify and, then, behave toward people they encounter on patrol. A 'subjective career' similarly encompasses its incumbent's sense of becoming, which enables her to develop a narrative of and align herself with the events of her biography. Subjective careers are the tales people tell to themselves and others that

lend coherence to the strands of their life. More importantly for present purposes, such interpretations and enactments lay foundations for change in role behaviors and career trajectories that eventually modify a role's or a career's institutional face.

Unlike Linton (1936) and Parsons (1951), the Chicagoans did not conceive of roles as predefined sets of rights and duties that could be donned and doffed. Instead they subscribed to Mead's (1934) notion that roles emerge in an ongoing process of negotiation, a 'conversation of gestures', during which individuals develop a repertoire of behaviors and attitudes tailored to specific interactional partners. For interactionists, 'role-making' was as important as 'role-taking'. Role-making (among other dynamics) allowed for variations that might eventually reformulate a role's institutional face (Turner 1962, 1968, 1976, 1978; McCall and Simmons 1978).

Strauss further developed the interactionists' imagery of a reciprocal relationship between structure and action in his much overlooked body of work (at least in organization studies) on negotiated order. Strauss believed that unraveling the link between action and structure was one of sociology's primary tasks. Foreshadowing Giddens by over a decade, he and Schatzman wrote: 'Institutions impose limitations upon practices and ideas, but in turn are modified by them. The precise ways in which these are related is an important aspect of sociological inquiry' (Schatzman and Strauss 1966: 13).

Strauss' interest in negotiated order began with a field study of a psychiatric hospital in the late 1950s where he and his colleagues encountered competing ideologies of illness and treatment (Strauss et al. 1963, 1964). Proponents of these ideologies espoused different visions of a psychiatric hospital's mission and how such hospitals should be organized and administered. At roughly the same time, Rue Bucher (Bucher and Schatzman 1962; Bucher and Stelling 1977) documented analogous ideological disputes raging in pathology: some pathologists saw their field as a science, while others believed it should be treated as a medical specialty. In their jurisdictional battles, these two camps formed alliances with different groups of physicians, championed different systems of education, formed different professional associations, and politicked for different roles in the medical community. Strauss and his collaborators explicated and refined the idea of negotiated order throughout the 1960s (Bucher and Strauss 1961; Bucher and Schatzman 1962; Schatzman and Bucher 1964; Glaser and Strauss 1965, 1968; Schatzman and Strauss 1966; Bucher and Stelling 1969). Their effort culminated with the publication of Strauss' (1978a) *Negotiations*.

Strauss insisted that all social orders are negotiated: That is, all social systems are the sediments of a history of voting, decree, conflict, agreement, compromise, bargaining, persuasion, coercion and other forms of interaction by which humans seek to achieve their interests and legitimate their perspectives. Strauss wrote that the negotiated order of an organization, such as a hospital or firm, was 'the sum total of the organization's rules and policies, along with whatever agreements, understandings, pacts, contracts, and other working arrangements currently [obtain]. These include agreements at every level of organization, of every clique and coalition, and include covert as well as overt agreements' (1978a: 6). An important corollary is that negotiated orders are temporally bound. Over time every negotiated order is 'reviewed, reevaluated, revised, revoked or renewed' (1978a: 5). Strauss noted, however, that because structural conditions influence who can negotiate with whom, when and about what, negotiated orders ought not be viewed as products of unconstrained agency (1978a: 5). The arrival of new participants, a shift in a law, or the development of new technologies could exogenously trigger revisions of a current order.

Strauss argued that negotiated orders not only have scope or range, they are also

usually nested in the sense that concentric circles are nested. The negotiated order of an accounting firm, for example, operates within the negotiated order of accounting as a profession. The former cannot ignore the latter and still remain an accounting firm in good standing. Some aspects of a negotiated order are, therefore, likely to be local, while others have wider scope. Those with the widest scope may be created from the top down by people with either the authority to direct others or a mandate to act on their behalf, as would be the case, respectively, with the imposition of a regal decree or an agreement forged through collective bargaining. Alternately, negotiated orders with a wide scope may bubble up from below, as Strauss described for institutions of mental health:

> In what sense can it be said that [the negotiations he observed in the hospital he studied] ... had a determinable impact on the larger social setting [national or professional]? Obviously, no single negotiation or even one hospital had much impact. Yet the many such 'experiments' taking place simultaneously or over a very few years must have had considerable impact – in giving new kinds of training to professionals; changing their attitudes toward professional partners, toward their own work and toward themselves; altering their ideologies; opening up new types of careers; and so on. Negotiated agreements and actions were very much a part of that consequential ferment. Said another way, the negotiations were integral to the subsequent changes in the state of the mental health professions and their associated institutions. (Strauss 1978a: 122)

In fact, in some cases, top-down and grassroots forms of action may work in concert.

Strauss proposed a three-level 'paradigm' (or model) for studying negotiated order (Strauss 1978a: 98–99). The paradigm's purpose was to ensure that researchers would not forget to tie situated action to macro-social contexts. At the lowest level – the level of ongoing action – were *negotiations*, whose attributes might vary systematically by the type of actors involved, by their strategies and tactics, and by other characteristics of people's actions and inter-actions. Negotiations might yield many types of outcomes, including organizations, conventions, practices, rules, understand-ings or working agreements. Second, Strauss claimed that all negotiations occurred within a *negotiation context*, a set of local condi-tions that shaped the actions and interactions that comprised the negotiations. For Strauss, the analytically relevant aspects of negotia-tion contexts included the number of actors involved, whom they represented, their rela-tive balance of power, whether negotiations occurred once or were ongoing, whether sessions occurred sequentially or simultane-ously on multiple fronts, whether the nego-tiations were visible or hidden, the number and complexity of the issues involved, and the legitimacy of those issues (Strauss 1978a: 100).

Finally, Strauss claimed that negotiation contexts were, in turn, situated within a *structural context*, a system of more encom-passing institutions. The larger institutions that were relevant for a set of negotiations would vary considerably across negotiation contexts. For instance, the institutions that constrain the negotiations of a corporate executive would differ from those that con-strain how and for what high school princi-pals negotiate. On this point Strauss (1978a: 98) wrote, 'The structural context for covert negotiations engaged in by a corrupt judge includes features of the American judiciary system and of marketplaces, while the struc-tural context of the negotiations that occur in a mental hospital includes the properties of American medical care, the subspecialty of psychiatry, specialization among the car-ing professions, and the division of labor in mental hospitals.'

Curiously, Giddens and others have depicted structuration using three-layered models analogous to Strauss' paradigm of negotiated order (see Giddens 1984: 12; Barley 1986: 82; Barley and Tolbert 1997: 97; Yates and Orlikowski 1992: 307). Negotiations that occur in the here and now

belong to what Giddens (1984: 11), Barley and Tobert (1997: 97) and Orlikowski (2000: 410), respectively, called 'systems of inter-action', 'the realm of action', and the realm of 'ongoing situated human action'. Strauss' notion of a structural context parallels what Giddens (1984: 31) called the 'structure of the institutional order' or what Barley and Tolbert (1997) called the 'realm of institu-tions'. Negotiation contexts mediate between negotiations and structural contexts, as do scripts in Barley's (1986) model of structur-ing or modalities in Giddens' model of struc-turation (1984: 29). In fact, Barley argued that scripts were exteriorized social forms that comprise part of the negotiation con-text. Finally, in Strauss' paradigm, as in all structuration models, influence moves up and down levels. As Maines put it in his exegesis of negotiated order theory:

> Strauss emphasizes that the lines of influence can go both ways, in which the consequences of nego-tiations can be measured (eventually) in changes in structural contexts, and in which structural con-texts condition how people will act ... Negotiation contexts are created insofar as certain elements of [the structural context] are incorporated into or become relevant to negotiations, but negotiations may work their way back through negotiation contexts 'up' to structural contexts. (1982: 270)

In sum, taken as a whole, it is fair to say that negotiated order theory is more accessible, but less well developed, than structuration theory. Compared to Giddens' encyclopedic coverage of sociological thought, Strauss' work on negotiations was far less sweeping, but his language was decidedly less obscure.[17] Yet, negotiated order theory trumps structuration theory in at least one important regard: it emphasizes the impor-tance of *observing situated behaviors* in specific social and temporal contexts to determine how institutions shape actions and how actions, in turn, form, sustain and change institutions. Thus, unlike structura-tion theory, negotiated order theory tells researchers what to look for. The notion of a social world suggests where to look.

SOCIAL WORLDS: ARENAS, NETWORKS, MATRICES, WEBS AND FIELDS

Although Chicagoans had used the term 'social world' for decades, aside from Shibutani (1955, 1962) few did so analytically before Strauss (1978b, 1982, 1984) and Becker (1978, 1982). In his first paper on social worlds, Strauss (1978b: 119–121) wrote: 'Since the early days of Chicago-style interactionism, the term "social worlds" has been used sporadically, sometime descriptively, rarely conceptually … We have not developed a general view of social worlds as a widespread, significant phenomenon, nor have we developed a program for studying them systematically.' By developing the concept more systematically, Strauss hoped to push interactionists to acknowledge that structural phenomena were as important as interpretive phenomena in shaping the institutional order.[18] 'Though the idea of social worlds may refer centrally to universes of discourse,' he cautioned his fellow interactionists, 'we should be careful not to confine ourselves to looking merely at forms of communication, symbolization … but also examine palpable matters like activities, memberships, sites, technologies and organizations typical of social worlds' (1978b: 121). In subsequent papers, Strauss (1982, 1984) elaborated:

> Social worlds refer to a set of common or joint activities or concerns, bound together by a network of communication … One can point to such social worlds as those of opera, ballet, baseball, surfing, art, stamp collecting, mountain climbing, homosexuality, and medicine, although the concept also is probably useful in conceptualizing and studying industries and the sciences. These social worlds vary considerably in size, types, number and varieties of central activities, organizational complexity, technological sophistication, ideological elaboration, geographical dispersion, and so on … One of the most important features of social worlds is their inevitable differentiation into subworlds … The conceptual imagery here is of groups emerging within social worlds, evolving, developing, splintering, disintegrating or pulling

> themselves together, or parts falling away and perhaps coalescing with segments of other groups to form new groups, often in opposition to older ones – in short, of subworlds intersecting, in powerful contact with other subworlds both within the parent social world and with those 'inside' other social worlds. (1982: 172)

To begin unpacking this fluid notion of social worlds, notice first that Strauss (as well as Becker 1978) used the plural rather than the singular form of the noun. Plurality is crucial. Rather than see social worlds as distinct units, interactionists viewed social worlds as fuzzy sets composed of elements, which Strauss called subworlds. Subworlds are themselves social worlds that are connected through their joint involvement in *a primary activity*. It is this joint involvement that warrants speaking of the elements as a set. Illustrative activities that serve as the basis for social worlds include the production of a form of art, such as a painting or play (Becker 1978, 1982), the manufacturing of computers (Kling and Gerson 1978a, 1978b; Kling and Sacchi 1982), the production of books (Coser et al. 1982; Powell 1985), the making of musical scores (Faulkner 1987), the manufacturing of wafer fabrication equipment (Bechky 2003a, 2003b), the hiring and placing of technical contractors (Barley and Kunda 2004), or the playing of games like Dungeons and Dragons and Little League Baseball (Fine 1983, 1987).

Second, Strauss emphasized that social worlds cleave around sites (places where activities routinely occur and where key actors are found), technologies (tools, techniques and procedures for carrying out key activities) and most importantly, divisions of labor.[19] For example, the thespian world requires theaters where plays can be performed and audiences can be seated, workshops for making props, dressing rooms for actors to prepare their bodies, box offices for selling tickets, print shops for printing programs, and so on. The thespian world also must have lighting, sound systems, curtains, wrenches and pulleys, printing presses, carpenter's tools, etc.

Most importantly, to pull off plays there must be actors, directors, producers, stage hands, lighting engineers, printers, patrons, advertisers, janitors, ticket agents, critics, electricians, manufacturers of cosmetics, costume designers, and seamstresses among others.

These structural features (sites, technologies and divisions of labor) are usually the nuclei around which 'subworlds' form. Subworlds control and are responsible for providing materials and services that are crucial for accomplishing the world's overarching activity. Because of differentiation, representatives of subworlds are linked via webs of patterned interaction, communication and transaction that allow them to pull off the world's primary activity. The existence of social worlds, therefore, implies the existence of social networks, which are usefully understood as a social world's essential structure. However, social worlds cannot be reduced to networks. Doing so would focus attention tightly on structures and flows to the exclusion of culture and action.

Accordingly, and third, Strauss held that interpretive and political phenomena are integral to the organization of social worlds. Ideologies, perspectives, theories, agendas, points of view, interests and languages differentiate the participants who are bound together by networks and their joint contribution to a central activity. Interpretive differences – which are rooted in the social world's division of labor – engender conflicts, tensions, alliances, movements and disputes. Thus, the interplay between networks and notions is central to any analysis of social worlds. The idea that social worlds have interpretive and political as well as structural topographies is what links the analysis of negotiated order to the study of social worlds. As Strauss et al. (1964) showed for psychiatric hospitals, differences in perspectives and interests motivate negotiations that configure and reconfigure institutions.

Political and interpretive phenomena are essential for understanding the dynamics of social worlds because they manufacture and sustain the legitimacy of a social world's institutions and practices:

> One can initially imagine something of the nature of legitimation problems which arise in that kind of social matrix. Questions of 'authenticity' of performance and product, of genuineness and purity, real and fake, but questions also of propriety and impropriety, even morality and immorality, and legality and illegality arise in kaleidoscopic, rapid and intricate fashion – not merely in areas like 'the arts' with their perennial legitimacy arguments and dilemmas, but in presumably less problematic, seemingly less ideologically-ridden areas like medicine, the sciences, industry and business. Imagery for what occurs in these rapidly changing social worlds and subworlds should be the very opposite of what is called up by the term 'stable' society ... legitimacy in these worlds pertains to issues like what, how, when, where, and who can legitimately or properly do certain things, with certain means and materials, at appropriate places and times, and in certain acceptable ways ... understanding of the legitimation process associated with social worlds will require a close look at the arenas in which such issues are fought out. (Strauss 1982: 172–173)

Struggles for legitimacy in social worlds were, for Strauss, the engine of action and a source of intrigue. In other words, legitimacy was always the product of negotiations.

Fourth, Strauss emphasized that social worlds are always in process; the only question is the rate at which the process unfolds. Strauss claimed that segmentation and intersection were central processes of the structuring in social worlds. The former is equivalent to the organizational theorist's notion of differentiation; the latter fuses the organizational theorist's concept of integration with the idea of overlapping jurisdictions. Ultimately the imagery of segmentation and intersection invokes a shifting institutional landscape. Examined over time, analysts should see social worlds and subworlds form around new technologies or ideas, split, fuse, challenge each other's bids for expertise, forge alliances and so on.

Writing before the spread of microcomputers, Kling and Gerson (1978a) claimed that the world of computing cleaved along four axes.

The first axis was type of computing: specifically, scientific, commercial, industrial and academic computing. The second axis was the kind of technology or equipment used. The third was type of application: for example, financial, medical or government applications. Interestingly, the fourth dimension was where actors positioned themselves relative to IBM. Since the 1970s, the landscape of the world of computing has changed. Personal computers have replaced mainframes and minicomputers in most, but not all, computing subworlds. COBOL and FORTRAN have died, and other languages have taken their place. New areas of application have arisen, including gaming and animation. Applications that were once separated are now integrated: for instance, financial and human resources databases (by SAP, Oracle, etc.) or word processing and presentation software (Microsoft$^{(R)}$ Office). Perhaps most telling, positioning relative to IBM is arguably far less important today than positioning relative to Microsoft.

Finally, for Strauss and other interactionists, social worlds constituted a unique unit of analysis. Accomplishing a primary activity usually involves actors from a variety of industries, social sectors, subcultures, occupations, firms, interest groups, organizations and so on. Social worlds, therefore, enroll participants who cut across the units of analysis that have traditionally preoccupied organizational theorists and other social scientists. For this reason, researchers who set their sights solely on organizations, industries or occupations, are unlikely to find social worlds. Seeing social worlds requires greater focal length.

By now it should be clear that the interactionists' notion of social worlds bears an uncanny resemblance to what institutionalists have called organizational fields. Indeed, it is not unreasonable to argue that the interactionists and institutionalists arrived at roughly the same analytic destination at more or less the same time unbeknownst to each other. Consider, for example, DiMaggio and Powell's (1983) definition of an organization field in light of the foregoing discussion:

> By organizational field, we mean those organizations that, in the aggregate, constitute a recognized area of institutional life: key suppliers, resource and product consumers, regulatory agencies, and other organizations that produce similar services or products. The virtue of this unit of analysis is that it directs our attention not simply to competing firms ... or to networks of organizations that actually interact ... but to the totality of relevant actors. In doing this, the field idea comprehends the importance of both connectedness and structural equivalence. The structure of an organizational field cannot be determined a priori but must be defined on the basis of empirical investigation. (1983: 148)

DiMaggio and Powell tell us that an organizational field 'constitute[s] a recognized area of institutional life', which echoes Strauss' notion of a 'primary activity'. Also like Strauss, DiMaggio and Powell note that fields have divisions of labor that bind a field's actors into a network of relations. Finally, DiMaggio and Powell portray field as a unique unit of analysis in precisely the same sense that Strauss saw a social world as a crosscutting unit.

Nevertheless, there seem to be three important differences between the concepts of social world and organizational field. First, Strauss and other interactionists portrayed social worlds as populated by a variety of collectives (occupations, associations, subcultures, organizations, etc.), while the institutionalists, being organizational theorists, have written as if fields comprise primarily organizations. While accurate, this difference is less important than it might first appear to be. Although Strauss was not an organizational theorist and was apparently as unaware of what the neo-institutionalists were doing as they were of him, he would have applauded their agenda. In his first paper on social worlds, Strauss explicitly noted that research on social worlds of organizations was sorely lacking:

> Organizations are commonly viewed as relatively closed in their boundaries, and there are few good analyses of interorganizational relations. The social world perspective tells us that some organizations

are relatively embedded within a social world, while others stand at intersections, indeed may have been intentionally constructed that way. The understanding of organizational evolution, change, and functions requires an examination of relations embedded in the same or intersecting worlds ... Organizational theory which ignores these considerations is likely to sell us very short. (Strauss 1978b: 125)

Second, the notion of a social world draws attention to interpretive phenomena that join as well as delineate and divide actors involved in the pursuit of a primary activity. In contrast, field has a stronger overtone of structure, especially that of network structure. Accordingly, students of social worlds are more likely to view legitimation as a problem of constructing, contesting and defending interpretations rather than a problem of acquiring status or standing in the eyes of others. Students of social worlds, therefore, have paid more attention to struggles for legitimacy than have institutionalists, who more commonly study sources of legitimacy.

Finally, in social world analysis the various strands of an institutional order – rhetoric, political action, organizations, laws, ideologies and so on – implicate each other. Thus, rather than treat institutions as well-bounded practices, interactionists typically speak of institutions as forming the 'web', 'matrix', or 'fabric' of a social world. These differences point to two topics about which interactionists still have much to offer institutionalists: the social construction of legitimacy, especially in the course of ongoing action, and the study of institutional complexes.

WHAT INSTITUTIONALISTS CAN LEARN FROM INTERACTIONISTS

Doing Legitimacy

No concept is more central to institutional theory than legitimacy. Yet, as Suchman (1995: 571) noted, 'Despite its centrality ... the literature on organizational legitimacy provides surprisingly fragile conceptual moorings. Many researchers employ the term ... but few define it.'[20] Furthermore, even though institutionalists continually remind us that legitimation is a process, until recently they have written more about sources of legitimacy, about whom or what bestows it, than about how it is bestowed. Sources of legitimacy commonly mentioned in the literature include public opinion, the educational system, laws, courts and, of late, higher-status others.

Although, the Chicagoans understood well that socialization, reputation, power, position and authority meant that some actors had greater (and perhaps final) say over what is legitimate, they trained their eyes less on sources and more on struggles for legitimacy. Histories of how a modus operandi, a law, a practice, or even an organizational form acquired legitimacy are ultimately tales of how people deploy ideas, ideologies, frames and arguments in negotiations, persuasions and political contests that unfold over time, often across multiple places and arenas. From this perspective, meaning and action are both crucial for constructing legitimacy. Legitimacy hinges not only on the substance of ideas and claims, but also on where, when, how and why people wield ideas and lodge claims.

Strauss (1982) argued that actors use five strategies for building for what Hughes (1971 [1962]: 287–292) would have called a mandate and license: (1) discovering, claiming and promoting the worth of their agenda, belief or stance; (2) developing theories that bolster their interests or perspectives with a veneer of rational, moral and even scientific respectability; (3) distancing themselves from rivals and alternate ideas; (4) setting standards of practice or belief that can be employed in evaluative accounts; and (5) establishing the boundaries of their jurisdiction. As actors struggle over legitimacy, they employ a wide range of resources ranging from court rulings, prophecies, scientific theories and high status allies to books, editorials, films and even the occasional payoff.

Institutionalists have spent much of the last decade rediscovering the role that interpretations and negotiations play in the social construction of legitimacy. Some have drawn inspiration from contemporary social movement theory, which emphasizes the importance of competing frames or ways of making sense out of situations, conditions and events (Rao 1998; Creed et al. 2002; Rao et al. 2003). Others have turned to rhetorical, narrative and discourse analysis (Hoffman 1999; Edelman et al. 2001; Greenwood et al. 2002; Lawrence and Phillips 2004; Munir and Phillips 2005; Suddaby and Greenwood 2005; Colyvas and Powell 2006; Greenwood and Suddaby 2006). Regardless of their starting point, however, all have explored how individuals, occupations, organizations, or coalitions deploy language, symbols, assumptions, theories, or frames to develop and promote their agendas or views of the world. In these papers, interests, politics and contestation are always front and center, regardless of whether the institution under construction be a new organizational form (Lawrence and Phillips 2004; Suddaby and Greenwood 2005; Greenwood and Suddaby 2006), a redefinition of an institution's mission and boundaries (Colyvas and Powell 2006), the passage of a law (Creed et al. 2002), the reinterpretation of a law (Edelman et al. 2001), the emergence of an occupation (Lounsbury and Kaghan 2001), or the promotion of a set of practices that define the role of a product in everyday life (Munir and Phillips 2005).

Nevertheless, despite the common emphasis on interpretation, the new institutional scholarship on legitimation differs from the interactionists' work in important ways. First, the institutionalists almost always employ textual rather than observational data. Second, because the texts are drawn from archives, they afford longitudinal analysis. Consequently, recent interpretive scholarship on institutions covers longer periods of time than even the most dedicated fieldworker could hope to cover. Taking the long view allows institutionalists the necessary resolve for identifying what Hughes might have called the stages and turning points in an institution's career. In fact, for institutions with broad range, analysis of texts may be the only way to study the protracted twists and turns of legitimation over the longue durée.

Yet, precisely because textual analysis opens up the panorama of history, it has difficulty focusing on how struggles for legitimacy played themselves out in daily life. To be sure, texts offer clues to how people interpreted a phenomenon at some point in time, and they can point to the perspectives of different factions. Texts often have relatively little to say, however, about how people arrived at those interpretations or what the members of various factions did to each other. Furthermore, texts are almost always silent on what led to the creation of the document in the first place. To answer questions about legitimation in action, one must examine behavior *in situ* and in real time. This is where the Chicagoans excelled. For an appreciation of how interactionist studies could enrich our understanding of the situated dynamics of legitimation, consider Nelsen and Barley's (1997) account of how paid and volunteer emergency medical technicians (EMTs) vied over who should deliver emergency medical services in local communities.

By 1970, volunteer rescue squads provided emergency transportation in most American communities. Towns and cities across the country had formed volunteer squads during the 1950s and 1960s in response to a social movement and subsequent legislation designed to reduce highway fatalities. Growing pressure to medicalize emergency services culminated, in 1973, with the Emergency Medical Services Act, which required that all responders have formal training in emergency medicine. Although the Act took no stance on whether volunteers or 'professionals' should deliver such services, by the 1990s private firms employing professional, fulltime EMTs had begun to compete with volunteer squads. Jurisdictional dramas over the proper delivery of emergency medicine were being played out on a daily basis on the streets of villages, towns and cities. Although advocates of voluntary and professional services recorded their perspectives in documents amenable to textual analysis, no documents recorded the type of behavior that Nelsen observed while riding with paid and voluntary squads in two upstate New York communities.

Nelsen and Barley (1997) recount, among other tactics, how paid EMTs pushed volunteers aside on arriving at the scene of an accident, how they belittled volunteers' skills before patients, doctors and nurses, and how they rewrote paperwork to expunge evidence that volunteers had ever been involved in responding to an accident. In these and other ways, paid EMTs actively fostered the perception that they were more competent than volunteers and that they were more deserving of a mandate to provide emergency medical services to the community. Without behavioral data, researchers examining the jurisdictional dispute would have difficulty discovering that the battle to legitimate professional emergency medical service (EMS) was waged with more than ideology and rhetoric. Worse, because hospital records often did not mention the volunteers who had been on the scene, researchers might conclude that no volunteers had been active.

In short, grounded studies of action and interaction are crucial for developing adequate accounts of the social construction of legitimacy, if for no other reason than that they inoculate us against assuming that struggles for legitimacy are largely battles of rhetoric. As institutional analysis takes its interpretive turn, it is well worth remembering that writing, reading and rhetoric are important for negotiating legitimacy, but words break no bones.

Institutional Complexes

In inventory of neo-institutional organizational studies will reveal that researchers have often treated institutions as well-bounded entities and their construction as a matter of diffusion. For instance, institutionalists have studied the spread of formal evaluation and performance systems in municipal governments (Tolbert and Zucker 1983), personnel offices (Dobbin and Sutton 1998), maternal leave policies (Kelly and Dobbin 1999) and poison pills (Davis 1991). Even the interpretive studies of legitimacy discussed above treat institutions as discrete phenomena. For instance, Suddaby and Greenwood (2005) focused on the rise of multidisciplinary accounting firms. Lounsbury and Kaghan (2001) examined the spread of recycling programs across universities. Lawrence and Phillips (2004) explored how a particular set of whale-watching practices emerged in Victoria, Canada. Studying well-specified forms and practices makes pragmatic, epistemological sense: A clear focus on an identifiable phenomenon allows researchers to target specific institutional processes. Focusing on discrete phenomena also makes for a more manageable story, especially within the constrained space of a journal article. However, should the image of institutions as well-bounded phenomena become an ontological assumption, organization studies would be left with a thin view of institutional reality.

Chicago sociologists took a thicker view. They typically portrayed institutions as complexes of related practices, conventions and understandings. Social worlds are always more than the sum of distinct institutions. Consider, for example, what makes a school. Surely a school needs teachers and students, yet teachers and students are found in other settings, including the boot camps run by the US Army and Al-Qaeda. Tests and books are also necessary for schools as we know them. Yet, libraries have books and employment offices give tests, neither of which we would confuse as a school. Even teachers, students, books and tests are not sufficient for making a school; one needs a host of other actors, laws, practices and so on. All institutional orders are similarly complex in this regard.[21]

To acknowledge precisely this sort of multiplexity, interactionists routinely described social worlds as 'webs', 'matrices', or 'clusters' of institutions (Hughes 1971 [1962]: 52; Strauss 1978a: 172; Kling and Sacchi 1982). The image of a 'web' or a 'matrix' draws attention to two key aspects of social worlds or organizational fields. First, institutions cluster in the sense that what distinguishes one social world from another is an integrated and unique set of institutionalized forms, practices and conventions. The idea is analogous to cliquing in social network analysis: members of a social world share more institutions with fellow members than they do with members of other worlds. In other words, the density of shared institutions should be higher within than across social worlds. Second, institutions form webs (or they cluster) in the sense that one institution is likely to implicate others. Analysts should, therefore, beware of treating institutions as discrete phenomena for any purpose other than analytic convenience. In reality, a change in one institutional parameter is likely to occasion, and perhaps even require, change in others.

Interactionists routinely pointed to the complexity of institutional connectedness. For instance, in an important paper that tied occupational commitment to an occupation's institutional order, Geer (1968) noted that teachers lacked the kind of occupational commitment evinced by doctors, scientists and lawyers. Geer argued the institutions of teaching were responsible. Unlike a functionalist, who might urge teachers to pursue the traits of a profession (Etzioni 1969), or a Marxist, who might advocate the politics of monopoly (Larson 1979), Geer recognized that changing the commitment of teachers would require altering the larger web of institutions in which teaching was suspended:

> Several of the mechanisms of commitment in other occupations which we have discussed suggest changes that might be brought about in the teaching profession if lifelong commitment on the part of more teachers is desired. But, as we have seen, commitment is a process so closely fitted to occupational structure that changes in it would necessarily involve structural change in teaching as a profession, which would, in turn, affect the organization of the school system in ways that might prove disruptive to other desirable goals. (Geer 1968: 233)

In other words, to change teachers' commitment to the occupation would require changing institutionalized relationships between schools, communities, families, local governments and school boards.

Because the Chicagoans were primarily ethnographers, their thick descriptions tended to capture the web of institutions that enveloped the social worlds they studied. But the Chicagoans did not usually call attention to how these various institutions were connected. Consequently, tracing the web of institutions that is laced throughout a Chicago-style ethnography usually requires readers to do their own analysis. Nevertheless, in most ethnographies the material for recovering the web lies near enough to hand.

Consider, for example, Barley and Kunda's (2004) ethnography of the contract labor market for skilled technical professionals. Contracting in high technology escalated during the 1980s when Microsoft and other firms realized that they could significantly reduce employment costs by firing employees and hiring them back as independent contractors. Because the practice spread quickly, the Internal Revenue Service (IRS) soon entered the picture and brought suit against Microsoft for tax evasion. Although the suit did not slow the use of contractors, it did reshape the way contractors were employed. On the advice of corporate lawyers, firms began to acquire contractors through staffing agencies rather than cut deals directly with individuals. Agencies protected the firms from the IRS, because they served as the contractor's employer of record. As a result, foundings of staffing agencies devoted to high-tech contracting burgeoned in the 1990s. At this point, we have an institutional story of the construction and diffusion of two institutions, a type of employment (contracting) and an organizational form (the high-tech staffing agency), each of which, in turn, reflects a larger institutional development, the rise of finance capitalism.[22] There are, however, more strands to the institutional web that envelops and defines the social world of contracting.

To reinforce the perception that contractors were not employees, employers began to institute an array of practices for differentiating contractors from permanent employees. These practices spread through mimesis and though the intervention of consultants, accountants and lawyers who advised firms on how to protect themselves from the IRS. As a result firms began to force contractors to wear distinct badges, to assign them to less desirable space than employees enjoyed, to prohibit contractors from attending meetings in which topics unrelated to their project were discussed, to prohibit contractors from attending company sponsored social functions and so on. In short, a series of institutionalized work practices spread throughout and across industries that hired contractors.

As more and more contractors were forced to go through staffing agencies, contractors also devised practices that spread by word of mouth and that were promoted by magazines, books and websites designed to help contractors better manage their careers. For example, contractors discovered that to minimize downtime (time between contracts) and to maximize earnings, they usually needed to change agencies to acquire their next contract. To dissuade contractors from switching, agencies began to offer health care and 401k's.[23] But, because most agencies also hesitated to find contractors new jobs before the current contract ended, few contractors remained with an agency long enough to secure health care or pension funds. Thus, large numbers of contractors saved little or nothing for retirement and relied on their fully employed spouse for heath insurance.

As in the case of contracting, institutionalization – whether defined as the construction of meaning or the acceptance and diffusion of practices – yields a web of conventions, procedures, laws and organizations that jointly shape an arena of social life into a social world or organizational field. The emergence of webs of institutions and the interplay between a web's various strands remains a fertile and largely unexplored opportunity for research that could enrich institutional theory. Although interactionism points institutionalism in this direction, no interactionist has yet explicitly attempted to develop concepts for analyzing webs of institutions. A particularly fruitful line of inquiry would be to examine the various reasons for why one institution tends to beget, alter, amplify, or specify other institutions.

CONCLUSION

I began this chapter by arguing that neo-institutionalism is unique in organization studies, because it represents the only macro-sociology of organizations rooted in micro-social concepts. Although the early institutionalists turned to ethnomethodology and constructionism for their micro-social grounding, the perspective forged at the University of Chicago by Everett C. Hughes, Anselm Strauss and their students is potentially more compatible with the institutionalists' agenda. The Chicagoans were themselves institutionalists, and unlike most ethnomethodologists and constructionists, they were concerned with institutions at the same levels of analysis that have intrigued the neo-institutionalists. In fact, as I have attempted to show, using a different language, the Chicagoans anticipated and developed many of the stances and perspectives that neo-institutionalists have had to reinvent as they struggled to incorporate social action into their analyses. My agenda in revisiting the Chicago School has been to point to how interactionism might help neo-institutionalists resolve important puzzles concerning action, legitimation and the social construction of institutional fields.

The Chicagoans held that sociology's job is to study social organization in action, which they conceived of as the link between institutions and the person. Institutions and actors meet in the throws of everyday life. In this sense, as the British might say, everyday life is institutional theory's coalface; it is where the rubber of theory hits the road of reality. For over 30 years, the coalface has lain largely idle while institutionalists have sought their fortunes in the cities of macro-social theory. As a result, there is plenty of coal left to mine. What we need are more miners.

Notes

1 Since this chapter focuses entirely on neo-institutionalism in organizational theory, I often drop the prefix, 'neo', to make the text less clumsy.

2 As phenomenologists, Berger and Luckmann had top pedigrees. Both studied at the New School of Social Research under the tutelage of Alfred Schultz, who was mentored by (but not formally a student of) Edmund Husserl (www.soci.canterbury.ac.nz/resources/biograph/schul tz.shtml). Garfinkel (1967: 36) also drew heavily on Schultz's thought, but was not a phenomenologist by training or intent. Garfinkel was a student of Talcott Parsons at Harvard. He rejected Parsons' structural functionalism, claiming, among other things, that internalized social norms and values could not be responsible for social structure. Garfinkel and other ethnomethodologists vigorously rejected logical positivism, yet remained decidedly realist in their hardnosed empiricism.

3 In contrast, ethnomethodologists have had much to say about work and work practices (Emerson 1970; Lynch 1985; Garfinkel 1986; Cicourel 1987, 1990; Suchman 1987; Heath and Luff 1992, 1996; Button 1993).

4 This assumes, of course, that the early institutionalists were actually interested in micro-social dynamics. Aside from Zucker, this was probably not the case. Hallett and Ventresca (2006: 215) have suggested that Meyer and Rowan turned to micro-sociology primarily for its vocabulary of motive: 'Given the new institutionalist focus on macro environments,' they wrote, 'we can turn Meyer and Rowan's legacy on its head to say that organizational sociology has been "decoupled" from its foundations in social interaction: Passing references to micro-sociology are a form

of "myth and ceremony" that create academic "legitimacy".'

5 Chicago School sociology covers at least two generations of scholars. The first included Robert Park, Ernest Burgess, Albion Small, and W. I. Thomas, who were most active in the first three decades of the twentieth century. The second included Everett Hughes, Anselm Strauss and Herbert Blumer, who wrote mostly from the 1930s through the 1960s. When I speak of the Chicago School in this chapter, unless otherwise noted, I am referring to the second group.

6 Ironically, Hughes and his colleagues paid more attention to organizations than did the ethnomethodologists. *Boys in White* (Becker et al. 1961) and *Psychiatric Ideologies and Institutions* (Strauss et al. 1964) were ethnographies of a medical school and a psychiatric hospital, respectively. Strauss conducted a famous set of studies on how nurses, doctors and patients construct and manage awareness of dying on cancer wards (Glaser and Strauss 1965). Dalton (1950) wrote about everyday life among managers in a firm. Roy studied union organizing (1964, 1965). Van Maanen studied police organizations (1973, 1975). Fine (1996) has written about restaurants and Kunda (1992) about high-tech firms. In fact, the hallmark of these studies is the weaving together of work and organization. By contrast, when ethnomethodologists studied life in organizations their focus was almost exclusively on how people do their work (Lynch 1985; Garfinkel 1986; Suchman 1987).

7 Athens, who was Blumer's student at Berkeley, claims that Blumer mistook the higher rate of change of institutions in contemporary society for their increasing irrelevance.

8 Furthermore, as Becker (1999: 7) revealed, 'Hughes and Blumer ... had very low opinions of one another. Blumer thought Hughes had a second-rate mind, and Hughes was openly contemptuous of Blumer's inability or unwillingness to do research.'

9 Blumer, however, did have this agenda (see Athens 2005).

10 Although the work of Hughes and his students is often categorized as 'symbolic interactionism', I avoid that term because it is more properly applied to Blumer's (1962) work. In this chapter I will use 'interactionist' and 'interactionism', since Hughes and his students certainly did examine social relations in everyday life.

11 See Rock (1979) and Lewis and Smith (1980) for extended discussions of Simmel's importance to the Chicagoans' concept of social structure.

12 Although Strauss received his PhD at Chicago in 1945, Strauss did not align himself with Hughes

until after he joined the faculty in 1952 (Strauss 1968: 265).

13 The term entrepreneur also raises ontological problems. Entrepreneurs are people who usually have some idea of what they are doing. As speakers of English commonly use the term, it is difficult to imagine how an entrepreneur could accidentally found a business. Yet, as Berger and Luckmann make clear, institutions sometimes (maybe, most of the time) emerge with anyone intending them.

14 Although DiMaggio (1988) and DiMaggio and Powell (1983, 1991) also used the term structuration, they did so primarily to speak of how people create institutions. Thus, their use of the term is closer to Berger and Luckmann's idea of sedimentation.

15 Barley (1986) spoke of structuring rather than structuration to emphasize agency. Gerunds have the utility of nouns while maintaining connotations of action. Barley used the concept of scripts to track structuring over time. Although scripts surely have a cognitive component, Barley emphasized the actions and interactions that instantiated scripts because the latter could be observed. Besides, if people don't do things because of their thoughts, thoughts cannot be real in their consequences, at least for people who are not having the thought. With the exception of Johnson, Smith and Codling (2000), most commentators assume Barley (1986; Barley and Tolbert 1997) saw scripts as cognitive rather than behavioral phenomena. Orlikowski and her colleagues (1992, 1996, 2000; Orlikowski and Yates 1994) have pushed behavioral studies of structuration further than any other scholar with their research on the structuring of technology and technical practice.

16 It is worth noting that when interactionists speak of accounts, interpretations, definitions of the situation and so on, they are surely referring to cognitions, but they almost always assume that these cognitions are instantiated in behavior. Accounts occur in speech; speech is a behavior and, hence, a way of doing something. Importantly, speech can be heard and recorded by observers, but thoughts and cognitions cannot. The interactionists were, above all else, empiricists.

17 Like most interactionists, Strauss shied away from Latinate nouns and wrote in a discursive, colloquial style. Could this help explain why organizational theorists have paid so little attention to the interactionists? How can sociologists be erudite, when they are so breezy to read? As Mark Knophler put it, 'sociologists invent words that mean industrial disease'.

18 Ironically, sociologists from other traditions, including many institutionalists, require precisely the opposite advice: interpretive phenomena are as important as structural phenomena.

19 One might argue that with the rise of life on the screen (Turkle 1995), tangible sites for action are no longer necessary for social worlds to form. Be this as it may, it is quite interesting to note that even virtual worlds like *Second Life* and *Warcraft* are marked by virtual places, virtual divisions of labor and virtual technologies. In fact sometimes the divisions of labor are real, as in the case of *Warcraft* where real people spend time creating virtual characters and accumulating virtual money which they sell to real people for real dollars so the buyers can participate in a virtual division of labor.

20 Suchman went on to define legitimacy as 'a generalized perception or assumption that the actions of an entity are desirable, proper, or appropriate within some socially constructed system of norms, values, beliefs, and definitions … Legitimacy is a perception or assumption in that it represents a reaction of observers to the organization as they see it; thus, legitimacy is possessed objectively, yet created subjectively. An organization may diverge dramatically from societal norms yet retain legitimacy because the divergence goes unnoticed. Legitimacy is socially constructed in that it reflects a congruence between the behaviors of the legitimated entity and the shared (or assumedly shared) beliefs of some social group; thus, legitimacy is dependent on a collective audience, yet independent of particular observers. An organization may deviate from individuals' values yet retain legitimacy because the deviation draws no public disapproval. In short, when one says that a certain pattern of behavior possesses legitimacy, one asserts that some group of observers, as a whole, accepts or supports what those observers perceive to be the behavioral pattern, as a whole, despite reservations that any single observer might have about any single behavior, and despite reservations that any or all observers might have, were they to observe more' (1995: 574).

21 Garfinkel (1967) played off this complexity in his analysis of Agnes, a young transsexual soon to undergo a sex change. As Garfinkel noted, there was no one institutionalized practice, convention or understanding that allowed Agnes to pass as female. Neither dress, nor stance, nor gait, nor even attitude was adequate for Agnes being seen as a woman. Rather Agnes had to display and was adept at displaying these and many other gendered traits and behaviors in a highly integrated fashion. In other words, the institution of gender is a multifaceted concept, no one strand of which is sufficient for defining a person

as male or female, however necessary that facet may be.

22 Finance capitalism matters because contracting is about turning the fixed cost of labor into a variable cost. Wall Street not only encourages firms to maximize variable costs, but also rewards them for doing so. Shifting to contractors boosts a firm's stock price, at least temporarily, because contractors are not included in the denominators of productivity ratios. Thus, shifting from employees to contractors not only makes a firm appear more flexible but more productive than it is.

23 A 401k is a pension plan that allows individuals to shelter money from each paycheck for retirement free of taxation until the individual has retired, begins to withdraw the funds and is presumably subject to a lower tax rate.

REFERENCES

Athens, Lonnie (2005). 'Mead's lost conception of society.' *Symbolic Interaction*, 28: 305–325.

Barley, Stephen R. (1986). 'Technology as an occasion for structuring: Evidence from observations of CT scanners and the social order of radiology departments.' *Administrative Science Quarterly*, 31: 78–108.

Barley, Stephen R. (1989). 'Careers, identities, and institutions: The legacy of the Chicago School of sociology.' In Michael B. Arthur, Douglas T. Hall and Barbara S. Lawrence (eds.), *Handbook of Career Theory*. New York: Cambridge University Press. pp. 41–66.

Barley, Stephen R. and Kunda, Gideon (2004). *Gurus, Hired Guns and Warm Bodies: Itinerant Experts in a Knowledge Economy*. Princeton, NJ: Princeton University Press.

Barley, Stephen R. and Tolbert, Pamela S. (1997). 'Institutionalization and structuration: Studying the links between action and institution.' *Organization Studies*, 18: 93–117.

Basu, Onker N., Dirsmith, Mark W. and Gupta, Parveen P. (1999). 'The coupling of the symbolic and the technical in an institutionalized context: The negotiated order of the GAO's audit reporting process.' *American Sociological Review*, 64(4): 506–526.

Battilana, Julie. (2006). 'Agency and institutions: The enabling role of individuals' social position.' *Organization*, 13: 653–676.

Bechky, Beth A. (2003a). 'Object lessons: Workplace artifacts and occupational jurisdiction.' *American Journal of Sociology*, 109: 720–752.

Bechky, Beth A. (2003b). 'Sharing meaning across occupational communities.' *Organization Science*, 14: 312–330.

Becker, Howard S. (1952). 'The career of the Chicago public schoolteacher.' *American Journal of Sociology*, 57: 470–477.

Becker, Howard S. (1953). 'Some contingencies of the professional dance musician's career.' *Human Organization*, 12: 22–26.

Becker, Howard S. (1963). *Outsiders: Studies in the Sociology of Deviance*. New York: Free Press.

Becker, Howard S. (1978). 'Arts and crafts.' *American Journal of Sociology*, 83: 862–889.

Becker, Howard S. (1982). *Art Worlds*. Berkeley, CA: University of California Press.

Becker, Howard S. (1999). 'The Chicago School, so-called.' *Qualitative Sociology*, 22(1): 3–12.

Becker, Howard S., Geer, Blanche, Hughes, Everett C. and Strauss, Anselm L. (1961). *Boys in White*. Chicago, IL: University of Chicago Press.

Berger, Peter L. and Luckmann, Thomas (1967). *The Social Construction of Reality*. New York: Doubleday.

Bittner, Egon (1965). 'The concept of organization.' *Social Research*, 32: 239–255.

Blumer, Herbert (1962). ' Society as symbolic interaction.' In Arnold M. Rose (ed.), *Human Behavior and Social Process: An Interactionist Approach*. Boston: Houghton Mifflin. pp. 179–193.

Braude, Lee. (1975). *Work and Workers: A Sociological Analysis*. New York: Praeger.

Bucher, Rue and Schatzman, Leonard (1962). 'The logic of the state mental hospital.' *Social Problems*, 9(4): 337–349.

Bucher, Rue and Stelling, Joan (1969). 'Characteristics of professional organizations.' *Journal of Health and Social Behavior*, 10(1): 3–15.

Bucher, Rue and Stelling, Joan (1977). *Becoming Professional*. Beverly Hills, CA: Sage Publications.

Bucher, Rue and Strauss, Anselm L. (1961). 'Professions in process.' *American Journal of Sociology*, 66: 325–334.

Button, Graham (1993). *Technology in Working Order: Studies of Work, Interaction and Technology*. London: Routledge.

Cicourel, Aaron V. (1967). *The Social Organization of Juvenile Justice*. New York: Wiley.

Cicourel, Aaron V. (1970). 'The acquisition of social structure: Toward a developmental sociology of language and meaning'. In Jack D. Douglas (ed.), *Understanding Everyday Life: Toward the Reconstruction of Sociological Knowledge*. Chicago, IL: Aldine. pp. 136–168.

Cicourel, Aaron V. (1972). 'Basic and normative rules in the negotiation of status and role'. In David Sudnow (ed.), *Studies in Social Interaction*. New York: Free Press. pp. 229–258.

Cicourel, Aaron V. (1974). *Cognitive Sociology: Language and Meaning in Social Interaction*. New York: Free Press.

Cicourel, Aaron V. (1981). 'The role of cognitive-linguistic concepts in understanding everyday social interactions'. *Annual Review of Sociology*, 7: 87–106.

Cicourel, Aaron V. (1987). 'The interpenetration of communicative contexts: Examples from medical encounters'. *Social Psychology Quarterly*, 50: 217–226.

Cicourel, Aaron V. (1990). 'The integration of distributed knowledge in collaborative medical diagnosis'. In Jolene Galegher, Robert E. Kraut and Carmen Egido (eds), *Intellectual Teamwork: Foundations of Cooperative Work*. Hillsdale, NJ: Lawrence Erlbaum Associates. pp. 221–242.

Colyvas, Jeannette A. and Powell, Walter W. (2006). 'Roads to institutionalization: The remaking of boundaries between public and private science.' *Research in Organizational Behavior*, 27: 305–353.

Coser, Lewis A., Kadushin, Charles and Powell, Walter W. (1982). *Books: The Culture and Commerce of Publishing*. New York: Basic Books.

Creed, W. E. D., Scully, Maureen A. and Austin, John R. (2002). 'Clothes make the person? The tailoring of legitimating accounts and the social construction of identity.' *Organization Science*, 13(5): 475–496.

Dalton, Melville. (1950). *Men Who Manage*. New York: John Wiley.

Davis, Gerald. (1991). 'Agents without principles: The spread of the poison pill through the intercorporate network.' *Administrative Science Quarterly*, 36: 583–613.

DiMaggio, Paul J. (1988). 'Interest and agency in institutional theory.' In Lynne G. Zucker (ed.), *Institutional Patterns and Organizations: Culture and Environment*. Cambridge, MA: Ballinger. pp. 3–22.

DiMaggio, Paul J. and Powell, Walter W. (1983). 'The iron cage revisited: Institutional isomorphism and collective rationality in organizational fields.' *American Sociological Review*, 48: 147–160.

DiMaggio, Paul J. and Powell, Walter W. (1991). 'Introduction.' In Walter W. Powell and Paul J. DiMaggio (eds.), *The New Institutionalism in Organizational Analysis*. Chicago, IL: University of Chicago Press. pp. 1–40.

Dobbin, Frank and Sutton, Frank R. (1998). 'The strength of a weak state: The rights revolution and the rise of human resources management divisions.' *American Journal of Sociology*, 104(2): 441–476.

Dobbin, Frank, Sutton, John R., Meyer, John W. and Scott, W. R. (1993). 'Equal opportunity law and the construction of internal labor markets.' *American Journal of Sociology*, 99: 265–316.

Edelman, Lauren B., Fuller, Sally R. and Mara-Drita, Iona (2001). 'Diversity rhetoric and the mangerialization of law.' *American Journal of Sociology*, 106(6): 1589–1641.

Emerson, Joan (1970). 'Nothing unusual is happening.' In Tomatsu Shibutani (ed.), *Human Nature and Collective Behavior*. New Brunswick, NJ: Transaction Books. pp. 208–222.

Etzioni, Amitai (1969). *The Semi-Professions and their Organization*. New York: Free Press.

Faulkner, Robert R. (1974). 'Coming of age in organizations: A comparative study of career contingencies and adult socialization.' *Sociology of Work and Occupations*, 1: 131–173.

Faulkner, Robert R. (1987). *Music on Demand: Composers and Careers in the Hollywood Film Industry*. New Brunswick, NJ: Transaction Books.

Fine, Gary A. (1983). *Shared Fantasy: Role Playing Games as Social Worlds*. Chicago: University of Chicago Press.

Fine, Gary A. (1987). *With the Boys: Little League Baseball and Preadolescent Culture*. Chicago, IL: University of Chicago Press.

Fine, Gary A. (1991). 'On the macrofoundations of microsociology: Order, meaning and comparative context.' *The Sociological Quarterly*, 32(2): 161–177.

Fine, Gary A. (1996). *Kitchens: The Culture of Restaurant Work*. Berkeley, CA: University of California Press.

Fligstein, Neil (1993). *The Transformation of Corporate Control*. Cambridge, MA: Harvard University Press.

Fligstein, Neil (2001). 'Social skill and the theory of fields.' *Sociological Theory*, 19(2): 105–125.

Garfinkel, Harold. (1967). *Studies in Ethnomethodology*. Englewood Cliffs, NJ: Prentice Hall.

Garfinkel, Harold. (1986). *Ethnomethodological Studies of Work*. London: Routledge and Kegan Paul.

Geer, Blanche (1968). 'Occupational commitment and the teaching profession.' In Howard S. Becker, Blanche Geer, David Reisman and Robert A. Weiss (eds.), *Institutions and the Person*. Chicago, IL: Aldine. pp. 221–234.

Giddens, Anthony. (1984). *The Constitution of Society*. Berkeley, CA: University of California Press.

Glaser, Barney G. and Strauss, Anselm L. (1965). *Awareness of Dying*. Chicago, IL: Aldine.

Glaser, Barney G. and Strauss, Anselm L. (1967). *The Discovery of Grounded Theory: Strategies for Qualitative Research*. Chicago, IL: Aldine.

Glaser, Barney G. and Strauss, Anselm L. (1968). *Time for Dying*. Chicago, IL: Aldine.

Goffman, Erving. (1961). 'The moral career of the mental patient.' In *Asylums*. New York: Anchor. pp. 125–170.

Goffman, Erving. (1967). *Interaction Ritual: Essays on Face-to-Face Behavior*. Garden City, NY: Doubleday.

Goffman, Erving. (1981). *Forms of Talk*. Philadelphia, PA: University of Pennsylvania.

Goffman, Erving. (1983). 'The interaction order.' *American Sociological Review*, 48:1–17.

Greenwood, Royston and Suddaby, Roy (2006). 'Institutional entrepreneurship in mature fields: The Big Five accounting firms.' *Academy of Management Journal*, 49(1): 27–48.

Greenwood, Royston, Suddaby, Roy and Hinings, C. R. (2002). 'Theorizing change: The role of professional associations in the transformation of institutionalized fields.' *Academy of Management Journal*, 45(1): 58–80.

Grimshaw, Allen D. (1981). 'Talk and social control.' In Morris Rosenberg and Ralph H. Turner (eds.), *Social Psychology: Sociological Perspectives*. New York: Basic. pp. 200–232.

Grodal, Stine. (2007). 'The emergence of an organizational field – labels, meaning and emotions in nanotechnology.' Unpublished dissertation, Stanford University, Stanford, CA.

Hallett, Tim and Ventresca, Marc J. (2006). 'Inhabited institutions: Social interactions and organizational forms in Gouldner's Patterns of Industrial Bureaucracy.' *Theoretical Sociology*, 35: 213–236.

Hannan, Michael T. and Freeman, John H. (1977). 'The population ecology of organizations.' *American Journal of Sociology*, 82: 929–964.

Heath, Christian and Luff, Paul (1992). 'Collaboration and control: Crisis management and multimedia technology in London Underground line control rooms.' *Computer Supported Cooperative Work*, 1: 69–94.

Heath, Christian and Luff, Paul (1996). 'Convergent activities: Line control and passenger information on the London Underground.' In Yrjo Engestrom and David Middleton (eds.), *Cognition and Communication at Work*. New York: Cambridge University Press. pp. 96–129.

Heritage, John (1993). *Garfinkel and Ethnomethodology*. London: Blackwell.

Hoffman, Andrew J. (1999). 'Institutional evolution and change: Environmentalism and the U.S. chemical industry.' *Academy of Management Journal*, 42(4): 351–371.

Hughes, Everett C. (1936). 'The ecological aspects of institutions.' *American Sociological Review*, 1: 180–189.

Hughes, Everett C. (1937). 'Institutional office and the person.' *American Journal of Sociology*, 43: 404–413.

Hughes, Everett C. (1942). 'The study of institutions.' *Social Forces*, 20(3): 307–310.

Hughes, Everett C. (1971 [1962]). 'Going concerns: The study of American institutions.' In Everett C. Hughes (ed.), *The Sociological Eye*. Chicago, IL: Aldine. pp. 52–64.

Johnson, Gerry, Smith, Stuart and Codling, Brian (2000). 'Microprocesses of institutional change in the context of privatization.' *Academy of Management Review*, 35: 572–580.

Kelly, Erin and Dobbin, Frank (1999). 'Civil rights law and work: Sex discrimination and the rise of maternity leave policies.' *American Journal of Sociology*, 105(2): 455–492.

Kling, Rob and Gerson, Elihu M. (1978a). 'Patterns of segmentation and intersection in the computing world.' *Symbolic Interaction*, 1: 24–43.

Kling, Rob and Gerson, Elihu M. (1978b). 'The social dynamics of technical innovation in the computing world.' *Symbolic Interaction*, 1: 132–146.

Kling, Rob and Sacchi, Walt (1982). 'The web of computing: Computer technology as social construction.' *Advances in Computers*, 21: 1–90.

Kunda, Gideon. (1992). *Engineering Culture: Control and Commitment in a High Tech Corporation*. Philadelphia, PA: Temple University Press.

Larson, Magali S. (1979). 'Professionalism: Rise and fall.' *International Journal of Health Services*, 9: 607–627.

Lawrence, Thomas B. and Phillips, Nelson. (2004). 'From Moby Dick to Free Willy: Macrocultural discourse and institutional entrepreneurship in emerging institutional fields.' *Organization*, 11(5): 689–711.

Leca, Bernard. (2006). 'A critical realist approach to institutional entrepreneurship.' *Organization*, 135(5): 627–651.

Lewis, J. D. and Smith, Richard L. (1980). *American Sociology and Pragmatism: Mead, Chicago Sociology, and Symbolic Interaction*. Chicago, IL: University of Chicago Press.

Linton, Ralph (1936). *The Study of Man*. New York: Appleton-Century-Crofts.

Lounsbury, Michael and Kaghan, William N. (2001). 'Organizations, occupations and the structuration of work.' *Research in the Sociology of Work*, 10: 25–50.

Lynch, Michael E. (1985). *Art and Artifact in Laboratory Science: A Study of Shop Work and Shop Talk in a Research Laboratory*. London: Routledge and Kegan Paul.

Maines, David R. (1982). 'In search of mesostructure: Studies in the negotiated order.' *Urban Life*, 11: 267–279.

McCall, George J. and Simmons, George L. (1978). *Identities and Interactions: An Examination of Human Association in Everyday Life*. New York: Free Press.

McCallion, Michael J. and Maines, David R. (2002). 'Spiritual gatekeepers: Time and the rite of Christian initiation of adults.' *Symbolic Interaction*, 25: 289–302.

Mead, George H. (1934). *Mind, Self, and Society*. Chicago, IL: University of Chicago Press.

Merton, Robert K. (1957). *Social Theory and Social Structure*. New York: Free Press.

Meyer, John W. and Rowan, Brian (1977). 'Institutionalized organizations: Formal structure as myth and ceremony.' *American Journal of Sociology*, 83: 340–363.

Munir, Kamal A. and Phillips, Nelson (2005). 'The birth of the "Kodak Moment": Institutional entrepreneurship and the adoption of new technologies.' *Organization Studies*, 26: 1665–1687.

Nelsen, Bonalyn J. and Barley, Stephen R. (1997). 'For love or money: Commodification and the construction of an occupational mandate.' *Administrative Science Quarterly*, 42: 619–653.

Orlikowski, Wanda J. (1992). 'The duality of technology: Rethinking the concept of technology in organizations.' *Organization Science*, 3: 398–427.

Orlikowski, Wanda J. (1996). 'Improvising organizational transformation over time: A situated change perspective.' *Information Systems Research*, 7: 63–92.

Orlikowski, Wanda J. (2000). 'Using technology and constituting structures: A practice lens for studying technology in organizations.' *Organization Science*, 11: 404–428.

Orlikowski, Wanda J. and Yates, Joanne. (1994 'Genre repertoire: The structuring of communicative practices in organizations.' *Administrative Science Quarterly*, 39: 541–574.

Park, Robert E. and Burgess, Ernest W. (1921). *Introduction to the Science of Sociology*. Chicago, IL: University of Chicago Press.

Parsons, Talcott (1951). *The Social System*. New York: Free Press.

Powell, Walter W. (1985). *Getting into Print: The Decision Making Process in Scholarly Publishing*. Chicago, IL: Chicago University Press.

Rao, Hayagreeva. (1998). ' Caveat emptor: The construction of nonprofit consumer watchdog organizations.' *American Journal of Sociology*, 103(4): 912–961.

Rao, Hayagreeva, Monin, Philippe and Durand, Rodolphe (2003). 'Institutional change in Toque Ville: Nouvelle cuisine as an identity movement in French gastronomy.' *American Journal of Sociology*, 108(4): 795–843.

Rock, Paul (1979). *The Making of Symbolic Interactionism*. Totowa, NJ: Rowman and Littlefield.

Roy, Donald F. (1964). 'Unionization in the South: The organizational campaign in the social and cultural context of the South.' *Labor Law Journal*, 15(7): 451–468.

Roy, Donald F. (1965). 'Change and resistance to change in the Southern labor movement.' In John McKinney and Edgar T. Thompson (eds.), *The South in Continuity and Change*. Durham, NC: Duke University Press. pp. 225–247.

Sachs, Harvey, Schegloff, Emanuel A. and Jefferson, Gail (1974). 'A simplest systematics for the organization of turn-taking for conversations.' *Language*, 50(4): 696–735.

Sandfort, Jodi R. (2003). 'Exploring the structuration of technology within human service organizations.' *Administration and Society*, 34(6): 605–631.

Schatzman, Leonard and Bucher, Rue (1964). 'Negotiating a division of labor among professionals in a state mental hospital.' *Psychiatry*, 27: 266–277.

Schatzman, Leonard and Strauss, Anselm L. (1966). 'A sociology of psychiatry: A perspective and some organizing foci.' *Social Problems*, 14(1): 2–16.

Scott, Marvin B. and Lyman, Stanford M. (1968). 'Accounts.' *American Sociological Review*, 33: 46–62.

Scott, W. Richard (1995). *Institutions and Organizations*. Thousand Oaks, CA: Sage.

Seo, M. G. and Creed, W. E. D. (2002). 'Institutional contradictions, praxis and institutional change: A dialectical perspective.' *Academy of Management Journal*, 27(2): 1–29.

Shibutani, Tomatsu (1955). 'Reference groups as perspectives.' *American Journal of Sociology*, 60: 522–529.

Shibutani, Tomatsu (1962). 'Reference groups and social control.' In Arnold M. Rose (ed.), *Human Behavior and Social Processes: An Interactionist Approach*. Boston: Houghton Mifflin Company. pp. 128–147.

Silverman, David (1971). *The Theory of Organisations*. New York: Basic.

Simmel, Georg. (1964). *The Sociology of Georg Simmel*. New York: Free Press.

Strauss, Anselm L. (1968). 'Some neglected properties of status passage.' In Howard S. Becker, Blanche Geer, David Riesman and Robert S. Weiss (eds.), *Institutions and the Person*. Chicago, IL: Aldine Publishing Company. pp. 235–251.

Strauss, Anselm L. (1978a). *Negotiations: Varieties, Processes, Context and Social Order*. San Francisco: Jossey–Bass.

Strauss, Anselm L. (1978b). 'A social world perspective.' *Studies in Symbolic Interaction*, 1: 119–128.

Strauss, Anselm L. (1982). 'Social worlds and legitimation processes.' *Studies in Symbolic Interaction*, 4: 171–190.

Strauss, Anselm L. (1984). 'Social worlds and their segmentation processes.' *Studies in Symbolic Interaction*, 5: 123–139.

Strauss, Anselm L., Schatzman, Leonard, Bucher, Rue, Ehrlich, Danuta and Sabshin, Melvin (1963). 'The hospital and its negotiated order.' In Elliot Freidson (ed.), *The Hospital in Modern Society*. New York: Free Press.

Strauss, Anselm L., Schatzman, Leonard, Bucher, Rue, Ehrlich, Danuta and Sabshin, Melvin (1964). *Psychiatric Ideologies and Institutions*. Glencoe, IL: Free Press.

Suchman, Lucy A. (1987). *Plans and Situated Action: The Problem of Human–Machine Communication*. Cambridge: Cambridge University Press.

Suchman, Mark C. (1995). 'Managing legitimacy: Strategic and institutional approaches.' *The Academy of Management Review*, 20(3): 571–610.

Suddaby, Roy and Greenwood, Royston (2005). 'Rhetorical strategies of legitimacy.' *Administrative Science Quarterly*, 50: 53–67.

Tolbert, Pamela S. and Zucker, Lynne G. (1983). 'Institutional sources of change in the formal structure of organizations: The diffusion of civil service reform, 1880–1935.' *Administrative Science Quarterly*, 28: 22–39.

Tolbert, Pamela S. and Zucker, Lynne G. (1996). 'The institutionalization of institutional theory.' In Stewart R. Clegg, Cynthia Hardy and Walter W. Nord (eds.), *Handbook of Organization Studies*. Thousand Oaks, CA: Sage. pp. 175–190.

Turkle, Sherry (1995). *Life on the Screen: Identity in the Age of the Internet*. New York: Simon and Schuster.

Turner, Ralph H. (1962). 'Role taking: Process versus conformity.' In Arnold M. Rose (ed.), *Human Behavior and Social Processes*. Boston: Houghton Mifflin. pp. 20–40.

Turner, Ralph H. (1968). 'Role: Sociological aspects.' In David L. Sills (ed.), *International Encyclopedia of the Social Sciences*. New York: Macmillian. pp. 552–557.

Turner, Ralph H. (1976). 'The real self: From institution to impulse.' *American Journal of Sociology*, 81: 989–1016.

Turner, Ralph H. (1978). 'Role and the person.' *American Journal of Sociology*, 84: 1–23.

Van Maanen, John (1973). 'Observations on the making of policemen.' *Human Organization*, 32: 407–418.

Van Maanen, John (1975). 'Breaking in: A consideration of organizational socialization.' In Robert Dubin (ed.), *Handbook of Work, Organization, and Society*. Chicago, IL: Rand–McNally.

Van Maanen, John (1978). 'The asshole.' In Peter K. Manning and John Van Maanen (eds.), *Policing: A View from the Street*. Los Angeles: Goodyear Press. pp. 221–238.

Venkatesh, Murali and Shin, Dong H. (2005). 'Extending social constructivism with institutional theory: A broadband civic networking case.' In Peter V. D. Besselaar, Giorgio de Michelis, Jenny Preece and Carla Simore (eds.), *Communities and Technologies 2005: Proceedings of the Second Communities and Technologies Conference*. Milan/New York: Springer.

Weick, Karl E. (1979). *The Social Psychology of Organizing*. Reading, MA: Addison–Wesley.

Williamson, Oliver E. (1975). *Markets and Hierarchies: Analysis and Antitrust Implications*. New York: Free Press.

Yates Joanne and Orlikowski, Wanda (1992). 'Genres of organizational communication: A structurational approach to studying communication media.' *Academy of Management Review*, 17: 299–326.

Zucker, Lynne G. (1977). ' The role of institutionalization in cultural persistence.' *American Sociological Review*, 42: 726–743.

Zucker, Lynne G. (1987). 'Institutional theories of organization.' *Annual Review of Sociology*, 13: 443–464.

Towards a Practice-Driven Institutionalism

Michael Smets, Angela Aristidou and Richard Whittington

INTRODUCTION

Recent years have seen an increasing mutual engagement between institutional and strategy-as-practice scholars who realize that they can learn from each other to address critical blind spots in their respective theories (Smets, Greenwood, & Lounsbury, 2015a; Suddaby, Seidl, & Lê, 2013; Vaara & Whittington, 2012). In this chapter, we argue that this nascent dialogue is bringing about a *practice-driven institutionalism* (PDI) that more truthfully reflects the intellectual heritage of institutional theory and, in doing so, sheds a more comprehensive light on modern-day issues of organizing and work (Barley & Kunda, 2001; Feldman & Orlikowski, 2011).

Institutional theorists are thereby following the 'practice turn' which has characterized much of organization theory in the last twenty years (Barrett, Oborn, Orlikowski, & Yates, 2012; Sandberg & Tsoukas, 2011; Schatzki, Knorr-Cetina, & Savigny, 2001;

Whittington, 2006). Especially, they build on strong process- and practice-driven ontologies which the literatures on routines (e.g., Feldman, 2016; Feldman & Pentland, 2003; Parmigiani & Howard-Grenville, 2011), technology-as-practice (and as institution) (e.g., Orlikowski, 1996, 2000; Orlikowski & Barley, 2001) and strategy-as-practice (for reviews, see: Smets et al., 2015a; Suddaby et al., 2013) have carried into the organizational literature. In following this turn, institutionalists seek to enhance their understanding of how institutions play out on the 'coalface' of everyday life (Barley, Chapter 13 this volume). Specifically, PDI advances their theorizing of institutional logics (e.g., Ocasio, Thornton & Lounsbury, Chapter 19 this volume; Thornton, Ocasio, & Lounsbury, 2012), the complexities that occur when incompatible logics clash (e.g., Greenwood, Raynard, Kodeih, Micelota, & Lounsbury, 2011; Kraatz & Block, Chapter 20 this volume), and the institutional work required to create, change, or maintain institutions under those conditions (e.g., Hampel, Lawrence and Tracey, this volume, Chapter 21; Lawrence, Leca, & Zilber, 2013; Lawrence & Suddaby, 2006). In this sense, PDI cuts across and informs the dominant conversations of current institutionalist theorizing.

Simultaneously, strategy-as-practice scholars have begun to look beyond the intra-organizational activities that have traditionally preoccupied them (Johnson, Langley, Melin, & Whittington, 2007) and earned themselves the critique of obsessing over minute details of activities such as strategy-making without attending to their broader meaning and significance (Geiger, 2009; Whittington, 2011). They are therefore now calling for 'more precise and contextually sensitive theories about the enactment and impact of practices' (Jarzabkowski, Kaplan, Seidl, & Whittington, 2015). Such contextual sensitivity, especially to broader social norms and prescriptions, has always characterized institutional research, albeit often to the neglect of those activities that sustain them. Whittington (2006: 617) has therefore long called for 'closer connections between what goes on deep inside organizations and broader phenomena outside', suggesting that practice and institutional theorists have simply been looking at opposite sides of the same coin and are now both calling for engagement with the other.

Notably, bringing together institutional and practice scholarship not only advances our understanding of phenomena with which scholars in both camps currently grapple; judiciously combining the 'best of both worlds' also unlocks new phenomena that previously eluded investigation with either of the two conceptual toolkits alone. In short, the two perspectives 'can open each other's eyes to new phenomena and start looking at familiar phenomena in new ways' (Smets et al., 2015a: 283).

The emergent strand of theorizing that springs from this dialogue is what we call a *practice-driven institutionalism (PDI)*, in which the everyday work of practitioners 'on the ground' is the engine room of social order and the practices by which jobs get done – its driving force. In this sense, we reconnect institutional theory with its practice-theoretical roots in order to (i) foreground the collective performance of institutions through situated, emergent and generative *practices*, (ii) acknowledge the institutional significance of *praxis*, the everyday work performed by and in organizations, and (iii) draw attention to the role of frontline *practitioners*, ordinary people doing ordinary work in the constitution of institutional orders. PDI differs from practice-based studies in general because it engages them specifically in relation to institutional theory and the supra-organizational orders that it attends to. As such, it acknowledges the need for onto-epistemological consistency when bringing together two communities with distinct traditions, even though they may share common ancestry, as we discuss next. Second, PDI draws attention to practice as 'driving' further developments in institutional theory. It does not simply refer to practice as the basis for theorizing, but highlights how a more comprehensive engagement with practice-theoretical thought may generate a new perspective on phenomena that puzzle institutional theorists.

We develop PDI on the basis of Schatzki's (2001: 2) definition of practices as 'embodied, materially mediated arrays of human activity centrally organized around shared practical understanding'. Any given practice comprises multiple interrelated and interdependent activities. To be *relevant* to a given practice, these activities should be intelligible for participants in a specific situation or spatio-temporal context (Feldman & Orlikowski, 2011), be collectively meaningful and accomplishable, and also be recurrently performed and recognized by multiple people (Schatzki, 2012). Opacity continues to surround the practice concept as different theorists draw on various philosophical underpinnings. However, two key onto-epistemological assumptions provide coherence: First, like institutionalists, practice theorists subscribe to a non-individualist view of the world (Barnes, 2001). For practice theorists, the basic unit of analysis is 'the practice', not practitioners (Nicolini, 2012; Osterlund & Carlile, 2003). Second, practice theories adopt a 'framework of practical rationality' (Sandberg & Tsoukas, 2011: 339) to explore how people actually get on with their work and how organizational practices are constituted and enacted in everyday life – which is of particular appeal and relevance for institutional scholars.

Institutional scholars have recently paid more attention to practice, but often in a more colloquial and unreflexive way to simply capture what people 'do' without embracing the onto-epistemological assumptions underpinning practice theory. Differentiating *practices* as norms and routines from their everyday performance in *praxis*, and insisting on *practitioners* as the active embodiment of practices rather than simply asocial 'individuals' (e.g., Jarzabkowski, Balogun, & Seidl, 2007; Whittington, 2006) adds much-needed conceptual clarity to the currently somewhat loose use of 'practice' in institutional scholarship. It is this additional granularity which holds great promise for adding nuance and conceptual rigour to institutionalists' understanding of practice.

To reconnect contemporary institutional theory with its intellectual heritage, we use the next section to trace the theoretical evolution that got us to the intellectual status quo. We remind ourselves of the common roots institutional and practice theorists share in the seminal works of Bourdieu (1977, 1990), Giddens (1984) and Foucault (1980), the different paths they have taken since then, and the common interests that have sparked the recent dialogue. In the third section, we lay the groundwork for PDI. We explore the conceptual touchpoints at which institutional and practice scholars can enrich each other's conversations and review new insights that recent work at these intersections has generated. We follow up in section four with some words of caution about pitfalls to avoid in the general excitement of theoretical integration. Finally, we conclude with a research agenda for PDI.

COMMON ORIGINS, DIFFERENT DESTINATIONS: A BRIEF OVERVIEW OF PRACTICE AND INSTITUTIONAL THEORY

Both institutional and practice scholars trace their intellectual heritage to the same seminal philosophers, foremost among them Bourdieu (1977, 1990), Giddens (1984) and Foucault (1980), but both have since selectively borrowed different theoretical tenets as 'figure' or 'ground' for their respective theorizing. As a result, they have come to occupy virtually opposite positions on multiple theoretical touchpoints: where one emphasized structure, the other focused on agency; where one foregrounded stability, the other highlighted the potential for change; and where one rose to the macro-social heights of field-level studies, the other dug into everyday activity.

Giddens' (1984) structurationist conception of structural rules and resources offers a common framework to analyse the disparate social influences on managerial action, to highlight the role of human agency and its recursive relationship to structure. Foucault (1980) views the social as a field of interconnected, recurrent and novel doings, materials and statements. Bourdieu (1977) explains social dynamics by focusing on how agents produce and re-produce the social structures they inhabit through their everyday activities – or praxis. In this sense, all three are quintessentially fascinated with explaining social order, much in the same way institutional theorists have been – and still are. Citing these seminal theorists as their 'forefathers', the practice and institutional communities have in the last decades foregrounded different aspects of their work in theorizing organizational life.

Large Ontologies

Practice theorists endorse 'large' ontologies (Seidl & Whittington, 2014), in which no episode of activity is self-standing and no entity is privileged as the origin of all others. Such large ontologies are expressed in different ways in the work of contemporary practice theorists. Some take 'flatter' positions. Thus Schatzki (2002; 2012) treats practices as extended bundles that stretch horizontally over time and space rather than as predetermined, fixed and hierarchical structures. Similarly, some practice theorists (e.g., Gehman, Treviño, & Garud, 2013) have endorsed Latour's (2005) conceptualization of networks that stretch horizontally and are sustained through heterogeneous association. Others take 'taller' ontological positions, as for example Giddens (1984) does when he distinguishes the structural properties of social systems from the specific activities of human agents. However, Giddens' structurationist theory simultaneously insists that the vertical relationship between larger social system and local activity is not one of top-down determination, but one of reciprocal duality. Order is not imposed from above by some overbearing social institution, but continuously reproduced through practices as 'regularized types of activity, produced by knowledgeable actors' (Giddens, 1976: 75). Whether tall or flat, all these practice ontologies recognize relationality in the sense of mutual interconnections extending beyond some singular practice or activity. The local has a larger reach and relationships are not simply hierarchical.

In such larger ontologies, the common denominator is that there is no prevalence of one practice over another, no sense of hierarchy. Rather, interrelated activities compose practices and, hence, all practices are interrelated in open-ended, spatially–temporally dispersed ways (Schatzki, 2012), transcending geographical, organizational and structural boundaries. Even more, individuals are viewed as existing in a state of 'entwinement' with others and with things (Sandberg & Dall'Alba, 2009: 1351; Sandberg & Tsoukas, 2011), as well as with any notions of 'structure'. In this vein, Orlikowski (2000) takes

'technology structure' to emerge from the recursive, repeated and situated interaction among technologies and humans, using the term 'technology-in-practice'. Individuals, practices and structures exist in a continuously emerging state of reciprocity and interconnectedness by which they generate, re-produce, maintain and change social order. This view that practices span traditionally conceived levels of analysis echoes relational sociologies that reject the idea that the world comes neatly divided into levels and fixed structures, or that there is a fundamental distinction between micro and macro phenomena (Reckwitz, 2002).

In the meantime, however, the fascination with how institutions persist and prescribe human conduct has led early institutionalists to adopt a more top-down ontology. Inspired by Foucault's (1980) attentiveness to how society's forces shape behaviour and expectations, the focus among institutional theorists has been on explaining micro-level phenomena by reference to reified macro-social structures or systems, which impose on social life like 'some external force or legislative deus ex machina' (Clemens & Cook, 1999: 447). Foregrounding Giddens' (1976) structuralist notions of rules and resources as forming systems, over his concern for individual agency (Giddens, 1984), the institutional community has adopted institutions as a putatively objective reality that actors accept as natural to the extent that alternatives become 'literally unthinkable' (Zucker, 1983: 25).

Committed to more hierarchical ontologies than practice theorists, institutionalists have construed social norms as exogenous to and imposing upon human interaction, rather than emerging from it (e.g., Hirsch & Lounsbury, 1997; Whittington, 1992). Replete with differentiations of macro- and micro-level phenomena, institutional accounts depict organizations as very much at the mercy of their institutional – often regulatory – context (e.g., Meyer & Rowan, 1977; Scott, 1987; Tolbert & Zucker, 1983). Thus, as critics have noted, this early focus of the institutional community ran directly counter to the theory's structurationist origins – and practice theorists' readings of those common origins. As Barley and Tolbert (1997: 95) note, institutions – at the time – were conceived of as 'demands of centralized authorities or regulatory agencies and only secondarily [of] widespread beliefs, practices, and norms'. In a practice ontology, institutions would be perceived as enacted in their ongoing performance – thoughts that have only recently taken hold again in institutional theory, as scholars examine the instantiation of 'logics in action' (e.g., Lounsbury & Boxenbaum, 2013; McPherson & Sauder, 2013).

Fields

Bourdieu draws on the analogy of soccer to illustrate his concept of a 'field' (Bourdieu, 1977; 1993): All players engage in the same game and their relative positions to each other are the result of their past activities, and opportunity for future ones. In short, their positions – and potential actions – are driven by their prior engagement with others in the practice. Endorsing relational ontologies, practice theorists have defined fields as 'the total nexus of *interconnected* human practices' (Schatzki, 2002: 2); that is as the social space that is defined by what practitioners *do* – and *do together* – on an everyday basis (Emirbayer & Johnson, 2008; Schatzki, 2005; Tsoukas & Chia, 2002). Such practice-based fields are held together by a shared 'interest' (Bourdieu & Wacquant, 1992: 117), akin to Hoffman's (1999) issue-based field.

Among institutional theorists, though, the concept of field has taken a different turn. Departing from their roots in practice theory, institutional theorists draw on DiMaggio and Powell's (1983: 148–149) now seminal definition of fields as 'those organizations that, in the aggregate constitute a recognized area of institutional life'. Thus, institutionalists' definitions of fields are very much centred on the actors who inhabit them – and the rules and regulations that yoke them together (for an overview, see Wooten & Hoffman, Chapter 2 this volume). Accordingly, fields in celebrated empirical works mostly comprise geographically bounded sets of actors, such as US art museums (DiMaggio, 1991) or the 'Big Five' accounting firms (Greenwood & Suddaby, 2006).

Nonetheless, while institutional scholars paid less attention to the activities in which actors engage and through which they connect, they did retain the notion of fields as systems of social positions (e.g., Bourdieu, 1977; Bourdieu & Wacquant, 1992). This topographical understanding of fields as positional systems in which actors compete for various forms of capital has taken hold among institutionalists, especially in discussions of how social position influences actors' motivation and ability to act as institutional entrepreneurs (e.g., Battilana, 2011; Battilana, Leca, & Boxenbaum, 2009). While the common understanding had long been that disadvantaged organizations on the field periphery are more motivated to act entrepreneurially because they stand to gain more, while risking less (e.g., Kraatz & Zajac, 1996; Leblebici, Salancik, Copay, & King, 1991), later research established conditions under which even central players would challenge the institutional status quo (e.g., Greenwood & Suddaby, 2006).

Embeddedness and Situatedness

The question of where change could originate gained particular salience in the context of the so-called 'paradox of embedded agency'(Seo & Creed, 2002), the question of how actors can become motivated and enabled to challenge supposedly taken-for-granted practices, structures and norms. We trace this puzzle to institutionalists' reading of Bourdieu's (1977) concept of 'habitus'; players' subconscious 'sense of the game'. It allows them to improvise according to the local, temporal, social norms within the field, and destines most activities of everyday life to go virtually unnoticed. However, while Bourdieu (1977: 59) defined habitus as 'the precondition not only for the coordination of practices, but also for practices of coordination', practice scholars and institutionalists – very simply put – focused on either part of this equation.

Practice scholars have traditionally foregrounded 'situatedness' and the need for practices of coordination. They maintain that, as practices are composed of interdependent activities, a practice can only be examined and understood within a specific context: temporal, spatial, historical and – above all – relational (Schatzki, 2006, 2012). Sandberg and Pinnington (2009) as well as Gherardi (2000) bring situatedness to life by drawing on Heidegger's notion of 'being-in-the-world' to highlight how actors respond to situations at hand as these evolve within a specific context. In Nicolini's (2011) work, situatedness is akin to a 'site' in time and place, echoing Giddens' (1979: 53) dictum that 'agents' action is always situated in time and space'. Accordingly, in recent applications of practice theory, authors have strongly emphasized that practitioners must be sensitive to the exigencies of specific situations to accomplish their work (Feldman & Orlikowski, 2011; Howard-Grenville, 2005; Nicolini, 2011). They have also recently urged researchers in the practice community to link 'what, who, and how' when examining practices in organizations (Jarzabkowski et al., 2015). In any particular situation, it is the participants' 'practical understanding' (Schatzki, 2006: 1864), their personal, tacit know-how, that allows them to select and competently perform specific actions that they consider pertinent to that particular situation. Wittgenstein's (1953) argument that, at some point, practitioners 'know how to go on' is echoed by Giddens (1984: 43) and – through Schatzki (2002, 2006) – is formulated as the collective and 'general understanding' which practice theorists accept

as guiding the appropriateness of specific actions in any given context or situation.

This line of thought is akin to institutional logics, but for early institutional theorists the institutional context is stringently perceived as an 'external' persuasive force, rather than part of the 'relational whole'. Therefore, institutionalists have traditionally given precedence to embeddedness over situatedness. Specifically, emphasizing the constraining effects of institutions on human conduct has denied actors the capacity to engage in self-determined action and to 'make a difference' to the institutional status quo (Giddens, 1984: 14). Thus, early institutional theorists have attacted a common criticism levied at those adopting Bourdieu's (1977) original formulation as lacking clarity on how habitus and field may recursively change each other (Crossley, 2001). Notably, de Certeau (1984) highlights how habitus accounts for predominant practices, but is unable to capture the micro-tactics of resistance, local deformations and reinvention that occur in enacting habitus.

Hence, while practice scholars followed Wittgenstein's (1953) train of thought on the open-endedness of rules, institutionalists limited agency to unreflective rule following that routinely reproduced existing institutional arrangements (DiMaggio & Powell, 1991). Essentially, it was this narrow conceptualization of practitioners' agentic capacities that produced the paradox of embedded agency. It therefore seems apposite to take a closer look at how institutional and practice camps conceive of agency, structure and change.

Agency, Structure and Change

The core tenet of institutional theory has always been that organizations conform to social expectations because doing so provides legitimacy which, in turn, provides access to material and symbolic resources that support organizational survival. This common quest for legitimacy, produces an 'inexorable push toward homogenization'

(DiMaggio & Powell, 1983: 148), meaning that *individual* responses to institutional forces *collectively* homogenize the field, reducing its organizational variety and increasing institutional stability (e.g., DiMaggio & Powell, 1983; Scott, 1995). This early focus on the resultant 'isomorphism' (DiMaggio & Powell, 1983; see also Boxenbaum & Jonsson, Chapter 3 this volume) critics noted, rendered institutional theory unable to conceptualize the conditions and mechanisms for divergent, interest-driven agency and change (e.g., Hirsch & Lounsbury, 1997; Oliver, 1991, 1992; Selznick, 1996). Therefore, with social norms conceptualized as the objective '"way things are" and/or the "way things are to be done"' (Scott, 1987: 496), the only conceivable origin of change in stable organizational fields is 'some kind of shock' (Sewell, 1992: 3). With an exogenous shock 'smacking into stable institutional arrangements', their taken-for-grantedness is undermined and actors are given cognitive space to conceive of alternatives (Clemens & Cook, 1999: 447). Lounsbury (2002) and Thornton (2002) offer illustrative examples of these dynamics through their respective studies of new forms of investing and the transformation of the higher education publishing industry.

However, as Sewell (1992: 2) noted very astutely, 'what tends to get lost in this language of structure is the efficacy of human action – or agency'. While structure was often perceived by early institutional theorists to exist apart from – but nevertheless determinant of – the shape of human action, researchers adopting a practice perspective foregrounded the role of agency in the constant becoming of organizations and social phenomena (Schatzki, 2006; Tsoukas & Chia, 2002). From practice perspectives, the world and phenomena within it come about only by being performed (Feldman, 2000; Feldman & Orlikowski, 2011) and are generated, reinforced and changed continuously through the situated and recurrent nature of everyday activities. Drawing on Giddens' (1984: 116–117) structuration concept, practice theorists emphasize that we should and could not separate 'individuals' and 'activity' from the contexts that they themselves participate in constituting. Building on Wittgenstein's (1953) original thought that any rule is open to being applied in multiple, differing ways and any rule to impose a dictated interpretation would itself constitute another rule, practice theorists celebrate a world of endless improvisation and potential for change.

Whereas institutional theorists chose to attend to the 'ostensive' homogeneity and stability of institutionalized practices, scholars in a practice tradition – such as those studying routines – have remained more attuned to the 'performative' variation that characterizes everyday praxis (e.g., Feldman & Pentland, 2003; Howard-Grenville, 2005; Spee, Jarzabkowski, & Smets, 2016). Routines rely 'neither on mindless, habitual performance as a source of stability, nor on exogenous shocks as a source of change' (Parmigiani & Howard-Grenville, 2011: 421). Routines from a practice perspective are generative – they hold the seeds of their own continuity or change (Feldman, 2016; Feldman & Pentland, 2003). If, in Wittgenstein's (1953) words, 'there is always the possibility of following the same one rule in multiple, differing ways', then similarly, there is always the possibility of performing the same routine in different ways. This recent literature on routines exemplifies what practice perspectives endorse: that 'stability and change are different outcomes of the same dynamic, rather than different dynamics' (Feldman & Orlikowski, 2011: 6). Change and stability are both effortful accomplishments of multiple actors engaged in a practice (Schatzki, 2012). It takes work to remain unchanged, as much as it takes work to change. Hence, rather than confronting the 'paradox of embedded agency' that has vexed institutional scholars for so long, practice scholars face what Cohen (2007: 781) calls the '(n) ever changing world paradox'.

Contemporary practice perspectives are, hence, in part a counterpoint to those early institutionalist positions that the social world is external to actors. They highlight human actors and agency to the extent that they perceive people's everyday actions as consequential in 'producing the structural contours of social life' (Feldman & Orlikowski, 2011: 2) and reassert the processes of mutual constitution in which structures are the result of human action, but at the same time enable and constrain said human action. Notably, thanks to the aforementioned interconnectedness of bundles of practice(s), change can originate in the inglorious level of praxis, but trigger ripples that reverberate throughout space, time and interrelated phenomena.

Divergent understandings of fields, agency, structure and change, as well as varying emphases on situatedness and embeddedness, should not deter dialogue between practice and institutional scholars, but rather highlight the potential for 'creative friction' and mutual learning at these touchpoints. Critical for such dialogue, however, is the recognition of common roots and shared interests as we outlined above. As both strands of literature focus on patterning and interdependence, on improvisation, change and emergence, and on the tension between agency and structure, we discuss recent development in institutional theory that have prompted their (re)-convergence. We point to the potential for equal sensitivity to both, what has previously been 'figure' or 'ground' in the respective literatures to develop an equally rich understanding of the everyday praxis of frontline practitioners, its institutional ramifications and their mutual constitution.

TOWARDS A PRACTICE-DRIVEN INSTITUTIONALISM

Given this temporary estrangement between practice and institutional theorists, what are the common interests and related concepts

that motivate scholars from both camps to reach out to the other? As outlined above, the evolution of institutional theory suggests several areas in which practice-driven scholarship could significantly contribute. These include a richer conceptualization of institutional logics and their enactment, dynamics of change and (institutional) work, and the management of institutional complexity which – so far – has been largely addressed at the level of the field or through organizational structures. We argue that a more stringent PDI holds great potential to add to these current debates. Specifically, it helps with the pervasive struggle to reconnect the 'macro-worlds' of institutions and the 'microworlds' of the individuals within them in a more ontologically consistent and theoretically accurate fashion (Kaghan & Lounsbury, 2011: 75; see also, Whittington, 2006). In doing so, PDI productively complements current strands exploring 'institutional work' (see Hempel, Lawrence, & Tracey, Chapter 21 this volume) and delving into the 'microfoundations' (see Powell & Rerup, Chapter 12 this volume) of institutional dynamics. It avoids the separation or juxtaposition of 'micro' and 'macro' and takes 'work' literally to explore the recursive influence through which institutional dynamics are constituted in the everyday work of practitioners on the ground – and vice versa. Below, we explore the key analytic nodes around which the two communities of institutional and practice scholars have come together so far and present some of the mutual learning they have developed from a joint conceptual toolkit.

Institutional Logics – and the 'Shared Understanding' Underpinning Practice

Institutional theory experienced a sea change when attention shifted from institutions to logics (Ocasio, Thornton, & Lounsbury, Chapter 19 this volume) and discovered a way to conceive of endogenous institutional change as motivated by 'contradictions' or 'ruptures' between institutional prescriptions (Seo & Creed, 2002: 233–234). Thereby, institutional scholars took a step back towards their intellectual roots: They began to more actively acknowledge the mutual constitution of structure and agency and to recognize societal orders as a potential source of agency and variation – rather than just stability.

Friedland and Alford's initial formulation defined institutional logics as '*symbolic* systems, ways of ordering reality, and thereby rendering experience of time and space meaningful' (1991: 243; emphasis added), or simply put, the 'rules of the game' of any given field (Ocasio et al., Chapter 19 this volume). The key question to address in order to demonstrate the power of logics, though, is the question of how these rules and principles materialize *in people's everyday praxis*. While Schatzki (2005: 482) concurs with institutionalists that 'symbolic elements [...] are vital to organizations', he adds that they only pervade organizational fields, industries, or societies, by virtue of being instantiated either in many practice bundles, or in particularly pervasive ones. It is this particular issue of instantiation that has brought some institutionalists to more actively consider practice-theoretical ideas (Lounsbury, 2007; Lounsbury & Boxenbaum, 2013; McPherson & Sauder, 2013; Smets, Jarzabkowski, Spee, & Burke, 2015b; Smets, Morris, & Greenwood, 2012; Zietsma & Lawrence, 2010). In this context, Thornton (2004: 69, emphasis added) explicitly defines logics as expressed in '*material practices*, assumptions, values, beliefs and rules' and, in her work with Ocasio, goes as far as specifying logics as 'socially constructed, *historical pattern of material practices*, assumptions, values, beliefs, and rules by which individuals produce and reproduce their material subsistence, organize time and space, and provide meaning to their social reality' (Thornton & Ocasio, 1999: 804, emphasis added). Logics are, hence, a natural conceptual segue

between institutional and practice theories. Even though Bourdieu's (1977) concept of fields already contained some early inklings of what institutionalists later conceptualized as logics, their current definitions most strongly resonate with the 'shared' or 'general' understandings studied by practice theorists (Schatzki, 2002, 2006). Both concepts inject bundles of otherwise trivial activities with order and meaning, turning them into a recognizable and legitimate practice. Barley and Tolbert (1997) – vocal advocates of a more structurationist approach to institutions and thereby forerunners of PDI – liken institutions and their logics to grammar. They suggest analogies of practices as sentences and words as activities. Notably, resonant with Schatzki's (2002) 'practical understanding', grammar can be played with in the circumstances of particular situations; for instance for artistic effect. Such improvisations and modifications are possible, but come at the expense of intelligibility in the case of grammar, and legitimacy in the case of institutions. Yet, as much as grammar, sentence and words are indistinguishable as 'levels' in Barley and Tolbert's (1997) linguistic image, logics, practices and activities do not make sense without the other, but mutually constitute each other. Hence, more actively attending to both the logics that provide meaning and the activities in which they are instantiated, produces the kind of 'flatter' ontology practice theorists advocate and institutional theory was originally steeped in.

Lounsbury and Crumley (2007) were among the first to explicitly reassert this link in their study of new practice creation in financial services. To make their point, they illustrate that pounding a nail is – in isolation – a trivial activity, but it assumes broader meaning in the practice of professional carpentry as underpinned by a logic of craft. Building on this idea, Smets and colleagues (2012) in their study of banking lawyers in a newly-merged global law firm exposed how the phoning, conversing, typing and negotiating lawyers engaged in only became meaningful in the context of legal practice, as governed by a distinct professional logic or 'shared understanding' of what it means to be a lawyer *in a particular jurisdiction*. In contrast and extension to aforementioned earlier, field-level treatments of institutional 'contradictions' (Greenwood & Suddaby, 2006; Seo & Creed, 2002), conflicts between those locally shared understandings only surfaced and played out in everyday *praxis* on cross-border deals. Similarly, Battilana and Dorado (2010) as well as Pache and Santos (2013a), albeit in a more colloquial use of 'practice', highlight how practices, in their case organizations, are the material enactments of institutional logics. However, as McPherson and Sauder (2013) or Venkataraman and colleagues (2016) show, these enactments may be politically embroiled in the sense that logics are 'used' strategically, and not necessarily enacted in some pure and disinterested form.

Therefore, both theory strands stand to benefit from this practice-driven approach to logics. On the one hand, practice, routine and strategy-as-practice scholars benefit from greater attention to broader cultural frameworks; that is, to institutional – rather than organizational – logics (Chia & Holt, 2009; Vaara & Whittington, 2012). In this sense, 'zooming out' to broader societal logics offers a useful corrective to balance the 'zooming in' that has commonly characterized contemporary applications of practice theory. The institutional component of PDI, hence, offers practice scholars richer insights into where local practices come from and are 'anchored' outside the organization, offering also deeper insights into supra-organizational sources of change. On the other hand, institutionalists can develop a more accurate and granular understanding of these logics that are instantiated in everyday praxis. Doing so would help address a pervasive issue in the current literature: the proliferation of logics. Attending to the various activities in which logics may be instantiated differently in different contexts respects logics as ideal-types

(Thornton et al., 2012), reduces the need to invent ever-new, context-specific 'logics', and lends greater conceptual coherence to the field. Tapping into societal-level logics as originally envisaged by Friedland and Alford (1991) and specifying in detail how they play out in everyday praxis across different empirical settings, strengthens the explanatory power of both logics and praxis, closes the gap between institutions and actions, and attends more closely to the structuration of social orders *in action*.

Institutional Change – Its Origins in Everyday Praxis

As alluded to above, the rise of the institutional logics perspective (Thornton et al., 2012) is closely intertwined with institutionalists' efforts to theorize endogenous change in stable institutionalized fields. Organizations caught in the 'interstitial spaces' (Furnari, 2014) between different fields and their respective logics experience the aforementioned 'contradictions' and become either aware of alternative institutional arrangements or sufficiently reflective to consider them. Yet, we know relatively little about how actors move from awareness to action. Existing studies predominantly use imagery of planned change in situations where actors encounter an alternative institutional arrangement and purposively pursue its adoption (Greenwood et al., 2011; Greenwood & Suddaby, 2006; Seo & Creed, 2002). Critics note, however, that this approach 'fails to consider the process through which new complexities are experienced and responses developed, rather than selected' (Smets & Jarzabkowski, 2013: 1283). This is especially true when novel complexities arise, expose inadequate institutional arrangements, but do not offer a suitable 'ready-to-wear' alternative.

Tapping into the practice-theoretical notions of 'becoming', emergence and continuous change (e.g., Schatzki, 2006; Tsoukas

& Chia, 2002), however, helps institutional scholars to address two conceptual blind spots implicit in this critique: First, it allows them to attend to 'the earliest moments of new practices emerging and gradually taking shape', which have typically been bracketed from conventional approaches to institutional change (Lounsbury & Crumley, 2007: 993; see also Furnari, 2014). Second, in so doing, institutionalists can develop a richer understanding of the improvisations and experimentations through which new solutions are discovered (Orlikowski, 1996) and the various types of agency through which they come to fruition (Emirbayer & Mische, 1998).

On both counts, practice-driven approaches to institutional change take seriously March's (1981: 564) call to resist the 'search for drama' regarding both the origin and unfolding of change. PDI locates the origin of institutional change in praxis. It is neither dramatic events such as social upheaval or technological disruption, nor 'heroic' entrepreneurship from which institutional change originates. Instead, it may be the mundane 'doing' of everyday work in which practitioners stumble upon – or construct – novel complexities and may develop the need as well as the destination for change (Bridwell-Mitchell, 2016; Lounsbury & Crumley, 2007; Reay, Golden-Biddle, & Germann, 2006; Voronov & Yorks, 2015). In this sense, the seeming mundanity of everyday work is by no means trivial. It is the source and site of 'situated improvising' as the earliest instance of change (Smets et al., 2012: 893; see also Dalpiaz, Rindova, & Ravasi, 2016). The seeds for macro-social change are always endogenous, emergent from and inherent to praxis, during which people 'invent, slip into, or learn new ways of interpreting and experiencing the world' (Orlikowski, 2002: 253). Accordingly, PDI celebrates the generative power of both ordinary practitioners and the work they perform.

Importantly, as an extension to existing theories of situated change and evolving routines, PDI specifically attends to institutional changes that originate in seemingly mundane praxis, but unfold effects beyond the organization in which they started. In short, they move 'from practice to field' (Reay et al., 2013; Smets et al., 2012). The way they escalate, though, is a counterpoint to earlier studies of theorization and macro-level change, insofar as the exigencies of praxis typically muffle the noise and conflict usually associated with the introduction of new practices (Lounsbury & Crumley, 2007; Zilber, 2002). In practice-driven accounts of change, theorization, thus, is more 'unobtrusive' (Smets et al., 2012: 895) or 'allusive' (Delmestri & Greenwood, 2016), because praxis itself – the joint performance of a new practice – implicitly coordinates diffusion. As organizations are conceptualized as interrelated and interdependent bundles of practices, altering one practice may have potentially significant direct and indirect consequences for other practices within the same social space (Emirbayer & Johnson, 2008; Gray, Purdy, & Ansari, 2015; Tsoukas & Chia, 2002). Improvisations that emerge in an uncoordinated fashion, yet with the intention of addressing the same issue, do not accumulate entirely 'accidentally' (Plowman et al., 2007), nor are they explicitly orchestrated by a planned strategy or institutional design. Instead, they are implicitly coordinated by communities of practice (Bridwell-Mitchell, 2016) or, as Dorado (2005: 396) puts it, the 'heedful interrelating of practitioners doing work'. Hence, taking seriously the generative power of praxis not only gives the institutionalist more nuanced insights into the origins, but also into the unfolding of institutional change.

Beyond explaining the diffusion of new practices to the field, however, PDI also offers helpful insights into the (re)-configuration of fields themselves. In this instance, it demonstrates the powerful apparatus practice theories provide to theorize larger social phenomena through smaller ones. Delmestri and Greenwood (2016: 4), for instance, explain the radical status re-categorization of the Italian liquor Grappa as a luxury good through its association with high-status micro-practices and argue that 'associating products with certain practices, actors can effect a change in the symbolic status order within the field'. In this sense, they liken Grappa to Champagne, whose status rests on its association 'with particular socio-cultural behaviors and practices, such as happiness, gaiety, and success […] visibly expressed and reinforced through widespread use at celebrations such as weddings, births, and awards'. Likewise, Faulconbridge and Muzio's (2016) work on Italian corporate law firms shows how their shared practice essentially formed a new, practice-based field with Milan at its centre and strong links into the corporate centres of other jurisdictions, rather than into other disciplines of law in Italy. A key question, as in Lounsbury and Crumley's (2007) comparable case in the US finance field, is when practices are deemed sufficiently different to constitute a new field, rather than a (gentle) variation on existing practice. As an extension of this work, casting a strategy-as-practice lens at field-configuring events such as conferences (Ansari, Wijen, & Gray, 2013; Schüssler, Rüling, & Wittneben, 2014) could direct attention away from the discourses and logics that dominate these events and to the role that their staging and performance have on the eventual outcome (Zilber, 2011).

Institutional Work – Its Intentionality and Multi-dimensional Agency

Calls for a broader and more nuanced perspective on agency have been particularly vocal in the 'institutional work' strand of the institutional literature (Hampel, Lawrence & Tracey, Chapter 21 this volume; see also: Lawrence et al., 2013; Lawrence, Suddaby, & Leca, 2009, 2011). In their original formulation, Lawrence and Suddaby (2006: 220) deeply grounded 'institutional work' in a practice-theoretical ontology, arguing that macro-level phenomena exist 'in the practices people engage in as part of those macro-phenomena,

rather than emerging from and existing independent of them'. Thereby, they have sought to redirect attention from institutions *per se* to the 'purposive action' by which they are accomplished (Lawrence & Suddaby, 2006: 217); in short, to redirect attention from structures and actors to practices and their role in creating, altering or maintaining institutions. The extent to which literature in the institutional work strand has leveraged the practice-theoretical toolkit, however, has remained partial.

On the one hand, this strand of literature produced an antidote to the simplified images of either relatively disembedded institutional entrepreneurship or of mindless institutional reproduction (Delbridge & Edwards, 2008; Smets & Jarzabkowski, 2013). Its concept of actorhood is undoubtedly closer to that of a practitioner, an individual as embodiment of practice who accomplishes work in relation with others (Whittington, 2006). As the 'the self (and intentionality) cannot be understood without reference to the particular "others" in which the acting individual is embedded' (Kaghan & Lounsbury, 2011: 75), such relational approaches add greater granularity to the positional dynamics of institutional work (Topal, 2015). Likewise, the practices driving institutional processes have become much clearer, thanks to studies of, for example, the 'boundary work' required in renegotiating forestry practices (Zietsma & Lawrence, 2010), the role of rules and rituals in maintaining institutions (Dacin, Munir, & Tracey, 2010), or the 'repair work' required after practice disruptions or legitimacy challenges (Lok & De Rond, 2013; Patriotta, Gond, & Schultz, 2011).

On the other hand, though, the sense in which this work has penetrated to the 'micro-level routines' (Lawrence & Suddaby, 2006: 247) of institutional agency, embraced attention to the everyday praxis of frontline practitioners and broadened our sense of agency is less clear. So far, it appears that the institutional work literature has primarily produced a more 'micro' perspective in the sense of

providing a more granular view on practice as the 'internal life of process' (Brown
& Duguid, 2000: 95), but not the mundane
praxis of practitioners. The practices under
investigation are typically performed by
organizations (e.g., Gawer & Phillips, 2013)
or field-level entities (e.g., Helfen & Sydow,
2013; Micelotta & Washington, 2013), not
individual practitioners. It is at this point that
institutional work and PDI diverge insofar as
the latter takes institutional *work* literally and
puts 'getting the job done', frontline practitioners accomplishing seemingly mundane
work – and its institutional ramifications –
front and centre of its theorizing.

Furthermore, but relatedly, the original
definition of institutional work as '*purposive* action [...] *aimed at* creating, maintaining and disrupting institutions' (Lawrence &
Suddaby, 2006: 215 emphasis added), has
retained strong overtones of planned change
and, hence, 'projective' agency (Emirbayer
& Mische, 1998). By focusing on field-level
purposive action, *institutional* work remains
detached from individuals' *practical* work.
Most people do not set out to affect the institutional arrangement that surround them, but
to cope with the practical exigencies of the
situation they find themselves in. This is by
no means to deny that such coping may have
institutional reverberations – this is exactly
the point of PDI – but these reverberations
are not a practitioner's primary interest and
focus of agency. As Bjerregaard and Jonasson
(2014: 1508) so poignantly put it, day-to-day
work is 'rather trivial, yet highly consequential'. The closer interplay and deeper engagement between institutional work and the
practice-theoretical legacy it claims (Kaghan
& Lounsbury, 2011), thus, opens up broader
avenues for building a broader understanding
of agency and intentionality.

In the recent past, Emirbayer and Mische's
(1998) differentiation of iterative, projective and practical-evaluative dimensions of
agency has informed the institutional conceptualization of agency. So far, however,
the literature has remained dominated by the
iterative and projective dimensions, which
respectively underpin institutional reproduction and entrepreneurship. This is perplexing
as, arguably, the practical-evaluative dimension that allows actors to exercise judgement
and 'get things done' in the here and now
should be particularly relevant, especially
in situations of institutional complexity (see
below). Yet, it has so far received relatively
little attention (for exceptions, see: Dalpiaz,
Rindova, & Ravasi, 2016; Smets et al.,
2012; Tsoukas & Cummings, 1997). A more
comprehensive adoption of Emirbayer and
Mische's (1998) framework and increased
attention to practical-evaluative agency not
only helps with the discovery of the earliest moments of change as discussed above.
It also reveals the dynamic interaction, and
changing order of dominance, between different dimensions of agency, as demonstrated
by Dalpiaz and colleagues (2016) in their longitudinal study of Alessi's multiple efforts to
combine logics of industrial and cultural production. They confirm how practitioners progress through a stage of practical-evaluative
experimentation from which they develop the
preferred solution which they subsequently
pursue with purpose (Smets & Jarzabkowski,
2013). Similarly, Raaijmakers and colleagues
(2014: 40) find that decision-makers faced
with a proposed new practice do not switch
directly from iterative to projective agency
but, instead, buy time 'to learn more about the
practice itself, about others' reactions to it,
and about potential ways to reduce complexity by adapting the practice to balance constituents' interests'. Such experimentation,
PDI highlights, is not driven by the future-
orientation of projective agency, but primarily by the need to resolve present issues in
the moment. It is driven by practice. This
is intuitive, insofar as 'most individuals are
not grand entrepreneurs, but practical people
doing practical work to get a job done' (Smets
& Jarzabkowski, 2013: 1304). The critical
role of practical-evaluative agency is likely to
be overlooked when institutional studies shy
away from studying everyday work. That is

why we advocate that PDI take 'work' more literally and apply an established practice-theoretical toolkit so as to enhance the nuance and granularity of our understanding of these micro-social institutional dynamics.

An important positive side effect of refining our understanding of agency is a corresponding closer look at intentionality. Notably, the practical-evaluative experimentations we discussed above remain focused on accomplishing work in the moment. They lack the intention of changing institutional arrangements and are, thus, not 'purposive' in the narrow sense of being '*aimed at* creating, maintaining, and disrupting institutions' (Lawrence and Suddaby, 2006: 217; emphasis added). Yet, while these actions are not intentional in this narrow sense, it seems wrong to deem them as unintentional, because they are firmly aimed at accomplishing practical work, a motivation for change more systematically acknowledged in the practice literature (Feldman, 2000; Kellogg, Orlikowski, & Yates, 2006; Orlikowski, 1996). Smets and Jarzabkowski (2013), therefore, suggest the need to transcend dichotomies of (un)-intentional institutional work by more clearly examining the object of that intentionality. Specifying that object is not only important for understanding the original motivation for initiating change, irrespective of its outcome, but also for understanding its unfolding, because the intention of accomplishing work coordinates dispersed change agents.

Institutional Complexity – Its Relationality, Constitution and Experience

Finally, studies of 'institutional complexity' (Besharov & Smith, 2014; Greenwood et al., 2011; Pache & Santos, 2010), focusing on the coexistence of incompatible prescriptions, their sources and consequences, provide a particularly fruitful interface for more deeply connecting research on institutions and practices. The encounter of 'incompatible prescriptions

from multiple institutional logics' (Greenwood et al., 2011: 317), the definitional characteristic of institutional complexity, naturally complicates the accomplishment of organizational tasks. Attention to *organizational* responses to institutional complexity has corrected for institutionalists' earlier fascination with field-level phenomena and brought into focus mechanisms and processes that unfold inside organizations. Especially those organizations that voluntarily embrace complexity to become 'hybrids' have recently attracted a lot of attention (for an overview, see: Battilana et al., this volume; Battilana & Lee, 2014). However, despite this increasing interest in intra-organizational phenomena, institutional theory has not traditionally developed a strong conceptual toolkit or vocabulary to attend to these.

A PDI, however, offers a powerful conceptual toolkit to understand those settings in which conflicting prescriptions collide in everyday operations, and institutional complexity must be managed continuously. Strategy-as-practice scholars in particular have built a powerful beachhead for these conversations through their studies of strategizing in pluralistic settings (e.g., Denis, Langley, & Rouleau, 2007; Jarzabkowski, Lê, & Van de Ven, 2013a). Especially, practice-based thought can enrich discussions of institutional complexity by drawing on their relational ontology[1] (Emirbayer, 1997; Hosking, 2011; Mutch, Delbridge, & Ventresca, 2006).

Drawing on Bourdieu's (1977) early relational approach to fields, this ontology provides a useful corrective to the binary approach to coexisting logics that largely dominates current discussions of institutional complexity. With a few exceptions (e.g., Fincham & Forbes, 2015; Goodrick & Reay, 2011; Greenwood, Magàn Diaz, Li, & Céspedes Lorente, 2010), institutional scholars have attended to pairs of two logics and predominantly portrayed them in a binary fashion. They are either compatible or contradictory. The relational ontology which practice theorists endorse more fundamentally acknowledges that – irrespective of their contradictions or complementarities – 'things seldom make sense when considered in isolation' and should be considered in dynamic interplay (Nicolini, 2011: 604). Thereby, PDI helps respond to calls for studies that 'delve deeper into the dynamic patterns of complexity' (Greenwood et al., 2011: 334). It provides the conceptual toolkit to study the active construction of 'others' (Emirbayer, 1997; Hosking, 2011; Mutch et al., 2006), and their construction as more or less compatible.

In this sense, as Smets, Jarzabkowski and colleagues (2013; 2015b) discovered in their work on lawyers and reinsurance underwriters respectively, institutional complexity or the paradoxes that result – when viewed from a practice perspective – are typically not encountered, but constructed. PDI hence corrects simplistic ideas that certain logics, or at least some of their elements (Pache & Santos, 2013b; Sauermann & Stephan, 2013) are *per se* compatible or conflicting. Instead, they are constructed as such through practitioners' skilful praxis. Accordingly, Jarzabkowski and Lê (forthcoming) foreground 'the role of micro-practices in shaping constructions of and responses to paradox', Mair and Hehenberger (2014) focus on practices of front-stage and back-stage convening, and Besharov (2014: 1486, emphasis added) emphasizes how relationalities between competing logics are formed when managers 'interpret *and enact* these values for frontline employees *through practices of developing integrative solutions, routinizing ideology, and removing ideology'*. That is why, more often than not, their relationality is also reported as far from stable. Several studies document how social enterprises seemingly successfully bridged conflicting logics of for-profit work and social impact, but later slipped back into a more conflictual rendering of both logics, leading to profound change or the organization's demise (Jay, 2013; Tracey, Phillips, & Jarvis, 2011). The relationality of coexisting logics, hence not only depends on what aspects of logics clash, but also on

how they are situationally brought together in practice.

Thus, attention to individual practitioners, the situatedness of their actions and the relationality of the logics they enact not only reveals new mechanisms of managing complexity, but also alerts us to potentially more instances of complexity than we have previously considered. As Smets and colleagues (2012: 892; emphasis in original) highlight, 'it is not the existence of institutional complexity per se that precipitates change, but the *novelty* of this complexity'. The permanent balancing of competing logics, and hence the absence of change, then, should be studied during times of *apparent stability* when complexities are no longer novel, but either settled in routines that allow individuals to continuously and dynamically balance competing demands (Smets et al., 2015b) or repaired instantly in response to practice breakdowns (Lok & De Rond, 2013).

We highlight 'apparent stability' above because, as Bjerregard and Jonasson (2014) expose, institutional complexity may well be *permanent, yet 'unstable'*. They argue that adopting a practice-theoretical ontology of organizational 'becoming' is particularly helpful in these situations as it provides a much-needed handle on 'the practice of managing institutional complexity in the course of everyday work' and a conceptual toolkit to note whether praxis, thanks to its institutional significance, 'is likely to result in higher or lower volatility within – on the surface – an otherwise seemingly stable institution' (Bjerregaard & Jonasson, 2014: 1508). In a similar vein, Heimer (1999) reports a compelling example of how individual practitioners may face unpredictable changes in the salience of the different institutional demands. She found that neonatal intensive care physicians need to balance the competing demands of medicine, family and the law every time they attend to a new-born in critical condition. The balance they strike, however, may be different every time, depending on the nature of the case at hand and the presence of those representing the different logics: parents, doctors and childcare workers. In these situations, structural, organization-level responses to institutional complexity necessarily fail, as they cement a relatively static balance between competing demands (e.g., Dunn & Jones, 2010; Pache & Santos, 2013b).

PDI can help address this issue through its sensitivity to people's 'practical understanding' (Schatzki, 2006: 1864); that is, their personal, tacit 'feel' for how to competently perform, even in a particular, complex situation in which different logics collide. Hence, while institutionalists have commonly emphasized the 'embeddedness' of individuals in 'logics', practice theorists offer a more balanced view in which a logic, or 'general understanding', is complemented by a 'practical understanding' that allows individuals to skilfully navigate situations in which different general understandings appear pertinent.

Such sensitivity to the practical origins of complexity – and its volatility – adds greater specificity to our understanding of how organizations which, by their very nature, face permanent institutional complexity, but also fluctuations in their specific demands can dynamically manage 'constellations' of two or more competing logics (e.g., Besharov & Smith, 2014; Fincham & Forbes, 2015; Goodrick & Reay, 2011). PDI is particularly suited for the study of such 'institutionalized complexity' (Smets et al., 2015b) because it is attuned to the accommodation of complexity in less notable, yet effortful, routines, rather than overtly strategic responses (Chia & Holt, 2009; Smets & Jarzabkowski, 2013). Paradoxically, though, as no 'drama' will alert scholars to these situations, spotting the instances in which competing logics are routinely balanced may be particularly difficult.

Institutional Agents – Practitioners as Carriers of Logics

By now, we know a lot about how organizations can structurally facilitate the accommodation of

institutional complexity (e.g., Battilana & Dorado, 2010; Pache & Santos, 2013b; Tracey et al., 2011). However, besides a few select studies we review below, we know very little about how the individuals inside those organizations employ those structures and continuously cope with the complexities they face. This is surprising insofar as there is active recognition that it is individual practitioners who 'represent' (Pache & Santos, 2010) logics inside organizations and more and more of them, from professionals, to physicians, to academics, regularly work across institutional boundaries (e.g., Faulconbridge & Muzio, 2016; Reay & Hinings, 2009; Sauermann & Stephan, 2013).

In this dialogue, practice theory offers the conceptual toolkit to take seriously the role of individuals as 'carriers of institutions' (Zilber, 2002: 234) and to discover how they experience institutional complexity as 'part of the ordinary, everyday nature of work, rather than exceptional phenomena' (Jarzabkowski, Matthiesen, & Van de Ven, 2009: 289; see also, Smets et al., 2015b). Just as institutional logics are enacted in practice, their incompatibilities are problematized in practitioners' everyday praxis. Therefore, practice theorists' sensitivity to how people 'go on' in the face of complexity and tension is particularly instructive here (Chia & Holt, 2009; Giddens, 1984). This emphasis on the work-level actions and interactions of individuals – and the understandings they reproduce and modify – suggests that a practice perspective is particularly suitable for connecting individual, organizational and institutional levels of analysis.

Primarily, practitioners are not individuals as such, but embodiments of practice, those doing the 'praxis'. Therefore, the focus has been on their collective efforts as part of a recognized practice, rather than the 'hypermuscular' activities, individual characteristics, skills and interests that have dominated work on institutional entrepreneurship (Lawrence et al., 2009: 1; see also Hardy & Maguire, Chapter 10 this volume).

The practice perspective, in other words, is not simply about observing people at work; it implies respecting each individual and what individuals do as socially constructed – and significant (Bertels & Lawrence, 2016; Bjerregaard & Nielsen, 2014; Smets et al., 2012). Taking this perspective takes the institutional context of agency seriously and addresses recent critiques that much analysis has lost sight of the institutional framing of individual action and behaviour (Delbridge & Edwards, 2008; Delmestri, 2006).

Building on Reay and colleagues' (2006: 979) early recognition of 'individuals at the front line' as potent institutional agents, more practice-driven institutionalists have since included them more actively as a new class of relevant actors. In their study of reinsurance underwriters in Lloyd's of London, for instance, Smets and colleagues (2015b) recently highlighted that ordinary people doing their everyday work may manage institutional complexity or, more generally, shape the social order they inhabit and it need not be '*leaders* who are able to understand ... requirements of constituencies of multiple logics' (Greenwood et al., 2011: 356, emphasis added), as is the dominant position in the institutional literature. Blomgren and Waks (2015), in their study of institutional complexity in healthcare, go as far as to suggest that the translational work of professionals at the intersection of competing logics produces 'hybrid professionals'. Importantly, they argue, this new identity springs from their daily practice and is, as such, institutionally embedded.

The profound insight here, though, is that – contrary to prevailing institutional thought – individuals, and not just organizations, can 'carry' multiple logics. While DiMaggio (1997) and Delmestri (2006) have highlighted that individuals may have this capacity, it is the attention to their praxis that reveals how they can do so. Zilber (2011), for instance, showed how participants at an industry conference used language and situational cues to switch between logics and promote different discourses. More recently, Smets and colleagues (2015b) develop a process model of three interrelated mechanisms, labelled 'segmenting', 'bridging' and 'demarcating', which allow individuals to balance conflicting logics in a state of dynamic tension in which they fruitfully feed off each other. Rather than the organization developing structures and practices to differentiate and integrate competing logics, individuals use their practical understanding to 'not only know *how* to enact multiple logics, but also *where* and *when*' (Smets et al., 2015b: 960; emphasis in original).

Finally, both institutional and practice scholars stand to gain from their joint engagement in the exploration of identities and emotions (see Glynn, Chapter 9 this volume; Lok, Creed, DeJordy, & Voronov, Chapter 22 this volume). While the latter have typically been bracketed from practice-theoretical explorations, except for their material instantiations in praxis, they have recently attracted some interest, for instance in the form of humour as mechanism for dealing with competing institutional demands (Jarzabkowski & Lê, forthcoming), but also in Voronov and colleagues' (2014, 2015, 2016) work on 'emotionalizing institutional theory' to breed greater sensitivity to how emotions influence the disruption or reproduction of institutions.

Further, emotions are clearly central to the study of emotional labour surrounding institutional compliance, change and their impact on practitioners' identification (Besharov, 2014), but also identity (e.g., Creed, DeJordy, & Lok, 2010; Grant, 2013; Lok, 2010; Vince & Broussine, 1996). Typically, though, while individual actors' skills and identities have been central to entrepreneurial arguments as proposed by Maguire and colleagues (2004) in their study of HIV advocacy, the institutional biographies that afford actors these identities have rarely been problematized. However, reminiscent of Bourdieu's (1977) football match example, how players got to where they are on the pitch matters, both for the moment and their future moves. Therefore, a richer interest in practitioners, neither as mere embodiments of practice, nor as disembedded individuals, but as skilled performers with institutional biographies and concomitant identities (Bertels & Lawrence, 2016) would also address recent critiques that practice scholars' focus on practice and not practitioners has inadvertently silenced individuals in practice-based studies (Reckwitz, 2002).

SOME NOTES OF CAUTION

For scholars turning towards PDI, there are many refreshing opportunities. Research is less about broad shifts in institutions, more about the creative effort involved in achieving such shifts. PDI research can be more vivid. However, we recognize that there are potential pitfalls in taking this turn, conceptual territories that we label 'danger-zones'. Such zones are not proscribed, simply flagged as requiring heightened care. The three concepts we highlight here as particularly tricky are 'micro', 'levels' and 'individuals'.

To start with 'micro', this is indeed an inspiring concept after the overly broad accounts of earlier institutional theory. As above, it has found powerful expression in contemporary appeals for research on the microfoundations of institutions (Powell & Rerup, Chapter 12 this volume). However, without care, two dangerous possibilities may emerge. First, a microfoundational approach can be easily confused with seeking to identify the fundamental component out of which all else may be built. In a relational view of the world, however, there is no foundational component: everything 'becomes' through the relations of multiple components (see Emirbayer's 1997: 286–287 discussion on 'relations' vs. 'elements'). In a relational ontology, such as the one PDI puts forward, the focus is on the relationships. Different patterns of relationships give emergence to different positions for the phenomenon under

investigation creating fluid configurations which constantly shift. Second, the micro interests of the typical microfoundational approaches can easily be confused with an all-absorbing fascination for the local, the particular and the detailed. This would be to reproduce the earlier strategy-as-practice error, sometimes called the burger-flipping problem of obsession with the trivialities of food mass-production. 'Micro' activity is of interest in a PDI only insofar as it reflects, reproduces and even changes larger practices. The micro activity of burger-flipping is important to the extent that it reveals something about the more extensive practices of, for example, McDonaldization (Ritzer, 1994). For PDI, 'micro' is never enough: it must always be connected to wider practices. The danger otherwise is of 'micro-isolationism' (Seidl & Whittington, 2014).

This takes us to the second tricky concept, 'levels'. 'Micro' is often differentiated from 'macro', the first operating on the ground, the second operating at some superior level. Activity is supposedly at one level; institutions at another. Proponents of flat ontologies scorn such talk of distinct levels (Latour, 2005): For them, all have equal status, differentiated primarily by the density of lateral connections. More moderately, Giddens (1984) does not deny the distinction between micro and macro levels, but warns us that it is potentially profoundly unhelpful. It can trap micro-sociology in the trivial and tempt macro-sociologists into top-down determinism. For Giddens (1984), the two levels do not exist apart as a dualism, but as essentially combined as a duality. The concept of levels may be provisionally useful as analytical construct, but ultimately they have no separate existence. Whether Latourian or Giddensian in orientation, either way it is clear that for PDI, the terminology of levels must be applied with caution.

The final potential pitfall is the concept of the actor as individual. Of course, an agency-sensitive PDI is bound to identify key actors. It may be natural to speak of individuals therefore. However, the danger with talk of individuals is slippage towards methodological individualism (Chia & MacKay, 2007) and the heroic imagery that plagued much of the institutional entrepreneurship literature. Here individuals are guided simply by their own private interests, personal histories or idiosyncratic cognitive biases; there is no role for shared practices. For Fligstein (2001), for instance, the solution when identifying the roles of key individuals is to insist on their 'social skills'. Yet in PDI, individual actors are essentially carriers and enactors of social practices. The individual actor is a social being, driven by practices. This embodiment of practices in individuals is captured in their conceptualization as practitioners.

LOOKING AHEAD: WHERE NEXT FOR PRACTICE-DRIVEN INSTITUTIONALISM

In this chapter so far we have laid out possible contours of a PDI and have erected signposts where a closer dialogue between the previously separate communities of institutional and practice scholars would be particularly fruitful. Beyond those already dominant themes we covered, however, there are some additional avenues for future research which we think deserve special mention on our agenda for approaching the future of PDI.

Looking at Institutions Comparatively

While comparative perspectives on organizational and national cultures abound in the management literature, we rarely attend to professional or institutional ones. If we take seriously that logics are enacted in praxis then we need to attend to how the putatively 'same' logics are enacted in different locales and contexts (e.g., Boxenbaum, 2006; Czarniawska & Joerges, 1996; Czarniawska

& Sevon, 2005; Wedlin & Sahlin, Chapter 4, this Volume). What 'family' means in different geographic regions and social strata varies widely, yet – so far – we pretend to be able to use the family logic (and all others) in a 'one size fits all' fashion. With such a bounded understanding in place, a logical next step to a richer comparative perspective would be to develop an understanding of what we call 'translation-as-practice'. Rather than take translation as a punctuated event, a specific point in time at which an institutional arrangement or practice is fitted into a new context, we should think of translation as an ongoing process that many boundary spanners have to perform as a matter of course in their everyday work.

Looking at the 'Stuff' of Institutions

As institutionalists grow more attuned to how logics are enacted and adapted in praxis, their logical next step should be to also attend to the 'stuff' involved in those activities (Jarzabkowski, Spee, & Smets, 2013c; Orlikowski & Scott, 2008). As Jarzabkowski and colleagues (2013b: 367) point out: The context of practice is 'not only institutional but also mundanely material'.

Practice theorists have long argued for the dissolution of analytical boundaries between the material and the social, or technologies and humans (Barley, 1986; Latour, 2005; Orlikowski & Barley, 2001). Such traditional divisions, as Orlikowski and Scott (2015) argue, excessively privilege the social and in doing so displace the vital contribution of materiality (see Jones, Meyer, Jancsary, & Höllerer, Chapter 23 this volume). Strategy-as-practice offers a promising conceptual toolkit for redressing this balance by drawing attention to the tools, methodologies and materials practitioners employ in their everyday actions and interactions (Lê & Spee, 2015; Orlikowski, 2010; Spee & Jarzabkowski, 2009, 2011).

One possibility in this direction may be found in the work of Levina and Arriaga (2014) whose work reveals the mechanisms linking the collective contributions of anonymous individuals, through – what they have termed – an 'online field', to the production of social status for individuals. Their work introduces the notion of online field and uniquely proposes an integrative analytical lens for studying social status production processes on and through online platforms.

Pushing this agenda further, we point to the exciting twist evident in Pickering's (1995) notion of the 'mangle of practice', whereby humans 'accommodate' by revising goals, changing their activities, adjusting the social or political context, whenever technology 'resists'. In a mode akin to 'tuning', Pickering (1995) argues, practices and technologies may configure, reconfigure and transform each other. Barrett and colleagues (2012), for example, yield novel insights into the understanding of robotics by replacing the traditional ontological primacy of human agency with a nuanced attention to 'tuning'. Another push to the frontier comes through the collaborative work of Orlikowski and Scott (2008; 2015; 2012). The authors not only explicitly assign agency to non-human actors, but also resist the distinction between human and non-human. Instead of seeking 'a-priori relationships among self-contained entities' (Scott & Orlikowski, 2014: 878), the authors put forward what they call 'entangled material discursive practices' as the centre of research priorities. This opens up possibilities for redrawing analytical boundaries, which institutional theorists might find especially useful for studying temporal, fluid and emergent phenomena. Anything less, we argue, would be adopting a disabling starting point for theorizing in a world where meaning and matter are increasingly entangled through social media, user-generated content, digital convergence, cloud computing, automated trading, mobile platforms and robotic assistance.

Looking at the 'Box'

Notably, and somewhat counterintuitively, *both* institutional *and* practice scholars appear to have lost sight of organizations for much of their recent empirical work. While institutionalists have for long black-boxed (intra)-organizational dynamics to focus on fields, strategy-as-practice scholars especially have done the opposite and opened that black box to look inside it. Surprisingly, despite the recent coming-together of these two perspectives, few scholars appear to be looking *at* the box; more precisely, at organizations and their specific properties. To be true to the core of a PDI, we need to understand the 'gear box', the mechanism by which the drive of everyday praxis hits the road of institutional context and resistance is signalled back to the engine. This gear box, we argue, represents organizational parameters such as size, identity, reputation, internationalization, organizational form or mode of governance that filter, mute, or amplify interactions between institutional demands and praxis (Battilana & Dorado, 2010; Kodeih & Greenwood, 2014; Pache & Santos, 2010, 2013b; Smets et al., 2015b; Smets et al., 2012). The ways in which they do so, however, are often relegated to boundary conditions of broader mechanisms. PDI should make every effort to move these closer to the centre of the stage. Doing so, would look beyond various organizational responses to isomorphic or complex demands (e.g., Oliver, 1991) and explain why particular organizations respond in particular ways, while others respond differently. It would also remind us – and helps us reassert – that at its core institutional theory is an *organizational theory*.

Looking towards Impact

Its original focus on lofty field-level dynamics has firmly positioned institutional theory among the sociological approaches to organizations – supposedly with limited managerial relevance. Recent trends that PDI seeks to continue and reinforce give greater presence to organizational dynamics and questions of practice – both in the conceptual and empirical sense. The CEO Report by Saïd Business School and Heidrick & Struggles found that of the 152 CEOs they interviewed around the world, the majority felt they were 'leading at the intersection' of competing demands and grappling with 'finding balance', both for themselves and their organizations. An entire section of this handbook is devoted to the consequences of institutions – whether they play out in organizations or broader society. The time seems ripe for an institutionalism that engages practice head-on – through its full conceptual apparatus and keen attention to the pressing questions practitioners pose. PDI, thus, has the potential to significantly narrow the theory–practice gap within management and organization studies and to provide 'a good theory', described by Latour (2005: 172) as one that does not 'designate what is being mapped, but how it is possible to map anything from such a territory'.

Note

1 We acknowledge that practice-informed scholars discuss relationality in many facets, such as the relationality and inseparability of the social and the material (Orlikowski & Scott, 2008), elements of a practice (Reckwitz, 2002), or the mutual orientation of interconnected actors to each other (Barnes, 2001; Nicolini, 2011). Here we confine ourselves to the dynamic positioning of coexisting logics relative to each other.

REFERENCES

Ansari, S., Wijen, F., & Gray, B. 2013. Constructing a climate change logic: An institutional perspective on the 'tragedy of the commons'. *Organization Science*, 24(4): 1014–1040.

Barley, S. R. 1986. Technology as an occasion for structuring: Evidence from observations of CT scanners and the social order of radiology departments. *Administrative Science Quarterly*, 31(1): 78–109.

Barley, S. R., & Kunda, G. 2001. Bringing work back in. *Organization Science*, 12(1): 76-96.

Barley, S. R., & Tolbert, P. S. 1997. Institutionalization and structuration: Studying the links between action and institution. *Organization Studies*, 18(1): 93–118.

Barnes, B. 2001. Practice as collective action. In T. R. Schatzki, K. Knorr-Cetina, & E. v. Savigny (Eds.), *The practice turn in contemporary theory*: 17–28. London: Routledge.

Barrett, M., Oborn, E., Orlikowski, W. J., & Yates, J. 2012. Reconfiguring boundary relations: Robotic innovations in pharmacy work. *Organization Science*, 23(5): 1448–1466.

Battilana, J. 2011. The enabling role of social position in diverging from the institutional status quo: Evidence from the UK national health service. *Organization Science*, 22(4): 817–834.

Battilana, J., & Dorado, S. 2010. Building sustainable hybrid organizations: The case of commercial microfinance organizations. *Academy of Management Journal*, 53(6): 1419–1440.

Battilana, J., Leca, B., & Boxenbaum, E. 2009. How actors change institutions: Towards a theory of institutional entrepreneurship. *The Academy of Management Annals*, 3(1): 65–107.

Battilana, J., & Lee, M. 2014. Advancing research on hybrid organizing – insights from the study of social enterprises. *Academy of Management Annals*, 8(1): 397–441.

Bertels, S., & Lawrence, T. B. 2016. Organizational responses to institutional complexity stemming from emerging logics: The role of individuals. *Strategic Organization*, 14(4): 336–372.

Besharov, M. 2014. The relational ecology of identification: How organizational identification emerges when individuals hold divergent values. *Academy of Management Journal*, 57(5): 1485–1512.

Besharov, M., & Smith, W. 2014. Multiple logics in organizations: Explaining their varied nature and implications. *Academy of Management Review*, 39(3): 364–381.

Bjerregaard, T., & Jonasson, C. 2014. Managing unstable institutional contradictions: The work of becoming. *Organization Studies*, 35(10): 1507–1536.

Bjerregaard, T., & Nielsen, B. 2014. Institutional maintenance in an international bureaucracy: Everyday practices of international elites inside UNESCO. *European Management Journal*, 32(6): 981–990.

Blomgren, M., & Waks, C. 2015. Coping with contradictions: Hybrid professionals managing institutional complexity. *Journal of Professions and Organization*, 2(1): 78–102.

Bourdieu, P. 1977. *Outline of a theory of practice*. Cambridge: Cambridge University Press.

Bourdieu, P. 1990. *The logic of practice*. Cambridge: Polity.

Bourdieu, P. 1993. *The field of cultural production*. Cambridge: Polity Press.

Bourdieu, P., & Wacquant, L. J. D. 1992. *An invitation to reflexive sociology*. Cambridge: Polity.

Boxenbaum, E. 2006. Lost in translation: The making of Danish diversity management. *American Behavioral Scientist*, 49(7): 939–948.

Bridwell-Mitchell, E. N. 2016. Collaborative institutional agency: How peer learning in communities of practice enables and inhibits micro-institutional change. *Organization Studies*, 37(2): 161–192.

Brown, J. S., & Duguid, P. 2000. *The social life of information*. Boston, MA: Harvard Business School Press.

Chia, R. C. H., & Holt, R. 2009. *Strategy without design: The silent efficacy of indirect action*. Cambridge: Cambridge University Press.

Chia, R. C. H., & MacKay, R. B. 2007. Post-processual challenges for the emerging strategy-as-practice perspective: Discovering strategy in the logic of practice. *Human Relations*, 60(1): 217–242.

Clemens, E. S., & Cook, J. M. 1999. Politics and institutionalism: Explaining durability and change. *Annual Review of Sociology*, 25(1): 441–466.

Cohen, M. 2007. Reading Dewey: Reflections on the study of routine. *Organization Studies*, 28(5): 773–786.

Creed, W. E. D., DeJordy, R., & Lok, J. 2010. Being the change: Resolving institutional contradiction through identity work. *Academy of Management Journal*, 53(6): 1336–1364.

Crossley, N. 2001. The phenomenological habitus and its construction. *Theory and Society*, 30(1): 81–120.

Czarniawska, B., & Joerges, B. 1996. Travels of ideas. In B. Czarniawska, & G. Sevon (Eds.), *Translating organizational change*: 13–48. Berlin: de Gruyter.

Czarniawska, B., & Sevon, G. 2005. *Global ideas: How ideas, objects and practices travel in a global economy*. Malmo: Liber & Copenhagen Business School Press.

Dacin, M. T., Munir, K., & Tracey, P. 2010. Formal dining at Cambridge colleges: Linking ritual performance and institutional maintenance. *Academy of Management Journal*, 53(6): 1393–1418.

Dalpiaz, E., Rindova, V., & Ravasi, D. 2016. Combining logics to transform organizational agency: Blending industry and art at alessi *Administrative Science Quarterly*, 61(3): 347–392.

de Certeau, M. 1984. *The practice of everyday life*. Berkeley, CA: University of California Press.

Delbridge, R., & Edwards, T. 2008. Challenging conventions: Roles and processes during nonisomorphic institutional change. *Human Relations*, 61(3): 299–325.

Delmestri, G. 2006. Streams of inconsistent institutional influences: Middle managers as carriers of multiple identities. *Human Relations*, 59(11): 1515–1541.

Delmestri, G., & Greenwood, R. 2016. How cinderella became a queen: Theorizing radical status change. *Administrative Science Quarterly*.

Denis, J.-L., Langley, A., & Rouleau, L. 2007. Strategizing in pluralistic contexts: Rethinking theoretical frames. *Human Relations*, 60(1): 179–215.

DiMaggio, P. 1991. Constructing an organizational field as a professional project: US art museums, 1920-1940. In W. W. Powell, & P. DiMaggio (Eds.), *The new institutionalism in organizational analysis*: 267–292. Chicago, IL: University of Chicago Press.

DiMaggio, P. 1997. Culture and cognition. *Annual Review of Sociology*, 23(1): 263–287.

DiMaggio, P., & Powell, W. W. 1983. The iron cage revisited: Institutional isomorphism and collective rationality in organizational fields. *American Sociological Review*, 48(2): 147–160.

DiMaggio, P., & Powell, W. W. 1991. Introduction. In W. W. Powell, & P. DiMaggio (Eds.), *The new institutionalism in organizational analysis*: 1–38. Chicago, IL: University of Chicago Press.

Dorado, S. 2005. Institutional entrepreneurship, partaking and convening. *Organization Studies*, 26(3): 385–414.

Dunn, M. B., & Jones, C. 2010. Institutional logics and institutional pluralism: The contestation of care and science logics in medical education, 1967–2005. *Administrative Science Quarterly*, 55(1): 114–149.

Emirbayer, M. 1997. Manifesto for a relational sociology. *The American Journal of Sociology*, 103(2): 281–317.

Emirbayer, M., & Johnson, V. 2008. Bourdieu and organizational analysis. *Theory and Society*, 37(1): 1–44.

Emirbayer, M., & Mische, A. 1998. What is agency? *The American Journal of Sociology*, 103(4): 962–1023.

Faulconbridge, J., & Muzio, D. 2016. Global professional service firms and the challenge of institutional complexity: 'Field relocation' as a response strategy. *Journal of Management Studies*, 53(1): 89–124.

Feldman, M. 2000. Organizational routines as a source of continuous change *Organization Science*, 11(1): 611–629.

Feldman, M. 2016. Routines as process: Past, present and future. In J. Howard-Grenville, C. Rerup, A. Langley, & H. Tsoukas (Eds.), *Organizational routines: How they are created, maintained and changed*: 23–47. Oxford: Oxford University Press.

Feldman, M. S., & Orlikowski, W. J. 2011. Theorizing practice and practicing theory. *Organization Science*, 22(5): 1240–1253.

Feldman, M. S., & Pentland, B. T. 2003. Reconceptualizing organizational routines as a source of flexibility and change. *Administrative Science Quarterly*, 39(1): 309–331.

Fincham, R., & Forbes, T. 2015. Three's a crowd: The role of inter-logic relationships in highly complex institutional fields. *British Journal of Management*, 26(4): 657–670.

Fligstein, N. 2001. Social skill and the theory of fields. *Sociological Theory*, 19(2): 105–125.

Foucault, M. 1980. *Power/knowledge: Selected interviews and other writings, 1972–1977*. NY: Pantheon Books.

Friedland, R., & Alford, R. R. 1991. Bringing society back in: Symbols, practices and institutional contradictions. In W. W. Powell, & P. DiMaggio (Eds.), *The new institutionalism in organizational analysis*: 232–263. Chicago, IL: University of Chicago Press.

Furnari, S. 2014. Interstitial spaces: Microinteraction settings and the genesis of new practices between institutional fields. *Academy of Management Review*, 39(4): 439–462.

Gawer, A., & Phillips, N. 2013. Institutional work as logics shift: The case of Intel's transformation to platform leader. *Organization Studies*, 34(8): 1035–1071.

Gehman, J., Treviño, L. K., & Garud, R. 2013. Values work: A process study of the emergence and performance of organizational values practices. *Academy of Management Journal*, 56(1): 84–112.

Geiger, D. 2009. Revisiting the concept of practice: Toward an argumentative concept of practicing. *Management Learning*, 40(2): 129–142.

Gherardi, S. 2000. Practice-based theorizing on learning and knowing in organizations. *Organization*, 7(2): 211–223.

Giddens, A. 1976. *New rules of sociological method: A positive critique of interpretative sociologies*. London: Hutchinson.

Giddens, A. 1979. *Central problems in social theory: Action, structure and contradiction in social analysis*. Basingstoke: Macmillan.

Giddens, A. 1984. *The constitution of society: Outline of the theory of structuration*. Cambridge: Polity.

Goodrick, E., & Reay, T. 2011. Constellations of institutional logics. *Work and Occupations*, 38(3): 372–416.

Grant, A. M. 2013. Rocking the boat but keeping it steady: The role of emotion regulation in employee voice. *Academy of Management Journal*, 56(6): 1703–1723.

Gray, B., Purdy, J. M., & Ansari, S. S. 2015. From interactions to institutions: Microprocesses of framing and mechanisms for the structuring of institutional fields. *Academy of Management Review*, 40(1): 115–143.

Greenwood, R., Magàn Diaz, A., Li, S., & Céspedes Lorente, J. 2010. The multiplicity of institutional logics and the heterogeneity of organizational responses. *Organization Science*, 21(2): 521–539.

Greenwood, R., Raynard, M., Kodeih, F., Micellota, E., & Lounsbury, M. 2011. Institutional complexity and organizational responses. *Academy of Management Annals*, 5(1): 1–55.

Greenwood, R., & Suddaby, R. 2006. Institutional entrepreneurship in mature fields: The big five accounting firms. *Academy of Management Journal*, 49(1): 27–48.

Heimer, C. A. 1999. Competing institutions: Law, medicine, and family in neonatal intensive care. *Law & Society Review*, 33(1): 17–66.

Helfen, M., & Sydow, J. 2013. Negotiating as institutional work: The case of labour standards and international framework agreements. *Organization Studies*, 34(8): 1073–1098.

Hirsch, P. M., & Lounsbury, M. 1997. Ending the family quarrel: Toward a reconciliation of 'old' and 'new' institutionalisms. *The American Behavioral Scientist*, 40(4): 406–418.

Hoffman, A. J. 1999. Institutional evolution and change: Environmentalism and the US chemical industry. *Academy of Management Journal*, 42(4): 351–371.

Hosking, D. M. 2011. Telling tales of relations: Appreciating relational constructionism. *Organization Studies*, 32(1): 47–65.

Howard-Grenville, J. A. 2005. The persistence of flexible organizational routines: The role of agency and organizational context. *Organization Science*, 16(6): 618–636.

Jarzabkowski, P., Balogun, J., & Seidl, D. 2007. Strategizing: The challenges of a practice perspective. *Human Relations*, 60(1): 5–27.

Jarzabkowski, P., Kaplan, S., Seidl, D., & Whittington, R. 2015. On the risk of studying practices in isolation: Linking what, who, and how in strategy research. *Strategic Organization*, doi:10.1177/1476127015604125.

Jarzabkowski, P., & Lê, J. forthcoming. We have to do this and that? You must be joking: Constructing and responding to paradox through humour. *Organization Studies*, DOI: 10.1177/0170840616640846.

Jarzabkowski, P., Lê, J. K., & Van de Ven, A. H. 2013a. Responding to competing strategic demands: How organizing, belonging, and performing paradoxes coevolve. *Strategic Organization*, 11(3): 245–280.

Jarzabkowski, P., Matthiesen, J., & Van de Ven, A. 2009. Doing which work? A practice approach to institutional pluralism. In T. B. Lawrence, R. Suddaby, & B. Leca (Eds.), *Institutional work: Actors and agency in institutional studies of organizations*: 284–316. Cambridge: Cambridge University Press.

Jarzabkowski, P., Smets, M., Bednarek, R., Burke, G., & Spee, A. P. 2013b. Institutional ambidexterity: Leveraging institutional complexity in practice. In M. Lounsbury, & E. Boxenbaum (Eds.), *Institutional logics in action*: 37–61. Bingley: Emerald.

Jarzabkowski, P., Spee, A. P., & Smets, M. 2013c. Material artifacts: Practices for doing strategy with 'stuff'. *European Management Journal*, 31(1): 41–54.

Jay, J. 2013. Navigating paradox as a mechanism of change and innovation in hybrid organizations. *Academy of Management Journal*, 56(1): 137–159.

Johnson, G., Langley, A., Melin, L., & Whittington, R. 2007. *Strategy as practice: Research directions and resources*. Cambridge: Cambridge University Press.

Kaghan, W., & Lounsbury, M. 2011. Institutions and work. *Journal of Management Inquiry*, 20(1): 73–81.

Kellogg, K. C., Orlikowski, W. J., & Yates, J. 2006. Life in the trading zone: Structuring coordination across boundaries in postbureaucratic organizations. *Organization Science*, 17(1): 22–44.

Kodeih, F., & Greenwood, R. 2014. Responding to institutional complexity: The role of identity. *Organization Studies*, 35(1): 7–39.

Kraatz, M. S., & Zajac, E. J. 1996. Exploring the limits of the new institutionalism: The causes and consequences of illegitimate organizational change. *American Sociological Review*, 61(5): 812–836.

Latour, B. 2005. *Reassembling the social*. Oxford: Oxford University Press.

Lawrence, T. B., Leca, B., & Zilber, T. B. 2013. Institutional work: Current research, new directions and overlooked issues. *Organization Studies*, 34(8): 1023–1033.

Lawrence, T. B., & Suddaby, R. 2006. Institutions and institutional work. In S. Clegg, C. Hardy, T. Lawrence, & W. Nord (Eds.), *The Sage handbook of organization studies*: 215–253. London: Sage.

Lawrence, T. B., Suddaby, R., & Leca, B. 2009. Introduction: Theorizing and studying institutional work. In T. Lawrence, R. Suddaby, & B. Leca (Eds.), *Institutional work: Actors and agency in institutional studies of organizations*: 1–28. Cambridge: Cambridge University Press.

Lawrence, T. B., Suddaby, R., & Leca, B. 2011. Institutional work: Refocusing institutional studies of organization. *Journal of Management Inquiry*, 20(1): 52–58.

Lê, J. K., & Spee, P. 2015. The role of materiality in the practice of strategy. In D. Golsorkhi, L. Rouleau, D. Seidl, & E. Vaara (Eds.), *The Cambridge handbook of strategy as practice*: 582–597. Cambridge: Cambridge University Press.

Leblebici, H., Salancik, G. R., Copay, A., & King, T. 1991. Institutional change and the transformation of interorganizational fields: An organizational history of the US radio broadcasting industry. *Administrative Science Quarterly*, 36(3): 333–363.

Levina, N., & Arriaga, M. 2014. Distinction and status production on user-generated content platforms: Using Bourdieu's theory of cultural production to understand social dynamics in online fields. *Information Systems Research*, 25(3): 468–488.

Lok, J. 2010. Institutional logics as identity projects. *Academy of Management Journal*, 53(6): 1305–1335.

Lok, J., & De Rond, M. 2013. On the plasticity of institutions: Containing and restoring practice breakdowns at the Cambridge university boat club. *Academy of Management Journal*, 56(1): 185–207.

Lounsbury, M. 2002. Institutional transformation and status mobility: The professionalization of the field of finance. *Academy of Management Journal*, 45(1): 255–266.

Lounsbury, M. 2007. A tale of two cities: Competing logics and practice variation in the professionalizing of mutual funds. *Academy of Management Journal*, 50(2): 289–307.

Lounsbury, M., & Boxenbaum, E. (Eds.). 2013. *Institutional logics in action*. (Vol. 39A/B). Bingley: Emerald.

Lounsbury, M., & Crumley, E. T. 2007. New practice creation: An institutional perspective on innovation. *Organization Studies*, 28(7): 993–1012.

Maguire, S., Hardy, C., & Lawrence, T. 2004. Institutional entrepreneurship in emerging fields: HIV/AIDS treatment advocacy in Canada. *Academy of Management Journal*, 47(5): 657–679.

Mair, J., & Hehenberger, L. 2014. Front-stage and backstage convening: The transition from opposition to mutualistic coexistence in organizational philanthropy. *Academy of Management Journal*, 57(4): 1174–1200.

March, J. G. 1981. Footnotes to organizational change. *Administrative Science Quarterly*, 26(4): 563–577.

McPherson, C. M., & Sauder, M. 2013. Logics in action: Managing institutional complexity in a drug court. *Administrative Science Quarterly*, 58(2): 165–196.

Meyer, J. W., & Rowan, B. 1977. Institutionalized organizations: Formal structure as myth and ceremony. *American Journal of Sociology*, 83(2): 340–363.

Micelotta, E. R., & Washington, M. 2013. Institutions and maintenance: The repair work of Italian professions. *Organization Studies*, 34(8): 1137–1170.

Mutch, A., Delbridge, R., & Ventresca, M. 2006. Situating organizational action: The relational sociology of organizations. *Organization*, 13(5): 607–625.

Nicolini, D. 2011. Practice as the site of knowing: Insights from the field of telemedicine. *Organization Science*, 22(3): 602–620.

Nicolini, D. 2012. *Practice theory, work and organization. An introduction*. Oxford: Oxford University Press.

Oliver, C. 1991. Strategic responses to institutional processes. *Academy of Management Review*, 16(1): 145–179.

Oliver, C. 1992. The antecedents of deinstitutionalization. *Organization Studies*, 13(4): 563–588.

Orlikowski, W., & Scott, S. 2008. Sociomateriality: Challenging the separation of technology, work and organization. *The Academy of Management Annals*, 2(1): 433–474.

Orlikowski, W., & Scott, S. V. 2015. The algorithm and the crowd: Considering the materiality of service innovation. *MIS Quarterly*, 39(1): 201–216.

Orlikowski, W. J. 1996. Improvising organizational transformation over time: A situated change perspective. *Information Systems Research*, 7(1): 63–92.

Orlikowski, W. J. 2000. Using technology and constituting structures: A practice lens for studying technology in organizations. *Organization Science*, 11(4): 404–428.

Orlikowski, W. J. 2002. Knowing in practice: Enacting a collective capability in distributed organizing. *Organization Science*, 13(3): 249–273.

Orlikowski, W. J. 2010. The sociomateriality of organisational life: Considering technology in management research. *Cambridge Journal of Economics*, 34: 125–141.

Orlikowski, W. J., & Barley, S. R. 2001. Technology and institutions: What can research on information technology and research on organizations learn from each other? *MIS Quarterly*, 25(2): 145–165.

Osterlund, C., & Carlile, P. R. 2003. How practice matters: A relational view of knowledge sharing. In M. Huysman, E. Wenger, & V. Wulf (Eds.), *Communities and technologies*: 1–22. Amsterdam: Kluwer Academic Publishers.

Pache, A.-C., & Santos, F. 2010. When worlds collide: The internal dynamics of organizational responses to conflicting institutional demands. *Academy of Management Review*, 35(3): 455–476.

Pache, A.-C., & Santos, F. 2013a. Embedded in hybrid contexts: How individuals in organizations respond to competing institutional logics. In M. Lounsbury, & E. Boxenbaum (Eds.), *Institutional logics in action, Part b*, Vol. 39b: 3–35. Bingley: Emerald.

Pache, A.-C., & Santos, F. 2013b. Inside the hybrid organization: Selective coupling as a response to competing institutional logics. *Academy of Management Journal*, 56(4): 972–1001.

Parmigiani, A., & Howard-Grenville, J. 2011. Routines revisited: Exploring the capabilities and practice perspectives. *Academy of Management Annals*, 5(1): 413–453.

Patriotta, G., Gond, J.-P., & Schultz, F. 2011. Maintaining legitimacy: Controversies, orders of worth, and public justifications. *Journal of Management Studies*, 48(8): 1804–1836.

Pickering, A. 1995. *The mangle of practice: Time, agency and science*. Chicago, Ill.: University of Chicago Press.

Plowman, D. A., Baker, L. T., Beck, T. E., Kulkarni, M., Solansky, S. T., & Travis, D. V. 2007. Radical change accidentally: The emergence and amplification of small change. *Academy of Management Journal*, 50(3): 515–543.

Raaijmakers, A., Vermeulen, P., Meeus, M., & Zietsma, C. 2014. I need time! Exploring pathways to compliance under institutional complexity. *Academy of Management Journal*, doi:10.5465/amj.2011.0276

Reay, T., Chreim, S., Golden-Biddle, K., Goodrick, E., Williams, B. E., Casebeer, A., Pablo, A., & Hinings,

C. R. 2013. Transforming new ideas into practice: An activity based perspective on the institutionalization of practices. *Journal of Management Studies*, 50(6): 963–990.

Reay, T., Golden-Biddle, K., & Germann, K. 2006. Legitimizing a new role: Small wins and microprocesses of change. *Academy of Management Journal*, 49(5): 977–998.

Reay, T., & Hinings, C. R. 2009. Managing the rivalry of competing institutional logics. *Organization Studies*, 30(6): 629–652.

Reckwitz, A. 2002. Toward a theory of social practices: A development in cultural theorizing. *European Journal of Social Theory*, 5(2): 234–263.

Ritzer, G. 1994. *The McDonaldization of society*. Thousand Oaks, CA: Pine Forge Press.

Sandberg, J., & Dall'Alba, G. 2009. Returning to practice anew: A life-world perspective. *Organization Studies*, 30(12): 1349–1368.

Sandberg, J., & Pinnington, A. 2009. Professional competence as ways of being: An existential ontological perspective. *Journal of Management Studies*, 46(7): 1138–1170.

Sandberg, J., & Tsoukas, H. 2011. Grasping the logic of practice: Theorizing through practical rationality. *Academy of Management Review*, 36(2): 339–360.

Sauermann, H., & Stephan, P. 2013. Conflicting logics? A multidimensional view of industrial and academic science. *Organization Science*, 24(3): 889–909.

Schatzki, T. R. 2001. Introduction: Practice theory. In T. R. Schatzki, K. Knorr-Cetina, & E. v. Savigny (Eds.), *The practice turn in contemporary theory*: 1–14. London: Routledge.

Schatzki, T. R. 2002. *The site of the social: A philosophical account of the constitution of social life and change*. University Park, PA: Penn State University Press.

Schatzki, T. R. 2005. The sites of organizations. *Organization Studies*, 26(3): 465–484.

Schatzki, T. R. 2006. On organizations as they happen. *Organization Studies*, 27(12): 1863–1873.

Schatzki, T. R. 2012. A primer on practices: Theory and research. In J. Higgs, R. Barnett, S. Billett, M. Hiutchings, & F. Trede (Eds.), *Practice-based education: Perspectives and strategies*: 13–26. Rotterdam: Sense Publishers.

Schatzki, T. R., Knorr-Cetina, K., & Savigny, E. v. (Eds.). 2001. *The practice turn in contemporary theory*. London: Routledge.

Schüssler, E., Rüling, C.-C., & Wittneben, B. B. F. 2014. On melting summits: The limitations of field-configuring events as catalysts of change in transnational climate policy. *Academy of Management Journal*, 57(1): 140–171.

Scott, S. V., & Orlikowski, W. J. 2012. Reconfiguring relations of accountability: Materialization of social media in the travel sector. *Accounting, Organizations & Society*, 37(1): 26–40.

Scott, S. V., & Orlikowski, W. J. 2014. Entanglements in practice: Performing anonymity through social media. *MIS Quarterly*, 38(3): 873–893.

Scott, W. R. 1987. The adolescence of institutional theory. *Administrative Science Quarterly*, 32(4): 493–512.

Scott, W. R. 1995. *Institutions and organizations*. Thousand Oaks, CA: Sage.

Seidl, D., & Whittington, R. 2014. Enlarging the strategy-as-practice research agenda: Towards taller and flatter ontologies. *Organization Studies*, 35(10): 1407–1421.

Selznick, P. 1996. Institutionalism 'old' and 'new'. *Administrative Science Quarterly*, 41(2): 270–277.

Seo, M. G., & Creed, W. E. D. 2002. Institutional contradictions, praxis, and institutional change: A dialectical perspective. *Academy of Management Review*, 27(2): 222–247.

Sewell, W. H. 1992. A theory of structure: Duality, agency, and transformation. *American Journal of Sociology*, 98(1): 1–29.

Smets, M., Greenwood, R., & Lounsbury, M. 2015a. An institutional perspective on strategy as practice. In D. Golsorkhi, L. Rouleau, D. Seidl, & E. Vaara (Eds.), *The Cambridge handbook of strategy as practice*, 2 ed.: 283–300. Cambridge: Cambridge University Press.

Smets, M., & Jarzabkowski, P. 2013. Reconstructing institutional complexity in practice: A relational model of institutional work and complexity. *Human Relations*, 66(10): 1279–1309.

Smets, M., Jarzabkowski, P., Spee, A. P., & Burke, G. 2015b. Reinsurance trading in Lloyd's of London: Balancing conflicting-yet-complementary logics in practice. *Academy of Management Journal*, 58(3): 932–970.

Smets, M., Morris, T., & Greenwood, R. 2012. From practice to field: A multilevel model of practice-driven institutional change. *Academy of Management Journal*, 55(4): 877–904.

Spee, A. P., & Jarzabkowski, P. 2009. Strategy tools as boundary objects. *Strategic Organization*, 7(2): 223–232.

Spee, A. P., & Jarzabkowski, P. 2011. Strategic planning as communicative process. *Organization Studies*, 32(9): 1217–1245.

Spee, A. P., Jarzabkowski, P., & Smets, M. 2016. The influence of routine interdependence and skillful accomplishment on the coordination of standardizing and customizing. *Organisation Science*, 27(3): 759–781.

Suddaby, R., Seidl, D., & Lê, J. K. 2013. Strategy-as-practice meets neoinstitutional theory. *Strategic Organization*, 11(3): 329–344.

Thornton, P. H. 2002. The rise of the corporation in a craft industry: Conflict and conformity in institutional logics. *Academy of Management Journal*, 45(1): 81–101.

Thornton, P. H. 2004. *Markets from culture: Institutional logics and organizational decisions in higher educational publishing*. Stanford, CA: Stanford University Press.

Thornton, P. H., & Ocasio, W. 1999. Institutional logics and the historical contingency of power in organizations: Executive succession in the higher education publishing industry, 1958–1990. *American Journal of Sociology*, 105(3): 801–844.

Thornton, P. H., Ocasio, W., & Lounsbury, M. 2012. *The institutional logics perspective: A new approach to culture, structure and process*. Oxford: Oxford University Press.

Tolbert, P. S., & Zucker, L. G. 1983. Institutional sources of change in the formal structure of organizations: The diffusion of civil service reform, 1880–1935. *Administrative Science Quarterly*, 28(1): 22–39.

Topal, C. 2015. A relational perspective of institutional work. *Journal of Management & Organization*, 21(4): 495–514.

Tracey, P., Phillips, N., & Jarvis, O. 2011. Bridging institutional entrepreneurship and the creation of new organizational forms: A multilevel model. *Organization Science*, 22(1): 60–80.

Tsoukas, H., & Chia, R. 2002. On organizational becoming: Rethinking organizational change. *Organization Science*, 13(5): 567–582.

Tsoukas, H., & Cummings, S. 1997. Marginalization and recovery: The emergence of Aristotelian themes in organization studies. *Organization Studies*, 18(4): 655–683.

Vaara, E., & Whittington, R. 2012. Strategy-as-practice: Taking social practices seriously. *The Academy of Management Annals*, 6(1): 1–52.

Venkataraman, H., Vermeulen, P., Raaijmakers, A., & Mair, J. 2016. Market meets community: Institutional logics as strategic resources for development work. *Organization Studies*, 37(5): 709–733.

Vince, R., & Broussine, M. 1996. Paradox, defense and attachment: Accessing and working with emotions and relations underlying organizational change. *Organization Studies*, 17(1): 1–21.

Voronov, M. 2014. Toward a toolkit for emotionalizing institutional theory. In N. M. Ashkanasy, W. J. Zerbe, & C. E. J. Härtel (Eds.), *Emotions and the organizational fabric*: 167–196. Bingham: Emerald.

Voronov, M., & Weber, K. 2016. The heart of institutions: Emotional competence and institutional actorhood. *Academy of Management Review*, 41(3): 456–478.

Voronov, M., & Yorks, L. 2015. 'Did you notice that?' Theorizing differences in the capacity to apprehend institutional contradictions. *Academy of Management Review*, 40(4): 563–586.

Whittington, R. 1992. Putting Giddens into action. *Journal of Management Studies*, 29(6): 693–713.

Whittington, R. 2006. Completing the practice turn in strategy research. *Organization Studies*, 27(5): 613–634.

Whittington, R. 2011. The practice turn in organization research: Towards a disciplined transdisciplinarity. *Accounting, Organizations & Society*, 36(1): 183–186.

Wittgenstein, L. 1953. *Philosophical investigations*. Oxford: Blackwell Publishing.

Zietsma, C., & Lawrence, T. B. 2010. Institutional work in the transformation of an organizational field: The interplay of boundary work and practice work. *Administrative Science Quarterly*, 55(2): 189–221.

Zilber, T. B. 2002. Institutionalization as an interplay between actions, meanings, and actors: The case of a rape crisis center in Israel. *Academy of Management Journal*, 45(1): 234–254.

Zilber, T. B. 2011. Institutional multiplicity in practice: A tale of two high-tech conferences in Israel. *Organization Science*, 22(6): 1539–1559.

Zucker, L. G. 1983. Organizations as institutions. In S. B. Bacharach (Ed.), *Research in the sociology of organizations*: 1–47. Greenwich, CN.: JAI Press.

15

Language, Cognition and Institutions: Studying Institutionalization Using Linguistic Methods

Nelson Phillips and Namrata Malhotra

Institutionalization occurs whenever there is a reciprocal typification of habitualized actions by types of actors. Put differently, any such typification is an institution. (Berger & Luckmann, 1967)

Early work in institutional theory[1] focused explicitly on the socially constructed nature of institutions, arguing that they arise out of the meaningful interactions of actors and shape behavior by conditioning cognition. Meyer and Rowan (1977: 341), for example, argued that '[i]nstitutionalization involves the processes by which social processes, obligations, or actualities, come to take on a rulelike status in social thought and action'. According to this definition, institutions are cognitive structures and institutionalization is the process whereby institutions are constructed in social interaction through the production of what Berger and Luckmann (1967: 54) call 'shared typifications'. This view of institutions drove much of the early work in new institutional theory (e.g., Tolbert & Zucker, 1983), as researchers worked to understand the effects of cognitive institutions on individuals and organizations.

In many ways, it is this cognitive focus that provides the distinctiveness of institutional theory. According to DiMaggio and Powell (1991), institutional theory is characterized by 'a scepticism toward rational-actor models of organization' (1991: 12) which are replaced by 'an alternative theory of individual action, which stresses the unreflective, routine, taken-for-granted nature of most human behavior and views interests and actors as themselves constituted by institutions' (1991: 14). By moving beyond arguments regarding rational action in contexts characterized by various forms of resource dependency, institutional theory provides explanations of patterns of behavior that make little sense from other perspectives. Perhaps more importantly, these explanations go well beyond the remit of these theories in examining the sources of interests and identities that determine the preferences that frame rational action in the first place.

Despite the retention of a general interest in what Douglas (1986: 11) calls the 'social basis of cognition', the emphasis of this early work, and the source of much of the distinctiveness of institutional theory, has become diluted. Rather than clearly focusing on cognitive institutions and continuing to develop this unique contribution, the conceptualization of an institution has blurred and, as a result, significant analytical power has been lost. In fact, the perspective that has dominated much of new institutionalism is that institutions are seemingly most recognizable by their effects and a number of mechanisms that produce isomorphism have been lumped together to form the focus of institutional analysis.

However, such an all-encompassing approach neglects critical theoretical and philosophical distinctions among the different mechanisms that lead to isomorphism. For example, an organizational form that is widely adopted in order to gain access to a government grant is seen as equally the result of institutional processes as an organizational form that is adopted due to its taken-for-grantedness in a field. Yet, the first case is simply a rational and conscious decision by managers to allow their organizations access to resources that they value. This is clearly not the sort of taken-for-grantedness originally associated with institutions.

From our perspective, defining an institution based on its effects is problematic for at least two reasons. First, in failing to clearly focus on cognitive institutions, institutional theory has conflated institutional processes with resource dependency and the coercive application of power. The fact that isomorphism occurs in an organizational field does not necessarily mean that taken-for-granted cognitive structures are the cause and it is only by examining the actual micro-processes through which organizations become more alike that we can differentiate between truly institutional forms of isomorphism and the multitude of other pressures that can lead to increasing similarities but which do so in fundamentally different ways. Put another way, it is only by being very clear about the nature of institutions, and by ensuring that what we study fits that definition, that we can hope to

develop deeper understandings of what are legitimately institutional processes.

Second, this lack of clarity about the nature of institutions is related to a lack of attention to explaining the process of institutional production. As Zucker (1991: 105–106) observed:

> Without a solid cognitive, micro-level foundation we risk treating institutionalization as a black box at the organizational level, focusing on content at the exclusion of developing a systematic explanatory theory of process, conflating institutionalization with resource dependency, and neglecting institutional variation and persistence. Although important insights can be gained by examining the content of institutions, there is an ever-present danger of making the neo-institutionalist enterprise a taxonomic rather than explanatory theory-building science. Institution theory is always in danger of forgetting that labeling a process or structure does not explain it.

By adopting a view of institutions that looks all too much like the taxonomic exercise that Zucker feared, we have left ourselves with no way to explain how they come to be. The fact that very different kinds of things are treated as different forms or elements of institutions leaves us without any common understanding of the process of institutional production and consequently, the nature of institutions. In other words, a 'taxonomic' approach has come to dominate institutional theory while there has been little attention paid to developing an explanation for the process of production of institutions in the first place.

In this chapter, we argue that there is a significant opportunity for institutional theorists to clarify the nature of institutions and to develop the sort of 'solid cognitive, micro-level foundation' for institutional theory that Zucker envisaged. More specifically, we explore the potential of linguistic methods[2] in the study of the processes of social construction through which institutions are constituted. As Phillips, Lawrence and Hardy (2004: 648) argue, '[u]nderstanding institutional phenomena requires a broader, more comprehensive theory that encompasses stability *and* change in institutions, institutional fields, and institutional effects'. Including a much more developed linguistic conceptualization of social construction is one important step toward understanding and exploring these issues.

We contribute to discussions of institutional theory in three ways. First, we make a plea for a return to a strong form of social construction in institutional theory. If we accept Meyer and Rowan's (1977) argument that institutions take on a rule-like status in thought, then no matter what the mechanism of their genesis, they are social facts and are fundamentally cognitive. Institutional theory therefore must focus on developing a deep understanding of the genesis, maintenance, change and effects of cognitive institutions.

Second, building on the previous point, we argue that we need to de-institutionalize the tripartite understanding of institutions as regulative, normative and cultural-cognitive. We stress the need to differentiate between simple isomorphism which can be caused by a variety of mechanisms and the institutional processes that drive isomorphism by structuring cognition. At the moment we lack that clarity, and call for more rigor in distinguishing between mechanisms or pressures for institutionalization and the actual process of institutionalization itself.

Finally, if institutional theory is going to take social construction seriously, we need a much more developed understanding of how the process of social construction occurs. We therefore highlight the potential of linguistic methods to provide both a theoretical and a methodological framework for explaining and investigating processes of social construction. Constructing institutionalized meanings is not a straight-forward journey, but rather meaning is continuously shaped and reshaped by the interaction among different actors. Fundamentally, linguistic methods such as discourse analysis, rhetorical analysis, narrative analysis and semiotics share a common purpose in that they allow researchers to explore how meaning is constituted in social interaction.

We present our arguments in three steps. We begin by discussing the social constructivist roots of new institutional theory and further explain why we believe the tripartite view of institutions that has developed in institutional theory is problematic. We then discuss how linguistic methods provide a theoretical and methodological frame for understanding the processes of social construction that underpin institutionalization. We draw on linguistic methods to provide an alternative perspective on the nature of institutions and the micro-institutional processes upon which they depend. Finally, we conclude with implications of this view of institutions for empirical research in institutional theory. We outline how a linguistic perspective can expand our understanding in current areas as well as be extended to emerging themes in institutional research.

INSTITUTIONS AND THE SOCIAL NATURE OF COGNITION

In the first part of this section, we revisit the roots of institutional theory and follow the development of the cognitive view of institutions in institutional analysis. Our purpose here is to show that various kinds of social constructionism have played a central role in institutional theory from its earliest development and that this constructionism points directly to the cognitive nature of institutions. We then discuss the development of the tripartite conception of institutions as regulative, normative and cultural-cognitive that has come to dominate institutional analysis and argue that this framework has distracted us from the processes of social construction that underpin cognitive institutions.

Early Notions of Institutions in Economics

As far back as the late nineteenth century, institutional economists began challenging economic assumptions about rational individual behavior. Veblen (1909: 245), for example, argued that behavior is governed by habit and convention and that an individual's conduct is directed by his or her habitual relations to other members of his or her group. He defined institutions as 'settled habits of thought common to the generality of man' (1909: 239). In doing so he foreshadowed the development of the cognitive view of institutions that came to characterize new institutionalism many years later. This definition is particularly striking as we can already see a strong cognitive understanding of institutions at such an early stage of development of institutional thought.

Even Menger (1981 [1871]), who stoutly defended the utility of overarching simplifying assumptions in economics, acknowledged the importance of broader institutional forces and, in fact, argued that institutions themselves were social phenomena in need of theoretical explanation (Scott, 2001: 2). Similarly, Commons (1924) in emphasizing that a transaction was the appropriate unit of analysis alluded to the rules of conduct governing a transaction. By rules of conduct he meant something very much like a social institution characterized by a degree of adherence to collective norms of reasonable behavior (Van de Ven, 1993).

Early Sociological Conceptions of Institutions

While modern institutional theorists may find significant aspects of this work quite sympathetic to their views, organizational institutionalism was predominantly built on more sociological foundations. The earliest forms of institutionalism in sociology started with a more functionalist flavor than characterizes institutional theory today, but with a clear cognitive orientation. Sumner (1906), for example, defined an institution simply as a concept or idea. Scott (2001) summarizes Sumner's conceptualization of institutions as

evolving from individual activities to folkways, to mores and to full-fledged institutions, although he also recognized that institutions can also be enacted as products of rational invention and intention. Similarly, Davis (1949) defined an institution as a set of interwoven folkways, mores and laws built around one or more functions. In both cases, the cognitive nature of institutions is clear although underpinned by a functionalist understanding of social processes.

But there was also important early work clearly emphasizing the cognitive and socially constructed nature of institutions from a less functionalist perspective. Cooley (1956 [1902]: 313–314), for example, observed that institutions are developed through interactions and exist 'as a habit of mind and of action, largely unconscious because largely common to all the group … the individual is always cause as well as effect of the institution'. Hughes (1936: 180) further emphasized the social production of institutions when he defined them as the 'establishment of relative permanence of a distinctly social sort'. Mead (1934) drew attention to the role of symbolic systems, arguing that meaning is created in interaction through gestures, particularly vocal gestures in the form of language – an argument that is particularly interesting to us here as it foreshadows a linguistic approach to the analysis of social construction. Schutz (1967 [1932]) similarly examined ways in which common meanings are constructed through interaction by individuals and become taken-for-granted assumptions.

Berger and Luckmann's (1967) conceptualization of institutions as cognitive structures was arguably the most influential. Their approach focused on the creation of shared knowledge and belief systems through meaningful interaction. They saw their work as being about developing a sociology of knowledge that would explain how objectified social knowledge arose through meaningful and subjective interaction. In doing so, they brought cognitive frameworks for conceptualizing institutions centre-stage. Berger and Luckmann (1967: 58), in their commonly cited definition, describe an institution as 'a reciprocal typification of habituated actions by types of actors'. In other words, institutions arise when groups of people come to understand an activity in a certain way and that understanding becomes shared across a group. From their perspective, institutions are cognitive constructions and the process of institutionalization is a process of social construction.

Early Organizational Institutionalism

While there were many early discussions of institutions in the literature, systematic attempts to connect organizations and institutions only appeared much later. Selznick (1948) was the first major contributor to the institutional theory of organizations. Selznick (1957) described institutionalization as a process that happens to an organization over time, reflecting its own distinctive history, the people who have been members, the vested interests members have created, and the way it has adapted to its environment. From his perspective, to institutionalize is to 'infuse with value beyond the technical requirements of the task at hand' (1957: 16).

This early approach to institutional analyses of organizations was followed by the emergence of new institutional approaches to organizational sociology. Scott (2001: 39) points out that attention to cognitive frames and cultural frameworks rather than to normative systems was a critical defining feature of this new form of institutional theory in sociology. The most significant difference between the old and the new institutionalisms lies in the conception of the cognitive bases of institutionalized behavior. According to the old institutionalists, organizations became institutionalized when they were 'infused with value' as ends in themselves (Selznick, 1957). Individuals' preferences were shaped

by values and norms emphasizing normative-evaluative judgments. New institutionalism departed from a moral framing in terms of norms and values and drew attention to the taken-for-granted scripts, rules and classifications as the basis of institutions (DiMaggio & Powell, 1991).

The work of Meyer and Rowan (1977) and Zucker (1977) grounded new institutional theory firmly in the sociological realm and conspicuously in the work of Berger and Luckmann (1967). Meyer and Rowan (1977) provide a macro-perspective on institutionalized organizations, arguing that formal structures of organizations reflect the myths of their institutional environments instead of the demands of their work activities. They draw on Berger and Luckmann's (1967) notion of institutionalized rules as classifications built into society as reciprocated typifications or understandings when they argue that 'formal structures are not only creatures of their relational networks in the social organization ... the elements of rationalized formal structure are deeply ingrained in, and reflect, widespread understandings of social reality' (Meyer & Rowan, 1977: 54).

In describing institutionalization as a process by which social processes, obligations, or actualities take on a rule-like status in social thought and action, they implied that the rules become taken-for-granted. From their conceptualization of institutionalization one could deduce that they perceived the nature of institutions to be primarily cognitive. They state, 'such elements of formal structure are manifestations of powerful institutional rules which function as highly rationalized myths that are binding on particular organizations' (Meyer & Rowan, 1977: 343). In other words, these shared understandings result in certain organizations having to perform specific activities regardless of their rationale because of the taken-for-granted nature of those understandings. The fact that we understand an organization to be of a particular kind means that a set of taken-for-granted rules must be followed.

It is not that some outside actor is enforcing these rules. But, rather, the fact that they are broadly accepted makes them unavoidable. Meyer and Rowan (1977) therefore provide one of the strongest statements about the cognitive nature of institutions.

Zucker (1977) provides a complementary characterization of institutions as primarily cognitive. In her study of the role of institutionalization in cultural persistence, Zucker argues that 'internalization, self-reward, or other intervening processes need not be present to ensure cultural persistence because social knowledge once institutionalized exists as a fact, as part of objective reality, and can be transmitted directly on that basis' (1991: 83).

Most importantly, Zucker's study comes closest to developing Berger and Luckmann's (1967) work in that it deals with the *process of institutionalization*, especially highlighting the social constructivist nature of the process: '[i]t is the process by which individual actors transmit what is socially defined as real, and at the same time, at any point in the process the meaning of an act can be defined as more or less a taken-for-granted part of this social reality' (Zucker, 1977: 85). In other words, institutionalized acts are perceived as *objective* because they can be repeated by other actors with a common understanding of the act. Further, institutionalized acts are *exterior* when 'subjective understanding of acts is reconstructed as intersubjective understanding so that the acts are seen as part of the external world' (1977: 85). Most critically, institutionalized acts do not require monitoring and enforcement, as deviation from them is literally unthinkable.

More Recent Organizational Institutionalism

Following Meyer and Rowan (1977) and Zucker (1977), several significant contributions to institutional theory developed a macro-level perspective on institutionalization

(e.g., DiMaggio & Powell, 1983; Meyer & Scott, 1983). However, there seemed to be little attention to clarifying and developing, theoretically and empirically, an understanding of the nature of institutions and the process by which they come to be. Rather, the line of enquiry changed from institutions and how they are constructed to the effects of institutionalization.

DiMaggio and Powell (1983), for example, addressed the question of why there is such striking homogeneity of organizational forms and practices, the phenomenon of isomorphism. They elucidated three key mechanisms by which institutional effects are diffused through a field of organizations resulting in structural isomorphism: coercive, mimetic and normative.

Tolbert and Zucker (1983) investigated the diffusion of civil service employment practices across US local governments arriving at a two-stage model of diffusion encompassing early adopters and late adopters. Early adoptions were motivated by functional imperatives but as an increasing number of organizations adopted the innovation, the authors surmised that it became progressively institutionalized. They concluded that social legitimacy was a driver for late adopters.

Fligstein (1987) also examined the rise of finance personnel to the position of president in large US corporations between 1919 and 1979. He posited a mimetic explanation of diffusion. Anti-trust legislation pushed firms toward unrelated diversification thus creating the conditions for the rise in finance officers, but as these actors established themselves in one set of firms, their counterparts in other firms were able to use that as a basis for gaining power (Fligstein, 1987).

Several studies in the 1980s pursued cross-category comparisons, for example, between commercial and non-profit organizations suggesting that the former were less sensitive to institutional influences (e.g., Baron & Bielby, 1986; Eisenhardt, 1988; Fennell & Alexander, 1987; Pfeffer & Davis-Blake, 1987; Tolbert, 1985). Further studies made cross-national comparisons analyzing the effect of cultural institutional effects (e.g., Carroll, Goodstein, & Gyenes, 1988; Hamilton & Biggart, 1988; Lincoln, Hanada, & McBride, 1986). All of these studies covered a variety of different agents of diffusion, including government agencies, professional networks, senior executives; a wide array of practices including personnel procedures, boundary-spanning strategies and accounting practices; and a diverse range of settings including municipalities, hospitals, universities and corporations.

The 1980s saw an impressive expansion of the realm of institutional theory, both theoretically and empirically. However, there appeared to be continued ambiguity about the nature of an institution and the processes through which it is constituted. For example, Baron and Bielby (1986) conceptualized the term institution in three fundamentally different ways in their empirical study. Their study depicts mimetic, coercive and normative mechanisms underpinning the spread of modern personnel administration in the United States during and after World War II. In one sense, they use the term institution as constituting cultural prescriptions but in another usage they describe it as reflecting the activities of regulatory agencies. The first usage resonates closely with Meyer and Rowan (1977) and Zucker (1977), but the description of institutions as a framework of regulatory policies leans more toward the sort of perspective developed in institutional economics (e.g., North, 1990). This example illustrates that in spite of significant advances in institutional research, the nature of the foundational concept – the institution – remains unclear. And, to make matters worse, these contradictory conceptualizations of the nature of institutions remained unresolved and, in fact, if anything have become exacerbated.

To summarize, impressive theoretical and empirical advances have been made in institutional theory over the past three decades. At the same time, much of this work has sidestepped the issue of what an institution actually is and how it comes to be. Although the cognitive nature of institutions is ostensibly the foundation of institutional theory, established clearly in the early works of Meyer and Rowan (1977) and Zucker (1977), we see that very aspect gets muddied through the 1980s and 1990s. A conspicuous absence of citations to Meyer and Rowan (1977), Zucker (1977) and Berger and Luckmann (1967) in much of the work reflects this lack of clarity. The process of institutionalization and the role of social construction in that process – the very basis for understanding that institutions are fundamentally cognitive – are often neglected.

CHALLENGING THE THREE PILLARS

As we discussed above, several influential contributions to institutional theory soon followed the foundational works of Meyer and Rowan (1977) and Zucker (1977). In one of the most often cited articles, DiMaggio and Powell (1983) identified the now ubiquitous three mechanisms of isomorphic change. However, while this framework is very valuable in identifying sources of pressure for organizational isomorphism, the mechanisms they propose shed little light on the actual process of institutionalization – a prerequisite for understanding institutions – nor on the nature of institutions.

Furthermore, there is an underlying tension in their framework. They begin by clearly indicating that they are interested in something other than simple rational actor explanations for isomorphism:

> Today, however, structural change in organizations seems less and less driven by competition or by the need for efficiency. Instead, we will contend, bureaucratization and other forms of organizational change occur as the result of processes that make organizations more similar without necessarily making them more efficient. (DiMaggio & Powell, 1983: 147)

Yet at the same time, they mix together acting in a taken-for-granted way in the face of the cognitive institutions of Meyer and Rowan (1977) and acting purposefully and rationally in the face of coercion or normative pressure. Furthermore, they indicate that, in fact, the sorts of cognitive institutions that Meyer and Rowan (1977) are interested in may actually be a *result* of these other mechanisms. They argue that while the 'institutional approach associated with John Meyer and his students posits the importance of myths and ceremony', it 'does not ask how these models arise' (DiMaggio & Powell, 1983: 157). They then go on to suggest that their mechanisms may provide some explanations for how and why cognitive institutions arise.

The work of DiMaggio and Powell (1983), and the ambiguity of their framework, was taken up and developed by Scott (2001) in his highly influential book *Institutions and Organizations*. Scott's book has played a significant role in shaping the broad conception of institution that has come to dominate in institutional theory and has also had an important influence more broadly across adjacent fields such as international management. We believe, however, that this conceptualization may in fact be a distraction from actually understanding the process of institutional production that is essential to completely comprehend the nature of institutions.

In his book, Scott develops a typology of what constitutes an institution comprising three component elements or pillars: the regulatory, normative and cultural-cognitive pillars. He draws on DiMaggio and Powell's (1983) typology to describe the mechanisms of control – coercive, normative and mimetic – underpinning the regulatory, normative and cultural-cognitive pillars respectively. The regulatory pillar emphasizes explicit regulatory processes involving 'the capacity to establish rules, inspect others' conformity to them, and as necessary, manipulate sanctions – rewards and punishments – in an attempt to influence future behavior' (Scott, 2001: 52). He goes on to explain that '[f]orce, fear, and expedience are central ingredients of the regulatory pillar' (Scott, 2001: 53). Powerful

actors may impose their will on others, based on the threat of sanctions or by offering inducements. In summary, the basis for compliance underlying a regulatory pillar is expedience, the mechanism is coercive and the basis of legitimacy is socially sanctioned.

The normative pillar emphasizes 'normative rules that introduce a prescriptive, evaluative and obligatory dimension into social life' (Scott, 2001: 55). Norms specify how things *should* be done and provide legitimate ways of pursuing valued ends. The basis of compliance is social obligation, the mechanism is normative and the basis of legitimacy is moral. Sometimes, the regulative and normative pillars can be mutually reinforcing, especially when coercive power is legitimated by a normative framework that both supports and constrains the exercise of power (Scott, 1987). Scott (2001) points to the normative conception of institutions embraced by early sociologists such as Durkheim, Parsons and Selznick, who focused on types of institutions such as kinship groups, social classes and religious systems that are usually underpinned by common beliefs and values.

The cultural-cognitive pillar is what Scott (2001) considers central to the thinking of scholars such as Berger, Meyer and Zucker. The basis of compliance underlying the cultural-cognitive pillar is taken-for-grantedness based on shared understandings, the mechanism is mimetic and the basis of legitimacy is something that is comprehensible, recognizable and socially supported (Scott, 2001). Compliance occurs because other types of behavior are inconceivable; it becomes the 'way we do things around here'. The socially mediated construction of a common framework of meaning is central to the cultural-cognitive pillar.

Scott's typology of the three pillars provides a comprehensive all-inclusive framework combining the different perspectives on isomorphism emanating from different theoretical disciplines. While such a typology serves that purpose of integrating different perspectives, conceptualizing institutions as comprising these three disparate elements raises a number of problems. First, the processes by which these three pillars come to be are different. Scott (2001) himself points out that the three pillars are based on very different philosophical assumptions about the nature of social reality. This is problematic for the development of a unified theory of institutions as it is difficult to see how to bridge the ontological differences between the underlying perspectives on which the pillars rest.

Second, the dynamics arising out of the three pillars are very different. The regulative and normative aspects of institutions are 'the products of human design, and the outcomes of purposive action by instrumentally oriented individuals' (DiMaggio & Powell, 1991). Consequently, there is an opportunity for deviance and contestation as agents work to resist pressures that they recognize and which they believe not to be in their interests (Hirsch, 1997). Questions of power and politics are central to these pillars as actors work purposively and consciously to advance their own interests. Furthermore, the literature that is most useful in understanding these dynamics lies largely in work on power, resource dependency and other related work.

The cognitive aspect of institutions, on the other hand, is very different from the other two pillars (DiMaggio & Powell, 1991; Hirsch, 1997; Hoffman, 1997). Hirsch (1997) argues that the basic assumptions and mechanisms underpinning the regulative and normative pillars are, in fact, rejected in the cognitive pillar. In the first two pillars stability and compliance is assured through values and norms that provide individuals and corporate actors consciously understood legal, social or moral rules and guidelines for behavior (Hirsch, 1997). On the other hand, within a cognitive frame conformity is driven unreflectively. As Hirsch puts it, the cognitive pillar works with 'no questions asked and without deviation' (Hirsch, 1997: 1710). The underlying questions that arise around this pillar and the sorts of theoretical perspectives useful in answering these questions are

fundamentally different from the other two pillars.

Third, if an institution is enduring and stable then it does not need regulatory sanctions or other social controls to support it – it is simply taken for granted. In a discussion of various avenues for institutional reproduction, Powell (1991) alludes to the exercise of power in ensuring persistence of certain practices but acknowledges that practices can take on a life of their own and not require any active elite support. Zucker (1991: 86) succinctly argues that 'direct social control through norms or sanctions (incentives or negative) is not necessary ... applying sanctions to institutionalized acts may have the effect of deinstitutionalizing them ... the act of sanctioning may indicate that there are other possible, attractive alternatives'. Berger and Luckmann, similarly, contrast institutions with other forms of social control:

> To say that a segment of human activity has been institutionalized is already to say that this segment of human activity has been subsumed under social control. Additional control mechanisms are required only in so far as the processes of institutionalization are less than completely successful. (1967: 73)

This is a powerful argument, suggesting that institutions are best thought of as fundamentally cognitive and that these other two pillars not be combined into a 'theory of institutions'. When something has become institutionalized no outside sanctions or controls are required. These other forces can create social order and lead to isomorphism, but they are of a very different nature from cognitive institutions.

Furthermore, this raises an interesting theoretical question: are the regulative and normative pillars, in fact, important *pressures* in the process of institutionalization rather than elements of an institution? It would seem that most of us, for example, obey traffic laws unthinkingly rather than because we are concerned about the potential punishment. Traffic laws are a cognitive institution for most of us most of the time. However, the appearance of a new law often leads to changes in behavior because of the potential punishment that is associated with the new law. But soon it too becomes taken-for-granted. It is important to note that there is no way to differentiate between the two motivations for behavior by only examining the behavior itself. We need to study intentions at an individual level to understand which sort of mechanism is functioning here. Much of the empirical work in institutional theory has failed to do this, leaving us without any clear indication of what is actually happening.

In sum, we are not arguing for a separate institutional theory of cognitive institutions or claiming that one type of institution is better than another. Rather we are posing a question central to the theoretical foundation of institutional theory – what is an institution and how does it come to be? Furthermore, we are highlighting the problems with the three pillars approach to isomorphism in helping address this question.

We believe we need to delve into the processes of institutional production in order to provide insight into how an institution comes to be. And, we will argue in the next section that a linguistic perspective on institutions and institutionalization provides a practical foundation for developing a more powerful theory of institutions. Linguistic methods help to empirically capture the social constructivist nature of the process of institutionalization and the understanding that when compliance comes naturally and automatically without the active intervention of sanctions or norms an institution comes to be. But they also serve as a theoretical foundation to support the investigation of the micro-processes of institutionalization at the field level.

USING LINGUISTIC METHODS TO STUDY INSTITUTIONIZATION

Linguistic methods are a family of related research approaches including discourse analysis, rhetorical analysis, narrative analysis and semiotics.[3] They share a common purpose in that they allow researchers to explore how meaning is constituted in social interaction. Given that the constitution of meaning plays a central role in the construction of social reality, linguistic methods are useful in understanding how the social reality that members experience comes to be, identifying the key actors involved and exploring the social impact of the reality that is produced.

Linguistic methods focus on language broadly defined. More specifically, research from this perspective involves the analysis of one or more texts defined as 'any kind of symbolic expression requiring a physical medium and permitting of permanent storage' (Taylor & Van Every, 1993: 109). Texts may take a variety of forms, including written documents, spoken words, artwork, pictures, videos, blogs, tweets, buildings and songs. What is important is that the 'symbolic expression' to be studied is inscribed in some material way that gives it a lasting physical form. At the same time, while linguistic methods can be used to study a variety of texts, even a cursory examination of the literature will show that most studies focus on words, or combinations of words and images, as these sorts of texts are the most common, and generally the most important, in processes of social construction.

Linguistic methods are distinguished from other methods in their focus on meaning as a social accomplishment. By this we mean that they foreground the process through which particular meanings become taken-for-granted and naturalized by members of a social group rather than investigating the collection of meanings that are in place at any particular time. What is interesting for researchers working from this perspective is how and why certain ways of thinking about the world become taken-for-granted and the impact of this on the particular social world that is being investigated.

The usefulness of these methods in studying institutionalization grows directly out of the points made in our discussion above. The process of social construction that underlies institutionalization is, at its most basic, a linguistic process. Language lends meaning and legitimacy to material practices and in doing so constructs the cognitive structures that underpin institutions (e.g., Berger & Luckmann, 1967). A linguistic conceptualization of institutionalization is, therefore, directly compatible with the cognitive focus that lies at the heart of institutional theory.

In summary, from a cognitive perspective institutions are taken-for-granted understandings (Zucker, 1977) and we need better ways of unpacking the journey toward taken-for-grantedness – the process of social construction – that leads to institutionalization. We propose that linguistic methods – and in particular discourse analysis, rhetorical analysis, narrative analysis and semiotics – have the potential to capture different aspects of this process of social construction. In the following subsections we discuss each of these methods in turn and explain how they can facilitate investigation of the social production of cognitive institutions. We provide a summary of our discussions in Table 15.1.

Discourse Analysis

Discourse analysis was one of the first, and arguably is still the most important, of the linguistic methods used in institutional theory (Phillips & Di Domenico, 2009). The linguistic turn that led to the widespread use of discourse analysis in organization theory more broadly (Alvesson & Karreman, 2000; Phillips & Oswick, 2012), also provided the impetus for institutional theorists to begin using discourse analysis to unpack the processes of social construction that underpin institutionalization. This process was further accelerated by the publication of 'Discourse and Institutions' in the *Academy of Management Review* in 2004, which provided a framework for thinking about institutions as discursive constructions (Phillips, Lawrence, & Hardy, 2004). Building on this framework, a number of different empirical studies have been conducted into the discursive construction of institutions. All in all, discourse analysis has proven to be popular and useful in the development of institutional theory and so we will begin here.

Table 15.1 Using linguistic methods in institutional theory

Form of analysis	Definition	Use in the study of institutionalization	Exemplar studies
Discourse analysis	The study of how sets of interrelated texts produce social objects	Useful for studying how meaningful actions produce texts that accrete and in doing so constitute institutions	Maguire & Hardy, 2009; Lawrence & Phillips, 2004; Munir & Phillips, 2005
Rhetorical analysis	The study of how arguments are constructed in an effort to shape understandings of social reality	Useful for studying the production of 'theorizations' meant to legitimate or delegitimate social arrangements	Green, Li & Nohria, 2009; Heracleous & Barrett, 2001; Suddaby & Greenwood, 2005; Oakes, Townley, & Cooper, 1998
Narrative analysis	The study of the construction of stories and how stories influence understandings of social reality	Useful for studing the 'myths' that underpin institutions. Also useful to study the stories produced by actors in an effort to create institutional change	Hardy & Maguire, 2010; Vaara & Tiernari, 2011
Semiotic analysis	The study of signs and the ways in which signs carry meaning and structure social reality	Useful for studying the institutionalization as a cultural process and connecting with semiotic theories of culture	Zilber, 2002, 2006; Brannen, 2004

An introduction to discourse analysis

Understanding what discourse analysis is about begins with an understanding of what discourse *is* (Phillips & Oswick, 2012). Discourse, in general terms, refers to an interrelated set of texts and the associated practices of production, dissemination and reception that bring a social object into being. Discourse analysis, by extension, is the study of these interrelated sets of texts.

For example, at one point in history the concept of endangered species did not yet exist, and by extension there were no 'endangered species' as we understand them today. Through a long and complex process, a body of texts were produced that made the concept of endangered species meaningful and accepted. Furthermore, the concept became applied to certain species of animals and endangered species as something in the material world came into being. This process occurred in and through discourse and the study of how this occurred is discourse analysis.

It is important to point out that discourses can never be examined in their entirety. Discourse analysts are therefore limited to examining selections of texts that they believe sufficiently embody a particular discourse to be worthy of study. At the same time, discourse analysts do not simply focus on individual texts; rather, in analyzing discourse researchers refer to *bodies* of interrelated texts since it is the interrelations between texts, changes in texts, new textual forms and new systems of distributing texts that constitute a discourse over time.

Similarly, discourse analysis requires researchers to make reference to the social context in which texts are found and the discourses of which they are a part are produced. From a social construction point of view, discourse analysis explores how texts are *made* meaningful and also how they contribute to the constitution of social reality by *making* meaning. These processes do not occur in single texts. It is only when complex and interrelated collections of texts develop that the social reality represented in the texts becomes a taken-for-granted facticity.

Discourse analysis and institutional theory

There has been growing interest among institutional scholars in the discursive perspective and its potential to further explicate and expand institutional theory. As we mentioned above, much of this work can be linked back to the work of Phillips et al. (2004). The authors argued that the processes underlying institutionalization were not well understood. Specifically, they proposed a discursive perspective to understand institutions as social constructions constituted through discourse (Phillips et al., 2004). Discourse analysis is not just a method of analysis, but also a theoretical approach with underlying theoretical assumptions that relate specifically to the social construction of reality (e.g., Chia, 2000; Gergen, 1999; Grant & Hardy, 2004; Phillips & Hardy, 2002) making it a potentially powerful and useful lens in the context of institutional theory.

In their article, Phillips et al. (2004) propose a model linking action and discourse that begins to explain the process of institutionalization. Institutionalization does not occur through the simple imitation of an action by immediate observers, but through the creation of supporting texts that range from conversational descriptions among colleagues to more elaborate and widely distributed texts such as manuals, books and magazine articles. This is particularly true in the organizational realm where many actions are not directly observable but must rather be learned about through accounts in various texts (think of Total Quality Management and its institutionalization as a common organizational practice).

Accordingly, the actions of individual actors affect the discursive realm through the production of texts, some of which leave meaningful traces that become embedded in new or existing discourses. Not all, or even most, actions lead to the production of texts. But some do and some of these go on to influence the discourse (and the institutions it constitutes) in important ways.

For example, Maguire & Hardy (2009) examined the role of discourse in outsider-driven deinstitutionalization of taken-for-granted practices of DDT use between 1962 and 1972. They theorized the process as one of 'translation' where different parties interact and negotiate to significantly reshape what is finally transmitted (Zilber, 2006). Discourse and translation are therefore linked because 'meaning is created from collections of texts – discourses – that evolve from the ongoing production, distribution and consumption of individual texts' (Maguire & Hardy, 2009: 149). Their study is a vivid depiction of how outsiders produced and distributed texts – claims, arguments, stories, examples, statistics, anecdotes – that 'problematized' the current institutionalized practices and, over time, built a case for abandonment. In a nutshell, meaning was negotiated between the text's author and its readers as it was consumed and, over time, there was a change in discourse at the macro-level but also power relations in the field were reconfigured.

In summary, discourses provide the socially constituted, self-regulating mechanisms that enact institutions and shape the actions that lead to the production of more texts. The bodies of texts that accumulate lead to the production of 'shared typifications' and institutions are produced through processes of social construction. Thus, the discursive realm acts as the background against which current actions occur – enabling some actions, constraining others. This then is the discursive explanation of how particular sorts of actions become institutionalized.

Rhetorical Analysis

Rhetorical analysis is not as commonly used as discourse analysis in organization theory, but recently 'organizational researchers have increased their interest in rhetorical theory as an additional lens through which to understand organizational actions and phenomena' (Green, 2004: 654). When used to understand institutional processes, rhetorical analysis focuses attention on the arguments that are used by actors as they seek to influence institutional processes, the characteristics of the actors that shape their potential to influence, and the outcome of their attempts to persuade other actors to think about the world differently. As such, rhetorical analysis provides an important and insightful way of understanding key institutional processes, and in particular institutional change, through the analysis of the structure of the arguments that underpin new theorizations.

An introduction to rhetoric

While rhetorical analysis is a less commonly used method in organization theory (and in social science more broadly), it has a long and illustrious history in the humanities. In fact, until quite recently, rhetoric was a central part of a classical Western education and is still a commonly used method of textual analysis in the humanities and social sciences. And, like discourse analysis, following the linguistic turn it has become an increasingly well developed and popular approach to studies of organizational phenomena, including the study of institutionalization.

The study of rhetoric is, at its most basic, the study of the structure of arguments in order to better understand their ability to persuade. Aristotle was an early proponent and his writings on rhetoric (Aristotle, 1991) – and particularly on logos, pathos and ethos – still form an important part of the theoretical infrastructure of this approach. Its application to the study of texts in organization theory provides another way to understand how social reality is constituted through production of texts of various kinds, but with a focus on the construction of logical arguments and on how various rhetorical moves are more persuasive and therefore have greater effects on the social reality where they occur.

What is distinctive about rhetorical analysis compared to other linguistic methods is that it focuses on the deliberate use of persuasion. The driving mechanism underlying rhetorical explanations is that actors manage their limited cognitive and attention resources through persuasion to construct and manipulate meaning (Green & Li, 2011). Rhetorical analysis is therefore helpful for delving into the structure of different communication strategies to better understand the contestation between actors underpinning the process of social construction (e.g., Burke, 1969 [1945]; Toulmin, 1958; Sillince & Suddaby, 2008).

Rhetorical theory, while quite complex and broad, has typically been classified under two domains: classical rhetoric and new rhetoric. Classical rhetoric focuses on persuasion as influence (Aristotle, 1991) and new rhetoric focuses on persuasion as communication (Green & Li, 2011). New rhetoric considers language as epistemic, but also a route to capturing the meaning generated through human interaction. In that sense, a combination of classical and new rhetoric is especially suited to capturing processes of social construction that often entail negotiation and contestation between opposing actors who engage in deliberate manipulation of meaning. Classical rhetoric's focus on *how we use words* combined with new rhetoric's focus on how *words use us* suggests that language has the potential to constrain *as well as* enable actors' thoughts and actions (Green & Li, 2011).

Therefore, analysing persuasive texts generated during times of institutional change is an effective way to track the unfolding of the process of social construction of new meaning. In this way, rhetorical analysis can capture the different stages of legitimacy building that underpin institutionalization. We will consider how rhetorical analysis has been used in the study of institutions in the next section.

Rhetorical analysis and institutional theory

Legitimacy lies at the heart of institutionalization and, importantly, the process of acquiring legitimacy is a process of social construction through which a practice becomes taken-for-granted. The adoption of practices and social arrangements may be driven by complex combinations of regulative, normative and mimetic pressures, but it is language that is pivotal to the production and acquisition of legitimacy through the production of theorizations (e.g., Phillips et al., 2004). We know this, yet there is continuing concern that we need a better understanding of *how* legitimacy, the desirability or appropriateness of an action or idea, emerges or is produced (Harmon et al., 2015; Suchman, 1995). Changing legitimacy assumptions through theorization is an important part of the process of social construction that underpins institutions, and rhetoric plays an important role in theorization.

Rhetoric as a linguistic method offers both a theoretical and an empirical approach to study legitimacy-building as a cognitive process. There are two critical aspects in building new legitimacy criteria that, we argue, rhetorical analysis has the potential to capture: first, it entails creative and persuasive arguments in support of the new practice and, second, it involves intense contests and extensive negotiation. As Green, Li and Nohria (2009) argued, before a practice is institutionalized it must make sense. By constructing an argument for what a practice means and why it makes sense, the actor provides theorizations intended to build shared cognition and meaning (e.g., Green, 2004; Strang & Meyer, 1993).

Green et al. (2009) applied a syllogistic model to capture how the structure of an argument evolves and morphs as the process of institutionalization progresses. They noted that the initial claim justifying a material practice is linked to the major premise and the minor premise that are two critical elements of a syllogism. As the process of institutionalization continues, one would expect a change in the structure of the argument, supporting that material practice, in the form of a collapse of the syllogism into an 'enthymeme', that is, the major premise would be suppressed.

Heracleous and Barrett (2001) identified the 'enthymemes', or arguments in use, used by competing stakeholders during the process of adopting digital communication in the London insurance market. Suddaby and Greenwood (2005) examined rhetorical strategies at play as the accounting and legal professions struggled to make sense of multidisciplinary practices and the resulting new organizational form where a law practice was subsumed within an accounting firm. They identified two elements: the use of institutional vocabularies as a critical mechanism to surface contradictions that in their study was inherent in the notion of professionalism and, second, how language is used to theorize change by connecting to broader cultural templates.

Oakes, Townley and Cooper (1998) showed how new vocabularies were instrumental in facilitating a shift from a cultural to an economic logic in a study examining change in a provincial museum in Alberta, Canada. Harmon et al. (2015) developed a model of rhetorical legitimation that specifies the communicative and cognitive structure underlying the maintenance and change of institutions. They point to two structurally distinctive forms of rhetoric – intra-field and inter-field – as appropriate to capture institutional maintenance and institutional change respectively.

In summary, rhetorical analysis provides an important analytical approach that allows institutional theory researchers to conceptualize processes of institutionalization in a way that highlights the role of agents in producing arguments to support processes of institutionalization as well as the tools to unpack these processes through the structured investigation of texts. The existing work we have discussed begins to show the potential of rhetorical analysis in institutional theory but we

also believe that there is much more potential to use rhetorical analysis in understanding cognitive institutions.

Narrative Analysis

Narrative analysis is a common linguistic method used to study a broad range of topics, including culture, identity and gender (see Rhodes & Brown, 2005 for a summary). In organizational research, narrative analysis focuses (either literally or more metaphorically) on how stories are used in the construction of organizational reality (Boje, 2001; Phillips, 1995). This has proven to be a highly productive research approach in studies of organizational phenomena, and is becoming increasingly common in institutional theory where narrative analysis provides another way to examine the narrative strategies (basically the patterns in the stories) used by actors as they seek to shape the way others understand and interpret the social world.

An introduction to narrative analysis

A narrative is 'an oral, written, or filmed account of events told to others or to oneself' (Smith, 2000: 328). They are complex social artifacts in that they are 'storylike constructions containing description, interpretation, emotion, expectations, and related material' (Harvey, 1995: 3). Narratives can be accounts of personal experience, accounts of the experiences of others, or explicitly fictional stories such as novels, fairy tales, or myths. Furthermore, the historical truth of narratives ('what really happened') is often unimportant, with narrative analysts being more concerned with narrative truth – 'the criterion we use to decide when a certain experience has been captured to our satisfaction' (Spence, 1982: 31).

A narrative is a 'meaning structure that organizes events and human actions into a whole, thereby attributing significance to individual actions and events according to their effect on the whole' (Polkinghorne, 1988: 18). Simply put, narratives are a form of purposeful storytelling that can facilitate managing meaning (Gabriel, 2000). In particular, narratives are able to effectively capture temporality – the past, present and future of an organization (Czarniawska, 2004) – through 'temporal chains of interrelated events or actions' (Gabriel, 2004: 63). Different narrative approaches can be used to capture different aspects of the process of social construction.

Narrative analysis, at its simplest, is the study of narratives and of the ways in which narratives shape social reality. While discourse analysis focuses on collections of texts of any sort, narrative analysis focuses on the use and impact of narratives (or, more simply, stories) in the production of social reality. Narrative analysis includes a set of tools for examining narratives in a structured way in order to better understand their role in shaping understandings. For example, narrative analysis is increasingly used by scholars interested in identity as a method for exploring how individuals construct their identities through an examination of the stories that individuals tell about themselves.

Narrative analysis in institutional theory

Several studies of institutional change explore narratives as a type of linguistic resource in order to highlight the dynamics of social construction underlying institutional processes. Hardy & Maguire (2010), for example, examined the role of narratives in the field-configuring events that have been identified as important sources of change in institutional fields. Focusing on the field of persistent organic pollutants, especially the insecticide DDT, they delineated different discursive spaces in which different sets of actors interacted and explored how the patterns of text production, consumption and distribution varied across these spaces.

More specifically, they teased out the emerging narratives underpinning the different mechanisms that facilitated the field configuration process. First, domination by a particular narrative at the conclusion of the field-configuring event enabled new field-level rules; second, the interpretation of new narratives by organizations helped shift relational and discursive activities toward new field-level positions; and, third, the ongoing translation of the narratives by organizations led to new field-level understandings. From their study it is clear that narratives have the potential to shape the process of social construction in a way that is much more profound than simply 'telling a story'. Narrative analysis allows us to understand how the story may advantage or disadvantage different people, generate counternarratives, get translated by other actors, all of which together may result in new meaning structures.

In another interesting example, Vaara & Tiernari (2011) elucidated the use of narratives as 'central discursive resources in times of change' (p. 370). They specifically drew on antenarrative analysis (Boje, 2001, 2008) to make sense of an unfolding merger process in an organization. They argued that unlike conventional narrative analysis, an antenarrative approach focuses on ongoing prospective sense-making and sense-giving. Antenarratives are conceptualized as fragments of organizational discourse and are mobilized through intentional storytelling. They applied Bakhtin's (1981) notion of alternative and competing antenarratives that may be in a dialogical relationship.

Vaara & Tiernari (2011) showed that in the context of change, organizational storytelling encompasses, on the one hand, antenarratives expressed to control the meaning of events and changes (legitimation) and, on the other hand, to challenge or break that control apart (resistance). Antenarrative analysis is potentially powerful in making sense of a process of social construction by focusing on fragments of text, communication and conversation to construct identities and interests. It is, indeed, a linguistic resource that through storytelling acts to bridge the linguistic realm and the material realm.

In summary, narrative analysis supports and complements discourse analysis and rhetorical analysis. All three share an interest in how social construction occurs through language, but each focuses on a different aspect of this process. Where discourse highlights the way in which sets of texts bring social objects into being and rhetoric focuses on the structure of arguments found in text, narrative sensitizes us to the fundamental role of narratives in making the social meaningful. Together these methods are able to illuminate how institutions are constituted through processes of social construction that occur as actors produce texts of various kinds in various ways.

Semiotic Analysis

While semiotic analysis has been less commonly used in organization theory than discourse analysis or narrative analysis, it is a fairly common method in the humanities and social sciences more broadly. And while its impact as a method may be somewhat less in the study of organizations, its influence as an ontology is significant both in institutional theory and in organization theory more broadly.

The reason for this is simple. Semiotics as a philosophical perspective underpins the semiotic perspective on culture or the idea that culture is made up of a system of signs. As Geertz (1973: 5) argued, 'Believing, with Max Weber, that man is an animal suspended in webs of significance he himself has spun, I take culture to be those webs, and the analysis of it to be therefore not an experimental science in search of law but an interpretative one in search of meaning.' Semiotics, and the semiotic conception of culture that it supports, are therefore compatible with and supportive of interpretive approaches to organization studies and also to the cognitive view of institutions and institutionalization that we have discussed here. It is therefore important to understand semiotics both as a

method and as a way of understanding the composition of the social world in order to better understand its potential as a method in institutional theory.

An introduction to semiotic analysis

Semiotics suggests that human beings are inextricably embedded in webs of meaningful signs through which they act, interact and otherwise experience the world: 'Indeed, at the heart of semiotics is the realization that the whole of human experience, without exception, is an interpretive structure mediated and sustained by signs' (Deely, 1990: 5).

Central to the study of social semiotics is the phenomenon of representation – the ways in which things stand for or substitute for other things. The potential phenomena of interest for semiotics are therefore quite extensive, including spoken and written language, gestures, pictures, traffic lights, clothing, consumer goods, architecture and food. This perspective has been used with some success in the examination of organizational phenomena (Barley, 1983; Fiol, 1989) but has not been extensively used to explore institutions or institutionalization.

At its most basic, then, semiotics is the study of signs, which, according to Saussure (1974 [1916]), are the conjunction of a signifier and a signified, where a signifier is some physical manifestation such as a sound or a visible mark and a signified is a concept or an idea. The signifier and signified coexist as a sign; no sign exists without both and neither can exist separately from a sign. It is important to stress that the signified is not part of the material world, but rather a concept that can then be linked to something in the world – this 'something in the world' is called the referent – through the sign (Hodge & Kress, 1988).

Central to this conception of signs is the idea that signs are arbitrary, historical constructs. It is not the world that gives them meaning but the active participation of individuals who apply shared sets of conventions in their construction and reception.

As a result, signs have meaning only by convention. Taking spoken language as an example, there is no necessary relation between things in the world and the system of language that we use. Rather, the relationship is a practical and historical one.

These signs can be joined together to produce meta-signs or myths (Barthes, 1967, 1988). These myths are built using existing signs as signifiers in the development of another level of signification. It is not as if the signs were placed together like words in a sentence, but rather that they form another whole, another combination of signifier and signified. It is at this level that complex texts produce sets of cultural understandings that underpin our social conventions. Ideas such as patriotism, ethnic identity and religious belief are often associated with complex signs – flags, religious symbols, styles of dress – that come to represent these important cultural myths.

This, of course, can extend to organizations where the Nike logo or the Microsoft name, for instance, becomes the signifier of a complex signified or myth developed through years of careful effort. It is not the signifier that is important, but the myth associated with the signifier – the complex collection of meanings produced by linking groups of simpler signs. It is not the 'fat check mark' that makes Nike more or less attractive and legitimate to its customers and critics, but the complex set of meanings that have become attached to that once meaningless mark. It is the process of producing this complex sign that is interesting from the point of view of semiotics.

Semiotic analysis in institutional theory

The ramifications of a semiotic perspective for the study of institutionalization are significant: to the degree that the 'social' depends on language or other forms of communication for its production, it depends on an analyzable semiotic system (Eco, 1976). Adopting this perspective for the study of institutions would mean examining them as social semiotic phenomena that arise out of the communication of signs and that are constructed and maintained through ongoing interpretation. In other words, to adopt a social semiotic perspective is to approach institutionalization as symbolic constructions created and sustained through semiotic practices.

For example, Zilber (2006) decoded signs through semiotic analysis to explore how the meanings associated with the growth in high tech in Israel, around the millennium, emerged from broader Israeli meaning systems and how they evolved through time in two institutional arenas – the societal and at the level of the organizational field.

Specifically, she explored the work of rational myths in institutionalization of high tech – generic rational myths in Israeli society at large, rational myths specific to high tech at the societal level, and expressed at the high tech organizational field level. The author used press articles and 'want ads' as sources of data to serve as systems of signs, which comprised a signifier – a word or a visual image – and the signified, which is the meaning attached to the signifier within a specific social, cultural and historical context (Zilber, 2006: 287). Decoding a sign entailed first distilling a 'denotative meaning' of visual images, words etc. that focused on the literal, common-sense meaning. She then moved to deriving the 'connotative meaning' by identifying the dominant values associated with the signs. In other words, how the denotative meaning of a text was embedded in a cultural context. The next step was to cluster the various signifiers into unified themes and track how the connotative meanings of these themes related to each other. We argue that semiotic analysis can help capture a process of social construction by decoding signs to see how shared meaning is constructed over time.

In another example, Brannen (2004) explored the different receptions that the Walt Disney Company received when it entered

Japan compared to when it entered France. She used semiotic analysis to understand the varied reactions to highly institutionalized practices and symbols and proposed the notion of 'semantic fit' to describe how the meaning of a symbol shifts from one cultural context to another. The same product (i.e., Mickey Mouse) or practice (i.e., service orientation) meant very different things when recontextualized into another culture and reinterpreted through a different cultural system. As a result, Disney's attempt to create meaning in the two cultural contexts had very different results and extensive semiotic activity was required to rescue the attempt to enter France.

In sum, semiotic analysis is an important toolkit for institutional analysis and also provides the philosophical underpinnings for understanding and theorizing about institutions as taken-for-granted social constructions. As a toolkit, it provides a proven set of concepts and approaches to analyze and unpack processes of institutionalization and institutional change. But perhaps more importantly, semiotics as an ontology provides the philosophical foundation for cultural institutionalism. A semiotic view of culture provides a broad foundation for thinking about what institutions are and how they relate to culture more broadly. It helps institutional scholars avoid 're-inventing the wheel' when it comes to thinking through and extending the focus of early institutionalism on the 'myths and ceremonies' that are so important from an institutional point of view.

DEVELOPING THE LINGUISTIC PERSPECTIVE IN INSTITUTIONAL THEORY

In the previous section we introduced linguistic methods as a family of methods that are useful in studying processes of social construction. We then discussed four linguistic methods that we believe are particularly

useful as a toolkit for institutional theory researchers and explored how they can be used to understand and explore the social construction of institutions.

But what are the broader implications of adopting a linguistic perspective to theorize and conduct research on processes of social construction underpinning institutional processes? And what are the next steps in the development of institutional theory from this perspective? We now turn our attention to three areas where we believe our arguments have particularly important ramifications for institutional theory: (1) how a linguistic perspective on social construction contributes to the ongoing change of focus in empirical research in institutional theory; (2) how a linguistic perspective expands our understanding of cultural institutionalism and cultural entrepreneurship; and (3) how it deepens our understanding of institutional change.

Changing the Research Focus

We believe that a linguistic perspective on institutions and institutionalization provides the tools (and perhaps more importantly the motivation) to help researchers refocus their attention from simply categorizing the outcomes of institutional processes to trying to understand the process of institutionalization itself. In fact, the various linguistic methods that we have introduced provide an underlying framework for identifying and analyzing texts in order to understand how the linguistic processes in question are impacting the social context in which they occur. This has two important consequences. First, by using linguistic methods researchers can open Zucker's (1991) 'black box' of institutionalization and delve into the micro level foundations of institutionalization processes. They enhance our ability to reveal different aspects of institutionalization and deepen our understanding of key institutional phenomenon.

Second, refocusing attention on the actual process of institutionalization helps to further redress the problem of agency in institutional theory. There has been a growing interest in institutional work (Lawrence, Suddaby, & Leca, 2011) that explores the role of purposeful action in institutional processes. The methods we have outlined above provide tools to help unpack the institutional work done by actors in a rigorous and well-grounded way. Texts are produced by agents acting purposefully, and focusing on the production of texts leads us directly to a concern for intention and an appreciation for agency. The further adoption and development of these methods is therefore an important next step in the development of the institutional work perspective.

In our pursuit of a finer-grained understanding of the processes of social construction, underlying institutionalization, we also have an opportunity to provide a more nuanced understanding of the relationship between the cognitive, regulative and normative pillars. As we argued above, the existence of three pillars has become taken-for-granted in institutional theory but the relationship between these different processes continues to be ambiguous. Scott (2001: 51) has suggested that 'one possible approach would be to view all of these facets as contributing, in interdependent and mutually reinforcing ways, to a powerful social framework'. But in order to do this effectively, distinguishing among these elements is critically important.

In a later review of developments in institutional theory Scott acknowledges that the three pillars are found together but it is the cultural-cognitive pillar that provides the 'deeper foundations of institutional forms … the infrastructure on which not only beliefs, but norms and rules rest' (2004: 5). Perhaps, as Hoffman (1997: 36) suggests, the three pillars form a continuum 'from the conscious to the unconscious, from the legally enforced to the taken-for-granted'.

So how are the three pillars related? From the perspective we have presented here, we would argue that in many ways the differentiation between the normative and cognitive is

overdrawn. That is, norms are basically cognitive when they are closely held and deeply felt. The regulative pillar, on the other hand, is both a reflection of the cognitive beliefs and norms of a group but can also lead to the formation of cognitive institutions. Laws and regulation, when regularly followed, become 'institutionalized' in the sense that they become taken-for-granted. The linguistic methods we have presented provide the tools to unravel and explore this relationship.

Cultural Institutionalism and Cultural Entrepreneurship

In addition to changing the focus of institutional theory research from the effects of institutions to underlying processes through which they are produced, a linguistic perspective also reconnects us back to the early focus in institutional theory on culture. Ideas about the nature of culture drawn from sociology and anthropology formed the foundation for Meyer & Rowan's (1977) arguments that formal structures of organizations reflect 'myth and ceremony'. The adoption of a linguistic perspective brings us full circle and connects institutional theory right back to concerns about culture and, in particular, to ideas of cultural entrepreneurship and cultural bricolage.

More recently, there has been a growing interest in understanding the role of macro culture Lawrence & Phillips, 2004) in institutional processes at the field level. This is perhaps most obvious in the work on institutional logics, but is also evident in work on categories (Weber, Heinze, & DeSoucey, 2008) and organizational change (Vaara & Tienari, 2011). Linguistic methods provide the tools and underlying philosophical frame to extend and develop this research.

In addition, there is now a growing literature on 'cultural entrepreneurship' (Lounsbury & Glynn, 2001; Wry, Lounsbury, & Glynn, 2011; Zott & Huy, 2007), which explores the use by entrepreneurs of cultural material such as narratives and symbols in the creation and legitimation of new ventures. While this work in organization theory has played an important role in pushing entrepreneurship research forward, the focus has been quite narrow and mostly concerned with the role of legitimacy in resource acquisition. One idea that has been neglected is the notion that culture might play a critical role in the process of new venture creation itself. This is perhaps surprising given the growing research in organization theory that draws on Swidler's (1986) conception of culture as a 'tookit' available to actors to shape organizational strategy and create market opportunities (Weber & Dacin, 2011). More specifically, little attention has been paid to one important form of new venture creation: the use by entrepreneurs of an organizational form – a 'combination of cultural material' (David, Sine, & Havenam, 2013: 356) – associated with successful ventures from another context as a template in order to establish a venture in their own context.

At its core, this approach to entrepreneurship seeks to 'deindividuate' (Steyaert & Katz, 2004) research on new venture creation and to conceptualize more fully the role of context more generally and cultural context more specifically. By helping to reconnect institutional theory to culture, the ideas we have presented here also provide an opportunity to further develop the relationship between institutional entrepreneurship and cultural entrepreneurship.

Institutional Change and Emotions

The ebb and flow of research situated in the new institutionalism era reflects a definitive shift from a macro, structural perspective to the micro-level, resurfacing the notion that people are the carriers of institutional processes (e.g., DiMaggio, 1988; Scott, 2001). Importantly, this shift automatically casts light on meaning creation through social interaction. As Hallett & Ventresca (2006:

215) eloquently put it, 'social interactions are the beating heart of institutions'. The turn in scholarly attention toward micro-level social processes has accompanied advances in institutional change research, from a dominant focus on field-level change toward encompassing multiple levels, including the organization and individuals. Further, it is now acknowledged that it is not just institutional logics that shape cognition and behaviors but organizations and individuals, in turn, shape and challenge values and beliefs resulting in change (e.g., Thornton & Ocasio, 2008). All of these developments reconnect with the social constructivist roots of institutions but also open a greater opportunity and need for linguistic methods to capture the dynamic interplay between institutional fields, organizations and individual practices. Notably, recent work examines institutional processes inside hybrid organizations, embodying multiple logics with different degrees of incompatibility, and by their nature are 'arenas of contradictions' (Pache & Santos, 2013: 972). We argue that underlying these dynamics is the agency of organizational and individual actors that manifests through a linguistic process. A linguistic framework offers the potential to capture mechanisms to mitigate conflict and enhance compatibility. Rhetorical analysis, for example, could delve into the different communication and influence processes as groups of actors reconcile differences in the logics they hold.

In keeping with the increasing focus on the micro-level social processes in institutional research, the role of emotions in institutional change is another area of growing interest. Importantly, it presents an opportunity to add an emotional dimension to the strong cognitive flavor that currently dominates our conceptualization of social construction of institutions. As Voronov & Vince (2012: 59) note, ignoring emotional processes in institutional research may result in institutional theory falling back on a 'cognitive miser' conceptualization of individuals (Fiske & Taylor, 1991). Processes of social construction are not devoid of people's feelings, passions and interests that are bound to influence the creation of shared understandings.

In other words, emotional and cognitive dimensions inter-weave. In a process of social construction, emotions need to be captured not just as 'individual, psychological reactions but as intersubjective collective experiences' (Goodwin & Pfaff, 2001: 283). Recent work in the social movements realm draws attention to the role of emotions in the maintenance and transformation of institutions (e.g., Goodwin, Jasper, & Poletta, 2004) but only recently have institutional theorists started exploring the role of emotions at the micro level. For example, Creed, DeJordy and Lok (2010) show how dispersed actors resolve their personal and highly emotional experiences of institutional contradiction and marginalization, through identity construction work, by selectively amplifying institutionally available narratives and meanings.

There is much scope for systematic analysis of how emotions connect to cognitive processes in shaping institutional change. Specifically, we need more empirical work on how individuals' emotions affect the process of institutional reproduction and change in organizational hybrids when different groups of individuals experience internal dilemmas as they feel conflicted between logics or when they need to sever ties with entrenched beliefs. We suggest that discursive and narrative analyses could help to tease out the cognitive and emotional bases of resistance to change (Creed et al., 2010) and inform how it could be managed. Accordingly, there is an opportunity to build on nascent work on how organizations may use emotion-laden rhetorical strategies to persuade groups of actors to buy into a particular institutional logic (Brown, Ainsworth, & Grant, 2012).

Institutional work is another area where there has been increasing awareness of the importance of combining rational as well was emotional elements of human agency (e.g., Voronov & Vince, 2012). In fact, institutional work scholars have incorporated 'emotions'

in their definition of institution as 'providing templates for action, cognition and emotion' (Lawrence et al., 2011: 53). Discursive processes, narratives and rhetoric are infused with emotion but there is a methodological challenge to understand how to recognize and isolate the influence of emotions in a process of social construction. We argue that linguistic methods offer a way forward.

CONCLUSIONS

In this chapter we have explored how linguistic methods can advance our theoretical and empirical grasp of the cognitive construction of institutions. We believe the recent shift in focus from stability and conformity to institutional change and an interest in redressing the balance between structure and agency have been important in directing scholarly attention toward the microfoundations of institutional processes. Consequently, we believe it is timely to restate and defend a cognitive conceptualization of institutions and to highlight the importance of social construction as fundamental to the process of institutionalization. We also believe that the growing awareness of language in institutional theory bodes well for pursuing the social constructivist perspective of institutions and institutionalization and wish to contribute to this stream of work.

In restating the arguments for a cognitive view of institutions and exploring the potential of linguistic methods in their conceptualization and investigation, we make three main contributions. First, we explain why we run the risk of losing touch with the cognitive nature of institutions and why we need to take this risk seriously. We point out that if institutions are fundamentally cognitive, then the three pillars framework of Scott (2001) that has become so dominant in institutional analysis has been more limiting than helpful in developing our understanding of the nature of institutions. By combining the regulatory, normative and cultural-cognitive pillars that can lead to isomorphism into the definition of an institution, the framework has something for everyone, but it raises critical theoretical and philosophical problems. The fact that coercive and normative mechanisms are externally managed by other actors makes them very different from the taken-for-grantedness of cognitive mechanisms.

Douglas (1986: 10) makes this argument very clearly when she says that '[e]pistemological resources may be able to explain what cannot be explained by the theory of rational behavior'. In other words, theories of rational behavior explain the responses of actors to coercive and normative mechanisms; cognitive mechanisms explain something very different and this is the proper domain of institutional theory.

Second, we describe the merits of adopting a linguistic perspective on the process of institutionalization. A number of linguistic methods – rhetorical analysis, narrative analysis, discourse analysis and semiotics – provide both a theoretical and methodological toolkit to explain the cognitive nature of institutions and expose the unresolved tensions around the nature of an institution. We illustrate how different linguistic methods have been used in institutional research and highlight their potential to further expand our understanding of current theoretical issues as well as emerging ones.

Third, in reconnecting institutional theory with social construction we re-emphasize the broad interest in culture and language that has played such an important part in new and neo-institutional theory. Even a cursory examination of the literature reveals a preponderance of empirical studies and theoretical discussion focused on taken-for-grantedness and the dynamics of the underlying cognitive processes. The connection with social construction and linguistic methods provides new opportunities for studying institutions and institutionalization from a cultural perspective.

In closing, we hope that the themes we have explored in this chapter explain some of our enthusiasm for the subject. We believe

that institutional theory is at a crossroads and risks in some ways trying to be everything to everyone. While a multiplicity of approaches and views is a sign of robust health, it can also wear away at the infrastructure that provided the impetus for discussion in the first place. In some ways, perhaps we have overshot – in trying to move away from a theory that was unnecessarily narrow we have developed one that is impractically broad. We believe that institutional theory needs to return to its roots in social constructionism and the wellspring of creative thought that this produced. While this will necessitate a narrowing of our understanding of what an institution *is*, it will also provide a renewed ability to understand how it works. Zucker's call to focus on the microprocesses of institutional production at the macro-level has been ignored for too long!

Notes

1   We use the term institutional theory in this chapter to refer to the stream of literature running from new institutional theory down through more recent developments in neo-institutional theory. When we wish to differentiate between new and neo-institutionalism we will identify them explicitly. References to other forms of institutionalism will be made explicitly (e.g., old institutionalism or institutional economics).

2   We refer to the family of related methods including discourse analysis, narrative analysis, rhetorical analysis and semiotics as 'linguistic methods' as they are all based on the insights into the role of language in social construction developed during the linguistic turn in the humanities and social sciences.

3   There are, of course, a number of other linguistic methods, such as hermeneutics, content analysis and conversation analysis. However, given the limited space we have for our discussion here, we will focus on the four methods that we feel are most useful for institutional research.

REFERENCES

Alvesson, M., & Karreman, D. (2000). Taking the linguistic turn in organizational research: Challenges, responses, consequences. *Journal of Applied Behavioral Science*, *36*(2), 136–158.

Aristotle (1991). *The art of rhetoric*. New York: Penguin Books.

Bakhtin, M. M. (1981). *The dialogic imagination: Four essays by MM Bakhtin* (M. Holquist, Ed.; C. Emerson & M. Holquist, Trans.). Volume 1 of University of Texas Press Slavic Series.

Barley, S.R. (1983). Semiotics and the study of occupational and organizational cultures. *Administrative Science Quarterly, 28*(3): 393–413.

Baron, J. N., & Bielby, W. T. (1986). The proliferation of job titles in organizations. *Administrative Science Quarterly, 31*(4), 561–586.

Barthes, R. (1967). *Elements of semiology*. New York: Hill & Wang.

Barthes, R. (1988). *The semiotic challenge*. New York: Hill & Wang.

Berger, B., & Luckmann, T. (1967). *The social construction of reality: A treatise on the sociology of knowledge*. Garden City, NY: Anchor.

Boje, D. M. (2001). *Narrative methods for organizational and communication research*. London: Sage.

Boje, D. M. (2008). *Storytelling organizations*. London: Sage.

Brannen, M. Y. (2004). When Mickey loses face: Recontextualization, semantic fit, and the semiotics of foreignness. *Academy of Management Review, 29*(4), 593–616.

Brown A. D., Ainsworth S., & Grant D. (2012). The rhetoric of institutional change. *Organization Studies, 33*(3), 297–321.

Burke, K. (1969 [1945]). *A grammar of motives*. New York: Prentice-Hall.

Carroll, G. R., Goodstein, J., & Gyenes, J. (1988). Organizations and the state: Effects of the institutional environment on agricultural cooperatives in Hungary. *Administrative Science Quarterly, 33*, 233–256.

Chia, R. (2000). Discourse analysis as organization analysis. *Organization, 7*(3), 513–518.

Commons, J. R. (1924). *The legal foundations of capitalism*. New York: Macmillan.

Cooley, C. H. (1956 [1902]). *Social organization*. Glencoe, IL: Free Press.

Creed, W. D., DeJordy, R., & Lok, J. (2010). Being the change: Resolving institutional contradiction through identity work. *Academy of Management Journal, 53*(6), 1336–1364.

Czarniawska, B. (2004). *Narratives in social science research*. London: Sage.

David, R. J., Sine, W. D., & Haveman, H. A. (2013). Seizing opportunity in emerging fields: How institutional entrepreneurs legitimated the professional form of management consulting. *Organization Science, 24*(2), 356–377.

Davis, K. (1949). *Human society*. New York: Macmillan.

Deely, J. (1990). *Basics of semiotics*. Bloomington, IN: Indiana University Press.

DiMaggio, P. (1988). 'Interest and agency in institutional theory'. In L. G. Zucker (Ed.), *Institutional patterns and organizations: Culture and environment* (pp. 3–21). Cambridge, MA: Ballinger Publishing Co./Harper & Row Publishers.

DiMaggio, P. J., & Powell, W. W. (1983). The iron cage revisited: Institutional isomorphism and collective rationality in organizational fields. *American Sociological Review, 48*, 147–160.

DiMaggio, P., & Powell, W. (1991). Introduction. In W. W. Powell and P. J. DiMaggio (Eds.), *The new institutionalism in organizational analysis* (pp. 1–38). Chicago, IL: University of Chicago Press.

Douglas, M. (1986). *How institutions think*. Syracuse, NY: Syracuse University Press.

Eco, U. (1976). *A theory of semiotics*. Bloomington, IN: Indiana University Press.

Eisenhardt, K. M. (1988). Agency-theory and institutional theory explanations: The case of retail sales compensation. *Academy of Management Journal, 31*(3), 488–511.

Fennell, M. L., & Alexander, J. A. (1987). Organizational boundary spanning in institutionalized environments. *Academy of Management Journal, 30*(3), 456–476.

Fiol, C. M. (1989). A semiotic analysis of corporate language: Organizational boundaries and joint venturing. *Administrative Science Quarterly, 34*(2), 277–303.

Fiske, S. T., & Taylor, S. E. (1991). *Social cognition*, 2nd edn. New York: McGraw-Hill.

Fligstein, N. (1987). The intraorganizational power struggle: The rise of finance presidents in large corporations, 1919–1979. *American Sociological Review, 52*, 44–58.

Gabriel, Y. (2000). *Storytelling in organizations. Facts, fictions and fantasies*. Oxford: Oxford University Press.

Gabriel, Y. (2004). Narratives, stories and texts. In D. Grant, C. Hardy, C. Oswick, & L. Putnam (Eds.), *The handbook of organizational discourse* (pp. 61–78). London: Sage.

Geertz, C. (1973). *The interpretation of cultures: Selected essays*. New York: Basic Books.

Gergen, K. (1999). *An invitation to social construction*. London: Sage.

Goodwin, J., & Pfaff, S. (2001). Emotion work in high-risk social movements: Managing fear in the US and East German civil rights movements. In J. Goodwin, J. M. Jasper, & F. Polletta (Eds.), *Passionate politics: Emotions and social movements* (pp. 282–302). Chicago, IL: University of Chicago Press.

Goodwin, J., Jasper, J. M., & Polletta, F. (2004). *Emotional dimensions of social movements*. Oxford: Blackwell.

Grant, D., & Hardy, C. (2004). Introduction: Struggles with organizational discourse, *Organization Studies, 25*(1), 5–13.

Green, S. E. (2004). A rhetorical theory of diffusion. *Academy of Management Review*, *29*(4), 653–669.

Green Jr, S. E., & Li, Y. (2011). Rhetorical institutionalism: Language, agency, and structure in institutional theory since Alvesson 1993. *Journal of Management Studies*, *48*(7), 1662–1697.

Green Jr, S. E., Li, Y., & Nohria, N. (2009). Suspended in self-spun webs of significance: A rhetorical model of institutionalization and institutionally embedded agency. *Academy of Management Journal*, *52*(1), 11–36.

Hallett, T., & Ventresca, M. J. (2006). Inhabited institutions: Social interactions and organizational forms in Gouldner's patterns of industrial bureaucracy. *Theory and Society*, *35*(2), 213–236.

Hamilton, G., & Biggart, N. W. (1988). Market, culture and authority: A comparative analysis of management and organization in the Far East. *American Journal of Sociology*, *94* (Supplement), S52–S94.

Hardy, C., & Maguire, S. (2010). Discourse, field-configuring events, and change in organizations and institutional fields: narratives of DDT and the Stockholm convention. *Academy of Management Journal*, *53*(6), 1365–1392.

Harmon, D. J., Green, S. E., & Goodnight, G. T. (2015). A model of rhetorical legitimation: The structure of communication and cognition underlying institutional maintenance and change. *Academy of Management Review*, *40*(1), 76–95.

Harvey, J. H. (1995). Accounts. In A. S. R. Manstead and M. Hewstone (Eds.), *The Blackwell Encyclopedia of Social Psychology* (pp. 3–5). Oxford: Basil Blackwell.

Heracleous, L., & Barrett, M. (2001). Organizational change as discourse: Communicative actions and deep structures in the context of information technology implementation. *Academy of Management Journal*, *44*, 755–778.

Hirsch, P. (1997). Sociology without social structure: Neo-institutional theory meets brave new world. *American Journal of Sociology*, *102*, 1702–1723.

Hodge, R., & Kress, G. (1988). *Social semiotics*. Cambridge: Polity Press.

Hoffman, A. (1997). *From heresy to dogma: An institutional history of corporate environmentalism*. San Francisco: New Lexington Press.

Hughes, E. C. (1936). The ecological aspect of institutions. *American Sociological Review*, *1*, 180–189.

Lawrence T.B., & Phillips, N. (2004). From Moby Dick to Free Willy: Macro-cultural discourse and institutional entrepreneurship in emerging institutional fields, *Organization*, 11, 689–711.

Lawrence, T. B., Suddaby, R., & Leca, B. (2011). Institutional work: Refocusing institutional studies of organization. *Journal of Management Inquiry, 20*(1) 52–58.

Lincoln, J. R., Hanada, M., & McBride, K. (1986). Organizational structures in Japanese and United States manufacturing. *Administrative Science Quarterly*, *31*(3), 403–421.

Lounsbury, M., & Glynn, M. A. (2001). Cultural entrepreneurship: Stories, legitimacy, and the acquisition of resources. *Strategic Management Journal*, *22*(6–7), 545–564.

Maguire, S., & Hardy, C. (2009). Discourse and deinstitutionalization: The decline of DDT. *Academy of Management Journal*, *52*(1): 148–178.

Mead, H. (1934). *Mind, self and society*. Chicago, IL: University of Chicago Press.

Menger, C. (1981 [1871]). *Problems of economics and sociology* (F. J. Nock, Trans.). Urbana, IL: University of Illinois Press.

Meyer, J., & Rowan, B. (1977). Institutionalized organizations: Formal structure as myth and ceremony. *American Journal of Sociology*, *83*, 340–363.

Meyer, J. W., & Scott, W. R. (1983). *Organizational environments*. Beverley Hills, CA: Sage.

Munir, K., & Phillips, N. (2005). The birth of the 'Kodak moment': Institutional entrepreneurship and the adoption of new technologies. *Organization*, *26*: 1665–1687.

North, D. R. (1990). *Institutions, institutional change, and economic performance*. Cambridge: Cambridge University Press.

Oakes, L. S., Townley, B., & Cooper, D. J. (1998). Business planning as pedagogy: Language and control in a changing institutional field. *Administrative Science Quarterly*, *43*, 257–292.

Pache, A-C., & Santos, F. (2013). Inside the hybrid organization: Selective coupling as a response to competing institutional logics. *Academy of Management Journal*, *56* (4), 972–1001.

Pfeffer, J., & Davis-Blake, A. (1987). The effect of the proportion of women on salaries: The case of college administrators. *Administrative Science Quarterly*, *32* (1), 1–24.

Phillips, N. (1995). Telling organizational tales: On the role of narrative fiction in the study of organizations. *Organization Studies*, *16*(4), 625–649.

Phillips, N., & Di Domenico, M. (2009). Discourse analysis in organizational research: Methods and debates. In David Buchanan and Alan Bryman (Eds.), *The SAGE Handbook of Organizational Research Methods* (pp. 549–565). London: Sage.

Phillips, N., & Hardy, C. (2002). *Discourse analysis: Investigating processes of social construction*. Thousand Oaks, CA: Sage.

Phillips, N., Lawrence, T. B., & Hardy, C. (2004). Discourse and institutions. *Academy of Management Review*, *29*, 635–652.

Phillips, N., & Oswick, C. (2012). Organizational discourse: Domains, debates, and directions. *Academy of Management Annals*, *6*, 435–481.

Polkinghorne, D. (1988). *Narrative knowing and the human sciences*. Albany, NY: State University of New York Press.

Powell, W. (1991). Expanding the scope of institutional analysis. In W. W. Powell and P. J. DiMaggio (Eds.),

The new institutionalism in organizational analysis (pp. 183–203). Chicago, IL: University of Chicago Press.

Rhodes, C., & Brown, A. D. (2005). Narrative, organizations and research. *International Journal of Management Reviews, 7*(3), 167–188.

Saussure, F. de (1974 [1916]). *Course in general linguistics*. London: Fontana.

Schutz, A. (1967 [1932]). *The phenomenology of the social world* (George Walsh and Frederick Lehnart, Trans.). Evanston, IL: North Western University Press.

Scott, W. R. (1987). The adolescence of institutional theory. *Administrative Science Quarterly, 32*, 493–511.

Scott, W. R. (2001). *Institutions and organizations*. Thousand Oaks, CA: Sage.

Scott, W. R. (2004). Reflections on a half-century of organization sociology. *Annual Review of Sociology, 30*, 1–21.

Selznick, P. (1948). Foundations of the theory of organization. *American Sociological Review, 13*, 25–35.

Selznick, P. (1957). *Leadership in administration*. Evanston, IL: Row, Peterson.

Sillince, J. A., & Suddaby, R. (2008). Organizational rhetoric: Bridging management and communication scholarship. *Management Communication Quarterly, 22*, 5–13.

Smith, C. P. (2000). 'Content analysis and narrative analysis', in T. Reis and C. Judd (Eds.), *Handbook of research methods in social and personality psychology* (pp. 313–335). Cambridge: Cambridge University Press.

Spence, D. P. (1982) *Narrative truth and historical truth: meaning and interpretation in psychoanalysis*, New York: Norton.

Steyaert, C., & Katz, J. (2004). Reclaiming the space of entrepreneurship in society: geographical, discursive and social dimensions. *Entrepreneurship & Regional Development, 16*(3), 179–196.

Strang, D., & Meyer, J. W. (1993). Institutional conditions for diffusion. *Theory and Society, 22*, 487–511.

Suchman, M. C. (1995). Managing legitimacy: Strategic and institutional approaches. *Academy of Management Review, 20*(3), 571–610.

Suddaby, R., & Greenwood, R. (2005). Rhetorical strategies of legitimacy. *Administrative Science Quarterly, 50*, 35–67.

Sumner, G. (1906). *Folkways*. Boston: Ginn & Co.

Swidler, A., (1986). Culture in action: Symbols and strategies. *American Sociological Review, 51*(2), 273–286.

Taylor, J. R., & Van Every, E. J. (1993). *The vulnerable fortress: Bureaucratic organization in the information age*. Toronto: University of Toronto.

Thornton, P., & Ocasio, W. (2008). 'Institutional logics'. In R. Greenwood, C. Oliver, R. Suddaby, &

K. Sahlin-Andersson (Eds), *The SAGE handbook of organizational institutionalism* (pp. 99–129). Thousand Oaks, CA: Sage.

Tolbert, P. S. (1985). Institutional environments and resource dependence: Sources of administrative structure in institutions of higher education. *Administrative Science Quarterly, 30*(1), 1–13.

Tolbert, P. S., & Zucker, L. G. (1983). Institutional sources of change in the formal structure of organizations: The diffusion of civil service reform, 1880–1935. *Administrative Science Quarterly, 30*, 22–39.

Toulmin, S. E. (1958). *The uses of argument*. Cambridge: Cambridge University Press.

Vaara, E., & Tiernari, J. (2011). On the narrative construction of multinational corporations: an antenarrative analysis of legitimation and resistance in a cross-border merger. *Organization Science, 22*(2), 370–390.

Van de Ven, A. H. (1993). The institutional theory of John R. Commons: A review and commentary. *Academy of Management Review, 18*, 129–152.

Veblen, T. B. (1909). The limitations of marginal utility. *Journal of Political Economy, 17*, 235–245.

Voronov, M., & Vince, R. (2012). Integrating emotions into the analysis of institutional work. *Academy of Management Review, 37*(1), 58–81.

Weber, K., & Dacin, M. T. (2011). The cultural construction of organizational life: Introduction to the special issue. *Organization Science, 22*(2), 287–298.

Weber, K., Heinze, K. L., & DeSoucey, M. (2008). Forage for thought: Mobilizing codes in the movement for grass-fed meat and dairy products. *Administrative Science Quarterly, 53*(3), 529–567.

Wry, T., Lounsbury, M., & Glynn, M. A. (2011). Legitimating nascent collective identities: Coordinating cultural entrepreneurship. *Organization Science, 22*(2), 449–463.

Zilber, T. B. (2002). Institutionalization as an interplay between actions, meanings, and actors: The case of a rape crisis center in Israel. *Academy of Management Journal, 45*(1), 234–254.

Zilber, T. B. (2006). The work of meaning in institutional processes: Translations of rational myths in Israeli Hi-Tech. *Academy of Management Journal, 49*(2), 279–301.

Zott, C., & Huy, Q. N. (2007). How entrepreneurs use symbolic management to acquire resources. *Administrative Science Quarterly, 52*(1), 70–105.

Zucker, L. (1977). The role of institutionalization in cultural persistence. *American Sociological Review, 42*, 726–743.

Zucker, L. (1991). The role of institutionalization in cultural persistence. In W. W. Powell and P. J. DiMaggio (Eds.), *The new institutionalism in organizational analysis* (pp. 83–107). Chicago, IL: University of Chicago Press.

16

The Evolving Role of Meaning in Theorizing Institutions

Tammar B. Zilber

The interest in the role of meanings in institutional theory has fluctuated throughout the years. Meanings were at the heart of early neo-institutional thinking, as scholars were arguing that organizations tend to imitate what they conceive to be the idea of a good organization (e.g., DiMaggio & Powell, 1983; Meyer & Rowan, 1977; Zucker, 1977). Contrary to other open-system theories, which underscored the technical, resource-based influences of the environment on organizations, neo-institutionalism's unique contribution has been the articulation of how shared meanings, rules and ideas constitute institutions and their power over organizations (Scott, 2001). Yet, in subsequent studies, which aimed at fleshing out the main arguments of this line of theorizing, the empirical exploration of meaning – and its nuanced theoretical implications – were somewhat neglected. In the 1980s and 1990s, meaning was assumed and taken for granted rather than explored, as scholars were focusing mainly on institutionalized structures and

practices. The explicit discussion of the actual work of meaning in institutional processes had been thus quite limited in that period (Dobbin, 1994a; Friedland & Alford, 1991; Hasselbladh & Kallinikos, 2000). Since the mid-1990s we have seen a renewed interest in the ideational aspects of institutional processes (Zilber, 2008) and still, such studies were quite peripheral to the dominant study of structures and practices. Scholars tended to remain focused on the empirical aspects of meanings rather than rethinking institutions in light of them. Only in the mid-2000s do we see a surge of new theoretical sub-streams along with empirical work that place meanings at the center of theoretical attention. So much so, that these days, critical voices urge institutional theorist to problematize taken-for-granted understating of meaning as a linguistic phenomenon, and go beyond verbal – spoken or written – texts, to explore how meanings are mediated through the emotional, the corporeal, the visual and the material in institutional dynamics (e.g., Meyer, Höellerer, Jancsary, & Van Leeuwen, 2013; Voronov & Vince, 2012).

In this chapter, I explore how meaning has been figuring in theorizing institutions throughout the years. My aim is twofold: offering a reading of institutional processes as depicted by studies that deal with meanings; and, on another level of analysis, pointing to the institutionalization of the study of meanings by the community of scholars who work within neo-institutional theory and its paradigmatic assumptions. Based on a review of empirical studies and conceptual formulations, I argue that studies that examine the dynamics of meanings in institutionalization moved from the periphery to the center of our discipline, and on the way re-claimed the social constructionist approach from which institutional theory had originated in the late 1970s. Looking forward, the study of meaning holds promise to further expand scholars' view of institutional dynamics, and to change our understanding of the inhabitants of institutions.

I start with a short exposition of what I mean by 'meaning', and then offer a review of three phases in the study of meanings in institutional theory – early conceptualizations (mid-1960s to 1990s); empirical surge (1990s to mid-2000s); and a conceptual-driven surge (since the mid-2000s). While in reality these stages are of course not that cut and clear, the historical-analytical timeline and the distinctions I suggest are helpful, I believe, in understanding how the conceptual and empirical treatment of meanings within institutional theory evolved throughout the years. Finally, I will discuss a few new directions in rethinking meaning in institutional theory.

THE MEANING OF 'MEANING'

While the role of meanings was central to early theoretical formulations of neo-institutional thinking, to date we do not have an agreed-upon terminology for 'meaning' or a clear definition thereof. Thus, I chose to craft this review using a bottom-up approach. Rather than offer a conclusive definition of 'meaning', I follow the way meanings (expressed through a family of terms) were dealt with by scholars who publish their work within the community of institutional scholars. Through a content analysis of published works that deal with 'meaning' and institutionalization, I came to (one possible) understanding of what institutional scholars consider as 'meaning' and what they conceive as its role in institutional processes.

Since reference to 'meanings' can be made without using the word *meaning*, and given the multitude of concepts used to denote the ideational (e.g., meaning, culture, myth, discourse, text), my selection of articles was not based on linguistic markers alone, but on a wide definition of meaning and careful, contextualized reading. Meaning is defined as 'what is intended to be, or actually is, expressed or indicated' (Random House Webster's 1998: 1191). Accordingly, I use the term 'meaning' to denote those aspects of institutions that are ideational and at times even symbolic, to distinguish them from the material aspects of institutions, like structures and practices. Of course, meaning and the material are intertwined. In the empirical world they constitute each other. Meanings are encoded in structures and practices, while structures and practices express and affect those meanings. Still, for analytical purposes, it is worthwhile to focus our attention on meaning alone, and take stock of how we theorize its dynamics, and its implications for understanding institutional processes.

I looked for empirical studies and theoretical formulations that explicitly deal with meanings in institutional processes. Many, if not most, publications in the area of institutional theory pay respect to meaning, as part of the institutional explanatory model, without directly measuring it or dealing with its dynamics (Mohr, 1998: 347). I looked for articles that treat 'meanings' – broadly defined – as their *main* concern. These include theoretical conceptualizations that deal with the role of meanings in institutional processes, as well as empirical investigations that use a case study to explore meanings and their dynamics. I started my search with a central database of journals, the 'Web of Science', using the key word 'institution*' and looking for papers that were published in the various outlets included in this database in the field of organizational theory (e.g., *Academy of Management Journal, Academy of Management Review, Administrative Science Quarterly, Organization Studies, Organization Science, Human Relations, Journal of Management, Journal of Management Inquiry, Journal of Management Studies*) as well as in sociology (*American Journal of Sociology, American Sociological Review*). Next, since works that deal with meanings are somewhat peripheral in our field (using qualitative research methods,[1] and often carried out by European scholars), I tried to be more inclusive by following the bibliographies of journal articles in a snowball manner, to trace articles that were published elsewhere, as well as relevant books and book chapters.

Once the data set was compiled, I used the tools of my trade to analyze it. I conducted a content analysis (Lieblich, 1998) of these works, looking for the specific ways they define and use 'meaning'. I read each paper, noting its theoretical question, methodological approach and the way it portrays the role of meanings in institutional processes. I then analyzed the collection of articles, looking for similarities between these depictions and compiling those clusters of articles along a timeline.

While I am interested in the role of meaning in institutional processes, I am not interested in meanings for their own sake. Rather, my focus is on how the exploration of meanings sheds light on institutions and institutional processes. The very study of meanings informed, and even changed, I argue, our understanding of institutions and institutionalization. Thus, my review will revolve around meanings, institutions and institutionalization. While meaning is my main focus and central concept, in order to highlight how it enriches our understanding of institutions and institutionalization, these concepts will at times take over.

MID 1960s TO 1990s: EARLY BEGINNINGS

The emphasis on meaning was at the heart of neo-institutional thinking in its early formulations in the 1970s. Neo-institutionalism was anchored in the idea that organizations are embedded in institutions and much reference was made to shared meanings, knowledge, culture and myths. Institutions were understood as social constructions (Berger & Luckmann, 1966), that is, shared structures, practices and meaning systems that come to be taken for granted through their repeated social enactment – which involves, first and foremost, language and other symbolic expressions and artifacts. More specifically, Meyer and Rowan underscored the constructivist aspects of organizations by using the notion of 'institutionalized *myths*', relating to 'rationalized and impersonal prescriptions that identify various social purposes as technical ones and specify in a rule-like way the appropriate means to pursue these technical purposes rationally … [These myths are] beyond the discretion of any individual participant or organization … [they are] taken for granted as legitimate, apart from evaluations of their impact' (1977: 343–344). In sharp contrast to functionalist theories of organizational structure, Meyer and Rowan (1977) claimed that organizations are 'dramatic enactments of the rationalized myths pervading modern societies' (p. 346). In the face of modern pride in efficiency, objectivity and logical, scientific reasoning, the main idea of institutions as social construction allowed then to explicate the paradoxical nature of institutions as mere shared myths. While the adoption of institutionalized elements (structures and practices) may not ensure the effective operation of an organization, it will confer legitimacy upon it, and this legitimacy is critical to its survival: 'vocabularies of structure which are isomorphic with institutional rules provide prudent, rational, and legitimate accounts. Organizations described in legitimated vocabularies are assumed to be oriented to collectively defined, and often collectively mandated, ends' (p. 349).

Zucker, in her study of cultural persistence (1977), highlighted the specific role of meaning in institutionalization. Treating institutionalization as a dependent variable and looking for independent variables to explain it, she claimed that it is the meaning of an act – the degree to which it is '*perceived* to be more or less exterior and objective' (p. 728) – that determines the degree of its institutionalization. Moreover, she also studied the effect of institutionalization on the transmission, maintenance and resistance of cultural understandings.

In their quest to define the isomorphic forces at play in institutionalization, DiMaggio and Powell (1983) followed suit with an inquiry into the role of ideational elements in structuring organizations (and organizational fields). Specifically, they explicated mechanisms through which meanings influence organizations. Each of the isomorphic pressures on organizations they outlined – the coercive, mimetic and normative – was extracted from, and built upon, *cultural expectations, shared cognitions and beliefs*. The isomorphic forces were described then as 'great rationalizing' forces in action.

And finally, in his 'omnibus' conceptualization of institutions, Scott argued early on and throughout the years (most lately 2014) that institutions have regulative, normative and *cultural-cognitive* elements. The latter 'involves the creation of shared conceptions that constitute the nature of social reality and the frames through which meaning is made' (Scott, 2003: 880). The cultural-cognitive pillar of institutions directs explicit theoretical attention to the taken-for-granted meanings that underlie the institutional order.

The emphasis on meaning is further reflected in Scott's (2001) conceptualization of four types of 'institutional carriers' – artifacts (material culture), routines (habitualized behavior), relational systems (personal and organizational networks) and symbolic systems. Symbolic systems carry institutions, Scott explains (2003: 882), through diverse 'schemata into which meaningful information is coded and conveyed'.

Meaning, then, had a central place in the development of early neo-institutional thinking. In fact, it is the attention to meanings, knowledge, culture and symbols – the non-technical environment, as it was termed – that is considered to distinguish the neo-institutional school from its 'old' predecessor, as well as from other open system theories in our discipline that underscore the material, technical and functional aspects of organizational environments (Scott, 2001). Notwithstanding this theoretical emphasis on meaning, most empirical studies of institutionalization during the 1980s–1990s focused on structures and practices, relegating meaning to the background (see also, Farashahi, Hafsi, & Molz, 2005; Glynn & Abzug, 2002; Hasselbladh & Kallinikos, 2000; Jepperson, 1991; Suddaby, 2010; Zilber, 2002, 2008).

How may we explain this empirical neglect of meanings? I suggest three explanations, all framed in neo-institutional terms. The first has to do with a taken-for-granted assumption about the central social carrier of institutions, the second is an outcome of a taken-for-granted epistemological assumption about the connection between meanings and their signifiers, and the third is related to the legitimate method for exploring institutions within Organizational Studies. First, the neglect of meanings may be related to the 'typical American version' of institutional theory, which perceives the 'rational actor' as a central carrier of institutions: 'These actors have prior purposes, clear boundaries, definite technologies, unified sovereignty, clear internal control systems, and definite and discrete resources to employ. This starting point makes it difficult to think about institutional processes as involving the travel of *ideas*' (Meyer, 1996: 241–242). Rational actors are in full control over their actions, motivated by goals that they pursue through the use of technologies and the resources at their disposal. While they do act in relation to meaning systems, such meanings and symbolic worlds have hardly any power of their own, and so have little place in exploring institutions.

Second, since neo-institutionalists hold that 'institutional beliefs, rules and roles come to be coded into the structure' of organizations (Scott, 1987: 506), in most institutional studies, the very institutionalization of a structure or practice is taken to testify that it won legitimacy – without probing into the meanings and ideational processes involved. Researchers studied structural and practical dimensions of institutions, assuming – rather than directly studying – their symbolic, meaningful character.

Third, methodological preferences may be responsible as well (Bowring, 2000; Schneiberg & Clemens, 2007). Again, in the lingo of institutional theory itself, longitudinal, quantitative studies are the taken-for-granted best-practices in our discipline (Bluhm, Harman, Lee, & Mitchell, 2011). Beyond their own epistemological, intrinsic justifications, they serve as a social resource that confers legitimacy, whereas qualitative studies, by contrast, do not quite fit within 'the way things are regularly done'. In particular, meanings elude quantification, do not allow for causal inferences and explanations in the form of correlations between clear-cut causes and effects. Instead, meanings call for 'after the fact' interpretations, and for case studies with thick contextualized descriptions and analytic, rather than empirical, generalizations (Schwandt, 2001) – all of which do not fit nicely with the positivistic paradigm current in our discipline (Amis & Silk, 2008).

As a result of the above institutionalized assumptions and pressures, many studies of the 1980s and early 1990s were based on, and contributed to, the conceptualization of institutionalization as *diffusion* (Creed, Scully, &

Austin, 2002; Czarniawska & Joerges, 1996; for reviews, see Boxenbaum and Jonsson, 2008; Strang & Soule, 1998; Whitson, Weber, Hirsch, & Bermiss, 2013). They followed the diffusion of clearly defined structures and practices across an institutional field, using quantitative, longitudinal and macro-level methodologies based on a positivistic paradigm. The imagery of institutionalization created by such studies was of a universal and deterministic process, made of separate steps (Sahlin-Andersson, 1996): More and more firms adopt – sooner or later – a certain institutionalized structure or practice. Adoption itself was evaluated and measured using quantitative means. So, while institutionalization was understood as a dynamic process, the process itself, once set forth, was not problematized. It was understood instead as moving smoothly along a path, with no changes occurring from source to target. It was thus considered as a question of volume (how many firms adopted it) rather than quality (what does it mean to adopt, what is exactly adopted). Moreover, the focus on diffusion 'across a single community' (Strang & Soule, 1998: 279) created a sense of a universal, homogeneous process of diffusion, one that is affected by characteristics of organizations and their interrelations, no matter where these organizations reside. Furthermore, since these studies were carried on the macro-level, usually focusing on the organizational field level, they neglected micro-processes and issues of power and politics within and without organizations (DiMaggio, 1988).

1990s TO MID 2000s: UNPACKING MEANING FROM THE PERIPHERY

Between the 1990s and the mid-2000s, we see a renewed interest in meanings in institutionalization. The linguistic turn (Alvesson & Karreman, 2000), the insistence on the importance of qualitative research methods (Van Maanen, 1998), and of critical approaches

(Alvesson & Deetz, 1996) within our discipline, all related also to the influence of European-based scholars (Usdiken & Pasadeos, 1995), contributed much to this change. Still, while a surge in studies was evident, it was also characterized by a somewhat peripheral position, in at least two ways. First, studies of meanings were peripheral to the mainstream studies in the North American tradition. Second, analytically, there were many studies, but hardly any integration of the new formulations about the work of meanings in institutional dynamics. As well, hardly any new overarching conceptual vocabulary to discuss institutions was developed – which could have been instrumental to that end. Rather, each study of meaning seemed quite isolated, and each scholar seemed busy refining our understanding of institutionalization by creating his or her own language and terms in order to explore that which is not the diffusion of structures or practices as such.

These limitations notwithstanding, when taken together, studies of meaning in the 1990s and early 2000s complicated our understanding of the work of meanings in institutionalization. Using mostly qualitative data – interviews, archival texts and participant observations, and drawing mostly on analyzing the contents of meaning– these studies probe into meanings as important sources upon which institutionalization rests. Breaking down and dissecting meanings in new and innovating analyses, these studies highlight four dimensions of institutions – their particularity, embeddedness within specific contexts, political and on-going nature. These attributes are of course interconnected, but for the sake of analytical clarity I will explain and exemplify each separately.

The Particularities of Institutionalization

Rather than depicting institutionalization as governed by universal laws, studies of meanings in the 1990s and early 2000s highlighted the particularities of the process, and the importance of *specific*, locally interpreted, meanings in explaining the micro-processes of (de)institutionalization, both on the organizational (Prasad & Prasad, 1994; Ritti & Silver, 1986; Wicks, 2001; Zilber, 2002) and field levels (e.g., Clark & Jennings, 1997; DiMaggio & Mullen, 2000; Ferguson, 1998; Hargadon & Douglas, 2001; Quaid, 1993; Rao, Monin, & Durand, 2003; Scheid-Cook, 1992; Townley, 2002).

For example, exploring a mine explosion, Wicks (2001) pointed out the crucial role of institutionalizing a 'mindset of invulnerability' embodied in these Canadian coal miners' masculine identity, and thus the embrace or downplaying of risk in their job. Exploring the rise of nouvelle cuisine in French gastronomy, Rao and colleagues (2003) highlighted the role of identity – meanings ascribed to the role of chefs and the various practices they employ – as central to the diffusion of a new institutional logic within the field.

Further, scholars started looking more carefully at what actors within organizations field actually do with shared meanings. Townley (2002) shows how the introduction of a new practice of business planning and performance evaluation to a division of the provincial government in Alberta, Canada, was affected by the meanings relevant actors saw in them. Using Weber's typology of four types of rationality as an interpretative schema, she follows the ways her informants made sense of the changes, and how these different understandings shaped their reactions to it.

No less important, once the particularities of institutionalization were explored more closely, it was found that the seemingly same institutional practices and structures may be infused with different meanings by different actors, and hence have differential institutional effects. In her study of a rape crisis center, Zilber (2002) demonstrated how as the center evolved under the dual, sometimes competing, institutional pressures of a feminist ideology and a therapeutic worldview, the same institutionalized practices were understood differentially by different members. Practices that originated from a feminist ideology and were understood as such by members who carried the feminist institution, were reinterpreted by therapeutically oriented members as reflecting a therapeutic rationale. Based on this ethnographic study, Zilber argued that the difference in interpretation – the work of meaning – allowed for the co-existence of the two quite different institutions in one organization. At the field level as well, DiMaggio and Mullen (2000) showed how the seemingly same practice – the ritual of 'music week' – was celebrated differentially in different communities across the United States. They connected the various constructions of the 'music week' as a civic ritual to various characteristics of the local communities. These studies show, then, that to fully understand the dynamics of institutionalization, one must attend not only to institutionalized structures and practices, but to their specific and diverse meanings as well.

Institutionalization in Context

Studies of meaning in institutional processes in the 1990s and early 2000s underscored the complex connections and interactions between institutions and the meaningful environments within which they are embedded – both at the organizational field and the societal levels (e.g., Holm, 1995; Lawrence & Phillips, 2004; Zilber, 2006a, 2006b). In her study of Israeli hi-tech industry, Zilber (2006a) followed the imagery of Israeli hi-tech in two social arenas (the societal versus the field level), and through time (the boom and bust of the hi-tech industry world-wide). Zilber connects the prevalent myths of Israeli hi-tech to generic myths in Israeli society and demonstrates how the same cultural building blocks were used differentially in different institutional arenas and in different points in time. This process of translation of generic into specific myths in the process of institutionalization, argued

Zilber, was related to material fluctuations over time and to the dynamics of the different institutional arenas. The broad context of meaning was also explored by Lawrence and Phillips (2004), who studied the emergence of commercial whale-watching in Canada showing how the emergence of this new institutional field was associated with a dramatic transformation in what they call 'macro-cultural discourse' concerning the nature of whales. They further argued that for a new institutional field to emerge, entrepreneurial action was needed, including the manipulation of these macro-cultural discourses. Lawrence and Phillips', (2004) study shows the embeddedness of an emerging institutional field, and of entrepreneurial activity, within various meaningful contexts. Studying the structural and practical dynamics alone would not have allowed tracking the crucial role played by meanings and the ways actors used them. Thus, studies of the meaningful aspects of institutionalization called our attention to local contexts and the embeddedness of organizational meanings within inter-organizational and societal meanings systems, and to the ways local actors work to align with such broad meanings.

Institutionalization as a Political Process

Power relations were always part of the institutional model. However, early formulations highlighted the overwhelming, deterministic power of the institutional order over anyone operating within it. Only after DiMaggio's (1988) call for a perspective that takes politics into account do we start to see explorations and more explicit theorizing of power and politics by and between various actors. Oliver's work on strategic responses (1991) was also important in the move to 'empower' the actors *vis-à-vis* the institutionalized structure. From the mid-1990s onward, studies have been following the ways meanings are intertwined with power and power relations.

Scholars argued then that since relevant institutional meanings are like multiple cultural building blocks (Friedland & Alford, 1991) and nested within each other (Holm, 1995), actors must choose and manipulate them in a process of (contested) interpretations. Actors do so in relation to conflicting interests and in alignment with their different subject positions (Maguire, Hardy, & Lawrence, 2004). Instilling institutional structures and practices with (specific) meaning is thus interest-driven and carried out through power relations dynamics.

These dynamics are especially apparent in the midst of institutional change (e.g., Arndt & Bigelow, 2000; Borum, 2004; Carruthers & Babb, 1996; Creed et al., 2002; Oakes, Townley, & Cooper, 1998), as well as in the creation of new institutions (e.g., Dejean, Gond, & Leca, 2004; Lounsbury & Pollack, 2001). Munir and Phillips (2005), for example, demonstrated how, in order to push forward its new roll-film technology, Kodak, as an institutional entrepreneur, 'engage[d] in discursive strategies to transform the "meaning" embodied by particular technologies, by producing new concepts, objects and subject positions' (p. 1666). Similarly, Oakes, Townley and Cooper (1998) demonstrated how business planning introduced in the provincial museums and cultural heritage sites of Alberta, Canada, was a political tool, by virtue of its 'monopoly of legitimate naming', – its ability to define meanings – 'actively construct the seeable and the sayable by specifying what will be documented and what will be ignored ... Through a process of naming, categorizing, and regularizing, business planning replaced one set of meanings, defined by the producers within the field, with another set that was defined in reference to the external market' (pp. 273, 277).

The ways struggles over meanings are carried out in institutionalization is especially apparent in studies that follow discursive efforts of competing institutional actors. Creed, Scully and Austin (2002) showed how various actors offered different 'legitimating accounts' for and against policies that ruled-out workplace discrimination on the basis of sexual orientation and identity. They identified five different frames used by different parties, each connected to different cultural building blocks, and invoking different social identities (for another example, see Etzion & Ferraro, 2010).

Accordingly, meanings are understood anew not as fixed entities but as flexible institutional resources (Rao, Morrill, & Zald, 2000). Rather than seeing institutions as all-encompassing, deterministic and hegemonic forces, these studies highlighted the importance of using particular languages in the processes of institutional change and emergence. In particular, actors construct social reality by specific uses of linguistic tools that align with their agenda. This is not a simple process. Institutional actors need to balance novelty and tradition, as they try to frame new (or changing) practices in ways that will provide them legitimacy and will not raise too much resistance (Lounsbury & Pollack, 2001). Various parties strive then to further their interests by manipulating these resources, creatively tailoring accounts that they hope would serve their interests (Arndt & Bigelow, 2000; Hargadon & Douglas, 2001).

Institutionalization as a Work in Progress

Studies in the 1990s and early 2000s also argued that meanings are fluid, dynamic and changing:

> The essence of a sign is that its meaning can never be determined once and for all by a given linguistic system, but always has the capacity to break with a context and take on different connotations. The sign is thus overflowed by a plurality of signification, which cannot be finally stabilized. (Howarth, 1998: 273; cf. Derrida, 1982: 320–321)

A focus on meanings, therefore, highlighted the ongoingness of institutions (DiMaggio, 1988). Studies of the institutionalization of law serve as a good example. As Edelman, Uggen and Erlanger (1999) showed in their study of the institutionalization of grievance procedures, 'the meaning of law regulating organizations unfolds dynamically across organizations, professional, and legal fields … the content and meaning of law is determined within the social field that it is designed to regulate' (pp. 406–407). In the same vein, Grattet and Jenness (2001) follow the construction of 'hate crimes' as a policy domain in the United States over a period of four decades, highlighting the interrelations of multiple interpretations of various actors in the process and over time. This and other studies (e.g., Anand, 2005; Anand & Peterson, 2000; Christensen & Westenholz, 1997; Edelman, 1992; Edelman, Abraham, & Erlanger, 1992; Phillips & Hardy, 1997) testify to how re-interpretations and the unfolding of any given meanings are crucial in institutionalization processes. Moreover, scholars also showed that such transformations are often tied with field-level or environmental changes (e.g., Reay & Hinings, 2005) that also call for more interpretations and theorizing, as the reshuffling of the institutional order needs to be (re)legitimated (e.g., Greenwood, Suddaby, & Hinings, 2002).

While the meaningful dynamics of institutionalization are especially apparent in the emergence of new institutions or change of existing ones, many studies show that even after structures and practices are institutionalized, their meaning still undergoes changes. In an early study that set the path to many ideational explorations of institutionalization, Hirsch (1986) showed how the 'normative framing' of corporate takeovers changed in tandem with the growing spread of the practice. With time, the depiction of takeovers – 'the language used, the rituals followed, and the meanings attributed to the event sequence by participants and close observers' turned from negative to positive (Hirsch, 1986: 802). This linguistic framing, Hirsch argued, served various cognitive, social-psychological and institutional functions, all facilitating the diffusion of the practice. This and other studies (e.g., Baron, Dobbin, & Jennings, 1986; Baron, Jennings, & Dobbin, 1988; Dobbin, Sutton, Meyer, & Scott, 1993; Kelly & Dobbin, 1998) show how cultural framings change with the institutionalization of structure and practices, influencing the very process of institutionalization.

As awareness to the dynamic of meaning have been growing, scholars started unpacking the underlying discursive processes. Ocasio and Joseph (2005) provide an historical account of the changing meanings attached to 'corporate governance'. Using an evolutionary model of vocabulary change, they show how mechanisms of variation, selection and retention work on the linguistic level. Inquiring into service learning in US higher education, Lounsbury and Pollack (2001) showed that the institutionalization of a new way of learning and knowing – through personal experience in the community, termed service-learning – changed the framing of those services. Whereas in the 1960s, service-learning was portrayed in revolutionary terms, as a means to transform higher education, in the 1980s it was framed within a functional discourse that highlighted its capacity to improve students' learning. The researchers explain this change in relation to the dialectics of a change in the broader higher-education field in which such services are embedded, as well as changes in the specific field of service-learning itself. The field of higher education changed from closed- to open-system logic, thus enabling the institutionalization of the innovative service-learning. And, the very institutionalization of service-learning entailed a change in its packaging. In its early days, a revolutionary framing made sense, and was in line with the norms of the era. As service-learning became the mainstream, such framing became too threatening, and thus the transformation into a more functional framing, which again, was also in line with the spirit of the time. This study shows that the very process of institutionalization changes the relevant field in ways that require further changes in the framing of those institutionalized structures and practices.

The surge of studies of meanings in institutional theory between the 1990s to the mid-2000s offered then a new understanding of institutions and institutionalization, highlighted the particularities of meanings in institutionalization, their embeddedness in local and broader contexts, their being part of political struggle and the on-going nature of institutionalization. This second phase of studies of meaning offered then a deeper understanding of the diverse ways they are significant in institutionalization.

MID-2000s TO MID-2010s: RE-PROBLEMATIZING MEANING

While empirically impressive, the theoretical contributions and implications of the second wave of studies of meanings were not fully spelled out. Why so? Their reliance on qualitative case studies may be one reason. As mentioned above, this method is probably still somewhat peripheral in our discipline, compared to the study of structures and practices using longitudinal, macro-level and quantitative methodologies (Bluhm et al., 2011; Bowring, 2000; Schneiberg & Clemens, 2007). Organization studies, like the social sciences more generally, strive to 'appear like the natural sciences through quantification and thus profit from the sciences' image' (Bort & Kieser, 2011). Another difficulty was the polyphony of terms relating to 'meaning' used to outline diverse theoretical arguments. Apparently with some nuanced-yet-important differences between them, scholars used many terms: 'rational myths' (Meyer & Rowan, 1977), 'linguistic framing' (Hirsch, 1986), 'theorizing' (Greenwood et al., 2002; Strang & Meyer, 1993), 'analogies' (Davis, Diekmann, & Tinsley, 1994), 'management rhetoric' or 'rationales' (Kelly & Dobbin, 1998), 'legitimating accounts' (Creed et al., 2002),

'rationalities' or 'institutional myths' (Townley, 2002). Only since the early 2000s do we see clearer overall and more systematic theoretical efforts to reconceptualize meanings in new ways that allow for the accumulations of discrete empirical studies into a well-defined stream of thinking within institutional theory. Further, especially since the mid-2000s, we see the study of meanings moving from the periphery to the foreground of the intellectual landscape of institutional theory, including within the North American scene.

Meanings are at the center of attention of an ever-growing community of institutional scholars and they are currently articulated within five explicit and distinct theoretical perspectives. First and quite early, Strang and Meyer (1993) offered the concept of 'theorization' as a critical component to understand diffusion of practices and structures. Second, Czarniawska and Joerges (1996) and Sahlin-Andersson (1996) argued we should depart from 'diffusion' altogether and use 'translation' and 'editing' instead as depictions of institutionalization. Third, Phillips, Lawrence and Hardy (2004) conceptualized institutions as 'discourse' and thus offered a new way to understand institutionalization as combining practices, structures and meanings all interacting within an overarching discourse. And, of late, the intellectual terrain of institutional theory in the American scene is dominated by two additional streams of thought, each trying to offer an overall reconceptualization of institutions (Zilber, 2013): institutional logics (Thornton & Ocasio, 1999) and institutional work (Lawrence & Suddaby, 2006). Each conceptualization highlights the role of meaning in its own distinct way.[2] I offer then a short analytical review of each of these five approaches, and the inquiries they inspire.

Theorization

Early on, institutionalization was conceptualized as *diffusion* of structures and practices, a process 'rich in structural mechanisms' (Strang and Soule, 1998: 270). Strang and Meyer (1993: 492) claimed that pointing to such underlying mechanisms is not enough. Social practices, they argued, are also always accompanied by 'theorized accounts' which play a central role in the very process of diffusion. 'Theorized accounts' chart abstract categories and outline the relationships between them (e.g., cause-and-effect). They are produced as part of the efforts to make sense of the world, and are the result of both individual-specific theorizing, and the influence of globally available theories and models, promoted by 'culturally legitimated theorists' (Strang & Meyer, 1993: 494–495) – like scientists, intellectuals and professionals. Strang and Meyer (1993) hypothesized that theorizing contributes to diffusion: the more theorization is complex and rich, diffusion will be more rapid, and less dependent on social relations.

Most studies of theorization depict meanings as 'things' rather than as an 'action', carried out by actors and part of social action and interaction. In other words, studies of theorization assume a process but the empirical focus is on the theorized: analyzing the structure or form of theorized accounts, or looking at how they operate once they had been produced. Greenwood, Suddaby and Hinings (2002), for example, studied the role of theorization in the jurisdictional changes in the practice of accounting firms in Canada in the 1980s–90s. They show how regulatory bodies were central in theorizing both the need for change by constructing a problem, and the change itself by constructing a solution. More broadly, they offer a process model of institutional change, within which theorization of new practices is center-stage, preceding and influencing the chances for actual diffusion. Analyzing so-called social responsibility in the financial sector in Austria, Höllerer (2013) argued that theorization in one important process that affects the diffusion of global ideas into local context, as labels and framings 'are instrumentalized

to challenge, replace, expand, reinterpret, or explicitly evoke the autochthonous idea of social/societal responsibility' (2013: 585). Others, as well, argued that theorization is especially relevant in times of institutional change, usually triggered by jolts or disruptive events, and carried out by experts (e.g., Carberry & King, 2012). Munir (2005: 94) argued, based on his study of institutional changes in the field of photography occurring with the advent of digital technology, that theorization is not only about making sense of such jolts, but rather about constructing these events as disruptive and thus triggering the process of change. Studies also differentiated between field-level circumstances – like mature versus emergent fields (Covaleski, Dirsmith, & Weiss, 2013; David, Sine, & Haverman, 2013) – and between different kinds of entrepreneurs. And, researchers pointed out the role of theorization at the micro level. For example, based on a comparative study of the adoption of the idea of interdisciplinary teamwork in four health care organizations in Canada, Reay et al. (2013) show that management theorization was a vital first stage in transforming new ideas into new practices as well as in proselytizing the ideas among relevant audiences (see also Borum, 2004).

In the main, those studies focus on the *impacts* of theorizations. They do not delve into the actual dynamics of their production. Suddaby and Greenwood (2005) is a rare example of a study offering an in-depth analysis of the various rhetorical strategies used by competing parties in their efforts to (de)legitimate an institutional change. Using the emergence of a new organizational form – multidisciplinary partnership – as their case study, they explore the jurisdictional struggle between proponents and opponents of the innovation. They show that this struggle was taking place on a rhetorical level. The two parties – each comprised by a multitude of organizational actors – made up two discursive communities. They used different institutional vocabularies (arguments and words) and relied upon different texts to invoke two different logics of professionalism, thus connecting 'prevailing and potential alternatives to broader cultural templates' (Suddaby & Greenwood, 2005: 57). By using this language, actors aimed at conferring legitimacy on the innovation and the institutional change it entailed. As well, each party relied upon and invoked different understandings of change. Proponents and opponents of the new organizational form deployed, then, various institutional vocabularies, and relied upon various understandings of change, as part of a political effort to further their interests through this discursive struggle.

Translation

Building on Latour (1986), Czarniawska and Joerges (1996) went a step beyond theorizing by suggesting 'translation' as an explicit new metaphor to articulate the spread of ideas across organizations. The 'diffusion' metaphor comes from physics and connotes a transmission of a given intact entity from one sphere to the other. The 'translation' metaphor, by contrast, comes from linguistics and connotes a break and transformation, so that whatever is translated is being reshaped in a specific new context (Czarniawska & Sevon, 1996). Thus, instead of thinking of adoption of fixed structures, practices and meanings as they move across various boundaries, we are dealing with adaptation, and the transformations of ideational and material objects in the process of their movement. Sahlin-Andersson (1996) highlighted especially the role of meaning in this process. Since most organizations do not have a direct experience with the original structures or practices they now implement, what they actually imitate are 'rationalizations – stories constructed by actors in the "exemplary" organization, and their own translation of such stories. The distance between the supposed source of the model – a practice or an action pattern – and the imitating organization forms a space for

translating, filling in and interpreting the model in various ways' (Sahlin-Andersson, 1996: 78–79).

Studies within the institutional translation perspective usually focus on the macro level, and look on how meanings, embedded in diverse texts, are adopted and adapted in new contexts (for a review, see Sahlin and Wedlin, 2008). Most translation studies use a before-and-after design, following the 'travel of ideas' (Czarniawska & Jorges, 1996) across various borders – across organizations (e.g., Doorewaard & van Bijsterveld, 2001; Ledderer, 2010; Morris & Lancaster, 2006), fields (Haedicke, 2012), geographically bounded communities (Waldorff & Greenwood, 2011) and national borders (e.g., Boxenbaum, 2006; Boxenbaum and Battilana, 2005; Czarniawska and Sevon, 2005; Frenkel, 2005; Mazza, Sahlin-Andersson, & Pedersen, 2005; Meyer & Hammerschmid, 2006; Meyer & Höllerer, 2010; Sahlin-Andersson & Engwall, 2002; Saka, 2004). Frenkel (2005), for example, studied how management ideas that originated in the United Stateswere adopted and adapted in Israel (see Ozen & Berkman, 2007 for the case of Turkey). A more dynamic and longitudinal approach to translation was taken by Zilber (2006a), who demonstrated how the meanings of Israeli high-tech changed before, during and after the year 2000 economic crisis. Zilber also showed how field-level meaning systems are derived from broad cultural frameworks echoing global economic fluctuations, yet are differentially translated into local societal and field-level understandings (see also Maguire & Hardy 2009; Hardy & Maguire, 2010).

Scholars also provided insights into the 'editing rules' (Sahlin-Andersson, 1996) that govern the process of translation, and the factors that shape the differences between 'original' and 'translated' versions. These include pre-existing perceptions and expectations held by organizational members (Doorewaard & Bijsterveld, 2001; Johnson & Hagström, 2005); organizational level behavioral norms (Ledderer, 2010); local culture and shared collective understandings (Haedicke, 2012; Meyer & Höllerer, 2010); discursive spaces within which translations occur (Hardy & Maguire, 2010), and the political dynamics motivating the actors involved (Frenkel, 2005).

As the study of translation grew in magnitude – and traveled from Europe (where it originated) into North American outlets – a fruitful dialogue between the translation and diffusion camps ensued. On the one hand, the particularistic emphasis in studies of translation affected the acknowledgment of 'practice variation' within studies of diffusion, and encouraged paying closer attention to the dynamic ways practices and structure are implemented in institutionalization (e.g., Ansari, Fiss, & Zajac, 2010; Fiss, Kennedy, & Davis, 2012; Lounsbury, 2001, 2007). On the other hand, the longitudinal emphasis in the study of diffusion may have helped in reshaping scholars' understanding of translation as a continuous process, which stretches throughout a long dynamic process, rather than as a one-time transformation from one site to another (e.g., Zilber, 2006a; Zilber & Zanoni, 2016).

Discourse

Phillips, Lawrence and Hardy (2004) offered a conceptualization of institutions as discourse, thus complementing the translation metaphor with a more comprehensive theoretical foundation, that of discourse analysis (Phillips & Hardy, 2002). Discourse serves as an all-encompassing concept that allows to combine anew various components and processes of institutions around the production, dissemination and consumption of texts. Institutions, they argue, are 'social constructions constituted through discourse … the structured collections of texts that exist in a particular field and that produce the social categories and norms that shape the understandings and behaviors of actors' (p. 638).

Producing texts is central to any institutional action and is carried out especially by actors who strive to make sense of reality and gain legitimacy for themselves and for their enterprises. In order for these texts to affect institutional processes, they need to become part of the relevant discourse. The genre of the texts, their producers, and the links between focal text and other relevant texts all influence their institutional impact. Once texts are embedded in a discourse, and as much as that discourse is structured, coherent and supported by other discourses, it produces 'institutions', which in their turn enable and constrain the production of other actions and texts in a cyclic process. The conceptualization of institutionalization as discourse highlights, over and beyond the idea of the text, the role of language and of meanings in the process, and offers new ways to study institutional fields and institutional entrepreneurship.

Empirical studies within this school examine the production and dissemination of texts – serving as carriers of meanings – in a variety of institutional contexts: mature fields undergoing change (Hardy & Maguire, 2010; Maguire et al., 2004); emerging fields (Khaire & Wadhwani, 2010); new global fields (Maguire & Hardy, 2009); and fields in crisis (Desai, 2011; Zilber, 2007). Taken together, these studies offer a new detailed picture of the chain of (discursive) events and actions leading to institution formation. To begin with, discursive activity depends on the subject position of actors. Thus, a first step in institutional action is occupying or acquiring a legitimate subject position (Maguire et al., 2004; Munir & Phillips, 2005). For texts to have impact, they need to relate to broader discourses (Khaire & Wadhwani, 2010; Maguire et al., 2004), and thus new discourses do not simply replace old ones, but rather overlap and interact with them, in a (discursive) struggle championed by diverse actors (Maguire & Hardy, 2006). More generally, discursive activity may construct meanings through various strategies – by producing new concepts, objects and subject positions (Munir & Phillips, 2005) or condi-tions of possibility (Maguire & Hardy, 2006); by redefining values in the field (Khaire & Wadhwani, 2010); by rhetoric (Green, Li, & Nohria, 2009); by using explicit and latent content to deliver contradictory messages (Zilber, 2007); and by the ongoing interpre-tation and translation of meanings (Hardy & Maguire, 2010). Not only meanings, how-ever, are mediated through discursive activ-ity. Practices (Maguire et al., 2004) and events (Desai, 2011; Munir, 2005) need to be discursively constructed as well, and it is this construction that turns them consequential.

Finally, discursive activity takes place within discursive spaces (Hardy & Maguire, 2010) and social spheres (Zilber, 2007) that enable, but also constrain, the types and con-tent of texts that can be produced and dissem-inated within them. As well, scholars pointed to specific discursive mediums – like narra-tives – as key features for institutional entre-preneurship, because they enable, and limit, the kinds of meanings that can be constructed (Hardy & Maguire, 2010; Zilber, 2007).

Institutional Logics

Following a diverse set of ideas drawn from the sociology of culture (DiMaggio, 1997; Giddens, 1984; Swidler, 1986) and specifi-cally further developing Friedland and Alford's (1991) notion of 'logics', Thornton and Ocasio (1999, 2008), Thornton (2004), and Thornton, Ocasio and Lounsbury (2012) offered the so-called institutional logics per-spective. 'Institutional logics' emphasize institutions in the plural. Society is always comprised, these scholars argue, of an inter-institutional system that includes diverse institutional orders – especially the family, community, religion, state, market, profes-sions and corporations. These orders are the origins of symbols and practices that shape different institutional logics, 'the socially constructed, historical patterns of material practices, assumptions, values, beliefs, and

rules by which individuals produce and reproduce their material subsistence, organ-ize time and space, and provide meaning to their social reality' (Thornton & Ocasio, 1999). As there are multiple institutional logics – governing different societal sectors – they represent competing and complemen-tary ways of thinking and acting. Individuals and organizations exploit these contradic-tions and complementarities resulting in dynamics of institutional stability and change.

The institutional logics perspective offers then yet another comprehensive theory of the work of meaning with a unique empha-sis on the wide and multiple social contexts. The institutional logics perspective aims at integrating agency and structure, the micro and macro, and – most relevant to our dis-cussion of the role of meanings – the idea-tional and the material. Further, institutional logics draws special attention to the histori-cal contingencies and complexities of institu-tions. The emphasis on the complexity of the institutional order may be seen as a mature development of the early studies of meanings in institutionalization, which depicted mean-ings as specific, context-dependent, contested and ever-transforming. The issue of *multi-plicity* in the institutional order was picked up and is now further developed within the institutional logics perspective (Greenwood, Raynard, Kodein, Micelotta, & Lounsbury, 2011).

Most studies of institutional logics relate to either the field or organizational level of ana-lysis, and treat institutional logics as the inde-pendent variable. Scholars try to uncover then how changes in institutional logics, or logics multiplicity, affect institutionalization (for rare exceptions that treat institutional logics as a dependent variable, see Ansari, Wijen, & Gray, 2013; Dunn & Jones, 2010). Logics are often defined as ideal types, broad meaning systems, shared in the organizational field or society at large. While they are not observed directly, they are assumed to be reflected in structures, practices and behaviors (Thornton

& Ocasio, 2008: 121), and thus their effect is measured by the diffusion of such structures, practices and behaviors. Empirically, the effort is not placed on identifying those meanings as such, since they are understood to derive from the limited set of known and given institutional orders (Thornton et al., 2012: 68–72). While these meanings, in their local manifestations, need to be explicated, their empirical and theoretical exploration is usually relegated to the background (Zilber, 2013: 82). Accordingly, the research impetus is mainly dedicated to explicate how certain logics affect macro-level outcomes (like the diffusion of practices across the field) or meso-level phenomenon (e.g., organizational response). Wright and Zammuto (2013), for instance, studied how a change in the competing institutional logics that governed the field of English County Cricket, affected organizational and field-level dynamics. The two logics – 'Cricket-as-art' and 'Cricket-as-business' – were identified and analyzed in the first stage of data analysis. Yet, the central empirical effort was not to further explicate these logics as such but to identify the various dynamics that ensue, and the main theoretical effort was to come up with a process model that integrates them into a coherent understanding of change in a mature field.

Conceiving institutional logics as macro-level ideal types of meanings is apparent in many field-level studies (e.g., Jones, Maoret, Massa, & Svejenova, 2012; Kennedy & Fiss, 2009; Lounsbury, 2002; Lounsbury, 2007; Marquis & Lounsbury, 2007; Purdy & Gray, 2009; Rao et al., 2003; Reay & Hinings, 2005, 2009; Sauermann & Stephan, 2013; Thornton & Ocasio, 1999; Thornton, 2001, 2002; Thornton, Jones, & Kury, 2005). It can be found, however, in studies of organizational daily practices as well. For example, Yu (2013) studied how one organization – the Service Employees International Union – responded when a long-standing 'occupational' logic was joined by a relatively new 'social movement' logic. The author explicated the two logics, and directly measured

the prevalence of the new logic in the field and tried to depict, both empirically and theoretically, a process model of the institutionalization of a new template under such elusive conditions of logic multiplicity. Likewise, Battilana and Dorado (2010) studied two microfinance organizations, and demonstrated how establishing pioneering hybrid organizations requires an organizational identity that explicitly celebrates and is built upon competing logics. The authors identify two competing logics – 'banking' and 'developmental' – which were blended into an emerging 'commercial microfinance logic'. Their main effort was to identify the mechanisms – like hiring practices and socialization processes – that allow the organizations to establish themselves as hybrids.

The study by Pache and Santos (2013) is a rare example of an effort to explicate the contents and the meanings encompassed within certain logics, instead of treating them as a 'black box'. The researchers identify the characteristics of the competing 'social welfare' and 'commercial' logics governing the field of 'work integration social enterprises'. They closely follow the 'organizational elements on which logics prescribe conflicting demands' (Pache & Santos, 2013: 979–983), thus setting the ground for the identification of response patterns, and their possible interpretations. Even in this case, however, the logics themselves are taken as given, unified and stable. The same goes for McPherson and Sauder's (2013) study of logics 'on the ground' based on an ethnographic, in-depth study of the internal dynamics within a drug court. The researchers outline how different actors creatively deploy, in micro-level interactions, different logics to further their interests. Still, the four logics they identify are taken, in themselves, to be clear-cut and given.

Studies of institutional logics emphasize then the effects of a multiplicity of meanings in the process of institutionalization and how such multiplicity changes practices and structures. So far, the price of this emphasis on multiplicity is that most studies of institutional logics treat meanings as reified, as given things – instead of further problematizing and unpacking each of the competing institutional logics (Smets & Jarzabkowski, 2013; Voronov, De Clercq, & Hinings, 2013).

Institutional Work

The emphasis in institutional logics has been on meaning and the ideational as such, and less so on who produces such meanings and how they are produced. Another recent conceptualization of meaning in institutional theory seems to have taken its starting point precisely from these issues of agency and social action. In tandem with conceptualizations of the role of actors in institutionalization (DiMaggio, 1988; Oliver, 1991, 1992), and building on the sociology of practice (Bourdieu, 1977, 1993; de Certeau, 1984; Giddens, 1984), Lawrence and Suddaby (2006: 215) developed the concept of 'institutional work' as 'the purposive action of individuals and organizations aimed at creating, maintaining, and disrupting institutions'. Institutions, they argued, are not self-perpetuating (Jepperson, 1991), but rather require constant labor (Lawrence, Suddaby, & Leca, 2009). Such efforts are conscious, and aim – though not necessarily successfully – at creating new institutions, and maintaining or disrupting existing ones. Giving institutional maintenance a central role – as much as institutional creation and change – is a unique contribution of the institutional work perspective, which may be traced back to the emphasis given to the continuous processes of meaning construction.

Meaning is important to any kind of institutional work. Although actors are using a variety of practices in such efforts, many of them are meaning- or 'language-centered', carried out through 'composing legislation, telling stories, writing histories, making jokes and insults, writing memos and letters, writing legal opinions, writing and making speeches and making announcements' (Lawrence & Suddaby, 2006: 239). Typologies of actions became crucial for this new analysis of meaning in institutions. Each type of institutional work demands its own set of practices. For example, work aimed at creating new institutions may involve 'constructing identities': 'defining the relationship between an actor and the field in which that actor operates'; as well as theorizing (pp. 221, 223, 226–227). Work aimed at maintaining institutions may involve 'valorizing and demonizing': 'providing for public consumption positive and negative examples that illustrates the normative foundations of an institution', as well as 'mythologizing': 'preserving the normative underpinning of an institution by creating and sustaining myths regarding its history' (pp. 230, 232–233). Work aimed at disrupting institutions may involve 'undermining assumptions and beliefs': 'decreasing the perceived risks of innovation and differentiation by undermining core assumptions and beliefs' (pp. 235, 237–238).

Following the influential typology offered by Lawrence and Suddaby (2006), many scholars pointed to additional nuanced kinds of institutional work. Perkmann and Spicer (2008), for instance, distinguished between political, technical and cultural work involved in the institutionalization of management fashions. Cultural work, for example, 'establishes or reframes belief systems and values, often by linking practices with more widely anchored discourses' (Perkmann & Spicer, 2008: 813). Scholars further contextualize the different types of institutional work by suggesting, for example, that 'calculative framing, engaging and valorizing' are three types of institutional work involved especially in standardization processes (Slager, Gond, & Moon, 2012: 763); evangelizing and adaptive emulation are called upon in institutionalizing new modes of construction (Jones & Massa, 2013); and in relational legitimacy-building (Daudigeos, 2013; see also Drori & Honig, 2013; Whittle, Suhomlinova,

& Mueller, 2010). Others distinguished between disruptive and defensive institutional work in deinstitutionalization, demonstrating how both kinds of institutional work involve manipulation of meanings in regard to the positive or negative impacts of certain practices (Maguire & Hardy 2009; see also Lefsrud & Meyer, 2012).

Furthermore, in analyzing institutional maintenance, scholars pointed to various mechanisms. Dacin, Munir and Tracey (2010), for instance, focused on organizational rituals that allow, they argued, for creation and transmission of meaning. Others showed that institutional repair work is carried out through manipulation of shared beliefs and understandings (Heaphy, 2013; Lok & de Rond, 2013; Micelotta & Washington, 2013; Ramirez, 2013). And, in regard to institutional change, scholars highlighted how a new role identity is legitimized by manipulating meanings through 'naturalizing the past, normalizing new meanings, altering identity referents, connecting with the institutional environment, and referencing authority' (Goodrick & Reay, 2010: 55; see also Creed, DeJordy, & Lok, 2010; Zietsma & Lawrence, 2010).

Aside from shedding new light on the structure and types of social actions, institutional work has been instrumental in highlighting the role of social actors in institutionalization of meaning. Hence, while focusing on how institutional work occurs by referring to the manipulation of meanings in creating, disrupting and maintaining institutions, scholars focused in particular on agency (Lawrence, Leca, & Zilber, 2013: 1024). Following early studies of meanings, which (as noted above) highlighted the political dynamics involved in institutional processes, the institutional work perspective broadened the conceptualization of 'power' and 'cultural entrepreneurship' (Lounsbury & Glynn, 2001). Interpretation (meaning-making) is understood here anew as a form of agency and part of contestations within an organizational field (Zilber, 2002).

In line with the original insight of neo-institutionalism according to which institutions hold tremendous power over the social order, institutional work studies mostly stay away from depicting such work as the productions of some individual 'heroic entrepreneurs'. Scholars try instead to strike a better balance between the initiative and creativity of individual entrepreneurs and the social settings within which they operate. Thus scholars have been looking at social actions and sense-making in which many actors (e.g., Empson, Cleaver, & Allen, 2013), and even collectives (e.g., Dorado, 2013) participate in shaping up institutions. Riaz, Buchanan and Bapuji (2011), for example, followed the different kinds of rhetoric used by different actors in mainstream media, in response to the global financial crisis of 2007. Their research highlights the 'experimental' nature of any institutional project (Malsch & Gendron, 2013), for they depict the ideational aspects of institutions as emerging and worked out in a complex web of meanings, actors and registries. In particular, they identify different actors (academics, bankers, the regulator), who took different positions (enhancing the status quo, keeping neutral and aiming at change) *vis-à-vis* central issues (policy, practice, recovery and regulation). They further highlight how actors communicated through different rhetorical devices (appeals to expert authority, blame, use of scenarios and avoidance of critical discussion), and how all these actions were creatively used as this institutional work evolved within and in reference to the institutional order.

In line with efforts to stay away from glorifying entrepreneurship and isolating the context of their actions, scholars also explored the conditions that enable agency (e.g., pointing to 'micro institutional affordances', van Dijk, Berends, Jelniek, Romme, & Waggeman, 2011). Desai (2011), for example, offers a rare quantitative exploration of the conditions that affect the motivation of organizations to engage in defensive institutional work in response to field-level crisis that may affect them as well. Many studies focused on the role of professionals in institutional work, both on organizational and field levels, as these actors are presumed to be central and well-resourced to manipulate meaning (see Suddaby & Viale, 2011 review, and Currie, Lockett, Finn, Martin, & Waring, 2012).

Many studies of institutional work are based on in-depth case studies, archival data and interviews (e.g., Zietsma & Lawrence, 2010; van Dijk et al., 2011) and *in situ* and *in vivo* observations (e.g., Dacin et al., 2010; Heaphy, 2013; Lok & de Rond, 2013; Raviola & Norback, 2013). In contrast to the institutional logics and the theorization approaches, which focus on how meanings are produced and enacted on the macro level, the methodological preference of institutional work are indicative of its focus on the more concrete dynamics of meanings and actions involved in institutionalization. Thus, scholars engaged in micro-level analyses (Kaghan & Lounsbury, 2011; Lawrence et al., 2009; Powell & Colyvas, 2008), and on meanings as social action (Polletta, Chen, Gardner, & Motes, 2011; e.g., Helfen & Sydow, 2013). Such methodologies fit well with the 'need to attend to meaning systems, symbols, myths and the processes by which organizations interpret their institutional environment' (Suddaby, 2010: 16). They allow for the exploration of the 'world inside' and the micro-level practices, discursive and material, that explain macro-level dynamics.

WHAT'S NEXT?: SUMMING UP AND LOOKING FORWARD

Theorization, translation, discourse, institutional logics and institutional work are current theoretical approaches that offer complementary ways to think about the role of meaning, language and interpretation in institutional processes, and they offer different (complementary and contrasting) takes on institutions and institutionalization.

These are new and exciting theoretical developments. While revolving around older questions in institutional theory they rethink them in innovative ways. As noted above, meanings were at the heart of the neo-institutional argument and contribution (Glynn & Abzug, 2002; Jepperson, 1991; Zilber, 2002). The new contributions are significant and nuanced partly because early treatments of meaning in early formulations of institutional theory were quite general, and hence partial and somewhat naïve. Thus, meanings in the early days of neo-institutionalism were mainly understood in their formal characteristic. Institutionalization meant that some structures, practices and understandings have become taken-for-granted. The content of institutions and the dynamics of such contents were not at center stage. Many early neo-institutional formulations were in fact assuming that regardless of the content of institutions, certain processes will take place (the same disregard for particularities was evident in the treatment of structures and practices). Early theorists were talking then about meanings, but in the abstract. In line with these depictions of meaning, most empirical studies of institutionalization focused on structural or practical aspects, using them as proxies of meaning, rather than exploring meaning directly (Farashahi et al., 2005; Hasselbladh & Kallinikos, 2000). The paradoxical argument of neo-institutionalism rested upon the implicit comparison between institutional myth and rationality. Yet, the meaning of rationality itself was quite overlooked, as rationality was treated as 'transparent and self-evident rather than meaningful' (Dobbin, 1994a: 218). The very content of institutions was neglected as students of institutional processes lacked 'the theoretical tools by which to understand the institutional *content* whose diffusion they [analyzed]' (Friedland & Alford, 1991: 243–244). Finally, the meaningful environment within which institutions reside were left unexplored: 'the social and cultural processes that make up the project of rationalization and shape the structure and functioning of work organizations have either been bypassed or given an exogenous status, reified to 'reality', 'society' or 'environment' and treated as independent variables in cross sectional or longitudinal empirical research' (Hasselbladh & Kallinikos, 2000: 697–698).

As I demonstrated above, much has changed since those early days. Already in the mid-1990s we have seen a surge of studies of meaning in institutional process, and while these studies were somewhat peripheral to the hegemonic emphasis on structures, practices and their diffusion, they nevertheless helped in adding pluralism and variety back into institutional theory (Glynn, Bar, & Dacin, 2000). In particular, they set forth new formulations of institutions and institutionalization – underscoring local and particularistic, context-sensitive, conflictual and on-going processes. They highlighted anew the social constructionist dimension of institutional processes, thus reconnecting to the roots of the neo-institutional school (though with modifications). They reminded scholars of institutions that neo-institutional theory 'seeks to grasp *not* the universal laws that generate social practice, but the social practices that generate universal laws' (Dobbin, 1994b: 123; emphasis in original). These studies, I suggest, invoked or at least served as the background for the more theoretically integrated conceptualizations of institutions since the mid-2000, all placing meaning at center-stage – theorization, translation, discourse and in particular the currently two dominant approaches: institutional logics and institutional work (Zilber, 2013). These theories are to be credited for a new and exciting wave of empirical works.

To further develop the meaningful understandings of institutional processes, I suggest that scholars of institutions need to pay attention to recent questioning of the meaning of meaning. In particular scholars should go beyond meanings as embodied in verbal (written and sometimes oral) texts, to include the interfaces of meaning with (broadly defined) material, visual and emotional aspects of institutions. Furthermore, scholars should delve more seriously and explicitly into the implications of such inquiries for our understanding of the institutional actor.

One potential avenue for further development of institutional theory through the study of meanings is by expanding our view to include various artifacts. Most of the studies reviewed in this chapter prioritized the dominant cognitive-linguistic reference and index of meaning and are thus based on the analysis of verbal or textual data. Language, discursive processes and textual interpretations have been at the center of institutional research in the past 15–20 years. Other modalities of institutional dynamics and of institutionalized meanings, however, have been quite neglected. Of late, there is a growing interest in three such modalities or registries of institutors – the material, the visual and the emotional.

As part of the 'material turn' in the social sciences (Latour, 2005), concrete material entities – like spaces, technologies, objects – are understood to be central to any process of organizing (Orlikowski & Scott, 2008). Whether taking a humanist approach, arguing that materiality mediates any human action, or a more extreme post-humanist stance that attributes materiality with active participation in social processes, the material turn has many implications for our understanding of the work of meaning in institutional theory and research. 'The same way a mason cannot construct a wall without cement and bricks, no institutions can be created, maintained, or disrupted without materials' (Monteiro & Nicolini, 2015: 74). A handful of studies that explore materiality in institutions testify to the potential of this new line of research. Sahlin and Wedlin (2008) and Czarniawska and Joerges (1996) underscore the role of materials as carriers of institutions; Czarniawska (2009) and Jones et al. (2012) highlight the importance of buildings in the creation of institutions; Monteiro and Nicolini (2015) and Svejenova, Mazza and Planellas (2007) show how institutional work involves materiality. To fully explore the "'silent" but essential role' of the material in institutional processes (Monteiro & Nicolini, 2015: 74), we need more empirical studies and elaborated conceptualizations. And, most relevant to the subject of this chapter, we need to explore how materiality encodes and interacts with meanings, and how actors decode these meanings – as part of the production of texts and other activities that constitute institutions.

Likewise, the role of visuals in institutional dynamics has slowly become a new focus of attention. Visual images – icons, typography, photographs, paintings, drawings – are all around us, especially given new communication technologies. How, then, is meaning embedded in the visual and how does the visual take part in institutional dynamics (Meyer et al., 2013)? In rare studies of visuals in institutionalization, Höllerer and colleagues (2013) explored the 'visual language' of institutional logics, arguing that each logic also carries specific legitimate visual accounts that are involved in its impact. Studying the iconography and brand images of universities, Drori, Delmestri and Oberg (2015) show how identity narrative relates to the trajectories of the institutionalization of organizations of higher education. The 'visual mode of meaning construction' is highlighted in these research projects. The visual is thus conceived as 'a specific way of constructing and expressing meanings: it is created, transformed, transferred, and put into practice by either the use of primarily visual objects and artifacts, or by integrating the visual and the verbal in such a way that neither can be fully understood without the other' (Meyer et al., 2013: 490–493). These formulations challenge institutional scholars to design new methodologies and new conceptual formulations that will account for the role of the visual in institutionalization.

Some new questions that arise from an emphasis on the material and visual, are: How do the material and the visual relate to the linguistic? Are specific kinds of meanings (e.g., positive versus negative) delivered through different modalities? Are different modalities more or less prevalent in different stages of an institutionalization process? Do they require different kinds of subject positions and institutional work?

A focus on the material and the visual as modes of meaning in institutional dynamics also relates and underscore the role of emotions, for such artifacts have 'repeatedly been found to transport and elicit strong emotional responses' (Meyer et al., 2013: 526). Yet meaning-full emotions, in contrast to meanings attached to cognitions and perceptions, have been quite neglected in institutional analysis (Voronov & Vince, 2012). This is regrettable, as 'institutional inhabitants are not merely carriers of institutions but, rather, are persons, with affective commitments and emotional stakes, who together instantiate and reproduce institutions through their symbolic interactions' (Creed et al., 2014: 293). Indeed, the few attempts to incorporate emotions into institutional theory point to new, fruitful directions. Creed et al. (2014) explored the role of shame in institutional processes, highlighting its impact on the construction of subjectivities. Shame and other emotions, they conclude, motivate the actions of institutional habitants, as they 'have not only shared cognitions about institutional prescriptions but also strong emotional impetus to preserve valued social bonds and their standing as valued persons within the communities constituted by those bonds' (p. 294). Voronov and Yorks (2015) explore the impact emotional investment has on actors' cognitions (specifically, apprehending institutional contradictions) and thus actors' ability to act on the institutional order. Creed, DeJordy, and Lok (2010) highlight the way emotions are part of processes of identity construction that underlie institutional work. These new inquiries into emotions thus open a set of new questions about meanings in the institutional drama. They suggest scholars should go beyond cognitive and social understanding of meaning-making to explore their deep, individual and collective affective base.

Underlying the efforts to push forward new threads in institutional theory lies a central challenge facing institutional theory today – how to broaden the concept of the actor operating at the heart of the institutional order. Voronov and Vince (2012) and Creed et al. (2014) urge scholars to 'replace the concept of the individual – with its connotations of atomized autonomy – with the construct of the person' (Creed et al., 2014: 278). Thus, I suggest that the study of institutional meanings as multifaceted, including verbal, material, visual and emotional – may help us reconceive actors as richer and more contextualized subjectivities.

More generally, the study of meanings in action, on various levels of analysis, working through and embedded in various modalities (verbal, material, visual and emotional), while being sensitive to the particularities of the institutional drama, its on-going nature and its political aspects, may help us further re-imagine and re-formulate institutional theory.

Notes

1 However, this was not a criterion in my search, as there are studies of meaning that use quantitative methods (e.g., Edelman, Uggen, & Erlanger, 1999; Rao, Monin, & Durand, 2003), and qualitative studies of institutional processes that do not explore meanings and their dynamics (e.g., Child & Tsai, 2005; Edwards, Almond, Clark, Colling, & Ferner, 2005).

2 I review here streams that already gathered some traction, while acknowledging others that are now being developed, like 'rhetorical institutionalism' (Green, 2004; Green & Li, 2011), and 'vocabularies' (Loewenstein, Ocasio, & Jones, 2012).

ACKNOWLEDGMENTS

I thank Tom Lawrence for his helpful comments on an earlier version of this chapter. Special thanks to Yehuda Goodman for the ongoing discussion of the ideas articulated in it. Research and writing were supported by the Leon Recanati Fund, at the School of Business Administration, the Hebrew University of Jerusalem.

REFERENCES

Alvesson, M., & Deetz, S. (1996). Critical theory and postmodernism approaches to organizational studies. In S. Clegg, C. Hardy & W. R. Nord (Eds.), *Handbook of organization studies* (pp. 191–217). London: Sage.

Alvesson, M., & Karreman, D. (2000). Varieties of discourse: On the study of organizations through discourse analysis. *Human Relations, 53*(9), 1125–1149.

Amis, J., & Silk, M. L. (2008). The philosophy and politics of quality in qualitative organizational research. *Organizational Research Methods, 11*(3), 456–480.

Anand, N. (2005). Charting the music business: Billboard magazine and the development of the commercial music field. In J. Lampel, J. Shamsie, & T. Lant (Eds.), *The business of culture: Strategic perspectives on entertainment and media*. Mahwah, NJ: Lawrence Erlbaum.

Anand, N., & Peterson, R. A. (2000). When market information constitutes fields: Sensemaking of markets in the commercial music industry. *Organization Science, 11*(3), 270–284.

Ansari, S. M., Fiss, P. C., & Zajac, E. J. (2010). Made to fit: How practices vary as they diffuse. *Academy of Management Review, 35*(1), 67–92.

Ansari, S., Wijen, F., & Gray, B. (2013). Constructing a climate change logic: An institutional perspective on the 'tragedy of the commons'. *Organization Science, 24*(4), 1014–1040.

Arndt, M., & Bigelow, B. (2000). Presenting structural innovation in an institutional environment: Hospitals' use of impression management. *Administrative Science Quarterly, 45*(3), 494–522.

Baron, J. N., Dobbin, F. R., & Jennings, P. D. (1986). War and peace: The evolution of modern personnel-administration in United States industry. *American Journal of Sociology, 92*(2), 350–383.

Baron, J. N., Jennings, P. D., & Dobbin, F. R. (1988). Mission control: The development of personnel systems in United-States industry. *American Sociological Review, 53*(4), 497–514.

Battilana, J., & Dorado, S. (2010). Building sustainable hybrid organizations: The case of commercial microfinance organizations. *Academy of Management Journal, 53*(6), 1419–1440.

Berger, P. L., & Luckmann, T. (1966). *The social construction of reality: A treatise in the sociology of knowledge*. Garden City, NY: Anchor Books.

Bluhm, D. J., Harman, W., Lee, T. W., & Mitchell, T. R. (2011). Qualitative research in management: A decade of progress. *Journal of Management Studies*, *48*, 1866–1891.

Borum, F. (2004). Means-end frames and the politics and myths of organizational fields. *Organization Studies*, *25*(6), 897–921.

Bort, S. & Kieser, A. (2011). Fashion in Organization Theory: An empirical analysis of the diffusion of theoretical concepts. *Organization Studies*, *32*(5): 655–681.

Bourdieu, P. (1977). *Outline of a theory of practice* (R. Nice, Trans. Vol. 16). Cambridge: Cambridge University Press.

Bourdieu, P. (1993). *Sociology in question*. London: Sage.

Bowring, M. A. (2000). De/Constructing theory: A look at the institutional theory that positivism built. *Journal of Management Inquiry*, *9*(3), 258–270.

Boxenbaum, E. (2006). Lost in translation: The making of Danish diversity management. *American Behavioral Scientist*, *49*(7), 939–948.

Boxenbaum, E., & Battilana, J. (2005). Importation as innovation: Transposing managerial practices across fields. *Strategic Organization*, *3*(4), 355–383.

Boxenbaum, E., & Jonsson, S. (2008). Isomorphism, diffusion and decoupling. In R. Greenwood, C. Oliver, K. Sahlin, & R. Suddaby (Eds.), *The SAGE Handbook of Organizational Institutionalism* (pp. 78–98). Los Angeles, CA: Sage.

Carberry, E. J., & King, B. G. (2012). Defensive practice adoption in the face of organizational stigma: Impression management and the diffusion of stock option expensing. *Journal of Management Studies*, *49*(7), 1137–1167.

Carruthers, B. G., & Babb, S. (1996). The color of money and the nature of value: Greenbacks and gold in Postbellum America. *American Journal of Sociology*, *101*(6), 1556–1591.

Child, J., & Tsai, T. (2005). The dynamic between firms' environmental strategies and institutional constraints in emerging economies: Evidence from China and Taiwan. *Journal of Management Studies*, *42*(1), 95–125.

Christensen, S., & Westenholz, A. (1997). The social/behavioral construction of employees as strategic actors on company boards of directors. *American Behavioral Scientist*, *40*(4), 490–501.

Clark, V., & Jennings, P. D. (1997). Talking about the natural environment: A means for deinstitutionalization? *American Behavioral Scientist*, *40*(4), 454–464.

Covaleski, M. A., Dirsmith, M. W., & Weiss, J. M. (2013). The social construction, challenge and transformation of a budgetary regime: The endogenization of welfare regulation by institutional entrepreneurs. *Accounting Organizations and Society*, *38*(5), 333–364.

Creed, W. E. D., DeJordy, R., & Lok, J. (2010). Being the change: Resolving institutional contradiction through identity work. *Academy of Management Journal*, *53*(6), 1336–1364.

Creed, W. E. D., Hudson, B. A., Okhuysen, G. A., & Smith-Crowe, K. (2014). Swimming in a sea of shame: Incorporating emotion into explanations of institutional reproduction and change. *Academy of Management Review*, *39*(3), 275–301.

Creed, W. E. D., Scully, M. A., & Austin, J. R. (2002). Clothes make the person? The tailoring of legitimating accounts and the social construction of identity. *Organization Science*, *13*(5), 475–496.

Currie, G., Lockett, A., Finn, R., Martin, G., & Waring, J. (2012). Institutional work to maintain professional power: Recreating the model of medical professionalism. *Organization Studies*, *33*(7), 937–962.

Czarniawska, B. (2009). Emerging institutions: Pyramids or anthills? *Organization Studies*, *30*(4), 423–441.

Czarniawska, B., & Joerges, B. (1996). The travel of ideas. In B. Czarniawska & G. Sevon (Eds.), *Translating Organizational Change* (pp. 13–48). Berlin: de Gruyter.

Czarniawska, B., & Sevon, G. (1996). Introduction. In B. Czarniawska & G. Sevon (Eds.), *Translating Organizational Change* (pp. 1–12). Berlin: de Gruyter.

Czarniawska, B. & Sevón, G. (2005) *Global Ideas: How Ideas, Objects and Practices Travel in a Global Economy*. Malmö, Sweden: Liber & Copenhagen Business School Press.

Dacin, M. T., Munir, K., & Tracey, P. (2010). Formal dining at Cambridge: Linking ritual performance and institutional maintenance. *Academy of Management Journal*, *53*(6), 1393–1418.

Daudigeos, T. (2013). In their profession's service: How staff professionals exert influence in their organization. *Journal of Management Studies*, *50*(5), 722–749.

David, R. J., Sine, W. D., & Haveman, H. A. (2013). Seizing opportunity in emerging fields: How institutional entrepreneurs legitimated the professional form of management consulting. *Organization Science*, *24*(2), 356–377.

Davis, G. F., Diekmann, K. A., & Tinsley, C. H. (1994). The decline and fall of the conglomerate firm in the 1980s: The deinstitutionalization of an organizational form. *American Sociological Review*, *59*(4), 547–570.

de Certeau, M. (1984). *The practice of everyday life* (S. Rendall, Trans.). Berkeley, CA: University of California Press

Dejean, F., Gond, J. P., & Leca, B. (2004). Measuring the unmeasured: An institutional entrepreneur strategy in an emerging industry. *Human Relations*, *57*(6), 741–764.

Derrida, J. (1982). *Margins of philosophy*. Brighton: Harvester Press.

Desai, V. M. (2011). Mass media and massive failures: Determining organizational efforts to defend field legitimacy following crisis. *Academy of Management Journal, 54*(2), 263–278.

DiMaggio, P. (1997). Culture and cognition. *Annual Review of Sociology, 23*, 263–287.

DiMaggio, P. J. (1988). Interest and agency in institutional theory. In L. G. Zucker (Ed.), *Institutional patterns and organizations: Culture and environment* (pp. 3–21). Cambridge, MA: Ballinger.

DiMaggio, P., & Mullen, A. L. (2000). Enacting community in progressive America: Civic rituals in national music week, 1924. *Poetics, 27*, 135–162.

DiMaggio, P. J., & Powell, W. W. (1983). The iron cage revisited: Institutional isomorphism and collective rationality in organizational fields. *American Sociological Review, 48*, 147–160.

Dobbin, F. R. (1994a). *Forging industrial policy*. Cambridge: Cambridge University Press.

Dobbin, F. R. (1994b). Cultural models of organization: The social construction of rational organizing principles. In D. Crane (Ed.), *The sociology of culture: Emerging theoretical perspectives* (pp. 117–141). Oxford: Blackwell.

Dobbin, F., Sutton, J. R., Meyer, J. W., & Scott, W. R. (1993). Equal opportunity law and the construction of internal labor-markets. *American Journal of Sociology, 99*(2), 396–427.

Doorewaard, H., & van Bijsterveld, M. (2001). The osmosis of ideas: An analysis of the integrated approach to IT management from a translation theory perspective. *Organization, 8*(1), 55–76.

Dorado, S. (2013). Small groups as context for institutional entrepreneurship: An exploration of the emergence of commercial microfinance in Bolivia. *Organization Studies, 34*(4), 533–557.

Drori, G. S., Delmestri, G., & Oberg, A. (2013). Branding the university: Relational strategy of identity construction in a competitive field. In L. Engwall & P. Scott (Eds.), *Trust in Higher Education Institutions* (pp. 134–147). London: Portland Press.

Drori, I., & Honig, B. (2013). A process model of internal and external legitimacy. *Organization Studies, 34*(3), 345–376.

Dunn, M. B., & Jones, C. (2010). Institutional logics and institutional pluralism: The contestation of care and science logics in medical education, 1967–2005. *Administrative Science Quarterly, 55*(1), 114–149.

Edelman, L. B. (1992). Legal ambiguity and symbolic structures: Organizational mediation of civil-rights law. *American Journal of Sociology, 97*(6), 1531–1576.

Edelman, L. B., Abraham, S. E., & Erlanger, H. (1992). Professional construction of law: The inflated threat of wrongful discharge. *Law & Society Review, 26*(1), 47–83.

Edelman, L. B., Uggen, C., & Erlanger, H. S. (1999). The endogeneity of legal regulation: Grievance procedures as rational myth. *American Journal of Sociology, 105*(2), 406–454.

Edwards, T., Almond, P., Clark, I., Colling, T., & Ferner, A. (2005). Reverse diffusion in US multinationals: Barriers from the American business system. *Journal of Management Studies, 42*(6), 1261–1286.

Empson, L., Cleaver, I., & Allen, J. (2013). Managing partners and management professionals: Institutional work dyads in professional partnerships. *Journal of Management Studies, 50*(5), 808–844.

Etzion, D., & Ferraro, F. (2010). The role of analogy in the institutionalization of sustainability reporting. *Organization Science, 21*(5), 1092–1107.

Farashahi, M., Hafsi, T., & Molz, R. (2005). Institutionalized norms of conducting research and social realities: A research synthesis of empirical works from 1983 to 2002. *International Journal of Management Reviews, 7*(1), 1–24.

Ferguson, P. P. (1998). A cultural field in the making: Gastronomy in 19th-century France. *American Journal of Sociology, 104*(3), 597–641.

Fiss, P. C., Kennedy, M. T., & Davis, G. F. (2012). How Golden Parachutes unfolded: Diffusion and variation of a controversial practice. *Organization Science, 23*(4), 1077–1099.

Frenkel, M. (2005). The politics of translation: How state level political relations affect the cross-national travel of management ideas. *Organization, 12*, 275–301.

Friedland, R., & Alford, R. R. (1991). Bringing society back in: Symbols, practice, and institutional contradictions. In W. W. Powell & P. J. DiMaggio (Eds.), *The new institutionalism in organizational analysis* (pp. 232–263). Chicago, IL: University of Chicago Press.

Giddens, A. (1984). *The constitution of society: outline of the theory of structuration*. Berkeley, CA: University of California Press.

Glynn, M. A., & Abzug, R. (2002). Institutionalizing identity: Symbolic isomorphism and organizational names. *Academy of Management Journal, 45*(1), 267–280.

Glynn, M. A., Barr, P. S., & Dacin, M. T. (2000). Pluralism and the problem of variety. *Academy of Management Review, 25*(4), 726–734.

Goodrick, E., & Reay, T. (2010). Florence Nightingale endures: Legitimizing a new professional role identity. *Journal of Management Studies, 47*(1), 55–84.

Grattet, R., & Jenness, V. (2001). The birth and maturation of hate crime policy in the United States. *American Behavioral Scientist, 45*(4), 668–696.

Green, S. E. (2004). A rhetorical theory of diffusion. *Academy of Management Review, 29*(4), 653–669.

Green, S. E., Jr., & Li, Y. (2011). Rhetorical institutionalism: Language, agency, and structure in institutional theory since Alvesson 1993. *Journal of Management Studies, 48*(7), 1662–1697.

Green, S. E., Jr., Li, Y., & Nohria, N. (2009). Suspended in self-spun webs of significance: A rhetorical model of institutionalization and institutionally embedded agency. *Academy of Management Journal, 52*(1), 11–36.

Greenwood, R., Raynard, M., Kodeih, F., Micelotta, E. R., & Lounsbury, M. (2011). Institutional complexity and organizational responses. *Academy of Management Annals, 5,* 317–371.

Greenwood, R., Suddaby, R., & Hinings, C. R. (2002). Theorizing change: The role of professional associations in the transformation of institutionalized fields. *Academy of Management Journal, 45*(1), 58–80.

Haedicke, M. A. (2012). 'Keeping our mission, changing our system': Translation and organizational change in natural foods co-ops. *Sociological Quarterly, 53*(1), 44–67.

Hardy, C., & Maguire, S. (2010). Discourse, field-configuring events, and change in organizations and institutional fields: Narratives of DDT and the Stockholm convention. *Academy of Management Journal, 53*(6), 1365–1392.

Hargadon, A. B., & Douglas, Y. (2001). When innovations meet institutions: Edison and the design of the electric light. *Administrative Science Quarterly, 46*(3), 476–501.

Hasselbladh, H., & Kallinikos, J. (2000). The project of rationalization: A critique and reappraisal of neo-institutionalism in organization studies. *Organization Studies, 21*(4), 697–720.

Heaphy, E. D. (2013). Repairing breaches with rules: Maintaining institutions in the face of everyday disruptions. *Organization Science, 24*(5), 1291–1315.

Helfen, M., & Sydow, J. (2013). Negotiating as institutional work: The case of labour standards and international framework agreements. *Organization Studies, 34*(8), 1073–1098.

Hirsch, P. M. (1986). From ambushes to golden parachutes: Corporate takeovers as an instance of cultural framing and institutional integration. *American Journal of Sociology, 91,* 800–837.

Höllerer, M. A. (2013). From taken-for-granted to explicit commitment: The rise of CSR in a corporatist country. *Journal of Management Studies, 50*(4), 573–606.

Höllerer, M. A., Jancsary, D., Meyer, R. E., & Vettori, O. (2013). Imageries of corporate social responsibility: Visual recontextualization and field-level meaning. *Research in the Sociology of Organizations, 39(B),* 139–174.

Holm, P. (1995). The dynamics of institutionalization: Transformation processes in Norwegian fisheries. *Administrative Science Quarterly, 40*(3), 398–422.

Howarth, D. (1998). Discourse theory and political analysis. In E. Scarbrough & E. Tanenbaum (Eds.), *Research strategies in the social sciences: A guide to new approaches* (pp. 268–293). Oxford: Oxford University Press.

Jepperson, R. L. (1991). Institutions, institutional effects, and institutionalism. In W. W. Powell & P. J. DiMaggio (Eds.), *The new institutionalism in organizational analysis* (pp. 143–163). Chicago, IL: University of Chicago Press.

Johnson, B. & Hagström, B. (2005). The translation perspective as an alternative to the policy diffusion paradigm: The case of the Swedish methadone maintenance treatment. *Journal of Social Policy, 34*(3), 365–388.

Jones, C., Maoret, M., Massa, F. G., & Svejenova, S. (2012). Rebels with a cause: Formation, contestation, and expansion of the de novo category 'modern architecture', 1870–1975. *Organization Science, 23*(6), 1523–1545.

Jones, C., & Massa, F. G. (2013). From novel practice to consecrated exemplar: Unity temple as a case of institutional evangelizing. *Organization Studies, 34*(8), 1099–1136.

Kaghan, W., & Lounsbury, M. (2011). Institutions and work. *Journal of Management Inquiry, 20*(1), 73–81.

Kelly, E., & Dobbin, F. (1998). How affirmative action became diversity management: Employer response to antidiscrimination law, 1961 to 1996. *American Behavioral Scientist, 41*(7), 960–984.

Kennedy, M. T., & Fiss, P. C. (2009). Institutionalization, framing and diffusion: The logic of TQM adoption and implementation decisions among US hospitals. *Academy of Management Journal, 52*(5), 897–918.

Khaire, M., & Wadhwani, R. D. (2010). Changing landscapes: The construction of meaning and value in a new market category-modern Indian art. *Academy of Management Journal, 53*(6), 1281–1304.

Latour, B. (1986). The powers of association. In J. Law (Ed.), *Power, action and belief* (pp. 264–280). London: Routledge and Kegan Paul.

Latour, B. (2005). *Reassembling the social.* Oxford: Oxford University Press.

Lawrence, T. B., Leca, B., & Zilber, T. B. (2013). Institutional work: Current research, new directions and overlooked issues. *Organization Studies, 34*(8), 1023–1033.

Lawrence, T. B., & Phillips, N. (2004). From Moby Dick to Free Willy: Macro-cultural discourse and institutional entrepreneurship in emerging institutional fields. *Organization, 11*(5), 689–711.

Lawrence, T. B., & Suddaby, R. (2006). Institutions and institutional work. In S. R. Clegg, C. Hardy, W. R. Nord, & T. Lawrence (Eds.), *Handbook of organization studies.* Thousand Oaks, CA: Sage.

Lawrence, T. B., Suddaby, R., & Leca, B. (Eds.) (2009). *Institutional work: Actors and agency in institutional studies of organizations.* Cambridge: Cambridge University Press.

Ledderer, L. (2010). Bringing about change in patient-centred preventive care. *International Journal of Public Sector Management, 23*(4), 403–412.

Lefsrud, L. M., & Meyer, R. E. (2012). Science or science fiction? Professionals' discursive construction of climate change. *Organization Studies, 33*(11), 1477–1506.

Lieblich, A. (1998). Categorical-content perspective. In A. Lieblich, R. Tuval-Mashiach, & T. Zilber (Eds.), *Narrative research: Reading, analysis and interpretation* (pp. 112–126). Newbury Park, CA: Sage.

Loewenstein, J., Ocasio, W., & Jones, C. (2012). Vocabularies and vocabulary structure: A new approach linking categories, practices, and institutions. *Academy of Management Annals, 6*, 41–86.

Lok, J., & de Rond, M. (2013). On the plasticity of institutions: Containing and restoring practice breakdowns at the Cambridge university boat club. *Academy of Management Journal, 56*(1), 185–207.

Lounsbury, M. (2001). Institutional sources of practice variation: Staffing college and university recycling programs. *Administrative Science Quarterly, 46*(1), 29–56.

Lounsbury, M. (2002). Institutional transformation and status mobility: The professionalization of the field of finance. *Academy of Management Journal, 45*(1), 255–266.

Lounsbury, M. (2007). A tale of two cities: Competing logics and practice variation in the professionalizing of mutual funds. *Academy of Management Journal, 50*(2), 289–307.

Lounsbury, M., & Glynn, M. A. (2001). Cultural entrepreneurship: Stories, legitimacy, and the acquisition of resources. *Strategic Management Journal, 22*, 545–564.

Lounsbury, M., & Pollack, S. (2001). Institutionalizing civic engagement: Shifting logics and the cultural repackaging of service-learning in US higher education. *Organization, 8*(2), 319–339.

Maguire, S., & Hardy, C. (2006). The emergence of new global institutions: A discursive perspective. *Organization Studies, 27*(1), 7–29.

Maguire, S., & Hardy, C. (2009). Discourse and deinstitutionalization: The decline of DDT. *Academy of Management Journal, 52*(1), 148–178.

Maguire, S., Hardy, C., & Lawrence, T. B. (2004). Institutional entrepreneurship in emerging fields: HIV/AIDS treatment advocacy in Canada. *Academy of Management Journal, 47*(5), 657–679.

Malsch, B., & Gendron, Y. (2013). Re-theorizing change: Institutional experimentation and the struggle for domination in the field of public accounting. *Journal of Management Studies, 50*(5), 870–899.

Marquis, C., & Lounsbury, M. (2007). Vive la resistance: Competing logics and the consolidation of US community banking. *Academy of Management Journal, 50*(4), 799–820.

Mazza, C., Sahlin-Andersson, K., & Pedersen, J. S. (2005). European constructions of an American model: Developments of four MEA programs. *Management Learning, 36*(4), 471–491.

McPherson, C. M., & Sauder, M. (2013). Logics in action: Managing institutional complexity in a drug court. *Administrative Science Quarterly, 58*(2), 165–196.

Meyer, J. W. (1996). Otherhood: The promulgation and transmission of ideas in the modern organizational environment. In B. Czarniawska & G. Sevon (Eds.), *Translating organizational change* (pp. 240–252). Berlin: de Gruyter.

Meyer, J. W., & Rowan, B. (1977). Institutionalized organizations: Formal structure as myth and ceremony. *American Journal of Sociology, 83*, 340–363.

Meyer, R. E., & Hammerschmid, G. (2006). Changing institutional logics and executive identities: A managerial challenge to public administration in Austria. *American Behavioral Scientist, 49*(7), 1000–1014.

Meyer, R. E., & Höllerer, M. A. (2010). Meaning structures in a contested issue field: A topographic map of shareholder value in Austria. *Academy of Management Journal, 53*(6), 1241–1262.

Meyer, R. E., Höellerer, M. A., Jancsary, D., & Van Leeuwen, T. (2013). The visual dimension in organizing, organization, and organization research: Core ideas, current developments, and promising avenues. *Academy of Management Annals, 7*(1), 489–555.

Micelotta, E. R., & Washington, M. (2013). Institutions and maintenance: The repair work of Italian professions. *Organization Studies, 34*(8), 1137–1170.

Mohr, J. W. (1998). Measuring meaning structures. *Annual Review of Sociology, 24*, 345–370.

Monteiro, P., & Nicolini, D. (2015). Recovering materiality in institutional work: Prizes as an assemblage of human and material entities. *Journal of Management Inquiry, 24*(1), 61–81.

Morris, T., & Lancaster, Z. (2006). Translating management ideas. *Organization Studies, 27*(2), 207–233.

Munir, K. A. (2005). The social construction of events: A study of institutional change in the photographic field. *Organization Studies, 26*(1), 93–112.

Munir, K. A., & Phillips, N. (2005). The birth of the 'Kodak moment': Institutional entrepreneurship and the adoption of new technologies. *Organization Studies, 26*(11), 1665–1687.

Oakes, L. S., Townley, B., & Cooper, D. J. (1998). Business planning as pedagogy: Language and control in a changing institutional field. *Administrative Science Quarterly, 43*(2), 257–292.

Ocasio, W., & Joseph, J. (2005). Cultural adaptation and institutional change: The evolution of vocabularies of corporate governance, 1972–2003. *Poetics, 33*, 163–178.

Oliver, C. (1991). Strategic responses to institutional processes. *Academy of Management Review, 16*, 145–179.

Oliver, C. (1992). The antecedents of deinstitutionalization. *Organization Studies, 13*(4), 563–588.

Orlikowski, W. J., & Scott, S. V. (2008). Sociomateriality: Challenging the separation of technology, work and organization. *Academy of Management Annals, 2*, 433–474.

Ozen, S., & Berkman, U. (2007). Cross-national reconstruction of managerial practices: TQM in Turkey. *Organization Studies, 28*(6), 825–851.

Pache, A. C., & Santos, F. (2013). Inside the hybrid organization: Selective coupling as a response to competing institutional logics. *Academy of Management Journal, 56*(4), 972–1001.

Perkmann, M., & Spicer, A. (2008). How are management fashions institutionalized? The role of institutional work. *Human Relations, 61*(6), 811–844.

Phillips, N., & Hardy, C. (1997). Managing multiple identities: Discourse, legitimacy and resources in the UK refugee system. *Organization, 4*(2), 159–185.

Phillips, N., & Hardy, C. (2002). *Discourse analysis: Investigating processes of social construction*. Thousand Oaks, CA: Sage.

Phillips, N., Lawrence, T. B., & Hardy, C. (2004). Discourse and institutions. *Academy of Management Review, 29*(4), 635–652.

Polletta, F., Chen, P. C. B., Gardner, B. G., & Motes, A. (2011). The sociology of storytelling *Annual Review of Sociology, 37*, 109–130.

Powell, W. W., & Colyvas, J. A. (2008). Microfoundations of institutional theory. In R. Greenwood, C. Oliver, R. Suddaby, & K. Sahlin-Andersson (Eds.), *The SAGE Handbook of Organizational Institutionalism* (pp. 276–298). Los Angeles, CA: Sage.

Prasad, P., & Prasad, A. (1994). The ideology of professionalism and work computerization: An institutionalist study of technological-change. *Human Relations, 47*(12), 1433–1458.

Purdy, J. M., & Gray, B. (2009). Conflicting logics, mechanisms of diffusion, and multilevel dynamics in emerging institutional fields. *Academy of Management Journal, 52*(2), 355–380.

Quaid, M. (1993). Job evaluation as institutional myth. *Journal of Management Studies, 30*(2), 239–260.

Ramirez, C. (2013). 'We are being pilloried for something, we did not even know we had done wrong!' Quality control and orders of worth in the British audit profession. *Journal of Management Studies, 50*(5), 845–869.

Random House Webster's Unabridged Dictionary (1998). New York: Random House.

Rao, H., Monin, P., & Durand, R. (2003). Institutional change in Toque Ville: Nouvelle cuisine as an identity movement in French gastronomy. *American Journal of Sociology, 108*(4), 795–843.

Rao, H., Morrill, C., & Zald, M. N. (2000). Power plays: How social movements and collective action create new organizational forms. *Research in Organizational Behavior, 22*, 237–281.

Raviola, E., & Norback, M. (2013). Bringing technology and meaning into institutional work: Making news at an Italian business newspaper. *Organization Studies, 34*(8), 1171–1194.

Reay, T., Chreim, S., Golden-Biddle, K., Goodrick, E., Williams, B. E., Casebeer, A., ... Hinings, C. R. (2013). Transforming new ideas into practice: An activity based perspective on the institutionalization of practices. *Journal of Management Studies, 50*(6), 963–990.

Reay, T., & Hinings, C. R. (2005). The recomposition of an organizational field: Health care in Alberta. *Organization Studies, 26*(3), 351–384.

Reay, T., & Hinings, C. R. (2009). Managing the rivalry of competing institutional logics. *Organization Studies, 30*(6), 629–652.

Riaz, S., Buchanan, S., & Bapuji, H. (2011). Institutional work amidst the financial crisis: emerging positions of elite actors. *Organization, 18*(2), 187–214.

Ritti, R. R., & Silver, J. H. (1986). Early processes of institutionalization: The dramaturgy of exchange in interorganizational relations. *Administrative Science Quarterly, 31*(1), 25–42.

Sahlin, K., & Wedlin, L. (2008). Circulating ideas: Imitation, translation and editing. In R. Greenwood, C. Oliver, R. Suddaby, & K. Sahlin-Andersson (Eds.), *The SAGE Handbook of Organizational Institutionalism* (pp. 218–242). Los Angeles, CA: Sage.

Sahlin-Andersson, K. (1996). Imitating by editing success: The construction of organization fields. In B. Czarniawska & G. Sevon (Eds.), *Translating organizational change* (pp. 69–92). Berlin: de Gruyter.

Sahlin-Andersson, K., & Engwall, L. (2002). Carriers, flows and sources of management knowledge. In K. Sahlin-Andersson & L. Engwall (Eds.), *The expansion of management knowledge: Carriers flows and sources* (pp. 3–32). Stanford, CA: Stanford Business Books.

Saka, A. (2004). The cross-national diffusion of work systems: Translation of Japanese operations in the UK. *Organization Studies, 25*(2), 209–228.

Sauermann, H., & Stephan, P. (2013). Conflicting logics? A multidimensional view of industrial and academic science. *Organization Science, 24*(3), 889–909.

Scheid-Cook, T. L. (1992). Organizational enactments and conformity to environmental prescriptions. *Human Relations, 45*(6), 537–554.

Schneiberg, M., & Clemens, E. S. (2007). The typical tools for the job: Research strategies in institutional analysis. In D. D. Powell & D. L. Jones (Eds.), *How Institutions Change*. Chicago, IL: University of Chicago Press.

Schwandt, T. A. (2001). *Dictionary of Qualitative Inquiry*. Thousand Oaks, CA: Sage.

Scott, W. R. (1987). The adolescence of institutional theory. *Administrative Science Quarterly*, *32*(4), 493–511.

Scott, W. R. (2001). *Institutions and organizations*. Thousand Oaks, CA: Sage.

Scott, W. R. (2003). Institutional carriers: Reviewing modes of transporting ideas over time and space and considering their consequences. *Industrial and Corporate Change*, *12*(4), 879–894.

Scott, W. R. (2014). *Institutions and organizations: Ideas, interests, and identities* (4th ed.). Thousand Oaks, CA: Sage.

Slager, R., Gond, J. P., & Moon, J. (2012). Standardization as institutional work: The regulatory power of a responsible investment standard. *Organization Studies*, *33*(5–6), 763–790.

Smets, M., & Jarzabkowski, P. (2013). Reconstructing institutional complexity in practice: A relational model of institutional work and complexity. *Human Relations*, *66*(10), 1279–1309.

Strang, D., & Meyer, J. (1993). Institutional conditions for diffusion. *Theory and Society*, *22*, 487–511.

Strang, D., & Soule, S. A. (1998). Diffusion in organizations and social movements: From hybrid corn to poison pills. *Annual Review of Sociology*, *24*, 265–290.

Suddaby, R. (2010). Challenges for institutional theory. *Journal of Management Inquiry*, *19*(1), 14–20.

Suddaby, R., & Greenwood, R. (2005). Rhetorical strategies of legitimacy. *Administrative Science Quarterly*, *50*(1), 35–67.

Suddaby, R., & Viale, T. (2011). Professionals and field-level change: Institutional work and the professional project. *Current Sociology*, *59*(4), 423–442.

Svejenova, S., Mazza, C., & Planellas, M. (2007). Cooking up change in haute cuisine: Ferran Adria as an institutional entrepreneur. *Journal of Organizational Behavior*, *28*(5), 539–561.

Swidler, A. (1986). Culture in action: Symbols and strategies. *American Sociological Review*, *51*, 273–286.

Thornton, P. H. (2001). Personal versus market logics of control: A historically contingent theory of the risk of acquisition. *Organization Science*, *12*(3), 294–311.

Thornton, P. H. (2002). The rise of the corporation in a craft industry: Conflict and conformity in institutional logics. *Academy of Management Journal*, *45*(1), 81–101.

Thornton, P. H. (2004). *Markets from culture: Institutional logics and organizational decisions in higher education publishing*. Stanford, CA: Stanford University Press.

Thornton, P., Jones, C., & Kury, K. (2005). Institutional logics and institutional change: Transformation in accounting, architecture, and publishing. In C. Jones & P. H. Thornton (Eds.), *Research in the sociology of organizations*. London: JAI.

Thornton, P. H., & Ocasio, W. (1999). Institutional logics and the historical contingency of power in organizations: Executive succession in the higher education publishing industry, 1958–1990. *American Journal of Sociology*, *105*(3), 801–843.

Thornton, P. H., & Ocasio, W. (2008). Institutional logics. In R. Greenwood, C. Oliver, R. Suddaby, & K. Sahlin-Andersson (Eds.), *The SAGE Handbook of Organizational Institutionalism* (pp. 99–129). Los Angeles, CA: Sage.

Thornton, P. H., Ocasio, W., & Lounsbury, M. (2012). *The institutional logics perspective: A new approach to culture, structure, and process*. Oxford: Oxford University Press.

Townley, B. (2002). The role of competing rationalities in institutional change. *Academy of Management Journal*, *45*(1), 163–179.

Usdiken, B., & Pasadeos, Y. (1995). Organizational analysis in North-America and Europe: A comparison of cocitation networks. *Organization Studies*, *16*(3), 503–526.

van Dijk, S., Berends, H., Jelinek, M., Romme, A. G. L., & Weggeman, M. (2011). Micro-institutional affordances and strategies of radical innovation. *Organization Studies*, *32*(11), 1485–1513.

Van Maanen, J. (Ed.). (1998). *Qualitative studies of organizations*. Thousand Oaks, CA: Sage.

Voronov, M., De Clercq, D., & Hinings, C. R. (2013). Institutional complexity and logic engagement: An investigation of Ontario fine wine. *Human Relations*, *66*(12), 1563–1596.

Voronov, M., & Vince, R. (2012). Integrating emotions into the analysis of institutional work. *Academy of Management Review*, *37*(1), 58–81.

Voronov, M., & Yorks, L. (2015). 'Did you notice that?' Theorizing differences in the capacity to apprehend institutional contradictions. *Academy of Management Review*, *40*(4), 563–586.

Waldorff, S. B., & Greenwood, R. (2011). The dynamics of community translation: Danish health-care centers. In C. Marquis, M. Lounsbury & R. Greenwood (Eds.), *Research in the sociology of organizations: Communities and organizations*, Vol. 33 (pp. 113–142). Bingley, UK: Emerald Group.

Whitson, J., Weber, K., Hirsch, P., & Bermiss, Y. S. (2013). Chemicals, companies, and countries: The concept of diffusion in management research. In B. M. Staw & A. P. Brief (Eds.), *Research in organizational behavior: An annual series of analytical essays and critical reviews*, *33*, 135–150.

Whittle, A., Suhomlinova, O., & Mueller, F. (2010). Funnel of interests: The discursive translation of organizational change. *Journal of Applied Behavioral Science*, *46*(1), 16–37.

Wicks, D. (2001). Institutionalized mindsets of invulnerability: Differentiated institutional fields and the antecedents of organizational crisis. *Organization Studies*, *22*(4), 659–692.

Wright, A. L., & Zammuto, R. F. (2013). Wielding the willow: Processes of institutional change in English cricket. *Academy of Management Journal*, *56*(1), 308–330.

Yu, K. H. (2013). Institutionalization in the context of institutional pluralism: Politics as a generative process. *Organization Studies*, *34*(1), 105–131.

Zietsma, C., & Lawrence, T. B. (2010). Institutional work in the transformation of an organizational field: The interplay of boundary work and practice work. *Administrative Science Quarterly*, *55*(2), 189–221.

Zilber, T. B. (2002). Institutionalization as an interplay between actions, meanings and actors: The case of a rape crisis center in Israel. *Academy of Management Journal*, *45*(1), 234–254.

Zilber, T. B. (2006a). The work of the symbolic in institutional processes: Translations of rational myths in Israeli high tech. *Academy of Management Journal*, *49*(2), 281–303.

Zilber, T. B. (2006b). Mythologies of speed and the shaping of Israeli hi-tech industry. In P. Case, S. Lilley, & T. Owens (Eds.), *The speed of organization* (pp. 147–160). Copenhagen: Copenhagen University Press.

Zilber, T. B. (2007). Stories and the discursive dynamics of institutional entrepreneurship: The case of Israeli high-tech after the bubble. *Organization Studies*, *28*(7), 1035–1054.

Zilber, T. B. (2008). The work of meanings in institutional processes and thinking. In R. Greenwood, C. Oliver, R. Suddaby, & K. Sahlin-Andersson (Eds.), *The SAGE Handbook of organizational institutionalism* (pp. 151–169). Thousand Oaks, CA: Sage.

Zilber, T. B. (2013). Institutional logics and institutional work: Should they be agreed? In Michael Lounsbury & Eva Boxenbaum (Eds.), *Institutional logics in action, Part A (Research in the sociology of organizations*, Volume 39A) (pp.77–96). Bingley, UK: Emerald Group.

Zilber, T. B., & Zanoni, P. (2016). *Institutionalization as a continuous process: The case of 'ethnography' in organization studies*. Unpublished Manuscript.

Zucker, L. G. (1977). Role of institutionalization in cultural persistence. *American Sociological Review*, *42*(5), 726–743.

17

Networks and Institutions[*]

Walter W. Powell and Achim Oberg

INTRODUCTION

We share a firm conviction that the traditions of research on networks and institutions ought to be brought into closer alignment. To pursue our agenda, we both selectively review past research that emphasizes their mutual influence and introduce an array of empirical studies and methodological tools that show how the two streams can be profitably joined. But before we build our argument about the commonalities in theory and the utility of methods, we take up why these lines of research are often treated, particularly among European organization scholars, as unrelated.

Networks are relational; they reflect webs of affiliation. They have a temporal element: a network exists only as long as a relationship endures. Networks are conduits that channel the flow of ideas and information. One might say that networks look more horizontal than

vertical. In contrast, institutions are obdurate structures. They reflect long-standing conventions and widely understood sources of power and influence. Institutions are 'sticky' (Clemens and Cook, 1999). They appear more vertical, either in the top-down form of research on the influences of the modern state or the professions, or bottom-up as in more recent studies that focus on building institutions. Nevertheless, in either respect, there is a strong constructivist imagery. Such differences in perception might well explain divergences in understanding.

But perhaps other sources account for the lack of common appreciation and awareness. In an important respect, institutions reflect widely accepted cultural understandings. They are imbued with legitimacy and taken for granted. In this regard, institutions are cognitive constructions. Networks, in contrast, are much more active forms of engagement. They can also invoke ideas of geometry, either in the form

[*] A full-colour version of this chapter can be found on the companion website for this *Handbook*, available at: https://study.sagepub.com/orginstitutionalism2e

of the distance or path link of networks or in their overall composition. Such imagery is not surprising given the early intellectual origins of network analysis in balance theory, or in its mathematical form, in graph theory (Diestel, 2010; Wasserman and Faust, 1994).

We want to disrupt the current division of intellectual labor. Indeed, we find it odd and wonder whether it reflects a kind of niche competition between organizational and economic sociology, or in management schools, between organizational behavior and strategy. Whatever its sources, we think a close reading of some of the early theoretical statements in institutional analysis and some of the most notable empirical papers suggest that the perceived disjuncture is flawed and unnecessary. To counter this view, we review three fruitful lines of work: (1) research on social relationships and the configuration of such larger entities as inter-organizational networks and fields; (2) studies that highlight relational aspects in meaning construction; and (3) a nascent direction that combines the two previous approaches via multi-level analyses that interweave the study of social relationships and meaning structures. For each of the three lines we provide empirical cases that demonstrate the co-constitutive relations between networks and institutions. Each case draws on empirical studies that we have been involved in. The benefit of drawing on our own past work is that we can provide visualizations of the processes that link relational and institutional factors. These concrete examples underscore the payoffs from thinking both relationally and institutionally. We turn now to locate our arguments in canonical writings on institutions, then begin our survey by drawing on Max Weber's fundamental early definitions of social relationships and their meanings.

NETWORKS AS SCAFFOLDS FOR INSTITUTIONS

In their classic paper, Meyer and Rowan (1977) observed that the formal structures of organizations 'dramatically reflect the myths of their institutional environments'. They argued that organizations are driven to incorporate practices and procedures defined and buttressed by widely prevalent, rationalized concepts in the larger society. These practices were institutionalized through professional standards and status hierarchies, and reinforced by public opinion. Meyer and Rowan also stressed that the complexity of relational networks in modern societies generates explosive organizing potential, which greatly increased the spread of rationalized myths.

The generative potential of networks as transmission channels was expanded on by DiMaggio and Powell (1983). Their ideas about organizational fields, and the mechanisms through which ideas are transferred, drew directly on three insights from network research. The concept of an organizational field built on research on inter-organizational networks (Laumann et al., 1978). The field image also drew on ideas of structural equivalence (White et al., 1976), which emphasized that people in common structural positions often experience similar pressures and possibly even think alike owing to these constraints, regardless of whether they have direct contact with one another. The third source of inspiration was French sociologist Pierre Bourdieu's provocative discussions of the role of fields in creating, assigning, and maintaining cultural capital. Perhaps no scholar has emphasized the relational character of fields more than Bourdieu. His vivid line, 'To think in terms of fields *is to think relationally*' (Bourdieu and Wacquant, 1992: 96) captures the linkage between networks and fields. Bourdieu insists that mechanisms of institutional influence should operate most strongly within fields, rather than at a diffuse societal level. These disparate ideas were foundational to DiMaggio and Powell's argument about how fields are formed, leading them to posit a four-step developmental process that involved: (1) increased interaction among participants; (2) the development of well-defined status orders and patterns of coalition; (3) heightened information sharing; and (4) mutual awareness and responsiveness.

Each of these four processes is inherently relational. Increased interaction among participants is facilitated by societal rules that smooth the establishing and deepening of social relationships; status orders emerge from vertical relationships, whereas coalitions are formed by horizontal relationships; information is shared within already established relationships; and awareness and responsiveness are bi-directional ties of mutual recognition and observation.

This strong connection between networks and fields does not mean that a field can easily be modeled as a 'flat' network consisting of only one type of social actor and one type of relationship. Instead, to model the four mechanisms we need different types of individuals and organizations, diverse types of social relationships (to wit, 'acquaintance relationships' that enable increased interaction among people without deep prior relationships, 'collaboration relationships' to form coalitions) and the variety of flows that follow these relationships (such as a flow of information, a flow of recognition, and a flow of endorsements). Before we turn to examples of complex network representations of fields, we begin with simple building blocks for these larger structures: the relationships between two individuals and the meaning construction that these relationships facilitate.

An Integrative View of Relationships and Meanings

When the German sociologist Max Weber summarized his conceptual and methodological ideas in *Wirtschaft und Gesellschaft* more than 100 years ago, he defined social relationships as:

The term 'social relationship' will be used to denote the behavior of a plurality of actors insofar as, in its meaningful content, the action of each takes account of that of the others and is oriented in these terms. The social relationship thus exists entirely and exclusively in the existence of a probability that there will be a meaningful course of social action – irrespective, for the time being, of the basis for this probability. (Weber, 1978: 26–27)[1]

Weber's definition of social relationships has proved robust. It captures the subjective elements of an interaction, the mutuality of expectations, and a temporal dimension as well. With relative ease, we can transpose Weber's definition into social network terms and also incorporate his writings about methodological issues (Ringer, 2009). Figure 17.1 illustrates a basic scenario consisting of two persons interacting with one another and two researchers observing their interaction.

Each of the focal persons has his/her own subjective understanding of how and why to interact with the other person and how the reaction of the other person could be understood. If a social relationship exists between the two, that attachment will guide them in interpreting the meaning of their interaction. Assuming that the two people are similarly aware, the likelihood of an overlap in their understanding is high. The result is a shared understanding based on an inter-subjective meaning construction.

A second aspect of Weber's definition is that the existence of a social relationship between two persons provides a chance for meaningful behavior. From a methodological point of view, a social relationship captures the likelihood of certain types of interactions. Moreover, a social relationship might exist even if neither individual was aware of it. For example, two members of the same large organization are joined by a 'colleague' relationship, even if they do not know each other. When they eventually meet, they recognize this relationship during a first introduction, and it can serve as a template for future behavior. This 'existence without knowing' aspect of social relations is a primary reason that reconstruction of such larger social entities as organizations, markets, or fields

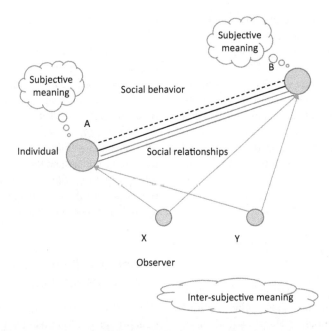

Figure 17.1   Subjective and inter-subjective meaning

as social networks enhances our understanding of the behavioral aspects of social and economic life. The idea of existence without knowing is captured in the concept of structural equivalence (Lorrain and White, 1971).

Weber also pointed out that a connection between people often entails more than one social relationship that provides meaning. When multiplex relations exist between two people, such as friend-to-friend, co-author-to-co-author, or senior-to-junior-scholar, each has to figure out which aspect of their relationship is relevant to understanding a particular interaction. Widely accepted social definitions of types of different relations are a useful guide to distinguishing meaning structures. For example, the father–son relationship is highly typified and captures a set of social expectations (which, of course, vary among cultures). Weber saw tradition and idealization as mechanisms to create types of relationships and their connected expectations of appropriate behaviors. As we will see later, such typification of social relationships becomes a critical building block

toward understanding the co-construction of networks and institutions.

In Weber's methodological thinking, types – especially ideal types – carry the potential for researchers to understand the interactions they observe. The difference between the use of types by interacting persons and their use by researchers is that researchers should explicate which types of relationships are best in explaining the observed behavior. The interacting persons themselves do not have to be aware of the relationship that best explains their behavior. Consequently, a purported 'objective' meaning could possibly deviate from the inter-subjective understanding shared by two persons.

The assumption that social relations provide meaning for interaction may strike some as static and deterministic. In his analysis of the spirit of capitalism, Weber (1904) described the connection between meaning and interaction as changing over time in different phases: In the first phase, the meaning of an interaction practice is clearly defined. In the second, a practice spreads among peers who share a similar cultural background and therefore understand the same meaning. In the third, the practice is disentangled from its local meaning, making it possible for it to spread to groups with different cultural backgrounds. In the final phase, the interaction practice becomes rationalized, and thus its meaning stabilizes again. Translated into modern terms, it is clear that Weber recognized the social and cultural construction of both types of relationships and categories of actors.

SOCIAL RELATIONS AS BUILDING BLOCKS FOR INSTITUTIONS

We take Weber's discussion as a starting point for our argument that social relations are the building blocks of larger social structures. This elemental, 'bottom-up' account rests on two premises.

First, the type of relationship influences the accompanying interaction. For example, gift-giving might be seen as a typical interaction in a 'friendship' relationship, whereas negotiations and haggling are less likely; in contrast, in an 'anonymous market relationship', negotiations and money transactions are expected, whereas gift-giving is unusual. Assuming that strong connections among types of relationships and interactions exist, one can deduce an expected interaction by knowing the type of relationship. Following this assumption, the social network algorithms model expected interactions between two participants, tracing a path across chains of actors and deducing indicators for the effect of different relations. Assuming a typical behavior for a specific type of relationship, the modeled social network generates expected behavioral outcomes for participants even though actual behavioral data are not collected. The second premise is that larger social entities are assembled from the social relations among individuals. For example, a social relation connects two individuals ('dyad') through employment contacts, they might become members of a company

('organization'). Because of the individuals' reputations, their organization is endorsed by other organizations in the same domain as a respected member ('organizational field'). In turn, this good reputation enables the organization to initiate business contacts with other organizations ('market'). By studying individuals and organizations as nodes and their relationships as links, social network analysis helps us to understand the flow of information, the aggregation of legitimacy, the diffusion of practices, and the embeddedness of individuals and organizations in larger networks.

Example 1: Foundation of an Organization

Our first example highlights relational construction processes that change the positions of individuals and organizations during the foundation of a new organization. The organization in question is a software company here called KnowledgeFactory, which was formally founded in January 2000 in Germany at the peak of the New Economy boom to produce knowledge management software that overcomes the limitations of hierarchical knowledge diffusion. Most studies interpret the formal founding date as the 'birth' of an organization, but we are also interested in contacts that existed before founding. We studied these relations, and the processes that changed them from 1998 to 2001, through repeat interviews with founders, funders, early clients, early employees and friends (Oberg and Walgenbach, 2008). In addition, we had access to the internal electronic messaging system that stored all messages, with their sender and receiver.

From the interviews, we created a database of all individuals and organizations that were mentioned as relevant to the founding process. Using interview data, we coded types of social relations that connected individuals (acquaintanceship, friendship, co-ownership, mentor–mentee), individuals and organizations (organizational membership ties), and organizations (market contract ties). We allowed for multiple ties between people. For example, the founders could be connected by both co-ownership and friendship. We also reconstructed the lifespan of each connection. We went through several iterations of interviews with participants to check the details for each person's relations.

The resulting database contains a two-mode network with nodes for individuals and organizations and edges for relations of different types and lifespan. To analyze the relational structure, we generated snapshots (see Figure 17.2) of the network of participants and their affiliations at particular times.

The first snapshot, two years before the formal founding, shows the participants embedded in two organizations. Some of the later founders and early employees were students at a university, and others had already founded a training company nearby. The organizational memberships within these organizations formed two dense clusters, as the respective contexts functioned as catalysts for contacts.

A striking feature of this example is the high number of multiplex ties in each cluster. The later founders have acquaintance relationships to other students and faculty. At the same time, they are members of the university where they acquired their first student consultancy jobs. One could interpret this high level of multiplexity as an indicator of the founders' social capital. The two clusters are weakly linked by acquaintance relationships and by the dual membership of one student of the university who was working part-time for the training company.

The lack of connections between the two organizations could be perceived as a structural hole that hinders information and knowledge from flowing between the two clusters (Burt, 1992). Nevertheless, the acquaintance relations provide a weak-tie structure for novel information to flow from one organization to the other (Granovetter, 1973).

One year later, the overall network structure had changed dramatically. The later founders at the university had successful

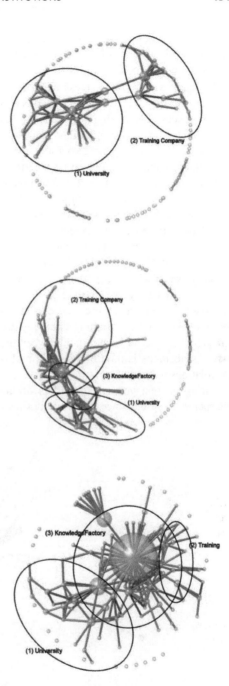

Figure 17.2   Founding of a company

consultancy projects; they learned through these projects that their clients were searching for easy-to-use knowledge management systems. Four of the later founders developed a software prototype for such a system. As they were still master's and PhD students, they searched for other potential co-founders with prior business experience. In doing so, they talked to many friends and acquaintances. Eventually, the student with the double affiliation proposed to introduce the university team to the two founders of the training company. After some meetings, they decided to collaborate and find potential customers for the new venture. Luckily, they found early customers and started initial knowledge management projects. As they worked on these projects, people from the training company and members of the team at the university formed deeper social relationships. Consequently, we observe in the second visualization that the previous clusters of the university and the training company are still relevant, but the former gap between the two organizations is now bridged via multiple relationships.

During its first year, the founders of the Internet start-up convinced several 'business

angels' to invest in them. At the same time, they received contracts from large companies in the same region for their knowledge management system. To fulfill these, nearly 60 employees were hired during the first month, initially close friends, then acquaintances, and later people without any connection to the founders or the initial organizations. Within the organization, the depth of the relations among individuals varied. Some members were connected through multiple relations, including co-ownership, friendship and mentorship, whereas others were linked only by formal mentorship relations. In sum, one year after the founding of the organization, the network structure was quite different. The new organization became the major node in this scenario, whereas the relevance of the university and the training company receded.

To uncover the internal communication connections, we reconstructed the network of sent messages from the company's internal electronic messaging system 18 months after its formation (see Figure 17.3). We observed

Figure 17.3 Communication network

a dense cluster of messages that connects all members of the organization, although the degree of involvement and the communication partners differ. Some employees form a strong core in which each member communicates with others. Other employees communicate infrequently with only a limited number of core members, and thus end up on the periphery.

When comparing the communication threads with the relations that existed before the company's creation, we observe that members with prior relationships are more likely to be in the core than those hired later. Furthermore, communication partners with multiplex relations – friendship combined with mentorship or ownership combined with mentorship – are less likely to use hierarchical signals in their communications than those with organizational membership and mentor–mentee ties as their only connection. Employees with multiplex relationships communicate in accordance with the company's avowed goal to implement knowledge management solutions that supplant more hierarchical modes of information diffusion. Members who lack social ties beyond their formal membership have a more limited set of communication partners, communicate most often with their mentors and evince signs of subordination. They do not embrace the company's goal to communicate non-hierarchically and use the mentor–mentee relations as a guide for orienting their interpersonal behaviors.

The example shows the strength and variation of the institutional expectations connected to social relations. Friendship and co-ownership both contain an expectation of non-hierarchical communication, whereas organizational membership and mentor–mentee relations come with stronger expectations of obedience and formal communication.

The study demonstrates both the flexibility and inflexibility of social relations. Relying on typical social ties, the network of affiliations was reconfigured extensively during the start-up phase. The non-idiosyncratic social relations operated as templates to configure and rewire social structures until the new company

was founded. But when it tried to change the behavioral expectations connected with social ties, the company failed to achieve its goal of establishing non-hierarchical modes of communication among all employees. In the short run, institutionalized relationships and their associated expectations provided a scaffolding to create a new entity, but highly institutionalized behavioral expectations about subsequent relations among new 'outside' hires hindered the effort to create an open workplace. The expectations inherent in social roles proved recalcitrant to attempts to build new work arrangements.

Inter-organizational Relations and Organizational Fields

After this example of relational processes within an organization, we turn now to relations among organizations. Analyses of relations across the same type of organization have been the stock-in-trade of network analysis. But to understand how fields form, and how field-wide norms and expectations develop, requires analyses of multiple types of organizations. It is at the intersection of different modes of activity that new fields emerge. Novelty often emerges at the intersection of two or more social worlds with divergent criteria of evaluation (Padgett and Powell, 2012; de Vaan et al., 2015). To illustrate the emergence of novelty, we draw on a two-decade project on the evolution of the field of life sciences (Powell et al., 2005, 2012). To exemplify how the intersection of social worlds leads to hybrid organizational forms, we present an example drawn from recent discussions of social impact (Korff, et al., 2015; Powell et al., 2017).

Example 2: Network Dynamics and Field Formation

We use a spatial analysis of Cambridge and Boston, Massachusetts, home to the largest

concentration of dedicated biotech companies and biomedical research in the world, to
illustrate how different types of organizations
interact, and in turn create a regional cluster.
Boston has a rich array of world-class
research organizations, including Harvard
University, MIT, Tufts and Boston University.
There are numerous world-class research
hospitals, including Massachusetts General
Hospital and Brigham and Women's Hospital.
There are also many cutting-edge medical
institutes, such as the Dana Farber Cancer
Center. Several of the first biotech companies
in the world were formed in Boston (Powell
and Sandholtz, 2012). These organizations
began collaborating on drug development in
the 1970s and 1980s, and by the 1990s the
Boston area also developed an active venture
capital sector that helped finance numerous
biotech companies.

At the start of the 21st century, Kendall
Square in Cambridge had become home to
a thriving cluster of biotech firms, as well
as MIT and the Whitehead Institute for
Biomedical Research, an international leader
in the Human Genome Project. In the early
part of this century, large pharmaceutical
firms, including Novartis and Pfizer, moved
their R&D facilities to Kendall Square, as
did the Los Angeles-based biotech company
Amgen. By one count, the larger Boston
region had 57 independent dedicated biotech
firms, 19 public research organizations and
37 venture capital firms, linked by an extensive network of relationships (Owen-Smith
and Powell, 2004).

In the course of our project on the evolution of the life science industry, we collected
detailed data on both formal and informal collaborative networks in Boston. The database
included information on founding teams,
strategic alliances, science advisory boards
and co-patenting, all of which helped build
a community of practice (Porter et al., 2006).
The most striking finding from this work is
that public research organizations were the
cornerstone on which the Boston community
was built (Owen-Smith and Powell, 2004).

To illustrate, more than half of the 131 people involved in creating biotech companies
between 1980 and 1999 were academics, and
the large majority (48 out of 67) were from
Boston-area universities. These founders all
retained some form of their university affiliations (Porter, 2004).

The public research organizations, notably MIT, BU, Harvard, Dana Farber,
Massachusetts General, and the New England
Medical Center, were densely interconnected,
formally through research partnerships and
informally through joint appointments of faculty and common grant funding. The biotech
network depended on these organizations,
and we have shown that if their presence is
removed, the larger network dissolves (Owen-
Smith and Powell, 2004, 2006). As the community matured, more and more participants
joined and the reliance on public research
organizations lessened. But the commitment
to open science, in which information, knowledge and human capital were widely shared,
persisted (Powell et al., 2007). The vitality of
the Boston community sprang from the universities acting as wellsprings of knowledge,
actively engaging in research partnerships
rather than pursuing only revenue-maximizing
activities. The Boston community was noted
for collaborative competition, a cornerstone of
the scientific ethos. Thus the inter-organizational networks that catalyzed the community
left a lasting institutional imprint.

Figure 17.4 represents the Boston network,
covering the years 1988–1999. The degree of
connectivity – that is, the number of alliances
that an organization engages in – is reflected
in the size of the node. The shape of the node
represents the type of organization; circles represent biotech companies, triangles universities,
and squares research institutes and hospitals. In
the upper left corner, we see alliances between
dedicated biotech firms, with the most connected companies represented by the larger
circles. The two largest circles are the first-gen-
eration companies Biogen and Genzyme, both
founded by academics. In the upper right, we
add universities, represented by triangles, and

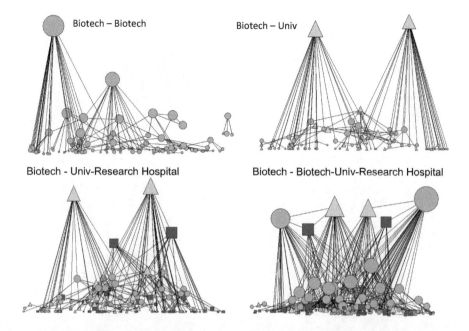

Biotech – Biotech

Biotech – Univ

Biotech - Univ-Research Hospital

Biotech - Biotech-Univ-Research Hospital

Figure 17.4   The Boston life sciences community, a field connected by different organizational forms (node size indicates number of alliances)

depict the network of ties between universities and biotech. The two largest nodes reflect the linkages of Harvard and MIT, on the left and right respectively. Research hospitals and medical institutes, the most active of which were Massachusetts General and Dana Farber, are added on the lower left as squares. The web of affiliations becomes much more complex and intermingled. On the lower left, we present a picture with all the organizations included. The full Boston community has something of the appearance of rival cliques, with two trios of firms, universities and hospitals at the head, vying with one another, and connected to an array of other organizations. This tightly connected, interdependent network is linked by multiple affiliations.

These network pictures illustrate how a set of individual relations among organizations of different types cohered into nested levels of affiliations that knitted the biomedical community in Cambridge and Boston; they created the dynamism that drove the evolution of the most productive biomedical

cluster in the world. Moreover, they illuminate how the joint engagement of universities, dedicated biotech firms, and research institutes and hospitals spawned a new era of life sciences research. These images collapse two decades of network data into four representations, so they do not capture the dynamics of the process. Nevertheless, they vividly illustrate how a web of affiliations spanned multiple types of organizations, private, public and non-profit, and suggest that the ethos of public research became the glue for the commercialization of the life sciences in the Boston cluster (Whittington et al., 2009).

How might such relationships evolve through time, and on a global level? Can we use network analysis to visualize how a field emerges and becomes a coherent entity? In Figure 17.5 we represent the evolution of the most connected set of participants in the worldwide field of biotechnology over a similar time span. To do so, we present four discrete-time visualizations to capture change and shift our focus from organizational forms

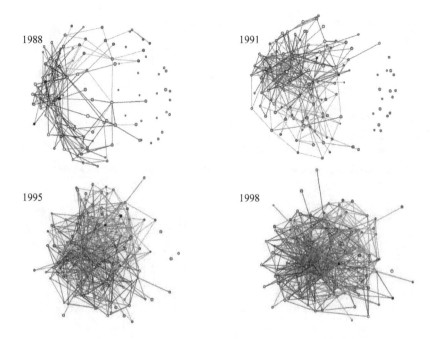

Figure 17.5   The dynamics of a field through time: the evolution of a biotech hub

Note: A full-colour version of this chapter can be found on the companion website for this *Handbook*, available at: https://study.sagepub.com/orginstitutionalism2e

to the type of relationships. We use Pajek, a free software package for the analysis and visualization of networks.

In this case, the networks are different types of formal inter-organizational relations, captured by data on contractual agreements between two parties. Pajek employs two powerful minimum-energy, network-drawing algorithms to represent data in two-dimensional Euclidian space. These algorithms simulate the network of collaborations as a system of interacting particles, in which organizational nodes repel one another unless network ties act as springs to draw the nodes closer together. These spring-embedded algorithms iteratively locate a network representation that minimizes the overall energy of the system by reducing the distance between connected nodes and maximizing distance between unconnected ones.

For this visualization, we include all members of the most connected component of the

overall network for the year 1998, represented in the lower right. We then go back in time to 1988 and depict a representation of the field a decade earlier. The links, or springs, are colored according to the functional activity reflected by a contractual inter-organizational tie. Red springs represent an R&D partnership, magenta a licensing agreement, green a financial relationship and dark blue an alliance involving one or more stages in the commercialization process, ranging from clinical trials to manufacturing to sales. All the nodes are scaled to the same size, so that we may focus on the evolution of relationships rather than the changing scale of nodes as in Figure 17.5. The nodes are colored according to their organizational form, with light blue a biotech firm, yellow a pharmaceutical corporation and brown a government institute or agency. Gray nodes represent venture capital firms; their growing importance is clearly seen in 1995 and 1998. One might think of the representation as an image of participants with different identities who engage in diverse activities with a variety of partners.

Several key features stand out in the 1988 image. The predominant color is blue, and the most active participants are small bio-tech firms, pharmaceutical corporations and government research agencies. The strong presence of commercialization ties (blue) indicates the dominant strategy of mutual need during the early years of the biotechnology industry. Young firms lacked the ability to bring new medicines to market, whereas large firms trailed behind in understanding new developments in molecular biology (Gambardella, 1995). Finance ties (green) are less prevalent, and very few venture capital firms (gray) are present. Most young companies supported themselves by selling their lead products to large corporations, who subsequently marketed the medicines and pocketed the lion's share of the revenues. In the lower half of the figure, one can see red springs between biotech firms and a brown node, representing the US National Institutes of Health. These reflect research collaborations between start-up companies and the NIH as well as its National Cancer Institute branch. The disconnected nodes on the right of the figure represent organizations that were not yet affiliated, but became so by 1998.

Move ahead to 1991 and notice several important changes. Many more green springs reflect a new form of financing from venture capital rather than large corporations. A few orange nodes enter the picture, reflecting the growing importance of universities in R&D collaborations and licensing efforts. The top of this image now has a mixture of blue, red and magenta, indicating that research partnerships were becoming as important as commercialization ties.

Fast-forward to 1995, and the importance of venture capital, reflected in the green springs, grows even more. Blue springs have declined in number, whereas red and magenta have also increased. The field is much more interconnected. Finally, in 1998,

we see a densely linked field in which organizations have multiple affiliations with a large number of different partners. Near the center is a brown node, again the NIH, and red is the dominant color in the middle, highlighting the increasing salience of scientific collaborations.

What are we to make of these network images of a field's evolution, reflected in different kinds of partnerships and collaborations? These longitudinal snapshots tell the story of how a field moved from relations of dependence to alliances on more equal footing. This shift is reflected in the transition in the color of ties from blue to red. The underlying driver of the changes is the development of alternative sources of financing, reflected by the green ties, which represent venture capital funding. Blue springs represent late-stage commercial development, whereas green springs reflect early-stage new product development and companies that are at a pre-IPO stage. The centrality of red ties, associated with public research organizations, suggests that venture capital financing and government support of R&D supplanted small firms' dependence on multi-national corporations. The multi-national corporations that appear in the center (represented by yellow nodes) in 1998 also had to learn how to interact differently with small start-ups, engaging in research, licensing and co-financing with them, rather than simply cherry-picking their most promising products.

The field that emerged is tightly interwoven; it is like a high-speed autobahn, or a hub, in which connections among participants follow multiple independent pathways. In subsequent work, we continued these network maps into the 21st century. Powell and Owen-Smith (2012) show that the field evolved with an open elite structure, allowing fast access to new entrants with promising research ideas, but at the same time having intensive competition among the most densely interconnected organizations. Although each successful regional cluster – the wellsprings of the field – had a different type of organizational anchor, the underlying relations and processes were similar: fluid labor markets, open sharing of successful practices and the interweaving of public and private science. These institutionalized expectations distinguished the successful regions, and even though they were absent in other cities, they left a relational footprint on the entire field. In this Boston example, we see the co-constitutive aspects of both networks and institutions: the norms of public science shaped early collaborations, and in turn an open-access network structure imparted its stamp on the larger community.

Example 3: Organizational Hybridity

Early research on organizational fields was based on the assumption that fields typically had a dominant type of organization or occupation, along with various supporting organizations. Consequently, studies of health care focused on doctors, hospitals, insurance companies and government regulation, and higher education studies focused on universities, students and professors (Scott, 2014: ch. 5). These early studies were typically focused on products and services, not on issues (Hoffman, 1999). Now, however, in many realms of life, fields are defined by emerging issues, and debates sprawl across a host of domains. Consider environmental sustainability, climate change, or many areas of health care that merge with lifestyle awareness. All these are fields with active participants from a wide spectrum of sectors.

Studying emerging issue-based fields is challenging, requiring new methodological tools that allow potential participants to be identified on the basis of connectivity rather than ontological properties. One fruitful source of data is the analysis of hyperlinks – the incoming and outgoing references that organizations make to one another on their web pages. Such data can be gathered with a webcrawler that starts from one or more identified central websites and then follows and

captures the network of links between web pages, in a form similar to snowball sampling. The resulting hyperlinks create a type of reference network, comparable to citations in academic papers or friendship networks expressed on Facebook. Lists of affiliated organizations with hyperlinks also resemble alliance portfolios, common in the study of inter-organizational networks, or tombstone listings, typical of work on investment banks. Incoming links may represent an organization's status or recognition, whereas outgoing links may reflect an organization's aspirations – that is, to whom it wishes to be attached or to whom it is indebted. Reciprocated links indicate mutual recognition. The overall portrait of a network of hyperlinks suggests the position of an organization within a particular domain or issue field.

The fact that references are hyperlinks, rather than resource flows or formal contracts, might raise concerns that such connections are somehow less tangible. But we think weblinks are particularly suitable for the analysis of dispersed fields, where interactions may be hard to observe in formats other than in digital communication. Even though it requires little financial investment, linking to an organization's website implies a willingness to alert one's audience to its existence and activities. Mutual bidirectional references reflect common awareness and a willingness to share traffic and a critical resource: attention.

To study the global debate on social impact that is bringing together organizations from international development, the non-profit sector and social entrepreneurship, we developed a weblink analysis of those involved in this discussion (Korff et al., 2015; Powell et al., 2017). Using a webcrawler we traced and recorded the hyperlinks to reveal a relational network of this emerging issue-based field. Our resulting sample, drawn in 2011, was remarkably interconnected. The 369 entities in our analysis had an average of 32 unidirectional connections to one another and shared 13 mutual references. With an average distance of just 2.2 degrees of separation between any two members, the issue field of performance evaluation is highly cohesive. Nevertheless, the boundaries of the field were exceedingly porous: they spanned non-profit, for-profit, government and international organizations. Even non-organizational entities, such as blogs, conferences and social movements, were involved. And within the non-profit domain there was great variety as well: associations, foundations, non-profit consulting firms and various service intermediaries, operating charities, public research organizations and churches.

We use a circular connection graph to illustrate the features of connectivity and diversity (see Figure 17.6). Graphs of this type were originally developed for the representation of genomic data, but they have since been used to represent global migration flows by world regions (Abel and Sander, 2014), the spread

of epidemics (Guo et al., 2013), and even patterns of musical beats (Lamere, 2012). The beauty of this method is that a plot of hierarchically structured nodes, in our case different types of organizations, forms a circular pattern with their weblinks displaying the relations between the various members of the field. When drawing the paths of connections, our script bundles ties with regard to organizational form. The resulting visualization shows how nascent fields bring together different types of organizations, thus offering a tool to capture membership in a possible emerging field.

We take a single organization, Acumen, from the full sample and display its hyperlinks, representing all ties between it and other organizations. We are able to show incoming, outgoing and bidirectional ties. Compared to more typical network visualizations, the circular display has the advantage of

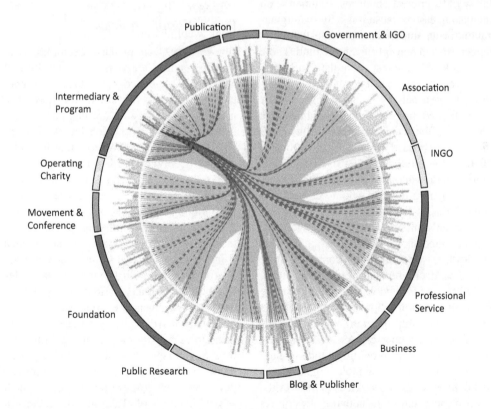

Figure 17.6 Relational definitions of organizational forms – Acumenfund as an example

conveying the distribution of types of organizations within the sample, thus highlighting diversity, and simultaneously representing ties among organizations, also depicting connectivity. We think these visualizations allow for a fast appraisal of the configuration of a field and the relationships among different types of organizations. This type of visualization is particularly appropriate for the analysis of nascent fields or fields in transition, where connections are made between organizations of diverse legal form. To be sure, a precondition for applying this method is the availability of information on organizations' legal status, but typically such information is easily obtainable.

The visualization depicts the hyperlinks that appeared in December 2011 on the web page of Acumen, a global non-profit venture fund created in 2001 to invest in social entrepreneurs working on solutions to poverty in the world's poorest countries. Acumen is an interesting case because it is a hybrid organization, or an amphibian, as suggested by its legal form as a non-profit venture fund. There is considerable interest these days in hybrid organizations (see Battilana et al., Chapter 5 this volume), but the focus of research has been limited to individual organizations rather than the wider environment in which they are embedded (Battilana and Dorado, 2010; Pache and Santos, 2013). Our network representation allows us to see the diverse set of organizations to whom Acumen has connections.

Acumen's mission is to build new organizational models for alleviating poverty. It employs a wide array of communication strategies, from regular email newsletters, to Twitter and Facebook accounts with more than half a million followers, to blogs. It also offers a fellowship program and has numerous free online courses. As an investment fund, it focuses on providing funds to help create financially sustainable organizations that deliver goods and services to the world's poorest communities. Its network of weblinks spans an array of organizational forms, with particular depth in contacts with financial services companies and other funders. It has relationships with operating charities and international non-governmental organizations (NGOs), such as Bangladesh Rehabilitation Assistance Committee (BRAC), Teach for America and Room to Read, all organizations with an emphasis on entrepreneurial leadership. Acumen also shares bidirectional ties with leading consultancies, non-profit intermediaries such as Bridgespan, and for-profits such as Deloitte and McKinsey. In sum, we see a combination of links that involve financial support, consulting, training and mobilization. These affiliations suggest that Acumen seeks to establish itself as a central contributor to debates on social impact, and it is able to put considerable financial weight behind its vision.

Research Potential for Institutional Analysis

As we have seen in these examples, relational structures are vehicles for the flow of information, knowledge, resources and reputation. But networks are much more than mere conduits; they do not just pass things. Networks do 'transformational work' (Padgett and Powell, 2012: 9). We saw that individuals are deeply embedded in multiple networks through their connections to friends, collaborators and mentors. These webs of affiliations create various demands and expectations, and identities are forged out of these divergent expectations. To act in such complex positions and switch roles in order to fulfill the linguistic and social rules attached to various relationships is part of daily life. Humans are often very good at managing such complexity, precisely because many roles and rules are deeply institutionalized. Social network analysis provides a rich toolkit to analyze micro-level institutional processes at the level of real-life data – such as with analyses of electronic interactions in organizations.

Meanings – both in terms of typifying a relationship and with respect to the identities of the participants – emerge out of intermittent switching across activities and relations. Such stories (to use Harrison White's language, 1992) are the cultural and discursive face of networks. To focus solely on pipes and prisms (Podolny, 2001) or embeddedness (Granovetter, 1985) can elide the myriad ways in which networks and institutions are intertwined.

We can also study how organizations are embedded in a network of relationships with other organizations in a similar way. As we have seen in the examples, variation in relational position affects legitimacy, growth and rates of innovation, even when we control for other organizational characteristics such as size, age and form (Powell et al., 1996; Maurer and Ebers, 2006). Although early network studies reduced this thick relational embeddedness to a simple count of the number of partners, more recent work examines the expected variety of environments that comes with differing types of relationships and partners. Such fine-grained measures for the heterogeneity of environments are helpful to study the complexity with which organizations are confronted (Beckman et al., 2014).

In addition to individuals or organizations, we can also analyze the types of relationships that facilitate interaction and govern exchange. When looking at affiliations among partners, we observed in many of the examples two parties who were connected through multiple types of relationships. These multiplex ties help to both initiate and govern formal transactions. From a broader institutional point of view, the character and complexity of relationships makes participants more receptive to new ideas. Which kinds of relationships can emerge from prior ones, and how these relationships interact with each other, are fertile topics for studying how congruent and conflicting institutional expectations emerge (Zaheer and Soda, 2009).

Limitations

One premise of this research direction is that institutionalized behavioral expectations can be proxied by capturing relevant types of social relationships. By relying on types of social relationships, this line of research does face several limitations. First, the same type of relationship might have divergent meanings for different participants. For example, within the field of biotechnology, a contract for a joint research program between a university and a big pharmaceutical company might be a highly detailed formal document regulating who contributes what and who owns the intellectual property. In contrast, a contract for a research collaboration between a university and a start-up could involve only a short letter of intent discussing shared problems. Thus the same activity has divergent meanings, depending on whom it is conducted with. Second, when we study social relationships in larger fields or in different and overlapping fields, the cultural sphere of these fields might lead to different understandings of the same type of relationship. For instance, an 'organizational membership' relationship is strongly connected to a work contract in the business sphere, whereas 'organizational membership' in a non-profit setting is more similar to belonging to a club. Third, even within the same sphere, the meaning of a type of relationship may vary depending on the historical era. Marriage in the 1950s in the United States and Europe was strongly associated with a hierarchical difference between husband and wife, whereas marriage or cohabitation today is on more equal terms. And, obviously, the very meaning of marriage has changed profoundly in recent years.

In principle, social network methods have the ability to capture information about differences in meanings. But it is no easy task. The above-mentioned problems could be handled by increasing the amount of stored information on the cultural and temporal specificities of each relationship. Such efforts have been rare because of data storage challenges, but we expect to see future research that makes use of fine-grained differences in the representation of types of relationships.

Another potential concern arises with the idea that social relationships 'transport' resources between actors, as if these resources are always commodities. The question is twofold. First, to what extent do tacit resources such as information or knowledge stay unchanged when traveling from actor to actor (Czarniawska and Joerges, 1996)? Resources may be altered as they travel across fields, social domains, or countries (Sahlin-Andersson, 1996). Transpositions might be the result of editing and translation practices that lead to local adaptations distinct from the originally transmitted idea (see Wedlin and Sahlin, Chapter 4 this volume). Indeed, a good deal of innovation occurs when ideas are transported from familiar ground to unfamiliar domains (Westney, 1980).

Second, social relationships are not the only vehicle for transporting tacit knowledge. The mass media and various high-status organizations are also crucial to the diffusion of ideas and legitimation (Meyer and Bromley, 2013; Meyer and Rowan, 1977). The World Wide Web, and if we think back to the past century, books, newspapers and radios, are crucial to the transmission of ideas and practices. Networks of relationships are important but surely not the only means through which ideas are shared and legitimated.

RELATIONAL MEANING STRUCTURES

A different, albeit smaller, line of research focuses on the meaning of relationships. Research in cultural sociology on narrative networks and historical reconstructions of relationships should be of keen interest to institutional scholars (Franzosi, 1998; McLean, 2007; Mische and White, 1998). Of special interest is the construction of meaning of typified relationships, types of roles and organizational forms, and transmitted content. To capture these different entities, we use the term 'concept' as a placeholder.

An underlying premise of this research is that the meaning of one concept cannot be understood without acknowledging its relationship to others. For example, the concept of a specific organizational role such as 'manager' is understood by taking into account its relation to other organizational roles such as 'employee' or 'owner'. Similarly, the meaning of types of social relationships is influenced by other concepts. For example, the meaning of the 'manager–employee' relationship is sharpened when compared with 'colleague' relationship or 'friendship'.

The similarity of concepts to each other can be captured via semantic relationships of the type 'A is similar to B'. Other types of relationships represent hierarchical categorical memberships ('A belongs to B') or contrasting ones ('A is opposite of B'). Together, concepts of a specific domain and their semantic relationships form a semantic network. In general, these networks share core structural features with social networks that allow the application of network analysis methods. Just as individuals are embedded in a network, concepts are embedded in a network of semantic relationships (Carley and Kaufer, 1993). Nevertheless, some differences have to be understood before applying social network methods to semantic networks. Although the metaphor of flow is helpful to study the transport of resources that is attached to social relationships, semantic relationships capture the similarity, rivalry, membership and connectivity between ideas. This difference in the content of relationships leads to a shift in the unit of analysis: instead of the flows that accompany social relationships, semantic distances are most relevant. Analyzing semantic distances is fruitful when we study divergent understandings of debated topics or when we try to understand cultural differences between individuals, organizations, or even fields.

Semantic network analysis can be applied to diverse phenomena, building on a range of ontological and epistemological assumptions. For example, in computer science, semantic networks are applied to summarize the content of documents with the assumption that the resulting network reflects a stable inter-subjective knowledge structure (Maedche, 2012). In sociology, semantic networks have been used to reconstruct subjective mental models and perceptions of individuals (Carley and Palmquist, 1992; Doerfel, 1998). In organizational sociology, semantic networks were discussed as ontologies that are 'systems of categories, meanings, and identities within which actors and actions are situated' (Ruef, 1999: 1403). For institutional research, the potential of semantic networks to capture processes of meaning construction is appealing. Researchers have analyzed how new organizational forms are understood (Ruef, 1999), market categories created (Kennedy, 2008) and organizational practices accepted (Meyer and Hoellerer, 2010).

To conceptualize meaning-construction processes with semantic networks, we draw on phenomenological traditions in the sociology of knowledge (Berger and Luckmann, 1966; Schutz, 1967). In this view, social interaction is possible only because individuals work with reciprocal typifications of actors, actions and relations (Schutz and Luckmann, 1973). Whether, for instance, we are writing an email or interacting directly with others in the workplace, we use typifications of actors (e.g., CEO, manager), actions (e.g., bookkeeping, meeting) and relations (e.g., colleague, business partner). In so doing, we assume that our counterparts have similar understandings. Through tradition, taken-for-grantedness and legitimation, these typifications become cultural categories for both thought and action.

Typifications – or, as we suggested above, concepts – are thereby the result of processes of collective construction through which people achieve agreement on the meaning of a concept. These processes are inherently relational because, in order to become part of the social stock of knowledge, concepts must be encapsulated in existing ideas. Thus, the relations to other concepts contribute to creating meaning for a focal concept in several ways. These linkages can be used to signal that the focal concept is a recognized part of the stock of knowledge. They can also be used to describe what the concept is and what it is not. Thus by differentiating a concept from others, its boundaries can be specified.

Although early proponents of the sociology of knowledge did not discuss connections among concepts in detail, Mohr and Duquenne (1997) have translated these ideas into relational terms. They examined how cultural categories of the poor were influenced by the treatment practices of Progressive Era poverty-relief organizations during the early 20th century in New York City. In an analysis of person-role interactions, Mohr (1994) demonstrated the historical contingencies of social roles and how the dominant moral discourse of poverty evolves. Later, writing with Harrison White, he argued that an institution is a link that interpenetrates the social and cultural realms (Mohr and White, 2008). Renate Meyer and colleagues applied a similar approach to the analysis of the semantic networks of the offices of the city of Vienna and the role identities they assign to citizens, customers and clients (Jancsary et al., 2016).

Example 4: Meaning Construction as a Relational Process

To explore relational aspects of meaning construction, we draw on Wikipedia for illustration. Wikipedia has become an integral part of our common knowledge sources today. Students, employees and managers look up terms when they hear them for the first time or when they need a short description of known concepts. Wikipedia articles are written by thousands of – mostly anonymous – authors. In the absence of extensive

Companies
and individuals

Societal and
legal concepts

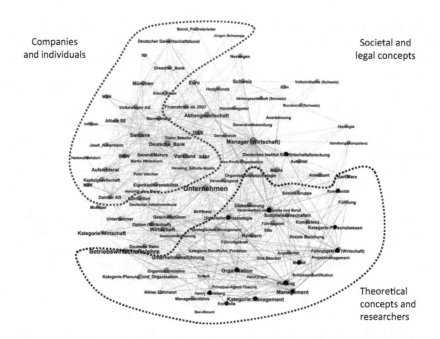

Theoretical
concepts and
researchers

Figure 17.7   Ego-network of the 'Manager (Wirtschaft)' page on the German Wikipedia in 2008

quality-checking mechanisms for authors and articles before publication, readers are invited to add and correct articles. The aggregation and constant refinement of everyday knowledge by many for many is an interesting source to study how concepts develop over time.

From a methodological point of view, Wikipedia is an interesting and well-structured source for studying relational meaning construction (Jemielniak, 2014; Benkler et al., 2015; Etter and Nielsen, 2015). In general, each article tries to define one concept. For instance, we find articles defining organizational concepts such as 'management', 'hierarchy' and 'employee'. Many of these are available in multiple languages. In the description section of an article, other articles are linked. The description of 'hierarchy' links to 'superior', 'subordinate', 'span' and 'member'. By transforming the articles into concept nodes and their links into semantic relationships, we can draw a semantic network that captures the concepts and references among them. To illustrate, we select

the ego-network of the article on 'Manager (Wirtschaft [Business])' in the German Wikipedia (see Figure 17.7).

The 'manager' concept is surrounded by three clusters. In the purple area on the left side we find pages of (mostly German) companies and individuals that provide factual examples of the role of a manager: influential managers like Dieter Zetsche (Daimler) and Josef Ackermann (Deutsche Bank) who have influenced the common understanding of what a top manager in Germany is. In the blue area on the bottom we see an interconnected group of theoretical/scientific concepts that frame the definition of a manager: business administration (*Betriebswirtschaftslehre*), management (*Unternehmensführung*) and organizational leadership (*Führung*) are the fields of research and teaching that are engaged in theorizing the concept of 'manager' and training managers. Prominent thinkers ranging from Karl Marx to Niklas Luhmann to Henry Mintzberg are embedded in this group. In between these two groups are societal and legal concepts that position the managerial role between other social entities, including companies (*Unternehmen*), board (*Verwaltungsrat*), stakeholders' meeting (*Generalversammlung*) and entrepreneur (*Unternehmener*). Additionally, normative aspects such as legitimacy (*Anerkennung*), corruption (*Korruption*), authority (*Autorität*) and responsibility (*Handlungskompetenz*) are connected to the managerial role.

Although the semantics of links is limited to 'concept A mentions concept B', without any classification of the character of the relationship (no 'concept A is a sub-concept of concept B' or any other precision), the references to and from a concept are simple but relevant indicators: (1) the number of references from a concept's description to other concepts can be interpreted as an indicator for the degree of attachment of the focal concept to a network of concepts; and (2) the number of incoming references indicates the relevance of the focal concept for the definition of other concepts.

Wikipedia stores all edits of articles, including changes of the description and changes in references to other articles. The stored versions can be downloaded for research purposes. We reconstruct a dynamic network based on the stored changes, including all changes to the concepts' descriptions and incoming/outgoing references for a sample of managerial topics (Schoellhorn et al., 2016). Staying with the same example of 'Manager (Business)', we select the development of central indicators for this article over time (see Figure 17.8). The values on the *y*-axis are scaled to make the processes visible.

We first examine the number of other articles referenced, reflected in 'Outdegree' and trend line 'Polynomic (Outdegree)'. We observe a relatively high number of outgoing references right after the creation of the article on 'Manager (Business)'. The first authors of this article located the new article by acknowledging other articles for the definition of the focal concept. 'Acknowledging' can mean that another concept is mentioned either as a similar concept or as a hierarchically higher one, or that the concept is clearly different. After nearly 2 years, we observe a steep drop in references to other concepts. Such pruning of references to other articles

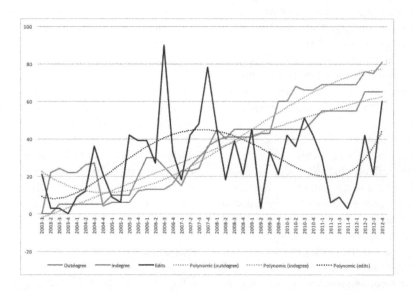

Figure 17.8   Processes affecting the 'Manager (Wirtschaft)' page on the German Wikipedia between 2003 and 2012 – processes are scaled on the *y*-axis to map them within the same diagram

limits the breadth of the focal article's context. The linkages are now selected more carefully, leading to a steady decrease in breadth. These processes can be interpreted as a form of boundary definition and maintenance.

From the start, the 'Manager (Business)' article aggregates the incoming references from other articles ('Indegree' and trend line 'Polynomic (Indegree)'). The steady increase shows that more articles written by authors who are largely independent from the original authors acknowledge the 'Manager (Business)' article as relevant. This development should indicate that the concept is increasingly recognized as part of the knowledge base.

During the 9-year time line the number of edits varies. In the initial introduction phase during the first six quarters, activity is relatively low. Then in a second growth phase lasting 3.5 years, the concept is redefined extensively, including pruning outgoing references. The heightened activity is connected with a significant growth in aggregating references from other articles. After that, we observe a stabilizing phase where editing takes place less often than in the growth phase, while outgoing and incoming references increase steadily. The initial increase in the number of changes in the article can be conceived of as editing and theorizing processes. The later reduction in the number suggests that, after a while, a certain agreement on the meaning of the concept has been realized.

The development of one concept in a semantic network with other concepts on Wikipedia reflects meaning construction. The achievement of agreement on the meaning of the concept is indicated by the reduced number of edits, boundaries are established through pruning and the recognition of the concept as part of the stock of knowledge or meaning system is observable by the steady increase in incoming references. Not all concepts on Wikipedia go through such a smooth development. Many are not recognized as relevant. Others show a high number of edits even after many years, a sign that they are either hotly debated or still developing. Either way, such discussion indicates that the ideas are not 'settled'.

Research Potential for Institutional Analysis

Using semantic networks to study processes of theorizing, objectification, institutionalization and deinstitutionalization has several promising applications. First, individual semantic networks can be created from the discursive actions of individuals or organizations. Then they reflect the speakers' positions in a cultural topography (DiMaggio et al., 2013; Mohr and Bogdanov, 2013). Comparing such portraits helps us to understand the similarities and differences between positions within a broader discourse. Similarities reveal which aspects of a discourse are taken for granted, whereas differences show what is challenged or which new ideas are debated. Second, semantic networks analysis enriches study of the diffusion of ideas and practices (see Boxenbaum and Jonsson, Chapter 3 this volume). The spread of single ideas is often theorized in institutional research (Strang and Meyer, 1993) and analyzed for single practices such as ISO 9000 (see Guler et al., 2002; Neumayer and Perkins, 2005). How nascent ideas are embedded into an existing ecology of concepts and how the successful institutionalization of a practice might affect congruent or competing others is seldom studied. By incorporating semantic relationships, we learn how the formation of ideas influence their diffusion (Höllerer et al., 2014; Wruk et al., 2016).

Limitations

Although highly promising, the application of semantic networks in institutional research does face challenges. The first is methodological: in order to model semantic relationships, we need a detailed qualitative coding of the connections between concepts (Phillips and Hardy, 2002). Alternatively, we might use automatic machine learning to identify semantic relationships, but this is currently possible only for simple semantic connections such as references or co-occurrences (Carley, 1993). Automatic identification can process large data corpora, albeit with a loss of subtlety. Qualitative coding is richer in capturing semantic depth but is applicable only to small samples. The methodological limitations of automated identification will decline as machine learning capabilities advance.

A second set of problems concerns the strong focus on semantic relationships and discourse in some research projects within this line of research: By capturing relations among concepts, such studies have focused on texts and have ignored the authors who created them. By ignoring the authors, the reconstructions of meaning structures become easily disconnected from understanding actors and social relationships. The last research direction that we present offers a solution to this problem.

A FRONTIER: MULTI-LEVEL ANALYSES OF CULTURE AND RELATIONSHIPS

Weber distinguished social interaction and meaning structures conceptually, but he proposed to study the dynamic between social relationships and meaning empirically. The two lines of research we have discussed focused either on the relational construction of social entities or on the relational construction of meaning. The third line of research we review attempts to overcome this divide by layering various units of analysis to study interactions among levels.

A relatively simple approach to adding a different level of meaning to a relational analysis is a multi-modal network, which combines two or more types of actors and their relationships. We gave an example earlier in this chapter when we explained the founding process of an organization as an interplay of individuals and organizations. In a multi-modal setting, the social entities of higher order – in our example, organizations – provide a meaningful context for the relationships of lower order – in our example, individuals.

Multi-level networks go further than multi-modal networks by distinguishing network levels that are meaningful as independent levels and, at the same time, allow an interlocking of levels. This interlocking can happen via two mechanisms. First, the same set of actors can appear on each level. In this case, an actor's network characteristics on various levels are compared. A vivid example is Padgett and Ansell's analysis of the Medici family in Renaissance Florence (Padgett and Ansell, 1993). Second, when we use different sets of nodes on different levels, inter-level relationships can capture the connections. For instance, when the social relationship level contains organizations and their connections and the semantic network level captures labels for management practices and their semantic relationships, then a relation 'used by' connects management practices and organizations. By connecting nodes of two different network levels, this multi-level network analysis combines relational and semantic networks.

Example 5: Research on Social Impact

Shared symbols help create both membership and distinction within organizational fields. The idea of shared symbols connects the relational organizational field of DiMaggio and Powell (1983) with the organizational field understanding of Bourdieu (1985). Such a synthesis requires that we distinguish social relationships and the cultural expressions of organizations. Our next example undertakes a dual analysis of social relationships and cultural expressions.

As we described earlier, we captured the discourse on social impact in the United States by collecting the text on the websites of organizations that contributed to the discussion. We also collected the hyperlinks of references among the websites. After we identified the relevant websites, we analyzed them for keywords that signal a certain position in the debate on metrics. We identified three sets of keywords: a first set highlights 'associational' values such as 'social justice' and 'charity'; a second focuses on 'scientific' concerns, including 'survey' and 'data'; a third mentioned 'managerial' aspects such as 'impact' and 'performance'. To be sure, all participants in the metrics debate used the keywords to some extent, but their usage differed significantly. Organizations that wanted to improve the measurement of social impact talked about it much more often than those focused on social justice.

To quantify the relevance of certain keywords for each organization, we stored all texts from each website and counted the number of appearances for each keyword. Then we aggregated the single-keyword counts to the number of occurrences within the 'associational', 'scientific' and 'managerial' domains. To control for the differing amounts of text on websites, we divided the columns by the number of all occurrences on a site. The results were three percentage values for the relative usage of associational, scientific and managerial keywords for each website. This 'discursive fingerprint' for each organization can be visualized in a triangle in which each position marks a particular mixture of the three perspectives (see Figure 17.9). In the center of the triangle, the three perspectives are used equally.

The distribution of organizations across the triangle shows a broad variety of positions in

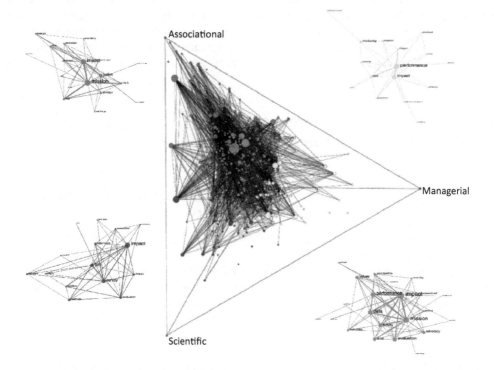

Figure 17.9 Overlay of semantic and social networks

Note: A full-colour version of this chapter can be found on the companion website for this *Handbook*, available at: https://study.sagepub.com/orginstitutionalism2e

the discourse on metrics. We can group the positions into three domains, each with a dominant voice: an associational community (colored red in Figure 17.9), a scientific community (colored blue), and a managerial community (colored yellow). Organizations in these communities use the keywords of their respective perspectives much more than keywords of the other two. We also find a fourth community of organizations that combines the three languages more equally (colored magenta).

As a next step, we add a relational layer. From the weblinks we collected, we extract the pairs of organizations that reference each other publicly on their websites. Figure 17.9 contains these social relationships of mutual public endorsement. As one can observe, many relationships connect organizations in the central community with organizations in one of the three 'home' communities. Analyzing the links in detail shows that the community of organizations that mixes discourses more equally forms a bridge to each of the other three communities of organizations with less balanced discursive positions (Korff et al., 2015).

In a final step, we identify how linguistic connections among the three perspectives function on a semantic level. We computed the co-occurrences of keywords for each community and drew co-occurrence graphs for each of the four communities (see Figure 17.9). In these graphs the keywords that coincide most often are connected via heavier lines. The organizations in the associational community strongly link *impact* with *mission* and add *trust* and *justice* as often-mentioned values. In the scientific community, impact is mentioned in combination with tools like survey and data, and with such purposes as performance and evaluation. In the managerial community, *performance* is most relevant and strongly combined with *impact*.

Overall, the semantic networks of the three home communities resemble prototypical ideas associated with their origins: Values such as justice, participation and mission

are discussed in the associational domain; data, methods and randomized control trials predominate in the scientific domain; and efficiency and outcomes typify the managerial domain. Organizations in the interstitial community combine *impact* and *mission*, as do members of the associational community; reference *data* and *survey*, as members of the scientific community do; and focus on *performance*, which is crucial for the managerial community. By picking up key terms of each of the other communities, organizations in the interstitial community create a synthesis of positions understandable to those in the other three communities.

In analyzing the backgrounds of members of the sample, we observed that the well-connected organizations in the interstitial community are neither ones with the highest status nor those with the longest history. Nor are they peripheral. Instead, the central interstitial community has a more equal composition of organizational forms and age cohorts than the other three communities. Therefore, what looks like a typical observation of a center–periphery structure is really an unexpected bridge. The interstitial organizations combine discursive positions in a way that connects positions in the same debate and facilitates mutual recognition among like-minded organizations as well as those from the other three domains.

Research Potential for Institutional Analysis

The combined analysis of social relationships and semantic networks expands the analysis of processes within fields. First, the semantic layer can, as we saw above, capture the cultural positions of organizations. By comparing an organization's positions in a relational network and at the same time on a cultural level, we can conceptualize and measure the cultural embeddedness of an organization. Comparison of relational and cultural distances for pairs of organizations provides insight into the degree of structuration of a field. Accordingly, in a highly structured field, we would expect a strong correlation between highly valued cultural expressions (Bourdieu, 1985) and an organization's centrality in a relational field (DiMaggio and Powell, 1983). On the other hand, if we observe that relational distances are low, whereas cultural distances are high, we can assume that interactions occur in a culturally fragmented field. Second, instead of capturing the cultural positions of organizations, a semantic level could entail the discursive positions of organizations in a specific debate. In such a multi-level analysis, the issue field (Hoffman, 2001) 'hovers' above a relational field. It would be interesting to explore how the structural positions of organizations affect their positions in an issue-driven debate or how the distribution of issue positions shapes the patterns of relationships among field members.

In addition to these two intra-field possibilities, a multi-level network approach allows us to study interactions among diverse fields. As in the previous example, the overlap of fields can be described in detail on relational and cultural aspects at the same point in time. This example is a snapshot of one point, but it would be enlightening to see dynamic analyses of overlapping fields that compare relational and semantic developments. Such analyses would deepen understanding of the causal mechanisms in the interaction between cultural and relational embeddedness of organizations and fields. As one example, it is possible to identify social connections where the cultural distance between fields would make it unlikely to have social connections. Instead of assuming homophily as a basic social rule that transforms quasi-deterministic culture into relationships (McPherson et al., 2001), we could observe where and why relations are created despite a low level of similarity.

Furthermore, if we assume that some fields are nested in other fields (Fligstein and McAdam, 2012), different levels for specific fields and their semantic specificities could be captured in multi-level networks. Hierarchical relationships among organizations in different levels would need to be introduced to link the nested fields with overarching fields. Relational and semantic relations can then be analyzed as either 'horizontal' within one field or 'vertical', connecting higher and lower fields.

Studying cultural and relational dynamics within and among fields will deepen our understanding of how rewiring, emergence and stability occur. By analyzing the location of new ideas or new practices on a cultural layer, we can observe settings in which similar new concepts show up in areas that are relationally distant from each other. Such emergence without traces of diffusion following relational structures would fit the expectation that some ideas travel via communication media and are independent of social relationships. In the long run, we could capture, measure and explain mechanisms such as editing and adaptation via multi-level network analysis comparing the semantic differences of the adopted ideas and relational positions of the adopting organizations.

Limitations

As much as a multi-level perspective is valuable theoretically and methodologically, applications to empirical settings are not easy. Data on social relationships and meaning structures have to be collected at the same time and in matching quality. But with the advancement of computer science and linguistics, we have tools to collect, store and analyze large amounts of high-quality data. In some research settings, such tools can be applied to real-life data, which are generated independent of the research process.

The web pages of organizations contain data that can be split into social relationships among organizations and concepts mentioned by organizations. As we show above, hyperlinks can be interpreted as social relationships of endorsement or, if they are bi-directional, mutual recognition between respective organizations. The published texts and even the images and icons on the web pages can be transformed into semantic data that capture an organization's cultural position (see Powell, et al., 2016).

Social networks such as Facebook and Twitter store data that can be transformed into multi-level networks as well (Golder and Macy, 2014). In addition to individual representations, relations among users are also stored. Such data would, in principle, allow a comparison of semantic, relational and behavioral interaction. In practice, access to such data is sometimes limited to a small set of cooperating or in-house researchers. Nevertheless, other publicly available sources can supply behavioral data. Wikipedia is an interesting source, as it stores edits on concepts next to the text and references as well. Yelp offers restaurant and other reviews, and Netflix has extensive film reviews (see Goldberg et al., 2016).

TOWARDS INTEGRATION

We have discussed three lines of research on networks and institutions: social network analysis, semantic networks and multi-level networks. Figure 17.10 sketches how these approaches are connected.

Research on social networks has emphasized the relational configurations of both people and organizations. The mantra of this work is perhaps best summarized as: 'in the short run, actors make relations, but in the long run, relations make actors' (Padgett and Powell, 2012: 2). In our analysis of the start-up company, we saw that individuals transformed acquaintance and friendship relationships into business relationships and then into organizational affiliations as they formed a new organization. This example underlines the observation that actors make relations in the short run, but in time those choices form their new identities. Looking at the community involved in discussions of non-profit evaluation, we saw that organizations can be defined by their connections to different types of organizations. In the biotechnology industry, the strategic trajectories of organizations were heavily shaped by their relational positions. Both examples underscore that the character of relationships molds both opportunities and worldviews, thus rendering some actions more legitimate and valuable.

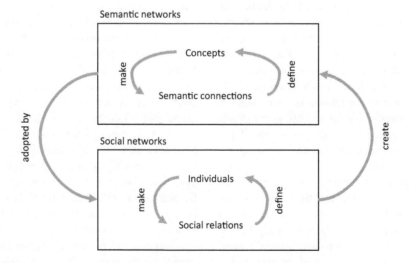

Figure 17.10   Multi-level relations between social and semantic networks

The second line of research we reviewed focuses on the discursive and cultural origins of meaning structures. The tagline of this work could be: 'In the short run, concepts reference other concepts via semantic connections, but in the long run, these semantic connections define concepts.' As the Wikipedia example shows, descriptions of concepts contain semantic connections that either help us compare concepts or create hierarchical relations among them. Semantic references from other concepts can further frame or reduce the meaning of a focal concept. The synchronous construction of concepts can be highly aligned in cases of well-theorized ideas or totally askew in cases of controversial topics. Attention to conceptual elaboration or the construction of narratives, especially for such emotion-laden topics as love or politics, is at the frontier of this line of research (Franzosi, 2010; Friedland et al., 2014).

The third research program focuses on the interplay of relational and semantic networks. To summarize it, one might say: 'In the short run, concepts are adopted by actors, but in the long run, actors create and change concepts.' In our nonprofit example, we observe the embrace of evaluation and other management concepts by social sector organizations. Furthermore, relational distance explains the mix of adopted concepts: the shorter the relational distance between organizations, the more similar the mix of adopted concepts. Reciprocally, organizations with longer relational distances combine concepts differently. They form communities in which central concepts are framed similarly within the community, but quite differently from other communities. In the long run, these alternative frames change the meaning of focal concepts.

A focus on the mechanisms outlined in Figure 17.10 would enable the study of complex institutional processes such as proto-institutionalization or changes in legitimate classifications. Proto-institutionalization may start when individuals form new types of relationships. For instance, 'Facebook

friends' became a new type of social relationship when more and more people made connections to distant acquaintances via the Facebook 'friend' function. This new practice – ironically a misuse of the software's function – led to an adaptation of the 'friendship' concept by introducing a distinction between 'friendship' and 'Facebook friendship'. After this new concept of friendship was extensively discussed in the media and integrated into a common stock of knowledge, people easily distinguished between 'real-life friendship' and 'Facebook friendship'. This new understanding even changes the way many people now make and maintain personal relationships. In this example, the proto-institutionalization was driven by changes in everyday practices, but this is not necessarily always the case. Influential institutional change of social relationships can start at the conceptual level, too. The reframing of concepts might expand or reduce the legitimate applicability of concepts even before practices have changed. For instance, disconnecting 'homosexuality' from 'sodomy' in the public discourse helped gays and lesbians to make existing committed relationships publicly visible. Public visibility changed the quality of relationships even before a formal recognition of homosexual partnership became possible.

A core assumption in our review of networks and institutions is that the situated meaning of relations matters a great deal. Individuals, groups, concepts, values, even fields take on meanings in and through their connections to others. In this regard, we argue that relations are the flows that both create and sustain identities. This duality of individuals and their relations to others and the meanings that adhere to such linkages is fundamental to the view, first offered by Simmel (1955) and later developed by Breiger (1974), that individuals are often defined by the social groups they belong to *and* those social groups are defined by their members. We think it is a short step, but a powerful one, to connect one level of social structure (individuals and their relations, individuals and organizations, organizations and organizations) to larger social and cultural spheres. In this view, institutions are the products of differing network configurations. The relational structures are the scaffolding on which cultural, political and economic institutions rest. The persistence and resilience of these macro-structures depends, we believe, at least in part on the character of the networks that shape them.

We began our chapter with the conviction that the traditions of research on networks and institutions ought to be brought into closer alignment. After showing that canonical institutional work incorporated both relational and cultural concepts, we provided examples of three lines of research that connect network analysis and institutional analysis empirically. The three streams highlight the variability of relational structures to form new social entities quickly, emphasize the deeply institutionalized and hard-to-alter expectations connected with social relations, and illustrate the dynamic interplay between relational and meaning structures that forge divergent paths of institutional change. We showed, in the first line, that social relations are building blocks for institutions within organizations at the micro-level (see Schneiberg and Lounsbury, Chapter 11 this volume) as well as between organizations within organizational fields (see Wootten and Hoffman, Chapter 2 this volume). We then turned to a second burgeoning line of research on the relational aspect of meaning structures (see Phillips and Malhotra, Chapter 15 this volume). The third line of multi-level analyses is located at the frontier, bringing together both cultural and relational analyses. We are convinced that all three avenues have propitious futures; each will benefit from the expansion of big data sources becoming available for relational analyses, the advancement of social network methods, and theoretical progress in both network analysis and institutionalism.

Note

1 Original version in German: Soziale «Beziehung» soll ein seinem Sinngehalt nach aufeinander gegenseitig eingestelltes und dadurch orientiertes Sichverhalten mehrerer heißen. Die soziale Beziehung besteht also durchaus und ganz ausschließlich: in der Chance, daß in einer (sinnhaft) angebbaren Art sozial gehandelt wird, einerlei zunächst: worauf diese Chance beruht. (Weber, 2002: 13)

ACKNOWLEDGMENTS

We are grateful to Stefan Berwing, Royston Greenwood, Renate Meyer and Dominika Wruk for their very helpful comments on early drafts of the manuscript. Several of the visualizations were done by Jason Owen-Smith, co-author of the chapter that appeared in the first edition. We appreciate his help and generosity.

REFERENCES

Abel, G. J. and Sander, N. (2014). Quantifying global international migration flows. *Science* 343(6178): 1520–1522.

Battilana, J. and Dorado, S. (2010). Building sustainable hybrid organizations. *Academy of Management Journal* 53(6): 1419–1440.

Beckman, C. M., Schoonhoven, C. B., Rottner, R. M. and Kim, S.-J. (2014). Relational pluralism in de novo organizations. *Academy of Management Journal* 57(2): 460–483.

Benkler, Y., Shaw, A. and Hill, B.M. (2015). Peer production: A form of collective intelligence. In M. Bernstein and T. Malone (eds), *Handbook of Collective Intelligence*. Cambridge, MA: MIT Press.

Berger, P. L. and Luckmann, T. (1966). *The Social Construction of Reality*. New York: Doubleday.

Bourdieu, P. (1985). The social space and the genesis of groups. *Theory and Society* 14(6): 723–744.

Bourdieu, P. and Wacquant, L. J. D. (1992). The logic of fields. In *An Invitation to Reflexive Sociology*. Chicago, IL: University of Chicago Press. pp. 95–115.

Breiger, R. (1974). The duality of persons and groups. *Social Forces* 53: 181–190.

Burt, R. S. (1992). *Structural Holes: The Social Structure of Competition*. Cambridge, MA: Harvard University Press.

Carley, K. (1993). Coding choices for textual analysis: A comparison of content analysis and map analysis. *Sociological Methodology* 23: 75–126.

Carley, K. and Kaufer, D. (1993). Semantic connectivity: An approach for analyzing symbols in semantic networks. *Communication Theory* 3(3): 183–213.

Carley, K. and Palmquist, M. (1992). Extracting, representing, and analyzing mental models. *Social Forces* 70(3): 601–636.

Clemens, E. S. and Cook, J. M. (1999). Politics and institutionalism: Explaining durability and change. *Annual Review of Sociology* 25: 441–466.

Czarniawska, B. and Joerges, B. (1996). Travels of ideas. In B. Czarniawska and G. Sevón (eds), *Translating Organizational Change*. Berlin: Walter de Gruyter. pp. 13–48

de Vaan, M., Stark, D. and Vedres, B. (2015). Game changer: The topology of creativity. *American Journal of Sociology* 120(4): 1144–1194.

DiMaggio, P. J. and Powell, W. W. (1983). The iron cage revisited: Institutional isomorphism and collective rationality in organizational fields. *American Sociological Review* 48(2): 147–160.

DiMaggio, P., Nag, M. and Blei, D. (2013). Exploiting affinities between topic modeling and the sociological perspective on culture. *Poetics* 41(6): 570–606.

Diestel, R. (2010). *Graph Theory*. Berlin and Heidelberg: Springer.

Doerfel, M. L. (1998). What constitutes semantic network analysis? A comparison of research and methodologies. *Connections* 21(2): 16–26.

Etter, M. and Nielsen, F. (2015). Collective remembering of organizations: co-construction of organizational pasts in Wikipedia. *Corporate Communications: An International Journal* 20(4): 431–447.

Fligstein, N. and McAdam, D. (2012). *A Theory of Fields*. New York: Oxford University Press.

Franzosi, R. (1998). Narrative analysis – or how (and why) sociologists should be interested in narrative. *Annual Review of Sociology* 24: 517–554.

Franzosi, R. (2010). Sociology, narrative, and the quality versus quantity debate (Goethe versus Newton): Can computer-assisted story grammars help us understand the rise of Italian fascism (1919–1922)? *Theory and Society* 39(6): 593–629.

Friedland, R., Mohr, J., Roose, H. and Gardinali, P. (2014). The institutional logics of love: Measuring intimate life. *Theory and Society* 43(3–4): 333–370.

Gambardella, A. (1995). *Science and innovation: The US pharmaceutical industry during the 1980s*. Cambridge: Cambridge University Press.

Goldberg, A., Hannan, M. and Kovacs, B. (2016). What does it mean to span cultural boundaries? Variety and atypicality in cultural consumption. *American Sociological Review* 81(2): 215–241.

Golder, S. A. and Macy, M.W. (2014). Digital footprints: Opportunities and challenges for online social research. *Annual Review of Sociology* 40: 6.1–6.24.

Granovetter, M. S. (1973). The strength of weak ties. *American Journal of Sociology* 78(6): 1360–1380.

Granovetter, M.S. (1985). Economic action and social structure: The problem of embeddedness. *American Journal of Sociology* 91(3): 481–510.

Guler, I., Guillén, M. F. and Macpherson, J. M. (2002). Global competition, institutions, and the diffusion of organizational practices: The international spread of ISO 9000 Quality Certificates. *Administrative Science Quarterly* 47(2): 207–232.

Guo, Z., Tao, X., Yin, C., Han, N., Yu, J., Li, H., Liu, H., Fang, F., Adams, J., Wang, J., Liang, G., Tang, Q. and Rayner, S. (2013). National borders effectively halt the spread of rabies. *PLoS Neglected Tropical Diseases* 7(1): e2039.

Hoellerer, M. A., Jancsary, D., Barberio, V., Meyer, R. E. (2014). Birds of a feather: Management knowledge as interlocking vocabularies. In Academy of Management Best Paper Proceedings. Philadelphia. pp. 873–878.

Hoffman, A. J. (1999). Institutional evolution and change: Environmentalism and the U.S. chemical industry. *Academy of Management Journal* 42(4): 351–371.

Hoffman, A. J. (2001). Linking organizational and field-level analyses: The diffusion of corporate environmental practice. *Organization & Environment* 14(2): 133–156.

Jancsary, D., Meyer R.E., Hollerer, M. and Barberio, V. (2016). Recursive categorization and enactment of role identities in pluralistic institutional contexts. Working paper, WU-Vienna.

Jemielniak, D. (2014). *Common Knowledge? An Ethnography of Wikipedia*. Stanford, CA: Stanford University Press.

Kennedy, M. (2008). Getting counted: Markets, media, and reality. *American Sociological Review* 73(2): 270–295.

Korff, V. P., Oberg, A. and Powell, W. W. (2015). Interstitial organizations as conversational bridges. *Bulletin of the Association for Information Science and Technology* 41(2): 34–38.

Lamere, P. (2012). The infinite jukebox. Music Machinery. (Retrieved online on August 5, 2015: http://musicmachinery.com/2012/11/12/the-infinite-jukebox/).

Laumann, E. O., Galaskiewicz, J. and Marsden, P. V. (1978). Community structure as interorganizational linkages. *Annual Review of Sociology* 4: 455–484.

Lorrain, F. and White, H. C. (1971). Structural equivalence of individuals in social networks. *Journal of Mathematical Sociology* 1(1): 49–80.

Maedche, A. D. (2012). *Ontology learning for the semantic web.* New York: Springer Science+Business Media.

Maurer, I. and Ebers, M. (2006). The dynamics of social capital and their performance implications: Lessons from biotechnology start-ups. *Administrative Science Quarterly* 51(2): 262–292.

McLean, P. D. (2007). *The Art of Networking: Strategic Interaction and Patronage in Renaissance Florence.* Durham, N.C.: Duke University Press.

McPherson, M., Smith-Lovin, L. and Cook, J. M. (2001). Birds of a feather: Homophily in social networks. *Annual Review of Sociology* 27: 415–444.

Meyer, J. W. and Bromley, P. (2013). The worldwide expansion of 'organization'. *Sociological Theory* 31(4): 366–389.

Meyer, R. E. and Hoellerer, M. A. (2010). Meaning structures in a contested issue field: A topographic map of shareholder value in Austria. *Academy of Management Journal* 53(6): 1241–1262.

Meyer, J. W. and Rowan, B. (1977). Institutionalized organizations: formal structure as myth and ceremony. *American Journal of Sociology* 83(2): 340–363.

Mische, A. and White, H. C. (1998). Between conversation and situation: Public switching dynamics across network domains. *Social Research* 65: 695–724.

Mohr, J. W. (1994). Soldiers, mothers, tramps and ohers: Discourse roles in the 1907 New York City Charity Directory. *Poetics* 22: 327–357.

Mohr, J. W. and Bogdanov, P. (2013). Topic models: What they are and why they matter. *Poetics* 41(6): 545–569.

Mohr, J. W. and Duquenne, V. (1997). The duality of culture and practice: Poverty relief in New York City, 1888–1917. *Theory and Society* 26(2–3): 305–356.

Mohr, J. W. and White, H. C. (2008). How to model an institution. *Theory and Society* 37: 485–512.

Neumayer, E. and Perkins, R. (2005). Uneven geographies of organizational practice. *Economic Geography* 81(3): 237–259.

Oberg, A. and Walgenbach, P. (2008). Hierarchical structures of communication in a network organization. *Scandinavian Journal of Management* 24(3): 183–198.

Owen-Smith, J. and Powell, W. W. (2004). Knowledge networks as channels and conduits: The effects of spillovers in the Boston biotechnology community. *Organization Science* 15(1): 5–21.

Owen-Smith, J. and Powell, W. W. (2006). Accounting for emergence and novelty in Boston and Bay Area biotechnology. In P. Braunerhjelm and M. Feldman (eds), *Cluster Genesis*. Oxford: Oxford University Press. pp. 61–83.

Pache, A.-C. and Santos, F. (2013). Inside the hybrid organization: Selective coupling as a response to competing institutional logics. *Academy of Management Journal* 56(4): 972–1001.

Padgett, J. F. and Ansell, C. K. (1993). Robust action and the rise of the Medici, 1400–1434. *American Journal of Sociology* 98(6): 1259–1319.

Padgett, J. F. and Powell, W. W. (2012). *The Emergence of Organizations and Markets*. Princeton, NJ: Princeton University Press.

Phillips, N. and Hardy, C. (2002). *Discourse Analysis: Investigating Processes of Social Construction*. Thousand Oaks, CA: Sage.

Podolny, J. M. (2001). Networks as the pipes and prisms of the market. *American Journal of Sociology* 107(1): 33–60.

Porter, K. A. (2004). You can't leave your past behind: the influence of founders' career histories on their firms. PhD dissertation, Stanford University.

Porter, K. A., Bunker-Whittington, K. and Powell, W. W. (2006). The institutional embeddedness of high-tech regions. In Stefano Breschi and Franco Malerba (eds), *Clusters, Networks, and Innovation*. Oxford: Oxford University Press. pp. 261–296.

Powell, W.W., Brandtner, C. and Horvath, A. (2016). Click and mortar: Organizations on the Web. *Research in Organizational Behavior*. 36:101–120.

Powell, W. W., Koput, K. W. and Smith-Doerr, L. (1996). Interorganizational collaboration and the locus of innovation: Networks of learning in biotechnology. *Administrative Science Quarterly* 41(1): 116–145.

Powell, W. W., Oberg, A., Korff, V. P, Oelberger, C. and Kloos, K. (2017). Institutional analysis in a digital era. In G. Krücken, C. Mazza, R. Meyer and P. Walgenbach (eds), *New Themes in Institutional Analysis: Topics and Issues from European Research*. Cheltenham: Edward Elgar.

Powell, W. W. and Owen-Smith, J. (2012). An open elite. In J. F. Padgett and W. W. Powell (eds), *The Emergence of Organizations and Markets*. Princeton, NJ: Princeton University Press. pp. 466–495.

Powell, W. W., Owen-Smith, J. and Colyvas, J. A. (2007). Innovation and emulation: Lessons from American universities in selling private rights to public knowledge. *Minerva* 45(2): 121–142.

Powell, W. W., Packalen, K. A. and Whittington, K. (2012). Organizational and institutional genesis. In J. F. Padgett and W. W. Powell (eds), *The Emergence of Organizations and Markets*. Princeton, NJ: Princeton University Press. pp. 434–465.

Powell, W. W. and Sandholtz, K. W. (2012). Amphibious entrepreneurs and the emergence of organizational forms. *Strategic Entrepreneurship Journal* 6(2): 94–115.

Powell, W. W., White, D. R., Koput, K. W. and Owen-Smith, J. (2005). Network dynamics and field evolution: The growth of interorganizational collaboration in the life sciences. *American Journal of Sociology* 110(4): 1132–1205.

Ringer, F. K. (2009). *Max Weber's Methodology: The Unification of the Cultural and Social Sciences.* Cambridge, MA: Harvard University Press.

Ruef, M. (1999). Social ontology and the dynamics of organizational forms: Creating market actors in the healthcare field, 1966–1994. *Social Forces* 77(4): 1403–1432.

Sahlin-Andersson, K. (1996). Imitating by editing success: The construction of organizational fields and identities. In B. Czarniawska and G. Sevón (eds), *Translating Organizational Change*. Berlin: de Gruyter. pp. 466–495.

Schoellhorn, T., Wruk, D. and Oberg, A. (2016). The social construction of management vocabularies: An analysis of data from Wikipedia. Working paper. University of Mannheim.

Schutz, A. (1967). *The Phenomenology of the Social World*. Evanston, IL: Northwestern University Press.

Schutz, A. and Luckmann, T. (1973). *The Structures of the Life-world* (Vol. 1). Evanston, IL: Northwestern University Press.

Scott, W. R. (2014). *Institutions and Organizations*. Thousand Oaks, CA: Sage.

Simmel, G. (1955). *Conflict and the Web of Group-Affiliations*. New York: Free Press.

Strang, D. and Meyer, J. W. (1993). Institutional conditions for diffusion. *Theory and Society* 22(4): 487–511.

Wasserman, S. and Faust, K. (1994). *Social network analysis: Methods and applications.* Cambridge: Cambridge University Press.

Weber, M. (1904). Die protestantische Ethik und der Geist des Kapitalismus. In *Archiv für Sozialwissenschaft und Sozialpolitik* 20 (1):1–54; 21 (1): 1–110.

Weber, M. (1978). *Economy and Society: An Outline of Interpretive Sociology*. Berkeley, CA: University of California Press.

Weber, M. (2002). *Wirtschaft und Gesellschaft: Grundriss der Verstehenden Soziologie*. Tübingen: Mohr Siebeck.

Westney, E. (1980). *Imitation and Innovation: The Transfer of Western Organizational Patterns to Meiji Japan*. Cambridge, MA: Harvard University Press.

White, H. C. (1992). *Identity and Control*. Princeton, NJ: Princeton University Press.

White, H. C., Boorman, S. A. and Breiger, R. L. (1976). Social structure from multiple networks. I. Blockmodels of roles and positions. *American Journal of Sociology* 81(4): 730–780.

Whittington, K. B., Owen-Smith, J. and Powell, W. W. (2009). Networks, propinquity, and innovation in knowledge-intensive industries. *Administrative Science Quarterly* 54(1): 90–122.

Wruk, D., Bort, S., Oberg, A. and Woywode, M. (2016). How relational theorizing influences the popularity of management concepts. Working Paper, University of Mannheim.

Zaheer, A. and Soda, G. (2009). Network evolution: The origins of structural holes. *Administrative Science Quarterly* 54(1): 1–31.

18

Power, Institutions and Organizations

Thomas B. Lawrence and Sean Buchanan

INTRODUCTION

The relationship between power and institutions is an intimate one. Institutions exist to the extent that they are powerful – the extent to which they affect the behaviors, beliefs and opportunities of individuals, groups, organizations and societies. Institutions are enduring patterns of social practice (Hughes, 1936), but they are more than that: institutions are those patterns of practice for which 'departures from the pattern are counteracted in a regulated fashion, by repetitively activated, socially constructed, controls – that is, by some set of rewards and sanctions' (Jepperson, 1991: 145). Thus, power, in the form of repetitively activated controls, is what differentiates institutions from other social constructions (Phillips, Lawrence, & Hardy, 2004). The relationship between power and institutions is also bi-directional. A significant stream of research has documented the processes through which actors, individual and collective, affect the institutional contexts within which they work (Lawrence & Suddaby, 2006; Lawrence, Suddaby, & Leca, 2009). This brings agency and interests directly into the relationship between power and institutions (DiMaggio, 1988).

Even with the close connection between power and institutions, a longstanding critique of organizational institutionalism is that it tends to downplay the role of power (Clegg, 2010; Hirsch & Lounsbury, 1997; Khan et al., 2007; Lawrence & Suddaby, 2006; Munir, 2015; Suddaby, 2010). As the focus in institutional research shifted from isomorphism, legitimacy and institutionalization to change, interests and conflict in the evolution of organizational fields, it sparked a renewed interest in the relationship between power and institutions. Research on institutional entrepreneurship (Hardy & Maguire, 2008), institutional work (Lawrence & Suddaby, 2006;

Lawrence et al., 2009), institutional logics (Thornton, Ocasio, & Lounsbury, 2012) and research at the intersection of institutional theory and social movement studies (Fligstein & McAdam, 2012) have assigned a more important and explicit role to power in their institutional analyses. As productive as these efforts have been, the explicit integration of existing theories of power in organizational institutionalism is still underdeveloped (Munir, 2015). Although recent theoretical developments in organizational institutionalism have created room for power and interests, there has still been little formal engagement with existing insights on power – a lamentable condition since new directions in organizational institutionalism offer the potential for integration in ways that could enhance both the power and institutional literatures.

Our objective in this chapter is to take a step in this direction by developing an organizing framework for understanding the multidimensional relationship between power and institutions, and exploring some of the implications of that framework. Specifically, we argue that there are two overarching dynamics that describe the

relationship between power and institutions – institutional control and institutional agency – each of which describes an aspect of how institutions and actors relate to each other in terms of power relations. Institutional control involves the effects of institutions on actors' beliefs and behavior; institutional agency describes the work of actors to create, transform, maintain and disrupt institutions. These two dynamics form the core of this chapter: we describe and illustrate each of them, examine the mode and forms of power with which each is associated and explore them in terms of three key dimensions – the role of decision-making, the presence or absence of conflict and the nature of resistance (see Figure 18.1).

We first outline the notion of institutional politics and introduce the concepts of institutional control and institutional agency. We then examine institutional control and institutional agency in more detail, with specific attention to how they connect to existing writing on power and politics. We conclude by exploring a set of issues that emerge from the framework and some future directions for research on power, organizations and institutions.

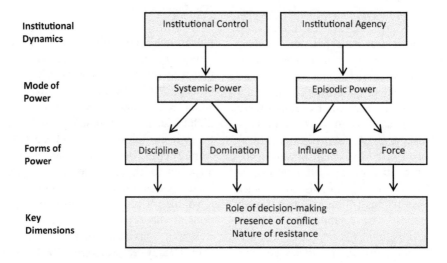

Figure 18.1   Institutional politics

THE POLITICS OF INSTITUTIONS

Overview

Holm's (1995) study of institutional change in Norwegian fisheries highlights the potential analytical power of adopting an explicitly political stance on institutions and institutional change, as well as suggesting the contours of what a political perspective on institutions might look like. Holm's (1995: 398) analysis explains the 'rise and fall of a specific institutional form, the mandated sales organization (MSO), in Norwegian fisheries', focusing on the 'interconnection between the practical and political levels of action' and the 'interaction of practices, interests and ideas'. This work highlights the power of a number of institutions and a range of political/institutional strategies. We draw on it here to illustrate the theoretical framework for connecting power and institutions that we develop in the rest of the chapter.

The central institutional battle in Holm's (1995) story is between the fishers and the fish merchants of Norway. Holm's (1995: 404) first example of institutional change in this battle provides a clear example of the relationship between power and institutions.

> The fishermen's common interest lay in restricting the supply of herring, which would bring better prices. As long as they acted individually, this option was not available. To solve their dilemma, the fishermen had to set up a rule system that allowed them to market their herring collectively. ... If we simply assume that the fishermen in this situation were rational and acted individually, we cannot account for the fact that [the rule system] was established and successfully organized the herring trade for two years without legal protection. To explain this, we must look into the pattern of interaction among the fishermen. The herring fishery in question was largely concentrated both in time and geographically, and the fishermen largely came from the same area, had the same social background and operated the same type of technology.

The rule system enacted by the fishermen is a classic example of an institution – a set of practices, for which compliance is enforced through social and cultural mechanisms, in this case implicitly through mechanisms of surveillance and shaming that are made possible by dense patterns of interaction and common cultural backgrounds (Douglas, 1973). This institution effected a set of power relations, directly between the rules and the fishermen, and indirectly between the fishermen and the fish merchants who now faced a powerful, organized collective actor, rather than a set of relatively weak, unorganized individual fishermen.

In further describing this example, Holm (1995) points to a second type of relationship between power and institutions.

> A rule making all fishermen sell their catch through the organization, enforced by police and the legal apparatus of the Norwegian state, would immediately solve the free-rider problem. Mobilizing the state's power behind the fishermen's institutional project in this way was not a simple matter, however. It would require, first, that the fishermen's problem could be made so important that it warranted a place on the political agenda; second, that the fishermen's solution would survive through the various stages of the decision-making process; and third, that the required number of votes be cast in their favor.

Thus, the system of rules that would bind the fishermen together and unite them against the fish merchants did not just appear, but required significant, complex forms of institutional work (Lawrence & Suddaby, 2006). In order to institutionalize the rule in law, the fishermen would need to engage in discursive strategies intended to frame the problem as important, as well as building and leveraging relationships with governmental actors who could shepherd the project through the bureaucracy. Thus, as much as institutions are connected to power through their impact on the beliefs and behaviors of actors, they are also connected to power through the strategies of actors that are intended to transform institutional arrangements through political means.

The contours of power and institutions in Holm's (1995) study illustrate the theoretical framework that guides the exploration of power and institutions in the rest of this chapter. These contours represent what we refer to as the 'institutional politics' of a situation. The concept of institutional politics, we argue, involves two primary dynamics, each of which describes a role that power plays in shaping the relationship between institutions and actors. Institutional control describes the impact of institutions on the behaviors and beliefs of individual and organizational actors. In research that has highlighted this role, power is present but usually appears only indirectly, observable primarily through the compliance of organizational actors to institutional rules and norms (DiMaggio & Powell, 1983; Meyer & Rowan, 1977; Tolbert & Zucker, 1983). Institutional agency is conceived of here as the work of individual and collective actors to create, transform, maintain and disrupt institutions. Research that has highlighted this role has made power explicit, highlighting the connection between power and agency and the influence of actors on institutional arrangements (DiMaggio, 1988; Greenwood & Suddaby, 2006; Maguire, Hardy, & Lawrence, 2004; Rojas, 2010; Zietsma & Lawrence, 2010). The interplay of these two roles in an organizational field can be described as the 'institutional politics' of a situation.

Power and Institutional Politics

Before exploring each dimension of institutional politics, we provide an overview of the approach we take to power and the terminology we employ. The study of power has long been a central element of organization studies, with a large and long-standing literature on what leads to individuals, groups and organizations gaining power relative to others (Bachrach & Lawler, 1980; Brass, 1984; Clegg & Dunkerly, 1980; Hickson, Hinings, Schneck, & Pennings, 1972; Jermier, Knights, & Nord, 1994; Mintzberg, 1983; Pfeffer, 1981; Pfeffer & Salancik, 1978). The variety of approaches and theories has meant

that the concept of power has been defined in a wide range of ways. In this chapter, we take the view that power is a property of relationships such that the beliefs or behaviors of an actor are affected by another actor or system. Thus, power is a relational phenomenon, rather than a commodity (Clegg, 1989; Clegg, Courpasson, & Phillips, 2006; Foucault, 1977): it is an effect of social relations, rather than something an actor can 'have', 'hold' or 'keep in reserve'. So, when we talk about power in this chapter, we do not refer to a capacity for effect, but rather the aspect of relationships in which there is an effect.[1]

This definition of power leads to a distinction between two basic modes in which power operates and which corresponds in large part to the dynamics of institutional politics described above. The first mode of power is 'episodic', which refers to relatively discrete, strategic acts of mobilization initiated by self-interested actors (Clegg, 1989). Historically, this mode of power has dominated the study of power in organizations through the development of two streams of theory (Hardy & Clegg, 1996), one focusing on power as domination through ownership and control of the means of production (Braverman, 1974; Burowoy, 1979; Clegg, 1975; Clegg & Dunkerly, 1980); and, one focusing on the role of power as an alternative to formal authority in organizations (Hickson et al., 1972; Mintzberg, 1984; Thompson, 1956). The second mode of power is 'systemic' – power that works through routine, ongoing practices to advantage particular groups without those groups necessarily establishing or maintaining those practices (Clegg, 1989; Foucault, 1977; Hardy, 1994; Laclau & Mouffe, 1985). Systemic forms of power are associated with a wide range of phenomena, including socialization and accreditation processes (Covaleski, Dirsmith, Heian, & Samuel, 1998), technological systems (Noble, 1984; Shaiken, 1984) and insurance and tax regimes (Simon, 1988). These forms of power tend to work in an ongoing, prosaic fashion, such that they are often not apparent as forms of power (Covaleski et al., 1998; Townley, 1993).

As illustrated in Figure 18.1, we argue that institutional agency is underpinned by episodic forms of power. Institutional agency requires actors to mobilize resources, engage in institutional contests over meanings and practices, develop, support or attack forms of discourse and practice – all involving discrete, strategic acts of mobilization. We further argue that institutional control is associated with systemic forms of power. As discussed above, Jepperson (1991) argues that institutions are associated with automatic forms of regulation that enforce compliance, without involving episodes of action on the part of interested actors. Regulations, norms and taken-for-granted understandings have their roots, of course, in self-interested behavior, but once established and associated with sets of social, cultural or cognitive 'stakes' (Bourdieu, 1993), institutional control operates as if significantly independent of any particular agent, or at least independent of the interests of such an agent. The differences between episodic and systemic power are observable in the concrete ways in which power is exercised. In this chapter, we explore two forms of episodic power – influence and force – that we believe are fundamental to institutional agency and two forms of systemic power – discipline and domination – that we believe are fundamental to institutional control.

For each of the four forms of power that we examine, we explore three distinct dimensions (see Figure 18.1): the role of decision-making; the role of conflict; and the nature of resistance. Our interest in decision-making is rooted in Lukes' (1974) argument that the study of power should not be limited to concrete decision-making, but must also include non-decision-making, which refers to instances where potential courses of action are 'suffocated before they are even voiced; or kept covert; or killed before they gain access to the relevant decision-making arena'

(Bacharach & Baratz, 1970: 44), as well as broader forms of agenda setting and control. Lukes' central argument is that power is exercised not only when an actor's decision is influenced by another; but also when certain courses of action are prevented from entering the decision-making arena.

The second dimension – the role of conflict – is also drawn from Lukes' (1974), who argues that the exercise of power can involve observable conflict but can also exist without any directly observable conflict. Although the exercise of power often sparks some kind of contestation, in some cases power can be exercised in ways that prevent conflict from emerging in the first place. Lukes (2005: 27) suggests that 'the supreme exercise of power [is] to get another or others to have the desires you want them to have – that is, to secure their compliance by controlling their thoughts and desires'.

The third dimension of each form of power we explore is its relationship to resistance. The first prominent recognition of institutional resistance was in Oliver's (1991) discussion of potential responses to institutional pressures: 'organizational responses [to institutional pressures] will vary from conforming to resistant, from impotent to influential, and from habitual to opportunistic' (Oliver, 1991: 151). Oliver argues that actors potentially respond to institutional pressures with five basic strategies that range from the most passive to the most active: 'acquiesce', 'compromise', 'avoid', 'defy' and 'manipulate'. All but the end points of this set involve attempting to impose limits on institutional control and thus constitute forms of institutional resistance. Despite Oliver's (1991) clear and influential statement regarding the importance of institutional resistance, it has remained the most neglected aspect of institutional politics. The 'acquiesce' strategy has been the dominant response described in studies of institutional control (e.g., Hinings & Greenwood, 1988; Tolbert & Zucker, 1983); and the 'manipulate' strategy has been the focus of research on institutional agency (e.g., DiMaggio, 1988; Garud, Jain, & Kumaraswamy, 2002; Maguire et al., 2004). There is, however, a relative dearth of research on the 'middle ground' strategies of 'compromise', 'avoid' and 'defy'.

Although studies of resistance in the social sciences are not rare, they tend to focus on resistance to either broad, societal norms and values (Kirsch, 2000), or to managerial control in organizations (Jermier et al., 1994). Much less well understood is the resistance of individuals and organizations to field-level rules, norms and beliefs. In this chapter, we adopt Barbalet's (1985: 531) position, that 'resistance imposes limits on power. Indeed, it is through its limitations on power that resistance contributes to the outcome of power relations'. Thus, institutional resistance is understood as the work of actors to impose limits on institutional control and institutional agency.

Table 18.1 provides an overview of how each of the elements of power is related to institutional control and institutional agency. In the following sections, we discuss institutional control and agency in more detail with a specific emphasis on their relationship with the modes, forms and dimensions of power we have described.

INSTITUTIONAL CONTROL

Overview

The concept of institutional control parallels the classic sociological notion of 'social control', which 'referred to the capacity of a society to regulate itself according to desired principles and values' (Janowitz, 1975: 82). Working from an institutional perspective, our concern is not with the ability of societies to regulate themselves, but with the ways in which institutions organize, encourage and diminish particular forms of thought and action in organizational fields. Thus, there are two important conceptual shifts in moving from a focus on social control to institutional control. First, consistent with the more general shift in discussions of power (Clegg et al., 2006), institutional control is not understood as a capacity but as a relational effect of institutions on actors. The second shift is toward an understanding of social systems as fragmented, contested arenas in which coherent sets of 'desired principles and values' are less likely than are competing and conflicting principles and values enacted in discourse and action (Dyck & Schroeder, 2005; Hoffman, 1999).

In order to clarify the nature and scope of institutional control, we can contrast it with resource dependence as a basis for interorganizational control. Drawing on exchange theory (Emerson, 1962), Pfeffer and Salancik (1978) argue that the critical determinant of power among organizations is the control of the flow of resources, such as money, physical resources, capital and human resources. Institutional theories also recognize the importance of resource flows as a control mechanism (Meyer & Rowan, 1977; Scott, W. R., 2001), but resource dependence theory is not a theory of institutional control: theories of institutional control focus on those aspects of a field that regulate behavior on an

Table 18.1   Elements of power in institutional agency and control

Element of power	Institutional agency	Institutional control
Mode of power	Episodic	Systemic
Forms of power exercised	Force, influence	Domination, discipline
Conflict and contestation	Observable	Not observable (Latent)
Decision-making	Yes	No
Nature of resistance	Active (explicit)	Passive (implicit)

ongoing basis and set 'the rules of the game' (Holm, 1995; Lawrence, 1999), including coercive and resource-based forms of control, but also including many other forms of control, such as social and professional norms and taken-for-granted assumptions about the world. Resource dependence arguments also go beyond institutional concerns, dealing with any actor-to-actor relationship shaped by mutual resource interdependence, whether it is an institutional phenomenon or an ad hoc, momentary negotiation (Pfeffer & Salancik, 1978). Thus, institutional and resource dependence theories constitute overlapping domains of concern rather than competing explanations; both approaches deal with resource-based institutional control, but each also includes other non-overlapping areas of interest.

Early neo-institutional writing on organizations, beginning with Meyer and Rowan's (1977) and DiMaggio and Powell's (1983) classic pieces, focused significantly on institutional control, but left out an explicit consideration of power. Meyer and Rowan's (1977) discussion of 'formal structure as myth and ceremony' provided a powerful set of images for understanding the nature of institutional control. Their central argument was that 'organizations are driven to incorporate the practices and procedures defined by prevailing rationalized concepts of organizational work and institutionalized in society' (Meyer & Rowan, 1977: 340). Most critical to how research on institutional control developed is their idea that organizational environments are constituted by powerful myths that are 'highly institutional and thus in some measure beyond the discretion of any individual participant or organization' (Meyer & Rowan, 1977: 344). DiMaggio and Powell's (1983) examination of institutional isomorphism and collective rationality extended the focus on compliance with powerful institutions, which led both to compliance and the homogenization of organizational fields. DiMaggio and Powell's (1983) three sources of institutional control – mimetic, normative,

coercive – have become a taken-for-granted feature of institutional theories of organization. Each of these describes a class of mechanisms that regulate the behavior of actors in a field through social and cultural systems rather than through enforcement by a self-interested actor.

The first stream of empirical research that emerged out of these theoretical discussions focused on the diffusion of innovation within fields and also largely ignored the role of power (Baron, Dobbin, & Jennings, 1986; Leblebici, Salancik, Copay, & King, 1991; Mezias & Scarselletta, 1994; Slack & Hinings, 1994; Strang & Soule, 1998; Tolbert & Zucker, 1983; Westphal, Gulati, & Shortell, 1997). This work demonstrated that the adoption of innovations depends significantly on the influence of social and cultural systems that reduce uncertainty and provide legitimacy and other resources to adopting organizations. The classic institutional argument regarding the diffusion of innovation has been that as new practices are adopted for technical reasons by leading organizations, the practices gain legitimacy that spurs adoption by other organizations who avoid cognitive uncertainty and normative sanction by mimicking the early adopters (Tolbert & Zucker, 1983).

Mode of Power

Looking across the theoretical and empirical writing on institutional control, it is clear that much of this work has left out any explicit consideration of power. There is, however, an image of power that is consistent with, though often implicit in, this work. Both the earlier institutional discussions of control that largely ignored power and the more recent work that brings it in directly are consistent with a conception of power as vested in social and cultural systems, rather than in individual actors. This approach to power is consistent with recent work in the sociology of power that describes it as 'systemic' –

power that works through routine, ongoing practices to advantage particular groups without those groups necessarily establishing or maintaining those practices (Clegg, 1989; Foucault, 1977; Laclau & Mouffe, 1985). Understanding power as potentially systemic is not intended to attribute 'will' or 'agency' to systems (social or technological), but rather to break any simple association between agency and power (Clegg, 1989; Foucault, 1977). From an institutional perspective, it seems important to embrace a definition of power that recognizes the power of the courts, professional associations, language and social customs, as well as the actors that occupy roles within these structures and who enact these routines. Indeed, a cornerstone of an institutional perspective is the idea that actors are subject to forms of power that are disconnected from the interests and actions of specific others (Meyer & Rowan, 1977).

Forms of Power

It is useful to differentiate between two major forms of institutional control, one of which has received attention in the institutional literature and one that has largely been ignored. The concept of power that is most closely connected to studies of institutional control is Foucault's (1977) notion of discipline; although not explicitly evoked in most institutional research, the idea of power exercised through mundane practices that revolve significantly around the constitution of identity is core to much writing on institutional control. Discipline as a form of power involves an ongoing, systemic engagement with the target of power and relies on the agency of that target to have an effect (Clegg, 1989; Covaleski et al., 1998; Jacques, 1995; Knights & Wilmott, 1989). Discipline works through the micro-techniques, practices and procedures of everyday life (Sewell, 1998; Sewell & Wilkinson, 1992; Townley, 1993) and consequently is often overlooked as a

form of power in organizations. An aspect of discipline that is critical for its role as a basis for institutional control is its capacity to provide a basis for agency through the formation of identity (Knights & Willmott, 1989). Discipline is concerned with shaping the actual formation of the subject, such that: 'subjects come to recognize themselves as discrete and autonomous individuals whose sense of a clear identity is sustained through participation in social practices which are a condition and consequence of the exercise of power' (Knights & Wilmott, 1989: 538). Thus, disciplinary practices involve a form of power that can be understood as positive in its provision of identity and motivation to organizational actors (Foucault, 1984).

A wonderful example of discipline as a basis for institutional control comes from its use in the Ford Motor Company in the early 20th century, as recounted in Stephen Meyer III's (1981), *The Five Dollar Day*. Although Henry Ford ran the Ford Motor Company and was responsible for many of its effects, he was particularly aware of the need to embed power in institutions which could control the behavior of employees (and others) without direct episodes of managerial agency. The Ford Motor Company's use of discipline as a means of institutional control stemmed from the problems it was facing with respect to its employees that were created in part by the assembly line technology. In 1914, the company's annual turnover rate was 416 percent and daily absenteeism ran between 10 and 20 percent. In response, Ford established another corporate institution, when it launched the 'Five Dollar Day' – a profit-sharing plan that would apply to 90 percent of its workforce, a plan so out of the ordinary that the *Wall Street Journal* accused Ford of promoting socialism. A central aspect of the program was the set of conditions that dictated who was eligible to benefit from it. Ford would only provide the profit sharing to those it deemed to be living a moral life, including 'every male employee over 22 years of age who leads a clean, sober and industrious life, and who can prove he has thrifty habits', and '[a]ll women employed by the company who are deserving and who have some relatives solely dependent upon them for support'. Alongside these rules, Ford established a Sociological Department, which investigated the home lives of Ford workers in order to ascertain eligibility and which actively intervened with training and advice intended to lift standards of morality and living conditions. The Sociological Department focused particularly on Ford's newly immigrated workers, who as Henry Ford expressed, 'must be taught American ways, the English language, and the right way to live'. To that end, compulsory courses at the Ford English School included 'industry and efficiency', 'thrift and economy', 'domestic relations' and 'community relations'.

Although disciplinary power is an important and pervasive mechanism underpinning institutions, other important forms of systemic power have been largely overlooked in institutional studies of organization. In particular, institutional research has tended to ignore systemic power that works by altering the range of options available to actors – a form of power we describe as domination[2] (Lawrence, Winn, & Jennings, 2001). This form of power can be embedded in a wide variety of social systems including material technologies (Noble, 1984; Shaiken, 1984), information systems and actuarial practices (Simon, 1988). In the context of institutional control, systems of domination often take the form of physical and social technologies that provide the context for action. The physical layouts of office building, factories and universities, for example, institutionalize particular patterns of interaction among workers and are often overlooked as political mechanisms (Brown, Lawrence, & Robinson, 2005). Winner's (1986) examination of the politics of artifacts examines numerous instances of this, with the most famous being the many overpasses on Long Island, New York, which are so low that they do not permit 12-foot high public buses to use the parkways over which those overpasses go. Winner (1986: 23) argues that this effect is not happenstance, but rather, that it was an intentional control strategy of Robert Moses, the chief architect of New York public works from the 1920s to the 1970s. Winner argues that Moses' specified the overpasses in this way so that: 'Poor people and blacks, who normally used public transit, were kept off the roads because the twelve-foot tall buses could not handle the overpasses' and were consequently limited in their access to 'Jones Beach, Moses' widely acclaimed public park' (Winner, 1986: 23).

A more subtle form of institutional control through domination is that which is embedded in systems that restrict the effects of action, rather than restrict action itself, as illustrated by a wide range of actuarial practices. Actuarial practices involve the use of statistics to represent the characteristics of a population, including the use of standardized tests of intelligence, aptitude or personality, the construction of probability tables reflecting life expectancies and other life chances and the definition of demographic categories (Simon, 1988). While these familiar practices seem relatively banal and benign, they represent a significant shift in the production and structuring of power relations in societies:

> Through the lens of representations thrown off by these practices, individuals, once understood as moral or rational actors, are increasingly understood as locations in actuarial tables of variations. This shift from moral agent to actuarial subject marks a change in the way power is exercised on individuals by the state and other large organizations. Where power once sought to manipulate the choice of rational actors, it now seeks to predict behavior and situate subjects according to the risks they pose. (Simon, 1988: 772)

Thus, actuarial practices involve a form of restrictive institutional control in which the lives of individuals are transformed, not through their own actions, but through their placement in a social order abstracted from their lived experiences.

Although discipline and domination both work though routines practices and systems, there is a critical difference between the two. Whereas disciplinary practices involve 'knowing' the individual through regimes of surveillance and training (Foucault, 1977; Townley, 1993), systems of domination work by 'knowing' the population. Disciplinary mechanisms of surveillance, normalization and examination all work to construct an image of the 'normal' subject in any defined social space, move actors toward uniformity and punish deviants. In contrast, systems of domination 'map out the distribution and arrange strategies to maximize efficiency of the population as it stands' (Simon, 1988). While the disciplinary practices replaced techniques of coercion and intimidation that were less precise and engendered overt conflict (Clegg, 1989; Foucault, 1977), systems of domination draw on our knowledge of populations to extend this process even further, constructing even more precise systems of institutional control which engender even less overt conflict.

Role of Decision-Making

To better understand the ways in which different forms of power affect the dynamics of institutional control, we explore three key dimensions of each, beginning with the role of decision-making. The two forms of power we have argued underpin institutional control have very different relationships to decision-making. Key to discipline is the assumption of agency, and in fact the construction of agency (Lawrence et al., 2001). This affects the assumptions about decision-making under conditions of discipline: disciplinary techniques involve ongoing interaction with the subject in ways that shape their subjectivities such that the decisions they make and the decisions they do not make conform with the institutions that underpin power (Foucault, 1977). As Lawrence et al. (2001: 636) state, disciplined actors are 'those that have

internalized the external demands and made them their own'. Thus, an objective of discipline is to prevent some issues from entering the decision-making arena; shaping the identities of targets such that certain courses of action are not considered, either because they simply seem impossible or because they are so repugnant as to be outside of the realm of serious contemplation. At the same time, discipline also works by ensuring that when decisions are made, they are done so intuitively in institutionally prescribed ways (Lawrence, Mauws, Dyck, & Kleysen, 2005). Thus, through surveillance, examination and other disciplinary practices, discipline affects decision-making through the continuous shaping of people's identities.

In contrast, domination constructs the target as an object, excluding the potential for agency (Lawrence et al., 2001), avoiding issues of decision-making not through the shaping of identities but through the shaping of circumstances. In systems of domination, including the layout of physical spaces, actuarial practices and some production technologies, power works by restricting the choice set available to people. Thus, domination controls targets in ways that render the ability of people to make decisions irrelevant.

Presence of Conflict

Although conflict and decision-making have been historically linked in the study of power (community power studies) contrasting the presence of conflict associated with discipline and domination shows the potential disconnect. A consistent and important finding in studies of institutional control has been the lack of visible conflict associated with successful instances of institutional control (Covaleski et al., 1998; Lawrence et al., 2001; Oakes et al., 1998; Townley, 1997). We argue that a lack of visible conflict is associated with institutional control based on both discipline and domination, but that this is achieved in very different ways.

In the case of discipline, the prevention of visible conflict is rooted in people's experience of discipline as a positive, productive form of power. As Foucault argues,

> If power were never anything but repressive, if it never did anything but say no, do you really think one would be brought to obey it? What makes power hold good, what makes it accepted, is simply the fact that it doesn't only weigh on us as a force that says no, but that it traverses and produces things, it induces pleasure, forms knowledge, produces discourse. It needs to be considered as a productive network which runs through the whole social body, much more than as a negative instance whose function is repression. (Foucault, 1980: 119)

The relationship between discipline and conflict is inherent in the multiple, related meanings of the term: discipline as a form of power is tightly tied to its meanings connected to knowledge (the discipline of sociology), professions (accounting as a discipline) and self-regulation (disciplined bodies). It is not that discipline as a basis for institutional control does not involve any conflict, but rather that the kinds of conflict we associate with discipline are not so much overt, visible conflict among parties, but rather the internal conflicts and tensions that are associated with individuals struggling with tensions between their self-identities and the prescribed identities that are engendered by the disciplinary system. In organizations, conflict stemming from discipline is similarly likely to involve internal tensions and contradictions rooted in the differential attachment of subgroups to the values in play, and differential exposure of subgroups to surveillance and examination. In Oakes et al.'s (1998) study of business planning as a mechanism of discipline in museums and cultural heritage sites in Alberta, Canada, they found that the pedagogic function of business plans in this field helped to prevent conflict that would have likely arisen if the changes engendered by the business planning had simply been implemented. The introduction of business planning made the managers actively involved – and

complicit – in practices that reduced their organizational power and cultural capital.

Conflict in institutional control underpinned by domination is similarly invisible, though for different reasons and with different dynamics. Domination works through structures and systems that limit the range of alternatives available to people as they confront different situations. Such structures and systems by their nature limit the scope for people to engage in conflict. Structures of domination rule out conflict by limiting potential interactions with other people: the creators and sponsors of physical infrastructure, information systems, actuarial systems and material technologies are often well removed from people's experience of those structures and systems, making conflict, at least in terms of social conflict between human actors, difficult or impossible to effect. Moreover, systems of domination often appear as 'technical' solutions rather than 'political' moves. In Noble's (1984) study of machine automation, the particular system of automation that was implemented – numerical control – wrested control from skilled workers, but did so immediately and silently, such that potential workplace conflict never emerged significantly because the technology appeared both neutral and inevitable. Similarly, actuarial practices are likely to be viewed as apolitical statistical systems (Simon, 1988) and physical layouts can appear as practical responses to organizational requirements (Gieryn, 2002). An understanding of systems as neutral and apolitical can prevent conflict because they are constructed as part of the technical environment that evolves in ways rational and inevitable (Holm, 1995). Although we argue that systems of domination are associated with relatively little overt conflict, we are not suggesting people necessarily 'like' or accept them, only that they tend not to engender direct, visible conflict. People's negative reactions to such systems are not without consequences, however, as we discuss below in terms of resistance.

Nature of Resistance

Scholarly attention to resistance to institutional control has increased significantly with the emergence of institutional pluralism and complexity (Greenwood, Raynard, Kodeih, Micelotta, & Lounsbury, 2011; Kraatz & Block, 2008) as important areas of institutional research. This stream of research has pointed to the potential, and even necessity, for organizational actors to strategically and creatively resist as they negotiate among competing sources of institutional control (Pache & Santos, 2010; Smets, Morris, & Greenwood, 2012). These studies, however, underplay the importance of resistance to institutional control regardless of the level of institutional complexity. We have known since Oliver's (1991) articulation of strategic responses to institutional control that organizational actors respond heterogeneously, including engaging in multiple forms of resistance. Our focus on discipline and domination as bases of institutional control helps to clarify how and under what conditions people will resist institutional control. The dynamics of resistance to discipline and domination stem from the role of decision-making and the presence of conflict tied to each.

When looking at resistance to discipline as a form of institutional control, space for potential resistance strategies is opened up by two key requirements of discipline: enclosure and surveillance. A key aspect of disciplinary systems is that they are 'inward' looking: discipline works through routine practices and structures that shape the choices of actors by establishing boundaries of appropriate and inappropriate behavior, but only for actors who understand themselves as members of the community, society or field within which those norms apply (DiMaggio & Powell, 1983; Douglas, 1986). In the Ford example, the Sociological Department developed powerful systems and routines that shaped the identities and actions of Ford employees, but for the most part, it only affected Ford employees (and perhaps their families), and in fact only those who were both eligible for and desirous of the Five Dollar Day. So, to the extent that Ford employees were professionally mobile (based on skills or family connections), they would have been able to avoid or deny the control of the Five Dollar Day and its associated disciplining systems.

A second requirement of discipline is continuous surveillance or members' perceptions of continuous surveillance (Barker, 1993; Sewell, 1998). The range of forms and intensities of surveillance associated with institutions is wide, but consistent across the range is the potential for noncompliance to be registered by systems that will automatically punish, shame, embarrass, or penalize. In describing the role of surveillance in the historical development of discipline, Foucault (1977: 175) argues that as large factories developed, it became 'a decisive economic operator both as an internal part of the production machinery and as a specific mechanism in the disciplinary power'. The importance of surveillance in effecting institutional control has only become more important and more effective since the industrial revolution described by Foucault. As Sewell (1988: 401) argues,

> New technology has enabled the erection of a surveillance superstructure throughout society that unobtrusively influences almost all aspects of daily life, especially work life. ... The impact of this surveillance, especially its ability to instill a profound sense of self-discipline and self-control in many social settings, is so subtle that it often goes unnoticed.

Sewell's argument notwithstanding, surveillance cannot be taken for granted in systems of institutional control. It must be effected in some manner and to the degree that actors can avoid or ignore it, institutional control will be undermined. An example of this dynamic and the potential for institutional resistance it raises comes from Fox-Wolfgramm, Boal and Hunt's (1998) examination of the reaction of two West Texas banks with distinct strategic orientations (one defender, one prospector) to new regulation which demanded the banks not 'discriminate against any so-called red-lined areas considered high risk in terms of loan repayment' (Fox-Wolfgramm et al., 1998: 91). Both banks resisted the institutional pressure associated with the new law, but in different ways and seemingly with distinct motivations. Fox-Wolfgramm et al. argue that the defender bank initially engaged in 'identity resistance' – an attempt to ignore the new regulation, operating on a 'business as usual' basis, because of a lack of congruence between the regulation and the bank's current and envisioned identity and image. The bank resisted by adopting a strategy of 'minimal technical compliance', so that 'the bank complied with the letter of the law', spending 'minimal time and effort' (1998: 104). Although the bank then moved some way towards accepting and implementing the new regulations, it reverted to old routines once it had passed the regulatory inspection associated with the new laws. The prospector bank also initially resisted the new regulation, again minimally complying with the letter of the law and largely carrying on with business as usual. The motivation for this resistance, however, differed significantly from that of the defender bank: in the case of the prospector bank, it 'seemed to resist change because top management believed that the bank was already fulfilling institutional expectations consistent with its "first to lead the way" identity and thus did not think change was needed' (1998: 117). The prospector bank's approach to the legislation changed significantly, however, when it failed a formal test of its compliance:

> management interpreted the examination performance as an indication of identity and image incongruence ... [and] responded by internalizing the changes needed to pass the test and incorporating these into [the bank's] ideology, strategy and other organizational and issue aspects of its 'community leadership' so as to be isomorphic with institutional forces. (1998: 120)

The resistance of the banks described by Fox-Wolfgramm et al. (1998) illustrates the limits of surveillance in many institutional systems, and especially those that are highly distributed and involve large numbers of actors. In this case, managers in both banks were able to simply avoid making any substantive changes in their operations for significant time periods with no significant repercussions, largely because the processes through which compliance was monitored occurred only periodically and with substantial prior warning.

Resistance to discipline may also take more active forms, as documented in Symon et al.'s (2008) study of academic publishing. In their study, Symon et al. show how academics resist the institutionalized practices of quantitative research by publishing qualitative research. The engagement in qualitative research, the authors argue, is a form of legitimate resistance to the illegitimate institutionalization of the academic working practices which favors quantitative research. In contrast to Fox-Wolfgramm et al.'s study, this study shows that resistance to discipline goes beyond avoidance and instead highlights the importance of active, albeit legitimate resistance to disciplinary practices.

Resistance to domination has distinctly different dynamics than does resistance to discipline. These differences stem from the differential effects of discipline and domination on actors, and particularly groups of actors. When systems of domination are effective, the potential for actors to resist, at least directly, may be significantly reduced in comparison to disciplinary systems. Taking actuarial practices as an example illustrates this dynamic. The most central technique in the development of actuarial practices is the classification of the individual within a population based on some set of relevant variables. The relevance of these variables is dependent, however, on the task at hand, rather than on any phenomenological significance for the individuals so classified. The same is true for physical and technological infrastructures, which effect power relations based on 'objective' characteristics of populations, which may or may not connect to their lived experiences. Simon (1988: 744) argues that this aspect of actuarial practices has significant consequences for our politics and our identities: 'By placing people in groups that have no experienced meaning for their members and therefore lack the capacity to realize common goals or purposes, ... [people] may be stripped of a certain quality of belongingness to others that has long played a role in our culture'. These classifications provide little basis for political action and even potentially work to usurp the political foundations of existing groups. Lawrence and Robinson argue that an important effect of this dynamic is the potential to provoke more significant, destructive resistance, because in contrast to discipline, it can 'entail a greater loss of autonomy, pose more serious threats to organizational members' identities and, may be perceived as less procedurally just'. Because direct, assertive resistance is problematic in reaction to systems of domination, Lawrence and Robinson (2007) argue that domination will be associated with relatively severe, 'deviant' forms of resistance directed at organizations or society as a whole, what Robinson and Bennett (1995) refer to as 'property deviance', which involves harmful behavior directed at the organization as a whole, such as theft, sabotage or intentional mistakes.

Institutional resistance to systems of domination, thus, present a paradox – although the ability of actors to compromise, avoid and defy institutional control based on domination may be less than it is under systems of discipline, the resistance that actors engage in is likely to be more severe and potentially more destructive. It may be difficult to avoid the effects of overpass heights, but it is possible to vandalize overpasses and buses. This dynamic is an unexplored one in institutional studies of organization, but could be a major issue when trying to understand the effects and side-effects of forms of institutional

control that might seem benign to the designers and implementers of those systems.

INSTITUTIONAL AGENCY

Overview

The second dynamic of institutional politics is 'institutional agency' – the work of actors to create, transform, maintain or disrupt institutions. Power and agency have been tied tightly to each other in organization theory, and more generally in the social sciences (Giddens, 1976, 1984). The capacity of individual and collective actors to attempt to realize their own interests was centrally important to the 'old institutionalism' and has re-emerged as an important focus for institutional research, particularly with respect to institutional entrepreneurship and social movements (see Hardy and Maguire, Chapter 10 and Schneiberg and Lounsbury, Chapter 11 this volume). Significant findings in this literature include the importance of relational and discursive strategies in effecting institutional change (Garud et al., 2002; Lawrence & Suddaby, 2006; Maguire et al., 2004; Maguire & Hardy, 2009; Suddaby & Greenwood, 2005), the impact of field development (Greenwood & Suddaby, 2006; Lawrence & Phillips, 2004; Maguire et al., 2004; Munir & Phillips, 2005), the role of actors' identities in affecting their institutional strategies (Fligstein, 1997; Greenwood, Suddaby, & Hinings, 2002; Hensmans, 2003; Lok, 2010) and the processes through which practices move across space and time (Boxenbaum & Battilana, 2005; Czarniawska & Joerges, 1996).

Research on institutional entrepreneurship (DiMaggio, 1988; Eisenstadt, 1980) describes the process through which new institutions are created when 'organized actors with sufficient resources (institutional entrepreneurs) see in them an opportunity to realize interests that they value highly'

(DiMaggio, 1988: 14). Power in this stream of research is tied to the ability of actors to create new institutions, through the mobilization of resources. This work has examined the processes and practices associated with the creation of practices (Boxenbaum, 2006; Lawrence, 1999; Munir & Phillips, 2005), technologies (Aldrich & Fiol, 1994; Hargadon & Douglas, 2001; Leblebici et al., 1991) and forms of organizing (Greenwood et al., 2002; Suddaby & Greenwood, 2005) that go against the institutional norms or rules within which they are embedded. Research on institutional entrepreneurship has shown that actors effect institutional agency in a broad set of ways, including technical and market leadership, lobbying for regulatory change and discursive action (Fligstein, 1997; Garud et al., 2002; Hoffman, 1999; Maguire et al., 2004).

A more recent stream of institutional research in this vein focuses on institutional work, which expands the scope of actor/institution relations by incorporating the ways that institutions are created, maintained and disrupted by actors (Lawrence & Suddaby, 2006; Lawrence et al., 2009; Lawrence, Leca, & Zilber, 2013). Like institutional entrepreneurship, the concept of institutional work emphasizes the deliberate strategies of actors as they skillfully and reflexively engage in activities to influence the institutional environments in which they operate (Lawrence et al., 2009). The study of institutional work, however, more clearly highlights the ways in which the agency of actors is shaped and influenced by the institutional environment(s) in which they are embedded (Battilana & D'Aunno, 2009). The literature on work thus views institutional agency as less 'heroic' than research on institutional entrepreneurship and seeks to uncover the ongoing, routinized and often mundane ways in which actors exercise power in their institutional environments (Lawrence & Suddaby, 2006).

Research on social movements has many similarities to the work on institutional entrepreneurship, particularly in their shared focus on the role of agents in effecting changes in institutional arrangements and a tendency to examine this role through the deep analysis of individual cases of institutional agency. What separates the two literatures, however, is their understandings of the form and the roots of that agency. Whereas institutional agency focuses significantly on the traits, strategies and positions of individual actors (Battilana, 2006; Maguire et al., 2004), social movements research highlights the role of collective action motivated by structural inequalities (Clemens, 1993; McAdam, 1988). The strategies that each literature highlights differ in ways that reflect their emphasis on individual versus collective action. While institutional entrepreneurship research highlights strategies focused specifically on institutional rules (Garud et al., 2002; Greenwood & Suddaby, 2006; Lawrence, 1999; Maguire et al., 2004), research on social movements focuses on strategies aimed at fostering and leveraging collective action, such as framing (Snow & Benford, 1988; Snow, Rochford, Worden, & Benford, 1986) and resource mobilization (Jenkins, 1983; McCarthy & Zald, 1977).

What is common across studies of institutional entrepreneurship, institutional work and social movements is a concern for how interested actors work to affect the institutions and fields that provide the institutional context within which they operate. More clearly than in the case of institutional control, the study of institutional agency is the study of a set of political processes and practices in which power in many forms is necessarily and obviously implicated.

Mode of Power

Most research and writing on institutional agency is explicitly political in its accounts of how actors create, transform and disrupt institutions (Beckert, 1999; DiMaggio, 1988; Hensmans, 2003). The dominant image of power in this work is as an 'episodic' phenomenon, constituted in relatively discrete, strategic acts of mobilization initiated by self-interested actors (Clegg, 1989). Research on institutional entrepreneurship and social movements both describe actors mobilizing resources, engaging in institutional contests over meanings and practices, developing, supporting or attacking forms of discourse and practice – all practices involving discrete, strategic acts of mobilization. Similarly, the research on institutional work has tended to concentrate on episodes of power, in which actors marshal resources and engage in tactics that allow them to shape their institutional environments. Thus, a key distinction between institutional agency and institutional control is the mode of power: whereas institutional control involves systemic forms of power, institutional agency represents episodic power.

Forms of Power

Although institutional agency is described by a single mode of power, it manifests in multiple forms. And like institutional control, the study of institutional agency has maintained a relatively narrow focus with respect to forms of power, in this case focusing primarily on influence. The concept of influence is typically described as the ability of one actor to persuade another actor to do something they would not otherwise do (Clegg, 1989; French & Raven, 1959; Lukes, 1974). It potentially involves a wide range of tactics, including moral suasion, negotiation, rational persuasion, ingratiation and exchange (Clegg, 1989; Lawrence et al., 2001; Maslyn, Farmer, & Fedor, 1996). The literatures on institutional entrepreneurship and social movements provide numerous examples of influence as a basis for institutional agency. Fligstein's (1997: 398) essay on the importance of social skills in institutional entrepreneurship, for example, positions influence as central to institutional entrepreneurship, which, as a form of 'skilled social action',

'revolves around finding and maintaining a collective identity of a set of social groups and the effort to shape and meet the interests of those groups'. Fligstein goes on to articulate a list of tactics available to 'strategic actors', most of which are examples of either influence or establishing conditions under which influence is possible: 'agenda setting', 'framing action', 'wheeling and annealing', 'brokering', 'asking for more, settling for less', 'maintaining goallessness and selflessness', 'maintaining ambiguity', 'aggregating interests', 'trying five things to get one', 'convincing people one holds more cards than one does', 'making others think they are in control' and 'networking to outliers'.

Fligstein (1997: 403) goes on to argue that the use of these influence tactics will depend significantly on how 'organized' the fields are in which they operate. He argues that:

> When fields are less organized, their tactics are to bring together disparate groups in a large number of ways. As a frame begins to cohere to organize the field, they act to propagate that frame and the social order it implies. Once in place, skilled strategic actors defend a status quo by deftly manipulating accepted meanings and making sure that the 'goods' are being delivered to those who dominate the organizational field. Under situations of crisis, actors committed to the status quo will continue to try to use dominant understandings to structure action as long as they can. Skilled strategic actors in challenger groups will offer new cultural frames and rules to reorganize the field.

Studies of institutional entrepreneurship (e.g., Garud et al., 2002; Maguire et al., 2004) have demonstrated the importance of influence tactics similar to, or a subset of, those delineated by Fligstein (1997). Moreover, the issue of field development has become an important theme in examining different forms of institutional agency and the question of what kinds of actors will engage in such action (Greenwood & Suddaby, 2006; Lawrence & Phillips, 2004; Maguire et al., 2004).

In organization studies, a significantly overlooked form of institutional agency is the use of force, which works by directly overcoming another actors' intentions or behavior (French & Raven, 1959; Lukes, 1974). The legitimate use of physical force is generally restricted by communities and societies to specific agencies, such as prisons, psychiatric hospitals, the military and police forces. Other organizations, however, use what might be described as 'bureaucratic force' on a regular basis: corporations fire employees; bars forcibly remove disruptive patrons; schools confiscate contraband substances; universities expel poorly performing students; and editors reject the submissions of aspiring authors.

The use of force, and especially of physical force, is perhaps the most under-examined aspect of institutional politics in the organizational literature. Although explicit physical force may be relatively rare in many of the institutional settings we study, this may be more of a reflection of the constrained empirical focus we have adopted in organization studies, than the relative importance of force in creating, maintaining and disrupting institutions. If we consider institutional change from a historical perspective, it is clear that force has been a critically important means by which states and state institutions have been created, maintained and disrupted (Mann, 1993), and not only in the past (Mann, 2003). In a broad array of institutional arenas, including health care, education and, more obviously, policing and the prison system, the use of force by the state or state-sanctioned agencies maintains many contemporary institutions.

The use of force as a basis for institutional agency is associated both with attempts to disrupt institutionalized practices and with attempts to maintain institutions. On June 26th, 2010, thousands of protesters, including many prominent organizations including the Canadian Labour Congress and Greenpeace International, gathered in downtown Toronto to protest the G-20 Summit. As the protest began, a small number of protesters broke off from the main march and began to engage in property damage aimed at retail locations for large corporate outlets such as Nike, Starbucks and American Apparel as well as the headquarters of media outlets such as the Canadian Broadcasting Corporation and CTV News. This triggered a response from the Toronto Police Service that included the use of tear gas – the first time in the city's history – as well as rubber bullets and pepper spray aimed at protesters. By the end of the summit, 1,118 people had been arrested. Over 800 of these individuals were held in temporary holding cells for the duration of the summit and then released without charge afterwards.

The events at the G-20 summit reveal a number of insights about the use of force as a form of institutional agency. For protesters, the specific targets of the vandalism (Nike, McDonald's, Toronto Dominion Bank) were significant in their symbolic connection to global capitalism and its connection to the G-20 organization; at one level, the protesters' use of force was focused on effecting property damage, but it was done with broader institutional rules and assumptions in mind. In turn, the Toronto Police Service used force to subdue the protestors, but in doing so were protecting the institutional arrangements symbolized and enacted by the G-20. Although the most dramatic uses of force by the police involved tear gas and rubber bullets, the most important use of force by the police was the mass arrests that kept more than 1,100 protesters in holding cells for the duration of the summit. The arrests and incarceration prevented people deemed potentially disruptive from participating in demonstrations without the police having to formally charge them; indeed, the vast majority of those arrested were later released without charges being laid. So, although it is rarely the focus of empirical attention in organizational institutionalism, force can be an important form of power used in institutional agency: at the 2010 G-20 summit in Toronto, as in many other clashes between anti-globalization protestors and transnational trade meetings, force was used by protesters to disrupt institutions while police services and other government agencies used force to try to maintain those same institutional arrangements.

Role of Decision-Making

Institutional agency is primarily associated with intentionality, purpose and interests (Lawrence et al., 2009). As a result, in studies of institutional agency, the use of power is often displayed within the decision-making arena. In other words, actors make conscious and strategic decisions to exert or resist power and are largely aware of the potential outcomes of doing so. This differs from institutional control that tends to focus on the realm of non-decision-making, in which power prevents particular choices from entering the agenda. The role of decision-making varies, however, between different forms of institutional agency. With regards to influence, the objective is to shape both decision making and non-decision-making (Bacharach & Baratz, 1962), affecting the decisions actors make as well as suppressing certain courses of action from entering the decision-making arena (Lukes, 1974). Maguire and Hardy's (2009) study of DDT use in the US chemical industry illustrates both of these possibilities, providing a rich example of how influence in organizational fields can disrupt or defend the pillars that underpin existing institutions as a means of influencing other actors in the field.

Influence can also exist outside of the decision-making realm (Bacharach & Baratz, 1962; Lukes, 1974). Barley (2010) details how US corporations sought to influence government policy through the creation of an 'institutional field' around government. Barley highlights the role of corporations in funding and structuring of organizations such as trade and peak associations, ad hoc organizations, foundations, think-tanks, Political Action Committees (PACs), public relations firms, lobbying firms and public affairs

offices. This 'field' of organizations works to influence government by lobbying, staffing, funding, providing personnel and testifying for different government branches including Congress, administration and advisory committees. The outcome of this diverse and complex realm of corporate political influence not only influences the decisions of government; it also prevents certain courses of action from entering the realm of decision-making. For instance, potential policies that are deemed as potentially harmful to corporate interests are unlikely to be considered given the embeddedness of corporate interests in and around government. In this way, influence is not confined to the realm of decision-making and may also be observable in situations of non-decision-making.

The use of force as a form of institutional agency also has an important relationship to decision-making but one distinctively different from that of influence. The use of force works by denying agency on the part of its target, removing them from decision-making opportunities. It shares this quality with domination, but force prevents decision-making in more direct and overt means. When a company dismisses an employee, for instance, the company prevents that individual from making a decision to stay (or not stay) in the organization. At the 2010 G-20 summit, the police arresting protesters and incarcerating them in holding cells for the duration of the summit rendered the potential decisions of protesters irrelevant; the relationship of protestors to the institutions in question was structured not by their aims or desires, but by the physical force exerted on them by the police.

Thus, institutional agency tends to focus on the realms of decision-making and non-decision-making. But, influence and force differ in the role they assign to decision-making. Influence is based on the assumption that targets of power can make decisions and thus focuses on shaping their decision-making by affecting their interpretation of the choices available, sometimes affecting the costs and benefits of potential choices and sometimes moving those choices out of the decision-making arena. The use of force works by removing the ability of targets to make decisions and so is less concerned with how those targets might interpret the value of choices or the composition of choice sets.

Presence of Conflict

Research on institutional agency has tended to include detailed descriptions of visible and, often dramatic, conflict in organizational fields (Hoffman, 1999; Maguire et al., 2004; Maguire & Hardy, 2009; Rojas, 2010; van Wijk et al., 2013; Zietsma & Lawrence, 2010). Hoffman (1999: 352) notably argues that organizational fields often witness periods of 'institutional war' in which field members 'compete over the definition of issues and the form of institutions that will guide organizational behavior'. Institutional research that focuses on influence tends to portray competing sets of actors all working to influence the actions of other actors in an organizational field. Battilana's (2011) study of institutional change in Britain's National Health Service illustrates these dynamics and demonstrates the important role of differential social positions in affecting who and how influence is effected in relation to institutionalized rules and practices. Similarly, Zietsma & Lawrence (2010) document a series of battles for influence in the British Columbia coastal forestry industry, in which activists, First Nations, forestry companies, government agencies and corporate buyers all engaged in influence strategies in order to transform or protect existing approaches to logging and the right to make decisions about BC forests.

Although studies of influence tend to focus on observable conflict, influence – in the form of manipulation – can also be used as a means to prevent conflict from arising (Lukes, 1974; Oliver, 1991). As Oliver argues, organizations may use a number of strategies, including co-optation, influence, or controlling, in response to institutional pressures. In cases of successful manipulation, no conflict will be present because the target will be controlled by the party exercising power. Although a number of studies have shown how corporate political activity and lobbying can effectively ensure compliance without overt conflict (Barley, 2010), there is still little research in organizational institutionalism on the exercise of influence as a means to prevent conflict and contestation.

The use of force as a form of institutional agency differs from influence with regards to the presence of conflict in that force can be accompanied by, result from, or trigger significant, overt conflict. Although many instances of firing employees, arresting citizens and expelling students go off without a hitch, other instances involve or trigger noisy or even violent clashes between the actors involved. The use of force, much like domination, can provoke strong emotional reactions on the part of targets, but unlike domination the source of power in cases of force are more visible and identifiable, making direct resistance more likely (Lawrence & Robinson, 2007). To return to our example of the G-20 meetings, although police were using force against protesters in the form of tear gas and rubber bullets, the protesters were also using force as a means to disrupt the meetings. Thus, force can be used by a wide variety of actors in organizational fields; not just the largest and most powerful.

Nature of Resistance

Resistance to institutional agency involves reaching compromises with institutional agents, avoiding their gaze or their ability to punish non-compliance, or defying their aims. Although its basic nature is similar to resistance to institutional control, the flux and uncertainty tied to institutional agency opens up more room for resistance and more potential for creativity in effecting forms of resistance. Dirsmith, Heian and Covaleski (1997) provide a detailed description of resistance to institutional agency in Big Six accounting firms. This study focused on the attempt by large, professional accounting firms to shift internal power relations by importing 'a legitimated form of formal organizational practice, MBO … in the hope of legitimating the actual application of control to the firm's professional cadre' (Dirsmith et al., 1997: 20). Dirsmith et al. (1997: 20) argue that the use of MBO as a tool is important because it represents a 'familiar, abstract, objective, proceduralized, client-sanctioned form of control' and thus challenges traditional, professional autonomy based on a discourse of 'business focus' and 'meritocracy'. Institutional resistance, in this case, emerged from the professionals in the firms who recognized MBO as a political tool, rather than a neutral technology. Interestingly, resistance did not involve direct refusal, but rather an indirect subversion of the aims and effects of MBO through the use of mentor relationships:

> mentors recognized MBO for the political as opposed to instrumental practice it was and transformed it into a means for advocating for their protégés, by enabling them to game the formal system, as in partnership proposal orchestration to display the 'right numbers'. (Dirsmith et al., 1997: 21)

This study highlights the need for both resources and skills in effecting institutional resistance. The mentors who helped their protégés game the MBO system had access to the information necessary to know when and how to manipulate the MBO system and held senior enough positions in their firms that their subversions would likely go unpunished.

Resistance to institutional agency also differs depending on the form of power that is being exercised. For example, the potential for resistance to institutional agency based on influence stems significantly from the uncertainty and complexity of attempts to create or transform institutional arrangements.

Attempts to create, maintain or disrupt institutions through influence are fraught with unintended consequences. These stem from the often indirect nature of institutional agency, as actors affect institutions by, for instance, working through third parties such as the state or professional bodies (Orssatto et al., 2002; Russo, 2001), or developing (or delegitimating) vocabularies of action and belief which are only effective to the extent that they are picked up and adopted by others (Angus, 1993; Lawrence & Suddaby, 2006). Unintended consequences also result from the intersection of multiple organizational fields and sets of institutional arrangements (Phillips et al., 2004).

Dirsmith et al.'s (1997) study of resistance to the implementation of MBO in accounting firms illustrates these dynamics. First, the MBO system that senior management attempted to implement in the accounting firms provides a good example of a complex, multi-party system in which the sponsors of the innovation are significantly dependent on a range of other parties if it is to be successfully implemented and institutionalized. Such situations invite the possibility of resistance from others who perceive these new systems as not serving their interests. In this case, resistance came significantly from professionals in the firm who saw the introduction of MBO as an opportunity to advance their own interests and resist the aims of the system sponsors. The resistance evidenced in this case also hinged on the interaction of MBO with an existing institution – mentoring – in the firms. The institutionalized positions and practices associated with mentoring provided both the motivation and the means for actors to compromise the newly implemented MBO system: the mentoring process provided a set of interests to actors that were in conflict with the MBO system and became the tool through which professionals gamed the new system. We describe this as an example of institutional resistance, rather than institutional agency, because it seems that the accountants who were gaming the system were not so much attempting to either create or disrupt an organizational institution, as compromise and avoid its effects on themselves and those whom they supported through mentorship programs.

More generally, the reliance of institutional agency on third parties and its situation within overlapping fields and institutions provides the foundation for a range of strategies for institutional resistance. The problems of surveillance associated with reliance on third parties opens up space for avoidance by institutional actors. Influence depends on the ability of one actor to observe the degree of compliance of another (Pfeffer, 1981; Pfeffer & Salancik, 1978) and so working through the state or other third party to effect institutional change or maintain a set of institutional arrangements may necessitate developing some complex scheme for surveillance. The involvement of third parties also invites the possibility of co-optation where targeted actors are able to influence the actions of the third parties and thus undermine institutional agency. Social movement organizations, for instance, often attempt to transform institutional arrangements by influencing the state, which might in turn enact new legislation or enforce existing laws and rules (Benford & Snow, 2000). These attempts, however, can lead to resistance on the part of targeted actors and result in framing contests in which each party attempts to convince the state agencies of the greater legitimacy of their own claims. A range of institutional resistance strategies is also connected to the webs of organizational fields and institutions within which institutional agency occurs. These webs provide space for targeted actors to reposition themselves when institutional pressures change.

While institutional agency based on influence engenders resistance because of its attendant uncertainty and complexity, we argue that the use of force as a basis for institutional agency has its own distinctive effects on institutional resistance. The

nature of institutional resistance to force as a basis for institutional agency stems from the reaction that force can tend to engender in its targets. The use of force treats the targets of power as 'objects' in the sense that the exercise of power is not dependent on the agency or potential agency of targets (Lawrence et al., 2001; Scott, J. R., 2001). Unlike influence, the use of force does not shape the will of the target, but rather achieves its ends despite that will. Such forms of power, we argue, tend to lead to greater resistance on the part of targets, because they 'entail a greater loss of autonomy, pose more serious threats to [actors'] identities and may be perceived as less procedurally just' (Lawrence & Robinson, 2007). Moreover, unlike systems of domination, which also treat targets as objects, the episodic nature of force means that it is easily associated with specific agents, at whom the resistance will likely be directed. This is because targets of force tend to aim their resistance at the perceived source of the harms that they perceive themselves as suffering (Berkowitz, 1993; O'Leary-Kelly, Griffin, & Glew, 1996). The resistance that the use of force tends to engender may limit its potential as an effective tool for institutional agency, both because targeted actors will attempt to compromise, avoid or defy the aims associated with its use and even when direct resistance is difficult, they will tend to quickly revert to previous behaviors (Lawrence et al., 2001).

STUDYING POWER AND INSTITUTIONS

The framework we have described here suggests that the institutional politics of an organizational field can be conceived of in terms of an interplay between institutional control and institutional agency. In the sections above, we attempted to provide a set of ideas from the literatures on power that can inform a more sophisticated political analysis of institutions and organizations, focusing particularly on the forms of systemic and episodic power that underpin institutional control and institutional agency, and the role of decision-making, the presence of conflict and the nature of resistance associated with each. We conclude by exploring a set of issues that emerge from this analysis.

Revisiting Institutional Control

A perhaps overly simplistic narrative of organizational institutionalism since Meyer and Rowan's (1977) and Zucker's (1977) seminal works is that after several years of examining stability, isomorphism and institutionalization, the literature was criticized for not being able to explain change in organizational fields. A sea change followed these criticisms, where the preponderance of institutional research focused on incorporating change and with it came a re-injection of agency, interests and conflict into the literature. Interpreting this shift with power in mind, the dominant focus of the literature shifted from institutional control to institutional agency, and with this shift a new understanding of institutions as more malleable, dynamic and contestable (Suddaby, 2010). This shift also helped re-establish a more explicit consideration of power in organizational institutionalism, but this renewed focus on power centered on institutional agency, largely overlooking the relationship between power and institutional control. Yet, the work of scholars such as Foucault and Winner (and many others) on discipline, domination and other forms of systemic power suggests otherwise; it suggests that the role of power in institutional control is more significant and more complex than current institutional writing acknowledges and that many important details regarding the dynamics of institutional control remain to be worked out.

Thus, it is time for a renewed focus on institutional control with more explicit acknowledgment of power. Although early institutional research emphasized institutional control, it did so without any formal consideration of power. The shift in focus to institutional agency demonstrated the compatibility between institutional research and power, but research has only begun to bring this incorporation of power to the study of institutional control. We believe that a more explicit integration of power in the study of institutional control could offer insights into some of the foundational arguments of organizational institutionalism and rebalance the control/agency dichotomy in the literature. A starting point would be the development of empirically grounded analyses of how discipline and domination support institutions, how specific instances of those forms of power work in different contexts and the overall limits of their effectiveness. Fully incorporating discipline domination into our research on institutions and organizations may require an expansion of both our conceptual frameworks and our research methods. We discuss these opportunities and the challenges associated with them below.

The lack of attention to domination in particular and systemic power in general might arguably be connected to a view of institutions as primarily cognitive or discursive phenomena (Lawrence & Phillips, 2004; Phillips et al., 2004), which might suggest that social practices held in place by physical or technological systems are not 'real institutions'. Such an argument, however, overlooks the distinctions between institutions, the mechanisms that underpin those institutions and the streams of action that create them. Phillips et al. (2004: 638) argue that institutions are best understood as 'social constructions constructed through discourse' that are associated with 'self-regulating socially constructed mechanisms that enforce their application'. Thus far institutional research has maintained a relatively restricted understanding of what those socially constructed mechanisms might involve, with a distinct focus on 'social' systems that rely on normative and regulative mechanisms to maintain compliance. We argue that our analysis of those socially constructed institutional mechanisms needs to expand to include the built environment, including mechanical and technological systems. Such systems, whether built from concrete or silicon, are often a critical element in the institutionalization of social practice.

This relates to a broader conceptual issue that is largely a holdover from early work in the area. Specifically, foundational organizational institutional research created an analytical distinction between 'technical' and 'institutional' environments (Meyer and Rowan, 1977; Meyer & Scott, 1983) that was useful for showing how organizational actors, striving for legitimacy in their institutional environment, were likely to be constrained in their actions by various institutional pressures that could be seen as not rational from some kind of technical standpoint (DiMaggio and Powell, 1983; Meyer and Rowan, 1977; Meyer & Scott, 1983). The widely adopted distinction between the technical and institutional environments in early organizational institutionalism (Dacin, 1997; Meyer & Rowan, 1977; Meyer & Scott, 1983; Zucker, 1987) may have led to the marginalization in institutional analysis of phenomena more obviously associated with technical environments. This marginalization is problematic because, as Holm (1995) argues, separating the institutional and technical environments 'excludes some of the most important phenomena in modern societies – market forces, competition, professionalization and science – from institutional analysis' (1995: 417). In revisiting institutional control achieved through forms of systemic power like discipline and domination, we believe it is critically important to focus on the practices, procedures and systems that appear to be neutral, apolitical and technical in nature.

Unintended Consequences, Marginalized Actors and Problematic Uses of Power

For all the progress that organizational institutionalism has made toward a more formal consideration of power, research in the area still tends to focus primarily on the actions of powerful actors in organizational fields with strong strategic intentions aimed at shaping existing institutions. As a result of this focus, three areas tend to be kept at the margins (Munir, 2015). These include the unintended consequences of institutional politics, the role of marginalized actors and problematic uses of power.

All institutions affect the distribution of power, resources and risk in the organizational fields they structure (Bourdieu, 1993; Clegg, 1989; Douglas & Wildavsky, 1983). This is a central tenet of this chapter and is consistent with much of the research on institutional entrepreneurship and social movements that has informed the study of institutional agency. Studies of institutional control have also moved toward recognizing the power effects of competing logics and institutional change (Amenta & Halfmann, 2000; Amenta & Zylan, 1991; Bartley & Schneiberg, 2002; Stryker, 2002; Thornton & Ocasio, 1999). What none of these studies accounts for in any detail, however, are the 'side effects' of institutions – the impacts of institutionalized practices and structures on the myriad of actors who are neither party to their creation nor are contemplated in their design. While it is clear, for instance, that the institutions that emerge out of occupational contests (e.g., between medical doctors and midwives) have a direct impact on the practitioners of those occupations, there are a host of other actors, such as patients and their families, other medical practitioners, nurses, public health officers and health policy-makers who are also affected but whose interests are less well attended to institutional research. Similarly, research on the work of HIV/AIDS activists and advocates has documented the significant impacts on the power of doctors, pharmaceutical companies and HIV/AIDS community groups (Maguire et al., 2004). Missing in this analysis, however, is the impact on HIV-positive individuals who were largely left out of this process, such as intravenous drug users, as well as its impact on other individuals living with other diseases. This example points to the heterogeneous nature of institutional side-effects. Although intravenous drug users were largely sidelined in the institutional contests around HIV/AIDS treatments, they later gained significant discursive resources in their attempts to construct drug addiction as a health, rather than a criminal, issue. Similarly, members of other disease groups benefited from the lessons learned in the HIV/AIDS arena and from the templates for action and collaboration that the HIV/AIDS community forged in their struggles for rapid access to new treatments and alternative experimental designs. Others, however, seem to have fared less well in this institutional battle. People living with HIV/AIDS in the third world, for instance, continue to suffer without the political resources to effect institutional change that the community had access to in the North. Moreover, research and treatment dollars are a scarce resource which shifted significantly toward work on HIV/AIDS, potentially incurring significant costs to advancement in other disease areas.

Khan et al. (2007) provide a vivid example of attending to the unintended consequences of institutional agency for marginalized actors in their study of child labor in the manufacturing of soccer balls in Pakistan. They show how institutional entrepreneurship aimed at disrupting rules, norms and practices that supported child labor in manufacturing soccer balls in Pakistan, ignored broader issues related to widespread poverty and women's issues. Although the institutional entrepreneurs in Khan and colleagues' (2007) study eliminated child labor in ball stitching, an unintended consequence of doing so was worsening the economic conditions of families involved in the industry: the new rules intended to protect children forced women to work in factories rather than at home, which limited their job flexibility and ultimately drove them from the workforce. This example highlights three important issues. First, it focuses on the unintended consequences of institutional agency which are so often neglected. Khan et al. could have developed a case study of successful institutional entrepreneurship aimed at disrupting practices relating to child labor, but by focusing on the unintended consequences of these actions, they open up an unexamined aspect of the institutional environment. Second, the study incorporates the voices of marginalized actors – the families involved in the ball stitching – in addition to the large corporations, NGOs and other actors involved in the process. That most of these families were opposed to the changes underscores the importance of including their voices because it illustrates the potential costs of ignoring the wisdom of the people institutional entrepreneurs may be intending to help. Third, it sheds light on problematic uses of power. As Munir (2015: 91) argues, for all the advances of organizational institutionalism, our studies end up 'painting a rather sanitary view of the world, skirting around, or simply accepting at face value, what more critical theorists consider to be highly problematic uses of power'.

Attending to these 'side effects' in institutional research would require a much widened lens in our research designs and data collection and analysis strategies, and could be facilitated by drawing across boundaries on work focused on issues of gender, race, age and class. Research designs that would be sensitive to the effects of institutions on marginalized actors would need to ask broader questions than how did particular institutions emerge and how do they control specific groups; instead, they would need to seek out the consequences of institutions more broadly in a society, following the traces of institutional impact outwards, as well as 'inverting' the process by taking on perspectives well outside of the assumed fields of influence to try to see the institutions from the margins. Data collection and analysis in such a process would need to be flexible enough to capture unexpected sets of findings and follow them through to their natural conclusions, a process that might be difficult in tightly designed qualitative or quantitative studies. Attending to and understanding the side effects of institutions might demand a long and deep engagement in a field, not only observing a population of organizations, but also connecting with the individuals, groups and communities affected by those organizations.

CONCLUSION

Since the initial publication of this chapter in the first edition of the Handbook, there have been significant advances in the incorporation of power into institutional research, stemming particularly from the emergence of vibrant discussions of institutional logics, institutional complexity and institutional work, all of which point to the importance of power and politics in fields and organizations. Even with these advances, however, we believe that the analysis of power and institutions remains underdeveloped, especially in terms of explicit empirical studies of this fundamental relationship. We have tried in this chapter to provide a framework that might encourage and facilitate such studies, beginning with the articulation of a situation's institutional politics – the interplay of institutional control and institutional agency in organizational fields. Institutional control represents the impact of institutions on the behaviors and beliefs of actors; institutional agency involves the work of actors to create, transform, maintain and disrupt institutions. Together, these describe the forms of power in play in organizational fields; their interaction significantly determines the evolution of institutions, networks and subject positions that structure the experiences and opportunities of actors.

Notes

1 A relational understanding of power is in part an attempt to avoid the distraction of a physical metaphor for social power, as established by French and Raven's (1959) distinction between power (capacity) and influence (the use of that capacity). This distinction provides a problematic foundation for discussions of power and institutions, since discussions of power easily become conflated with resources or other sources of power and the forms of power become narrowed to those that occur through influence.

2 Although the concept of domination has a long and varied history in the social sciences and has been used in a wide variety of ways (Arendt, 1970; Marx & Engels, 1906), we use it here to describe a general category of forms of power. While the term has been used in reference to 'false consciousness' (Jermier, 1985; Marx & Engels, 1906), 'manipulation' (Clegg, 1975; Lukes, 1974), the overwhelming use of power, we use it simply to describe forms of power that support institutional control through systems that restrict the range of options available to actors (Lawrence et al., 2001).

REFERENCES

Aldrich, H. E., & Fiol, C. M. (1994). Fools rush in? The institutional context of industry creation. *Academy of Management Review, 19*, 645–670.

Amenta, E., & Halfmann, D. (2000). Wage wars: Institutional politics, WPA wages, and the struggle for U.S. social policy. *American Sociological Review, 65*(4), 506–528.

Amenta, E., & Zylan, Y. (1991). It happened here: Political opportunity, the new institutionalism, and the Townsend movement. *American Sociological Review, 56*(2), 250–265.

Angus, L. B. (1993). Masculinity and women teachers at Christian Brothers College. *Organization Studies, 14*(2), 235–260.

Arendt, H. (1970). *On violence*. London: Allen Lane.

Bachrach, P., & Baratz, M.S. (1962). Two faces of power. *American Political Science Review, 56*(4), 947–952.

Bachrach, P., & Baratz, M.S. (1970). *Power and poverty: Theory and practice*. Oxford: Oxford University Press.

Bachrach, S. B., & Lawler, E. J. (1980). *Power and politics in organizations*. San Francisco: Jossey–Bass.

Barbalet, J. M. (1985). Power and resistance. *British Journal of Sociology, 36*(4), 531–548.

Barker, J. R. (1993). Tightening the iron cage: Concertive control in self-managing teams. *Administrative Science Quarterly, 38,* 408–437.

Barley, S.R. (2010). Building an institutional field to corral a government: A case to set an agenda for organization studies. *Organization Studies, 31*(6), 777–805.

Baron, J. N., Dobbin, F. R., & Jennings, P. D. (1986). War and peace: The evolution of modern personnel administration in U.S. industry. *American Journal of Sociology, 92,* 350–383.

Bartley, T., & Schneiberg, M. (2002). Rationality and institutional contingency: The varying politics of economic regulation in the fire insurance industry. *Sociological Perspectives, 45*(1), 47–79.

Battilana, J. (2006). Agency and institutions: The enabling role of individuals' social position. *Organization, 13*(5), 653–676.

Battilana, J. (2011). The enabling role of social position in diverging from the institutional status quo: Evidence from the UK National Health Service. *Organization Science, 22*(4), 817–834.

Battilana, J. and D'Aunno, T. (2009). Institutional work and the paradox of embedded agency. *Institutional Work: Actors and Agency in Institutional Studies of Organizations,* pp. 31–58.

Beckert, J. (1999). Agency, entrepreneurs and institutional change: The role of strategic choice and institutionalized practices in organizations. *Organization Studies, 20*(5), 777–799.

Benford, R. D., & Snow, D. A. (2000). Framing processes and social movements: An overview and assessment. *Annual Review of Sociology, 26,* 611–638.

Berkowitz, L. (1993). *Aggression: Its causes, consequences, and control.* New York: McGraw-Hill.

Boxenbaum, E. (2006). Lost in translation: The making of Danish diversity management. *American Behavioral Scientist, 49*(7), 939–948.

Boxenbaum, E., & Battilana, J. (2005). Importation as innovation: transposing managerial practices across fields. *Strategic Organization, 3*(4), 355–383.

Bourdieu, P. (1993). *Sociology in question.* London: Sage.

Brass, D. J. (1984). Being in the right place: A structural analysis of individual influence in an organization. *Administrative Science Quarterly, 29,* 518–539.

Braverman, H. (1974). *Labor and monopoly capital.* New York: Monthly Review Press.

Brown, G., Lawrence, T. B., & Robinson, S. L. (2005). Territoriality in organizations. *Academy of Management Review, 30*(3), 577–594.

Burowoy, M. (1979). *Manufacturing consent.* Chicago, IL: University of Chicago Press.

Clegg, S. R. (1975). *Power, rule and domination.* London: Routledge.

Clegg, S. R. (1989). *Frameworks of power.* London: Penguin Books.

Clegg, S. (2010). The state, power, and agency: missing in action in institutional theory? *Journal of Management Inquiry, 19*(1), 4–13.

Clegg, S. R., Courpasson, D., & Phillips, N. (2006). *Power and organizations.* London: Sage.

Clegg, S. R., & Dunkerly, D. (1980). *Organization, class and control.* London: Routledge.

Clemens, E. (1993). Organizational repertoires and institutional change: Women's groups and the transformation of American politics, 1890–1920. *American Journal of Sociology, 98,* 755–798.

Covaleski, M. A., Dirsmith, M. W., Heian, J. B., & Samuel, S. (1998). The calculated and the avowed: Techniques of discipline and struggle over identity in Big Six public accounting firms. *Administrative Science Quarterly, 43,* 293–327.

Czarniawska, B., & Joerges, B. (1996). Travel of ideas. In B. Czarniawska & G. Sevon (Eds.), *Translating organizational change* (pp. 13–48). Berlin: de Gruyter.

Dacin, M.T. (1997). Isomorphism in context: The power and prescription of institutional norms. *Academy of Management journal, 40*(1), 46–81.

DiMaggio, P. J. (1988). Interest and agency in institutional theory. In L. G. Zucker (Ed.), *Institutional patterns and organizations: Culture and environment* (pp. 3–22). Cambridge, MA: Ballinger.

DiMaggio, P. J., & Powell, W. W. (1983). The iron cage revisited: Institutional isomorphism and collective rationality in organizational fields. *American Sociological Review, 48,* 147–160.

Dirsmith, M. W., Heian, J. B., & Covaleski, M. A. (1997). Structure and agency in an institutionalized setting: The application and social transformation of control in the Big Six. *Accounting, Organizations and Society, 22*(1), 1–27.

Douglas, M. (1973). *Natural symbols.* New York: Pantheon Books.

Douglas, M. (1986). *How institutions think.* New York: Syracuse University Press.

Douglas, M., & Wildavsky A. (1983). *Risk and culture: An essay on the selection of technological and environmental dangers.* Berkeley, CA: University of California Press.

Dyck, B., & Schroeder, D. (2005). Management, theology and moral points of view: Towards an alternative to the conventional materialist-individualist ideal-type of management. *Journal of Management Studies, 42*(4), 705–735.

Eisenstadt, S. N. (1980). Cultural orientations, institutional entrepreneurs, and social change: Comparative analysis of traditional civilizations. *American Journal of Sociology, 85,* 840–869.

Emerson, R. M. (1962). Power-dependence relations. *American Sociological Review, 27*(1), 31–41.

Fligstein, N. (1997). Social skill and institutional theory. *American Behavioral Scientist, 40*(4), 197–405.

Fligstein, N., & McAdam, D. (2012). *A theory of fields*. Oxford: Oxford University Press.

Foucault, M. (1977). *Discipline and punish: The birth of the prison*. New York: Vintage Books.

Foucault, M. (1980). *Power knowledge: Selected interviews and other writings, 1972–1977* (C. Gordon, Ed.). New York: Vintage.

Foucault, M. (1984).*The Foucault reader* (P. Rabinow, Ed.). New York: Pantheon Books.

Fox-Wolfgramm, S. J., Boal, K. B., & Hunt, J. G. (1998). Organizational adaptation to institutional change: A comparative study of first-order change in prospector and defender banks. *Administrative Science Quarterly, 43*, 87–126.

French, J. R. P., & Raven, B. (1959). The bases of social power. In D. Cartwright & A. Zander (Eds.), *Studies in social power* (pp. 15–167). Ann Arbor. MI: University of Michigan, Institute of Social Research.

Garud, R., Jain, S., & Kumaraswamy, A. (2002). Institutional entrepreneurship in the sponsorship of common technological standards: The case of Sun Microsystems and Java. *Academy of Management Journal, 45*(1), 196–214.

Giddens, A. (1976). *New rules of sociological method: A positive critique of interpretative sociologies*. London: Hutchinson.

Giddens, A. (1984). *The constitution of society: Outline of a theory of structuration*. Cambridge: Polity Press.

Gieryn, T.F. (2002). What buildings do. *Theory and society, 31*(1), 35–74.

Greenwood, R., Raynard, M., Kodeih, F., Micelotta, E.R., & Lounsbury, M. (2011). Institutional complexity and organizational responses. *Academy of Management Annals, 5*(1), 317–371.

Greenwood, R., & Suddaby, R. (2006). Institutional entrepreneurship in mature fields: The big five accounting firms. *Academy of Management Journal, 49*(1), 27–48.

Greenwood, R., Suddaby, R., & Hinings, C. R. (2002). Theorizing change: The role of professional associations in the transformation of institutionalized fields. *Academy of Management Journal, 45*, 58–80.

Hardy, C. (1994). *Managing strategic action: Mobilizing change*. London: Sage.

Hardy, C., & Clegg, S. R. (1996). Some dare call it power. In S. R. Clegg, C. Hardy, & W. R. Nord (Eds.), *Handbook of organization studies* (pp. 622–641). London: Sage.

Hardy, C., & Maguire, S. (2008). Institutional entrepreneurship. In R. Greenwood, C. Oliver, R. Suddaby, & K. Sahlin-Andersson (Eds.), *The SAGE handbook of organizational institutionalism* (pp.198–217). London: Sage.

Hargadon, A., & Douglas, Y. (2001). When innovations meet institutions: Edison and the design of the electric light. *Administrative Science Quarterly, 46*, 476–501.

Hensmans, M. (2003). Social movement organizations: A metaphor for strategic actors in institutional fields. *Organizational Studies, 24*, 355–381.

Hickson, D. J., Hinings, C. R., Schneck, R. E., & Pennings, J. M. (1972). A strategic contingencies theory of intra-organizational power. *Administrative Science Quarterly, 16*, 216–229.

Hinings, C. R., & Greenwood, R. (1988). The normative prescription of organizations. In L. Zucker (Ed.), *Institutional patterns and organizations: Culture and environment* (pp. 53–70). Cambridge, MA: Balinger.

Hirsch, P. M., & Lounsbury, M. (1997). Ending the family quarrel toward a reconciliation of 'old' and 'new' institutionalisms. *American Behavioral Scientist, 40*(4), 406–418.

Hoffman, A. J. (1999) Institutional evolution and change: Environmentalism and the U.S. chemical industry. *Academy of Management Journal, 42*, 351–371.

Holm, P. (1995). The dynamics of institutionalization: Transformation processes in Norwegian fisheries. *Administrative Science Quarterly, 40*, 398–422.

Hughes, E.C. (1936). The ecological aspect of institutions. *American Sociological Review, 1*, 180–189.

Jacques, R. (1995). *Manufacturing the employee: Management knowledge from the 19th to 21st Centuries*. London: Sage.

Janowitz, M. (1975). Sociological theory and social control. *American Journal of Sociology, 81*(1), 82–108.

Jenkins, J. C. (1983). Resource mobilization theory and the study of social movements. *Annual Review of Sociology, 9*, 527–553.

Jepperson, R. L. (1991). Institutions, institutional effects, and institutionalism. In W. W. Powell & P. J. DiMaggio (Eds.), *The new institutionalism in organizational analysis* (pp. 143–163). Chicago, IL: University of Chicago Press.

Jermier, J. M. (1985). 'When the sleeper wakes': A short story extending themes in radical organization theory. *Journal of Management, 11*(2), 67–80.

Jermier, J. M., Knights, D., & Nord, W. (1994). *Resistance and power in organizations*. New York: Routledge.

Khan, F. R., Munir, K. A., & Willmott, H. (2007). A dark side of institutional entrepreneurship: Soccer balls, child labour and postcolonial impoverishment. *Organization Studies, 28*(7), 1055–1077.

Kirsch, M. H. (2000). *Queer theory and social change*. London: Routledge.

Knights, D., & Wilmott, H. (1989). From degradation to subjugation in social relations: An analysis of power and subjectivity at work. *Sociology, 23*, 535–538.

Kraatz, M. S. and Block, E. S. (2008). Organizational implications of institutional pluralism. In R. Greenwood, C. Oliver, R. Suddaby, & K. Sahlin-Andersson (Eds.), *The SAGE handbook of organizational institutionalism* (pp. 243–275). London: Sage.

Laclau, E., & Mouffe, C. (1985). *Hegemony and socialist strategy: Towards a radical democratic politics*. London: Verso.

Lawrence, T. B. (1999). Institutional strategy. *Journal of Management, 25*, 161–187.

Lawrence, T. B., Leca, B., & Zilber, T.B. (2013). Institutional work: Current research, new directions and overlooked issues. *Organization Studies, 34*(8), 1023–1033.

Lawrence, T. B., Mauws, M. K., Dyck, B., & Kleysen, R. F. (2005). The politics of organizational learning: integrating power into the 4I framework. *Academy of Management Review, 30*(1), 180–191.

Lawrence, T. B., & Phillips, N. (2004). From Moby Dick to Free Willy: Macro-cultural discourse and institutional entrepreneurship in emerging institutional fields. *Organization, 11*(5), 689–711.

Lawrence, T. B., & Robinson, S. L. (2007). Ain't misbehavin: Workplace deviance as organizational resistance. *Journal of Management, 33*(3), 378–394.

Lawrence, T. B., & Suddaby, R. (2006). Institutions and institutional work. In S. R. Clegg, C. Hardy, T. B. Lawrence, & W. R. Nord (Eds.), *Handbook of organization studies* (2nd ed.) (pp. 215–254). London: Sage.

Lawrence, T. B., Suddaby, R., & Leca, B. (2009). *Institutional work: Actors and agency in institutional studies of organizations*. Cambridge: Cambridge University Press.

Lawrence, T. B., Winn, M., & Jennings, P. D. (2001). The temporal dynamics of institutionalization. *Academy of Management Review, 26*, 624–644.

Leblebici, H., Salancik, G. R., Copay, A., & King, T. (1991). Institutional change and the transformation of interorganizational fields: An organizational history of the U.S. radio broadcasting industry. *Administrative Science Quarterly, 36*, 333–363.

Lok, J. (2010). Institutional logics as identity projects. *Academy of Management Journal, 53*(6), 1305–1335.

Lukes, S. (1974). *Power: A radical view*. London: Macmillan.

Lukes, S. (2005). *Power: A radical view* (2nd ed.). Hampshire: Palgrave Macmillan.

Maguire, S., & Hardy, C. (2009). Discourse and deinstitutionalization: The decline of DDT. *Academy of Management Journal, 52*(1), 148–178.

Maguire, S., Hardy, C., & Lawrence, T. B. (2004). Institutional entrepreneurship in emerging fields: HIV/AIDS treatment advocacy in Canada. *Academy of Management Journal, 47*, 657–679.

Mann, M. (1993). *The sources of social power, Volume II: The rise of classes and nation-states, 1760–1914*. Cambridge: Cambridge University Press.

Mann, M. (2003). *Incoherent empire*. London: Verso Books.

Marx, K., & Engels, F. (1906). *Manifesto of the communist party*. CH Kerr.

Maslyn, J. M., Farmer, S. M., & Fedor, D. B. (1996). Failed upward influence attempts: Predicting the nature of subordinate persistence in pursuit of organizational goals. *Group & Organization Management, 21*(4), 461–480.

McAdam, D. (1988). *Freedom summer*. New York: Oxford University Press.

McCarthy, J. D., & Zald, M. N. (1977). Resource mobilization and social movements: A partial theory. *American Journal of Sociology, 82*(6), 1212–1241.

Meyer, J. W., & Rowan, B. (1977). Institutionalized organizations: Formal structure as myth and ceremony. *American Journal of Sociology, 83*, 340–363.

Meyer, J.W., Scott, W.R. (1983). Centralization and the legitimacy problems of local government. *Organizational Environments: Ritual and Rationality, 199*, 215.

Meyer, S., III (1981). *The Five Dollar Day*. Albany, NY: State University of New York Press.

Mezias, S., & Scarselletta, M. (1994). Resolving financial reporting problems: An institutional analysis of the process. *Administrative Science Quarterly, 39*(4), 654–658.

Mintzberg, H. (1983). *Power in and around organizations*. Englewood Cliffs, NJ: Prentice–Hall.

Mintzberg, H. (1984). Power and organizational life cycles. *Academy of Management Review, 9*, 207–224.

Munir, K. A. (2015). A loss of power in institutional theory. *Journal of Management Inquiry, 24*(1), 90–92.

Munir, K. A., & Phillips, N. (2005). The birth of the 'Kodak Moment': Institutional entrepreneurship and the adoption of new technologies. *Organization Studies, 26*(11), 1665–1687.

Noble, D. (1984). *Forces of production: A social history of industrial automation*. New York: Knopf.

Oakes, L., Townley, B., & Cooper, D. J. (1998). Business planning as pedagogy: Language and control in a changing institutional field. *Administrative Science Quarterly, 43*, 257–292.

O'Leary-Kelly, A. M., Griffin, R. W., & Glew, D. J. (1996). Organization-motivated aggression: A research framework. *Academy of Management Review, 21*, 225–253.

Oliver, C. (1991). Strategic responses to institutional processes. *Academy of Management Review, 16*, 145–179.

Orssatto, R. J., den Hond, F., & Clegg, S. R. (2002). The political ecology of automobile recycling in Europe. *Organization Studies, 23*(4), 639–665.

Pache, A. C., & Santos, F. (2010). When worlds collide: The internal dynamics of organizational responses to conflicting institutional demands. *Academy of Management Review, 35*(3), 455–476.

Pfeffer, J. (1981). *Power in organizations*. Marshfield, MA: Pitman.

Pfeffer, J., & Salancik, G. R. (1978). *The external control of organizations: A resource dependence perspective*. New York: Harper & Row.

Phillips, N., Lawrence, T. B., & Hardy, C. (2004). Discourse and institutions. *Academy of Management Review, 29*, 635–652.

Robinson, S. L., & Bennett, R. J. (1995). A typology of deviant workplace behaviors: A multidimensional scaling study. *Academy of Management Journal, 38*(2), 555–572.

Rojas, F. (2010). Power through institutional work: Acquiring academic authority in the 1968 third world strike. *Academy of Management Journal, 53*(6), 1263–1280.

Russo, M. V. (2001). Institutions, exchange relations and the emergence of new fields: Regulatory policies and independent power production in America, 1978–1992. *Administrative Science Quarterly, 46*, 57–86.

Schneiberg, M., & Lounsbury, M. (2008). Social movements and institutional analysis. In R. Greenwood, C. Oliver, R. Suddaby, & K. Sahlin-Andersson (Eds.), *The SAGE handbook of organizational institutionalism* (pp. 648–670). London: Sage.

Scott, J. R. (2001). *Power*. Oxford: Blackwell.

Scott, W. R. (2001). *Institutions and organizations* (2nd ed.). Thousand Oaks, CA: Sage.

Sewell, G. (1998). The discipline of teams: The control of team-based industrial work through electronic and peer surveillance. *Administrative Science Quarterly, 43*, 397–428.

Sewell, G., & Wilkinson, B. (1992). 'Someone to watch over me': Surveillance, discipline and the just-in-time labour process. *Sociology, 26*(2), 271–289.

Shaiken, H. (1984). *Automation and labor in the computer age*. New York: Holt, Rinehart & Winston.

Simon, J. (1988). The ideological effects of actuarial practices. *Law & Society Review, 22*(4), 771–800.

Slack, T., & Hinings, C. R. (1994). Institutional pressures and isomorphic change: An empirical test. *Organization Studies, 15*(6), 803–827.

Smets, M., Morris, T.I.M., & Greenwood, R. (2012). From practice to field: A multilevel model of practice-driven institutional change. *Academy of Management Journal, 55*(4), 877–904.

Snow, D. A., & Benford, R. D. (1988). Ideology, frame resonance and participant mobilization. *International Social Movement Research, 1*, 197–218.

Snow, D. A., Rochford, E. B., Worden, S. K., & Benford, R. D. (1986). Frame alignment processes, micromobilization, and movement participation. *American Sociological Review, 51*, 464–481.

Strang, D., & Soule, S. A. (1998). Diffusion in organizations and social movements: From hybrid corn to poison pills. *Annual Review of Sociology, 24*, 265–290.

Stryker, R. (2002). A political approach to organizations and institutions. In M. Lounsbury & M. J. Ventresca (Eds.), *Research in the sociology of organizations* (pp. 169–191). Oxford: JAI Press.

Suddaby, R. (2010). Challenges for institutional theory. *Journal of Management Inquiry, 19*(1), 14–20.

Suddaby, R., & Greenwood, R. (2005). Rhetorical strategies of legitimacy. *Administrative Science Quarterly, 50*, 35–67.

Symon, G., Buehring, A., Johnson, P., & Cassell, C. (2008). Positioning qualitative research as resistance to the institutionalization of the academic labour process. *Organization Studies, 29*(10), 1315–1336.

Thompson, J. D. (1956). Authority and power in 'identical' organizations. *American Journal of Sociology, 62*(3), 290–301.

Thornton, P. H., & Ocasio, W. (1999). Institutional logics and the historical contingency of power in organizations: Executive succession in the higher education publishing industry, 1958–1990. *American Journal of Sociology, 105*(3), 801–843.

Thornton, P. H., Ocasio, W., & Lounsbury, M. (2012). *The institutional logics perspective: A new approach to culture, structure, and process*. Oxford: Oxford University Press on Demand.

Tolbert, P. S., & Zucker, L. G. (1983). Institutional sources of change in organizational structure: The diffusion of civil service reform, 1880–1935. *Administrative Science Quarterly, 28*, 22–39.

Townley, B. (1993). Foucault, power/knowledge and its relevance for human resource management. *Academy of Management Review, 18*, 518–545.

Townley, B. (1997). The institutional logics of performance appraisal. *Organization Studies, 18*(2), 261–285.

Van Wijk, J., Stam, W., Elfring, T., Zietsma, C., & Den Hond, F. (2013). Activists and incumbents structuring change: The interplay of agency, culture, and networks in field evolution. *Academy of Management Journal*, *56*(2), 358–386.

Westphal, J. D., Gulati, R., & Shortell, S. M. (1997). Customization or conformity? An institutional and network perspective on the content and consequences of TQM adoption. *Administrative Science Quarterly*, *42*, 366–394.

Winner, L. (1986). *The whale and the reactor: A search for limits in an age of high technology*. Chicago, IL: University of Chicago Press.

Zietsma, C., & Lawrence, T. B. (2010). Institutional work in the transformation of an organizational field: The interplay of boundary work and practice work. *Administrative Science Quarterly*, *55*(2), 189–221.

Zucker, L. G. (1977). The role of institutionalization in cultural persistence. *American Sociological Review*, *42*(5), 726–743.

Zucker, L. G. (1987). Institutional theories of organization. *Annual Review of Sociology*, *13*, 443–464.

PART IV

Conversations

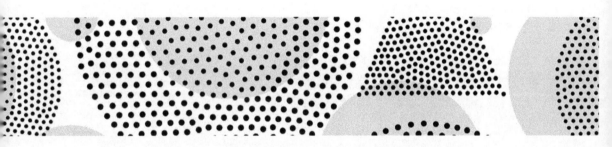

19

Advances to the Institutional Logics Perspective

William Ocasio, Patricia H. Thornton and
Michael Lounsbury

INTRODUCTION

The study of institutional logics has become, in the more than twenty years since Friedland and Alford's (1991) seminal article, one of the key theoretical perspectives in organizational institutionalism (Thornton et al., 2012). In particular, research on institutional logics has exploded since 2011 and 2012, when approximately 40 articles on the subject appeared in Web of Science each year, increasing to approximately 120 per year in 2014 and 2015. Research on institutional logics has influenced not only organizational theory and sociology, but is increasingly applied to other areas of management, including strategy, technology management and business ethics, as well as to political science, marketing, education and communication, among others. The more than 700 articles published with institutional logics as a key topic (with thousands of other articles

also citing the concept) has led to both an accumulation of knowledge on the determinants and consequences of institutional logics, as well as a divergence, and at times confusion, regarding the concept, the perspective and its application. The objective of this chapter is to address issues and ambiguities in this rapidly expanding literature in order to better position scholars for future research and theoretical development.

The institutional logics perspective has advanced and transformed itself considerably since Friedland and Alford's (1991) exploration of how the logics associated with the various institutional orders of society enabled and constrained organizations and individuals. While retaining the cultural emphasis of neo-institutionalism (Meyer and Rowan, 1977; Zucker, 1977; DiMaggio and Powell, 1983), the institutional logics perspective emphasizes cultural differentiation and pluralism, rather than isomorphism. Building on, yet going beyond, an emphasis on societal logics, Thornton and Ocasio (2008) reviewed and synthesized the theory and research on institutional logics and established five key principles for the metatheory: embedded agency, society as an inter-institutional system, the material and cultural foundations of institutions, institutions at multiple levels, and historical contingency. Thornton et al. (2012) further developed the perspective in our theoretical treatise. Advances included: an explicit cross-level model with microfoundations; a reformulation of the ideal types of institutional logics at the societal level, including the addition of community as an institutional order; and a more explicit development of how logics are embodied in practices, both at the level of the organization and the organization field. We believe the institutional logics perspective, as it has developed, provides a novel theory of agency that has importantly broadened institutional theory.

In this chapter we will not review in detail these advances and theoretical developments. The current chapter is not intended as revision or substitute for these prior efforts (Thornton and Ocasio, 2008; Thornton et al., 2012), but as a complement to them. However, we do seek to clarify key aspects of the institutional logics perspective and detail key impacts it has had on the field. In the next section, we discuss and clarify the nature of institutional logics. We then provide a brief overview of how the institutional logics perspective has developed from early ideas to current developments on institutional pluralism and complexity, institutional emergence and change, and applications to areas such as strategy. Next, we discuss methodological issues and promising advances for institutional logics research, and encourage the use of mixed-method approaches. We then highlight the important ways in which the institutional logics perspective has advanced institutional theory, and conclude with an invitation for scholars to advance our understanding of microfoundations and bridges to different disciplinary conversations and problems.

WHAT IS THE INSTITUTIONAL LOGICS PERSPECTIVE?

We begin by clarifying key aspects of the institutional logics perspective and how it is used and, in our view, should be used in future theory and research (see also Thornton et al., 2012). One of the most cited definitions of institutional logics is that provided by Thornton and Ocasio (1999: 804): 'the socially constructed, historical patterns of cultural symbols and material practices, assumptions, values, and beliefs by which individuals produce and reproduce their material subsistence, organize time and space, and provide meaning to their daily activity'. Building from this foundational imagery, the institutional logics perspective 'is a metatheoretical framework for analyzing the interrelationships among institutions, individuals, and organizations in social systems' (Thornton et al., 2012: 2). To further clarify the nature of the perspective, we offer the following observations to guide future research.

(1) Institutional logics are both symbolic and material (Friedland and Alford, 1991; Thornton et al., 2012), by which we mean that they are simultaneously embodied through both symbolic representations and material practices and artifacts. Institutional logics are communicated through language and other semiotic signs but are also materially observable. This signifies that institutional logics are more than theories but are concretely experienced and made durable through practices (Thornton et al., 2012).

(2) The organizing principles of institutional logics are multidimensional and institutional logics are configurations of distinct, yet interrelated dimensions. Thornton and Ocasio (2008) identified four dimensions common to all institutional logics: sources of collective identity; determinants of power and status; systems of social classification and categorization; and allocation of attention. Thornton et al. (2012) provided examples

of nine dimensions for the analysis of institutional orders of society: root metaphor; sources of legitimacy; sources of authority; sources of identity; bases of norms; basis of attention; basis of strategy; informal control systems; and economic systems. In a recent paper, Pahnke, Katila and Eisenhardt (2015) provided a simplified representation of these dimensions useful for their empirical analysis of financing of innovations: basis of norms, basis of strategy and basis of attention. While the dimensionality of institutional logics is at the core of the perspective, they remain provisional; that is, the particular dimensions that are relevant to different contexts, or empirical studies may vary. It is up to individual scholars to justify the existence of logics and their relevant dimensions with respect to a particular study.

(3) Institutional logics can be defined at various levels of analysis: world systems (Ansari et al., 2013); societies (Friedland and Alford, 1991); institutional fields (Rao et al., 2003) and organizations (Spicer and Sewell, 2010), among others. While societal logics permeate other levels (Thornton, 2004; Thornton and Ocasio, 2008), institutional logics at other levels are not merely variants or combinations of societal logics, but are also shaped by local variations and cultural adaptations that emerge from within that level (Lounsbury, 2007: Ocasio et al., 2015; Quattrone, 2015). We can identify an institutional logic at a particular level of analysis to the extent that we identify an associated institution[1] at that level (Thornton and Ocasio, 2008) and that the organizing principles of that institution have a certain degree of unifying coherence (i.e., 'logic'), albeit not complete, as institutional logics are subject to some internal contradictions (Seo and Creed, 2002). In other words, institutional logics are the organizing principles of institutions, where institutions can be identified at various level of analysis, including, but not limited to, the institutional orders of society. More research is needed on the degree of coherence of institutional logics, on how logics at other

levels of analysis are influenced by, yet differentiated from societal logics.

(4) We are making the ontological claim that institutional logics are real phenomena. Institutional logics are real in the same way bureaucracy is real, social networks are real and culture is real. We understand that not all users of institutional logics follow a realist ontology (e.g., Zilber, 2013), but some consider them instead as analytical constructs defined by researchers to make sense of a complex world. Our assumption is that institutional logics exist independently of researcher's analysis of them, and have causal powers upon individuals, groups and organizations. The analytical representation of an institutional logic is defined by researchers, but the validity of that representation is an empirical question, subject to the strengths and limitations of empirical methods (see discussion of methods below).

(5) One useful and well-established analytical representation of institutional logics is through ideal types (Thornton and Ocasio, 1999; Thornton, 2004; Thornton et al., 2012). But ideal types are not institutional logics, but a particular method for measuring logics. Here is an area where we have heard much misunderstanding of what we intended and perhaps we were not clear. The societal ideal types in Thornton et al. (2012) provide an ideal-typical model of societal-level logics from a reading of canonical texts such as Weber's (1978 [1922]) *Economy and Society* and contemporary organization theory. They are meant to be an example and not the only possible model. Other forms of representing and measuring logics besides ideal types are both possible and desirable, as further discussed in the methods section.

(6) As institutional orders change, and institutions at other levels change, so do the institutional logics associated with them. Institutional logics are historically contingent and evolve and change over time (Thornton and Ocasio, 2008; Ocasio et al., 2016). More research is needed in examining historical changes in institutional logics, both at the

level of the institutional orders of society, as well as at other levels of analysis.

(7) In defining and characterizing institutional logics it is also useful to note what are not institutional logics. Theories, frames, narratives, practices and categories are all building blocks of institutional logics but are not themselves institutional logics (Thornton et al., 2012; Ocasio et al., 2015). Ideologies, which provide an espoused normative ideal that guides political mobilization, are also not institutional logics. For example a market logic, which provides the operating principles that guide actual market practices, is distinguishable from a market ideology, which provides a political justification for mostly unregulated markets, without characterizing their real-word limitations. Institutional logics should also be distinguished from various measures or indicators of logics, including ideal types, as noted above, but also organizational forms, vocabularies of practice, functional backgrounds and governance structures.

THE DEVELOPMENT AND EXPANSION OF INSTITUTIONAL LOGICS RESEARCH

Early Development

The concept of institutional logics was first introduced by Alford and Friedland's (1985) treatise in political sociology to analyze how the conflicting logics of capitalism, bureaucracy and democracy shape the formation of the modern state. In the study of organizations, Jackall (1988) independently introduced a complementary approach, one that the literature has not engaged as much with. We believe, however, that Jackall's approach remains quite relevant to the continuing development of the institutional logics perspective, particularly with respect to the embodiment of logics in organizational practices. In his field research, Jackall examines the complex, ambiguous reality facing corporate managers, one where managers' goals and actions are shaped by institutional logics.

While placing the institutional logics of corporate managers within secularized versions of the Protestant ethos, Jackall's focus is not on society or its institutional orders, but on the institutional logics that guide situated action and decision-making. His definition of institutional logics is revealing of his underlying meta-theory:

> [By institutional logic] I mean the complicated, experientially constructed, and therefore contingent, set of rules, premiums and sanctions that men and women in a particular context create and re-create in such a way that their behavior and accompanying perspectives are to some extent regularized and predictable. Put succinctly, institutional logic is the way a particular social world works; of course, although individuals are participants in shaping the logic of institutions, they often experience this logic as an objective set of norms. And, of course, managers' own fate depends on how well they accomplish the defined goal in accordance with the institutional logic of the situation. (Jackall, 1988: 112)

Friedland and Alford (1991), building on their earlier work (Alford and Friedland, 1985), introduced the concept of institutional logics to organizational institutionalism as a means to bring to the forefront the role of society in shaping organizations. Rather than viewing society as monolithic, they describe it in terms of a variety of institutional orders, each with its own institutional logic. Elsewhere, Thornton et al. (2012) described at length the importance of this seminal contribution, not only for our own work, but for practically all subsequent work on institutional logics. While Friedland and Alford's emphasis on societal logics has not been the focus of most subsequent research, it influenced important pieces such as Haveman and Rao's (1997) analysis of how change in societal logics led to ecological changes in the savings and loan industry, as well as Mohr and Duquenne's (1997) innovative study of institutional logics in poverty relief at the turn of the twentieth century.

Thornton and Ocasio (1999) shifted the level of analysis of institutional logics from society to industry in their study of executive succession in higher education publishing. This change to the industry or field level has been quite influential in subsequent research. Their study examines how the change from an editorial logic to the market logic changes the determinants of succession. While very directly influenced by Friedland and Alford (1991), linking industry logics to societal logics of the profession and the market and emphasizing the symbolic and material basis of logics, Thornton and Ocasio's view is also heavily influenced by Jackall's (1988) characterization of logics as describing how a particular social world works, and his emphasis on how institutional logics shape organizational decision-making. Following Ocasio's (1997) attention-based view of the firm, Thornton and Ocasio emphasize the role of organizational attention as mediating the effects of logics on decision-making. Thornton and Ocasio further emphasize the historical contingency of institutional logics.

After publication of the Thornton and Ocasio (1999) study, interest in institutional logics began to grow, and theoretical development flowered. In a 2002 *Academy of Management Journal* Special Research Forum on Institutional Theory and Institutional Change edited by Dacin, Goodstein and Scott, Thornton (2002) and Lounsbury (2002) published papers on changes in institutional logics and their relationship to key transformations in the social organization of the fields of higher education publishing and finance respectively. Building on the developing conversation on social movements and organizational change that was beginning to occur at around the same time (e.g., Davis and Thompson, 1994; Lounsbury, 2001), Rao, Monin and Durand (2003) adopted a social movement perspective to study the abandonment of classical cuisine for nouvelle cuisine in France. Their field-level analysis emphasizes the role of identity movements and theorization

in explaining the shift from an institutional logic to another, both variants of the professional logic. Much of the effort here was to harness the concept of institutional logic to shed light on the general theoretical problem of how institutional change happens.

In 2004, Thornton provided a book-length analysis of changes in institutional logics in the higher education publishing industry and relies on this research to further extend and develop an emerging institutional logics perspective. Three theoretical developments are given extended treatment, including the use of typologies in theory construction, and an extended treatment of the institutional logics of societal sectors, or institutional orders. Second a more explicit link between industry-level logics and societal logics, and third, a more extensive treatment of a theory of how institutional logics shape attention. This book was especially important to the advance of institutional logics research because of its novel theorizing as well as its effort to bring coherence to a growing but still nascent theoretical conversation. This provided a platform for the broadening of institutional logics research to account for institutional pluralism, to expand our understanding of emergence and change in logics, and to develop implications for varied topics in fields such as strategic management. Thornton's 2004 book and the subsequent empirical and theoretical flowering of institutional logics research has coalesced into what has come to be known as the institutional logics perspective (Thornton et al., 2012).

Pluralism and Complexity

Over the past decade, scholarly development of logics has blossomed with an increased focus on institutional pluralism and complexity (Suddaby and Greenwood, 2005; Lounsbury, 2007; Kraatz and Block, 2008; Greenwood et al., 2011). Of course, this research builds on the key original insights of how multiple societal orders provide the foundation for the mobilization of various logics that enable institutional multiplicity, contestation and change (Friedland and Alford, 1991; Seo and Creed, 2002). Thus, institutional logics research has focused a great deal on how multiple logics enable change and provide the institutional sources of organizational heterogeneity (Thornton et al., 2012). In doing so, the institutional logics perspective provides a theory of agency and approach to micro-processes.

While institutional pluralism refers to contexts where actors are confronted with a variety of institutional logics that may be more or less complementary, enabling cooperation or competition (Kraatz and Block, 2008), institutional complexity refers more specifically to how individual and collective actors cope with and respond to conflicting demands associated with different logics (Greenwood et al., 2011). Although the literature to date has placed great emphasis on the competing nature of logics, we believe that more scrutiny is required to understand the conditions under which as well as the mechanisms by which logics are indeed competing versus complementary. Recent theoretical and empirical scholarship on logics has begun to do this, focusing on the different ways in which multiple logics are configured and reconfigured (e.g., Reay and Hinings, 2009; Almandoz, 2012; Lee and Lounsbury, 2015).

Building on research that focused on the sources and consequences of co-existent (often competing) logics (e.g., Rao et al., 2003; Lounsbury, 2007), research has aimed to advance our understanding of the mechanisms by which multiple logics take shape, interrelate and have effects. For instance, Glynn and Lounsbury (2005) examine how field-level shifts in institutional logics from aesthetic to market logics changed the discursive practices of critics of the Atlanta Symphony Orchestra. They distinguish between stable and changing institutional fields, and characterize the former by dominant logics and the latter by competing logics, shifts to a new logic, and logic blending.

This paper, while directly building on the work on historical changes in logics by Thornton and Ocasio (1999) and Rao et al. (2003), highlights the relevance of cultural entrepreneurship (Lounsbury and Glynn, 2001) to the dynamics of logics, and provides an early emphasis on competing logics and implicitly on hybridization and logic pluralism.

Dunn and Jones (2010) highlight how the medical profession is constituted by multiple logics – care and science – which were supported by distinct groups and interests, providing a competitive tension that expressed itself in the educational infrastructure of the profession. Thus, this chapter suggests how competition between field-level logics consequentially takes shape in the vocabularies and content of professional knowledge, and how shifts in the nature of vocabularies may lead to corollary shifts in the valorization of logics. Almandoz (2012) showed how institutional logics rooted in the backgrounds of founding team members had consequential effects on new bank creation. Founders with prior experiences in a community logic were better at resource acquisition and bank establishment, while those informed by a financial logic were more likely to disband before establishment in turbulent times.

Greenwood et al. (2010) examined how multiple logics shaped organizational decisions to downsize in Spain. In particular, they showed regions in which the Catholic church was influential in supporting a family logic, which moderated organizational responses to an overarching market logic by pressuring firms to downsize their workforces. This paper importantly advanced the notion of institutional complexity, highlighting how non-market institutions, especially those rooted in geographic community, can counterbalance market logics. In a similar vein, Lee and Lounsbury (2015) show how different kinds of community logics filter how field-level logics are interpreted and responded to by organizational actors. They emphasize the need to further understand the role of community logics, how logics at different levels of analysis relate (compete versus cooperate), and the conditions under which logic manifestations at different levels (e.g., individual, organization, region, nation-state) become more salient and potent with respect to key outcomes of interest.

Since research on institutional pluralism has been especially focused on field-organization cross-level dynamics, it is not surprising that researchers have begun to probe more deeply into the practices and intra-organizational dynamics related to institutional pluralism and complexity (Lounsbury and Crumley, 2007; Lok, 2010; Pache and Santos, 2010; Lounsbury and Boxenbaum, 2013; Smets, Greenwood et al., 2015). For instance, focusing on the development of collaborative relationships within and across healthcare organizations, Reay and Hinings (2009), in the context of state-mandated institutional change, identified four mechanisms by which institutional logics co-exist, yet distinctively guide the behavior of different actors. Relying on an embedded case study of a global law firm, Smets, Morris and Greenwood (2012) develop a model of practice-driven institutional change that specifies mechanisms by which change that emerges from everyday work can concatenate and enable shifts in field-level logics.

Sauermann and Stephan (2013) show that while industrial and academic science are often characterized as conflicting institutional logics in the literature, this conventional view ignores heterogeneity within those domains as well as connections between them (see also Wry et al., 2014). Relying on survey data on more than 5,000 research-active scientists, they develop a conceptual framework to compare and contrast industrial and academic science along four interdependent dimensions of work practice and show how differences in the nature of work better explain heterogeneity in how work is organized and results are disclosed. This research highlights the importance of more critically examining relationships among logics and variance within institutional fields through a more situated analysis of practice. For instance, we need more research on the conditions under which different logics may become organized in a more competitive or complementary manner.

Emphasizing a toolkit approach to logics (Swidler, 1986), McPherson and Sauder (2013) study how people with different professional backgrounds employ a variety of logics in their micro-level negotiations in a drug court. They find that actors not only employ their own professional logics, but are also able to access and use logics associated with other institutional and professional backgrounds in the context of negotiations where multiple logics are understood and routinely invoked. However, they also provide evidence that suggests that there are procedural, definitional and dispositional constraints that limit actors' discretion in the use of different logics. We need more research on how different logics can be drawn upon in different situations, as well as how actors may develop the social skill (Fligstein, 1997) and creative capacity (Lounsbury and Glynn, 2001) to access and use a wider variety of logics.

Another notable development in the literature focuses on hybrid organizing (Battilana and Lee, 2014; Battilana, Besharov and Mitzinneck, Chapter 5 this volume). For instance, relying on an in-depth comparative organizational case study, Battilana and Dorado (2010) showed how organizations can successfully combine distinct logics by creating a common 'hybrid' organizational identity via human resource practices. This paper importantly contributes to our understanding of the mechanisms by which organizations might go about using different HR practices for employees to manage the tensions they experience when impacted by different logics. Based on an inductive comparative case study of four work integration social enterprises that struggled to cope with competing social welfare and commercial logics, Pache and Santos (2013) show that, instead of keeping logics compartmentalized, their organizations selectively coupled elements prescribed by each logic. By doing so strategically, they can create hybrid organizations that can gain and maintain legitimacy.

Based on an ethnography of a public–private hybrid organization, the Cambridge Energy Alliance, Jay (2013) highlighted how multiple, competing field-level logics did not result in overtly competing interests or factions inside the organization. Instead, he highlights how they provided distinct interpretive schemes that provide contradictory interpretations of outcomes – what he refers to as the performance paradox where the same outcome might be deemed a success or failure depending on the sense-making logic used. He develops a novel process model that highlights how intra-organizational sense-making processes related to this paradox can result in a shift in dominant logics or a novel synthesis between them, enabling a reinterpretation of an organization's identity.

Besharov and Smith (2014) develop a theoretical framework of logic multiplicity within organizations, highlighting how logic compatibility and centrality might vary across organizations. They argue that field, organizational and individual factors will influence these two dimensions that characterize the relationship of logics. Drawing on a year-long ethnographic study of reinsurance trading in Lloyd's of London, Smets, Jarzabkowski et al. (2015) identify three balancing mechanisms – segmenting, bridging, and demarcating – which allow individuals to dynamically balance co-existing logics in ways that maintain their distinctiveness. Such practice-based approaches to the study of logics have not only greatly enhanced our understanding of the workings of logics, but further reinforce the need to more carefully probe the multiplex relationship of logics in and across different levels of analysis. As Vaerlander et al. (2016) show in their longitudinal ethnographic study of a large multinational software development company, such practice-based approaches can also be illuminating at more macro levels. They highlight how the global transfer of practices within a multi-site organization is importantly shaped

by the constellation of logics at a specific organization site that guides how employees experience and respond to practice transfer. They probe how such practice recontextualization affects performance, what makes a particular logic or constellation of logics salient for a particular practice at a particular time, and how logics and their constellations might change, especially in the context of global collaborations when different logics are invoked at different locations.

The key thread that runs through all this work is a focus on uncovering the cross-level mechanisms by which multiple institutional logics become instantiated, interrelate and have effects at the level of institutional fields, organizations and social interactions (Thornton et al., 2012). As such, the institutional logics perspective embraces the mechanism-based approach to theorizing (Davis and Marquis, 2005; Swedberg, 2014). Our understanding of the mechanisms that underlie institutional pluralism and complexity remains in its infancy, and will provide a vibrant area of development for the future.

Emergence and Change in Logics

Another prominent area of research on institutional logics that remains vibrant is the emergence and change in field-level logics. In Chapter 7 of our 2012 book, we provided an extensive review of this literature until 2011 and proposed a typology of change based on existing research. Three forms of transformational change were identified: replacement (Thornton and Ocasio, 1999; Rao et al., 2003), blending or hybridization, combining elements of different logics (Glynn and Lounsbury, 2005), and segregation – the separation of logics from a common origin (Purdy and Gray, 2009). But the research further shows that not all changes in field-level logics are transformative, but instead four forms of developmental change were identified: *assimilation*, which has to do with the incorporation of external elements into existing logics (Murray, 2010), *elaboration*, which refers to endogenous reinforcement (Shipilov et al., 2010), *expansion*, which involves shifts from one field to another (Nigam and Ocasio, 2010), and *contraction*, which refers to a decrease in a logic's scope (Reay and Hinings, 2009). The literature further highlights a variety of mechanism involved in the logic change: theorization, translation, sense-making, sense-giving, attention to events, categorization, vocabulary use and reification (Thornton et al., 2012).

Since 2012, research and theory development on the emergence and change in field-level logics has continued apace. The importance of language change is a common theme in both empirical research and theory development. For example, Ansari and colleagues (2013) examine the impact of frame shifts in the emergence of a transnational climate change logics, further expanding research on the importance of language use on changes in logics. Harmon, Greene and Goodnight (2015) theorize about the importance of inter-field rhetoric in fostering institutional change. Ocasio et al. (2015) examine how vocabulary changes must reflect not only the symbolic underpinning of institutional logics, but also the material ones, and that vocabulary changes must therefore reflect vocabularies used in coordinating practices and translating these practices across contrasts, as well as vocabularies employed for sense-giving and theorizing.

The role of practices and their variation was highlighted in several studies, For example, Gawer and Phillips (2013) examined the role of practices and identity work on changing institutional logics at Intel. Joseph, Ocasio and McDonnell (2014) examined structural elaborations in corporate governance practices, in particular the adoption of the CEO as the only insider in the board of directors – a new practice that is consistent with the theory of shareholder value maximization, yet diverges from its intent by increasing the power of CEOs over external directors. Quattrone (2015) examines

changing procedures in Jesuit accounting, reflecting the interplay between spiritual self-accountability and administrative accounting and recordkeeping. While this fascinating historical study purports to be distinct from prior approaches to the emergence and change in logics, in many ways it reminds us of Jackall's (1988) account, where the focus is less on societal-level logics, but the actual practices and procedures that guide management, or in the case of Quattrone, accounting.

Strategic Management

Space limitations preclude us from a full examination of the variety of topics, research questions and applications both within and outside organization theory, generated through the institutional logics perspective, for example in marketing (Scaraboto and Fischer, 2013). We would like to briefly highlight one area: the recent, but increasing, application of institutional logics to the study of strategic management. The work here is varied. Some relates to the effects of alternatives to the shareholder value logic. For example, Miller, Brenton-Miller and Lester (2013) found that firms with a family logic were more likely to conform to industry standards in strategic choices than other firms. Ioannou and Serafeim (2015) found that weakening of a shareholder value logic led to more positive analysts' evaluation of firms adopting corporate social responsibility practices.

Another area is the effects of alternative institutional logics for technology strategy and innovation. For example, Vasudeva, Alexander, and Jones (2014) examine how country-level differences in institutional logics shape inter-organizational learning in standard-setting organizations. Pahnke and colleagues (2015) examine how the different institutional logics of venture capitalists, internal corporate ventures and government funding agencies lead to differences in patenting and product introductions.

Finally, both theory and research in strategy examine field-level institutional logics as building blocks for corporate and business strategies. Durand and colleagues (2013) examined how French industrial design firms used institutional logics as strategic resources; awareness of a managerialist logic led to changes in strategy that prevailed along with the pre-existing logics of modernism and formalism. Ocasio and Radoynovska (2016) examine how increased institutional pluralism in a field increases heterogeneity across firms in their business models and governance, as organizations vary in their commitments to the variety of institutional logics in the field. Zhao et al. (2017) highlight how the institutional logics perspective provides a foundation for a renewed approach to optimal distinctiveness research that focuses on how firms strategically respond to conformity and differentiation pressures, and how their strategic responses appeal to various audiences and affect performance outcomes. They argue that research on optimal distinctiveness informed by the institutional logics perspective has important implications for many core strategy topics such as ambidexterity, competitive advantage, product-market scope and market entry.

Overall, there has been a proliferation of, and conceptual advance in research on institutional logics over the past two decades. While the dimensionality of the core theory continues to be fleshed out particularly with regards to micro-foundations and multi-level mechanisms, the institutional logics perspective has proven to be generative across a variety of empirical research sites and theoretical questions. To enable further progress, increased attention needs to be given to improving and expanding available methods of analysis. As a community of researchers, we must be appreciative of the usefulness and the limitations of different methodological approaches – from qualitative case studies, to large sample quantitative studies, to experimental designs. It is important to not valorize methods on ideological

grounds, but to understand how a variety of research approaches is needed to accumulate and assess the strength of research findings and to generate new knowledge and insights. To this end, we develop in the next section an extended discussion of methods used to study institutional logics.

METHODS OF ANALYSIS

Our students and more senior colleagues inform us of the need to clarify the methods used to study institutional logics. Given this feedback, we review institutional logics studies with a focus on the methods, discuss why it is complicated to measure institutional logics and suggest the use of methods from sister literatures to advance methods development.

Institutional logics research has generated a diversity of methods to measure institutional logics. These methods range from identifying time periods (Thornton and Ocasio, 1999; Thornton, 2001, 2002), actors' functional backgrounds (Almandoz, 2012; Thornton et al., 2012: ch. 5), geographic regions (Lounsbury, 2007; Greenwood et al., 2010; Lee and Lounsbury, 2015) and actors' vocabularies associated with institutional logics (Suddaby and Greenwood, 2005; Jones and Livne-Tarandach, 2008; Dunn and Jones, 2010), the reading of canonical texts (Thornton, 2004), experimental designs (Glaser et al., 2016) and visual imageries (Höllerer et al., 2013).

Researchers employ a variety of ontological approaches, including inductive, abductive and deductive, and use one or more of these approaches in a single study. Inductive and abductive methods are useful for developing theory; they enable researchers to substantively describe and interpret empirical observations that prior theory may be unable to explain. Inductive interpretative methods reveal emergent phenomena that might not be possible to measure in large-sample representative studies in which theory is tested.

Interpretive and Text Analytical Methods

There are a variety of interpretive methods, including ethnography, historical comparative methods, and content and discourse analysis (Phillips, Lawrence and Hardy, 2004). These methods use a coherent or canonical collection of texts, including interviews, archival documents, focus groups, naturally occurring conversations, political speeches, newspaper articles, novels, cartoons, photographs, or any written or visual form of information.

Precursor research set the groundwork for a focus on written information (words), known as vocabularies of motive (Mills, 1940), which are a way to explain the influences of differences in legitimacy, identity and authority. Vocabularies also are a way to measure these attributes of institutional logics because words are used by actors to persuade audiences (rhetoric) to embrace institutional change and stability (Suddaby and Greenwood, 2005). This genre of research examines how actors connect their words to the broader culture (e.g., institutional orders) to activate and given meaning to them, that is to theorize a strategy (Strang and Meyer, 1993).

This idea of 'culture and cognition', that is, measuring the underlying dimensions of how micro elements of institutional logics link to more macro or societal level logics is not new; but it has presented measurement challenges with respect to how smaller units of cultural knowledge such as words aggregate to larger cultural structures (DiMaggio, 1997). There are several standards or conventions for the micro and macro analysis of content, including manual content coding (Reay and Hinings, 2009), ideal types (Thornton and Ocasio, 1999), software counts of word frequency and co-occurrence (Jones and Livne-Tarandach, 2008; Dunn and Jones,

2010), correspondence analysis (Meyer and Höllerer, 2010) and cognitive mapping of the connections between categories (nouns) and relations (verbs) (Bingham and Kahl, 2013).

Varieties of interpretive analysis are continuing to advance with developments marrying the digital humanities and computer science enabling automated content coding of large corpora word texts (Mohr and Bogdanov, 2013: 564; Gardiner and Musto, 2015). While the traditional practice of researcher immersion in the actual context is still required for well-informed human interpretation of machine-generated codes or topics, the human subjectivity of the interpretive process particularly for large corpora is diminished by the use of software such as NVivo, Atlas TI (Reay and Jones, 2016), topic categorization with R (Jockers and Mimno, 2013) and Automap (Carley, 1993). In essence, automation of texts shifts the subjective moment of interpretation to the post-modeling stage (Mohr and Bogdanov, 2013: 560).

There are other recent developments in the measurement of situated cognition that hold promise for advancing interpretive methods useful to examining institutional logics. Cultural analytic methods combine existing online and survey-based data collection strategies with computerized text mining tools, as well as observational techniques to discern differences in actors' perceptions (e.g., DiMaggio et al., 2013; Hannigan, 2015). Other approaches such as productive methods (McDonnell, 2014) allow researchers to observe people creating cultural objects to reveal difficult to access cognitive processes including categorization and category development, automatic and deliberative cognition, sensory-motor schema, tacit knowledge, and resonance.

Composite Methods

Institutional logics can be examined with composite measures. For example, Lee and

Lounsbury (2015), in measuring two types of logics instantiated at the community level of analysis, politically conservative and pro-environmental, created a proxy variable from five related measures to represent the underlying concept of the logics. They were further able to substantiate the underlying variation in these two logics by tracing the logics' attributes back to their origin in institutional orders of the state and the market. Using these qualitative data, the pro-environmental logic was traced to the state logic and the politically conservative logic was traced to the market logic.

Comparative Methods

Comparative methods are central to the institutional logics perspective because its subsystem framework (inter-institutional system) lends itself to contrasting the effects of institutional logics across institutional orders (Friedland and Alford, 1991). While the subsystem framework has been widely used by scholars to describe society (Merton et al., 1959; Zucker, 1977: 84; Weber, 1978 [1922]; Friedland and Alford (1991) were the first to use it comparatively as a conflict theory of institutional change. Some scholars have contrasted logics across institutional orders (Thornton and Ocasio, 1999; Thornton, 2001, 2002; Lounsbury, 2002, 2007; Marquis and Lounsbury, 2007; Greenwood et al., 2010). Others have contrasted different variants of logics within an institutional order such as the professions (Suddaby and Greenwood, 2005; Dunn and Jones, 2010; McPherson and Sauder, 2013).

Ideal types are often used in this type of comparative analysis in particular to show how the elemental categories of institutional logics are a coherent set as distinct from independent variables (Pahnke et al., 2015). Ideal types are simplified, synthetic, analytical, abstract representations of institutional logics based in empirical observation. For example bureaucracy and professionalism are ideal types that represent ontologically distinct categories (Blau and Scott, 1962). What is important here is not what is true or not, but that the incompatibility of these two categories form part of an argument that assumes a logical difference or conflict between the categories (Suddaby and Greenwood, 2005: 46).

The ideal-type method stems from Weber (1978 [1922]), who suggested that abstracting from the complexity and specificity of concrete events is useful to guide comparative analysis. In constructing ideal types, the researcher deliberately departs from reality by focusing on certain attributes for analytically comparative purposes (Astley, 1985: 502). As a typological method of theory construction ideal types can be developed inductively (Glaser, 2001), deductively (Thornton, 2004) and abductively.

Ideal types are used for the purpose of theory construction and hypothesis generation. They are useful for comparison of multiple configurations of institutional logics and nonlinear patterns of logics in cross-sectional and longitudinal studies. Ideal types are not ahistorical; it is the data that are either historical or not depending on the research question and design. Subjectivity and observer bias can be ruled out in this qualitative analysis by using an independent data source to empirically test the ideal types.

The ideal types presented in Thornton and Ocasio (1999), Thornton (2001) and Thornton (2002) are instantiations, that is realizations of conceptual abstractions in concrete instances that are specific to the publishing industry. One would not expect the matrix cell contents to be relevant to some other domain. Some of the y-axis categorical elements may be relevant across different substantive domains, but the specific instantiations (matrix cell contents) can vary as research questions, domains and historical time periods vary. The cell contents of the ideal types in Thornton et al. (2012) are 'examples' from prior institutional logics research and are not meant to be reified robust attributes applicable to other institutional domains.

Actor Dispositions

Measuring actors' functional backgrounds is another reemerging approach. Almandoz (2012) measured logics by coding founders' functional backgrounds from bank charter applications submitted to regulators. Note this method is similar to coding the backgrounds of corporate CEOs in precursor research (Fligstein, 1985). To understand how to code founders' biographical profiles, Almandoz (2012) first engaged interpretive methods to familiarize himself with the banking industry and the process of founding a bank. He employed participant observation by attending a workshop for prospective bank founders, interviewed individuals contemplating starting a bank, and read archival documents on banking compiled by the FDIC. He conducted word searches of regulatory documents describing the mission, goals and opportunities of prospective banks and the founding team as noted by regulators. This native immersion into bank founding practices enabled Almandoz (2012) to identify a theme that the backgrounds of founders represent two contrasting ideal types, a financial and a community logic. Almandoz then showed that these two logics, measured by the ratio of founders' team member backgrounds in a community and a financial logic produced significantly different consequences for the success of bank founding.

Time Dependence

Because institutional logics are historically contingent and historically constituted, measuring the effects of time is important if researchers want to be able to understand causal patterns, longer-term trends and to generalize their findings (Thornton and Ocasio, 1999; Ocasio et al., 2016). Ecological and neo-institutional research developed advanced methods to measure various parameterizations of time with dynamic event history models, including calendar years, organization age and event sequencing

(Tuma and Hannan, 1984). A number of institutional logics studies build on these conventions in using longitudinal research designs and quantitative modeling (e.g., Haveman and Rao, 1997; Thornton and Ocasio, 1999; Thornton, 2001, 2002; Marquis and Lounsbury, 2007; Dunn and Jones, 2010). The strongest studies combine quantitative and qualitative methods to account for constitution, contingency and consequences of institutional effects over time. These studies advance beyond frequency distribution graphs and descriptive calendars of events to show event sequencing in hazard rate graphs.

Real and Ideal Boundaries

The growing study of conflicting institutional logics and how actors manage this conflict through hybrid practices and organizational forms (Lounsbury, 2007; Purdy and Gray, 2009; Battilana and Dorado, 2010; Dunn and Jones, 2010) highlights the need to further develop methods that aid researchers in defining boundaries and measuring the relative distance between them. Do sources of identity stem from a single institutional order or logic, or multiple ones (Rao et al., 2003)? How hybrid or how pure is the logic or element of a logic relative to the ideal type (Goodrick and Reay, 2011)? Geographic boundaries can distinguish institutional logics as shown by differences in the strategies of financial analysts in Boston versus New York (Lounsbury, 2007), and regional differences in the management strategy of manufacturing firms (Greenwood et al., 2010).

Another avenue to advance understanding of how boundaries affect the measurement of institutional logics lies in the affinity between institutional logics and categorization (Loewenstein et al., 2012; Durand and Boulongne, Chapter 24 this volume) and organizational ecology and categorization (Kennedy and Fiss, 2013: 10–11). Ecologists have used set theoretic approaches, such as fuzzy sets, to model grade-of-membership in multiple categories or full membership in a focal category (Hannan et al., 2007). To illustrate our point, substitute the concept of categorical elements of a logic for the concept of category; set theoretical approaches may be well-suited to this task. Negro, Hannan and Rao (2010), for example, used crisp and fuzzy membership in overlapping categories as evidence of category emergence and change. Their research design suggests that it may be possible in a more fine-grain fashion to examine overlapping logics and the degree to which actors' behaviors align with one logic versus another. For example, Lander et al. (2017) use set theoretic methods to explore how organizational design elements congruent with different institutional logics are combined to contribute to achieving organizational goals in Dutch law firms.

Some combinations of institutional logics are argued to be more complimentary, others are more incommensurate (Thornton et al., 2012), but this proposition is speculative. In theory, the logics of the professions and the state are resource dependent in the sense that the professions produce knowledge and the state enacts legislation to codify and enforce knowledge. Given this argument the question remains which combinations of logics or institutional orders are more interdependent and which are more autonomous? Qualitative Comparative Analysis (QCA) (Ragin, 1987, 2000, 2008; Ragin and Fiss, 2016) used in sociology, political science and management (Fiss, 2011; Fiss et al., 2013) could help address these types of questions. This method uses truth tables to combine measures of multiple qualities or attributes into matrices that capture how cases are distributed in an n-dimensional property space defined by these attributes (Kennedy and Fiss, 2013).

Socially Constructed Truth as Methods Bias

Even the most rigorous methods have limitations, which is why confidence in findings can be bolstered by the use of mixed methods approaches that triangulate, i.e., validate, findings across different methods (Creswell, 2003; Kaplan, 2015). As Eisenhardt (1989) notes, methods bias can be counteracted by the triangulation of methods of analysis and studies that engage both inductive and deductive approaches in single studies. Eisenhardt (1989), for example, states, 'we build on existing theory because a prior specification of constructs can also help to shape the initial design of theory building research ... If these constructs prove important as the study progresses, then researchers have a firmer empirical grounding for the emergent theory ... In a description of her own study, Eisenhardt (1989) states 'there were strong, triangulated measures on which to ground the emergent theory' (1989: 536).

One of the virtues of the institutional logics perspective is that it is a mixed method subfield that embraces deduction, which accumulates advances in theory, as well as induction which privileges contextual understanding and development of new theory. Depending on the research question and setting, researchers engage the objective world and beliefs in universal interpretation stemming from theory testing and positivist grounded theory. Researchers also engage the enacted world and beliefs in particular interpretation from grounded theory. All ontologies present some type of a bias to data collection and researchers' conclusions. We encourage researchers to be ambidextrous in their ontologies and methods as the distinctions between types are analytical and not an ideological badge of identity.

Accumulating Generalizable Findings

While each method has its strengths and weaknesses, we are not aware of a single method that is superior to mixed methods studies. As we consider advances, there is only one set of generalizable findings in the institutional logics literature based on a meta-analysis; these findings indicate that the market logic is colonizing professional domains (Thornton et al., 2015). Achieving greater accumulation of findings across diverse studies is an ultimate goal that requires researchers to give greater care to the selection of their research practices in a number of ways. This involves more careful citations to avoid confusing theoretical and empirical papers. It requires researchers to better distinguish those papers that are focused on determining institutional logics from those that are focused on the consequences of logics. It means discriminating the value of novel inductive analyses with limited generalizability as distinct from hypothesis testing studies that cumulate findings (Barley, 2016; Davis, 2015). Future efforts require greater attention to identifying the mechanisms that link institutional logics across levels of analysis and developing hypothesis testing studies using mixed methods and longitudinal research designs.

Ultimately, the continued vibrancy of institutional logics research is dependent upon how well researchers bring together the findings of more interpretive analysis, which emphasizes the historical and situational context, with more quantitative analysis, which emphasize generalizability and the testing of theory.

DISCUSSION AND CONCLUSION

The institutional logics perspective is a highly productive research program, which employs a diverse set of methods, emphasizes different levels of analysis, focuses on a variety of dependent variables and outcomes, and identifies multiple mechanisms to explain the determinants, consequences and variability of logics. This research is quite diverse and not always consistent with respect to underlying assumptions, theoretical emphasis, methods, or in research findings. In our book (Thornton et al., 2012), we provide an integrative metatheory to bring a common context to prior work and to set foundations for the future. Differences remain, are welcomed and are to be expected, but there is not always full engagement with prior theory and research in the perspective.

We do not expect or argue for a closed scientific research paradigm (Kuhn, 1962), as is common in the natural sciences. Yet despite, or perhaps because of, the continuing heterogeneity, the quarter century of research and theory development in the institutional logics perspective has led to fairly radical change in how organizational scholars understand institutions and organizations, which builds on yet departs from neo-institutional theory (Meyer and Rowan, 1977; DiMaggio and Powell, 1983; DiMaggio and Powell, 1991). Ironically, Friedland and Alford (1991), which was published in the 'orange' volume (Powell and DiMaggio, 1991) that brought together and provided a synthesis of the new institutionalism, was the seminal contribution that allowed for that transformation.

Here we outline three major changes in how researchers view institutions and organizations that, in our judgment, have either been a direct result or greatly influenced by the institutional logics perspective.

1 From Isomorphism to Institutional Pluralism

Isomorphism was termed the master proposition of neo-institutional theory (Meyer and Rowan, 1977; DiMaggio and Powell, 1983; Scott, 2008). Organizations, particularly formal organizational structures, became isomorphic with their institutionalized environments in order to gain legitimacy and survive (Meyer and Rowan, 1977). In the Meyer version, isomorphism was a property of the world system and the Western cultural account (Meyer and Rowan, 1977). In DiMaggio and Powell (1983), it was the focal point for the theorization of field structuration.

The institutional logics perspective has not only theorized the prevalence of institutional pluralism rather than isomorphism at various levels: society (Friedland and Alford, 1991; Thornton, 2004), institutional fields (Greenwood et al., 2011) and organizations (Pache and Santos, 2010; Ocasio and Radoynovska, 2016), but, as we reviewed above, provided compelling empirical evidence of continuing pluralism at multiple levels (Lounsbury, 2007; Dunn and Jones, 2010; Greenwood et al., 2010; McPherson and Sauder, 2013). Note that the perspective does not negate the existence of isomorphic pressures. Under the perspective, shared commitments or conformity to institutional logics will lead to isomorphism among organizations or social groups that share the same logics. But the institutional logics perspective differs from the neo-institutional view on isomorphism in multiple ways, including: (i) field-level heterogeneity due to competing logics (Lounsbury, 2007; Dunn and Jones, 2010); (ii) local variations in institutional logics (Purdy and Gray, 2009; Lee and Lounsbury, 2015); (iii) organizational heterogeneity due to diverse strategic commitments (Kraatz and Block, 2008; Ocasio and Radoynovska, 2016); (iv) power differentials, conflict and contestation leading to organizational heterogeneity (Pache and Santos, 2010; Besharov and Smith, 2014).

2 From Structural Theory to Embedded Agency

Closely related to the focus on isomorphism, a significant issue for both critics (e.g., Kraatz and Zajac, 1996) and proponents (DiMaggio, 1986) of neo-institutional theory was the limited role for agency at both the individual and organizational levels. The institutional logics perspective shifted away from a structuralist approach to embrace a theory of embedded agency (Thornton and Ocasio, 2008; Thornton et al., 2012). Embedded agency rests on the foundational assumption that institutional logics are both enabling and constraining of individual actions, and that individuals exercise agency in the formation, reproduction and transformation of organizations (Friedland and Alford, 1991). With the Weberian influences in the specification of institutional orders (Thornton, 2004), the institutional logics perspective is a theory of action, albeit action shaped by and shaping social and cultural structures. Note for example that Thornton and Ocasio (1999) is a study of organizational actions: executive succession events, as shaped by institutional logics. Organizational actions, shaped by logics, are critical in the determination of organizational structures: e.g., acquisitions (Thornton, 2001), and multidivisional structures (2002).

The embedded agency generated by institutional logics departs from structural determinism in multiple ways. Given institutional pluralism, a variety of logics are available to actors, and this multiplicity provides a source of agency (Thornton et al., 2012; Pache and Santos, 2013). The principles of institutional logics are guideposts for action but allow for local variations (Lounsbury, 2001), a variety of structural elaborations (Shipilov et al., 2010; Joseph et al., 2014) and are subject to significant ambiguity (Jackall, 1988; Quattrone, 2015). Consequently the so-called paradox of embedded agency (Battilana and D'Aunno, 2009) is not really a paradox, as embeddedness does not imply oversocialized behavior (cf., Granovetter, 1985), and adaptive change and intentional action is a property of embedded agency and the institutional logics perspective (Thornton et al., 2012). Overall, a focus on embedded agency shifts institutional theory from a top-down structural perspective to incorporation of cross-level (both top-down and bottom-up) mechanisms in research and theory development.

While the core embedded agency assumption is a fundamental change from structural determinism, it is also distinct from the overly agentic, undersocialized approach that is characteristic of some varieties of organizational institutionalism. For example, although we believe that the institutional logics perspective can be productively combined with an analysis of institutional work (e.g., Lok, 2010), at times theory and research on institutional work appears undersocialized, particularly with respect to the constitution of actors' interests (e.g. Lawrence et al., 2009). Unlike theories of rational choice, interests and preferences are not individual-level phenomena, but are shaped by institutional logics that actors have learned, experienced through practices, and with which they identify. Similarly, an embedded agency approach differs from a resource dependence perspective on institutions (cf., Oliver, 1991), one that has also been applied to interpret the determinants and consequences of institutional logics (e.g., Wry et al., 2013).

3 From an Alternative to Rational Choice Economics to the Institutional Contingency and Multiplicity of Economic and Market Orientations

Neo-institutional theory began as an attempt to explain organizations as a product of institutional environments distinct from technical environments (Meyer and Rowan, 1977) and economic and market forces (DiMaggio and Powell, 1983; Tolbert and Zucker, 1983).[2] This distinction between institutional and technical environments actually dates back to Parsons (1956), and is also reflected in precursors to neo-institutional theory, such as Hirsch's (1975) account of how the institutional environment shaped industry performance.

The institutional logics perspective takes a different view of the relationship between economics and markets and institutions. Markets and institutions are not two different spheres but markets are shaped by institutions and institutional logics (Thornton, 2004). At the same time, competitive and market forces have a material existence that is not predetermined by institutions or logics but itself shapes the formation of institutional logics (Thornton et al., 2012). For example the

merger waves in the publishing industry and the market for corporate control facilitated the rise of the market logic in higher education publishing (Thornton and Ocasio, 1999).

Anthropologists provide evidence of the near-universal existence of market exchange in all societies (Fiske, 1991), along with other forms of governance: authority relationships, reciprocity and communal sharing. Societies differ, however, in both the extent and organization of different forms of governance. Friedland and Alford (1991) posited market capitalism as one of the key institutional orders, with its own distinct logic. Thornton and Ocasio (1999) shifted the emphasis from capitalism to market orientation as a distinct institutional logic, implicitly arguing that market logics, associated with economic market orientations, are not universally dominant, but their prevalence is a historical contingency.

A key finding of the institutional logics perspective (Thornton et al., 2015), as previously noted, is the rise of a market logic across different sectors during the last decades of the twentieth century. An extreme form of the market logic has prevailed in many economies, particularly the United States: the shareholder maximization logic (Lazonick and O'Sullivan, 2000). More generally, market orientations and the economic way of thinking and viewing the world have become increasingly shaped by a variety of institutions across society. From this perspective, economic reasoning and market structures are deeply embedded in institutional structures and guided by institutional logics (Thornton, 2004). Institutional environments are not distinct from economic or technical environments but rather how technical and market forces operate is shaped by the historical contingencies of institutional logics (Thornton and Ocasio, 2008; Ocasio et al., 2016).

In addition to the historical contingency of market logics, institutional logics research has also highlighted how markets are socially constructed, and that market logics can be instantiated in different ways across time and space. For instance, Lounsbury (2007) showed how different regional markets for mutual funds were guided by the different competitive orientations of efficiency versus maximizing performance outcomes. Thus, despite the overarching rise of the market logic, we need more research on instantiation of market logics and the social construction of different markets. This calls for more direct engagement with economic sociologists (e.g., Swedberg, 1990; Granovetter and Swedberg, 1992; Smelser and Swedberg, 2010; Du Gay and Morgan, 2013) who are interested in understanding the sources and consequences of varieties of markets and capitalisms. In this regard, it would be especially helpful to develop a cross-national comparative agenda on how market logics get translated, altered and resisted in different cultural contexts (Djelic, 2001).

While the influence of the institutional logics perspective in reformulating organizational institutionalism has been significant, other areas remain fertile for further theoretical and empirical development. One area, highlighted in our book (Thornton et al., 2012) is the microfoundations of institutional logics and its integration with both top-down and bottom-up cross-level models. In our book, we introduced the availability–accessibility– activation model to explain how multiple logics available to individuals and organizations, yet a more limited number of logics are readily accessible to them, and different logics become activated in any particular situation. Logic activation is a cross-level phenomenon further shaped by the negotiated order among individuals who may vary in the logics most accessible to them (cf., McPherson and Sauder, 2013). The availability– accessibility–activation model has been employed by Pache and Santos (2013) to explain political responses to multiple logics but further empirical research is required to test, validate, or modify the theory.

Given the development of theory and research on microfoundations and understanding culture as a toolkit (Swidler, 1986;

Thornton et al., 2012; McPherson and Sauder, 2013), we have argued that the institutional logics perspective provides a novel approach to agency that appreciates the constitutive power of broader socio-cultural structures. However, many open questions remain, including the conditions under which actors are able to invoke or combine different logics, and with what effects. In this regard, it would be useful to engage contemporary developments in the sociology of culture (e.g., Vaisey, 2009; Lizardo, 2014; Mohr and Ghaziani, 2014).

More generally, we encourage institutional logics scholars to engage problems and ideas across disciplines from sociology, political science and economics, to domains of strategy, entrepreneurship and international business. While not every study need (or should) engage the institutional logics perspective, we believe the perspective will continue to shed light on important, yet heretofore unexplored, aspects of organizations, society, politics and the economy. We believe that research on institutional logics remains in the early stages, and we invite efforts to contribute to its shaping and the continued vitality of institutional analysis.

Notes

1 Despite the varieties of institutional theory employed in organizational studies, the term 'institution' is rarely defined. A useful definition for our purposes is that an institution is a taken-for-granted, normatively sanctioned set of roles and interaction orders for collective action. Accordingly we can consider publishing (Thornton and Ocasio, 1999), French cuisine (Rao et al., 2003), mutual funds (Lounsbury, 2007) and Jesuit accounting (Quattrone, 2015) as examples of institutions, each with its own set of organizing principles and institutional logics. The institutional logics that may compete or are relatively dominant within each of these institutions are shaped by the societal logics associated with the institutional orders (Friedland and Alford, 1991), but also by factors unique to the analysis of the organization, industry and institutional field.

2 Meyer and Rowan (1977) contrast institutional environments with technical environments with functional demands for efficiency and boundary-spanning exchange. They are implicitly contrasting

institutional theory from then prevalent contingency views of organization, such as Thompson's (2003 [1967]). For DiMaggio and Powell (1983) the contrast is with neoclassical economics and its emphasis on competitive market forces. While contingency theory differs from economic theory, for the purpose of subsequent discussion we will treat them as equivalent, as both focus on rationality and efficiency.

REFERENCES

Alford, Robert R. and Friedland, Roger (1985). *Powers of Theory: Capitalism, the State, and Democracy.* Cambridge: Cambridge University Press.

Almandoz, Juan (2012). Arriving at the starting line: The impact of community and financial logics on new banking ventures, *Academy of Management Journal,* 55: 1381–1406.

Ansari, Shaz, Wijen, Frank and Gray, Barbara (2013). Constructing a climate change logic: An institutional perspective on the 'tragedy of the commons', *Organization Science,* 24: 1014–1040.

Astley, W. Graham (1985). Administrative science as socially constructed truth, *Administrative Science Quarterly,* 30: 497–513.

Barley, Stehen R. (2016). 60th anniversary essay ruminations on how we became a mystery house and how we might get out, *Administrative Science Quarterly,* 61: 1–8.

Battilana, Julie and D'Aunno, Thomas (2009). Institutional work and the paradox of embedded agency. In Thomas B. Lawrence, Roy Suddaby and Bernard Leca (eds), *Institutional Work: Actors and Agency.* Cambridge: Cambridge University Press. pp. 31–58.

Battilana, Julie and Dorado, Silvia (2010). Building sustainable hybrid organizations: The case of commercial microfinance organizations, *Academy of Management Journal,* 53: 1419–1440.

Battilana, Julie and Lee, Mathews (2014). Advancing research on hybrid organizing – insights from the study of social enterprises', *Academy of Management Annals,* 8: 397–441.

Besharov, Marya L. and Smith, Wendy K. (2014). Multiple institutional logics in organizations: Explaining their varied nature and implications, *Academy of Management Journal,* 39: 364–381.

Bingham, Christopher and Kahl, Stephen J. (2013). The process of schema emergence: Assimilation, deconstruction, unitization and the plurality of analogies, *Academy of Management Journal,* 56(1): 14–34.

Blau, Peter and Scott, W. Richard (1962). *Formal Organizations.* San Francisco: Chandler.

Carley, Kathleen M. (1993) Coding choices for textual analysis: A comparison of content analysis and map analysis, *Sociological Methodology,* 75–126.

Creswell, John W. (2003). *Designing and Conducting Mixed-Method Research,* London: Sage Publications.

Davis, Gerald F. (2015). Editorial essay: What is organizational research for? *Administrative Science Quarterly,* 60(2): 179–188.

Davis, Gerald F. and Marquis, Christopher (2005). Prospects for organization theory in the early twenty-first century: Institutional fields and mechanisms, *Organization Science,* 16: 332–343.

Davis, Gerald. F. and Thompson, Tracy (1994). A social movement perspective on corporate control, *Administrative Science Quarterly,* 39: 141–173.

DiMaggio, Paul J. (1986). Structural analysis of organizational fields: A blockmodel approach, *Research in Organizational Behavior,* 8: 335–370.

DiMaggio, Paul J. (1997). Culture and cognition, *Annual Review of Sociology,* 23(1): 263–287.

DiMaggio, Paul J., Nag, Manish and Blei, David (2013). 'Exploiting affinities between topic modeling and the sociological perspective on culture: Application to newspaper coverage of U.S. government arts funding', *Poetics,* 41: 570–606.

DiMaggio, Paul J. and Powell, Walter W. (1983). The iron cage revisited: Institutional isomorphism and collective rationality in organizational fields, *American Sociological Review,* 48: 147–160.

DiMaggio, Paul J. and Powell, Walter W. (1991). Introduction. In Walter W. Powell and Paul J. DiMaggio (eds), *The New Institutionalism in Organizational Analysis.* Chicago, IL: University of Chicago Press. pp. 1–40.

Djelic, Marie-Laure (2001). *Exporting the American Model: The Postwar Transformation of European Business.* Oxford, UK: Oxford University Press.

Du Gay, Paul and Morgan, Glenn (2013). *New Spirits of Capitalism?: Crises, Justifications, and Dynamics.* Oxford, UK: Oxford University Press.

Dunn, Mary B. and Jones, Candace (2010). Institutional logics and institutional pluralism: The contestation of care and science logics in medical education, 1967–2005, *Administrative Science Quarterly,* 55: 114–149.

Durand, Rodolphe, Szostak, Berangere, Jourdan, Julien and Thornton, Patricia H. (2013). Institutional logics as strategic resources. In *Institutional Logics in Action: Research in the Sociology of Organizations,* Volume 39A. Bingley, UK: Emerald Group. pp. 165–201.

Eisenhardt, Kathleen M. (1989). Building theories from case study research, *Academy of Management Review,* 14: 532–550.

Fiske, Alan (1991). *Structures of Social Life: The Four Elementary Forms of Human Relations.* New York: Free Press.

Fiss, Peer C. (2011). Building better causal theories: A fuzzy set approach to typologies in organization research, *Academy of Management Journal*, 54: 393–420.

Fiss, Peer C., Cambré, B. and Marx, A. (eds) (2013). *Configurational Theory and Methods in Organizational Research: Research in the Sociology of Organizations*, Volume 38. Bingley, UK: Emerald Group.

Fligstein, Neil (1985). The spread of the multidivisional form among large firms, 1919–1979. *American Sociological Review,* 50: 377–391.

Fligstein, Neil (1997). Social skill and institutional theory, *American Behavioral Scientist*, 40: 397–405.

Friedland, Roger and Alford, Robert (1991). Bringing society back in: Symbols, practices, and institutional contradictions. In Walter W. Powell and Paul J. DiMaggio (eds), *The New Institutionalism in Organizational Analysis*. Chicago, IL: University of Chicago Press. pp. 232–263.

Gardiner, Eileen and Musto, Ronald G. (2015). *The Digital Humanities: A Primer for Students and Scholars*. Cambridge: Cambridge University Press.

Gawer, Anabelle and Phillips, Nelson (2013). Institutional work as logics shift: The case of Intel's transformation to platform leader, *Organization Studies*, 34(8): 1035–1071.

Glaser, Barney G. (2001). *The Grounded Theory Perspective: Conceptualization Contrasted with Description*. Mill Valley, CA: Sociology Press.

Glaser, Vern L., Fast, Nathaniel, Harmon, Derek J. and Green, Sandy E. Jr. (2016). Institutional frame switching: how institutional logics shape individual action. In *Research in the Sociology of Organizations*, Volume 49A. Bingley, UK: Emerald Group.

Glynn, Mary Ann and Lounsbury, Michael (2005). From the critics' corner: Logic blending, discursive change and authenticity in a cultural production system, *Journal of Management Studies*, 42: 1031–1055.

Goodrick, Elizabeth and Reay, Trish (2011). Constellations of institutional logics: changes in the professional work of pharmacists, *Work and Occupations*, 38: 372–416.

Granovetter, Mark (1985). Economic action and social structure: the problem of embeddedness, *American Journal of Sociology*, 91: 481–510.

Granovetter, Mark and Swedberg, Richard, Eds. (1992). The Sociology of Economic Life. Boulder, CO, Westview Press.

Greenwood, Royston, Díaz, Amalia Magán, Li, Stan Xiao and Lorente, José Céspedes (2010). The multiplicity of institutional logics and the heterogeneity of organizational responses, *Organization Science*, 21: 521–539.

Greenwood, Royston, Raynard, Mia, Kodeih, Farah, Micelotta, Evelyn R. and Lounsbury, Michael (2011). Institutional complexity and organizational responses, *Academy of Management Annals*, 5: 317–371.

Hannan, Michael T., Pólos, László and Carroll, Glenn R. (2007). *Logics of Organization Theory: Audiences, Codes, and Ecologies*. Princeton, NJ: Princeton University Press.

Hannigan, Timothy (2015). Close encounters of the conceptual kind: Disambiguating social structure from text, *Big Data and Society*, July–December: 1–6.

Harmon, Derek, Greene, Sandy and Goodnight, G. Thomas (2015). A model of rhetorical legitimation: The structure of communication and cognition underlying institutional maintenance and change, *Academy of Management Review*, 40(1): 76–95.

Haveman, Heather A. and Rao, Hayagreeva (1997). Structuring a theory of moral sentiments: Institutional and organizational coevolution in the early thrift industry, *American Journal of Sociology,* 102: 1606–1651.

Hirsch, Paul M. (1975). Organizational effectiveness and the institutional environment, *Administrative Science Quarterly,* 20(3): 327–344.

Höllerer, Markus A., Jancsary, Dennis, Meyer, Renate E. and Vettori, Oliver (2013). Imageries of corporate social responsibility, visual recontextualization, and field-level meaning. In *Institutional Logics in Action: Research in the Sociology of Organizations*, Volume 39B. Bingley, UK: Emerald Group. pp. 139–174.

Ioannou, Ioannis and Serafeim, George (2015). The Consequences of Mandatory Corporate Sustainability Reporting: Evidence from Four Countries, *Strategic Management Journal*, 36(7): 1053–1081.

Jackall, Robert (1988). *Moral Mazes: The World of Corporate Managers*. New York: Oxford University Press.

Jay, Jason (2013). Navigating paradox as a mechanism of change and innovation in hybrid organizations, *Academy of Management Journal*, 56: 137–159.

Jockers. Mathew L. and Mimno, David (2013). Significant themes in 19th-century literature, *Poetics*, 41(6): 750–769.

Jones, Candace and Livne-Tarandach, Reut (2008). Designing a frame: rhetorical strategies of architects, *Journal of Organizational Behavior*, 29: 1075–1099.

Joseph, John, Ocasio, William and McDonnell, Mary-Hunter (2014). The structural elaboration of board independence: Executive power, institutional logics, and the adoption of CEO-only board structures in U.S. corporate governance, *Academy of Management Journal*, 57: 1834–1858.

Kaplan, Sarah (2015). Mixing qualitative and quantitative research methods. In K. Elsbach and R. Kramer (eds), *Handbook of Innovative Qualitative Research Methods: Pathways to Cool Ideas and Interesting Papers*. London: Taylor and Francis. pp. 423–433.

Kennedy, Mark T. and Fiss, Peer C. (2013). An ontological turn in categories research: From standards of legitimacy to evidence of actuality, *Journal of Management Studies*, 50: 1138–1154.

Kraatz, Mathew S. and Block, Emily S. (2008). Organizational implications of institutional pluralism. In R. Greenwood, C. Oliver, R. Suddaby and K. Sahlin-Andersson (eds), *The SAGE Handbook of Organizational Institutionalism.* Thousand Oaks, CA: Sage. pp. 243–275.

Kraatz, Mathew S. and Zajac, Edward J. (1996). Exploring the limits of the new institutionalism: The causes and consequences of illegitimate organizational change, *American Sociological Review*, 61: 812–836.

Kuhn, Thomas (1962). *The Structure of Scientific Revolutions.* Chicago, IL: University of Chicago Press.

Lander, Michel W., Heugens, Pursey P. M. A. R. and van Oosterhout, J. (Hans) (2017) Drift or alignment? A configurational analysis of law firms' ability to combine profitability with professionalism, *Journal of Professions and Organization*, doi:10.1093/jpo/jow011

Lawrence, Thomas B., Suddaby, Roy and Leca, Bernard (eds) (2009). *Institutional Work: Actors and Agency.* Cambridge: Cambridge University Press.

Lazonick, William and O'Sullivan, Mary (2000). Maximizing shareholder value: A new ideology for corporate governance, *Economy and Society*, 29: 1.

Lee, M.D.P. and Lounsbury, Michael (2015). Filtering institutional logics: community logic variation and differential responses to the institutional complexity of toxic waste, *Organization Science*, 26: 847–866.

Lizardo, Omar (2014). Omnivorousness as the bridging of cultural holes: A measurement strategy, *Theory and Society*, 43: 395–419.

Loewenstein, J., Ocasio, William and Jones, Candace (2012). Vocabularies and vocabulary structure: A new approach linking categories, practices, and institutions, *Academy of Management Annals*, 6: 41–86.

Lok, Jaco (2010). Institutional logics as identity projects, *Academy of Management Journal*, 53: 1305–1335.

Lounsbury, Michael (2001). Institutional sources of practice variation: Staffing college and university recycling programs, *Administrative Science Quarterly*, 46: 29–56.

Lounsbury, Michael (2002). Institutional transformation and status mobility: The professionalization of the field of finance, *Academy of Management Journal*, 45: 255–266.

Lounsbury, Michael (2007). A tale of two cities: Competing logics and practice variation in the professionalizing of mutual funds, *Academy of Management Journal*, 50: 289–307.

Lounsbury, M. and Boxenbaum, Eva (2013). *Institutional Logics in Action: Research in the Sociology of Organizations*, Volume 39. Bingley, UK: Emerald Group.

Lounsbury, Michael and Crumley, E.T. (2007). New practice creation: An institutional approach to innovation, *Organization Studies*, 28: 993–1012.

Lounsbury, Michael and Glynn, Mary Ann (2001). Cultural entrepreneurship: Stories, legitimacy, and the acquisition of resources, *Strategic Management Journal*, 22(6/7): 545–569.

Marquis, Christopher and Lounsbury, Michael (2007). Vive la resistance: Competing logics and the consolidation of U.S. community banking, *Academy of Management Journal*, 50: 799–820.

McDonnell, Terence E. (2014). Drawing out culture: productive methods to measure cognition and resonance, *Theory and Society*, 43(3–4): 247–274.

McPherson, Chad and Sauder, Michael. (2013). Logics in action: Managing institutional complexity in a drug court, *Administrative Sciences Quarterly*, 58: 165–196.

Merton, Robert K., Brown, L. and Cottrell, L.S. Jr. (1959). *Sociology Today: Problems and Prospects.* New York: Basic Books.

Meyer, John W. and Rowan, Brian (1977). Institutionalized organizations: formal structure as myth and ceremony, *American Journal of Sociology*, 83: 340–363.

Meyer, Renate E. and Höllerer, Markus A. (2010). Meaning structures in a contested issue field: A topographic map of shareholder value in Austria, *Academy of Management Journal*, 53: 1241–1262.

Miller, Danny, Brenton-Miller, Isabelle, and Lester, Richard H. (2013). Family firm governance, strategic conformity, and performance: Institutional vs. strategic perspectives, *Organization Science*, 24(1): 189–209.

Mills, C.W. (1940). Situated action and vocabularies of motive, *American Sociological Review*, 5: 904–913.

Mohr, John W. and Bogdanov, Petko (2013). Introduction – topic models: What they are and why they matter, *Poetics*, 41: 545–569.

Mohr, John W. and Duquenne, Vincent (1997). The duality of culture and practice: Poverty relief in New York City, 1888–1917, *Theory and Society* 26: 305–356.

Mohr, John W. and Ghaziani, Amin (2014). Problems and prospects of measurement in the study of culture, *Theory and Society*, 43: 225–246.

Murray, Fiona (2010). The oncomouse that roared: Hybrid exchange strategies as a source of distinction at the boundary of overlapping institutions, *American Journal of Sociology*, 116 (2): 341–388.

Negro, Giacomo, Hannan, Michael T. and Rao, Hayagreeva (2010). Category reinterpretation and defection: modernism and tradition in Italian winemaking, *Organization Science*, 22: 1449–1463.

Nigam, Amit and Ocasio, William (2010). Event attention, environmental sensemaking, and change in institutional logics: An inductive analysis of the effects of public attention to Clinton's health care reform initiative, *Organization Science*, 21(4): 823–841.

Ocasio, William (1997). Towards an attention-based view of the firm, *Strategic Management Journal*, 18: 187–206.

Ocasio Willam, Loewenstein, Jeffrey and Nigam, Amit (2015). How streams of communication reproduce and change institutional logics: The role of categories, *Academy of Management Review*, 40: 28–48.

Ocasio, William, Mauskapf, Michael and Steele, Christopher W.C. (2016) History, society, and institutions: the role of collective memory in the emergence and evolution of societal logics, *Academy of Management Review*, 41(4): 676–699.

Ocasio, William and Radoynovska, Nevena (2016). Strategy and commitments to institutional logics: Organizational heterogeneity in business models and governance, *Strategic Organization*, 14(4): 207–209.

Oliver, Christine (1991). Strategic responses to institutional processes, *Academy of Management Review*, 16: 145–179.

Pache, Anne and Santos, Felipe (2010). When worlds collide: The internal dynamics of organizational responses to conflicting institutional demands, *Academy of Management Review*, 35(3): 455–476.

Pache, Anne and Santos, Felipe (2013). Inside the hybrid organization: Selective coupling as a response to competing institutional logics, *Academy of Management Journal*, 56: 972–1001.

Pahnke, Emily C., Katila, Riitta and Eisenhardt, Kathleen M. (2015). Who takes you to the dance? How partners' institutional logics influence innovation in young firms, *Administrative Science Quarterly*, 60: 596–633.

Parsons, Talcott (1956). Suggestions for a sociological approach to the theory of organizations-I, *Administrative Science Quarterly*, 1(1): 63–85.

Phillips, Nelson and Hardy, Cynthia (2002). *Discourse Analysis: Investigating Processes of Social Construction*. London: Sage Publications.

Phillips, Nelson, Lawrence, Thomas B. and Hardy, Cynthia (2004). Discourse and institutions, *Academy of Management Review*, 29: 635–652.

Powell, Walter W. and DiMaggio, Paul J. (eds) (1991). *The New Institutionalism in Organizational Analysis*. Chicago, IL: University of Chicago Press.

Purdy, Jill M. and Gray, Barbara (2009). Conflicting logics, mechanisms of diffusion, and multilevel dynamics in emerging institutional fields, *Academy of Management Journal*, 52: 355–380.

Quattrone, Paolo (2015). Governing social orders, unfolding rationality, and Jesuit accounting practices: A procedural approach to institutional logics, *Administrative Science Quarterly*, 60: 411–445.

Ragin, Charles C. (1987). *The Comparative Method: Moving Beyond Qualitative and Quantitative Strategies*. Berkeley, CA: University of California Press.

Ragin, Charles C. (2000). *Fuzzy-Set Social Science*. Chicago, IL: University Chicago Press.

Ragin, Charles C. (2008). *Redesigning Social Inquiry: Fuzzy Sets and Beyond*. Chicago, IL: University of Chicago Press.

Ragin, Charles C. and Fiss, Peer C. (2015). *Intersectional Inequalities: A Fuzzy-Set Analysis of Race, Test Scores, and Poverty*. Chicago: The University of Chicago Press.

Rao, Hayagreeva, Monin, Philippe and Durand, Rodolphe (2003). Institutional change in Toque Ville: Nouvelle cuisine as an identity movement in French gastronomy, *American Journal of Sociology*, 108: 795–843.

Reay, Trish and Hinings, C. Robert (2009). Managing the rivalry of competing institutional logics, *Organization Studies*, 30: 629–652.

Reay, Trish and Jones, Candace (2016). Qualitatively capturing institutional logics, *Strategic Organization*, 14(4): 441–454.

Sauermann, Henry and Stephan, Paula (2013). Conflicting logics? A multidimensional view of industrial and academic science, *Organization Science*, 24, 889–909.

Scarabato, D. & Fischer, E. (2013). Frustrated 'fatshionistas': An institutional theory perspective on consumer quests for greater choice in mainstream markets. *Journal of Consumer Research*, 39(6): 1234–1257.

Scott, W. Richard (2008). *Institutions and Organizations: Ideas and Interests*. Los Angeles: Sage.

Seo, Myeong-Gu and Creed, W.E. Douglas (2002). Institutional contradictions, praxis, and institutional change: A dialectical perspective, *Academy of Management Review*, 27: 222–247.

Shipilov, Andrew V., Greve, Henrich R. and Rowley, Timothy J. (2010). When do interlocks matter? Institutional logics and the diffusion of multiple corporate governance practices, *Academy of Management Journal*, 53: 846–864.

Smelser, Neil, J. and Swedberg, Richard, Eds. (2010). *Handbook of Economic Sociology*. Princeton, NJ: Princeton University Press.

Smets, Michael, Greenwood, Royston and Lounsbury, Michael (2015). An institutional perspective on strategy as practice. In Damon Golsorkhi et al. (eds), *The Cambridge Handbook of Strategy as Practice*, 2nd ed. Cambridge: Cambridge University Press. pp. 283–300.

Smets, Michael., Jarzabkowski, Paula., Spee, A. Paul., and Burke, Gary (2015). Reinsurance trading in

Lloyd's of London: Balancing conflicting-yet-complementary logics in practice. *Academy of Management Journal*, 58: 932–970.

Smets, Michael, Morris, Tim, and Greenwood, Royston (2012). From practice to field: A multilevel model of practice-driven institutional change, *Academy of Management Journal, Academy of Management Journal*, 55: 877–904.

Spicer, Andre and Sewell, Graham (2010). From national service to global player: Transforming the organizational logic of a public broadcaster, *Journal of Management Studies*, 47(6): 913–943.

Strang David and Meyer, John W. (1993). Institutional conditions for diffusion, *Theory and Society*, 22: 487–512.

Suddaby, Roy and Greenwood, Royston (2005). Rhetorical strategies of legitimacy, *Administrative Science Quarterly*, 50: 35–67.

Swedberg, Richard (1990). *Economics and Sociology: Redefining Their Boundaries: Conversations with Economists and Sociologists*. Princeton, NJ: Princeton University.

Swedberg, Richard (2014). *The Art of Social Theory*. Princeton, NJ: Princeton University Press.

Swidler, Ann (1986). Culture in action: Symbols and strategies, *American Sociological Review*, 51: 273–286.

Thompson, James D. (2003 [1967]). *Organizations in Action: Social Science Bases of Administrative Theory*. New Brunswick, NJ: Transaction Publishers.

Thornton, Patricia H. (2001). Personal versus market logics of control: A historically contingent theory of the risk of acquisition, *Organization Science*, 12: 294–311.

Thornton, Patricia H. (2002). The rise of the corporation in a craft industry: Conflict and conformity in institutional logics, *Academy of Management Journal*, 45: 81–101.

Thornton, Patricia H. (2004). *Markets from Culture: Institutional Logics and Organizational Decisions in Higher Education Publishing*. Stanford, CA: Stanford University Press.

Thornton, Patricia H. and Ocasio, William (1999). Institutional logics and the historical contingency of power in organizations: Executive succession in the Higher Education publishing industry, 1958–1990, *American Journal of Sociology*, 105: 801–843.

Thornton, Patricia H. and Ocasio, William (2008). Institutional logics. In R. Greenwood, C. Oliver, R. Suddaby and K. Sahlin-Andersson (eds), *The SAGE Handbook of Organizational Institutionalism*. London: Sage. pp. 99–129.

Thornton, Patricia H., Ocasio, William and Lounsbury, Michael (2012). *The Institutional Logics Perspective: A New Approach to Culture, Structure, and Process*. Oxford: Oxford University Press.

Thornton, Patricia H., Ocasio, William and Lounsbury, Michael (2015). The institutional logics perspective. In Robert Scott and Stephen Kosslyn (eds), *Emerging Trends in the Social and Behavioral Sciences*. New York: Wiley On-line Reference.

Tolbert, Pamela S. and Zucker, Lynn G. (1983). Institutional sources of change in the formal structure of organizations: The diffusion of civil service reform, 1880–1935, *Administrative Science Quarterly*, 28: 22–39.

Tuma, Nancy Brandon and Hannan, Michael (1984). *Social Dynamics: Models and Methods*. Orlando, FL: Academic Press.

Vaerlander, Sara, Hinds, Pamela, Thomason, Bobbi, Pearce, Brandi and Altman, Heather (2016). Enacting a constellation of logics: How transferred practices are recontextualized in a global organization, *Academy of Management Discoveries*. 2(1): 79–107.

Vaisey, Stephen (2009). Motivation and justification: A dual process model of culture in action. *American Journal of Sociology*, 114: 1675–1715.

Vasudeva, Gurneeta, Alexander, Elizabeth A., and Jones, Stephen L. (2014). Institutional logics and interorganizational learning in technological arenas: Evidence from standard-setting organizations in the mobile handset industry, *Organization Science*, 26(3): 830–846.

Weber, Max (1978 [1922]). *Economy and Society: An Outline of Interpretive Sociology* (Guenther Roth and Claus Wittich, Eds). Berkeley, CA: University of California Press.

Wry, Tyler, Cobb, Adam and Aldrich, Howard E. (2013). More than a metaphor: Assessing the historical legacy of resource dependence and its contemporary promise as a theory of environmental complexity, *Academy of Management Annals*, 7: 439–486.

Wry, Tyler, Lounsbury, Michael and Jennings, P. Devereaux (2014). Hybrid vigor: Securing venture capital by spanning categories in nanotechnology. *Academy of Management Journal*, 57: 1309–1333.

Zhao, Eric, Fisher, Greg, Lounsbury, Michael and Miller, Danny (2017). Optimal distinctiveness revisited: Broadening the interface between institutional theory and strategic management. *Strategic Management Journal*. 38(1): 93–113

Zilber, Tammar B. (2013). Institutional logics and institutional work: should they be agreed? In *Institutional Logics in Action: Research in the Sociology of Organizations*, Volume 39. Bingley, UK: Emerald Group. pp. 77–96.

Zucker, Lynne G. (1977). The role of institutionalization in cultural persistence. *American Sociological Review*, 42: 726–743.

20

Institutional Pluralism Revisited[1]

Matthew S. Kraatz and Emily S. Block

In the fall of 2006, we wrote a chapter for the first edition of this Handbook introducing the concept of institutional pluralism and developed a set of arguments about the 'organizational implications' of this phenomenon (Kraatz & Block, 2008). That chapter was an important milestone on our own intellectual journey, and we still view it with some satisfaction and pride for this reason. We are also pleased that it seems to have resonated with many readers and to have played some role in altering the trajectory of contemporary institutional theory and research. The growing literature on institutional complexity (Dunn & Jones, 2010; Greenwood, Raynard, Kodeih, Micelotta, & Lounsbury, 2011; Besharov & Smith, 2014) and hybrid organizations (e.g., Battilana & Dorado, 2010; Pache & Santos, 2010; Battilana & Lee, 2014) has emerged from a confluence of different sources and developed in ways that we could not and did not anticipate. But, our chapter was among the earliest contributions to this stream of work and it appears to be somehow implicated in much of what has come since.

In light of its personal significance and apparent influence, we were very pleased to be given an opportunity to revisit our original chapter and rejoin the conversation about the topics that we first confronted therein. The present chapter represents our effort to do just this. It will proceed as follows. First, we will briefly review our initial work, explaining both its basic substance and its underlying aims (i.e., what we said and why we said it). Second, we will dig below the surface with the intent of identifying some overlooked arguments and themes. While these ideas were not necessarily hidden within our original chapter, they have for whatever reason failed to manifest themselves in the contemporary literature. By bringing them back to the foreground, we hope to enrich and inform the current discourse. Finally, we will identify a few key mistakes and omissions in our earlier work and make an effort to amend these flaws. This last piece, which constitutes a disproportionate share of the present chapter, focuses especially on the role of values. While our original chapter said very little about values, they are a critically important facet of institutional pluralism and institutional reality more generally. When we bring this normative dimension back to the foreground, our understanding of pluralism and its consequences changes in a number of important ways.

We will close our chapter by discussing its possible implications for future theory and research. These implications are somewhat bifurcated and uneven in their felt importance. On the one hand, our chapter develops a number of ideas that could be readily imported into the current literature on complexity and hybrids. We would certainly be pleased if this were to occur, and we offer these ideas partly in that spirit. However, we will also emphasize that our true aims lie elsewhere. For us, pluralism is just one part of a more comprehensive value-centric approach toward institutional analysis. This envisioned approach is not necessarily oppositional to the complexity literature (which is now effectively subsumed within the hugely popular institutional logics perspective). It is also not necessarily better. But, it is substantially different – in terms of its premises, its empirical focus and its ultimate purposes. We will try to explain these differences and their importance. We will also suggest that our value-centric approach is a 'live option' for those who are interested in an alternative. Our chapter does not aim to challenge, critique, or reform the dominant understanding of institutions and their effects. Instead, it merely aims to present an alternative and to create a space for a different sort of work.

INSTITUTIONAL PLURALISM REVISITED

Defining the Construct

We began our original chapter by defining and elucidating its central construct:

Institutional pluralism is the situation faced by an organization that operates within multiple institutional spheres. If institutions are broadly understood as 'the rules of the game' that direct and circumscribe organizational behaviour, then the organization confronting institutional pluralism plays in two or more games at the same time. Such an organization is subject to multiple regulatory regimes, embedded within multiple normative orders, and/or constituted by more than one cultural logic. It is a participant in multiple discourses and/or a member of more than one institutional category. It thus possesses multiple, institutionally derived identities which are conferred upon it by different segments of its pluralistic environment. (Kraatz & Block, 2008: 243)

While this lengthy definition is mainly self-explanatory, it does have a few features that merit special attention. First, it is explicitly organization-centric (defining the phenomenon of pluralism from the perspective of a sentient actor looking out at a heterogeneous environment). Second, it is inclusive (taking pains to avoid favouring and reifying any one dimension of institutional reality). Third, it posits a direct link to organization identity (viewing identities as the things that derive from societal institutions and connect the actor back to them). These features are architectural components of the larger perspective that we developed, and their significance should become more clear as we summarize the perspective itself.

Implications for Legitimacy, Governance and Change

We devoted much of our original chapter to explaining pluralism's implications for our understanding of three important organizational phenomenon – legitimacy, governance and change. We were interested in these phenomena for two reasons. The first was substantive. By 2006, we had spent much time studying these particular phenomena and trying to develop explanations for them. They were things that we cared about as ends in themselves. The second was more distinctly theoretical. These three topics were a central focus within the neo-institutional literature, and this perspective had ascended to dominance largely because it appeared to offer better explanations of them (DiMaggio & Powell, 1991; Dobbin, 1994; Suchman, 1995; Greenwood & Hinings, 1996, 2006; Ruef & Scott, 1998; Thornton & Ocasio, 1999). We believed that pluralism undermined these theoretical understandings. We also believed that it demonstrated the need for a new and different kind of theory.

Our specific arguments about these three phenomena are quite varied and difficult to explain without more contextual background. For this and other reasons, we believe that the present chapter is best read as a companion to the earlier one.[2] Nevertheless, our arguments did all share a common structure, and each proceeded in basically the same way. The first step was simply to stress the basic importance of the phenomenon in question and to acknowledge neo-institutionalism's genuine contributions to our understanding of it. In the case of legitimacy, this meant recognizing the reality of isomorphic pressures and affirming the basic idea that audience approval rests partly on cultural conformity. In the case of governance, it meant acknowledging that organizational purpose and control are often shaped by cultural forces that operate at higher levels of society (e.g., field-level logics). In the case of change, it meant linking organizational-level change processes back to the societal or field level, and acknowledging the causal influence of the latter things. It also meant acknowledging the partially symbolic character of many organization-level changes. In this latter sense, our interest in legitimacy and change converged.

The second step was merely to introduce the 'wrinkle' of institutional pluralism into each of these three familiar and widely accepted accounts. For legitimacy, this meant that the organization seeking societal approval needed to conform to multiple isomorphic pressures (which emanated from different sources and often pushed it in different directions). For governance, it meant that field-level logics could not wholly determine the purpose

and control of the individual organization. This organization was not simply a unit of a more encompassing institutional system. It was, at minimum, a sort of an 'arena' where competing logics came into conflict and vied for control. For change, the implications were very similar. While field-level forces might impel an organization to follow certain courses of action (and reward them for their conformity), these forces did not dictate any particular outcome. Conforming to them was also no guarantee of organizational success. This is because efforts to please one external constituency were apt to displease others.

Organizational Responses to Pluralism

Having elaborated the basic problem of institutional pluralism, we went on to consider how organizations could best adapt to it. These conceptual arguments were introduced within the aforementioned sections on legitimacy, governance and change, and they presented themselves mostly as solutions to these particular problems. Nevertheless, they were also linked back to an integrated and encompassing perspective on the more general relationship. The concept of identity was at the core of this perspective. Accepting the basic idea that societal institutions are often 'constitutive' of organizations, we proposed that institutional pluralism had the effect of imposing multiple identities on the organization and requiring it to be 'multiple things to multiple people'.[3] The problem of adapting to institutional pluralism thus became a problem of managing multiple institutionally ascribed identities.

With this foundation in place, we were then able to identify four archetypal responses to the phenomenon we had identified. In the first, the organization merely shed problematic or unwanted identities (responding to pluralism by eliminating the problem itself). In the second, it engaged in 'loose coupling' and 'compartmentalized' these identities so as to avoid overt conflict. In the third, disparate identities were brought into ongoing, dynamic tension with one another (in the effort to achieve and maintain 'a balance'). In the last, they were more deeply fused and reconciled (while maintaining their essential separateness).

In developing our arguments about this last archetypal response, we were much influenced by the work of Philip Selznick and by pragmatist theories of the social self. These influences — which are themselves deeply intertwined — will be explained more deeply in the next section. In developing this more general framework of organizational responses to pluralism, we also benefited greatly from our conversations with Mike Pratt (who was then our colleague at the University of Illinois). We spent a great deal of time talking with Mike, and his earlier work on multiple identities in organizations deeply and positively affected our own thinking (Pratt & Foreman, 2000). Mike was also the first author of a subsequent paper which further developed the concept of the organizational self (Pratt & Kraatz, 2009). We turn to that concept next.

Organization as Self

Our chapter's most important and ambitious creation was a new theoretical model of the organization and its relationship to society. Specifically, we proposed that the organization could be usefully seen as a 'self' that possesses the same basic characteristics as the social selves featured in pragmatist theory (Mead, 1934; Joas, 1993, 1996; Wiley, 1994; Callero, 2003). Sociological identity theorists have long recognized that people possess identities that are imposed upon them by their societal roles (e.g., parent, husband, teacher, scholar). They have also argued that each individual possesses multiple identities, and concerned themselves with the problems and potentialities that this multiplicity creates. Within this tradition, the self is seen as the place wherein these identities meet

(Stryker, 1980, 2008; Stryker & Burke, 2000; Burke, Owens, Serpe, & Thoits, 2003). It is, at once, a collection of different socially ascribed identities and a higher order entity (with an inner life of its own). This self serves a number of manifest and logically necessary functions (e.g., activating identities, assigning them relative priority, and mediating conflicts between them) (Stets & Burke, 2000; Gecas & Burke, 1995). It also seems to possess a number of more distinctly human potentialities (though these are latent and not discussed in much of the sociological identity literature) (Hitlin, 2003).

Our main theoretical 'move' was simply to transfer this understanding of the individual self to the organizational context. For instance, we explicitly argued that:

> organizational governance can be usefully thought of as a process through which an 'organizational self' selects, prioritizes, and/or integrates its various institutionally-given identities (and also as the process through which these identities conjointly construct an organizational self. (2008: 246)

This reasoning, which also deeply affected our arguments about legitimacy and change, was a bit of a creative leap. But, most of the work had already been done for us. Neo-institutional theorists had previously drawn the link from institutions to identity. Pratt, Whetten and others had dealt with the problem of multiple identities at the organization level (Albert & Whetten, 1985; Pratt & Foreman, 2000). All that was left for us to do was to pick up the theoretical tools in front of us and redeploy them as a means toward slightly different ends. While our interest in institutional pluralism was the impetus for this work, most of the rest of it seemed to follow more or less automatically.

Our development of this concept was made even easier (and more exciting) by the strong influence of Selznick's institutionalism. Selznick had also been deeply influenced by Mead, and he had memorably described the process of institutionalization as one of self formation.[4] In his view, this self was born in conflict, emerging as a response to the 'anxiety laden problems' of organizational life (e.g., struggles over power, purpose, mission and societal role) (Selznick, 1957: 39). He had also described this mysterious process as one that could yield a number of desirable outcomes (e.g., self-understanding, distinctive competence, internal solidarity, and the capacity for self-determination). We were quite excited by these arguments as they seemed to suggest a hopeful resolution to the problems that institutional pluralism can obviously engender. They also seemed to suggest a path toward a deeper theoretical reconciliation – between Selznick's 'old' institutionalism and its neo-institutional successor (DiMaggio & Powell, 1991; Selznick, 1996; Stinchcombe, 1997). More specifically, they seemed to suggest that Selznick's purposive, distinctive, autonomous and self-governing institution could actually emerge in direct response to the very forces that were at the core of the neo-institutional perspective. Put differently, it seemed as though neo-institutional identities could be the very stuff of which Selznickian institutions (selves) were ultimately made. We recognized that this transformative outcome did not inevitably occur (and in fact said very little about the process itself). Still, this connection did seem to bring us full circle and to answer some questions that had nagged us for a long time. While it was not exactly where we thought pluralism would lead us, the discovery seemed remarkably serendipitous.

Aims and Motivations

In addition to leading us in directions we did not expect, our chapter also emerged for reasons that we cannot easily crystallize or convey. It was, most directly, an effort to express ourselves and respond to our own 'anxiety laden problems'. Because these concerns were all bound up together, they are quite difficult to parse or prioritize. Nevertheless, we are able to identify at least

three partially separable motives that figured in to the development of our chapter.

Pluralism as an interesting empirical phenomenon. A large part of our interest in pluralism was conventionally scientific and empirically motivated. Much of our earlier work had examined colleges and universities (Kraatz & Zajac, 1996; Kraatz, 1998; Kraatz & Moore, 2002), and this experience had led us to two ostensibly contradictory realizations. The first was that these organizations were highly institutionalized in virtually all senses of this term (being deeply embedded in society and subject to a great many regulative, normative and cognitive influences emanating therefrom). The second was that these institutional forces did not align with each other or flow from a single, centralized source. Instead, they appeared to come from all quarters of our pluralistic society and to push/pull these organizations in many different directions. This seemed like an interesting and rather neglected problem. It also seemed like one that was not limited to American higher education. This motivation should be evident in our earlier discussion of legitimacy, governance and change. It was also clearly expressed in our chapter:

> Prior empirical research has uncovered numerous instances of organizations facing institutional environments which appear to exert pluralistic demands. However … there has to date been little apparent effort to systematically assess its practical and theoretical implications. What are the characteristic challenges and opportunities faced by organizations that operate in pluralistic environments? How do organizations typically adapt to these challenges and opportunities (structurally, politically, symbolically, rhetorically)? What broader and more general lessons might researchers take away from the methodical and sustained analysis of organizations that dwell in pluralism's midst? These are the broad questions that we set out to address in this chapter. (2008: 243)

Pluralism as an Achilles' heel for neo-institutionalism. A second and rather less innocent motivation was to expose the limitations of the neo-institutional perspective and sow the seeds of theoretical discontent.

In addition to being an interesting and important empirical phenomenon, pluralism also appeared to be a sort of 'Achilles' heel' for this fast-growing and increasingly hegemonic perspective. Neo-institutionalism had steadily advanced by encompassing its theoretical competition and finding progressively more distant and abstract explanations for actions and outcomes that were once thought to be the product of proximate and tangible forces. While this explanatory strategy is remarkably powerful, it stops working when we position the organization within a pluralistic milieu and highlight the tensions and interactions between these disparate forces. These limitations were also explained in our earlier discussion of legitimacy, governance and change.

It is difficult to say how much this competitive and somewhat unseemly motivation affected our original chapter. We would like to believe that it was not the dominant force. But, it certainly cannot be discounted or overlooked altogether. By 2006, we had a track record of criticizing neo-institutionalism and trying to expose its soft spots (Kraatz & Zajac, 1996). Part of our hope was that pluralism would succeed where these prior efforts had failed.

Pluralism as an occasion for a different kind of theory. A final goal was to build (or perhaps rebuild) an organization theory of a different sort. Though we certainly did critique neo-institutionalism, our chapter did not actually propose any reforms or changes to the theory itself. Instead, we merely tried to declare our own independence from the perspective and to make a case for bringing back the sort of organization-centric theories which it had displaced. As part of this case, we emphasized the need to incorporate the many lessons learned from neo-institutionalism. But, our main argument was for a sort of anti-Copernican shift that would restore the individual organization to its former place – at the centre of our theory and research.[5] We saddled this envisioned perspective with the name 'institutional

organizationalism' (a rather unfortunate label that merely reversed the ordering of the words in the Handbook's title). Our hopes for this perspective were well-expressed in the chapter's discussion.

> We think that field-level and societal-level institutions are certainly an appropriate focus for sociological research, and we have learned much from studies examining them ... Nonetheless, we think it is essential to clearly distinguish the neo-institutional research endeavor from the program of research that we inherited and have tried to further in this chapter. Scholars committed to understanding organizations as ends in themselves will never discover answers to the questions that legitimately preoccupy neo-institutionalists. But, we think the obverse is equally true and perhaps much less well-understood. We hope that our chapter provides some evidence of the great potential symbiosis between neo-institutionalism and the 'organization-centric theories of organizations. But, we also hope that it demonstrates the continued need for separation ... (2008: 265)

SOME IDEAS AND THEMES WORTH RECOVERING

As we went back through our original chapter and held it up against the contemporary literature, we saw a great many points of agreement and convergence. While we claim no responsibility for any of the changes that have unfolded over the last decade, we cannot help but feel some sense of satisfaction from this state of affairs. Today's institutional theory is very different from the one that we critiqued back then. Some of the most important changes seem to have occurred around the 'soft spots' that we tried to expose and irritate through our introduction of pluralism. At the same time, we were also struck by a number of disconnects and made aware of some things that our chapter might still add to this contemporary literature. These ideas are offered in a spirit of humility and goodwill, and with a recognition that they may not appeal to everyone.

Pluralism

In the contemporary literature, the concepts of pluralism and complexity are sometimes used interchangeably. More often, people just use the latter term. We have largely given up on trying to explain or maintain the difference. Nevertheless, the word pluralism is a very meaningful one and we chose it for a reason. In using this word, we were not just naming an empirical phenomenon. We were also: (a) advocating a particular way of looking at this phenomenon and (b) attempting to establish a connection to pluralist traditions that have long existed in other areas (e.g., philosophy, religion, politics etc.). The integral connection between pluralism and pragmatism was especially salient and important from our perspective (James, 1909; Bernstein, 1987; Selznick, 1992). Whatever one may think of that particular philosophy, the larger point is simply that pluralism is an 'ism'. While this may be seen as a liability, it also has a number of critical strengths. Chief among these is that this distinctive way of thinking does not require one to assume conflict or incommensurability. Thus, to say that institutions are plural is not to propose that they are oppositional. We underscored this point in our chapter's conclusion:

> Institutional pluralism is itself a metaphor. It is not an innocent one. We have willfully used it to name an apparent reality which could be (and has been) described much differently (e.g. as fragmentation or the postmodern condition). We find the pluralism metaphor compelling because it suggests the possibility of symbiosis and latent cooperation among distinct identity groups, even in organizations where conflict and dissensus are very real and perhaps much more clearly evident. It is also appealing because it suggests the possibility of an emergent organizational whole that is capable of accommodating, encompassing, and governing its various distinct parts. (2008: 266)

In surfacing this issue, we do not aim to critique the institutional complexity formulation or to assert the superiority of our own concept. Instead, we merely wish to stress its distinctiveness and its independent merits.

If some students of institutional multiplicity were to approach the phenomenon from a pluralist perspective, it would likely lead them to ask different questions and (thus) produce a rather different sort of research. Our own sense is that this would enrich the literature.

Inclusive View of Institutional Reality

Our chapter was also distinctive in its catholic approach toward conceiving the institutional world. In our omnibus definition (see above), pluralism contains all of the different 'institutional stuff' that comes to bear on organizations and enters into the consciousness of their leaders. In the contemporary literature, the focus is more typically on tensions between discrete logics (Pache & Santos, 2010; Greenwood et al., 2011; Besharov & Smith, 2014). While these logics are themselves inclusive (containing multiple elements), they are generally viewed as self-contained and internally consistent. They are also usually seen to be in direct conflict with other logics that possess similar properties. In most empirical research, only two such logics are at work.

We see no necessary problem with this approach. The literature on institutional complexity is a subsidiary of the institutional logics perspective, and this approach to the study of institutional multiplicity clearly serves the interests of advancing that powerful and encompassing theory. This said, we do question whether this is the only or best way to approach the more general phenomenon of multiplicity. Institutional reality is, in at least some instances, more like the 'blooming and buzzing confusion' that William James (the original pluralist) first described (James, 1890; 1909). Those who are interested in understanding the subjective experience of this reality might do well to focus on this raw and unmediated experience (rather than processing and packaging it into discrete institutional logics). This pragmatic approach might also help to produce knowledge that is more directly relevant to the concerns of institutional inhabitants. While we certainly do not deny the existence or importance of institutional logics, they do not appear to be especially salient to most people outside of our own theoretical discourse. Reparsing the institutional world and focusing renewed attention on its constituent elements might help us to re-engage with these constituencies.

Legitimacy, Governance and Change

Though our chapter found important problems with the neo-institutional literature on legitimacy, governance and change, we also affirmed the crucial importance of these phenomena and tried to develop revised explanations of them (ones that incorporated institutional insights and adapted them to a pluralistic world). As we survey the current literature, we see relatively little attention to these particular arguments – or to these phenomena themselves. Current research on complexity and hybrids does, of course, deal with issues of legitimacy, governance and change. But, the overall focus of institutional research has clearly shifted away from these real and substantive phenomena and toward a set of more abstract and synthetic questions (ones that flow from the internal logic of the theory itself). Scholars who are interested in doing empirical research on organizational legitimacy, governance and change might still find some value and inspiration in our chapter. We put much effort into developing these arguments, and many of them could easily be applied and/or extended.

The Organizational Self

In our frank and inescapably subjective opinion, our arguments about the nature, origins and functions of the organizational self are the very best part of our original chapter. It is possible that we gave insufficient attention to this concept and failed to convey its felt importance and significance within the larger scheme of our work. It is also possible that these arguments have already been thoroughly examined and found to be wanting (for whatever reason). Either way, they were truly the core of our chapter and the glue that held the rest of it together. Ten years later, we still see organizations as 'coalitions of identities' that hang together more or less effectively. We still see strong and compelling parallels between the individual self and the organizational one. We also continue to believe that this metaphor is worthy of further examination and development. In light of this abiding enthusiasm, we are particularly disappointed that the concept has not caught on and found more traction in the literature. We are hopeful that the revised model of the organizational self that we will put forward in the pages below will help to change this.

Selznick and Pragmatism

Our chapter was, among other things, an effort to more fully reconcile the new and old institutionalisms. It was also an effort to bring back pragmatism (the philosophy at the heart of both Selznick's institutionalism and sociological identity theory). For us, the connections between these different elements of our chapter were compelling and largely self-evident. Pluralism led us to identity theory, and this led us back to Selznick (with a deeper understanding of what he had actually said). The fact that these outwardly disparate elements (pluralism, pragmatism, identity, self, institutionalism) could all be traced back to the same original sources (the geniuses of William James and George Herbert Mead) seemed to prove that we were on the right track. The connections between these various 'parts' were not just ones that we had made up and cobbled together. They were real ones which we had somehow unearthed and rediscovered.

Looking back, we can see that we may have been overly optimistic about the self-evident nature of these connections. We also see that we could have done much more to articulate these connections and hammer them home (in our original chapter and in the years since). Still, we are rather surprised that the study of institutional multiplicity has proven to be so easily (and perhaps completely) separable from the intellectual influences that essentially defined our own understanding of the phenomenon. While this has been a bitter pill to swallow, there is no reason it could not change. To the extent that others are also interested in redeveloping these connections, they are still there waiting to be found. Our original chapter's discussion section contained a long discussion of pragmatism and its influence on our thought. The following passage provides a good taste of the larger argument:

> Pragmatism highlights the continuities between thought and action, and between academic and practical knowledge. It also emphasizes that the practical consequences of academic ideas can be momentous. Taking pragmatism seriously thus has the effect of putting scholars and organizational participants on the same side of the fence (as fellow humans trying to understand and live in an ambiguous and unfolding world). We believe that this both ennobles and humbles the theoretical enterprise. The ennoblement comes from the recognition that theories can and do matter. Organizational scholars have the opportunity to participate in the ongoing construction of reality by creating metaphors that escape the academia and 'become true' as people use them to make sense of themselves and their ambiguous organizational worlds. The humility has the same essential source. Bad metaphors can have frightening consequences for people and institutions ... (2008: 265)

MISTAKES AND OMISSIONS

We have spent a great deal of time reflecting on our chapter, thinking about the errors that we may have made, and speculating on their possible consequences. The list which this reflection has produced is very long, and we are confident that we are doing our readers a favour by keeping it mostly to ourselves. We would, however, like to highlight three notable mistakes. While we do not know what would have happened if these had been avoided, we are pretty sure that they have played some role in getting us to the present point.

Failure to Articulate a Positive Vision for Institutional Theory

Our chapter seems to have diagnosed a key weakness in neo-institutionalism and helped to foment a subsequent series of innovations and reforms. However, it did not map out a new or different course that institutional theorists could follow. This was by design. We saw pluralism mostly as a problem *with* institutional theory, rather than a problem *for* it. Our expressed concern was with developing something called 'institutional organizationalism'. Whatever the possible merits of that idea, it had at least two critical flaws. The first was that it relied on a nostalgia for a theoretical past that no one else seemed to miss very much. The second is that it made no effort to capture the remarkable energy that institutional theory had by then amassed (a force that has only continued to grow in the years since). The institutional complexity approach suffered from neither of these liabilities. Its founders effectively endogenized the phenomenon that we had tried to describe from our sceptical, 'outside' position. In so doing, they set a clear agenda and told institutional theorists what they could (and should) do next. While this agenda excluded many items on our own wish list, it has clearly moved the field forward. In this sense, it represents a clear achievement.

Lack of Follow Through

Our second major error was not in the chapter itself. Over the years since it was published, we have had many opportunities to rejoin the conversation that we helped to start. We have also had plenty of chances to 'stand up' for our own point of view (by clarifying, restating, extending, and/or differentiating it). It is very difficult to say why we have not done this. Perhaps it was because we (initially) considered complexity to be 'close enough' to pluralism, and did not wish to engage in a petty conflict over a mere label. Perhaps it was because we were flattered by the steady flow of citations and pleased to find ourselves on the inside of a fast-growing intellectual movement (even though it was not really ours). Perhaps it was because we were honestly unsure how to re-enter this conversation and what exactly it was that we needed to say. Regardless of the cause, the basic point is the same. Our chapter was merely an initial statement in a vital theoretical conversation that continues to this day. Unfortunately, it was our only substantive contribution to this dialogue. We bear all responsibility for this silence.

Inattention to Values

Our final and most important oversight was that we said virtually nothing about values in our original chapter. This was regrettable for at least three reasons. The first is that values are widely accepted to be an important facet of institutional life. Though we conceptualized pluralism in an inclusive fashion, we said nothing explicit about the 'normative pillar' of institutional thought (Scott, 2014). The second is that values are an integral part of pluralism (broadly conceived). There are, of course, a variety of different pluralisms, and they are not all equally concerned with moral issues (Bernstein, 1987; Eisenberg, 1995; Crowder, 2004; Lassman, 2011). But, when people say 'pluralism', 'value pluralism' is often what they have in mind (Kekes, 1996; Gill & Nichols, 2008; Graham et al., 2013). Finally, it was also a mistake because our understanding of institutional pluralism's 'organizational implications' is misshapen and impoverished when we conceptualize the phenomenon in a way that excludes or marginalizes this important dimension.

We have also spent much time pondering this error and wondering how we could have missed something that now seems so obvious. Part of the answer may be that we believed values were implicit in our argument (and did not require separate treatment). Part of it may be that we viewed value-based reasoning as a losing approach (in comparison with arguments relying on cognition, symbolism and power etc.). It may also be that we were simply uncomfortable with this dimension of institutional life and not yet ready to incorporate it into our theorizing. Whatever the reason, it was a consequential error. It is particularly bothersome given our strong affinity for Selznick's value-focused institutionalism and our expressed concern with reconciling this theory with the contemporary one. While we still feel that we achieved a reconciliation of sorts, we can now see that it was badly one-sided. A pluralism without values is one that Selznick would have been unlikely to accept (or even recognize). The same can be said for institutional theory more generally. While it took us a long time to see this for ourselves, it has now sunk in quite deeply.

INSTITUTIONS, VALUES AND PLURALISM

The preceding section explains the basic reasons why values should be included in our understanding of pluralism. Our main objective in the space remaining is to elaborate this case and to explain how it can be done. We will also spend some time discussing the potential consequences of this theoretical move and considering its implications for future research. Before we proceed through these steps, we first need to say a bit about values themselves.

About Values

Values are an exceptionally complex social phenomena, and many problems and misunderstandings can emerge when they are defined in an overly sharp and simplistic way. As such, we are with Selznick and other pragmatists in our general preference for relatively loose and inclusive concepts (which can sustain conversation and connect different strands of empirical inquiry). Despite this general preference, we nevertheless recognize the need to explain our basic understanding of this central concept. The following subsections serve this basic function.

Values as part of the institutional fabric

The easiest and most natural place to begin our discussion is within the existing institutional literature. The institutional world is widely recognized to contain normative elements as well as cultural-cognitive and regulative ones. This understanding is well reflected in Scott's universally known 'Three Pillars' framework. It is also much apparent in other influential formulations (e.g., Suchman's (1995) tripartite model of legitimacy and DiMaggio and Powell's (1983) discussion of coercive, mimetic and normative isomorphism). These morally informed (and implicitly pluralistic) conceptualizations of institutional reality have clearly been challenged by more recent formulations. The institutional logics perspective (Thornton et al., 2012), for instance, appears to assign a preeminent role to cognition and to subsume other elements within the cultural–cognitive realm. But, even logics theorists agree that values are a part of their master construct, and some within this camp have recently taken a renewed interest in them (Friedland, 2013; Hinings & Greenwood,

2015). Thus, our case for reinfusing values is partly just an effort to refocus something that has been there all along.

Values as personal beliefs

While values clearly exist 'out there' in society, this is not their only location or (arguably) their true home. They are also, and perhaps more importantly, personal beliefs that reside in the heads and hearts of individual human beings. These beliefs focus on conceptions of the good – ideals about what is worth having, doing and being. They define purpose and 'ends'. As such, they also have strong links to action. This understanding of values is much apparent in the large (and recently resurgent) literature on the sociology of values (Rokeach, 1979; Hechter, 1993; Hitlin & Piliavin, 2004; Hitlin & Vaisey, 2013). This work is deeply attentive to the collective dimension of values (as would be expected in any form of sociology). But, it has generally studied the values of individual persons (and conceived these persons as social selves in the Meadian sense we have already described). An additional, and critically important, feature of this work is that it highlights values' 'trans-situational' and 'non-coerced' qualities (Schwartz, 1994; Joas, 2000; Hitlin, 2003). Sociological theory and research has shown that personal values are relatively stable and capable of influencing behaviour across a range of different contexts. It also suggests that these values are generally experienced as things that are unforced and arise from within. For this reason, values have been closely connected to processes of moral agency and self-formation. Values enable internally directed action and personal autonomy. To know one's values is, in some sense, to know oneself. In the absence of such knowledge, people are unlikely to flourish and realize their potentialities.

Values as the core of organizational institutions

Lastly, it is also important to discuss the values of specific organizations (in addition to those of individual persons and society at large). These values were, of course, the main focus of Selznick's organization-centric institutionalism, and we shall rely mainly on his insights in discussing their nature, origins and functions (Selznick, 1957, 1992, 1996, 2000). Selznick's theory of the organizational institution said a great many different things about values, and we will dig more deeply into it later on. At this point, three basic points should suffice. The first is that organizational-institutions do indeed possess values that are distinctly their own. While these values are of course affected by the values of their members on the one hand and the broader society on the other, they are not reducible to either. The second critical point concerns the historically accreted and particularistic nature of these values. Selznick saw institutionalization (aka value infusion) as a diachronic and development process that occurred in the life course of a specific organization. This process does create a sort of reconciliation between the organization and society, but the society in question is a unique, local and directly experienced one. In order to see this process (and the values it produces), we need to look at organizations up close and over time. We also need to recognize the existence and importance of these local and meaning-laden histories even when they are not directly observed in our research. When organizations are viewed only as units of larger institutional systems, their values are apt to disappear from view. Conceptualizing them as hybrid entities that simultaneously inhabit multiple systems does not fix this problem. The final point concerns the many and varied functions of these distinctly organizational values. In Selznick's view, values matter in many different ways. These include: (a) providing direction, meaning and purpose, (b) creating social solidarity, (c) legitimating the power of organizational elites, (d) defining the organization's place in society and (e) serving as the foundations of distinctive competence.[6]

Anticipating questions about values

We recognize that the foregoing discussion will not answer all of our readers' questions, and we have explained that it is still a work in progress. This said, we would like to highlight a few of its positive features and anticipate some possible questions and concerns.

To begin, it is important to re-emphasize that we are not proposing a radical rethinking of the institutional world or the organization's relationship thereto. Values are only one part of the institutional fabric and this dimension is already a part of most institutional theory. While we clearly think values matter, they are obviously not the only thing that matters. Indeed, part of what motivates our interest in this moral dimension is the fact that it is often so weak, distant and ineffectual. It is not just tensions between values that we are concerned with. It is also the tension between values and other parts of the institutional world.

It also seems quite important to note that we are not proposing a 'consensus' theory of the organization – or of society more generally. Values are, without question, socially integrative in their effects. They bind people together into moral communities large and small. They also play some role in binding organizations back to the larger society. In so much as society itself coheres, values would seem to have something to do with it (as the basic things upon which we all can more or less agree). None of this questions the reality of conflict, domination, fragmentation, rationalization, or other unpleasant facts of contemporary social life. It also does not negate the existence of conflicts *over* values. As pluralists, we are keenly attuned to these latter tensions. Organizational institutions can be accurately described as moral orders, and we are much interested in repopularizing and further developing this conceptualization. We do not propose that they are just moral orders. Nor do we propose that these moral orders are always (or even usually) harmonious.

Finally, we also feel compelled to confront the spectre of exploitation and manipulation and to frankly acknowledge the 'dark side' of values-based organizing. Many managers and practitioners seem to be interested in values for reasons that are something less than humanistic. Moreover, it is all too easy to produce examples of organizations and leaders who have done evil in the name of values in which they appeared to have sincerely believed. We think that this chequered history may have played some role in pushing values to the back of our collective theoretical consciousness. We also recognize the dangers and risks involved in bringing them back. We think these risks are both manageable and worth taking. Expunging values from our theoretical discourse has done nothing to change their power and ubiquity within the world of affairs. It has only made our discourse more arid, more obscure and more irrelevant to that world. Organizational theories that focalize values and generate knowledge about their nature and functions could, of course, be abused. This is a responsibility we must accept and a risk that we need to guard against. Fortunately, it may be partially self-correcting. Values-based theorizing is also a powerful resource for criticism and reconstruction. We shall have much more to say about this function in the conclusion to our chapter.

How Values Affect our Conception of Institutional Pluralism

We still view institutional pluralism as the 'situation faced by an organization that operates within multiple institutional spheres'. While values are an important and previously neglected part of this experienced reality, they are only one part of it. In some cases, they are a weak part. In others, they are more salient. The arguments that follow focus especially on these latter instances. Much of the discussion will be focused on value pluralism (situations wherein multiple values are at stake). Some of it will also focus on tensions between values and other dimensions of the institutional world. We see these twin concerns as interdependent and equally important.

The organization's relationship to society

When we recognize that values are a part of the institutional fabric, it changes our understanding of the organization's relationship to society in a number of ways. To begin, it draws our attention to the normative character of audience evaluations. External evaluators bring values to bear in judging organizations (Suchman, 1995; Love & Kraatz, 2009; Mishina, Block, & Mannor, 2012). Organizations are also required to make normative commitments and claims (i.e., to say what they value and what they contribute to society). These value claims become organization-specific standards against which their subsequent actions are judged. Value sceptics may, of course, question the sincerity and substantive importance of these claims. While some appear deeply meaningful and real, others are harder to take seriously. Still, this basic argument does at least help us understand their ubiquity and felt importance. If there was no moral dimension to institutional reality, it seems quite unlikely that organizations and their leaders would spend so much time constructing value statements and fiddling with their content. The same argument helps us understand variations in the evaluative process. When organizations make strong value claims, it changes the way in which they are judged (inviting moral praise and blame). For some organizations, these claims appear to be the primary basis of evaluation. They set themselves apart by declaring values and striving to 'embody' them in their actions.

A second and closely related implication concerns the moral content of the various identities that society ascribes to the organization. When we focalize the moral dimension of institutional life, we see that these identities are not only categorical memberships or group attachments. They do not just require the organization to engage in symbolic conformity and adopt culturally appropriate structures and practices. They also compel it to declare commitments to normative ideals – and to deliver upon their substantive commitments to these declared ends. Thus, when an organization admits a new member into its 'coalition of identities', it is also admitting new values, new ideals and new objectives. These changes can be hugely consequential – affecting the purpose and 'character' of the organization as a whole (Selznick, 1957; King, 2015; Kraatz & Flores, 2015).

A third and final change regards our conception of society itself. When we see values, we also see people. They are the ones applying moral standards in their legitimacy judgements. They are also the ones who are articulating ideals, making value claims, and pursuing particular aims and aspirations inside the organization. In Stinchcombe's (1997) memorable phrase, they are the 'guts of institutions'.[7] When we tune out the moral dimension of institutional reality, these fellow humans are apt to disappear from view altogether.

Relations between institutional identity groups

Values also change our understanding of the relationships between identity groups inside the organization. These changes are complex and may be either positive or negative in nature. We shall discuss both possibilities further in the following sections (which revise our original arguments about adaptations to pluralism and the nature of the organizational self). For now, we just need to highlight that values permeate these relationships and are an inescapable part of them. Identity groups do, of course, fight over power, resources and status. They also fight because their cognitive models, logics and taken for granted assumptions fail to align. But, these material and cognitive factors are only part of a bigger, holistic picture. As values come into focus, this picture changes quite remarkably.

The subjective experience of pluralism

Finally, values also change our understanding of the subjective experience of pluralism. When we focus on the regulative dimension of the institutional world, pluralism appears as confusion over which rules to follow and which authorities to obey. When we focus on the cognitive dimension, it appears as ambiguity over which roles to play and which logics to enact. When people confront value pluralism, they are apt to face questions about their commitments, responsibilities, duties and moral identities. They may also face much deeper existential questions (about the nature and existence of true morality and the very possibility of being a good person). These latter questions are, quite fortunately, unlikely to be triggered by most instances of mundane value pluralism. They are also far beyond the scope of this present chapter. We mention them only to highlight the distinctive quality of this experience and the kinds of issues it can present. Unless we make a deliberate effort to bring values to the forefront of our thinking, this sort of moral experience is likely to remain hidden and unexamined. People have a well-documented tendency to rationalize their choices and to 'tune out' the moral dimension of social life (Bandura, 1999; Tenbrunsel & Messick, 2004). We believe that this occurs within our own theoretical world as well as the empirical world that our theories attempt to describe and explain. Selznick described his value-focused institutionalism as a 'voice of resistance' to this troubling but persistent propensity. This chapter is written in that same spirit.

Responses to Value Pluralism

Our original chapter was centrally concerned with understanding organizational responses to pluralism, and especially focused on identifying adaptations of a positive and socially integrative variety. At first glance, values would seem to create a significant barrier to this search. Morality is (by many accounts) an emotional, primal and deeply irrational phenomenon (Haidt, 2012; Greene, 2013). Conflicts with an overtly moral component are often the most bitter and intractable ones. For this and other reasons, there seems to be a discernible bias towards institutional designs that adapt to pluralism by creating and maintaining barriers. The theory, it seems, is that 'good fences make for good neighbors'. There also appears to be a parallel tendency to suppress the normative dimension in managing intergroup conflicts (e.g., by focusing on interests and material objectives and 'keeping morality out of it'). This general orientation is understandable and in some ways functional. If nothing else, it probably helps organizations hang together and ensures a basic level of civility. But, it also has at least three critical flaws. The first is that it does not make the underlying tensions go away. Values remain latent in the experiences of the people involved in these situations, and they continue to affect their actions and perceptions of those on the other side (of a particular conflict or an organizational chart). The second is that it seems to drain the meaning out of organizational life and to create a 'lowest common denominator' mentality. Imagine, as an extreme example, two groups who are divided over their respective commitments to beauty and truth, and thus decide to found their organization upon a shared interest in money. The final, and related, problem is that this approach forgoes all opportunities for the realization of synergies and deeper forms of cooperation. Dialogue is no sure route to transcending differences and finding common ground. But, silence ensures that there will be no forward movement along this path.

Realizing the Promise of Pluralism

The problems that we have just described are real and perennial. They do not just exist because people are thinking about their identities and relationships in the wrong way (Bernstein, 1987; Joas, 2004). They are also not going to magically disappear as a result of a new theoretical formulation. Nevertheless, we do believe that theory is some significant part of the larger problem. We also believe that it has an ameliorative potential. These beliefs are key parts of our pragmatist philosophy.

In order to begin to realize this potential, two small but significant steps are required. The first step involves a deeper affirmation of the values that we have been discussing. This means that we need to see them not only in a social scientific sense (as elements of an institutional order that find purchase in the minds of individual persons and organizations). Instead, we also need to see them in a deeper, normative sense (as things that are valuable in some genuine sense and thus worthy of their name). The second step involves recognizing the plurality of these genuine human goods. This means acknowledging their particularity and contingency. While the values we are now discussing are real and genuine, they are not unitary or mutually exclusive. Both these moves are difficult. Neither can be made without internal struggle and self-reflection. But, they are both defensible, reasonable and entirely possible. They are also mutually supportive. Embracing a normative perspective is an uncomfortable and seemingly transgressive leap for many social scientists (ourselves included). But, it is apt to be made easier when we recognize the plurality and fundamentally human character of the values we are studying. Selznick provides a very apt and revealing account of the sensibility that we are struggling here to describe:

> The alternative to radical relativism on the one hand and absolutism on the other is a pluralist view of truth and morality. The lesson of diversity is not that anything goes or that variation has no limits. 'Plurality' refers to an indefinite number greater than one, but it is not a synonym for 'infinity' or 'boundlessness.' In the context of moral

ordering, pluralism rejects the idea of one right answer but leaves open the question of how many are valid or justified. (Selznick, 1992: 111)

Isaiah Berlin's value pluralism was quite distinct from Selznick's, and it emerged from very different sources. But it also conveys the same affirmative, hopeful and deeply human message:

I am not a relativist; I do not say 'I like my coffee with milk and you like it without; I am in favor of kindness and you prefer concentration camps'— each of us with his own values, which cannot be overcome or integrated. This I believe to be false. But I do believe that there is a plurality of values which men can and do seek, and that these values differ. There is not an infinity of them: the number of human values, of values that I can pursue while maintaining my human semblance, my human character, is finite – let us say 74, or perhaps 122, or 26, but finite, whatever it may be. And the difference it makes is that if a man pursues one of these values, I, who do not, am able to understand why he pursues it or what it would be like, in his circumstances, for me to be induced to pursue it. Hence the possibility of human understanding. (Berlin, 2001: 12)

Our original chapter was deeply affected by the spirit and sensibility which is evident in these two passages. We really thought that we had adequately conveyed it at the time. Looking back, we can see that we failed in this regard. Without an explicit discussion of values, pluralism is ultimately indistinguishable from relativism. While it might still be called pluralism, it is apt to become pluralism of the 'wild' or 'degenerate' variety that Bernstein (1987) has aptly described. When we embrace a normative view of values, this troubling condition is alleviated. People may still be deeply divided by the particular values that they pursue, but they are at least united in the sense that they are people (moral agents who can choose genuine values, experience meaning and community, and live their lives in pursuit of worthy ends). They are also united in the sense that they can communicate values and understand the values of other people with whom they disagree. Indeed, they can even respect and

deeply admire these strange and otherwise uninterpretable creatures: 'Hence the possibility of human understanding.'

This understanding of values and human beings is at the very core of Selznick's institutionalism. It also thoroughly infuses everything that he wrote for over four decades thereafter (in legal sociology and pragmatist social theory). His organizational-institution was a pluralistic moral order that provided its inhabitants with all of the opportunities just discussed. His vision of the good society (as a 'Moral Commonwealth') was basically just a larger and messier version of the same thing (Selznick, 1992, 2002). He saw this larger entity as a 'community of communities', and he recognized that it must provide its myriad inhabitants with the all important opportunity for 'self-affirming participation in a moral order' (Selznick, 1992: 218). He also recognized this social whole would have to be a patchwork of many different moral orders and realized that it could only be realized through a 'union of solidarity and respect' (Selznick, 2008: 52). This required, among many other things, a proper mix of 'civility and piety' (Selznick, 1992: 387). As we look out at the contemporary world, we do not see any surplus of people who appear to possess this curious combination of virtues. But, we know that there are many and we are encouraged by this fact. We are also resolved to increase their numbers. Bringing values back into our understanding of institutional pluralism may not make much difference in the big picture, but it does seem like at least a small step in the right direction.

Building a Better Self

If there is an immediate and tangible payoff to be gained from embracing the perspective that we have just tried to describe, it is most evident in our understanding of the organizational self (the central construct in our original model). When we allow values into our understanding of this theoretical entity, it obtains a number of desirable qualities that were not obviously present in our initial formulation. These include the following.

Inherent capacity for agency and change

The value-infused identities that make up the organizational self are a source of energy and dynamism. Whereas categorical or group based-identities mostly appear as constraints, value-based identities create aspirations and push the organization forward through time. Because the values at the core of these identities are necessarily abstract and ideal, they do not impose hard limitations on adaptive change and innovation. Because they belong to the organization itself, they can be reinterpreted, updated and amended. They can also be changed (within limits imposed by the history and evolving character of the institution itself). The self we described in our original paper was an objective one (the organization level analogue of Mead's 'me'). The value-infused self that we describe here is a subject and a moral actor (a 'we' that corresponds to Mead's 'I').

Organic solidarity

Value-based identities can also be brought together and connected in ways that are not possible in other theoretical constructions. The reasons for this are mostly evident in the prior section on realizing pluralism's potential. While group-based values create inevitable divisions within the organization, people have the remarkable ability to communicate their values and to understand and respect values that are not their own. They also have the opportunity to develop shared values which transcend (but do not eliminate) group divisions. The net effect of these potentialities is to create the theoretical possibility of organizational integrity (in the sense of 'wholeness' rather than mere consistency). When we see the organization in this way, it really is a living, human entity.

Capacity for moral choice and responsibility

The self at the centre of our model also possesses a capacity for moral choice and responsible action. This capacity stems partly from the tensions between values. As it confronts and responds to these 'right vs. right' dilemmas, the organizational self makes moral decisions (and so defines its moral character) (Dewey, 1932; Selznick, 1957; Badaracco, 1997). Its responsibility also stems from the deeper tension between the moral dimension of institutional reality and its value-free counterparts. When these different dimensions are both present in consciousness, organizations have a capacity to make morally informed judgements. They also have the ability to neglect and wilfully disregard these concerns. In either case, attributions of responsibility are entirely appropriate. While it is a categorical error to ascribe responsibility to a socially controlled object, the entity we are describing does not fall into this category.

Distinctiveness

Organizations are situated in modern society, and this society contains many forces that push them towards homogeneity, rationalization and commodification. These forces, which were the central focus of neo-institutionalism's first wave, are real and cannot be ignored. The good news is that they are countered by other forces that continue to persist and operate within the normative realm (Kraatz & Flores, 2015). Because values emerge within a unique and directly experienced life-world, they are necessarily unique, particularistic and self-possessed. They make each organization distinctive, and separate it from others that are (outwardly) of the same basic type. Following these values is, of course, no guarantee of organizational success. Value claims may not be accepted, and they are also likely to create conflicts and misunderstandings in many instances. Nevertheless, values are a critical (and perennial) source of distinctiveness, and a key resource for those who are interested in maintaining it. While this idea does not appear to be well understood within our theoretical discourse, many managers and practitioners appear to understand it quite well.

Purpose and direction

Finally, the organizational self that we have described here also has a purpose. This purpose comes partly from its unique historical trajectory, partly from its morally infused identities and partly from its avowed commitments and its accepted roles within society. In the idealized vision we have presented, these seemingly disparate elements all converge. In this convergence, the self is reconciled with its surroundings. We began our original chapter with a hopeful and evocative quote from Mead:

> Hence, social control, so far from tending to crush out the human individual or to obliterate his self-conscious individuality, is, on the contrary, actually constitutive of and inextricably associated with that individuality; for the individual is what he is, as a conscious and individual personality, just in so far as he is a member of society... (Mead, 1934: 255)

Having reinfused values into our own understanding of 'Mind, Self and Society', we have a much deeper sense of what this actually means.

Fragility

While there is much more to be said about the organizational self, most of it will have to wait for another paper. There are two things that need to be said now. The first is that this is just a theory. It builds on ideas that have a very distinguished pedigree, and it attempts to respond to a problem that is not merely academic. Still, it is mainly an analytical abstraction and not a mirror of nature. The second point is that this abstraction relies wholly on the assumption of 'goodwill' (in Kant's language) and 'fellowship' (in Selznick's). If we assume the worst about people and their motives, it immediately

dissolves. While cynicism and misanthropism are surely the strongest solvents, they are not really required. Value-free scientism and vulgar utilitarianism serve the same essential function. Selznick was well aware of this potentiality, and he expressed it in many different ways. We find the closing paragraph of his study of the TVA to be particularly meaningful. Having provided a deeply cutting analysis which exposed the anti-democratic reality of this putatively 'grassroots' organization, he left his readers with the following sentiment:

> For the things which are important in the analysis of democracy are those that bind the hands of good men. We then learn that something more than virtue is necessary in the realm of circumstance and power. (Selznick, 1949:266)

We do not know exactly what Selznick meant by 'more than virtue'. But it has always seemed quite relevant to the pluralist sensibility we are trying here to convey.

DISCUSSION AND FUTURE DIRECTIONS

The arguments that we have put forward here are in some sense incremental with respect to our original chapter. Our main focus has been on resurfacing some neglected elements of our original model and correcting one particularly notable flaw (the exclusion of values). In doing this, we have relied mainly on familiar concepts and resources that have long been present in the institutional tradition. Values have been there all along. We have simply tried to bring them back to the foreground and to rearrange their relationship with other elements of the institutional world. Despite this deliberate incrementalism, the collective effect of our small changes may appear rather large. Our chapter also seems likely to provoke many questions about future implications and directions.

We have two short answers to these questions. The first is that we do not really know. The second is that we would very much like to talk about it. At this point, our goals are quite modest. We would mainly just like to open up a space (large or small) for institutional research that addresses some of the questions we have put on the table and which embodies the pluralist sensibility that we have tried to convey. We would also like to rejoin the broader institutional conversation and perhaps spread a few of these ideas more broadly. The following suggestions are offered in this collegial spirit.

Organizational Responses to Institutional Multiplicity

Our chapter's most direct implications are for future research examining organizational responses to institutional multiplicity (very broadly conceived). We began by reviewing the arguments of our original chapter and highlighting several overlooked ideas and themes. In the process, we stressed their distinctiveness and independent merits. We continue to see much value in the basic concept of pluralism and in other key aspects of our initial formulation. These include its inclusive conceptualization of institutional reality, its close connections to sociological theories of identity and self, its problem-centred orientation and its strongly Selznickian/pragmatist flavour. We were careful to note that we do not perceive this approach as a competitor or a critic of the complexity formulation (or of institutional logics theory more generally). Instead, we see it as a (still) viable alternative that proceeds from different premises and pursues different aims.

By amending our earlier mistakes and including values into our theory, we tried to further enhance its viability and attractiveness. Values are a critical part of the larger institutional world, and our understanding of pluralism's organizational implications is substantially enriched and deepened when

we bring them back into focus. Empirical research, which more closely attends to this neglected aspect of institutional life, may produce valuable insights that are not otherwise available. Many inter-institutional clashes have a palpable normative component, and the subjective experience of multiplicity has a strong (if variable) moral aspect. This aspect is often obscured and easy to miss if we do not go looking for it.

We would definitely like to see research that focuses on the experience of moral ambiguity and angst (the most obvious effects of value pluralism). However, we also hope to see work that examines experiences of a more positive nature. Pragmatist theory suggests that human selves have a remarkable ability to internalize a range of outwardly discordant values (including those that are apt to seem irreconcilable when we view the person from a distant, theoretical perspective). Close evaluation of our own experiences and relationships seems to produce many examples of this ability. While this capacity appears quite essential to realizing the 'promise of pluralism', we seem to know remarkably little about the thing itself.

Research examining these and other adaptations to value pluralism could be conducted in virtually any organizational setting. However, the context of social-business hybrids seems particularly apt. These organizations are largely populated by extremely idealistic people who are striving to realize a plurality of overtly moral aims. Though research approaching these organizations through the institutional logics lens has certainly produced many useful insights, it often appears to be handicapped by its lack of a moral vocabulary. Our pluralistic and value-based approach seems like one way to fill this void. It is also possible that some of the ideas that we have put forward here could be incorporated into the logics perspective itself. While we would be pleased if this were to occur, we do not know how it could be done and do not consider it to be a central part of our own agenda.

Second-Order Pluralism and the Problem of Means and Ends

We also see an important opportunity for research that looks beyond value vs. value tensions and examines values' relationship with other dimensions of the institutional world. We have repeatedly observed that the normative dimension is only one part of a larger institutional reality, and also stressed values' tenuous connection with action and choice. While moral standards and ideals are generally available to people, they do not invariably enter into decisions and are often overridden by institutional forces of a different stripe (e.g., rules, authority structures, or pressures for social conformity).

We believe that research examining this tension (which we have labelled as 'second-order pluralism') would be useful for at least two different reasons. The first is conventionally scientific. Though we have long understood that there are multiple dimensions to institutional reality, we do not seem to have thought systematically about the tensions and interactions between them. This was certainly true in our original chapter. Research examining this interface would thus seem novel and interesting. The second reason is more ethical and humanistic. If we are willing to acknowledge that the normative realm is home to values that are genuinely valuable and worthy of our endorsement, it follows that we should typically favor normative forces when they come into conflict with other institutions. More plainly, we should generally hope that people and organizations will bring their values to bear in making decisions. This support must, of course, be tempered by an awareness of the plurality of values, and informed by some knowledge of the particular values in question. Not all values are equally meritorious, and not everything that is claimed as a value can withstand closer scrutiny. Nevertheless, a 'pro values' bias is clearly indicated by everything else we have thus far written. If readers have followed us this far, this suggestion should

not be particularly controversial. The larger aim is to cultivate what Selznick described as 'moral competence' and what Aristotle called phronesis (practical moral judgement).

We are also excited by the idea of second-order pluralism because it provides a way to refocus and redescribe the central tension that was at the heart of Selznick's institutionalism. Selznick saw formal organizations mostly as 'means' – structural tools or devices that were created for the purpose of realizing various substantive values ('ends'). But he also recognized organizations' maddening tendency to subvert their own goals and undermine the very values that provided their reason for being.[8] They were 'recalcitrant tools' that tended to 'tyrannize' the people and values they were meant to serve. His institutionalism was, above all else, an effort to address this problem (both theoretically and practically). Selznick did not think that this problem could ever be fully solved or eliminated. But he did believe that it could be controlled and ameliorated (Krygier, 2012, 2015). While this required many things, the most important was a recognition of the basic problem itself: If people didn't see it, they couldn't hope to address it.

We have long been disturbed by contemporary institutionalism's inattention to this problem (which is in some deep sense the theory's very own reason for being). We have also been haunted by the fact that our theoretical formulations often seem to obscure the very existence of the problem itself. Bringing values back into the theoretical discourse will not immediately fill this void, and our concept of second-order pluralism does not begin to capture the many subtleties and nuances of Selznick's institutionalism and pragmatist social theory. But, it does at least create an opening for researchers who are interested in rediscovering this critical human problem and picking up where Selznick left off. While this research could go in many different directions, we are especially keen to promote research that examines the tension between the normative and cognitive dimensions of the institutional world (Kraatz, Ventresca, & Deng, 2010; Kraatz & Flores, 2015). Selznick's theory was all about the tension between the regulative and normative realms (i.e., between the organizational body and its institutional soul). These problems persist and merit our renewed attention. But institutional values are also threatened by cultural forces that operate in the broader society. These problems are largely unexplored, and contemporary institutional theorists would appear 'distinctly competent' to address them. The critical need, as Kraatz and Flores (2015) have suggested, is to position Selznick's institution within its broader institutional environment. When this is done, we can begin to see how the latter thing affects the well-being of the former one.

Institutional Leadership

Reintroducing values also opens a door for serious research on the phenomenon of institutional leadership (Besharov & Khurana, 2015; Raffaelli & Glynn, 2015). When we imagine an institutional world without values, institutional leadership is neither necessary nor possible. The would-be leader has no meanings to convey and affirm, no mission to protect and promote, no integrity to defend, and no distinctive competence to realize. This hypothetical person is not even able to 'default' on his/her responsibilities and botch the job (because there is really no job to do). We know all of these things in part because we have previously tried to restore the concept of institutional leadership without an explicit discussion of values (in a companion piece to our original chapter) (Kraatz, 2009). While that paper may have made some very minor progress, it suffered from the same handicaps as our original description of institutional pluralism. This is probably why that paper has had such limited influence – and why the concept of leadership remains largely absent from the burgeoning literature on institutional work.

We believe that the theory we have forwarded here could help change this. People who occupy positions of formal power have a huge ability to affect the moral lives of their institutions. Some of this work is transparently symbolic and institutional in character. But, much of it crosses between institutional realms (Besharov & Khurana, 2015). The things that people do (and fail to do) in their narrow administrative capacity also send powerful moral signals. When they strive to embody values in their decisions and practise 'leadership in administration', their institutions are more apt to flourish. Selznick well described what happens when they do not:

> The default of leadership shows itself in an acute form when organizational achievement or survival is confounded with institutional success ... A university led by administrators without a clear sense of values to be achieved may fail dismally while steadily growing larger and more secure. (Selznick, 1957: 27)

In advocating a renewed focus on leadership, we are not advocating hero-worship or fuzzy, mystical thinking. Institutional leadership is a type of work done by ordinary people in response to the sociological realities we have discussed throughout this paper. Leaders are flawed and ordinary people just like the rest of us. We are also not denigrating or overlooking the experiences and contributions of other institutional inhabitants who do not occupy elite roles. As people, all institutional members matter equally, and we all have opportunities to rise above our roles and live our values (or not). Our case for refocusing attention on elites rests solely on their (vastly) disproportionate ability to help or harm the moral communities entrusted to their care. Power and responsibility go hand in hand. We see a tremendous need (and opportunity) for research that embodies and conveys this simple human truth. While we believe that this research could be tremendously 'relevant' and appealing to managerial audiences, the relevance we envision is not the type that is most typically sought and prized within management research.

Critical Scholarship

A value-centric institutionalism could also be an important resource for criticism. Whatever their other merits, value-free social scientific theories are essentially useless in this regard (Cooper, Ezzamel, & Willmott, 2008; Willmott, 2015). The reasons for this have already been largely explained. When we conceptualize organizations and their leaders as socially controlled objects whose actions are dictated by external forces, we can scarcely blame them for the things they do (or realistically hope for a different outcome) (Margolis, 2001). When we push the normative dimension into the deep background of our thought, we rob ourselves of the basic human language and moral resources that are needed to expose, critique and ultimately change these disturbing realities. While we may still be deeply and rightly troubled by the things we observe in our research, we are forced to describe them in neutral scientific language (or retreat into ourselves and watch in mute horror).

The pluralistic, value-based institutionalism we have described here does not completely solve these problems. It contains a mix of scientific and humanistic concerns that may not satisfy the requirements of many critical minds. It also suggests a need to reserve judgement in many instances and to recognize any number of moral trade-offs (these being characteristic features of pluralist thought). The standard of judgement which our perspective offers (moral integrity) is also less objective and demanding than some critics may prefer. With all this said, it is at least a standard. It is also a substantial improvement over what is currently on offer within institutional theory. By bringing values back in, we regain an ability to critique and to expect more from our subjects. We also begin to regain our moral voice.

In proposing this possible application of our perspective, we feel obligated to note that we are largely ignorant of the critical management literature (and somewhat surprised to realize that our work may be relevant thereto). We should also note that our own objectives are not mainly critical in their orientation. We have always been predisposed to approach organizational problems from a managerial perspective, and we are constitutionally unable to apologize for this. It is a value and a deeply felt responsibility. With this said, we also recognize the contingent nature of this value and the dark consequences that might ensue when it is held up above all others. Institutional theory has a legitimate role to play in the improvement and maintenance of institutions, and we strongly believe it should offer a message that speaks to those in positions of authority. We do not believe this is its only legitimate role or its only constituency.

We have tried here to articulate a perspective that might enable leadership as well as criticism and reform; one that can help us improve and maintain our valued institutions at the same time that it exposes their flaws and failings. We have also tried to show that these objectives are not as oppositional as they often appear. Institutional theory will surely remain divided along many lines, but these divides do not negate the possibility of communication and solidarity. Properly understood, they might even be seen as the very source of the thing itself.

Humanist Science

In 2008, Philip Selznick published his last book, entitled *A Humanist Science*. Two years later, he passed away at the age of 91. While he described the basic idea of humanist science in a variety of different ways, the following passage is perhaps the most succinct:

> Facts are the conditions affecting human achievement; Values are ideals ... realized or undermined by these conditions. A discipline that brings out this interdependence is a humanist science. (Selznick, 2008: xviii)

Though he did not introduce this term until this last book, it was in some sense just a new way to describe what he had actually been doing his entire life. Krygier (2012) has provided a brilliant analysis of Selznick's thought, which reveals its deep character and shows the remarkable continuity of its themes across a career that spanned nearly seven decades. Selznick himself also summarized and reiterated these master themes in a number of different places (Selznick, 1992, 1996, 2000). We find the following quote to be especially evocative and revealing:

> I have in mind the fate of ideals in the course of social practice. Most of my specialized writings in the sociology of law and the sociology of organizations have been preoccupied with the conditions and processes that frustrate ideals or instead give them life and hope. (Selznick, 1992: x)

We have been deeply influenced by these words, and tried (with uncertain success) to embody Selznick's vision in this chapter. We have also been captivated by the broader idea of a 'humanist science' and spent a great deal of time reflecting on what such a thing is (or could be). If we may be indulged, we would like to close our chapter by offering a few of our own speculative thoughts on this very large question.

To begin, we think that a humanist science would have to be *about humans*. This means that we have to acknowledge people's ability to form and pursue values. It also means that we have to acknowledge their capacity to make choices, moral and otherwise. While we may be able to predict human behaviour with some reliability, we can never fully explain it. People have their own reasons which are not fully knowable, and this seems like something that we must respect. The 'human factor' cannot be resigned to the error term of our models or our thinking. Second, we think that a humanist science would have to be *for humans*. This means that our scholarship must speak to real human problems (rather than just addressing tensions between abstract theoretical postulates). It also means

that it must have some real world constituency. Human problems and constituencies are hugely varied, and they are all fair game so far as we can see. But, these people and their problems would have to be represented in our work. It can't just be for us.[9] Finally, we think that that a humanist science would have to be conducted *by humans*. This means that we need to look inward and consider our own biases and motivations. It also means that we need to recognize the limits of our own theories and to avoid presenting them as something more than they really are. While our *own values* are almost sure to come to bear in our scholarship, this influence is not necessarily a corrupting one (Selznick, 2000).

In the closing pages of our first chapter, we said that pragmatism both 'humbles and ennobles the theoretical enterprise'. Looking back, we can see that our own personal mix of humility and nobility was still somewhat out of whack. The foregoing discussion of humanist science might come a little closer to conveying the proper combination. We do not, of course, know if Selznick himself would have approved of this interpretation of his concept. We also don't know whether this ideal will resonate with anyone else, or find a home in other minds besides our own. We do believe that it is a very nice ideal in its own right. If we were to follow it, it is at least possible that some good may occur as a result.

Notes

1   This chapter was written while the first author was on sabbatical at the University of Oxford's Saïd Business School. We gratefully acknowledge the support and encouragement of Tom Lawrence, Marc Ventresca and many other Oxford colleagues.

2   The first edition is available online.

3   We owe this useful formulation to Clark Kerr (1963: 8), who had observed that 'the American university is so many different things to so many different people that it must, of necessity, be partly at war with itself'.

4   'As an organization acquires a self, a distinctive identity, it becomes an institution. This involves the taking on of values, ways of acting and

believing that are deemed important for their own sake' (Selznick, 1957: 21).

5   King, Felin and Whetten (2010) made a somewhat similar case for 'finding the organization in organization theory'.

6   Kraatz & Flores (2015) provide a more thorough discussion of Selznick's institutionalism and the various roles that values play therein. This brief summary is distilled from that chapter.

7   'The guts of institutions is that somebody, somewhere really cares to hold an organization to the standards and is often paid to do that. Sometimes that somebody is inside the organization, maintaining its competence. Sometimes it is in an accrediting body, sending out volunteers to see if there is really any algebra in the algebra course. And sometimes that somebody, or his or her commitment, is lacking, in which case the center cannot hold, and mere anarchy is loosed upon the world' (Stinchcombe, 1997: 115).

8   'Institutions embody values, but they can do so only as operative systems or going concerns. The trouble is that what is good for the operative system does not necessarily serve the standards or ideals that the institution is supposed to uphold. Therefore institutional values are always at risk. Insofar as organizational, technological and short-run imperatives dominate decision-making, goals and standards are vulnerable. They are subject to displacement, attenuation, and corruption' (Selznick, 1992: 244).

9   John Dewey famously remarked that 'philosophy recovers itself when it ceases to be a device for dealing with the problems of philosophers and becomes a method, cultivated by philosophers, for dealing with the problems of men'. Our chapter carries no message for philosophy or social science, *per se*. But, we do think that this pragmatist advice is profoundly relevant to organizational theory (as an applied field).

REFERENCES

Albert, S., & Whetten, D.A. (1985). Organizational identity. In L.L. Cummings & B.M. Staw (Eds.), *Research in organizational behavior*, *7*, 263–295. Greenwich, CT: JAI Press.

Badaracco, J.L. (1997). *Defining moments: When managers must choose between right and right*. Boston, MA: Harvard Business School Press.

Bandura, A. (1999). Moral disengagement in the perpetration of inhumanities. *Personality and Social Psychology Review*, *3*, 193–209.

Battilana, J., & Dorado, S. (2010). Building sustainable hybrid organizations: The case of commercial microfinance organizations. *Academy of Management Journal*, *53*, 1419–1440.

Battilana, J., & Lee, M. (2014). Advancing research on hybrid organizing: Insights from the study of social enterprises. *Academy of Management Annals*, *8*, 397–441.

Berlin, I. (2001). My intellectual path. In H. Hardy (Ed.), *The power of ideas* (pp. 1–23). Princeton, NJ: Princeton University Press.

Bernstein, R.J. (1987). The varieties of pluralism. *American Journal of Education*, *95*, 509–525.

Besharov, M.L., & Khurana, R. (2015). Leading amidst competing technical and institutional demands: Revisiting Selznick's conception of leadership. In M.S. Kraatz (Ed.), *Institutions and ideals: Philip Selznick's legacy for organizational studies* (pp. 53–88). *Research in the sociology of organizations*, Volume 44. Bingley, UK: Emerald Group.

Besharov, M.L., & Smith, W.K. (2014). Multiple institutional logics in organizations: Explaining their varied nature and implications. *Academy of Management Review*, *39*, 364–381.

Burke, P.J., Owens, T.J., Serpe, R., & Thoits, P.A. (Eds.) (2003). *Advances in identity theory and research*. New York: Kluwer–Plenum Press.

Callero, P. (2003). The sociology of the self. *Annual Review of Sociology*, *29*, 115–33.

Cooper, D.J., Ezzamel, M., & Willmott, H. (2008). Examining institutionalization: A critical theoretic perspective. In R. Greenwood, C. Oliver, R. Suddaby, & K. Sahlin-Andersson (Eds.), *The SAGE handbook of organizational institutionalism* (pp. 673–701). London: Sage.

Crowder, G. (2004). *Isaiah Berlin: Liberty and pluralism*. Cambridge: Polity Press.

Dewey, J. (1932). *Ethics*. New York: Henry Holt & Company.

DiMaggio, P., & Powell, W.W. (1983). The iron cage revisited: Institutional isomorphism and collective rationality in organizational fields. *American Sociological Review*, 48: 147–160.

DiMaggio, P.J. & Powell, W.W. (1991). Introduction. In Powell, W.W. and P. J. DiMaggio (Eds.). *The New Institutionalism in Organizational Analysis*. Chicago, IL: University of Chicago Press.

Dobbin, F. (1994). *Forging industrial policy: The United States, Britain and France in the railway age*. New York: Cambridge University Press.

Dunn, M.B., & Jones, C. (2010). Institutional logics and institutional pluralism: The contestation of care and science logics in medical education, 1967–2005. *Administrative Science Quarterly*, *55*, 114–149.

Eisenberg, A. (1995). *Reconstructing political pluralism*. Albany, NY: SUNY Press.

Friedland, R. (2013). God, love, and other good reasons for practice: Thinking through institutional logics. In M. Lounsbury & E. Boxenbaum (Eds.), *Institutional logics in action* (pp. 25–50). *Research in the sciology of organizations*, Volume 39A. Bingley, UK: Emerald Group.

Friedland, R., & Alford, R.R. (1991). Bringing society back in: Symbols, practices, and institutional contradictions. In Walter W. Powell & Paul J. DiMaggio (Eds.), *The new institutionalism in organizational analysis* (pp. 232–263). Chicago, IL: University of Chicago Press.

Gecas, V., & Burke, P.J. (1995). Self and identity. In K.S. Cook, G.A. Fine, & J.S. House (Eds.), *Sociological perspectives on social psychology* (pp. 41–67). Needham Heights, MA: Allyn & Bacon.

Gill, M., & Nichols, S. (2008). Sentimentalist pluralism: Moral psychology and philosophical ethics. *Philosophical Issues, 18*, 143–163.

Graham, J., Haidt, J., Koleva, S., Motyl, M., Iyer, R., Wojcik, S., & Ditto, P.H. (2013). Moral foundations theory: The pragmatic validity of moral pluralism. *Advances in Experimental Social Psychology, 47*, 55–130.

Greene, J. (2013). *Moral tribes: Emotion, reason, and the gap between us and them.* New York: Penguin.

Greenwood, R., & Hinings, C.R. (1996). Understanding radical organizational change: Bringing together the old and the new institutionalism. *Academy of Management Journal, 21*, 1022–1054.

Greenwood, R., & Hinings, C.R. (2006). Radical organizational change. In S. Clegg, C. Hardy, W.W. Nord, & T. Lawrence (Eds.), *The SAGE Handbook of Organization Studies.* London: Sage.

Greenwood, R., Raynard, M., Kodeih, F., Micelotta, E.R., & Lounsbury, M. (2011). Institutional complexity and organizational responses. *Academy of Management Annals, 5*, 317–371.

Haidt, J. (2001). The emotional dog and its rational tail: A social intuitionist approach to moral judgment. *Psychological Review, 108*, 814–834.

Haidt, J. (2012). *The righteous mind: Why good people are divided by politics and religion.* New York: Pantheon.

Hechter, M. (1993). Values research in the social and behavioral sciences. In M. Hechther, L. Nadel, & R.E. Michod (Eds.), *The origin of values* (pp. 1–28). New York: Aldine de Gruyter.

Hinings, C.R., & Greenwood, R. (2015). Missing in action: The further contribution of Philip Selznick to contemporary institutional theory. In M.S. Kraatz (Ed.), *Institutions and ideals: Philip Selznick's legacy for organizational studies* (pp. 121–148). *Research in the sociology of organizations*, Volume 44. Bingley, UK: Emerald Group.

Hitlin, S. (2003). Values as the core of personal identity: Drawing links between two theories of self. *Social Psychology Quarterly, 66*, 118–137.

Hitlin, S., & Piliavin, J.A. (2004). Values: Reviving a dormant concept. *Annual Review of Sociology, 30*, 359–393.

Hitlin, S., & Vaisey, S. (2013). The new sociology of morality. *Annual Review of Sociology, 39*, 51–68.

James, W. (1890). *The Principles of Psychology.* New York: Henry Holt and Company.

James, W. (1979 [1907]). *Pragmatism.* Cambridge, MA: Harvard University Press.

James, W. (1909). *A pluralistic universe.* New York: Library of America.

Joas, H. (1993). *Pragmatism and social theory.* Chicago, IL: University of Chicago Press.

Joas, H. (1996). *The creativity of action.* Chicago, IL: University of Chicago Press.

Joas, H. (2000). *The genesis of values.* Chicago, IL: University of Chicago Press.

Joas, H. (2004). Morality in an age of contingency. *Acta Sociologica, 47*, 392–399.

Kekes, J. (1996). *The morality of pluralism.* Princeton, NJ: Princeton University Press.

Kerr, C. (1963). *The uses of the university.* Cambridge, MA: Harvard University Press.

King, B.G. (2015). Organizational actors, character, and Selznick's theory of organizations. In M.S. Kraatz (Ed.), *Institutions and ideals: Philip Selznick's legacy for organizational studies* (pp. 149–174). *Research in the sociology of organizations*, Volume 44. Bingley, UK: Emerald Group.

King, B.G., Felin, T., & Whetten, D.A. (2010). Perspective – finding the organization in organizational theory: A meta-theory of the organization as a social actor. *Organization Science, 21*, 290–305.

Kraatz, M.S. (1998). Learning by association? Interorganizational networks and adaptation to environmental change. *Academy of Management Journal, 41*, 621–643.

Kraatz, M.S. (2009). Leadership as institutional work: A bridge to the other side. In T.B. Lawrence, R. Suddaby, & B. Leca (Eds.), *Institutional work: Actors and agency in institutional studies of organization* (pp. 59–91). Cambridge: Cambridge University Press.

Kraatz, M.S., & Block, E. (2008). Organizational implications of institutiomal pluralism. In R. Greenwood, C. Oliver, R. Suddaby, & K. Sahlin-Andersson (Eds.), *The SAGE Handbook of Organizational Institutionalism* (pp. 243–275). London: Sage.

Kraatz, M.S., & Flores, R.G. (2015). Reinfusing values. In M.S. Kraatz (Ed.), *Institutions and ideals: Philip Selznick's legacy for organizational studies* (pp. 353–381). *Research in the sociology of organizations*, Volume 44. Bingley, UK: Emerald Group.

Kraatz, M., & Moore, J.D. (2002). Executive migration and institutional change. *Academy of Management Journal, 45*, 120–143.

Kraatz, M.S., Ventresca, M.J. and Deng, L. (2010). Precarious values and mundane innovations:

Enrollment management in American liberal arts colleges. *Academy of Management Journal*, 53, 1521–1545.

Kraatz, M.S., & Zajac, E.J. (1996). Exploring the limits of the new institutionalism: The causes and consequences of illegitimate organizational change. *American Sociological Review*, 61, 812–836.

Krygier, M. (2012). *Philip Selznick: Ideals in the world*. Stanford, CA: Stanford University

Krygier, M. (2015). Selznick's Hobbesian idealism: Its nature and origins. In M.S. Kraatz (Ed.), *Institutions and ideals: Philip Selznick's legacy for organizational studies* (pp. 21–52). *Research in the sociology of organizations*, Volume 44. Bingley, UK: Emerald Group.

Lassman, P. (2011). *Pluralism*. Cambridge: Polity Press.

Love, E.G., & Kraatz, M.S. (2009). Character, conformity or the bottom line? How and why downsizing affected corporate reputation. *Academy of Management Journal*, 52, 314–335.

Margolis, J.D. (2001). Responsibility in organizational context. *Business Ethics Quarterly*, 11, 431–454.

Mead, G.H. (1934). *Mind, self, and society*. Chicago, IL: University of Chicago Press.

Mishina, Y., Block, E.S., & Mannor, M.J. (2012). The path dependence of organizational reputation: How social judgment influences assessments of capability and character. *Strategic Management Journal*, 33, 459–477.

Pache, A., & Santos, F. (2010). When worlds collide: The internal dynamics of organizational responses to conflicting institutional demands. *Academy of Management Journal*, 35, 455–479.

Pratt, M.G., & Foreman, P.O. (2000). Classifying managerial responses to multiple organizational identities. *Academy of Management Review*, 25, 18–42.

Pratt, M.G. and Kraatz, M.S. (2009). E pluribus unum: Multiple identities and the organizational self. In Dutton, J., and Roberts, L.M. (Eds.), *Exploring Positive Identities and Organizations*. Mahwah, NJ: Lawrence Erlbaum and Associates, 385–410.

Raffaelli, R., & Glynn, M.A. (2015). What's so institutional about leadership? Leadership mechanisms of value infusion. In M.S. Kraatz (Ed.), *Institutions and ideals: Philip Selznick's legacy for organizational studies* (pp. 283–316). *Research in the sociology of organizations*, Volume 44. Bingley, UK: Emerald Group.

Rokeach, M. (1979). *Understanding human values: Individual and societal*. New York: Free Press.

Ruef, M., & Scott, W.R. (1998). A multidimensional model of organizational legitimacy: Hospital survival in changing institutional environments. *Administrative Science Quarterly*, 43, 877–904.

Schwartz, S. (1994). Are there universal aspects in the structure and content of human values? *Journal of Social Issues*, 50, 19–45.

Scott, W.R. (2014). *Institutions and organizations: Ideas, interests and identities*. Thousand Oaks, CA: Sage.

Selznick, P. (1949). *TVA and the grass roots*. Berkeley, CA: University of California Press.

Selznick, P. (1957). *Leadership in administration*. New York: Harper & Row.

Selznick, P. (1992). *The moral commonwealth: Social theory and the promise of community*. Berkeley, CA: University of California Press.

Selznick, P. (1996). Institutionalism 'old' and 'new'. *Administrative Science Quarterly*, 41, 270–277.

Selznick, P. (2000). On sustaining research agendas: Their moral and scientific basis. *Journal of Management Inquiry*, 9, 277–282.

Selznick, P. (2002). *The communitarian persuasion*. Washington, DC: Woodrow Wilson Center Press.

Selznick, P. (2008). *A humanist science: Values and ideals in social inquiry*. Stanford, CA: Stanford University Press.

Stets, J.E., & Burke, P.J. (2000). Identity theory and social identity theory. *Social Psychology Quarterly*, 63, 224–37.

Stinchcombe, A.L. (1997). On the virtues of the old institutionalism. *Annual Review of Sociology*, 23, 1–18.

Stryker, S. (1980). *Symbolic interactionism: A social structural version*. Menlo Park, CA: Benjamin/Cummings.

Stryker, S. (1987). Identity theory: Developments and extensions. In K. Yardley and T. Honess (Eds.) *Self and identity: Psychosocial perspectives*. New York: Wiley.

Stryker, S. (2008). From Mead to a structural symbolic interactionism and beyond. *Annual Review of Sociology*, 34, 15–31.

Stryker, S., & Burke, P.J. (2000). The past, present, and future of an identity theory. *Social Psychology Quarterly*, 63, 284–297.

Suchman, M. (1995). Managing legitimacy: Strategic and institutional approaches. *Academy of Management Review*, 20, 571–611.

Tenbrunsel, A.E., & Messick, D.M. (2004). Ethical fading: The role of self-deception in unethical behavior. *Social Justice Research*, 17, 223–235.

Thornton, P.H., Ocasio, W., & Lounsbury, M. (2012). *The institutional logics perspective: A new approach to culture, structure, and process*. Oxford: Oxford University Press.

Thornton, P., & Ocasio, W. (1999). Institutional logics and the historical contingency of power in organizations: Executive succession in the higher education publishing industry, 1958–1990. *American Journal of Sociology*, 105, 801–843.

Wiley, N. (1994). *The semiotic self*. Chicago, IL: University of Chicago Press.

Willmott, H. (2015). Why institutional theory cannot be critical. *Journal of Management Inquiry*, 24, 105–111.

21

Institutional Work: Taking Stock and Making It Matter

Christian E. Hampel, Thomas B. Lawrence and
Paul Tracey

INTRODUCTION

'Institutional work' has evolved from a concept introduced to capture a set of actions described in institutional research, to a perspective on the relationship between institutions and actors associated with a distinctive set of questions, assumptions, findings and theoretical claims. The questions at the heart of the institutional work perspective focus on understanding how, why and when actors work to shape sets of institutions, the factors that affect their ability to do so, and the experience of these efforts for those involved. Built into these questions are a set of assumptions: that social reality is socially constructed, mutable and dependent on as well as embedded in the behavior, thoughts and feelings of people and collective actors. There is also a key assumption that people and collective actors have the potential to act in ways that involve an awareness of their relationship to institutions. Rather than accepting institutions as innately enduring and their effects as immutable, research on institutional work explores the practices and processes associated with actors' endeavors to build up, tear down, elaborate and contain institutions, as well as amplify or suppress their effects. Pursuing research on institutional work has led to important findings that have identified a wide range of forms of institutional work, documented the complex interplay of different forms of institutional work (Creed, DeJordy, & Lok, 2010; Granqvist & Gustafsson, 2016; Leung, Zietsma, & Peredo, 2014), demonstrated the important work of actors to maintain institutions (Currie, Lockett, Finn, Martin, & Waring, 2012; Micelotta & Washington, 2013; Trank & Washington, 2009) and shown the potentially powerful intended and unintended consequences of institutional work (Singh & Jayanti, 2013; Zietsma & Lawrence, 2010). Scholars have explored how actors employ institutional work across different levels, including individual (Tracey, 2016), organizational (Gawer & Phillips, 2013; Tracey, Phillips, & Jarvis, 2010), community (Lawrence & Dover, 2015; Mair, Marti, & Ventresca, 2012), field (Suddaby & Viale, 2011; Trank &

Washington, 2009) and national levels of analysis (Hirsch & Bermiss, 2009). An important set of findings describes how the interplay of institutional work by groups of actors can lead to institutional change that combines conflicting and competing interests in newly negotiated institutional orders (Helfen & Sydow, 2013; Helms, Oliver, & Webb, 2012; Maguire & Hardy, 2009; Smets, Morris, & Greenwood, 2012; Zietsma & Lawrence, 2010).

The institutional work perspective has, we argue, shifted the conversation around institutions and organizations, both within the confines of the institutional work literature and more broadly across organizational institutionalism: it has been a significant catalyst for the integration of a practice perspective on institutions (see Smets, Aristidou, & Whittington, Chapter 14 this volume), greater attention to 'micro' institutional concerns (though we will argue that this may be at the cost of understanding the institutional work to influence large institutions; see Powell & Rerup, Chapter 12 this volume), a renewed concern for politics and contestation in institutional change (see Lawrence & Buchanan, Chapter 18 this volume), and especially a deeper, more nuanced investigation of the relationship between agency and institutions. As research on institutional work has progressed, the perspective has also acted as a gateway to introduce or extend new concerns for institutional scholars, including the relationship between emotions and institutions (Creed, Hudson, Okhuysen, & Smith-Crowe, 2014; Voronov & Vince, 2012; see also Lok, Creed, DeJordy, & Voronov, Chapter 22 this volume), the lived experienced of institutional life (Creed et al., 2010; Tracey et al., 2010), the interplay of institutions and materiality (Jones & Massa, 2013; Lawrence & Dover, 2015; Raviola & Norbäck, 2013; see also Jones, Meyer, Jancsary, & Höllerer, Chapter 23 this volume), the oppressive potential of institutions (Creed et al., 2010; Martí & Fernández, 2013), and the connection between changes in fine-grained practices and larger institutions (Jarzabkowski, Matthiesen, & Van de Ven, 2009; Smets & Jarzabkowski, 2013).

THEORETICAL FOUNDATIONS OF INSTITUTIONAL WORK

Originally defined as 'the purposive action of individuals and organizations aimed at creating, maintaining and disrupting institutions' (Lawrence & Suddaby, 2006: 215), institutional work contrasts with most other institutional approaches by placing the spotlight on the role of actors and their efforts to interact with and influence institutions. The study of institutional work is founded on two primary theoretical ideas. The first is embedded agency (Battilana & D'Aunno, 2009), which from an institutional work perspective is less a paradox than simply a description of how people confront institutions on a day-to-day basis (Creed et al., 2010; Leung et al., 2014). From an institutional work perspective, institutions shape every facet of human existence, providing meaning and motivation to our actions, and holding together the material and symbolic structures that trigger and shape those actions; at the same time, however, institutions are ongoing human accomplishments, constructed and maintained by people's behavior, thoughts and feelings, often in ways that are unreflexive and unintended, but just as often in ways that reflect people's institutional awareness, their desires to affect institutional arrangements, and the skills and resources they marshal to achieve those desires. The idea of embedded agency has become a part of nearly all research on institutions and organizations, but it is at the heart of the institutional work perspective. The location of embedded agency in the institutional work perspective builds directly on the foundational writing of DiMaggio (1988) and Oliver (1991, 1992) that clarified the need to integrate a sophisticated and heterogeneous understanding of agency when considering the relationship between institutions and organizations. An important move in the institutional work literature beyond these foundations has been to explore the whole gamut of outcomes of actors' work, including achieving one's objectives, failing at them, and triggering unintended consequences.

A second key concept for the institutional work perspective is the idea of practice. The study of institutional work draws significantly on the sociology of practice that has been an important part of the broader practice turn in the social sciences (De Certeau, 1984; Giddens, 1984; Schatzki, Knorr-Cetina, & Von Savigny, 2001; Whittington, 2006). In this tradition, practices represent 'embodied, materially mediated arrays of human activity centrally organized around shared practical understanding' (Schatzki et al., 2001: 2). Practice-theoretic approaches to social life bring with them a specific ontology within which 'phenomena of various complexities are not made of transcendental elements such as forces, logics or mental models. When it comes to the social world, it is practicing all the way down' (Nicolini & Monteiro, 2017). Although this may seem like an extreme position, it brings with it the potential for fantastic theoretical clarity. The institutional work perspective relies heavily on the concept of practice as a bridge between people's reflexive, purposive efforts and the institutions at which those efforts are aimed: concrete instances of institutional work are simultaneously practices – embodied, materially mediated arrays of human activity – that are organized around institutions and people's intentions to shape those institutions. Thus, the institutional work perspective builds on the sociology of practice by focusing on particular sets of practices aimed at affecting the institutional arrangements within which they are situated. In so doing, institutional work encourages a shift in attention from field-level patterns, to the specific practices that underpin them, and at the same time offers a path along which institutional and practice scholars might enjoy a shared journey and benefit from the strengths of each other's approaches.

OUR AIMS IN THIS CHAPTER

Three main aims motivate this chapter. First, we aim to take stock of the institutional work perspective as it has developed since 2006. We limit our review to research that has explicitly adopted the 'institutional work' label, rather than including all research concerned with the relationship between agency and institutions more broadly. So, for instance, although research on social movements, hybrid organizations and paradox examines forms of social action that could be understood from an institutional work perspective, we leave a discussion of those literatures to others (including other chapters in this Handbook – see Schneiberg and Lounsbury, Chapter 11 and Battilana, Besharov, & Mitzinneck, Chapter 5 this volume). We also realize that our review overlaps with Hardy and Maguire's review of institutional entrepreneurship in this volume (Chapter 10), and so we leave a detailed exploration of the concept to their chapter. Our first aim of taking stock is represented by the chapter's first main section, which investigates the institutional work literature in terms of 'what' (the institutions highlighted in research on institutional work), 'who' (the actors on which institutional work research has focused) and 'how' (the strategies through which actors influence institutions).

Our second aim is to highlight what we see as important gaps in the development of the institutional work perspective, focusing in particular on the 'what', 'who' and 'how' of institutional work. With respect to 'what', we found an important gap in our understanding of institutional work aimed at large-scale institutions. A consistent focus in institutional work research has been on how actors influence what might be described as 'middle-range' institutions – institutionalized beliefs, rules and values that exert a significant influence within an organization, community or field. This is despite dramatic shifts in large-scale institutions over the past few decades, much of which has been the result of intentional, effortful work by a wide range of individuals, groups, organizations and networks. The second gap we address concerns 'who' – the range of actors that research on institutional work has included. Largely missing in research to date has been the collaborative work of heterogeneous networks of actors, which may be especially important in institutional work that is concerned with shaping large-scale institutions. The third gap we examine concerns 'how' institutional work is done. Despite a range of studies that have explored a wide variety of strategies for institutional work, there has remained a focus on symbolic forms of institutional work, at the expense of understanding the role of relational and material forms. For each of these gaps, we explore an allied literature that we believe could provide theoretical and methodological insights that would provide insight and energy if integrated into the institutional work perspective.

Our third aim in this chapter is to use the study of institutional work to move organizational institutionalism toward a more practical, impactful connection with audiences outside of the academy. Thus, in the chapter's final main section, we explore the possibility of an applied program of institutional work research. We approach this challenge first by examining the potential for institutional work research to shift towards a focus on institutions 'that matter' – institutions tied to major social challenges. We then explore two ways in which an applied program of institutional work research might be constructed: as a policy science; and as a form of participatory action research. We argue that an applied program of institutional work would provide an important practical, prescriptive addition to the current focus on theoretical novelty and empirical precision. It would, however, necessitate broad changes to the way we conduct research projects, interact with policy-makers and conceptualize our relationships with those we study. We encourage scholars to use and develop institutional work to tackle the challenges surrounding the institutions that matter.

INSTITUTIONAL WORK AT 10

In the decade that the institutional work perspective has been an active ingredient in organizational institutionalism, it has been incorporated in a wide variety of empirical and conceptual articles. At the time of this writing, Google Scholar lists more than 1,500 works citing either Lawrence and Suddaby (2006) or Lawrence, Suddaby and Leca (2009). The concept of institutional work has been connected closely to a number of the topics and issues that motivate chapters of this volume, including legitimacy (Dansou & Langley, 2012; Trank & Washington, 2009), (Hardy & Maguire, 2010; Suddaby & Viale, 2011), emotions (Creed, Hudson, Okhuysen, & Smith Crowe, 2014; Moisander, Hirsto, & Fahy, In press; Voronov & Vince, 2012), identity (Creed, Dejordy, & Lok, 2010; Leung, Zietsma, & Peredo, 2014), discourse (Maguire & Hardy, 2009a; Zilber, 2007a), community (Lawrence & Dover, 2015), inhabited institutions (refs), power (Currie, Lockett, Finn, Martin, & Waring, 2012; Rojas, 2010a) and institutional logics (Gawer & Phillips, 2013). Along with organization studies research, the concept has gained traction in related fields, including the study of strategic management (Durand, 2012; Paroutis & Heracleous, 2013), business ethics (J. Gond & Boxenbaum, 2013; Vadera & Aguilera, 2015), public administration (Cloutier, Denis, Langley, & Lamothe, 2016; Coule & Patmore, 2013), accounting (Arroyo, 2012; Modell, 2015), business history (Smothers, Murphy, Novicevic, & Humphreys, 2014), and communication (Bartlett, Tywoniak, & Hatcher, 2007; Pallas & Fredriksson, 2011).

Our aim in this section is not to provide a comprehensive summary of the literature or an examination of the broader relationship between agency and institutions. Rather, we seek to provide a snapshot of research on institutional work. To do so, our review draws primarily from a set of 53 empirical studies that were explicitly framed in terms of institutional work and published in major organization studies journals. In reviewing these articles, we pose three questions. First, we ask *what* institutions actors try to influence through work. In brief, we find that research on institutional work has tended to focus on "middle-range" institutions – those specific to particular fields, such as discourses in the

Israeli high-tech field (Zilber, 2007b) and the platform logic within the semiconductor field (Gawer & Phillips, 2013). Second, we ask *who* engages in institutional work. Our review suggests that institutional work research has focused primarily on actors who either work alone or cooperate with relatively similar partners, as in the case of a Nordic university creating a new blueprint for higher education institutions (Granqvist & Gustafsson, In press) and Italian journalists integrating the offline and online content of their newspaper (Raviola & Norbäck, 2013). Finally, we ask *how* actors do institutional work. Mirroring institutional theory more broadly, we find that most research on institutional work highlights symbolic and discursive strategies, such as the use of narratives (Zilber, 2009) and discourse (Maguire & Hardy, 2009b).

THE INSTITUTIONS IN 'INSTITUTIONAL WORK'

The question of what kinds of institutions are examined in research on institutional work is a complex one. A common way to differentiate institutions in organizational research is in terms of the particular form they take – such as practices (Hiatt, Sine, & Tolbert, 2009; Lok & De Rond, 2013), boundaries (Åkerström, 2002; Zietsma & Lawrence, 2010), values (Gehman, Trevino, & Garud, 2013; Wright, Zammuto, & Liesch, 2015), rules (Heaphy, 2013), or standards (Slager, Gond, & Moon, 2012). In strategy and international business, a more common categorization focuses on formal versus informal institutions (Peng, Wang, & Jiang, 2008; Stiglitz, 1999). In looking across the research on institutional work, we found studies that incorporated all of these different kinds of institutions.

An important, but under-examined, basis for differentiating studies of institutional work is the 'level' of the institution that is the target of institutional work. The issue of levels is a surly one in organizational institutionalism. Some

scholars posit a distinctly institutional level, often focusing on the rules, practices and beliefs institutionalized across societies or fields. By contrast, others suggest that institutions can exist at any level of analysis, including the organization, group and individual levels. In reviewing the literature on institutional work, it is apparent that there has been a clear tendency to focus on the field and organization levels. Indeed, 44 out of the 53 studies in our review fall into this category.

Field-Level Institutions

Following DiMaggio and Powell's (1983) lead and mirroring institutional theory more broadly, research on institutional work has often focused on characteristics of fields as the main target for institutional work. The concept of a field is, of course, a contested one (see Wooten & Hoffman, Chapter 2 this volume). Broadly defined as 'a community of organizations that partakes of a common meaning system and whose participants interact more frequently and fatefully with one another than with actors outside the field' (Scott, 1995: 56), fields have been the focus of a vibrant stream of research that examined the institutional work associated with efforts to create, maintain and transform them. Studies have shown the challenges that field actors face in finding agreement for the internal arrangements of the field: they need to decide which roles to allow, which practices to adopt and which logics to follow (e.g., Jones & Massa, 2013; Wright & Zammuto, 2013a; Zietsma & McKnight, 2009a). In terms of external work, studies have shown that actors need to build or maintain the field's legitimacy, its boundaries and its relations to other fields (Boxenbaum & Strandgaard Pedersen, 2009; Riaz, Buchanan, & Bapuji, 2011). These actions are vital to secure the continued support from key resource providers, such as regulators, the media, or investors, many of which are usually external to the field.

By far the most commonly examined object of institutional work has been field-level practices – 34 of the 53 studies that we review here fall into this category. Indeed, investigations of how actors affect the status of field-level practices have been a consistent focus for institutional work research throughout the past decade. In looking across these studies, it is interesting to observe that researchers have continued to dedicate more attention to the creation and maintenance of practices, rather than to their disruption (some notable exceptions, such as Maguire & Hardy, 2009, notwithstanding). Early examples include Perkmann and Spicer's (2008) analysis of the institutionalization of management fashions, in which the authors identified three forms of institutional work – political work, technical work and cultural work – and showed that the advocates of such fashions are more likely to be successful in institutionalizing them when they increase the types of institutional work that they deploy and when the skill sets of the actors involved are heterogeneous. Another early study of institutional work aimed at field-level practices was Zietsma and McKnight's (2009b) analysis of the efforts of actors in the British Columbia coastal forestry industry to promote competing proto-institutions in the face of contestation. They find that actors in contested fields often need to collaborate with the proponents of opposing ideas to jointly co-create novel solutions that can protect them against external attacks. More recently, institutional work research has examined field-level practices in a range of contexts, including financial services regulation (Riaz et al., 2011), microfinance (Dorado, 2013), architecture (Jones & Massa, 2013), capital markets (Clark & Newell, 2013) and housing (Lawrence & Dover, 2015).

Roles constituted the second most commonly studied field-level object of institutional work. The study of roles as objects of institutional work emerged later than the study of practices and has focused primarily on professional roles, including changes in the role identities of nurses from 1955 to 1992 (Goodrick & Reay, 2010), efforts to maintain power by elites in response to the emergence of new roles in the UK healthcare

system (Currie et al., 2012), the institutional work of pharmaceutical companies to control internal professional staff (Singh & Jayanti, 2013), the strategies of Italian professionals to maintain the power and privileges associated with their roles (Micelotta & Washington, 2013), and the institutional experimentation inside accounting firms struggling to define the role of auditors in the wake of financial and professional crises (Malsch & Gendron, 2013). The interest in professional roles as objects of institutional work follows a long tradition of examining professions as arenas of institutional change (Greenwood, Suddaby, & Hinings, 2002; Kitchener & Mertz, 2012; Scott, Ruef, Caronna, & Mendel, 2000). Research that has focused specifically on professional roles has added important nuance to our understanding of institutional work dynamics in these domains by explaining how and why professionals work to effect or resist change. For example, in Ramirez's (2013) study of the British audit profession, the trigger for institutional work was a perceived injustice stemming from institutional change that threatened the sense of 'equity in a community of peers': in an effort to increase accountability in the audit profession, the professional body introduced a monitoring scheme that created an 'uproar' among the smaller firms.

A third field-level institution examined in institutional work research is the organizational form – 'archetypal configuration of structures and practices given coherence by underlying values regarded as appropriate within an institutional context' (Greenwood & Suddaby, 2006a: 30). Despite organizational forms being a long-standing concern in institutional theory and organizational research more broadly (Child & McGrath, 2001; Davis, Diekmann, & Tinsley, 1994; DiMaggio, 1991), there have been relatively few studies of the institutional work associated with their creation, and none of their disruption or maintenance. The small number of institutional work studies that has focused on organizational forms have shown that they require specific types of work to become legitimate, with cooperation between like-minded organizations especially important (e.g., Empson, Cleaver, & Allen, 2013; Perkmann & Spicer, 2007; Tracey, Phillips, & Jarvis, 2011). For example, David, Sine and Haveman (2013) showed that collective action amongst related firms and relationships with high-profile actors such as prestigious universities, played a key role in the emergence of management consulting as a new organizational form.

A small set of institutional work studies have examined the efforts of actors to affect standards and standard-setting processes. Standards represent mechanisms of control that 'facilitate coordination by defining the appropriate attributes of the standardized subject, rendering these aspects visible to external inspection and opening up the possibility of sanctioning non-compliance' (Slager et al., 2012: 765). Despite much public and scholarly discussion of the increasing roles that standards play in contemporary society, the institutional work that goes into their formation has been relatively neglected. The research of Slager, Gond and Moon (2012) on the creation of the FTSE4Good index, which 'emerged as a standard for socially responsible corporate behaviour', and of Helfen and Sydow (2013) on global labor standards shows that the institutional work underpinning such standards involves a combination of forms undertaken in complex, collaborative and competing relationships. Standards provide a particularly useful context for studying institutional work because of the public and often heated contests and debates that occur around them, which expose the varied institutional strategies used by interested actors.

Although a range of other field-level institutions exist, the bulk of institutional work research has focused on the practices, roles, organizational forms and standards described above. A minority of studies, however, have examined the institutional work associated with more varied institutions, including social boundaries (Zietsma & Lawrence, 2010), values (Wright et al., 2015), discourses (Zilber, 2007), network configurations (Bertels, Hoffman, & DeJordy, 2014), and field-level

logics (Gawer & Phillips, 2013). The paucity of research on these objects of institutional work is unfortunate because they all represent key facets of organizational fields.

One of the most notable – and perhaps disappointing – outcomes of our review is the lack of attention to field-level logics as potential targets of institutional work. This is especially surprising given the significant attention that institutional scholars have paid to logics more broadly (see Ocasio, Thornton, & Lounsbury, Chapter 19 this volume). Institutional logics are frames of reference through which actors make sense of the world, construct their identities, and interact with the world around them (Thornton, 2002; Thornton, Ocasio, & Lounsbury, 2012). Thus it is clearly very important to explore how logics can be shaped by institutional work. Gawer and Phillips (2013) is a rare example of a study that considers how actors affect field-level logics. These authors documented the strategies through which Intel introduced the platform logic into the semiconductor field to replace the traditional supply chain logic. Importantly, they show that change in field-level logics may require simultaneous internal work at the organizational level to change local identities and practices, and external work at the field level to change field-wide practices and build legitimacy (see also Tracey et al., 2011). We return to this issue in the next major section when we discuss gaps in our understanding of institutional work.

Organization-Level Institutions

Although not as abundant as research on institutional work that targets field-level institutions, there have also been a significant number of investigations of institutional work focused on organization-level institutions, including organizational practices, logics, values, and rules (Daudigeos, 2013; Rojas, 2010a; Van Wijk, Stam, Elfring, Zietsma, & Den Hond, 2013; Zilber, 2009). The practical and political effects of organization-level institutions often lead to ongoing negotiations that result in oscillations between peaceful co-existence and conflict-ridden clashes. Consequently, some organization-level institutions are associated with frequent breakdowns and breaches, and thus work to repair and restore their status and legitimacy (Bjerregaard & Jonasson, 2014; Heaphy, 2013; Lok & De Rond, 2013). Two kinds of institutions have been particularly prominent in institutional work research: rules and logics.

Rules – both formal and informal – matter in organizations. They motivate, facilitate and constrain behavior, and they help shape the construction of organizational history and culture (March & Olsen, 1976; Zhou, 1993). Rules also distribute resources and provide or limit opportunities for organizational members, and thus act as both the incentive and means for institutional work aimed at their maintenance or transformation (Heaphy, 2013; Raviola & Norbäck, 2013). The institutional work of members to influence organizational rules includes a wide array of possibilities. One particularly radical form of institutional work in this regard involves acquiring sufficient power to change the rules. This kind of work is at the center of Rojas' (2010a) study of how the president of San Francisco State College responded to the 1968 Third World Strike, namely by using the dramatic situation to gain more powers and create draconian new rules as well as stricter punishments. A small number of studies have also looked at the maintenance, rather than the transformation, of organizational rules. Most notably, Heaphy (2013) explored how staff at US teaching and veteran hospitals struggled to treat patients in the face of physical threats that seemed to nullify formal rules. This study focused on the important role of patient advocates, who helped hospital staff by providing them with strategies so that they could protect themselves in such situations.

Finally, a third form of institutional work in relation to organizational rules involves amending particular rules while maintaining the spirit underlying them. Such an approach might prove especially appropriate in cases where rules represent sources of conflict or disagreement. Lok and De Rond (2013), for example,

describe such a situation in their study of the Cambridge University Boat Club. An informal but important Club rule declared that members were to devote all their efforts to the shared goal of beating Oxford University in the annual rowing competition. But, in 2007, the crew's most experienced coxswain made the controversial and unexpected decision to train for the varsity boxing team at the same time as training with the rowing team. Lok and De Rond (2013: 198) describe how the situation triggered 'negotiation work between Russ and the squad to come to an acceptable working agreement that fell outside of the scope of the normal selection script'. This negotiation work served to contain the breach and thus preserve the sanctity of the informal commitment rule.

Very different institutional work is needed in novel situations, in which actors are confronted with new activities. While conflict about existing rules has been the subject of some scholarly attention, we know very little about the work involved in deciding how new domains should be governed, the processes underpinning the creation of these rules and how new rules interact with prevailing ones. Raviola and Norbäck (2013) suggest that in such situations actors can try to identify existing rules in analogous domains of activity and transfer them to new situations. For example, when negotiating the new domain of online newsmaking, Italian journalists were able to draw on the rules supporting the print edition of their newspaper as a 'law book' to guide the behavior of organizational members and help them adjust. This study also highlights that the cautious adaptation and selective application of existing rules provides actors with a non-confrontational approach through which they can navigate institutional challenges and employ rules to their own advantage (see also Seo & Creed, 2002).

Although institutional logics are more typically thought of as field-level or societal phenomena, a small number of studies have shown that logics can represent the targets of organization-level institutional work. These studies take the perspective that institutional logics are 'constructed rather than given' (Smets & Jarzabkowski, 2013: 1279) inside organizations. Logics may be grounded in extra-organizational structures and cultures, but to be meaningful and impactful in organizations they need to be made local – rendered interpretable and actionable in the face of organizational routines, structures, values, beliefs and relationships. This dynamic is especially visible in the context of institutional complexity, where organizational members struggle with the concurrent impact of multiple competing logics, such as the market logic and the family logic, in the same organization (Greenwood, Raynard, Kodeih, Micelotta, & Lounsbury, 2011; Kraatz & Block, 2008). Although organizational responses to institutional control has emerged as a vibrant research domain, relatively few studies (e.g., Smets, Jarzabkowski, Burke, & Spee, 2015; Toubiana & Zietsma, forthcoming) have drawn on the concept of institutional work to tackle this thorny challenge. One such exception is Jarzabkowski, Matthiesen and Van de Ven's (2009) study of institutional complexity in a utility firm whose members sought to reconcile opposing market and regulatory logics through a wide array of institutional work. Interestingly, this study showed that organizational members can engage in different types of seemingly conflicting institutional work simultaneously – creation work was used to augment certain aspects of the logics inside the firm, while disruption work was used to contest other aspects. More broadly, research on institutional work directed at shaping logics inside organizations has illustrated various approaches to tackling this issue, including slowly integrating emerging logics into an established logic, combining multiple logics and continuously recalibrating the relationship between existing logics (Bjerregaard & Jonasson, 2014; Empson et al., 2013; Smets & Jarzabkowski, 2013; Tracey et al., 2010).

These studies highlight two important, broader phenomena within institutional work research at the organization-level: first, scholars make increasingly explicit and prominent use of practice-theory for explaining institutional work, and second, scholars increasingly

suggest that the process and outcomes of institutional work may differ. Thus, while actors are usually concerned with only one institutional outcome (creation, maintenance or disruption), they often need to draw on all three institutional work processes (creation, maintenance and disruption) to achieve that outcome – as Jarzabkowski, Matthiesen and Van de Ven (2009), among others, have shown.

Individuals and Institutions

The relationship between individuals and institutions could be central to the study of institutional work if one follows Giddens (1984) and Bourdieu (1998) who locate social structure in the memory traces of individuals. This perspective suggests that actors can engage in a critically important form of institutional work by shaping the memories (and identities and emotions) of individuals, including their own. Despite the tremendous potential, and the repeated calls for scholars to investigate the microfoundations – the coalface – of institutions, relatively little research on this kind of institutional work has been undertaken. An exception is Tracey's (2016) study of the Alpha course, 'an evangelizing movement designed to convert agnostics to a particular – and contested – interpretation of Christianity'. This study asks how organizations persuade individuals to internalize a new logic, and documents four key kinds of 'micro-institutional work' (framing work, identity work, affective work and performative work). A key finding of this study is the precariousness of such institutional work: Tracey argues that effectively enacting 'these forms of work is challenging and requires high levels of skill', and that even then, 'the outcomes of the persuasive process [are] uncertain – conversion is by no means guaranteed'.

The institutional work connecting individuals and institutions has also been explored as a 'bottom-up' phenomenon, in which people experience their identities as in conflict with or constrained by broader institutions, and consequently engage in institutional work to reclaim, redefine or justify their identities (Creed et al., 2010; Leung et al., 2014). Creed, DeJordy and Lok (2010), for example, found in their study of GLBT ministers that individuals can use embodied identity work to reconcile clashes between their identity and dominant institutions. The GLBT ministers in this study used self-narratives based on salient experiences to justify their institutional role and challenge their marginalization. Although these studies have begun to show how actors can work to accommodate their own identities in different institutional settings, the forms of work needed to resist or shed identities that result from institutional pressures have not yet been subject to systematic analysis.

More broadly, the first steps towards individual-level studies highlight various intriguing possibilities for moving institutional work research forward. First of all, they are starting to explore the important – and mostly overlooked – role that emotions play when actors interact with institutions. Second, they also alert us to the vastly different forms of commitment that individuals have to institutions – from ardent support to lukewarm compliance – and suggest scope for interesting research into why individuals increase or decrease their commitment to institutions.

Societal Institutions

We have discussed how research on institutional work has made significant advances in understanding efforts to shape field- and organization-level institutions, and some progress on understanding institutional work that targets individuals. Institutional work designed to shape societal institutions, however, has been a distinct blind spot. Only six of the 53 papers in this review focus on institutions that can reasonably be described as being anchored at the societal level. What these papers bring to the conversation around institutional work is a consideration of institutions that are often more complex and distal than the simpler, more proximal institutions located in fields and organizations.

Hirsch and Bermiss (2009), for example, explore how actors in the Czech Republic used preservation work to maintain the old societal rules, while transitioning into the emerging post-Communist economic system. During this period, the Czech Republic privatized the majority of state-owned enterprises and appeared to move to an economy of market-driven enterprises with dispersed ownership. In practice, however, many of the enterprises were controlled by Investment Privatization Funds, which in turn were under the influence of state-owned banks. Thus, the old rules of state-planned enterprise remained in force, despite a seemingly smooth transition to a market economy. This study highlights the complexity faced by actors when seeking to influence societal institutions, and suggests that institutional workers operating in this context need to be particularly skilled at negotiating countervailing forces. In a study focused on a very different set of dynamics, Dacin, Munir and Tracey (2010) examine a long-standing societal institution in British society – the class system. These authors show how formal dining rituals in Cambridge colleges contribute to the maintenance of social class structures in Britain. Specifically, the repeated performance of these rituals legitimizes for participants the concept of social stratification, transform (or in some cases reinforce) the self-perception of Cambridge students and elevate their social position by providing access to (and a sense of identification with) an elite professional–managerial class. A third example of institutional work aimed at societal institutions is Wijen and Ansari's (2007) research on the creation of the Kyoto Protocol. This study suggests a key challenge facing actors seeking to influence societal institutions involves uniting large numbers of diverse actors, which requires distinctive types of institutional work, such as the construction of 'enrolling bandwagons' in order to rapidly recruit a critical mass of supporters.

Taken together, these studies offer only preliminary insights into the distinctive dynamics of institutional work at the societal level. But they also reveal the gaps in our knowledge and highlight the importance of, and potential for, additional research in this area – societal-level institutions arguably exert greater influence on social behavior compared to institutions at the meso and micro levels. Intriguingly, existing studies suggest that actors may be able to use forms of institutional work that have been shown to be effective at other levels of analysis for the maintenance of societal institutions (e.g., Dacin et al., 2010) but that they may need to deploy distinct types of work to create or disrupt them (e.g., Mair & Marti, 2009; Wijen & Ansari, 2007). This insight offers an interesting initial direction for future institutional work research at the societal level.

In sum, this section has shown that our understanding of institutional work directed at institutions operating at different levels of analysis is uneven. The societal level arguably offers most promise for future research given the limited attention it has received to date and the sheer scale of the influence on social behavior exerted by institutions at this level. Clearly, however, there are many important issues that would benefit from sustained research attention across the levels that we have considered.

THE ACTORS: WHO ENGAGES IN INSTITUTIONAL WORK?

The second question we use to structure our review of the institutional work literature focuses on the actors – the people, organizations and networks that engage in institutional work. This question is an important one because different constellations of actors have been shown to face different challenges and opportunities, experience different emotions and conflicts, and are able to achieve different institutional outcomes. The early institutional studies that underpinned the development of institutional work as a concept focused primarily on individual people and organizations, and especially those conceived of as institutional entrepreneurs who marshal resources to shape institutions in a way that furthers their interests (Battilana, Leca, & Boxenbaum, 2009; Garud, Jain, &

Kumaraswamy, 2002; Greenwood & Suddaby, 2006b; Maguire, Hardy, & Lawrence, 2004a), a tendency that shaped much of the work since 2008 as well. Institutional work scholars have often explored how individual actors influence the institutions under whose influence they find themselves – a phenomenon known as 'the paradox of embedded agency' (Seo & Creed, 2002). This stream of research describes individual actors engaging in progressive bottom-up change, building subject positions, and drawing on broader societal elements in order to achieve their goals (Maguire, Hardy, & Lawrence, 2004b; Rojas, 2010a; Tracey et al., 2011). For example, in their study of the creation of a new hybrid organizational form that bridged for-profit retailing and non-profit charity, Tracey, Phillips and Jarvis (2010) show how institutional entrepreneurs can leverage emerging macro-cultural discourses. In their case, the two proponents drew on increased public acceptance for social enterprises and for responsible business to establish their type of organization. Much of the research about institutional entrepreneurs has (at least implicitly) adopted a strong form of Swidler's (1986) 'culture-as-a-toolkit' perspective that treats cultural elements as resources to be used for change, while downplaying the concomitant constraints that impede agency.

Despite its roots in the study of institutional entrepreneurship, one of the key elements of the institutional work agenda has been to move away from the somewhat heroic notions of institutional entrepreneurship, to a more social image of actors and agency – one that was variously more fragmented, distributed, partial and collective. This move was a reaction to the image of 'hypermuscular institutional entrepreneurs' (Lawrence, Suddaby, & Leca, 2009: 1) who were singularly able to transform what seemed for others to be intractable institutional structures (Battilana et al., 2009). Thus, a second set of institutional work studies has explored the efforts of relatively similar groups of actors, who were usually drawn from the same field of activity and shared similar interests. Indeed,

40 of the 53 studies in our review fall into this category. This research shows that relatively homogeneous groups can influence institutions by engaging in collective action, adopting favorable social positions and enacting desired practices in the face of resistance (Clark & Newell, 2013; Currie et al., 2012; Dorado, 2013). The relatively homogeneous actor groups in institutional work research primarily fall into two categories.

One set of studies explores groups of homogeneous actors who engage in institutional work within a specific organization. In contrast to field-level groups, coalitions of organizational actors tend to focus inwards by negotiating intra-organizational practices and aligning their own identities with their roles. In so doing they often affect how the organization relates to its broader institutional environment (e.g., Daudigeos, 2013; Jarzabkowski et al., 2009; Leung et al., 2014). Lok and De Rond's (2013) study of the Cambridge University Boat Club is a case in point. The homogeneity of the actor group helped to ameliorate conflict relating to the Club's goal of defeating Oxford University. Nonetheless, conflict still ensued as actors disagreed about the best approach and level of commitment for achieving this goal – a common phenomenon among homogeneous actor groups (e.g., Jarzabkowski et al., 2009; Zilber, 2009).

Another set of studies about homogeneous actors explores highly organized groups within a specific field; this set is dominated by professionals, such as nurses and lawyers (e.g., Empson et al., 2013; Micelotta & Washington, 2013; Rainelli Weiss & Huault, 2016). These groups of actors are often concerned with protecting jurisdictional claims, fending off challenges to their field, and adapting their roles to new situations (e.g., Currie et al., 2012; Trank & Washington, 2009). For example, Currie, Lockett, Finn, Martin and Waring (2012) study how specialist doctors in the English NHS were able to neutralize the status threat that resulted from the introduction of a new role. These elite actors used their command of resources and control over service delivery to shape the new role to their benefit and to co-opt actors from

other professional groups to support them. This study highlights a key theme among studies of homogeneous actor groups: these – usually professional – actors can employ their privileged positions, power and status to maintain and extend their interests. This parallels the 'Matthew effect' – the idea that the 'rich get richer' and 'the poor get poorer' as the advantages of a favorable starting position compound evermore (Merton, 1968). However, institutional work research has yet to systematically explore the circumstances under which homogeneous groups (of professionals) can see their sphere of influence curtailed, their practices removed and their status demoted. Thus many interesting research opportunities exist for exploring the limits of professional power.

The third main set of actors upon which institutional work scholars have focused are heterogeneous actor groups, usually from different fields of activity characterized by different – and often divergent – objectives. A notable feature of these studies is that the actors on which they focus are nearly always engaged in significant, and sometimes dramatic, conflicts with one another (e.g., Zietsma & Lawrence, 2010). Maguire and Hardy (2009), for instance, explore how scientists and activists went on the offensive to successfully de-legitimate the use of DDT in the face of widespread industry opposition. This study highlights that conflicts between heterogeneous actors are often decided by actors' ability to overcome power imbalances and challenge widely accepted institutional norms.

Interestingly, studies that concern heterogeneous actor groups who are in conflict tend to focus mainly on one side of the conflict – usually the 'winning' side. While this may be an inevitable consequence of data access constraints, the result is that these studies often emphasize one perspective of a struggle to the detriment of others, which clearly limits the insights that can be generated and conclusions that can be drawn. A notable exception is Zietsma and Lawrence's (2010) study of the British Columbia forestry field. By collecting extensive data across the field – from forestry companies, environmentalists and government officials – these authors are able to paint a more even-handed picture of each stage of the field's transformation. In particular, their multi-vocal data allow them to show how initial confrontation gave way to small-scale collaborations between the conflicted parties. Future institutional work research would benefit from more balanced accounts such as this one that take into consideration the perspectives of all the groups involved in conflict situations. This would allow researchers to provide more nuanced accounts of the dynamics of conflict as they unfold, and the of role institutional work in resolving them.

TYPES OF INSTITUTIONAL WORK: HOW DO ACTORS INFLUENCE INSTITUTIONS?

The foundational book chapter by Lawrence and Suddaby (2006) divided institutional work according to its intended *outcomes*, i.e., into the work of creating, maintaining and disrupting institutions. In this chapter, we provide an alternative perspective by classifying institutional work based on the *means* that are used to achieve particular institutional objectives. This leads us to distinguish between three types of institutional work: first, symbolic work that uses symbols, including signs, identities and language, to influence institutions; second, material work that draws on the physical elements of the institutional environment, such as objects or places, to influence institutions; and third, relational work that is concerned with building interactions to advance institutional ends.

Symbols dominate institutional work. The popularity of symbolic work can be explained by institutional theory's strong roots in symbolic interactionism, particularly the influential work of Berger and Luckmann (1966). This long tradition has inspired many studies that show how actors can strategically interact with symbols

to achieve their institutional objectives. Indeed, nearly all of the studies in our review discussed symbolic work to some extent, with 46 out of 53 placing particular emphasis on it. In these papers it is apparent that scholars have drawn on a wide range of symbols, including categories, identities, narratives, rhetoric, rules and scripts, among others (e.g., Leung et al., 2014; Raviola & Norbäck, 2013; Singh & Jayanti, 2013). While actors have a huge array of symbols available to them, deploying these symbols so that they resonate with key actors is far from straightforward – connecting to existing institutional arrangements, adapting broader themes and neutralizing oppositional symbols have been identified as important skills in this regard (e.g., Riaz et al., 2011; Ruebottom, 2013; Trank & Washington, 2009).

The role of narratives and identities features especially strongly in the literature on symbolic forms of institutional work. Actors construct narratives through the 'selection, combination, editing, and molding of events into a story form' (Zilber, 2009: 208). These narratives can become powerful symbols that actors can use to explicate situations, justify actors and defend different courses of actions. Closely related is the concept of rhetoric, which involves the use of 'persuasive language' (Ruebottom, 2013: 100). Studies have shown that actors employ narratives (and rhetoric) in different ways to pursue institutional work (e.g., Riaz et al., 2011; Zilber, 2007). One approach is for actors to draw on meta-narratives that exist across multiple fields and thus resonate with many salient audiences. For example, Zilber (2009) found in her study of a rape crisis center that actors translated and re-interpreted societal meta-narratives to justify feminist and therapeutic practices. This included using them to socialize new members by, for instance, embedding narratives into routines. As a result, the center was able to justify its activities with stories that resonated widely across society. A second approach involves the creation of new stories that invoke widely accepted tropes, vocabularies or rhetorical devices rather than specific societal meta-narratives. For example, Ruebottom (2013) shows that social entrepreneurs in Bangladesh were able to build legitimacy for their ventures by constructing narratives that depict themselves in the role of heroic protagonists standing up to the villainous antagonists.

Identity – a self-referential statement of 'who we are' or 'who I am' (Albert & Whetten, 1985) – is the second main type of symbolic institutional work that researchers have focused on. Specifically, scholars have explored how actors construct and reconstruct identities at different levels – both individual and organizational – to influence institutions. This research suggests that identities and institutions are in a constant interplay. As a result, actors can sometimes use their identities to influence broader institutions and, in turn, sometimes adapt their identities to fit these institutions (e.g., Creed et al., 2010; Goodrick & Reay, 2010). The former case is highlighted by Jones and Massa's (2013) study of Frank Lloyd Wright's Unity Temple church building which moved from 'entrepreneurial anomaly' to 'consecrated exemplar'. They show how actors had to publicly express and defend their novel architectural identity to attain legitimacy for their work. The latter case is highlighted by Gawer and Phillips' (2013) observation that Intel had to adapt its identity to introduce the platform logic across its industry. Specifically, it had to make new identity claims, and resolve tensions between its established identity and new platform practices. These studies highlight that institutional workers are often required to renegotiate their identities as they seek to shape the institutional landscape.

Despite a rich vein of existing research, symbolic work continues to offer much promise for students of institutional work. For example, Granqvist and Gustafsson (2016) extended institutional work to account for the temporal realm. Through a study of the creation of a new university blueprint in Finland, they find that the strategic manipulation of notions of time – for instance by creating urgency or enacting momentum – can have a powerful bearing on the outcomes of institutional projects. Two underexplored types of symbols that offer much promise are the visual and the sonic. Despite the

old adage that a picture says more than a thousand words, it is unclear how institutional workers can effectively employ image-based symbols (see Meyer, Höllerer, Jancsary, & Van Leeuwen, 2013, for an overview). Similarly, despite being constantly surrounded by them, scholars have been largely silent about the role of sounds in institutional dynamics (see Schwarz, 2015, for an exception). For example, chants are often instrumental for mobilization during political revolutions or anti-corporate protests. Research that explores the potency of the sonic realm for institutional action has the potential to make an important contribution.

The exploration of the tangible side of institutional life has also proven a less well trodden path. In particular, we know little about material work, which involves the manipulation of physical aspects of the institutional environment, and more specifically about the role of materiality in shaping institutional work. Indeed, only five studies in our review explored the material dimension in any detail. This, admittedly small, body of work has suggested three roles for the material realm. First, actors can draw on material objects to interpret situations that they face. In this instance, objects contain institutional information that can guide decision-making. For example, in their study of technological change in an Italian newspaper business, Raviola and Norbäck (2013) showed that actors can use the material functions of technology – in which institutions are inscribed – to navigate new situations. In their case, journalists used their experiences of working with paper-based version of newspapers to make sense of proposals for a digital version. Second, actors can use material objects to extend their agency by using them to perform institutional work. For example, in their study of the introduction of new prizes into the Italian public sector, Monteiro and Nicolini (2015) show that actors can use material objects for many types of institutional work, such as educating others, theorizing institutions, or reconfiguring normative networks. Third, material objects can complicate institutional work. For example, in their study of the role of place in Vancouver support programs for the hard-to-house, Lawrence and Dover (2015) show that the unique materiality of a daycare facility led to significant shifts in how actors approached their institutional work.

As these studies show, material work offers much promise for the study of institutional work. One possible route forward would be to engage with theoretical ideas and perspectives from elsewhere in the social sciences that place greater emphasis on the role of the material. For example, institutional work researchers might consider drawing on actor-network theory or theories of socio-materiality to help extend and refine their thinking (Latour, 2005; Orlikowski & Scott, 2008).

Relational work is another important type of symbolic institutional work. The study of relational work explores how actors can influence institutions through their interactions with others. To date this has been studied in two different ways. In a first stream of research, scholars have explored how actors can gain followers for their cause. Studies have suggested that to this end actors can build networks, amplify each other's initiatives through indirect work and suppress alternatives (Bertels et al., 2014; Boxenbaum & Strandgaard Pedersen, 2009; Rojas, 2010b). For example, in a study of Bolivian microfinance, Dorado (2013) finds that actors can use group dynamics to recruit supporters: the presence of a group helps to motivate others to join it, inspires members to identify opportunities, and facilitates access to yet more potential members. Other studies have shown that actors may engage in relational institutional work in a variety of ways in order to entangle others in their institution – ranging from the subtle use of rituals to aggression and other forms of coercive behavior (Dacin et al., 2010; Martí & Fernández, 2013).

In a second stream of research, scholars have explored how actors can engage in collaborations with others in their field. This work has focused in particular on the role of factors such

as status, social position, goal alignment and role clarity in collaboration success (Bertels et al., 2014; Empson et al., 2013; Singh & Jayanti, 2013; Sminia, 2011; Wright & Zammuto, 2013b). It has also considered the challenges of coordination and control (Clark & Newell, 2013; Zietsma & McKnight, 2009a). For example, Dorado (2005) suggested that large groups of loosely connected actors can influence institutions when these actors are 'convened' to act in concert – a process by which big collectives work in a seemingly independent manner towards a common goal with minimal formal coordination.

It is notable, however, that existing research on relational institutional work has focused primarily on the work involved in influencing like-minded actors from the same field. We know much less about the work needed to marshal support from actors in different fields, who may have vastly different goals and occupy very different roles. In a notable exception, Wijen and Ansari (2007) draw on regime theory to explain how collective inaction was overcome to realize the Kyoto Protocol to limit emissions. They identify several drivers that enabled heterogeneous actors to reach a productive agreement. Another blindspot in current research is the work involved in negotiating formal institutional standards. One interesting exception is Helfen and Sydow's (2013) study of the negotiation of new labor framework agreements between global trade unions and multinational corporations. These authors show that relational work can yield vastly different outcomes and illustrate both the potential and the pitfalls of 'negotiation work' for institutional change.

Taken together, the research on institutional work has in its maiden decade played an important role in moving forward our understanding of the relationship between agency and institutions. In particular, it has provided a new vocabulary and way of thinking about a range of institutional dynamics, and the purposive action required to influence them. But … there is still much to be done to fulfill the potential of this perspective. In the rest of this chapter, we address two sets of issues: the theoretical holes in the fabric of institutional work research that have been left by selective attention to some sets of dynamics while ignoring others; and the even larger gap between the theoretical contributions of the institutional work perspective and its impact outside the academy.

MISSING IN ACTION: LOGICS, NETWORKS AND OBJECTS

In reviewing the existing literature on institutional work, we found it prioritized field- and organization-specific institutions rather than institutions that cut across fields. It also focused on actors who either act on their own or collaborate in relatively homogenous alliances but said much less about collaborations between diverse groups of actors. Moreover, symbolic forms of institutional work were dominant, with institutional work related to the material aspects of institutional life seldom considered. Next we explore the potential for research on institutional work to move beyond each of these tendencies.

Institutional Work, Institutional Logics and 'Big' Institutions

The study of institutional work has primarily focused on the work of actors to affect field- or organization-specific institutions, but this tendency, we argue, is neither inevitable nor helpful. In this section, we consider how the institutional work perspective might be broadened to incorporate a concern with more expansive institutional configurations. We begin by exploring the existing and potential connection between the study of institutional work and the study of institutional logics. We then discuss some of the 'big' institutions not addressed within an institutional logics perspective and how these might be brought into the study of institutional work.

There has emerged a curious, and we suggest artificial, schism over the past decade between the two most dynamic and vital areas of institutional research and writing: institutional work and institutional logics. Each of these concepts has generated a plethora of theory and empirical research, exploring the core of the ideas and elaborating their dynamics in a range of contexts, but there has been relatively little systematic effort to examine the relationship between the two. In an essay exploring this divide, Zilber argues that these two streams of work 'each developed within a distinct tradition and with its own trajectory' but share an impetus to 'bridge the tension between structure and agency that undergirds the development of neo-institutional theory for decades now' (Zilber, 2013: 89). She goes on to argue that the 'tension' between these two streams represents 'the most recent incarnation of a long series of theoretical conundrums within neo-institutionalism, each igniting deep and ongoing discussions that pushed the theory forward', including diffusion vs. translation, stability vs. change, structure vs. agency and the heroic institutional entrepreneur vs. the cultural dope. Zilber suggests that this tension is a healthy one such that institutional research and writing might best be served by keeping the streams separate, appreciating what they each bring to our understanding of organizations and institutions, and recognizing their limitations.

Although we appreciate Zilber's arguments, we believe there may be significant insight gained by integrating the concept of institutional logics more deeply into the study of institutional work. More specifically, we argue that the concept of logics could provide a way into understanding how actors work to shape large-scale, cross-field institutions. In their pivotal essay, Friedland and Alford (1991) argued that in contemporary Western societies there exist five major institutions each with an associated institutional order, which Thornton et al. (2012) built on to articulate a set of seven institutional orders: family, community, religion, state, market, profession, corporation. Shaping the meaning of these major institutions represents a form of institutional work largely unexamined in the literature on institutional work, and the literature focused on institutional logics reveals the same gap – both literatures tend to ignore how actors purposefully and skillfully affect the meaning and status of major institutions. Instead, the study of institutional logics has focused primarily on the movement of these logics into new domains (Reay & Hinings, 2009; Thornton, 2002), and the ways in which competition among logics plays out in fields (Lounsbury, 2007) and organizations (McPherson & Sauder, 2013; Pache & Santos, 2013). Even in their exhaustive articulation of an institutional logics perspective, Thornton et al. (2012) pay little attention to the potential for actors to engage in work aimed at shaping major societal institutions.

This gap is unnecessary and unhelpful. Examining how actors work to shape the meaning and status of institutional orders could provide the basis for a productive and interesting, though challenging, extended research program. Important to such an investigation would be shifts in the kinds of actors on which we usually focus in institutional work research, and the kinds of strategies and tools in play. If we take, for instance, the institutional order of the corporation, we might look historically or recently at the efforts of actors to shape the meaning and status of this institutional order, rather than any particular instantiation of it. We might also look at how the corporation takes markedly varied forms around the world and the institutional work that has helped to sustain such divergence. These differences become apparent not only by comparing the corporate form in the West with its counterparts in emerging economic giants like China and India, but by considering the stark disparities between corporations within the West itself (see Dore, 2000). The concept of a corporation, its meaning and its role in society have been the objects of sustained

institutional work in the West since at least the 18th century, when they began to be constructed as private economic entities, rather than state-chartered entities. Over the 20th and 21st centuries, the definition of a corporation and its relationship to the societies in which it operates have continued to be objects of institutional work, focusing on a range of dimensions including criminal culpability, civil liability and social responsibility. Despite the enactment of a broad range of institutional work that has shaped the corporation as a fundamental institutional pillar of societies globally, relatively little institutional research has examined this work.

As a second example, take the family. This institutional order has been a battleground for complex, conflictual institutional work for centuries. Even looking back at only the last few decades, we see institutional work by individuals, organizations, networks, states and branches of government all attempting to shape societal definitions of what constitutes a family, its sources of authority and legitimacy, mechanisms of control, and its relationship to the economy. In the United States, recent institutional work has resulted in highly pitched political and cultural contests referred to as the 'family wars' (Stacey, 1993: 545). At the heart of these 'wars' is the argument that 'The family, far more than government or schools, is the institution we draw the most meaning from. From the day we are born, it gives us our identity, our language and our expectations about how the world should work' (Goldberg, 2015). What 'the family' is, though, and how it relates to other institutional orders in society, are significantly contested, with contestants including politicians, policymakers, religious leaders, media figures and social scientists. Looking just at the institutional work of social scientists in this war, we see at least two distinct roles. One traditional role of social scientists in the debates over what constitutes a proper and effective family has been to contribute and interpret scientific 'facts' – the results of empirical studies that tend to focus on the relationship between family structure and a particular outcome, such as the educational achievement of children, or the economic success of family members (Biblarz & Gottainer, 2000; Biblarz & Raftery, 1999). A second role has been to focus on the concept of 'family' itself, as illustrated by Judith Stacey (1993: 545), a University of California sociologist, who argues that: 'no positivist definition of the family, however revisionist, is viable', because it is 'an ideological, symbolic construct that has a history and a politics'. The work of academics to define the concept of a family is important for our discussion because it so clearly illustrates the potential for even individual actors to shape the nature of institutional logics.

Although we have drawn on the concept of institutional logics as a response to the lack of attention in the study of institutional work to 'big' institutions – institutionalized practices, beliefs and norms that cut across fields and seem to endure over long periods of time – this perspective draws our attention to only a particular set of institutions. This appears to ignore other major institutions, some of which seem even more basic and enduring than the logics articulated in the various formulations. The institutions of race and gender, for instance, are undeniably central to people's lives, communities, cultures and political economies, but somehow sit outside of the institutional logics identified by Friedland and Alford (1991) or Thornton, Ocasio and Lounsbury (2012). For the study of institutional work, understanding how actors work to shape definitions of race and gender, their place in societies and their relationship to organizational life represents a profoundly important direction for future research. Though not explicitly focused on institutional work, the chapters in this volume by Rojas (Chapter 30) and by Dobbin and Kalev (Chapter 31) provide important contributions, helping us move in this direction. These institutions matter in their own right, not least because they are fundamental to understanding processes of marginalization and discrimination – why some groups are excluded from opportunities while others have privileged access to them. More fundamentally, all institutions are both gendered and racialized (Hawkesworth, 2003). This includes the 'big' logics discussed above (for example, it is surely impossible to study the institutional dynamics of the family without considering gender roles, and mixed race marriage remains taboo in many parts of the world), but also meso-level institutions such as development, social enterprise and the professions.

Institutional Work by Networks of Heterogeneous Actors

A second significant gap in the study of institutional work concerns the actors that have been studied – our review shows a tendency to focus either on individual actors or on relatively similar sets of actors working together. Indeed, it is striking that institutional work has very little to say about collaborations between heterogeneous actors who hail from different fields or who hold radically different worldviews; only a handful of studies in our review explored such situations. Where heterogeneous actors are considered, it tends to be in the context of conflict and division – with the relevant actors competing over the institutionalization of rules, norms, practices and boundaries. Although these situations are certainly common, they ignore the important possibility of cooperation among diverse sets of actors.

Two institutional work studies covered in our review do offer significant insights into heterogeneous collaboration and are worth highlighting. First, Wijen and Ansari (2007) draw on regime theory in their analysis of the emergence of the Kyoto Protocol to suggest that the creation of common ground is imperative for disparate actors to join forces. While common ground is usually not a major concern among homogeneous actors who share fields, worldviews and objectives, the lack of common ground can be a major impediment to heterogeneous collaborations that cut across fields. Second, Zietsma and Lawrence (2010) suggest an alternative approach for building collaboration between heterogeneous actors: the creation of safe spaces for small-scale experimentation, in which seemingly oppositional actors can cautiously learn to collaborate. These studies notwithstanding, the lack of attention to collaborations between heterogeneous actors leaves many important questions unexplored. Much research remains to be done to explain how such difficult, yet important, collaborations can influence institutions. For example, we lack answers to very practical questions that institutional work research could inform, such as: how can NGOs partner with governments to improve global health? And how can charities collaborate with multinationals to change long-held notions of gender? To tackle this shortcoming, institutional work scholars can learn much from other domains that have explored how heterogeneous actors can work together.

Research on cross-sector partnerships provides a useful starting point, given its focus on explaining alliances between heterogeneous actors that tackle complex social issues (Selsky & Parker, 2005). This work has shown that goal conflict is perhaps the core tension that lies at the heart of most cross-sector partnerships: the involved actors likely have vastly different objectives, as well as time horizons, resources and capabilities (Huxham & Vangen, 1996). For example, while government actors may be concerned with improving the efficiency of the provision of public services, non-profit organizations may be focused on achieving social and environmental goals, and at the core of corporate forms is, ultimately, a concern with how partnerships feed into overarching commercial objectives such as profits and market share (Seitanidi, Koufopoulos, & Palmer, 2010; Selsky & Parker, 2005). The precise nature of these tensions is likely to differ depending on the

type of partnership in question – public–private, public–nonprofit, private–non-profit, or trisector (Selsky & Parker, 2005).

Regardless of the type of partnership, scholars have suggested a number of practices that can support effective collaboration across sectors and which may be of particular interest to institutional work scholars. Perhaps the most important practice – or type of institutional work – is the creation of 'meta-goals' that apply to the entire partnership and are designed to override, or at least place in perspective, the goals of the individual partners (Huxham & Vangen, 1996). The construction of shared goals can be painful for the parties involved, and include 'recurring episodes of problematic negotiation activity' (Ackermann, Franco, Gallupe, & Parent, 2005: 312). Eden and Huxham (2001) describe in detail the social processes underpinning 'the negotiation of purpose' in the context of different partnership dynamics and the trauma that can be experienced when these negotiations do not follow a smooth path. Soundararajan and Brammer (2015) begin to reveal some of these dynamics from an institutional work perspective. Their analysis of global production networks in garment manufacturing reveal how suppliers must negotiate a complex web of relationships with governmental organizations, non-governmental organizations and other companies in the supply chain as part of efforts to ensure ethical labor practices. The authors further reveal a distinct set of strategies that suppliers engage in to manage the complexities of these relationships, ranging from 'intentional deception' to 'consensual cooperation'.

A second key practice, or type of institutional work, that has been identified in the cross-sector partnership literature as underpinning effective collaboration is the construction of a coherent partnership identity (Hardy, Lawrence, & Grant, 2005). Koschmann, Kuhn, & Pfarrer (2012) argue that cross-sector partnerships 'must continually manage individual and collective interests alongside efforts to create novel solutions to complex social issues' (p. 340–341). They further suggest that 'It is the managing – not resolving – of these tensions that increases the value potential' of such partnerships (p. 341). This requires partners to engage in complex identity work – while a coherent partnership identity can increase meaningful participation with stakeholders and help manage tensions, such an identity also needs to be flexible. The reason is that partnership effectiveness 'hinges on members' capacity to avoid inserting their own assumptions regarding others, asserting their sectional interests, and believing that their backgrounds provide special insight into the "correct" answers to partnerships' objectives' (p. 341). Given the increasing importance of identity work as a type of institutional work (Creed et al., 2010), these dynamics are potentially of much interest to institutional theorists.

Interestingly, and more broadly, an important outcome of cross-sector partnerships is not only their 'direct impact' – the immediate, practical outcomes of the partnership – but also their 'indirect impact' – their influence on the values, beliefs and practices within a given problem domain (Selsky & Parker, 2005). This emerging focus on 'indirect impact' resonates with the ambition that we have set out for institutional work scholars to explore how actors can influence the truly 'big' institutions. More broadly, cross-fertilization between scholars of institutional work and cross-sector partnerships would be fruitful, given the complementary expertise of the two fields. From the point of view of our arguments in this chapter, research on cross-sector partnerships offers institutional work scholars a detailed understanding of how heterogeneous alliances can emerge and the nature of the unique challenges between different types of partnerships – two essential areas about which institutional work has been notably silent (Koschmann et al., 2012; Selsky & Parker, 2005).

Institutional Work Involving Material Objects

The last major gap we identify in the literature on institutional work is the role of material objects in motivating and shaping institutional work. The significance of this gap has been made clear in recent years by the burgeoning literature on materiality in organization studies and sociology. Despite this growth in interest, research connecting material objects and institutional work is still relatively scarce, reflecting a more general problem in organizational institutionalism (see Jones, Meyer, Jancsary, & Höllerer, Chapter 23 this volume).

One of the first detailed discussions of the relationship between materiality and institutions was Pinch's (2008) essay rooted in the social studies of science and social construction of technology literatures. Pinch (2008: 461) argues that the 'traditional sociological approach carves up the world' into separate social and material domains, with sociologists dealing only with social things, leaving the 'world of objects, machines, and materials ... left unanalyzed or considered the territory of others'. Central to Pinch's argument is the mutual constitution of the material and the social, which he suggests is nodded to in sociological reasoning but not taken seriously or examined in detail with respect to how such mutual constitution might occur or with what consequences.

A basis for integrating materiality into institutional analysis might be the sociology of technology that emerged in the 1980s (Bijker, Hughes, & Pinch, 2012; Latour, 1987; Latour & Woolgar, 1986). From this perspective, unpacking the mutual constitution of the social and material involves research that can 'uncover and analyze the choices embedded within technologies and technological regimes and show how these choices are tied to wider societal concerns' (Pinch, 2008: 469). A key strategy in this tradition is to focus on specific technologies, examining their histories and particularly the interplay of the engineering practices and decisions involved in their creation and the societal interests that were embedded in those practices and decisions. From the institutional literature, a fascinating example is Munir and Phillips' (2005) study of the 'birth of the 'Kodak Moment', that involved the introduction of the roll-film camera and the transformation of photography from a specialist practice into an everyday activity. Munir and Phillips argue that Kodak acted both as a technological innovator and an institutional entrepreneur and that these roles were tied tightly to each other. In 1882, Kodak introduced the roll-film camera, which made photography much more convenient, but came with a significant loss of image quality unacceptable to the professional photographers. Kodak's eventual success with this design depended on four discursive strategies through which they re-shaped the institution of photography, including tying photography to the institutionalized notion of a holiday, and creating new roles, such as 'the Kodak girl' who carried a camera in her handbag. Munir and Phillips' (2005) analysis of these changes in photography powerfully illustrates the ways in which materiality, meaning and society are interpenetrated, and – importantly for our discussion – how that nexus is the object of significant work on the part of interested actors.

In the institutional work literature, the role of the material has only begun to be examined in a systematic manner. Raviola and Norbäck's (2013) study of an Italian business newspaper that integrated its online and offline news offerings represents an important step in this direction. Raviola and Norbäck focus on the agencement (Callon, 2008) – 'arrangements of humans and non-humans, which have the capacity to act' – that operate in the news room, which in this case is constituted by the journalists, the website and the newspaper. In exploring the role of these socio-technical arrangements in institutional work, they argue that, 'The new technology (website) offers possibilities for action – indeed proposes action – to the journalists that differ from the action the print proposes and the journalists engage in on the newspaper' (Raviola & Norbäck,

2013: 1178–1179). This idea of the website proposing possible actions is core to their analysis of how material objects become included in the institutional work of human actors. They show through three different episodes how the website proposes action that then requires deliberation and institutional work on the part of the journalists, and how the old technology (the newspaper) inserts itself into the process as a resource for that institutional work. Raviola and Norbäck (2013) thus present an image of materiality in institutional work in which technology plays an active part – triggering institutional work by proposing actions that cause dilemmas, constructing how these dilemmas are interpreted by framing understandings of the present and the past, and shaping action to resolve such dilemmas. We have highlighted in this section that scholarship would benefit from a detailed investigation into the work involved in changing big institutions, collaborating with networks of heterogeneous actors, and employing objects. While institutional work research has somewhat neglected these important topics, cross-fertilization with other fields has much to offer. We suggest that institutional work scholars can particularly connect to research on institutional logics, cross-sector partnerships and materiality in order to illuminate these relative blind spots.

MAKING RESEARCH ON INSTITUTIONAL WORK MATTER

One of the most common complaints among institutional scholars is the lack of impact their research has on the world outside of universities. Management practice and government policy are heavily influenced by academic research, but this research is typically rooted in disciplines directly connected to the issue at hand, such as epidemiology in healthcare (e.g., Upshur, VanDenKerkhof, & Goel, 2001), criminology in law enforcement and correction (e.g., Mastrofski & Parks, 1990), and education research in schooling (e.g., Lee & Barro, 2001). And then there is the transdisciplinary influence of economics; more than any other discipline, research on economics has infiltrated and profoundly influenced nearly every facet of management practice and government policy (Franklin, 2016).

The debate about organization theory's (lack of) relevance to the issues and challenges facing managers, policy-makers and society more broadly, has ebbed and flowed for many years. Hinings and Greenwood (2002), for instance, note that organization theory has the potential to offer distinctive insights about contemporary society, the nature of the problems it faces and the varied effects of organizational action on these problems. But they conclude that organizational research has consistently failed to address such 'grand themes' or to take seriously its role as a 'policy science' (Hinings & Greenwood, 2002: 419–420). Unfortunately, this critique applies to institutional theory at least as much as to other areas of organizational research. This is disappointing because institutional theory comprises, in our view, a sophisticated set of theoretical tools and an associated vocabulary that endows it with significant potential to contribute to our understanding of the grand themes and challenges to which Hinings and Greenwood refer. This point is reinforced by Munir (2011: 115), who argues that although the 2008 financial crisis represents a 'treasure chest' for institutional theorists, offering the chance to engage with one of the most significant global events in recent decades, we have shown relatively little interest in studying this tumultuous period and learning from it.

Within the domain of organizational institutionalism, the study of institutional work is particularly well placed to tackle pressing real-world challenges. By exploring the highly practical question of how actors can shape institutions it is uniquely positioned to not only provide academic answers for the ivory towers but to create tangible change in practice. At the same time, and as implied by our discussion in the previous section, the questions that institutional work scholars typically address, how the analysis of institutional work is connected to empirical worlds, and the conclusions that institutional work research typically provides would all need to shift significantly in order for institutional work research to realize its practical potential.

Where to Start: Institutions that Matter

To create a body of institutional work research with greater social impact, one way forward is to begin to address institutions and institutional work of greater consequence – those that have the most profound effects related to global social challenges. According to the United Nations, the international community must grapple with no fewer than 30 fundamental global issues, including global health, gender inequality, the continent of Africa, access to potable water, peace and security, and refugees and migration (United Nations, 2016). For the sake of illustration, we consider one issue that has been a key concern of the United Nations: slum dwelling in the global south. More than one billion people live in slums, around 14 percent of the world's population. More than 100,000 people move from rural areas to urban slums every day. The high cost of medicines in the global south, acute shortages of potable water, and poor nutrition mean non-communicable diseases that are mostly treatable and/or preventable kill millions of slum dwellers every year. From our perspective, these slums and their consequences represent not only a global challenge, but a nexus of institutionalized practices, beliefs, values and assumptions tied to complex combinations of institutional work, as are the potential remedies for the harms they currently effect. These dynamics offer opportunities to build novel theoretical insights and, perhaps more importantly, to shed light on deep-rooted, intractable global problems that shape the lives of many millions of people. Such a focus would begin to render obsolete any questions about institutional theory's relevance to 'real world' issues and problems (Nicolai & Seidl, 2010).

Following the pattern set in the earlier sections of this chapter, we turn from 'what' to 'who'. Investigating the institutional work connected to slums in the global south would, we suspect, involve two complex sets of actors. The first set of actors concerns those whose institutional work maintains the institutions that underpin slums. This is, of course, a potentially challenging group to study. It is unlikely that anyone is going to readily admit to engaging in institutional work that maintains the wide array of harms inflicted on people due to living in slums. At the same time, this is a critically important set of actors to identify; one of the most important insights that has emerged from the study of institutional work over the past decade is that complex institutions do not simply endure, but require significant maintenance efforts in the face of potential disruption and entropy. The second set of actors concerns those engaged in efforts to disrupt the institutions associated with slums, and create new institutions that might provide people living in slums with better access to key resources, routes out of slum living, and perhaps alternative forms of community that could replace slums. Identifying and investigating the institutional work of this second set of actors would be associated with its own challenges, as it is likely to involve diverse, complex networks of actors spanning sectors and countries, and include kinds of actors, such as governments, less familiar to many institutional work scholars.

Finally, we ask whether studying institutions that matter might lead us to consider differently the question of 'how' institutional work is accomplished in these contexts. Clearly, the study of institutional work will lead to continued identification of distinct forms of work as it explores new empirical contexts, regardless of whether those contexts feature 'big' or 'small' institutions. We believe, though, that while much current research focuses on symbolic or relational or material work, research on major social issues is likely to involve complex combinations of all three. Consider again our slum dwelling example. One of the key problems that blights the lives of slum dwellers is open defecation. In response, NGOs have invested billions of dollars in the construction of toilets (material work), a complex task given that many slums are built illegally on land not owned by the residents. Yet even where they have been built, toilets often remain largely unused. This is partly because using a toilet is an institutionalized practice that is learned through socialization into culturally specific meaning systems that construct a relationship between sanitation and wellbeing. In many cases, NGOs have responded to this problem by engaging community workers to deploy narratives that make the link between sanitation and personal and community health (symbolic work). Moreover, as noted above, addressing the problem of sanitation in isolation will have a relatively marginal impact on the lives of slum dwellers. Thus, organizations dealing with this problem need to ally with other actors working on, for example, nutrition, potable water and healthcare (relational work). Each issue poses formidable challenges in its own right but is also intimately connected and interwoven with other, broader issues. This renders the task of studying and changing the institutions that matter particularly difficult – and very important.

What it might look like: Applied Institutional Work as a Policy Science

Focusing on institutions and institutional work of global significance only begins to answer how we might make institutional work research matter; still in question is what our own research activity would look like, and how we would convert our interest and attention into impact. Earlier, we lamented the limited engagement by institutional researchers in large-scale social problems and issues. Interestingly, there have emerged conversations among organizational scholars that point to the potential for such engagement in domains as diverse as democracy (Barley, 1990; Zald & Lounsbury, 2010), financial crises (Lounsbury & Hirsch, 2010; Munir, 2011), and climate change (Hoffman & Jennings, 2015; Knox-Hayes & Levy, 2011). What these authors suggest, however, is an analytical engagement – a role for institutional scholars in *explaining* these grand institutional challenges – rather than an activist engagement. With a few exceptions (Davis, 2015; Zuckerman, 2010), even when institutional scholars have engaged with grand institutional challenges, we have tended to remain at our desks, not leaving our offices to apply our tools and insights to change the world.

We propose an alternative: an active, engaged, political program of applied institutional work research, the aim of which is not only to understand grand social challenges but to affect them and in so doing change the world. In particular, we suggest that sets of institutional scholars establish organized mechanisms through which they can intentionally and programmatically work on affecting the world's grand challenges. We noted Hinings and Greenwood's (2002: 420) argument that organizational research has failed as a 'policy science'. It is this exact failure that could provide the space and motivation for scholars to develop applied institutional work research as a policy-focused arena of discourse and action.

What we are not suggesting is that applied institutional work emulate the dominant applied social science – economics – in its research methods, political methods or epistemology. It has been suggested that the certainty with which economics research articulates its findings and prescriptions is key

to its attractiveness in policy circles – easy to follow, clear and simple prescriptions when compared with the often 'self-indulgent' and jargon-laden findings associated with institutional research, and organizational research more broadly (Starbuck, 2003; Walsh, Meyer, & Schoonhoven, 2006). Similarly, economic theory, and especially the neo-liberal variants that have dominated transnational policy organizations, is appealing to political and corporate elites in the most affluent countries because it reinforces the wisdom of the markets that are currently rewarding and maintaining those same elites. Where neo-liberal economic policy has failed, however – and those spaces are vast and growing – there exists fertile ground for an alternative policy science and an alternative scientific politics. A program of policy-focused applied institutional work research could bring to those spaces a powerful and energizing approach to the integration of research and public policy. Rather than simple prescriptions that are decontextualized and ahistorical, applied institutional work research could provide culturally, socially and historically situated policy prescriptions. And rather than echoing the assumptions and anxieties of elites, applied institutional work could provide a medium for a complex chorus of voices that would cut across social, demographic and economic divides.

Another Possibility: Institutional Work as Participatory Action Research

Although imagining institutional work research as a policy science creates exciting possibilities, another, more hands-on approach is suggested by Dover and Lawrence (2010) in their essay on applied institutional work as a foundation for participatory action research. This form of action research revolves around the co-construction of practical knowledge by researchers and community members together in cycles of research, action and reflection (Greenwood, Whyte, & Harkavy, 1993; Kemmis & McTaggart, 2005). Although, there has been almost no conversation connecting institutional work and participatory action research, important points of potential connection exist. First, both emphasize the role of agency in understanding the dynamics of social systems, especially how, when and why significant social change occurs. Both approaches adopt a view of actors as 'intelligent, creative, and purposive' (Dover & Lawrence, 2010: 308). Participatory action research, however, suggests a significant shift in the epistemology of action, replacing a view of actors and action as objects of research, to one in which the relationship between researcher and researched is a subject–subject relationship (Fals-Borda, 1991). Participants in this form of research are engaged with as competent and capable partners who participate in exploring their social worlds and realizing change (McIntyre, 2008). Participatory action research suggests a more intimate and equal relationship than is usually adopted in institutional research, with participants involved in every step of the process – identifying the research question, collecting and making sense of data, developing interventions or responses to the findings, and coming back to the theory that guided the research in order to reflect on what the findings might suggest for those ideas.

In practical terms, institutional scholars could either draw on participatory action research as a method or as an orienting perspective that forms part of their broader research philosophy. To draw on participatory action research as a method would involve using its many creative modes of engagement such as storytelling, photography, poetry, drawing, sculpture, drama and popular theatre (e.g., Ospina, Dodge, Foldy, & Hofmann-Pinilla, 2008). Such approaches might provide a powerful basis for applied institutional work research: they could facilitate engaging with the embeddedness of individuals and groups in their institutional context, facilitating their awareness of institutions

as well as a belief in their ability to affect those institutions. This first approach would thus likely open up much deeper and more varied insights into the institutions inhabited by the people we study. The second approach of engaging with the philosophy of participatory action research might provide an even more powerful foundation for applied institutional work, allowing us to bring our theoretical tools and empirical wisdom with us into the field, but then work in collaboration with members to identify our research questions, establish our goals in terms of impact and knowledge generation, and develop ways of knowing that ensure the validity of our findings is consistent with the working epistemologies of researchers and members.

Tackling Grand Challenges: A New Type of Scholarship?

In sum, thinking about grand challenges – such as slum dwelling in the global south – from an institutional work perspective is both fascinating and intimidating. The complexity of the issues involved poses profound challenges with respect to research design, data collection and analysis, skills and networks needed, and links to academic careers. Moreover, there will be important limits to what can be uncovered in individual studies, and so institutional work scholars may need to think differently about how research is funded and organized. The study of grand social challenges from multiple perspectives may also require large teams of researchers working as part of an overarching initiative rather than small groups working independently.

THE PAST, PRESENT AND FUTURE OF INSTITUTIONAL WORK RESEARCH

The first decade of institutional work research has been an exciting journey. Our image of institutions has shifted, with an increasing recognition that although institutions are powerful forces in society, they are also subject to the agency of individuals and collective actors who create, shape and disrupt them. Our conceptions of institutional agency have broadened considerably, with research documenting the complex range of long-term and day-to-day strategies through which actors craft and cope with institutional arrangements. As much as institutional work research has progressed, however, important blind spots remain. We now know a great deal about how actors shape field- and organization-level institutions, but relatively little about the institutional work associated with truly 'big' institutions that span society and wield disproportionate influence over us all. We have a growing understanding of the inhabited worlds of individuals and collective actors that engage in institutional work, but a much less developed appreciation of when, why and how networks of heterogeneous actors work together to shape institutions. Our research has described and analyzed symbolic forms of institutional work in detail, while we still know much less about relational and material work. Taken together, institutional work research is on its way towards its own adolescence but is experiencing growing pains as vital parts lag behind.

We have pointed to three sets of ideas with tremendous potential for integration into the study of institutional work: the institutional logics perspective, research on cross-sector partnerships and scholarship on the role of materiality in organization studies and sociology. More broadly, we have proposed an agenda for institutional work research that expands its aims to include contributing to efforts to address the world's grand challenges by shaping policy and practice.

The image we have in mind for applied institutional work research is inspired by the pioneering careers of Paulo Freire and Myles Horton. Freire was an educator whose ideas were rooted in his work with Brazil's 'illiterate poor' (Torres, 2014). These early experiences provided the foundation for his most influential book – the Pedagogy of the Oppressed (Freire, 2000) – which focused on the relationship between knowledge and social class, and had a profound influence on the study and practice of teaching throughout the world. Freire advocated a relationship between learners and educators based on a view of knowledge as mutually co-created. Similar in many ways, Myles Horton's ideas were inspired by his involvement in the US civil rights movement, and led to his co-founding of the Highlander Folk School, which was based on an appreciation of situated knowledge and fought against segregation within the American schooling system.

While the thinking of Freire and Horton was rooted in practice, their work also addressed fundamental theoretical issues including whether education can ever be ideologically neutral, the role of authority in education, the role of charismatic leadership in teaching and the similarities and differences between 'educating' and 'organizing' (Bell, Gaventa, & Peters, 1990). While Horton and Freire are in one sense 'extreme' examples – both were what now would probably be termed social innovators and both clashed with the authorities (Freire spent time in prison for his views, Horton was stigmatized as a communist during the McCarthy era and forced to close the school he co-founded) – they capture our imagination and offer a glimpse of what might be possible as institutional researchers if we first engage with significant institutions and social issues, and then immerse ourselves in empirical settings that we not only try to study but also work to change for the better.

Whether the agenda that we advocate can be realized in a business school world that increasingly embraces narrow metrics based on publication in a small number of elite journals is not clear. The need for management researchers to 'bridge the relevance gap' (Starkey & Madan, 2001) has been much discussed over several decades, but little progress has been made. A quick glance at the major management journals reveals only a small subset of papers that speak to significant organizational and societal issues. The anodyne nature of the so-called 'rigor versus relevance' debate has hardly helped matters.

Despite these profound and longstanding challenges, there are small signs of hope and some grounds for optimism. In the UK, 'impact' (an admittedly vague concept) is now explicitly considered when measuring the research performance of university departments, including business schools. Crucially, here 'impact' is not understood by how our research fares in journal rankings and citation counts within academia, but instead by how our studies create benefits for the world beyond academia, such as by improving society, the environment, or quality of life. Similarly, the *Academy of Management Journal* has actively encouraged the submission of manuscripts focused on issues and parts of the world that have been almost completely ignored by mainstream management research, including the 'grand challenges' of our time. And for a new generation of younger scholars there is a growing dissatisfaction with the status quo and a strong desire to promote a different type of scholarship – one that resonates more closely with the ideas discussed above.

For scholars who share the desire to employ their research to contribute to the world, we think that the theoretical apparatus provided by the concept of institutional work offers a possible way forward. The concept is rooted in practice and has a strong focus on purposive action, but at the same time it is part of an institutional perspective that seeks to understand how systems of language and meaning perpetuate social structures that work in favor of some groups and against others. We hope that organizational researchers will build on our ideas to make organizational research in general, and institutional research in particular, more engaged with issues such as poverty, inequality and the environment, and less focused on the notion of 'theoretical contribution' for its own sake.

REFERENCES

Ackermann, F., Franco, L. A., Gallupe, B., & Parent, M. (2005). GSS for multi-organizational collaboration: Reflections on process and content. *Group Decision and Negotiation*, 14(4): 307–331.

Åkerström, M. (2002). Slaps, punches, pinches – but not violence: Boundary-work in nursing homes for the elderly. *Symbolic Interaction*, 25(4): 515–536.

Arroyo, P. 2012. Management accounting change and sustainability: an institutional approach. *Journal of Accounting & Organizational Change*, 8(3): 286–309.

Albert, S., & Whetten, D. A. (1985). Organizational identity. In L. L. Cummings & B. M. Staw (Eds.), *Research in organizational behavior*, vol. 7 (pp. 263–295). Greenwich, CT: JAI Press.

Barley, S. R. (1990). The alignment of technology and structure through roles and networks. *Administrative Science Quarterly*, 35: 61–103.

Bartlett, J., Tywoniak, S., & Hatcher, C. (2007). Public relations professional practice and the institutionalisation of CSR. *Journal of Communication Management*, 11(4): 281–299.

Battilana, J., & D'Aunno, T. A. (2009). Institutional work and the paradox of embedded agency. In T. B. Lawrence, R. Suddaby, & B. Leca (Eds.), *Institutional work: Actors and agency in institutional studies of organizations* (pp. 31–58). Cambridge: Cambridge University Press.

Battilana, J., Leca, B., & Boxenbaum, E. (2009). How actors change institutions: Towards a theory of institutional entrepreneurship. *Academy of Management Annals*, 3(1): 65–107.

Bell, B., Gaventa, J., & Peters, J. (1990). *We make the road by walking: Conversations on education and social change: Myles Horton and Paulo Freire*. Philadelphia, PA: Temple University Press.

Berger, P., & Luckmann, T. (1966). *The social construction of reality: A treatise in the sociology of knowledge*. New York: Doubleday.

Bertels, S., Hoffman, A. J., & DeJordy, R. (2014). The varied work of challenger movements: Identifying challenger roles in the US environmental movement. *Organization Studies*, 35(8): 1171–1210.

Biblarz, T. J., & Gottainer, G. (2000). Family structure and children's success: A comparison of widowed and divorced single-mother families. *Journal of Marriage and Family*, 62(2): 533–548.

Biblarz, T. J., & Raftery, A. E. (1999). Family structure, educational attainment, and socioeconomic success: Rethinking the 'pathology of matriarchy'. *American Journal of Sociology*, 105(2): 321–365.

Bijker, W. E., Hughes, T. P., & Pinch, T. J. (Eds.). (2012). The social construction of technological systems: New directions in the sociology and history of technology (Anniversary). Cambridge, MA: MIT Press.

Bjerregaard, T., & Jonasson, C. (2014). Managing unstable institutional contradictions: The work of becoming. *Organization Studies*, *35*(10): 1507–1536.

Bourdieu, P. (1998). *Practical reason: On the theory of action*. Cambridge: Polity Press.

Boxenbaum, E., & Strandgaard Pedersen, J. (2009). Scandinavian institutionalism: A case of institutional work. In T. B. Lawrence, R. Suddaby, & B. Leca (Eds.), *Institutional work: Actors and agency in institutional studies of organization* (pp. 178–204). Cambridge: University of Cambridge Press.

Callon, M. (2008). Economic markets and the rise of interactive agencements: From prosthetic agencies to habilitated agencies. In T. J. Pinch & R. Swedberg (Eds.), *Living in a material world: Economic sociology meets science and technology studies* (pp. 29–56). Cambridge, MA: MIT Press.

Child, J., & McGrath, R. G. (2001). Organizations unfettered: Organizational form in an information-intensive economy. *Academy of Management Journal*, *44*(6): 1135–1148.

Clark, C. E., & Newell, S. (2013). Institutional work and complicit decoupling across the U.S. capital markets: The work of rating agencies. *Business Ethics Quarterly*, *23*(1): 7–36.

Cloutier, C., Denis, J.-L., Langley, A., & Lamothe, L. (2016). Agency at the Managerial Interface: Public Sector Reform as Institutional Work. *Journal of Public Administration Research and Theory*, *26*(2): 259.

Coule, T., & Patmore, B. (2013). Institutional Logics, Institutional Work, and Public Service Innovation in Non-Profit Organizations. *Public Administration*, *91*(4): 980–997.

Creed, W. E. D., Dejordy, R., & Lok, J. (2010). Being the change: Resolving institutional contradiction through identity work. *Academy of Management Journal*, *53*(6): 1336–1364.

Creed, W. E. D., Hudson, B. A., Okhuysen, G. A., & Smith-Crowe, K. (2014). Swimming in a sea of shame: Incorporating emotion into explanations of institutional reproduction and change. *Academy of Management Review*, *39*(3): 275–301.

Currie, G., Lockett, A., Finn, R., Martin, G., & Waring, J. (2012). Institutional work to maintain professional power: Recreating the model of medical professionalism. *Organization Studies*, *33*(7): 937–962.

Dacin, M. T., Munir, K., & Tracey, P. (2010). Formal dining at Cambridge colleges: Linking ritual performance and institutional maintenance. *Academy of Management Journal*, *53*(6): 1393–1418.

Dansou, K., & Langley, A. (2012). Institutional Work and the Notion of Test. *Management*, *15*(5): 503–527.

Daudigeos, T. (2013). In their profession's service: How staff professionals exert influence in their organization. *Journal of Management Studies*, *50*(5): 722–749.

David, R. J., Sine, W. D., & Haveman, H. A. (2013). Seizing opportunity in emerging fields: How institutional entrepreneurs legitimated the professional form of management consulting. *Organization Science*, *24*(2): 356–377.

Davis, G. F. (2015). Editorial essay: What is organizational research for? *Administrative Science Quarterly*, *60*(2): 179–188.

Davis, G. F., Diekmann, K. A., & Tinsley, C. H. (1994). The decline and fall of the conglomerate firm in the 1980s: The deinstitutionalization of an organizational form. *American Sociological Review*, *59*(4): 547–570.

De Certeau, M. (1984). *The practice of everyday life*. Berkeley, CA: University of California Press.

DiMaggio, P. J. (1988). Interest and agency in institutional theory. In L. G. Zucker (Ed.), *Institutional patterns and organizations: Culture and environment* (pp. 3–21). Cambridge, MA: Ballinger.

DiMaggio, P. J. (1991). Constructing an organizational field as a professional project: U.S. art museums, 1920–1940. In W. W. Powell & P. J. DiMaggio (Eds.), *The new institutionalism in organizational analysis* (pp. 267–292). Chicago, IL: University of Chicago Press.

DiMaggio, P. J., & Powell, W. W. (1983). The iron cage revisited: Institutional isomorphism and collective rationality in organizational fields. *American Sociological Review*, *48*(2): 147–160.

Dorado, S. (2005). Institutional entrepreneurship, partaking, and convening. *Organization Studies*, *26*(3): 385–414.

Dorado, S. (2013). Small groups as context for institutional entrepreneurship: An exploration of the emergence of commercial microfinance in Bolivia. *Organization Studies*, *34*(4): 533–557.

Dore, R. P. (2000). *Stock market capitalism: Welfare capitalism: Japan and Germany versus the Anglo-Saxons*. Oxford: Oxford University Press on Demand.

Dover, G., & Lawrence, T. B. (2010). A gap year for institutional theory: Integrating the study of institutional work and participatory action research. *Journal of Management Inquiry*, *19*(4): 305–316.

Durand, R. (2012). Advancing strategy and organization research in concert: Towards an integrated model? *Strategic Organization*, *10*(3): 297–303.

Eden, C., & Huxham, C. (2001). The negotiation of purpose in multi-organizational collaborative groups. *Journal of Management Studies, 38*(3): 373–391.

Empson, L., Cleaver, I., & Allen, J. (2013). Managing partners and management professionals: Institutional work dyads in professional partnerships. *Journal of Management Studies, 50*(5): 808–844.

Fals-Borda, O. (1991). Remaking knowledge. In O. Fals-Borda & M. Rahman (Eds.), *Action and knowledge: Breaking the monopoly with participation action-research* (pp. 146–164). New York, NY: Apex Press.

Franklin, J. S. (2016). A history of professional economists and policymaking in the United States: Irrelevant genius. New York: Routledge.

Freire, P. (2000). *Pedagogy of the oppressed*. London: Bloomsbury Publishing.

Friedland, R., & Alford, R. R. (1991). Bringing society back in: Symbols, practices, and institutional contradictions. In W. W. Powell & P. J. DiMaggio (Eds.), *The new institutionalism in organizational analysis* (pp. 232–263). Chicago, IL: University of Chicago Press.

Garud, R., Jain, S., & Kumaraswamy, A. (2002). Institutional entrepreneurship in the sponsorship of common technological standards: The case of Sun Microsystems and Java. *Academy of Management Journal, 45*(1): 196–214.

Gawer, A., & Phillips, N. (2013). Institutional work as logics shift: The case of Intel's transformation to platform leader. *Organization Studies, 34*(8): 1035–1071.

Gehman, J., Trevino, L., & Garud, R. (2013). Values work: A process study of the emergence and performance of organizational values practices. *Academy of Management Journal, 56*(1): 84–112.

Giddens, A. (1984). *The constitution of society: Outline of the theory of structuration*. Cambridge: Polity Press.

Goldberg, J. (2015) Why the 'family wars' will never end. *New York Post*. October 27. http://nypost.com/2015/10/27/why-the-family-wars-will-never-end/.

Gond, J., & Boxenbaum, E. (2013). The Glocalization of Responsible Investment: Contextualization Work in France and Québec. *Journal of Business Ethics, 115*(4): 707–721.

Goodrick, E., & Reay, T. (2010). Florence Nightingale endures: Legitimizing a new professional role identity. *Journal of Management Studies, 47*(1): 55–84.

Granqvist, N., & Gustafsson, R. (2016). Temporal institutional work. *Academy of Management Journal, 59*(3): 1009–1035.

Greenwood, D. J., Whyte, W. F., & Harkavy, I. (1993). Participatory action research as a process and as a goal. *Human Relations, 46*(2): 175–192.

Greenwood, R., Raynard, M., Kodeih, F., Micelotta, E. R., & Lounsbury, M. (2011). Institutional complexity and organizational responses. *Academy of Management Annals, 5*(1): 317–371.

Greenwood, R., & Suddaby, R. (2006a). Institutional entrepreneurship in mature fields: The big five accounting firms. *Academy of Management Journal, 49*(1): 27–48.

Greenwood, R., & Suddaby, R. (2006b). Institutional entrepreneurship in mature fields: The Big Five accounting firms. *Academy of Management Journal, 49*(1): 27–48.

Greenwood, R., Suddaby, R., & Hinings, C. R. (2002). Theorizing change: The role of professional associations in the transformation of institutionalized fields. *Academy of Management Journal, 45*(1): 58–80.

Hardy, C., Lawrence, T. B., & Grant, D. (2005). Discourse and collaboration: The role of conversations and collective identity. *Academy of Management Review, 30*(1): 58–77.

Hardy, C., & Maguire, S. (2010). Discourse, field-configuring events, and change in organizations and institutional fields: Narratives of DDT and the Stockholm Convention. *Academy of Management Journal, 53*(6): 1365–1392.

Hawkesworth, M. (2003). Congressional enactments of race–gender: Toward a theory of raced–gendered institutions. *American Political Science Review, 97*(4): 529–550.

Heaphy, E. D. (2013). Repairing breaches with rules: Maintaining institutions in the face of everyday disruptions. *Organization Science, 24*(5): 1291–1315.

Helfen, M., & Sydow, J. (2013). Negotiating as institutional work: The case of labour standards and international framework agreements. *Organization Studies, 34*(8): 1073–1098.

Helms, W. S., Oliver, C., & Webb, K. (2012). Antecedents of settlement on a new institutional practice: Negotiation of the ISO 26000 standard on social responsibility. *Academy of Management Journal, 55*(5): 1120–1145.

Hiatt, S. R., Sine, W. D., & Tolbert, P. S. (2009). From Pabst to Pepsi: The deinstitutionalization of social practices and the creation of entrepreneurial opportunities. *Administrative Science Quarterly, 54*(4): 635–667.

Hinings, C. R., & Greenwood, R. (2002). Disconnects and consequences in organization theory? *Administrative Science Quarterly, 47*(3): 411–421.

Hirsch, P. M., & Bermiss, Y. S. (2009). Institutional 'dirty' work: Preserving institutions through strategic decoupling. In T. B. Lawrence, R. Suddaby, & B. Leca (Eds.), *Institutional work: Actors and agency in institutional studies of organizations* (pp. 262–283). Cambridge: University of Cambridge Press.

Hoffman, A. J., & Jennings, P. D. (2015). Institutional theory and the natural environment research in (and on) the Anthropocene. *Organization & Environment, 28*(1): 8–31.

Huxham, C., & Vangen, S. (1996). Working together: Key themes in the management of relationships between public and non-profit organizations. *International Journal of Public Sector Management, 9*(7): 5–17.

Jarzabkowski, P., Matthiesen, J., & Van de Ven, A. H. (2009). Doing which work? A practice approach to institutional pluralism. In T. B. Lawrence, R. Suddaby, & B. Leca (Eds.), *Institutional work: Actors and agency in institutional studies of organizations* (pp. 284–315). Cambridge: University of Cambridge Press.

Jones, C., & Massa, F. G. (2013). From novel practice to consecrated exemplar: Unity Temple as a case of institutional evangelizing. *Organization Studies, 34*(8): 1099–1136.

Kemmis, S., & McTaggart, R. (2005). Participatory action research: Communicative action and the public sphere. In N. K. Denzin & Y. S. Lincoln (Eds.), *The SAGE handbook of qualitative research* (3rd ed.) (pp. 559–604). London: Sage.

Kitchener, M., & Mertz, E. (2012). Professional projects and institutional change in healthcare: The case of American dentistry. *Social Science & Medicine, 74*(3): 372–380.

Knox-Hayes, J., & Levy, D. L. (2011). The politics of carbon disclosure as climate governance. *Strategic Organization, 9*(1): 91–99.

Koschmann, M. A., Kuhn, T. R., & Pfarrer, M. D. (2012). A communicative framework of value in cross-sector partnerships. *Academy of Management Review, 37*(3): 332–354.

Kraatz, M. S., & Block, E. S. (2008). Organizational implications of institutional pluralism. In R. Greenwood, C. Oliver, R. Suddaby, & K. Sahlin-Andersson (Eds.), *The SAGE Handbook of Organizational Institutionalism* (pp. 243–275). London: Sage.

Latour, B. (1987). *Science in action: How to follow scientists and engineers through society*. Cambridge, MA: Harvard University Press.

Latour, B. (2005). *Reassembling the social: An introduction to actor-network-theory*. Oxford: Oxford University Press.

Latour, B., & Woolgar, S. (1986). *Laboratory life: The construction of scientific facts*. Princeton, NJ: Princeton University Press.

Lawrence, T. B., & Dover, G. (2015). Place and institutional work: Creating housing for the hard-to-house. *Administrative Science Quarterly, 60*(3): 371–410.

Lawrence, T. B., & Suddaby, R. (2006). Institutions and institutional work. In S. R. Clegg, C. Hardy, T. B. Lawrence, & W. R. Nord (Eds.), *Handbook of organization studies* (2nd ed.) (pp. 215–254). London: Sage.

Lawrence, T. B., Suddaby, R., & Leca, B. (2009). Introduction: Theorizing and studying institutional work. In T. B. Lawrence, R. Suddaby, & B. Leca (Eds.), *Institutional work: Actors and agency in institutional studies of organizations* (pp. 1–27). Cambridge: University of Cambridge Press.

Lee, J., & Barro, R. J. (2001). Schooling quality in a cross section of countries. *Economica, 68*(272): 465–488.

Leung, A., Zietsma, C., & Peredo, A. M. (2014). Emergent identity work and institutional change: The 'quiet' revolution of Japanese middle-class housewives. *Organization Studies, 35*(3): 423–450.

Lok, J., & De Rond, M. (2013). On the plasticity of institutions: Containing and restoring practice breakdowns at the Cambridge University Boat Club. *Academy of Management Journal, 56*(1): 185–207.

Lounsbury, M. (2007). A tale of two cities: Competing logics and practice variation in the professionalizing of mutual funds. *Academy of Management Journal, 50*: 289–307.

Lounsbury, M., & Hirsch, P. M. (2010). *Markets on trial: The economic sociology of the U.S. financial crisis*. Bingley, UK: Emerald Group.

Maguire, S., & Hardy, C. (2009). Discourse and deinstitutionalization: The decline of DDT. *Academy of Management Journal, 52*(1): 148–178.

Maguire, S., Hardy, C., & Lawrence, T. B. (2004a). Institutional entrepreneurship in emerging fields: HIV/AIDS treatment advocacy in Canada. *Academy of Management Journal, 47*(5): 657–679.

Maguire, S., Hardy, C., & Lawrence, T. B. (2004b). Institutional entrepreneurship in emerging fields: HIV/AIDS treatment advocacy in Canada. *Academy of Management Journal, 47*(5): 657–679.

Mair, J., & Marti, I. (2009). Entrepreneurship in and around institutional voids: A case study from Bangladesh. *Journal of Business Venturing, 24*(5): 419–435.

Mair, J., Marti, I., & Ventresca, M. J. (2012). Building inclusive markets in rural Bangladesh: How intermediaries work institutional voids. *Academy of Management Journal, 55*(4): 819–850.

Malsch, B., & Gendron, Y. (2013). Re-theorizing change: Institutional experimentation and the struggle for domination in the field of public accounting. *Journal of Management Studies, 50*(5): 870–899.

March, J. G., & Olsen, J. P. (1976). *Ambiguity and choice in organizations*. Bergen, Norway: Universitetsforlaget.

Martí, I., & Fernández, P. (2013). The institutional work of oppression and resistance: learning from the Holocaust. *Organization Studies*, *34*(8): 1195–1223.

Mastrofski, S., & Parks, R. B. (1990). Improving observational studies of police. *Criminology*, *28*(3): 475–496.

McIntyre, A. (2008). *Participatory action research: Qualitative research methods*. Thousand Oaks, CA: Sage.

McPherson, C. M., & Sauder, M. (2013). Logics in action: Managing institutional complexity in a drug court. *Administrative Science Quarterly*, *58*(2): 165–196.

Merton, R. K. (1968). The Matthew effect in science. *Science*, *159*(3810): 56–63.

Meyer, R. E., Höllerer, M. A., Jancsary, D., & Van Leeuwen, T. (2013). The visual dimension in organizing, organization, and organization research: Core ideas, current developments, and promising avenues. *Academy of Management Annals*, *7*(1): 489–555.

Micelotta, E. R., & Washington, M. (2013). Institutions and maintenance: The repair work of Italian professions. *Organization Studies*, *34*(8): 1137–1170.

Modell, S. (2015). Making institutional accounting research critical: dead end or new beginning? *Accounting, Auditing & Accountability Journal*, *28*(5): 773–808.

Moisander, J., & Stenfors, S. (2009). Exploring the edges of theory-practice gap: Epistemic cultures in strategy-tool development and use. *Organization*, *16*(2): 227–247.

Monteiro, P., & Nicolini, D. (2015). Recovering materiality in institutional work: Prizes as an assemblage of human and material entities. *Journal of Management Inquiry*, *24*(1): 61–81.

Munir, K. A. (2011). Financial Crisis 2008–2009: What does the silence of institutional theorists tell us? *Journal of Management Inquiry*, *20*(2): 114–117.

Munir, K. A., & Phillips, N. (2005). The birth of the 'Kodak moment': Institutional entrepreneurship and the adoption of new technologies. *Organization Studies*, *26*(11): 1665–1687.

Nicolai, A., & Seidl, D. (2010). That's relevant! Different forms of practical relevance in management science. *Organization Studies*, *31*(9-10): 1257–1285.

Nicolini, D., & Monteiro, P. (2017). The practice approach: For a praxeology of organizational and management studies. In H. Tsoukas & A. Langley (Eds.), *The SAGE Handbook of Process Organization Studies*. London: Sage.

Oliver, C. (1991). Strategic responses to institutional processes. *Academy of Management Review*, *16*(1): 145–179.

Oliver, C. (1992). The antecedents of deinstitutionalization. *Organization Studies*, *13*(4): 563–588.

Orlikowski, W. J., & Scott, S. V. (2008). Sociomateriality: Challenging the separation of technology, work and organization. *Academy of Management Annals*, *2*(1): 433–474.

Ospina, S., Dodge, J., Foldy, E. G., & Hofmann-Pinilla, A. (2008). Taking the action turn: Lessons from bringing participation to qualitative research. *The SAGE Handbook of Action Research: Participative Inquiry and Practice* (pp. 420–434). London: Sage.

Pache, A.-C., & Santos, F. (2013). Inside the hybrid organization: Selective coupling as a response to competing institutional logics. *Academy of Management Journal*, *56*(4): 972–1001.

Pallas, J., & Fredriksson, M. (2011). Providing, promoting and co-opting. *Journal of Communication Management*, *15*(2): 165–178.

Paroutis, S., & Heracleous, L. (2013). Discourse revisited: Dimensions and employment of first-order strategy discourse during institutional adoption. *Strategic Management Journal*, *34*(8): 935–956.

Peng, M. W., Wang, D. Y. L., & Jiang, Y. (2008). An institution-based view of international business strategy: a focus on emerging economies. *Journal of International Business Studies*, *39*(5): 920–936.

Perkmann, M., & Spicer, A. (2007). 'Healing the scars of history': Projects, skills and field strategies in institutional entrepreneurship. *Organization Studies*, *28*(7): 1101–1122.

Perkmann, M., & Spicer, A. (2008). How are management fashions institutionalized? The role of institutional work. *Human Relations*, *61*(6): 811–844.

Pinch, T. J. (2008). Technology and institutions: Living in a material world. *Theory and Society*, *37*(5): 461–483.

Rainelli Weiss, H., & Huault, I. (2016). Business as usual in financial markets? The creation of incommensurables as institutional maintenance work. *Organization Studies*, *37*(7): 991–1015.

Ramirez, C. (2013). 'We are being pilloried for something, we did not even know we had done wrong': Quality control and orders of worth in the British audit profession. *Journal of Management Studies*, *50*(5): 845–869.

Raviola, E., & Norbäck, M. (2013). Bringing technology and meaning into institutional work: Making news at an Italian business newspaper. *Organization Studies*, *34*(8): 1171–1194.

Reay, T., & Hinings, C. R. (2009). Managing the rivalry of competing institutional logics. *Organization Studies*, *30*(6): 629–652.

Riaz, S., Buchanan, S., & Bapuji, H. (2011). Institutional work amidst the financial crisis: Emerging positions of elite actors. *Organization*, *18*(2): 187–214.

Rojas, F. (2010a). Power through institutional work: Acquiring academic authority in the 1968 third world strike. *Academy of Management Journal,* *53*(6): 1263–1280.

Rojas, F. (2010b). Power through institutional work: Acquiring academic authority in the 1968 third world strike. *Academy of Management Journal,* *53*(6): 1263–1280.

Ruebottom, T. (2013). The microstructures of rhetorical strategy in social entrepreneurship: Building legitimacy through heroes and villains. *Journal of Business Venturing, 28*(1): 98–116.

Schatzki, T. R., Knorr-Cetina, K., & Von Savigny, E. (2001). *The practice turn in contemporary theory.* London: Psychology Press.

Schwarz, O. (2015). the sound of stigmatization: Sonic habitus, sonic styles, and boundary work in an urban slum. *American Journal of Sociology, 121*(1): 205–242.

Scott, W. R. (1995). *Institutions and organizations,* vol. 2. Thousand Oaks, CA: Sage.

Scott, W. R., Ruef, M., Caronna, C. A., & Mendel, P. J. (2000). *Institutional change and healthcare organizations: From professional dominance to managed care.* Chicago, IL: University of Chicago Press.

Seitanidi, M. M., Koufopoulos, D. N., & Palmer, P. (2010). Partnership formation for change: Indicators for transformative potential in cross sector social partnerships. *Journal of Business Ethics, 94*(1): 139–161.

Selsky, J. W., & Parker, B. (2005). Cross-sector partnerships to address social issues: Challenges to theory and practice. *Journal of Management, 31*(6): 849–873.

Seo, M.-G., & Creed, W. E. D. (2002). Institutional contradictions, praxis, and institutional change: A dialectical perspective. *Academy of Management Review, 27*(2): 222–247.

Singh, J., & Jayanti, R. K. (2013). When institutional work backfires: Organizational control of professional work in the pharmaceutical industry. *Journal of Management Studies, 50*(5): 900–929.

Slager, R., Gond, J.-P., & Moon, J. (2012). Standardization as institutional work: The regulatory power of a responsible investment standard. *Organization Studies, 33*(5-6): 763–790.

Smets, M., & Jarzabkowski, P. (2013). Reconstructing institutional complexity in practice: A relational model of institutional work and complexity. *Human Relations, 66*(10): 1279–1309.

Smets, M., Jarzabkowski, P., Burke, G. T., & Spee, P. (2015). Reinsurance trading in Lloyd's of London: Balancing conflicting-yet-complementary logics in practice. *Academy of Management Journal, 58*(3): 932–970.

Smets, M., Morris, T., & Greenwood, R. (2012). From practice to field: A multilevel model of practice-driven institutional change. *Academy of Management Journal, 55*(4): 877–904.

Sminia, H. (2011). Institutional continuity and the Dutch construction industry fiddle. *Organization Studies, 32*(11): 1559–1585.

Smothers, J., Murphy, P. J., Novicevic, M. M., & Humphreys, J. H. (2014). Institutional entrepreneurship as emancipating institutional work: James Meredith and the Integrationist Movement at Ole Miss. *Journal of Management History, 20*(1): 114–134.

Soundararajan, V., & Brammer, S. (2015). Understanding resource-deprived actors' interaction with conflicting institutional demands. *Academy of Management Proceedings,* 2015 (Meeting Abstract Supplement): 16488.

Stacey, J. (1993). Good riddance to 'the family': A response to David Popenoe. *Journal of Marriage and Family, 55*(3): 545–547.

Starbuck, W. H. (2003). The origins of organization theory. In *The Oxford Handbook of Organization Theory* (pp. 143–182). Oxford: Oxford University Press.

Starkey, K., & Madan, P. (2001). Bridging the relevance gap: Aligning stakeholders in the future of management research. *British Journal of Management, 12*(s1): S3–S26.

Stiglitz, J. E. (1999). Formal and informal institutions. In P. Dasgupta & I. Serageldin (Eds.), *Social capital: A multifaceted perspective* (pp. 59–68). Washington, DC: The World Bank.

Suddaby, R., & Viale, T. (2011). Professionals and field-level change: Institutional work and the professional project. *Current Sociology, 59*(4): 423–442.

Swidler, A. (1986). Culture in action: Symbols and strategies. *American Sociological Review,* 51(2): 273–286.

Thornton, P. H. (2002). The rise of the corporation in a craft industry: Conflict and conformity in institutional logics. *Academy of Management Journal, 45*(1): 81–101.

Thornton, P. H., Ocasio, W., & Lounsbury, M. (2012). *The institutional logics perspective: A new approach to culture, structure, and process.* Oxford: Oxford University Press.

Torres, C. A. (2014). *First Freire: Early writings in social justice education.* New York: Teachers College Press.

Toubiana, M., & Zietsma, C. (forthcoming). The message is on the wall? Emotions, social media and the dynamics of institutional complexity. *Academy of Management Journal,* doi: 2014.0208.

Tracey, P. (2016) Spreading the word: The microfoundations of institutional persuasion and conversion. *Organization Science, 27*(4): 989–1009.

Tracey, P., Phillips, N., & Jarvis, O. (2010). Bridging institutional entrepreneurship and the creation of new organizational forms: A multilevel model. *Organization Science, 22*(1): 60–80.

Tracey, P., Phillips, N., & Jarvis, O. (2011). Bridging institutional entrepreneurship and the creation of new organizational forms: A multilevel model. *Organization Science, 22*(1): 60–80.

Trank, C. Q., & Washington, M. (2009). Maintaining an institution in a contested organizational field: The work of AACSB and its constituents. In T. B. Lawrence, R. Suddaby, & B. Leca (Eds.), *Institutional work: Actors and agency in institutional studies of organizations* (pp. 236–261). Cambridge: University of Cambridge Press.

United Nations (2016). Global issues overview. www.un.org/en/globalissues/ [Accessed 31/05/16].

Upshur, R. E. G., VanDenKerkhof, E. G., & Goel, V. (2001). Meaning and measurement: an inclusive model of evidence in health care. *Journal of Evaluation in Clinical Practice, 7*(2): 91–96.

Vadera, A. K., & Aguilera, R. V. (2015). The Evolution of Vocabularies and Its Relation to Investigation of White-Collar Crimes: An Institutional Work Perspective. *Journal of Business Ethics, 128*(1): 21–38.

Van Wijk, J., Stam, W., Elfring, T., Zietsma, C., & Den Hond, F. (2013). Activists and incumbents structuring change: The interplay of agency, culture, and networks in field evolution. *Academy of Management Journal, 56*(2): 358–386.

Voronov, M., & Vince, R. (2012). Integrating emotions into the analysis of institutional work. *Academy of Management Review, 37*(1): 58–81.

Walsh, J. P., Meyer, A. D., & Schoonhoven, C. B. (2006). A future for organization theory: Living in and living with changing organizations. *Organization Science, 17*(5): 657–671.

Whittington, R. (2006). Completing the practice turn in strategy research. *Organization Studies, 27*(5): 613–634.

Wijen, F., & Ansari, S. (2007). Overcoming inaction through collective institutional entrepreneurship: Insights from regime theory. *Organization Studies, 28*(7): 1079–1100.

Wright, A., & Zammuto, R. (2013a). Creating opportunities for institutional entrepreneurship: The Colonel and the Cup in English County Cricket. *Journal of Business Venturing, 28*(1): 51–68.

Wright, A., & Zammuto, R. (2013b). Wielding the willow: Processes of institutional change in English County Cricket. *Academy of Management Journal, 56*(1): 308–330.

Wright, A., Zammuto, R., & Liesch, P. (2015). Maintaining the values of a profession: Institutional work and moral emotions in the emergency department. *Academy of Management Journal,* amj.2013.0870.

Zald, M. N., & Lounsbury, M. (2010). The Wizards of Oz: Towards an institutional approach to elites, expertise and command posts. *Organization Studies, 31*(7): 963–996.

Zhou, X. (1993). The dynamics of organizational rules. *American Journal of Sociology, 98*(5): 1134–66.

Zietsma, C., & Lawrence, T. B. (2010). Institutional work in the transformation of an organizational field: The interplay of boundary work and practice work. *Administrative Science Quarterly, 55*(2): 189–221.

Zietsma, C., & McKnight, B. (2009a). Building the iron cage: Institutional creation work in the context of competing proto-institutions. In T. B. Lawrence, R. Suddaby, & B. Leca (Eds.), *Institutional work: Actors and agency in institutional studies of organizations* (p. 143). Cambridge: Cambridge University Press.

Zietsma, C., & McKnight, B. (2009b). Building the iron cage: Institutional creation work in the context of competing proto-institutions. In T. B. Lawrence, R. Suddaby, & B. Leca (Eds.), *Institutional work: Actors and agency in institutional studies of organizations* (pp. 143–177). Cambridge: Cambridge Universisty Press.

Zilber, T. B. (2007). Stories and the discursive dynamics of institutional entrepreneurship: The case of Israeli high-tech after the bubble. *Organization Studies, 28*(7): 1035–1054.

Zilber, T. B. (2009). Institutional maintenance as narrative acts. In T. B. Lawrence, R. Suddaby, & B. Leca (Eds.), *Institutional work: Actors and agency in institutional studies of organizations* (pp. 205–235). Cambridge: University of Cambridge Press.

Zilber, T. B. (2013). Institutional logics and institutional work: Should they be agreed? In M. Lounsbury & E. Boxenbaum (Eds.), *Institutional logics in action,* vol. 39. Bingley, UK: Emerald Group.

Zuckerman, E. W. (2010). What if we had been in charge? The sociologist as builder of rational institutions. In M. Lounsbury & P. M. Hirsch (Eds.), *Markets on trial: The economic sociology of the U.S. financial crisis,* vol. B (pp. 359–378). Bingley, UK: Emerald Group.

22

Living Institutions: Bringing Emotions into Organizational Institutionalism

Jaco Lok, W.E. Douglas Creed, Rich DeJordy and Maxim Voronov

INTRODUCTION

The historical development of organizational institutionalism has been marked by the so-called cognitive turn (DiMaggio & Powell, 1991), with a particular theoretical emphasis on people as cognitive 'carriers' of taken-for-granted institutional 'schemas' or 'scripts'. This emphasis on cognition as the primary modality of institutional processes has recently been challenged as a result of a reinvigorated effort to develop institutional theory's microfoundations. This has produced a view of institutions not only as cognitively 'carried' by people in organizations, but as 'inhabited' (Hallett, 2010; Hallett & Ventresca, 2006) by people who can actively engage in the work of maintaining, creating, or disrupting institutions (Lawrence & Suddaby, 2006).

These recent developments have triggered increasing attention to a modality of institutional life that has largely been ignored in the literature on organizational institutionalism until very recently: emotions. Institutions help to make our lives orderly and predictable. They spare us the need to rethink every encounter and every situation, and they enable us to operate relatively smoothly as citizens, employees and family members. But why do we heed institutional norms and conform to institutional prescriptions? And why do we, on occasion, rebel against them and seek to transform or overthrow them? Until the recent turn to institutional theory's microfoundations, people did not figure prominently in neo-institutional research, and these kinds of questions did not arise. In fact, as we argue in this chapter, people – as opposed to 'individuals', 'actors', or 'agents' – are still largely absent from neo-institutional analysis. Our primary motivation for considering the role of emotions in institutions is therefore animated by the fundamental question that Hallett and Ventresca (2006: 214) posed to contemporary institutionalism: 'What are we to do about people?'

Over the past three decades organizational institutionalism's increasing theoretical and methodological sophistication in its treatment of institutions has not been matched by its conceptualization of people, who have traditionally been characterized in a rather flat and one-dimensional manner, either as cognitive misers driven mainly by habit, or as interest-seeking agents. In this chapter, we will prompt scholars who agree that this mismatch presents a serious theoretical challenge to consider possible paths to better understanding institutional processes as 'lived'; as animated by persons with emotions, social bonds and commitments, by persons to whom institutional arrangements matter (Sayer, 2011). In order to better understand why some people engage in particular forms of institutional work and not others, 'we need to understand how people experience the institutional arrangements that not only shape the resources available to them, but also make their lives meaningful and prime how they think and feel' (Voronov & Yorks, 2015: 579). Thus, our focus is on 'the socially embedded, interdependent, relational, and emotional nature of persons' lived experiences of institutional arrangements' (Creed, Hudson, Okhuysen, & Smith-Crowe, 2014a: 278).

A more sophisticated theoretical treatment of people in organizational institutionalism has the potential to greatly enhance our understanding of the social processes producing institutional stability and change; this project necessarily involves a systematic integration of emotions into our theorizing. In their essence, institutions condition not only how we think and what actions we consider appropriate in a particular situation, they also condition how we feel about various people, events, practices and rules in our lives. We need to study why people care about certain institutions and despise others. We need to understand how they come to not only *understand* themselves as particular kinds of institutional 'actors', but also how they come to *feel* like those actors in particular

settings, because at no time are institutions more fragile than when people no longer feel what institutions prescribe them to feel (e.g., Creed, DeJordy, & Lok, 2010).

EMOTIONALITY IN ORGANIZATIONAL INSTITUTIONALISM, 2000–2010

To be sure, our review of a broad sample of institutionalist studies published between 2000 and 2010 suggests that emotions have long been implicitly present in organizational institutionalism. Below we discuss six examples to illustrate this implicit emotionality in organizational institutionalism, prior to 2010, in addition to highlighting early work in which emotions did already feature more explicitly.

Emotions in Intra-organizational Logic Conflicts

First, in her well-known piece on a labor strike at the Atlanta Symphony Orchestra (ASO), Glynn (2000) offers a process model of how identity claims and counterclaims can shape the construction of strategic issues, and the different definitions that competing groups have of institutional identity, organizational purpose and purpose-critical core resources. While Glynn highlights her contributions to resource-based theory, her analysis has much to tell us about how emotions are implicated in the construction and embodiment of institutionalized meaning systems and how institutional hybridity can complicate this process.

Embedded in the labor conflict she analyzes was a battle over the ASO's future and over the relative importance of competing logics – on the one hand, the logic of artistry/aesthetics, and, on the other, the logic of financial stewardship. Indeed, the conflict hinged on the fact that different groups of professionals – musicians versus administrators – identified with different cultural codes and systems of values associated with these competing logics (see Brown & Humphreys, 2006 and Lok & Willmott, 2014 for very similar examples). The groups' distinct emotional attachments and commitments to competing cultural codes and institutional logics translated into divergent strategic priorities and laid the basis for conflict. Glynn's rich depiction of this conflict shows how musicians experienced nearly insurmountable feelings of 'mistrust, disillusionment, and hurt' based on their perceived denigration of their aesthetic aspirations by administrators. This fed the musicians' sense that they were not understood, appreciated or even acknowledged, and amplified their sense that the administrators and board members were enemies of artistic excellence. In the other corner, the administrators and the many professionally accomplished benefactors, who peopled the ASO board, were incensed by what they saw as unfair caricatures of them as more concerned with their social status and the prestige of board membership. They in turn came to resent the musicians for their suspiciousness, their alleged willful misunderstanding of the financial picture, and their ingratitude. Each side denied the other ratification of core features of their desired identities, as musicians committed to artistic excellence on the one hand, and, on the other, as generous, civic-minded professionals committed to the longer-term financial health of the ASO. Emotional experiences of trust or betrayal, which hinged on attributions of trustworthiness or enmity, thus figured crucially in the particular interaction order that lay at the basis of the institution's disruption, and survival.

Emotions as a Basis for Proto-Institutions

A second example of the implicit acknowledgment of the importance of emotions for institutional dynamics is Lawrence, Hardy

and Philips' (2002) study on the emergence of proto-institutions. In it, these scholars ask 'what are the characteristics of those collaborations that are associated with the production of new practices, technologies, and rules and with their initial diffusion beyond the original collaboration' (p. 283)? They find that collaborations that have highly involved partners are most likely to generate proto-institutions, where levels of involvement pertain to the ways participating organizations relate to each other as determined by: (1) the depth of interaction among participants; (2) the nature of partnership arrangements; and (3) the bilateral flow of information. While the focal actors in this particular paper are organizations, and there is little to no explicit reference to emotions, a closer reading reveals that the notion of 'high involvement' actually refers to personal connections between people at many levels of the collaborating organizations, not just between the highest status people. We can reasonably speculate that to the extent that involvement of this sort gives rise to complex relational histories, replete with emergent feelings of mutual appreciation, respect and gratitude – as opposed to the feelings of distrust, suspicion, resentment and disillusionment seen in the ASO case – they would be more likely to generate proto-institutions.

Emotions in Institutional Change

Another example of implicit emotionality in organizational institutionalism is offered by Zilber's (2002) paper on an Israeli rape crisis center, which focuses on the dialectical nature of institutionalization, found in the interaction of practices, actors and meanings. As in Glynn's paper, in Zilber's study people are depicted as more than just passive carriers of particular institutional logics; their professional and political identities are implicated in *how* they participate in institutional processes. In other words, people can engage in what ostensibly look like the same practices, but the way they *feel* about these practices and their underlying values will shape *how* they engage with them. Zilber found that although feminism was the undisputed institutional framework of the center's founders, over time dialectical processes led to the partial deinstitutionalization and diminished importance of feminism in favor of a logic of therapeutic professionalism introduced by later waves of volunteer staff.

Given the emotionally fraught nature of rape as a crime, it is perhaps ironic that emotions do not figure expressly in Zilber's framing of the dialectical process of (de)institutionalization. The word emotion itself rarely appears in the paper and, when it does, it is usually in the context of volunteers' or clients' emotional disclosures and discussion of the way emotions can figure in effective or ineffective support for rape victims. Yet, emotions nonetheless clearly animated the dialectical interplay of practices, actors and meanings, shaping how meanings were attached to practices. For example, feminist political and emotional commitments and principles drove the founding design of the center and animated its culture of sisterhood. The feminist worldview infused practices at the center with emotional commitments and understandings: for example, empathetic understandings of the victims as no different from the volunteers, the centrality of sisterhood, the focus on helping rape victims regain feelings of self-control after experiencing violence, and a logic of action that entailed accompanying the victims practically and spiritually. Yet, as the demographics of the volunteer staff changed, such feminist logics and rationales for practices, including their emotional associations, went unmentioned in trainings and other features of volunteer socialization for fear that teaching the feminist rationales for specific practices would intimidate non-feminist newcomers from the therapeutic community. Thus, driving what might be called the slippage of the feminist institutional rationales and worldview was the conflict between non-feminists' fears of

feminism and feminists' fear of intimidating the new volunteers. Hence it is not only people's own direct experience of emotions that can shape institutional processes; their anticipation of how others will emotionally or ideologically respond to their expressing of their values, or their framing of the meanings and rationales associated with practices, can also play an important role in institutional maintenance or disruption. This suggests that the 'work of meaning' does not just involve changing interpretations, understandings and shared beliefs; it also implicates sentiments, ideological and moral commitments, emotional bonds and notions of solidarity.

Emotions, Identity and Field Membership

Lawrence's (2004) work on membership dynamics within a professional field offers yet another example of how emotionally fraught identity dynamics appear in earlier theorizing of institutional processes without explicit acknowledgment of emotions as critical to these processes. Drawing extensively on Collins' notions of ritual action chains and the associated idea of accumulated emotional energy, Lawrence offers a picture of how membership in professional fields, and the nature of subject positions in that field, are products of interaction rituals that 'structure the boundaries of fields, work to distribute power differentially within fields, and consequently engender strategies of resistance on the part of those not privileged by existing conditions' (2004: 115).

Lawrence's rich depiction of resistance to marginalizing arrangements or disadvantageous stratification also reveals – largely without expressly identifying or theorizing them – how emotions, identity and membership are interrelated in ways that have implications for thinking about the role of emotions in institutional dynamics more broadly. Not only do emotions create the necessary interpersonal space within which symbolic interactions unfold, they also are factors in establishing the meaning of these interactions, as well as in animating processes of institutional structuration, reproduction and change.

Professionally based 'feeling rules' both shape members' emotional expectations for what will unfold in an encounter and trigger in them emotions consistent with those expectations. In such encounters, rule-compliant emotional performances also accentuate the boundaries between members and non-members, with implication both for inclusion in, or exclusion from, professional interactions and for relative access to material and symbolic resources. Thus, culturally appropriate emotional performances are themselves a type of symbolic resource that institutional inhabitants deploy in order to claim and enact membership. More broadly, field-appropriate emotional repertoires are a form of capital, because they serve to infuse meaning into both identity claims and legitimating accounts.

Emotionality in Legitimating Accounts

Legitimating accounts, in turn, often rely on bolstering rational appeals with emotional frames that resonate with stakeholders' own concerns or commitments. This is particularly clear in Creed, Scully and Austin's (2002) study of the legitimating accounts that were used for and against policies precluding workplace discrimination against gay, lesbian, bisexual and transgender people (GLBT), although, as in the previous examples, emotionality is rarely addressed explicitly in this paper. Creed and colleagues show how both proponents and opponents used references to societal master frames in their legitimating accounts, which served the purpose of achieving 'cultural resonance' with their respective audiences in a way that would 'inspire and legitimate' a set of preferred actions. Gay rights activists also used

individuals' stories to 'put a human face' on abstractions about discrimination during legislative hearings, in an effort to get their target audience to 'identify and empathize' with victims of discrimination based on sexual orientation. Thus, legitimating accounts are more than scripted explanations designed to enhance or preserve legitimacy; they include attempts to construct empathy and a common identity between protagonists and their audience. In the case of supporters of the Employment Non-Discrimination Act, this consisted of portraying their target audience as heroic participants in the grand tradition of civil rights; their opponents used similar rhetorical strategies to construct supporters of their cause as 'Christian soldiers'. In effect, it is emotions that change mere strings of words into meaningful narratives that inform inspired practice.

Explicit References to Emotions in Organizational Institutionalism pre-2010

Building on this recognition of the importance of emotive value-based identity claims in legitimating accounts, Suddaby and Greenwood (2005: 56) explicitly argue that '[m]ost value-based rhetoric openly appeals, directly or indirectly, to emotion'. Weber, Heinze and DeSoucey's (2008) study of the emergence of a market for grass-fed meat also explicitly links value-based motivational frames with emotional commitment: 'Pioneering grass-fed producers chose and persisted with grass-based agriculture because they obtained *emotional energy* from connecting their work to a sense of self and moral values represented in the movement's codes' (Weber et al., 2008: 543; emphasis added).

Other early explicit references to emotions in organizational institutionalism can be found in Scott (2001) and Lok (2007). Scott (2001) suggests – in a footnote – that emotions could constitute a 'fourth pillar' of institutions in addition to the regulative, normative, and cognitive pillars. In Scott's (2013) more recent edition, he changes this position by arguing that affect operates across the three pillars, and that emotions 'are among the most important motivational elements in social life' (2013: 63). Lok (2007) uses the concept of 'role distance' to incorporate an explicit affective dimension into institutionalism's understanding of the drivers of practical action. Here role distance refers to a person's degree of affective commitment to, or identification with, a role identity. Lok (2007) argues that people can continue to reproduce the status quo when they become affectively committed to existing institutional arrangements through role identification, even when the taken-for-granted nature of their social reality is disrupted. At the same time, strong role identification does not necessarily mean that people become conservative in their actions; as long as their agentic disposition remains future-oriented, strong role identification can propel them to become 'zealous activists' who are wholly committed to changing the institutional order.

These examples of institutionalist studies published between 2000 and 2010 all show that emotions have long featured in institutional explanations, although hardly ever explicitly. They play a role in identity dynamics; they feature in high involvement relationships that can form the basis of proto-institutions; they animate the dialectical interplay of practices, actors, and meanings, shaping how meanings are attached to practices; they help regulate membership dynamics in professional fields through feeling rules; they feature in value-based legitimating accounts; and they are a motivating force in institutional projects. In other words, emotions have already implicitly appeared in just about every key explanatory mechanism used in institutionalist analysis over the past four decades.

Still lacking, however, is a coherent theoretical framework through which their role can be studied more explicitly. To provide us with a basic platform for developing such a framework, we now turn to a review of the literature on the sociology of emotions in order to distill some basic premises on which the study of emotions and institutions can be based. We follow this by showing how work on emotions and institutions that has been published since 2010 has drawn on these premises to advance our understanding of institutional dynamics.

BASIC PREMISES OF INTERACTIONIST PERSPECTIVES IN THE SOCIOLOGY OF EMOTIONS

Although research explicitly engaging emotions in institutional theory is still fledgling, we find that the primacy of affective experience in social contexts has been well established in the field known as the 'sociology of emotions' (Stets & Turner, 2007b). That there has been considerable research in this line of inquiry is evident in the sheer volume of published research in sociology that explicitly incorporates emotions, and the two handbooks dedicated to the subject (Stets & Turner, 2007a, 2014). Although work on the sociology of emotions spans many theoretical camps, we leave the comprehensive review to the handbooks dedicated to the topic. Further, while a broad range of theoretical approaches have obvious implications for the study of emotions in institutions, in the interest of space, we focus our discussion on theories built upon symbolic interactionist foundations that enable attending to self-processes and their link to the construction, maintenance or disruption of social arrangements and meaning systems. These sociological theories fall into three families – identity theory, justice theory and ritual theory – though we recognize many other areas of sociological thought (particularly expectation states theory, cultural theory and affect control theory) also have much to contribute to the study of emotions in institutions.

Emotions have been studied in such disparate fields as economics, neuroscience, sociology, psychology and economics, which makes the concept of emotions difficult to define in any singular way. Some of these traditions treat the biological individual as the natural and primary unit of analysis (Ekman, 1992). For example, Elfenbein (2007) summarizes the emotion process as beginning 'with intrapersonal processes when a focal individual is exposed to an eliciting stimulus, registers the stimulus for its meaning, and experiences a feeling state and physiological changes' (p. 317). She then moves to discussing interpersonal processes, classifying them as 'downstream'. In her view, it is downstream that society – in the form of tangible interaction partners – can intervene and influence some aspects of emotional expression and experience. We believe that this approach complicates an integration of emotion into institutional analysis because it puts the cart before the horse. If before experiencing a feeling state in response to a stimulus, the person must 'register' the stimulus for its meaning, we have to ask where those registers of meaning came from. Placing society downstream implies that social context plays a limited role as either trigger or moderator, rather than as the source of the registers of meaning invoked in Elfenbein's sequence of events. Consequently, we argue that the singular biological person cannot be the primary unit of analysis, however natural it may seem (Voronov, 2014).

Instead, we proffer a more relational approach to the study of emotions and institutions (Voronov & Vince, 2012), echoing recent arguments that institutions should be seen as relational and understood as a nexus of typifications of actors, situations and behaviors (Smets & Jarzabkowski, 2013; Weber & Glynn, 2006). Hence, our decision to focus broadly on interactionist theories, and on identity theory, justice theory and ritual theory in particular, reflects their close alignment with Berger and Luckmann's (1966) micro-sociology, which has played

an important role in the development of organizational institutionalism. These scholars emphasize that institutional roles carry with them prescriptions for performances of a distinctly social nature. In addition, while any person may internalize the meaning associated with an institutional order, these meanings only become manifest or concrete in interactions with others who can employ the same system of meaning in interpreting interactions and constructing social realities. It is through such symbolic interactions that patterned behaviors become infused with symbolic meaning, constructing social reality through 'reciprocal typifications' (Berger & Luckmann, 1966).

Thus, emotions are inherently social in their nature, in their expression and in their effects (Friedland, Mohr, Roose, & Gardinali, 2014; Kemper, 1978; von Scheve, 2012). Emotions are the 'personal expression of what one is feeling in a given moment, an expression that is *structured by social convention, by culture*' (Gould, 2009: 20; emphasis added). Building on the basic premise that emotions are intersubjective in nature, our micro-sociological perspective therefore holds that emotions have a transpersonal ontology, even though they have a personal or intra-personal phenomenology (i.e., people experience them as occurring internally). This fundamental premise of the interactionist perspective underpins the three micro-sociological perspectives on emotions and social structure we discuss below.

Emotions in Sociological Theories of Identity

Throughout Stets and Trettevik's (2014) review of the role of emotions in various sociological theories of identity, we find that at the heart of each is a process entailing identity claims, efforts to elicit mutual verification or 'reciprocal ratification' of those identity claims (Goffman, 1961), and affective responses to one's success or failure in eliciting verification. Stets and Trettevik (2014: 36) assert that emotions are 'based on identity performances and the extent to which individuals think that others see them as meeting the expectations tied to a particular identity in a situation'. While on the one hand this concept of identity clearly harkens back to Mead's (1967 [1934]) concept of the 'Me', or the self as knowable object, on the other hand, the notion of situational identity 'expectations' clearly recalls Berger and Luckmann's (1966) arguments regarding the role prescriptions that make up the institutional contexts that embed and channel people's role enactments.

Considerable work has linked the verification/ratification process not only to people's emotion experiences but also to other sociological concepts, such as status (Cast et al., 1999), power and access to resources (Burke, 2008) and social structure (Stryker, 2004). For example, Stryker (2004) suggests that social structure results, in part, because the positive emotions that result when people offer reciprocal ratification of each other's identity claims and enactments encourage continued interaction. These patterns of interaction can lead to the formation of social ties among like-minded (or perhaps like-hearted) inhabitants. In contrast, the withholding of verification/ratification yields negative affective responses that can hinder the recurring interactions that give rise to enduring social ties. Both processes influence the composition and structure of personal networks, which, in turn, affect the aggregate social structure. Persons' affective responses to identity verification and non-verification are grounded in Cooley's (1964 [1902]) concepts of the 'looking glass self' and 'living in the minds of others'. He suggests that persons perpetually imagine or anticipate others' assessment of the self in ways that translate into persons' self-regulation of their behaviors in order to either avoid shame or engender pride over the acceptability of one's role enactment.

Emotions in Sociological Perspectives on Justice

The second micro-sociological perspective that links emotions and social structure are justice theories. At the core of all sociological perspectives of justice processes is a comparison between what is expected and what is experienced, and the problems that arise from disparities between the two. Here, 'expectations stem from beliefs about normative principles regarded as fair in a particular context' (Hegtvedt & Parris, 2014: 104). Departures from expectations can be in terms of the distribution of benefits or costs, consideration in decision processes or other procedures, or the civility of interactions. There are two things implicit in this basic distillation of justice processes relevant to our discussion. First, justice processes are sociological in nature; the concern is for 'just' distribution and fair procedures for decision-making *within* and *among* a group engaged in some form of interaction. Second, the 'normative principles' that ground the expectations are both *about* social interactions and created *through* social interactions. And although traditional social psychological approaches to justice suggest that the creation of expectations used to evaluate fairness are cognitive in nature (Hegdvedt & Parris, 2014), the process of performing the evaluation against those criteria is actually rooted in affective identity processes. As Scher and Heise (1993: 227) write, evaluation 'depends crucially on the affective responses arising within the interaction, and that these affective responses emerge from the way the actors perceive the role-identities held by various interactants, the definitions of the various actions, and the ways that these meanings combine in ongoing social interaction'. Thus, while what is just is often framed as cognitively determined, evaluating or experiencing something as just or unjust entails a visceral, affective experience. And such visceral experiences arise through social interactions that unfold in webs of socially constructed role-identities and meaning systems. In short, assessments of justice are highly emotional and unfold in institutional contexts.

Building on this, Hegtvedt and Parris (2014) agree that perceptions of injustice are the result of a comparison between expectations and experience, but suggest that this comparison itself is triggered by a negative affective response to some form of identity disconfirmation (of either the self or another party or parties). Thus, while in identity theory, confirmation and disconfirmations produce affective responses that are implicated in the creation of social structures, justice theories suggest they also trigger evaluation of the justness of such arrangements. These evaluations are then potentially implicated in establishing normative principles of justice and can trigger collective action toward either retributive or restorative justice under conditions of perceived injustice. The interesting distinction between identity and justice theory is that, in identity theory, it is identity verification (or lack thereof) that directly generates the affective responses. In contrast, in justice theory, the affective response stems from the subjective evaluation of identity confirmations or disconfirmations (of the self or others) as being just or unjust according to intersubjective normative prescriptions.

Ritual theory, to which we now turn, focuses more explicit attention on emotions at play in these intersubjective processes.

Emotions in Ritual Theory

While traditional views of ritual, commonly associated with anthropology, suggest that meaning and belief systems emerge from social structure and give rise to ritual, ritual theory based in micro-sociology suggests the opposite: that rituals give rise to beliefs and infuse symbols with meaning, which subsequently become manifest in social structure (see, for example, Collins, 2004). The importance of ritual theories of emotion, and

particularly Collins' theory of ritual action chains, lies in the idea that macro structures are built from chains of micro-level interaction rituals strung across time and space. Although Turner and Stets (2005) suggest that these theories, and Collins' theory in particular, claim too much for themselves when they suggest that macro structure can be explained even primarily by the accumulation of ritual action chains, ritual theories nonetheless provide important insights for theorizing the roles of emotions in institutional processes.

Central to ritual theories (following Goffman, Durkheim and Collins) is attention to the effects of how ritual interactions synchronize or provide rhythm to people's response to each other. Ritual's responsiveness and rhythm arouse emotions in the moment, potentially creating a situational emotional effervescence that enhances a sense of solidarity (Durkheim, 1965 [1912]). However, while building on Durkheim, Collins' (1981, 2004) theory of ritual action chains focuses not so much on the potentially ephemeral experience of emotional effervescence in situ. Rather, he is primarily concerned with the longer-term consequences of the accumulation of an emotional energy that persists in persons' minds and informs and even shapes their internal conversations. Here emotional energy refers to 'the feelings, sentiments, and affect that individuals mobilize in a situation' (Turner & Stets, 2005: 83). Rituals give rise to additional emotional–cultural resources through the creation of symbols that bespeak group solidarity and elevate the group relations as special and even sacred (Turner & Stets, 2005). Persons' internal conversations reproduce the emotional energy created in ritual situations, in a sense creating a personal stock of sentiments, commitments and affect that can be deployed in subsequent interactions in a manner that reproduces solidarity, shared beliefs and values, and ultimately institutional arrangements (e.g., Dacin et al., 2010; Weber et al., 2008).

In addition, as the symbols of group solidarity circulate among group members outside the confines of the ritual, they become a form of particularized cultural capital that transcends face-to-face interactions. Here, by cultural capital, Stets and Turner mean 'stored memories of previous conversations, vocal styles, special types of knowledge and expertise, rights and privileges associated with power to make decisions, and rights to receive honor' (2005: 82). This build-up of sacred cultural capital enhances the moral quality of the group itself, making deviance a kind of moral violation of what is sacred. To put this in more institutionalist language, the sacralization through symbols of the group and its emotional solidarity institutionalizes a system of sacred moral commitments in what Friedland (2013) describes as an institutional value sphere. Drawn from Weber (2002), the idea of value spheres refers to domains of social life, or 'life spheres', each of which is governed by its own 'value rationality' (Friedland, 2013:16). This transforms persons from mere cognitive carriers of institutional logics into vessels of the sacred.

In sum, we can derive three basic premises from interactionist perspectives in the sociology of emotions. First, identity claims and enactments are intrinsically emotive in that they involve processes of intersubjective self-verification or non-verification that are implicated in institutionalized social structures in a variety of ways. Second, people emotionally evaluate these social structures as either just or unjust based on intersubjective normative expectations, particularly as they pertain to their own and others' identities. And third, emotions are intersubjective in nature, rooted in rituals of interaction that are maintained through performances that are animated by accumulated emotional energies and a shared sense of value.

These premises are closely linked to the work on institutions and emotions that has been developed since 2010, which we discuss next as a basis for developing a number of theoretical insights that can be drawn from across this recent work.

TOWARDS A MORE EXPLICIT CONSIDERATION OF EMOTIONS IN ORGANIZATIONAL INSTITUTIONALISM, 2010–2016

Over the past six years an increasing number of publications in the field of organizational institutionalism has built on some of the social theoretical foundations discussed above to develop a deeper theoretical understanding of the relations between institutions, emotions and people's practice engagement in organizations. Below, we discuss some of the particular insights that this recent research has generated, against the backdrop of four common threads that we believe run through this recent work. First, we point to the general focus in this recent literature on *social* emotions, and the need to study these in specific relation to institutional context. Second, we highlight work that has focused on the role of emotions in the disciplinary power of institutions. Third, we explain how such disciplinary power relates to agency and emotions in ways that produce an understanding of institutional stability and change that is different from the traditional cognitive approach to institutions. Finally, we conclude with a discussion of recent work that reveals some of the ways in which emotions can be strategically deployed to influence institutional dynamics.

A Focus on Social Emotions in Institutional Context

In line with the above-mentioned premise regarding the intersubjective nature of emotions, a primary focus in recent work on institutions and emotions has been on the institutional antecedents and effects of what are known in the social psychology literature as 'social' and 'moral' emotions, such as guilt, shame, jealousy, envy, empathy, pride and moral indignation. These specific emotions are inherently relational in nature, in the sense that they always occur in interactions with concrete or generalized others, and are both an outcome of – and intrinsic to – the process of negotiating and settling on a particular institutional order. For example, Creed et al. (2014a) argue that to the degree that institutions rely on microfoundations that entail symbolic interaction, *social* emotions are likely to be particularly important. This is because 'social emotions are implicated in the ways people make sense of and participate in the interactions that underpin the shared enactment of institutional arrangements'. Thus, from an institutionalist perspective, emotions do not belong to, or reside within, isolated individuals, but instead, exist in interactions that are constitutive of, and structured by, institutional orders (Emirbayer, 1997; Emirbayer & Goldberg, 2005). From this perspective, a primary focus on social emotions makes sense, because it offers a natural fit with the social constructionist foundations of institutional theory.

This approach also resonates strongly with the field of cultural psychology in the sense that one of its dictums is that 'culture and psyche make each other up' (Haidt, 2012). Just as we cannot adequately study the mind while ignoring the cultural substance that structures it, we cannot adequately study institutions while ignoring emotions and desires that are rooted deep within the human mind, because these help shape the social practices that form the basis of institutions by informing *why* and *how* people engage in these practices. Hence, from our institutionalist perspective social emotions should always be studied in relation to specific institutional contexts.

Of the recent studies that explicitly consider the role of emotions in institutional dynamics, Creed, DeJordy and Lok's (2010) study of GLBT church ministers perhaps most clearly shows this intricate relation between institutions, human emotions and practice engagement. The GLBT ministers in their study strongly identified themselves with their church, framing their role as a 'Calling' that they experienced as a deeply

personal animating force. This personal identification was so strong that it led them to deny or suppress their sexual orientation, which they perceived to be normatively illegitimate in the eyes of their church. These conditions produced strong emotions, such as shame and self-hatred, so that they engaged in a variety of practices that worked to leave their churches' institutionalized heterosexism intact. However, ultimately the GLBT ministers came to experience their situations as stemming from an untenable institutional contradiction, which led them to reassess both their GLBT identities and church doctrine, thereby creating a narrative space for themselves in which their contradictory identities as ministers and GLBT people could be reconciled. This, in turn, changed the way they engaged in their practice as church ministers, transforming themselves into embodiments of emergent change in the church.

Without an attentiveness to deeply rooted emotions and desires related to identification, it would be difficult to explain why the ministers could not simply compartmentalize their identities. And without an attentiveness to the power of institutions to shape people's sense of self, it would be difficult to explain why church doctrine should produce shame and self-hatred. And, finally, without an attentiveness to the relation between institutions, emotions and practice, it would be difficult to even notice the often subtle practice changes that were informed by changed role claims and role use that resulted from the ministers' identity work. Thus, a focus on social emotions in relation to specific institutional contexts can enable a better understanding of both how and why people come to experience particular emotions, as well as how these emotions can inform their practice.

A Focus on the Role of Emotions in the Disciplinary Power of Institutions

Considering the relations between social emotions, identity and practice in this way naturally invokes questions of power and agency, which have also featured prominently in recent work on institutions and emotions. This is because emotional experiences do not merely represent reactions to institutions that are 'out there'; rather, they are complicit with the institutional work of maintaining, creating and disrupting institutions (agency), and are shaped by, and constitutive of, systems of domination (power) (Friedland, forthcoming; Thompson & Willmott, 2016). Voronov and Vince (2012) argue in this regard that socialization processes ensure that people more or less automatically produce emotions, desires and fantasies that are prescribed and valued in relation to their particular position in institutional fields. This includes both outward emotional displays, as well as relatively private emotional experiences. The resulting internalized unconscious representations of what is good and bad and right and wrong 'help to generate self-imposed limitations on behavior. ... [T]o enter and remain in a particular field, agents must exhibit a degree of tacit acceptance of and conformity with the dominant institutional order both through *thinking* and *feeling* that are *compatible* with it' (Voronov & Vince, 2012: 64–65). Similarly, Jarvis (2015) argues that '[a]dherence to norms for emotional expression is ... integral to the perpetuation of institutional arrangements, while non-normative displays of emotion threaten the stability of meaning systems'. This is evident empirically in DeJordy and Barrett's (2014) study of the first co-ed classes at the United States Naval Academy. Upon entering the academy for formal orientation with their female colleagues, the male cadets exhibited solidarity with their female classmates; however, once the upperclassmen returned, they internalized the negative affective responses carried by upperclassmen in the institution. Toubiana and Zietsma (2016) also show how institutional logics can be associated with specific emotional 'registers' that regulate the use and expression of particular emotions.

Creed et al. (2014a) argue that this power of institutions to generate self-imposed limitations on behavior, through the emotions they induce in people as well as the emotional displays they require from people, often involves shame. In theorizing a constellation of related constructs that they label the 'shame nexus', they suggest that the experience of 'felt shame' can signal a threat to valued social bonds; because the maintenance of valued social bonds is considered a key human motive, shame is a particularly powerful social emotion. Such felt shame becomes systemic and (self)-disciplinary in nature when shared rules of what constitutes shameful behavior become taken-for-granted as objectively correct and natural. As a result, 'systemic shame enlists us in ubiquitous processes of self-surveillance and self-regulation that underpin its disciplinary power' (Creed et al., 2014a: 282). Thus, from an institutional point of view, shame is not simply a personal emotion, but rather acts as a social disciplinary mechanism that connects, on an ongoing basis, a person to an institutional order through the internalization of an institutional order's rules and values, and the (self-)sanctioning of deviations from these (Creed et al., 2010; Creed et al., 2014a).

A key concept in this argument is the notion of 'value' – in Creed et al.'s (2014a) case in the form of 'valued' social bonds. Indeed, scholars have long held that as systems of meaning, institutions reify underlying associations between power and commitment to particular values (Berger & Luckmann, 1966; Stinchcombe, 1987). Friedland (2012) has recently extended this to argue that institutions align power (and resources) with a particular hierarchy of values. Emotions are always directly implicated in these in the sense that positive affective experience – like, for example, the feeling of pride – results from congruence between the value system manifest in the institution and the values with which a person or group of persons have become identified (Kraatz, 2015; Toubiana, Greenwood, & Zietsma, forthcoming). Likewise, negative affective experience results from incongruence between value expectations and actual experience of manifest values in observed practice. This can produce feelings of injustice, shame and/or other negative social emotions, such as those associated with identity non-verification. For example, Wright, Zammuto and Liesch (2015) show how emergency department physicians experienced exasperation and anger when they felt that other specialists treated patients as low-priority 'unit[s] of work'. Their feelings of injustice were directly related to the breach of the professional value that prioritizes the patient's interests, which was central to their internalized professional identity.

Thus, it is when people become identified with particular value commitments by associating positive emotions with their personal desire for value fulfillment, and/or negative emotions with their fear of losing what is valued, that value-based desires become (self-) disciplinary in nature (Voronov & Vince, 2012). In essence, institutional orders govern their participating members by channeling the members' emotional investment toward fundamental institutional ideals. Institutions acquire their objective and external appearance as people become emotionally invested in, identified with, and committed to their underlying values (Friedland, 2013). It is in this sense that 'institutions depend, both in their formation and their core, on a passionate identification' (Friedland, 2012: 593). Thus, institutions, identity and emotions are closely tied together: 'We cleave to institutional ways of doing because of the way they make us feel; indeed *we are the way they make us feel*. Institutions are not only ways of doing, but of being' (Friedland, forthcoming; emphasis added). Once people become 'passionately identified' with institutional systems of meaning and their associated value hierarchy, it becomes increasingly difficult for them to deliberate the validity of those very arrangements that endow their lives with meaning, because such deliberation

can become 'distressing, anxiety provoking, anger inducing, or even terrifying' (Voronov & Yorks, 2015: 567). For example, De Rond and Lok (2016) show how military protocol in Camp Bastion's field hospital relating to the transfer of Afghan casualties diverged from war surgeons' value commitments to the point that it made such deliberations inescapable, and led to the surgeons experiencing profoundly distressing feelings of senselessness, futility and surreality.

Siebert, Wilson and Hamilton (2016) show that the (self-)disciplinary effects of emotions in institutions are not necessarily always tied up with such extreme emotional experiences. In a departure from literature that focuses primarily on highly activated 'hot' emotions – such as shame, pride, or fear – they explore affective aspects of 'enchantment' among those entering the profession of Scottish advocates. By discussing feelings of comfort or discomfort, of unease, and 'not feeling like a member', they show how more subtle emotional experiences can also affect and effect the reproduction of the institutional order.

Thus, a second thread that connects recent work on institutions and emotions is the emphasis on the power of institutions to shape people's value commitments and related positive and negative emotions in ways that channel their self-expectations and behavioral self-regulation.

A Focus on Emotions as Resources for Agency

Yet, recent work also shows that the power of institutions to employ both shared and personal emotions as self-regulative and self-disciplinary mechanisms in the pursuit of particular institutional ideals does not necessarily mean that there is little room left for agency. Indeed, agency is only possible *through* the pursuit of particular value commitments, because it is the value commitments underlying action that make such action purposive in its orientation. In other words, power, as manifest in internalized identifications, and agency are two sides of the same coin, with emotionally fraught value commitments tying the two sides together dialectically.

In addition to value commitments as a motivating force for agency, Jarvis (2015) suggests a second way in which emotion and agency are related. He argues that even if people genuinely *feel* emotions conducive to institutionally conformant behaviors, they still need to successfully *enact* appropriate emotional displays. He argues that such agentic displays of appropriate emotions often include the feigning of amplified or diminished emotions, even when felt emotions are congruent with institutional expectations. For example, beauty therapists may exaggerate genuine feelings of happiness, compassion, or love as they attempt to emotionally bond with clients based on a market logic. This implies that effective agency requires 'emotional competence (EC)' (Voronov & Weber, 2015): an understanding and ability to work with what Velho (1992) calls a particular community's institutional 'ethos', a concept based on Bateson (1936) and Geertz (1973) to mean a social group's style of life and characteristic way of organizing emotions and emotional experiences. Groups' institutionalized ethoi vary such that groups value some emotional experiences and expressions more than others (Siebert et al., 2016; Voronov & Weber, 2015). For example, Fan and Zietsma (2016) show how, in the context of institutional pluralism, emotionally competent actors must be able to perform in accordance with the ethoi of diverse communities, especially if their institutional work is oriented at transcending different institutional logics.

Hence, the relation between the disciplinary power of institutions, agency and emotions is far from straightforward. For example, DeJordy and Barrett (2014) show how some people, whose counter-normative identity performances invoked others' efforts to shame and police them, may not respond by feeling shame and renewing their self-regulation to correct their perceived deviance. Instead, they can respond with a sense of determination to achieve a state of pride, which challenges and can even disrupt the institutionalized role prescriptions that apply to them. Further, Voronov and Vince (2012) suggest the possibility of a paradoxical combination of emotional identification with a particular institutional order and disruptive practice. This combination becomes more likely when people's emotional investment in this order is high and their cognitive investment in it is low. They argue that becoming emotionally invested in a particular institutional order need not mean that people automatically work to maintain it (see also Lok, 2007), because when their cognitive investment is low they can still engage in behaviors that can disrupt the institutional order. As an example, they refer to Andreas' (2007) study of the Chinese Cultural Revolution, which shows that Mao Zedong inspired the student rebellion that attacked the Communist Party, without losing his desire to advance communism.

A further complicating factor is that people's lived experiences cross different institutional logics, communities and organizations, which results in them becoming emotionally invested in different systems of institutional arrangements and their associated institutional projects. Voronov and Yorks (2015) argue that the variety of experiences that people have in different institutional spheres result in them developing durable investments in particular institutional arrangements that are imprinted in people's minds and internalized in the form of more or less durable dispositions. The tensions and contradictions between the different personal and institutional projects any one person is engaged in at any one time may require them to engage in identity work in order to maintain a level of narrative self-coherence. This can inform why and how people engage in practice in a way that is unique to them as a person with a particular biography (Creed et al., 2010).

When people experience institutional contradictions, this may facilitate a change in a person's consciousness 'such that the relative dominance of some institutional arrangements is no longer seen as inevitable' (Seo & Creed, 2002: 233). Voronov and Yorks (2015) suggest in this regard that people's particular lifelong experiences make them differentially capable of apprehending, reflecting on and responding to, institutional contradictions. Specifically, they propose that people who have a dialogical conception of themselves are more amenable to re-examining institutional arrangements than people who become strongly identified with particular social bonds or desired identities that guide their feelings, thoughts and actions.

Thus, the relationship between emotional identification, institutionalization and agency is very different from the way cognitive institutional theories have theorized the relationship between cognitive embeddedness, institutionalization and agency. Whereas according to the latter, room for agency is necessarily reduced through increased cognitive embeddedness that renders institutional arrangements increasingly reified and taken-for-granted (cf. Barley & Tolbert, 1997; Jepperson, 1991), this direct relationship does not necessarily apply to increased emotional identification with the institutional order. This is because the effects of emotional identification on how people participate in institutional processes and projects depends on their different abilities to apprehend tensions and contradictions between different institutional projects (Voronov & Yorks, 2015), and on their agentic disposition in any given situation (Lok, 2007). Both of these depend, in turn, on the particularities of the person's biography, making some more, and others less, predisposed to accept, or engage in, change-oriented institutional work (Tracey, 2016).

In sum, a third theme in recent research on institutions and emotions focuses on emotions as resources for animating agency, thus offering an alternative to more traditional explanations in institutional theory of people's agentic orientations that are primarily based on cognitive embeddedness (cf. Thornton, Ocasio, & Lounsbury, 2012).

A Focus on the Strategic Use of Emotions for Conversion and Mobilization

Finally, recent research has shown how emotions can be strategically deployed to mobilize others into reproductive or change-oriented action. This research suggests that when people and organizations begin to reflexively engage with institutional arrangements with an eye for changing or defending them, they can use emotions strategically to induce support for their institutional projects. For example, Zietsma and Lawrence (2010) found that environmentalist and First Nation activist groups successfully used highly emotive, dramatic language in the media as a basis for challenging established logging practices in Canada. Similarly, Herepath and Kitchener (2016) show how the UK government deployed 'pathos' in the form of shame argumentation as a rhetorical mechanism for repairing perceived breaches of the institutionalized medical values and practices in the English NHS. In two separate studies of 'conversion', both Tracey (2016) and Massa, Helms, Voronov and Wang (2016) show how the strategic use of emotion in communication and rituals are important tools for connecting and committing people to particular institutional projects. Outside the realm of evangelism, Voronov, De Clercq and Hinings (2013) found that Ontario winemakers changed the emotive content of their messaging depending on the particular audience they were communicating to. Thus, one particular way in which emotions are strategically deployed in institutional projects is as resources in shaping the discursive spaces around such projects. For example, Moisander, Hirsto and Fahy (2016) examine how actors' evoke, eclipse and divert emotional responses to shape the 'rules of understandings'. They theorize such rules as enactments of power that may inhibit or organize the publicly felt legitimacy of alternative course of actions, including the ability to entertain such alternatives as a possibility in the first place.

These tactics are also well known in social movement theory, which has shown how activists draw on different emotional repertoires and can use them strategically to elicit support for their projects (Groves, 1997; Whittier, 2001). This is because they know that emotions play an important role in the processes by which people are mobilized, participate in, or otherwise express support for, social movements (Wood, 2001). For example, Jasper (2011: 296) argues that

> [a]ny flow of action throws up a constant stream of emotions, and the more positive they are ... the more likely participants are to continue. The satisfaction of action, from the joy of fusion to the assertion of dignity – become a motivation every bit as important as a movement's stated goals.

Yet, Schüssler, Rüling and Wittneben (2014) point out that the strategic use of emotion to rally people and organizations behind the urgency and importance of a particular cause may have important unintended consequences that can actually disrupt the institutional project. They show how the use of emotions in the staging of specific climate change summits into 'high stake events' successfully attracted a larger number and variety of observer organizations, which ended up increasing the complexity of climate change negotiations to the point where they failed.

In sum, people use emotions as agentic resources in a double sense. First, they use emotions to animate and fuel their own engagement in, and level of commitment to, any particular institutional project through the value congruence they associate with it. Second, people can strategically use emotions in others to advance certain institutional projects by appealing to the ethos of a particular

audience whose support they want to elicit, regardless of the level of emotional commitment to the project they themselves may feel. These two roles of emotions in agency appear vividly in Toubiana and Zietsma's (2016) study of members' responses to the Degenerative Disease Foundation's (DDF) decision not to promote a scientifically unproven new treatment of degenerative disease. In terms of the first role, the DDF had throughout its history leveraged members' empathy and love for people who suffered from the disease to cultivate members' commitment to its projects through financial support and ongoing volunteerism. However, a crisis of commitment arose when withholding support for the unproven treatment in line with the established norms of clinical science ran afoul of members' deeply held commitment to relieving the suffering of loved ones with the disease. This decision provoked strong emotions of betrayal and anger among many members. In terms of the second role, in response, distressed members strategically used social media to leverage a shared ethos of care and suffering reduction to propel broader collective action as a basis for the strategic use of shaming and shunning tactics to try to force the organization to change its stance.

A FRAMEWORK FOR ORGANIZING DIFFERENT POSSIBLE APPROACHES TO STUDYING EMOTIONS AND INSTITUTIONS

These different roles of emotions in institutional processes suggest that they can be studied in very different ways. In an effort to draw out some of these differences more systematically, we now present a heuristic framework that can be used to organize different approaches to the study of emotions and institutions. We believe it is important to acknowledge and even celebrate different possible approaches to the study of institutions and emotions in order to avoid the false impression that we think it is, or should be, based in a uniform hegemonic paradigm. Rather, our more modest aim in this chapter is to inspire an increased sensitivity to the importance of emotions in a broad range of institutional processes, without intending to foreclose any new avenues for research. In this spirit of welcoming diversity, we suggest six different approaches to studying institutions and emotions, which are summarized in Table 22.1.

These approaches draw on different research traditions and focus on different institutional dynamics, yet we think they are not necessarily mutually exclusive. Rather, they constitute ideal-type building blocks that can be combined depending on the particular research question a researcher may be interested in. Rather than aiming to stratify research on emotions and institutions into distinct niches, the idea behind this framework is therefore to help cognitively organize a range of possible approaches.

As such, the individual cells in Table 22.1 are intended to be specific entry points into research on emotions and institutions that naturally orient the researcher to different research questions (and possibly methods) as a starting point, without foreclosing the possibility of conducting research that spans several cells. Indeed, we believe the greatest potential for significant new contributions will probably lie in efforts to combine some of the cells in Table 22.1. We are aware, for example, that the analytical distinction between institutional maintenance and institutional change may not be appropriate for certain research projects that consider them to be dialectically related (Wright et al., 2017). Likewise, we are aware that institutional maintenance or change probably often involves structural *and* agentic processes at the same time. Nevertheless, we do think that greater clarity on distinct theoretical traditions and empirical phenomena can be helpful in structuring specific future research projects.

Table 22.1 A framework for organizing different approaches to studying institutions and emotions

	Research tradition		
	---	---	---
	Structuralist *Emotions constituted in institutions*	People-centric *Emotions in response to institutions*	Strategic *Emotions as tools for institutional work*
Institutional dynamics — **Reproduction**	**I.** INSTITUTIONAL CONTROL THROUGH EMOTIVE SELF-REGULATION Studies that focus on institutional control through rationalization, subjectification and/or normalization involving emotional self-regulation in the pursuit of institutional projects	**III.** INSTITUTIONAL REPRODUCTION DESPITE NEGATIVE OR MIXED EMOTIONS Studies that focus on the ways in which people can end up maintaining the very institutional systems they feel unhappy about	**V.** EMOTIVE INSTITUTIONAL MAINTENANCE WORK Studies that focus on institutional work aimed at maintaining current institutional arrangements by actively and purposefully inducing particular emotions in target audiences
Change	**II.** SOCIETAL CHANGE THROUGH CHANGING COLLECTIVE ASPIRATIONS Studies that focus on changing collective emotions caused by broad societal changes and vice versa	**IV.** EMOTIONS AS A SOURCE OF RESISTANCE AND CHANGE Studies that focus on emotions that trigger resistance and/or change-oriented behavior in people	**VI.** EMOTIVE INSTITUTIONAL CHANGE WORK Studies that focus on institutional work aimed at changing current institutional arrangements by actively and purposefully inducing particular emotions in target audiences

Emotions as Institutional Effects: A Structuralist Approach to the Role of Emotions in Institutional Reproduction and Change

A structuralist approach to studying emotions and institutions focuses on the constitution of emotions *in* institutions, as integral to their purposive, animating force. The structuralist perspective is already well established in organizational institutionalism through the work of John Meyer and colleagues (Meyer, Boli, & Thomas, 1987; Meyer, Boli, Thomas, & Ramirez, 1997), although it appears to have increasingly faded into the background since organizational institutionalism's agentic turn in the early 1990s. This body of research has focused predominantly on broad societal changes, such as, for example, increased cultural rationalization through legal, accounting and professionalization principles that have led to the historically contingent construction of people and organizations as 'actors' who are increasingly held accountable for their agentic responsibilities (Meyer & Jepperson, 2000; Meyer et al., 1997). As such, this work shows important parallels to (post)structuralist work in Critical Management Studies that is oriented toward the processes and effects of subjectification and normalization, as informed by the work of Foucault (Covaleski et al., 1998).

When this approach is applied to the study of emotions and institutions, interesting new research possibilities immediately emerge. For example, researchers interested in institutional maintenance and reproduction (Table 22.1, Cell I) can deploy these perspectives to explore the processes through which institutions are reproduced through emotive self-regulation (e.g., Creed et al., 2014a). That is, how are institutions able to control human behavior by invoking emotions in people that ensure institutional reproduction? What social emotions play a particularly important role in this process? And what are the processes that ensure these social emotions are felt deeply enough to ensure

authentic reproduction? When drawing on the structuralist tradition in organizational institutionalism, the focus could be on what, if any, reproductive emotional effects the process of rationalization produces. When drawing on the poststructuralist tradition the focus could be on subjectification and normalization as the key processes through which people become identified with, and through, institutions (Moon, 2013).

Researchers interested in emotions and institutional change from a structuralist perspective (Table 22.1, Cell II) could focus on the way collective emotions can change due to broad societal changes. For example, contemporary Western societies have seen trends towards increasing individualism, financialization, social activism and a reduction of the relative powers of the nation-state. We strongly suspect that these trends must be having a significant impact on the collective emotions of the people living through these trends, yet we are not aware of research that explicitly focuses on these effects (for an exception, see Illouz, 2007). What are the emotional effects, for example, of the increased focus on the individual's responsibility for their happiness and success through self-help books and seminars, happiness indexes in the media, and schooling programs focused on happiness and health? And how do these emotional effects either hamper, or help fuel, these societal trends?

Another potential research path is to analyze the social construction in specific historical contexts of the dreams, hopes, or desires that animate societal changes. Just as 'actorhood' and the agentic responsibilities that come with it are historically contingent (Meyer & Jepperson, 2000), the emotions that animate such agency are likely to be as well. And if it is true that value rationality is the central driving force behind institutional dynamics (Friedland, 2012, 2013), more work is required on the specific value rationalities, and their associated emotive substance, that inform specific societal changes.

Emotions as Responses to Institutions: A People-Centric Approach to the Role of Emotions in Institutional Reproduction and Change

A second main approach that can be used to study emotions and institutions focuses on people's emotional *responses to* the disciplinary control of institutions, including emotions that can form a source of resistance to institutional arrangements. Goffman (1961: 320) famously concludes his study of a totalizing psychiatric institution by arguing that '[o]ur sense of being a person can come from being drawn into a wider social unit; our sense of selfhood can arise through the little ways in which we can resist the pull. Our status is backed by the solid buildings of the world, while our sense of identity often resides in the cracks.' Due to institutional pluralism (Berger & Luckmann, 1966) and the inevitability of practice breakdowns even in the most totalizing institutional environments (Lok & De Rond, 2013), socialization is never complete. The emotions that a people-centric approach to studying the role of emotions in institutions can therefore bring into focus are those through which people 'resist the pull' of institutions.

An obvious subclass of these emotions are those that can produce resistance to institutional arrangements, such as dissatisfaction, indignation, incredulity, moral outrage, resentment, contempt and/or envy. While 'dissatisfaction' with institutional arrangements that do not meet people's material or symbolic 'interests' is often theorized as an important trigger for resistance that can produce institutional change, we know very little about the conditions under which such dissatisfaction can mobilize resistance. When and why do some people opt to ignore, sublimate, or otherwise not act upon emotions associated with resistance and continue to reproduce the status quo, when others do not? Are some social emotions more powerful drivers of collective resistance than others?

A less obvious pathway for analyzing ways in which people 'resist the pull' is to consider the role of 'mixed emotions', the experiencing of different emotions together at the same time. Even though we all experience mixed emotions on a regular basis in relation to particular life events or choices, the phenomenon of mixed emotions has not been studied directly and explicitly in relation to institutional dynamics as far as we are aware. This is somewhat surprising given the increased recent interest in studying 'institutional complexity' (Greenwood, Raynard, Kodeih, Micelotta, & Lounsbury, 2011), which may be related to the notion of 'emotional complexity' in psychology (Grossmann, Huynh, & Ellsworth, 2016). One exception is Lok and De Rond's (2012) conference paper on the relations between institutional logics, identity and emotions, in which they focus on the sources and practice effects of the emotional tensions that Cambridge University rowers experienced in their season preparations for the annual Boat Race. They show how people can have dual self-defining loyalties (e.g., winning versus friendship), and that choosing between these two 'pulls' can be agonizing due to the guilt it invokes for betraying one of them (see Creed et al., 2010 for a similar example).

Importantly, Lok and De Rond (2012) argue that these mixed emotions are often not reducible to tensions between different institutional logics. Rather, they theorize institutional logics as 'perpetually underspecified guides, into which particular emotions are introjected depending on the particular people involved in a particular interaction sequence'. Hence, an explicit focus on the sources and effects of mixed emotions may lead to a different understanding of the ways in which institutional logics inform action. The question under what conditions people experience mixed emotions, where they come from, and how they inform practice engagement, therefore requires greater research attention.

When these types of questions are focused on institutional maintenance and reproduction

(Table 22.1, Cell III) the main issue becomes how it is possible that social emotions that produce resistance, skepticism, or doubt can sometimes paradoxically end up reproducing the status quo. For example, Voronov and Vince (2012) refer to Zizek's notion of 'false disidentification' as a basis for arguing that many forms of private and unobtrusive resistance can actually lead to a subconscious complicity in institutional reproduction (cf., Contu, 2008). On the other hand, emotions such as fear, when felt or deployed in reaction to perceived threats to the values embedded in institutions, can trigger reactions that work to promote the status quo (DeJordy, 2010; DeJordy & Barrett, 2014; Hirschman, 1991).

When the focus is on institutional change (Table 22.1, Cell IV), the main question appears more straightforward: How and which social emotions can become a source for disidentification to the point where they lead to the mobilization of resistance to institutional arrangements? Voronov and Vince (2012) point out in this regard that even when people see the current institutional order as consistent with their interests, they may not necessarily act as enthusiastic defenders of it when they are emotionally disinvested. Hence, an explicit focus on people's emotional investment in a particular order holds the promise of better understanding how institutional disruption can eventuate, even when people appear cognitively committed to preserving the status quo.

Emotions as Tools for Institutional Work: A Strategic Approach to the Role of Emotions in Institutional Reproduction and Change

Finally, a strategic approach to the role of emotions would see emotions primarily as resources or tools through which different types of institutional work can be affected or effected. Institutional work has been defined as active and purposive in nature,

strategically oriented at creating, disrupting, or maintaining institutions (Lawrence, Suddaby, & Leca, 2009). As discussed above, emotions can play an important role in these processes as they can be used to elicit support from particular target audiences. Obvious open questions in this regard are which social emotions are particularly effective in supporting particular types of institutional work, and why? What are the institutional conditions under which the strategic use of emotions in institutional work is more or less effective? And what are some of the limits of the strategic use of emotion in institutional work in relation to particular audiences, who may receive such attempts cynically instead of being open to them?

For example, when the researcher's primary interest is in processes of institutional maintenance (Table 22.1, Cell V), her focus is likely to be on the relative effectiveness, under various institutional conditions, of the purposive use of active shaming or fear in disciplining and policing, as a way of maintaining the institutional order. The purposive use of fear, or other negative social emotions, can be compared to, for example, the relative effectiveness of institutional maintenance through attempts to increase people's emotional investment in the institutional order by instilling pride (e.g., nationalism) or by invoking nostalgia.

Researchers may also want to explore the emotional substance of key concepts in institutional theory that are closely linked to the understanding of institutional reproduction, such as 'taken-for-grantedness' or 'legitimacy'. As Jepperson (1991) has pointed out 25 years ago, the phenomenology of the concept of taken-for-grantedness is ambiguous and underanalyzed, and deserves greater attention. We believe it still does. What does it actually mean, both cognitively *and* emotionally, to take something for granted, and, if taken-for-grantedness has a somatic substance, how can agentic maintenance work be deployed to induce it? Similarly, Suchman (1995) has included 'desirability' as part of his widely cited definition of legitimacy, and explicitly refers to the importance of value judgments for what he calls 'moral legitimacy'. Yet we know relatively little about what makes particular institutional arrangements *feel* more desirable than others, and what role active maintenance work plays in inducing the feeling that a current institutional order is 'desirable, proper, or appropriate' (Suchman, 1995: 574) as a basis for their perceived legitimacy.

When the primary research interest turns to institutional change (Table 22.1, Cell VI), the focus is likely to be on the relative effectiveness of different strategies for invoking positive or negative emotions that lead to collective mobilization to disrupt and change existing institutions, or create new ones. Recent research on the use of rhetoric in processes of institutional change has pointed to the importance of 'pathos' in rhetorical arguments for change, arguing that different rhetorical strategies can influence people's legitimacy assumptions on which institutions are based (e.g., Green, 2004; Green, Li, & Nohria, 2009; Harmon, Green, & Goodnight, 2015). Similarly, social movement theory has begun to pay much more explicit attention to the role of emotions in collective action for change (Goodwin, Jasper, & Polletta, 2004).

Not only do we see potential for combining these strands of research, we also see possibilities for extending them by exploring, for example, the relative effectiveness of different media strategies for creating a collective sense of injustice, fear, or even mass hysteria, as a basis for institutional change. Moreover, rather than focusing predominantly on the use of rhetorical arguments, it would be of great interest to consider the strategic use of symbols or other visual materials in inducing emotions for change (Meyer, Höllerer, Jancsary, & Van Leeuwen, 2013). The important concept in institutional theory of 'theorization' still has a very cognitive connotation, yet social change is often associated with strong emotions that are not just tied to the nature and structure of particular

rhetorical arguments or 'theories'. Rather, they also involve attempts at collective emotional identification by communicating the need for institutional change in a way that resonates with people's value commitments. Such communication often includes the use of visual images and symbols as somatic markers around which a collective mood for change can crystallize. For example, many media observers noted that the shocking image of a drowned boy on a Turkish beach in September 2015 appears to have marked a turning point in the Syrian refugee crisis in the sense that it created a greater sense of collective urgency and willingness to find a resolution. This was likely based on shared feelings of empathy that humanized the victims of the refugee crisis in a way that cut through the political stalemate that had developed (Reich & Amis, 2016). We believe that a deeper empirical and theoretical exploration of such processes holds the promise to greatly enrich our understanding of institutional disruption and change.

FINAL THOUGHTS: BEYOND THE INDIVIDUAL ACTOR AS A BASIS FOR ORGANIZATIONAL INSTITUTIONALISM'S MICROFOUNDATIONS

Building on the theoretical foundations that have been developed over the past ten years or so, the aim of the previous section was to inspire a broad range of approaches to exploring institutions as 'lived', without intending to foreclose any new avenues for research. In order to begin taking up this general invitation, we now turn to some of our own more specific thoughts on further developing this research agenda. Specifically, we call on institutional researchers to move beyond the 'individual actor' as a naturalized basis for organizational institutionalism's microfoundations. We suggest that a turn to symbolic interactions as the primary unit of analysis may be a particularly fruitful avenue for studying institutional dynamics as 'lived'. And we also draw attention to the possible use of psychoanalytic concepts as a basis for further deepening understanding of the relations between emotions and institutions.

Moving Beyond the 'Individual' in Understanding Institutions and Emotions

In our view, institutional theory challenges the assumption that persons and contexts are separable (e.g., Meyer & Jepperson, 2000). Rather, a relational conceptualization of persons and institutions has been central to institutional theory since Berger and Luckmann's (1966: 54) foundational assertion that 'institutionalization occurs whenever there is a typification of habitualized actions by types of actors'. Thus, we echo Willmott's (2011) observation that the notion of 'individual' itself is a 'socio-cultural formation' – an institution. We would therefore challenge organizational scholars to question their taken-for-granted references to, and reified use of, the 'individual level of analysis'. This is more than semantics because 'the individual level of analysis' is not simply descriptive. Rather, the term 'individual' inherently *presumes* a bounded and atomized entity, with the societal context conceived as something that impinges on and constrains its individuality. Hence, the 'individual actor' is a tacitly ideological term to the degree that it ascribes autonomy to, and atomizes people as certain kinds of 'actors' who are attributed a certain type of 'agency'. This can obscure the operation of systemic power, whereby institutions classify people into stratified actor roles and enable them to inhabit these roles by endowing them with appropriate subjective experiences of the world that animate their practice engagement.

The implication of this is that confining emotions to the intrapersonal realm that is mediated or moderated by 'external' context is not easily justifiable from an institutionalist perspective. Rather, emotions should be seen as intersubjective, as residing in transpersonal exchanges that are double embedded in systems of relationships and in institutionalized systems of meaning. This means that institutions and other persons are necessarily implicated in any one person's emotional experience. Even though this argument has been made by others (Emirbayer, 1997; Emirbayer & Goldberg, 2005), institutional theory is particularly well positioned to advance these ideas empirically through the emerging research program we have outlined in this chapter.

For example, rather than seeing emotions as originating 'inside' people and being only mediated by interpersonal and societal contextual variables (e.g., Elfenbein, 2007), institutional researchers have begun to show how certain emotions might be rooted in particular kinds of institutional logics (Toubiana & Zietsma, 2016) and institutionalized aesthetic codes (Taylor, Creed, & Hudson, 2015). Wright and colleagues (2017) also effectively use institutional theory to contextualize insights from moral psychology about emotions by linking moral emotions to professional values and institutional norms of ER physicians. Rather than being rooted in universal moral codes (Rozin et al., 1999), these moral emotions appeared to originate in the strongly internalized institutional norms pertaining to duties and obligations of emergency physicians.

To be sure, our objection to the term 'individual' does not imply a wholesale rejection of valuable insights generated by researchers in the psychological tradition. Rather, we suggest that these insights need to be thoroughly contextualized. This can open up a variety of new and important lines of inquiry that revolve around exploring how institutions shape people into particular kinds of 'individuals', the emotional conflicts and tensions that necessarily arise in this process, and how people negotiate these in practice. Thus, we think it is important to return to the notion of the person as profoundly social rather than individualized; a human being who derives a sense of self from participating in a variety of practices in different institutional spheres in which she or he is active. This redirection is of course far from new, but instead takes us back to the early work of William James (1890), whose notion of the 'social self' emphasized that people are inherently social creatures who 'have an innate propensity to get ourselves noticed, and noticed favorably, by our kind. No more fiendish punishment could be devised, were such a thing physically possible, than that one should be turned loose in society and remain absolutely unnoticed by all the members thereof.'

Focusing on Symbolic Interactions as the Primary Unit of Analysis

Analytically, such a move from the common conceptualization of people as autonomous 'individuals' to that of personhood as profoundly lived through social relations and bonds, invites refocusing on symbolic interactions as the modality through which institutional processes play themselves out. No social realities, including and perhaps especially institutional arrangements, emerge or persist without symbolic interactions. Further, the symbolic interactions that give rise to social realities unfold between and among embodied persons, which means that emotions must necessarily be implicated in all of the intersubjective processes through which institutions are lived, sustained, and changed. An analytical focus that toggles back and forth between macro-level 'institutional forces' that contextualize on the one hand, and micro-level 'agency' by institutional 'actors' on the other, essentially omits this mediating role of embodied symbolic interactions. As Hallett and Ventresca (2006) have said, for institutionalists it is not so much what people do that matters, as what they do together. And what they do

together, they do through symbolic interactions.

By focusing on what people do together in systems of social relations such as groups (Fine, 2012) or communities (Creed et al., 2014b), institutionalists will be better able to explore how persons' lived experiences unfold, their identities are constructed and systems of meaning are made knowable. Thus, we echo Creed et al's (2014b) call for more careful theorizing of the socio-emotional locations where institutions become real in the lives of persons. Our view is that it is through symbolic interactions that social emotions become manifest, and, through them, institutional processes unfold. This understanding challenges the more traditional perspective that decomposes structuration into situational mechanisms (macro to micro), action formation mechanisms (micro to micro), and transformational mechanisms (micro to macro) (Hedstrom & Swedberg, 1998; Thornton, Ocasio and Lounsbury, 2012). We believe that the latter perspective can be advanced by delving into how emotions and institutional processes are implicated and intertwined in the symbolic interactions that mediate micro–macro linkages.

Of course, the question remains, how might we engage in such an intersubjective, symbolic interactionist project? One approach may be to focus on how a community's institutional ethos – its characteristic way of organizing and manifesting emotions (Velho, 1992) – shapes interactions in ways that both affect the subjectification and self-regulation of its members, thus reproducing institutional arrangements. Two studies in the existing institutional literature, both qualitative, stand out as offering very worthy models for further developing this approach. First, Angus' (1993) ethnographic study of masculinity and the gender regime at a Christian Brothers College in Australia offers an often distressing depiction of how the fear of threatened and actual violence can operate to reproduce a culturally specific version of masculinity.

In Angus' case study, this masculinity spanned the masculinity peculiar to the boys' working class roots and the school's image of a masculinity congruent with upward mobility. At the same time, intersubjective enactments of the masculine ethos of the Christian Brothers College in its classrooms and playing fields normalized and reproduced a gender regime – with gender-based differences in 'power relations, cultural expectations and access to resources' – that legitimated the denigration, exclusion and emotional and sexual harassment of female teachers in the previously all-male school.

A second example is Dacin, Munir and Tracey's (2010) examination of dining rituals at Cambridge University. This study brings to the reader details of the ritual enactments that socialize lower-class students into the ethos and practices of British class privilege. These rituals unfold through symbolic interactions, while their effects take hold in participants' personhood, their systems of social relations, as well as the broader society. At the personal level, students become not only acclimated but co-opted into a specific institutional order, with the effect that their relations with, and self-regulation around, their families and communities of origin are changed, even to the point of creating friction among them. In addition, the students learn to master the etiquette and knowledge needed to traverse class boundaries and enter the elite strata of British society. Thus, this paper is noteworthy for its rich depiction of how symbolic interactions figure in the intertwined processes of institutional reproduction and subjectification (Cooper, Ezzamel, & Willmott, 2008; Creed et al., 2014a).

Following such examples, researchers might study the different ways the institutional ethos of any particular community can pattern encounters in ways that give life to the notion of taken-for-grantedness. At the same time, in both of these cases, we see how practices shape the conditions under which interactions unfold and the ratification of identity happens, with implications

for subjectification and subsequent identity enactments. Hence, 'personhood' that effects identity enactments is created, refined and sustained through participation in shared social practices grounded in a shared 'ethos' (Creed et al., 2014a, 2014b; Massa et al., 2016).

Studying Fantasy and Anxiety in the Context of Increased Rationalization

A different, alternative way to move beyond the individual level of analysis in organizational institutionalism is to further develop Voronov and Vince's (2012) use of psychoanalytic theory to conceptualize the relations between emotions and institutions. They argue that people may not always understand their own motives, and, as a result, their automatic and unconscious actions can 'reflect their emotional experience of coping with the anxieties and traumas associated with the ongoing work of navigating the fields in which they are embedded' (p. 61). Their references to the importance of 'anxiety' and 'fantasy' as drivers of actions that can reproduce or disrupt institutions sharply differentiate this approach from the interactionist perspective that we have predominantly drawn on throughout this chapter. This is because the latter perspective focuses primarily on concrete social emotions experienced through embodied social relations, and does not deploy the concepts of fantasy, desire and anxiety. The psychoanalytic perspective thus offers an alternative pathway for future research on emotions and institutions, which, despite its primary psychological focus, does not treat the 'individual' as primary.

Relatively few sociologists in the field of the sociology of emotions have sought to draw on the psychoanalytic tradition (see Turner, 2007 for an exception). However, the perspective is already receiving increasing attention in the field of organization studies, particularly in relation to the work of the French psychoanalyst Jacques Lacan (e.g., Driver 2009, 2014; Lok & Willmott, 2014; Thompson & Willmott, 2016; Vidaillet & Gamot, 2015). Even though this perspective may seem quite foreign to organizational institutionalism at first glance, it is important to remember that both Berger and Luckmann (1966) and Giddens (1984) explicitly pointed to the crucial role of institutions in keeping existential anxiety at bay. Berger and Luckmann (1966) consider the staving off of existential doubt and dread to be one of the primary 'nomic functions' (1966: 59) of institutions in the sense that their 'normality' serves to existentially ground us. Likewise, Giddens (1984, 1991) attributes an important existential purpose to institutions by arguing that the routinization that is central to institutionalization addresses a fundamental human psychological need for what he calls 'ontological security'. He defines this as 'confidence or trust that the natural and social worlds are as they appear to be, including the basic *existential parameters* of self and social identity' (Giddens, 1984: 375; emphasis added).

According to the psychoanalytic perspective, such 'ontological security' is very fragile, leading us to invest ourselves in fantasies that help sustain the institutional order because they hold out the impossible promise of self-closure (Lok & Willmott, 2014; Voronov & Vince, 2012). Friedland (2013) deploys a similar psychoanalytic argument when he notes that the value rationality on which institutional identification is based

never completes us; it is a *pleasurable agony* to which we aspire over and over again ... We live for those moments of possession, returning over and over to the prospect of this becoming. *Animated by desire, it is also fraught with danger that one will be destroyed*, found not worthy, able only to go through the motions, remaining untouched, untransformed and transforming nothing. (p. 44; emphasis added)

In the context of more traditional themes in organizational institutionalism we see great

potential to apply this perspective to the global trend towards increased rationalization that has been observed and theorized by John Meyer and colleagues. The unintended negative consequences of the increased prevalence of the use of ranking systems, for example, are becoming increasingly well known (e.g., Tourish & Willmott, 2015; Willmott, 2007), yet their diffusion appears to continue unabated. Not only would it be interesting to empirically explore the fantasies and related desires that help sustain them, but, perhaps more importantly, we believe empirical research is needed on the emotional *effects* of their increased diffusion. Following psychoanalytic theory, we suspect that if people continue to invest their selves into an increasingly rationalized institutional order, that this should produce a significant amount of anxiety. This is because the institutional value that appears central to the rationalization project is 'accountability', which increases the anxious feeling that one might be found 'not worthy' (Friedland, 2013). Hence, there may be an unexplored link between rationalization and the production of collective anxiety at a societal level, with possible real consequences for our understanding of the increased prevalence of clinical depression as a 'disease of modernity' (Hidaka, 2012).

This highly speculative, and probably oversimplified, link between societal rationalization, the production of anxiety and clinical depression is not meant here as a formal, fully developed proposition. Rather, it is meant to show that incorporating the psychoanalytic tradition into the study of emotions and institutions need not be a strictly abstract, theoretical exercise (cf. Lok & Willmott, 2014). Indeed, we believe that an increased focus on emotion in organizational institutionalism, including through the lens of psychoanalytic theory, can significantly increase its perceived relevance for speaking more directly to pressing societal issues and challenges, as is exemplified in recent studies on post-traumatic stress disorder

(De Rond & Lok, 2016) and degenerative disease (Toubiana & Zietsma, 2016).

CONCLUSION

In this chapter, we have advanced an 'emotionally lived' conceptualization of institutions in a modest attempt to offer an alternative to the institutionalist orthodoxy that conceives of people as fundamentally cognitive 'actors'. Rather than treating emotions as an added surface dimension that can enrich our existing understanding of what people do to, or in, institutions, we have argued that people's lived experience of institutions lies at the core of processes of institutional creation, disruption and maintenance. We therefore need to expand our understanding of how the processes and practices through which institutions are accomplished, are animated by a more complete range of human experience, particularly affective experiences, and unravel their connection to broader societal forces. With few exceptions, institutional scholars have yet to acknowledge the lived experience of people as of inherent research interest in and of itself. Yet it is only by studying this lived experience more directly that we can hope to address important questions such as 'what to do about people in institutional theory' and 'how and why people become complicit in institutional creation, maintenance, and disruption'. This is because institutions reveal themselves not through the abstract norms, rules and beliefs that we bestow on them as researchers, but, rather, through the hopes, fears and fantasies of the people who live them.

REFERENCES

Andreas, J. (2007). The structure of charismatic mobilization: A case study of rebellion during the Chinese cultural revolution. *American Sociological Review, 72,* 434–458.

Angus, L.B. (1993). Masculinity and women teachers at Christian Brothers College. *Organization Studies, 14,* 235–260.

Barley, S.R., & Tolbert, P.S. (1997). Institutionalization and structuration: Studying the links between action and institution. *Organization Studies, 18,* 93–117.

Bateson, G. (1936) *Naven.* Stanford, CA: Stanford University Press.

Berger P.L., & Luckmann, T. (1966). *The social construction of reality: A treatise in the sociology of knowledge.* New York: Doubleday.

Brown, A.D., & Humphreys, M. (2006). Organizational identity and place: A discursive exploration of hegemony and resistance. *Journal of Management Studies, 43*(2), 231–257.

Burke, P.J. (2008). Identity, social status, and emotion. In D.T. Robinson and J. Clay-Warner (Eds.), *Social structure and emotion* (pp. 69–92). Burlington: Elsevier.

Cast, A.D., Stets, J., & Burke, P.J. (1999). Does the self conform to the views of others? *Social Psychology Quarterly, 62,* 68–82.

Cherniss, C. (2010). Emotional intelligence: Toward clarification of a concept. *Industrial and Organizational Psychology, 3,* 110–126.

Collins, R. (1981). On the micro-foundations of macro-sociology. *American Journal of Sociology, 86,* 984–1014.

Collins, R. (2004) *Interaction ritual changes.* Princeton, NJ: Princeton University Press.

Contu, A. (2008). Decaf resistance – on misbehavior, cynicism, and desire in liberal workplaces. *Management Communication Quarterly, 21,* 364–379.

Cooley, C.H. (1964 [1902]) *Human nature and the social order.* New York: Schocken Books.

Cooper, D.J., Ezzamel, M., & Willmott, H. (2008). Examining institutionalization: A critical theoretic perspective. In R. Greenwood, C. Oliver, R. Suddaby, & K. Sahlin-Andersson (Eds.), *The SAGE handbook of organizational institutionalism* (pp. 673–701). London: Sage.

Covaleski, M.A., Dirsmith, M.W., Heian, J.B., & Samuel, S. (1998). The calculated and the avowed: Techniques of discipline and struggles over identity in big six public accounting firms. *Administrative Science Quarterly, 43,* 293–327.

Creed, W.E.D., DeJordy, R., & Lok, J. (2010). Being the change: Resolving institutional contradiction through identity work. *Academy of Management Journal, 53,* 1336–1364.

Creed, W.E.D., Hudson, B.A., Okhuysen, G.A., & Smith-Crowe, K. (2014a). Swimming in a sea of shame: Incorporating emotion into explanations of institutional reproduction and change. *Academy of Management Review*, *39*, 275–301.

Creed, W.E.D., Hudson B.A., Okhuysen G.A., & Smith-Crowe, K. (2014b). Institutional communities and the constitution of the self: The intersection of social bonds, institutional prescriptions, and affective commitments. *European Group for Organization Studies*, July 2014, Rotterdam, Netherlands.

Creed, W.E.D., Scully, M.A., & Austin, J.R. (2002). Clothes make the person? The tailoring of legitimating accounts and the social construction of identity. *Organization Science*, *13*, 475–496.

Dacin, M.T., Munir, K., & Tracey, P. (2010). Formal dining at Cambridge Colleges: Linking ritual performance and institutional maintenance. *Academy of Management Journal*, *53*, 1393–1418.

DeJordy, R. (2010). Institutional guardianship: The role of agency in preserving threatened institutional arrangements. Doctoral dissertation, Boston College.

DeJordy, R., & Barrett, F. (2014). Emotions in institutions: Bullying as a mechanism of institutional control. *Research on Emotions in Organizations*, *10*, 219–243.

de Rond, M., & Lok, J. (2016). Some things can never be unseen: The role of context in psychological injury at war. *Academy of Management Journal*, *59*(6), 1965–1993.

DiMaggio, P.J., & Powell, W. (1991). Introduction. In P.J. DiMaggio & W. Powell (Eds.), *The new institutionalism and organizational analysis* (pp. 1–38). Chicago, IL: University of Chicago Press.

Driver, M. (2009). Struggling with lack: A Lacanian perspective on organizational identity. *Organization Studies*, *30*(1), 55–72.

Driver, M. (2014). The stressed subject: Lack, empowerment and liberation. *Organization*, *21*(1), 90–105.

Durkheim, E. (1965 [1912]). *The elementary forms of religious life*. New York: Free Press.

Ekman, P. (1992). An argument for basic emotions. *Cognition & Emotion*, *6*, 169–200.

Elfenbein, H.A. (2007). Emotion in organizations. *Academy of Management Annals*, *1*, 315–386.

Emirbayer, M. (1997). Manifesto for a relational sociology. *American Journal of Sociology*, *103*, 281–317.

Emirbayer, M., & Goldberg, C.A. (2005). Pragmatism, Bourdieu, and collective emotions in contentious politics. *Theory and Society*, *34*, 469–518.

Fan, G.H., & Zietsma, C. (2016). Constructing a shared governance logic: The role of emotions and cognitive processes in enabling dually embedded agency. *Academy of Management Journal*. doi: 10.5465/amj.2015.0402

Fine, G.A. (2012). Group culture and the interaction order: Local sociology on the meso-level. *Annual Review of Sociology*, *38*: 159–179.

Friedland, R. (2012). Book review: Patricia H. Thornton, William Ocasio & Michael Lounsbury, The Institutional logics perspective: A new approach to culture, structure, and process. *M@n@gement*, *15*(5), 582–595.

Friedland, R. (2013). Divine institution: Max Weber's value spheres and institutional theory. *Research in the Sociology of Organizations*, 39A: 25–50.

Friedland, R. (forthcoming). Moving institutional logics forward: Emotion and meaningful material practice. *Organization Studies*.

Friedland, R., Mohr, J. W., Roose, H., & Gardinali, P. (2014). The institutional logics of love: measuring intimate life. *Theory and Society*, *43*(3-4), 333-370.

Geertz, C. (1973) *The interpretation of cultures: Selected essays*. New York: Basic Books.

Giddens, A. (1984). *The constitution of society: Outline of the theory of structuration*. Berkeley, CA: University of California Press.

Giddens, A. (1991). *Modernity and self-identity: Self and society in the late modern age*. Stanford, CA: Stanford University Press.

Glynn, M.A. (2000). When cymbals become symbols: Conflict over organizational identity within a symphony orchestra. *Organization Science*, *11*, 285–298.

Goffman, E. (1961) *Asylums. Essays on the social situation of mental patients and other inmates*. Garden City, NY: Doubleday Anchor.

Goodwin, J., Jasper, J.M., & Polletta, F. (2004) *Emotional dimensions of social movements*. London: Blackwell Publishing.

Gooty, J., Gavin, M., & Ashkanasy, N.M. (2009). Emotions research in OB: The challenges that lie ahead. *Journal of Organizational Behavior*, *30*, 833–838.

Gould, D. B. (2009). *Moving politics: Emotion and ACT UP's fight against AIDS*. University of Chicago Press.

Green, S.E. Jr. (2004). A rhetorical theory of diffusion. *Academy of Management Review*, *29*, 653–669.

Green, S.E. Jr., Li, Y., & Nohria N. (2009). Suspended in self-spun webs of significance: A rhetorical model of institutionalization and institutionally embedded agency. *Academy of Management Journal*, *52*, 11–36.

Greenwood, R., Raynard, M., Kodeih, F., Micelotta, E.R., & Lounsbury, M. (2011). Institutional complexity and organizational responses. *Academy of Management Annals*, *5*(1), 317–371.

Grossmann, I., Huynh, A.C., & Ellsworth, P.C. (2016). Emotional complexity: Clarifying definitions and cultural correlates. *Journal of Personality and Social Psychology*, *111*(6), 895–916.

Groves, J. M. (1997). *Hearts and minds: The controversy over laboratory animals*. Temple University Press.

Haidt, J. (2012). *The righteous mind: Why good people are divided by politics and religion*. New York: Penguin.

Hallett, T. (2010). The myth incarnate: Recoupling processes, turmoil, and inhabited institutions in an urban elementary school. *American Sociological Review*, 75(1), 52–74.

Hallett, T., & Ventresca, M.J. (2006). Inhabited institutions: Social interactions and organizational forms in Gouldner's): Patterns of industrial bureaucracy. *Theory and Society*, 35, 213–236.

Harmon, D.J., Green, S.E. Jr., & Goodnight, G.T. (2015). A model of rhetorical legitimation: The structure of communication and cognition underlying institutional maintenance and change. *Academy of Management Review*, 40(1), 76–95.

Hedstrom, P., & Swedberg, R. (1998). *Social mechanisms: An analytic approach to social theory*. Cambridge: Cambridge University Press.

Hegtvedt, K.A., & Parris, C.L. (2014). Emotions in justice processes. In J. Stets and J. Turner (Eds.), *Handbook of the sociology of emotions*, Volume II. New York: Springer.

Herepath, A., & Kitchener, M. (2016). When small bandages fail: The field-level repair of severe and protracted institutional breaches. *Organization Studies*, doi: p.0170840615622065.

Hidaka, B.H. (2012). Depression as a disease of modernity: Explanations for increasing prevalence. *Journal of Affective Disorders*, 140(3), 205–214

Hirschman, A.O. (1991). *The rhetoric of reaction: Perversity, futility, jeopardy*. Cambridge, MA: Harvard University Press.

Illouz, E. (2007). *Cold intimacies: The making of emotional capitalism*. Malden, MA: Polity.

James, W. (1890). *The principles of psychology*. New York: Dover.

Jarvis, L. (2015). Feigned versus felt: Feigning behaviors and the dynamics of institutional logics. *Academy of Management Review*, doi:10.5465/amr.2014.0363.

Jasper, J.M. (2011). Emotions and social movements: Twenty years of theory and research. *Annual Review of Sociology*, 37, 285–303.

Jepperson, R.L. (1991). Institutions, institutional effects, and institutionalism. In W.W. Powell & P.J. DiMaggio (Eds.), *The new institutionalism in organizational analysis* (pp. 143–163). Chicago, IL: University of Chicago Press.

Kemper, T. D. (1978). *A social interactional theory of emotions* (p. 933). New York: Wiley.

Kraatz, M.S. (2015). *Institutions and ideals: Philip Selznick's legacy for organizational studies. Research in the Sociology of Organizations*, Volume 44. Bingley, UK: Emerald.

Lawrence, T.B. (2004). Rituals and resistance: Membership dynamics in professional fields. *Human Relations*, 57, 115–143.

Lawrence, T.B., Hardy, C., & Phillips, N. (2002). Institutional effects of interorganizational collaborations: The emergence of proto-institutions. *Academy of Management Journal*, 45, 281–290.

Lawrence, T.B., & Suddaby, R. (2006). Institutions and institutional work. In R. Clegg, C. Hardy, T. B. Lawrence, & W. R. Nord (Eds.), *The SAGE handbook of organization studies* (2nd ed.) (pp. 215–254). London: Sage.

Lawrence, T.B., Suddaby, R., & Leca, B. (2009). Introduction: Theorizing and studying institutional work. In T.B. Lawrence, R. Suddaby, & B. Leca (Eds.), *Institutional work: Actors and agency in institutional studies of organizations* (pp. 1–27). Cambridge: Cambridge University Press.

Lewin, K. (1951). *Field theory in social science: Selected theoretical papers*. New York: Harper.

Lok, J. (2007). Fetishists, politicians and resistors: Role theory as a lens for understanding institutional actors. *Academy of Management Proceedings* (Meeting Abstract Supplement), 1–7.

Lok, J., & De Rond, M. (2012). The relations between institutional logics, identity and emotions. Presented at the Academy of Management Annual Meeting, Boston, 3–7 August 2012.

Lok, J., & De Rond, M. (2013). On the plasticity of institutions: Containing and restoring practice breakdowns at the Cambridge University Boat Club. *Academy of Management Journal*, 56(1), 185–207.

Lok, J., & Willmott, H. (2014). Identities and identifications in organizations: Dynamics of antipathy, deadlock, and alliance. *Journal of Management Inquiry*, 23(3), 215–230.

Massa, F., Helms, W., Voronov, M., & Wang, L. (2016). Emotions uncorked: Inspiring evangelism for the emerging practice of cool climate winemaking in Ontario. *Academy of Management Journal*, doi:10.5465/amj.2014.0092.

Masuda T., Ellsworth, P.C., Mesquita, B., Leu, J., Tanida, S., & Van de Veerdonk, E. (2008). Placing the face in context: Cultural differences in the perception of facial emotion. *Journal of Personality and Social Psychology*, 94, 365.

Mead, G.H. (1967 [1934]). *Mind, self, & society from the stand-point of a social behaviorist*. Chicago, IL: University of Chicago Press.

Meyer, J.W., Boli, J., & Thomas, G.M. (1987). *Ontology and rationalization in the western cultural account*. Beverley Hills, CA: Sage.

Meyer, J.W., Boli, G., Thomas, G.M., & Ramirez, F.O. (1997). World society and the nation-state. *American Journal of Sociology*, 103(1), 144–181.

Meyer, J.W., & Jepperson, R.L. (2000). The 'actors' of modern society: The cultural construction of social agency. *Sociological Theory, 18*, 100–120.

Meyer, R.E., Höllerer, M.A., Jancsary, D., & Van Leeuwen, T. (2013). The visual dimension in organizing, organization, and organization research: Core ideas, current developments, and promising avenues. *Academy of Management Annals, 7*(1), 489–555.

Moisander, J.K., Hirsto, H., & Fahy, K.M. (2016). Emotions in institutional work: A discursive perspective. *Organization Studies*, doi: p.0170840615613377.

Moon, D. (2013). Powerful emotions: Symbolic power and the (productive and punitive) force of collective feeling. *Theory and Society, 42*, 261–294.

Reich, J., & Amis, J. (2016). From 'cockroaches' to 'refugees': Images, emotions, and institutional change during the migration crisis. *EGOS*, Naples.

Rozin, P., Lowery, L., Imada, S., & Haidt, J. (1999). The CAD triad hypothesis: A mapping between three moral emotions (contempt, anger, disgust) and three moral codes (community, autonomy, divinity). *Journal of Personality and Social Psychology, 76*, 574–586.

Sayer, A. (2011). *Why things matter to people: Social science, values and ethical life*. Cambridge University Press.

Scher, S.J., & Heise, D.R. (1993). Affect and the perception of injustice. *Advances in Group Processes, 10*, 223–252.

Schüssler, E., Rüling, C.C., & Wittneben, B.B. (2014). On melting summits: The limitations of field-configuring events as catalysts of change in transnational climate policy. *Academy of Management Journal, 57*(1), 140–171.

Scott, W.R. (2001). *Institutions and organizations* (2nd ed.). London: Sage.

Scott, W. R. (2013). *Institutions and organizations: Ideas, interests, and identities*. Sage Publications.

Seo, M.G., & Creed, W.E.D. (2002). Institutional contradictions, praxis, and institutional change: A dialectical perspective. *Academy of Management Review, 27*, 222–247.

Siebert, S., Wilson, F., & Hamilton, J. (2016). 'Devils may sit here': The role of enchantment in institutional maintenance. *Academy of Management Journal*, doi:10.5465/amj.2014.0487.

Smets, M., & Jarzabkowski, P. (2013). Reconstructing institutional complexity in practice: A relational model of institutional work and complexity. *Human Relations, 66*(10), 1279–1309.

Suddaby, R. & Greenwood, R. (2005). Rhetorical strategies of legitimacy. *Administrative Science Quarterly, 50*(1), 35–67.

Stets, J., & Trettevik, R. (2014). Emotions in identity theory. In J. Stets & J. Turner (Eds.), *Handbook of the sociology of emotions*, Volume II. New York: Springer.

Stets, J., & Turner, J. (2007a). *Handbook of the sociology of emotions*. (*Handbooks of sociology and social research*, H. Kaplan, Ed.). New York: Springer.

Stets, J., & Turner, J. (2007b). Introduction. In J. Stets & J. Turner (Eds.), *Handbook of the sociology of emotions* (pp. 1–7). New York: Springer.

Stets, J., & Turner, J. (2014). *Handbook of the sociology of emotions*, Volume II (*Handbooks of sociology and social research*, K. DeLamater, Ed.). New York: Springer.

Stinchcombe, A. (1987). *Constructing social theories*. Chicago, IL: University of Chicago Press.

Stryker, S. (2004). Integrating emotion into identity theory. *Advances in Group Processes, 21*, 1–23.

Suchman, M.C. (1995). Managing legitimacy: Strategic and institutional approaches. *Academy of Management Review, 20*(3), 571–610.

Taylor, S.S., Creed, W.E.D., & Hudson, B.A. (2015). Institutional aesthetics: Rethinking the constraints of organizational creativity. Paper presented at the 10th Organizational Studies Summer Workshop, Chenia, Crete.

Thompson, M., & Willmott, H. (2016). The social potency of affect: Identification and power in the immanent structuring of practice. *Human Relations, 69*(2), 483-506.

Thornton, P.H., Ocasio, W., & Lounsbury, M. (2012). *The institutional logics perspective: A new approach to culture, structure, and process*. Oxford: Oxford University Press.

Toubiana, M., Greenwood, R., & Zietsma, C. (forthcoming). Beyond ethos: Outlining an alternate trajectory for emotional competence and investment. *Academy of Management Review*.

Toubiana, M., & Zietsma, C. (2016). The message is on the wall? Emotions, social media and the dynamics of institutional complexity. *Academy of Management Journal*, doi:10.5465/amj.2014.0208.

Tourish, D., & Willmott, H. (2015). In defiance of folly: Journal rankings, mindless measures and the ABS Guide. *Critical Perspectives on Accounting, 26*(1), 37–46.

Tracey, P. (2016). Spreading the word: The microfoundations of institutional persuasion and conversion. *Organization Science*, http://dx.doi.org/10.1287/orsc.2016.1061.

Turner, J.H. (2007). Psychoanalytic sociological theories and emotions. In J.E. Stets & J.H. Turner (Eds.), *Handbook of the sociology of emotions* (pp. 276–294). New York: Springer.

Turner J.H., & Stets. J.E. (2005). *The sociology of emotions*. Cambridge: Cambridge University Press.

Velho, G. (1992). Project, Emotion, and Orientation in Complex Societies. *Sociological Theory, 10*(1), 6–20.

Vidaillet, B., & Gamot, G. (2015). Working and resisting when one's workplace is under threat of being shut down: A Lacanian perspective. *Organization Studies*, doi: 10.1177/0170840615580013.

von Scheve, C. (2012). The social calibration of emotion expression: An affective basis of micro-social order. *Sociological Theory, 30*(1), 1–14.

Voronov, M. (2014). Toward a toolkit for emotionalizing institutional theory. *Research on Emotion in Organizations, 10*, 167–196.

Voronov, M., De Clercq, D., & Hinings, C.R. (2013). Institutional complexity and logic engagement: An investigation of Ontario fine wine. *Human Relations, 66*, 1563–1596.

Voronov, M., & Vince, R. (2012). Integrating emotions into the analysis of institutional work. *Academy of Management Review, 37*(1), 58–81.

Voronov, M., & Weber, K. (2015). The heart of institutions: Emotional competence and institutional actorhood. *Academy of Management Review*, doi: 10.5465/amr.2013.0458.

Voronov, M., & Yorks, L. (2015). 'Did you notice that?' Theorizing differences in the capacity to apprehend institutional contradictions. *Academy of Management Review, 40*(4), 563–586.

Weber, M. (2002). *The Protestant Ethic and the Spirit of Capitalism: and other writings*. Penguin.

Weber, K., & Glynn, M. A. (2006). Making sense with institutions: Context, thought and action in Karl Weick's theory. *Organization Studies, 27*(11), 1639–1660.

Weber, K., Heinze, K.L., & DeSoucey, M. (2008). Forage for thought: Mobilizing codes in the movement for grass-fed meat and dairy products. *Administrative Science Quarterly, 53*(3), 529–567.

Whittier, N. (2001). Emotional strategies: The collective reconstruction and display of oppositional emotions in the movement against child sexual abuse. In J. Goodwin, J.M. Jasper, & F. Polletta (Eds.), *Passionate politics: Emotions and social movements*. University of Chicago Press: 233–250.

Willmott, H. (2007). Journal list fetishism and the perversion of scholarship: Reactivity and the ABS list. *Organization, 18*(4), 429–442.

Willmott, H. (2011). 'Institutional work' for what? Problems and prospects of institutional theory. *Journal of Management Inquiry, 20*, 67–72.

Wood, E.J. (2001) The emotional benefits of insurgency in El Salvador. In J. Goodwin, J.M. Jasper, & F. Polletta (Eds.), *Passionate politics: Emotions and social movements*. University of Chicago Press: 267–281.

Wright, A.L., Zammuto, R.F., & Liesch, P.W. (2017). Maintaining the values of a profession: Institutional work and moral emotions in the emergency department. *Academy of Management Journal, 60*(1), 200–237.

Zietsma, C., & Lawrence, T.B. (2010). Institutional work in the transformation of an organizational field: The interplay of boundary work and practice work. *Administrative Science Quarterly, 55*, 189–221.

Zilber, T.B. (2002). Institutionalization as an interplay between actions, meanings, and actors: The case of a rape crisis center in israel. *Academy of Management Journal, 45*, 234–254.

23

The Material and Visual Basis of Institutions

Candace Jones, Renate E. Meyer, Dennis Jancsary and Markus A. Höllerer

Institutions have a 'relative permanence of a distinctly social sort' (Hughes, 1936: 180), which means that they are resilient social structures that provide stability and meaning to social life (Scott, 2003, 2008), influencing which organizational practices and arrangements are utilized and with what consequences (Greenwood, Oliver, Sahlin, & Suddaby, 2008). One of the most basic assumptions of institutional theory is that this relative permanence is achieved through sedimentation in a sign system that is a central resource for the social construction of reality (Berger & Luckmann, 1967). Institutional scholars have until now focused on verbal language as the primary sign system and on 'linguistic artifacts' (Czarniawska, 2008; Zucker, 1977), which does not provide a theoretical account of how other sign systems – such as the material or visual and their specific modes – create artifacts and representations, interact with ideation and, ultimately, lead to durable institutional effects. When beliefs and ideas

are made exterior and objective, they endure to influence practices and arrangements (Berger & Luckmann, 1967; Zucker, 1977). Materiality and visuality are crucial to institutions and institutional processes. On the one hand, they constitute 'embodied' aspects of all experiences, including the creation and interpretation of signs and institutions, which are bound to material properties of the sensory apparatus, such as vocal chords, retinas, the brain, etc. On the other hand, materiality and visuality are central media by which ideas, beliefs and values are expressed, shared and stored to endure over time and across space.

Materiality is the reality of our everyday life, grounded in our senses and the material properties of objects, which appear already objectified and ordered by means of vocabulary. Thus, 'language marks the coordinates of my life in society and fills that life with meaningful objects' (Berger & Luckmann, 1967: 22). Even though Berger and Luckmann recognize the crucial role of objects, they highlight them *vis-à-vis* (verbal) language. Material objects, however, preceded verbal and written texts and 'even literature societies recorded their aspirations and hopes not only in writing but in things' (MacGregor, 2010: xvi). Yet, 'materiality is an inherently polysemic concept and ... different ways of conceiving materiality matter differently in practice' (Carlile, Nicolini, Langley, & Tsoukas, 2013: 4). In short, matter has consequences. Materiality shapes not only which ideas, beliefs and values endure or decay over time, but also how they move across space. Visuality is less concerned with the actual physicality – the haptic properties – of artifacts, but instead focuses on the way material and immaterial objects are composed spatially, positioned with regard to the 'gaze' of audiences, and how aspects of, for instance, social distance, abstraction, color, or perspective are reflected in core constructs and processes to influence processes of meaning-making (Meyer, Höllerer, Jancsary, & van Leeuwen, 2013).

Although the social construction of institutions is tethered to the material world and relies on visual representations of the latter, the material and visual basis of institutions appears to be taken for granted within institutional theory. Few institutional scholars consider the material and visual representations by which humans create, stabilize and reproduce the understandings and meanings that comprise institutions and influence institutional processes (for exceptions see, e.g., Jones, Boxenbaum, & Anthony, 2013; Meyer et al., 2013). The relatively stable, shared understandings and meanings of institutions provide the contextual dynamics for organizations (Greenwood et al., 2008), circumscribing what is legitimate for whom (Suchman, 1995), which institutional logics are utilized when and by whom (Dunn & Jones, 2010; Meyer & Höllerer, 2010; Thornton, Ocasio, & Lounsbury, 2012), how ideas are theorized (Strang & Meyer, 1993) and translated as they move across contexts (Czarniawska & Joerges, 1996; Wedlin & Sahlin, Chapter 18

this volume) and which identity is salient and invoked (Glynn, Chapter 9 this volume; Jones & Massa, 2013; Kraatz & Block, Chapter 20 this volume). Institutional scholarship has rich, extensive theorizing about, and empirical studies on, these core constructs and processes; yet, how the material and visual underpin institutions and institutional processes by enabling shared meanings that move across space and endure over time, remains under-explored and under-theorized.

In this chapter, we first explore materiality and visuality in general. Subsequently, we examine how material and visual properties of artifacts influence core institutional constructs and processes such as legitimacy, institutional logics, theorization, translation and identity. Finally, we present our conclusions and offer potential directions for future research.

THE MATERIAL AND VISUAL AS BASIS AND EXPRESSION OF INSTITUTIONS

Institutional scholars have privileged the role of cognition (e.g., ideas and beliefs) and culture (e.g., shared meanings) in creating, sustaining and changing institutions (DiMaggio, 1997; Lawrence & Suddaby, 2006; Selznick, 1996). This cognitive focus is grounded in Weber, who provided a 'common start' for both North American and Scandinavian institutionalism (Czarniawska-Joerges & Joerges, 1990: 3) and likened ideas to 'switchmen', determining 'the tracks along which action has been pushed by the dynamic of interest' (Weber, 1958 [1946]: 280).

Institutions are sedimentations of social meanings, or, as Berger and Kellner (1981: 31) have put it: 'a crystallization of meanings in objective form'. This sedimentation, or crystallization, of meaning is accomplished in socially shared sign systems. Berger and Luckmann built upon Weber's and Schütz's insights that bestow upon verbal language – vocal and written signs – preeminent relevance in modern societies. For Berger and Luckmann (1967), institutions primarily rely on linguistic signification. We argue here that they, and the institutional research that follows them, are preoccupied with cognitive aspects of institutions and interpretation processes, and with linguistic artifacts. Thus, they have considerably underestimated other sign systems, especially material or visual significations, in their capacity to organize, communicate, store and transmit social meanings.

The ability to signify in shared sign systems is more than an add-on to interpretation processes. It gives objectifications the power to transcend the here and now and is central to the durability and transferability of institutions across time and space. But how the properties and features of the different sign systems, especially those other than verbal language, may impact on meanings and interpretation processes, as well as on the institutional architecture of a field or society, have been largely ignored. We argue that the workings of different modes of signification must be disentangled, if we are to understand their interplay and deepen our understanding of institutions.

Institutions and Materiality: Making Ideas and Meanings Durable and Transferable

Our knowledge and experience of the world is fundamentally material; it is mediated through our bodily senses – sight, hearing, touch, smell and taste – and the properties of objects (e.g., weight, texture, strength, rates of decay etc.). Even when institutional scholars acknowledge the material world, they place it in the service of cognitive symbolic systems. Scott (2003: 883) elaborates symbolic systems by discussing how materials enable ideas to endure and travel: '[W]riting on stone or clay is preserved longer than that on papyrus, and the latter outlasts paper, but paper can be readily transported and more widely distributed.' Material objects are not simply institutional carriers, but also boundary objects that are 'flexibly interpretative' to enable coordination among diverse social actors (Star & Griesemer, 1989; Bechky, 2003), transfer knowledge across groups (Carlile, 2002) and generate locally situated meanings from abstract knowledge (Thurk & Fine, 2003).

The interplay of human and material was first illuminated by Durkheim (1951: 313): '[I]t is not true that society is made up only of individuals; it also includes material things, which play an essential role in the common life' because [s]ocial life...is...crystallized... and fixed on material supports...and acts upon us from without'. Material artifacts enable societies to stabilize and endure over time because when a social fact is made material, i.e., becomes durable, it is no longer tied to individuals and thus it can exist across time and space. Despite the vital role of material objects, sociologists neglected materiality because they 'would rather deal with people than with things' (Berger, 1963: 1). Material objects, however, help to anchor and reproduce the culture's ideas and meanings, constraining their drift and flux; thus, materiality stabilizes and enables the institutionalization of shared ideas, values, beliefs and meanings.

Scholars of Science and Technology Studies (STS) and material culture have elaborated on Durkheim's core insight that society is mutually constituted of things and people; this insight can be applied usefully to institutions. For example, Jones, Boxenbaum and Anthony (2013) extend our understanding of institutional logics by applying insights from anthropology (e.g., exchange theory, consumption) and Science and Technology Studies (e.g., Social Construction of Technology [SCOT], Actor-Network-Theory [ANT] and textuality). Just as an object has stable networks of relations (e.g., a functioning ship has oars, sails, crew, water, wind) (Law, 2002: 95), institutions, to have relative permanence, depend upon the stable relations among ideas, people and material artifacts. A religion has a deity and beliefs, worshippers and clergy, as well as special buildings and objects. This relationality creates polyvocality and 'enables different meanings or uses' for material objects (McDonnell, 2010: 1806). By examining these relational networks, we reveal a material vocabulary, which offers important insights into the foundations of institutions and institutional dynamics (e.g., change and stability) (Jones & Vaara, 2014).

Jones, Anthony and Boxenbaum (2013) develop a framework for analyzing materiality by examining how two core dimensions of materials – their durability and transferability – influence institutional processes. Durability is a property of material artifacts (e.g., tensile and compressive strength, or rates of decay, such that reinforced concrete has stronger tensile and compressive strength and lower rates of decay than wood), but also beliefs about the durability of materials, which may be valid or invalid (e.g., e-mails are ephemeral until government agencies use them to trace our communication history). The configuration and use of material objects shape social action (Dourish & Mazmanian, 2013). The more durable material artifacts such as buildings are, the more likely they will 'give structure to social institutions, durability to social networks, [and] persistence to behavior patterns' (Gieryn, 2002: 35). Durability is not static; material artifacts not only decay, but they are also reinterpreted over time and across cultural contexts. An AIDS campaign in Ghana found that AIDS prevention ads, such as billboard or bus stops, were routinely used for either hawking goods or pasted over with other posters, such that the legibility and visuality of the message was completely disrupted. In other cases, the ads had eroded so words and images had decayed, fundamentally altering the meaning of the original ad (McDonnell, 2010). Thus, the durability or decay of materials can alter ideas and their communication.

Transferability refers to the portability or mobility of material artifacts, which influences how easily ideas are shared within groups and translated across different groups (Latour, 1986). For instance, contemporary communications systems depend on commonly shared material infrastructure that enhances transferability, such as transmitting towers for cell phones or fiber optic lines for computers, which if absent, cause communication to cease (Dourish & Mazmanian, 2013). Material artifacts, whether with the human body (e.g., voice, movement) or instruments and tools (e.g., pen, telescope or computer) provide the foundation upon, and the means by which ideas, values and meanings are expressed, shared, transmitted and stored. The symbolic – ideas, beliefs and schemas – must be made material in order to signify (Friedland, 2001). In this way, the material is the foundation for institutions and shapes key institutional processes such as how acts and actors are legitimized, how identity is evoked and invoked, which logics are stabilized and durable due to encoding into material form and how ideas are translated, theorized and transported across space and time.

Institutions and Visuality: Making the Invisible Visible

Following social semiotics (e.g., Kress & van Leeuwen, 2006; Meyer et al., 2013), the visual constitutes a specific sign system and semiotic mode. Akin to the grammar and vocabulary of verbal language, it has its own specific way of organizing, transmitting and storing meanings. As 'a socially shaped and culturally given semiotic resource for making meaning' (Kress, 2010: 79), the visual mode is part of a group, field, or society's shared stock of knowledge (e.g., Berger & Luckmann, 1967; Jewitt, 2009; Jewitt & Oyama, 2001; Schütz & Luckmann, 1973). It is, as are the institutions that it signifies, situated in particular social, cultural and ideological contexts, which implies that different eras and cultures, but also different lifespheres and institutional orders, engender distinct forms of visual expression.

More systematically, semiotic modes and their sign systems can be distinguished with regard to how they distinctively accomplish signification, how they communicate and establish relationships between the actors involved and, finally, how they merge individual signs into a coherent message. Hence, the differences between, for example, the visual, the material and the verbal mode, essentially lie in the ways in which they organize information and meaning, address audiences and connect meaningful elements within and across representations and broader discourses, rather than in the activation of particular sensory equipment. In this respect, the visual mode builds on specific characteristics that differentiate it from other sign systems, such as spatial ordering and composition (as opposed to the sequential and linear ordering of verbal language), holistic presentation and storage of information, immediacy of perception, the ability to strongly condense information, and a tendency towards polysemy. These characteristics make visual signification particularly suited to attracting attention (e.g., Bloch, 1995), creating involvement and/or detachment through an embodied perspective (Kress & van Leeuwen, 2006), eliciting or suppressing emotions (e.g., Raab, 2008; Schill, 2012), and making facticity claims by presenting its objects as 'real' (e.g., Mitchell, 1984). Moreover, visual signs grant access to those parts of a collective stock of knowledge that are primarily available in a non-discursive form.

Up until now, with very few exceptions, the reliance of institutions on sign systems other than verbal language, especially on visual signs, has, although regularly acknowledged (e.g., Cooren, Kuhn, Cornelissen, & Clark, 2011; Phillips, Lawrence, & Hardy, 2004; Phillips & Oswick, 2012), remained under-developed, and explicit elaborations are scarce. This is unfortunate, since the visual has become a dominant form of communication in society in general, and in and around organizations, in particular (e.g., Bell, Schroeder, & Warren, 2014; Kress & van Leeuwen, 2006; Mitchell, 1994), to an extent that a 'visual turn' has been proclaimed by observers (e.g., Boehm, 1994; Fellmann, 1995; Mitchell, 1994). In addition, in modern Western culture, the visual mode is currently less scrutinized than, for example, the verbal mode (e.g., Kress & van Leeuwen, 2006; Meyer et al., 2013). McQuarrie and Phillips (2005; see also Messaris, 1997), for instance, stress that claims that could not be verbalized for cultural or even legal reasons can easily be visualized without invoking sanctions. This underlines the potential of visual images and artifacts, especially in instances of change or subtle resistance.

What has increased is not only the quantity of images, in a way that we are constantly flooded with visual information in everyday life, but also the quality of what can be depicted, and how malleable visual signs have become. For instance, means for visual composition and manipulation have become ever more accessible to broader parts of society, and the Internet as a platform has furthered the widespread dissemination of 'amateur' visual discourse (e.g., Kress, 2010). When Berger and Luckmann first wrote their treatise in 1966, verbal discourse was certainly dominant; however, it is time to update institutional theory in accordance with more recent developments of today. As Meyer et al. (2013) emphasize, this may well change the way in which we understand such central topics as processes of institutionalization, legitimation, theorization and translation, institutional logics or responses to institutional complexity.

LEGITIMACY AND LEGITIMATION THROUGH MATERIAL FORM AND VISUAL REPRESENTATION

Legitimacy is a central concept in institutional thinking, dating back to Weber (1978 [1922]) and Berger and Luckmann (1967), who argue that legitimation is the process of explaining and justifying institutions: Legitimation 'explains the institutional order by ascribing cognitive validity to its objectivated meanings. Legitimation justifies the institutional order by giving a normative dignity to its practical imperatives' (1967: 111). Similarly, institutional theory has defined the concept of legitimacy as *the perceived appropriateness of an organization to a social system in terms of rules, values, norms, and definitions* (Deephouse, Bundy, Plunkett Tost, & Suchman, Chapter 1 this volume). Aldrich and Fiol (1994) differentiated between cognitive and socio-political legitimacy, whereas Suchman (1995) distinguishes between three different forms of legitimacy: Pragmatic legitimacy basically rests on evidence of usefulness; moral legitimacy requires integration with accepted norms and values. Cognitive legitimacy demands normalization through assimilation into established and taken-for-granted symbolic systems. More recently, an elaborate body of literature has focused on how legitimacy is gained and lost from a more agentic and processual perspective. Such research has focused on legitimacy judgments (e.g., Bitektine, 2011), legitimation strategies such as authorization, rationalization, moralization, narrativization, or normalization (e.g., Lefsrud & Meyer, 2012; Suddaby & Greenwood, 2005; Vaara & Tienari, 2008; van Leeuwen & Wodak, 1999).

As 'second-order objectivation of meaning' (Berger & Luckmann, 1967: 110), legitimation may be built upon the use of any conventionalized shared sign system. However, by accepting that the 'edifice of legitimation is built upon [verbal] language' (1967: 82), institutional research has hitherto failed to acknowledge how each of the forms of legitimacy can be invoked through material and visual display.

Materiality

Institutions are materially anchored (Pinch, 2008), even though Berger and Luckman focus on institutions as being legitimized – that is explained and justified – through language. We experience institutions daily through objects such as buildings (homes, schools, offices) and work implements (computers to surgical knives). Thus, our first experiences of the appropriateness and desirability of institutions is pragmatic legitimacy: being nourished, sheltered and loved. Normative legitimacy is anchored and learned materially: whether to convey food to our mouths with forks or hands and which clothing to wear for what occasions. Cognitive legitimacy is established through material objects that teach and integrate us into established sign systems, such as books that justify and explain institutions. Our argument is that the materiality of objects or practices, specifically its durability and transferability, shapes our perceptions of legitimacy and influences legitimation processes.

By materializing ideas, it heightens their perceived facticity; they are experienced as exterior and objective. For example, religious institutions materialize the ineffable God and spirit with icons; they materialize aspirations to reach the unseen and unknowable in spires for Christian churches or minarets for Muslim mosques, which not only act symbolically as conduits between heaven and earth, but also as boundary markers that locate religious buildings for adherents and the community to gather. Humans believe that materiality adds power and legitimacy to prophetic or protective words; they transcribe these words into objects and wear them to gain 'safe passage through a precarious world' (Skemer, 2006). When we perceive material objects as illegitimate, we strike at them, such as burning books deemed pornographic, destroying cultural artifacts associated with a rival legal and moral order, or banning icons to reinforce religious beliefs such as in the Protestant Reformation. By destroying the materiality of the object, we may inhibit the capacity of an idea to endure and may precipitate institutional change in belief and normative systems. Psychological experiments demonstrate that when people write down their evaluative ideas and then physically tear up their notes, they more easily alter their opinions than those who only imagine ripping up their notes (Briñol, Gascó, Petty, & Horcajo, 2013). Material culture, such as museums and building preservation, is premised on the idea that culture and institutions are irrevocably lost when the durability of material artifacts is altered or destroyed (Barthel, 1996; MacGregor, 2010). Materiality offers unique perspectives into cultural meaning and institutions beyond linguistic explanation (Hicks & Beaudry, 2010).

When material objects and practices can be transferred to other actors, they are more likely to become standards that shape the future. Certification contests, material mimicry and camouflage are three examples of material legitimation strategies. Certification authenticates that verbal or written claims correspond to material realities (e.g., the company that claims to sell organic fruits engages in the material practices of organic farming, the signature corresponds to the person signing the document). *Certification* contests are mechanisms that demonstrate the pragmatic legitimacy of material objects and their properties by authenticating and comparing claims of superior performance. For example, when cars were a new invention, the superiority of cars, as compared to horses, in terms of speed and durability had to be demonstrated. Once the superiority of cars was accepted, the features of cars that demonstrated enhanced durability such as speed and hill climbing, were compared among cars to demonstrate superiority (Rao, 1994). By comparing material objects and their features, those material objects that win certification contests are more likely to be adopted by competitors and consumers to become industry standards.

Material *mimicry* legitimates networks of people, practices and objects, which not only stabilizes understandings, but also generates normative legitimacy for new practices and objects in new industries. In the early film industry, the industry clientele were poor immigrants. To shift normative understandings of the film industry from illegitimate to legitimate, film entrepreneurs imitated the Broadway Theater's network of people (actors), ideas (stories with narratives and genres), and material and visual forms (ostentatious theaters with porticos, plush red seats and carpets). By doing so, they destabilized the normative understanding of the industry as appealing to poor immigrants who viewed films through peepboxes in warehouses and stabilized the meaning of the new film industry as a form of fine arts that is for the upper class (Jones, 2001).

Entrepreneurs may also *camouflage* – assimilating the new into the familiar – to gain cognitive legitimacy by enhancing comprehension and familiarity. For example, Edison camouflaged his electric lightbulb into the familiar forms of the gas lamp (shape of the bulb, flickering light), imitating its visual appearance and surface features to gain acceptance for the early electricity industry (Hargadon & Douglas, 2001). These surface features were taken-for-granted material and visual forms, but had completely distinct infrastructural and institutional foundations. Edison needed to 'overcome the institutions – the existing understandings and patterns of action – that had, over the fifty years of the gas industry's existence, accreted around these fundamental physical properties and now maintained the stability of the gas system' (Hargadon & Douglas, 2001: 492). These three forms of material legitimation are non-verbal explanations and justifications that legitimate new actors and practices. Since institutions are complex and materiality is both layered and relational (Dourish & Mazmanian, 2013), the coherence among material elements may be as important as their durability and transferability in influencing which type of legitimacy (e.g., pragmatic, cognitive, normative) is conferred and most successful. A critical question for future research is how relations among material artifacts and institutional contexts influence forms of legitimacy and legitimation strategies.

Visuality

Due to their ability to provide seemingly 'factual' evidence (e.g., Graves, Flesher, & Jordan, 1996), specific visual forms, like photographs or technical sketches, are highly conducive to enhancing what Berger and Luckmann (1967: 112) call 'incipient legitimation' – the most basic assertion that this is how things are, which in turn forms the foundation for self-evidence and taken-for-grantedness. Photographs, in particular, may hide persuasive statements behind a 'veil' of 'objective and neutral' representation (e.g., Kress & van Leeuwen, 2006; Mitchell, 1994), for instance in visualizations found in corporate reports (e.g., Preston, Wright, & Young, 1996). The depiction of prestigious figures (e.g., global, local, and/or historical 'heroes'), symbols (e.g., the section sign '§' to connote the power of the law, the Red Cross, or the Statue of Liberty), renowned experts (see Höllerer, Meyer, Jancsary, & Vettori, 2013), or even God and religious figures (see Carruthers & Espeland, 1991; Quattrone, 2004) embeds the idea in holistic compositions that provide non-verbal justifications and enhance the appeal of, for example, novel organizational practices. Consequently, it legitimizes both practice and organization. A normative fit is exhibited, for instance, through the material and visual aspects of dress codes (e.g., Rafaeli & Pratt, 1993). Due to their ability to connect divergent elements inconspicuously in spatial arrangements, visuals can create 'legitimacy spillovers' (e.g., Benford & Snow, 2000; Haack, Pfarrer, & Scherer, 2014; Kostova & Zaheer, 1999) from familiar, socially shared and already institutionalized values and ideologies (e.g., modern working standards) to the new and/or potentially problematic (e.g., new employment laws), and are, therefore, uniquely suited to increase the familiarity and comprehensibility required for cognitive

legitimacy (e.g., Höllerer et al., 2013; Rämö, 2011). The same is true for illegitimacy spillovers, when objects are brought in relation to illegitimate objects or practices (e.g., delegitimating abortion practices through horrifying imagery) (e.g., Lefsrud, Graves, & Phillips, 2013).

More recently, attempts have been made to connect legitimacy to affection and aesthetics. Meyer et al. (2013) suggest that *aesthetic* legitimacy builds on a shared 'aesthetic code' (Gagliardi, 2006) of a community or field, and specifies the distinction between the 'beautiful' and the 'ugly', when and how the 'triad of the good, the true, and the beautiful' unfolds, and how this influences legitimacy judgements (Bitektine, 2011; Tost, 2011) across different institutional orders. Haack et al. (2014) have suggested that legitimacy also has an *affective* component. Both aesthetic and affective legitimacy build, to a certain degree, on emotionality. Visuals are particularly well suited for eliciting emotional reactions (e.g., Phillips, 2000; Schill, 2012; Scott & Vargas, 2007). Since visual communication transmits information with a high degree of immediacy (e.g., Mitchell, 1984; see also Rowley-Jolivet, 2004; Smith and Taffler, 1996), affective and aesthetic evaluations based on visuals become salient before verbal text has been processed and more elaborate pragmatic, normative, or cognitive evaluations set in. Aesthetic and affective appeal has been found to be particularly relevant when dominant models have not yet been established (e.g., Eisenman, 2013).

Although most research on legitimation strategies (e.g., Lefsrud and Meyer, 2012; Suddaby & Greenwood, 2005; Vaara & Tienari, 2008) acknowledges that discourse includes multiple sign systems, only very few studies actually go beyond verbal strategies to include visual rhetorics. Visual images and artifacts can support *authorization* (legitimation through tradition, law, or persons or organizations upon whom or which authority of some kind has been bestowed) by visually invoking proximity to authorities, and experts, such as, for instance, photographs of politicians, activists, or experts that provide powerful testimonials and signal external approval (e.g., Höllerer et al., 2013). Visual images also enhance *rationalization* (legitimation through reference to utility) by projecting detachment and objectivity (for instance, by removing perspective and affective style or by presenting diagrams and charts). They could employ cosmological rhetoric (e.g., Suddaby & Greenwood, 2005) by claiming facticity through iconic representation. Visual images and material artifacts can facilitate *moralization* (legitimation through references to specific value systems) by subtly evoking broadly shared and established norms, values and belief systems (see above). They perform *mythopoiesis* (legitimation through narratives) through visual storytelling, the proliferation of visual stereotypes (e.g., Hardy & Phillips, 1999), and providing visual 'evidence' for the truth of such narratives. Similarly, visuals subtly and powerfully link complex phenomena to established cultural myths (e.g., Zilber, 2006), by 'fitting' them into established cultural formats featuring heroes, villains and victims, and framing them as heroic quests, stories of survival, or tragic narratives of downfall. Finally, by virtue of their inherent truth claims, visual images display normality and established imagery, thereby supporting legitimation strategies building on *normalization*. Further, complex and globally distributed phenomena (like the Global Financial Crisis; see Höllerer, Jancsary, & Grafström, 2014) are cognitively normalized by combining sophisticated verbal text with established imagery in order to encapsulate them in a comprehensible idea. While verbal rhetoric is widely studied, how legitimation is accomplished by other semiotic modes has rarely been tackled. The specific features and affordances of the visual mode – especially its ability to allude without providing grounds or logical conjunctions, the immediacy of its impact and the tendency towards polysemy – provide visual legitimation strategies with

room to maneuver that deserve much more scholarly attention.

INSTITUTIONAL LOGICS, VOCABULARIES AND INSTITUTIONAL PLURALITY

Institutional logics are composed of cognitive schema, normative expectations and material practices; they are socially shared, deeply held assumptions and values that form a framework for reasoning, provide criteria for legitimacy and help organize time and space (Friedland & Alford, 1991; Thornton et al., 2012). In short, institutional logics are cultural rules that provide practical guides for action (Rao, Monin, & Durand, 2003; Dunn & Jones, 2010). Scholars conceptualize logics as originating within societal sectors – such as professions, corporations, community, the market, the state, the family and religions (Friedland & Alford, 1991; Thornton et al., 2012) – because in modern, differentiated societies, knowledge is distributed, and social reality is segmented into distinct 'provinces' of meaning (e.g., Berger & Luckmann, 1967) or 'value spheres' (Weber, 1978 [1922]). However, these logics do not exist in isolation from each other, but may interpenetrate, and societies are characterized by specific constellations of institutional logics (e.g., Goodrick & Reay, 2011; Jones & Livne-Tarandach, 2008) that become institutionally complex when contradictions between them arise (e.g., Besharov and Smith, 2014; Greenwood, Raynard, Kodeih, Micelotta, & Lounsbury, 2011; Raynard, 2016).

Although scholars of institutional logics emphasize both the ideational (e.g., language, cognitive frames and symbols) and material dimension (e.g., structures and practices) (e.g., Thornton et al., 2012), research tends to privilege the ideational, especially in terms of language and cognition as demonstrated by Jones, Boxenbaum and Anthony's

(2013) analysis of the most influential institutional logics articles. Scholars emphasize empirical analysis of logics through written language (e.g., Jones & Livne-Tarandach, 2008; McPherson & Sauder, 2013; Meyer & Höllerer, 2010; Mohr & Duquenne, 1997; Nigam & Ocasio, 2010; Ruef, 1999). As Friedland (2013: 26) notes, institutional logics are 'tied to vocabularies of both motive and belief'; vocabulary structure is language-centric, involving the frequency of key words, their relationship to one another and their relationship to exemplars that render vocabularies concrete and understandable (Loewenstein, Ocasio, & Jones, 2012). We argue here that institutional logics are symbolically represented also by material and visual vocabularies (e.g., Höllerer et al., 2013; Jones, Maoret, Massa, & Svejenova, 2012; Jones, Boxenbaum & Anthony, 2013). However, the role material and visual resources play and whether they engender distinct mechanisms has received only scarce attention.

Materiality

Institutional logics scholars rarely theorize the role that objects play in institutions and institutional processes. In examining vocabularies of seminal institutional logics articles, Jones, Boxenbaum and Anthony (2013) found a rate of only 0.003% where material and practice co-occurred; thus, 'the materials that underpin, or concretely convey, certain structures and practices seem either implicit or peripheral in many studies of institutional logics' (p. 54). Empirical studies of institutional logics hint at materiality, but focus on governance (e.g., Reay & Hinings, 2009; Scott, Martin, Mendel, & Caronna, 2000; Thornton, 2002), contested practices in professions (Dunn & Jones, 2010; Lounsbury, 2007; Smets, Morris, & Greenwood, 2012; Suddaby & Greenwood, 2005) and classification of actors and practices (Mohr & Duquenne, 1997; Ruef, 1999). It is unclear whether any material objects were mobilized

or changed by shifts in organizational structure or contested practices. How material objects change is central to understanding human history: we create, what MacGregor (2010) calls a 'biography of things' that reveals institutional transformations and material transformations, thus enabling us to revise history by how we interrogate material objects. For example, the development of X-rays for medicine were used on Egyptian mummies, revealing the specific talisman Egyptian pharaohs took into their afterlife and the trade routes associated with a jade (MacGregor, 2010). Friedland (2013: 37) advocates that '[u]nobservable substances must be transmuted into observable objects – nested and interlocked – which are the means by which practices are anchored, affected and oriented'. Thus, material artifacts reflect tensions, settlements and transformations of institutional order (Roger Friedland, 2016 personal communication). Scholars should 'examine how material objects and their physical properties anchor and carry logics' (Jones, Boxenbaum, & Anthony, 2013: 64). To reveal how materiality anchors logics that enable them to endure or change over time and transfer across contexts, scholars use a relational approach to examine the patterns of co-occurrences within material elements as well as with language and actors (Mohr & White, 2008). For example, using French restaurants as a case study, Rao et al. (2003) analyzed the ingredients of dishes and key roles (e.g., waiter and chef) to illuminate the shift in logics from classical to nouvelle cuisine. Jones et al. (2012) demonstrated that modern functional architects, who catered to business clients, used a linguistic vocabulary of technical, efficiency and industry coupled with a restricted set of materials: concrete, steel and glass. In contrast, modern organic architects, who served a wider mix of clients, deployed a linguistic vocabulary of organic, nature and technical coupled with a variety of materials: wood, brick, concrete, steel and glass. These stable relations of linguistic vocabularies, construction materials and clients revealed two logics of modern architecture that were fought over and finally reconciled later by architects who integrated functional and organic modernism. Thus, semiotic codes and material bases are key dimensions of logics that offer an insight into institutional change and stability (Jones, Anthony & Boxenbaum, 2013; Jones, Lorenzen, & Sapsed, 2015). Relationships among material objects or aspects thereof reveal a material vocabulary similar to the vocabulary structure described by Loewenstein et al. (2012). The relationality of material objects form a language. Architectural and religious books explain how to decode and read the material form of churches (e.g., spatial plan and layout, arches, windows etc.) (Kieckhefer, 2004). Thus, material forms, like written text, need to be read and require a different form of literacy (Woolgar & Cooper, 1999).

Material objects are a particularly important means for the translation, diffusion and institutionalization of logics over time (Jones, Boxenbaum and Anthony, 2013). For example, Jones and Massa (2013) show how Unity Temple became a boundary object that framed novel practices for Unitarians (e.g., a building that expressed their unique beliefs and practices) in a way quite distinct from how it was framed for modern architects (e.g., how to reconceptualize space, form and a new material of concrete by using site pouring, rather than blocks that imitate stone) even though it was the same building. Ocasio, Mauskapf and Steele (2016) propose that logics are constituted through collective memory, which is stored in material artifacts. Latour (1986) asserts that materials support the durability of social arrangements. Similarly, Pinch (2008) stresses the importance of materiality in producing and reproducing institutions. As such, material objects can be important carriers of and mechanisms by which logics are sustained and transformed over time. Material artifacts as boundary objects enable and reflect pluralism within the institutional environment. For example, Stave churches in Norway capture the transition from paganism to Christianity (Christie, 2016). They were 'patterned on a foreign Romanesque style', housed 'a new religion conceived in distant Mediterranean lands … [and] were adorned with dragons and heroes from Norse myth and legend' (Byock, 1990). Jones and Massa (2013) demonstrate that variations in Christian church architecture mirror variations in beliefs (ideas), people and practices. These beliefs are encoded in material form such as spires and church layout that stabilize beliefs (God as outside of, or immersed in, human lives) and reproduce practices (priest as intermediary between faithful and God). Drawing on Norberg-Schulz's (1986) framework, Jones and Vaara (2014) start to sketch out the grammar of a material vocabulary – topology (place and spatial arrangement), morphology (formal structure) and typology (figural quality) – that illuminates institutional logics, as well as their stability and change.

Visuality

Building on Mills' (1940) understanding that typical vocabularies are woven into the institutionalized fabrics of specific institutional orders and their logics, Meyer et al. (2013) argue that visual signification is a central resource for the constitution, encoding and instantiation of macro-level meaning structures. Visual signs are more immediately perceived, less socially controlled and are able to evoke implicit parts of social knowledge. They are able to 'recall complex systems of knowledge through a minimal sign' (Meyer et al., 2013: 508; see also Quattrone, 2009), and are more quickly and easily processed (e.g., Edell & Staelin, 1983; Mitchell & Olson, 1981). In an analogy to 'vocabularies-of-practice' (Loewenstein et al., 2012, building on Mills, 1940), Höllerer et al. (2013) introduce the concept of 'imageries-of-organizing'. Similar to work that has underlined the substantial role vocabulary structure plays in the maintenance and change of institutional logics (e.g., Ocasio, Loewenstein & Nigam, 2015), they show – based on their in-depth analysis of images in corporations' CSR reports – that such shared imageries-of-organizing at least match the written word in their ability to materialize the unobservable, unknowable substances of institutional logics (Friedland, 2009; Friedland, Mohr, Roose, & Gardinali, 2014) and, in the literal sense of the word, make the invisible visible. Höllerer et al. (2013) find typical imageries that represent different structural semiotic opposites (e.g., Greimas, 1983) and organize the visual CSR discourse in distinct field-level logics. Akin to studies on occurrences and co-occurrences of verbal semantic cues, visual typology mostly focuses on the content of the images. In order to fully grasp the visual potential, future research needs to address how different institutional or field-level logics are encoded and evoked through variations in style, perspective, color, or, more general, through different aesthetic codes.

According to Höllerer et al. (2013), perhaps the greatest unexplored potential of a visual perspective lies in the ability of visual images and artifacts to act as a 'bridging device'. In their study, visuals align globally theorized ideas with local examples and symbols, allow for the simultaneous communication of potentially irreconcilable ideas and ideational systems, and bridge the past, present and future. These findings complement and extend earlier research in science and technology studies on visual images as 'boundary objects' (e.g., Henderson, 1995) that connect different realms of meaning, epistemic communities and activities (e.g., Ewenstein & Whyte, 2007, 2009; Justesen & Mouritsen, 2009). This makes visuals highly useful for research on institutional pluralism and complexity (e.g., Greenwood et al., 2011; Kraatz and Block, Chapter 20 this volume). Höllerer et al. (2013) show how visuals, due to their substantial polysemy, holistic impression and lower level of social scrutiny, 'resolve, bridge, and/or conceal

existing inconsistencies between different institutional spheres and their underlying logics' (p. 140). In a similar vein, this capacity of visual images and artifacts to reduce perceived incommensurability and facilitate the maneuvering of overlaps and ruptures may play a considerable role in creating and sustaining hybrid organizations (e.g., Battilana & Dorado, 2010), or for the reconfiguration and transposition activities of amphibious entrepreneurs or organizations (Powell & Sandholtz, 2012; Korff, Oberg, & Powell, 2015). It requires 'visual literacy' to decode such meaning, but also to unveil manipulation and power that, given our lack of knowledge about its working, often 'fly under the radar' with visual signification.

THEORIZING, TRANSLATING AND FRAMING PROCESSES

A core focus within institutional theory is how ideas and practices are theorized, diffused, adopted and adapted (DiMaggio & Powell, 1983). Theorizing is a 'strategy for making sense of the world' and most effective when promulgated by legitimated theorists (e.g., scientists, professionals) (Strang & Meyer, 1993: 493, 487–496). For example, the Canadian accounting profession instigated change through theorization: they began by identifying problems, specifically organizational failings, and providing possible solutions, and subsequently justified these new solutions by 'invoking' professional values (Greenwood, Suddaby, & Hinings, 2002). Theorization provides ready-made, abstracted and simplified accounts that explain and justify the 'who', 'what' and 'why' and are thought to be more persuasive because 'actual practices are interpreted as partial, flawed, or corrupt implementation of theorized ones' (Strang & Meyer, 1993: 499).

Research on translation reveals that as ideas and practices and their theorizations travel, they are edited (Sahlin-Andersson, 1996) and adapted to local needs and situations (Czarniawska and Joerges, 1996; Wedlin & Sahlin, Chapter 4 this volume). Translation is a linguistic analogy first proposed by Latour (1992) to map the dynamics of artifacts (e.g., AND statements reveal complementary elements whereas OR statements identify substitutions and translations). Although it is acknowledged that ideas are often materialized, the focus is mostly on 'linguistic artifacts' whose 'repetitive use in unchanged form ... [such as] labels, metaphors, platitudes objectifies them' (Czarniawska & Sévon, 1996: 33).

Following Goffman (1986), frames are socially constructed guides to interpretation, and framing means the 'socially situated process of meaning construction' (Cornelissen & Werner, 2014: 183). Framing defines a situation (Goffman, 1986) and scholars who study frames emphasize either the strategies for, or content of, frames (Benford & Snow, 2000). Institutional scholars explore frames, for instance, in relation to identity constructions (Creed, Scully, & Austin, 2002; Lefsrud & Meyer, 2012), architects' rhetorical strategies (Jones & Livne-Tarandach, 2008) or the interpretation of globally diffusing concepts (Fiss & Zajac, 2006; Meyer & Höllerer, 2010) to reveal how meaning varies within and across different contexts.

Studies on theorizing, translating and framing within institutional theory are primarily, if not exclusively, language-centric and espouse the goal of moving beyond 'the brute material "facts"' (Cornelissen, Durand, Fiss, Lammers, & Vaara, 2015: 10). Thus, they tend to edit out the material world and its visual representations. Institutional scholars view language as performative – that is, producing and reproducing institutions. What institutional theory still lacks is how material artifacts and visual representations influence processes of theorizing, translating and framing to shape meaning construction and transmission that are at the center of institutional theory.

Materiality

Material objects play a central role in theorization through symbols and narratives. The cross in Christianity theorizes the spiritual journey (enlightenment), where the vertical represents God to earth and the horizontal human crossing the divine to the other side (Roberts, 2011). Gospel stories in stained glass are material objects that provide visual narratives that act as readymade accounts of religious values and beliefs. A building may theorize and make tangible a different kind of relationship with, and experience of, God. Jones and Massa (2013: 1117) in their study of Unity Temple showed how Reverend Johonnot and architect Frank Lloyd Wright theorized 'a new ecclesiastical aesthetic by marrying Unitarian and modern rational, scientific ideas into symbolic and material form' and by translating the four key ideas of the Unitarian faith – love, reason, community, and free expression – into the material. Although translation was originally a linguistic analogy for Latour, he emphasized its material base: to translate '[y]ou have to go and to come back *with* the "things" if your moves are not to be wasted. But the "things" have to be able to withstand the return trip without withering away' (Latour, 1986: 7). Thus, material objects, which may or may not include visual representations, are at the heart of theorization, translation and framing, but relatively invisible within institutional theory.

Translation enables ideas and practices to move and demands material objects that are immutable mobiles such as books, maps and graphs (Latour, 1986). Immutability means that the material object is durable: it withstands travel, enhances storage and reduces corruption through error. Mobility means that the material object is portable so that it can travel, enabling transfer, comparison, translation and innovation of ideas. Translation processes of material artifacts also reshape work practices, such as Frank Gehry adapting airplane design software to the design of buildings, which, as it rippled through interdependent suppliers, sparked 'waves of innovation' when organizations revised their work practices to adapt to the technology (Boland, Lyytinen, & Yoo, 2007). Within institutional theory, few scholars examine how the immutability and mobility of material artifacts influences institutions and institutional processes.

Framing processes also involve material objects, which act as boundary objects, such as museum artifacts, prototypes or blueprints. Boundary objects 'are both plastic enough to adapt to local needs and constraints of the several parties employing them, yet robust enough to maintain a common identity across sites' (Star & Griesemer, 1989: 393). For example, engineers, technicians and assemblers created shared meaning by using prototypes that enabled them to move beyond the knowledge of their discrete occupational communities and coordinate action (Bechky, 2003). Frames tap into existing social categories and institutions to capture 'the social underpinnings of society' (Goffman, 1986) and link organizational actors to their social context (Bielby & Bielby, 1994; McLean, 1998). For example, blueprints coordinate actions among architects, engineers and contractors, but are also flexible enough to facilitate distinct frames: the architect spatial relations, the engineer load bearing and mechanical conduits, the contractor material needs and subcontractor specialties. Material artifacts may trigger institutional change when they become exemplars that reframe action and possibilities. For example, Unity Temple as a material exemplar was worthy of emulation, which not only enhanced stable interpretations among social actors, but also diffused ideas and practices (Jones & Massa, 2013). The church is not an immutable mobile, but its material and visual representations in the form of sketches, photos, plans and books of the church are immutable mobiles. The combination, the immutable immobile church and the immutable mobiles of the church, can diffuse new beliefs,

practices and understandings that transform the institution of church architecture, such as concrete moving from a despised profane material to the most widely used material for churches. When material artifacts do not survive in physical form or visual representation, they are hard pressed to survive in collective memory (Jones, 2010; Jones & Massa, 2013) and thus cannot act as a means to reframe beliefs, practices or symbolic systems that may guide future action.

Visuality

Despite the emphasis in institutional theory that it is not practices that travel, but rather theorized models and their framings (e.g., Strang & Meyer, 1993; Strang & Soule, 1998), the potential of visual images and artifacts has to date not been systematically explored. Theorization involves defining a 'problem' and a 'solution', including practices, role identities for a particular cast of actors and clarifications of causal relationships between categories (Greenwood et al., 2002). Due to its immediacy of perception, facticity and emotional impact, visuals are able to powerfully communicate problems and failings cognitively and affectively. NGOs and activist groups rely strongly on shocking imagery in order to point at societal and environmental problems, such as human rights violations, animal suffering or environmental disasters. Similarly, the media employ imagery in order to make problems concrete and tangible, and endow them with facticity (e.g., Höllerer et al., 2014). With regard to explaining the benefits of the proposed solution, visual representations suggest relationships through spatial juxtaposition of means and ends (e.g., showing a modern factory as integrated in unspoiled nature; Höllerer et al., 2013), abstract ways of establishing causal chains (e.g., in flow-charts, figures, blueprints, or sketches of prototypes), or by providing visual 'evidence' of effectiveness (e.g., various forms of charts or infographics). Meyer, Jancsary, Höllerer and Boxenbaum (2016) elaborate how visual text enables initial framing, theorization, and sedimentation, and thereby supports the institutionalization of shared ideas, values and beliefs.

Similarly, framing cues (Goffman, 1986) or contextualization cues (Gumperz, 1982) clearly have substantial material and visual components that deserve much more attention in our theory development. In real life contexts, situated interpretations of meaning are hardly effected on the basis of verbal signs only, but integrate multimodal signs, i.e., visual, verbal and material components. More systematically extending framing theory by integrating visuality might, for instance, build on Snow and Benford's (1988) 'core framing tasks' of diagnostic framing, prognostic framing and motivational framing. *Prognostic* framing could be expected to build more on neutral and technical visual artifacts, such as flow-charts and causal models, while *motivational* framing (and, to a lesser degree, *diagnostic* framing) might rely more on highly symbolic and emotional visual artifacts in order to put 'fire in the belly and iron in the soul' (Gamson, 1992: 32).

The potential of visual representations to act as 'bridging devices' (Höllerer et al., 2013) is equally relevant for framing and translation processes. In their study on the visual translation of CSR, visuals align globally theorized ideas with local examples and symbols, allow for the simultaneous communication of potentially irreconcilable ideas and ideational systems, and bridge the past, present and future. This bridging capacity is related to particular visual affordances. First, due to their iconicity, their content is more broadly understood, increasingly constituting a kind of global visual language (Machin, 2004). Second, visuals are able to transport complex meaning in a restricted space, enabling them to travel far without requiring intense engagement and adaptation. Third, their persuasive appeal is more subtle,

allowing for more implicitness and ambiguity (e.g., McQuarrie & Phillips, 2005; Phillips, 2000). Visuals facilitate translation not only vertically (global/local), but also horizontally (e.g., between fields or logics). Justesen and Mouritsen (2009), for example, show how different types of visual artifacts invoke different conceptions of time and are able to connect epistemic communities within and across organizations and professions. Finally, translation – similar to legitimacy – may also have an *affective* and/or *aesthetic* dimension: Local audiences not only understand the novel concepts cognitively, but also develop emotional attitudes towards them and evaluate their desirability on the basis of their own aesthetic codes.

IDENTITY AND IDENTIFICATION

Identities answer the questions 'who are we' or 'who am I' through the lens of social categories and social comparison (Albert & Whetten, 1985; Brewer & Gardner, 1996; Brickson, 2005; Cerulo, 1995) and have long been a central topic in organizational institutionalism (e.g., Glynn, 2000; Kodeih & Greenwood, 2014). Research has studied social identities (e.g., Creed & Scully, 2000), role identities (e.g., Chreim, Williams, & Hinings, 2007; Goodrick & Reay, 2010), and collective identities (e.g., Wry, Lounsbury, & Glynn, 2011) on the individual, organization and field levels. More recent debates have been devoted to the relationship between identities and the larger (pluralistic) institutional environments in which they are embedded (e.g., Rao et al., 2003; Meyer & Hammerschmid, 2006) or to 'identity work' (e.g., Creed, DeJordy, & Lok, 2010) that denotes the active engagement of actors in constructing a favorable, legitimate and coherent self-identity. Issues of identity and identification are strongly related to feelings and emotions (e.g., Albert, Ashforth, & Dutton, 2000). However, the role of emotion for institutional topics is, as yet, rather under-theorized, and a related body of literature is only just emerging (e.g., Creed, Hudson, Okhuysen, & Smith-Crowe, 2014; Haack et al., 2014; Voronov & Vince, 2012). Material artifacts and visual representations signify identities in manifold ways: They mediate between the individual and his or her identities, materialize/manifest role identities (e.g., stethoscope and white coat signify medical doctors) and enhance their cultural 'fit', cue social identities and establish criteria for membership, symbolize adherence to broader social categories and, at the same time, allow for differentiation and individualization. Material and visual artifacts facilitate 'doing' identities and elicit identification through an emotional connection to objects (Höllerer et al., 2013; Jones & Massa, 2013; Rafaeli & Pratt, 2006).

Materiality

When studying identity, scholars tend to highlight their ideational or symbolic elements that provide cultural resources for identity claims (e.g., Lounsbury & Glynn, 2001; Rao et al., 2003). For example, gay and lesbian ministers use cultural resources to manage contradictions between professional roles and marginalized social identities (Creed et al., 2010). This raises the fundamental question of how identity claims based on cultural or symbolic resources can be 'self-replicated and persist beyond the lifetime of their creators' (Lawrence & Suddaby, 2006: 234). The materialization of identities – whether individual (e.g., Picasso's paintings), organizational (e.g., Sidmore, Owings and Merrill's buildings), or collective (the city of Boston or Barcelona's unique architecture and parks) – enable these identities to endure over time and transfer across space. For example, the Eiffel Tower is a material symbol of Parisian identity that is widely recognized beyond Paris or France. Although institutional scholars recognize material

artifacts as carriers of institutions (Scott, 2008), research has not explored what key dimensions and scope conditions of material artifacts influence institutions and institutional processes.

Identity scholars have highlighted the central role of artifacts in expressing identity and engendering identification (as well as dis-identification) for individuals, organizational members and collectives such as logos (Baruch, 2006), built spaces (Berg & Kreiner, 1992; Wasserman & Frenkel, 2010; Jones & Massa, 2013; Yanow, 2006), dress (Elsbach & Pratt, 2007; Miller, 2009; Rafaeli & Pratt, 1993) and office décor (Elsbach, 2004) to express 'collective values, beliefs and feelings' (Yanow, 2006: 42). Material artifacts express values and beliefs, enabling 'people [to] understand themselves, their organizations and their institutions' (Rafaeli & Pratt, 2006: 279).

The few studies that reveal institutional processes of materiality in identity expression, and identification processes, show that when individuals are allowed to personalize their office through décor such as photos and memorabilia, they identify more with the organization (Elsbach, 2004). When designers develop a recognizable, though unsigned, signature style, even in a commoditized product such as toy cars, it enables the organization to create desirable products for the market, while affirming the individual's self-concept (Elsbach, 2009). These self concepts of designers varied in their desire for idealism and control over the design; strong idealism and control enacted an individual identity whereas receiving and building on others' ideas expressed a more collective or collaborative identity (Elsbach & Flynn, 2013). When a collective's distinctive history is encoded into a material artifact, such as a church building, it becomes a collective identity marker. For example, Frank Lloyd Wright customized Unity Temple by marrying Unitarian ideas with novel materials to express a coherent identity of a progressive Unitarian church, triggering the identification of Unitarians with the church building and enabling the church to be supported by the congregation for over 100 years (Jones & Massa, 2013). The key insight is that, in order to signify identity and engender identification, collective material artifacts, similar to personal identity markers (Elsbach, 2004), depend on customizing and embedding what is distinctive about an individual's, organization's or collective's history into the material artifact.

When buildings, whether church or commercial, do not engender identification by its organizational members, the building is destroyed along with its organizational community. In this way, the material artifact enables the institution to persist over time. Just as importantly, a material artifact does not automatically engender identification. As Wasserman and Frenkel (2010) show, a building can spawn acts of resistance when it is seen to be encoding beliefs, symbols and activities that contradict or offend its occupants.

Future research can explore whose identity is materialized (or omitted through not being materialized) when there are multiple identities within an organization or collective. Do various identities hive off into distinct material artifacts and does this lead to identity conflict, expansion or organizational fragmentation and demise? The role of durability and its influence on identity markers is equally important. How does the decay rate and variance in materiality influence whose identity persists or is forgotten? Can material artifacts help transfer identities across time and space as presumed by most global enterprises in terms of their branding and advertising?

Visuality

Visual communication plays a substantial role in creating and performing identities due to their potential to express adherence and deviance simultaneously, through aspects such as color, perspective or subtle reference to shared symbols. Such effect is often more latent and not consciously noticed (e.g., McQuarrie & Phillips, 2005), meaning that visuals, if designed carefully, may reproduce identities, or deviate from them with a substantially lower risk of triggering legitimacy discounts. Visual images and artifacts evoke stereotypes, but also facilitate subtle variation due to the fact that they always need to exemplify social categories. For instance, a photograph can never visualize 'an academic' in a purely abstract way, so any depiction necessarily displays other categories (e.g., gender, race, age, or dress). Outside institutional theory, this has been acknowledged in research on image, reputation and branding (e.g., Schroeder, 2012). Schill (2012) argues that visual images are particularly useful for differentiating actors immediately from each other and providing heuristics about background, personality and demeanor in very short spaces of time. Such affordance is useful for reinforcing collective identities on the field level, but also for stressing the idiosyncratic nature of the identity on the organizational or individual level which is, as Navis and Glynn (2010) have shown, particularly important once a new category has achieved broad legitimacy. One strand of literature has focused on the construction of corporate identity through CEO portraiture and has claimed, for instance, that visualization may communicate intangible aspects of identity, such as intellectual and social capital (e.g., Davison, 2010), create or reinforce brands through narrativization (e.g., Boje & Smith, 2010), and help to maneuver the tricky waters of authenticity (e.g., Guthey & Jackson, 2005). Going beyond portraiture, Pratt and Rafaeli (1997) have also shown how social identities are related to corporate dress codes. This ability of visuals to communicate conformity, as well as uniqueness, can also be observed in the construction of organizational logos (Drori, Delmestri, & Oberg, 2015). Similarly, Vaara, Tienari and

Irrmann (2007) investigate how organizations employ visuals, among other resources, to resolve identity tensions during mergers and acquisitions. Due to their bridging potential and ability to encode messages inconspicuously, visuals may also facilitate role integration (e.g., Ashforth, Kreiner, & Fugate, 2000). Role integration implies porous boundaries between multiple role identities, meaning that roles are either permeable (i.e., an actor can perform one role identity while currently invested in another), or role referencing is common (i.e., an actor can reference one role identity while in the domain of another). Visuals may increase both role permeability (e.g., by visually naturalizing the 'home-office') and role referencing (e.g., a manager displaying family photographs on her desk).

Besides issues of conformity and differentiation, existing research has pointed to the fact that identities may encompass elements that are either distinctly non-discursive or, at the very least, difficult to verbalize (Giddens, 1984). Researchers utilize what Meyer et al. (2013) have labelled 'dialogical approaches' to capture such identity work. For instance, Slutskaya, Simpson and Hughes (2012) use photoelicitation techniques to materialize the more physical elements of butchers' identities. As visuals, due to their spatial ordering, are able to create particular positions for themselves in distinct environments, Shortt and Warren (2012) use participant-taken photographs to reconstruct elements of hairdressers' identities. Such pioneering research shows that neglecting the visual, material and aesthetic aspects of identity work cannot holistically capture the lived experience of actors in the field.

We further suggest that research on the emotional aspects of identification needs to incorporate the affective qualities of visuals. Visuals trigger (dis-)identification with organizations, social roles and particular values by suggesting distinct attitudes towards objects and issues much more easily, directly and subtly than verbal text. Photographs, in particular, impose particular perspectives and social distance (e.g., Kress & van Leeuwen, 2006), thereby creating either engagement or dis-engagement between the viewer and the viewed, as well as constituting power relations. Additionally, the visual depiction of roles and types allows for direct interactions between audiences and depicted people (e.g., through eye contact) and may adjust both similarity and difference between the ideal type and the assumed audience, thereby increasing the potential for identification. Schill (2012), for instance, argues that visual depictions of politicians aim at creating similarity to their audiences, and thereby increase identification. Such identification is facilitated by strongly emotional symbolism.

CONCLUSION

In this chapter we started from the observation that scholars in institutional theory have been remiss in addressing material and visual aspects of institutions and institutional processes. Whereas most institutional inquiry still focuses on verbal language, we have argued that materiality and visuality are at least equally relevant and have therefore discussed the value of such 'multimodality' (Jancsary, Höllerer, & Meyer, 2016; Kress, 2010) in central topics of institutional theory: legitimacy and legitimation, institutional logics, vocabularies and pluralism, theorization, translation and framing, and identity and identification. In this final section, we will summarize the main learnings from our engagement with the material and visual.

First, we suggest that institutions are multimodal achievements. The meanings we encounter in our daily organizational lives are created, manifested, shared, stored and transmitted in a variety of forms that clearly transcend the spoken or written word. Materiality shapes the very way we encounter institutions – through our bodies and senses – and through material objects in our physical environment. Visual images are almost 'omnipresent' in our daily (private as well as professional) lives. It is therefore negligent to assume that institutional theory can or should be a theory of spoken and written language only. Materiality reshapes our institutional world by altering the durability and transferability by which meanings and practices are experienced and shared across time and space. For example, materials have always mediated our communication, but changes in materiality, such as new technologies have transformed when, where and how we communicate such as speeding it up and creating virtual interactions via email, Skype, Google hangouts, Facebook, tweets, texting and IM chats. We have greater transferability by communicating and sharing understandings with more people more quickly and across more time zones, but may increasingly have less durability in those understandings and meanings, as we communicate in shorter and more limited ways (e.g., thousands of 140-character tweets daily). The ease with which visuality in the digital age is available and malleable for almost everybody (e.g., Kress, 2010) makes it an increasingly dominant resource for meaning-making. In fact, with the rise of technologies like the 'emoji' (i.e., ideograms and/or smileys used primarily in electronic communication) or 'snapchat' (i.e., electronic communication through temporary photography) which replace large amounts of verbal information with immediate visual cues, an increasing relevance of visual images and artifacts is to be expected. Consequently, materiality and visuality need to be integrated much more systematically and thoroughly in institutional thinking.

Second, we have shown that – although the material and the visual (and the verbal) are usually strongly intertwined in the creation, dissemination and perception of images and artifacts – the modes can, and should, be distinguished by their specific characteristics and workings. Materiality expresses itself through the properties such as durability and transferability of objects and artifacts.

Visuality is constituted through spatial ordering and composition, holistic presentation, immediacy of perception and substantial polysemy. Such a perspective stresses that the visual and the material have distinct potentials for meaning-making that are different to those of the verbal. Such difference needs to be accounted for in our theories if we are to understand the 'multimodal construction of reality' and its implications for organizational institutionalism.

Third, while we see that both materiality and visuality provide novel insights into a large number of institutional constructs and processes, they do so in different ways. Materiality influences institutional constructs and processes by the way in which it shapes the durability and transferability of ideas, practices and embedded meanings such that they can exist beyond an individual, specific time or place, and by how materials are relationally embedded with one another and with ideas, thereby providing not only (in)coherence but also (in)stability in meaning systems. Visual images provide higher credibility in our Western culture, are more evocative of emotion, and more broadly comprehensible across cultural and linguistic boundaries than verbal text. Combined with a high potential for polysemy, fast cognitive processing and spatial construction of relations, they are a crucial means of meaning construction and rhetoric. We have outlined the particular workings of both materiality and visuality for core institutional processes and have highlighted the need for future research in these areas. A full understanding of institutional processes, consequently, does not only need to take multiple sign systems and their specific modes into account, but also their interaction and the particular 'division of labor' between them.

Fourth, and finally, we must be aware that despite their performative role in the creation, sustenance and challenge of institutions, material and visual artifacts are not 'simple tools' that can be applied strategically for institutional purposes. On the one hand, they are historically and culturally bounded, which implies that their role and workings are also institutionally enabled and restricted. On the other hand, as are all sign systems, materiality and visuality are subject to power and interest. What is needed, therefore, is an increased material and visual literacy of not only practitioners, but especially of researchers. This requires adequate sets of analytical knowledge and methodological tools that are conducive to capturing the particularities of materiality and visuality (e.g., Carlile et al., 2013; Jancsary et al., 2016; McDonnell, 2010).

Summing up, since institutions have relative permanence of a distinctly social sort, institutional research will benefit from further elaboration on how materiality and visuality shape this relative permanence and enable (or disable) the meaning making that underpins and colors institutions.

ACKNOWLEDGMENTS

We gratefully acknowledge financial support from the Danish Research Council: DFF-1327-00030.

REFERENCES

Albert, S., Ashforth, B. E., & Dutton, J. E. (2000). Organizational identity and identification: Charting new waters and building new bridges. *Academy of Management Review, 25*(1), 13–17.

Albert, S., & Whetten, D. A. (1985). Organizational identity. *Research in Organizational Behavior, 7*, 263–295.

Aldrich, H. E., & Fiol, C. M. (1994). Fools rush in? The institutional context of industry creation. *Academy of Management Review, 19*(4), 645–670.

Ashforth, B. E., Kreiner, G. E., & Fugate, M. (2000). All in a day's work: Boundaries and micro role transitions. *Academy of Management Review, 25*(3), 472–491.

Barthel, D. (1996). *Historic preservation: Collective memory and historical identity*. New Brunswick, NJ: Rutgers University Press.

Baruch, Y. (2006). On logos and business cards: The case of UK universities. In A. Rafaeli & M. G. Pratt (Eds.), *Artifacts and organizations: Beyond mere symbolism* (pp. 181–198). Mahwah, NJ: Lawrence Erlbaum.

Battilana, J., & Dorado, S. (2010). Building sustainable hybrid organizations: The case of commercial microfinance organizations. *Academy of Management Journal, 53*(6), 1419–1440.

Bechky, B. A. (2003). Sharing meaning across occupational communities: The transformation of understanding on a production floor. *Organization Science, 14*(3), 312–330.

Bell, E., Schroeder, J. E., & Warren, S. (Eds.) (2014). *The Routledge companion to visual organization*. Abingdon: Routledge.

Benford, R. D., & Snow, D. A. (2000). Framing processes and social movements: An overview and assessment. *Annual Review of Sociology, 26*(1), 611–639.

Berg, P. O., & Kreiner, K. (1992). Corporate architecture: turning physical setting into symbolic resources. In P. Gagliardi (Ed.), *Symbols and artifacts: View from the corporate landscape* (pp. 41–47). New York: Aldine de Gruyter.

Berger, P. L. (1963). *Invitation to sociology: A humanistic perspective*. New York: Doubleday.

Berger, P. L., & Kellner, H. (1981). *Sociology reinterpreted: An essay on method and vocation*. New York: Anchor Books.

Berger, P. L., & Luckmann, T. (1967). *The social construction of reality. A treatise in the sociology of knowledge*. New York: Anchor Books.

Besharov, M. L., & Smith, W. K. (2014). Multiple institutional logics in organizations: Explaining their varied nature and implications. *Academy of Management Review, 39*(3), 364–381.

Bielby, W. T., & Bielby, D. D. (1994). 'All hits are flukes': Institutionalized decision making and the rhetoric of network prime-time program development. *American Journal of Sociology, 99*, 1287–1313.

Bitektine, A. (2011). Toward a theory of social judgments of organizations: The case of legitimacy, reputation, and status. *Academy of Management Review, 36*(1), 151–179.

Bloch, P. H. (1995). Seeking the ideal form: Product design and consumer response. *Journal of Marketing, 59*(3), 16–29.

Boehm, G. (1994). Die Wiederkehr der Bilder. In G. Boehm (Ed.), *Was ist ein Bild?* (pp. 11–38). Munich: Fink.

Boje, D., & Smith, R. (2010). Re-storying and visualizing the changing entrepreneurial identities of Bill Gates and Richard Branson. *Culture and Organization, 16*(4), 307–331.

Boland, R. J., Jr., Lyytinen, K., & Yoo, Y. (2007). Wakes of innovation in project networks: The case of digital 3-D representations in architecture, engineering, and construction. *Organization Science, 18*(4), 631–647.

Brewer, M.B., & Gardner, W. (1996). Who is this 'We'? Levels of collective identity and self representations. *Journal of Personality and Social Psychology, 71*(1), 83–93.

Brickson, S. L. (2005). Organizational identity orientation: Forging a link between organizational identity and organizations' relations with stakeholders. *Administrative Science Quarterly, 50*(4), 576–609.

Briñol, P., Gascó, M., Petty, R. E., & Horcajo, J. (2013). Treating thoughts as material objects can increase or decrease their impact on evaluation. *Psychological Science, 24*(1), 41–47.

Byock, J. (1990). Sigurðr Fáfnisbani: An Eddic hero carved on Norwegian stave churches. In T. Pàroli (Ed.), *Poetry in the Scandinavian Middle Ages. The Seventh International Saga Conference* (pp. 619–628). Spoleto, Italy: Centro Italiano di Studi Sull'Alto Medioevo.

Carlile, P. R. (2002). A pragmatic view of knowledge and boundaries: Boundary objects in new product development. *Organization Science, 13*(4), 442–455.

Carlile, P. R., Nicolini, D., Langley, A., & Tsoukas, H. (2013). How matter matters: Objects, artifacts, and materiality in organization studies: Introducing the third volume of 'Perspective on Organization Studies'. In P. R. Carlile, D. Nicolini, A. Langley, & H. Tsoukas (Eds.), *How matter matters: Objects, artifacts, and materiality in organization studies*. Oxford: Oxford University Press.

Carruthers, B. G., & Espeland, W. N. (1991). Accounting for rationality: Double-entry bookkeeping and the rhetoric of economic rationality. *American Journal of Sociology, 97*(1), 31–69.

Cerulo, K. (1995). *Identity designs: The sights and sounds of a nation.* The Arnold and Caroline Rose Book Series of the American Sociological Association. New Brunswick, NJ: Rutgers University Press.

Chreim, S., Williams, B. E., & Hinings, C. R. (2007). Interlevel influences on the reconstruction of professional role identity. *Academy of Management Journal, 50*(6), 1515–1539.

Christie, H. (2016). The stave churches of Norway. Retrieved from www.reisenett.no/norway/facts/culture_science/stave_churches_of_norway.html [Accessed 30/11/2016].

Cooren, F., Kuhn, T., Cornelissen, J. P., & Clark, T. (2011). Communication, organizing and organization: An overview and introduction to the special issue. *Organization Studies, 32*(9), 1149–1170.

Cornelissen, J. P., Durand, R., Fiss, P. C., Lammers, J. C., & Vaara, E. (2015). Putting communication front and center in institutional theory and analysis. *Academy of Management Review, 40*(1), 10–27.

Cornelissen, J. P., & Werner, M. D. (2014). Putting framing in perspective: A review of framing and frame analysis across the management and organizational literature. *Academy of Management Annals, 8*(1), 181–235.

Creed, W. E. D., DeJordy, R., & Lok, J. (2010). Being the change: Resolving institutional contradiction through identity work. *Academy of Management Journal, 53*(6), 1336–1364.

Creed, W. E. D., Hudson, B. A., Okhuysen, G. A., & Smith-Crowe, K. (2014). Swimming in a sea of shame: Incorporating emotion into explanations of institutional reproduction and change. *Academy of Management Review, 39*(3), 275–301.

Creed, W. E. D., & Scully, M. A. (2000). Songs of ourselves: Employees' deployment of social identity in workplace encounters. *Journal of Management Inquiry, 9*(4), 391–412.

Creed, W. E. D., Scully, M. A., & Austin, J. R. (2002). Clothes make the person? The tailoring of legitimating accounts and the social construction of identity. *Organization Science, 13*(5), 475–496.

Czarniawska, B. (2008). How to misuse institutions and get away with it: Some reflections on institutional theory(ies). In R. Greenwood, C. Oliver, R. Suddaby, & K. Sahlin-Andersson (Eds.), *The SAGE handbook of organizational institutionalism* (pp. 769–782). London: Sage.

Czarniawska, B., & Joerges, B. (1996). Travel of ideas. In B. Czarniawska & G. Sevón (Eds.), *Translating organizational change* (pp. 13–48). Berlin: de Gruyter.

Czarniawska, B., & Sevón, G. (1996). Introduction. In B. Czarniawska & G. Sevón (Eds.), *Translating organizational change* (pp. 1–12). Berlin: de Gruyter.

Czarniawska-Joerges, B., & Joerges, B. (1990). Linguistic artifacts at service of organizational control. In P. Gagliardi (Ed.), *Symbols and artifacts: Views of the corporate landscape* (pp. 339–379). Berlin: de Gruyter.

Davison, J. (2010). [In]visible [in]tangibles: Visual portraits of the business élite. *Accounting, Organizations and Society, 35*(2), 165–183.

DiMaggio, P. J. (1997). Culture and cognition. *Annual Review of Sociology, 23*(1), 263–287.

DiMaggio, P. J., & Powell, W. W. (1983). The iron cage revisited: Institutional isomorphism and collective rationality in organizational fields. *American Sociological Review, 48*(2), 147–160.

Dourish, P., & Mazmanian, M. (2013). Media as material: Information representations as material foundations for organizational practice. In P. R. Carlile, D. Nicolini, A. Langley, & H. Tsoukas (Eds.),

How matter matters: Objects, artifacts, and materiality in organization studies (pp. 92–118). Oxford: Oxford University Press.

Drori, G. S., Delmestri, G., & Oberg, A. (2015). The iconography of universities as institutional narratives. *Higher Education, 71*(2), 163–180.

Dunn, M. B., & Jones, C. (2010). Institutional logics and institutional pluralism: The contestation of care and science logics in medical education, 1967–2005. *Administrative Science Quarterly, 55*(1), 114–149.

Durkheim, É. (1951). *Suicide: A study in sociology*. Glencoe, IL: The Free Press.

Edell, J. A., & Staelin, R. (1983). The information processing of pictures in print advertisements. *Journal of Consumer Research, 10*(1), 45–61.

Eisenman, M. (2013). Understanding aesthetic innovation in the context of technological evolution. *Academy of Management Review, 38*(3), 332–351.

Elsbach, K. D. (2004). Interpreting workplace identities: The role of office decor. *Journal of Organizational Behavior, 25*, 99–128.

Elsbach, K. D. (2009). Identity affirmation through 'signature style': A study of toy car designers. *Human Relations, 62*(7), 1041–1072.

Elsbach, K. D., & Flynn, F. J. (2013). Creative collaboration and the self-concept: A study of toy designers. *Journal of Management Studies, 50*(4), 516–544.

Elsbach, K.D., & Pratt, M.G. (2007). The physical environment in oganizations. *Academy of Management Annals, 1*(1), 181–224.

Ewenstein, B., & Whyte, J. (2007). Beyond words: Aesthetic knowledge and knowing in organizations. *Organization Studies, 28*(5), 689–708.

Ewenstein, B., & Whyte, J. (2009). Knowledge practices in design: The role of visual representations as 'Epistemic Objects'. *Organization Studies, 30*(1), 7–30.

Fellmann, F. (1995). Innere Bilder im Licht des imagic turn. In K. Sachs-Hombach (Ed.), *Bilder im Geiste: Zur kognitiven und erkenntnistheoretischen Funktion piktorialer Repräsentationen* (pp. 21–38). Amsterdam: Rodopi.

Fiss, P. C., & Zajac, E. J. (2006). The symbolic management of strategic change: Sensegiving via framing and decoupling. *Academy of Management Journal, 49*(6), 1173–1193.

Friedland, R. (2001). Religious nationalism and the problem of collective representation. *Annual Review of Sociology, 27*(1), 125–152.

Friedland, R. (2009). Institution, practice, and ontology: Toward a religious sociology. In R. E. Meyer, K. Sahlin, M. J. Ventresca, & P. Walgenbach (Eds.), *Institutions and ideology: Research in the sociology of organizations* (Vol. 27, pp. 45–83). Bingley, UK: Emerald Group.

Friedland, R. (2013). God, love, and other good reasons for practice: Thinking through institutional logics. In M. Lounsbury & E. Boxenbaum (Eds.), *Institutional logics in action*, Part A (pp. 25–50). *Research in the Sociology of Organizations*, Vol. 39. Bingley, UK: Emerald Group.

Friedland, R., & Alford, R. R. (1991). Bringing society back in: Symbols, practices, and institutional contradictions. In W. W. Powell & P. J. DiMaggio (Eds.), *The new institutionalism in organizational analysis* (pp. 232–263). Chicago, IL: University of Chicago Press.

Friedland, R., Mohr, J. W., Roose, H., & Gardinali, P. (2014). The institutional logics of love: measuring intimate life. *Theory and Society, 43*(3–4), 333–370.

Gagliardi, P. (2006). Exploring the aesthetic side of organizational life. In S. R. Clegg, C. Hardy, T. Lawrence, & W. R. Nord (Eds.), *The SAGE handbook of organization studies* (2nd ed., pp. 701–724). London: Sage.

Gamson, W. A. (1992). *Talking politics*. Cambridge: Cambridge University Press.

Giddens, A. (1984). *The constitution of society: Outline of the theory of structuration*. Berkeley, CA: University of California Press.

Gieryn, T. F. (2002). What buildings do. *Theory and Society, 31*(1), 35–74.

Glynn, M. A. (2000). When cymbals become symbols. Conflict over organizational identity within a symphonic orchestra. *Organization Science, 11*(3), 285–298.

Goffman, E. (1986). *Frame analysis. An essay on the organization of experience*. Boston, MA: Northeastern University Press.

Goodrick, E., & Reay, T. (2010). Florence Nightingale endures: Legitimizing a new professional role identity. *Journal of Management Studies, 47*(1), 55–84.

Goodrick, E., & Reay, T. (2011). Constellations of institutional logics: Changes in the professional work of pharmacists. *Work and Occupations, 38*(3), 372–416.

Graves, O. F., Flesher, D. L., & Jordan, R. E. (1996). Pictures and the bottom line: The television epistemology of U.S. annual reports. *Accounting, Organizations and Society, 21*(1), 57–88.

Greenwood, R., Oliver, C., Sahlin, K., & Suddaby, R. (2008). Introduction. In R. Greenwood, C. Oliver, R. Suddaby, & K. Sahlin-Andersson (Eds.), *The SAGE handbook of organizational institutionalism* (pp. 1–46). London: Sage.

Greenwood, R., Raynard, M., Kodeih, F., Micelotta, E. R., & Lounsbury, M. (2011). Institutional complexity and organizational responses. *Academy of Management Annals, 5*(1), 317–371.

Greenwood, R., Suddaby, R., & Hinings, C. R. (2002). Theorizing change: The role of professional associations in the transformation of institutionalized fields. *Academy of Management Journal, 45*(1), 58–80.

Greimas, A. J. (1983). *Structural semantics: An attempt at method.* Lincoln, NE: University of Nebraska Press.

Gumperz, J. J. (1982). *Discourse strategies.* Cambridge: Cambridge University Press.

Guthey, E., & Jackson, B. (2005). CEO portraits and the authenticity paradox. *Journal of Management Studies, 42*(5), 1057–1082.

Haack, P., Pfarrer, M. D., & Scherer, A. G. (2014). Legitimacy-as-feeling: How affect leads to vertical legitimacy spillovers in transnational governance. *Journal of Management Studies, 51*(4), 634–666.

Hardy, C., & Phillips, N. (1999). No joking matter: Discursive struggle in the Canadian refugee system. *Organization Studies, 20*(1), 1–24.

Hargadon, A. B., & Douglas, Y. (2001). When innovations meet institutions: Edison and the design of the electric light. *Administrative Science Quarterly, 46*(3), 476–501.

Henderson, K. (1995). The political career of a prototype: Visual representation in design engineering. *Social Problems, 42*(2), 274–299.

Hicks, D., & Beaudry, M. C. (2010). Introduction: Material culture studies: A reactionary view. In M. C. Beaudry & D. Hicks (Eds.), *The Oxford Handbook of Material Culture Studies* (pp. 1–21). Oxford: Oxford University Press.

Höllerer, M. A., Jancsary, D., & Grafström M. (2014). 'A picture is worth a thousand words': Visually assigned meaning and meta-narratives of the Global Financial Crisis. Paper presented at European Group for Organization Studies (EGOS), Rotterdam, The Netherlands, July 3–5.

Höllerer, M. A., Jancsary, D., Meyer, R. E., & Vettori, O. (2013). Imageries of corporate social responsibility: Visual recontextualization and field-level meaning. In M. Lounsbury & E. Boxenbaum (Eds.), *Institutional logics in action*, Part B (pp. 139–174). *Research in the Sociology of Organizations*, Volume 39. Bingley: Emerald Group.

Hughes, E. C. (1936). The ecological aspect of institutions. *American Sociological Review, 1*, 180–189.

Jancsary, D., Höllerer, M. A., & Meyer, R. E. (2016). Critical analysis of visual and multimodal texts. In R. Wodak & M. Meyer (Eds.), *Methods of critical discourse studies* (3rd ed., pp. 180–204). Los Angeles, CA: Sage.

Jewitt, C. (Ed.) (2009). *The Routledge handbook of multimodal analysis.* London: Routledge.

Jewitt, C., & Oyama, R. (2001). Visual meaning: a social semiotic approach. In T. van Leeuwen & C. Jewitt (Eds.), *Handbook of visual analysis* (pp. 134–156). London: Sage.

Jones, C. (2001). Co-evolution of entrepreneurial careers, institutional rules and competitive dynamics in American film, 1895–1920. *Organization Studies, 22*(6), 911–944.

Jones, C. (2010). Finding a place in history: Symbolic and social networks in creative careers and collective memory. *Journal of Organizational Behavior, 31*(5), 726–748.

Jones, C., Anthony, C., & Boxenbaum, E. (2013). Let's get physical: Materiality and institutional theory. Paper presented at European Group for Organization Studies (EGOS), Montreal, Canada, July 3–6.

Jones, C., Boxenbaum, E., & Anthony, C. (2013). The immateriality of material practices in institutional logics. In M. Lounsbury & E. Boxenbaum (Eds.), *Institutional logics in action*, Part A (pp. 51–75). *Research in the Sociology of Organizations*, Volume 39. Bingley, UK: Emerald Group.

Jones, C., & Livne-Tarandach, R. (2008). Designing a frame: Rhetorical strategies of architects. *Journal of Organizational Behavior, 29*(8), 1075–1099.

Jones, C., Lorenzen, M., & Sapsed, J. (2015). Creative industries: A typology of change. In C. Jones, M. Lorenzen, & J. Sapsed (Eds.), *The Oxford handbook of creative industries* (pp. 3–32). Oxford: Oxford University Press.

Jones, C., Maoret, M., Massa, F. G., & Svejenova, S. (2012). Rebels with a cause: Formation, contestation, and expansion of the de novo category 'Modern Architecture,' 1870–1975. *Organization Science, 23*(6), 1523–1545.

Jones, C., & Massa, F. G. (2013). From novel practice to consecrated exemplar: Unity Temple as a case of institutional evangelizing. *Organization Studies, 34*(8), 1099–1136.

Jones, C., & Vaara, E. (2014). Material vocabularies in institutional stability and change: An analysis of religious buildings in early and late modernism. Presented at European Group for Organization Studies (EGOS), Rotterdam, Netherlands, July 4–8.

Justesen, L., & Mouritsen, J. (2009). The triple visual: Translations between photographs, 3-D visualizations and calculations. *Accounting, Auditing & Accountability Journal, 22*(6), 973–990.

Kieckhefer, R. (2004). *Theology in stone: Church architecture from Byzantium to Berkeley.* Oxford: Oxford University Press.

Kodeih, F., & Greenwood, R. (2014). Responding to institutional complexity: The role of identity. *Organization Studies, 35*(1), 7–39.

Korff, V. P., Oberg, A., & Powell, W. W. (2015). Interstitial organizations as conversational bridges. *Bulletin of the Association for Information Science and Technology, 41*(2), 34–38.

Kostova, T., & Zaheer, S. (1999). Organizational legitimacy under conditions of complexity: The case of the multinational enterprise. *Academy of Management Review, 24*(1), 64–81.

Kress, G. (2010). *Multimodality. A social semiotic approach to contemporary communication.* Abingdon: Routledge.

Kress, G., & van Leeuwen, T. (2006). *Reading images: The grammar of visual design* (2nd ed.). London: Routledge.

Latour, B. (1986). Visualization and cognition: Thinking with eyes and hands. In H. Kuklick (Ed.), *Knowledge and society: Studies in the sociology of culture. Past and present* (Volume 6, pp. 1–40). London: JAI Press.

Latour, B. (1992). Where are the missing masses? The sociology of a few mundane artifacts. In W. E. Bijker & J. Law (Eds.), *Shaping technology/building society: Studies in sociotechnical change* (pp. 225–258). Cambridge, MA: MIT Press.

Law, J. (2002). Objects and spaces. *Theory, Culture & Society, 19*(5–6), 91–105.

Lawrence, T. B., & Suddaby, R. (2006). Institutions and institutional work. In S. R. Clegg, C. Hardy, T. B. Lawrence, & W. Nord (Eds.), *The SAGE handbook of organization studies* (pp. 215–254). London: Sage.

Lefsrud, L. M., Graves, H., & Phillips, N. (2013). Dirty oil, ethical oil: Categorical illegitimacy and the struggle over the Alberta oil sands. Working Paper. University of Alberta.

Lefsrud, L. M., & Meyer, R. E. (2012). Science or science fiction? Professionals' discursive construction of climate change. *Organization Studies, 33*(11), 1477–1506.

Loewenstein, J., Ocasio, W., & Jones, C. (2012). Vocabularies and vocabulary structure: A new approach linking categories, practices, and institutions. *Academy of Management Annals, 6*(1), 41–86.

Lounsbury, M. (2007). A tale of two cities: Competing logics and practice variation in the professionalizing of mutual funds. *Academy of Management Journal, 50*(2), 289–307.

Lounsbury, M., & Glynn, M. A. (2001). Cultural entrepreneurship: Stories, legitimacy, and the acquisition of resources. *Strategic Management Journal, 22*(6/7), 545–564.

MacGregor, N. (2010). *A history of the world in 100 objects.* New York: Viking.

Machin, D. (2004). Building the world's visual language: The increasing global importance of image banks in corporate media. *Visual Communication, 3*(3), 316–336.

McDonnell, T. E. (2010). Cultural objects as objects: Materiality, urban space, and the interpretation of AIDS campaigns in Accra, Ghana. *American Journal of Sociology, 115*(6), 1800–1852.

McLean, P. D. (1998). A frame analysis of favor seeking in the renaissance: Agency, networks, and political culture. *American Journal of Sociology, 104*, 51–91.

McPherson, C. M., & Sauder, M. (2013). Logics in action: Managing institutional complexity in a drug court. *Administrative Science Quarterly, 58*(2), 165–196.

McQuarrie, E. F., & Phillips, B. J. (2005). Indirect persuasion in advertising: How consumers process metaphors presented in pictures and words. *Journal of Advertising, 34*, 7–20.

Messaris, P. (1997). *Visual persuasion: The role of images in advertising.* Thousand Oaks, CA: Sage.

Meyer, R. E., & Hammerschmid, G. (2006). Changing institutional logics and executive identities. A managerial challenge to public administration in Austria. *American Behavioral Scientist, 49*(7), 1000–1014.

Meyer, R. E., & Höllerer, M. A. (2010). Meaning structures in a contested issue field: A topographic map of shareholder value in Austria. *Academy of Management Journal, 53*(6), 1241–1262.

Meyer, R. E., Höllerer, M. A., Jancsary, D., & Van Leeuwen, T. (2013). The visual dimension in organizing, organization, and organization research. *Academy of Management Annals, 7*(1), 487–553.

Meyer, R. E., Jancsary, D., Höllerer, M. A., & Boxenbaum, E. (2016). Power of images: The role of visual text in the process of institutionalization. Paper presented at the Fifth European Theory Development Workshop, Helsinki, Finland, June 30–July 1.

Miller, D. (2009). *Stuff.* Cambridge: Polity Press.

Mills, C. W. (1940). Situated actions and vocabularies of motive. *American Sociological Review, 5*(6), 904–913.

Mitchell, A. A., & Olson, J. C. (1981). Are product attribute beliefs the only mediator of advertising effects on brand attitude? *Journal of Marketing Research, 18*(3), 318–332.

Mitchell, W. J. T. (1984). What is an image? *New Literary History, 15*(3), 503–537.

Mitchell, W. J. T. (1994). *Picture theory. Essays on verbal and visual representation.* Chicago, IL: University of Chicago Press.

Mohr, J. W., & Duquenne, V. (1997). The duality of culture and practice: Poverty relief in New York City, 1888–1917. *Theory and Society, 26*(2), 305–356.

Mohr, J. W., & White, H. C. (2008). How to model an institution. *Theory and Society, 37*(5), 485–512.

Navis, C., & Glynn, M. A. (2010). How new market categories emerge: Temporal dynamics of legitimacy, identity, and entrepreneurship in satellite radio, 1990–2005. *Administrative Science Quarterly, 55*(3), 439–471.

Nigam, A., & Ocasio, W. (2010). Event attention, environmental sensemaking, and change in institutional logics: An inductive analysis of the effects of public attention to Clinton's Health Care Reform Initiative. *Organization Science*, *21*(4), 823–841.

Norberg-Schulz, C. (1986). The demand for a contemporary language of architecture. *Art & Design*, *2*, 14–21.

Ocasio, W., Loewenstein, J., & Nigam, A. (2015). How streams of communication reproduce and change institutional logics: The role of categories. *Academy of Management Review*, *40*(1), 28–48.

Ocasio, W., Mauskapf, M., & Steele, C. (2016). History, society, and institutions: The role of collective memory in the emergence and evolution of societal logics. *Academy of Management Review*, *41*(4), 676–699.

Phillips, B. J. (2000). The impact of verbal anchoring on consumer response to image ads. *Journal of Advertising*, *29*(1), 15–24.

Phillips, N., Lawrence, T. B., & Hardy, C. (2004). Discourse and institutions. *Academy of Management Review*, *29*, 635–652.

Phillips, N., & Oswick, C. (2012). Organizational discourse: Domains, debates, and directions. *Academy of Management Annals*, *6*(1), 435–481.

Pinch, T. (2008). Technology and institutions: living in a material world. *Theory and Society*, *37*(5), 461–483.

Powell, W. W., & Sandholtz, K. W. (2012). Amphibious entrepreneurs and the emergence of organizational forms. *Strategic Entrepreneurship Journal*, *6*(2), 94–115.

Pratt, M. G., & Rafaeli, A. (1997). Organizational dress as a symbol of multilayered social identities. *Academy of Management Journal*, *40*(4), 862–898.

Preston, A. M., Wright, C., & Young, J. J. (1996). Imag[in]ing annual reports. *Accounting, Organizations and Society*, *21*(1), 113–137.

Quattrone, P. (2004). Accounting for God: accounting and accountability practices in the Society of Jesus (Italy, XVI–XVII centuries). *Accounting, Organizations and Society*, *29*(7), 647–683.

Quattrone, P. (2009). Books to be practiced: Memory, the power of the visual, and the success of accounting. *Accounting, Organizations and Society*, *34*(1), 85–118.

Raab, J. (2008). *Visuelle Wissenssoziologie: Theoretische Konzeption und materiale Analysen*. Konstanz: UVK Verlagsgesellschaft.

Rafaeli, A., & Pratt, M. G. (1993). Tailored meanings: On the meaning and impact of organizational dress. *Academy of Management Review*, *18*(1), 32–55.

Rafaeli, A., & Pratt, M. G. (Eds.). (2006). *Artifacts and organizations: Beyond mere symbolism*. Mahwah, NJ: Lawrence Erlbaum.

Rämö, H. (2011). Visualizing the phronetic organization: The case of photographs in CSR reports. *Journal of Business Ethics*, *104*(3), 371–387.

Rao, H. (1994). The social construction of reputation: Certification contests, legitimation, and the survival of organizations in the American automobile industry: 1895–1912. *Strategic Management Journal*, *15*(S1), 29–44.

Rao, H., Monin, P., & Durand, R. (2003). Institutional change in Toque Ville: Nouvelle cuisine as an identity movement in French gastronomy. *American Journal of Sociology*, *108*(4), 795–843.

Raynard, M. (2016). Deconstructing complexity: Configurations of institutional complexity and structural hybridity. *Strategic Organization*, *14*(4), 310–335.

Reay, T., & Hinings, C. R. (2009). Managing the rivalry of competing institutional logics. *Organization Studies*, *30*(6), 629–652.

Roberts, M. S. (2011). The cross. *Religions*. www. bbc.co.uk/religion/religions/christianity/symbols/cross_1.shtml [Accessed 12/09/2011].

Rowley-Jolivet, E. (2004). Different visions, different visuals: A social semiotic analysis of field-specific visual composition in scientific conference presentations. *Visual Communication*, *3*(2), 145–175.

Ruef, M. (1999). Social ontology and the dynamics of organizational forms: Creating market actors in the healthcare field, 1966–1994. *Social Forces*, *77*(4), 1403–1432.

Sahlin-Andersson, K. (1996). Imitating by editing success: The construction of organizational fields. In B. Czarniawska & G. Sevón (Eds.), *Translating organizational change* (pp. 69–92). Berlin: de Gruyter.

Schill, D. (2012). The visual image and the political image: A review of visual communication research in the field of political communication. *Review of Communication*, *12*(2), 118–142.

Schroeder, J. E. (2012). Style and strategy: Snapshot aesthetics in brand culture. In F.-R. Puyou, P. Quattrone, C. McLean, & N. Thrift (Eds.), *Imagining organizations: Performative imagery in business and beyond* (pp. 129–151). New York: Routledge.

Schütz, A., & Luckmann, T. (1973). *The structures of the life-world*. London: Heinemann.

Scott, L. M., & Vargas, P. (2007). Writing with pictures: Toward a unifying theory of consumer response to images. *Journal of Consumer Research*, *34*(3), 341–356.

Scott, W. R. (2003). Institutional carriers: reviewing modes of transporting ideas over time and space and considering their consequences. *Industrial and Corporate Change*, *12*(4), 879–894.

Scott, W. R. (2008). *Institutions and organizations: Ideas and interests* (3rd ed.). Thousand Oaks, CA: Sage.

Scott, W.R., Martin, R., Mendel, P.J. & Caronna, C.A. (2000). *Institutional change and healthcare organizations: From professional dominance to managed care*. Chicago, IL.: University of Chicago Press.

Selznick, P. (1996). Institutionalism 'old' and 'new'. *Administrative Science Quarterly*, *41*(2), 270–277.

Shortt, H., & Warren, S. (2012). Fringe benefits: Valuing the visual in narratives of hairdressers' identities at work. *Visual Studies*, *27*(1), 18–34.

Skemer, D. C. (2006). *Binding words: Textual amulets in the middle ages*. University Park, PA: Pennsylvania State University Press.

Slutskaya, N., Simpson, A., & Hughes, J. (2012). Lessons from photoelicitation: Encouraging working men to speak. *Qualitative Research in Organizations and Management: An International Journal*, *7*(1), 16–33.

Smets, M., Morris, T., & Greenwood, R. (2012). From practice to field: A multilevel model of practice-driven institutional change. *Academy of Management Journal*, *55*(4), 877–904.

Smith, M., & Taffler, R. (1996). Improving the communication of accounting through cartoon graphics. *Accounting, Auditing & Accountability Journal*, *9*(2), 68–85.

Snow, D. A., & Benford, R. D. (1988). Ideology, frame resonance, and participant mobilization. In B. Klandermans, H. Kriesi, & S. Tarrow (Eds.), *From structure to action: Comparing social movement research across cultures* (pp. 197–217). Greenwich, CT: JAI Press.

Star, S. L., & Griesemer, J. R. (1989). Institutional ecology, 'translations' and boundary objects: Amateurs and professionals in Berkeley's Museum of Vertebrate Zoology. *Social Studies of Science*, *19*(3), 387–420.

Strang, D., & Meyer, J. W. (1993). Institutional conditions for diffusion. *Theory and Society*, *22*(4), 487–511.

Strang, D., & Soule, S.A. (1998). Diffusion in organizations and social movements: From hybrid corn to poison pills. *Annual Review of Sociology*, *24*(1), 265–290.

Suchman, M. C. (1995). Managing legitimacy: Strategic and institutional approaches. *Academy of Management Review*, *20*(3), 571–610.

Suddaby, R., & Greenwood, R. (2005). Rhetorical strategies of legitimacy. *Administrative Science Quarterly*, *50*(1), 35–67.

Thornton, P. H. (2002). The rise of the corporation in a craft industry: Conflict and conformity in institutional logics. *Academy of Management Journal*, *45*(1), 81–101.

Thornton, P. H., Ocasio, W., & Lounsbury, M. (2012). *The institutional logics perspective: A new approach to culture, structure and process*. Oxford: Oxford University Press.

Thurk, J., & Fine, G. A. (2003). The problem of tools: Technology and the sharing of knowledge. *Acta Sociologica*, *46*(2), 107–117.

Tost, L. P. (2011). An integrative model of legitimacy judgments. *Academy of Management Review*, *36*(4), 686–710.

Vaara, E., & Tienari, J. (2008). A discursive perspective on legitimation strategies in multinational corporations. *Academy of Management Review*, *33*(4), 985–993.

Vaara, E., Tienari, J., & Irrmann, O. (2007). Crafting an international identity: The Nordea case. In L. Lerpold, D. Ravasi, J. van Rekom, & G. Soenen (Eds.), *Organizational identity in practice* (pp. 215–231). Abingdon: Routledge.

van Leeuwen, T., & Wodak, R. (1999). Legitimizing immigration control: A discourse-historical analysis. *Discourse Studies*, *1*(1), 83–118.

Voronov, M., & Vince, R. (2012). Integrating emotions into the analysis of institutional work. *Academy of Management Review*, *37*(1), 58–81.

Wasserman, V., & Frenkel, M. (2010). Organizational aesthetics: Caught between identity regulation and culture jamming. *Organization Science*, *22*(2), 503–521.

Weber, M. (1958 [1946]). Essays in Sociology. In M. Weber, H. Gerth, & C. W. Mills (Eds.), *From Max Weber*. New York: Oxford University Press.

Weber, M. (1978 [1922]) *Economy and society: An outline of interpretive sociology*. Berkeley, CA: University of California Press.

Woolgar, S., & Cooper, G. (1999). Do artefacts have ambivalence? Moses' bridges, winner's bridges and other urban legends in S&TS. *Social Studies of Science*, *29*(3), 433–449.

Wry, T., Lounsbury, M., & Glynn, M. A. (2011). Legitimating nascent collective identities: Coordinating cultural entrepreneurship. *Organization Science*, *22*(2), 449–463.

Yanow, D. (2006). Studying physical artifacts: An interpretive approach. In A. Rafaeli & M. G. Pratt (Eds.), *Artifacts and organizations: Beyond mere symbolism* (pp. 41–60). Mahwah, NJ: Lawrence Erlbaum.

Zilber, T. B. (2006). The work of the symbolic in institutional processes: Translations of rational myths in Israeli high tech. *Academy of Management Journal*, *49*(2), 281–303.

Zucker, L. G. (1977). The role of institutionalization in cultural persistence. *American Sociological Review*, *42*(5), 726–743.

24

Advancing Research on Categories for Institutional Approaches of Organizations

Rodolphe Durand and Romain Boulongne

Over the past two decades, research on categories has grown rapidly in the management literature. In their review some years ago, Durand and Paolella (2013: 1100) indicated that 'categories represent a meaningful consensus about some entities' features as shared by actors grouped together as an audience'. They noted that etymologically, the word *katègorein* in ancient Greek means to accuse publicly (i.e., to make an argument in the agora) and to come to a consensus under public scrutiny. Today, the category concept retains its public (marketplace) nature in the exchange of arguments around features and entities. As such, categories can be defined as interfaces of cognitive agreement about a considered object. In a seminal paper, Zuckerman (1999) found evidence in asset markets that analysts better acknowledge and prefer firms with identifiable industry categories. In a contemporary study, Rosa et al. (1999) documented the emergence of a new product category (minivans) as borrowing from prior existing categories, diffusing and stabilizing around a product prototype through a process of producer–consumer interactions.

In addition to their cognitive component, categories embody semantic content and relationships; thus, they play an important role in institutional maintenance and change (Maguire et al., 2004; Hiatt et al., 2009). For institutions to emerge and be maintained, different audiences must share and sustain agreement over time. Indeed, institutions can be seen as systems of sustained 'common cognitive understandings' (Cornelissen et al., 2015: 14) and social perceptions of semantic objects across different audiences. Categories are a fundamental component of institutions' cognitive and normative pillars; they are the bond between 'collections of communicative events [that] can converge to yield the meaningful and durable higher-order cultural structures' (Ocasio et al., 2015: 31) necessary for institutions to exist and endure. Without categories as 'social agreements about the meanings of labels applied to them'

(Negro et al., 2010: 1450), neither institutional consensus nor exchanges (economic, symbolic, or otherwise) are likely to be achieved.

Thus far, category studies have been based largely on the premise that 'audiences navigate better across markets and social worlds when categories are clearly marked and unambiguous' (Durand and Paolella, 2013: 1101). Building on the idea from population ecology that there exists a tradeoff between the breadth of a niche wherein an organization positions itself and the relative performance the organization can obtain, Hsu (2006) explained that producers that cross and span categories receive less attention and positive rewards from their audiences, as illustrated by the feature movie industry. Hannan, Polos and Carroll (2007) systematized the linkages between the population ecology tradition and category research. They noted how categories discipline producers through a cognitive selection process, and by framing expectations and associating rewards and sanctions with conforming and deviating behaviors, respectively. Indeed, category spanners face specific challenges compared to those that do not straddle multiple categories. Audiences are confused by what category spanners offer (cognitive ambiguity), who they are (identity ambiguity) and how well they multi-task (competence ambiguity). Thus, the more organizations deviate from existing prototypical categories, the less audiences are able to understand the meanings associated with what they offer. In more recent research, scholars have contextualized this main theoretical thread, that of a 'categorical imperative' disciplining producers toward clear and acceptable categories that facilitate comprehension of who is operating and what is being exchanged (Ruef and Patterson, 2009; Pontikes, 2012; Negro and Leung, 2013).

Inspired by the population ecology research stream, this ecological approach to categories is grounded in the prototypical view of categorization (Rosch and Mervis, 1975). A prototype captures the essential characteristics shared by all members of a category

and is used to evaluate an entity. Therefore, the more an entity acquires categorical characteristics from distant prototypes, the more cognitive, identity and competence ambiguity it generates, and the less the entity is noticed and rewarded by audiences. The prototypical view of categories has been complemented by other approaches recently, resulting in a stretch of the 'categorical imperative' for three reasons (Durand and Paolella, 2013). First, producers continuously combine category features and create new labels and categories in markets. They cannot all be wrong or blind or oblivious to the categorical imperative, so category spanning must provide some benefits. Second, audiences must have existing prototypes in mind for the ecological perspective to apply; however, audience members may face situations that are original, specific or unprecedented, for which they would not seek a typical supplier but an atypical one. Choices and preferences may not always be the most typical, as an audience's theory of value, defined as 'how audiences identify issues and solutions, ascribe value, and rank solution providers' (Paolella and Durand, 2016: 333), does not unilaterally coincide with proximity to a prototype (Barsalou, 1983). Third, categories belong to category systems (i.e., associations with other categories, features and labels); beyond the horizontal ordering and combining of categories (represented by spanning across categories), there exist vertical layers of category inclusiveness and embeddedness. Spanning is therefore just one of the many modalities of feature combination and sensemaking in categorical associations (Wry and Lounsbury, 2013).

In this chapter, we describe this new territory that researchers need to explore. We first review the two main approaches to categories (understood from a cognitive perspective) found in the current literature. The ecological and the goal-based approaches to categories vary in terms of premises (prototypes vs. ideals), processes (central tendency and family resemblance vs.

conceptual combination and goal achievement), and economic and institutional consequences. We then present three modes of reconciliation between the two approaches (intra-audience, inter-audience and as a function of field evolution) and integrate them more broadly into the institutional literature. Finally, in the last section, we expose fruitful areas for future research: we account for the domain validity of each approach; emphasize ignored research avenues at the field, organizational and individual levels; and finally make stronger connections between category research and strategy research.

TWO MAIN APPROACHES TO CATEGORIES

Categories as ambiguity alleviators

Organizational and management scholars research the cognitive and institutional underpinnings of fields and markets and seek to understand how firms and organizations navigate the potential areas of ambiguity that contaminate social and economic exchanges. Categories are the interfaces enabling these exchanges. As 'cognitive infrastructures of markets' (Schneiberg and Beck, 2010: 257), categories help alleviate the three sources of ambiguity faced by audiences: What is the offering? Who is the producer? What inferences can be made about its competences? Understanding how actors come to make sense, agree and trade is therefore of fundamental importance for organization and strategy studies, entrepreneurship and the related activities of innovation, financing and distribution of new services and products (Hiatt et al., 2009; Navis and Glynn, 2010; Pontikes, 2012; Granqvist et al., 2013). Moreover, clearly understanding category functions and categorization processes in fields creates opportunities to better comprehend institutional processes such as legitimacy judgments and

change (Bitektine, 2011). The evolution of category systems drives as much as it echoes the cognitive and institutional modes and practices that enable social phenomena (Durand, 2012, 2014). Understanding how categories and their attached meanings evolve enables exploration of the two main forces that nurture economic evolution and social transformation: legitimacy and competition.

Conditions and moderators

Several scholars have made recent research contributions to the main theoretical stream of category research. The ecological approach is primarily rooted in the prototypical view of categories. Empirical results confirm the premise of higher sanctions against producers with cognitive, identity and competence ambiguity (Hsu et al., 2009; Negro et al., 2010; Negro and Leung, 2013; Leung and Sharkey, 2014). Several conditions moderate this disciplining principle levied against category spanners. As such, the negative effects of category spanning on audiences' evaluations vary depending on:

1 **Contrast between categories**. Kovács and Hannan (2010) argued that the effect of category spanning on audience reception depends on the fuzziness of the categories being spanned. They suggested that penalties for associating high contrast categories are more severe than for associating low contrast categories. The wider the distance between the corresponding prototypes of the spanned categories, the stronger the associated negative effects of category spanning on evaluation.

2 **Actors' status and legitimacy conferred to spanning**. Phillips and Zuckerman (2001) theorized and found evidence that high-status actors are given more latitude when violating membership norms. They can deviate more from expectations without paying as high a penalty for spanning as lower status actors. Accordingly, Zhao et al. (2013) showed that the legitimacy granted to a movie sequel by the first movie's success helps offset the 'categorical imperative' (Zuckerman, 1999): in such cases, films that are associated with highly legitimate past productions can straddle multiple categories without

suffering major penalties. Durand and Kremp (2016) further decomposed the organizational and individual effects of status on the misalignment and unconventionality of offerings by investigating the history of American symphonic orchestras and disentangling the constraining and liberating effects of status (for middle-status and high-status organizations, respectively). At the organizational level, orchestras seek alignment and respect within the category system. At the individual level, conductors care about conventionality. As a result, high-status orchestras are misaligned relative to their peer organizations, and high-status conductors more unconventional than their peers.

3 **Audiences.** Pontikes (2012) wondered whether all audiences share the same aversion for ambiguity. Some audiences may prefer organizations that do not have clear and crisp categorical identities. She distinguished market-takers (e.g., end consumers) for whom ambiguity is deleterious, from market-makers (e.g., venture capitalists [VCs]) who can strategically use the ambiguity of category spanning as an asset and advantage to promote their own agendas. As a venture's business model evolves, VCs and the start-up redefine its membership, identity and products, and hence benefit from a certain amount of flexibility in its original categorical identification. On a similar note, Smith (2011) found that investors attach a significant premium to atypical hedge funds after (short) periods of positive performance.

4 **Combined categories, categorical combination.** Audiences make different sense of different category combinations; members of a combined category do not all play the same role. For instance, a category combination can be decomposed into a 'header category' that anchors perceptions and a 'category modifier' that modifies perceptions by adding other categories' features. Wry, Lounsbury and Jennings (2014) argued that the spanning direction (i.e., the degree to which header versus modifier identity markers are affected) impacts audiences' perceptions. For instance, the words 'house' and 'cat' can be combined in two different ways to indicate a domestic animal or a house of ill-repute. Thus, associating commercial competences to a core technology for a start-up produces better results than the opposite association (i.e., a core commercial competence to which some scientific expertise is added).

5 **Category hierarchies.** Category spanners do not face harsh penalties, provided such categories share linkages with accepted and recognized superordinate categories. In this sense, 'categories can also be linked vertically in a "stem and branch" type hierarchy where higher level categories encompass a series of lower level ones' (Wry and Lounsbury, 2013: 120). Paolella and Durand (2016) found corroborative evidence that categorical inclusiveness positively moderates the relationship between category spanning and social evaluations of category spanners.

6 **Category system's maturity.** Ruef and Patterson (2009) studied R.G. Dun & Company's system of industrial classification and credit rating evaluation from its inception in the 19th century. They compared early institutionalization (1864 to early 1880s) with mature institutionalization (late 1880s to 1900) of the industrial taxonomy used to assess businesses' credit worthiness. The authors showed that Dun's evaluators tolerated category spanning during the early period because the categorical boundaries separating activities were neither precisely established nor socially legitimate.

Central tendency and family resemblance

Accounting for these various conditions, it is possible to provide a nuanced explanation of the main prescription provided by scholars who have taken an ecological approach to category research: minimize the penalties associated with the various sorts of ambiguity generated by deviating from the central tendencies expressed in prototypes. Crisp and clear category memberships alleviate the cognitive, identity and competence ambiguity that category spanning activates by reducing the family resemblance between the spanner and the prototype(s) to which audiences compare it (Hsu, 2006; Hannan et al., 2007; Hsu et al., 2009). Barsalou (1985) defined family resemblance as 'an exemplar's average similarity to other category members and its average dissimilarity to other members of contrast categories' (Barsalou, 1985: 630). An apple is a typical exemplar of the category 'fruit', as it is likely that most people have encountered many apples during their lifetimes. Thus, family resemblance relies on the core mechanism of central tendency (Barsalou, 1985, 1991) – individuals learn about categories as they encounter many such items in their experiences. The comparative mechanism of central tendency underlying family resemblance is based on repeated exposure over time to instances of the considered category. As individuals who assess offerings such as movies, wines and restaurants have clear representations and memories of what constitutes a 'good' movie or a 'good' restaurant, they penalize deviant offerings because they differ from the typical exemplars that audiences usually find in such contexts (Hsu, 2006; Hsu et al., 2009; Negro et al., 2010, 2011; Negro and Leung, 2013; Kovács et al., 2014).

Categories Based on Goals

Importance of audiences' theories of value

Despite its merits, the ecological approach to categories is based on overly strict assumptions, which recently has hindered the development of relevant research in organization and management studies. This approach assumes the pre-existence of prototypes used as a baseline to assess family resemblance and bestows on audiences a selective role in evaluation: they react to the offers and producers they encounter. Anecdotal evidence from multiple studies contradicts these assumptions; recently, scholars have considered the ecological approach to be an important but simplified application of a more general theory of categories based on different mechanisms and principles (Durand and Paolella, 2013; Paolella and Durand, 2016). Indeed, judgments and assessments are not necessarily predetermined to favor prototypical producers: exemplars may not exist, or may exist but not be applicable to given situations. Audience members may also face unique situations for which they have no

comparable previous experiences or expertise. In these frequent cases, instead of relying on preexisting exemplars, audience members categorize producers and their offerings as active functions of their needs – that is, they develop different theories of value.

In some past studies, researchers assumed that theories of value (rather than prototypes) are at the core of an audience's attention to offerings and solutions in social and economic contexts. For instance, in his seminal paper on the categorical imperative, Zuckerman (1999: 1431) stated that the:

> industry-based category structure analyzed in this article is contingent on the prevalence of a particular theory of value … The possibility of alternative theories of value and classification schemes persists, as indicated by the welcome received by the conglomerate firm in the 1960s.

Here and in his other works (Zuckerman et al., 2003; Phillips et al., 2013), Zuckerman drew attention to the importance of understanding which theory of value prevails within a context. Thus, Zuckerman (1999) has been rather inappropriately associated with the ecological approach to categories, because the functioning and theory of value prevalent in asset markets (an extreme case) has been misapplied as a rule for all contexts.

Conceptual combination and goal-based categories

By putting an audience's theory of value at the center of the analysis, we render audience members active in both the classification and evaluation phases of categorization processes. Depending on their needs, audiences group distinct solution providers into ad hoc categories (Barsalou, 1983). This active role of categorical ascription establishes a goal-based model of categories (Murphy, 2002), whereby 'category members are items that most suit *an ideal*, even if they greatly differ from each other – category structure is driven more by goal pursuit than by family resemblance' (Durand and Paolella, 2013: 1109). In the ecological approach (Hannan et al., 2007), categories perform their function almost independently of audiences; the ecological approach does not take into consideration the interactions that individuals nurture with the categories and the entities they face, value and evaluate. In the goal-based approach, interactions between individuals and categories are viewed as expanding individuals' 'conceptual systems' (Kahl, 2015). In this view, ideals transform categories' functioning, from alleviating ambiguity to becoming means for goal achievement.

For instance, Ruef and Patterson (2009) described that Dun's agents responsible for evaluating the profiles of companies in 19th century America were either untrained local correspondents or professional traveling credit reporters. Since the principal objective in 19th century credit rating 'was to minimize risk, not to encourage it as a source of growth or innovation' (Ruef and Patterson, 2009: 494), combining businesses (e.g., drugstores and alcoholic beverage distributors) and hence spanning categories of activities appeared to meet the requirements of business solvency, thus such activity combinations attracted positive attention. During this early period, therefore, category spanners were not sanctioned, but favorably evaluated, illustrating the fact that raters conceived spanning industrial categories as a means to achieve a certain goal (i.e., credit trustworthiness). In the same vein, Ross and Murphy (1999) investigated how people make inferences from categories that are 'readily cross-classified'. Using food product categories as their setting of choice, they demonstrated the existence of categories based on interactions with the food rather than on the composition of the food product categories. For instance, while bananas, grapes, oranges and pomegranates are all categorized as 'healthy foods', among those four items only bananas and grapes are categorized as 'healthy foods that can be eaten in a car'.

Hence, contrary to central tendency and family resemblance as the basis of the prototypical view, the goal-based view of categories relies on ideals formed through conceptual combination whereby 'people derive new categories by manipulating existing knowledge in memory' (Barsalou, 1991: 4). Conceptual combination does not rely on exemplars that capture the central tendencies of the category, but on ideals.

> First, ideals generally do not appear to be the central tendencies of their categories (although they may occasionally be) ... Ideals tend to be extreme values that are either true of only a few category members or true of none at all. Instead of lying at the center of categories (as does central tendency), they generally lie at the periphery ... Central tendency and ideals also differ in origin. Central tendency depends directly on the exemplars of a category, and more specifically, on the particular exemplars a person has experienced. Although people may form impressions of a category's central tendency through hearsay, they may generally acquire such information through experience with exemplars. In contrast, ideals may often be determined independently of exemplars, being acquired through the process of planning how to achieve goals before exemplars are ever encountered. (Barsalou, 1985: 631)

As a result, depending on the audience's goals, the cognitive mechanism of comparing distance from prototypical features is thwarted by conceptual combination. Illustrating this aspect, several scholars analyzed how venture capitalists (VCs) associate and recombine features to fit their goals around some idealized investments in technological start-ups (Pontikes, 2012; Wry et al., 2014). VCs invest money in ambiguous targets because they value the capacity to reinterpret ambiguity to their own advantage: 'for market-takers, ambiguous classification makes organizations unclear. But for market-makers, this same ambiguity represents flexibility' (Pontikes, 2012: 82). Indeed, as market makers, VCs ascribe value to offerings that are uneasy to classify with the promise of potential exceptional performance and rewards (Hsu et al., 2012). As a matter of fact, 'conceptual combination often produces idealized knowledge about how the world should be rather than normative knowledge about how it is' (Barsalou, 1991: 4). Hence, VCs see the world as it could be, not as it is, foreseeing and forecasting potential (new) revenue streams once markets stabilize around a dominant category (Suarez et al., 2015).

The fact that conceptual combination often overcomes similarity calculation is of fundamental importance for organization studies. As an illustration, Bitektine (2011) described the cognitive processes associated with social judgment formation. In such a context, conceptual combination helps explain why audiences grant cognitive as well as sociopolitical legitimacy based on 'different forms of analytical processing' (Bitektine, 2011: 156) to agents as a function of what audiences pursue – not just what they recognize or assess. Furthermore, both audiences and producers can import, modulate and create labels and vocabularies that coincide with their ideals and goals, and as such, contribute to a field's evolution beyond the product categories that have been studied by the ecological perspective. There is therefore ample application of the goal-based perspective to other objects of social significance, from the legitimation of death (Livne, 2014) and social tastes (Goldberg, 2011), to the redefinition of gender and race categories and associated cultural and social practices (Telles and Paschel, 2014; Davenport, 2016). A final illustration concerns the conflicting logics operating at the field level, and how vocabularies, repertoires and communication associated with goal-based categorization serve as the basis for making an institutional logic more prevalent (Jones et al., 2012; Cornelissen et al., 2015; Ocasio et al., 2015).

RECONCILING APPROACHES

We have seen so far that the ecological and goal-based approaches to categories vary in their premises (prototypes vs. ideals),

processes (central tendency and family resemblance vs. conceptual combination and goal achievement) and consequences (e.g., penalties vs. rewards for category spanners; market functioning vs. institutional field evolution). In this section, we propose three main ways to reconcile the current approaches, rather than maintain their separation. First, audiences' theories of value explain how they categorize organizations and the consequences that ensue. Second, there exist not only intra-audience, but also inter-audience variations in theories of value: not all actors share the same theory of value about an organization and what it offers. Investors, consumers and mediators may differ in this respect, and the validity of either approach can be more or less applicable to one or another audience. Third, depending on a field's developmental stage, one approach can be more relevant than the other. In a nascent field, categories are not yet fixed, and actors' multiple goals are expressed; however, when the field is settled, most actors rely on a stabilized category system, triggering family resemblance and proximity with exemplars more than ad hoc categorization.

One Audience Does Not Mean Only One Theory of Value

The first reconciliation between the two main approaches to categorization lies in the possibility that audiences activate different theories of value depending on circumstances. There is no reason to assume that audiences always apply the same theory of value for all of their needs. Actually, Paolella and Durand (2016) explained that audiences have diverse theories of value depending on their requirements; some are anchored in crisp prototypes (e.g., for well-established consumption products), whereas others evade typecasting (for more complex requirements). They argued that when issues are complex (e.g., sophisticated, singular and high stakes) clients' theories of value shift from type-based to goal-based; hence, clients assess producers as holistic entities that could potentially address their complex requirements before assessing whether individual product offerings are proto-typical (Paolella and Durand, 2016). To illustrate, when audiences aim to address less complex needs (e.g., a desire to indulge in a fine dining experience) they rely on proto-types (e.g., starred restaurants in a specific culinary genre). When audiences aim to address complex needs (e.g., a desire to implement a multi-billion dollar cross-border merger), they form an ideal (e.g., the best team of specialists across diverse practices) and categorize suppliers based on their capabilities to achieve their goal. In the former case, audiences are likely to select a proto-typical restaurant in a given genre, whereas in the latter they will value suppliers with multiple capabilities (i.e., category spanners). Therefore, depending on the goal and the type of transaction implied by the exchange, theories of value vary, and so do categorization processes, from identification to evaluation and sanctions.

Accordingly, Tost (2011) highlighted the importance of the selected mode of evaluation chosen by audiences (either passive or evaluative), and its subsequent impact on legitimacy judgments during the stage of judgment formation:

> In the passive mode ... rather than engage in effortful information processing, individuals either use validity cues as cognitive shortcuts to reach a legitimacy judgment or passively assume the legitimacy of entities that conform to cultural expectations (or some combination of the two). (2011: 696)

In the evaluative mode, audience members are more engaged and compare the phenomenon to abstracted expectations because 'in this mode the individual is actively motivated to construct an evaluation of the entity' (2011: 695). To put it differently, relying either on central tendency or conceptual combination significantly influences legitimacy judgments about categories across members within an audience.

Audiences' theories of value are also in flux; as such, a considered theory of value amongst an audience can evolve, leading to a change in the perception of the category *per se*. As an illustration, Delmestri and Greenwood (2016) built on the case of the status redefinition of grappa in Italy during the second half of the 20th century. They explained how categorical systems evolve to ultimately incorporate new social practices, thus extending the meaning associated with the category and leading to a redefinition of the categorical system. Indeed, the radical recategorization of grappa is an illustration of how theories of value can evolve over time: grappa, initially a low-status product, was gradually repositioned as a high-status category through the intervention of an elite (Delmestri and Greenwood, 2016). The role of politicians, writers, journalists and local producers was to conceptually recombine the grappa offering with existing categories but not through a direct comparison with other high-status categories such as whisky or cognac. Instead, allusions to neighboring categories, especially that of French wine (Delmestri and Greenwood, 2016), helped grappa benefit from favorable associations. Categories are embedded in a system of institutions and practices and grappa was progressively reclassified as a product used in the context of high social practices (Delmestri and Greenwood, 2016). The case of grappa showcases how identity, legitimacy and categorization processes are structurally interconnected and evolve over time (Ruef and Patterson, 2009; Alexy and George, 2013). As explained by Wry and colleagues (2011), categories acquire cognitive crispness when used repeatedly by a well-identified group of recognized actors:

> legitimation is facilitated when a nascent group of actors agree on a *collective identity defining story* that outlines their group's core purpose and practices, theorizing their meaning and appropriateness ... Once understood, accepted, and repeated by members, defining collective identity stories can become institutionalized, accounts that create a symbolic boundary. (Wry et al., 2011: 450, 452; see also Lamont and Molnár, 2002)

Within an audience, different members possess different theories of value that evolve through social processes that modify categories' identity perceptions, elaborate their symbolism and associate novel or traditional social practices and usages with them.

Multiple Actors Means Multiple Categorization Processes

Audience members use either a prototypical or a goal-based approach to categories depending on the ideals they generate and the theories of value they activate. As discussed before, investors and (cultural and institutional) entrepreneurs are not averse to categorical ambiguity; they rely on the cognitive mechanism of conceptual combination when evaluating organizations, and therefore tend to use the goal-based approach more than the prototypical approach. Other actors such as mediators (i.e., media, raters, NGOs and other observers) may prefer to anchor their judgments in prototypes and value producers' new offerings by activating the mechanism of central tendency (Barsalou, 1991). Contrary to investors like VCs and entrepreneurs, many mediators assess conformity to extant categories in order to facilitate information exchange in a field (Glynn and Lounsbury, 2005; Rao et al., 2005). As such, mediators rely on central tendency and family resemblance. They value the presence of exemplary features because of 'the need of stakeholders to communicate meaningfully with other stakeholders regarding their activities' (Suarez et al., 2015: 440). Indeed, industry commentators value conformity to the offerings already experienced in the past that 'speak to them' and their readers or listeners:

Industry commentators and users are likely to be more influential than producers in driving the process of categorical selection. Unlike producers, who have an incentive to promote the particular categories in which they position their designs, commentators and users are generally less invested

in any particular category. *For them, the primary purpose of categories is to help them make sense of the evolving industry and to reduce uncertainty regarding the traits of competing products.* (Grodal et al., 2015: 432; emphasis added)

Evaluators' judgments of categories are central to understanding any institutional order (Bitektine and Haack, 2015). Mediators are legitimacy providers and, as such, maintain and confer legitimacy to established or rising categories that are the fabric of institutions: they are the 'critical sources of validity that fundamentally influence other evaluators' judgments' (Bitektine and Haack, 2015: 51). Through valuation and evaluation, mediators produce discourses and narratives that influence an audience's theory of value (Hardy and Phillips, 1998; Phillips et al., 2004). Some organizations and mediators can choose to create new categories or mix and match references and features alien to past exemplars. In so doing, they aggregate new communities of users, initiate trends and facilitate the emergence of entirely novel categories or branches in the category system, as we see in the cases of modern Indian art (Khaire and Wadhwani, 2010) or grass-fed beef (Weber et al., 2008), for instance. Overall, researchers have relied on a simplified theorization of categories and assumed that audiences respond uniformly, or when studying two audiences, have ignored the interferences that may exist across audiences. However, VCs can diffuse the reliance and interest of goal-based categories to other field participants through their multiple investments. In the computer industry, VCs were able to influence other field participants to prefer more malleable categories, notably 'organizations that are in constraining categories [which], when they receive VC investment, are more likely to enter a lenient category' (Pontikes and Barnett, 2015: 1426).

Beyond diffusion of goal-based categories, another phenomenon explains the prevalence of one form of categorization over the other: rivalry among actors. For instance, in the culinary industry studied by Durand, Rao and Monin (2007), the Michelin guide opted for the preservation of categories while Gault and Millau promoted nouvelle cuisine and new categories. It is crucial to keep in mind that as much as there is competition for producers who strive to be categorized, highly ranked and rewarded, there is competition for mediation. Which rater, critic or media format imposes its criteria, analysis, rankings, vocabulary and so forth? Here again, it is critical to not blindly associate one approach with one type of audience, but to scrupulously link each audience member with a preferred approach. This hints at the strategic importance of categorization processes, which we discuss later.

Furthermore, theories of value vary among actors of a given type (i.e., producers, mediators or consumers). Across actor types, there is variance too; some types of actors might be closer to other types of representative entities than to their peers. For instance, some mediators typecast producers as much as some consumers (and hence function as conventional market-takers), whereas others share common ideals and goal-based categories with some consumers and producers. This novel representation therefore opens rich new research opportunities.

Different Stages Imply Different Approaches to Categories

In fields and markets, categories enable producers and audiences to create more or less efficient exchanges (in terms of information quality, time and satisfaction). However, new fields and markets spawn over time and necessitate adjusted category systems to guarantee information flows, access and quality evaluation between parties. In turn, in existing fields and markets, incumbent and/ or entrant producers generate innovative offerings that impose novel feature associations, trigger cognitive surprises and imply the creation, emergence, fusion and grafting of new categories. In either case, there exist situations where field maturity does not coincide with the prevalent category system, opening spaces for the predominance of one or the other approach to categories.

The ecological approach, rooted in prototypes, explains the matching process between maturity stages and categories by the role of 'enthusiasts', the driving force for category emergence; indeed, 'enthusiasts within the audience likely do the hard work of clustering, labeling and schematizing' (Hannan et al., 2007: 111). From this perspective, enthusiasts participate in the formation of a new category and rapidly achieve an equilibrium state whereby actors categorize novelties and identify, assess and reward producers. However, this rapid equilibration between novelty and the category system eschews both the cognitive processes and actors' intents associated with novelty. Here again, considering actors' goals matters.

First, Alexy and George (2013) stated that in lieu of discounting a repeatedly observed mismatch between existing categories and a novel reality, some audiences attempt to redefine categorical boundaries without the mobilization of enthusiasts. Such a mismatch, prompted by novelty, triggers a learning process that leads audiences to revise the categorization process and schema associated with the observed reality: 'the outcome of this updating process may be either the redefinition of the boundaries of the old category to include the newly observed behavior, or the subdivision of the old category with the divergent behavior attaining legitimate category status in its own right' (Alexy and George, 2013: 182). According to the ecological view, a mismatch between categorization and what is observed in reality should lead to either the devaluation and sanctioning of such deviant offerings or to a rapid constitution of a new exemplar, sponsored by enthusiasts and shared and used by audiences to discipline producers (Hannan et al., 2007). Alexy and George (2013) observed nonetheless that audiences learn and rethink 'their causal modelling of category membership' (Alexy and George, 2013: 193; see also Durand and Paolella (2013) on the causal-model approach to categories). In other words, audiences are able to conceptually approach novelty, modify the category system's internal boundaries and branching, and update their identification and evaluation processes accordingly.

Second, actors' intentions are a crucial component of the emergence of new markets and categories (Granqvist and Ritvala, 2016). By definition, novelty is introduced by something that differs significantly from a prototype, a typical exemplar. In markets, novelty is intentional and aimed at providing a differentiation advantage. The essence of strategic behavior is striking the balance between conformity to expected features and deviance that is acceptable and legitimate (Durand, 2012, 2014; Durand and Kremp, 2016). Therefore, when actors strive to facilitate the emergence of new categories, they pursue an ideal, group and link some features together, and divide and dissociate others; in a nutshell, they create and project ad hoc categories in the field.

These ad hoc categories violate previously accepted correlational structures and are not recognized by most people (Barsalou, 1983). For instance, Barsalou (1983) illustrated an ad hoc category of 'things to take from one's home during a fire', which contains items as diverse as children, a dog, a stereo and a blanket (Barsalou, 1983: 214). Items in this category do not appear to share correlated properties. In such a context, it would not make sense to penalize category spanners. That is why 'it is worth noting that whereas common categories are primarily disciplinary, ad hoc categories serve as a medium for coordination among producers and audiences, and they do not penalize deviance' (Etzion, 2014: 424). With novelty in fields and markets (e.g., Apple's iPod, iPad, etc., which created new product categories and facilitated the emergence of new market segments within a few years), the same absence of correlated properties amongst a set of categorical features can be observed

during category emergence since there are 'no widely shared prototypes' (Kennedy and Fiss, 2013: 1143) of the emerging category.

Since 'our understanding of categories is limited to established categories in market settings and focuses on how audiences shape product categories and highlight features as a basis for categorizing artifacts' (Jones et al., 2012: 1525), it is likely that the ecological approach to categories is more applicable in settled fields. The approach based on prototypes sheds light on the identification and evaluation processes of producers and offerings when categories are well-established among field actors, producers, consumers and mediators. Central tendency and family resemblance both imply that actors have encountered entities and stored enough information to constitute exemplars. As shown, the ecological perspective is not well-suited to explain market and category emergence. It cannot be used to theorize (voluntary) distancing from exemplars. Why would actors evade positive rewards by deviating from prototypes? Also, from this perspective, evaluation is fundamentally thought of as an immanent principle – audiences are supposed to have an immediate and intuitive sense of the category being proposed and should consequently mentally derive and somehow compute whether or not the proposed object, product or service aligns with the prototype of a given category (Hsu, 2006; Hsu et al., 2009). Finally, the role of audience enthusiasts is exaggerated but necessary to the theory in order to justify the copresence of a stable field and a stable category system through which the disciplinary role of the categorical imperative can operate. In other words, the ecological approach is relevant to explain the evaluative outcomes of well-institutionalized fields and well-recognized categories.

When fields are nascent, or in existing markets where actors introduce novelty, the goal-based approach to categories appears to be more relevant. Whether producers disrupt a field, mediators reshuffle categories or customers' theories of value differently link features of past and current supply, field members face novel situations that trigger original processes and reactions. Such novelties prompt associations with categories that are not clearly established in audience members' minds, thereby preventing them from relying on prototypes to evaluate a newly formed proposal. Again, if one thinks of a fruit, an apple is a typical instance of such a category; in other words, it could be considered a prototype of the category 'fruit' because there is a strong concept-to-instance association. Conversely, if a person is asked to categorize an apple, the answer will likely be 'fruit;' in such a context, there is also a strong instance-to-concept association. Those who have adopted a prototype-based approach have mainly dealt with established categories and products (e.g., beer, wine, movie, etc.) with high instance-to-concept and concept-to-instance associations in well-established and settled industries. However, to use one of Barsalou's (1983) examples, if a person is asked to respond to an ad hoc category such as 'what to bring to a picnic', and she has never been to a picnic before (i.e., there is a weak instance-to-concept association), how would she react if she was unable to rely on an existing prototype stored in memory? In such a context, when categories are weakly established in audience members' minds, conceptual combination and goal achievement become the relevant mechanisms for identifying fitting candidates and valuing them.

During the field emergence and early market stages, actors recombine and build new relationships between existing categories, encapsulated in the words used to describe and name them. For instance, Grodal et al. (2015: 430) identified compounding, the process that 'recombine[s] existing words or phonemes [as] the most common type of linguistic recombination'. Conceptual combination is thus central for the semantic construction of new fields or product categories in early stages. Loewenstein, Ocasio and Jones (2012: 66) emphasized 'word-to-word

frequencies', 'word-to-word relationships' and 'word-to-example relationships' to account for the semantic structure of the new categorical system in formation.

In sum, the ecological and goal-based approaches are valid in different domains depending on the degree of field maturity and the establishment level of the category system in use.

DISCUSSION AND RESEARCH AGENDA

In this last section, we structure the discussion around three main areas of development for future research. We suggest projects that would help delineate the validity domains for the two main approaches to categories. Then, we focus on ignored aspects of category research. Finally, we link category research to the economic dimensions of production, and prompt researchers to examine the relationships between strategy and categorization processes.

Validity Domains

Based on our previous sections, three main areas of research need to be investigated. First, we must account for intra-audience heterogeneity in the use of various theories of value. What are the conditions that explain the fact that certain audience members expect more or less complex characteristics from producers and pursue distinct goals? What are the links between theories of value mobilized by decision-makers (at the cognitive level) and the institutional logics that surround and influence them (at the normative level)? Further, depending on the proportion of audience members who adopt one or the other approach to categories and on the social or institutional importance of audience members, what would explain the predominance of one theory of value over the other in a field? Imagine an industry in which all peripheral audience members have simple goals and needs, but a few central members pursue more complex ideals. What are the consequences for the category system prevalent in this industry? Which producers will create or facilitate the emergence of new categories? And for which audience members (i.e., central or peripheral)?

Second, we need a better theorization of the consequences resulting from the existence of a plurality of actors that participate in maintaining or upending a category system. In addition to intra-audience variation, the inter-audience component opens unexplored research areas. When some portions of an audience pursue a prototypical approach in their categorization of a field's actors (e.g., producers), they may be more similar to members of another audience who do the same than to their peers. What are the consequences of such inter-audience proximities for (market) exchanges, producers' identities and performance, and the category system *per se*? Said differently, what matters more for a producer in its efforts to impose its product categories, offerings and innovations? That one audience's members (e.g., consumers) all concur about its products' categories (i.e., low cognitive, identity and competence ambiguity) but disagree with another audience (e.g., mediators); or that a sufficient portion of both consumers and mediators share the same approach to categorization, whatever it is? When does the former proposition invalidate the latter, and vice versa? We need to better relate how producers (or any field actors) choose vocabulary, use rhetorical strategies and evoke inherent institutional logics to how other actors mobilize similar or different categorization processes across audiences (Durand et al., 2013; Ocasio et al., 2015; Suddaby and Greenwood, 2005; Thornton et al., 2005).

Once some of these questions have been answered, a fascinating research project would focus on the transition from one approach to categorization to the other as a field matures. We simplified the analysis previously by associating field maturity with the ecological approach of categories. But how and why do fields and markets follow a path where emergent categories are goal-based, find their audiences and stabilize as exemplars, or another path in which category spanning, for instance, becomes the prototype (Paolella and Durand, 2016) even though a specific category combination appears to remain a severe prototypical violation or even a betrayal (Phillips et al., 2013)? There is a rich area of investigation that connects institutional literature, categories, semantic and vocabulary structure (Cornelissen et al., 2015; Green et al., 2009; Loewenstein et al., 2012; Ocasio et al., 2015) that would help to explain the legitimization of goal-based categories. Reciprocally, fields do not settle forever, and material as well as cognitive and symbolic structures shift and disrupt them. Therefore, there is a shift from stable category systems where the ecological approach to categories is valid to a situation where category systems evolve and other approaches to categories become more valid. Hence, what are the factors that explain this change in the validity domain of either approach? Does the change in categorical approach validity follow field disruption, or cause it?

Ignored Aspects

At the field level, the goal-based approach appears to be a relevant theoretical apparatus for understanding how 'a new category becomes stable [and] relevant audiences collectively recognize the meanings that define its identity' (Khaire and Wadhwani, 2010: 1283). Research efforts have been undertaken to better understand category emergence at the conceptual level. For instance, Grodal and colleagues (2015) identified different stages of categorical evolution. The authors highlighted: (a) a period of categorical divergence where linguistic recombination prevails and where new category labels are created, followed by (b) a period of convergence characterized by categorical deepening where 'semantic connections of a particular category become denser' (Grodal et al., 2015: 426). Such longitudinal considerations would gain traction by integrating considerations about audiences' theories of value and the influence of categorization mechanisms (central tendency vs. conceptual combination). In other words, what role do central tendency and conceptual combination play during the linguistic recombination stage? What roles do they play during the categorical deepening phase? Furthermore, additional research is needed that tracks the values associated with goal-based categories and how field agents develop discourses in support of or against these categories. For instance, Meyer and Höllerer (2010) scrutinized the introduction of the 'shareholder value' category within the Austrian economy and the struggles to define meaning in confrontation with local institutions throughout the 1990s.

At the firm level, further research needs to be undertaken to recognize when and how producers rely on different audiences' theories of value to position their offerings; arguably, factoring in the ability of audiences to rely on either central tendency or conceptual combination has implications for strategic categorization (Vergne and Wry, 2014). Producers have leeway to present their offerings in ways that favor the cognitive mechanism of central tendency (prototype-based categories) or conceptual combination (goal-based categories). Hsu and Grodal (2015) showed how audiences balance different goals, health concerns and taste-related concerns during the emergence of the light cigarette category between 1964 and 1993. Producers duped consumers with the 'light' category while maintaining very high tar and nicotine levels. Consequently, we need more research that investigates how producers strive to have their offerings identified and valued by consumers, and which strategies

they employ to do so – either by matching their audiences' prototypes and ideals or by deceiving them (see works on market identity and conventionality by Kim and Jensen, 2011 and Durand and Kremp, 2016). Finally, such an approach would help us to understand not only why and how categories appear and diffuse but also why and how they disappear as a function of producers' actions (Kuilman and Van Driel, 2013).

Furthermore, Vergne and Wry (2014) identified that 'opportunities abound to explore the ways in which organizations strategically signal their affiliation(s) within an existing category system' (2014: 78). Sharkey (2014) showed how the status of a producer's industrial affiliation matters when evaluating corporate moves that are usually discounted; as such, firms issuing earning restatements are less penalized if they are 'from a higher-status industry' (2014: 1411). To acknowledge the full potential of a producer's affiliations, such affiliations need to be connected to other field participants' (e.g., audiences, mediators) theories of value. In particular, when actors combine different sources of legitimacy such as institutional logics, mediators play a crucial role by enforcing the hybridization of categories or failing to do so. Organizations hybridize by modifying their core governance structures, organizational routines, identities and even institutional logics (Borys and Jemison, 1989; Pache and Santos, 2010; Besharov and Smith, 2014). For instance, social enterprises mix the logics of the welfare sector and the private sector into a new form of organizational arrangement (Battilana and Dorado, 2010; Pache and Santos, 2013). Such an uncommon institutional disposition leads to cognitive, identity or competence ambiguity for external audiences. But mediators' theories of value evolve, leading to a reconfiguration of how category blending is perceived and evaluated. In another example, Ioannou and Serafeim (2015) depicted how mediators gradually adopted a stakeholder perspective and its subsequent logic in their evaluation judgments in lieu of the traditional agency perspective, leading to a stronger evaluation of firms that hybridize their practices by integrating CSR concerns.

At the individual level, Hannan and colleagues (2007) stressed the 'considerable cognitive load' that categorization processes require in the context of category creation, which implies that people need to be in 'a high-energy state;' hence, these people are called enthusiasts or activists (Hannan ct al., 2007: 45). To make sense of new categories, Glynn and Navis (2013: 1126) also emphasized that it takes 'cognitive effort for participants to think differently about a given fact, and not apply their usual schemes, derived from their own logics'. This demanding cognitive effort was also illustrated by Bingham and Kahl (2013), who studied how groups in the life insurance industry built a new schema between 1945 and 1975 that later became the business computer category. Likewise:

> in the early stages of a category's development, market participants must attempt to determine which membership claims they regard as valid even as they are still making sense of and updating their category-level beliefs. As a result, the process of evaluating potential category members is likely to require considerable time and effort. (Hsu and Grodal, 2015: 37)

However, these efforts have not been qualified, studied and theorized in the organization and management field. What are the individual characteristics that explain the fact that some people are more likely to pay attention to and spend considerable time and effort engaging in such categorization processes (Bowers, 2015)? What are the social and network conditions that explain whether or not category emergence or creation will spread? Network studies and psychology experiments are promising avenues to nurture category research and better account for the apprehension of category features, positioning of categories in a category system, triggering of certain theories of value and acceptance of new categories at the individual level. Another potentially fruitful area

concerns the connection with the sociology of culture and taste, so as to understand how novelty (and not just category combination) can conflict with individual and group-defined taste and influence both the identification and evaluation phases (Goldberg, 2011; Lizardo and Skiles, 2012).

Strategic Perspectives

A last promising avenue for advancing research on categories associates category creation and categorization processes with strategy-making and outcomes. In existing research on categories, scholars typically have ignored which organizations preserve category systems or attempt to upend them. They have studied existing categories, but have not associated specific actors with the emergence, use, diffusion or abandonment of categories. Therefore, some questions surface: Which producers are more likely to preserve extant categories? What resources and means are required to create a new category in a field? What are the relationships between the cognitive aspects of categorization (whether central tendency or conceptual combination) and an organization's material aspects (i.e., structure, tangible resources, identity) in relationship with the organization's involvement in creating, using, diffusing or dropping a category? Some researchers began to explore the strategic positioning of actors and their choices of logics. For instance, Durand and colleagues (2013) provided evidence of how the competences, industry focuses and statuses of French industrial design agencies explained why they had or had not adopted new management logics relative to the two historical logics of modernism and formalism. More effort is required to associate these organizational strategic characteristics with the ways in which organizations mobilize categories, associated features and cues, and semantic relationships from within the categorical system to alter their positioning, blend dimensions of logics or strive for purity. Works that have tackled the heterogeneity of responses chosen by organizations when facing institutional complexity (for a review, see Greenwood et al., 2011) have paved the way in this direction.

We suggest a way to represent the expected prevalence of organizational approaches to categories (central tendency and family resemblance vs. conceptual combination and goal achievement) based on a market logic, but it is generalizable to other institutions and institutional logics. In general, categories exist to facilitate exchanges, and in markets, economic transactions. In some markets, producers benefit from 'economies of reproduction' (i.e., they have access to standardization advantages, scale and volume matter, learning is exploitative and innovation is incremental). One research insight poses that the presence of such economies of reproduction influences which type of categorization approach is better suited to a context. Crossing this dimension with the theory of value used by an audience (which depends on the goal and the type of transaction implied by the exchange) yields distinct scenarios:

1 When economies of reproduction are weak and theories of value rely on ideals and complex transactions, the best approach for producers is one that is goal-based. This corresponds to the case of the corporate law industry mentioned earlier (Paolella and Durand, 2016): each legal case is specific, hence no economies of reproduction are attainable and the ideal coincides with a complex need.

2 As economies of reproduction strengthen and become more accessible, goal-based categories tend to solidify in the sense that concept-to-instance associations (Barsalou, 1983) become recurrent, identifiable and sought after by audiences. Lo and Kennedy's (2015) work on patent adoption and categorical blending illustrates this phenomenon, since expert patent examiners evaluate more easily category combinations when they use patterns seen before in other inventions. As the repetition of an unusual categorical combination unfolds, concept-to-instance associations cement to facilitate the acceptance

of the new mix. For a given complex goal, audiences begin to believe that certain instances (elements, features extolled by a producer) coincide with the expected category, and that there will be causal associations between the presence of these elements and features and an expected outcome. This is what Murphy (2002) and Durand and Paolella (2013) called the 'causal model approach of categories'. This approach has been under-researched, yet applies to many concrete cases. For instance, the presence of certain quality labels or stamps on products triggers a causal association that the producers have been controlled and tested on selective criteria (hygiene, components, environmental footprint, etc.). These causal associations between features and categories do not obey the central tendency mechanism *per se* since products can be prototypical, but convey cues that trigger the causal associations or not. By the same token, the goal-based approach only partially captures the causal associations, since they require more than the capacity to meet a goal for a specific case: causal associations imply repeated exposures to situations that induce storage of a cause-and-effect relationship into memory; that is, the observation that products or producers with a given feature have a certain characteristic (e.g., a quality stamp implies an independent process of quality control).

3 Finally, as the theory of value relies on less complex goals and the existence of exemplars, the ecological approach to categories takes the lead, based on prototypes and family resemblance.

Figure 24.1 represents this graphically.

This mapping of the expected prevalence of organizational approaches to categories is tentative, complements what has been presented earlier and can lead to some new research inquiries. Figure 24.2 revisits the consequences of category spanning for each approach in terms of social evaluation and performance. While the upper part of the matrix consecrates positive evaluations of category spanning, the right-hand part (i.e., where the goal-based approach is more relevant) shows that performance is not directly impacted positively due to weak economies of reproduction (e.g., Paolella and Durand, 2016). However, an unexplored area of the

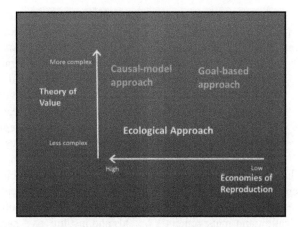

Figure 24.1 Strategic mapping of market category approaches

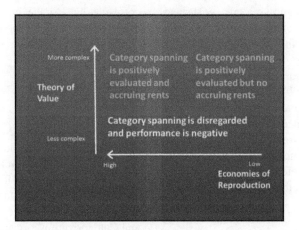

Figure 24.2 Consequences of category spanning

matrix is where the causal-model approach to categories is prevalent and where positive impacts on performance should materialize. Therefore, it is important to study an industry with strong enough economies of reproduction, and identify the choices of different producers related to their categorization approaches and concurrently test whether or not a direct positive impact on producers follows a causal-model approach relative to the other possibilities.

This mapping is parsimonious and amenable to other perspectives, beyond the market logic. Depending on the logic (state, profession, etc.), the prototypes and goals pursued by audiences will differ, as will categories. By the same token, economies of reproduction need to be adjusted to the determinants of organizational survival defined from within a logic, and to the theories of value that determine what audiences expect from the candidate organizations (Phillips and Zuckerman, 2001). After adjusting for the setting specificities (prototypes and goals in use, sources of economies of reproduction and theories of values), we think that at the cognitive level, the validity domains of the three categorization approaches as represented in Figure 24.1 and the consequences of category spanning (or logic blending or hybridization) as represented in Figure 24.2 do not change.

CONCLUSION

In this chapter we have exposed two main approaches to categories, proposed three ways to reconcile the two dominant approaches in organization and management studies, and sketched new research avenues that consider both prior research and the proposed reconciliations. Our attempt has been to delineate a 'cognitive core' enshrined within the corpus of institutional research that characterizes the norms, vocabularies and logics that surround the cognitive determinants of category evaluation: central tendency and family resemblance for the ecological perspective of categories based on prototypes, and conceptual combination and goal achievement for the goal-based perspective. An audience's theories of value determine their preferences, and organizations either address their preferences well or not. Organizations' solutions that fit nicely with shared common categorical features activate audiences' central tendencies and prototypical comparisons. When they deviate significantly from expected prototypical features, organizations' solutions that correspond to an audience's more complex ideals trigger conceptual combinations of dissimilar categorical features in a meaningful way.

Such a distinction has implications for organization and strategy scholars: (a) audience members' preferred categorization frameworks vary based on their own theories of value; (b) these different cognitive mechanisms exist between and across field participants (i.e., producers, consumers and mediators) and influence legitimacy judgments; and finally, (c) such a divide can evolve over time (i.e., as categories become more mature and institutionalized into systems). More terrain needs to be covered at the intersection of category, strategy and neo-institutional research. Organizations' actions must be better associated with the evolution of category systems. Furthermore, preserving or transforming categories and categorical boundaries is of strategic importance, and connects with performance implications at the organizational, institutional and social levels. Therefore, we conclude this chapter with a call to investigate the fundamental role of organizations in upending the cognitive infrastructure of fields and institutions – particularly markets – and relatedly, both the field structure itself (as per the advantages and penalties associated with these actions) and the social practices corresponding to the novel uses, meanings and identity elements sponsored and enacted through the organizations' work on categories.

ACKNOWLEDGMENT

The slides in Figures 24.1 and 24.2 were presented by R. Durand at the Academy of Management Conference, 2014, in the OMT Division Professional Development Workshop 'From Stable and Static Categories: To a Dynamic View on Categories and Categorization' organized by R. Durand, N. Granqvist and A. Tyllstrom.

REFERENCES

Alexy, O. and George, G. (2013). Category divergence, straddling, and currency: Open innovation and the legitimation of illegitimate categories. *Journal of Management Studies*, 50: 173–203.

Barsalou, L.W. (1983). Ad hoc categories. *Memory & Cognition*, 11: 211–227.

Barsalou, L.W. (1985). Ideals, central tendency, and frequency of instantiation as determinants of graded structure in categories. *Journal of Experimental Psychology: Learning, Memory, and Cognition*, 11: 629–654.

Barsalou, L.W. (1991). Deriving categories to achieve goals. In G.H. Bower (ed.), *The Psychology of*

Learning and Motivation: Advances in Research and Theory, Vol. 27. San Diego, CA: Academic Press. pp. 1–64.

Battilana, J. and Dorado, S. (2010). Building sustainable hybrid organizations: The case of commercial microfinance organizations. *Academy of Management Journal*, 53: 1419–1440.

Besharov, M.L. and Smith, W.K. (2014). Multiple institutional logics in organizations: Explaining their varied nature and implications. *Academy of Management Review*, 39(3): 364–381.

Bingham, C. and Kahl, S.J. (2013). The process of schema emergence: Assimilation, deconstruction, unitization and the plurality of analogies'. *Academy of Management Journal*, 56(1): 14–34.

Bitektine, A. (2011). Towards a theory of social judgments of organizations: The case of legitimacy, reputation, and status. *Academy of Management Review*, 36: 151–179.

Bitektine, A. and Haack, P. (2015). The 'macro' and the 'micro' of legitimacy: Toward a multilevel theory of the legitimacy process. *Academy of Management Review*, 40: 49–75.

Borys, B. and Jemison, D.B. (1989). Hybrid arrangements as strategic alliances: Theoretical issues in organizational combinations. *Academy of Management Review*, 14(2): 234–249.

Bowers, A. (2015). Relative comparison and category membership: The case of equity analysts. *Organization Science*, 26(2): 571–583.

Cornelissen, J.P., Durand, R., Fiss, P.C., Lammers, J.C. and Vaara, E. (2015). Putting communication front and center in institutional theory and analysis. *Academy of Management Review*, 40(1): 10–27.

Davenport, L. (2016). The Role of Gender, Class, and Religion in Biracial Americans' Racial Labeling Decisions. *American Sociological Review*, 81(1): 57–84.

Delmestri, G. and Greenwood R. (2016). How Cinderella Became a Queen: Theorizing Radical Status Change. *Administrative Science Quarterly*, 61(4): 507–550.

Durand, R. (2012). Advancing strategy and organization research in concert: Towards an integrated model? *Strategic Organization*, 10(3): 297–303.

Durand, R. (2014). *Organizations, Strategy and Society: The Orgology of Disorganized Worlds*. London: Routledge.

Durand, R. and Khaire, M. (2017). Where Do Market Categories Come From and How? Distinguishing Category Creation From Category Emergence. *Journal of Management*, 43(1): 87–110.

Durand, R. and Kremp, P.-A. (2016). Classical deviation: Organizational and individual status as antecedents of conformity. *Academy of Management Journal*, 59: 65–89.

Durand, R. and Paolella, L. (2013). Category stretching: Reorienting research on categories in strategy, entrepreneurship, and organization theory. *Journal of Management Studies*, 50(6): 1100–1123.

Durand, R., Rao, H. and Monin, P. (2007). Code and conduct in French cuisine: Impact of code changes on external evaluations. *Strategic Management Journal*, 28: 455–472.

Durand, R., Szostak, B., Jourdan, J. and Thornton, P.H. (2013). Institutional logics as strategic resources. In E. Boxenbaum and M. Lounsbury (eds), *Institutional Logics in Action*, Part A. *Research In the Sociology of Organizations*, Volume 39A. Bingley, UK: Emerald Group. pp. 165–201.

Etzion, D. (2014). Diffusion as classification. *Organization Science*, 25(2): 420–437.

Glynn, M.A. and Lounsbury, M. (2005). From the critics' corner: Logic blending, discursive change and authenticity in a cultural production system. *Journal of Management Studies*, 42(5): 1031–1055.

Glynn, M.A. and Navis, C. (2013). Categories, identities, and cultural classification: Moving beyond a model of categorical constraint. *Journal of Management Studies*, 50(6): 1124–1137.

Goldberg, A. (2011). Mapping shared understandings using relational class analysis: The case of the cultural omnivore reconsidered. *American Journal of Sociology*, 116: 1397–1436.

Granqvist, N., Grodal, S. and Woolley, J.L. (2013). Hedging your bets: Explaining executives' market labeling strategies in nanotechnology. *Organization Science*, 24: 395–413.

Granqvist, N. and Ritvala, T. (2016). Beyond prototypes: Drivers of market categorization in functional foods and nanotechnology. *Journal of Management Studies*, 53 (2): 210–237.

Green, S., Li, Y. and Nohria, N. (2009). Suspended in self-spun webs of significance: A rhetorical model of institutionalization and institutionally embedded agency. *Academy of Management Journal*, 52(1): 11–36.

Greenwood, R., Raynard, M., Kodeih, F., Micelotta, E.R. and Lounsbury, M. (2011). Institutional complexity and organizational responses. *Academy of Management Annals*, 5(1): 317–371.

Grodal, S., Gotsopoulos, A. and Suarez, F.S. (2015). The co-evolution of categories and designs during industry emergence. *Academy of Management Review*, 40(3): 423–445.

Hannan, M.T., Pólos, L. and Carroll, G.R. (2007). *Logics of Organization Theory: Audiences, Codes, and Ecologies*. Princeton, NJ: Princeton University Press.

Hardy, C. and Phillips, N. (1998). Strategies of engagement: Lessons from the critical examination of collaboration and conflict in an interorganizational domain. *Organization Science*, 9: 217–230.

Hiatt, S., Sine, W. and Tolbert, P. (2009). From Pabst to Pepsi: The deinstitutionalization of social practices and the emergence of entrepreneurial opportunities. *Administrative Science Quarterly*, 54: 635–667.

Hsu, G. (2006). Jacks of all trades and masters of none: Audiences' reactions to spanning genres in feature film production. *Administrative Science Quarterly*, 51: 420–450.

Hsu, G. and Grodal, S. (2015). Category taken-for-grantedness as a strategic opportunity: The case of light cigarettes, 1964–1993. *American Sociological Review*, 80(1): 28–62.

Hsu, G., Hannan, M.T. and Kocak, O. (2009). Multiple category memberships in markets: An integrative theory and two empirical tests. *American Sociological Review*, 74: 150–169.

Hsu, G., Negro, G. and Perretti, F. (2012). Hybrids in Hollywood: A study of the production and performance of genre spanning films. *Industrial and Corporate Change*, 21: 1427–1450.

Ioannou, I. and Serafeim, G. (2015). The impact of corporate social responsibility on investment recommendations: Analysts' perceptions and shifting institutional logics. *Strategic Management Journal*, 36: 1053–1081.

Jones, C., Maoret, M., Massa, F.G. and Svejenova, S. (2012). Rebels with a cause: The formation, contestation and expansion of the de novo category modern architecture, 1870–1975. *Organization Science*, 23: 1523–1545.

Kahl, S.J. (2015). Product conceptual systems: Toward a cognitive processing model. In Giovanni Gavetti and William Ocasio (eds), *Cognition and Strategy. Advances in Strategic Management*, Volume 32. Bingley, UK: Emerald Group. pp.119–146.

Kennedy, M.T. and Fiss, P.C. (2013). An ontological turn in categories research: From standards of legitimacy to evidence of actuality. *Journal of Management Studies*, 50: 1138–1154.

Khaire, M. and Wadhwani, R.D. (2010). Changing landscapes: The construction of meaning and value in a new market category – modern Indian art. *Academy of Management Journal*, 53: 1281–1304.

Kim, B. and Jensen, M. (2011). How product order affects market identity repertoire ordering in the US opera market. *Administrative Science Quarterly*, 56: 238–256.

Kovács, B., Carroll, G. and Lehman, D. (2014). Value and categories in socially constructed authenticity: Empirical tests from restaurant reviews. *Organization Science*, 25(2): 458–478.

Kovács, B. and Hannan, M.T. (2010). The consequences of category spanning depend on contrast. In G. Hsu, G. Negro and O. Kocak (eds), *Categories in Markets: Origins and Evolution. Research in the Sociology of Organizations*, Volume 31. Bingley, UK: Emerald Group. pp. 175–201.

Kuilman, J.G. and Van Driel, H. (2013). You too, Brutus? Category demise in Rotterdam warehousing, 1871–2011. *Industrial and Corporate Change*, 22(2): 511–548.

Lamont, M. and Molnár, V. (2002). The study of boundaries across the social sciences. *Annual Review of Sociology*, 28: 167–195.

Leung, M.D. and Sharkey, A.J. (2014). Out of sight, out of mind? The audience-side effect of multi-category membership in markets. *Organization Science*, 25(1): 171–184.

Livne, R. (2014). Economies of dying: The moralization of economic scarcity in U.S. hospice care. *American Sociological Review*, 79(5): 888–911.

Lizardo, O. and Skiles, S. (2012). Reconceptualizing and theorizing 'omnivorousness' genetic and relational mechanisms. *Sociological Theory*, 30(4): 263–282.

Lo, J.Y.C., Kennedy, M.T. (2015). Approval in nanotechnology patents: Micro and macro factors that affect reactions to category blending. *Organization Science*, 26: 119–139.

Loewenstein, J., Ocasio, W. and Jones, C. (2012). Vocabularies and vocabulary structure: A new approach linking categories, practices, and institutions. *Academy of Management Annals*, 6(1): 41–86.

Maguire, S., Hardy, C. and Lawrence, T.B. (2004). Institutional entrepreneurship in emerging fields: HIV/AIDS treatment advocacy in Canada. *Academy of Management Journal*, 47(5): 657–679.

Meyer, R.E. and Höllerer, M.A. (2010). Meaning structures in a contested issue field: A topographic map of shareholder value in Austria. *Academy of Management Journal*, 53(6): 1241–1262.

Murphy, G.L. (2002). *The Big Book of Concepts*. Boston, MA: The MIT Press.

Navis, C. and Glynn, M.A. (2010). How new market categories emerge: Temporal dynamics of legitimacy, identity, and entrepreneurship in satellite radio, 1990–2005. *Administrative Science Quarterly*, 55: 439–471.

Negro, G., Hannan, M.T. and Rao, H. (2010). Categorical contrast and niche width: Critical success in winemaking. *Industrial and Corporate Change*, 19: 1397–1425.

Negro, G., Hannan, M.T. and Rao, H. (2011). Reinterpretation and defection: Modernism and tradition in Italian wine making. *Organization Science*, 22: 1449–1463.

Negro, G. and Leung, M.D. (2013). 'Actual' and perceptual effects of category spanning. *Organization Science*, 24: 684–696.

Ocasio, W., Loewenstein, J. and Nigam, A. (2015). How streams of communication reproduce and change institutional logics: The role of categories. *Academy of Management Review*, 40(1): 10–27.

Pache, A.C. and Santos, F. (2010). When worlds collide: The internal dynamics of organizational responses to conflicting institutional demands. *Academy of Management Review*, 35: 455–476.

Pache, A.C. and Santos, F. (2013). Inside the hybrid organization: Selective coupling as a response to competing institutional logics. *Academy of Management Journal*, 56(3): 971–100.

Paolella, L. and Durand, R. (2016). Category spanning, evaluation, and performance: Revised theory and test on the corporate law market. *Academy of Management Journal*, 59: 330–351.

Phillips, D., Turco, C. and Zuckerman, E.W. (2013). Betrayal as market barrier: Identity-based limits to diversification among high-status corporate law firms. *American Journal of Sociology*, 118: 1–32.

Phillips, D.J. and Zuckerman, E.W. (2001). Middle-status conformity: Theoretical restatement and empirical demonstration in two markets. *American Journal of Sociology*, 107(2): 379–429.

Phillips, N., Lawrence, T.B. and Hardy, C. (2004). Discourse and institutions. *Academy of Management Review*, 29: 635–652.

Pontikes, E.G. (2012). Two sides of the same coin: How ambiguous classification affects multiple audiences' evaluations. *Administrative Science Quarterly*, 57(1): 81–118.

Pontikes, E.G. and Barnett, W.P. (2015). The persistence of lenient market categories. *Organization Science*, 26: 1415–1431.

Rao, H., Monin, P. and Durand, R. (2005). Border crossing: Bricolage and the erosion of categorical boundaries in French gastronomy. *American Sociological Review*, 70: 968–991.

Rosa, J.A., Porac, J.F., Runser-Spanjol, J. and Saxon, M.S. (1999). Sociocognitive dynamics in a product market. *Journal of Marketing*, 63: 64–77.

Rosch, E. and Mervis, C.B. (1975). Family resemblances: Studies in internal structure of categories. *Cognitive Psychology*, 7: 573–605.

Ross, B.H. and Murphy, G.L. (1999). Food for thought: Cross-classification and category organization in a complex real-world domain. *Cognitive Psychology*, 38: 495–553.

Ruef, M. and Patterson, K. (2009). Credit and classification: The impact of industry boundaries in 19th century America. *Administrative Science Quarterly*, 54: 486–520.

Schneiberg, M. and Berk, G. (2010). From categorical imperative to learning by categories: cost accounting and new categorical practices in American manufacturing, 1900–1930. In Hsu, G., Kocak, O.

and Negro, G. (eds), *Categories in Markets: Origins and Evolution. Research in the Sociology of Organizations*, Volume 31. Bingley, UK: Emerald. pp. 255–292.

Sharkey, A.J. (2014). Categories and organizational status: The role of industry status in the response to organizational deviance. *American Journal of Sociology*, 119(5): 1380–1433.

Smith, E.B. (2011). Identities as lenses: How organizational identity affects audiences' evaluation of organizational performance. *Administrative Science Quarterly*, 56(1): 61–94.

Suarez, F.S., Grodal, S. and Gotsopoulos, A. (2015). Perfect timing? Dominant category, dominant design and the window of opportunity for firm entry. *Strategic Management Journal*, 36(3): 437–448.

Suddaby, R. and Greenwood, R. (2005). Rhetorical strategies of legitimacy. *Administrative Science Quarterly*, 50(1): 35–67.

Telles, E. and Paschel, T. (2014). Who is black, white or mixed race? How skin color, status and nation shape racial classification in Latin America. *American Journal of Sociology*, 120(3): 864–907.

Thornton, P., Jones, C. and Kury, K. (2005). Institutional logics and institutional change: Transformation in accounting, architecture, and publishing. In Candace Jones and Patricia H. Thornton (eds), *Transformation in Cultural Industries. Research in the Sociology of Organizations*, Volume 23. Bingley, UK: Emerald Group. pp. 125–170.

Tost, L.P. (2011). An integrative model of legitimacy judgments. *Academy of Management Review*, 36: 686–710.

Vergne, J.P. and Wry, T. (2014). Categorizing categorization research: Review, integration, and future directions. *Journal of Management Studies*, 51(1): 56–94.

Weber, K., Heinze, K. and DeSoucey, M. (2008). Forage for thought: Mobilizing codes in the movement for grass-fed meat and dairy products. *Administrative Sciences Quarterly*, 53(3): 529–567.

Wry, T. and Lounsbury, M. (2013). Contextualizing the categorical imperative: Category linkages, technology focus, and resource acquisition in nanotechnology entrepreneurship. *Journal of Business Venturing*, 28: 117–133.

Wry, T., Lounsbury, M. and Devereaux Jennings, P. (2014). Hybrid vigor: Securing venture capital by spanning categories in nanotechnology. *Academy of Management Journal*, 57: 1309–1333.

Wry, T., Lounsbury, M. and Glynn, M.A. (2011). Legitimating new categories of organizations: Stories as distributed cultural entrepreneurship. *Organization Science*, 22: 449–463.

Zhao, E.Y., Ishihara, M. and Lounsbury, M. (2013). Overcoming the illegitimacy discount: Cultural entrepreneurship in the U.S. feature film industry. *Organization Studies*, 34(12): 1747–1776.

Zuckerman, E.W. (1999). The categorical imperative: Securities analysts and the illegitimacy discount. *American Journal of Sociology*, 104: 1398–1438.

Zuckerman, E.W., Kim, T.-Y., Ukanwa, K. and Rittmann, J.V. (2003). Robust identities or nonentities? Typecasting in the feature-film labor market. *American Journal of Sociology*, 108: 1018–1074.

PART V

Consequences

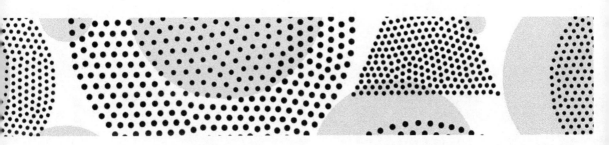

25

Institutional Theory and Entrepreneurship: Taking Stock and Moving Forward[1]

Robert J. David, Wesley D. Sine
and Caroline Kaehr Serra

INTRODUCTION

Entrepreneurship, defined here in a general sense as the process of creating a new organization, contributes to both economic and social renewal. Yet, until recently, institutional theorists have not shown concerted interest in this phenomenon, and research on entrepreneurship has largely relied on theories rooted in psychology (e.g., cognition, personality) or economics (e.g., theory of the firm, resource-based view). Even sociological approaches to entrepreneurship have generally neglected institutional factors, emphasizing instead the role of social networks and population demographics. Over the last ten or so years, however, an institutional-theory approach to entrepreneurship has taken shape. This approach focuses on how institutions shape entrepreneurial opportunities and behaviors and on how actors leverage and build institutions to create new organizations. Attention is shifted away from the personal traits of 'heroic' entrepreneurs on the one hand, and from the (in)efficient functioning of markets on the other, towards how the institutional environment affects entrepreneurial organizations and how entrepreneurs act on their institutional environment. The premise of this approach is that institutional theory's emphasis on regulatory structures, normative expectations and cultural-cognitive beliefs (Scott, 1995) draws attention to important factors that have been neglected in the study of entrepreneurship.

The institutional-theory approach to entrepreneurship has its roots in Stinchcombe's (1965) discussion of the 'liability of newness' and the importance of legitimacy for new organizations, and the subsequent calls by organizational sociologists to complement the dominant focus on entrepreneurs' traits with attention to the environmental context in which entrepreneurs operate (Aldrich and Wiedenmayer, 1993; Aldrich and Fiol, 1994; Thornton, 1999). Early work suggested a number of institutional factors that could influence rates of organizational founding (Tucker et al., 1990; Aldrich and Wiedenmayer, 1993; Thornton, 1999), and highlighted the legitimacy challenges faced by entrepreneurs (DiMaggio, 1991; Aldrich and Fiol, 1994). Following these leads, scholars elaborated the institutional-theory approach to entrepreneurship by delineating a variety of institutional influences and legitimating processes, and suggesting fertile areas of inquiry (e.g., Hwang and Powell, 2005; Brandl and Bullinger, 2009; Sine and David, 2010; Tolbert et al., 2011). Empirically, evidence has accumulated on how institutions create entrepreneurial opportunity (e.g., Lounsbury et al., 2003; Sine and David, 2003; Hiatt et al., 2009; David, 2012); how institutions influence the kinds of organizations that are founded (e.g., Sine et al., 2005; Marquis and Lounsbury, 2007; Sine and Lee, 2009; Tolbert and Hiatt, 2010; Almandoz, 2012); and how entrepreneurs interact with their institutional environments (Lawrence and Phillips, 2004; Navis and Glynn, 2010; Jones et al., 2010; Tracey et al., 2011; David et al., 2013; Khaire, 2014). As Figure 25.1 illustrates, the number of published articles taking an institutional-theory perspective on

the phenomenon of entrepreneurship shows an upward trend, with only two articles published in a sample of leading management journals in the decade 1990–1999, 14 published in the decade 2000–2009, and 13 published in the five years from 2010 to 2014.[2]

Despite the recent accumulation of research captured in Figure 25.1, this literature remains fragmented and incipient. In what follows, we take stock of the theoretical and empirical developments to date, and by doing so consolidate our knowledge. We clarify first that our focus is on entrepreneurship *as the creation of a new organization*, as opposed to other treatments that focus on opportunity detection and give little or no consideration to organizational creation (e.g., Kirzner, 1973; Casson, 1982). Rather than define entrepreneurship as the identification, evaluation and exploitation of future goods and services (e.g., Venkataraman, 1997; Shane and Venkataraman, 2000; Eckhardt and Shane, 2003; Shane, 2012), we follow Aldrich and Ruef (2006: 65) in conceptualizing entrepreneurship as 'activities that are intended to culminate in a viable organization' (see also Gartner, 1988; Thornton, 1999). In other words, we focus less on

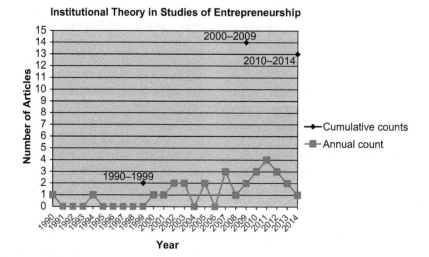

Figure 25.1   Number of articles taking an institutional-theory approach to entrepreneurship in four leading management journals

how entrepreneurs formulate a 'profitable conjecture about an opportunity' (Eckhardt and Shane, 2003: 339) and more on where opportunities for new organizations come from, why some opportunities lead to new organizations while others do not, and how institutions both enable and constrain the creation of new organizations. At the same time, we distinguish our conceptualization of entrepreneurship from that of 'institutional entrepreneurship', which generally refers to actions undertaken to change existing institutions (Greenwood et al., 2002; Maguire et al., 2004). While the two constructs overlap, they are distinct: some, but not all, institutional entrepreneurs create new organizations as part of their change efforts, and some, but not all, founders of new organizations engage in institutional change projects (David et al., 2013: 358).[3] Finally, we exclude from our analysis 'corporate entrepreneurship', or innovative activity within existing organizations (Burgelman, 1983; Sharma and Chrisman, 1999), as such activity does not entail starting a new organization *per se*.

After reviewing existing research within the perspective, we propose fruitful avenues for advancing the institutional approach to entrepreneurship, and conclude with a discussion of the promise of institutional theory as both a lens for studying entrepreneurship and as a toolkit that entrepreneurs can draw from.

THE INSTITUTIONAL-THEORY APPROACH TO ENTREPRENEURSHIP: ACCUMULATED KNOWLEDGE

Despite the relatively small size of the literature taking an institutional-theory approach to the study of entrepreneurship, papers vary widely in their focus. As explained above, our search of leading management journals returned 29 articles published since 1990 (all but two published since 2000). In addition, we searched for relevant articles in three specialized entrepreneurship journals (*Journal of Business Venturing*, *Entrepreneurship Theory and Practice* and *Strategic Entrepreneurship Journal*). We searched for the words ['institution*' OR 'legitimacy'] in the title, abstract and keywords using ABI/INFORM, and then read the abstracts and scanned the reference lists for use of institutional theory.[4] Finally, we identified a small number of papers (some unpublished or forthcoming) from conference programs or by using the reference lists of papers we read. In what follows, we distill the major themes that emerged from our reading of these articles. Our goal is not to review all findings or assess levels of support for the various relationships posited, and not all articles we read are included in our discussion below. Rather, our goal is to outline the major lines of inquiry present in the literature and highlight key findings under each theme.

Logics and Entrepreneurship

Early work on the relationship between institutions and entrepreneurship focused on institutional logics, or 'the socially constructed, historical patterns of material practices, assumptions, values, beliefs, and rules by which individuals produce and reproduce their material subsistence, organize time and space, and provide meaning to their social reality' (Thornton and Ocasio, 1999: 804). The institutional logics perspective is well suited to the study of entrepreneurship, as it directs attention to the contradictions in the institutional environment that provide opportunities for entrepreneurship on the one hand, and to the strategic agency inherent in entrepreneurship on the other (Thornton et al., 2012). Drawing on the logics perspective, a number of empirical studies have shown that shifts in or clashes between logics are generative of entrepreneurship. For example, Sine and David (2003) found that logic change in the electric power generation sector had a mutually reinforcing relationship with entrepreneurship. For over 40 years, the 'natural monopoly' logic limited cognitive awareness and search processes for alternative means of electricity generation, and resulted in little entrepreneurial activity. Environmental jolts in the form of the oil crisis ultimately led to the erosion of this logic and to an avalanche of entrepreneurial activity, with more than 5,000 independent power firms founded. Entrepreneurial activity, in turn, reinforced the shift in logic.

Rather than focusing on logic change, as Sine and David (2003) did, Marquis and Lounsbury (2007) explored the presence of two competing logics and their effects on organizational foundings in the banking sector. They found that acquisitions of banks espousing a 'community logic' by banks espousing a 'national logic' led to increased foundings of banks following the former logic. In other words, entrepreneurship arose to resist the dominance of one banking logic over another. In subsequent research on the effects of interactions between logics on entrepreneurship, Jain and Sharma (2013) showed in their study of the Indian telephony sector that the evolution from a state-based to a market-friendly logic involved three 'provisional logics' that each resulted in unique industry dynamics. Specifically, the first provisional logic led to a so-called 'predatory' market that raised the costs of doing business and led to the exit of most newly entered ventures. The subsequent 'tangled' market logic was characterized by a limbo state with limited entrepreneurial growth before giving way to the final, 'supportive' market logic under which the institutional arrangements were sufficiently robust to reduce sector uncertainty and risk, thus facilitating entrepreneurial entry. In brief, extant research suggests that the logics present in a field importantly shape both the amount and the type of entrepreneurial activity within the field.

At a more micro level of analysis, research also shows that the logics subscribed to by entrepreneurs and their key stakeholders affect both entrepreneurial behavior and outcomes. Almandoz (2012) found that banks with founding teams embedded in a community logic were more likely to be successfully established than those with founding teams subscribing to a financial logic. Most recently, Pahnke, Katila and Eisenhardt (2015) found that the institutional logics of different types of funding partners influence the type of innovations produced by new ventures. Specifically, venture capitalists, corporate venture capitalists and government agencies take different approaches to the relationships they have with the firms they fund, and these relationships affect the likelihood of commercial (vs. technical) innovation produced by these funded firms. This suggests that the choice among types of funding partners may have unanticipated effects on entrepreneurial firms beyond the financial resources gained through the relationship. In sum therefore, institutional logics affect not only the types of organizations that are founded, but also their behaviors and outcomes.

Social Movements and Entrepreneurship

There is an extensive literature within sociology on social movements, dating from the foundational work of Zald and Ash (1966) and McCarthy and Zald (1977). While definitions vary, central to all perspectives is that social movements are 'change-oriented struggles' involving collective action that challenges the status quo (McAdam et al., 1996: 21; King and Pearce, 2010: 251). Early work focused on 'shared grievances' and 'generalized beliefs' about the causes and possible means to reduce grievances, whereas later work adopted a 'resource mobilization' perspective that focuses on the variety and sources of resources mobilized by social movements (McCarthy and Zald, 1977). This literature has taught us much about how movements mobilize resources, organize and recruit participants, and maintain activist energy (Lounsbury et al., 2003: 74). More recently, scholars have explored the intersection of social movement theory and organization theory, particularly institutional theory (Davis et al., 2005; Schneiberg and Lounsbury, Chapter 11 this volume).

Whereas one line of research at this intersection conceives of social movements as threats to existing organizations and examines how organizations respond to these threats (e.g., King and Soule, 2007; King, 2008; Waldron et al., 2013; Hiatt et al., 2015), a smaller body of research sees social movements as generative of entrepreneurship and new market categories. A core line of argument is that social movements provide collective action frames and facilitate resource mobilization by entrepreneurs (Swaminathan and Wade, 2001; Lounsbury et al., 2003). Two related mechanisms have emerged as particularly salient: increased motivation to participate and persist in entrepreneurship, and a freeing of resources for its pursuit. For example, Weber et al. (2008) showed how the social movement for grass-fed meat and dairy products motivated entrepreneurs to produce these products and increase their commitment to the category, even in the face of obstacles. These entrepreneurs 'obtained emotional energy from connecting their work to a sense of self and moral values' represented by the movement (Weber et al., 2008: 543). Hiatt and colleagues (2009) described how the temperance movement in the United States at once deinstitutionalized breweries, created demand for a new category of 'soft' drinks, and increased the availability of resources for entrepreneurs in the nascent category. Sine and Lee (2009) showed how the environmentalism movement mobilized members *and* non-members of the movement to support the emerging wind power sector. Emphasizing the motivational potential of social movements, David, Sine and Haveman (2013) explained how the Progressive movement's valorization of efficiency and scientific logic provided a source of inspiration and cultural material for entrepreneurs in the nascent management consulting field.

Recent work has pointed to a complex and nuanced relationship between social movements and entrepreneurship. Taking a co-evolutionary perspective on the relationship between social movements and the nascent wind power sector, Pacheco, York and Hargrave (2014) showed how generalist social movement organizations initially spurred sector growth by advocating institutional change; this growth then led to the emergence of specialized, technology-focused social movement organizations that further leveraged distinct knowledge, capabilities and strategies to provide support for the sector, thus fueling its continued growth. Recent research has also highlighted the role of social movements in shaping the identity of emerging market categories and influencing audiences' expectations. For instance, Hiatt and Carlos (2016) showed how the US biodiesel industry developed an agrarian identity due to the actions of farmer activists who carefully crafted market narratives of biodiesel made from virgin seed oils. Boghossian and David (2016) described how market intermediaries such as retailers and critics projected a 'patriot' identity onto artisan cheese producers in Quebec and in doing so linked them to the Quebec nationalist movement. Lee, Hiatt and Lounsbury (2016) showed how the legitimacy-seeking behaviors of the organic food movement actually *diluted* the initial collective identity and founding ethos of the original category members by emphasizing the product over the producer. Collective identities can also arise in response to social movements rather than flow from them. Hiatt and Park (2016) found that social movements opposing emerging markets significantly affected the degree to which wood pellet entrepreneurs worked together to promote a coherent collective identity, a key factor in audience recognition and market legitimation.

In sum, existing research suggests that social movements can promote shared notions of which kinds of organizations are desirable. This can motivate entrepreneurs who are sympathetic to the values of a given movement, persuade consumers to accept certain products and services as valuable (thus creating market opportunities that even non-sympathizing entrepreneurs may pursue), and affect policies and create infrastructures that facilitate certain entrepreneurial activities (Tolbert et al., 2011). Social movements can also play an important role in the formation (and sometimes erosion) of a collective identity for emerging market categories, by supporting (or sometimes opposing) these new categories.

Regulatory Institutions and Entrepreneurship

Until recently, few studies have explored how regulatory institutions affect entrepreneurship, specifically who becomes an entrepreneur, the distribution of entrepreneurial opportunities and the legitimating impact of government policies and practices on entrepreneurship (Sine and David, 2010). An initial finding is that laws directly permitting or supporting an activity can spur entrepreneurship. Sine and colleagues (2005) showed that a law requiring electric utilities to purchase and distribute power from independent power plants in the heavily regulated US power industry increased founding of independent power plants, especially those using novel technologies. Dowell and David (2011) found that the number of private liquor stores in Alberta increased dramatically in the wake of an abrupt regulatory change. Whereas prior to 1993 only state-run liquor stores were permitted, deregulation allowed private stores to open. Interestingly, founders of private liquor stores followed the location patterns of the government-run stores, suggesting that entrepreneurs rely on institutionalized templates to deal with the inherent uncertainty of the founding process. Surprisingly, however, following this template conferred no survival advantage to private liquor stores (Dowell and David, 2011).

Regulation can also be generative of entrepreneurship indirectly. Specifically, legal institutions can promote supportive conditions that foster business creation. Kim, Lee and Reynolds (2012) showed how policies that protect individuals against economic risk can spur entrepreneurial action in highly coordinated economies by orienting economic activity toward a system of highly skilled and productive labor. Kim and Li (2014) found that in emerging economies, however, individuals may be discouraged from taking entrepreneurial action because of the difficulties in accessing legal protections efficiently even when these exist. Kim and Li (2014) also examined the moderating role of generalized social trust and argued that generalized trust between strangers exerts positive moderating effects on the direct relationship between legal protections and entrepreneurship. Further explicating the complex relationship between regulatory institutions and entrepreneurship, Thébaud (2015) investigated how regulatory policies fuel gender differences in entrepreneurship by creating gender-differentiated incentives to start a business. In contexts where institutional arrangements (e.g., publicly funded childcare, paid family leave) mitigate work–family conflict, Thébaud found that women are less likely than men to opt for business ownership as a 'fallback' employment strategy. As a result, women in these contexts are relatively less well represented among entrepreneurs as a whole, but comparatively better represented among entrepreneurs in riskier, high-growth sectors.

Another line of research investigates regulatory regimes surrounding financial markets. Using data from Japan, Eberhart, Eisenhardt and Eesley (2013) studied the complex effects of IPO (initial public offering) regulatory reform. Specifically, they found that lowering the barriers to 'successful' entrepreneurial exit by lowering IPO requirements makes IPOs more likely, attracts more capital investment in subsequent ventures (in some industries), and improves some venture performance. These reforms may also pull investment away from other sectors and help elite founders to launch high-performing firms; but, they can also damage the performance of firms founded by 'average' entrepreneurs. In related work, Eberhart and colleagues (2016) found that relaxing bankruptcy laws not only increases the number of bankruptcies, but also amplifies the entry of elite individuals into entrepreneurship and the performance of new firms, particularly by creating a greater proportion of exceptionally fast-growing firms. In other words, lowering failure barriers reduces the risks of starting firms, risks that would otherwise 'push' away elite individuals who have other career choices. In sum, these authors extend the institutional perspective on entrepreneurship to the closing of a firm's 'entrepreneurial life' and show that institutions that condition the exit of a firm have material effects on who founds new firms, the amount invested in new firms, the kinds of firms that receive investments and their subsequent performance (Eberhart et al., 2013: 34).

Recent research investigates the relationship between regulatory context and entrepreneurship in the informal economy.[5] De Castro, Khavul and Bruton (2014) found that entrepreneurs' decisions to formally register their firms depended not only on cost–benefit considerations but also on the normative environment. Entrepreneurs decided to operate informally (i.e., not register their business) for fear of being perceived as outliers among their communities of practice. The decision to not register their business was further reinforced by the fact that penalties for failing to do so were remote and that collaboration with formal organizations such as banks was still possible. In fact, it appears that in the absence of a belief in the enforcement powers of the central government, the normative institutional context plays a stronger role in influencing entrepreneurial behavior than the regulatory context. Lee and Hung (2014) examined the reciprocal relationship between nascent Chinese entrepreneurs active in the mobile telephone sector and the regulatory regime. Given that the Chinese state had exclusive license control over mobile telephony until 2007, entrepreneurial activity in that sector was considered informal – that is, illegal (i.e., outside of formal institutions) yet legitimate (i.e., accepted by certain social groups). Based on three kinds of strategic actions – framing to appeal to the public, aggregating to foster support based on collective action and bridging to offer alternative rules and practices – Chinese entrepreneurs brought about regulatory change that not only increased the legitimacy of their activities but also their legal standing (Lee and Hung, 2014). Entrepreneurship can thus bring about changes in the regulatory environment that represent a first step in the transition from informal to formal economy.

Academic Institutions and Entrepreneurship

For the present purposes, we refer to academic entrepreneurship as the creation of a firm with the objective to commercially exploit an innovation or body of expertise developed in a university setting (Shane, 2004; Perkmann et al., 2013). This is a distinct mode of commercializing academic knowledge, for example as compared to licensing inventions to existing firms. While a large literature has applied traditional economic theories of entrepreneurship (i.e., focusing on resources, incentives) to academic entrepreneurship (Rothaermel et al., 2007), a small number of recent papers have taken an institutional-theory approach to this endeavor. The core insight of these papers is that norms at different levels of analysis have a strong effect on academic entrepreneurship. In her case study of Stanford University, Colyvas (2007) found that norms of the academy shaped the uses of resources and the conditions of their appropriation, while in turn, the currency of industrial science prompted the rethinking of academic norms. In fact, she found that the norms and rewards of science define the very meaning and uses of revenues and resources (Colyvas, 2007: 471). Ultimately, Colyvas described an institutionalization process of technology transfer (the codification of standard, enforceable policies) that reflected the selective retention of some features of early models and the demise of others. She concluded that 'Stanford's celebrated model was neither the result of purposeful design, nor driven solely by pecuniary goals on the part of key individuals' (Colyvas, 2007: 474).

Stuart and Ding (2006) studied the predictors of entrepreneurship among academic scientists, noting that 'whereas in the early years of biotechnology the scientists who participated in private ventures risked the disapproval of their peers, those who do so today typically act without concern for adverse professional consequence' (p. 98). Adopting a normative approach, they found that faculty members were more likely to become entrepreneurs – to found or join advisory boards of for-profit biomedical firms – when they worked in university departments that employed other scientists who had previously ventured into the commercial sector. Patterson, Carlos and Sine (2015) found that university spin-out rates, or foundings of new firms, were higher among universities having a technology transfer office (TTO), and that university norms and prestige played an important role in explaining which universities were more likely to be early adopters of TTOs. At the field level of analysis, Agung (2014) explores normative differences across academic fields, and finds that the relationship between research 'appliedness' and start-up establishment likelihood changes across academic fields: some academic fields exhibit a positive relationship between scientists' research appliedness and start-up formations, whereas others show, surprisingly, a negative relationship. While clearly nascent, the literature on academic entrepreneurship from an institutional-theory perspective suggests that the number and type of firms founded out of a university setting depends on the normative institutional environment.

Legitimacy Work and Entrepreneurship

The largest body of research within the institutional-theory perspective on entrepreneurship deals with the legitimating activities undertaken by entrepreneurs. While institutional theorists generally reject notions of charismatic, hyper-muscular entrepreneurs, they do not deny the role of agency in building legitimacy – including for new ventures (Lounsbury and Crumley, 2007; Barley, 2008). Legitimacy, or 'a generalized perception or assumption that the actions of an entity are desirable, proper, or appropriate within some socially constructed system of norms, beliefs, and definitions' (Suchman, 1995: 574), is essential for new venture viability. Work on new venture legitimation often takes a discursive approach, and examines the rhetoric and 'stories' told by entrepreneurs in their attempts to legitimate their activities. An early instantiation of this approach is Lounsbury and Glynn's (2001: 545) elaboration of 'cultural entrepreneurship' as the 'process of storytelling that mediates between extant stocks of entrepreneurial resources and subsequent capital acquisition and wealth creation'. Building on the notion of cultural entrepreneurship, Martens, Jennings and Jennings (2007) studied initial public offering prospectuses in the high-tech sector and found that entrepreneurs' narratives helped build clear identities for their firms, thereby facilitating resource acquisition. However, Drori, Honig and Shaeffer (2009) found that the identity created through such (early) narratives may also constrain an organization's ability to adapt its business model in light of environmental change. In their study of a multimedia dotcom start-up, they showed how an initial 'aesthetic script' became institutionalized and constrained the firm from adapting to new business practices that became requisite as the Internet evolved. Expressing a similar cautionary note, Garud, Schildt and Lant (2014) found that the very expectations created through 'projective stories' to gain venture legitimacy can also serve as the source of future disappointments (due, for example, to environmental jolts), resulting in lower venture legitimacy.

Subsequent research in this stream has focused on the field level of analysis and has examined the role of discourse in the legitimation of new *market categories* as fertile areas of entrepreneurial activity. A new market category arises when 'substantial collective agreement' exists about the meaning of the category label among the audiences who use it (Kennedy et al., 2010).[6] Category labels provide a means of describing the core features or underlying concept of the category, as well as its 'shared identity' (Navis and Glynn, 2010: 441). Organizational theorists emphasize that new market categories do not emerge on their own, but rather require the mobilization of economic, cultural and sociopolitical resources (Weber et al., 2008). In their research on the emergence of satellite radio as a new market category, Glynn and Navis (2010; see also Navis and Glynn 2010) analyzed the public statements of executives from start-up firms XM and Sirius, and found these statements helped construct a distinctive identity for new ventures, and, in the process, lent credibility to the nascent market category. Importantly, this 'institutional leadership' activity was more pronounced in the emergence stage of the category, whereas statements of a more firm-specific nature increased as the category moved from emergence to growth. Further in this tradition, Wry, Lounsbury and Glynn (2011: 449) argued 'that legitimacy is more likely to be achieved when members [of an entrepreneurial group] articulate a clear defining collective identity story that identifies the group's orienting purpose and core practices'. This involves telling stories that emphasize the

similarities among entrepreneurial group members and their core practices, and theorizing the value and distinctiveness of the identity relative to other collective identities. Finally, in their study of the emergence of the nanotechnology field, Grodal and Granqvist (2014) focused on the affective content of entrepreneurial discourse, and found that in the early stages of the field's emergence affective discourses 'inspire and stimulate participation' in the category; importantly, the effect of these discourses in stimulating field emergence 'does not only depend on legitimate claims, but also on emotionally activating claims' (p. 163).

Legitimacy work goes beyond discursive activity, however, and encompasses a range of other symbolic actions. For example, Delmar and Shane (2004) found that two symbolic actions help new ventures to gain legitimacy: the establishment of a legal entity, as this constitutes a visible adherence to legal norms and thus underlines the founder's intentions, and the completion of a business plan, as this signals that the venture has an envisioned future. Another symbolic action is explained in Rao's (2004) work on the emergence of the American automobile industry. Car enthusiasts organized so called 'demonstration events' (i.e., reliability contests) as a means of demonstrating that the car was a reliable means of transportation, thus conferring legitimacy to entrepreneurs' endeavor of founding an organization in this emerging industry. In their study of symbolic management by entrepreneurs in Britain, Zott and Huy (2007) identified a variety of symbols that entrepreneurs deployed and that facilitated their acquisition of resources: business school degrees, fashionably decorated front offices and impressive buildings, dress codes and 'name dropping' of prestigious stakeholders. Sine and colleagues (2007) showed how entrepreneurs in the independent electric power industry worked to create a certification that raised the confidence of resource holders in the entrepreneurs' activities; importantly, the certification was entirely symbolic, and provided no new information to stakeholders that was not otherwise available at little or no cost.

David et al. (2013) identified a number of symbolic elements deployed by entrepreneurs in the early management consulting industry, such as ties to prestigious universities and scientific associations. Finally, Khaire (2014: 50) found that entrepreneurs in the emergent high-end fashion industry in India incorporated traditional textiles and clothing styles to signal that their activities were consistent with 'ancient skills and traditions', thereby increasing acceptance among a population skeptical of elitist fashion.

Finally, it is important to note that legitimacy work often takes place collectively and involves the construction of formal or informal associations of entrepreneurs. For example, Granovetter and McGuire (1998: 154) described how the National Electric Light Association (NELA) and the Association of Edison Illuminating Companies (AEIC) helped define the boundaries of the emerging independent electricity industry by denouncing city-owned electric firms, excluding them from their meetings, and organizing boycotts against this competing form. Similarly, David et al. (2013) explained how early management consulting entrepreneurs banded together to found the Association of Consulting Management Engineers (ACME) in 1929, and through this association defined their 'professional' model of consulting in a way that mimicked established (i.e., legitimate) professions and mounted scathing attacks against alternative forms of management consulting.

FUTURE RESEARCH OPPORTUNITIES

As our review above suggests, knowledge has begun to accumulate about the relationship between institutions and entrepreneurship. Much remains to be learned, however,

and we point here to three areas of inquiry that we believe to be particularly promising.

First, while we have gained insight into how regulatory change can influence entrepreneurship, there is ample scope for research on how entrepreneurs, particularly those in new market categories, influence regulation in ways that further their interests. Entrepreneurs must often overcome regulatory barriers or otherwise obtain political support for their activities (e.g., Sine and David, 2003). This process is important because the way a market category is regulated – whether by a patchwork of local regulations, national or international standards, national legislation, etc. – can have a profound effect on consumer confidence, category meaning, innovation and ultimately the growth and survival of the category (Lee, 2009; Gurses and Ozcan, 2015; Lee et al., 2016). Yet, most research on regulatory capture, or organizational activities to influence regulation, has been conducted in the context of established firms and industries (e.g., Hillman et al., 2004; Bonardi et al., 2006; Ahuja and Yayavaram, 2011; Hiatt and Park, 2013). We know far less about the attempts of entrepreneurs – here, the creators of new organizations – to shape the regulatory regimes of new market categories. One need look no further than the regulatory struggles present in the 'sharing economy' for rich examples: how these new markets are regulated will determine new venture success and even survival. Another promising line of inquiry would be to explore how entrepreneurs in new market categories influence the development of standards and certifications for their products or activities. This question is complicated by the fact that such regulatory regimes would likely advantage some entrepreneurs over others within the category, making regulatory capture contentious and collective action difficult.

The question of regulatory capture is further complicated in nascent markets inspired by social movements. While the research we reviewed above suggests that movements can spawn markets, the goals and values of movements are often imperfectly instantiated in the corresponding markets (McInerney, 2014). Struggles over regulatory capture (e.g., instituting a set of standards) can be expected not only between entrepreneurs in nascent markets, but also between entrepreneurs and other social movement actors who may object to profiting from the movement. How will such struggles play out, and what implications do they have for the category? Further, how is the emergent regulatory regime of movement-inspired markets affected by the 'mix' of entrepreneurs in the market? As a category grows and attracts entrepreneurs with looser connections to the social movement, we might expect conflict over how strongly the goals and values of the social movement should be reflected in market regulation. Such contests are important to understand, as a dissociation between a movement's values and the regulation of a nascent market can lead to a decline in consumer and producer commitment, migration from the market, and even the rise of counter-movements promoting alternative market categories.

A second promising area of research on how institutions affect entrepreneurship lies within the informal economy. The Organization for Economic Co-operation and Development (OECD) concluded that in 2009 about half of the world's workers (1.8 billion people) were working in the informal economy, and that by 2020, this will rise to two-thirds of the world's workers (Neuwirth, 2011). Yet, our theories about the formal economy are often not readily applicable to the informal economy (Godfrey, 2011; Hiatt and Sine, 2014). In particular, we know little about entrepreneurship in the informal economy (Webb et al., 2009). How do regulatory, normative and cultural-cognitive institutions (and changes in them) affect informal entrepreneurship? Here again, recent studies such as the work of Lee and Hung (2014) point to the importance of regulatory capture as part of entrepreneurs' attempts to enhance the legitimacy and legal standing of their

activities. Another important question is how do institutions (or lack thereof) shape an entrepreneur's decision to exploit an opportunity formally versus informally? Recent findings suggest considering formality versus informality along a multidimensional continuum rather than as a binary system (De Castro et al., 2014). Further, might there be certain opportunities that could only be exploited by those operating within the informal sector? Could certain contexts be seen as arenas for only formal activity, other contexts with opportunities that could be exploited formally or informally, and yet others where one could only exploit them informally? In brief, there are avenues for future research on both the explanans (X) and explained (Y) side of theory. On the explanans (X) side of theory, we know little about how different regulative, normative and cultural-cognitive institutions shape informal entrepreneurship. On the explained (Y) side of theory, we need to understand both general variation in informal entrepreneurship across contexts, as well as who in a given context engages in it and how.[7]

Third, we point to the promise of studying how collective identities are formed in new market categories. While a small body of research has shed light on identity formation at the organizational level (e.g., Gioia et al., 2010; Ashforth et al., 2011; Glynn and Watkiss, 2012; Kroezen and Heugens, 2012; for a review, see Gioia et al., 2013) we know less about how identity is formed at higher levels of analysis. Only a handful of studies have analyzed how a collective identity emerges for entrepreneurial organizations that form a new market category (Weber et al., 2008; Khaire and Wadwhani, 2010; Navis and Glynn, 2010; Wry et al., 2011; Boghossian and David, 2016). These studies have revealed the important role that discourse plays in forming a collective identity, particularly a discourse that establishes the distinctiveness of the nascent category. We suggest two ways in which this stream of research can be extended. First, research on collective identity formation should go beyond its current focus on discourse. What other cultural symbols can be deployed in the construction of a collective identity for a new market category? How do struggles over the collective identity of a new market category unfold? And, related to our suggestion above about regulatory capture, how might emergent collective identities for nascent market categories be instantiated in laws, regulations and standards?

Finally, we encourage more attention to place as a basis for collective identity. The importance of place is suggested by a number of organizational scholars. Romanelli and Khessina (2005: 344) argued that regions may come to have a 'regional industrial identity' that 'arises from the shared understandings of residents and external audiences about the suitability of a region for particular kinds of business activity'. Marquis and Battilana (2009) unpacked the market, regulative, social and cultural mechanisms that result in the enduring influence of local communities on organizations (see also Lounsbury, 2007; Greenwood et al., 2010; Howard-Grenville et al., 2013; Dalpiaz et al., 2015). Yet, we know little about how place provides cultural material for the collective identity of nascent market categories (i.e., beyond the effects of local resource endowments and social networks that have dominated considerations of geography in entrepreneurship studies). Place is invested with its own meaning and reflects collective histories, memories and identities (Gieryn, 2000; Zukin, 2011). The 'emotional, sentimental bonds between people and place' serve as a 'wellspring of identity' in the same way as do race, class and gender (Thomas and Meyer, 1984; Gieryn, 2000: 481). How then might the shared identity associated with place – or regional collective identity – become embedded in the collective identities of new market categories? Do regional collective identities serve a legitimating function for new market categories, and if so, for which constituents and under what conditions? And might new organizations or market categories

embodying a regional collective identity reinforce that identity? These are just some of the questions that await future research on institutions and entrepreneurship.[8]

CONCLUSION: INSTITUTIONAL THEORY AS A LENS AND A TOOLKIT

The study of entrepreneurship is part of institutional theory's larger struggle to explain change, and in particular the role of agency in change (Dacin et al., 2002; David and Bitekine, 2009). While our discussion above suggests the fruitfulness of studying entrepreneurship through an institutional-theory lens, this approach is not without tension. Entrepreneurship is fundamentally about change – creating a new organization or even a new kind of organization – whereas early statements of neo-institutional theory emphasized constraint over change (Meyer and Rowan, 1977; DiMaggio and Powell, 1983). Indeed, from the viewpoint of any individual entrepreneur the institutional environment seems immutable. It would seem imprudent, therefore, for future research to depict institutions as easily transformed, leveraged, or circumvented by entrepreneurs in pursuit of their interests, and doing so would in fact bestow the 'hyper-muscularity' to entrepreneurs that the institutional approach sought to avoid in the first place (Aldrich, 2011). Instead, the institutional approach to entrepreneurship might be most useful in helping us understand where opportunities come from (as opposed to how entrepreneurs 'discover' them), why some contexts produce more entrepreneurs than others, why certain types of organizations arise in some places but not others, and how entrepreneurs can 'build' institutions into their organizations (Selznick, 1957). While the research reviewed above has made strides in addressing these questions, the avenues for future research that we propose present fruitful opportunities to extend our knowledge further.

Finally, it is important to consider what institutional theory might offer to entrepreneurs and policy-makers. If theories rooted in economics direct entrepreneurs to look for information asymmetries, clusters of available resources and disruptive technologies, what more might institutional theory tell them? For one, it might help them understand where to look. For instance, research reviewed above suggests that institutional change provides a context rich in entrepreneurial opportunity, and that regulatory changes are an important instance of institutional change. But institutional change happens in other ways; for example, 'institutional collisions' (Leatherbee and Eesley, 2015) in which groups subscribing to different normative systems meet in time and space may provide other, perhaps less apparent, kinds of opportunity for entrepreneurship. Second, research within the institutional-theory perspective directs entrepreneurs to pay as much attention to 'symbolic value' as they do to traditional notions of 'economic value'. While providing a solid economic 'value proposition' is central to any new organization, incorporating cultural elements with little obvious economic value may be critical to entrepreneurial success or even survival. This, moreover, may well be true at the category level, not only at the organizational level. And third, institutional theory might help entrepreneurs to better understand the nature of the constraints they face. Often overconfident and focused on 'building a better mousetrap', entrepreneurs may lose sight of why doing so might not be enough. With its deep, multidimensional understanding of the environment in which entrepreneurs operate, institutional theory can help entrepreneurs to more fully contextualize their activities.

Notes

1   W. Sine and C. Kaehr Serra contributed equally and are joint second authors of this chapter. The authors thank Howard Aldrich, Shon Hiatt, Renate Meyer, Donald Palmer, Patricia Thornton, and the participants at the 2015 Alberta Institutions Conference (Banff) for helpful comments on a first draft of this chapter. Robert David gratefully acknowledges the Cleghorn Faculty Scholar Award and the Brodje Faculty Scholar Award for generous funding.

2   The journals are *Academy of Management Journal*, *Academy of Management Review*, *Administrative Science Quarterly* and *Organization Science*. We used the database ABI/INFORM Complete for the period 1990 to the present, with the search string [all(entrepreneur*) AND all(institution* OR legitima*) AND pub(academy of management journal OR academy of management review OR administrative science quarterly OR organization science)], where the search term 'all' refers to 'anywhere except full text' (thus title, abstract, and keywords). We then went through each of the 65 articles retrieved (in October, 2015) to assess relevance to new organization creation and the use of institutional theory in the sense meant here, resulting in 29 articles. The goal was not to capture comprehensively all articles within the perspective, but to get a sense of the trend in number of publications over time.

3   As David et al. (2013) pointed out, an important instance of overlap between entrepreneurship and institutional entrepreneurship occurs in cases of new organizational forms that are the subject of an institutionalization project.

4   We clarify that we restricted our focus to organizational institutionalism. As Scott (1995) explained, there are other institutionalisms in other disciplines (e.g., political science, economics, law), but we limit our consideration here to institutional theory within organization studies.

5   Defined most simply, the informal economy consists of those economic activities that produce legal products, but the sales of which are unrecorded (Nichter and Goldmark, 2009). Other definitions, such as that of Webb et al. (2009: 492), include legitimate yet illegal activities.

6   We note that the emergence of new market categories need not necessarily require the founding of new organizations, but often does.

7   We thank Ryan Coles for contributing ideas to this paragraph.

8   We thank Johnny Boghossian for contributing to the ideas in this paragraph.

REFERENCES

Agung, S. D. (2014). Academic scientists and startup formations: The role of the industry institutional environment. Working Paper, Drexel University.

Ahuja, G. and Yayavaram, S. (2011). Explaining influence rents: The case for an institutions-based view of strategy. *Organization Science*, 22(6):1631–1652.

Aldrich, H. E. (2011). Heroes, villains, and fools: Institutional entrepreneurship, NOT institutional entrepreneurs. *Entrepreneurship Research Journal*, 1(2): 1–4.

Aldrich, H. E. and Fiol, M. (1994). Fools rush in? The institutional context of industry creation. *Academy of Management Review*, 19(4): 645–670.

Aldrich, H. E. and Ruef, M. (2006). *Organizations Evolving*, 2nd edn. London: Sage.

Aldrich, H. G. and Wiedenmayer, G. (1993). From traits to rates: An ecological perspective on organizational foundings. *Advances in Entrepreneurship, Firm Emergence, and Growth*, 1: 145–195.

Almandoz, J. (2012). Arriving at the starting line: The impact of community and financial logics on new banking ventures. *Academy of Management Journal*, 55(6): 1381–1406.

Ashforth, B. E., Rogers, K. M. and Corley, K. G. (2011). Identity in organizations: Exploring cross-level dynamics. *Organization Science*, 22(5): 1144–1156.

Barley, S. R. (2008). Coalface institutionalism. In R. Greenwood, C. Oliver, R. Suddaby and K. Sahlin-Andersson (eds), *The SAGE Handbook of Organizational Institutionalism*. London: Sage. pp. 491–518.

Boghossian, J. and David, R. J. (2016). Artisans of authenticity: The construction of collective identity in a nascent market category. Working Paper, Université Laval.

Bonardi, J. P., Holburn, G. L. F. and Vanden Bergh, R. G. (2006). Nonmarket strategy performance: Evidence from U.S. electric utilities. *Academy of Management Journal*, 49(6): 1209–1228.

Brandl, J. and Bullinger, B. (2009). Reflections on the societal conditions for the pervasiveness of entrepreneurship in Western societies. *Journal of Management Inquiry*, 18(2): 159–173.

Burgelman, R. A. (1983). Corporate entrepreneurship and strategic management: Insights from a process study. *Management Science*, 29(12): 1349–1364.

Casson, M. (1982). *The Entrepreneur*. Totowa, NJ: Barnes & Nobles Books.

Colyvas, J. A. (2007). From divergent meanings to common practices: The early institutionalization of technology transfer in the life sciences at Stanford University. *Research Policy*, 36(4): 456–476.

Dacin, M. T., Goodstein, J. and Scott, W.R. (2002). Institutional theory and institutional change: Introduction to the special research forum. *Academy of Management Journal*, 45(1): 43–56.

Dalpiaz, E., Tracey, P. and Phillips, N. (2015). New venture creation and the translation of organizational forms: The case of H-Farm. Paper presented at the 4th Alberta Insitutions Conference in Banff, Alberta.

David, R. J. (2012). Institutional change and the growth of strategy consulting in the United States. In M. Kipping and T. Clark (eds), *The Oxford Handbook of Management Consulting*. Oxford: Oxford University Press. pp. 71–92.

David, R. J. and Bitektine, A. B. (2009). The deinstitutionalization of institutional Theory? Exploring divergent agendas in institutional research. In D. Buchanan and A. Bryman (eds), *The SAGE Handbook of Organizational Research Methods*. London: Sage. pp. 160–175.

David, R. J., Sine, W. D. and Haveman, H. A. (2013). Seizing opportunity in emerging fields: How institutional entrepreneurs legitimated the professional form of management consulting. *Organization Science*, 24(2): 356–377.

Davis, G. F., McAdam, D., Scott W. R. and Zald, M. N. (eds) (2005). *Social Movements and Organization Theory*. Cambridge: Cambridge University Press.

De Castro, J. O., Khavul, S. and Bruton, G. D. (2014). Shades of grey: How do informal firms navigate between macro and meso institutional environments? *Strategic Entrepreneurship Journal*, 8(1): 75–94.

Delmar, F. and Shane, S. (2004). Legitimating first: Organizing activities and the survival of new ventures. *Journal of Business Venturing*, 19(3): 385–410.

DiMaggio, P. J. (1991). Constructing an organizational field as a professional project: U.S. art museums, 1920–1940. In W. W. Powell and P. J. DiMaggio (eds.), *The New Institutionalism in Organizational Theory*. Chicago: University of Chicago Press. pp. 267–292.

DiMaggio, Paul J. and Powell, Walter W. (1983). The iron cage revisited: Institutional isomorphism and collective rationality in organizational fields. *American Sociological* Review, 48(2): 147–160.

Dowell, G. and David, R. J. (2011). Effects of ancestral populations on entrepreneurial founding and failure: Private liquor stores in Alberta, 1994–2003. *Industrial and Corporate Change*, 20(3): 825–853

Drori, I., Honig, B. and Shaeffer, Z. (2009). The life cycle of an internet firm: Scripts, legitimacy, and identity. *Entrepreneurship Theory and Practice*, 33(3): 715–738.

Eberhart, R. N., Eesley, C. E. and Eisenhardt, K. M. (2016). Failure is an option: Institutional change, entrepreneurial risk and new firm growth. Working paper. Available at https://ssrn.com/abstract=1982819 or http://dx.doi.org/10.2139/ssrn.1982819.

Eberhart, R. N., Eisenhardt, K. M. and Eesley, C. E. (2013). How making it easier to succeed reduces success: IPO reform and new firm performance. Working paper (SSRN-id2316342).

Eckhardt, J. T. and Shane, S. (2003). Opportunities and entrepreneurship. *Journal of Management*, 29(3): 333–349.

Gartner, W. B. (1988). Who is an entrepreneur? Is the wrong question. *Entrepreneurship Theory Practice*, 13(4): 47–68.

Garud, R., Schildt, H. A. and Lant, T. K. (2014). Entrepreneurial storytelling, future expectations, and the paradox of legitimacy. *Organization Science*, 25(5): 1479–1492.

Gieryn, T. F. (2000). A space for place in sociology. *Annual Review of Sociology*, 26: 463–496

Gioia, D. A., Patvardhan, S. D., Hamilton, A. L. and Corley, K. G. (2013). Organizational identity formation and change. *Academy of Management Annals*, 7: 123–193.

Gioia, D. A., Price, K. N., Hamilton, A. L. and Thomas, J. B. (2010). Forging an identity: An insider–outsider study of processes involved in the formation of organizational identity. *Administrative Science Quarterly*, 55(1): 1–46.

Glynn, M. A. and Navis, C. (2010). Entrepreneurship, institutional emergence, and organizational leadership: Tuning in to 'the next big thing' in satellite radio. In W. D. Sine and R. J. David (eds), *Institutions and Entrepreneurship: Research in the Sociology of Work*, Volume 21. Bingley, UK: Emerald Group. pp. 257–286.

Glynn, M. A. and Watkiss, L. (2012). Exploring cultural mechanisms of organizational identity construction. In M. Schultz, S. Maguire, A. Langley and H. Tsoukas (eds), *Constructing Identity in and around Organizations*. Oxford: Oxford University Press. pp. 63–88.

Godfrey, P. (2011). Toward a theory of the informal economy. *Academy of Management Annals*, 5(1): 231–277.

Granovetter, M. and McGuire P. (1998). The making of an industry: Electricity in the United States. In M. Callon (ed.), *The Law of Markets*. Oxford: Blackwell. pp. 147–173.

Greenwood, R., Diaz, A. M., Li, S. X. and Lorente, J. C. (2010). The multiplicity of institutional logics and the heterogeneity of organizational responses. *Organization Science*, 21(2): 521–539.

Greenwood, R., Suddaby, R. and Hinings, C. R. (2002). Theorizing change: The role of professional associations in the transformation of institutionalized fields. *Academy of Management Journal*, 45(1): 58–80.

Grodal, S. and Granqvist, N. (2014). Great expectations: Discourse and affect during field emergence. In Neal M. Ashkanasy, Wilfred J. Zerbe, Charmine E. J. Härtel (eds), *Emotions and the Organizational Fabric. Research on Emotion in Organizations*, Volume 10. Bingley, UK: Emerald Group. pp. 139–166.

Gurses, K. and Ozcan, P. (2015). Entrepreneurship in regulated markets: Framing contests and collective action to introduce pay TV in the U.S. *Academy of Management Journal*, 58(6): 1709–1739.

Hiatt, S. R. and Carlos, W. C. (2016). From farms to fuel tanks: Differential effects of collective action on firm entry in the emergent U.S. biodiesel sector. Marshall School of Business Working Paper No. MOR 03.16. Available at SSRN: http://ssrn.com/abstract=2601798.

Hiatt, S. R., Grandy, J. and Lee, B. (2015). Organizational responses to public and private politics: An analysis of climate change activists and U.S. oil and gas firms. *Organization Science*, 26(6): 1769–1786.

Hiatt, S. R. and Park, S. (2013). Lords of the harvest: Third-party influence and regulatory approval of genetically modified organisms. *Academy of Management Journal*, 56(4): 923–944.

Hiatt, S. R. and Park, S. (2016). The impact of external market threats on entrepreneurial collective action in the emergent U.S. wood pellet industry. Available at SSRN: http://ssrn.com/abstract=2766733.

Hiatt, S. R. and Sine, W. D. (2014). Clear and present danger: Planning and new venture survival amid political and civil violence. *Strategic Management Journal*, 35(5): 773–785.

Hiatt, S. R., Sine, W. D. and Tolbert, P. S. (2009). From Pabst to Pepsi: The deinstitutionalization of social practices and the creation of entrepreneurial opportunities. *Administrative Science Quarterly*, 54(4): 635–667.

Hillman, A. J., Keim, G. D. and Schuler, D. (2004). Corporate political activity: A review and research agenda. *Journal of Management*, 30(6): 837–857.

Howard-Grenville, J., Metzger, M. and Meyer, A. (2013). Rekindling the flame: Processes of identity resurrection. *Academy of Management Journal*, 56(1): 113–136.

Hwang, H. and Powell, W. W. (2005). Institutions and entrepreneurship. In S. Alvarez, R. Agarwal and O. Sorenson (eds), *Handbook of Entrepreneurship Research: Disciplinary Perspectives*. New York: Springer. pp. 201–232.

Jain, S. and Sharma, D. (2013). Institutional logic migration and industry evolution in emerging economies: The case of telephony in India. *Strategic Entrepreneurship Journal*, 7(3): 252–271.

Jones, C., Livne-Tarandach, R. and Balachandra, L. (2010). Rhetoric that wins clients: Entrepreneurial firms use of institutional logics when competing for resources. In W.D. Sine and R.J. David (eds), *Institutions and Entrepreneurship: Research in the Sociology of Work*, Volume 21. Bingley, UK: Emerald Group. pp. 183–218.

Kennedy, M. T., Lo, J. and Lounsbury, M. (2010). Category currency: The changing value of conformity as a function of ongoing meaning construction. In M. Lounsbury (ed.), *Research in the Sociology of Organizations*, Volume 31. Bingley, UK: Emerald Books. pp. 369–397.

Khaire, M. (2014). Fashioning an industry: Socio-cognitive processes in the construction of worth of a new industry. *Organization Studies*, 35: 41–74.

Khaire, M. and Wadhwani, R. D. (2010). Changing landscapes: The construction of meaning and value in a new market category – modern indian art. *Academy of Management Journal*, 53(6): 1281–1304.

Kim, P. H., Lee, C. and Reynolds, P. D. (2012). Backed by the state: Social protection and starting businesses in knowledge-intensive industries. In J. Katz and A. C. Corbett (eds), *Advances in Entrepreneurship, Firm Emergence and Growth. Entrepreneurial Action*, Volume 14. Bingley, UK: Emerald Group. pp. 25–62.

Kim, P. H. and Li, M. (2014). Seeking assurances when taking action: Legal systems, social trust, and starting businesses in emerging economies. *Organization Studies*, 35(3): 359–391.

King, B. G. (2008). A political mediation model of corporate response to social movement activism. *Administrative Science Quarterly*, 53(3): 395–421.

King, B. G. and Pearce, N. A. (2010). The contentiousness of markets: Politics, social movements, and institutional change in markets. *Annual Review of Sociology*, 36: 249–267.

King, B. G. and Soule, S. A. (2007). Social movements as extra-institutional entrepreneurs: The effect of protests on stock price returns. *Administrative Science Quarterly*, 52(3): 413–442.

Kirzner, I. (1973). *Competition and Entrepreneurship*. Chicago, IL: University of Chicago Press.

Kroezen, J. J. and Heugens, P. P. M. A. R. (2012). Organizational identity formation: Processes of identity imprinting and enactment in the Dutch microbrewery landscape. In M. Schultz, S. Maguire, A. Langley and H. Tsoukas (eds), *Constructing Identity in and around Organizations*. Oxford: Oxford University Press. pp. 89–128.

Lawrence, T. B. and Phillips, N. (2004). From Moby Dick to Free Willy: Macro-cultural discourse and institutional entrepreneurship in emerging institutional fields. *Organization*, 11(5): 689–711.

Leatherbee, M. and Eesley, C. (2015). Remodeling the iron cage: Micro-level effects of institutional collisions. Paper presented at the 2015 Academy of Management Meeting, Vancouver.

Lee, B. (2009). The infrastructure of collective action and policy content diffusion in the organic food industry. *Academy of Management Journal*, 52(6): 1247–1269.

Lee, B., Hiatt, S. and Lounsbury, M. (2016). Market mediators and the tradeoffs of legitimacy-seeking behaviors in a nascent category. Marshall School of Business Working Paper No. MOR 04.16. Available at SSRN: http://ssrn.com/abstract=2615964.

Lee, C. K. and Hung, S. -C. (2014). Institutional entrepreneurship in the informal economy: China's Shan-Zhai mobile phones. *Strategic Entrepreneurship Journal*, 8(1): 16–36.

Lounsbury, M. (2007). A tale of two cities: Competing logics and practice variation in the professionalizing of mutual funds. *Academy of Management Journal*, 50(2): 289–307.

Lounsbury, M. and Crumley, E. T. (2007). New practice creation: An institutional perspective on innovation. *Organization Studies*, 28(7): 993–1012.

Lounsbury, M. and Glynn, M. A. (2001). Cultural entrepreneurship: Stories, legitimacy, and the acquisition of resources. *Strategic Management Journal*, 22(6): 545–564.

Lounsbury, M., Ventresca, M. and Hirsch, P. (2003). Social movements, field frames and industry emergence: A cultural-political perspective on U.S. recycling. *Socio-Economic Review*, 1(1): 71–104.

Maguire, S., Hardy, C. and Lawrence, T. B. (2004). Institutional entrepreneurship in emerging fields: HIV/AIDS treatment advocacy in Canada. *Academy of Management Journal*, 47(5): 657–679.

Marquis, C. and Battilana, J. (2009). Acting globally but thinking locally? The enduring influence of local communities on organizations. *Research in Organizational Behavior*, 29: 283–302.

Marquis, C. and Lounsbury, M. (2007). Vive le resistance: Competing logics and the consolidation of U.S. community banking. *Academy of Management Journal*, 50(4): 700–820.

Martens, M. L., Jennings, J. E. and Jennings, P. D. (2007). Do the stories they tell get them the money they need? The role of entrepreneurial narratives in resource acquisition. *Academy of Management Journal*, 50(5): 1107–1132.

McAdam, D., Tarrow, S. and Tilly, C. (1996). To map contentious politics. *Mobilization*, 1(1): 17–34.

McCarthy, J. D. and Zald, M. N. (1977). Resource mobilization and social movements: A partial theory. *American Journal of Sociology*, 82(6): 1212–1241.

McInerney, P.-B. (2014). *From social movement to moral market: How the circuit riders sparked an IT revolution and created a technology market*. Stanford, CA: Stanford University Press.

Meyer, J. W. and Rowan, B. (1977). Institutionalized organizations: Formal structure as myth and ceremony. *American Journal of Sociology*, 83(2): 340–363.

Navis, C. and Glynn, M. A. (2010). How new market categories emerge: Temporal dynamics of legitimacy, identity, and entrepreneurship in satellite radio, 1990–2005. *Administrative Science Quarterly*, 55(3): 439–471.

Neuwirth, Robert (2011). *The Stealth of Nations*. New York: Pantheon.

Nichter, Simeon and Goldmark, Lara (2009). Small firm growth in developing countries. *World Development*, 37(9): 1453–1464.

Pacheco, D. F., York, J. G. and Hargrave, T. J. (2014). The co-evolution of industries, social movements, and institutions: The case of wind power. *Organization Science*, 25(6): 1609–1632.

Pahnke, E. C., Katila, R. and Eisenhardt, K. (2015). Who takes you to the dance? How partners' institutional logics influence innovation in young firms. *Administrative Science Quarterly*, 60(4): 596–633.

Patterson, K., Carlos, W. C., Sine, W. D. (2015). Identity constraints: The diffusion of commercialized science in higher education. Working Paper, Marshall School of Business.

Perkmann, M., Tartari, V., McKelvey, M., Autio, E., Brostrom, A., D'Este, P., Fini, R., Geuna, A., Grimaldi, R., Hughes, A., Krabel, S., Kitson, M., Llerena, P., Lissoni, F., Salter, A., Sobrero, M. (2013). Academic engagement and commercialisation: A review of the literature on university–industry relations. *Research Policy*, 42(2): 423–442.

Rao, H. (2004). Institutional activism in the early American automobile industry. *Journal of Business Venturing*, 19(3): 359–384.

Romanelli, E. and Khessina, O. M. (2005). Regional industrial identity: Cluster configurations and economic development. *Organization Science*, 16(4): 344–358.

Rothaermel, F. T., Agung, S. D. and Jiang, L. (2007). University entrepreneurship: A taxonomy of the literature. *Industrial and Corporate Change*, 16(4): 691–791.

Scott, W. R. (1995). *Institutions and Organizations*. Thousand Oaks, CA: Sage.

Selznick, P. (1957). *Leadership in Administration*. New York: Harper and Row.

Shane, S. (2004). *Academic Entrepreneurship: University Spinoffs and Wealth Creation*. Aldershot: Edward Elgar.

Shane, S. (2012). Reflections on the 2010 AMR Decade Award: Delivering on the promise of entrepreneurship as a field of research. *Academy of Management Review*, 37(1): 10–20.

Shane, S. and Venkataraman, S. (2000). The promise of entrepreneurship as a field of research. *Academy of Management Review*, 26(1): 217–226.

Sharma, P. and Chrisman, S. J. J. (1999). Toward a reconciliation of the definitional issues in the field of corporate entrepreneurship. *Entrepreneurship Theory and Practice*, 23(3): 11–27.

Sine, W. D. and David, R. J. (2003). Environmental jolts, institutional change, and the creation of entrepreneurial opportunity in the U.S. electric power industry. *Research Policy*, 32(2): 185–207.

Sine, W. D. and David, R. J. (2010). Introduction. In W. Sine and R. David, *Institutions and Entrepreneurship: Research in the Sociology of Work*, Volume 21. Bingley, UK: Emerald Group. pp. 1–26.

Sine, W. D., David, R. J. and Mitsuhashi, H. (2007). From plan to plant: Effects of certification on operational start-up in the emergent independent power sector. *Organization Science*, 18(4): 578.

Sine, W. D., Haveman, H. A. and Tolbert, P. S. (2005). Risky business? Entrepreneurship in the new independent-power sector. *Administrative Science Quarterly*, 50(3): 200–232.

Sine, W. D. and Lee, B. H. (2009). Tilting at windmills? The environmental movement and the emergence of the U.S. wind energy sector. *Administrative Science Quarterly*, 54(1): 123–155.

Stinchcombe, A. L. (1965). Social structure and organizations. In J. March (ed.), *Handbook of Organizations*. Chicago: Rand-McNally. pp. 142–193.

Stuart, T. E. and Ding, W. W. (2006). When do scientists become entrepreneurs? The social structural antecedents of commercial activity in the academic life sciences. *American Journal of Sociology*, 112(1): 97–144.

Suchman, M. C. (1995). Managing legitimacy: Strategic and institutional approaches. *Academy of Management Review*, 20(3): 571–610.

Swaminathan, A. and Wade, J. B. (2001). Social movement theory and the evolution of new organizational forms. In C. Schoonhoven and E. Romanelli (eds), *The Entrepreneurship Dynamic*. Stanford, CA: Stanford University Press. pp. 286–313.

Thébaud, S. (2015). Business as Plan B? Institutional foundations of gender inequality in entrepreneurship across 24 industrialized countries. *Administrative Science Quarterly*, 60(4): 671–711.

Thomas, G. M. and Meyer, J. W. (1984). The expansion of the state. *Annual Review of Sociology*, 10: 461–482.

Thornton, Patricia H. (1999). The sociology of entrepreneurship. *Annual Review of Sociology*, 25: 19–46.

Thornton, P. H. and Ocasio, W. (1999). Institutional logics and the historical contingency of power in organizations. Executive succession in the higher education publishing industry, 1958–1990. *American Journal of Sociology*, 105(3), 801–843.

Thornton, P. H., Ocasio, W. and Lounsbury, M. (2012). *The Institutional Logics Perspective*. Oxford: Oxford University Press.

Tolbert, P. S., David, R. J. and Sine, W. D. (2011). Studying choice and change: The intersection of institutional theory and entrepreneurship research. *Organization Science*, 22(5): 1332–1344.

Tolbert, P. S. and Hiatt, S. (2010). The shape of things to come: Institutions, entrepreneurs, and the case of hedge funds. In W. Sine and R. David, *Institutions and Entrepreneurship: Research in the Sociology of Work*, Volume 21. Bingley, UK: Emerald Group. pp. 157–182.

Tracey, P., Phillips, N. and Jarvis, O. (2011). Bridging institutional entrepreneurship and the creation of new organizational forms: A multilevel model. *Organization Science*, 22(1): 60–80.

Tucker, D. J., Singh, J. V. and Meinhard, A. G. (1990). Organizational form, population dynamics, and institutional change: The founding patterns of voluntary organizations. *Academy of Management Journal*, 33(1): 151–178.

Venkataraman, S. (1997). The distinctive domain of entrepreneurship research: An editor's perspective. In J. Katz and R. Brockhaus (eds), *Advances in Entrepreneurship, Firm Emergence and Growth*, Volume 3. Greenwich, CT: JAI Press. pp. 119–138.

Waldron, T. L., Navis, C. and Fisher, G. (2013). Explaining differences in firms' responses to activism. *Academy of Management Review*, 38(3): 397–417.

Webb, J. W., Tihanyi, L., Ireland, R. D. and Sirmon, D. G. (2009). You say illegal, I say legitimate: Entrepreneurship in the informal economy. *Academy of Management Review*, 34(3): 492–510.

Weber, K., Heinze, K. L. and DeSoucey, M. (2008). Forage for thought: Mobilizing codes in the movement for grass-fed meat and dairy products. *Administrative Science Quarterly*, 53(3): 529–567.

Wry, T., Lounsbury, M. and Glynn, M. A. (2011). Legitimating new categories of organizations: Stories as distributed cultural entrepreneurship. *Organization Science*, 22(2): 339–463.

Zald, M. N. and Ash, R. (1966). Social movement organizations: Growth, decay, and change. *Social Forces*, 44(3): 327–340.

Zott, C. and Huy, Q. N. (2007). How entrepreneurs use symbolic management to acquire resources. *Administrative Science Quarterly*, 52(1): 70–105.

Zukin, S. (2011). Reconstructing the authenticity of place. *Theory & Society*, 40(2): 161–165.

26

How Institutions Create Income Inequality

Gerald F. Davis

Evidence of inequality is pervasive in social life, from race-based microaggressions at work to disparities in the growth rates of national economies. Every social science has something to say about inequality. Scholars who tell you they study inequality might be examining the experience of low-wage work (anthropology) or the rise of CEO compensation (management); occupational sex segregation in the California civil service (sociology) or the dispersion of incomes within Danish firms (strategy); tax policies on inheritances (economics) or how child-rearing practices influence children's job choices (psychology). Since the birth of the Occupy movement in 2011 and the publication of Thomas Piketty's (2014) *Capital in the 21st Century*, however, attention has focused on inequality understood as the uneven spread of incomes within national economies and the gap between the top 1% and the rest. This chapter focuses on the role of organizations and institutions in creating national income inequality.

Organization theory has a distinctive contribution to make to understanding income inequality (Baron, 1984; Bapuji and Neville, 2015). The distribution of income in industrialized societies happens primarily through organizational processes. Who gets hired, how they are evaluated, how they are paid and how they are promoted or fired all happen in organizations through the employment relation. Organizational structures are therefore the fulcrum for the distribution of individual rewards. To know who gets what, we need to know how employing organizations are structured. In particular, I argue here that organizational size plays a paradoxical role in the creation of income inequality: economies with big organizations tend to have low income inequality, and vice versa (Davis and Cobb, 2010).

Institutions play a central part in shaping organizations and the employment relation (Cobb, 2016). Organizations come to be structured as they are due to economy-wide institutions that govern labor markets, product markets, financial markets, educational systems and the social safety net. Institutions provide the raw materials and the conditions of possibility for creating organizations, which explains why firms look so different around the world. Just as skyscrapers require structural steel and elevators powered by electricity, formal organizations require a set of institutional preconditions (cf. Stinchcombe, 1965). More specifically, the kinds of organizations an economy gets depend on the kinds of economic institutions in place: stock markets are essential for creating public corporations, and smartphones are required for ride-hailing apps staffed by independent contractors. This is where the explanatory heavy lifting for income inequality takes place, by explaining how economic institutions and technological raw materials shape the demography of organizations and their employment practices.

This chapter argues that the drive-train of economic inequality runs from national institutions, to organizational structures, to the distribution of individual rewards. To explain economy-wide inequality we need to understand how institutions shape the organizations that allocate income and wealth, a topic that has received less attention than it merits in organizational scholarship. For the purpose of this chapter, I will focus on just one dimension of organizations: their size, and specifically the number of people they employ. Size is perhaps the single most basic feature of organizations, yet there is surprisingly little scholarship on how organizational size varies around the world, how size is influenced by institutions and how the size of an economy's organizations is connected to the unequal distribution of incomes. This is an area ripe for comparative institutional research.

In this chapter, I first describe the wide variety of processes and outcomes that come under the heading of 'inequality,' and then narrow the focus to the distribution of income at the level of the national economy. I briefly summarize how sociologists have studied

inequality, and how organizations have taken on a role as the central explanatory mechanisms for inequality. I explain how inequality at the national level is measured, and summarize the many social ills that are correlated with high inequality. Next is a discussion of how organizations cause inequality through how they hire, pay, evaluate, promote and fire employees. This leads to a question: why do organizations look the way they do (e.g., why are some bigger than others), and how is it linked to national institutions? I propose a 'drive train of inequality': national institutions shape the kinds of organizations that thrive in an economy, and these organizations in turn shape the distribution of incomes. I then close with a description of some of the forces changing national institutions and the researchable questions these raise for changes in organizations and, thus, inequality.

WHAT DO WE MEAN BY 'INEQUALITY'?

Scholars who study economic inequality typically focus on a few specific outcomes. These include:

- **Poverty**: Why are some people or groups in society poor? Why do some countries have higher poverty rates than others?
- **Mobility**: How do some people become (or stay) rich? Why do some societies have higher class mobility than others?
- **Global inequality**: Why are some nations consistently richer than others? What accounts for different trajectories of GDP growth (that is, divergences in the 'wealth of nations')?
- **Comparative inequality**: Why do some nations have greater internal inequality of income (or wealth)? What accounts for national trends in income distributions?

More recently, scholars have sought to examine income distributions at the global level, finding that the middle-income groups of low-income countries (particularly China) have fared well in recent times; the middle-income groups of high-income countries have fared poorly; and the global 1% has done surpassingly well over the past generation relative to the rest of the population (Milanovic, 2016). (Those who seek to obfuscate inequality might also refer to 'equality of opportunity', which unlike poverty rates or income disparities, is impossible to measure and serves more as a rhetorical device than an empirically tractable concept.)

Economic inequality can be analyzed using different conceptual tools. Inequality can be examined within different units of analysis, from groups to the global economy. Economists such as Thomas Piketty (2014) focus on *inequality within or across countries*, that is, how wealth and income are distributed within society as a whole. But organizational researchers have also examined *pay dispersion within firms* or other organizations (e.g., Pfeffer and Langton, 1988), or the distribution of rewards among top management team members, or the ratio of CEO pay to the average pay of workers.

Dispersion itself can be conceptualized in different ways. Piketty and others have drawn attention to *concentration*: how much accrues to, say, the top 10% or the top 1%. This is most commonly examined in terms of *income* (how much the top individuals or households earn in a given year). In the United States, 21.2% of the nation's income went to the top 1% in 2014, compared with just 8% in 1980. As noted by President Obama, the top 25 hedge fund managers in America take home more income than all of the kindergarten teachers in the country combined. *Wealth* is even more concentrated than income. The six heirs of the Walmart fortune had a net worth greater than that of the bottom 42% of the population combined. Stated differently, the net worth of the Walton family was more than one million times greater than that of the median US family.

Researchers also examine *economy-wide distributions*. Like concentration, distributions can be examined in terms of income or wealth, at one point in time or over an extended period. Below we describe the Gini coefficient (Gini, 1913), a measure that allows comparisons across societies and over time. As with income and wealth concentration, the Gini measure has been going up almost continuously since 1980 in the United States, but not everywhere.

Scholars of inequality also examine *social divides*. It is frequently reported than women earn on average only 80% of what men earn in the US, a gap that has only modestly declined over the past 30 years. Racial differences are also stark: in 2013, the net worth of the median African-American family was just $11,000, compared to $141,900 for the median white family, following a catastrophic drop during the Great Recession.

This brief tour of the landscape highlights that 'inequality' is like a multidimensional Rubik's Cube. People who study inequality in the abstract can be examining radically different topics on the ground, from national differences in the concentration of wealth in the top 1% to pay differences among men and women within the same occupation (e.g., Chan and Anteby, 2016).

Sociologists who study inequality have generally aimed to explain income differences: why do some people earn more than others? While economists such as Piketty aim to explain aggregates such as economy-wide inequality in terms of other aggregates (say, the rate of GDP growth relative to the rate of return on investments), sociological research evolved from an initial focus on individual attainment, to examinations of the organizational structures and practices that allocated rewards to individuals, to a more recent focus on economy-wide institutions that shape these organizational structures and practices.

The first wave of stratification research in sociology in the 1960s and 1970s relied heavily on survey research methods to explain individual attainment. Survey respondents might be asked about their income, occupation, race, sex, education and fathers' and mothers' educational background. Income (or socio-economic status, a composite of income and occupational factors) was modeled as a function of individual characteristics and parental attainments, which represented intergenerational mobility. Blau and Duncan's *The American Occupational Structure* (1967), a landmark in sociology, perhaps represents the high-water mark of this approach. Although massively influential within sociology, this approach had its critics. Baron and Bielby (1980) pointed out a critical fact: it is arrangements within the firm that allocate incomes and occupational outcomes, and these were largely absent from the models of Duncan and followers. Who gets hired, and how they move up, are critical, and these happen within organizations. Throwing a dummy variable for 'female' into a regression modeling income might very well yield a statistically significant coefficient, but it will not explain exactly how and why women end up earning less. 'Concepts, methods, and findings are unlikely to be cumulative without systematic comparative analyses that identify the crucial dimensions of organizations along which reward structures and sorting processes vary' (Baron, 1984: 41).

Thus, beginning in the 1980s, a second wave of stratification research asked, 'What explains variation in hiring practices and career ladders in organizations?' Rather than examining individuals as autonomous actors, this structural approach sought to examine the features of organizations that underlay unequal rewards. For instance, one reason that women might earn less than similarly-qualified men is that women were systematically channeled into segregated jobs categorized as 'women's work', or if men and women held the same jobs, they might be geographically segregated such that direct comparisons were unlikely (Bielby and Baron, 1986). This core insight led to a large body of work illuminating the organizational practices most directly responsible

for income inequality and mobility. Features of firms such as their size, growth, demography, technology, unionization and business environments were linked to their hiring, pay, and promotion practices (Baron, 1984). It was not individual 'race' or 'sex' *per se*, but the existence of job ladders, or different approaches to affirmative action that helped explain who got ahead in society. One of the limitations of this line of work is that it was surprisingly difficult to gain access to data across a large sample of organizations comparing promotion practices across the organization. 'Job ladder' is an evocative metaphor, but to actually track organization-wide patterns of pay and upward mobility was largely a dream; most research ended up being, in effect, detailed case studies of particular organizations (e.g., a state civil service corps; a large bank; see Baron and Newman, 1990).

A third wave of inequality research aimed to locate the processes at work further back. Why do some firms have elaborate formal practices around equal opportunity, others have a 'diversity' office with little formal authority and still others have nothing at all? Most broadly, how do institutional configurations shape income and mobility within and across organizations? Much of this work in the 1990s sought to explain how corporate employers responded to legal mandates around equal opportunity (e.g., Edelman, 1992; Dobbin et al., 1993). Subsequent studies dug into the outcomes to examine which programs actually worked to increase the representation of women and minorities at higher levels of the organization (e.g., Dobbin, 2009). What distinguished some of this later work was the availability of comprehensive time-series data at the establishment level from the US Equal Employment Opportunity Commission. Although creating maps of career ladders within organizations still remains beyond the horizon, these data allowed scholars to understand, for instance, which affirmative action practices actually resulted in women and minorities subsequently achieving positions in upper management.

The most recent work in this domain takes a broader view of the institutions that shape organizational employment practices and asks, for instance, 'How do cities' politics, norms, business cultures, and elite networks influence occupational segregation and attainment?' Why is the glass ceiling higher in Minneapolis than in Phoenix (Stephens, 2016)? Local 'business culture' turns out to be crucial in shaping how outposts of the same firm are organized in different parts of the country. Stainback et al. (2010: 241) point out that 'the relative power of culturally legitimate actors (corporate executives, human resource managers, men, credentialed employees) can vary with the national, institutional, and market environment of the firm'.

At the broadest level, this work intersects with theories about 'varieties of capitalism' from political science (Hall and Soskice, 2001; Amable, 2003). The varieties-of-capitalism approach asks, How do national institutions shape what a 'firm' is? How do different national institutions channel what kinds of firms arise and survive, and how do different kinds of firms shape individual economic outcomes? It becomes clear from reading this work that the vast majority of the published research on organizations and inequality focuses on very particular kinds of organizations: large, American, publicly traded corporations. This is an important group, but hardly representative of what 'organizations' are or do. If we want to understand cross-national patterns of inequality and how they relate to organizations, we need to take a broader institutionalist view.

This chapter will focus on inequality at the economy-wide level. What accounts for the compression or dispersion of incomes in national economies? And what does it have to do with organizations and institutions? I will argue that the proper level of analysis to explain income distributions in national economies is at the institutional

level. The configuration of institutions in a country's economy shapes the kinds of enterprises that arise, and these enterprises in turn shape who gets what.

HOW DO WE MEASURE INEQUALITY?

The Gini coefficient is the most widely used measure of national income inequality. The Gini index measures the extent to which the distribution of income deviates from a perfectly equal distribution. Imagine lining up people's annual incomes on a grid from the lowest on the left to the highest on the right on an x axis. On the y axis, plot the cumulative amount of income. If you draw a line through all of these points, it gives you the 'Lorenz curve'. If all incomes were equal, the Lorenz curve would be a 45 degree line. The more unequal the distribution of incomes, however, the lower the Lorenz curve sags downward. The Gini coefficient represents the percentage of the area that lies between a country's Lorenz curve and the line of perfectly equality. It varies between 0 (perfect equality) and 1 (perfect inequality, in which one person gathers all the income). One of the advantages of the Gini measure is that it is purely about distribution, and not about levels of income. It is therefore comparable across levels of economic size and growth: countries can be rich and relatively equal (Norway), poor and unequal (South Africa), poor and equal (Belarus), rich and unequal (Singapore), or combinations in between.

Although the Gini measure is conceptually straightforward, it is not always easy to gather the data to calculate it. Scandinavian countries often have detailed individual and household data on incomes going back decades; Latin American countries are considerably less fastidious. A basic requirement for calculating the Gini is to have good data on individual or household incomes: either a large random sample or, ideally, a complete census. The idea of sampling households to learn about their incomes is a 20th-century innovation that is not universally adopted, making it difficult to do long-term studies using the Gini. Comprehensive income tax data can provide a complete census, but the availability of tax data varies widely around the world: the United States did not have a routine federal income tax until 1913, and the records are not always available in a form that lends itself to computer analysis. It turns out that even having data available on inequality is related to a country's variety of capitalism.[1]

Measured by the Gini coefficient, inequality varies widely across countries and over time. The Scandinavian countries habitually occupy the low end, with relatively low levels of inequality. Latin American countries and some parts of sub-Saharan Africa occupy the top end. But levels of inequality change over time. Sweden has substantially increased in inequality over the past 35 years, albeit from a very low base. In contrast, France has actually declined in inequality during the same period. Policies around labor markets and in income transfers can raise or lower inequality.

One of the most striking things is just what an outlier the United States is. One recent review of the evidence notes that 'nowhere is the US more exceptional than in its level of economic inequality' (Fisher and Smeeding, 2016: 32). The US has the highest level of inequality in disposable income among rich countries, and has done so for decades; moreover, inequality has been increasing almost continuously since 1980. The rich are richer in the US, and the poor are poorer, than in other countries: for instance, 'The poor in Norway (i.e., 10th percentile) enjoy more than twice the real incomes of the poor at our [US] 10th decile' (2016: 34). The US also has by far the most unequal distribution of wealth among industrialized countries. This in turn correlates with a lower level of mobility over time, as the rich are good at provisioning their

children for economic success and pulling up the ladder behind them. As with its idiosyncratic corporate sector, the US is an outlier when it comes to inequality. These two are, I will argue, connected.

IS INEQUALITY BAD?

Why do we care about inequality? Other than prurient interest in the lives of the wealthy, or concerns about the lives of those in poverty, is there something about inequality in itself that merits concern?

Research demonstrates that inequality is associated with a wide variety of social ills. Wilkinson and Pickett (2009) show strong correlations between the Gini index and negative social outcomes at the national level, including rates of infant mortality, homicide, mental illness, drug use and incarceration. Many of these relations also hold within smaller geographic units, such as among the 50 American states. If you had to choose a country to be born into from behind a veil of ignorance, by which you would be randomly assigned to birth parents, a good heuristic would be to choose the country with the lowest income inequality. Countries with low inequality tend to score high on many of the most important quality-of-life measures. On this basis, you might choose one of the more equitable Scandinavian or Western European countries over one of the more 'pathological' English-speaking countries.

Yet it is extremely difficult to show a causal relation between economic inequality and other outcomes. That is, we cannot easily say that inequality in itself *causes*, say, higher rates of infant mortality or mental illness. The fact that so many social pathologies are correlated with inequality hints at the problem: many bad things tend to go together, and locating the 'effective ingredient' in what causes what is nearly impossible. In a world with a surplus of research funding and a shortage of ethics, we could imagine creating field experiments in which different economies were endowed with different levels of inequality in order to examine whether inequality led to social pathologies. We might also compare countries that are similar on many dimensions but differ in their level of inequality. The United States and Canada share many similarities in terms of language, history, culture, ethnic diversity and level of economic development. Yet Canada has far lower income inequality than the US, and also experiences lower levels of almost every social pathology (other than Nickelback). Whether it is inequality or other factors that lead to these differences (universal health insurance? low-cost higher education? widespread politeness?) is impossible to tell.

On the other hand, some popular defenses of inequality are also insupportable on these grounds. One moral rationale for inequality is that it promotes economic growth and job creation. According to this account, growth happens when entrepreneurs take bold risks that have a chance to pay off big, and it is this chance at a big payoff that motivates economic innovation. If we want more Larry Pages and Mark Zuckerbergs, we need to hold out the opportunity for fabulous riches. Not only is greed good; envy is good too, because of its motivating power. This story is popular among the billionaire demographic (e.g., Paul Graham of Y Combinator), but has little basis in reality. Colombia's highly unequal economy is not well known for its (legal) entrepreneurship; Denmark, on the other hand, has one of the most entrepreneurial economies on Earth, in spite of (or perhaps because of) its low level of inequality and a comprehensive social safety net. Rapaciousness may not be the primary motivation of innovators. Moreover, there is no evidence that inequality increases rates of growth at the national level: if anything, rich economies tend to be more equal than poor economies.

Although it is intuitively plausible that inequality would have negative consequences for individuals, it is quite difficult to provide persuasive causal evidence. On the other hand, its influence on democracy is evident. We might leave the last word on this to Angus Deaton, winner of the 2015 Nobel Prize in economics:

> The political equality that is required by democracy is always under threat from economic inequality, and the more extreme the economic inequality, the greater the threat to democracy. If democracy is compromised, there is a direct loss of wellbeing because people have good reason to value their ability to participate in political life, and the loss of that ability is instrumental in threatening other harm. ...
>
> The very wealthy have little need for state-provided education or health care ... They have even less reason to support health insurance for everyone, or to worry about the low quality of public schools that plagues much of the country. They will oppose any regulation of banks that restricts profits, even if it helps those who cannot cover their mortgages or protects the public against predatory lending, deceptive advertising, or even a repetition of the financial crash. To worry about these consequences of extreme inequality has nothing to do with being envious of the rich and everything to do with the fear that rapidly growing top incomes are a threat to the wellbeing of everyone else. (Deaton, 2013)

DO ORGANIZATIONS CAUSE INEQUALITY?

Scholars have offered a number of competing explanations of inequality at a national level. Simon Kuznets (1955) famously proposed that inequality varied with the level of industrialization in an inverse U-curve fashion. That is, during the early stages of industrialization, inequality rose as the demand for new skills increased compensation for some industrial laborers, while perhaps decreasing the pay for those left behind in agriculture. As industry advanced, however, inequality declined. This idea is echoed in contemporary accounts of 'skill biased technological change', which attributes recent increases in inequality to the high wages paid to those with tech skills that are demanded by the new information economy. Piketty (2014) proposes an alternative interpretation that hinges on the relative magnitude of economic growth and returns to investment. When the rate of economic growth is greater than investment returns, the concentration of wealth declines. When investment returns outstrip economic growth, wealth becomes ever more concentrated.

Cobb (2016) reviews several alternative accounts that have been proposed for societal income inequality, including skill-biased technological change (new technologies raise the productivity and pay of workers having relevant skills while potentially lowering the pay of workers without the new skills); globalization (low-skilled jobs migrate to low-pay countries, reducing wages at the low end in developed countries); unionization (declining rates of unionization reduce the bargaining power of labor and reduce wages for less-skilled workers); and public policy (increasing minimum wages reduces overall inequality; income transfers reduce after-tax inequality). Although each has merit, none is sufficient to explain the diverse patterns of change in inequality in countries around the world since 1980. Moreover, accounts at a purely aggregate level give little sense of the mechanisms that lead to greater or lesser inequality. It is one thing to know that eating salt increases blood pressure; it is quite another to know exactly how this happens. This is where organization theory fits in.

Since the work of Jim Baron and Jeff Pfeffer in the 1980s, organizational scholars have tended to see the organization and its practices as the most direct source of income inequality. A recent annual review opened with the statement, 'Contemporary stratification scholars are unlikely to deny the claim that organizations are the primary site of the production and allocation of inequality in modern societies' (Stainback et al., 2010: 226). Most individuals earn most of their income through jobs with organizations. To understand the spread of incomes in society, we need to know how those people came to occupy those jobs, and why jobs pay what they do. Thus, the most immediate cause of income inequality is the social organization of the economy. How do different kinds of people come to be hired for jobs? How is employment allocated within and among formal organizations, and what is the 'shape' of those organizations?

The implication of this line of reasoning is that if we want to explain income inequality at a national level, we should look to the demography of organizations, that is, the prevalence of organizations with different kinds of structures and strategies.

The post-War American economy illustrates the link between the shape of the corporate sector and income inequality. Davis and Cobb (2010) define 'employment concentration' as the proportion of a country's labor force employed by the largest corporate employers (the biggest 10, 25, 50, or 100 domestic corporations). This measure is a simple way to assess the tendency toward large size, perhaps the most basic indicator of organizational structure. Davis and Cobb find that employment concentration has varied greatly since 1950, reaching a peak around 1970, when the 25 largest US corporations employed the equivalent of 10% of the civilian labor force. Inequality also varied widely over this period. But what is most remarkable is the correlation between these two, at about −0.9. That is, as corporate size increased, inequality went down almost in lockstep, and vice versa. The dominance of large and growing firms in the 1950s and 1960s reduced inequality; the disaggregation of large corporations in the 1980s and 1990s increased it. Similar tendencies held around the world: the countries with the lowest inequality (e.g., Sweden, Denmark, Switzerland) were often the home of huge firms, while countries with high inequality (Colombia, South Africa, Honduras) hosted tiny domestic firms.

This finding is paradoxical: bigger firms generally have more levels of hierarchy, greater inequality internally and higher-paid top executives than small firms (see Simon, 1957), yet an economy composed of larger firms has lower inequality than an economy composed of smaller firms. Why? Two reasons: first, organizations beyond a small size tend to adopt systems of compensation that attach pay to positions in relation to each other. In the most extreme case, jobs are evaluated and paid according to set schemes (e.g., the Hay System) that may be detached from market prices. Second, the boundaries of the firm define relevant social comparisons and create pressures for equity. Faculty in institutions with salary transparency routinely compare their pay to the person down the hall but not to colleagues at the private institution up the road. We often hear about how a CEO's compensation compares to the average worker; how often do we hear comparisons between the CEOs of Coke and Pepsi, or between branch managers at Bank of America and Home Depot?

Income inequality in society is most directly attributable to the organizational demography of the economy. Moreover, if we want to understand the prevalence of different kinds of organizations at different times and in different countries, we need to understand the institutions that underlie them. Institutions provide the soil in which organizations grow, and changes in institutions lead to changes in organizations that in turn shape the distribution of incomes. When American corporations valued size and growth as their primary objectives, organizations grew almost without limit, gathering more employees under the same organizational umbrella and typically paying them according to rationalized processes that reduced pay dispersion. During the 1960s, GM grew by 100,000 employees, AT&T grew by 200,000 and ITT grew by 260,000. Not coincidentally, this growing concentration of employment corresponded with the greatest compression in incomes in American history. When the 'shareholder value' fad overtook the sector in the 1980s, corporations

went on an ongoing spree of layoffs and outsourcing, drastically shrinking many of the largest corporate employers. Low-wage big box stores replaced high-wage manufacturers as the biggest employers, and inequality soared. In the next section, I sketch an account for how to attack this task.

HOW DO NATIONAL INSTITUTIONS SHAPE ORGANIZATIONS?

One of the striking things about our knowledge of organizations and inequality is just how heavily it is based on small samples of large American organizations – often Fortune 500 corporations – from the post-War period. It is as if our understanding of biology depended entirely on species observed on the Galapagos Islands. We know about internal labor markets, the provision of benefits such as health insurance and pensions, the effect of industry-based labor unions – features that are sometimes utterly idiosyncratic to a particular place, time and form of organization. Fast food chains do not have elaborate internal labor markets. French corporations do not need to provide health insurance. Chinese firms do not face free-standing industrial labor unions.

Corporations and other business organizations vary widely around the world. Consider one of the most basic aspects: size, as measured by employment. One might imagine that organizational size corresponds to country size, and that big countries grow big firms, while small countries grow small firms. This turns out to be incorrect: the biggest domestic company in Colombia (population 48 million) is Grupo Exito, a supermarket chain with 63,000 employees, while the biggest company in Denmark (population 5.6 million) is facility services company ISS, with 522,000 employees (albeit not all in Denmark). Walmart is the biggest private employer in the United States, with 1.4 million domestic workers. It is also the biggest private employer in Canada and Mexico, but has abandoned Germany and South Korea because its business practices evidently did not fit local customs. The ability to grow and sustain a big organization evidently depends on local conditions.

Table 26.1 lists the five largest employers headquartered in Dominica, China, the United States, Denmark, Brazil and Bangladesh. Not surprisingly, Dominica's largest employers are tiny, and China's are huge. But compare Denmark's relatively vast corporations with those of Brazil (population 200 million) and Bangladesh (population 157 million). Or consider the types of organizations that make up the largest employers. In the US, they are dominated by retailers. In other countries, it tends to be resources, banking and heavy manufacturing. Most striking of all, however, is the sheer variation in terms of size and industry, and what that implies for the variation in pay distributions.

Even within the same industry, corporate size varies widely around the world. Toyota, Volkswagen and General Motors manufacture the same number of cars (roughly 10 million apiece in 2015) in the same price range. But Toyota employed 344,000 people, Volkswagen employed 593,000 and GM employed only 215,000.

Or consider corporate governance, that is, how the board of directors is structured and staffed. Generations of corporate governance researchers have published tens of thousands of papers on the boards of public corporations – how big they are, how they are staffed, how many insiders and outsiders, how these connect to performance – and if there is any domain in which researchers should have figured out global best practices, it is here. Yet consider the boards of leading firms in the global automotive industry: 'In the US, the board of General Motors includes the CEO and ten outsiders, who are mostly retired CEOs of other companies. In Japan, the board of Toyota includes 21 directors, most of whom are current or former Toyota executives. Under German law,

half of the supervisory board is elected by employees to represent labor, as are 10 of the 20 board members at Daimler. China's Geely Automotive board, in contrast, includes eight executive and six non-executive directors' (Davis, 2016a).

Why do firms vary so widely around the world, even in the same industry? Consider an analogy. In the pre-modern period, the kinds of buildings one encountered reflected locally available materials and geography. In the Cotswolds one might see cottages made of stone; in Kentucky, the preferred building material was logs; in Japan, bamboo. Available materials constrained the kinds of structures that were possible; vernacular styles and local needs shaped what they looked like. The tallest structure in any given country might be a cathedral made of marble. Technological advances in the 19th century, such as the industrial production of plate glass, structural steel and reinforced concrete, allowed low-cost construction on a grand scale; electrification and elevators in the early 20th century enabled a new age of skyscrapers. Organizational structures are also built from available raw materials. Stinchcombe (1965) noted that different historical eras produced different kinds of organizations, just as the 18th century produced log cabins and the 20th century produced skyscrapers. But what is the equivalent of steel and glass for business organizations? The 'varieties of capitalism' program in political science suggests some possibilities (Hall and Soskice, 2001; Amable, 2003).

National economies include institutions that guide each of five broad domains that shape the kinds of firms they get. The first dimension is *product market competition*: how are rivalries or collaborations among producers regulated? The US has a long history of antitrust regulation aimed at preventing monopolies or oligopolies from charging high prices to American consumers, which limited the size of firms, while South Korea was more oriented toward growing national champions to compete on a global market,

Table 26.1 Largest domestic employers in six selected countries, 2015

Dominica	No. emp.	China	No. emp.	US	No emp.	Denmark	No. emp.	Brazil	No. emp.	Bangladesh	No. emp.
J Astaphan & Co.	350	Petrochina Company Limited	534,652	Wal-Mart Stores	2,200,000	ISS A/S	522,258	Itaú Unibanco Holdings	93,175	Janata Bank	14,413
HHV Whitchurch and Co.	220	Aviation Industry Corp.	500,000	US Postal Service	488,000	AP Moller– Maersk	89,209	Petróleo Brasileiro	80,908	Zahintex Industries	13,400
Dominica Electricity Services	219	Agricultural Bank of China	493,583	Kroger Co.	400,000	Novo Nordisk	51,059	Vale SA	76,531	Bangladesh Export Import Co.	7,852
National Bank of Dominica	149	Industrial & Commercial Bank of China	462,282	Home Depot Inc.	371,000	Carlsberg A/S	46,832	Marfrig Global Foods SA	45,243	Pubali Bank	7,645
Fine Foods Inc.	130	China Construction Bank	372,321	Target Corp.	347,000	Lundbeckfonden	32,135	Telefônica Brasil SA	26,598	Advanced Chemical Industries Ltd	6,930

encouraging grand scale. The second dimension is *labor market regulation*: how is the employment relation organized, and what obligations does it include? American firms generally operate under employment-at-will, allowing firms to hire and fire workers with few limitations, while many Chinese firms are expected to provide an 'iron rice bowl' of relatively permanent employment. The third dimension is *capital market structure*: how do firms fund their operations, and how is ownership organized? American corporations were distinctively reliant on stock markets to raise capital, whereas half the world's economies do not have a local stock market, and half of those that do have domestic stock markets only created them in the past generation. In such economies, banks or wealthy families rather than markets often play a crucial role in financing business. The fourth is *education systems*: how are workers prepared for jobs? The US emphasizes general education and college preparation, while Germany has a strong system of technical training that supports high-end manufacturing. The fifth is *social welfare provision*: how are things like health care, unemployment security and retirement income provided? Since the 1950s, American corporations have been the primary source of health insurance and retirement security for employees and their families, creating costly obligations for firms, whereas Denmark has an elaborate system of social welfare provision for all citizens, independent of employment.

The major insight of the varieties of capitalism program is that these economy-level institutional conditions decisively shape what firms can and will look like, and what kinds of industries are likely to thrive (or fail). A growth-oriented business created in the US today can expect to be funded by venture capitalists who hope the firm will eventually list on a stock market. It will hire workers who expect to get health insurance and a 401(k) retirement plan, who can be fired at will, and whose preparation is likely to be fairly general and in need of some firm-specific

training. This might be a great environment for a software or biotech company, but not so great for precision manufacturing, which requires highly skilled operatives with specialized training who might prefer the employment security of a family-owned firm.

The five institutional domains at the national level can be complementary and often form more or less coherent configurations, at least among highly successful economies. There are, in short, *varieties of capitalism* that are conducive for particular kinds of firms. Amable (2003) analyzed 21 OECD countries and uncovered five broad clusters of national institutional configurations, each of which typically provided a favorable climate for particular kinds of firms and industries.

In *market-based systems*, such as the US, UK, Canada and Australia, product competition and financial markets are predominant forces. World-leading research universities and vast capital markets make these systems fruitful for industries such as software, biotech and electronics. The *social-democratic model* includes countries like Sweden, Finland and Denmark. Here, coordinated wage bargaining and robust social protection give comparative advantages in health-related industries and industries that draw on their natural resources, like paper and printing. The *Continental European* model describes France, Germany, Austria, Belgium, Ireland, Norway and, arguably, Switzerland and the Netherlands. This model is similar to the social-democratic model but less reliant on coordinated wage bargaining. The *Mediterranean model* applies in Italy, Spain, Portugal and Greece. These economies offer more employment protection and less social protection than Continental Europe, and the education system produces workers with lower skills and wages on average. These economies often specialize in light industry and lower-tech activities. Finally, the *Asian model* describes Japan and South Korea, where large corporations

Figure 26.1 Employment concentration and inequality by varieties of capitalism

historically coordinated with the national government in an export-oriented system. This model includes employment protection and a limited welfare state, and provides advantages in computers, electronics and machines (Amable, 2003: 22).

To a remarkable degree, these different varieties of capitalism correspond both to the sizes of domestic corporations and to the level of inequality (see Figure 26.1). Social democratic countries have low levels of inequality and very large domestic corporations. Mediterranean countries have higher inequality and smaller corporations. Continental Europe is somewhere in the middle.

This suggests a 'drive train of inequality': national institutions shape the kinds of organizations that thrive in an economy, and these organizations in turn shape the distribution of incomes. Thus, to understand inequality, one needs to understand how institutions shape the kinds of choices made around organizations. Moreover, to understand changes in inequality over time, we should look to changes in national-level economic institutions that shape the configuration of organizations in an economy.

WHAT SHAPES NATIONAL INSTITUTIONS?

Thus far I have aimed to establish that formal organizations are the proximal cause of income inequality through their hiring, pay and promotion practices; that organizational size is a particularly important aspect of formal organizations; and that economic institutions at the societal level decisively shape organizational size and structure. To explain income inequality, we need to explain the distribution, size and structure of employing organizations, and that requires mapping the institutions governing product markets, labor markets, financial markets, education and social welfare provision.

At the risk of causing social science vertigo, it is important to note that national institutions are not static. The preceding account suggests that we can explain income inequality by examining how changes in institutions lead to changes in the prevalence of different kinds of organizations. This is beyond the scope of this chapter, but it does suggest a research agenda going forward.

Institutional scholarship in recent years often seems unmoored, as if it lacked an agenda beyond filling a gap in the prior literature, and research is driven more by the internal concerns of the discipline than by problems in the world. But not all gaps are worth filling. Explaining inequality, on the other hand, is an area where institutional theory can bring its insights to bear, by explaining how national-level institutions shape the kinds of organizations that are created and the distribution of rewards they offer. My concern is not original, and it is not new. Stinchcombe (1997) noted 20 years ago that modern institutionalists (in contrast to predecessors like Commons and Schumpeter) imagine institutions as collective representations that generate themselves through some opaque process. We now have a bit more insight into the institutional manufacturing process, but we lack a strong agenda to explain the institutions that create the organizations that generate inequality.

The varieties-of-capitalism programs provides a good starting point for the institutions worth studying. Inequality provides the why; organizational creation provides the how. One example of how this work might be done is Bruce Kogut's (2012) collaborative effort with roughly two dozen scholars to track how changes in financial markets led to changes in the structure of ownership and director networks around the world. The next step is to track how such changes connect with other institutional domains, and to the shape of firms and to inequality.

In recent years we have witnessed substantial changes in all five domains that are certain to change the shape of business organization, and thus the level of inequality in different economies. Information and communication technologies have changed each of these domains, and each is worthy of investigation by organizational scholars (Davis, 2016b).

- In financing, market-based finance has become increasingly accessible around the world, and traditional distinctions between commercial banking (taking in deposits, making loans) and investment banking (underwriting securities) have evaporated as loans are frequently 'securitized' (bundled together and sold as bonds to global investors). Moreover, platforms for peer-to-peer lending and crowdsourcing expand the range of possibilities for funding firms, with unknown long-term consequences for organizational structures. *How do changes in financing options change the goals, governance, and structure of employing organizations around the world?*

- In product markets, firms are increasingly subject to 'Nikefication', in which design and marketing are organizationally separated from production and distribution. Supply chains are increasingly dispersed and global; new entrants are able to scale up and down rapidly by renting rather than buying capacity, which enables radically tiny organizations to have large impacts and outcompete large-scale incumbents. *How does the availability of contractors for essential organizational activities change the distribution of incomes across the enterprise? How does it change the sizes of organizations across the value chain?*

- In social welfare provision, states are under great budget pressures due in part to 'Baumol's disease', by which services increase in cost much faster than manufactured products. Traditional methods of financing social welfare and retirement are facing strains around the world, while in the United States functions previously provided by firms (health insurance, retirement security) are increasingly taken on by states or individuals. *How does the location of social welfare provision (public or private) influence the size of organizations and the creation of new enterprises?*

- In education, the rising cost of higher education (due in part to Baumol's disease) leaves many college students weighed down by debt as they enter the labor force. New technologies enable on-demand training for very specific skills and hold out the possibility of job training being offered just-in-time by outside providers. *How does educational funding influence the kinds of training provided and the kinds of firms that are possible? How does the privatization of education change the priorities of scholarship?*

- Labor markets face perhaps the biggest disruption of all through 'Uberization', by which labor is hired by the task rather than by the job. Online platforms increasingly allow workers to bid for the performance of specific tasks for set fees. The career was replaced by the job; now the job is increasingly being replaced by the task, with dire implications for career mobility. *What kinds of new forms of enterprise will be enabled by 'Uberization', and what impact will these new forms have on inequality?*

In combination, these changes are poised to reshape business enterprise itself. Where the traditional corporation entailed boundaries, members and goals, with career ladders providing mobility for long-term employees, the new enterprise increasingly resembles a web page, consisting of a set of calls on resources (including labor) that may be housed outside the firm (Davis, 2016b). As the components of enterprise are available for short-term contracts, businesses come to look like impromptu constructions for specific performances. This will play out differently around the world, as is evident from the starkly divergent receptions to Uber in North America, France, Germany, China and Indonesia.

CONCLUSION

Income inequality results from the employment practices of organizations, and organizations are shaped by institutions, particularly those at the level of the national economy. Institutional scholars can contribute to our understanding of income inequality around the world by rigorously analyzing national institutions and their effect on organizational hiring practices and reward structures. As new technologies change the institutional backdrop for organizations in the 21st century, we are witnessing a wholesale reformulation of what an enterprise looks like, and even whether it counts as an 'organization' at all. The most productive organizational research on inequality today will take up the task of analyzing changing technologies, changing institutions and the changing architecture of enterprise as careers are replaced by jobs and jobs are replaced by tasks.

Note

1 Scholars interested in cross-national data on inequality can find links at http://worldinequality.org/.

REFERENCES

Amable, Bruno (2003). *The Diversity of Modern Capitalism.* New York: Oxford University Press.

Bapuji, Hari and Neville, Lukas (2015). Income inequality ignored? An agenda for business and strategic organization. *Strategic Organization,* 13(3): 233–246.

Baron, James N. (1984). Organizational perspectives on stratification. *Annual Review of Sociology,* 10: 37–69.

Baron, James N. and Bielby, William T. (1980). Bringing the firms back in – stratification, segmentation, and the organization of work. *American Sociological Review,* 45: 737–765.

Baron, James N. and Newman, Andrew E. (1990). For what it's worth: Organizations, occupations, and the value of work done by women and nonwhites. *American Sociological Review,* 55: 155–175.

Bielby, William T. and Baron, James N. (1986). Men and women at work: Sex segregation and statistical discrimination. *American Journal of Sociology,* 91: 759–799.

Blau, Peter and Duncan, Otis Dudley (1967). *The American Occupational Structure.* New York: John Wiley.

Chan, Curtis K. and Anteby, Michel (2016). Task segregation as a mechanism for within-job inequality: women and men of the transportation security administration. *Administrative Science Quarterly,* 61: 184–216.

Cobb, J. Adam. (2016). How firms shape income inequality: Stakeholder power, executive decision-making, and the structuring of employment relationships. *Academy of Management Review,* 41: 324–348.

Davis, Gerald F. (2016a). Can an economy survive without corporations? Technology and robust organizational alternatives. *Academy of Management Perspectives,* 30 (2): 129–140.

Davis, Gerald F. (2016b). *The Vanishing American Corporation: Navigating the Hazards of a New Economy.* Oakland: Berrett–Koehler.

Davis, Gerald F. and Cobb, J. Adam (2010). Corporations and economic inequality around the world: The paradox of hierarchy. *Research in Organizational Behavior,* 30: 35–53.

Deaton, Angus (2013). *The Great Escape: Health, Wealth, and the Origins of Inequality.* Princeton, NJ: Princeton University Press.

Dobbin, Frank (2009). *Inventing Equal Opportunity*. Princeton, NJ: Princeton University Press.

Dobbin, Frank, Sutton, John R., Meyer John W. and Scott, Richard (1993). Equal opportunity law and the construction of internal labor markets. *American Journal of Sociology*, 99: 396–427.

Edelman, Lauren B. (1992). Legal ambiguity and symbolic structures: Organizational mediation of civil rights law. *American Journal of Sociology*, 97: 1531–1576.

Fisher, Jonathan and Smeeding, Timothy M. (2016). Income inequality. *Pathways: The Poverty and Inequality Report 2016*. Stanford Center on Poverty and Inequality, Stanford University. pp. 32–38.

Gini, C. (1913). Variabilita e mutabilita. *Journal of the Royal Statistical Society*, 76(3): 326–327.

Hall, Peter A. and Soskice, David W. (2001). *Varieties of Capitalism: The Institutional Foundations of Comparative Advantage*. Oxford: Oxford University Press.

Kogut, Bruce (ed.) (2012). *The Small Worlds of Corporate Governance*. Cambridge, MA: MIT Press.

Kuznets, Simon (1955). Economic growth and income inequality. *American Economic Review*, 45: 1–28.

Milanovic, Branko (2016). *Global Inequality: A New Approach for the Age of Globalization*. Cambridge: Harvard University Press.

Pfeffer, Jeffrey and Langton, Nancy (1988). Wage inequality and the organization of work – the case of academic departments. *Administrative Science Quarterly*, 33(4): 588–606.

Piketty, Thomas (2014). *Capital in the 21st Century*. Cambridge, MA: Belknap.

Simon, Herbert A. (1957). The compensation of executives. *Sociometry*, 20: 32–35.

Stainback, Kevin, Tomaskovic-Devey, Donald and Skaggs, Sheryl (2010). Organizational approaches to inequality: Inertia, relative power, and environments. *Annual Review of Sociology*, 36: 225–247.

Stephens, Flannery G. (2016). Community matters: Uncovering the societal mechanisms undergirding workplace inequality. Unpublished paper, University of Utah.

Stinchcombe, Arthur L. (1965). Social structure and organizations. In James G. March (ed.), *Handbook of Organizations*. Chicago, IL: Rand McNally. pp. 142–193.

Stinchcombe, Arthur L. (1997). On the virtues of the old institutionalism. *Annual Review of Sociology*, 23: 1–18.

Wilkinson, Richard and Pickett, Kate (2009). *The Spirit Level: Why More Equal Societies Almost Always Do Better*. London: Allen Lane.

27

Institutions and Economic Inequality[1]

John Amis, Kamal Munir and Johanna Mair

INTRODUCTION

The global rise of economic inequality has become an increasingly prevalent theme in the economics and sociology literatures. Much of the focus of this work has been on the uncovering of statistical evidence that economic inequality exists, and is increasing. A growing body of research, including Atkinson (2015), Dorling (2011, 2014), Jencks et al. (1979), Piketty (2014) and Stiglitz (2013), overwhelmingly suggests that overall improvements in aggregate wealth are in fact associated with increases in inequality. For example, the share of wealth in the United States enjoyed by the top 0.1% grew from 7% in 1979 to 22% in 2012 (Saez & Zucman, 2014). In 1965, CEOs of major American companies earned 10 or 18 times more than the typical worker, depending on the compensation measure; by 2012, it had increased to 202-to-1 or 273-to-1 respectively (Mishel & Sabadish, 2013). These figures become even more extreme in the financial

sector. In 2004, for example, the combined income of the top 25 hedge fund managers was greater than the combined income of all CEOs of S&P 500 firms (Kaplan & Rauh, 2010). Further, of the top 0.1% of income earners, 18.4% worked in finance or were executives, managers and supervisors of financial firms (Bakija, Cole, & Heim, 2012).

The extreme levels of inequality are starkly borne out in the anti-poverty charity Oxfam's (2017) report that the proportion of the world's wealth owned by the top 1% has continued to dramatically increase. In fact, Oxfam (2017) reports that the eight wealthiest people in the world own the same amount as the least well off 3.5 billion, or 50% of the world's population. When juxtaposed with Oxfam's (2016) research that stated that the wealth of the richest 62 people in the world increased by 44% between 2010 and 2015 while that of the bottom 3.5 billion fell by 41% over the same period, it can be seen that there appears to be an ever-increasing concentration of wealth among the richest members of our society.

If the recent rise in inequality is now well established, what is also increasingly recognized is that it appears to have hugely detrimental consequences. Wilkinson and Pickett (2010) have demonstrated that higher levels of inequality are correlated with a wide variety of undesirable consequences including lower life expectancies, greater levels of community dysfunction, greater levels of drug use, more mental health problems, poorer physical health, greater obesity rates, increased levels of violence, lower levels of educational performance, higher rates of imprisonment and lower levels of social mobility.

Such patterns of inequality seem to perpetuate themselves not just in society in general but within organizations too. The 'working poor', while 'seemingly indispensable to the value creation model for firms in developed economies' (Leana, Mittal, & Stiehl, 2012: 901), appear to have little chance of advancing beyond their current circumstances (see also Mair, Martí, & Ventresca, 2012 for a similar argument in developing economies). Further, despite decades of awareness, women remain discriminated against in many organizations, leading to a perpetuation of unequal pay and severe under-representation in senior management positions (Belliveau, 2012; Ryan & Haslam, 2007). Racial disparities (Carton & Rosette, 2011; Cortina, 2008), sexual harassment (Berdahl, 2007; Raver & Gelfand, 2005), discrimination against stigmatized and marginalized individuals and groups (Martí & Fernández, 2013; Soule, 2012) and exploitation that leads to 'body breakdowns' (Michel, 2011) have also been reported as outcomes of formal and informal policies of exploitation and inequality.

These patterns of inequality are engendered by deeply entrenched power structures that are manifest in institutionalized beliefs and rules that dominate social and economic life. These include economic and political ideologies, the class system, gender

roles, social structures, discourses and subject positions that have themselves reified societal inequalities. Mair et al. (2012: 820), for example, provide an evocative analysis of the ways in which social inequalities in developing countries are reinforced as market access and opportunities are governed by local institutional arrangements that 'consist of complex interlocks of formal institutions, such as constitutions, laws, property rights, and governmental regulations, and informal institutions, such as customs, traditions, and religious beliefs'. To date, however, the institutional arrangements underpinning, and dynamics of, inequality have been largely overlooked (for an exception see Mair, Wolf & Seelos, 2016).

It is this agenda that we take up in our chapter. In doing so, we are responding to recent polemics, prescriptions and calls to engage more with substantive societal problems (e.g., Bapuji, 2015; Dover & Lawrence, 2010; George, McGahan, & Prahbu, 2012; Gulati, 2007; Hinings & Greenwood, 2002; Lorsch, 2009; Mair & Martí, 2006; Munir, 2011, 2015; Riaz, 2015; Seelos & Mair, 2007, 2017; Starkey & Madan, 2001; Von Glinow, 2005). We believe that the potential for institutional scholars to inform understanding of the mechanisms that exacerbate or reduce inequality is significant; similarly, the study of inequality poses fundamental questions for institutional theory.

The problem of increasing inequality appears to stem, at least in part, from the growing disparity between stagnating wages of lower-level employees on the one hand and rapid wealth accumulation by the rich on the other (e.g., Lansley, 2012; Piketty, 2014; Stiglitz, 2013). This in turn has been causally linked to two related phenomena, the first of which is the influence of corporations. Barley (2007) argued that many corporations wield inordinate influence over policy-making, hamper the performance of institutions created to protect the public from corporate excesses and, together with various multilateral institutions, push for increased privatization of public services. One example of a firm that is arguably intent on increasing its influence on public policy in the United States and Europe is Google. Concerns have been raised, on the one hand, about the firm's strategy of recruiting former government insiders, and, on the other, of how several former Google employees have been recruited to fill prominent political positions (Doward, 2016). While Barley (2007) particularly emphasizes the effects of large corporations, Davis (2016) argues that in fact an economy dominated by a number of large corporations has been replaced by the so-called 'gig economy', with an emphasis on flexible work produced by self-employed contractors. However, these organizations designed to be more responsive to environmental changes also have the potential to increase disparities between those in professional or senior leadership positions, and those reliant on short-term, temporary and non-guaranteed contracts. Thus, whether large, traditional employers, or technology-intensive firms intent on constructing highly flexible workforces, corporations, in varied ways, are employing strategies that are apparently increasing levels of inequality.

The second antecedent for the increasing prevalence of inequality has been the financialization of the economy (Davis, 2009; Lansley, 2012; Stiglitz, 2013). Precipitated most notably by the emphasis on deregulation of the financial industry in the 1980s by the governments of Margaret Thatcher in the UK and Ronald Reagan in the United States, financial institutions became characterized by the aggressive pursuit of short-term policies aimed at increasing wealth maximization. Such an approach, inevitably, spilled over into other industries such that shareholder return has become, in many cases, the sole driver of corporate strategies. As Burgin (2012: 214) documented, 'the rise of deregulation in the 1970s and the subsequent election of Ronald Reagan had ushered in nearly thirty years during which the primacy of free markets was largely assumed'. Chang

(2011) is among those who have pointed to the ways in which such a philosophy is explicitly oriented to have a positive impact on minority shareholders and senior managers at the expense of lower-level employees and long-term corporate well-being. In this environment, imperatives such as employment conditions, economic mobility and employee benefits are consistently overlooked (Stout, 2012).

In the context of these observations, our purpose in this chapter is to open up possibilities for developing institutional explanations for the persistence of inequality. We believe this will lead to a more holistic understanding of the causes of inequality, and in turn a more robust conceptualization of possible prescriptions. To this end, we draw upon four different streams of work to provide a conceptual framework for an institutional understanding of inequality. Our intent is not to provide detailed theoretical expositions of each stream – these are carried out in detail elsewhere in this book – but rather to uncover the ways in which an institutional infrastructure has emerged to create a society in which inequality is widely seen as inevitable. The four perspectives are selected, and ordered, to cumulatively build a detailed understanding of how institutions and inequality are inextricably interlinked. We begin by examining the institutional microfoundations of inequality. Our focus here is on uncovering the ways in which inequality becomes reified in everyday actions and interactions by and among individuals. We build out from a focus on individuals to consider how the discourse that people produce structures social life and in so doing creates a context in which systems of inequality can flourish but can also be potentially challenged. The third section focuses upon institutional logics, the material and symbolic constructions underpinned by a shared set of values, norms and assumptions that help determine what are considered to be appropriate, and inappropriate, courses of action. In so doing, the taken-for-granted social structures that have resulted in inequality are investigated. This allows us, in our final section, to examine the role of identity in the creation and maintenance of inequality. Implicated here are the ways in which social constructions such as gender, class, race, disability and status create expectations of how we and others should behave in particular situations. In adopting this structure, we show how four of the most dominant perspectives in institutional theory are mutually interlinked to create an environment in which inequality has become a taken-for-granted feature of everyday life, and how those institutions that underpin inequality might be reframed.

THE MICROFOUNDATIONS OF INEQUALITY

> The ideas of economists and political philosophers, both when they are right and when they are wrong are more powerful than is commonly understood. Indeed, the world is ruled by little else. Practical men, who believe themselves to be quite exempt from any intellectual influences, are usually slaves of some defunct economist. (Keynes, 1936: 383)

An important consideration for those interested in the perpetuation of inequality is how the dynamics of everyday life in organizational and field settings can reify and institutionalize particular social structures. Resonating with efforts to attend to the microfoundations of institutions and institutional processes (e.g., see Barley, Chapter 13 this Volume; Powell & Rerup, Chapter 12 this Volume), this is a broader theoretical concern at the forefront of institutional scholarship and one that we consider here. In particular, we first investigate the ways in which inequality is experienced and reinforced from repeated, often mundane, everyday organizational practices. Second, we assess the ways in which practices that lead to, and accentuate, inequality spread within and across institutional fields.

Reproducing Practices of Inequality

Understanding how practices become institutionalized has long been at the heart of institutional theory. However, as Martí and Mair (2009: 98) explained in their discussion of the perpetuation of poverty, 'there is a need to unpack the institutional forces that make policies so persistent and to understand how to act upon them ... Studying how the wide array of legacy institutions, traditions, myths and customary practices that underlie policy are reproduced and maintained, and by whom, is of utmost importance.' Understanding how such 'institutions, traditions, myths, and customary practices' are constructed and reproduced will, we contend, provide insight into the escalation and perpetuation of inequality.

Institutions are produced, and reproduced, through the situated, everyday activities of individuals. Members of organizations ascribe meaning to actions and, in so doing, develop taken-for-granted understandings (Powell & Rerup, Chapter 12 this Volume). Thus, when becoming institutionalized, practices that would otherwise be considered quite banal and unremarkable are imbued with a meaning informed by broader cultural beliefs (Lounsbury & Crumley, 2007; Thornton, Ocasio, & Lounsbury, 2012). Powell and Covylas (2008) suggested that insights from ethnomethodology, sensemaking, interaction rituals, performativity and status expectations can help us understand how this process takes place. In each case, they argue, we gain exposure to the sequences of individual actions and decisions that constitute the building blocks of microfoundations of institutions and institutional processes. We argue that the unveiling of the microfoundations underpinning inequality would have great utility in helping us understand the ways in which inequality becomes established and subsequently reproduced, and how they might also be unpicked. For example, in contrast to the popular image of processes underpinning institutional change as muscular, radical or triggered by external jolts, Mair and Hehenberger (2014) provide insight into the mundane and gradual processes that became rationalized and taken-for-granted as strategies to alleviate poverty and fight inequality. In particular, they show the importance of collective action by dissimilar actors in bringing about change, but also demonstrate how such action is only possible by reframing constituents' practices in such a way that neutralizes opposition from groups with disparate interests.

Further insight into the microfoundations of inequality can be gained by examining the ways in which changes to the socioeconomic environment in which firms operate has led to a change in the structure of workforces in many firms. At the operational level, firms have engaged in strategies that have led to the outsourcing of manufacturing, the employment of staff on temporary rather than full-time contracts, and the general stagnation of wages. By contrast, senior and chief executives have seen their wages and bonuses climb, particularly in the United States (Stiglitz, 2013). On the one hand, such steps can be seen as straightforward responses to competitive pressures. However, as such practices are repeated within and across organizations, are permeated by interlocking boards, become reinforced by complementary practices, are reported on by the media, become topics of conversation inside and outside organizations, and so on, they become constituted within a broader cultural understanding of what is considered normal, and become *meaningful*. In other words, practices take on a symbolic value of being representative of good management practice. In fact, not following such practices is seen as unusual, even bizarre. A good illustration of the way in which new micro-practices became institutionalized and had a major impact on inequality is provided by the recent financial crisis. Ray Perman's (2013) book on the rise and fall of the Bank of Scotland in the UK is beautifully illustrative in this regard.

The Bank of Scotland

Perman (2013) starts out by pointing out how banks have traditionally been highly conservative organizations that ascribed to the maxim 'lend short and borrow long'. In other words, capital to be borrowed by a bank should be on terms that allow repayment over a relatively long period, while money should be lent only over short timeframes. The principle underlying this was that any bank that fails to maintain its liquidity is extremely vulnerable. Of course, such a value proposition mitigates against practices such as mortgage lending in which lent capital is typically tied up for periods of up to, and beyond, 25 years. Following the deregulation of financial services in 1986, the UK financial industry fundamentally changed. Among other things, building societies, the traditional mortgage lenders, saw opportunities to engage in the provision of other financial services that had been the preserve of banks. By contrast, leaders of banks also began to look at how they might expand their services, and began to view mortgages and other forms of lending as potentially lucrative. In 1995, the Bank of Scotland celebrated its tercentenary, an occasion marked by the *Financial Times* calling it 'the most boring bank in Scotland', something that it noted had allowed it to enjoy 300 years of consistent profitability and to 'outperform the sector by nearly 100 per cent since 1980' (quoted in Perman, 2013: 50). A series of decisions illustrates how the bank's operating values subsequently changed, to disastrous effect.

In 2001 the Bank of Scotland merged with the Halifax Building Society to create HBOS. Rather than slow, organic 'boring' growth, this marked a strategy of aggressive expansion in an attempt to compete with the 'big four' banks in the UK: HSBC, Lloyds, Barclays and the Royal Bank of Scotland. James Crosby, the new CEO, instructed his staff to pursue rapid growth in each of their main market areas. To achieve this, the previous conservatism was replaced by a much greater tolerance for risk. Lending standards were relaxed, with decisions taken to offer unsecured personal loans, increased credit card lending and high-risk 'specialist' mortgages – including self-certified, buy-to-let and 125 per cent mortgages. In fact, to achieve sales targets, it was common practice – at HBOS and elsewhere – for bank staff to help potential mortgage customers lie on their applications about their income levels in order to secure bigger loans.

Another action that further entrenched the new way of banking was the appointment in June 2005 of a new Chief Operating Officer (COO). Rather than banking stalwart George Mitchell, the bank appointed Andy Hornby, a 38-year-old with limited banking experience, as COO and heir apparent to Crosby. Hornby had brought with him to HBOS the sales approach he had developed during his retailing experience with grocery chain Asda. Among other things, he was (in)famous for his monthly staff newsletter, which always ended with the instruction to 'Keep smiling, keep selling'. To further improve market share, prices on new products were cut wafer thin as the bank pursued market share at any price. Those staff at the bank who tried to instill a more cautious approach were fired, actions that were as much symbolic as instrumental in the further reification of the new values. Despite the looming recession, and increasing numbers of bank customers suffering financial hardships, bank employees were still expected to hit their sales targets primarily by selling new products to existing customers; in some cases, the already difficult-to-hit targets were increased for retail staff.

In retrospect, the constellation of actions described above served as microfoundations for institutional change in the banking industry. While at one level, each of the changes in practice could be considered a response to competitive market forces, we can see clear institutional drivers and effects. There were pronounced changes to the values that had guided banking practices, from a conservative attitude to lending allied with careful organic growth, to a very aggressive pursuit of profits and desire for rapid growth in market share. This value change – unsurprisingly – was accompanied with shifts in norms of behavior and assumptions about how a modern bank should act. Further, these changes went almost entirely unchallenged. Chang (2011: 4) explains that the 'free market' is anything but free. Rather practices are underpinned by expectations, understandings and rules of engagement that are established and reified. 'We accept the legitimacy of certain regulations so totally that we don't see them. More carefully examined, markets are revealed to be propped up by rules – and many of them.' While some of these 'rules' were codified in legislative changes, others emerged from the day-to-day practices that become accepted and taken-for-granted as appropriate ways of acting.

If HBOS had been the only bank to embrace this new ideology of capital accumulation, then its impact on the economy might have been relatively minor. However, the new approach to banking had spread like a contagion across the industry. The upshot was a failure in the banking system from Iceland to Ireland, the US to the UK, eventually leading to a worldwide financial collapse.

This collective outcome was not a direct result of market liberalization policies. It was mediated and made possible by rituals, subcultures and identities that emerged to make it all intelligible and indeed desirable to the participants. Those in the financial industries were lauded, particularly investment bankers who regarded themselves as Masters of the Universe, occupying the commanding heights of the economy. Their identities were reinforced by their military-like intense socialization in a 'white collar sweatshop', convincing them that they were the smartest, and hardest-working, young people in society who deserved every ounce of success that came their way (Ho, 2009). In her brilliant ethnography of Wall Street, Ho (2009: 152) described how the concept of shareholder value became 'decontextualized, naturalized and globalized' by institutional actors, particularly economists. 'Reckless expediency' and shifting risk on to other people became an institutionalized practice on Wall Street. Any talk of 'redistribution' of the massive amounts of wealth being generated was openly derided and derogatively labeled as being socialist.

As the financial crisis played out, the effects of decisions made in banks such as HBOS became apparent. In a very sobering manner, the financial crisis illustrated how seemingly isolated decisions made in response to a perceived business pressure or opportunity can become exponentially magnified as new practices become institutionalized. The emergence of these new practices, of course, did not take place in a vacuum, but in a culture in which, particularly in the UK and the US, people had been encouraged from 1980 on to buy shares, borrow money to purchase houses that were almost unaffordable, and pursue wealth-generating opportunities. This was a socioeconomic environment in which greed was not seen as problematic, and in which the financial industry was lauded as traditional industries, such as manufacturing and mining, declined (Collins, 2007; Dobbin & Zorn, 2005; Thompson, 2007). The shifts in banking practice ultimately resulted in hundreds of thousands of people losing their jobs as banks struggled to survive, loans were called in, and lines of credit for business closed; thousands more defaulted on their mortgages and lost their homes. Many of those remaining lower-level employees who did retain their jobs in the banking industry were given pay cuts. Following the worst of the crisis, executive pay quickly rebounded in banking, and in other sectors; share prices also recovered to exceed their pre-2008 highs (Dorling, 2014). Thus, those with senior positions, who could afford to retain their shares, regained most if not all of their losses; those at the lower end, who lost jobs, homes and earning power over an extended period, will likely never recover in the same way

(Stiglitz, 2013). Thus, the financial gap has been extended by changes at both ends of the spectrum.

The Institutionalization of New Practices

As the types of new practices and processes that we lay out above become repeated and gradually adopted across a field, there is a 'typification of habitualized action' (Berger & Luckmann, 1967: 54) that leads to practices gaining legitimacy and becoming institutionalized. There are several, mutually reinforcing, mechanisms through which this happens, and that generally distinguish between those actions that are institutionalized and those that are not. First, those in positions of power usually feel that it is in their best interest to maintain the inequity and thus utilize their bases of power to ensure that systems are established to protect their position. Thus, some practices are encouraged and reinforced, while others are condemned and curtailed. While work on power in the establishment and development of institutionalized practices is relatively limited (Munir, 2015; Willmott, 2015), Lawrence (2008; see also Lawrence & Buchanan, Chapter 18 this Volume) is among the few who has theorized how episodic and systemic forms of power are utilized to establish particular institutional practices.

Second, while those in power can take decisions of the type we saw at HBOS that can create what become microfoundations of new institutionalized practices, institutions rely on the wider repetition of actions for their reproduction (Barley, Chapter 13 this Volume; Berger & Luckmann, 1967; Powell & Rerup, Chapter 12 this Volume). Thus, it becomes apparent that institutionalization is dependent on the situated actions of those at all levels of society. Lawrence and Suddaby (2006: 215) termed this 'institutional work – the purposive action of individuals and organizations aimed at creating, maintaining and disrupting institutions'. For example, Dacin, Munir and Tracey (2010: 1406) described how social class structures are perpetuated, at least in part, by ritualized formal dining practices at Cambridge University. These practices are maintained in part by the institutional work carried out by staff 'performing a role akin to that of servants during England's Victorian era'. A student in the study recalled an example of this: 'At our first formal [dinner], a couple of people got up to go out and have a cigarette in between the courses and the sort of the head waiter came up to them and said loudly, "You are not peasants! Getting up and smoking in between meals is for peasants!" That incident has just stuck in my mind.' Such repeated microactivity helps to maintain a system of inequality that, in societal terms at least, often disadvantages those who are reinforcing it. As Willmott (2015) pointed out, even relatively mundane forms of oppression can become institutionalized in ordinary work situations.

The role of day-to-day practices in organizations in maintaining particular courses of action leads to our third point that the ways in which organizations are structured can ensure that hierarchical divisions are reinforced and taken-for-granted. In this way, not only do organizational practices that promote inequality become reified through the establishment of ritual and repetition, but those who are disadvantaged often see no way to challenge the accepted orthodoxy and, as we see above, often actively participate in the practice reproduction. Gray and Kish-Gephart (2013) described the processes that lead to this as a particular form of institutional work that they term 'class work'. Drawing on Goffman (1967), they define class work as the interpretive processes and interaction rituals that organization members individually and collectively engage in to conform to 'class rules' and reinforce class distinctions. As they explain, 'one's social class and attendant behavior is not simply a function of one's self-construed social

class but is also constructed and reinforced (often unconsciously) through routines and practices that perpetuate inequality ... Class work constructs and legitimates organizational norms and routines as appropriate and expected behavior ... In this way, inequities become institutionalized and maintained over time' (Gray & Kish-Gephart, 2013: 672). A significant component of this reinforcement of unequal status comes from those who self-ascribe to a lower social class feeling threatened, and even stigmatized. According to Eitzen and Smith (2003), this in turn can lead to feelings of shame, humiliation and self-blame for their position, and 'a constant fear of never having "got it right"' (Skeggs, 1997: 6). In sum, many of those in the upper and lower classes see their positions as inevitable outcomes of inherent characteristics: the upper class have no desire to alter the *status quo*, the lower class lack the means to do so. This underpins Wilkinson and Pickett's (2010) analysis of why inequality is so pernicious in its societal outcomes.

While these mechanisms remain underexamined in the institutional literature, they are central to our understanding of how inequality becomes established in often seemingly mundane organizational practices. Equally important is how these practices spread from one organization, and field, to another. It is to this that we now turn.

Disseminating Practices of Inequality

Barley (2007), building on the arguments that he espoused over a decade earlier (Stern & Barley, 1996), contended that while we have attended to the ways in which society influences organizations, we have paid much less attention to how organizations enact the world around them and shape society. Of course, this entire chapter explores this in one way or another, but it is an observation that is particularly apposite when we think about how particular institutional microfoundations serve as platforms for enacting new mechanisms for the production and perpetuation of inequality. As the financial crisis illustrated, individual actions can quickly spread across institutional fields, and from one field to another. For this to happen, as Zucker (1977: 728) explained, actions must be perceived as being *objective* and *exterior*: 'Acts are *objective* when they are potentially repeatable by other actors without changing the common understanding of the act, while acts are *exterior* when the subjective understanding of acts is reconstructed as intersubjective.' A key component to this is the process of theorization whereby a particular practice is seen as being a legitimate solution to a particular organizational failing (Greenwood, Suddaby, & Hinings, 2002; Strang & Meyer, 1993). Thus, a decision at the Bank of Scotland to shift from being conservative guardians of people's money to aggressive purveyors of a range of banking services is constructed as a rational act with moral and pragmatic legitimacy. This is because other banks confronted with similar circumstances are carrying out similar activities, and in so doing establishing perceived economies for their organizations and greater returns for shareholders. In this process, 'the objectivity of institutional arrangements "hardens" as individuals internalize these objective social realities, take them for granted and recreate them in their ongoing interactions' (Dolfsma & Verbürg, 2008: 1036).

While earlier institutional accounts failed to problematize the diffusion of practices across a field, with their attendant microprocesses and issues of power and politics (Zilber, 2008), it has since been established that ideas are not passively transmitted from one organization to another. Rather, the concepts of theorization and translation (Czarniawska & Sevon, 1996; Zilber, 2006; Wedlin & Sahlin, Chapter 4 this volume) established the idea that practices are adapted to suit local circumstances. In particular, practices established in one context are never fully understood, and thus the gaps

in understanding lead to interpretations – translations – based on the meanings that are attributed to particular aspects of the practice and how they might fit in a different organizational context (Sahlin-Andersson, 1996; Sahlin & Wedlin, 2008; Wedlin & Sahlin, Chapter 4 this Volume). Importantly, this process is *intentional* rather than accidental, and *collective* in that there is broad agreement or acceptance in how the practice is to be adopted (Gondo & Amis, 2013; Searle, 2005). Thus, new practices are not 'imprinted literally' into organizations or professions by external parties, such as a government, regulator, or other dominant organization, but are rather interpreted and enacted by those within an organization (Dunn & Jones, 2010). For example, the adoption of more risky banking practices, while broadly accepted, was interpreted and enacted differently in different banks. Thus, some banks emphasized different products, or developed different loan application processes, but were still hit with common catastrophic effects (Martin, 2013; Perman, 2013). The acceptance of particular power structures, large CEO salaries, part-time contracts for lower-skilled workers, and sub-contracting of manufacturing to overseas factories, takes place at the field level where practices are theorized as viable solutions to common problems: local translation takes place within organizations to make the solution contextually specific. As Powell and Colyvas (2008: 285) explained:

> micro-level consensus is generated through a process in which values and beliefs from the larger society are pulled down into local circumstances, creating differential expectations about the performance of individuals in task groups. These expectations can become taken-for-granted features of organizations, and persist even if they are unjust or unproductive, thus giving them an 'objective' quality.

However, as Meyer and Höllerer (2010) have pointed out, selection options are limited by the situation in which the action is to occur. Thus, for our purposes, actions that increase inequality have become in many cases seemingly inevitable outcomes derived from the perceived scarcity of 'legitimate' policies of banks, large corporations and governments. Those who rail for change – the 'Occupy' movements, living wage proponents, those who argue for wealth distribution from more progressive taxation regimes – find themselves marginalized: while they may attract sympathy from (some) decision-makers, the actions they propose are usually seen as not viable in the construed value frameworks in which they would have to be implemented. In order to be seen as having utility, therefore, problems within the field normally need to be reframed in some way, as we saw, for example, with the Arab Spring; however, such reframing is exceptional.

Our intent in this section has been to show the interplay between activities at the individual, organizational and field levels. While practices, rules, norms and values are transmitted through fields, they are initially constructed, and then subsequently translated, by individuals in organizations. It is at the organizational level that policies and actions that perpetuate inequality are enacted, often resulting in income levels becoming stratified (see, e.g., Cobb, 2016), and wealth accumulating in a small proportion of the population (Chang, 2011; Piketty, 2014; Stiglitz, 2013). We have demonstrated the ways in which everyday activities can become reified, sometimes quite rapidly in the case of the banking industry, and how these can create an interlocking system of structures, systems, values and norms of behavior in which increased inequality becomes an almost inevitable outcome. Aligned to these activities, of course, are the modes of language and other communicative practices that individuals use that help to coordinate social activities. We assess the influence of such discursive devices in the next section.

DISCOURSE AND INEQUALITY

In a society such as ours, but basically in any society, there are manifold relations of power which permeate, characterise, and constitute the social body, and these relations of power cannot themselves be established, consolidated, nor implemented without the production, accumulation, circulation, and functioning of a discourse. There can be no possible exercise of power without a certain economy of discourses of truth which operates through and on the basis of this association. We are subjected to the production of truth through power and we cannot exercise power except through the production of truth. (Foucault, 1980: 93–94)

The ideas of the ruling class are in every epoch the ruling ideas: i.e., the class which is the ruling material force of society is at the same time its ruling intellectual force. The class which has the means of material production at its disposal, has control at the same time over the means of mental production, so that thereby, generally speaking, the ideas of those who lack the means of mental production are subject to it. (Marx & Engels, 1970 [1932]: 64)

Inequality is different from winning or losing in a race, although that is how it is often portrayed. Rather, inequality is a long-term condition, and its continued existence necessarily means domination of some groups over others. Given the problematic nature of visible privilege or domination, which can lead to rebellion or resistance by the oppressed, it is not surprising that the continuation of inequality needs continuous legitimation. This is made possible by an interrelated system of discourses that collectively serve to justify a particular social order (Fairclough, 2010; Fallon, 2006; Van Dijk, 1994). Indeed, over centuries, discourse has played a central role in institutionalizing inequality. Previously, we mentioned the unprecedented concentration of wealth in the world and the fact that inequality has been increasing rapidly. Why have people not resisted it? How have they come to accept their inferior status?

Our hierarchical societies are not maintained by brute force. Although physical force is often necessary in establishing a social structure, the everyday maintenance of the institutional order is carried out principally through the establishment of a belief system that bestows moral and pragmatic legitimacy upon it. In other words, those in inferior positions must somehow be made to accept their fate. Thus, surveys show that while American class mobility has diminished greatly over the years, especially in comparison to Western Europe, faith in the American Dream continues to exist. As Wilkinson and Pickett (2010) suggest, if one wants to live the American Dream, one should move to Denmark or Finland. Still, discourses based on rags-to-riches stories of billionaires and celebrities, who through their vision or never-say-die attitude attain heights that are supposedly within the grasp of everyone if only they tried hard enough, go a long way towards sustaining and perpetuating this myth.

The same discourses serve to legitimize the exponential growth in CEO salaries reported at the opening of the chapter. The myth of meritocracy, springing once again from a willingness to work hard, intelligence and the courage to take risks, provides crucial support to our acceptance of stark inequality in income. Similarly, gender inequality manifest in differing pay for men and women is able to continue because we believe that men are clearly able to do things women cannot, and that if the 'value-neutral' institution of the market pays men more, they must deserve it. Before we describe how the production and dominance of various discourses has been instrumental in the creation and perpetuation of inequality, we briefly examine the rise in attention paid to discourse analysis within institutional theory.

Institutionalism and Discourse

With discourse central to the creation and persistence of particular social orders, the use of discourse analysis has increased among institutional theorists (Hardy & Maguire, 2010; Munir & Phillips, 2005; Phillips, Lawrence, & Hardy, 2004; Phillips & Oswick, 2012; Phillips & Malhotra,

Chapter 15 this Volume). This is, of course, unsurprising given that the roots of institutionalism lie in social constructivism (Berger & Luckmann, 1967), a perspective that privileges discourses as building blocks of social life and suggests that perhaps the best method to deconstruct institutional formation is discourse analysis. In fact, Phillips et al. (2004) claim that institutions are constructed primarily through the production of texts. Texts include written documents, speech acts, pictures and symbols (Grant, Keenoy, & Oswick, 1998; Taylor & Van Every, 2000) and combine symbolic and material elements.

For example, the institutional process of theorization, referred to in the previous section, could be seen as a process in which texts are produced that collectively form discourses which in turn render particular institutional arrangements sensible, meaningful and legitimate. The HBOS example above provides a good example of this as the new approach to creating, promoting and selling financial products was imbricated in an array of electronic, printed, audio and video materials that were circulated to staff and customers. Similarly, in their study of popular photography, Munir and Phillips (2005) described how institutional entrepreneurship was in fact a discursive process rooted in the production of texts, which constituted new objects, concepts and subject positions that changed the dynamics of the institutional field. More recently, Khaire and Wadhwani (2010) used organizational discourse analysis to investigate the production of a new category in the global market for art. Discourse analysis thus provides an epistemological foundation and a methodological approach for exploring the processes of social construction that privilege certain discourses and social groups over others, thereby continuously legitimizing particular institutionalized practices. We now briefly describe how various discourses are produced and go on to examine their role in institutionalizing inequality.

Discursive Legitimization of Inequality

As mentioned above, sustained domination requires continuous legitimation for which the production and acceptance of texts is essential. An interesting example is that of British rule in India, which was underpinned by discourses that privileged everything that the colonial masters stood for and convinced the natives of their inferiority (Said, 1977). One example of such a text is the English Education Act of 1835. The Act took away support from indigenous curricula and educational institutions and reallocated it to Western curriculum, with English as the medium of instruction. As Cutts (1953) has pointed out, this Act was the result of long discussions, which are most famous for the memorandum produced by Thomas Macaulay, a historian and high-ranking member of the British government, in February 1835. The memorandum, known as Macaulay's Minute, laid the basis for an educational policy whose effects can be seen even today. Cutts (1953) reported that, in his Minute, Macaulay stated, 'I have conversed both here and at home with men distinguished by their proficiency in the Eastern tongues. ... I have never found one among them who could deny that a single shelf of a good European library was worth the whole native literature of India and Arabia.'

Macaulay argued that the need of the hour was to produce in India, 'a class of persons, Indian in blood and color, but English in taste, in opinions, in morals and in intellect'. Such arguments were decisive in the adoption of this policy in India and in completely transforming the educational system of the vast country to one that affirmed Western supremacy and established the useless nature of locally produced knowledge.

The dismantling of the traditional schooling system and the privileged position of the English language and Western knowledge provided the bedrock on which a new stratification of India took place, helping to ensure continuous deference by Indians to their Western rulers. The durability of such structures depends on the success with which imperialist discourses are diffused and internalized (Bhabha, 2004; Said, 1977). The effect of such discourses is to sustain a 'regime of truth' such that a particular 'object of discourse', or social objectivity, is effectively institutionalized (Foucault, 1977).

Religious discourses have also played a significant role in justifying sustained inequalities and the legitimization of particular social orders (Berger, 1967). While various religious movements have, over the years, undoubtedly led to more egalitarian social orders, they have also been used to legitimize highly unequal relations and institutions by 'bestowing upon them an ultimately valid ontological status, that is, by locating them within a sacred and cosmic frame of reference' (Berger, 1967: 33).

To take another example from India, a religious stratification was juxtaposed on society pinning down each individual's place in the social order depending on their social category, or caste. Conveniently, this social stratification placed the powerful on top, and precluded the weak from ever rising to the higher castes. Moreover, the concept of karma justified one's plight in terms of deeds in a past life. Good karma could only be accumulated through obedience and acceptance of the existing social order. This process is not confined to India of course. A similar process took place in the West where, when Catholicism was seen to provide inadequate justification for capitalism, Protestantism, much friendlier towards private property and the social divides that markets created, was ushered in (Wisman & Smith, 2011). Such forms of analysis have been taken on by Mair et al, (2016), who highlight the importance of religious texts in explaining the difficulty in overcoming deeply entrenched social practices such as open defecation that reify patterns of inequality in rural India.

We can also trace the role of discourse in the perpetuation of racial and gender-based inequality. The legacy left behind by the institution of slavery and historical power relations between racial groups is pervasive and persistent in the United States. Compared to whites, African Americans have significantly lower incomes, less wealth, higher mortality rates, greater levels of incarceration, and poorer health (Bobo & Smith, 1998). For a long time, this inequality was justified by dominant scientific and other discourses that suggested African Americans were somehow biologically inferior. Thanks to the Civil Rights movement in America and other struggles, explicit racism has become illegal. Few, other than far right extremists, admit to being racist in public. However, while greatly diminished, the practice of racism continues, with many whites still preferring to maintain social distance from African Americans – though they would not admit it is because of racism. While overtly racist discourses have now been marginalized, other essentialist and culturally deterministic ones have taken their place, arguing that much of these individuals' social and economic condition is not due to race but simply because of lack of hard work or attitude problems. For many, affirmative action is seen to only exacerbate this laziness and dependence (Bobo & Smith, 1998). As van Dijk (1992) shows, reporting in the media often reinforces such beliefs, constructing and then playing to stereotypes.

Research on gender shows similar patterns. Several scholars have shown organizations to be profoundly gendered places to work (Acker, 1990; Gherardi, 1995). Calás and Smircich (1993), for example, explain how the management literature constructs a masculine image of the leader. Ogbor (2000) and Ahl (2006) show how entrepreneurship discourse is similarly gendered. The gendering of the workplace continues at least partially due to the texts that describe the workplace and women's role in it. In most of these, women are represented as the only gendered subjects, disturbing the smooth running of otherwise gender-free organizations, a problem to be fixed (Calás & Smircich, 1993). Similarly, the debate is confined to the capitalist paradigm in which a firm must function in particular ways, and our job is simply to make it possible for women to play the roles that are available. Sheryl Sandberg's bestselling *Lean In* (2013) is a case in point. Sandberg's feminism essentially rests on the notion that if women get the same rights as men, the problem is solved. She does not see that the gender 'problem' is inextricably linked with other issues, such as capitalism, which create certain corporate dynamics and organizational forms. Thus, even if privileged white men choose to share the benefits of corporate capitalism with privileged white women who 'lean in', the systemic inequality does not go away (see also Dobbin & Kalev, Chapter 31 this volume).

These discourses matter because they are instrumental in constructing reality (Fairclough, 1992). Management texts, popular books, media reports and television programs all shape perceptions of reality (Calás & Smircich, 1993; Hardy, Palmer, & Phillips, 2000; Phillips & Hardy, 1997) and the gendered language, concepts and tropes that are used act as powerful transmitters of meaning about how an ideal workplace should function and who is appropriate for a job.

The Discourse of Markets and Inequality

Perhaps the most powerful discourse justifying inequality now is that of the supremacy of markets. As we have seen above, even institutionalized practices of gender or race-based discrimination are increasingly supported by resorting to the fundamental 'truth' of the market. Gray (2001) similarly suggests that the types of religious doctrines that were pervasive more than a hundred years ago have now been replaced for many people by those of a more 'scientific' persuasion – neo-classical economics. This notion served to entrench the myth of 'free' markets and justi-fied the consequent concentration of wealth. The wealth accumulated by the elites was seen to be legitimately acquired and funda-mental to the progress of the entire society. Indeed, so powerful was the discourse that promoted a neoliberal agenda that any coun-try, or individual, who professed anything other than a belief in the primacy of free markets was derided and marginalized (Chang, 2011). Discourses portraying the elite as superior in ability and fortitude and as producers of livelihoods for the less fortunate members of society were similarly created.

Inequality is justified by this discourse as being essential to motivating investments in human and material capital, rewarding effort and getting talented individuals to fully use their abilities. Thus, in a recent issue of *The Economist*, a magazine known for articulat-ing free market arguments, raising the mini-mum wage was presented as a dangerous thing to do for it might end in job losses for the very workers that it purported to help. The argument goes back to the productivity incentives logic enshrined in neoclassical economics discourse.

A similarly dominant discourse that informs our understanding of corporate gov-ernance is agency theory (Fama & Jensen, 1983; Jensen & Meckling, 1976; Shleifer & Vishny, 1997). This discourse developed not only to explain the longevity of corpora-tions despite the self-interested proclivities of managers, but also to justify it. This has led to sustained redistribution of profits to shareholders and corporate managers leading to concentration of wealth not only across organizations but also across geographi-cal locations. The pressure that this system exerts has also led to the erosion of labor laws that circumscribed minimum employment conditions, and marked increases in inequal-ity (Chang, 2011).

Corporate devices to further entrench top management and enrich shareholders, often at the expense of other stakeholders, have been institutionalized by new discourses. For example, Hirsch's (1986) landmark study of golden parachutes and ambushes showed convincingly how discursive strategies aimed at glamorizing financial instruments and portraying firms as assets contributed to a transformation of practices on Wall Street (see also Collins, 2007). The enrichment of CEOs and shareholders over workers is fur-ther sustained by discourses of meritocracy and exceptionalism which provide justifica-tions for the elite's position at the top. Over the past three decades, discourses celebrating successful CEOs have led to the legitimiza-tion of their pay, which according to some, has now reached 'Marie Antoinette propor-tions' (Lublin, 1996).

An important manifestation of the central-ity of language to such issues is seen in the debate on welfare. From an ideal, a social contract and an aspiration in the 1960s, by the 1990s, the term 'welfare' had become associated with one of the most unpopu-lar social programs in America (Jacoby, 1994), with welfare recipients one of the least respected groups (Fiske, Xu, Cuddy, & Glick, 1999). This transformation was under-pinned by discourses that categorized the poor as undeserving (Katz, 1993; Piven & Cloward, 1993).

The powerful free market discourse is so pervasive that it is constantly evoked in dis-cussions of gender or race-based inequal-ity too. Serbian tennis champion Novak Djokovic's remarks about women tennis players' lower wages being a fair reflection of their market demand is a good illustra-tion of the intersection of gender and market discourses (*Guardian*, 2016). Djokovic sug-gested that men should get paid more because men's television ratings are higher than women's. In other words, whoever is able to attract more coverage should get paid more. What he overlooked was that other factors are often at work other than popularity. The US women's soccer team's World Cup victory against Japan in 2015 was the most-watched soccer match in American history. Yet on average, American women soccer players earn far less than the male players. The salary cap in the National Women's Soccer League is $265,000, over 13 times less than the cap in men's Major League Soccer.

Thanks to powerful, deeply entrenched discourses that color reality, empirical evidence and impressions are often at odds, be it CEO salaries, proportion of women on boards, or the proportion of white males in executive positions. If inequality is to be challenged the discourses underpinning these social orders and their taken-for-grantedness need to be dismantled.

Understanding how power operates and how discourses assume hegemony is a challenge for institutional theorists. While power is always implicit in these analyses, with institutional entrepreneurs producing and leveraging discourses to achieve their ends (Hirsch, 1986; Munir & Phillips, 2005) the lack of explicit attention to power constitutes a noteworthy lacuna (see Lawrence, 2008, for a review). As Willmott (2015) suggested, power may occasionally be invoked as a relevant focus or concept of analysis (e.g., Zald & Lounsbury, 2010; Lawrence & Buchanan, Chapter 18 this Volume), but its operation and significance is disassociated from structures of domination and oppression. Understanding how discourses perpetuate social inequality provides fertile ground for understanding the location and operation of power in an institutional setting and is a subject to which institutional theorists can thus make an important contribution.

INSTITUTIONAL LOGICS AND INEQUALITY

[N]ew instruments are needed to regain control over a financial capitalism that has run amok. (Piketty, 2014: 474).
To what extent do we wish to make ours a market-centered world? (Burgin, 2012: 226)

The dominant theme in institutional theory in recent years has been the turn to institutional logics. An institutional logic refers to 'a set of material practices and symbolic constructions – which constitutes its organizing principles and which is available to organizations and individuals to elaborate' (Friedland & Alford, 1991: 248). As Friedland and Alford (1991) explained, and Thornton, Ocasio and Lounsbury (2012; see also Thornton, 2004) later elaborated, each society contains an inter-institutional system that is composed of several institutional orders – family, community, religion, state, market, profession and corporation[2] – that vary in scope and prominence across societies. Central to these orders are institutional logics. 'These logics are symbolically grounded, organizationally structured, politically defended, and technically and materially constrained, and hence have specific historical limits' (Friedland & Alford, 1991: 249). A logics perspective recognizes that institutions cannot be analyzed in isolation from each other but rather that they must be understood in their mutually interdependent relationships, even if this implies dealing with contradiction and conflict. Extending neo-institutional theorizing (e.g., DiMaggio & Powell, 1983, 1991; Meyer & Rowan, 1977) that emphasized structure over agency, the institutional logics perspective seeks to understand how institutions both constrain and enable action. More recently, this has been used to show how the socially constructed patterns of cultural symbols, beliefs and values shape the dynamics, actions and decision outcomes in organizations and across organizational fields (Lounsbury, 2007; Ocasio, Thornton, & Lounsbury, Chapter 19 this volume).

While, as a theoretical perspective, the turn to logics has generated significant insights on a range of social phenomena, as with other streams within institutional theory it has hardly been used to engage with some of the major social issues of our time, including the financial crisis, exploitation of workers, corporate power and inequality (e.g., Munir, 2011, 2015; Willmott, 2015). In this section, we explain why and how institutional logics can offer a potentially revelatory route to uncovering why systems of inequality have become entrenched in our society, and in so doing offer useful avenues that interested scholars might profitably pursue.

Martí and Mair (2009: 100) argued that 'poverty is multidimensional and its causes are rooted in a set of practices, rules, and technologies institutionalized in a determinate context'. We suggest that the same is true of inequality. Primarily, this is because logics shape what issues are considered problematic, what should be attended to, and thus what should be considered during decision-making (Thornton et al., 2012). Recent work on institutional logics has pointed to the ways in which institutional fields are subject not to simple struggles whereby proponents of one logic are pitted against those of another until one group is able to assert its dominance. Rather, decision-makers in social settings are subject to more complex arrangements of logic 'constellations' (Goodrick & Reay, 2011) in which multiple sets of values, beliefs and assumptions assume influence from different parts of, and beyond, the field. This has reaffirmed a characteristic of 'old' institutionalism that emphasized the plural nature of institutions (e.g., Kraatz & Block, 2008; Selznick, 1949), something that was often lost as attempts focused on the exposition of a struggle for dominance among competing logics. Kraatz and Block (2008) developed the idea of institutional pluralism (see also Kraatz & Block, Chapter 20 this Volume), a theoretical understanding that was elaborated by Greenwood, Raynard, Kodeih, Micelotta and Lounsbury (2011), who contended that the degree of 'institutional complexity' in a particular field is dependent upon the number of salient logics and their degree of incompatibility. This point was taken up by Uzo and Mair (2014), who found that organizations in institutionally complex settings, including developing countries such as Nigeria, are often born at the interstices of formal and informal institutions. In these settings, organizational life and outcomes are critically shaped by the incongruence between 'what the law prescribes as legal and what informal systems of beliefs foresee as socially acceptable' (Uzo & Mair, 2014: 57). The impact of this institutional pluralism becomes apparent when we consider the working conditions in many developing countries that result in factory owners and senior brand managers garnering large sums while those doing the physical work frequently operate in dangerous conditions for low rates of pay (e.g., Chamberlain, 2012; Chan, 2013; Khan, Munir, & Willmott, 2007; Pattisson, 2015).

Recent work suggests that while societies in many parts of the world are characterized by a constellation of competing logics, the dominant logic is often an extreme form of capitalism that values the maximization of self-interest and accompanying wealth accumulation above anything else. Piketty's (2014) treatise *Capital*, Danny Dorling's (2011, 2014) critiques of a society that permits the wealthiest 1% to continue to accumulate wealth at an increasing rate, and other similar pieces (e.g., Chang, 2011; Lansley, 2012; Stiglitz, 2013) make a compelling case for this. Indeed, the change in practices at HBOS were reflective of a dominant institutional logic in which the maximization of profits, rather than more conservative accrual of capital, became taken-for-granted. It also clearly demonstrates the reciprocal interaction between micro-processes and field-level logics. While we certainly acknowledge that the case for the dominance of such a market logic is undeniable, we contend that an examination of the institutional dynamics that have produced such an outcome provides useful insights for theorists and policy-makers alike. As Munir (2011) suggests, institutional theorists could add great value by exploring how logics shifted from one that placed markets within society to one that understands society in terms of markets.

Society has not always been dominated by a market logic (Biggart & Castanias, 2001). Pre-capitalist economic thought in the West was deeply influenced by a strong sense of the social and even the religious. Prices did not only have to be 'right' but also 'just' and the economy was often envisioned as a moral order. Even when later liberal thought, exemplified in the writings of David Hume and Adam Smith, went about creating a new moral order from the perspective of the public rather than the monarch, institutional relations still had to be 'correct' in terms of morality. Further, as Chang (2011) contends, if we look historically, those countries that currently are biggest proponents for free market systems, such as the US and the UK, benefitted from strongly protectionist regimes that they now tout as anathema to modern economies. How we moved from systems predicated on government intervention to an institutional order where it has become accepted that whatever social order results from market forces is 'just' (see Burgin, 2012, for a historical exposition of this) is thus an extremely important and significant challenge for institutional theorists.

Despite our point about the apparent predominance of the market logic, it is certainly not some form of monolithic hegemony. Even countries that emphasize free market economies, such as the United States, Sweden, Germany, Japan and South Korea, have variations in the degree and location of government intervention. Further, there are of course conflicting logics enacted in countries with different ideological regimes – for example, China, Russia, Cuba, North Korea, Greece, Iran and Saudia Arabia. The rise of Jeremy Corbyn in the UK and Bernie Sanders in the US as populist socialist figureheads also points to the problematizing of market logics. There was also, of course, a questioning of market logics in the aftermath of the 2007–2008 global financial crisis, even if it has not immediately resulted in any large-scale ideological shifts in government philosophies in most major economies around the world.

Again, it is important to understand the complexity of institutional logics when it comes to understanding the persistence of inequality and the (in)effectiveness of measures designed to address it. For example, Martí and Mair (2009: 112) described how attempts to engage women in rural Bangladesh in commercial activities involved not only,

juggling financial and business logics ... it also requires the entrepreneurial actor to navigate subtly between a range of other logics since the provision of loans for productive purposes challenges existing cultural and religious norms that sanction the seclusion of these women in their houses, the patriarchal system, or the gendered division of labor that restricts the involvement of women to a very limited range of public activities.

Building on this line of thought, Venkataraman, Vermeulen, Raaijmakers, and Mair (2016) showed how logics can be deployed as strategic resources to alter institutional arrangements that underpin deeply entrenched inequality. Studying a development project targeting women in rural India, they showed how the simultaneous enactment of both community and market logics was critical in the development of new social structures – Self-Help Groups – to break existing patterns of dominance and economic exclusion. Thus, while we can see the prominence of a market logic, we also need to account for the ways in which constellations of logics interact in messy, often unanticipated ways.

There are, of course, other situations in which conflicting logics should draw attention from institutional theorists. For example, in the field of Islamic Banking, while practices may vary, the system is premised on fairness rather than simply an efficiency of capital. Work must be done to accrue profits: simply lending money to someone who needs it does not count as work as, under the Islamic banking logic, money must not be allowed to simply create more money. Thus, instead of traditional accounts with set interest rates, Islamic banks offer accounts in which the bank uses deposits to purchase assets that in turn can generate profits or losses. Similarly, market speculation is disallowed. Islamic finance prohibits the selling of something one does not own, since that introduces the risk of its unavailability later on. Finally, Islamic finance requires that investments are restricted to ethical causes or projects. Anything unethical or socially irresponsible, from weapons to gambling to adult entertainment, is considered inappropriate for investment. The continued presence of such principles in societies dominated by a market logic raises questions such as how and why traditional logics based on fairness and principles of justice are resisted and suppressed.

Below, we discuss two mutually constitutive societal characteristics that have resulted in the current dominance of the market logic. The first is the development of values and norms that have rendered capital accumulation not only legitimate but unquestionably appropriate for a functioning member of society. The second is the creation of policies and laws that render any other form of functioning as irrational and difficult to comprehend. We take each of these in turn.

Inequality, Logics and Society

Barley (2008, see also Chapter 13 this Volume) provides compelling encouragement for institutionalists to 'study social organization in action'. Drawing in particular on the Chicago School sociology of Everett Hughes, Barley argued that, 'institutions are tied to ideologies championed by specific segments of society that lend the institution legitimacy. As ideologies change, legitimacy will change and, hence, so will the institution' (2008: 497). Scott, Ruef and Caronna (2000) similarly argued that changes in institutional logics are accompanied by changes in the structures of field governance. It is our contention that such societal changes in what constitutes legitimate courses of action, has led, over time, to an increase in levels of inequality. For example, as has been widely reported, many if not most developed economies have been characterized by a shift from, among other things, a strong manufacturing base to a reliance on service sector jobs. One outcome of this has been, drawing on Barley, a new societal ideology with an accepted bifurcation. Leana et al. (2012: 888), building on Craypo and Cormier (2000), similarly argued that, as a consequence, 'many firms are structured like an hourglass, characterized by large wage disparities. At the top is a set of highly skilled professionals (e.g., doctors, chefs), and at the bottom is a far larger group of frontline support staff with fewer qualifications (e.g., nurse aides, waiters) and nowhere to move up.' This has created an accepted reality in which 'poverty, like culture, provides a context with systematic and persistent influences that are substantial to the individuals living in it' (Leana et al., 2012: 891). This points to the revived interest in cultural perspectives of inequality (see, for example, Cohen, 2010; Small, Harding, & Lamont, 2010). This increasingly polarized societal structure is sustained and perpetuated by a shared understanding and acceptance of inequality based on a set of widely held beliefs, material practices and symbolic constructions. The pervasiveness of inequality is reinforced by a strong emphasis on the role of professions and professional workers in our society. This runs across the financial industries, including banks, financial traders, accounting firms, and so on, with an emphasis on the maximization of financial returns for clients, shareholders and senior employees.

Stinchcombe (1997: 8) argued that the influence of institutions stems from the fact that they 'embody a value that the people also accept.' Lok (2010) goes further, stating that institutional logics not only direct what individuals want or how they should act, but indeed who or what they are. In this respect, the pervasiveness of logics becomes apparent. Importantly, while we have argued that there is often a dominant market logic, we must be attuned to the fact that inequality creates, and rests upon, different lived experiences, and different corresponding logics that are experienced in multiple ways. Thus, inequality will condition understanding and action in particular ways that are nonsensical to those from different socioeconomic strata. For example, according to Gray and Kish-Gephart (2013: 678),

Members of upper social classes adopt a privileged subject position that allows them to assume that, as successful people, they possess 'the right stuff' and deserve more than others. To hold this view they must develop a rationale that justifiably differentiates them from others.

As Dorling (2014) and other social commentators, such as *The Guardian*'s Polly Toynbee, have described, this allows those in positions of advantage to pursue courses of action that reinforce and extend that advantage, irrespective of the outcomes on others be they Nepalese construction workers in Qatar (Gibson, 2014), factory workers manufacturing Apple products in China (Agence France-Presse, 2014; Chan, 2013) or the working poor in the UK (Butler, 2015). In this respect, outcomes are not only the result of one group being more powerful than another and thus able to exert its will, but also of socially constructed and broadly accepted meanings that are attached to groups and actions. This, in turn, accounts for opportunity 'hoard and exclusion' practices that result in enduring patterns of inequality (Tilly, 1998). Thus, those in different societal positions will operate according to different institutional logics. That said, those in some groups will not be unaware of the logics that govern others. Indeed, the litany of social ills that have been correlated with inequality stem from the realization among those who have little that others adhere to a different set of rules and values (Wilkinson & Pickett, 2010).

Given that institutional logics are social constructions that place a heavy emphasis on broadly understood meanings (Berger & Luckmann, 1967; Zilber, Chapter 16 this Volume), and that the degree to which these

meanings are accepted determines their level of institutionalization, we can see that established understandings of what is appropriate – including assumptions that inequality is inevitable and that people are wealthy or poor as of right – have an extreme durability. Mutually understood schemas, frames and rules structure the sense-making of individuals: 'the shared nature of these cognitive frames makes it difficult to stray far from them in either thought or deed' (Garud, Hardy, & Maguire, 2007: 959).

Logics and Policy-Making

In addition to the centrality of institutional logics in our understandings of inequality being located within, and a product of, societal norms and expectations, logics also come to be embodied in prevailing political and legal structures. These can be at the macro governmental level or those that attend to more micro, situation-specific contextual imperatives. Not only do they exert a prescriptive effect on what is and is not legally acceptable (cf. Scott's [1995] regulative pillar), they also have a powerful symbolic impact on conveying what is legitimate in a particular societal setting. In this respect, as institutional scholars have explained, we can see mutually constitutive effects across levels, from the individual to the organizational to the field.

For example, as we have noted earlier, the predominance of the market logic can be attributed to the rise of Thatcherism in the UK and Reaganomics in the US (see, among others, Lansley, 2012; Levy & Temin, 2007; Stiglitz, 2013; Thompson, 2007). Accompanied by the withering away of the Soviet Union and fall of the Berlin Wall, a political ideology took root in the West that favored free-market principles above all else. This led to a number of policies that reduced government intervention in corporate activities, and brought in 'private sector discipline' to what were viewed as profligate public sector agencies. While the effects of these were manifold, one particularly important outcome was the so-called big bang in the UK in 1986 that allowed much greater operative freedom to financial institutions. Similar shifts in the financial services industry also occurred in the US, in particular with the repeal of the Glass–Stegall Act in 1999 that had separated commercial and investment banking.

Economic and social theorists have traced the relaxing of these regulative structures to the beginning of an increase in inequality (Chang, 2011; Dorling, 2011; Piketty, 2014; Stiglitz, 2013). To this point, the disparities of the early years of the 20th century had been successively overcome by forced redistribution of wealth and controls on top wage earners, primarily through taxation. This had seen levels of inequality decrease throughout the 20th century. However, from 1980 on, the Republicans in the US and the Conservatives in the UK began a policy shift that reflected the prevailing institutional logics. These changes led directly to the rapid increase in salaries in the financial sector that, it has been contended, have increased levels of inequality (e.g., Dorling, 2014; Stiglitz, 2013). While perhaps most obvious in their effect in the US and UK, the trend in other wealthy countries, such as Japan, Germany, France and other continental European states, 'is in the same direction' (Piketty, 2014). This was certainly not a one-way street – government policies in the early 1980s reflected large swathes of public sentiment on both sides of the Atlantic – as such, we can see policies as carriers of logics in that they reinforced a particular ideology.

While we can document the ways in which macro-level policies are carriers of logics, there are more localized effects that can also be powerful in their impact. For example, Barley (2007: 203) described how a decision by Chief Justice Waite in the 1886 Supreme Court hearing of an initially local property dispute in *Santa Clara County v. Southern Pacific Railroad Co.* led to corporations

being 'protected as if they were natural persons under the law … and has been subsequently used by U.S. Courts to decide cases and grant corporations additional rights.' By becoming ensconced in law, Barley argues that corporate protectionism has worked to the benefit of shareholders and owners, but is against the public good. Chang (2011) similarly points to how the prioritization of shareholders in various pieces of legislation over the past 30 years has exacerbated inequality. In contrast to shareholders, who are generally able to move their capital to maximum advantage relatively easily, other stakeholders such as employees and some suppliers, are much more vulnerable to downturns in corporate performance. As we pointed out with the HBOS example, shareholders and senior managers have generally recovered their losses caused by the financial crisis, but those who have lost jobs, lost homes, or been otherwise negatively impacted, will likely never be able to fully recover. Thus, the shift in logics, described by Barley (2007) and documented in detail by Burgin (2012), from a protection of the individual worker to a prioritization of shareholder interests, has increased levels of inequality.

Munir (2011: 116) similarly provides an example of how seemingly small policy shifts, in this case the creation in 1991 by Goldman Sachs of a food commodity index and subsequent deregulation of futures markets, can have large effects on inequality. As he explained, 'investors flocked toward the index, which led first to a gradual increase in food prices and then a rapid escalation. Riots broke out across numerous countries and the number of "food insecure" crossed a billion.' Again, we see the effects of an evolution in logics as other banks created their own indices, trading increased, and US government policy changed, such as dropping the restriction that futures trading in wheat should only be allowed by bona fide hedgers and increasing the number of contracts that could be held.

In sum, therefore, we see how changes in institutional logics over time have reflected increasing levels of inequality. As yet, however, we have not had sustained investigation by institutional theorists of how different logics emerge over time, why market logics have proved so resilient and what the long-term effects of these have been for levels of inequality across different countries.

IDENTITY AND INEQUALITY

The oppressed will believe the worst about themselves. (Fanon, 1963)
It is not the consciousness of men that determines their existence, but their social existence that determines their consciousness. (Marx, 1977 [1859])

Identity has emerged as a central concept in the social sciences (Anderson, 1991; Butler, 1990; Gilroy, 1997; Glynn, Chapter 9 this Volume). Very simply, it allows us to make sense of who is who and adapt our behavior accordingly. This is not to suggest that identities are static and fixed in place, or even something we can possess. As Laclau and Mouffe (2001) argued, it is only in our social relations that we acquire 'subject positions' and such subjective identities are multifaceted. Thus, the same woman might be a soldier, an ethnic immigrant, a Muslim, a mother and a wife. Likewise, a man and a woman might share the same identity in one context (e.g., members of the American elite) but might end up with different ones (man and woman) upon travelling to Saudi Arabia. Therefore, no identity is inherently privileged and the salience of particular identities depends on the social context and the existence of discursive practices that make such identities subjectively accessible.

Similarly, identity is malleable rather than fixed in time or space. It is thus an ongoing project. Among many other things, the construction of a particular identity might draw upon actions (e.g., consumerism), biology (skin color), inheritance (wealth or class), or membership of a particular category

(the communist party). As Gray and Kish-Gephart (2013) suggest, all these identities can play important roles in the structuring of social and organizational life. For example, who we hire, who rises through the ranks, who talks to who, and so on, all have much to do with identity. It is not surprising then that in organization studies, identity has also come to assume an increasingly important position as an interpretive frame in the analysis of organizations (Ashforth & Mael, 1989; Glynn, Chapter 9 this Volume; Haslam & Reicher, 2006). As Alvesson, Ashcraft and Thomas (2008: 7) suggested, 'identity research has already yielded insight on questions of motivation, individual and group behaviour, communication patterns, leadership and managerial work, organizational change, corporate image, inter-organizational interaction, dynamics of control and resistance, and relations of gender and race-ethnicity'. Even economists have found identity, especially stigmatized identity, to affect performance in organizations (Akerlof & Kranton, 2005, 2010; Hoff & Pandey, 2006).

Identity and the Maintenance of Inequality

While organization and institutional theorists have found identity to be a powerful construct, and even recognized how it is implicated in organizational dynamics (Gray and Kish-Gephardt, 2013), an aspect of identity that has been little explored in organization studies is its role as a key mechanism through which inequalities are sustained. Wider literature in sociology and history has linked identity to unequal social structures – mainly through discursive, symbolic and performative mechanisms, and it is important that institutional theorists recognize this dynamic.

The implication of identity in the perpetuation of inequality begins right from childhood. Lareau's (2011) seminal work argued that middle-class and working-class families raise their children completely differently, with the former cultivating attributes in children that will later help them get ahead in economic and social life, and the latter viewing a child's natural growth as an accomplishment in itself. Similarly, Aries and Seider (2005) demonstrated how social class plays an important role both as an independent variable that shapes the formation of identity and as a domain of identity exploration. Their study of college students reveals how pupils carry different identities depending on their socioeconomic class. Similarly, in a study of 5th–12th graders from US school districts in an economically depressed area, Alix and Lantz (1973) found high occupational aspirations varied positively with socioeconomic status. Other studies have confirmed these findings. For example, Cook et al. (1995) found that economically advantaged boys disproportionately anticipated that they would become doctors or lawyers while those from lower socioeconomic groups more expected to be policemen or firemen.

Particularly interesting here is the work of Bourdieu and Passeron (1990), who showed how the lower academic performance of working-class children is explained not by lower ability but by institutional biases against them resulting in a situation where the class in which one is born ends up determining one's probability of success in life. Bourdieu and Passeron (1990) suggested that schools evaluate all children on the basis of their cultural capital (familiarity with highbrow culture of the dominant class) and penalize lower-class students who lack familiarity with it. Schools value extensive vocabularies, wide-reading, knowledge of music and art, and general etiquette. Almost always, students from higher social backgrounds acquire these resources at home while working-class children have little access to them. Given the proliferation of texts that attribute success and failure to hard work and other personal qualities, lower-class children end up blaming themselves for their failure, which in turn leads to low performance and confidence wherever they go next. This is what Sennett and Cobb (1972) call the 'hidden injuries of class', in other words, the low self-esteem that plagues working-class identity.

Through 'symbolic violence' the dominant classes create meaning, control resources, enjoy privilege and status, and successfully hide the power relations that are the basis of its force (Bourdieu & Passeron, 1990). Once the lower classes internalize the hierarchy of 'taste' (Bourdieu, 1984), it becomes relatively easy for the upper class to maintain their privileges (Lamont & Molnár, 2002). Despite shared membership of a particular category (Tajfel, 1981) this dynamic prevents the lower class from seeing systemic oppression and thus from rebelling against this hierarchy in which they are consigned to the bottom. It is encouraging that some organizational theorists (e.g., Gray & Kish-Gephardt, 2013) are beginning to pay attention to class dynamics in the workplace but the role of social class in the production of different identities is still underexplored. As Aries and Seider (2005) point out, even in sociological literature when class is invoked it is generally done in material terms. More work needs to be done on the lived experience of class in organizations. In particular, discussions of inequality need to be enriched with insights into how social class position constrains decision-making (Aries & Seider, 2005).

While class is important in understanding the links between institutional identities and inequality, distinctions based on gender identities are also produced and sustained through discourse, language, symbolism and social performance (see Dobbin & Kalev, Chapter 31 this Volume). Once formed, such identities severely constrain human behavior, limiting spheres of prescribed action and expectation in organizations. Such distinctions are in turn maintained and reinforced by existing inequalities. Thus, as Ely (1995) pointed out, an overrepresentation of white men in high-status positions not only reinforces the devaluation of women and non-white subordinates but is also found to be detrimental to performance outcomes and treatment of women and ethnic minorities. Ely also found that compared to women in more gender-balanced firms, women in male-dominated firms tended to evaluate women's attributes less favorably in relation to firm requirements for success. Thus, the construction of gender identities does not stop after one is socialized in families, schools and through media and culture, but continues in work organizations. As Ely's research shows, proportional representation of women in power affects women's gender identity at work. There are clearly opportunities for institutional theorists to provide insight into the ways in which organizational forms are related to particular identities. Work that similarly examines links with race, disability, sexuality, age and so on would also be highly valued.

Exploitation and Creation of New Identities

Thanks to work on 'total institutions' we do have some knowledge of how certain organizational settings bestow particular identities on people (Wallace, 1971). For example, research has revealed how the military offers men unique resources for constructing a masculine identity defined by emotional control, physical fitness, self-discipline, the willingness to use violence and risk-taking. These characteristics are in line with the hegemonic ideal present in the wider institutional context (Hinojosa, 2010).

On the other hand, in order to survive in 'total' institutions, old, complex identities formed in the 'normal' world need to be covered up. Research on prisons highlights the radical identity changes that ensue there (Berger, 1963). Similarly, the Bank of Scotland case revealed how individuals had developed particular identities that were crucially compatible with the decisions they made, from being risk-averse, to aggressively pursuing merger opportunities, to embracing a strategy of high-pressure

selling of new products (Perman, 2013). Lipsky's (2003: 145) four-year ethnography of West Point vividly describes the process of identity construction, from how on their first day the cadets have to strip down to their underwear, have their hair cut off, put on a uniform and address an older cadet with the proper salute and the statement: 'Sir, New Cadet Doe reports to the cadet in the Red Sash for the first time as ordered.' The new cadets must stand and salute and repeat, and stand and salute and repeat, until they get it exactly right, all the while being reprimanded for every mistake. This is the beginning of the process in which they surrender their old identity and assume a new one.

Indeed, organizational membership often requires shedding old identities and assuming new ones. For instance, Sasson-Levy (2002) highlights how women in masculine roles are found to accept the model of hegemonic masculinity and employ a series of discursive and bodily practices to shape their identity accordingly. This 'identity work' has been observed in other organizations as well. Gray and Kish-Gephart (2013) have highlighted how employees carry their class identities into organizations, a phenomenon that results in visible identity-based dynamics in organizational life. Members of upper and lower classes experience and make sense of organizational life differently. For example, concerned about 'symbolic threats' to their identity in organizations, members of lower classes will often try to obscure their own class background, or devise coping strategies such as referring to middle and upper classes as incompetent but lucky. In this way, they counteract their own fear of denigration and negative evaluation by elites (Gray & Kish-Gephart, 2013).

At a societal level, identities are also created by the dominant classes to extend and legitimize their domination. The work on colonialism, for example, is particularly instructive in this regard. To justify the colonization of a people, images are often created so that the subjugation makes sense.

These images become the identity of the colonized. Amongst various things that the colonized come to believe are that they are lazy, backward and unimaginative. Such images become excuses for the colonial situation, with the white man's burden seeming a legitimate one. Such myths valorize the colonizers and humble those who are colonized. Meager wages for the colonized, lower privileges and a life of subordination are all justified through such discursive means.

These literatures highlight how colonization creates and is sustained by the creation of identities of both the colonized and the colonizer (Said, 1977). The colonized develop negative identities – coming to see themselves as lesser beings who do not deserve more resources or increased participation in societal affairs (Fanon, 1963). Such identities enable the colonial apparatus to go largely unchallenged, and are a result of affective behavioral, cognitive, linguistic and cultural mechanisms designed to solidify political domination (Prilleltensky & Gonick, 1996).

Other Mechanisms of Reinforcement of Inequality

Socialization and domination both require creation of identities, but there are other mechanisms for reinforcement and transmission of inequality too. The two that institutional theorists will be most familiar with are myth and ceremony (Meyer & Rowan, 1977).

Elites cultivate identities that allow them to sustain and legitimize their privileged position in organizations. The dominant discourse of meritocracy allows elites to reject the notion that 'the game is rigged' (Schwalbe, 2008). By invoking the meritocracy argument, which suggests that top management positions, fame and fortune are all 'earned' through hard work and cleverness, elites legitimize their identities. They rely on 'autobiographical reasoning' (Scully & Blake-Beard, 2006: 436) to project onto everyone their own experience of success, which they attribute to individual effort and ability, assuming that others' circumstances and capabilities are similar to their own.

Rituals play a key role in how the elites come to internalize their identities. Privileged and non-privileged positions are of course in part a result of societal logics that cultivate particular identities. For instance, in their study of formal dining at Cambridge University, Dacin et al. (2010) point out how the production of particular identities in organizations is central to the perpetuation of unequal social structures that allow privileged groups to maintain their positions at the top. They argue that rituals socialize participants into particular norms and values and teach them the roles they are expected to play. The ritual of college dining historically reflected the British class system in the sense that Fellows and students were drawn almost exclusively from its upper reaches and served by waiters and butlers whose primary objective was to protect the privilege of the former. Participants were therefore familiar with the performance and how to enact its main aspects *before* their arrival at Cambridge. Moreover, they essentially took for granted the notion of a class structure and their place in it. More recently, however, as the social backgrounds of participants became increasingly diverse, the purpose of the ritual changed: it now subtly socialized the participants into *adopting* the sensibilities that made the elite distinct. In particular, it legitimated social stratification and an explicit categorization of people according to rank and station. In short, it endorsed and reified the concepts that lay at the core of the class system. In this sense, organizational rituals were seen to produce and maintain identities that sustained wider inequalities.

Identity and Agency

In addition to being a device for categorization and legitimization, as we lay out above, identity can also serve as a mechanism for challenging existing classification systems.

Indeed, the assumption of new identities at a collective level is often a hallmark of revolutionary and social movements aimed at reducing inequality. Discourses creating and emphasizing particular collective identities aimed at ending the domination of the elites may become contentious. An example is Margaret Thatcher's aversion to the usage of the term 'class' – she preferred the terms 'individual' or 'family', viewing class as a 'divisive' term. Such distinctions may also be observed in organization theory, with labor process theorists preferring to use the term 'labor' where others would have used 'employees' or 'human resources' (Braverman, 2003). In short, assumptions about and consciousness of particular identities can serve to sustain or destabilize existing relations of inequality. Identity then is a crucial and understudied construct in understanding the creation, perpetuation and destabilization of unequal social orders. Institutional theorists are ideally poised to study the creation of particular identities and their implication in the maintenance of particular social orders. This requires a heightened sensitivity to the maintenance of unequal power relations underpinning particular institutional orders (Munir, 2015) and the factors constraining the agency of the oppressed.

CONCLUSION

Inequality has increased dramatically since 1980, with the ability of those with the most wealth to continue to capture more of it, at the expense of those with significantly less, being remarkable (Oxfam, 2016, 2017; Piketty, 2014; Saez & Zucman, 2014). Accompanying this rise in inequality has been a growing amount of commentary, predominantly from economists and sociologists, into the levels of inequality and the associated consequences for various groups in our societies. Organization theorists in general, and institutional theorists in particular, by contrast, have been largely absent from these debates. Thus, our purpose in this chapter has been to uncover where, and how, institutional theorists might effectively contribute to our understanding of inequality. In this concluding section, we offer a brief recapitulation of our theorizing and make suggestions as to where institutionalists might direct their lines of inquiry.

We have focused our attention on four strands of the institutional literature that have particular promise in opening up new understandings of why inequality has become so entrenched in society. The first of these involves examining the institutional microfoundations of inequality. Inequality is enacted and experienced through the everyday, often mundane, unquestioned activities of individual actors. These activities become routine and taken-for-granted over time through processes of habitualization and legitimization. As yet, however, we have little understanding of how these processes take place, and in particular how they impact inequality. We therefore feel that there are several questions that could be profitably addressed. First, it would be useful to know how elites are able to draw on existing power arrangements to reproduce practices that maintain their positions of advantage over others in society. Second, what forms of institutional work are engaged in by those in different strata in society – both deliberately and inadvertently – that reinforce inequality? A third useful point of investigation would be into how the structures and practices within organizations resulting in hierarchical divisions become reinforced and taken-for-granted.

Our second conceptual area of focus draws attention to the ways in which discourse helps reinforce societal divisions. Our central contention here is that inequality is not maintained by brute force, but rather requires continuous legitimization through the use of an interrelated system of discourses that collectively justify a particular social order. However, as yet we have little understanding of how discourses are deployed by powerful stakeholders to maintain their power. Thus, a useful first point of inquiry would be to map over time the ways by which different discourses are constructed and invoked to maintain intra and inter-organizational inequality. Second, institutional theorists could assume a more critical perspective and question the market-based paradigm that dominates most aspects of our society. This is important because there is an increasingly clear relationship between market-based exchanges and the creation of inequality. For example, the ways in which markets have been imposed on public sector organizations has been a notable feature of government policies in several countries over the last four decades. Understanding the discourses that are implicated in such transference would undoubtedly be a valuable addition to our understanding of inequality. A third line of investigation could be to uncover the ways in which power is used in the construction of, and becomes manifest through, different discourses in ways that retain systems of advantage and disadvantage.

Institutional logics, our third focal point, has become important in helping uncover how ways of thinking, decision-making and behaving combine to create courses of action that are not only viewed as the 'obvious' way to proceed, but that also establish others as illegitimate if not unthinkable. This, of course, is particularly important when we think about how the day-to-day activities that we described in the first section, and the discourse discussed in the second section, help reify structures of inequality. While there has been much discussion about how logics help determine particular courses of action, there has been virtually no explicit attention given to the links between institutional logics and inequality. There are several avenues of potentially valuable research that are open to exploration. First, investigation of the emergence of different logics and their corresponding connection to societal inequalities would be particularly useful. The rise, and dominance, of market logics is perhaps the most obvious starting point here, though there are other kinds of logics that also demand attention

for the ways in which they pervade organizational life and exacerbate inequality. Second, the processes by which policies in private, public and non-profit organizations are developed such that they not only reflect dominant societal logics, but also act as carriers of them, is also a theoretically important question into which we as yet have little insight. Third, the ways in which certain logics in complex fields become more or less influential over time is ill-understood: research in this area should thus have great potential for advancing not only our understanding of inequality, but institutional change processes more generally.

In the fourth theoretical component of the chapter, we demonstrate how the construction and legitimization of particular identities is inherently linked to unequal social structures. From class dynamics in the workplace through to distinctions based on gender, race, age, sexuality, disability and so on, it is clear that identity plays heavily into the processes through which inequalities are legitimized. Again, this leads to several potential areas by which institutional theorists can contribute to our understanding of inequality. First, it would be immensely useful if we could better understand the ways in which identities become ensconced from early childhood through the activities of institutions such as families, schools, universities – including business schools – and local communities. Second, the role of organizations in bestowing identities on particular stakeholders in ways that privilege some groups over others is not well understood and thus warrants attention. Third, while much work has viewed identity as stable and monolithic, there is undoubtedly the potential for flexibility and some level of malleability, so it is certainly possible that identity could be a mechanism for challenging existing systems of inequality. Again, this is a dynamic of which we have, as yet, little understanding.

As laid out above, each of the four areas upon which we have focused offers insights into inequality, and the potential for further fruitful lines of research. Moreover, as our institutional interpretations are made explicit, the policy implications should follow. In this respect, institutionalists are well positioned to make purposeful practical, as well as theoretical, interventions, something previously the preserve of other social scientists. It is also worth pointing out that, while we treat each of the four institutional topics in isolation, much as they have been developed in the literature, how they might be used in combination demands attention. While all four offer the potential to examine the antecedents and outcomes of inequality at different levels, from individual to societal, each tends to preference one level over another: logics, for example, have been considered more macro while microfoundations are, unsurprisingly, more micro in orientation. Similarly, we might find that discourse is consumed and interpreted individually in some settings whereas identity is collectively enacted. Adopting a multiperspective approach has, therefore, much potential. Whether singly or in combination, it is apparent that each of these aspects of institutionalism has much to contribute to our understanding of inequality. We hope that this chapter proves to be useful in providing impetus to such much-needed research.

Notes

1   Our thanks to editors Royston Greenwood and Tom Lawrence, along with David Cooper and Maureen Scully, for their encouragement and astute comments on earlier drafts of this chapter. Thanks also to the participants of sub-theme 16 at EGOS 2012 and sub-theme 24 at EGOS 2015, and those who attended the 2013 'Inequality, Institutions and Organizations' conference in Vancouver for their inspiration and insights
2   From Thornton, Ocasio and Lounsbury (2012).

REFERENCES

Acker, J. (1990). Hierarchies, jobs, bodies: a theory of gendered organisations *Gender and Society*, 4(2), 139–158.

Agence France-Presse. (2014). Apple under fire again for working conditions at Chinese factories. *The Guardian*, 19 December. www.theguardian.com/technology/2014/dec/19/apple-under-fire-again-for-working-conditions-at-chinese-factories?CMP=share_btn_link [Accessed 19/12/2014].

Ahl, H. (2006). Why research on women entrepreneurs needs new directions. *Entrepreneurship: Theory and Practice*, 30(5), 595–621.

Akerlof, G.A.,& Kranton, R.E. (2005). Identity and the economics of organizations. *The Journal of Economic Perspectives*, 19(1), 9–32.

Akerlof, G.A., & Kranton, R.E. (2010). Identity economics: How our identities shape our work, wages, and well-being. Princeton, NJ: Princeton University Press.

Alix, E.K., & Lantz, H.R. (1973). Socioeconomic status and low occupational aspirations: Resignation as an orientational variable. *Social Science Quarterly*, 53(3), 596–607.

Alvesson, M., Ashcraft, K.L., & Thomas, R. (2008). Identity matters: Reflections on the construction of identity scholarship in organization studies. *Organization*, 15(1), 5–28.

Anderson B. (1991). *Imagined communities* (2nd ed.). London: Verso.

Aries, E., & Seider, M. (2005). The interactive relationship between class identity and the college experience: The case of lower income students. *Qualitative Sociology*, 28(4), 419–443.

Ashforth, B., & Mael, F. (1989). Social identity theory and the organization. *Academy of Management Review*, 14(1), 20–39.

Atkinson, A.B. (2015). *Inequality: What can be done?* Cambridge, MA: Harvard University Press.

Bakija, J., Cole, A., & Heim, B. (2012). Jobs and income growth of top earners and the causes of changing income inequality: Evidence from U.S. tax return data. Working Paper. Williams College.

Bapuji, H. (2015). Individuals, interactions and institutions: How economic inequality affects organizations. *Human Relations*, 68(7), 1059–1083.

Barley, S.R. (2007). Corporations, democracy, and the public good. *Journal of Management Inquiry*, 16(3), 201–215.

Barley, S.R. (2008). Coalface institutionalism. In R. Greenwood, C. Oliver, R. Suddaby, & K. Sahlin-Andersson (Eds.) *The SAGE handbook of organizational institutionalism* (pp. 491–518). London: Sage.

Belliveau, M.A. (2012). Engendering inequity? How social accounts create vs. merely explain unfavorable pay outcomes for women. *Organization Science*, 23(4), 1154–1174.

Berdahl, J.L. (2007). Harassment based on sex: Protecting social status in the context of gender hierarchy. *Academy of Management Review*, 32(2), 641–658.

Berger, P. (1963). *Invitation to sociology: A humanistic perspective*. New York: Doubleday.

Berger, P. (1967). *The sacred canopy. Elements of a sociological theory of religion* (pp. 3–28). New York: Anchor Books.

Berger, P.L., & Luckmann, T. (1967). *The social construction of reality*. New York: Anchor.

Bhabha, H.K. (2004). *The location of culture*. London: Routledge.

Biggart, N.W., & Castanias, R. (2001). Collateralized social relations: The social in economic calculation. *American Journal of Economics and Sociology*, 60(2), 471–500.

Bobo, L.D., & Smith, R.A. (1998). From Jim Crow racism to laissez-faire racism: The transformation of racial attitudes. In W.F. Katkin, N. Landsman, & A. Tyree (Eds.), *Beyond pluralism: The conception of groups and group identities in America* (pp. 182–220). Champaign, IL: University of Illinois Press.

Bourdieu, P. (1984). *Distinction: A social critique of the judgement of taste*. Cambridge, MA: Harvard University Press.

Bourdieu, P., & Passeron, J.-C. (1990). *Reproduction in education, society and culture* (2nd ed.). London: Sage.

Braverman, M. (2003). Managing the human impact of crisis. *Risk Management*, 50(5): 10–14.

Burgin, A. (2012). *The great persuasion: Reinventing free markets since the depression*. Cambridge, MA: Harvard University Press.

Butler, J. (1990). *Gender trouble: Feminism and the subversion of identity*. New York: Routledge.

Butler, P. (2015). Food bank use tops million mark over the past year. *The Guardian*, 22 April. www.theguardian.com/society/2015/apr/22/food-bank-users-uk-low-paid-workers-poverty?CMP=share_btn_link [Accessed 22/04/2015].

Calás, M.B., & Smircich, L. (1993). Dangerous liaisons: The 'feminine-in-management' meets 'globalization'. *Business Horizons*, 36(2), 71–81.

Carton, A.M., & Rosette, A.S. (2011). Explaining bias against black leaders: Integrating theory on information processing and goal-based stereotyping. *Academy of Management Journal*, 54(6), 1141–1158.

Chamberlain, G. (2012). Olympic brands caught up in abuse scandal. *The Guardian*, 3 March. www.theguardian.com/business/2012/mar/03/olympic-brands-abuse-scandal [Accessed 11/03/2012].

Chan, J. (2013). A suicide survivor: The life of a Chinese worker. *New Technology, Work and Employment*, 28(2), 84–99.

Chang, H.J. (2011). *23 things they don't tell you about capitalism*. Harmondsworth: Penguin.

Cobb, J.A. (2016). How firms shape income inequality: Stakeholder power, executive decision-making, and the structuring of employment relationships. *Academy of Management Review*, 41(2), 324–348.

Cohen, P. (2010). Culture of poverty makes a comeback. *New York Times*, A1. www.nytimes.com/2010/10/18/us/18poverty.html?_r=0.

Collins, R.M. (2007). *Transforming America: Politics and culture in the Reagan years*. New York: Columbia University Press.

Cook, K.S., Fine, G.A., & House, J. (1995). *Sociological perspectives in social psychology*. Needham Heights, MA: Allyn & Bacon.

Cortina, L.M. (2008). Unseen injustice: Incivility as modern discrimination in organizations. *Academy of Management Review*, 33(1), 55–75.

Craypo, C., & Cormier, D. (2000). Job restructuring as a determinant of wage inequality and working-poor households. *Journal of Economic Issues*, 34(1), 21–42.

Cutts, E.H. (1953). The background of Macaulay's Minute. *American Historical Review*, 58(4), 824–853.

Czarniawska, B., & Sevon, G. (Eds.) (1996). *Translating the organizational change*. New York: Walter de Gruyter.

Dacin, M.T., Munir, K., & Tracey, P. (2010). Formal dining at Cambridge colleges: Linking ritual performance and institutional maintenance. *Academy of Management Journal*, 53(6), 1393–1418.

Davis, G.F. (2016). *The vanishing American corporation: Navigating the hazards of a new economy*. San Francisco: Berrett–Koehler.

Davis, G.F. (2009). *Managed by the markets*. Oxford: Oxford University Press.

DiMaggio, P.J., & Powell, W.W. (1983). The iron-cage revisited: Institutional isomorphism and collective rationality in organizational fields. *American Sociological Review*, 48(2), 147–160.

DiMaggio, P.J., & Powell, W.W. (1991). Introduction. In W.W. Powell & P.J. DiMaggio (Eds.), *The new institutionalism in organizational analysis* (pp. 1–40). Chicago, IL: University of Chicago Press.

Dobbin, F., & Zorn, D. (2005). Corporate malfeasance and the myth of shareholder value. *Political Power and Social Theory*, 17, 179–198.

Dolfsma, W., & Verbürg, R. (2008). Structure, agency and the role of values in processes of institutional change. *Journal of Economic Issues*, 42(4), 1031–1054.

Dorling, D. (2011). *Injustice: Why social inequality persists*. Bristol: Policy Press.

Dorling, D. (2014). *Inequality and the 1%*. London: Verso.

Dover, G., & Lawrence, T.B. (2010). A gap year for institutional theory: Integrating the study of institutional work and participatory action research. *Journal of Management Inquiry*, 19(4), 305–316.

Doward, J. (2016). Google: New concerns raised about political influence by senior 'revolving door' jobs. *The Guardian*, 4 June. www.theguardian.com/technology/2016/jun/04/google-influence-hiring-government-officials?CMP=share_btn_link [Accessed 4 June 2016].

Dunn, M.B., & Jones, C. (2010). Institutional logics and institutional pluralism: The contestation of care and science logics in medical education, 1967–2005. *Administrative Science Quarterly*, 55, 114–149.

Eitzen, D.S., & Smith, K.E. (2003). *Experiencing poverty: Voices from the bottom*. Belmont, CA: Thomson–Wadworth.

Ely, R.J. (1995). The power in demography: Women's social constructions of gender identity at work. *Academy of Management Journal*, 38(3), 589–634.

Fairclough, N. (1992). *Discourse and social change*. Cambridge: Polity Press.

Fairclough, N. (2010). *Critical discourse analysis: The critical study of language*. Harlow: Pearson.

Fallon, D. (2006). To 'raise dream and ambition' – The rhetorical analysis of a teenage pregnancy strategy. *Nursing Inquiry*, 13(3), 186–193.

Fama, E., & Jensen, M. (1983). Separation of ownership and control. *Journal of Law and Economics*, 26(2), 301–325.

Fanon, F. (1963). *The wretched of the earth*. New York: Grove Press.

Fiske, S.T., Xu, J., Cuddy, A.C., & Glick, P. (1999). (Dis)respecting versus (dis)liking: Status and interdependence predict ambivalent stereotypes of competence and warmth. *Journal of Social Issues*, 55(3), 473–491.

Foucault, M. (1977). *Discipline and punish: The birth of the prison*. Harmondsworth: Penguin.

Foucault, M. (1980). Two lectures. In C. Gordon (Ed.) *Power/Knowledge: Selected interviews and other writings, 1972–1977* (pp. 78–108). New York: Pantheon Books.

Friedland, R., & Alford, R. (1991). Bringing society back in: Symbols, practices and institutional contradictions. In P. DiMaggio & W.W. Powell (Eds.), *The new institutionalism in organizational analysis* (pp. 232–263). Chicago, IL: University of Chicago Press.

Garud, R., Hardy, C., & Maguire, S. (2007). Institutional entrepreneurship as embedded agency: An introduction to the Special Issue. *Organization Studies*, 28(7), 957–969.

George, G., McGahan, A.M., & Prabhu, J. (2012). Innovation for inclusive growth: Towards a theoretical framework and a research agenda. *Journal of Management Studies*, 49(4), 661–683.

Gherardi, S. (1995). *Gender, symbolism and organizational cultures*. London: Sage.

Gibson, O. (2014). The hundreds of migrant workers dying as a brand new Qatar is built. *The Guardian*, 14 May. www.theguardian.com/world/2014/may/14/migrant-workers-dying-qatar-world-cup [Accessed 22 September 2014].

Gilroy, P. (1997). Diaspora and the detours of identity. In K. Woodward (Ed.), *Identity and difference* (pp. 299–243). London: Sage.

Goffman, E. (1967). *Interaction ritual: Essays in face-to-face behavior*. New York: Pantheon.

Gondo, M., & Amis, J.M. (2013). Variations in practice adoption: The roles of conscious reflection and discourse. *Academy of Management Review*, 38(2), 229–247.

Goodrick, E., & Reay, T. (2011). Constellations of institutional logics: Changes in the professional work of pharmacists. *Work and Occupations*, 38(2), 372–416.

Grant, D., Keenoy, T., & Oswick, C. (1998). Organizational discourse: Of diversity, dichotomy and multidisciplinarity. In D. Grant, T. Keenoy & C. Oswick (Eds.), *Discourse and Organization* (pp. 1–13). London: Sage.

Gray, B., & Kish-Gephart, J.J. (2013). Encountering social class differences at work: How 'class work' perpetuates inequality. *Academy of Management Review*, 38(4), 670–699.

Gray, P. (2001). *Famine, land and politics: British government and Irish society, 1843–50*. Dublin: Irish Academic Press.

Greenwood, R., Raynard, M., Kodeih, F., Micelotta, E.R., & Lounsbury, M. (2011). Institutional complexity and organizational responses. *Academy of Management Annals*, 5(1), 317–371.

Greenwood, R., Suddaby, R., & Hinings, C.R. (2002). Theorizing change: The role of professional associations in the transformation of institutionalized fields. *Academy of Management Journal*, 45, 58–80.

Guardian (2016). 'Novak Djokovic: Men's tennis should fight for more prize money than women.' *The Guardian*, 21 March. www.theguardian.com/sport/2016/mar/21/novak-djokovic-indian-wells-equal-prize-money-tennis?CMP=share_btn_link [Accessed 04/06/2016].

Gulati, R. (2007). Tent poles, tribalism, and boundary spanning: The rigor-relevance debate in management research. *Academy of Management Journal*, 50, 775–782.

Hardy, C., & Maguire, S. (2010). Discourse, field-configuring events, and change in organizations and institutional fields: Narratives of DDT and the Stockholm Convention. *Academy of Management Journal*, 53, 1365–1392.

Hardy, C., Palmer, I., & Phillips, N. (2000). Discourse as a strategic resource. *Human Relations*, 53, 1227–1248.

Haslam, A., & Reicher, S. (2006). Social identity and the dynamics of organizational life. In C. Bartel, S. Blader, & A. Wrzesniewski (Eds.), *Identity and the modern organization*. Mahwah, NJ: Lawrence Erlbaum.

Hinings, C.R., & Greenwood, R. (2002). Disconnects and consequences in organization theory? *Administrative Science Quarterly*, 47, 411–421.

Hinojosa, R. (2010). Doing hegemony: Military, men, and constructing a hegemonic masculinity. *Journal of Men's Studies*, 18(2), 179–194.

Hirsch, P.M. (1986). From ambushes to golden parachutes: Corporate takeovers as an instance of cultural framing and institutional integration. *American Journal of Sociology*, 91, 800–837.

Ho, K. (2009). *Liquidated: An ethnography of Wall Street*. Durham, NC: Duke University Press.

Hoff, K., & Pandey, P. (2006). Discrimination, social identity, and durable inequalities. *American Economic Review*, 96, 206–211.

Jacoby, W.G. (1994). Public attitudes toward government spending. *American Journal of Political Science*, 38, 336–361.

Jencks, C., Bartlett, S., Corcoran, M., Crouse, J., Eaglesfield, D., Jackson, G., McClelland, K., Mueser, P., Olneck, M., Schwartz, J., Ward, S., & Williams, J. (1979). *Who gets ahead? The determinants of economic success in America*. New York: Basic Books.

Jensen, M., & Meckling, W. (1976). Theory of the firm: Managerial behavior, agency costs, and ownership structure, *Journal of Financial Economics*, 3, 305–360.

Kaplan, S.N., & Rauh, J. (2010). Wall Street and main street: What contributes to the rise in the highest incomes? *Review of Financial Studies*, 23, 1004–1050.

Katz, M.B. (1993). *The 'underclass' debate: Views from history*. Princeton, NJ: Princeton University Press.

Keynes, J.M. (1936). *The general theory of employment, interest and money*. London: Macmillan.

Khaire, M., & Wadhwani, D. (2010). Changing landscapes: The construction of meaning and value in a new market category – modern Indian art. *Academy of Management Journal*, 53, 1281–1304.

Khan, F.R., Munir, K.A., & Willmott, H. (2007). A dark side of institutional entrepreneurship: Soccer balls, child labour and postcolonial impoverishment. *Organization Studies*, 28, 1055–1077.

Kraatz, M.S., & Block, E.S. (2008). Organizational implications of institutional pluralism. In R. Greenwood, C. Oliver, R. Suddaby, & K. Sahlin-Andersson (Eds.), *The SAGE handbook of organizational institutionalism* (pp. 243–275). London: Sage.

Laclau, E., & Mouffe, C. (2001). *Hegemony and state socialism: Towards a radical democratic politics* (2nd ed.). London: Verso Books.

Lamont, M., & Molnár, V. (2002). The study of boundaries in the social sciences. *Annual Review of Sociology*, 28, 167–195.

Lansley, S. (2012). *The cost of inequality*. London: Gibson Square.

Lareau, A. (2011). *Unequal childhoods: Class, race, and family life*. Berkeley, CA: University of California Press.

Lawrence, T.B. (2008). Power, institutions and organizations. In R. Greenwood, C. Oliver, R. Suddaby, & K. Sahlin-Andersson (Eds.), *The SAGE handbook of organizational institutionalism* (pp. 170–197). London: Sage.

Lawrence, T.B., & Suddaby, R. (2006). Institutions and institutional work. In S.R. Clegg, C. Hardy, T.B. Lawrence, & W.R. Nord (Eds.) *The SAGE handbook of organization studies* (2nd ed.) (pp. 215–254). London: Sage.

Leana, C.R., Mittal, V., & Stiehl, E. (2012). Organizational behavior and the working poor. *Organization Science*, 23, 888–906.

Levy, F., & Temin, P. (2007). Inequality and institutions in 20th century America. National Bureau of Economic Research. Working Paper Series, Working Paper 13106. www.nber.org/papers/w13106.

Lipsky, D. (2003). *Absolutely American: Four years at West Point*. New York: Houghton Mifflin Harcourt.

Lok, J. (2010). Institutional logics as identity projects. *Academy of Management Journal*, 53, 1305–1335.

Lorsch, J.W. (2009). Regaining lost relevance. *Journal of Management Inquiry*, 18, 108–117.

Lounsbury, M. (2007). A tale of two cities: Competing logics and practice variation in the professionalizing of mutual funds. *Academy of Management Journal*, 50, 289–307.

Lounsbury, M., & Crumley, E.T. (2007). An institutional perspective on innovation. *Organization Studies*, 28, 993–1012.

Lublin, J.S. (1996). America's new continental divide! The executives vs. the rest. *Wall Street Journal*. 11 April. http://online.wsj.com/public/resources/Money-Investing/reference/b-div.html [Accessed 14 June 2016].

Mair, J., & Hehenberger, L. (2014). Front-stage and backstage convening: The transition from opposition to mutualistic coexistence in organizational philanthropy. *Academy of Management Journal*, 57, 1174–1200.

Mair, J., & Martí, I. (2006). Social entrepreneurship research: A source of explanation, prediction, and delight. *Journal of World Business*, 41(1), 36–44.

Mair, J., Martí, I., & Ventresca, M.J. (2012). Building inclusive markets in rural Bangladesh: How intermediaries work institutional voids. *Academy of Management Journal*, 55, 819–850.

Mair, J., Wolf, M., & Seelos, C. (2016). Scaffolding: A Process of Transforming Patterns of Inequality in Small-Scale Societies. *Academy of Management Journal*, 59(6): 2021–2044.

Martí, I., & Fernández, P. (2013). The Institutional work of oppression and resistance: Learning from the Holocaust. *Organization Studies*, 34, 1195–1223.

Martí, I., & Mair, J. (2009). Bringing change into the lives of the poor: Entrepreneurship outside traditional boundaries. In T.B. Lawrence, R. Suddaby, & B. Leca (Eds.), *Institutional work: Actors and agency in institutional studies of organizations* (pp. 92–119). Cambridge: Cambridge University Press.

Martin, I. (2013). *Making it happen: Fred Goodwin, RBS and the men who blew up the British economy*. London: Simon & Schuster.

Marx, K. (1977 [1859]). *A contribution to the critique of political economy*. Moscow: Progress Publishers.

Marx, K., & Engels, F. (1970 [1932]). *The German ideology* (Ed. C.J. Arthur). New York: International Publishers.

Meyer, J.W., & Rowan, B. (1977). Institutionalized organizations: Formal structure as myth and ceremony. *American Journal of Sociology*, 83: 340–363.

Meyer, R.E., & Höllerer, M.A. (2010). Meaning structures in a contested issue field: A topographic map of shareholder value in Austria. *Academy of Management Journal*, 53, 1241–1262.

Micelotta, E.R., & Washington, M. (2013). Institutions and maintenance: The repair work of Italian professions. *Organization Studies*, 34, 1137–1170.

Michel, A. (2011). Transcending socialization: A nine-year ethnography of the body's role in organizational control and knowledge workers' transformation. *Administrative Science Quarterly*, 56, 325–368.

Mishel, L., & Sabadish, N. (2013). CEO pay in 2012 was extraordinarily high relative to typical workers and other high earners. *Issue Brief*, 367. Washington, DC: Economic Policy Institute. Available at www.epi.org/files/2013/ceo-pay-2012-extraordinarily-high.pdf [Accessed 04/06/2016].

Munir, K.A. (2011). Financial crisis 2008–2009: What does the silence of institutional theorists tell us? *Journal of Management Inquiry*, 20(2), 114–117.

Munir, K.A. (2015). A loss of power in institutional theory. *Journal of Management Inquiry*, 24, 90–92.

Munir, K.A., & Phillips, N. (2005). The birth of the Kodak moment: Institutional entrepreneurship and the adoption of new technologies. *Organization Studies*, 26, 1665–1687.

Ogbor, J.O. (2000). Mythicizing and reification in entrepreneurial discourse: Ideology-critique of entrepreneurial studies. *Journal of Management Studies*, 37, 605–635.

Oxfam (2017). *An economy for the 99%: It's time to build a human economy that benefits everyone, not just the privileged few*. Oxford: Oxfam.

Oxfam (2016). *An economy for the 1%: How privilege and power in the economy drive extreme inequality and how this can be stopped*. Oxford: Oxfam.

Pattisson, P. (2015). Aid money for development projects in Nepal linked to child labour. *The Guardian*, 12 February. www.theguardian.com/global-development/2015/feb/12/aid-money-development-projects-nepal-child-labour?CMP=share_btn_link [Acessed 12/02/2015].

Perman, R. (2013). *Hubris: How HBOS wrecked the best bank in Britain*. Edinburgh: Birlinn.

Phillips, N., & Hardy, C. (1997). Managing multiple identities: Discourse, legitimacy and resources in the UK refugee system. *Organization*, 4, 159–185.

Phillips, N., Lawrence, T., & Hardy, C. (2004). Discourse and institutions. *Academy of Management Review*, 29, 1–18.

Phillips, N., & Oswick, C. (2012). Organizational discourse: Domains, debates and directions. *Academy of Management Annals*, 6, 435–481.

Piketty, T. (2014). *Capital in the Twenty-First Century*. Cambridge, MA: Belknap Press.

Piven, F.F., & Cloward, R.A. (1993). *Regulating the poor: The functions of public welfare*. New York: Vintage.

Powell, W.W., & Colyvas, J.A. (2008). Microfoundations of institutional theory. In R. Greenwood, C. Oliver, R. Suddaby, & K. Sahlin-Andersson (Eds.) (pp. 276–298). *The SAGE Handbook of organizational institutionalism*. London: Sage.

Prilleltensky, I., & Gonick, L. (1996). Polities change, oppression remains: On the psychology and politics of oppression. *Political Psychology*, 17, 127–148.

Raver, J.L., & Gelfand, M.J. (2005). Beyond the individual victim: Linking sexual harassment, team processes, and team performance. *Academy of Management Journal*, 48, 387–400.

Riaz, S. (2015). Bringing inequality back in: The economic inequality footprint of management and organizational practices. *Human Relations*, 68, 1085–1097.

Ryan, M.K., & Haslam, S.A. (2007). The glass cliff: Exploring the dynamics surrounding the appointment of women to precarious leadership positions. *Academy of Management Review*, 32, 549–572.

Saez, E., & Zucman, G. (2014). Wealth inequality in the United States since 1913: Evidence from capitalized income data. National Bureau of Economic Research. Working Paper 20625.

Sahlin, K., & Wedlin, L. (2008). Circulating ideas: Imitation, translation and editing. In R. Greenwood, C. Oliver, R. Suddaby, & K. Sahlin-Andersson (Eds.), *The SAGE handbook of organizational institutionalism* (pp. 218–242). London: Sage.

Sahlin-Andersson, K. (1996). Imitating by editing success: The construction of organizational fields. In B. Czarniawska & G. Sévon (Eds.), *Translating the organizational change* (pp. 69–92). New York: Walter de Gruyter.

Said, E. (1977). *Orientalism*. Harmondsworth: Penguin.

Sandberg, S. (2013). *Lean in: Women, work and the will to lead*. London: W.H. Allen.

Sasson-Levy, O. (2002). Constructing identities at the margins: Masculinities and citizenship in the Israeli army. *Sociological Quarterly*, 43, 357–383.

Scott, W.R. (1995). *Institutions and organizations*. Thousand Oaks, CA: Sage.

Scott, W.R., Ruef, M., Mendel, P., & Caronna, C. (2000). *Institutional change and healthcare organizations: From professional dominance to managed care*. Chicago, IL: University of Chicago Press.

Schwalbe, M. (2008). *Rigging the game: How inequality is reproduced in everyday life*. New York: Oxford University Press.

Scully, M.A., & Blake-Beard, S. (2006). Locating class in organisational diversity work. In A.M. Konrad, P. Prasad & J.K. Pringle (Eds.), *Handbook of workplace diversity* (pp. 431–454). London: Sage.

Searle, J.R. (2005). What is an institution? *Journal of Institutional Economics*, 1, 1–22.

Seelos, C., & Mair, J. (2007). Profitable business models and market creation in the context of deep poverty: A strategic view. *Academy of Management Perspectives*, 21(4), 49–63.

Seelos, C., & Mair, J. (2017). *Innovation and scaling for impact – how effective social enterprises do it*. Stanford, CA: Stanford University Press.

Selznick, P. (1949). *TVA and the grass roots: A study in the sociology of formal organization*. Berkeley, CA: University of California Press.

Sennett, R., & Cobb, J. (1972). *The hidden inquiries of class*. New York: Alfred A. Knopf.

Shleifer, A., & Vishny, R. (1997). A survey of corporate governance. *Journal of Finance*, 52, 737–783

Skeggs, B. (1997). *Formations of class and gender: Becoming respectable*. London: Sage.

Small, M.L., Harding, D.J., & Lamont, M. (2010). Reconsidering culture and poverty. *Annals of the American Academy of Political and Social Science*, 629(1), 6–27.

Soule, S.A. (2012). Social movements and markets, industries, and firms. *Organization Studies*, 33, 1715–1733.

Starkey, K., & Madan, P. (2001). Bridging the relevance gap: Aligning stakeholders in the future of management research. *British Journal of Management*, 12, S3–S26.

Stern, R.N., & Barley, S.R. (1996). Organizations and social systems: Organization theory's neglected mandate. *Administrative Science Quarterly*, 41, 146–162.

Stiglitz, J. (2013). *The price of inequality*. Harmondsworth: Penguin.

Stinchcombe, A.L. (1997). On the virtues of the old institutionalism. *Annual Review of Sociology*, 23, 1–18.

Stout, L. (2012). *The shareholder value myth: How putting shareholders first harms investors, corporations, and the public*. San Francisco, CA: Berrett–Koehler.

Strang, D., & Meyer, J.W. (1993). Institutional conditions for diffusion. *Theory and Society*, 22, 487–511.

Tajfel, H. (1981). *Human groups and social categories: Studies in social psychology*. Cambridge: Cambridge University Press.

Taylor, J.R., & Van Every, E.J. (2000). *The emergent organization: Communication as its site and surface*. Mahwah, NJ: Lawrence Erlbaum Associates.

Thompson, G. (2007). *American culture in the 1980s*. Edinburgh: Edinburgh University Press.

Thornton, P.H. (2004). *Markets from culture: Institutional logics and organizational decisions in higher education publishing*. Stanford, CA: Stanford University Press.

Thornton, P., Ocasio, W., & Lounsbury, M. (2012). *The institutional logics perspective: A new approach to culture, structure and process* New York: Oxford University Press.

Tilly, C. (1998). *Durable inequality*. Berkeley, CA: University of California Press.

Uzo, U., & Mair, J. (2014). Source and patterns of organizational defiance of formal institutions: Insights from Nollywood, the Nigerian movie industry. *Strategic Entrepreneurship Journal*, 8(1), 56–74.

Van Dijk, T.A. (1992). Discourse and the denial of racism. *Discourse & Society*, 3(1), 87–118.

Van Dijk, T.A. (1994). Discourse and inequality. Keynote address: International Conference of the International Communication Association. Dublin, 29 June 1990. *Lenguas Modernas*, 21, 19–37.

Venkataraman, H., Vermeulen, P., Raaijmakers, A., & Mair, J. (2016). Market meets community: Institutional logics as strategic resources for development work. *Organization Studies*, 37(5), 709–733.

Von Glinow, M.A. (2005). Let us speak for those who cannot. *Academy of Management Journal*, 48(6), 983–985.

Wallace, S.E. (Ed.) (1971). *Total institutions*. Piscataway, NJ: Transaction Publishers.

Wilkinson, R., & Pickett, K. (2010). *The spirit level: Why equality is better for everyone*. Harmondsworth: Penguin.

Willmott, H. (2015). Why institutional theory cannot be critical. *Journal of Management Inquiry*, 24(1), 105–111.

Wisman, J., & Smith, J. (2011). Legitimating inequality: Fooling most of the people all of the time. *American Journal of Economics and Sociology*, 70(4), 974–1013.

Zald, M.N., & Lounsbury, M. (2010). The wizards of Oz: Towards an institutional approach to elites, expertise and command posts. *Organization Studies*, 31(7), 963–996.

Zilber, T.B. (2006). The work of the symbolic in institutional processes: Translations of rational myths in Israeli high tech. *Academy of Management Journal*, 49(2), 281–303.

Zilber, T.B. (2008). The work of meanings in institutional processes and thinking. In R. Greenwood, C. Oliver, R. Suddaby, & K. Sahlin-Andersson (Eds.) (pp. 151–169). *The SAGE handbook of organizational institutionalism*. London: Sage.

Zucker, L. (1977). The role of institutionalization in cultural persistence. *American Sociological Review*, 42, 726–743.

28

Institutions, Institutional Theory and Organizational Wrongdoing

Donald Palmer

INTRODUCTION

Wrongdoing in and by organizations, hereafter for simplicity organizational wrongdoing, is increasingly a topic of interest to organization theorists.[1] Institutional theorists have conducted research on specific types of organizational wrongdoing. But no one has yet attempted to take stock of these efforts with the goal of articulating in a holistic way the implications that institutional theory holds for the study of organizational wrongdoing. This is my objective. I begin by elaborating working definitions of the three concepts central to the chapter: institutions, institutional theory and organizational wrongdoing. Then, I discuss six ways in which institutional theory can inform the analysis of organizational wrongdoing. I conclude by exploring three implications of my enquiry into theory on the relationship between institutions and organizational wrongdoing.

INSTITUTIONS, INSTITUTIONAL THEORY AND ORGANIZATIONAL WRONGDOING

What Are Institutions?

Institutions have been conceptualized in various and variably precise ways. In political science, where the concept has fluctuated in its significance over time, institutions are conceptualized as the forms that political activity can take. From this vantage point, institutions include political systems, such as democracy, socialism and communism, as well as their component parts, such as unions, political parties, legislatures and courts (Moe, 1990).

In economics, where the concept is more consistently invoked, institutions are sometimes characterized broadly, as 'humanly devised constraints that structure political, economic and social interactions' and that include both formal rules such as laws and informal sanctions such as customs

(North, 1991). More often, though, institutions are characterized more narrowly as arrangements that shape and regulate economic exchange. From this vantage point, the principal institutions are market and command economies. They also include the structures that establish the rules of the game within each form of exchange; perhaps most importantly, legal systems (Hodgson, 1998).

In sociology, where the concept reigns supreme, institutions are conceptualized in a variety of ways. Most generally, institutions are considered domains of human interaction that are distinguished from one another by their unique organizing principles that take the form of distinct values, beliefs and norms, and are manifest in typically occurring practices. From this vantage point, institutions include the economy, polity, family and religion (Turner, 1997), although bounded spheres of activity can be conceptualized in a more emergent and delimited way, such as interpersonal interaction in dyads and small groups (Berger and Luckmann, 1966).

In the subfield of organizational sociology, also referred to as 'organization theory', the term has taken on additional organization-specific meanings. Some organization theorists conceptualize organizations *as* institutions consisting of participants who share a value orientation and a desire to persist as a community independent of the goals the organization is pursuing at a particular moment in time (Gusfeld, 1955). Most, though, characterize organizations *as situated in* institutional environments, which consist of a variety of social structures that influence the forms that organizations take and the behaviors in which they engage (Stinchcombe, 1965). Some characterize institutional environments as constellations of constituencies upon which the organization depends for its social support or legitimacy (Parsons, 1956a, 1956b; Zald, 1967, 1969). Others characterize institutional environments more narrowly as networks of other organizations on which the organization depends for resources needed for survival (Hirsch, 1975; Pfeffer

and Salancik, 1978). These views are associated with the 'old' sociological institutionalism. Recently, though, organization theorists have reconceptualized the institutional environment in two more elaborate ways, which will be a primary focus of this chapter.

In the new institutional (or neo-institutional) view, codified by W.R. Scott (1987, 2001), institutions are conceptualized as regulative, normative and cognitive structures that shape the behavior of organizations and their members in a delimited 'field'. Regulative structures are legal and administrative rules, and the organizations that make and enforce those rules (e.g., governmental agencies). Normative structures are taken-for-granted assumptions and reflexively expressed expectations about appropriate ways of behaving and the organizations that promulgate and enforce those assumptions and expectations (e.g., professional associations). Cognitive structures are taken-for-granted ways of thinking about the required or most efficacious ways of behaving and the organizations that promulgate and enforce those mindsets (e.g., educational organizations). Finally, fields are territories within which actors interact around a common set of inputs and outputs. Fields can be conceptualized at various quasi-hierarchically ordered yet interpenetrating levels of analysis, such as the world economic system, national economies, industrial sectors and geographical areas.

In the institutional logics perspective, advanced by Thornton, Ocasio and Lounsbury (2012), institutions take the form of orders and logics that regulate the behavior of organizations and their participants in delimited fields. In this view, society is characterized as an inter-institutional system composed of seven broadly defined institutional orders: the family, religion, state, market, profession, corporation and community. Each of these seven orders contains nine ideal-typical elements: root metaphor, sources of legitimacy, sources of authority, sources of identity, basis of norms, basis of attention, basis of strategy, informal control mechanisms and economic system. A key distinguishing aspect of this perspective is that fields may be composed of multiple variably symbiotic or antagonistic logics, which represent realized combinations of institutional order elements.

What is Institutional Theory?

Institutional theory is any theory formulated to understand the causes, processes and consequences of institutions as they relate to the behavior of organizations and their members. There are more than a few somewhat ill-defined varieties of institutional theory in political science, economics, sociology and organization theory implied by the paragraphs above. In this chapter I will focus exclusively on economic and sociological theories of institutions (hereafter, institutional economics and institutional sociology or, interchangeably the economic and sociological institutionalisms), because these formulations are the ones most frequently invoked by this chapter's likely audience.[2] Further, I will privilege sociological institutionalism over economic institutionalism for the same reason. In reference to the range of work operating underneath the broad umbrella of sociological institutionalism, I will sometimes single out one or more of three specific types of institutional theory: the old institutionalism (Stinchcombe, 1965; Zald, 1967, 1969; Hirsch, 1975; Pfeffer and Salancik, 1978), the new institutionalism (Meyer and Rowan, 1977; DiMaggio and Powell, 1983; Scott, 2001, 2008), and the institutional logics perspective (Thornton et al., 2012). With this said, I will not be overly concerned about the accuracy of my categorizations of the institutional theory referenced here. My goal is to explore comprehensively the ways in which institutional theory can contribute to our understanding of organizational wrongdoing, rather than to categorize precisely those contributions.

What is Organizational Wrongdoing?

Organizational wrongdoing has been conceptualized broadly to include behavior that violates ethical principles, social norms, organizational rules and protocols, industry or professional guidelines and civil or criminal laws. In this chapter, I will focus primarily on behavior that violates civil or criminal laws for two reasons. First, wrongdoing that violates civil and criminal law is the most consequential form of wrongdoing in terms of its impact on perpetrators and victims as well as society at large. Civil and criminal laws are enacted to protect victims and society at large from the most significant harm and the most serious insults to shared moral sensibilities. Further, violations of civil and criminal law can result in large fines for organizations and long jail terms for organizational participants. Second, there is already considerable institutional theory focused on the causes and consequences of behavior that violates ethical principles, social norms, organizational rules, and industry and professional guidelines, sometimes referred to as 'organizational deviance' or 'illegitimate behavior' (cf., Kraatz and Zajac, 1996).

Organizational wrongdoing of the sort I focus on is typically subdivided into wrongdoing perpetrated by organizational participants on behalf of their organizations, referred to as 'corporate crime', and wrongdoing perpetrated by organizational participants at the expense of their organizations, referred to as 'white collar crime'. I will not honor this distinction in this chapter because it is based on two questionable implicit assumptions: (1) that organizational participants' wrongdoing advances *either* the interests of the perpetrators *or* the interests of the organizations of which they are members and (2) that organizational wrongdoing is always motivated behavior. I think many instances of organizational wrongdoing can advance *both* the interest of the perpetrators and the organizations of which they are members, such as Andy Fastow's fraudulent special purpose entities did at Enron Corporation (Eichenwald, 2005). Further, I think that much organizational wrongdoing is unintentional, as is the case in organizational accidents such as the Exxon Valdez oil spill (Lev, 1990).

STRONG INSTITUTIONS CURTAIL ORGANIZATIONAL WRONGDOING

Arguably the most well established current in institutional thought holds that strong institutions curb organizational wrongdoing. Institutional economics explicitly maintains that institutions reduce the incidence of malfeasance in economic exchange. It contends that robust institutions, by closely monitoring economic behavior and swiftly and harshly punishing actors that engage in behavior detrimental to the market's self-regulating operation, suppress corruption. This perspective has its roots in the work of Polanyi (1957), who was among the first to recognize that markets function smoothly only when institutional structures such as laws that hold in check deleterious behaviors such as transaction partner misrepresentations of facts and violations of agreements are in place and enforced. This view has its practical expression in rating systems of the sort developed by Transparency International that rank countries on a scale from most corrupt to least corrupt, with an eye to providing investors with guidance regarding the integrity of economic and political institutions in different countries and thus the riskiness of investment opportunities in those locales.

Institutional economics also explicitly maintains that robust governance structures reduce the incidence of malfeasance within organizations. The most well known variant of this outlook focuses on the unique problems created by the transition from owner capitalism to managerial capitalism and the institutional structures that arose to cope with these

problems. Business historians document the rise of new forms of organization, such as the multi-divisional form that minimizes opportunism (the pursuit of self-interest with guile) created by the separation of ownership and control (Chandler, 1962, 1980). Agency theorists analyze these problems in a formal way, identifying conflicts of interest within the uppermost levels of management-controlled firms, most importantly between top management and owners, and the types of governance structures that have arisen to mitigate these problems (Hillman and Dalziel, 2003; Peasnell et al., 2005; Dalton et al., 2007). Contracts that align the interests of owners and managers, and independent boards of directors that monitor managers on behalf of owners, feature prominently in this work as devices that reduce the incidence of managerial wrongdoing. Recently, these same ideas have been extended to understanding conflicts of interest within not-for-profit firms (Harris et al., 2015).

Institutional sociology implicitly holds that institutions curb wrongdoing in and by organizations of all types. This outlook has its roots in the old sociological institutionalism, which assumes that organizations require societal legitimacy as well as technical efficiency to survive and prosper. In Parson's (1956a, 1956b, 1961) classic formulation, the upper most level of organizational hierarchies, such as the boards of directors of private sector firms, primarily function not to control the organization's internal operations but rather to broker its relationship to the external environment, so as to guarantee the support of key environmental constituents.

This outlook also is manifest in the new sociological institutionalism, which adds that the need to obtain legitimacy results in the homogenization of organizational forms, if not the actual activities through which organizations conduct their business. Proponents of the new institutionalism characterize it as 'a theoretical perspective that focuses on organizational conformity with social rules' (Orru et al., 1997) and thus the suppression of deviation. Insofar as civil and criminal laws are the most widely acknowledged social rules in any society, new institutional theory implicitly holds that institutional structures inhibit organizational wrongdoing as here defined. For DiMaggio and Powell (1983), legitimacy constraints homogenize organizations within fields, such that they bend to specific coercive, normative and mimetic pressures that do not have a single impetus (e.g., efficiency, effectiveness, rationality, functionality, etc.).[3] But for Meyer and Rowan (1977), legitimacy constraints homogenize organizations such that they conform to general myths about the rationality of formal organization. And in related work, Drori, Yang and Meyer (2006) equate the rationalization of society throughout the world system with the inhibition of corruption.

The stance that institutions curb organizational wrongdoing also finds expression in the institutional logics perspective. Thornton and associates maintain that three of the seven institutional orders – the state, the professions and religion – 'provide constraint on the unbridled practices of capitalism' (2012: 119–120). Muzio et al. (2016), building on Abbott (1988), elaborate the role that the professions, especially the accounting profession, play in this regard. Of course, the actions, cognitions and emotions of human beings are the most fundamental basis of all organizational behavior. The institutional logics perspective goes beyond the new institutional view in specifying the 'microfoundations' of institutional structures and processes; that is, how institutional constraints are expressed at the level of the individuals who populate and lead organizations (Thornton et al., 2012: 76–102). For the most part, for the sake of simplicity, I will ignore this 'levels of analysis' issue in the remainder of this chapter.

In summary, institutional economics assumes that institutions arise to ensure that economic actors behave in efficient ways and that economic actors generally conform to institutions so as to avoid the consequences of inefficiency. Similarly, three variants of institutional sociology assume that institutions arise to ensure that organizations behave in ways that conform to social prescriptions about what is legitimate and that organizations generally conform to institutions so as to acquire and maintain social support, which is a condition of their existence. Thus, all four variants of institutional theory reviewed above presume that institutions patrol the economic and organizational landscape with an eye to keeping economic and organizational actors on the straight and narrow. This implies that organizations and those who lead them should eschew behaviors that cross the line separating right from wrong because crossing the line jeopardizes their survival chances, as long as the line is monitored closely and policed aggressively. But if institutions suppress wrongdoing in and by organizations, why is organizational wrongdoing so common? Institutional theory offers five answers to this question.

WEAK INSTITUTIONS COUNTENANCE ORGANIZATIONAL WRONGDOING

Of course, outlooks maintaining that robust institutions suppress organizational wrongdoing simultaneously imply that weak institutions countenance it. Institutional economists explicitly recognize that societies, industries and organizations vary in the robustness of their governance regimes. For example, weak governance structures have been cited as the underlying cause of such diverse instances of organizational wrongdoing as corruption in developing nations (Rose-Ackerman, 2004), the fraud that underpinned the US Savings and Loan crisis in the 1980s (Pizzo et al., 1991), and the various forms of malfeasance at Enron Corporation (Eichenwald, 2005).

Similarly, the new sociological institutionalism acknowledges that institutional pressures vary depending on the degree to which a field is 'structurated' and technical efficiency and performance constraints are weak (DiMaggio and Powell, 1983). Thus, some new institutional theorists have explored the weaknesses of regulatory regimes. For example, Gabbioneta and associates (2013) maintain that 'regulatory loopholes' in the rules governing the auditing of multi-layered subsidiaries, which Prechel and Hou (2016) contend provide unique opportunities for financial deception, allowed the Italian food conglomerate Parmalat to disguise its fraudulent accounting for an extended period of time.

INSTITUTIONS CAN STIMULATE ORGANIZATIONAL WRONGDOING

While much institutional theory holds that robust institutions curb wrongdoing in and by organizations (and thus, at the same time, implies that weak institutions countenance it), a well-established counter current in institutional thought holds that institutions also can stimulate wrongdoing. As already noted institutional economists maintain that a crucial development within capitalist societies, the transition from owner capitalism to managerial capitalism, created conditions that give rise to misconduct in public corporations. Berle and Means (1932) were the first to draw attention to this transition and its implications for economic behavior. They argued that as firms grew in size and complexity over the course of the 19th and early 20th centuries, their founders' financial capacity to generate capital sufficient to fuel growth as well as their intellectual capacity needed to manage operations became strained. As a result, founders increasingly reached out to dispersed outside investors to provide capital, and to professional managers to provide administrative expertise.

Institutional economists believe that these developments gave rise to a new economic order in which ownership was separated from control in the large corporation. In this mode of control regime, corporate managers (and the boards of directors that they assemble and orchestrate) command firms with little interference from their firms' owners. As a result, managers are free to pursue their parochial interests at the expense of stockholder welfare. Agency theorists formalized this argument by conceptualizing the problems presented by the transition from owner to managerial capitalism as stemming from the fact that the 'principals' (i.e., owners) in large firms are at a disadvantage in the monitoring and controlling of their 'agents' (i.e., managers) who are responsible for executing the firm's operations on their behalf (Fama, 1980; Fama and Jensen, 1983). It is precisely these arguments that laid the foundation for the institutional economics perspectives reviewed in the previous sections.

Coleman (1987, 1988) develops an institutional sociology argument that is analogous to the institutional economics argument outlined above, but that instead focuses on the transition from feudalism to capitalism. He maintains that capitalism is typified by a cultural imperative to pursue wealth and an economic environment that embraces competition and thus inherently constrains individuals' pursuit of wealth. Further, he argues that when economic actors fail to achieve their aspirations through legitimate channels, as will inevitably occur in a competitive system, they turn to illegitimate means to reach their aspirations; that is, they will engage in economic crime. Braithwaite (1988) shares this outlook, although he locates the institutional impetus for wrongdoing in industrialization rather than the transition to capitalism. Both arguments have commonalities with Merton's (1938) general theory of crime. Merton contended that societies characterized by cultures that place a supreme value on economic achievement but that employ economic structures that limit achievement to restricted subsets of the population have higher levels of crime, because those whose achievement goals are blocked by legitimate economic structures seek illegitimate means to attain their goals.

Thornton et al. (2012) provide an institutional logics argument that extends Coleman's line of reasoning about capitalism's affinity for economic crime to the specific capitalist form of the large corporation; they employ Jackall's (1988) analysis of the corporation in their characterization of the institutional order of the corporation. In *Moral Mazes* (1988) and elsewhere (1983, 1984), Jackall contends that the normative outlook and practical rules of the modern corporation transmute matters of ethics into matters of practical (i.e., economic and political) expediency, in the process making it likely that managers will make unethical decisions such as those that jeopardize worker safety and lead to environmental degradation. Consistent with this implicit general indictment of the corporate order, Thornton et al. (2012) speculate that Arthur Andersen's descent into criminally lax accounting practices can be attributed to its abandonment of key elements of the professional logic and its adoption of central features of the corporate logic.

A related sociological argument locates the cause of wrongdoing in imbalances in the inter-institutional system. This argument has its roots in Durkheim's (1997) classic analysis of social deviance. Durkheim speculated that societies in which the economy is self-regulating (i.e., disciplined only by market forces) and other institutions such as the family are weak; they suffer a condition he termed 'anomie', in which economic ambition is unchecked and deviance likely. This formulation, known today as 'institutional anomie theory', has been re-conceptualized at the individual level (Messner et al., 2008) and used to explain a wide variety of social deviance. For example, Stults and Falco (2014) show that students who strongly adhere to economic values are more prone to engage in delinquent behavior, a tendency muted by simultaneous adherence to non-economic values. Interestingly, proponents of the institutional logics perspective have taken up this line of reasoning as well. Thornton et al. (2012) contend that when one or more of the seven institutional orders comes to dominate the others, the inter-institutional system becomes imbalanced. And they opine that the dominance of the market order in the latter part of the 20th and early years of the 21st century may have been the root cause of the 2008 global financial crisis.

Others working under the broad umbrella of institutional theory maintain that cultural norms, cognitive frames and/or routinized practices underpin cross-national variation in organizational wrongdoing. For example, Fisman and Miguel (2007) analyzed the number of illegal parking citations and the number of unpaid such tickets attributed to foreign embassy personnel stationed in New York City. They found that wrongdoing in this domain was highest among personnel associated with embassies from countries rated as corrupt by Transparency International (TI). Similarly, Palmer and Yenkey (2015) studied the use of banned performance enhancing drugs (PEDs) among professional cyclists in advance of the 2010 Tour de France. They found that riders most likely to be using banned PEDs in advance of the Tour were citizens of countries ranked as corrupt by TI or members of teams home-based in countries similarly ranked as corrupt. In both studies, the authors maintain that the observed patterns at least partly reflected cross-national differences in normative orientations towards law violation.

It seems likely that cultural norms, cognitive frames and/or routinized practices also underpin inter-industry variation in organizational wrongdoing. For example, the use of banned PEDs was pervasive, considered appropriate and even thought to be an essential element of a successful training regimen in professional cycling in the late 1990s and the early 2000s. Indeed, some riders who later confessed to using banned PEDs during this period reported that their first use of PEDs left them feeling proud to have cleared the last hurdle to becoming a true professional, rather than guilty for breaking the rules of the sport (Millar and Whittle, 2011; Hamilton and Coyle, 2012). But available evidence suggests that PED use in other sports, such as tennis, in the same period was much less prevalent and considered an anathema (Rosen, 2008).

Finally, Gabbioneta et al.'s (2013) new institutional analysis of accounting fraud at Parmalat indicates that institutional arrangements also can give rise to wrongdoing in two more indirect ways. First, institutions can create conditions that breed other more proximate non-institutional causes of wrongdoing, such as performance strain. Performance strain, the gap between an actor's aspirations and its capacity to achieve those aspirations, is arguably the most frequently cited cause of wrongdoing in and by organizations (cf. Agnew et al., 2009). A number of studies show that firms that struggle to meet their historical performance levels (i.e., those with declining performance trajectories) are more likely to engage in wrongdoing (cf., Simpson, 1986; Palmer and Yenkey, 2015) and a few identify organizational characteristics that moderate this relationship (Mishina et al., 2010). Gabbioneta and associates (2013) show that the institutional relationships in which Parmalat was embedded led it to pursue policies that increased its motivation to engage in wrongdoing, a process they call 'institutional endorsement'. They contend that Parmalat pursued a strategy of growth via acquisition and fueled by debt because financial institutions upon which it depended for capital and financial analysts upon whom it depended for legitimacy endorsed this strategy. Further, they show that pursuit of this strategy, in vogue in the financial community at the time, resulted in declining profits that generated performance strain, which in turn motivated Parmalat's owner and top managers to pursue an escalating program of financial fraud.

Second, institutional arrangements can provide mechanisms through which other causes of organizational wrongdoing, such as differential association, are expressed. Differential association, the extent to which organizational actors are linked to other actors already engaged in wrongdoing, is arguably the oldest theorized cause of economic wrongdoing (Sutherland, 1949). Differential association is thought to expose actors to motivations that provide the impetus to embark on wrongdoing, the resources (e.g., skills and assistance) needed to perpetrate it, information on the potential costs and benefits of wrongdoing, and rationalizations that blunt the guilt that wrongdoers might otherwise experience as the result of engaging in wrongdoing. Numerous studies have surfaced evidence of the impact of differential association on actors' propensity to engage in wrongdoing (cf. Robinson and O'Leary-Kelly, 1998; Palmer and Yenkey, 2015). Gabbioneta and associates (2013) show that the institutional structures in which Parmalat was embedded provided for the transmission of skills it needed to engage in wrongdoing. Specifically, they show that Parmalat's principal accounting firm, Grant Thornton, provided crucial expertise needed to orchestrate its fraud – specifically, the types of accounting maneuvers needed to represent the firm as a financially healthy enterprise.[4]

INSTITUTIONS CAN SUSTAIN WRONGDOING (AND VICE VERSA)

Another emergent strain of institutional thought holds that intuitions can sustain wrongdoing in or by organizations, regardless of the factors responsible for its initiation. Diane Vaughan (1996) advanced this line of reasoning in her study of the Challenger space shuttle disaster. To simplify her complex and nuanced analysis, Vaughan maintained that pressures to reduce costs in the United States space shuttle program, which emanated from the US Congress, caused NASA and its subcontractors to progressively satisfice in the domain of technological perfection; in so doing, deprioritizing safety. When technical problems arose, such as the 'hot gas blow-by' that eroded the seals on the Challenger's solid rocket booster, and they did not immediately result in catastrophic failure, the problems were tolerated. This toleration of problematic technological processes constituted a 'normalization of deviance' that became part of the space program's culture. In the early years, NASA and its subcontractors operated according to the belief that they should proceed with a launch only when they could prove that their systems, both their hardware and procedures, were safe. As the space shuttle program evolved, though, NASA and its subcontractors came to operate according to the belief that they should postpone a launch only if they could prove that their systems were unsafe. The accumulation of unattended problems, though, increased the risk of system failure, which ultimately materialized in the Challenger disaster.

Several management theorists have extended Vaughan's argument, both with respect to theoretical scope and type of wrongdoing. Brief and associates (2001), Ashforth and Anand (2003) and Palmer (2008) elaborated a multi-stage process by which wrongdoing can become entrenched in organizations, a crucial phase of which consists of the institutionalization of wrongdoing. According to this model, after wrongdoing has been initiated by persons at the top of the organization and proliferated throughout the organization via a host of social influence mechanisms, it can become embedded in the organization's culture, cognitive maps and administrative routines. Cultural norms interpret the wrongdoing as acceptable. Cognitive schemas and scripts encode the wrongdoing as appropriate. Finally, rules and standard operating procedures concretize the wrongdoing as routine. Ultimately, organizational participants engage in the wrongdoing without giving it much thought. In Brief et al.'s (2001) terminology, they become 'amoral automatons'.

This framework accounts well for Ford Motor Company's production and marketing of its Pinto subcompact car, despite its fuel tank's known tendency to erupt in flames when the car was struck from behind even at relatively slow speeds. The firm's actions in this regard resulted in a landmark civil judgment and criminal indictments (albeit not convictions). Ford's CEO famously conceived the Pinto to occupy the price-conscious (i.e., low purchase price and fuel-efficient operation) consumer market niche. He disseminated the cultural mantra 'safety doesn't sell' that directed engineering attention away from safety considerations in the design of Ford's cars. He promulgated the 'rule of 2000', which stipulated that the Pinto should cost no more than $2000 to manufacture and weigh no more than 2000 pounds, which restricted its engineers' ability to add even relatively inexpensive safety devices that could reduce the fuel tank fire problem (Dowie, 1977). Tragically, when the Pinto's susceptibility to fuel tank fires came to the attention of the company's recall coordinators, the problem was discounted, partly because the fires did not fit the categorization scheme used to identify legitimate recall candidates. The cognitive schemas in place led coordinators to consider problems to be appropriate triggers for recall only when they were the immediate result of an automotive system failure (e.g., a faulty ignition switch). The Pinto fires, to the contrary, were the immediate result of another automobile driver's failure to avoid striking the car from behind (Gioia, 1992).

While most theory about the wrongdoing-sustaining effects of institutions has focused on institutional structures and processes within organizations, at least one group of theorists have argued that wrongdoing-sustaining effects also can operate at higher levels of analysis. Gabbioneta et al. (2013) contend that the institutionalized trust characterizing the network of relationships among key actors in Parmalat's environment amplified the legitimating effect of its accountant's faulty certification of Parmalat's accounting reports, insulating Parmalat's fraud from detection via a process that the authors refer to as 'institutional ascription'. When Parmalat's principal accountant, Grant Thornton, certified Parmalat's books, thereby legitimating its operations, other key institutional actors, such as Parmalat's other accounting firm, Deloit and Touche, trusted Grant Thornton's certification. Further, other high status actors with which Parmalat was associated, most importantly its prestigious bankers, Citigroup, Deutsche Bank, JPMorgan and UBS, trusted Grant Thornton's and Deloit and Touche's determinations (as well as each other's positive evaluations of those determinations) and as a result curtailed their own due diligence efforts.

Finally, while no institutional theorists have acknowledged this possibility, it is likely that wrongdoing can play a role in sustaining institutions. Granovetter, the progenitor of the 'embeddedness perspective', maintains that illegal black market exchange in the African continent's state socialist countries became 'economically necessary because the officially condoned activity as regulated by central planning was too rigid and unrealistic to provide goods and services that citizens considered necessary' (2007: 163). Further, he argues that corruption of this type can persist even in the face of liberal economic reform bolstered by what Thornton et al. (2012) might characterize as alternative institutional logics embodied in 'universalistic ideologies'. This is partly because the corruption is embedded in normative frameworks and concrete social relationships (e.g., friendship networks) that have substantial inertia. It is also partly because the corruption offers citizens concrete benefits that the free market reforms are yet unable to provide. Indeed, there is some evidence that liberal reforms can undermine the apparently necessary and effective economic and business–government exchanges that corruption makes possible in state socialist economies, as appears to be happening in China today (Denyer, 2015).

INSTITUTIONS SHAPE THE EXTENT AND FORM OF WRONGDOING THROUGH TIME AND SPACE

All varieties of institutional theory implicitly assume that institutions delineate the line separating acceptable from unacceptable behavior in a social order. But few institutional theorists have devoted much attention to an important implication of this assumption; namely, that institutions influence the extent and nature of wrongdoing in a society. Logically speaking, if institutions did not exist, there could be no wrongdoing. Practically speaking, when institutions elaborate few rules, norms, or cognitive models (to use new institutional theory terminology, when fields exhibit little 'structuration') there can be little wrongdoing. To simplify my exposition of this implication I confine my discussion to regulative institutions, although an analogous analysis could be extended to cultural norms, cognitive frames and other elements of the institutional system.

Institutions determine where the line separating right from wrong is drawn. Insofar as institutions vary over time and space, the position of the line separating right from wrong varies throughout history and across localities. For example, while one can be sent to prison for insider trading in the United Kingdom today, one could not be sent to prison for this behavior in 18th-century England, when insider trading was legal and commonplace. Further, while inside trading is illegal in the UK today, it is not prohibited in many other contemporary economies, such as Kenya. What is more, some behavior categorized as insider trading in the present-day UK is not considered insider trading in the contemporary United States.

Institutions also determine the manner in which and the vigorousness with which the line separating right from wrong is enforced. And insofar as institutions vary over time and space, the manner in which and the vigorousness with which the line separating right from wrong is enforced also varies through-out history and across localities. For exam-ple, today in the United States specialized formal organizations patrol the economic landscape in search of wrongdoing such as insider trading (the Securities and Exchange Commission), market manipulation (the Federal Trade Commission) and financial fraud (the Department of Justice). Further, for the most part these entities focus on organi-zations (e.g., corporations), rather the people who command them (e.g., corporate execu-tives). Finally, when they impose punishment on perpetrators, these specialized formal organizations typically levy fines meted out in proportion to the damage the malfeasance is presumed to have caused.

But the institutional apparatus that policed the line separating right from wrong in 18th-century England was quite different. Consider the prosecution of those believed to have been responsible for the misdeeds asso-ciated with the South Sea Bubble (Carswell, 2001). When the South Sea Corporation's stock price plummeted precipitating a global financial crisis, the two houses of Parliament, rather than agencies specializ-ing in the policing of economic crime, con-ducted investigations of the debacle. Further, these political bodies focused their attention on the managers and directors of the South Sea Corporation, rather than the firm itself. Finally, as punishment, these political bod-ies confiscated the accumulated property of the firm's managers and directors for the pur-pose of making repayment to those injured by the company's stock price collapse, rather than levy fines against the individuals. Then, after open debate, Parliament decided how much of each director's confiscated wealth would be returned to him as an 'allowance' with which to carry on his life.[5]

In the advanced societies such as the United States, there is considerable complexity even within specialized compartments of the regu-lative pillar. For example, the Environmental Protection Agency, Occupational Health and Safety Administration, Mine Safety and Health Administration, and the Food and Drug Administration all have jurisdiction over workplace safety. But these agencies vary substantially in the penalties they can impose on employers, with the EPA capable of imposing large fines and OSHA only small ones. They also vary substantially in the legal implications of the fines they impose, with the EPA violations treated as felonies and OSHA violations treated as misdemeanors. For this reason, the Justice Department is much more likely to pursue criminal prosecution of EPA violations than it is to pursue OSHA viola-tions, even though the OSHA violations are more likely to involve human injury and loss of life (Steinzor, 2014).

Those who study wrongdoing in and by organizations often proceed as if the line sep-arating right from wrong is etched in concrete and marked with bright red ink. But as this discussion indicates, the line varies in loca-tion over time and space, and can be difficult to discern. The crucial role that institutions play in delineating the line separating right from wrong is not just a matter of academic interest. The perpetrators of behavior at risk of being labeled as wrongful must take this fact into account if they wish to avoid detec-tion and punishment. And those who seek to control the perpetrators of behavior at risk of being labeled as wrongful must take this fact into account if they wish to collar those they consider wrongdoers. Further, members of society need to take this fact into account if they wish to curtail behavior that they find abhorrent. It sometimes happens that the per-petrators of behavior widely considered to be abhorrent go undetected and unpunished, because elements of the regulative pillar do not focus on them. To offer an extreme example, military contractors in Iraq enjoyed considerable leeway in the killing of Iraqi civilians simply because the contractors were under the sole jurisdiction of the Coalition Provisional Government established by the invading US forces, which stipulated very few rules regulating their behavior. In this context, contractor employees conformed to what they called 'big boy rules', which constrained them from engaging in only those behaviors that might endanger their fellow contract employees (Fainaru, 2008).[6]

KNOWLEDGE OF THE INSTITUTIONAL ENVIRONMENT CAN ENABLE WRONGDOERS

Finally, not much appreciated by scholars but likely well recognized by those charged with defending institutions, individuals and organizations prone to engage in wrongdoing often use their knowledge of the institutional environment as a resource. In all societies, economic exchange is facilitated by the social relationships in which exchange partners are embedded (Granovetter, 1985). These social relationships, which include acquaintance, friendship and stronger bonds, allow actors to develop reputations for being trustworthy; that is, for being persons or organizations that can be counted on to adhere to the norms of exchange in force in a particular time and place (Yenkey, 2016). They also allow other actors to monitor and discipline exchange partners when they violate shared norms of exchange, where discipline can at a minimum entail the loss of reputation and at a maximum can constitute exclusion from future exchanges. Ironically, the social relationships that facilitate economic exchange simultaneously create opportunities for malfeasance. When actors are tied to and thus trusted by one another, each actor has the opportunity to take advantage of the other actor's trust. Specifically, social ties allow actors to deceive one another, because tie partners are less likely to seek independent verification of one another's representations (Granovetter, 1985). Further, when an actor's tie to an exchange partner is strong, (i.e., characterized by frequent and intimate interaction), his/her opportunity to take advantage of his/her transaction partner is enhanced (Brass et al., 1998).

Persons engaged in organizational wrongdoing often use their implicit understanding of the ways in which social relationships facilitate trust between exchange partners to orchestrate their wrongdoing (Palmer and Moore, 2016). For example, Barry Minkow, who organized a phony investment scheme in connection with his ZZZZ Best carpet cleaning business, recruited investors from among his friends and acquaintances, and from among those associates' friends and acquaintances. Further, he strengthened his ties to the recruited investors over time, by arranging social occasions at which they could intimately interact. Finally, Minkow maintained that he was a personal friend of Apple Computer Company's founder Steve Jobs, a bogus claim that was never challenged, to provide prospective and current investors with the false sense of security that Minkow's actions were subject to the monitoring and discipline of an important third party (Domanick, 1991).

In modern societies, institutions supplement social relationships as facilitators of trust between exchange partners. These institutions, which include regulative, normative and cognitive structures as well as logics, when observed, legitimize the behavior of actors that are parties to exchanges, providing assurance that the behavior conforms to shared understandings of the distinction between right and wrong in a particular time and place. Perhaps most importantly, where regulative institutions are robust, enforcement consisting of economic penalties (e.g., fines) and criminal prosecution (e.g., jail sentences) are in place. Institutions arise to supplement social relationships as facilitators of economic exchange in modern societies because exchange is increasingly impersonal; that is, exchange increasingly links actors who lack intimate knowledge of one another (North, 1991). With this said, institutions never completely supplant social relationships in the regulation of market exchange. Typically, the two work side by side to insure that actors do not deviate from accepted practice.

Put simply, social relationships and institutions create trust that allows actors to embark on exchange with others.

Knowledge of the ways in which institutions facilitate trust between exchange partners, like knowledge of the ways social relationships can facilitate trust, can be used to orchestrate wrongdoing. While the old sociological institutionalism implicitly assumed that conformity to the institutional environment ensured that organizations behave in ways that are considered legitimate by society, the new sociological institutionalism allows that conformity can be symbolic rather than substantive. When this is the case, the structures and processes organizations adopt in conformity to institutional rules are only loosely coupled to their actual operating procedures. In its benign form, such symbolic conformity is cynical. In its malignant form, it is strategic. That symbolic conformity to institutional rules can facilitate wrongdoing is particularly evident in the case of accounting fraud. Accounting fraudsters often create false but rule-conforming accounting documents, reports that conform to Generally Accepted Accounting Principles, in order to mislead investors and in so doing obtain stakeholder support (e.g., in the form of investor loyalty and bank loans) that they otherwise might not obtain. The creation of false accounting documents is considered so essential for the perpetration of financial fraud that it is considered a crime in and of itself, independent of the misdirection it accomplishes.

Knowledge of the ways institutions facilitate trust between exchange partners can be used to facilitate wrongdoing in other ways as well. Institutions often stipulate that organizations establish formal relationships with other organizations that are charged with the verification of the organization's integrity. In modern societies, these other organizations, which include law and accounting firms, function according to professional codes and themselves are subject to the certification of professional bodies. Organizations that can

engineer relationships that appear to conform to institutional prescriptions, but that are in fact corrupt in one way or another, are in a superior position to engage in wrongdoing. For example, Parmalat was able to sustain its fraud for so many years partly because its prestigious and trusted accounting firms provided their stamp of approval (Gabbioneta et al., 2013).

Wrongdoers can also enhance their ability to engage in wrongdoing by faking conformity to institutionalized practices. Organizations that enact practices that appear to conform to institutional prescriptions, but that in fact fail to do so, are the beneficiaries of misplaced trust and reduced scrutiny that can be exploited for the purpose of reaping ill-gotten gains. For example, large firms sometimes simulate adoption of stock buyback programs that are believed to constitute good governance practice, by publically announcing plans to buyback large blocks of their outstanding shares but discretely failing to fulfill their stated course of action (Fiss and Zajac, 2004). If institutional economists are correct, such simulated conformity to good governance practices should provide top management with the trust (and associated reduced scrutiny) of stockholders and other key stakeholders such as financial institutions and thus with enhanced opportunities to engage in wrongdoing.

The historical evolution of the bases of trust in economic exchange and hence the strategy that wrongdoers use to exploit such trust are well illustrated by a comparison of financial fraud in 18th-century England and the contemporary United States. People who sought to defraud investors in 18th-century England (such as the promoters of the South Sea Corporation) manufactured lies to prospective investors, surrounded those investors with others who possessed information that reinforced their misrepresentations, and insulated them from those who possessed information that might disconfirm their claims and reveal their deceits. But today people who seek to defraud investors must falsify documentation such as accounting records, which did not exist in 18th-century England. This temporal progression of bases of trust and technologies of wrongdoing can also be observed on a more compressed time scale. While Barry Minkow embarked on his fraudulent investment scheme by tapping his social network, he expanded his fraudulent enterprise by creating elaborate institutional practices and associations. Minkow hired a full-time assistant to prepare entirely bogus accounting records. And he embarked on deceptions that brought him endorsements from a prestigious investment bank and law firm that oversaw ZZZZ Best's public stock offering, just before the scheme collapsed.[7]

In short, successful pursuit of illegitimate behavior requires intimate knowledge of the types of institutionalized structures, relationships and practices that lead others to view a wrongdoer as a legitimate actor. For this reason, those who seek to control wrongdoing aver to develop the expertise to uncover these deceptions. Indeed, the development of the audit profession and more recently forensic accounting were motivated by just this concern.

WHAT ARE THE SOURCES OF INSTITUTIONAL CHANGE?

If institutions and organizational wrongdoing are intimately related, as the above discussion suggests, then one must consider the sources of institutional change if one wishes to develop a comprehensive understanding of the causes of organizational wrongdoing. There is much theory in economics and sociology on the origins of institutional change. Here I discuss only aspects of this theory that pertain to organizational wrongdoing.

Institutional change is often characterized as an evolutionary phenomenon. In some evolutionary perspectives, functional imperatives play a crucial role in institutional change. This is the case with institutional

economics explanations, in which endogenous factors (such as initial conditions and path dependence) and exogenous developments (such as economic or technological innovations) jointly determine change. In one variant of this view, inexorable economic or technological innovation generates problems that threaten to rend the economic order. And institutions evolve to solve these problems and restore system equilibrium. Thus, as outlined above, economists who study the emergence of the joint stock corporation believe this organizational form was a response to the growing size and scope of economic enterprise. But they maintain that the emergence of this new form gave rise to the separation of ownership and control, which created new problems of organizational governance; namely, increased incentives and opportunities for managers to behave opportunistically vis-à-vis the firm's owners. And following the evolutionary logic, they contend that these problems laid the foundation for the development of the multi-divisional form variant of the corporation, the design of which serves to hold top management opportunism in check (Chandler, 1962).

When viewed from an analytical distance as above, evolutionary institutional change driven by functional imperatives appears to be smooth and unproblematic. When viewed up close, though, it can be seen to proceed in fits and starts. For example, the creation of the Internet facilitated communication and resource sharing between scientists. But it also created new opportunities to engage in wrongdoing, such as the unauthorized access to computers that the Internet linked – in popular terminology, 'hacking'. In the early years of the Internet, there were very few laws that distinguished between acceptable and unacceptable access to the Internet. Further, there were no formally constituted entities authorized to police access to the network. Thus, when system administrators at a handful of university computing centers discovered the first hackers in the early 1980s, they struggled mightily and with uneven success to enlist the help of the law enforcement community, which included the local police, FBI, CIA, NSA and even the armed forces, whose computers were among those compromised (Stoll, 1989). Since this time, though, a body of law related to computer security, an enforcement apparatus dedicated to policing that law, and a profession dedicated to information technology governance have emerged and proliferated.

In other evolutionary perspectives, functional imperatives do not play a significant role in institutional change. This is the case with new institutional theory, which portrays the world system as progressively adopting institutions considered rational and antithetical to corruption. This outlook derives its inspiration from Weber's (2001 [1930]) analysis of the Protestant ethic, which culminated in the prediction that modern society would evolve increasingly stringent constraints on human agency that he likened to an 'iron cage'. This view is well represented by Drori, Yong and Meyer's (2006) analysis of the cross-national diffusion of reforms designed to increase conformity in economic and political behavior to universalistic standards believed to be associated with efficiency and effectiveness. Drori and her associates showed that countries most thoroughly integrated into the peak organizations of the world economic system were most likely to adopt governance reforms of this type. The fact that this evolutionary process is far from smooth is evident in the emergence in recent years of charismatic and religious political movements that aspire to statehood, such as ISIS/Daesh, that have successfully undermined political regimes that had embraced 'rational' governance reforms.

Alternatively, institutional change can be considered an agentic process, in which actors' interests and power play key roles, albeit conditioned by institutional structures. The institutional logics perspective is unique among institutional theories in its explicit consideration of human agency, interests and power. Thornton et al. (2012) have elaborated

a theory in which actors dubbed institutional entrepreneurs pursue institutional change motivated by interests and enabled by power, but conditioned by the existing institutional context. They maintain that institutional entrepreneurs' prior exposure to unique combinations of institutional logics simultaneously conditions their outlooks and provides them with resources to pursue their goals. While Thornton and associates do not employ their theory to explain the emergence of institutional frameworks related to organizational wrongdoing, one can imagine how they might.

For example, Thornton and associates (2012) illustrate their theory of institutional change by analyzing how the public university professor John Sperling came to develop a new institutional form in the field of higher education. They maintain that Sperling's unique background as the son of Southern sharecroppers and later an organizer in a radical trade union, which in the institutional logics perspective constituted 'vertical specialization within and horizontal generalization across institutional orders', allowed him to both recognize the needs of adults seeking practical courses of higher education organized in ways that accommodated their work and family demands, and envision the institution arrangements that could satisfy those needs. Further, they contend that Sperling used this awareness and understanding to found the for-profit non-residential University of Phoenix and in the process created a new niche in the higher education market into which other enterprises such as Corinthian College quickly followed. In the language of the institutional logics perspective, the creation of this new form amounted to 'segregating (the dominant form in higher education) from the logics of the professions and blending the logics of the corporation and the market'. But recently colleges embracing this new institutional form, including the University of Phoenix itself, have become the target of regulators contending that colleges adopting this new form are guilty of a variety of frauds, including false advertising regarding student job placement rates, predatory lending and abusive debt-collection tactics (Lobosco, 2015). While Thornton and associates (2012) did not anticipate it, apparently this new institutional form is prone to these sorts of wrongdoing.[8]

Misangyi and associates (2008) have explicated how the institutional logics perspective might be mined to develop a recipe for eradicating wrongdoing in and by organizations. They maintain that institutional entrepreneurs can articulate and embed identities, roles, schemas and rules that are antithetical to corruption. However, in order to do so they must craft their anti-corruption institutional logics out of institutional material (e.g., schemas and symbols) considered legitimate by the existing dominant institutional order. Further, they must marshal social, political and economic resources to overcome entrenched interests. Finally, they must insure that the new anti-corruption logic is instituted substantively (i.e., with respect to actual practices) as well as symbolically (i.e., with respect to meanings), because loose coupling is an ever-present danger in institutional change efforts.

Of course, there are multiple non-institutional theories that also can explain institutional change. Elsewhere I have argued that the location of the line separating right from wrong in the regulative pillar of the institutional system is best considered the product of political conflict among collectivities (social classes and/or interest groups) in society and between these collectivities and the state (Palmer, 2013). Different collectivities, as well as the state, have different interests and capacities that largely determine the outcome of the political struggle at any moment in history. However, collectivities sometimes organize social movements to express their interests and translate their power into influence. Further, the relationship between collectivities and social movements on the one hand and the state on the other hand, is often mediated by media organizations that

transform newsworthy events into scandals. Perhaps in recognition of this dynamic, management theorists have recently turned their attention to developing theory about social movements (Davis et al., 2005) and media-induced scandals (Graffin et al., 2013; Clemente et al., 2016).

The way that political conflict of the sort described above shapes institutional change is well illustrated by the transformation of institutions regulating workplace safety in the United States. Labor and employer organizations waged war over workplace safety as early as the late 19th century. Labor won an important battle in this war in 1970 when the US congress passed the Occupational Safety and Health Act, which created a body of workplace safety statutes and an agency to enforce them. But the victory was partial. Politically conservative states that championed employers' interests ensured that the legislation left states the option to implement their own locally controlled OSHA plan, referred to as a 'state plan'. And as expected, these politically conservative states were most likely to avail themselves of this option, and in so doing implemented less stringent workplace protections. This aspect of the legislation influences where the line separating right from wrong is drawn when it comes to regulating an organization's behavior.

For example, OSHA law dictates that when firms with 10 or more employees experience an accident involving a fatality, an OSHA representative must conduct an investigation of the event. The violations assessed and the fines levied by OSHA against the employer are partly the product of a political contest between the employer and the dead worker's representatives, which in the case of organized workplaces includes the worker's union. But the institutional context in which the actors are situated conditions this contest. Most consequential, when OSHA investigators arrive at the scene of an accident, they have the option of conducting a partial inspection of the work site, confined to the immediate area where the accident occurred, or a complete inspection of the work site, expanded to areas that extend beyond the immediate area where the accident occurred. Not surprisingly, OSHA investigators identify fewer violations that lead to lower fines when they conduct partial inspections of the work site where an accident occurs than when they conduct complete inspections. And OHSA investigators are more likely to conduct partial inspections of a work site when the accident occurs in a state plan state. Ultimately, this can influence whether an employer is forced to pay hundreds of thousands of dollars in fines for the death of an employee or only a few hundred (Palmer, 2014).

CONCLUSION

I have argued that institutions, variably conceptualized and theorized, are intertwined with wrongdoing in and by organizations in at least six ways. Institutions can suppress wrongdoing when they are robust. But they can countenance it when they are weak. Further, institutions can be conducive to wrongdoing, such as when they embody contradictory tendencies (e.g., intense achievement aspirations in the context of limited mobility chances) or when they give rise to conditions that motivate wrongdoing (e.g., performance strain). In addition, institutions can sustain wrongdoing by incorporating it in the normal functioning of an organization or a field, regardless of the factors that might have given rise to the wrongdoing in the first place. More fundamentally, institutions determine where the line separating right from wrong is drawn, and in so doing influence the amount and nature of wrongdoing in any given time or place. Finally, actors can use their understanding of the ways in which institutions are believed to suppress wrongdoing to facilitate their pursuit of wrongdoing.

My analysis holds three implications for the analysis of organizational wrongdoing

and organizational behavior more generally. First, my analysis implies that scholars seeking to develop a comprehensive understanding of the relationship between institutions and organizational wrongdoing should consider the full range of institutional theories in use, rather than confine themselves to a favored theoretical approach, such as the new institutional view or the institutional logics perspective. For example, I have argued that several varieties of institutional theory can be marshaled to understand the ways in which institutions suppress wrongdoing. Economic institutionalism explicitly maintains that robust institutions curb wrongdoing so that economic actors can interact efficiently. The old sociological institutionalism implicitly assumes that robust institutions quash wrongdoing in order to integrate organizations into the larger social fabric of shared values, beliefs and norms. The new sociological institutionalism implies that robust institutions limit wrongdoing in order to allow actors to obtain legitimacy in the eyes of key constituencies, if not economic efficiency and functional social integration. Further, within the new institutionalism, there are competing teleological and non-teleological assumptions about the direction that institutional evolution tends to take. Failure to take each of these different perspectives into account forgoes the opportunity to develop a thorough understanding of how institutions can suppress wrongdoing in and by organizations.

Second, my analysis implies that scholars seeking to develop a comprehensive understanding of the causes of organizational wrongdoing should pay more attention to the ways in which institutions draw the line separating right from wrong in particular times and places. I argue that even when institutions do not affect an actor's propensity to engage in behavior that crosses the line separating right from wrong, they affect the extent to which social control agents will label their behavior as wrongful and them as wrongdoers. This fundamental aspect of the relationship between institutions and organizational wrongdoing tends to be ignored or treated as a methodological inconvenience by most who study wrongdoing in and by organizations. For example, most micro-organizational behavior researchers define wrongful behavior in general terms, as behavior that violates ethical principles or social norms. They then proceed to study behaviors that they implicitly assume most readers would consider unethical or socially deviant, such as cheating or lying. This ignores the fact that many of the behaviors they study are considered ethical and socially acceptable in many organizations much of the time. For example, organizational participants frequently misrepresent the truth, partly because lying increases the efficiency and effectiveness of organizational functioning (Shulman, 2007).

Similarly, most macro-organization theory researchers define wrongdoing as behavior that violates administrative or legal rules. They then proceed to study behaviors that have been sanctioned by administrative or legal entities. Many macro researchers acknowledge that administrative or legal entities do not sanction all rule-violating behaviors and rule violators and may be biased in the extent to which they identify wrongdoing and wrongdoers. But macro researchers treat this variation as a methodological problem; specifically, as resulting in an incomplete or biased identification of wrongdoing. This ignores a crucial aspect of the social process that generates the data they study, the labeling of behaviors as wrongful and perpetrators as wrongdoers. Expressed in the affirmative, this chapter suggests that a focus on institutions allows theorists and researchers to problematize an important dimension of organizational wrongdoing, the process by which behavior comes to be considered wrongful. In so doing, it allows researchers to ask why specific behaviors are characterized as wrongdoing in particular historical moments and places, and how this influences the amount

and type of wrongdoing that can be found in those moments and places.

Finally, my analysis implicitly calls into question the dominant theoretical objective motivating research in organization studies today: the formulation and evaluation of hypotheses that hold true across historical time and geo-political space. Academic journal editors and reviewers promote this objective when they exhort authors to formulate abstract hypotheses and restrict all discussion of historically and situationally specific processes to the methods section of papers. For example, in Graffin and associates' (2013) excellent journal article on the 2009 British Members of Parliament expenses scandal, the authors formulate abstract hypotheses about the way in which elite status, wrongdoing and scandalization interacted to influence elite punishment. For the most part the authors relegate consideration of the unique historical (contemporary) and national (United Kingdom) context of their study and the conceptualization of key explanatory variables – elite status (official title), wrongdoing (expense fraud), scandalization (media coverage) and punishment (failure to achieve re-election) – to the methods section of the paper.

I suspect that the ways in which elite status, wrongdoing and scandalization interact to influence elite punishment is highly dependent on the institutional context in which these constructs materialize. Thus, the appropriate conceptualization and associated measurement of these constructs, which hinges on the institutional context, is not a subordinate technical matter. My preliminary investigation into the South Sea Bubble suggests that the way in which elite status, wrongdoing and scandalization interacted to influence the punishment of South Sea Corporation directors in 18th-century England was much different than the way in which elite status, wrongdoing and scandalization interacted to influence the punishment of British MPs in the contemporary UK.

Clearly, there is much that remains to be done with respect to developing a comprehensive understanding of the relationship between institutions and wrongdoing. I hope this chapter provides a foundation for future work along these lines.

Notes

1   For recent literature reviews of theory on organizational wrongdoing at the micro level see Tenbrunsel and Smith-Crowe (2008) and at the macro level see Greve, Palmer and Pozner (2010).
2   For an excellent institutional analysis of wrongdoing in the political sphere, see Scott (1972).
3   There is a raft of research that suggests that organizational structures and practices conform to institutional prescriptions promulgated by coercive, normative and mimetic pressures emanating from the environment (cf., Palmer et al., 1993). Further, Deephouse (1996) has shown that conformity to institutionalized prescriptions leads to legitimacy. Finally, numerous studies suggest that institutional embeddedness enhances an organization's life chances (cf., Baum and Oliver, 1991, 1992).
4   In a related quantitative empirical study, Mohliver (2012) shows that firms are more likely to engage in stock option backdating when they contract for auditing services with accounting firms whose local offices provide auditing services to other firms that previously engaged in backdating. He argues that accounting firms whose clients engage in stock option backdating gain expertise in this form of wrongdoing and subsequently transfer this knowledge to their other clients interested in getting in on the game.
5   Interestingly, there is one similarity between 21st-century United States and 18th-century England in regards to meting out punishments in the wake of economic wrongdoing. In both times and places, the allocation of punishments is/was informed by consideration of the impact that the punishment might have on the national and world economy. Informed partly by a memo written in 1999 by then Deputy Attorney-General Eric Holder, the US Justice Department implemented what has come to be known as the 'too big to fail' policy in the wake of the 2008 financial crisis. According to this policy, the punishment inflicted on the institutions believed to have been at the center of the crisis was crafted to preserve these institutions' financial viability so as to avoid 'collateral consequences' that would eventuate were the institutions to enter bankruptcy. In some cases, the government facilitated the acquisition of presumed wrongdoers,

as was the case with Countrywide Financial. In other cases, the government bailed out the presumed wrongdoer, as was the case with American International Group (Taibbi, 2014). A similar logic informed the punishment of the South Sea Corporation's directors in 18th-century England. When calculating the extent of each director's wealth that was to be confiscated, a portion of which was to be returned as an allowance, Parliament first deducted the director's liabilities. This procedure was motivated by the desire to reduce the likelihood that a director's punishment would impair their ability to meet their obligations to other businesses and thus the likelihood that the collective punishment would generate negative externalities that would ripple throughout the world economy. This had the effect of privileging those directors who were members of the emerging mercantile capitalist class, whose wealth derived from trade and manufacture, over those directors who were members of the traditional landed gentry, whose wealth derived from land ownership.

6   The military contractors did not, though, enjoy complete leeway in the killing of Iraqi civilians, a fact attested to by the recent convictions in the case of the Nisoor Square massacre outside of Baghdad.
7   Gabbioneta and associates (2013) suggest that a similar evolution of techniques underpinned the Parmalat fraud, which was sustained over two decades. Parmalat's CEO Calisto Tanzi was a well-connected figure in the Italian business community, eventually achieving celebrity status within Italian society more generally. Gabbioneta and associates contend that Tanzi's connections and status insulated him and his firm from close scrutiny by key actors in the institutional environment who bestowed legitimacy on Tanzi and Parmalat. But at the same time, Parmalat's financial executives established relationships with key institutional actors who helped them fabricate legitimate-looking accounting reports.
8   A similar analysis could be applied to Jeff Skilling and his tenure at Enron Corporation. His unique background as a McKinsey consultant and his location in an era of deregulation could be referenced to explain why he was able to chart the firm's transition from a natural gas producer and distributor to a natural gas trader, to characterize this new organizational form as a 'gas bank', and then use this characterization to convince the US Securities and Exchange Commission to allow Enron to adopt mark-to-mark accounting (a type of accounting often employed by investment banks, but seldom used by industrial firms). Many observers contend that the adoption of

mark-to-mark accounting provided Enron with both the motivation and capacity to engage in the financial fraud that eventually did the company in.

REFERENCES

Abbott, A. (1988). *The System of Professions: An Essay on the Division of Expert Labor*. Chicago, IL: University of Chicago Press.

Agnew, R., Piquero, N. and Cullen F.T. (2009). General strain theory and white-collar crime. In S. Simpson and D. Weisburd (eds), *The Criminology of White-Collar Crime*. New York: Springer. pp. 35–60.

Ashforth, B.E. and Anand, V. (2003). The normalization of corruption in organizations. *Research in Organizational Behavior*, 25: 1–52.

Baum, Joel A.C. and Oliver, Christine (1991). Institutional linkages and organizational mortality. *Administrative Science Quarterly*, 36(2): 187–218.

Baum, Joel A.C. and Oliver, Christine (1992). Institutional embeddedness and the dynamics of organizational populations. *American Sociological Review*, 57(4): 540–559.

Berger, Peter and Luckmann, Thomas (1966). *The Social Construction of Reality*. New York: Anchor Books.

Berle, A.A. and Means, G.C. (1932). *The Modern Corporation and Private Property*. New York: Macmillan.

Braithwaite, J. (1988). White-collar crime, competition, and capitalism: Comment on Coleman. *American Journal of Sociology*, 94 (3): 627–632.

Brass, D.J., Butterfield, K.D. and Skaggs, B.C. (1998). Relationships and unethical behavior: A social network perspective. *Academy of Management Review*, 23(1): 14–31.

Brief, A.P., Bertram, R.T. and Dukerich, J.M. (2001). Collective corruption in the corporate world: Toward a process model. In M.E. Turner (ed.), *Groups at Work: Advances in Theory and Research*. Hillsdale, NJ: Lawrence Erlbaum and Associates. pp. 471–499.

Carswell, J. (2001). *The South Sea Bubble*. Gloucestershire: Sutton Publishing.

Chandler, A.D. Jr (1962). *Strategy and Structure*. Cambridge, MA: MIT Press.

Chandler, A.D. Jr (1980). *Managerial Hierarchies: Comparative Perspectives on the Rise of the Modern Industrial Enterprise*. Cambridge, MA: Harvard University Press.

Clemente, M., Durand, R. and Porac, J. (2016). Organizational wrongdoing and media bias. In D. Palmer, K. Smith-Crow and R. Greenwood (eds), *Organizational Wrongdoing: Key Perspectives and New Directions*. Cambridge: Cambridge University Press. pp.435–473.

Coleman, J.W. (1987). Toward and integrated theory of white-collar crime. *American Journal of Sociology*, 93(2): 406–439.

Coleman, J.W. (1988). Competition and the structure of industrial society: Reply to Braithwaite. *American Journal of Sociology*, 94(3): 632–636.

Dalton, D.R., Hitt, M.A., Certo, S.T. and Dalton, C.M. (2007). The fundamental agency problem and its mitigation: Independence, equity, and the market for corporate control. *Academy of Management Annals*, 1(1): 1–64.

Davis, G., McAdam, D., Scott, W.R. and Zald, M.N. (2005). *Social Movements and Organization Theory*. Cambridge: Cambridge University Press.

Deephouse, David (1996). Does isomorphism legitimate? *Academy of Management Journal*, 39(4): 1024–1039.

Denyer, S. (2015). Without corruption, some ask, can the Chinese Communist Party function? *The Washington Post*, 11 February. www.washingtonpost.com/world/asia_pacific/without-corruption-some-ask-can-the-chinese-communist-party-function/2015/02/10/69693e8-b12f-11e4-bf39-5560f3918d4b_story.html [Accessed 02/12/2016].

DiMaggio, P.J. and Powell, W.W. (1983). The iron cage revisited: Institutional isomorphism and collective rationality in organizational fields. *American Sociological Review*, 48(2): 147–160.

Domanick, J. (1991). *Faking it in America*. New York: Knightsbridge Publishing.

Dowie, M. (1977). How Ford put two million firetraps on wheels. *Business and Society Review*, 23: 46–55.

Drori, Gili, Yong Suk Jang and Meyer, John W. (2006). Sources of rationalized governance: Cross-national longitudinal analyses, 1985–2002. *Administrative Science Quarterly*, 51(2): 205–229.

Durkheim, E. (1997). *Suicide*. New York: The Free Press.

Eichenwald, K. (2005). *Conspiracy of Fools: A True Story*. New York: Broadway Books.

Fainaru, S. (2008). *Big Boy Rules*. Philadelphia, PA: Da Capo Press.

Fama, E.F. (1980). Agency problems and the theory of the firm. *Journal of Political Economy*, 88(2): 288–307.

Fama, E.F. and Jensen, M.C. (1983). The separation of ownership and control. *Journal of Law and Economics*, 26(2): 301–325.

Fisman, R. and Miguel, E. (2007). Corruption, norms, and legal environment: Evidence from diplomatic parking tickets. *Journal of Political Economy*, 115(61): 1020–1048.

Fiss, P.C. and Zajac, E.J. (2004). The diffusion of ideas over contested terrain: The (non) adoption of a shareholder value orientation among German firms. *Administrative Science Quarterly*, 49(4): 501–534.

Gabbioneta, C., Greenwood, R., Mazzola, P. and Minoja, M. (2013). The influence of institutional context on corporate illegality. *Accounting, Organizations, and Society*, 38(6–7): 484–504.

Gioia, D.A. (1992). Pinto fires and personal ethics: A script analysis of missed opportunities. *Journal of Business Ethics*, 11(5–6): 379–389.

Graffin, S.D., Bundy, J., Porac, J.F., Wade, J.B. and Quinn, D.P. (2013). Falls from grace and the hazards of high status: The 2009 British MP expense scandal and its impact on Parliamentary elites. *Administrative Science Quarterly*, 58(3): 313–345.

Granovetter, M.S. (1985). Economic action and social structure: The problem of embeddedness. *American Journal of Sociology*, 91(3): 481–493.

Granovetter, M.S. (2007). The social construction of corruption. In Nee V. and Swedberg R. (eds), *On Capitalism*. Stanford, CA: Stanford University Press. pp. 152–172.

Greve, H.R., Palmer, D. and Pozner, J.E. (2010). Organizations gone wild: The causes, processes, and consequences of organizational wrongdoing. *Academy of Management Annals*, 4(1): 53–108.

Gusfeld, J.L. (1955). Social structure and moral reform: A study of Women's Christian Temperance Union. *American Journal of Sociology*, 61(3): 221–232.

Hamilton, T. and Coyle, D. (2012). *The Secret Race*. New York: Bantam Books.

Harris, E., Petrovits, C. and Yetman, M. (2015). Why bad things happen to good organizations: The link between governance and asset diversions in public charities. https://papers.ssrn.com/sol3/papers.cfm?abstract_id=2604372 [Accessed 02/12/2016].

Hillman, A.J. and Dalziel, T. (2003). Boards of directors and firm performance: Integrating agency and resource dependence perspectives. *Academy of Management Review*, 28(3): 383–396.

Hirsch, P.M. (1975). Organizational effectiveness and the institutional environment. *Administrative Science Quarterly*, 20(3): 327–344.

Hodgson, G.M. (1998). The approach of institutional economics. *Journal of Economic Literature*, 36(1): 166–192.

Jackall, R.J. (1983). Moral mazes: Bureaucracy and managerial work. *Harvard Business Review*, 61(5): 118–130.

Jackall, R.J. (1984). The moral ethos of bureaucracy. *State Culture and Society*, 1(1): 176–200.

Jackall, R.J. (1988). *Moral Mazes: The World of Corporate Managers*. Oxford: Oxford University Press.

Kraatz, M.S. and Zajac, E.J. (1996). Exploring the limits of the New Institutionalism: The causes and consequences of illegitimate organizational change. *American Sociological Review*, 61(5): 812–836.

Lev, M. (1990). Hazelwood's acquittal clouds the Exxon case. *New York Times*, 28 March. www.nytimes.com/1990/03/28/us/hazelwood-s-acquittal-clouds-the-exxon-case.html [Accessed 02/12/2016].

Lobosco, K. (2015). University of Phoenix is the latest college under investigation. *CNNMoney*. http://money.cnn.com/2015/07/29/pf/college/university-of-phoenix-investigation/ [Accessed 02/12/2016].

Merton, R.K. (1938). Social structure and anomie. *American Sociological Review*, 3(5): 672–682.

Messner, S.E., Thome, H. and Rosenfeld, R. (2008). Institutions, anomie, and violent crime: Clarifying and elaborating institutional anomie theory. *International Journal of Conflict and Violence*, 2(2): 163–181.

Meyer, J.W. and Rowan, B. (1977). Institutionalized organizations: Formal structure as myth and ceremony. *American Journal of Sociology*, 83(2): 340–363.

Millar, D. and Whittle, J. (2011). *Racing Through the Dark: The Fall and Rise of David Millar*. London: Orion Books.

Mishina, Y., Dykes, B.J., Block, E.S. and Pollock, T.G. (2010). Why 'good' firms do bad things: The effects of high aspirations, high expectations and prominence on the incidence of corporate illegality. *Academy of Management Journal*, 53(4): 701–722.

Moe, T. (1990). Political institutions: The neglected side of the story. *Journal of Law, Economics, and Organization*, 6(April): 213–253.

Mohliver, A.C. (2012). The legitimacy of corrupt practices: Geography of auditors advice and backdating of stock option grants. Paper presented at the Academy of Management Annual Meeting, Boston, MA.

Misangyi, V., Weaver, G.R. and Elms, H. (2008). Ending corruption: The interplay among institutional logics, resources, and institutional entrepreneurs. *Academy of Management Review*, 33(3): 750–770.

Muzio, D., Falconbridge, J., Gabbioneta, C. and Greenwood, R. (2016). Bad apples, bad barrels, and bad cellars: A 'boundaries' perspective on professional wrongdoing. In D. Palmer, K. Smith-Crowe and R. Greenwood (eds), *Organizational Wrongdoing: Key Perspectives and New Directions*. Cambridge: Cambridge University Press. pp. 141–175.

North, D. (1991). Institutions. *Journal of Economic Perspectives*, 5(1): 97–112.

Orru, Marco, Woolsey Biggart, Nicole and Hamilton, Gary G. (1997). *The Economic Organization of East Asian Capitalism*. Thousand Oaks, CA: Sage.

Palmer, D. (2008). Extending the process model of collective organizational wrongdoing. *Research in Organizational Behavior*, 28: 107–135.

Palmer, D. (2013). *Normal Organizational Wrongdoing: A Critical Analysis of Theories of Wrongdoing in and by Organizations*. Oxford: Oxford University Press.

Palmer, D. (2014). The politics of right and wrong. Presented at the Annual Meeting of the Academy of Management, Vancouver, Canada.

Palmer, D. Jennings, P. D., and Zhou, X. (1993). Late adoption of the multidivisional form. *Administrative Science Quarterly*, 37: 100–131.

Palmer, D and Moore, C. (2016). Social networks and organizational wrongdoing in context. In D. Palmer, K. Smith-Crowe and R. Greenwood (eds), *Organizational Wrongdoing: Key Perspectives and New Directions*. Cambridge: Cambridge University Press. pp. 203–234.

Palmer, D. & Yenkey, C. (2015). Drugs, sweat and gears: An organizational analysis of performance enhancing drug use in the 2010 Tour de France. *Social Forces*, 94(2): 891–922.

Parsons, Talcott. (1956a). Suggestions for a sociological approach to the theory of organizations. I. *Administrative Science Quarterly*, 1(1): 63–85.

Parsons, Talcott. (1956b). Suggestions for a sociological approach to the theory of organizations. II. *Administrative Science Quarterly*, 1(2): 225–239.

Peasnell, K.V., Pope, P.F. and Young, S. (2005). Board monitoring and earnings management: Do outside directors influence abnormal accruals? *Journal of Business Finance & Accounting*, 32(7–8): 1311–1346.

Pfeffer, Jeffrey and Salancik, Gerald R. (1978). *The External Control of Organizations: A Resource Dependence Perspective*. Stanford, CA: Stanford University Press.

Pizzo, S., Fricker, M. and Muolo, P. (1991). *Inside Job: The Looting of America's Savings and Loans*. New York: HarperCollins.

Polanyi, K. (1957). *The Great Transformation*. New York: Rinehart.

Prechel, H. and Hou, D. (2016). Corporate and state politics: Creating financial markets and the FIRE sector, 1930s–2000. In D. Palmer, K. Smith-Crow and R. Greenwood (eds), *Organizational Wrongdoing: Key Perspectives and New Directions*. Cambridge: Cambridge University Press. pp. 77–113.

Robinson, S.L. and O'Leary-Kelly, A.M. (1998). Monkey see, monkey do: The influence of work groups on the antisocial behavior of employees. *Academy of Management Journal*, 41(6): 658–672.

Rose-Ackerman, S. (2004). Governance and corruption. In Bjorn Lomborg (ed.), *Global Crises, Global Solutions*. Cambridge: Cambridge University Press. pp. 301–344.

Rosen, D.M. (2008). *Dope: A History of Performance Enhancement in Sports from the Nineteenth Century to Today*, London: Praeger.

Scott, J. (1972). *Comparative Political Corruption*. Englewood Cliffs, NJ: Prentice-Hall.

Scott, W. Richard (1987). The adolescence of institutional theory. *Administrative Science Quarterly*, 32(4): 493–511.

Scott, W. Richard. (2001). *Institutions and Organizations*, 2nd ed. Thousand Oaks, CA: Sage.

Scott, W. Richard. (2008). Approaching adulthood: The maturing of institutional theory. *Theory and Society*, 37(5): 427–442.

Shulman, D. (2007). *From Hire to Liar: The Role of Deception in the Workplace*. Ithaca, NY: ILR Press.

Simpson, S.S. (1986). The decomposition of antitrust: Testing a multilevel, longitudinal model of profit-squeeze. *American Sociological Review*, 51(6): 859–975.

Steinzor, R. (2014). *Why Not Jail?* Cambridge: Cambridge University Press.

Stinchcombe, Authur L. (1965). Social structure and organizations. In James G. March (ed.), *Handbook of Organizations*. Chicago, IL: Rand McNally. pp. 142–193.

Stoll, C. (1989). *The Cuckoo's Egg: Tracking a Spy Through the Maze of Computer Espionage*. New York: Pocket Books.

Stults, B.J. and Falco, C.S. (2014). Unbalanced institutional commitments and delinquent behavior: An individual-level assessment of institutional anomie theory. *Youth Violence and Juvenile Justice*, 12(1): 77–100.

Sutherland, E.H. (1949). *White Collar Crime*. New York: Dryden Press.

Taibbi, M. (2014). *Divide: American Injustice in the Age of the Wealth Gap*. New York: Random House.

Tenbrunsel, A.E. and Smith-Crowe, K. (2008). Ethical decision making: Where we've been and where we're going, *Academy of Management Annals*, 2(1): 545–607.

Thornton, P.H., Ocasio, W. and Lounsbury, M. (2012). *The Institutional Logics Perspective*. Oxford: Oxford University Press.

Turner, Jonathan (1997) *The Institutional Order*. New York: Longman.

Vaughan, D. (1996). *The Challenger Launch Decision: Risky Technology, Culture, and Deviance at NASA*. Chicago, IL: University of Chicago Press.

Weber, M. (2001 [1930]). *The Protestant Ethic and the Spirit of Capitalism*. London: Routledge.

Yenkey, C. (2016). Wrongdoing and market development: An examination of the distinct roles of trust and distrust. In D. Palmer, K. Smith-Crow and R. Greenwood (eds), *Organizational Wrongdoing: Key Perspectives and New Directions*. Cambridge: Cambridge University Press. pp. 114–140.

Zald, M. (1967). Urban differentiation, characteristics of boards of directors and organizational effectiveness. *American Journal of Sociology*, 73(3): 261–272.

Zald, M. (1969). The power and function of boards of directors: A theoretical synthesis. *American Journal of Sociology*, 75(1): 97–111.

29

Institutional Theory and the Natural Environment: Building Research through Tensions and Paradoxes

P. Devereaux Jennings and Andrew J. Hoffman[1]

Why should we tolerate a diet of weak poisons, a home in insipid surroundings, a circle of acquaintances who are not quite our enemies, the noise of motors with just enough relief to prevent insanity? Who would want to live in a world which is just not quite fatal? (Carson, 1962)

The focus of institutional theory is directed towards an understanding of situations such as those depicted in Rachel Carson's quote above – situations where context is strong and binding, yet subtly experienced; where agency is often diffuse, embodied in an arrangement or system of actors rather than in an individual; and where action and inaction both matter, if in often unpredictable ways. One area in which these phenomena are notably pronounced is research in the area of the interaction between institutional systems and the workings of the natural environment; the ways in which human societies both understand their interface with that environment, and the ways in which the actions of one impact the other. In this chapter, we offer an overview of that domain of research, tracing

the evolution of efforts at combining the two since its beginnings in the early 1990s, when the Greening of Industry Network initiated its environmental management research collection (1989), the Organizations and the Natural Environment special interest group of the Academy of Management was formed (1994) and the seminal Special Issue on environmental management was published in the *Academy of Management Review* (1995).

As in our other recent work (Hoffman and Jennings, 2011, 2012, 2015), we use prior reviews, a literature search and our knowledge of the field to consider past and current work in institutional theory and the natural environment (ITNE). In this chapter, we structure that inquiry around the notion that fruitful research has come from tensions – indeed, at times, paradoxes – that exist from trying to combine institutional theory with natural environment studies. Below we discuss the tensions and paradoxes inherent in ITNE work and then examine how that work has been propelled forward by these tensions, all at the ontological, epistemological and normative levels. After using this framework for examining past and present studies, we turn to a new future challenge for ITNE: combining institutional complexity research with environmental and geophysical studies in the era of the Anthropocene.

TENSIONS AND PARADOXES WITHIN INSTITUTIONAL THEORIES AND NATURAL ENVIRONMENT STUDIES

Mixing institutional theory with natural environment studies leads to both tensions and paradoxes at the level of both grand and mid-range theory development. At the grand theory level, debate and tension allow for multiple theoretical approaches to develop, while avoiding the hegemony of any particular perspective (van Maanen, 1995). Vigorous debate among multiple approaches clarifies paradigms and exposes possible new combinations among them (Westwood and Clegg, 2009). At the mid-range level, debate about concepts and their relations is fundamental to better model building, and that debate can be enhanced by having to wrestle with multiple inconsistencies (Whetten, 1989).

This debate can vary in the extent to which it poses more or less fundamental questions and concerns. Less fundamental debate centers on issues in which two grand or mid-range theories may differ, but this difference does not challenge the premises of either theory. In contrast, more fundamental debate centers on an antimony between two theories because of a paradox generated between them (Smith and Lewis, 2011), where a paradox is 'a statement or proposition that, despite sound (or apparently sound) reasoning from acceptable premises, leads to a conclusion that seems senseless, logically unacceptable, or self-contradictory' (*Oxford Advanced Learner Dictionary*, 2012).

It is just such tensions and paradoxes that expose issues around what constitutes a field

and the nature of agency. More specifically, they expose questions around the degree to which an organizational field will be indexed and aligned with the natural ecosystems in which the organizations are embedded. This is a central element that has animated ITNE studies for decades, if not centuries. In fact, some of the key paradoxes in ITNE stretch back to the *Naturwissenschaften* versus *Geisteswissenschaften* debates of 19th-century German philosophy (Ermarth, 1981; Weber, 1978 [1919]). These debates explored the extent to which humans apprehend the natural environment and generate scientific knowledge. In particular, one issue that has animated this line of inquiry is whether *Verstehen* (putting oneself in the other shoes), which is so fundamental for social science, has any equivalent in the natural sciences. This debate emerges in multiple forms, not least of which was Catton and Dunlap's (1980) New Ecological Paradigm, which called for a shift away from anthropocentric (human-centered) thinking to ecocentric (environment-centered) thinking, where humans are one of many species inhabiting the earth and institutional and social development must consider other, non-human, considerations in its trajectory.

With this as a preamble to set the foundations of our inquiry, we proceed by examining more deeply the tensions and paradoxes in ITNE at three levels of theory development: (1) the ontological, (2) the epistemological and (3) the normative. These levels are used often for discussing theory and are readily applicable here.

Tensions at the Ontological Level

Ontology is the study of the nature of being and existence. As such, ontology includes the fundamental premises about the phenomena that constitute a domain of study, their nature or status of existence, and how they relate to human or other agents.

The ontological focus of institutional theory is about the gradual, widespread acceptance of ideas and practices such that they become taken-for-granted, i.e., 'legitimated' and 'institutionalized' (DiMaggio and Powell, 1991; Meyer et al., 1985). The process and the outcome of institutionalization depend on social construction. Social construction within institutional theory has its roots in phenomenology (Schutz, 1967) and semiotics (Searle, 1979). The social order that evolves from and supports social construction processes is argued, by some, to be at least moderately functional (Berger and Luckmann, 1966), although social orders are also shaped by the many unintended outcomes of institutional processes (McCarthy and Zald, 1977; Selznick, 1949). As an aside, it is worth noting that Parsons (1967, 1968) offered a much more structural and top-down account of social order, one that was quite functional in nature. Neo-institutional thinkers, for the most part, have not followed this line of thinking.

At the heart of these foundational approaches, is the need for individuals to grapple with the uncertainty of life. Humans must face this uncertainty, but the various ways of doing so can never overcome the felt sense of separation of the self and other, and the limited nature of experienced reality. To continue to operate, according to Schutz (1967) and Berger and Luckmann (1966), individuals rely on conventions of understanding of social interaction. These conventions, such as ceremonies and rituals, bring order to the relation of self and other and create some predictability to life.

> Habitualization carries with it the important psychological gain that choices are narrowed ... the background of habitualized activity opens up a foreground for deliberation and innovation [which demand a higher level of attention] ... The most important gain is that each [member of society] will be able to predict the other's actions. Concomitantly, the interaction of both becomes predictable ... (Berger and Luckman, 1966: 53–57)

In contrast, standard environmental studies approaches (i.e., Odum and Barrett, 2004) portray the natural and human worlds as a set of nested ecosystems, with a variety of niches and carrying capacities for interdependent, biological populations. These populations evolve via reproduction, selection and evolution driven by competition and cooperation among members and across populations. The evolutionary processes within ecosystems in mainstream environmental studies are believed to be best theorized using an objective and realist approach – i.e., as 'environmental science' (Gladwin, 2012; Meadows et al., 1972).

But some branches of environmental studies have embraced a more subjective and culturally attuned approach to ecosystem evolution. These branches recognize the extreme difficulty of comprehending the complex systems in a fine-grained, enduring fashion compared to a more holistic, situated one (Bramwell, 1989; Evernden, 1985, 1992). While human ecology and human settlement branches of environmental studies have made progress in convincing other eco-scientists to recognize their claims (Young and Dhanda, 2013), their ideas have not become mainstream nor is human 'flourishing' deeply embraced by those advancing ecological sustainability in environmental studies (Ehrenfeld and Hoffman, 2013).

The social views of the natural environment within the two (objective and subjective) theories are fundamentally at odds, with the former externalizing and the latter internalizing it. As a result, the ontological standing, modes of existence and roles of humans within the natural world are quite different in each theory (Hoffman and Jennings, 2015; Jennings and Zandbergen, 1995). On these two deep issues, then, institutional theory and its inquiry of environmental studies exists within a paradox as to the true nature of the linkages between social and environmental systems. Overall, this paradox illuminates tensions that have manifested themselves around the degree of integration and joint operation of the social and biophysical sphere and around the role of agency in each.

Tensions at the Epistemological Level

Epistemology refers to the methods for studying ontologically designated phenomena; that is, for building up and using knowledge. Even though epistemology is not fully separable, analytically or practically, from ontology, its focus is more on the 'how' to conduct intellectual inquiry than around what and why one does so, which is more clearly the ken of ontology. At the epistemological level, one can further observe the tensions and paradoxes that exist between institutional theory and research on the natural environment.

Institutional theory studies the institutionalization process, which occurs through diffusion (creation, theorization, objectification and acceptance) of ideas and practices and is based on gaining and maintaining legitimacy (Suddaby and Greenwood, 2005; Greenwood et al., 2002; Powell and DiMaggio, 1991; Scott, 2001). Institutionalization occurs within and across macro and micro levels (Thornton et al., 2012) and the institutional actors, adopted ideas and practices, and social situations condition one another in ways that are often difficult to disentangle (Lawrence et al., 2011). As a result, the social scientific knowledge generated about institutional dynamics is contextualized in both a temporal and relational sense.

Natural environment studies – given their belief in nested ecosystems driven by competition and (limited) cooperation among and within populations, according to the constraints of the niches in question – have devoted significant attention to examining the mechanisms of variation, reproduction and selection. This is mirrored within studies of the ecology of human systems (Hannan and Freeman, 1977), where commensal mechanisms are also at play (Astley, 1985). At the same time, environmental and social studies seek to understand the operation of multiple ecosystems and populations at the local, regional and international levels. Climate change research, for example, has pushed environmental scientists to consider the multiple levels of planetary ecosystems, often via models of particular dimensions, such as weather, biodiversity, or forests. Similarly, social studies of environmental phenomena seek to explore the multi-level relations and interactions among human populations both in identifying environmental issues and developing solutions (Perrow, 2010).

Not surprisingly, in light of its ontology, the epistemology of environmental studies revolves around objectivist techniques to create generalizable, enduring knowledge. The lower the levels of analysis and the more closed the boundaries of the particular ecosystem, the more objective and enduring the knowledge and modeled dynamics are deemed to be. For instance, there are many studies of aquatic environments within lake and stream systems that can be used to generalize to similar ecosystems (Healey, 1999). However, in the case of certain specific species, like salmon, that migrate across ecosystem boundaries, the generalizability and predictability of these models drop off immensely (Healey, 1999).

ITNE, then, has several tensions at the epistemological level, and at least one point of paradox. These tensions arise from the ways in which systematic and multi-level data on both the biosphere and social sphere should be collected and analyzed. Where institutional theory has traditionally focused more on top-down historical studies, environmental studies have been built more by bottom-up and temporally proximate case studies of different ecological units. There is also a tension around how durable the knowledge is from these studies and how literal a translation can be made from one domain to another.

An even more fundamental paradox, however, is around the nature of human action and meaning and how it should be incorporated into the method and type of knowledge generation in each discipline: institutional theory sees meaning as a central phenomenon to encode and to use as part of its methodology, whereas environmental studies sees meaning as lodged in a different domain from methodology – that of decision-making and policy.

Tensions at the Normative Level

The normative level refers to the normative systems and moral precepts of a particular line of theorizing. Theories of both social life and the natural environment each pose moral precepts, either directly or indirectly. Some do so by incorporating within them analyses of normative systems or normative dimensions, as is often the case with social science theories, along with some criteria for evaluating these systems relative to one another (i.e., in terms of richness, diversity, mobility, etc.). Others do so by specifying the operations of systems in which phenomena are embedded, with consideration for the implications in terms of better and worse operations or outcomes (i.e., more diverse and robust ecosystems, more efficient social processes, etc.).

Natural environment studies focus on the evolution of ecosystems as well as the human systems that depend on them, with notions of balance and preservation being key criteria, along with the need for richness and diversity. This balance requires, at the very least, human stewardship (Hawken, 1993). Some have argued that to pursue the difficult task of achieving and maintaining balance, the human stewards themselves require normative or moral systems of beliefs, generally found within the domain of spirituality (Suzuki, 1997). These views about balance and the natural environment are clearly prescriptive in seeking a particular and desirable end.

Institutional theory focuses on the gradual, widespread acceptance of ideas and practices such that they become taken for granted. But institutional theory is fundamentally agnostic about the moral nature of the process and its outcomes. Furthermore, institutional theory typically looks backward and seeks to explain; it does not seek to evaluate and judge the emergence of future outcomes. Nevertheless, the outcomes bear directly on our moral sense of who we are as humans, how we relate to other humans and how we relate to the natural world. The Pope's encyclical letter *Laudato Si* (Pope Francis, 2015) has opened up this set of issues for conversation in the religious domain. Yet, institutional theory is not prepared nor fully equipped to grapple with them – particularly in any moral or religious sense (Friedland et al., 2014).

So, at the normative level, the tensions between environmental and institutional studies are evident, even though the paradoxes are less so. Both theoretical approaches agree that seeking some types of social orders over others is *not* the primary goal of theory, and each approach is relativistic about how value and action should be judged; i.e., it should be judged from the point of the view of the social order being examined or raising the issue. Yet the two theories are in disagreement about the underlying implications of theory and research for society. The subtext of most environmental studies is that the preservation of nature and the balance between the biosphere and the social sphere is critical for both human society and the natural world; whereas institutional theory is relatively silent about such claims.

HOW THESE TENSIONS HAVE INFLUENCED ITNE RESEARCH

We have argued that ontological, epistemological, and normative tensions and paradoxes animate research on institutional theory and the natural environment (ITNE). Now, we would like to turn our attention to ways in which these tensions and paradoxes enrich and guide that work. One piece of evidence for this enrichment process is the growth rates in ITNE research, as depicted by Figure 29.1.[2] We see that research in

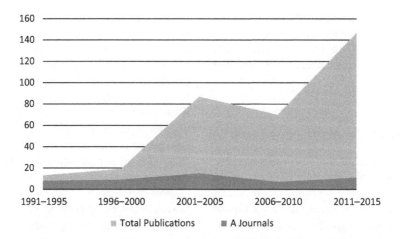

Figure 29.1   Publications rates for institutional theory and the natural environment, 1995–2015

ITNE began around 1995 and has grown steadily, though remaining fairly flat in the 'A' journals. Yet, it is also known that these 'A' journal pieces generate high citation counts and stimulate research by the wider community. This wider growth rate is reflected the number of articles on business and the natural environment in a similar time period, shown in Figure 29.2 (see Hoffman and Georg, 2013 and Hoffman and Bansal, 2012 for reviews).[3]

Embedded within these steady growth rates is the driving force of the tensions and paradoxes that have led to some of the distinctive features of ITNE research, even if they have not been resolved. The main tensions are displayed in Table 29.1 and discussed in detail below, particularly with regards to ITNE theory and empirics the tensions have helped generate

RESEARCH DIRECTIONS IN RESPONSE TO ONTOLOGICAL TENSIONS

The ontological tensions in ITNE have manifested themselves around the degree of integration and joint operation of the social and biophysical spheres and around the role

of agency in each. This leads to four topical areas where ITNE research is enriched by them: logics, triggers, social movements and institutional agents.

Logics

Originally, environmental ideas and practices were theorized and investigated as being part of the rationalization project of modern societies. Like other modern features, such as constitutions and education, ideas such as environmental stewardship and practices like ISO 14001 are part of the rationalization of all areas of human life (Meyer et al., 1997). This has been elaborated and demonstrated in David Frank's work (1997), which shows the adoption of environmental treaties by highly diverse countries based on their linkage to world-level bodies. Hironaka and Schofer (2002) refined these points in their study of the diffusion of environmental practices in the world system (also see Schofer and Hironaka, 2005). Mimicry (i.e., similar cognitive stances), rather than coercion (force or regulation), in many cases was sufficient for adoption of environmental practices by less centrally linked members in the system.

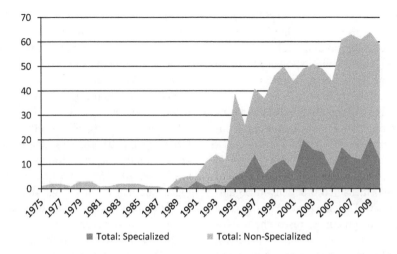

■ Total: Specialized   ▓ Total: Non-Specialized

Figure 29.2   Publication rates for business and the natural environment, 1975–2010 (Hoffman and Georg, 2013)

Table 29.1   Tensions, paradoxes and opportunities in ITNE research

	Tension and paradoxes	*Resultant research directions*
Ontological	• The degree of integration and joint operation of the social and biophysical spheres • The role of agency within each	• Logics • Triggers • Social movements • Institutional gents
Epistemological	• How to gather and analyze systematic, multi-level data on both the biosphere and social sphere • Transferring and generalizing from models and findings across levels and domains • Incorporating meaning and value ascribed by humans into the methodologies for generating knowledge	• Encoding ITNE phenomena • Assessing ITNE phenomena
Normative	• The contrast between the subtext of most environmental studies, which revolves around the preservation of nature and the balance between the biotic and social as critical for society versus that of institutional theory, which is typically silent (unsuccessfully) about such issues	• Does it pay to be green? • Experiments • Failures • Policy

In the 1990s, ITNE scholars came to view the environment as a unique domain where logics were given *in situ* expression. This expression, in the case of corporate logics, became embodied in a series of evolving structures, methodologies and motivational frames around concepts of environmental management, pollution prevention, waste minimization and the like. Hoffman (1999, 2001) documented a progression of logics used in the US chemical industry over a 40-year period, from industrial to regulatory to social responsibility to strategic. These environmental logics follow Scott's (1995) theorized transition from regulative to normative to cognitive and back to regulative, starting with the industrial as a cognitive approach in mainstream US manufacturing in the early 1960s. This 'three-pillar' approach was also influential in the works of Bansal and Clelland (2004) and Bansal (2005), which showed, through qualitative analysis, how different meanings of sustainability evolved, at the cognitive, normative or regulatory levels and how companies use them to influence environmental discourses.

Over the last ten years, however, as in all of institutional theory, ITNE has viewed environmental ideas and practices in organizations with a wider lens. Instead of focusing on management practices, researchers have considered how environmental processes, thinking and practice permeate a number of different social orders beyond the corporate. For instance, Weber, Heinze and De Soucey (2008), in their highly regarded study on organic beef, examine local alternative methods ('grassfed') meat production, from its inception with rearing practices through to grassfed beef's marketization. The community as a social order was central to defining the alternative, more environmentally friendly logic, even if the market logic was increasingly used as organic beef becomes popular. Similarly, in her study of a natural food store chain, Besharov (2014) has shown the importance of gradually blending (neither completely, nor uniformly) organic and corporate-market principles in the daily operation and roles in the main store. Ansari et al. (2013) examined the emergence from lower-level action of an overarching, hybrid 'commons logic' at the field level that has enabled a shift in thinking around the tragedy of the commons.

Nevertheless, while ITNE theorists use environmental logics, like institutional scholars more generally, they have stopped short of making environmental logics a generic form of social order (i.e., see Thornton et al., 2012). Environmental logics, instead, are instantiated in different social orders, ranging from the market to the community. On the one hand, this seems eminently sensible, for humans may not live in some ideal type

of 'environmental social order'. Such an order would likely be a combination of other orders in a unique configuration. On the other hand, if the environment as experienced by humans is essential socially constructed, then that social construction might be worth considering as a generic logic. Hoffman and Jennings (2011) in their study of logic changes possibly following the BP's Deepwater Horizon spill drew upon the work of Hulme (2009). Hulme has theorized a more generic environmental logic, one that considers the deeper assumptions of modern society with the contested elements exposed by this formative event, such as the relations of humans to the environment, the role of knowledge and the long range goals of society.

Triggers

The tension between the social and biosphere as depicted in ITNE's ontology has manifested itself in the use of triggers, anomalies and field-configuring events. As a matter of tradition, many ITNE researchers have used detailed case studies – exposés – of environmental incidents as examples to develop ITNE arguments about how the natural environment affects institutionalized ideas and practice. These include works like Perrow's *Normal Accidents* (1999), Weir's *The Bhopal Syndrome* (1986) and even Weick's work on the Mann Gulch fire (1993). Such incidents, which are grounded in the biosphere, act as 'shocks' or 'triggers' in the social sphere for institutional change (see Greenwood et al., 2002, 2008).

To this notion of triggers, Hoffman and Ocasio (2001) added considerations for attentional processes. Without key stakeholders recognizing and agreeing that the trigger is worth problematizing and theorizing in some reflexive way, then institutional change will often not be initiated. The assembling of attention may be structured by existing systems, such as found in legal rule systems (Jennings et al., 2002, 2005) or it must be generated via negotiation over its meaning (Hoffman et al., 2002).

Whereas triggers in this earlier line of thinking appear to be more exogenous to institutional systems, the consideration of attention and negotiation begins to make them more endogenous. The recognition and theorization of the triggers require reflexivity, which also requires recursion between the social and biophysical worlds. To understand this reflexive process around biophysical triggers, ITNE researchers have turned to environmental risk, cultural anomalies and field-configuring events. Environmental risk is very much a function of the framing of a potential trigger. Framing it in more human versus environmental terms is known to increase its effects (McDaniels et al., 1999; Thaler and Sunstein, 2008). Similarly, cultural anomalies, like the BP oil spill (Hoffman and Jennings, 2011), or temperature increase in climate change models (Hoffman, 2015; Lefsrud and Meyer, 2012) require modifying field-level systems and commensuration of biophysical processes. A field-level event is likely to be required to make sense of the risk and cultural anomaly posed, partly by adjusting field-level systems and measurement, and the attention engendered.

In spite of their importance, however, the impact of natural environment triggers on social change is frequently blunted by attention, interpretation and attendant action of those in the field (Misutka et al., 2014 for review). This has been the case in the Conference of the Parties (COP) meetings, as studied by Schüssler, Rüling and Wittneben (2014), who sought to explore more of the contextual factors that allow events to be catalysts for change. Analyzing how regular and high-stakes events in an event series interacted in producing and preventing institutional change in the transnational climate policy field, they found that growing field complexity and issue multiplication compromise the change potential of a field-configuring event series in favor of field maintenance. Triggers by themselves,

therefore, are insufficient for integrating elements of the biosphere with those of the social. In the end, the exploration of an emergent environmental logic has been central to ITNE research and promises to continue to be so.

Stakeholders and Social Movements

ITNE work has drawn on stakeholder and social movement research to help understand the role of agency in institutional changes affecting the environment. The stakeholder research in ITNE studies rests on stakeholder theory as elaborated by Mitchell, Agle and Wood (1997), which sees stakeholders as internal and external groups who are concerned with some set of issues (such as environmental) to varying degrees, and who have different degrees of legitimacy and power to deal with them. The array of stakeholder groups and their alignment around environmental versus economic issues has been shown to make a difference on activities such as technology choice and the long run returns for firms (Sharma and Henriques, 2005). Stakeholders associated with different types of firms also tend to be associated with different forms of environmental plans and practices (Henriques and Sadorsky, 1996).

Nevertheless, in and of themselves, stakeholders do not serve as a compelling institutional construct. Instead, it is important to understand their mindsets and how they construct interests and issues in order to act (Bansal, 2005). Those mindsets and the practices they entail have been shown to generate different meanings of 'sustainability', and those meanings unpin different environmental management schemes (Bansal and Clelland, 2004; Bansal and Roth, 2000).

In parallel with stakeholder theory, ITNE researchers have used social movement studies to offer yet another mechanism for institutional change as it relates to the natural environment, again tying the biophysical and social worlds together, along with human agency and environmental effects. Social movement theory draws on mobilization explanations, where interests and resource availability are concentrated in groups activated by social issues (Davis et al., 2005). Work in sociology on environmental movements, like studies of protests against the Santa Barbara oil spill (Molotch, 1970), have led ITNE researchers to consider movements around recycling (Lounsbury, 2001), alternative power (Russo, 2001; Sine et al., 2005; Sine and Lee, 2009), and climate change policy (McCright and Dunlap, 2003; Schüssler et al., 2014). This social movement work pushes agency up a level of analysis from stakeholders and makes agency more enduring across decisions and situations involving that particular environmental cause. In this way, the natural environment has a broader and more lasting connection to institutional field dynamics.

While ITNE has considered social movements around environmental issues and documented some effect of them, it has yet to consider social movements in the same way as many in environmental studies. In environmental studies, the most fundamental social movement is around the issues of human population growth, migration and expansion (Bramwell, 1989). These migrations and expansions have had a tremendous impact on the natural environment over the centuries, often through habitat and species loss (Diamond, 2005).

Institutional Agents

Stakeholders and social movement members are both types of institutional agents, though the degree of agency and amount of impact may range from diffuse and low to concentrated and high. More recent ITNE research has focused on agents who are more identifiable as a class, more directed in their interest and have a higher impact. Two types are

evident. The first is institutional entrepreneurs. These entrepreneurs, through bricolage that generates new ideas and practice and via negotiation with others – often leveraging social movements to which they belong – change the institutions in the field through directed and concerted action (Maguire and Hardy, 2009). Sometimes, multiple entrepreneurs and rounds of entrepreneurial effort are evident, as in the gradual de-legitimation of the use of the insecticide DDT (Maguire and Hardy, 2009). At other times, particular entrepreneurs are able to generate change relatively rapidly, often by developing not only new institutional artifacts and leveraging movements, but by creating new roles or organizations to aid the legitimation and adoption process.

For example, Bertels, Hoffman and DeJordy (2014) explore the heterogeneous nature of field-level membership, developing a method to identify configurations of social position, identity and work that result in a distinct set of challenger roles. Such has been the case in recycling, where university groups created formal recycling roles and committees and used the legitimacy of the university, in conjunction with the social movement for recycling, to institutionalize the practices on key campuses, then spread these practices elsewhere (Lounsbury, 2001). Besharov (2014) has gone on to show that by creating 'hybrid' roles in an organization (a natural food store) that blend environmental and business concerns, the organization may better adapt to both logics in the surrounding field.

The second type of agent is the advocacy organization. Like institutional entrepreneurs, the advocacy organization represents interests and groups in the field aligned with different institutional logics. Unlike institutional entrepreneurs – even those entrepreneurs with formalized change agent roles – advocacy groups are even more permanent and embedded within a field and reflective of it. For instance, Hoffman and Bertels (2010) mapped out the various networks and clusters of eNGOs in the United States over the last 15 years, and showed that four types of advocacy organizations exist, ranging from dark to light green and more versus less aligned with corporate interests. As Hoffman (2011) has gone on to show in the case of climate change, advocacy groups are either believers in or deniers of the phenomenon and line up in politically partisan ways to generate or thwart change. Lefsrud and Meyer (2012) examined the views of geo-scientists employed in different Alberta Oil Sands organizations to see how their professional roles would combine with advocacy pressures. They found a strong association of particular types of training and place of employment with views of climate change, even though all participants were surveyed using the same scenarios and questions about climate change.

It is evident, then, that in both stakeholder and social movement theory, while there is agency, the focus and direction of that agency may positively or negatively affect the natural environment. From an institutional theory point of view, ignoring environmental stakeholder groups, undermining environmental claims and denying the science of climate change is just as likely as the reverse. So agency as depicted in ITNE has only partly dealt with the documented negative effects of humans on many ecosystems.

Summary

As a result of wrestling with tensions about agency within the social and environmental domains as depicted by ITNE, human agency in diverse forms (via triggers, stakeholders, social movements, and specific institutional agents) has come to be viewed as a central driver in the relation of the social and biosphere order. Indeed, around this point, institutional studies of the natural environment may now have more agreement than tension or paradox, but how that driver operates with regard to the natural environment – and with what inevitable effects – is more debated.

But one issue remains to be addressed. In ITNE today, some degree of fundamentalism or essentialism exists about the role of the natural environment in society. ITNE sees nature as less malleable than other features of the social order, even if the natural environment is socially constructed. But this is problematic, given the scale and nature of the environmental problems being studied. Schüssler et al., in their article on the UN Conference of the Parties on climate change in Copenhagen, for example, comment that:

> The field of climate policy is an extreme case of a transnational field, because the need to substantially reduce greenhouse gas emissions … requires that millions of organizations and individuals change their production and consumption patterns, which implies changing an economic system to meet a threat that lies largely in the future. (2014: 142)

RESEARCH DIRECTIONS IN RESPONSE TO EPISTEMOLOGICAL TENSIONS

Epistemologically, ITNE studies have wrestled with several tensions. These include how to gather and analyze systematic, multilevel data on both the biosphere and social sphere, transferring and generalizing from models and findings across levels and domains, and incorporating meaning and value ascribed by humans into the methodologies for generating knowledge. The way in which ITNE scholars have handled these tensions can best be seen in how data are encoded and assessed.

Encoding ITNE Phenomena

Originally in institutional models, the natural environment was treated as simply a type of outcome affected by institutional processes. These outcomes were typically at the organizational level. Examples include environmental management practices (Espeland, 1998; Hoffman, 2001) and environmental performance (King and Lenox, 2000). There are face-valid, well-understood measures of these phenomena, and these measures had already been tied by other studies to the environment's health. As a result, the outcome variables themselves were not so much the focus as the institutional processes generating them. This is true even in more recent ITNE studies. However, what is also true in these more recent studies is that the meaning of those variables in both social and environmental terms is more evident. For example, alternative power has been studied as a point of contestation in the US energy industry, one that signals the progressiveness of communities and willingness to change on the one hand and an unsightly eyesore and government supported industry on the other (Sine et al., 2005; Sine and Lee, 2009). Indeed, ITNE scholars have begun to consider other textured outcomes, like policy (Marcus et al., 2013) and media opinion (Bansal and Clelland, 2004) in their studies.

The natural environment has also been encoded as an input – an independent variable – for institutional processes and outcomes. The difficulty has been squeezing the somewhat different meaning of environmental factors into institutional ones. As one clever move, institutionalists relied on the regulatory interface of institutions and the natural environment to generate useful input variables. For example, the natural environment's effects have been captured by environmental infractions (King et al., 2005) and scandals (Perrow, 1999, 2011; Vogel, 2012). These incidents, in turn, lead to compliance on the part of the firm and to repair attempts (Petriglieri, 2015). Now there is more of a move to examine the natural environment inputs as normal operating elements for organizations and industries. For example, firms measure their emissions in carbon cap-and-trade schemes and how their performance and response to emissions controls, in turn, affects the direction of R&D investments (Liesen, 2013).

In addition, the natural environment has been encoded as a context for institutional processes. Originally, the industry or region was used to proxy ecosystems and to simultaneously capture the organizational field, even if this transformation was only partial. One might view Selznick's study of water management in *TVA and the Grassroots* (1949) as an example. Studies of Responsible Care in the chemical industry (e.g., King and Lenox, 2000) also illustrate the encoding of the natural environment at the industry level through outcome variables (emissions). Increasingly, considerations of various environmental logics and policy regimes are injected into such studies. These period effects condition the relationship of the inputs and outputs, further bridging between environmental and social spheres. Indeed, as part of this contextualization, ITNE research now encodes more variation in practice and idea adoption within firms (i.e., Besharov, 2014 on natural foods) and fields (i.e., Sharifian, 2015 on clean technology use).

Perhaps the most subtle way of encoding and linking natural and social phenomena from an institutional angle is by using discourse. Discourse includes the terms used to refer to aspects of a phenomenon, the process for understanding these terms and the conventions for using them (Phillips and Hardy, 2002). Discourse in any field, according to institutional theory, is also embedded in wider, societal level discourse about related phenomena and processes (Lefsrud and Jennings, 2014). Early ITNE studies of discourse examined the corporate/natural environment linkage around terms for environmental practice, such as 'waste' (Clark and Jennings, 1997) or 'recycling' (Lounsbury, 2001). More recent studies, have considered how these terms are embedded in broader meaning systems, such as that revolving around 'sustainability' (Bansal, 2005). Building on Bansal's work, Soderstrom and Weber (2011a, 2011b) trace the evolution of sustainability's meaning at the global level, using media outlets and government documents. In another example, Lefsrud and colleagues (2014) focus on how 'oil' is encoded, and examine how the term has changed over time to influence local regulatory hearings and media perception of oil operations.

While all of these strategies for encoding and linking social and environmental processes help overcome some of the epistemological tensions between institutional and natural environment studies, they still suffer from encoding data from only one or two levels of analysis, by overlooking reciprocal relationships, and from relying on observations over relatively short time periods. Also, in our experience, natural scientists are often uncomfortable with the encoding effort in ITNE, commenting that something essential about ecosystems and processes is lost in translation. These are points to consider when we examine future ITNE work.

Assessing ITNE Phenomena

While encoding institutional and natural environmental observations has seen some unique epistemological moves in ITNE, especially around discourse, assessing the encoded information, for the most part, has relied on extant institutional methodologies, not new ones that wrestle in a deep way with natural environment phenomena. The encoding of the natural environment as independent variables, dependent, contextual and control variables, has led to the use of relatively standard quantitative methods. One type of model is based on panel analysis (Gehman et al., 2012; King and Lenox, 2000; Russo, 2001). Some models have focused on events (such as incidents, triggers, adoptions and periods). These models move somewhat closer to natural environment phenomena as these incidents or periods are often central to the specification of the model and type of modeling themselves. Such types include event history analyses of adoptions (Frank, 1997; Hironaka and Schofer, 2002; Jennings et al., 2005; Sine et al., 2005; Sine and Lee, 2009) and event history period models

(Jennings et al., 2005; Sine and Lee, 2009). Here ITNE researchers try to use time frames and distributions of events that capture the impact of human activity on the natural system, such as climate change and treaty adoption in the Frank (1997) study. The recent models by Sine et al. (2005) also are sensitive to spatial contagion (see Strang and Tuma, 1993). These too move in the direction of considering ecosystems, by characterizing political spaces (US states) in both social and environmental terms.

Qualitative analysis in ITNE also originally relied on assessment techniques already extant in the broader institutional literature, then moved to wrestle with the deeper tensions in doing so. The original techniques included content and discourse analysis, historical (longitudinal) case study and process modeling. The assessment of discourse translates and relates how the natural environment is viewed by different stakeholder groups (Bansal and Roth, 2000), communities (Hoffman and Jennings, 2011; Petriglieri, 2015) and societies in different periods (Djelic and Quack, 2010). Still, the action linked to this discourse and its follow-on effects on the natural environment are often implied (Bansal, 2005; Clark and Jennings, 1997; Soderstrom and Weber, 2011b), but less often examined directly. Now there is an effort to examine how language changes become encoded into regulation (Lefsrud, 2013; Maguire and Hardy, 2009) and policy (Schüssler et al., 2014).

Historical case analysis, such as Holm's (1995) study of the Norwegian fishing industry's transformation, blend the natural and social worlds in a more fine-grained fashion. Changes in the natural environment are stimuli for social changes, part of the discussion of change and influenced as a result of the institutional negotiations and transformations. Process models go further still. For instance, in Zietsma and Lawrence's (2010) study of 'The War of the Woods,' we see the development of a recursive process model based on historical case and field-configuration observations. This process illustrates how boundary shifting occurs to enfranchise more stakeholders, yet re-stabilizes again after intense periods of contestation. This process, while traced through a 15-year period in British Columbia, appears generic enough to transfer to other ITNE fields, especially those where there are battles around natural resources.

Summary

ITNE research, perhaps more than other organization theory approaches, requires consideration of the phenomenon being studied from at least two angles – the institutional and the environmental – choosing the most appropriate level of analysis for the institutional and ecological dynamics, bounding the study using natural systems boundaries and focusing on face valid outcomes that resonate in both environmental and institutional domains. Given these requirements, it is not surprising that it has been difficult to balance institutional and ecological factors when encoding and assessing ITNE phenomena. For instance, the study of chemical industry self- versus government regulation (King and Lenox, 2001) uses the industry as the organizational field and private firms as actors, with emissions as the main measured outcomes; but the emissions generation process is not part of the study, which is based on emissions standards developed in separate environmental studies of local and non-local ecosystem effects. Alternatively, in 'Tilting at Windmills', which examines the adoption of renewable wind power across US states, the adoption is about a clear, positively sanctioned, environmental investment by businesses in each political unit, but an adoption pattern whose environmental impact is not directly examined and whose effect on electrical power usage and greenhouse gas reduction is ambiguous, and, in the short run anyway, likely minimal. We return to this issue of aligning levels, boundaries, specificity of processes and different types of outcomes when we discuss specific research studies generated around this tension.

CURRENT AND RESEARCH DIRECTIONS IN RESPONSE TO NORMATIVE TENSIONS

The ITNE research involving normative (moral) tensions wrestles with the contrast between the subtext of most environmental studies and those in institutional theory. The former's subtext revolves around the need to preserve nature and the balance between the biotic and social as critical for society. Institutional theory, in contrast, is typically silent about such issues. As a result, most ITNE research suffers from an imbalance in the normative realm. The subtext in ITNE research tends to collapse into implicit statements about better versus worse natural environment outcomes. Rarely is a better or worse society, which is associated with those outcomes, also examined. Still, we think that there are four areas were the normative implications of outcomes along both environmental and institutional dimensions are considered: the market impact of being 'green', positive organization experiments in greening, organizational failures around the environment and institutional policy efforts to address environmental matters.

Does It Pay to Be Green?

This question has been central to much business and environment work, particularly up to 2005 (Hoffman and Georg, 2013). On the surface the question resembles an economics concern, but beneath is the pre-ordained belief of many undertaking the research that the answer would be 'yes' (Hart and Ahuja, 1996; Sharma and Vredenberg, 1998). Institutional theory has not been particularly well positioned to address the question directly, given that its main concern has tra-ditionally been with legitimacy rather than performance (Scott, 2001). However, the system for building green markets and rewarding green performance is more institutional in nature. Indeed, economists have long recognized the need for such institutional infrastructure for environmental innovation and performance, even if it has been pitched in formal terms; i.e., as sets of legal systems, market rules and associated polices (Porter and Van de Linde, 1995). Not surprisingly, some of the institutionalists who have examined the question also emphasized building markets to ensure the value of green products and services (Babiak and Trendafilova, 2011; Jones and Boxenbaum, 2012).

More recently, institutionalists have considered the beliefs that support different versions of sustainability and how these versions of sustainability frame what it means to 'pay'? Bansal's line of work on the meaning of sustainability documented the importance of different meanings (Bansal and Roth, 2000; Bansal and Clelland, 2004; Bansal, 2005). One popular theme is that of the 'triple bottom line', a focus on the economic, social and environmental dimensions of performance, with the economic typically being weighted the most heavily. A host of other broad schemes for assessing green performance also exist, such as ISO 14001, EMAS, the Global Reporting (GRI) Index and so on. Other schemes are more specific to the industry or community, such as the Sustainable Forestry Initiative, the US Green Building Council or Energy Star. One of the most elaborate systems for assessing green performance has been 'The Natural Step' (Karl-Henrik, 1997). It is a sweeping method of evaluating the inputs, throughputs and outputs of organisms and organizations at the spectrum between the micro and macro levels (i.e., using systems theory). At the organizational level it back-casts from an envisioned sustainable future and then re-orients purchasing, production and

distribution for organizations to help achieve that vision. Given its requirements for a fundamental mind-shift and building social consensus, the Natural Step is both institutional in nature, and a set of practices that has been commented upon by ITNE researchers (Bradbury and Clair, 1999).

In these broader, more recent schemes, the time horizon for assessing environmental management practice and sustainability as models for institutional change has shifted. A wide variety of scholars have now come to embrace the essence of the Rio definition of sustainability, which involves not compromising the needs of future generations with current practice (see Henderson et al., 2015 for a review). A more positive version of this message has been held out by Ehrenfeld and Hoffman (2013), whereby societies should not just preserve and pursue precautionary principles, but try to *flourish*. Flourishing refers to both material and immaterial existence, where innovative living around sustainable principles improves general well-being.

All in all, in spite of its emphasis on understanding systems and deeper culture in order to capture and improve environmental performance, the ITNE research on this area has greatly emphasized the socially constructed, consensually agreed upon measurements of performance, not wider measures as they exist in natural environment studies. The institutional measures, then, tend to weight the well-being and sustainable development of society instead of the health of extant ecosystems and the rights of their other inhabiting species to sustainable futures.

Experiments

One reading of ITNE research is as a set of investigations in institutional change (Greenwood et al., 2015). From a moral angle, these change efforts look like experiments to improve institutionalized thought or practice, if not necessarily so. The initial experiment to problematize and theorize a new artifact or create a prototypical organization is critical for the institutionalization process (Greenwood et al., 2002; Lawrence et al., 2002).

In the 1990s and early 2000s period, ITNE-related research focused on environmental management practices. The use of ISO 14001 and EMAS (Bansal and Hunter, 2003; Delmas, 2001, 2002; King et al., 2005) represent a shift in systems of operations in firms. The shift still works with standards of technical rationality held by many in firms, just as Total Quality Management and other quality-related practices do (Westphal et al., 1997). This makes adoption more palpable for the majority of firms' stakeholders, including representatives from government. These stakeholders in turn, by positively signaling and sanctioning the practices, help diffuse the experiment.

Observation of more extreme experiments by researchers, such as of outdoor clothing company Patagonia's efforts to re-design its products and to re-socialize consumers against unneeded (but wanted) purchase (Dacin et al., 2010), have led institutional theorists to think more about the deeper systemic change that might allow for such experiments to be created and adopted. Hoffman, in from *Heresy to Dogma* (2001), has shown that these experiments require reciprocal change in underlying logics, and that the natural progression of these logics is from the regulative to the normative to the cognitive (also see Scott, 1995). The logics, in other words, need to become ever more deeply imbedded in the managerial mindset for new, beneficial experiments to be created. Unfortunately, a host of more recent studies has shown that the terrain beneath such experiments is usually hotly contested, and, as a result, the outcomes are often the outcome of multiple compromises. This is so for the allocation of water management systems across dry US states (Espeland, 1998), for curbing the use of DDT (Maguire and Hardy, 2009) and for reducing greenhouse gases

affecting climate change (Hoffman, 2011; Schüssler et al., 2014).

With regards to experiments, ITNE research has recently spent as much time considering the role played by entrepreneurs and advocacy groups as change agents generating these experiments. In the study by Marti et al. (2013) of a local community in Argentina, for instance, the creation of more sustainable living arrangements in the barrio is as much the result of the actions of community members (i.e. the local priests and church members) as any set of legal and governmental systems aiding its creation (see Jennings et al., 2013 for review). Battilana and Dorado (2010) make a similar point in their study of actors involved in the creation of hybrid forms of financing organizations.

Atmospheric scientists have also played a key role in problematizing the climate change issue (Lefsrud and Meyer, 2012). Yet these experiments, particularly in legal and governmental systems, are unlikely to diffuse more broadly without advocacy groups promoting them. From an institutional and political point of view, such a claim seems completely logical; but from the normative perspective, advocacy groups seem to indicate some form of moral relativism. Their claims are simply based on their position in relational fields or social movements, and, thus, one position may be just as valid as the other, depending on one's point of view. Unless a stronger societal and environmental ethic is developed and injected into such ITNE work, accepting the experiments of groups and valorizing their leaders may lead us down the wrong path – or, alternatively, we could go back to trying to avoid signaling and sanctioning such efforts in the first place.

Failures

Like experiments, failures signal the potential for institutional change. ITNE scholars have used specific, high-profile cases of failures to dramatize the need for change.

Silent Spring (Carson, 1962), the Santa Barbara oil spill (Molotch, 1970), the Cuyahoga River fire (Hoffman and Ocasio, 2001), *The Bhopal Syndrome* (Weir, 1986), *Normal Accidents* (Perrow, 1999), the Fukushima disaster (Aoki and Rothwell, 2012) and other well-researched exposés question current practice and signal the urgent need to re-assess the institutions that help lead to such accidents. *Silent Spring*, for instance, has been used as one of the precursors assessing the side effects of chemical industry practice (Hoffman, 2001) and the *Exxon Valdez* oil spill has also been used in work on BP's Deepwater Horizon spill (Hoffman and Jennings, 2011) to allude to how in the past institutional systems in the oil industry have handled major spills.

Failures have also been used more directly, if still normatively, in ITNE research as triggers for institutional change in a field. General Electric (GE), while often lauded as a progressive firm, has been shown to shift polluting operations to subsidiaries and offshore locations (Gehman, 2012). Exposure of such greenwashing has led to changes in stakeholder support and corporate reputation (also see Delmas and Burbano, 2011). The BP Deepwater Horizon oil spill generated a lot of controversy, highlighting the anomalous nature of the event in the oil production field. From that point, its potential for changing practice could be traced through theorization and objectification to the stages where it began to lose momentum as a trigger. This appeared to be in the slow decision-making process around liability, the lack of social mobilization across (not just within) affected communities, and strong efforts by the BP Group to work with US government officials to forestall more sweeping changes and repair relationships (Hoffman and Jennings, 2011). The failure of the various Copenhagen Conference of the Parties (COP) meetings on climate change, particularly the 2009 negotiations that were highly visible in the media, illuminated the complex nature of policy-making in COP and the need to overhaul the system (Schüssler et al., 2014).

Yet highlighting failure in ITNE research has not addressed the underlying normative issue of what constitutes better thought and practice and how they might be encouraged. Nor does highlighting failure require that ITNE scholars discuss their motives for studying failure in the first place. Ironically, these, like many items in institutional theory, are left implicit.

Policy

Within any form of institutional analyses, the role of government is paramount. Indeed, any discussion of institutional fields without the inclusion of government would, in the eyes of many, be considered a glaring oversight. Research in ITNE is no exception, with much research being devoted to the role of government in setting norms to address and ameliorate environmental and social grievances (Hoffman and Ventresca, 2002). Further, many such ITNE studies also examine the outcome of regulation: on the economic performance of companies (Barnett and Salomon, 2006; King and Lenox, 2001; Waddock and Graves, 1997), the development of clean technology (Kemp, 1993; Schot, 1992), innovation (Ashford, 1993; OECD, 2000), and the introduction of environmental management systems (Dahlmann and Brammer, 2011; Delmas, 2001; Khanna and Anton, 2002).

In particular, ITNE studies consider context to be extremely important, with regulatory responses differing by private vs. public sectors (Jennings et al., 2011), industry characteristics (Dahlmann and Brammer, 2011), company characteristics (Prakash and Kellman, 2004) and the policy instrument being applied. For example, there has been a marked increase in research on the use of voluntary negotiated agreements and market-based instruments such as environmental taxes, and emission trading schemes which fit the regulatory and policy schemes within the dominant economic logics that are at play (Labatt and Maclaren, 1998; Potoski and Prakash, 2004). Further, there are important country differences in policy instruments (Sharifian, 2015). The use of negotiated voluntary agreements, for instance, is more common in Europe than in the United States (Glachant, 1994; OECD, 2003).

While many such policies have resulted in reduced environmental degradation, they are still culturally contentious. Adherents of opposing worldviews continue to debate and conflict over the role of government within market environments, particularly if such policies impose a dampening effect on economic activity. Regulations regarding the environment are often central to such debates and therefore stand as touchstones for deeper cultural debates and contests over the nature of society, the state of the natural environment and the interplay between the two (Hoffman, 2011; Hulme, 2009).

Summary

As a means of resolving some of the tensions between institutional and natural environment studies, ITNE research discusses moral issues indirectly and directly. Indirectly, when ITNE raises issues such as toxins or global climate change, a better and worse practice and outcome is implied. Less indirectly, this discussion of better ideas and practice can be the focus of research, such as in 'Talking trash' (Bansal and Clelland, 2004), where sustainability's meaning is investigated. Even more directly, environmental issues may be the focus of policy efforts (e.g., Hoffman and Jennings, 2011; Hoffman and Ventresca, 2002), in which case ITNE is more explicitly used to advocate for more sustainable outcomes.

CURRENT CHALLENGES DUE TO RENEWED TENSIONS

As discussed in each of the sections above, in spite of efforts to combine institutional

theory and natural environment studies, tensions between them are still evident in ITNE research. These range from: ontological tensions around integrating the social and biosphere through the use of environmental logics and the degree to which human agency drives environmental versus institutional issues; to epistemological tensions around how to encode and assess two complex systems simultaneously; to normative ones around whether direct, indirect or no moral stance should be taken by ITNE researchers on these subjects. These tensions may be even more evident if we add two more recent developments in each domain: the entry into the Anthropocene era (Crutzen and Stoermer, 2000) and the increasing use of institutional complexity theory (Greenwood et al., 2011; Thornton et al., 2012).

The Anthropocene

The Anthropocene era refers to the argument proposed by a large group of geophysicists, paleontologists, archeologists and climate change experts that we have entered a new geologic epoch, one that acknowledges that humans are now a primary operating element in the Earth's ecosystems (Crutzen and Stoermer, 2000). This era is argued to have started around the industrial revolution of the early 1800s, and has become more acute since 'the Great Acceleration' around 1950 onwards (Steffen et al., 2007). It is marked by the reality that:

> Human activity has transformed between a third and a half of the land surface of the planet; Many of the world's major rivers have been dammed or diverted; Fertilizer plants produce more nitrogen than is fixed naturally by all terrestrial ecosystems; Humans use more than half of the world's readily accessible freshwater runoff. (Crutzen, 2002: 23)

Offering more clarity to the concept, scientists have identified nine key biotic and geochemical markers or 'planetary boundaries' (Rockstrom et al., 2009) that represent 'thresholds below which humanity can safely operate and beyond which the stability of planetary-scale systems cannot be relied upon' (Gillings and Hagan-Lawson, 2014: 2). These include: climate change, ocean acidification, ozone depletion, atmospheric aerosol loading, phosphorous and nitrogen cycles, global freshwater use, land system change, loss of biodiversity and chemical pollution (Gillings and Hagan-Lawson, 2014). 'Unless there is a global catastrophe such as a meteorite impact, world war or pandemic,' these planetary boundaries will continue to be approached as 'mankind will remain a major environmental force for many millennia' (Crutzen, 2002: 23). Indeed, scientists believe that three have already been exceeded: climate change, biodiversity loss and the nitrogen cycle (Rockstrom et al., 2009).

The deterioration in each dimension is based on thresholds, some from which there is no return, and the joint consequence of deterioration, in the short run, is volatility and more spike events – in the long run, systems collapse (Gillings and Hagan-Lawson, 2014). This emergent reality compels research in ITNE with a new urgency, one that directly challenges its position on many of the ontological, epistemological and normative tensions just discussed.

Institutional Complexity

Institutional complexity is a variant of institutional theory, one that focuses on multiple, sometimes competing logics and complex organizational fields in which organizations may have multiple responses and feedback effects – hence the label 'complexity'. In the Thornton et al. (2012) framing, seven generic social logics and their instantiation and expression in different fields, combined with more micro dynamics around decisions, politics, social movements and entrepreneurial activity determine what thought and practice is adopted or abandoned in fields over time. In the Greenwood et al. (2011) framing, the

field infrastructure and the response of organizations based on their ownership, governance, structure and identity drive more of the institutional change (also see Greenwood et al., 2015).

Below we focus on the tensions in ITNE research, particularly those created by the use of Anthropocene theory and institutional complexity, and identify a few interesting areas for investigation (also see Hoffman and Jennings, 2015).

Ontological Tensions

The construct of the Anthropocene is based on the notion of an inter-connected, multi-domain system. On the face of it, this notion would seem to fit well with the multiple institutional logics that characterize complex organizational fields. In addition, the need to promote the construct and meaning of Anthropocene, partly using threshold shocks and partly with scientific discourse, would seem to fit with the need in institutional complexity to recognize and theorize triggers via reflexivity. Thus, it might be possible to fit elements of the Anthropocene as inputs and context for the institutional complexity model.

But the Anthropocene also has a long time horizon, many systems and non-linear threshold effects. As a result, the Anthropocene requires a different scale of social construction to capture it compared to, for example, capturing the notion of toxins in local aquatic environments (see Bansal and Knox-Hayes, 2013 for similar commentary). In addition, the Anthropocene re-inserts human agency into the ecological system as a prime cause of its dynamics and deterioration; whereas complexity theory sees agency as more of a response and less directly active. Therefore, at the ontological level, more work needs to be done to integrate the basic notion of the Anthropocene with that of institutional complexity.

As partly discussed in Hoffman and Jennings (2015), we see at least four areas as being fruitful for further integration: comparing the meaning of the Anthropocene with sustainability and considering the meaning and logic behind a resultant Anthropocene society, adjusting the idea of environment risk, re-considering the importance of organizational resilience and conceptualizing organizational ecosystems in institutional terms (also see Greenwood et al., 2015).

Epistemological Tensions

Because it involves long time horizons, carbon-related and usage data, studying the Anthropocene appears to require the use of big data. One cannot experience the multiple markers of this new era through one's senses or directly. Global scale increases in carbon dioxide or mean temperatures require complex aggregations of data and analysis, far beyond those available to individual citizens. Therefore, institutional efforts to recognize and address these changes are necessary. Alternatively, environment studies might require deeper, almost archeological-level interest in production/consumption patterns in organizations, households and other units.

Complexity theory requires multiple logics in a field, variation in field maturity, variable and modal firm responses to moderated field pressures and, eventually, an examination of the feedback loops. Macro and micro, along with qualitative and quantitative data, are useful. Perhaps the upswing in carbon use and greenhouse gas emissions since 1950 would be a good starting point for ITNE, particularly if paired with carbon trigger and multi-field data. Also, consideration (once again) of attention and problematization in relational fields would seem to be a critical part of reflexivity in these studies.

Normative Tensions

The environment study of the Anthropocene requires that we think about better versus worse Anthropocene societies and whether human survival is even possible (Ellis and Trachtenberg, 2013). In short, it challenges directly ITNE's moral and normative neutrality on the types of outcomes toward which institutional processes lead human societies. It calls for a more expansive assessment of the stakes of institutional processes and, again, compels a recognition of more or less competent actors in the debate and its outcome. Science and scientists are viewed as critical in making this assessment. Complexity appears, like its institutional theory predecessor, to be agnostic; but it does encourage the consideration of meaning and value as part of the reflexivity process, and also in identity-based responses to complex fields.

In ITNE work on the Anthropocene we might expect, then, greater consideration of happiness and survivability outcomes for fields and societies, whether positive institution-preserving responses to Anthropocene shocks are possible and what form of new institutions should be built.

We imagine that oscillations in institutional pressures and considerations of maintenance on the downside will become more prominent. One important moral question is whether the future should be viewed in apocalyptic terms, which may serve to create urgency, but also futility. Given the dire warning about carbon dioxide rising too rapidly by 2020, perhaps caution, and built-in pre-cautionary principles rather than specific outcomes, should be considered.

Further, considerations of the Anthropocene era compel a re-examination of the role and form of policy in a globalized context. For example, regulatory policies to address local or national environmental issues may be, and most likely are, inadequate for exploring the intricacies of creating a global market for carbon to address the global problem of climate change (Callon, 2009; MacKenzie, 2009). The examination of such issues could also help shape the ways in which markets are conceptualized and open questions over the very foundations of the existing social order (Rowan, 2014).

FINAL THOUGHTS

In the end, one might return to fundamentals and pose the question of whether the tensions between (and contraposition of) institutional theory of organizations with environmental science views of nature is really sufficiently enriching for either set of views to warrant the continued effort.

We have tried to persuade the reader that the tensions between the two are still giving rise to interesting theoretical and empirical avenues, but we have not considered the opportunity cost of trying to combine them. Suppose we were just to end the effort and search for a different social science theory to combine with natural environment studies, in general, and the Anthropocene, in particular. What characteristics would that theory need to have?

Any new approach would seem to require the use of multiple, interacting levels and long time horizons. It would also need to be sensitive to the needs of both natural systems and social orders to recognize and label Anthropocene phenomena. The role and responsibility of human agency would also be important to incorporate, but always within the context of a biotic reality that human knowledge does not understand nor even fully detect. Yet the bounded rationality and emotive sides of humans would need consideration, along with the likelihood of both intended and unintended consequences of action within ecosystem processes.

To us, this 'other' approach would likely look institutional in many ways, but with some amendments as we have laid out in this chapter. In fact, we believe that institutional theory is well suited to this task. The theory's vibrancy and visibility are due, in large part, to its distinctive stance on environmental phenomena. Institutional theory emphasizes

environmental problems as being not primarily technological or economic in character, but behavioral and cultural. While technological and economic activity may be the direct cause of environmentally destructive behavior, it is our individual beliefs, cultural norms and societal institutions that guide the development of that activity (Bazerman and Hoffman, 1999).

Therefore, we encourage ITNE researchers to continue with their efforts at combining the two theories. In this way we may be able to study and act on the ominous warning by Rachel Carson noted at the outset of this chapter. Indeed, we do not really have the luxury of turning away from this reality and waiting. We need all of our collective intellectual and community-based efforts in order to make any progress on improving the relationship between organizations and the natural environment as we enter the new epoch of the Anthropocene, one for which our species has no prior experience. As noted scientist Steven Jay Gould wrote:

> We have become, by the power of a glorious evolutionary accident called intelligence, the stewards of life's continuity on earth. We did not ask for this role, but we cannot abjure it. We may not be suited to it, but here we are. (Gould, 1985)

As humankind embarks on this new reality of assuming a guiding role in the operation of the world's natural systems, we must begin to ask what this means for the institutions of society and how we understand them. Institutional theory can help us create a structure for exploring what the cultural and institutional basis is for entering into a new social and environmental reality, and the tools for teasing apart the key questions of analyzing possible and – if our challenge in this chapter is taken seriously – desired outcomes.

Notes

1 We would like to thank our many colleagues and students at the University of Michigan and University of Alberta for their support and

feedback over the years on this line of theorizing and research, as well as our peers at the Academy for pushing us to develop our ideas. Nevertheless, this chapter has not been funded by any external or internal agencies or organizations.

2　The protocol for collecting these articles is available upon request. It uses standard keyword searches in journals around terms, such as 'institution*', for institutional theory, and 'climate' for environmental studies related to institutions, with intersection of these words in management journals to capture ITNE's growth rate.

3　The methodologies for generating each graph are different. The protocol for collecting these articles used a proxy of articles cited in the *Oxford Handbook of Business and the Natural Environment* and is not intended to be comprehensive. Therefore a direct comparison of scale along the vertical axis is not accurate for a direct comparison. That said, the trend lines in each graph can be used for comparison.

REFERENCES

Ansari, S., Wijen, F. and Gray, B. (2013). Constructing a climate change logic: An institutional perspective on the 'tragedy of the commons'. *Organization Science*, 24(4): 1014–1040.

Aoki, M. and Rothwell, G. (2012). A comparative institutional analysis of the Fukushima nuclear disaster: Lessons and policy implications. *Energy Policy*, 53(Feb): 240–247.

Ashford, N. (1993). Understanding technological responses of industrial firms to environmental problems: Implications for government policy. In K. Fischer and J. Schot (eds), *Environmental Strategies for Industry: International Perspectives on Research Needs and Policy Implications*. Washington, DC: Island Press. pp. 277–307.

Astley, W. G. (1985). The two ecologies: Population and community perspectives on organizational evolution. *Administrative Science Quarterly*, 224–241.

Babiak, K. and Trendafilova, S. (2011). CSR and environmental responsibility: Motives and pressures to adopt green management practices. *Corporate Social Responsibility and Environmental Management*, 18(1): 11–24.

Bansal, P. (2005). Evolving sustainably: A longitudinal study of corporate sustainable development. *Strategic Management Journal*, 26(3): 197–218.

Bansal, P. and Clelland, I. (2004). Talking trash: Legitimacy, impression management, and unsystematic risk in the context of the natural environment. *Academy of Management Journal*, 47(1): 93–103.

Bansal, P. and Hunter, T. (2003). Strategic explanations for the early adoption of ISO 14001. *Journal of Business Ethics*, 46(3): 289–299.

Bansal, P. and Knox-Hayes, J. (2013). The time and space of materiality in organizations and the environment. *Organization and Environment*, 26(1): 61–82.

Bansal, P. and Roth, K. (2000). Why companies go green: A model of ecological responsiveness. *Academy of Management Journal*, 43(4): 717–736.

Barnett, M. and Salomon, R. (2006). Beyond dichotomy: The curvilinear relationship between social responsibility and financial performance. *Strategic Management Journal*, 27(11): 1101–1122.

Battilana, J. and Dorado, S. (2010). Building sustainable hybrid organizations: The case of commercial microfinance organizations. *Academy of Management Journal*, 53(6): 1419–1440.

Bazerman, M. and Hoffman, A. (1999). Sources of environmentally destructive behavior: Individual, organizational and institutional perspectives. *Research in Organizational Behavior*, 21: 39–79.

Berger, P. and Luckmann, T. (1966). *The Social Construction of Reality*. New York: Random House.

Bertels, S., Hoffman, A. and DeJordy, R. (2014). The varied work of challenger movements: Identifying challenger roles in the U.S. environmental movement. *Organization Studies*, 35(8): 1171–1210.

Besharov, M. L. (2014). The relational ecology of identification: How organizational identification emerges when individuals hold divergent values. *Academy of Management Journal*, 57(5): 1485–1512.

Bradbury, H. and Clair, J. A. (1999). Promoting sustainable organizations with Sweden's natural step. *Academy of Management Executive*, 13(4): 63–74.

Bramwell, A. (1989). *Ecology in the 20th Century*. New Haven, CT: Yale University Press.

Callon, M. (2009). Civilizing markets: Carbon trading between in vitro and in vivo experiments. *Accounting, Organizations and Society*, 34(3–4): 535–548.

Carson, R. (1962). *Silent Spring*. Boston, MA: Houghton Mifflin.

Catton, W. and Dunlap, R. (1980). A new ecological paradigm for post-exuberant sociology. *American Behavioral Scientist*, 20(1): 15–47.

Clark, V. and Jennings, P. D. (1997). Talking about the natural environment. *American Behavioral Scientist*, 40(4): 454–464.

Crutzen, P. (2002). Geology of mankind. *Nature*, 415: 23.

Crutzen, P. and Stoermer, E. (2000). The 'Anthropocene'. *Global Change Newsletter*, 41: 17–18.

Dacin, P. A., Dacin, M. T. and Matear, M. (2010). Social entrepreneurship: Why we don't need a new theory and how we move forward from here. *Academy of Management Perspectives*, 24(3): 37–57.

Dahlmann, F. and Brammer, S. (2011). Exploring and explaining patterns of adoption and selection in corporate environmental strategies in the USA. *Organization Studies*, 32(4): 527–553.

Davis, G., McAdam, D., Scott, W. R. and Zald, M. (eds) (2005). *Social Movements and Organization Theory*. New York: Cambridge University Press.

Delmas, M. (2001). Stakeholders and competitive advantage: The case of ISO 14001. *Production and Operations Management*, 10(3): 343–358.

Delmas, M. (2002). The diffusion of environmental management standards in Europe and in the United States: An institutional perspective. *Policy Sciences*, 35(1): 91–119.

Delmas, M. A. and Cuerel Burbano, V. (2011). The drivers of greenwashing. *California Management Review*. 54(1): 64–87.

Diamond, J. (2005). *Collapse: How Societies Choose to Fail or Succeed*. New York: Penguin.

DiMaggio, P. and Powell, W. (1991). Introduction. In P. DiMaggio and W. Powell (eds), *The New Institutionalism in Organizational Analysis*. Chicago, IL: The University of Chicago Press. pp. 1–40.

Djelic, M. L. and Quack, S. (eds) (2010). *Transnational Communities: Shaping Global Economic Governance*. Cambridge: Cambridge University Press.

Ehrenfeld, J. and Hoffman, A. (2013). *Flourishing: A Frank Conversation on Sustainability*. Palo Alto, CA: Stanford University Press.

Ellis, M. and Trachtenberg, Z. (2013). Which Anthropocene is it to be? Beyond geology to a moral and public discourse. *Earth's Future*, 2: 122–125.

Ermarth, M. (1981). *Dilthey: The Critique of Historical Reason*. Chicago, IL: Chicago University Press.

Espeland, W. (1998). *The Struggle for Water: Politics, Rationality, and Identity in the American Southwest*. Chicago, IL: University of Chicago Press.

Evernden, N. (1985). *The Natural Alien: Humankind and Environment*. Toronto: University of Toronto Press.

Evernden, N. (1992). *The Social Creation of Nature*. Baltimore, MD: The Johns Hopkins University Press.

Frank, D. J. (1997). Science, nature, and the globalization of the environment, 1870–1990. *Social Forces*, 76(2): 409–435.

Friedland, R., Mohr, J. Roose, H. and Gardinali, P. (2014). The institutional logics of love: measuring intimate life. *Theory and Society*, 1–38.

Gehman, J. (2012). Categorical cleaning: Divestitures as a strategic response to sustainability concerns. Working Paper, University of Alberta.

Gehman, J., Mastrioianni, D., Grant, A. and Etzion, D. (2012). An analysis of unconventional gas well reporting under Pennsylvania's Act 13 of 2012. *Environmental Practice*, 14(4): 262–277.

Gillings, M. and Hagan-Lawson, E. (2014). The cost of living in the Anthropocene. *Earth Perspectives*, 1: 2.

Glachant, M. (1994). The setting of voluntary agreements between industry and government: Bargaining and efficiency. *Business Strategy & the Environment*, 3(2): 43–49.

Gladwin, T. (2012). Capitalism critique: Systemic limits on business harmony with nature. In P. Bansal and A. Hoffman (eds), *The Oxford Handbook of Business and the Environment*. Oxford: Oxford University Press. pp. 657–674.

Gould, S. J. (1985). *The Flamingo's Smile: Reflections in Natural History.* New York: WW Norton.

Greenwood, R. G., Hinings, C. R. and Jennings, P. D. (2015). Sustainability and organizational change: An institutional perspective. In R. Henderson, R. Gulati and M. Tushman (eds), *Leading Sustainable Change*. Oxford: Oxford University Press.

Greenwood, R., Oliver, C., Suddaby, R. and Sahlin-Andersson K. (2008). *The SAGE Handbook of Organizational Institutionalism*. London: Sage.

Greenwood, R., Raynard, M., Kodeih, F., Micelotta, E. R. and Lounsbury M. (2011). Institutional complexity and organizational responses. *Academy of Management Annals*, 5(1): 317–371.

Greenwood, R., Suddaby, R. and Hinings, C. R. (2002). Theorizing change: The role of professional associations in the transformation of institutionalized fields. *Academy of Management Journal*, 45(1): 58–80.

Hannan, M. T. and Freeman, J. (1977). The population ecology of organizations. *American Journal of Sociology*, 82(5): 929–964.

Hart, S. L. and Ahuja, G. (1996). Does it pay to be green? An empirical examination of the relationship between emission reduction and firm performance. *Business Strategy and the Environment*, 5(1): 30–37.

Hawken, P. (1993). *The Ecology of Commerce: A Declaration of Sustainability*. New York: Harper Collins.

Healey, M. (ed.) (1999). *Seeking Sustainability in the Lower Fraser Basin: Issues and Choices*. British Columbia: Institute for Resources and Environment, Westwater Institute.

Henderson, R., Gulati, R. and Tushman, M. (eds) (2015). *Leading Sustainable Change*. Oxford: Oxford University Press.

Henriques, I. and Sadorsky, P. (1996). The determinants of an environmentally responsive firm: An empirical approach. *Journal of Environmental Economics and Management*, 30(3): 381–395.

Hironaka, A. and Schofer, E. (2002). Decoupling in the environmental arena: The case of environmental impact assessments. In A. Hoffman and M. Ventresca (eds), *Organizations, Policy and the*

Natural Environment. Stanford, CA: Stanford University Press. pp. 214–234.

Hoffman, A. (1999). Institutional evolution and change: Environmentalism and the US chemical industry. *Academy of Management Journal*, 42(4): 351–371.

Hoffman, A. (2001). *From Heresy to Dogma: An Institutional History of Corporate Environmentalism*. Palo Alto, CA: Stanford University Press.

Hoffman, A. (2011). Talking past each other? Cultural framing of skeptical and convinced logics in the climate change debate. *Organization & Environment*, 24(1): 3–33.

Hoffman, A. (2015). *How Culture Shapes the Climate Change Debate*. Stanford, CA: Stanford University Press.

Hoffman, A. and Bansal, P. (2012). Retrospective, perspective and prospective: Introduction. In P. Bansal and A. Hoffman (eds), *The Oxford Handbook on Business and the Natural Environment*. Oxford: Oxford University Press. pp. 3–28.

Hoffman, A. and Bertels, S. (2010). Who is part of the environmental movement? In T. Lyon (ed.), *Good Cop Bad Cop: Environmental NGOs and their Strategies Towards Business*. Washington, DC: RFF Press. pp. 48–69.

Hoffman, A. and Georg, S. (2013). A history of research on business and the natural environment: Conversations from the field. In S. Georg and A. Hoffman (eds), *Business and the Environment: Critical Perspectives in Business and Management*, Volume I. Oxford: Routledge. pp. 1–58.

Hoffman, A. and Jennings, P. D. (2011). The BP Oil Spill as a cultural anomaly? Institutional context, conflict and change. *Journal of Management Inquiry*, 20(2): 100–112.

Hoffman, A. and Jennings, P. D. (2012). The social and psychological foundations of climate change. *Solutions*, 4(3): 58–65.

Hoffman, A. and Jennings, P. D. (2015). Institutional theory and the natural environment: research in (and on) the Anthropocene. *Organization and Environment*, 28(1): 8–31.

Hoffman, A. and Ocasio, W. (2001). Not all events are attended equally: Toward a middle-range theory of industry attention to external events. *Organization Science*, 12(4): 414–434.

Hoffman, A., Riley, H., Troast, J. and Bazerman, M. (2002). Cognitive and institutional barriers to new forms of cooperation on environmental protection: Insights from Project XL and Habitat Conservation Plans. *American Behavioral Scientist*, 45(5): 820–845.

Hoffman, A. and Ventresca, M. (eds) (2002). *Organizations, Policy and the Natural Environment: Institutional and Strategic Perspectives*. Stanford, CA: Stanford University Press.

Holm, P. (1995). The dynamics of institutionalization: Transformation processes in Norwegian fisheries. *Administrative Science Quarterly*, 40(3): 398–422.

Hulme, M. (2009). *Why We Disagree About Climate Change: Understanding Controversy, Inaction and Opportunity*. Cambridge: Cambridge University Press.

Jennings, P. D., Greenwood, R., Lounsbury, M. D. and Suddaby, R. (2013). Institutions, entrepreneurs, and communities: A special issue on entrepreneurship. *Journal of Business Venturing*, 28(1): 1–9.

Jennings, P. D., Schulz, M., Patient, D., Gravel, C. and Yuan, K. (2005). Weber and legal rule evolution: The closing of the iron cage? *Organization Studies*, 26(4): 621–653.

Jennings, P. D. and Zandbergen, P. (1995). Ecologically sustainable organizations: An institutional approach. *Academy of Management Review*, 20(4): 1015–1052.

Jennings, P. D., Zandbergen, P. and Martins, L. (2002). Complications in compliance: Variations in enforcement in British Columbia's Lower Fraser Basin, 1985–1996. In Andrew Hoffman and Marc Ventresca (eds), *Organizations, Policy, and the Natural Environment: Institutional and Strategic Perspectives*. Stanford University Press: Palo Alto. pp. 57–89.

Jennings, P. D., Zandbergen, P. and Martins, M. (2011). An institutional view of process strategy in the public sector. In Pietro Mazzola and Franz Kellermann (eds), *Handbook of Strategy Process Research*. Cheltenham, UK: Edward Elgar. pp. 492–517.

Jones, C. and Boxenbaum, E. (2012). Let's get concrete!: Revealing the symbolic, material and aesthetic within architects' professional logic. Paper presented at ABC Network 2012, Banff, Canada.

Karl-Henrik, R. (1997). *The Natural Step: A Framework for Achieving Sustainability in Our Organizations*. Westford, MA: Pegasus Communications.

Kemp, R. (1993). An economic analysis of clean technology. In K. Fischer and J. Schot (eds), *Environmental Strategies for Industry: International Perspectives on Research Needs and Policy Implications*. Washington, DC: Island Press. pp. 79–113.

Khanna, M. and Anton, W. (2002). Corporate environmental management: Regulation and market based incentives. *Land Economics*, 78(4): 539–558.

King, A. and Lenox, M. (2000). Industry self-regulation without sanctions: The chemical industry's Responsible Care Program. *Academy of Management Journal*, 43(4): 698–716.

King, A. and Lenox, M. (2001). Does it really pay to be green? An empirical study of firm environmental and financial performance. *Journal of Industrial Ecology*, 5(1): 105–116.

King, A., Lenox, M. and Terlaak, A. (2005). The strategic use of decentralized institutions: Exploring certification with the ISO 14001 management standard. *Academy of Management Journal*, 48: 1091–1106.

Labatt, S. and Maclaren, V. (1998). Voluntary corporate environmental initiatives: A typology and preliminary investigation. *Environment and Planning C: Government and Policy*, 16(2): 191–209.

Lawrence, T., Hardy, C. and Phillips, N. (2002). Institutional effects of interorganizational collaboration: The emergence of proto institutions. *Academy of Management Journal*, 45(1): 281–290.

Lawrence, T. B., Suddaby, R. and Leca, B. (eds) (2011). *Institutional Work: Actors and Agency in Institutional Studies of Organization*. Cambridge: Cambridge University Press.

Lefsrud, L. (2013). When worlds collide: The intersection of meaning-making between hearings and media for Alberta's oil sands. Unpublished thesis, University of Alberta.

Lefsrud, L., Graves, H. and Phillips, N. (2014). Dirty oil, ethical oil, legitimate or not? The struggle to categorize the Alberta oil sands. Alliance for Research on Corporate Sustainability (ARCS) Conference, Cornell University, May 7–9, Ithaca, NY.

Lefsrud, L. and Jennings, P. D. (2014.) Being entrepreneurial in your storytelling: An institutional tale. In S. L. Newbert, *Small Businesses in a Global Economy: Creating and Managing Successful Organizations*, 2 vols. Westport, CT: Praeger.

Lefsrud, L. and Meyer, R. (2012). Science or science fiction? Professionals' discursive construction of climate change. *Organization Studies*, 33(1): 1477–1506.

Liesen, A. (2013). Climate change and asset prices – evidence on market inefficiency in Europe. Unpublished dissertation, University of Leeds.

Lounsbury, M. (2001). Institutional sources of practice variation: Staffing college and university recycling programs. *Administrative Science Quarterly*, 46(1): 29–56.

MacKenzie, D. (2009). Making things the same: Gases, emission rights and the politics of carbon markets. *Accounting, Organizations and Society*, 34(3–4): 440–455.

Maguire, S. and Hardy, C. (2009). Discourse and deinstitutionalization: The decline of DDT. *Academy of Management Journal*, 52(1): 148–178.

Marcus, A., Malen, J. and Ellis, S. (2013). The promise and pitfalls of venture capital as an asset class for clean energy investment research questions for organization and natural environment scholars. *Organization & Environment*, 26(1): 31–60.

Marti, I., Courpasson, D. and Barbosa, S. D. (2013). 'Living in the fishbowl.' Generating an entrepreneurial culture in a local community in Argentina. *Journal of Business Venturing*, 28(1): 10–29.

McCarthy, J. and Zald, M. (1977). Resource mobilization and social movements: A partial theory. *American Journal of Sociology*, 82: 1212–1240.

McCright, A. M. and Dunlap, R. E. (2003). Defeating Kyoto: The conservative movement's impact on US climate change policy. *Social Problems*, 50(3): 348–373.

McDaniels, T., Gregory, R. and Fields, D. (1999). Democratizing risk management: Successful public involvement in local water management decisions. *Risk Analysis*, 19: 497–510.

Meadows, D., Randers, J., Meadows, D. and Behrens, W. (1972). *The Limits to Growth*. New York: Universe Books.

Meyer, J. W., Scott, W. R., Rowan, B. and Deal, T. (1985). *Organizational Environments: Ritual and Rationality*. London: Sage.

Meyer, J., Boli, J., Thomas, G. and Ramirez, F. (1997). World society and the nation state. *American Journal of Sociology*, 103(1): 144–181.

Misutka, P., Coleman, C., Jennings, P. D. and Hoffman, A. (2014). Processes for retrenching logics: The Alberta oil sands case, 2008–2011. In M. Lounsbury and E. Boxenbaum (eds), *Institutional Logics in Action: Research in the Sociology of Organizations*. Bingley, UK: Emerald Group. pp. 131–164.

Mitchell, R. K., Agle, B. R., & Wood, D. J. (1997). Toward a theory of stakeholder identification and salience: Defining the principle of who and what really counts. *Academy of Management Review*, 22(4): 853–886.

Molotch, H. (1970). Oil in Santa Barbara and power in America. *Sociological Inquiry*, 40(1): 131–144.

Odum, E. and Barrett, G. (2004). *Fundamentals of Ecology*, 5th edn. Boston, MA: Cengage Learning.

OECD (Organization for Economic Cooperation and Development) (2000). *Innovation and the Environment*. Paris: OECD.

OECD (Organization for Economic Cooperation and Development) (2003). *Voluntary Approaches for Environmental Policy: Effectiveness, Efficiency and Usage in Policy Mixes*. Paris: OECD.

Oxford Advanced Learner Dictionary (2012). 8th Edition. Oxford: Oxford University Press.

Parsons, T. (1967). *Sociological Theory and Modern Society*. New York: The Free Press.

Parsons, T. (1968). *The Structure of Social Action: A Study in Social Action with Special Reference to a Group of Recent European Writers*. New York: The Free Press.

Perrow, C. (1999). *Normal Accidents: Living with High Risk Technologies*. Princeton, NJ: Princeton University Press.

Perrow, C. (2010). Organizations and global warming. In Constance Lever-Tracy (ed.), *Routledge Handbook of Climate Change and Society*. New York: Routledge. pp. 59–77.

Perrow, C. (2011). *The Next Catastrophe: Reducing Our Vulnerabilities to Natural, Industrial, and Terrorist Disasters.* Princeton, NJ: Princeton University Press.

Petriglieri, J. L. (2015). Co-creating relationship repair: Pathways to reconstructing destabilized organizational identification. *Administrative Science Quarterly*, 60(3): 518–557.

Phillips, N. and Hardy, C. (2002). *Discourse Analysis: Investigating Processes of Social Construction.* London: Sage.

Pope Francis (2015). *Laudato Si.* Vatican City: Vatican Press.

Porter, M. E. and Van der Linde, C. (1995). Green and competitive: Ending the stalemate. *Harvard Business Review*, 73(5): 120–134.

Potoski, M. and Prakash, A. (2004). The regulation dilemma: Cooperation and conflict in environmental governance. *Public Administration Review*, 64(2): 152–163.

Powell, W. and DiMaggio, P. (eds) (1991). *The New Institutionalism in Organizational Analysis.* Chicago, IL: University of Chicago Press.

Prakash, A. and Kellman, K. (2004). Policy modes, firms and the natural environment. *Business Strategy & the Environment*, 13(2): 107–128.

Rockström, J., Steffen, W., Noone, K. et al. (2009). Planetary boundaries: Exploring the safe operating space for humanity. *Ecology and Society*, 14(2): 32. Available at www.ecologyandsociety.org/vol14/iss2/art32/.

Rowan, R. (2014). Notes on politics after the Anthropocene. In E. Johnson and H. Morehouse (eds), After the Anthropocene: Politics and geographic inquiry for a new epoch. *Progress in Human Geography*, 38(3): 439–456.

Russo, M. V. (2001). Institutions, exchange relations, and the emergence of new fields: Regulatory policies and independent power production in America, 1978–1992. *Administrative Science Quarterly*, 46(1): 57–86.

Schofer, E. and Hironaka, A. (2005). The effects of world society on environmental protection outcomes. *Social Forces*, 84(1): 25–47.

Schot, J. (1992). Constructive technology assessment and technological dynamics: The case of clean technology. *Technology and Human Values*, 17(1): 36–56.

Schüssler, E., Rüling, C. and Wittneben, B. (2014). On melting summits: The limitations of field-configuring events as catalysts of change in transnational climate policy. *Academy of Management Journal*, 57(1): 140–171.

Schutz, A. (1967). *The Phenomenology of the Social World.* Chicago, IL: Northwestern University Press.

Scott, W. R. (1995). *Institutions and Organizations.* Thousand Oaks, CA: Sage.

Scott, W. R. (2001). *Institutions and Organizations,* 2nd edn. Thousand Oaks, CA: Sage.

Searle, J. (1979). *Expression and Meaning: Studies in the Theory of Speech Acts.* Cambridge: Cambridge University Press.

Selznick, P. (1949). *TVA and the Grassroots.* Berkeley, CA: University of California Press.

Sharifian, M. (2015). The paths of clean technology: From innovation to commercialization. Unpublished dissertation, University of Alberta.

Sharma, S. and Henriques, I. (2005). Stakeholder influences on sustainability practices in the Canadian forest products industry. *Strategic Management Journal*, 26(2): 159–180.

Sharma, S. and Vredenburg, H. (1998). Proactive corporate environmental strategy and the development of competitively valuable organizational capabilities. *Strategic Management Journal*, 19(8): 729–753.

Sine, W. D., Haveman, H. A. and Tolbert, P. S. (2005). Risky business? Entrepreneurship in the new independent-power sector. *Administrative Science Quarterly*, 50(2): 200–232.

Sine, W. and Lee, B. (2009). Tilting at windmills? The environmental movement and the emergence of the US wind energy sector. *Administrative Science Quarterly*, 54 (1): 123–155.

Smith, W. K. and Lewis, M. W. (2011). Toward a theory of paradox: A dynamic equilibrium model of organizing. *Academy of Management Review*, 36(2): 381–403.

Soderstrom, S. and Weber, K. (2011a). Corporate sustainability agendas from the bottom. *European Business Review*, March/April: 6–9.

Soderstrom, S. and Weber, K. (2011b). Organizational sustainability agendas: An interaction ritual perspective on issue mobilization. Working paper, University of Michigan, Ann Arbor, MI.

Steffen, W., Crutzen, P. and McNeil, J. (2007). The Anthropocene: Are humans overwhelming the great forces of nature? *AMBIO*, 36(8): 614–621.

Strang, D. and Tuma, N. B. (1993). Spatial and temporal heterogeneity in diffusion. *American Journal of Sociology*, 99(3): 614–639.

Suddaby, R. and Greenwood, R. (2005). Rhetorical strategies of legitimacy. *Administrative Science Quarterly*, 50(1): 35–67.

Suzuki, D. (1997). *The Sacred Balance: Rediscovering Our Place in Nature.* Vancouver: Greystone Books.

Thaler, R. H. and Sunstein, C. R. (2008). *Nudge: Improving Decisions about Health, Wealth, and Happiness.* New Haven, CT: Yale University Press.

Thornton, P. H., Ocasio, W. and Lounsbury, M. (2012). *The Institutional Logics Perspective: A New Approach to Culture, Structure and Process.* Oxford: Oxford University Press.

Van Maanen, J. (1995). Crossroads style as theory. *Organization Science*, 6(1): 133–143.

Vogel, D. (2012). *The Politics of Precaution: Regulating Health, Safety and Environmental Risks in Europe and the United States.* Princeton, NJ: Princeton University Press.

Waddock, S. and Graves, S. (1997). The corporate social performance–financial performance link. *Strategic Management Journal*, 18: 303–319.

Weber, K., Heinze, K. L. and De Soucey, M. (2008). Forage for thought: Mobilizing codes in the movement for grass-fed meat and dairy products. *Administrative Science Quarterly*, 53(3): 529–567.

Weber, M. (1978 [1919]). *Economy and Society.* Berkeley, CA: University of California Berkeley Press.

Weick, K. E. (1993). The collapse of sensemaking in organizations: The Mann Gulch disaster. *Administrative Science Quarterly*, 38: 628–652.

Weir, D. (1986). *The Bhopal Syndrome.* San Francisco, CA: Sierra Club Books.

Westphal, J. D., Gulati, R. and Shortell, S. M. (1997). Customization or conformity? An institutional and network perspective on the content and consequences of TQM adoption. *Administrative Science Quarterly*, 42: 366–394.

Westwood, R. and Clegg, S. (eds) (2009). *Debating Organization: Point-Counterpoint in Organization Studies.* Oxford: Blackwell.

Whetten, D. A. (1989). What constitutes a theoretical contribution? *Academy of Management Review*, 14(4): 490–495.

Young, S. and Dhanda, K. (2013). *Sustainability: Essentials for Business.* Los Angeles, CA: Sage.

Zandbergen, P. A. (2009). Exposure of US counties to Atlantic tropical storms and hurricanes, 1851–2003. *Natural Hazards*, 48(1): 83–99.

Zietsma, C. and Lawrence, T. B. (2010). Institutional work in the transformation of an organizational field: The interplay of boundary work and practice work. *Administrative Science Quarterly*, 55(2): 189–221.

30

Race and Institutionalism

Fabio Rojas

INTRODUCTION

Race is a core sociological topic and institutionalism is a core paradigm in organizational theory. Surprisingly, there are relatively few attempts to explore the connections between race and institutional processes. A casual perusal of classic texts in neo-institutional theory reveals a genuine scarcity of research on how race and institutions interact. None of the early classic articles of institutional theory mention race, such as Stinchcombe's (1965) article on environmental imprinting, Meyer and Rowan's (1977) discussion of myth and ceremony, or DiMaggio and Powell's (1983) iron cage article. The edited volumes defining early neo-institutionalism, such as *The New Institutional Analysis* (DiMaggio and Powell, 1991), exhibit a similar lack of attention given to race. Even recent anthologies, such as *Institutional Work: Actors and Agency in Institutional Studies of Organization* (Lawrence et al., 2011), do not have sustained discussions of race.

This situation is starting to change. In the last ten years, a number of scholars in sociology, management and related areas have begun an earnest effort to integrate the study of race and institutional analysis. There are a number of motivating factors behind this new scholarship. Some scholars are interested in race as an issue of contention within organizations. These scholars use concepts from the study of social movements to formulate questions about the impact of race within organizational settings (Binder, 2002; Rojas, 2007, 2010). Social movement scholar Doug McAdam and organizational theorist Neil Fligstein used the Civil Rights movement to illustrate contention within organizational fields (Fligstein and McAdam, 2012). Other scholars are interested in race as an example of the regulating forces that shape organizations (Shiao, 2005). Diversity policies, employment law and other policies are all aimed at trying to force organizations to provide a public accounting for how they hire and manage employees (e.g., Dobbin, 2009;

Skrentny, 1996, 2014). Still other scholars are interested in race because social categories are basic ingredients to organizational fields (Wooten, 2015). As various actors strive to build and develop organizational fields, they react to the basic categories of the social world, which influence their decision making.

The chapter introduces the reader to the intersection between institutional analysis and the sociology of race. First, this chapter will provide a brief summary of what sociologists understand race to mean and why it is important for the study of organizations. Second, the chapter will review the emerging literature that illustrates the role of race in shaping organizations and institution. In the conclusion, I will present a synthesis and outline a series of open questions about how race affects institutional processes.

RACE AS A SUBJECT OF SOCIAL SCIENCE

The definition of race is one of the most contentious topics in the social sciences (see Morning, 2011 for a review). The debate focuses on whether race refers to a social convention or whether human beings can be classified into subgroups based on shared ancestry and physical traits. Those who argue that race is a social convention are often called 'constructivists' because they believe that terms like 'Black' or 'White' are historically specific categories. On this point, constructivists note that the definition of a racial group varies greatly over time, racial definitions vary across cultures, the boundaries of racial groups are vague, and they claim that the evidence for biologically defined racial groups is weak or inconclusive. In contrast, there is also a tradition of social science that asserts that 'race is real'. Scholars in this tradition point to the fact that there is detectable genetic drift within the human population. As people migrated out of East Africa, they became geographically distant, which allowed there to be differences between communities. Scholars in this tradition usually rely on studies of human genes collected from populations across the world and they try to establish that there is non-random clustering of genetic markers. For a recent review of this literature, see Shiao et al. (2012).

In general, most scholars in management, sociology, economics and related areas focus on the social dimensions of race and treat race as a socially constructed category guiding action. For example, in Gary Becker's (1957) economic analysis of employment discrimination, race acts as a proxy for people's beliefs about workers. As people interact, they must establish formal, and informal, criteria for who belongs in a specific category and what the categories mean. For example, in the United States, many people employ the 'one drop rule' to define 'Black' – a person with a single ancestor who was Black is also Black. In other contexts, race is very strictly defined. In the United States, membership in an indigenous tribe, such as the Cherokee, requires that a person have an ancestor on a government enumeration of tribe members called the 'Dawes Roll', which was finalized in 1907 (Cherokee Nation, 2015). Other tribes, such as the Navajo, require both ancestry and participation in a tribal community (Bardill, 2015).

Thus, for students of institutional theory, the social and behavioral aspects of race are very important. If the core insight of institutional theory is that organizations are subject to the pressures of their social and political environments, then it is extremely important to know that an organization's audience, workers and regulators have racial identities. These racial identities affect organizational behavior from the ground up. Workers might be separated based on racial groups. The government may create policies to protect, or harm, specific groups. Regulators may demand an explanation of the demography of their workforce. Thus, race should be a central concern for institutional scholars.

A FIELD-CENTRIC APPROACH TO RACE

Contemporary institutional analysis, often dated to Stinchcombe's (1965) article, is now approximately fifty years old and has resulted in many competing versions of the theory. In this section, I focus on a version of institutional theory that is useful for taking about race in the context of organizational studies and management. I start with field theory, as presented in Neil Fligstein and Doug McAdam's *A Theory of Fields* (2012), and then move on to describe the more interactional processes described by scholars working in the traditions of inhabited institutions, institutional work and institutional logics.

Fligstein and McAdam define a 'strategic action field' as a 'meso-level social order where actors interact with each other based shared understandings'. This definition speaks to multiple approaches to institutional theory that focus on specific industries or sectors. The definition is expansive in that interaction may be defined broadly – through interpersonal contact, organizational behavior, or state policy. Within a field, there may be all manner of social structures emerging. Formally, we might expect a wide range of coercive forces reflecting regulation by the state or accreditation agencies. Inter-personal and inter-organizational networks may appear to coordinate action within fields, and organizations may be created to pursue goals within a social domain. Thus, the theory of fields depicts social domains as having the following components: a population of organizations that are 'about' a specific type of activity (e.g., education); a cognitive dimension of the field such as beliefs about legitimate or illegitimate behavior; forms of status where participants can judge

who is influential; relations between groups; and relationships, or lack of relationships, between the field and the state.

In initially describing fields, it may appear that fields are domains of action that uniformly affect their participants. Indeed, in reading Bourdieu or Fligstein and McAdam's treatment of fields, there is relatively little attention given to the heterogeneity present in social fields. In fact, a number of institutional scholars have argued that their work has been misread. DiMaggio, for example, argued that too many readers were quick to focus on pressure for conformity within organizational communities and few remembered that DiMaggio and Powell (1983) concluded with a list of hypotheses that explained when organizations were subject to the 'iron cage'. Similarly, many have noted that readers often overlook the features of fields that may permit, or encourage, disruption and change. Here, I briefly review more of the complexities of fields that have been discussed in the literature with an emphasis on how they relate to race. For a more systematic exploration of this issue, readers should consult the chapter of this handbook dedicated to fields, which delves into the concept of fields as it has appeared in the history of institutionalist scholarship (Wooten and Hoffman, Chapter 2 this Volume).

Heterogeneity: Initially, it may appear as if fields are homogeneous entities. The organizations and actors within a field share behavioral scripts and structural templates. Instead, fields vary in how much organizations and actors are subject to these social pressures. The sources of variation are many. A young field may simply not have an established rule for behavior. The sector may be 'pre-institutional'. Consider the case of auto manufacturing. When automobiles were invented, there were few norms that needed to be obeyed. As the industry aged, activists entered the field to legitimize some types of automobiles while delegitimizing others (Rao, 2009).

Another process that contributes to field heterogeneity is uneven exposure to the actors and institutions that encourage order and uniformity (Lounsbury, 2001; Quirke, 2013). That is, not all organizations are routinely policed or inspected at the same rate. For example, it has often been noted by organizational scholars that high and low status organizations do not appear to be subject to the same pressures as those with intermediate status. According to the 'middle class conformity' hypothesis, low-status organizations have little to lose through deviance and high-status groups can afford to suffer criticism when they violate norms (Phillips and Zuckerman, 2001). The result is that institutional pressures are felt most strongly by organizations that are 'middle class' in their field.

Network structures: Social networks are an important element of field theory and institutionalism more generally. Throughout scholarly writings on fields, it has been noted that actors in fields can use social ties to their advantage and that larger patterns of relationships can structure and channel action within fields. Neil Fligstein (2001) includes the strategic employment of social ties in his broader concept of social skill, which denotes the strategic manipulation of an individual's social environment. The classic example in economic sociology is James Coleman's (1988) treatment of social capital – features of social relationships that facilitate the achievement of strategic goals. He uses the example of people from the same ethnic group: membership in the same community increases trust and boosts cooperation.

The work of Podolny and colleagues indicates the ways in which networks shape fields by concentrating attention, information and resources. In a classic article on how social actors employ networks, Podolny (2001) argues that networks may be interpreted as signals of status, which he calls 'prisms', or quality and networks are 'pipelines' for scarce information. This has suggested to many readers that fields and networks are endogenous. As fields develop, elites emerge and ties with these elites disproportionately

attract resources, which then perpetuates inequality in fields.

The main question for this section is how race should be included in institutional analysis. One intuitive approach is to treat race as a basic ingredient for all the field-level processes that I have just described. For example, a great deal of the literature in institutional analysis addresses coordination processes where organizations adopt similar forms, or policies, as a response to environmental pressures (e.g., DiMaggio and Powell, 1983; Rogers, 2003; Scott, 2001; Scott et al., 2000). Race, then, can be a factor that causes some organizational forms to be adopted over others, or causes policies to become the standard within a field. Similarly, another tradition within institutional analysis examines the creation of status within fields. This research literature describes the different ways that actors try to create forms of status or acquire status within fields (Bourdieu, 1977; Dezalay and Garth, 1996; Fligstein, 2001). Similarly, a race-based approach to institutionalism might ask how race shapes these status orders (Chiang, 2009; Wooten, 2015). Are forms of status within a field giving advantage to some groups? Do forms of capital take the characteristics of certain groups for granted? That is to say, are the 'right behaviors' the behaviors of dominant racial groups?

A second approach to race and institutionalism is to ask how institutional processes affect race. That is, how do environmental pressures, regulatory processes and institutional logics affect or change the classification of people into different ethnic groups? For example, if a political group lobbies the state to mandate ethnic diversity in firms, one can ask how this new rule changes racial attitudes or boundaries between racial or cultural groups. Thus, race can be an outcome of an institutional process, not just the cause.

These two broad approaches to race and institutions reflect an understanding that race and organizational processes co-evolve. However, one can move from this broad observation to a more specific understanding of the relationship. First, fields can be viewed from an interactional perspective (Emirbayer and Desmond, 2015). As many organizational theorists have pointed out, organizations are just places where organizing happens. Perhaps the classic expression of this view comes from the Carnegie School of organizational analysis, which focused on the routines and procedures that define organizations (March and Simon, 1958). The field-centric approach to race would amend this view and point out that an organization's routines and policies are responses to race or inevitably are shaped by their racial context. People take their views of race into account when they design and implement an organization's routines.

An informative example comes from the study of higher education and elite universities. At first, it might appear that college admissions policies do not reflect race. For example, many universities state that they accept students with specific credentials, such as a high school diploma, or a level of performance on a standardized test. These admissions policies are often developed by administrators that are trying to bolster or undermine racial barriers in the university system. Karabel's (2005) historical study of the admissions policies of Harvard, Yale and Princeton details how policies focusing on 'well-rounded' students and geographic diversity were attempts to limit Jewish and Asian applicants, who tended to score well on standardized tests but not have the resources needed to pursue extracurricular activities and who lived in large urban centers on the East and West Coasts. Earlier higher education leaders, ironically, promoted standardized tests to counter the anti-Semitism that prevented many qualified Jewish students from entering the university.

The interaction of race and institutional pressures can also be seen in recent studies of graduate education in the arts and sciences. Posselt's (2015) ethnographic study of graduate admissions committees shows how doctoral program admissions committees

are struggling to reconcile different institutional imperatives. They experience normative pressures; their discipline has norms for what constitutes a qualified candidate. But there are also university-level concerns about equity. This indicates the importance of 'inhabited institutions' for the study of race (Hallett, 2010). While universities may experience environmental pressures for racial diversity, they are mitigated by a myriad of organizational processes, such as disciplinary standards and department committees.

Second, the macro-level field-level dynamics described affect how race and institutions interact. For example, the 'patchiness' of institutions makes it possible for individuals to experiment with new meanings of race (Quirke, 2013). One example comes from the study of urban economies. In urban centers that are on the decline, there are fewer and fewer traditional retailers for food and many resort to low-quality food. In response to this, there are movements of Black 'urban farmers' who are using racial inequality as a framing for their agricultural work (White, 2011b). The crumbling and disintegration of urban economies has allowed race to become an important factor in reorganizing food production in some inner city neighborhoods. Disruptions in fields can also destabilize racial orders and undermine institutions. Foston's (2015) recent dissertation on the effects of segregation on organizational fields shows how the end of Jim Crow led to the vast reduction of all-Black high schools in the American South. The political disruption of Civil Rights meant that mono-racial schools were less legitimate and possibly illegal, even if they served students who might not otherwise obtain a quality high school education.

The preceding discussion draws attention to a very important aspect of race. It is something that is pervasive in social life. It is a cause and an outcome of other important processes. Thus, it is not something within a specific field, like the state or the non-profit sector, nor is there a distinct 'racial field'.

Race is a sorting of people, a social classification, whose presence can be felt in nearly all social contexts and itself can be changed by external events. Race is a system of meaning that is recursive in that its current definition relies on how race was articulated in previous eras and interacted with other economic and social orders.

Figure 30.1 presents a simplified version of this argument. The purpose is not to document all the ways that race shapes organizational fields and, in turn, might be shaped by institutional processes. The intuition is that race is a factor in the creation of fields and an outcome of fields. Furthermore, race and institutions exist in a dynamic relationship that institutional analysis must recognize.

In the next section, I will illustrate the general approach to how one might incorporate race into the study of institutions. The subsequent sections will explore different aspects of fields, such as institutional logics, contentious politics and the creation of organizational status orders.

RIVAL ORGANIZATIONAL FORMS IN FIELDS: THE FAILURE OF BLACK STUDIES COLLEGES AND THE SUCCESS OF BLACK STUDIES PROGRAMS

This section uses as an example recent scholarship on Black Power and student protest to examine the push and pull between race and organizations (Biondi, 2014; Kendi, 2012; Rojas, 2007). In the late 1960s, a number of students, educators and Civil Rights activists asserted that college curricula needed to change. They argued that college curricula were flawed because they excluded meaningful discussions of the African or African American experience. They also claimed that colleges were intentionally, or unintentionally, racist. The solution to this problem, in their view, was to create a new area of scholarly inquiry called 'Black Studies' and use activism to promote it on college campuses. From the 1960s to the 2000s, over 200 degree-granting programs were created at American campuses.

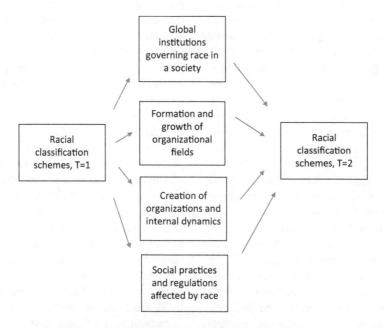

Figure 30.1 How race affects institutions and organizational fields

The evolution of Black Studies is a decades-long process that defies brief summary, but here I will focus on aspects that are relevant to the study of institutions. First, the victory of the Civil Rights movement entailed the de-institutionalization of many educational norms. For example, prior to Black Studies, the study of Black history was relegated to a few specialists and was considered to be a very low status type of scholarly activity. The desegregation of colleges meant that there was an influx of students into predominantly White campuses. Upon arrival, many students believed that Black topics were unfairly excluded from classes and that there were few faculty who conducted research in this area. In 1968, there was an important student strike at San Francisco State College where activists demanded the creation of multiple ethnic studies programs, such as Black Studies.

Second, the Black Studies movement generated a wide range of organizational forms that were designed to implement the new Black Studies curriculum. There were proposals for Black Studies courses, Black Studies interdisciplinary undergraduate programs, Black Studies doctoral programs, Black Studies research institutes, Black Studies colleges and independent Black Studies colleges. In other words, changes in the American racial order prompted new social practices, like desegregation, and the emergence of entirely new organizational fields. Activists created new organizations that re-appropriated existing forms and combined them with new educational practices.

Third, the higher education environment strongly affected the survival of organizations. Forms of Black Studies that were seen as consistent with the pre-existing logic of higher education were more likely to survive. A common theme from scholarship on these units is that administrators could accept them as long as they justified themselves by appealing to academic norms and the logic of interdisciplinary academic work. In other words, Black Studies activists had to assure

administrators that the program would not be a haven for political radicals. Instructors would teach courses that bore a strong resemblance to those taught in existing history, humanities and social science programs.

The strategy of isomorphism with the rest of academia worked. Even though Black Studies programs in universities are often harshly criticized, there have been very few closures, most occurring very early in the history of the field. In recent years, there has been an expansion of doctoral programs. The first doctoral program was founded at Temple University in the 1980s and now twelve programs offer doctoral degrees. These programs can be found at the most elite institutions, such as Harvard University, Yale University and the University of California, Berkeley. Perhaps the most popular form of Black Studies is the courses that focuses on African American history and culture. Such courses can be found in nearly all comprehensive institutions of higher education in the United States.

In contrast, forms of Black Studies that rejected the logic of de-politicized teaching and interdisciplinary academic organization often failed. For example, there was, at one time, a proposal that the University of Chicago establish a Black Studies institute that would reach out and help poor urban communities in Chicago. Almost at the same time, nearby University of Illinois at Chicago was presented with a similar proposal for an Ethnic Studies program that would be supervised by 'community members'. Both proposals were rejected. At the University of Chicago administrators felt that community outreach was simply incompatible with elite education, while at the University of Illinois administrators thought it was simply not appropriate for non-scholarly outsiders to have power over an academic unit.

Perhaps the most instructive failure in the history of Black Studies was the attempt to build freestanding colleges. At least two were built in 1969 and each operated for a few years. One was Malcolm X University in North Carolina and the other was Nairobi College in East Palo Alto, California (Belvin, 2004; Hoover, 1992). They were established by activists associated with Duke University and Stanford University. In each case, activists wanted an institution that would be completely free from the institutional pressures of higher education. Specifically, they did not want Black Studies to be forced into an interdisciplinary stance where students and faculty needed to justify their activities to White audiences. Rather, they wanted colleges that were free to develop courses suited for African American students. Instructors at Malcolm X College believed that they could train people who could help America's urban poor and countries in Africa develop stronger economies.

Malcom X University shut down by 1972 and Nairobi College persisted for a few more years. These educational organizations were undermined by a predictable set of factors. Both suffered from internal conflict. The more interesting observation is that freestanding Black Studies colleges were subject to harsh criticism in the media. This led to an abrupt drop in funding. Since there were few students, and facilities were expensive, even a modest decline in donations could force the collapse of these schools. What is important to note is that Black Studies degree programs were not immune to the same criticisms and they also suffered from internal conflict. The difference between independent Black Studies colleges and Black Studies degree programs is that the latter were integrated into larger universities and colleges, thus insulating them from turbulence. This was made possible by conforming to the institutional logics of higher education. By insisting on a community focus and thus obtaining independence, schools like Nairobi College and Malcolm X University exposed themselves to great risk.

This brief overview of the history of Black Studies indicates the different ways that race and fields affect each other. The early history of Black Studies is all about field disruptions.

Some disruptions 'come from above' and reflect national, or international, political processes. A common observation on the history of Civil Rights and Black Power is that these movements were affected by anti-colonial struggles. Minority groups within Western nations often modeled themselves after groups in African and Asian colonies that fought armed struggles against European powers. Most famously, Black radical groups in the 1960s were inspired by Castro's Cuban revolution and Mao's Chinese communist revolution. The Black Panthers, for example, explicitly claimed to be Maoists at their inception (Rojas, 2007). Thus, there is a 'trickle' down process. Larger racialized conflicts disrupt fields and create new models in close-by fields.

The struggle for Black Studies also illustrates the importance of the interactional elements of fields and how disruptions are caused, or altered, by race. For example, much of the conflict around Black Studies focused on the claim that college curricula were biased or intentionally excluded Black contributions. Thus, there was a lot of 'institutional work' aimed at persuading students, and sympathetic activists, that college courses needed to be challenged and reformed (Lawrence and Suddaby, 2006; Rojas, 2010). College administrators set the tone of conflict with their responses to protest. When confronted by activists, they could actively resist, appropriate student demands, or capitulate. Resisting students could allow the university administration to prevent curricular change, but exacerbate conflict in the long term. Giving in completely to students could make administrators appear illegitimate. It was common for administrators to attempt to tie in Black Studies protest into their own agendas. For example, Black Studies programs were sometimes used by deans to claim that the campus was successfully recruiting Black Students and faculty.

Black Studies protest also showed how the field of higher education touches and overlaps with 'close-by' fields, as suggested by the theory of strategic action fields. It was often the case that demands for Black Studies were bundled with related racial issues. It was not uncommon for activists promoting Black Studies to ask for more affirmative action on campus, or ask for the university to support the nearby Black community or reform 'town–gown' relations (Rojas, 2007). Similarly, activists who worked on non-academic issues would sometimes move to college campuses to help Black students mobilize. These two processes show how field-level events shape the outcomes of racial conflicts. Ruptures in close-by fields can be used to motivate political challenges within fields and overlaps can facilitate the transmission of people and resources between fields.

The field-centric approach to race can also help us understand the resolution of conflicts within fields. When incumbents in organizations, and fields, allow challengers to develop alternatives, there are multiple processes that select possible outcome. This section has indicated how this played out in Black Studies. Some activists wanted to institutionalize race inside of existing universities, while other more radical activists wanted completely independent Black Studies organizations, such as think-tanks and Black Studies colleges. Then, the question becomes which cultural and economic processes can support some types of social change while 'weeding out' others. In the case of Black Studies, a strong alignment with the structures and values of higher education, such as race neutrality and interdisciplinary collaboration, allowed Black Studies to survive. The radical audience for autonomous Black Studies did not have the financial resources and academic legitimacy needed to make this form of institutional reform viable.

To summarize, the history of Black Studies shows us how race and field dynamics are intertwined. The gap between stated ideals of equality in education and the situation in colleges promoted grievances. Broader national and international conflicts over race 'spilled over' into the higher education system. The overlap between higher education and city politics helped students come into contact with experienced activists. Then, students developed racialized alternatives to the curriculum of the 1960s and field-level processes 'selected out' those that were culturally or financially incompatible with the rest of the field.

MACRO-LEVEL INSTITUTIONAL CHANGE: THE CREATION OF LATINOS AND ASIAN AMERICANS

Here we examine two examples of recent research that explain how race is a factor in macro-institutional change that affects multiple organizational fields. The first is the emergence of the 'Latino' or 'Hispanic' category in the United States. G. Cristina Mora's (2014) recent book, *Making Hispanics: How Activists, Bureaucrats & Media Constructed a New American*, explains the political and economic processes that re-articulated the racial order of the United States. This account of a new social and political category has many lessons for institutionalists.

First, there is an institutional dimension of race, a taken-for-granted understanding of race that guides social interaction, organizational behavior and public policy. In the mid-1900s, the United States had White citizens, Black citizens, members of Native American tribes, and people from various other nations (e.g., 'Chinamen' or 'Mexicans'). Over time, those descended from European migrants retained an identity based on their nation of origin, as well as a larger pan-ethnic identity (e.g., Irish Americans were both White and Irish). This earlier classification treated Spanish-speaking people from Mexico, Central America, South America and the Caribbean as a sort of residual category. Pre-1970 censuses allowed people to indicate that they were Mexican or Peruvian, but it was rare for government agencies and private groups to have a larger pan-ethnic category for these people.

The Civil Rights movement created an opportunity for institutional entrepreneurs when it effectively changed race relations in the United States in the 1950s and 1960s. By showing that ethnic mobilization worked, other constituencies in the United States copied the style and tactics of the Civil Rights movement in pursuit of their own goals. Not surprisingly, Mexican American activists, and others, used the openness of the late 1960s to pursue a novel idea – Hispanic pan-ethnicity. That is, it was thought by various activists, business leaders and policy-makers that having a broad Hispanic ethnic category was tremendously useful.

Each constituency had a different reason for promoting the Hispanic ethnic category. Political activists found it easier to shape public policy if there was a large unified constituency that needed to be represented. A broadening of social categories increases influence. That is, it is easier to have influence if one represents tens of millions of Hispanics instead of one million Guatemalans. Actors with a cultural or economic interest eventually found that it was also valuable to promote Hispanic pan-ethnicity because it resulted in larger economic opportunities and facilitated marketing. Media, such as Univision, could be reorganized around a Hispanic market that was much easier to understand than an assembly of specific markets, which vary in their size across the country (e.g., Colombians are well represented in Texas and New York, but less so in San Francisco).

An important element of Mora's account is the focus on organizational processes. For example, much attention is paid to the US Census and its role in creating the policy infrastructure for the new Hispanic identity. The Hispanic identity project would be bolstered if the American government could say, with confidence, that millions of Hispanics did indeed live within the United States. Thus, it was very important for the US Census Bureau to create a Hispanic category and then ensure that people used that category in the decennial Census and other official forms.

The result of this intensive effort by activists, non-profits and the corporate community was the birth of a new racial category in the United States. The Hispanic category is now a standard, if contentious, element of the Census and it is used by policy-makers to describe a significant portion of the population (e.g., the 2010 Census reports that 16.3% of respondents indicated 'Spanish origin'). It is also a category that has great economic salience. Major media outlets present themselves as broadly oriented toward American Latino. *Hispanic* magazine was published from 1987 to 2010 and had a peak circulation of more than 300,000. *Latina*, which focuses on beauty and lifestyle, has a circulation of over 3 million.

The story I have presented is simplified and elides much of the contention around the Hispanic ethnic category. The Hispanic category was helped by the fact that migrants from South and Central American nations mostly spoke Spanish, were Christian or Catholic, and already recognized a shared Spanish heritage. In contrast, other episodes of macro-institutional racial change in the United States speak to the fact that reforming racial categories is very difficult, often resulting in an incompletely institutionalized racial identity.

The major example of this is the effort to create Asian pan-ethnicity in the United States in the 1970s and 1980s. Like the case of Hispanics, the Civil Rights movement encouraged activists to promote the idea of a common racial or ethnic group – 'Asian American.' This category is meant to include individuals who migrated from, or were descended from migrants from, China, Korea, India, the Philippines, Vietnam, and other parts of Central Asia, East Asia, South East Asia and the Pacific Islands. This discussion of Asian pan-ethnicity is drawn from Dina Okamoto's (2014) *Redefining Race: Asian American Panethnicity and Shifting Ethnic Boundaries*.

One of the major barriers to the Asian pan-ethnic category is that the cultural divide among Asian migrant populations is much larger than the one separating Latino migrant groups. There is no single language or religion that encompasses the Asian population. Exacerbating these differences, migrants would often carry over regional and national differences to the United States. The national and racial inequalities of Asia were often reconstructed completely in the United States. This is very apparent in the housing market. Rather than settle in majority Asian areas, Japanese would settle in neighborhoods that were separate from Chinese neighborhoods. One important factor that determined this pattern was that early Asian migration was about labor recruitment. Employers tended to draw from specific areas of Asia, which meant that early settlements were drawn from the same communities (e.g., the earliest Japanese settlers in the United States were often from Kumamoto, Hiroshima and Yamaguchi prefectures). The US legal system reinforced these boundaries. Consistently, courts supported laws and regulations that would prohibit Asian migrants from claiming the status of Whites and it was difficult to purchase housing outside of ethnic enclaves. The result is that Asian political and social organization was heavily dependent on Asian migrant communities that were stable and embodied longstanding national divisions.

Like Hispanic activists, Asians in the 1960s challenged this system by promoting the concept of an all-encompassing 'Asian American' category. One of the most important challenges was creating narratives that would appeal to a wide range of populations. Why would people in San Francisco's century-old Chinatown be part of an alliance with recent Vietnamese immigrants in Los Angeles? Activists employed multiple strategies. One was the simple strategy of using bridging ties, which speaks to interplay of structural holes and institutional processes. A Korean activist, for example, might not be able to directly speak to an Indian group, but he might work through mutual friends.

Another strategy is to rally around specific events that might threaten a wide range of Asian groups, such as the murder of Vincent Chin, a Chinese resident of Detroit who was killed by disgruntled auto-workers. Chin's murder, and the lenient sentencing of the killers, drew together a broad coalition of Asian groups. Other events that helped accelerate pan-ethnic coalition-building is the depiction of Asians in the media. Films or televisions shows that showed denigrating depictions of Asians would draw protest from these Asian American coalitions.

Overcoming these racial divisions required discursive work on the part of activists and a layering of narratives and identities. Activists had to actively fashion a narrative of their activities that would draw attention to commonalities. The murder of Vincent Chin highlighted the fact that people from any Asian nation could be targeted by anti-Asian violence. Presumably, the perpetrators were angry at Japanese firms who competed against Detroit's automakers. Yet, Chin was Chinese American, showing that anti-Japanese prejudice could be directed toward people of any Asian ancestry.

The creation of a broad Asian pan-ethnicity did not mean that people erased identities and categories based on nation of origin. People still identified as Korean or Filipino. What it did mean is that these national or regional identities had to be layered, or merged with, the broader Asian American narratives. Nation of origin categories were salient in some organizational fields (e.g., housing, religion, or labor markets) but pan-ethnic identities could be activated in other fields (e.g., social movement politics or Census politics). In fact, Okamoto presents some evidence about the interaction of traditional ethnic (e.g., Indian) identities and pan-ethnic identities (e.g., Asian American) for political organizations. The presence of ethnic organizations is negatively correlated with pan-Asian mobilization, suggesting that there is competition between ethnic and pan-ethnic identities.

The rise of pan-ethnic Hispanic and Asian categories in the US has multiple lessons for students of institutional theory. First, racial categories are the subject of massive amounts of institutional work. People have to actively make them and re-invent them. This work occurs both at the level of individual interactions and entire fields. The examples just mentioned above indicate the multi-level nature of this process. Latino activists, for example, had to argue to specific power holders in business and government that pan-ethnic categories were needed. This includes lobbying census officials for the right to create a broader Hispanic or Latino category and explaining to media executives that there was in fact a viable pan-ethnic market that could be catered to. Similarly, the renegotiation of pan-ethnic identity occurred at a broader field level. Once activists were able to persuade some elites of the value of pan-ethnic categories, they were able to diffuse throughout various sectors. For example, the spread of the Latino pan-ethnic category occurred in the media when magazines and broadcasters began offering 'Latino programming', as opposed to content aimed specifically at narrower groups like Mexicans or Puerto Ricans.

The revision of American Latino ethnicity from a collection of loosely related groups to a larger more coherent category entails a wide range of institutional work that has yet to be properly explored by scholars in either management or sociology. For example, much effort was spent deinstitutionalizing racial schema as they existed in the late 1950s. Mora's (2014) book provides an initial examination of this issue, but more can be done. Her analysis focuses mostly on institutional work that occurred within very elite situations – the US Census Bureau, leading Latino media outlets and major advertising agencies. In contrast, there is little literature that delves into how these categories were accepted, or rejected, and renegotiated 'on the ground'. The institutionalization of 'Latino' throughout the United States requires a more thorough account. In Texas, there were pan-Latino political parties that tried to employ the new Hispanic ethnicity and displace the Democratic party. These parties failed and the Democratic party of Texas was able to retain Latino voters. Aside from some historical treatments, there have been few attempts to explain how the new ethnic categories of the 1960s were, or were not, successful in shaping various political organizations. Similarly, there are few treatments of how specific organizations in various fields managed these new categories.

Second, the modification of macro-level racial categories allows for the emergence of new organizations and entire fields, such as pan-ethnic Asian political groups. That is, when there is conflict over ethnicity in a society, some organizations become delegitimized while others are allowed to appear. One very notable feature of pan-ethnic political groups in the United States is that few of them precede the 1960s. There were very few organizations before the 1960s that claimed to represent all Asians. A casual examination of the organizations discussed in Okamoto's book show that many are creations of the 1970s and 1980s. The creation of pan-ethnic organizational fields also reflects events that redefine ethnic politics. As noted above, the killing of Vincent Chin by enraged auto workers motivated the creation of anti-racist organizations that defended Asians of all nationalities, not just Japanese or Chinese Americans. This is why Okamoto notes that there appear to be 'generations' of pan-ethnic organizations that reflect shifting conceptions of racial solidarity.

Third, the modification of ethnic categories for economic and political purposes might require that new and old categories exist side-by-side. Thus, there is a possible 'layering' or 'overlapping of institutions'. Here, the example of Black Power organizations is instructive. In the late 1960s, there appeared many organizations that promoted Black independence from White institutions. One such organization was the Institute for the Black World, an independent think-tank and research center (White, 2011a). To survive, this organization had to cooperate with organizations that adhered to a more traditional view of race relations, such as the Ford Foundation, which funded the Institute in its earliest years. The interaction and co-existence between Black Power and liberal organizations resulted in persistent conflict. Okamoto's study shows that these identities may compete with each other and new categories may be salient in some cases but not others. For Asian pan-ethnic groups, the major issue that draws groups together is political challenge. When it is perceived that Asians are under threat, there is cooperation. On other issues, such as housing or cultural promotion, there is less cooperation; pan-ethnic and mono-ethnic groups act independently.

RACE AND INSTITUTIONAL LOGICS

A powerful new perspective in institutional theory comes from the literature on institutional logics (Thornton et al., 2012). The basic idea is that people use a shared framework for 'the socially constructed, historical patterns of material practices, assumptions, values, beliefs, and rules by which individuals produce and reproduce their material subsistence, organize time and space, and provide meaning to their social reality.' As people operate schools, gas stations, or hedge funds, they employ a system of beliefs that instructs them on how to survive, how to do things in a legally and socially legitimate way, and what the purpose of their actions is.

Race and institutional logic theory come together when scholars study the ideas that shape how organizations hire and promote workers, such as affirmative action, diversity and multiculturalism. J. Lee Shiao's (2005) analysis of diversity rhetoric and policy among philanthropic organizations is an instructive example. Lee situates his analysis in the immediate aftermath of the Civil

Rights movement. In the 1970s, Civil Rights advocates found themselves in an unusual position. Even though Civil Rights advocates had won major judicial and legislative victories, desegregation simply did not happen in the way they had anticipated. Civil Rights proponents often thought that the end of legal segregation and racist policies would entail a substantial entry of Blacks into previously White dominated institutions. This did not happen and activists noted the lack of progress. Education is an insightful example. Even though the US Congress banned racial discrimination in education and court cases affirmed it, many schools remained disproportionately White. Many of the education controversial policies of the 1970s were aimed specifically at trying to change this situation, such as busing policies that brought Black children to mainly White schools.

The institutional logics that guided non-profits in this era were modified to help philanthropic organizations operate in this environment. In the 1960s, the major logic of action was activism aimed at desegregation. The Ford Foundation, for example, set the tone by actively supporting various efforts to desegregate schools and housing. The Ford Foundation's leadership saw themselves as an ally of the social movement sector. The President of the Ford Foundation, McGeorge Bundy, directed program officers to give aid to groups that were fighting for desegregation (Rojas, 2007: ch. 5). In the 1970s, philanthropists found that an activist framing was no longer helpful. Instead, they found it more effective to shift from 'good causes' to 'good works' and 'good strategies' (e.g., shifting from supporting protest about education to supporting specific people and policies). The shift required that the non-profit sector become concerned with race less as a cause and more as a 'technical' issue that could be fruitfully addressed with support for personnel development and policy implementation.

The institutional logic that emerged in the 1970s and 1980s was 'diversity'. Rather than call for wholesale desegregation and the racial equalization of institutions, the logic of diversity emphasized inclusion (Shiao, 2005). This logic made it easy to justify a series of programs that developed leadership in education, business and politics. Instead of insisting that organizations have proportional racial representation among their leaders, non-profit actors could promote social change through programs aimed at increasing the population of qualified minorities, even if they were few relative to the population. For example, instead of immediately insisting that 14% of professors should be African American, it was more tractable to sponsor programs for minority graduate training. Similarly, a wide range of non-profit organizations began to develop programs that would encourage ethnic minorities to strive for leadership positions in the corporate sector, higher education and public policy. With cohorts of qualified minority professionals, it was possible to request that cultural and political institutions be more diverse in their leadership. Additionally, it was hoped that a diverse leadership would result in different policies.

The logic of diversity, in addition to being easier to implement, was also valuable in an age where counter-movement actors tried to roll back, or limit, the gains of the Civil Rights movement. A common theme in historical accounts of public policy in the 1980s is that various actors had effectively resisted the changes brought by Civil Rights. The most famous example is 'White flight', where White parents moved to racially homogenous neighborhoods so their children would not have to attend racially mixed schools. In such an environment, it would be nearly impossible to desegregate schools since people intentionally resided in places with few minority students or enrolled in all-White academies. Diversity is a logic that by-passed this political reality. Rather than directly confront behaviors that undermined desegregation, diversity initiatives focused on the elements of organizations that were subject to public scrutiny, like leadership.

Diversity and, later, multiculturalism are institutional logics that helped reformist organizations, such as non-profits and protest groups, develop strategies aimed at the mainstream. There are also institutional logics that emphasize social difference and, in a sense, acted against the mainstream. In American history one of the most famous examples was the Black Power movement, which was motivated by a logic of cultural autonomy. The principal idea behind the Black Power movement was that Black Americans should not have to wait for others in their search for freedom, equality and self-governance. Instead, Black Power activists believed that political, economic and cultural organizations for Blacks should be controlled by Blacks.

There were a wide range of organizations that embodied this basic logic (see Rojas and Carson, 2014 for detailed discussions of these groups). Some organizations, such as the Black Congressional Caucus, tried to create a 'safe space' for Blacks within mainstream institutions. Scholars have called such institutional 'counter-centers' because they try to coordinate a minority view inside a larger mainstream power center, such as the US Congress (Rojas, 2007: ch. 6). Other Black Power organizations operated on a strategy of parallelism. A group would form a more radical version of an existing group to represent a constituency that would normally be ignored. The Dodge Radical Union Movement was one such example. Created in 1968, DRUM was a Black union that demanded recognition from Detroit auto-makers and the United Auto Workers. There are similar 'parallel' groups in education and the professions, which will be discussed later in this chapter.

The most radical Black Power groups were revolutionary in nature. For example, the Republic of New Afrika was an armed group and they wanted African Americans to move to the South and form a break-off nation. The US Organization, based in Southern California, offered a completely different lifestyle for its member that was separate from White society. They had their own residences, cultural traditions and publications. Another group, which slightly preceded the Black Power era, was the Nation of Islam, which also provided an all-Black cultural institution. The most famous of the radical Black Power groups was the Black Panther Party. Initially formed as a defense against police harassment, the group soon adopted a socialist economic ideology. Later, the group provided housing, its own newspaper, social services and nearly won the 1973 mayoral election in Oakland, California.

The contrast between the organizational logic of diversity and cultural autonomy draws attention to a basic choice that all actors must make when dealing with race – do they choose to align, or integrate, themselves with the mainstream or do they opt to exit and manage their own affairs? Recent scholarship on Black Power suggests that it is possible to go quite far using the logic of cultural autonomy. The examples above show the range of possibilities. Some groups, like the Black Panthers or the freestanding Black Studies colleges, were short-lived because they were undermined by internal political conflict as well as institutional pressures. But numerous other 'Black conscious' organizations were successful.

The main difference between Black Power groups that survived and those that did not is that survivors tended to rely not just on a logic of cultural autonomy, but a version of that logic that permitted some flexibility in dealing with the American mainstream. For example, nearly all political groups that embraced political militancy disappeared by the late 1970s. These include the Black Panthers, the Republic of New Afrika, the US Organization and the Black Liberation Army (Bloom and Martin, 2014; Brown, 2003; Davenport, 2014). Educational groups that actively separated themselves from the mainstream also disappeared, such as Nairobi College, Malcolm X University and the Institute for the Black World. In contrast, organizational versions of Black Power that allowed activists to acquire some mainstream

support survived, such as Departments of Black Studies, various Black Power professional groups like the Association of Black Psychologists, and the Congressional Black Caucus.

Some of these groups existed within larger organizations, while others were independent. But what they shared was a belief that it was possible to assert Black interests while maintaining cultural autonomy and not completely attacking the mainstream. This allowed some types of Black Power organizations to embed themselves in larger organizations (e.g., Congress or the higher education system) and allowed independent groups to maintain a large enough constituency of Black, and some White, supporters. Through embedding and having a sufficiently large audience, these Black Power organizations were not the subject of repression, did not generate quite the same level of internal conflict, and had enough support so they could survive economic downtowns (e.g., the late 1970s).

To summarize, issues surrounding racial inequality can lead to the creation of institutional logics that framed new organizations, oriented them toward (or against) the mainstream, and gave them resources that facilitated, or undermined, their long term success. The logics can express an attempt to reduce rational inequality through inclusion, such as desegregation in the Civil Rights era, or an attempt to address inequality through ethnic control of organizations. Each has its own distinct collection of advantages and challenges. Those focused on inclusion might be co-opted, or simply work in a marginal way. Those focused on cultural autonomy invite repression and complete exclusion, especially if they adopt an extremely militant stance toward the mainstream.

The logics that emerge from struggles over race are not only about status and inclusion, they are collective judgments about the validity of the mainstream. For example, the institutional logics that motivated the Civil Rights movement and later non-profits articulated the belief that mainstream American society was open to reform and a desirable place for minorities. Racial integration implied that most distinctions between Blacks and Whites should be abandoned. Later, the call for diversity meant that Blacks and Whites would be working together, even though racial difference would be recognized. A similar logic applies to multiculturalism. In contrast, other logics focus on difference, such as Black Power or pan-ethnicity. These logics incorporate the idea that an organization, such as a school or political group, should resist complete incorporation into the mainstream.

The varying logics informing fields of ethnic organizations should have an effect on their organizational networks. Those employing more inclusive logics should become well incorporated into larger organizational networks. For example, educational institutions that try to integrate Black college graduates into the labor market should develop more ties with predominantly White institutions than more Black conscious institutions. An instructive example comes from recent research on historically Black Colleges, which had a strong tradition of sending their athletes to White sports teams, before a wave of anti-Black sentiment in the Depression severed those ties (Foston, 2015).

In contrast, the case of the Institute for the Black World illustrates how a Black Power logic could result in the severing of ties between organizations. As noted earlier, the Institute was a Black Power think-tank in the 1970s. Initially, it was aligned with integrationist organizations, such as the Ford Foundation, which was funding school reform in the United States. Quickly, the Institute's leadership came into conflict with the Ford Foundation over issues of Black autonomy. The Ford Foundation's program officers were very uncomfortable with an organization that openly criticized the Civil Rights movement's goals. Unsurprisingly, the social tie between the Institute and the Ford Foundation frayed and the two organizations ceased cooperating by the early 1970s (Rojas, 2007; White, 2011a).

These multiple, competing logics suggest that students and organizations should expend more effort in understanding the sequencing and layering of logics within fields. The history of American organizations shows the wide range of logics that have appeared: segregation, desegregation, Black Power, diversity and multiculturalism. J. Shiao Lee's analysis of philanthropic organizations shows how some of these logics (e.g., diversity) were responses to the failure of earlier logics (e.g., desegregation). Still, more can be done to understand the sequencing, layering and competition of the logics that are created when people reframe and contest existing racial classifications.

RACIALIZED FIELD DYNAMICS

Institutional logics like separatism, diversity and multiculturalism trigger long-term change in organizational fields. This section examines two instances of where institutional processes resulted in profound changes in existing fields. The first example is taken from Joyce Bell's (2014) analysis of the social work profession. The second is Melissa Wooten's (2015) analysis of historically Black colleges and universities (HBCUs). In each case, changing race relations created conflict that disrupted organizational fields and resulted in a readjustment that took decades to occur.

Bell looks at the profession of social work within the era of Black Power. The primary issue was that American social workers tended to see their work in terms that either downplayed or ignored the issues most relevant to Black clients. Activists also critiqued social workers for the tendency to see Black behavior as inherently problematic, and thus playing a role in perpetuating racial inequality. Bell's analysis focuses on a number of processes that are of interest to institutional scholars. When Black Power emerged, it provided a new framework for professionals who were frustrated with White-dominated professions. It allowed Black professionals to question the standards within their field (e.g., social work or the law) and then create alternatives.

In many cases, the result of questioning was a period of conflict, which was then followed by exit. In Bell's account, it was very difficult for Black social workers to have their criticisms taken seriously by their White colleagues. In some cases, claims that White social workers were inadvertently perpetuating Black inequality were immediately rejected and Black social workers became the focus of contention. After a series of events where Black social workers tried to mobilize during meetings of national social work associations, many felt that the White mainstream within their profession was simply not amenable to critique and change. As a result, the decision was made to form a parallel organization, the National Association of Black Social Workers. The NABSW became an alternative to the White mainstream in social work and it served various functions. One function was simply to provide a place where people with similar backgrounds and similar clienteles could meet. Another function was to be a place where the needs of the African American community could be focused on. A third function was to be an implicit criticism of the mainstream of American social work.

Melissa Wooten's analysis of HBCUs addresses different issues about race and organizational fields. Her story starts with the establishment of the HBCUs in the late 19th and early 20th century. These colleges were created to serve freedmen after the Civil War and to provide an avenue for mobility during the Jim Crow era, and they were often very underdeveloped. Academically, many were not different than high schools. Others did genuinely offer post-secondary education, but were severely underfunded. To resolve these problems, the HBCUs created forms of certification that allowed outsiders to judge which schools merited aid for development and improvement. The principal mechanism

is an organization known as the United Negro College Fund. In modern times, the UNCF is best known for soliciting donations for scholarships, but it is mainly a certification board within the HBCU field. One of Wooten's main claims about the UNCF was that, in an unintended way, the field of HBCUs became more stratified after the UNCF was established. Since participation required substantial resources, schools that direly needed assistance were not members. This resulted in a situation where most of the funds for HBCU development went to schools who needed it the least and made fund-raising efforts by lesser-status schools less effective.

Wooten also recounts the transformation of the HBCU field after the Civil Rights movement. The primary issue is that the desegregation of higher education removed one of the main reasons for having HBCUs. Black students now had access, in theory, to all institutions of higher education. This meant that HBCUs, as a group, had to adapt in order to survive. The institutional environment triggered a great deal of turbulence within these organizations. Some HBCUs simply did not attract enough students, which triggered automatic funding cuts from state governments. Other schools, ironically, found themselves in jeopardy when they found themselves potentially in violation of federal law. It was no longer permissible to serve students from one racial group. Others simply found that their traditional offerings were no longer sufficient to attract students and donors. Subsequently, HBCUs pursued a number of legal and political strategies to justify themselves. In terms of legal standing, advocates argued that HBCUs provided a method of diversifying higher education that would complement predominantly White institutions. With respect to the market for higher education, efforts were made to make HBCU degree offerings more similar to the rest of the higher education sector.

The examples of Black social workers and HBCUs highlight the way that race can trigger, or modify, the typical social change processes within organizational fields. The social workers case shows how contention over race can promote differentiation within fields, as competing actors struggle with each other. It is an excellent example of 'voice, then exit' in an organizational field. The HBCUs example highlights multiple dynamics: the unintentional magnification of status hierarchies and the encouragement of isomorphism following political reform.

CONSEQUENCES FOR INSTITUTIONS

Race is a very basic feature of human interaction because it guides so many of our actions. The most elemental aspect of race from an institutionalist perspective is that it guides and informs how people interact in organizations. Informally, people use race as a factor in deciding to hire and which customers to pursue. For organizations, race is important because it determines who the stakeholders are for an organization and the relationship between the organization and various racial and ethnic groups in society. Thus, all racial classifications will require the creation of formal and informal rules and behavioral patterns that reflect how people in an organizational field understand race.

One should not be surprised when changes in racial classifications erode and transform institutions. This may be unintentional. When Jewish students began entering competitive colleges in the early 20th century, this prompted administrators to create new rules and understandings of college admissions that excluded these students, which resulted in controversy (e.g., Karabel, 2005). In other cases, the transformation of racial schema can be intentional, with the explicit goal of changing institutions. As noted in the discussion of Latino pan-ethnicity, people can target the state and demand new racial categories with the purpose of encouraging new organizations and institutions to develop. In fact, this would appear to be the

necessary consequence of any successful challenge of racial classification schemes. If public opinion shifts and people adopt new ideas about race, organizations created earlier in time will have practices and routines that do not conform to their new environment. For example, in a post-Civil Rights era, White nationalist groups have low legitimacy. Even organizations whose goals might seem appropriate in a new era of racial egalitarianism would face trouble. Numerous scholars have noted that all Black educational institutions, meant to help those excluded from White dominated schools, may seem illegitimate and therefore experience declining enrollments.

Perhaps the most fundamental aspect of the relationship between race and institutions is that race is about inequality and institutions, which stabilize and govern behavior, by their nature solidify social inequality. Thus, any change in race is bound to alter institutions and changes in institutions have the potential to revise social inequalities. Throughout this chapter, we have seen this play out. Political challenges to race can trigger the process of de-institutionalization. Conversely, organizations that become institutionalized in society have the power to perpetuate racial inequalities. States can favor some groups over others. Courts and legislatures can be used to smother or bolster challenges to racial hierarchies. Schools, which have the power to award highly prized credentials and access to well-paid professions, can shape racial inequality.

The economist Joseph Schumpeter famously wrote that entrepreneurs were by their nature disruptive. Innovators create better and more efficient firms which bankrupt existing firms. A similar lesson can be applied to race and organizations. When social movements and other political entrepreneurs successfully formulate a new framing of race, good or bad, they can knock out the pillars of resources and legitimacy that allow organizations to survive. The goal for scholars analyzing the interplay of race, organizations and institutions is to use the tools of institutional theory to better understand the different ways that this process plays out.

OPEN QUESTIONS FOR RACE AND INSTITUTIONAL RESEARCH

This chapter has examined the different ways that race interacts with organizational fields. First, we examined race as a macro-institutional process where activists and political entrepreneurs struggle to preserve, or transform, racial categories that govern entire societies. This sort of process draws together two strands of theory: institutional work and polity theories. The former describes how people attack or maintain institutions, such as racial categories, while the latter discusses how these institutions are then used to create global order. Second, this chapter discussed institutional logics and examined racialized logics that tried to reform the mainstream (e.g., desegregation or diversity) or maintain autonomy (Black Power). Then, there was a discussion of the organizations that were motivated by the different logics. Third, this chapter discussed field dynamics – how specific fields changed in response to changing political or cultural environments. Some fields split (social work associations), while other fields were drawn closer to their 'mainstream' (HBCU mimicking predominantly White colleges post-1964).

For each of these processes, we can identify open questions. With respect to macro-institutional processes, one can ask if the processes observed in the United States have any analog elsewhere. For example, there have been pan-ethnic movements in other regions of the world, such as pan-Arabism. In that case, there was a movement in the Middle East to create a larger state, or social unit, from various nationalities and religious subgroups (Dawn, 1988). The movement did have a brief period of success when the states of Egypt and Syria formed a large, single

federation in 1958, which then disbanded in 1961. There was also an attempt to merge Egypt, Libya and Syria, which was approved by referenda in each nation, but the final merger did not occur. One can ask if the attempt to create pan-Arabic identity and political institutions affected various organizational fields.

Conversely, one can ask about variations within a single nation. As people restructure racial categories, which organizations are most likely to resist the new categorization? Already, this chapter encountered two forms resistance to new racial categories. Within the Asian communities of the United States, people often relied on their nation of origin for their identity, which, at times, made it difficult for inter-organizational collaboration to occur (Okamoto, 2014). Another example of resistance is the more militant wing of Black Power. While many scholars have situated Black Power as consistent with the larger Civil Rights movement, my view is that many Black Power organizations, especially the more militant ones, were pursuing a goal substantially different than that promoted by the Civil Rights movements. For example, the King Center in Atlanta, Georgia is a non-profit that was founded after Martin Luther King Jr's murder (Rojas, 2007: ch. 5; White, 2011a). The Center's mission is to preserve King's legacy by operating a museum, holding the archive of his personal papers and by sponsoring educational projects. By 1970, the King Center had distanced itself from educators and other professionals who embraced Black Power ideology. The relevant point is that Black Power activists promoted policies that were not immediately focused on racial desegregation, which was the intellectual focal point of decades of Civil Rights actions.

Nationalist movements from the majority are one type of resistance that is infrequently addressed in institutional analysis, but they are attracting more attention in other fields. In this context, majority nationalist movements would include White nationalism in the United States, Hindu nationalism in India, and Arab nationalism in the Middle East.

Often, majority nationalists are mobilized by the claiming of rights by minority groups. A research questions for scholars is how organizational fields of nationalists organizations intersect with other fields. In the United States, White nationalists tend to be fairly marginal and, in some cases, have had to modify their rhetoric in order to have influence (Hughey, 2012). In other polities, majority nationalists are the highest-status actors. For example, Hindu nationalists have achieved the highest political office and they define the political landscape in India. A question for research is to identify the conditions under which majority nationalist organizations occupy positions of high status, and when are they marginal.

A related issue regarding organizational fields and macro-level institutional change is which fields are the most likely to accept or resist change. In the US context, for example, one could ask if non-profit fields (like colleges or philanthropic organizations) are more accepting of racial integration or new categories (e.g., 'Asian American' or 'Hispanic') than other fields. The value of the 'multi-field' perspective offered by Fligstein and McAdam is that they emphasize that fields exist in relation to each other. They overlap and have avenues of influence and transmission of ideas. Thus, we would expect some fields to be 'closer' or 'farther' from the fields that define race in a society. A hypothesis for future research is to determine if a field's proximity to the state (or other fields that define race) has an effect on whether new racial categories are institutionalized in that field.

A second avenue of inquiry looks at institutional logics (Thornton et al., 2012). A simple, but unanswered, question concerns the types of logics that address race and organizations. In this chapter we have encountered desegregation (bringing groups together), segregation (separating groups), diversity (representing groups in important organizations), cultural autonomy (allowing groups to participate in the wider society but allowing them to control the organizations) and multiculturalism (ensuring equal representation of groups in

culture). It is probably not the case that this list exhausts the possibilities. Comparative analysis would help researchers discover the range of institutional logics that people use to define and implement race in organizations.

A related question concerns sequencing. A number of scholars have argued that, in the US case, there appears a specific sequence of racialized institutional logics. Originally, segregation is standard in that most ethnic groups, including many of European origin, are physically separated and subject to repression. Then, there is a period of liberalization where ideologies of freedom flourish and, sometimes, there are nationalist logics that appear as counterpoints. It may be the case that this sequencing only is possible in the American context and that rival logics are more common in other places. Another question about institutional logics is about layering. As racial categories change, and new logics are articulated, they may be merged, combined, or layered in some manner. More research can be done into how institutional logics are combined when people change their ideas about race.

A third sort of open question concerns field dynamics. One might ask if the sort of 'voice, then exit' process, as described by Bell, is common. Is it true that minority groups tend to first rely on asserting themselves within existing organizations before exiting? Not only was this the case for the National Association of Black Social Workers, but a similar pattern was seen in Black Power political groups that broke off from mixed White and Black Civil Rights groups and in Black Studies colleges which emerged from more traditional universities. An important question about exit is survival. Once groups decide to exit, they may not be able to sustain themselves if the larger movement that spawned them goes into abeyance. The two Black Studies colleges I mentioned suffered this fate, as did numerous political groups. The question for research is whether this is common or if fields that bifurcate in this way can find strategies for survival beyond embedding themselves in the mainstream.

CONCLUSION

Institutionalism is a theoretical tradition that is not normally associated with studies of race. However, recent scholarship by social movement researchers, political scientists, historians and others shows that race is a crucial factor influencing many institutional processes. Racial classifications surely are an example of an institution that provides meaning and coordinates behavior. The history of social movements abounds with cases of institutional work where activists, policy entrepreneurs and others actively tried to undermine, or bolster, racial categories. The consequence of racial categorizations is populations of organizations and the logics that guide them. These are extremely diverse, ranging from revolutionary groups to Black librarian associations.

The gap between institutional theory and race research speaks to a general theme in institutionalism. Though it is one of the most popular forms of organizational scholarship in management and sociology, there is relatively little overlap with other core areas of sociology. Hopefully, this survey suggests that institutionalism has a lot to say to studies of race and to other areas of sociology, such as social psychology, gender and inequality.

REFERENCES

Bardill, Jessica (2015). Tribal Sovereignty and Enrollment Determinations. National Congress of American Indians. http://genetics.ncai.org/tribal-sovereignty-and-enrollment-determinations.cfm [Accessed 11 August 2015].

Becker, Gary (1957). *The Economics of Discrimination*. Chicago, IL: University of Chicago Press.

Bell, Joyce (2014). *The Black Power Movement and American Social Work*. New York: Columbia University Press.

Belvin, Brent (2004). Malcolm X Liberation University: An experiment in independent black education. MA thesis, Department of History, North Carolina State University.

Binder, Amy (2002). *Contentious Curricula: Afrocentrism and Creationism in American Public Schools*. Princeton, NJ: Princeton University Press.

Biondi, Martha (2014). *The Black Revolution on Campus*. Berkeley, CA: University of California Press.

Bloom, Joshua and Martin, Waldo (2014). *Black Against Empire: The History and Politics of the Black Panther Party*. Berkeley, CA: University of California Press.

Bourdieu, Pierre (1977). *Outline of a Theory of Practice*. Chicago, IL: University of Chicago Press.

Brown, Scot (2003). *Fighting for US: Maulana Karenga, the US Organization, and Black Cultural Nationalism*. New York: New York University Press.

Cherokee Nation (2015). Tribal Citizenship. www.cherokee.org/Services/TribalCitizenship/Citizenship.aspx [Accessed 11 August 2015].

Chiang, Mark (2009). *The Cultural Capital of Asian American Studies: Autonomy and Representation in the University*. New York: New York University Press.

Coleman, James (1988). Social capital in the creation of human capital. *American Journal of Sociology*, 94: S95–S120.

Davenport, Chris (2014). *How Social Movements Die: Repression and Demobilization of the Republic of New Africa*. Cambridge: Cambridge University Press.

Dawn, C. Ernest (1988). The formation of pan-Arab ideology in the interwar years. *International Journal of Middle East Studies*, 20(1): 67–91.

Dezalay, Y. and Garth, B. G. (1996). *International Arbitration and the Construction of a Transnational Commercial Order*. Chicago, IL: University of Chicago Press.

DiMaggio, Paul and Powell, W. (1983). The iron cage revisited: Institutional isomorphism and collective rationality in organizational fields. *American Sociological Review*, 48: 147–160.

DiMaggio, Paul J. and Powell, Walter W. (1991). Introduction. In Walter W. Powell and Paul J. DiMaggio (eds), *The New Institutionalism in Organizational Analysis*. Chicago, IL: University of Chicago Press. pp. 1–38.

Dobbin, Frank (2009). *Inventing Equal Opportunity*. Princeton. NJ: Princeton University Press.

Emirbayer, Mustafa and Desmond, Matthew (2015). *The Racial Order*. Chicago, IL: University of Chicago Press.

Fligstein, N. (2001). Social skill and the theory of fields. *Sociological Theory*, 19: 105–125.

Fligstein, Neil and McAdam, Doug (2012). *A Theory of Fields*. Oxford: Oxford University Press.

Foston, Amia (2015). Catalysts and consequences: Understanding the organizational status dynamics of organizational desegregation. Dissertation, Department of Sociology, Indiana University, Bloomington, IN.

Hallett, Tim (2010). The myth incarnate: Recoupling processes, turmoil, and inhabited institutions in an urban elementary school. *American Sociological Review*, 75(1): 52–74.

Hoover, Mary Eleanor Rhodes (1992). The Nairobi Day School: An African American independent school, 1966–1984. *Journal of Negro Education*, 61(2): 201–210.

Hughey, Matthew (2012). *White Bound: Nationalists, Antiracists, and the Shared Meanings of Race*. Stanford, CA: Stanford University Press.

Karabel, Jerome (2005). *The chosen. The hidden history of admission and exclusion at Harvard, Yale and Princeton*. Boston: Houghton Mifflin.

Kendi, Ibram (2012). *The Black Campus Movement: Black Students and the Racial Reconstitution of Higher Education, 1965–1972*. London: Palgrave–Macmillan.

Lawrence, T. B. and Suddaby, R. (2006). Institutions and institutional work. In S. R. Clegg, C. Hardy, T. B. Lawrence and W. R. Nord (eds), *Handbook of Organization Studies* (2nd edn). London: Sage. pp. 215–254.

Lawrence, Thomas, Suddaby, Roy and Leca, Bernard (2011). *Institutional Work: Actors and Agency in Institutional Studies of Organization*. Cambridge: Cambridge University Press.

Lounsbury, Michael (2001). Institutional sources of practice variation: Staffing college and university recycling programs. *Administrative Science Quarterly*, 46: 29–56.

March, James G. and Simon, Herbert (1958). *Organizations*. New York: John Wiley and Sons.

Meyer, John and Rowan, Brian (1977). Institutionalized organizations: Formal structure as myth and ceremony. *American Journal of Sociology*, 83: 340–363.

Mora, G. Cristina (2014). *Making Hispanics: How Activists, Bureaucrats & Media Constructed a New American*. Chicago, IL: University of Chicago Press.

Morning, Ann (2011). *The Nature of Race: How Scientists Think and Teach about Human Difference*. Berkeley, CA: University of California Press.

Okamoto, Dina (2014). *Redefining Race: Asian American Panethnicity and Shifting Ethnic Boundaries*. New York: Russell Sage Foundation.

Phillips, Damon and Zuckerman, Ezra (2001). Middle status conformity: Theoretical restatement and empirical demonstration in two markets. *American Journal of Sociology*, 107: 379–429.

Podolny, Joel (2001). Networks as the pipes and prisms of the market. *American Journal of Sociology*, 107: 33–60.

Posselt, Julie R. (2015). *Inside Graduate Admissions: Merit, Diversity, and Faculty Gatekeeping*. Cambridge. MA: Harvard University Press.

Quirke, Linda (2013). Rogue resistance: Sidestepping isomorphic pressure in a patchy institutional field. *Organization Studies*, 34: 1675–1699.

Rao, Hayagreeva (2009). *Market Rebels: How Activists Shape Innovation*. Princeton, NJ: Princeton University Press.

Rogers, Everett (2003). *Diffusion of Innovations*, 5th edn. New York: Simon & Schuster.

Rojas, Fabio (2007). *From Black Power to Black Studies: How a Radical Social Movement Became an Academic Discipline*. Baltimore, MD: Johns Hopkins University Press.

Rojas, Fabio (2010). Power through institutional work: Building academic authority in the 1968 Third World strike. *Academy of Management Journal* 53:1263–80.

Rojas, Fabio and Byrd, Carson (2014). The four histories of black power: The black nationalist sector and its impact on American society. *Black Diaspora Review*, 4(1): 113–156.

Scott, W. Richard (2001). *Institutions and Organizations*, 2nd edn. Thousand Oaks, CA: Sage.

Scott, W. R., Ruef, M., Mendel, P. and Caronna, C. (2000). *Institutional Change and Healthcare Organizations: From Professional Dominance to Managed Care*. Chicago, IL: University of Chicago Press.

Shiao, Jiannbin Lee (2005). *Identifying Talent, Institutionalizing Diversity: Race and Philanthropy in Post-Civil Rights America*. Durham, NC: Duke University Press.

Shiao, Jiannbin Lee, Bode, Thomas, Beyer, Amber and Selvig, Daniel (2012). The genomic challenge to the social construction of race. *Sociological Theory*, 30(2): 67–88.

Skrentny, John (1996). *The Ironies of Affirmative Action: Politics, Culture and Justice in America*. Chicago, IL: University of Chicago Press.

Skrentny, John (2014). *After Civil Rights: Racial Realism in the New American Workplace*. Princeton, NJ: Princeton University Press.

Stinchcombe, A. L. (1965). Social structure and organizations. In J. G. March (ed.), *Handbook of Organizations*. Chicago, IL: Rand McNally & Co. pp. 142–193.

Thornton, Patricia H., Ocasio, William and Lounsbury, Michael (2012). *The Institutional Logics Perspective: A New Approach to Culture, Structure and Process*. Oxford: Oxford University Press.

White, Derrick (2011a). *The Challenge of Blackness: The Institute of the Black World and Political Activism in the 1970s*. Gainesville, FL: University of Florida Press.

White, Monica M (2011b). D-Town Farm: African American Resistance to Food Insecurity and the Transformation of Detroit. *Environmental Practice*, 13(4): 406–417.

Wooten, Melissa (2015). *In the Face of Inequality: How Black Colleges Adapt*. New York: SUNY Press.

31

Are Diversity Programs Merely Ceremonial? Evidence-Free Institutionalization

Frank Dobbin and Alexandra Kalev

Institutionalists describe large domains of corporate policy and practice as symbolic. The work of entire departments is carried out to convey a firm's commitment to efficiency (the now dismantled strategic planning unit) or to fairness (the Chief Diversity Officer and her cadre). Executives may deliberately choose purely symbolic policies that will not alter proven routines or traditions that employees hold dear. What distinguished institutional theory, from the start, was the recognition that while organizational practices are often ceremonial, they may nonetheless serve the very material purpose of conferring legitimacy on the firm, which helps executives to raise capital, win customers and attract talent.

Institutionalists have been interested in the rise and spread of corporate equal opportunity innovations precisely because they viewed those innovations as ceremonial. The performance rating system gives the human resources office the stamp of meritocracy, even if research shows that that raters favor white men. Formal hiring guidelines make the firm appear to be operating on principles of bureaucracy, not bias, even if we know that managers often circumvent guidelines to hire their cronies. From the start, new institutionalists have described such practices as window-dressing, adopted largely to win legitimacy: 'Employees, applicants, managers, trustees, and governmental agencies are predisposed to trust the hiring practices of organizations that follow legitimated procedures – such as equal opportunity programs' (Meyer and Rowan, 1977: 349).

Nonet and Selznick (1978) tell us that firms often adopt programs that symbolize conformity with new social norms when they have not yet made substantive changes. Meyer and Rowan (1977) and Edelman (1990, 1992) suggest that firms adopt policies to symbolize their commitment *instead of* making substantive changes. In describing diversity practices as symbolic, institutionalists suggest that innovations are put into place for show, rather than to actually promote equality of opportunity. The fact that executives have rarely embraced equal opportunity programs without pressure from social movements, regulators, or professional groups has led institutionalists to speculate that their hearts aren't in it.

We report from an outpost of new institutionalists that has begun to go beyond speculation about when equal opportunity innovations have real effects. Some of us have documented the effects of diversity programs in studies using intensive data from individual firms, through field experiments (Kelly et al., 2011) or analyses of archival personnel data (Castilla and Benard, 2010; Fernandez and Fernandez-Mateo, 2006). These scholars are part of a wider movement of social scientists who look at the effects of institutional innovations on such organizational outcomes as profitability and share price, and who are advancing evidence-based approaches to understanding the effects of organizational innovations (e.g., Jung and Dobbin, 2016; Pernell et al., forthcoming; Yermack, 1996; Zuckerman, 1999).

We make a novel argument about the relationship between the intentions of innovation adopters and the effects of those innovations. The 'symbolic compliance' (Edelman, 1990; Meyer and Rowan, 1977) literature suggests that executives knowingly adopt innovations that symbolize new goals such as equal opportunity, but that have no real effects. We suggest, instead, that groups develop myths of causality about innovations but rarely put those myths to empirical tests. Management myths are rarely tested, and when they are, they may be impervious to disconfirming evidence. Thus the myth that employees are best motivated with financial incentives remains strong, despite substantial evidence that incentives can prevent people from internalizing organizational goals (Pfeffer and Sutton, 2006). The myth that diversity training reduces bias, and promotes workforce diversity, remains strong despite hundreds of studies finding that bias is resistant to training (Paluck and Green, 2009).

If institutionalists are correct in arguing that executives adopt certain diversity programs to curry favor with the public, in full confidence that those programs will fail, those executives would have to know which programs work and which do not. Research shows some diversity innovations to be effective, and others to be useless or counter-productive. But our survey suggests that even ardent advocates of equal opportunity do not know which are which. Women in leadership, crusading regulators and liberal litigators have no idea what works. Thus one study shows that women in corporate management champion diversity practices that research has shown to be ineffective, such as diversity training, and neglect practices that typically work, such as mentoring (Dobbin et al., 2011; Dobbin et al., 2015). Others find that in negotiating discrimination suit settlements, liberal federal litigators ask for ineffective diversity practices but not for effective practices (Hegewisch et al., 2011; Schlanger and Kim, 2014). If women managers and federal litigators advocating for change do not know which innovations work and which don't, neither, we suggest, do corporate policy-makers.

We have arrived at this situation because, as institutionalists have been arguing, innovations diffuse based not so much on evidence as on 'theorization' (Davis and Greve, 1997; Johnson et al., 2006; Strang, 2010; Strang and Meyer. 1993). A good theory of how an innovation functions is all you need to get firms to buy in. Once institutionalized, the prevalence of a practice in leading organizations is taken to be proof that it must be effective (Meyer and Rowan, 1977). Thus today, unconscious bias training is all the rage because Google and Facebook are doing it – two companies with alarmingly low levels of diversity in management and tech positions according to their own widely publicized statistics.[1] Based on the evidence, if there are two companies that you should not emulate to promote diversity they are Google and Facebook. The paradox underlying the symbolic-adoption argument, then, is that if managers rely on theorization alone to determine the efficacy of a practice, their efforts to make mere symbolic efforts may backfire. While some practices are 'theorized' to have merely symbolic value (posting an equal opportunity statement) and others are 'theorized' to work (mandatory diversity training), practitioners do not know which really work (spoiler: neither works). Thus institutional theorists need to focus not only on whether innovations are theorized to have symbolic or substantive effects, but on the decoupling of means and ends (Bromley and Powell, 2012). This means we must examine the real-world evidence about the substantive effects of different innovations.

Next we review the literature on how diversity management institutions arose and diffused across US workplaces to demonstrate that the practices that diffused were championed by genuine advocates for workforce diversity. They were advocated by professional human resources and diversity managers, women in corporate management, and liberal federal officials and judges. These groups often got the innovations they wanted. They generally favored practices designed to stop bias through education, feedback or bureaucratic controls to quash managerial bias, such as mandatory job tests, formal performance ratings and grievance procedures.

After discussing the role of activists in promoting corporate change, we review evidence about the efficacy of three broad approaches to promoting diversity. We consider predictions from social science theories about the effects of management practices. These predictions often conflict with the managerial theories that are used to popularize innovations, such as the theory that anti-bias training can reduce bias. Thus job-autonomy and self-determination theories suggest that bias-control efforts, including training and bureaucratic controls, will backfire by sparking managerial resistance. Research confirms this expectation. By contrast, cognitive dissonance and self-perception theories suggest

that innovations designed to put managers in charge of promoting diversity will increase commitment and lead to change. Studies confirm that mentoring programs, special college recruitment programs and in-house management training programs have substantial positive effects on managerial diversity. Finally, accountability theory suggests that when corporate officials charged with hiring, promotion and pay decisions feel accountable to others, they will scrutinize their own behavior for signs of bias, and make personnel decisions based on evidence rather than stereotypes. Studies show that diversity taskforces, diversity managers and federal regulators activate 'evaluation apprehension' on the part of managers making personnel decisions, and thereby promote workforce diversity.

One of our goals is to provide a model of how organizational institutionalists might make their work even more relevant to managers by exploring what makes innovations effective. Thus, we demonstrate that, when coupled with performance measures, the kind of organizational diffusion data that institutionalists collect can help to determine the effects of innovations.

WHAT DIVERSITY ACTIVISTS WANTED

That employer recruitment, hiring, promotion, discharge and pay practices have been revolutionized since the 1960s is not in doubt. But why? Most analysts trace the rise of new practices designed to promote workforce diversity to the civil rights and women's movements of the 1950s and 1960s, and to the expansion of federal anti-discrimination regulation, notably John F. Kennedy's Executive Order 10925 from 1961, the Equal Pay Act of 1963 and the Civil Rights Act of 1964, signed by Lyndon Johnson the year after Kennedy was assassinated (Dobbin, 2009; Nelson and Bridges, 1999).

Why did the legislation unleash two generations of constant innovation in human resources practices? Because affirmative action and equal opportunity policies did not specify the terms of compliance, they left the door open to institutional entrepreneurs who created one wave after another of innovations, and who continue today apace. We detail findings from the research in this domain, which point to the entrepreneurs at the heart of this revolution and their allies in government and in corporations.

Corporate leaders in the United States have reached broad consensus on how to achieve equality of opportunity. That consensus revolves around a set of employer policies and programs that are widespread among leading firms (Dobbin, 2009), inscribed in federal 'best practices' lists (Kalev et al., 2006), and required by discrimination suit settlements negotiated by federal litigators and approved by federal judges (Schlanger and Kim, 2014). For the purposes of our argument – that employers could not have deliberately adopted ineffective diversity practices because they knew not which were effective – we trace the research on who was behind these innovations. The people who helped to diffuse these innovations were on a mission. But because they wrote their wish lists in an evidentiary vacuum, they often championed innovations that did not work. After detailing who pushed these innovations, we turn to research on the efficacy of different types of equal opportunity and diversity innovations. We show that some innovations that have been described as largely symbolic, such as diversity managers and diversity taskforces (Edelman and Petterson, 1999), are highly effective, while others that are costly or disruptive, such as diversity training, diversity score cards and networking programs, are not effective. We outline a three-part theory for predicting which innovations will be effective in this domain based in the evidence.

Crusaders in Personnel Management

Equal opportunity legislation and presidential affirmative-action orders left substantial latitude to employers to devise compliance measures. Here we review the literature on the forces that promoted compliance to make a simple point. Proponents of change were civil rights crusaders, and saw the innovations they were championing as weapons for putting an end to discrimination. Those who brought change to firms were not seeking mere symbolic compliance with the law. While some of the innovations they championed did not make the cut – the courts quickly ruled against quotas – crusaders often got what they wanted. As we argue below, neither the cheerleaders for change, nor the executives who went along kicking and screaming, knew which practices actually promoted diversity. So neither group could game the system. This understanding challenges the view that firms deliberately adopt ineffectual diversity innovations for the purpose of symbolic compliance. Instead, we suggest, key groups on both sides of the issue work with a common set of theories of what works that were, until recently, untested.

Uncertainty over how to comply with Kennedy's 1961 requirement that federal contractors take 'affirmative action' to end discrimination led contractors to band together and devise strategies, at first through the semi-public Plans for Progress group (Edelman, 1990; Graham, 1990). Then, when Title VII of the Civil Rights Act of 1964 prohibited employment discrimination at all private firms, Congress left the details of compliance to employers and the courts, choosing not to create a regulatory agency with independent authority to set compliance standards (Chen, 2009). Ambiguity in both laws thus stimulated 'endogenous' compliance, whereby the regulated helped to define compliance (Edelman et al., 1999). Executives perceived the law as a moving target, and the biggest employers hired full-time equal opportunity experts to track changes in the law and in judicial interpretation.

Personnel experts took charge of designing compliance systems. Lawyers might well have taken over, however their professional modus operandi was not to speculate wildly about what the courts would accept as compliance initiatives, but rather to come in on the back end of the problem, when suits had been filed and employers needed representation (Dobbin and Kelly, 2007).

The field of personnel management had been dominated by white men who had made careers in resisting, or negotiating with, unions. As unions declined and as the discipline came to focus on civil rights, women took over (Dobbin, 2009: 171). Personnel specialists grew tenfold between 1960 and 2000, while the labor force grew only threefold. Women were nearly unknown in personnel as of 1960, but they held half of specialist and manager jobs by 1980, and 70% by the late 1990s (Dobbin, 2009: 5, 169; Roos and Manley, 1996). This change in the profession's composition shaped its agenda, and corporate policies supporting gender equality came to take precedence. In the early 1970s, for instance, federal law did not require employers to offer maternity leave, but corporate personnel offices began to create programs. Thanks in large measure to the advocacy of women in personnel management, firms offering maternity leave nearly tripled between 1969 and 1978 – but not until 1993 did Congress mandate it (Bureau of National Affairs, 1975; Kamerman et al., 1983; Ruhm and Teague, 1997).

Women in personnel also fought to keep and expand equal opportunity programs in the face of the Reagan-era retrenchment of civil rights laws. From the early 1970s, experts had argued that equal opportunity was good for business (Boyle, 1973: 95; Edelman et al., 2001). When Reagan appointed Clarence Thomas to head the Equal Employment Opportunity Commission and announced plans to bring an end to affirmative action in employment, personnel experts rebranded their efforts as part of a new 'diversity management' program to create 'strategic advantage by helping members of diverse groups perform to their potential' (Conference Board, 1992: 11). Personnel experts picked up where the civil rights and women's movements had left off.

As personnel departments took charge of diversity management, and became dominated by women, the profession became the leading local advocate of diversity programs in most companies; firms with human resources departments, diversity staff and HR consultants became significantly more likely than their peers to adopt a range of different diversity measures (Dobbin et al., 1993, Dobbin and Kelly, 2007; Edelman, 1990, 1992).

Crusading Women Executives

Corporate diversity innovations were championed not only by human resources experts, but by women and minorities within firms. Surveys have long shown that these groups favor diversity programs. Bobo and Kluegel (1993) find that blacks are significantly more supportive than whites of opportunity enhancement policies, and white women are more supportive than white men. Cohen and Huffman (2007) report that in the 1996 General Social Survey, women managers were 1.3 times as likely as men to agree that 'employers should make special efforts to hire and promote qualified women'. Decades of research show, Steeh and Krysan (1996) conclude, that blacks are consistently more supportive of government aid for minorities and of hiring preferences.

It is no surprise, then, that when women gain ground in firms they advocate for diversity programs. Employers with more women are more likely to offer flexible work arrangements and childcare centers (Deitch and Huffman, 2001) and sexual harassment programs (Dobbin and Kelly, 2007). The support of women managers for diversity programs more generally (Dobbin et al., 2011) may help to explain the continuing popularity of diversity programs even after regulatory activity was cut back in the early 1980s, for women continued to gain ground in management through the 1990s (Anderson, 1996; Edelman et al., 2001; Kelly and Dobbin, 1998; Leonard, 1990).

One piece of evidence in support of our contention that corporate adoption of diversity programs that serve purely symbolic purposes is not entirely deliberate is that women executives often support policies that do not work. Quantitative studies show that they encourage the adoption of one program that has been shown to promote diversity – taskforces – but also three programs that have been shown to be ineffective – EEO advertisements, diversity training for managers and diversity training for non-managers. They do not help to spread mentoring programs, which are highly effective (Dobbin et al., 2007; Dobbin et al., 2011; Edelman and Petterson, 1999).

Crusading Officials and Liberal Judges

Kennedy's 1961 affirmative action order (Executive Order 10925, *26 Fed. Reg. 1961*) requiring federal contractors to end discrimination in employment stimulated extensive private-sector action, through the semi-public Plans for Progress group of federal contractors (Dobbin, 2009: 13). Contractors soon wrote non-discrimination policies of their own, changed their personnel manuals and announced in job advertisements that they were 'Equal Opportunity Employers' (Dobbin et al., 1993; Edelman, 1992).

By most accounts, the Civil Rights Act did not require specific hiring and promotion practices, or give the executive branch that power, because the bill's sponsors sought the votes of moderates (Chen, 2009; Graham, 1990). Hence compliance was a moving target because local, state and federal judges and regulators could weigh in on standards. The regulatory system was 'porous', in that citizens could appeal to various public authorities to interpret and reinterpret laws (Kelly, 2003; Lieberman, 2002).

In the 1960s and 1970s, the people drawn to work at the agencies overseeing the Civil Rights Act and presidential affirmative-action orders, the Equal Employment Opportunity Commission (EEOC) and Office of Federal Contract Compliance Programs (OFCCP), respectively, were mostly champions of change (Blumrosen, 1993). The federal judiciary was largely liberal. In the 1980s, Reagan appointed conservatives to those agencies – Clarence Thomas headed the EEOC from 1982 to 1990 – but it took Reagan many years to change the judiciary. EEOC litigation and investigation of complaints, and OFCCP compliance reviews of federal contractors, have been shown to promote the use of a number of different diversity programs (Edelman, 1992). Litigation and compliance reviews also led to increases in workforce diversity, although compliance reviews became ineffective in the Reagan years (Kalev and Dobbin, 2006). While Reagan appointees did not enforce the law vigorously, corporate reforms that had begun to spread, such as diversity training, continued to grow in popularity (Dobbin and Kelly, 2007; Dobbin and Sutton, 1998; Edelman, 1990, 1992; Kelly and Dobbin, 1999).

Federal agencies appear to have reduced pressure on employers during the 1980s. But the people who championed specific corporate diversity policies were proponents of change, not foot-draggers. When employers embraced innovations, they embraced those championed by crusaders. When conservatives controlled the executive branch they did not lobby for change, and thus when federal regulators did lobby firms, they advocated programs the left believed in. Liberal EEOC regulators recommended practices popular among leading employers[2] in the belief that those employers know what they are doing. Conservative judges rarely vetted diversity innovations, and liberal judges vetted innovations they expected to expand opportunity. Thus for instance liberal regulators and judges alike moved toward defining discrimination against pregnant workers as prohibited under

Title VII, encouraging firms to offer maternity leave long before Congress required it in 1993 (Kelly and Dobbin, 1999). As Guthrie and Roth (1999) show, liberal justices played a key role in promoting corporate work–family programs. Liberal judges also backed corporate anti-harassment policies, training and complaint systems (Dobbin and Kelly, 2007). Liberal regulators and judges actively promoted corporate innovations they expected to work.

Perhaps the best evidence that officials with the best of intentions promoted the wrong policies comes from studies of the behavior of career civil rights litigators representing plaintiffs. When discrimination suits are being settled, those litigators negotiate over terms. Thus private litigators, and litigators for the EEOC, have a say in what goes into agreements. Some settlements include only monetary awards, but large class action settlements usually include program changes ('injunctive relief'), in the form of anti-discrimination initiatives. The most common programmatic changes are posted equal opportunity policy (86%), equal opportunity training (87%), written anti-discrimination policy (33%) and civil rights grievance system (32%) (Schlanger and Kim, 2014: 1573). However, we show below that these initiatives have either no effect (true for policy posting and creation) or adverse effects (true for equal opportunity training and grievance system). In fact, none of the organizational initiatives found with any regularity in these settlements shows a positive effect on workforce diversity. A study of major consent decrees in discrimination cases concluded that settlements specify programmatic changes that have been shown to have little or no effect (Hegewisch et al., 2011). Do career civil rights litigators working for plaintiffs deliberately sabotage agreements? We suggest that like everyone else, they have no idea what works.

If diversity managers, women in management and liberal officials and judges promote diversity programs that do not increase diversity then we may need to understand policy failure as the consequence of a mismatch between means and ends (Bromley and Powell, 2012). By theorizing how new innovations work, management gurus give executives tools for achieving goals. But if their theorizations are flawed, and are never tested with evidence, innovations that are ineffective or counter-productive may prevail. Programs adopted with the best of intentions may not be effective, but may survive. This may explain why many American firms with elaborate diversity initiatives have made little progress in promoting diversity since the 1980s. Below we explore which diversity practices work and which fail. We offer a theory to explain these differences.

ARE DIVERSITY PROGRAMS MERELY CEREMONIAL?

Our core argument is that because no one has known which corporate diversity innovations have only symbolic value, executives who were secretly opposed to diversity could not systematically choose interventions that did not work. We have been arguing that the people who chose diversity measures were, by and large, advocates for change, and that even these advocates mostly chose ineffective measures. They were human resources managers who had been attracted by the field's civil rights mission, women who rose to management positions and liberal litigators and judges. We suggest that their core strategy of trying to control managerial bias through training, feedback and bureaucratic measures is wrong-headed. Next we review research on the effects of corporate anti-discrimination programs to assess which broad approaches work and which do not. Are diversity programs merely ceremonial? Some are. Some aren't. The control strategies we begin with are, for the average firm, worse than ceremonial – they have adverse effects on actual workforce diversity.

Bias Control

Everything we know from psychological and sociological studies of work suggests that efforts to control managerial bias through rules and rehabilitation will fail. Job-autonomy theorists in sociology and self-determination theorists in psychology tell us that such control strategies typically backfire. In the job autonomy literature, intrusive controls on workers predict job dissatisfaction and failure to perform (Hodson, 1996; Judge et al., 2001; Lamont, 2000). Lacking autonomy, workers often try to assert control through sabotage, goldbricking and resistance (Gouldner, 1954; Hodson, 1991a, 1991b; Roy, 1952). The self-determination literature shows that people respond to constraints and efforts to influence their decisions by rebelling to reassert personal control (Brehm and Brehm, 1981; Silvia, 2005). Studies of bias control confirm the general principle: whites resist external controls on racial prejudice (Galinsky and Moskowitz, 2000; Plant and Devine, 2001).

Diversity training and feedback comprise one control strategy, designed on the principle of thought control. Stereotyping is a natural cognitive mechanism, the thinking goes, but the associations we make between race, gender and workplace performance can have the effect of sustaining inequality (Gorman, 2005; Kanter, 1977; Lemm and Banaji, 1999). Since the 1960s, federal agencies such as the Social Security Administration and private companies such as General Electric have tried to give employees the tools to control their own biases. Diversity training is supposed to make managers aware of their own biases, and diversity performance ratings are supposed to provide them with feedback on their behavior (Bendick et al., 1998; Shaeffer, 1973). Anti-bias training is based in the intuition that knowledge about members of other groups, and an understanding of stereotyping, may reduce discrimination (Fiske, 1998; Nelson et al., 1996). Diversity performance evaluations are based on the intuition that feedback

can influence managerial attention and motivation (Reskin, 2003: 325), and that accountability can reduce bias (Tetlock, 1985). Resistance has been documented in a number of studies. They suggest that anti-bias training can activate rather than suppress bias (Kidder et al., 2004; Naff and Kellough, 2003; Rynes and Rosen, 1995; Sidanius et al., 2001). A review of over 900 anti-bias interventions finds that most have weak effects, and some backfire (Paluck and Green, 2009). For instance, when white subjects read anti-prejudice materials and feel pressured to agree, their anti-black prejudice *increases* (Legault et al., 2011).

Rules that govern personnel decisions represent a second control strategy for quashing bias. Early on, personnel managers built bureaucratic anti-discrimination practices, such as formal performance evaluations and civil rights grievance procedures, on the foundation of policies that unions championed to shield their leaders from retaliation (Baron and Bielby, 1980; Dobbin et al., 1993; Jacoby, 1984; Kochan et al., 1994). As noted, plaintiff attorneys in discrimination suits often ask for these practices in settlements (Edelman et al., 2011; Schlanger and Kim, 2014). And social scientists have argued that employers can 'reduce attribution errors by routinely collecting concrete performance data and implementing evaluation procedures [including performance ratings] in which evaluators rely exclusively on these data' (Reskin and McBrier, 2000: 235; see also Bielby, 2000). Job tests, written performance evaluations and grievance procedures are thought to achieve this purpose.

Mandatory job tests were popularized as a means of ensuring that managers select employees based on ability, not race or gender. For management jobs, most employers use standardized paper-and-pencil tests (Berry et al., 2011). However, hiring managers may resist the formal control of job tests by administering tests selectively (Mong and Roscigno, 2010: 10; Puma, 1966). Studies suggest that managers sometimes require only minority applicants to take tests (Purcell,

1953) or ignore test results that do not rein-force stereotypes (Rivera, 2015).

HR experts argue that quantitative per-formance rating systems can also quash bias, when firms tie promotions, pay and layoffs to employee scores. Yet manage-rial resistance against performance evalua-tions designed to control pay and promotion decisions shows up in biased scores. Studies suggest that raters often prefer white men to similarly productive women and non-whites (Hamner et al., 1974; Heilman, 1995; Kraiger and Ford, 1985; Oppler et al., 1992; Pulakos et al., 1989; Roth et al., 2003; Tsui and Gutek, 1984). Meta-analyses show a persis-tent gap in ratings of black and white work-ers (McKay and McDaniel 2006, Roth et al., 2003). In firms that use mathematical formu-las to link compensation to objective ratings, managers resist by interpreting scores sub-jectively to pay their cronies more (Castilla, 2008; Shwed and Kalev, 2014). It appears that managers try to circumvent performance rating systems to achieve their own purposes. Rules elicit rebellion.

A third control strategy is the civil rights grievance procedure, designed to rehabili-tate or remove discriminatory managers. Personnel experts created quasi-judicial

grievance systems modeled on union griev-ance procedures (Edelman et al., 2011: 919). These were designed to give workers a sys-tem for resolving complaints of discrimi-nation within the firm, and to ensure that managers who discriminate are rehabilitated. But managers appear to rebel against griev-ance systems, which threaten their autonomy by opening them to rebuke (Edelman, 1992: 1543). Of nearly 90,000 discrimination com-plaints to the EEOC in 2015, 45% included a charge of retaliation, suggesting that manag-ers do not respond to grievances with neutral-ity, but by punishing complainants.

Studies of the effects of these programs on the share of women and minorities in management suggest that they do not work. Obligatory diversity training backfires because it signals that the company is trying to control employees' thoughts. In the aver-age company that made training mandatory for managers, black women in management decreased by 10%, and Asian American men and women decreased by 4–5%, over about five years (see Figure 31.1; see Dobbin et al., 2007; Dobbin et al., 2015; Kalev et al., 2006 for details on model estimation). Making training mandatory appears to be particu-larly harmful; companies that made diversity

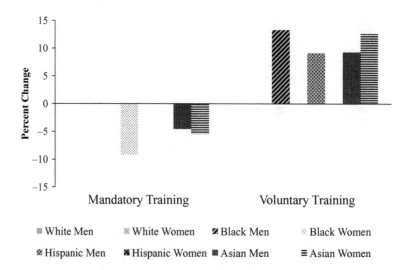

Figure 31.1   Effects of diversity training on managerial diversity

training *voluntary* saw some increases in managerial diversity. Companies that provided feedback to managers on their diversity performance appear to elicit resistance as well. Those that put in *diversity* performance ratings for managers see no positive effects, and negative effects of 6% for black men in management. We omit this policy from the figure because only one effect is significant.

Figure 31.2 shows the effects of one bureaucratic hiring procedure designed to constrain managerial discretion and one dispute-resolution program. We argued that managerial resistance to mandatory job tests has been shown to take several forms – managers can test only some applicants, or ignore test results, for instance. Companies creating written job tests for managers – about 10% have them today – see decreases of 4–10% in white women, black men and women, Hispanic men and women, and Asian women over the next five years. On average, companies that create performance rating systems see no change in minority managers over the next five years, and a 4% decrease in white women (we omit this policy from the figure). After companies adopt civil rights grievance systems, they see significant declines in white women

managers, and all minority groups except Hispanic men, ranging from 4% to 11%. This suggests that retaliation against complainants may be widespread.

These negative effects are entirely consistent with findings from the scholarly literature on job autonomy and self-determination. People resist obtrusive controls on their behavior in order to maintain autonomy in decision-making. The evidence suggests that they do so in different ways for different practices. Taken together these results point to the importance of testing managerial theories with evidence. Well-intentioned activists often backed practices that were worse than ineffective – that were counter-productive. We suggest that executives with the best of intentions could not have known that these innovations did not work. And thus that it would have been difficult for them to deliberately create anti-discrimination programs that would have only symbolic effects.

Managerial Engagement

The second broad approach championed by diversity activists and embraced by firms was

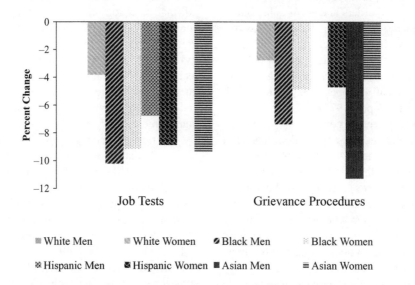

Figure 31.2 Effects of bureaucratic controls on management diversity

to engage managers in changing the workplace through mentoring programs, special college recruitment programs for women and minorities, and skill and management training with special nomination procedures for underrepresented groups. Any of these programs could elicit the same sort of rebellion we saw for the control tactics, and indeed, some firms have been reluctant to create special recruitment and training for fear of white male backlash (Dobbin 2009). But these programs share several key characteristics that, we argue, make them effective. They are voluntary – managers are asked to sign up, and while some may be nudged, they are not required to participate. These programs encourage managers to help address the the problem rather than labeling them as the cause of the problem. And they engage managers in active problem-solving.

Cognitive-dissonance and self-perception theories suggest that by encouraging them to help solve the problem, employers help managers to think of themselves as proponents of change (Bem, 1972; Festinger, 1957; Festinger and Carlsmith, 1959; Ito et al., 2006; Mori and Mori, 2013). This approach is better aligned with the managerial modus operandi than practices that require them to follow detailed orders and seem to lay blame for inequality on them – those we just discussed. Psychologists find that when people's attitudes and behaviors are out of sync, they face internal pressure to bring the two into alignment (Cooper and Fazio, 1984; Zanna and Cooper, 1974). Festinger argued that when behavior conflicts with beliefs, people experience cognitive dissonance. If you ask someone to write an essay in support of a view they do not hold, they come to see some merits in that view. So long as executives do not twist their arms, we suggest, even managers who are cool to the idea of promoting diversity will come to support diversity through policies that engage them in positive change.

Several innovations engage managers in promoting diversity, and we suggest that

participation will win them over. Mentoring programs grew in popularity in the 1980s as a way to groom talent for promotion (Roche, 1979), and diversity experts soon argued that they could provide special benefits to women and minorities (Vernon-Gerstenfeld and Burke, 1985: 67). Sociologists had argued that network contacts are key to finding jobs and moving up (Baron and Pfeffer, 1994; Granovetter, 1974), and that women and minorities often lack the ties to powerful executives that junior white men have to begin with, or develop outside of work through shared interests and activities (Burt, 1998; Ibarra, 1995; Petersen et al., 1998; Reskin and McBrier, 2000). Formal mentoring programs match junior employees with volunteer mentors, who are typically at least two rungs above them on the corporate ladder, in different departments (Neumark and Gardecki, 1996). By the early 1990s, 20–30% of big US firms had formal mentoring programs (Conference Board, 1992; Thomas, 2001). Among mid-size to large firms, about 10% had mentoring programs targeting women and minorities by 2002 (Kalev et al., 2006).

Special recruitment programs for blacks were popularized in the early 1960s as affirmative-action measures among federal contractors (Gordon, 2000). These programs use existing managers to find minority recruits. Companies now run special recruitment programs for entry-level production and service jobs in high schools, and special programs for professionals and management-track employees at colleges. By the mid-1960s, high-profile historically black schools were drawing large numbers of recruiters (Mattison, 1965). Today, some 15% of medium and large corporations run visits to colleges to draw minorities and women to management, including Target Stores and General Mills (Dobbin et al., 2015; Rodriguez, 2007: 69).

From the early 1960s, federal contractors subject to affirmative-action regulations created in-house training systems for skilled jobs, supervisory positions and management jobs, and coupled these with programs to draw in minorities and women (Boyle, 1973; Holzer and Neumark, 2000). Training programs are often designed and staffed by existing managers. While the courts struck down the idea of employer-initiated hiring quotas, they accepted employer quotas for training programs (Stryker, 1996). Management training programs, in particular, typically engage current managers in training aspiring managers in the latest methods in their own fields of specialization. Companies organize these on different models depending on the geographic dispersion of their employees; those with a single large location may spread training out over months in small doses, while those whose business units are small and farflung may train in a central location, in concentrated doses. Either way, existing managers are usually integral to the training, and are often asked to nominate women and minorities for participation.

Studies show that these programs promote workforce diversity. Cross-sectional studies suggest that special college recruitment, in-house management training, and special nomination guidelines to promote women and minorities, are associated with greater workforce diversity (Holzer and Neumark, 2000; Konrad and Linnehan, 1995). Our longitudinal studies of a national sample of firms, over the course of 30 years, suggest these engagement activities typically promote diversity, even in the hard-to-change ranks of management.

First, Figure 31.3 shows that firms that institute special college recruitment for women count 10% more white women, 8% more black women, 11% more Hispanic women, and 8% more Asian American women in management after 5 years. These programs also boost black and Asian American men (Dobbin et al., 2015). Special minority recruitment programs increase black men in management by 7% and black women by 9%. Second, Figure 31.4 shows that mentoring programs increase black women in management by over 15%, Hispanic men by about 10%, Asian Men by about 18% and Hispanic and Asian American women by over 23% each (Dobbin et al., 2007). Third, management training programs, not shown in the tables, boost white women in management by 12%, and special nomination procedures to enroll women boost white women by another 11% and Asian American men by the same amount (Dobbin et al., 2015).

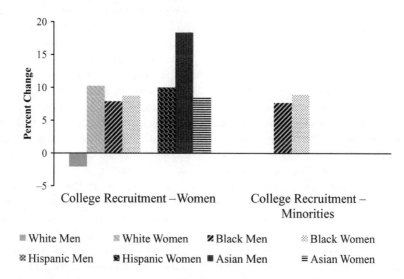

Figure 31.3 Effects of special college recruitment on management diversity

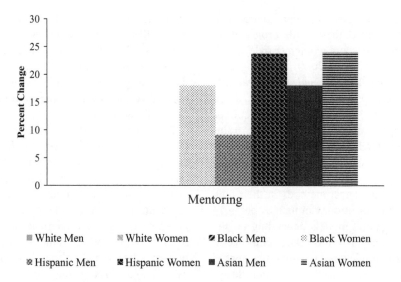

Figure 31.4   Effects of mentoring on management diversity

Just as the diversity-management literature gave executives little reason to think that control-oriented programs were counter-productive, the literature gave them little reason to think that engagement-oriented programs would work better (Dobbin, 2009). Thus well-meaning executives were clueless about which programs to adopt, as were executives hoping not to rock the boat.

Social Accountability

Institutionalists have long viewed accountability as a means of ensuring that organizational policies are carried out (Edelman, 1992). Yet, accountability mechanisms that smack of control appear to have adverse effects. Diversity report cards come off as controlling and show only negative effects. Civil rights grievance procedures hold managers accountable through an internal quasi-judicial system, and have broad negative effects. The accountability literature, however, suggests that another type of accountability can have positive effects – a type we will call social accountability. What we know from social psychological studies suggests that accountability of this sort can have positive

effects. If people think that others will evaluate their decision processes, they may censor their own biases. In their organizational theories of inequality, Reskin (2000) and Bielby (2000) build on accountability theory from psychology, which suggests that when people think they will be asked to account for a decision, they suppress bias (Tetlock, 1992; Lerner and Tetlock, 1999). Evaluation apprehension (Cottrell, 1972), or the concern that one's decisions will be reviewed, has been shown to reduce bias in assessments of individuals (Kruglanski and Freund, 1983).

Research suggests that several types of policies can elicit social accountability of this sort: diversity taskforces, diversity managers and federal contract oversight. In each case, managers charged with making hiring and promotion decisions know that they may be asked about those decisions. In the case of taskforces, they may be asked by taskforce members who are in their own departments. In the case of diversity managers, they may be asked when those managers review hiring, promotion and pay decisions. In the case of federal contractors, they may be asked to account for decisions during Department of Labor reviews of personnel practices and outcomes.

The first diversity taskforces appeared in the late 1960s, in firms such as General Electric, under the banner of equal opportunity (Dobbin, 2009). Today's taskforces typically bring together higher-ups from different departments in monthly meetings, at which they scrutinize hiring, promotion, retention and pay data to identify problem areas that need solutions (Sturm, 2001). Members brainstorm for solutions to weak recruitment of minorities, or poor retention of women professionals. Taskforces create accountability because members return to their departments, and are the first to notice when new initiatives are not being carried out. Firms design taskforces to get managers involved in problem-solving, and so taskforces have the added benefit of ratcheting up managerial engagement. By 1991, the Conference Board found that a third of big US firms had taskforces (Miller, 1994). Our own 2002 survey shows that taskforces began to spread in the wider population of firms in the late 1980s (Kalev et al., 2006).

Diversity managers first appeared after Kennedy's 1961 affirmative-action order, under an array of different titles – equal opportunity specialist, affirmative action manager, minority relations executive. Studies suggest that diversity managers improve the efficacy of equity reforms by activating accountability (Castilla, 2008; Hirsh and Kmec, 2009; Kalev et al., 2006). In line with accountability theory, diversity managers report that one of their primary duties is to question managerial decisions. According to a Massachusetts electronics industry diversity manager: '[My] role is making sure that we have not overlooked anybody. [We get] pushback from managers when we have internal postings for jobs, but [my job is] making sure [the manager has] really thought through their decision. I would keep asking – why *this* person, why not *that* person?' (quoted in Dobbin and Kalev, 2015: 180–181).

Taskforces and diversity managers should elicit 'evaluation apprehension' within the firm and thereby promote diversity. We expect regulatory oversight to have similar effects. The Department of Labor's Office of Federal Contract Compliance Programs (OFCCP) conducts on-site reviews of affirmative-action compliance in federal contractors, at its discretion (Anderson, 1996). Firms with contracts or subcontracts of at least $10,000 are subject to reviews scrutinizing personnel practices and results. It is 'evaluation apprehension', rather than the evaluation itself, that causes people to scrutinize their own behavior for signs of bias, and thus we expect federal contractors to see increases in diversity, whether or not they actually experience compliance reviews (Cottrell, 1972; Sturm, 2001).

Studies show positive effects of all three types of accountability on workforce diversity. We find that at the average company that puts in a diversity taskforce, white women and each of the minority groups grow in management by 8 to 30% over 5 years (see Figure 31.5) (Dobbin et al., 2015). Companies that appoint diversity managers see increases in white women, black men and women, Hispanic women and Asian American men and women in management ranging from 7% to 18% in the following five years. These interventions work well, but they are not common.

The effects of federal contractor status are a bit complex to show in a bar chart because they vary over time. Contractors saw better-than-average improvements in gender and racial diversity in the 1970s (Leonard, 1989, 1990). In those years, Washington was actively conducting compliance reviews. After the Reagan administration reduced enforcement, the positive effect of federal contractor status declined (Kalev and Dobbin, 2006). Since then, winning a federal contract predicts a decline in diversity in most firms (Kalev et al., 2006). This may be because contracts ensure employment stability and thus draw applicants; Reskin and Roos (1990) find that employers discriminate in favor of white men when they have long queues of applicants. Yet federal contracts catalyze a number of

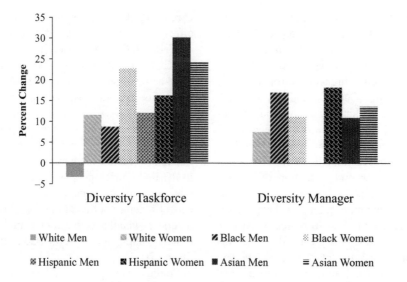

Figure 31.5   Effects of diversity taskforces and diversity managers on management diversity

equal opportunity practices in the years after the Reagan administration curtailed enforcement. In employers with federal contracts, diversity practices tend to work better due to evaluation apprehension (Kalev et al., 2006). When firms win federal contracts and managers realize that the Department of Labor may conduct inspections, for instance, the negative effects of job tests that we saw in Figure 31.2 disappear, as do all but two of the negative effects of grievance procedures (Dobbin et al., 2015).

CONCLUSION

We argue that because the effects of corporate innovations are typically based on untested theories, rather than on evidence, leaders who hope to make real change, as well as those who do not, operate in the dark. This throws a wrench into executive efforts to comply with the law by taking symbolic measures that will not affect workforce diversity. Window-dressing, or 'symbolic compliance', may have the unanticipated effect of actually changing workplaces. That is the

case for diversity taskforces for instance, which many expected to generate a lot of hot air and the occasional Mexican-themed cafeteria menu. In fact, we have found, taskforces lead to substantial improvements in managerial diversity.

The flip side is that even the most ardent of diversity champions promote innovations drawing on theorization by management gurus and leading firms, rather than on hard evidence. Some of the innovations they favor backfire. Practices can diffuse widely on the basis of compelling theorization (Strang and Meyer, 1993), and may then become impervious to disconfirming evidence. It took centuries following the scientific revolution for evidence-based medicine to take hold. Evidence-based management has yet to gain a substantial following, and thus the field of management is still rife with gurus and snake-oil salesmen. Their theories often smack of science, being based loosely on concepts from economics, psychology and sociology, but their theories are rarely tested in the field, and even when they are disproven, they are rarely rejected (Pfeffer and Sutton, 2006).

Perhaps the best evidence for our argument is that the people who decided which diversity programs would become popular were, by and large, champions of diversity. They were women drawn to human resources management by the mission of equal opportunity, who devised race relations training, formal performance evaluations and diversity scorecards for managers. They were women and minorities who reached leadership positions in corporations and lobbied successfully to have diversity training and formal equal opportunity policies put into place. They were plaintiff litigators in discrimination suits who helped to define diversity grievance procedures, and bureaucratic hiring and promotion systems, as tools for stopping discrimination. And they were federal regulators working in agencies devoted to equality of opportunity who put such measures at the top of their 'best practices' lists.

When the civil rights movement wound down, these were the groups that carried the banner of equal opportunity forward. What companies did was defined by these groups. Yet some of the programs they championed have proven to be ineffective or counterproductive. Research from various quarters supports this conclusion. In quantitative studies, we have examined large numbers of diversity practices at once, and have largely supported the findings from various studies of individual programs, such as field and lab studies of performance rating systems (which show evidence of bias in ratings), and field and lab studies of anti-bias training (which seldom show any long-term effects, and frequently evidence increased stereotyping and resistance).

Advocates do not necessarily know whether the programs they promote are effective or not because they operate in a faith-based, evidence-free zone. The result is that both for crusaders hoping to promote equality of opportunity, and for executives who want no more than symbolic measures that will not change their workforces, diversity programs may have unintended consequences that thwart their best (or worst) intentions. This suggests that institutionalists

should study not only policy–practice decoupling but also means–ends decoupling (Bromley and Powell, 2012). In the case at hand, decoupling between means and ends may have adverse effects when policies that do not have the advertised effects, such as mandatory diversity training, create managerial rebellion and crowd out other programs from the diversity budget.

The growing body of research on the effects of diversity programs provides proof of concept of a new area of research for institutionalists. Both psychologists and sociologists have begun to test the effects of diversity innovations (Castilla and Benard, 2010; Fernandez and Fernandez-Mateo, 2006; Kaiser et al., 2013), providing a foundation for an evidence-based approach to diversity management. Institutionalists typically have the ideal type of data to address questions of management efficacy. Whether they study shareholder value reforms, environmental initiatives, or diversity management, institutionalists track the spread of innovations across populations of firms, and over time. By coupling the data they use for diffusion studies with data on outcomes, such as firm performance, environmental degradation, or workforce diversity, institutionalists can examine the efficacy of innovations. In the process, they can not only explore the theories that are at the foundation of management fads, determining their veracity, they can also play a role in improving the performance of organizations, and ask a question that is particularly pressing for the paradigm – would executives go for innovations that are mere window-dressing if they knew better?

We offer a theory of organizational change wherein innovations that turn managers into change agents are effective while those that seek to constrain managers and control their discretion will lead to resistance to program goals. This theory is in keeping with research on new work practices oriented to commitment, and research on empowerment. Unfortunately, in the field of diversity management, more firms have programs that constrain managers and control discretion than have programs that engage managers or create social accountability. Taskforces and diversity managers activate both engagement and accountability, but only 20% of medium and large employers have taskforces, and just 10% have diversity managers. Efforts to control managers' thinking and decision-making are more common. Nearly half of firms have diversity training; over half have formal grievance systems. We have been arguing that firms have adopted the wrong policies not with malice aforethought, but because they were clueless. The question is, now that the research is beginning to provide a clearer picture of which diversity programs are effective, will employers flock to those that work, or to those that don't?

Notes

1   http://newsroom.fb.com/news/2015/06/driving-diversity-at-facebook/; www.google.com/diversity/

2   www.eeoc.gov/eeoc/initiatives/e-race/best practices-employers.cfm.

REFERENCES

Anderson, Bernard E. (1996). The ebb and flow of enforcing Executive Order 11246. *American Economic Review*, 86(2): 298–301.

Baron, James N. and Bielby, William T. (1980). Bringing the firms back in: Stratification, segmentation, and the organization of work. *American Sociological Review*, 45(5): 737–765.

Baron, James N. and Pfeffer, Jeffrey (1994). The social psychology of organizations and inequality. *Social Psychology Quarterly*, 57(3): 190–209.

Bem, Daryl J. (1972). Self-perception theory. In L. Berkowitz (ed.), *Advances in Experimental Social Psychology*. New York, NY: Academic Press. pp. 1–62.

Bendick, Mark, Egan, Mary Lou and Lofhjelm, Suzanne M. (1998). *The Documentation and Evaluation of Anti-Discrimination Training in the United States*. Washington, DC: Bendick and Egan Economic Consultants.

Berry, Christopher A., Clark, Malissa A. and McClure, Tara K. (2011). Racial/ethnic differences in the criterion-related validity of cognitive ability tests: a qualitative and quantitative review. *Journal of Applied Psychology*, 96(5): 881–906.

Bielby, William T. (2000). Minimizing workplace gender and racial bias. *Contemporary Sociology*, 29(1): 120–129.

Blumrosen, Alfred W. (1993). *Modern Law: The Law Transmission System and Equal Employment Opportunity*. Madison, WI: University of Wisconsin Press.

Bobo, Lawrence and Kluegel, James R. (1993). Opposition to race-targeting: Self-interest stratification ideology or racial attitudes. *American Sociological Review*, 58(4): 443–464.

Boyle, Barbara M. (1973). Equal opportunity for women is smart business. *Harvard Business Review*, 51: 85–95.

Brehm, S. S. and Brehm, J. W. (1981). *Psychological Reactance: A Theory of Freedom and Control*. New York, NY: Academic Press.

Bromley, Patricia and Powell, Walter W. (2012). From smoke and mirrors to walking the talk: Decoupling in the contemporary world. *Academy of Management Annals*, 6(1): 483–530.

Bureau of National Affairs. (1975). *Paid Leave and Leave of Absence Policies*. Vol. 111. Washington, DC: Bureau of National Affairs.

Burt, Ronald S. (1998). The gender of social capital. *Rationality and Society*, 10(1): 5–46.

Castilla, Emilio J. (2008). Gender, race, and meritocracy in organizational careers. *American Journal of Sociology*, 113(6): 1479–1526.

Castilla, Emilio J. and Benard, Stephen (2010). The paradox of meritocracy in organizations. *Administrative Science Quarterly*, 55(4): 543–576.

Chen, Anthony S. (2009). *The Fifth Freedom: Jobs, Politics, and Civil Rights in the United States, 1941–72*. Princeton, NJ: Princeton University Press.

Cohen, Philip N. and Huffman, Matt L. (2007). Working for the woman? Female managers and the gender wage gap. *American Sociological Review*, 72(5): 681–704.

Conference Board. (1992). In diversity is strength: Capitalizing on the new work force. 75th Anniversary Symposia Series. Report Number 994 (edited by J. Alster, T. Brothers and H. Gallo). New York: Conference Board, Inc.

Cooper, Joel and Fazio, Russell H. (1984). A new look at dissonance theory. *Advances in Experimental Social Psychology*, 17: 229–266.

Cottrell, Nicholas (1972). Social Facilitation. In C. McClintock (ed.), *Experimental Social Psychology*. New York, NY: Holt, Rinehart & Winston. pp. 185–236.

Davis, Gerald F. and Greve, Henrich (1997). Corporate elite networks and governance changes in the 1980s. *American Journal of Sociology*, 103(1): 1–37.

Deitch, Cynthia H. and Huffman, Matt L. (2001). Family-responsive benefits and the two-tiered labor market. In R. Hertz and N. Marshall (eds), *Working Families: The Transformation of the American Home*. Berkeley, CA: University of California Press. pp. 103–130.

Dobbin, Frank (2009). *Inventing Equal Opportunity*. Princeton, NJ: Princeton University Press.

Dobbin, Frank and Kalev, Alexandra (2015). Why firms need diversity managers and task forces. In M. Pilati, H. Sheikh, F. Sperotti and C. Tilly (eds), *How Global Migration Changes the Workforce Diversity Equation*. Newcastle upon Tyne: Cambridge Scholars. pp. 170–198.

Dobbin, Frank, Kalev, Alexandra and Kelly, Erin (2007). Diversity management in corporate America. *Contexts*, 6(4): 21–28.

Dobbin, Frank and Kelly, Erin (2007). How to stop harassment: The professional construction of legal compliance in organizations. *American Journal of Sociology*, 112(4): 1203–1243.

Dobbin, Frank, Kim, Soohan and Kalev, Alexandra (2011). You can't always get what you need: Why diverse firms adopt diversity programs. *American Sociological Review*, 76(3): 386–411.

Dobbin, Frank, Schrage, Daniel and Kalev, Alexandra (2015). Rage against the iron cage: The varied effects of bureaucratic personnel reforms on diversity. *American Sociological Review*, 80(5): 1014–1044.

Dobbin, Frank and Sutton, John R. (1998). The strength of a weak state: The employment rights revolution and the rise of human resources management divisions. *American Journal of Sociology*, 104(2): 441–476.

Dobbin, Frank, Sutton, John R., Meyer, John W. and Scott, W. Richard (1993). Equal opportunity law and the construction of internal labor markets. *American Journal of Sociology*, 99(2): 396–427.

Edelman, Lauren B. (1990). Legal environments and organizational governance: The expansion of due process in the American workplace. *American Journal of Sociology*, 95(6): 1401–1440.

Edelman, Lauren B. (1992). Legal ambiguity and symbolic structures: Organizational mediation of civil rights law. *American Journal of Sociology*, 97(6): 1531–1576.

Edelman, Lauren B., Fuller, Sally Riggs and Mara-Drita, Iona. (2001). Diversity Rhetoric and the managerialization of the law. *American Journal of Sociology*, 106(6): 1589–1641.

Edelman, Lauren B., Krieger, Linda H., Eliason, Scott, Albiston, Catherine R. and Mellema, Virginia (2011). When organizations rule: Judicial deference to institutionalized employment structures. *American Journal of Sociology*, 117(3): 888–954.

Edelman, Lauren B. and Petterson, Stephen M. (1999). Symbols and substance in organizations response to civil rights law. *Research in Social Stratification and Mobility*, 17: 107–135.

Edelman, Lauren B., Uggen, Christopher and Erlanger, Howard S. (1999). The endogeneity of legal regulation: Grievance procedures as rational myth. *American Journal of Sociology*, 105(2): 406–454.

Fernandez, Roberto M. and Fernandez-Mateo, Isabel (2006). Network, race, and hiring. *American Sociological Review*, 71(1): 42–71.

Festinger, Leon (1957). *A theory of cognitive dissonance*. Stanford, CA: Stanford University Press.

Festinger, Leon and Carlsmith, James M. (1959). Cognitive consequences of forced compliance. *Journal of Abnormal and Social Psychology*, 58(2): 203–210.

Fiske, Susan T. (1998). Stereotyping, prejudice and discrimination. In D. T. Gilbert, S. T. Fiske and G. Lindzey (eds), *The Handbook of Social Psychology*, 4th edn, volume 2. New York: McGraw Hill. pp. 357–411.

Galinsky, Adam D. and Moskowitz, Gordon B. (2000). Perspective taking: decreasing stereotype expression stereotype accessibility, and in-group favoritism. *Journal of Personality and Social Psychology*, 78(4): 708–724.

Gordon, Hugh L. (2000). Cobb County Oral History Series No. 75. Interview with Hugh L. Gordon conducted by Joyce A. Patterson.

Gorman, Elizabeth (2005). Gender stereotypes, same-gender preferences, and organizational variation in the hiring of women: Evidence from law firms. *American Sociological Review*, 70(4): 702–728.

Gouldner, Alvin W. (1954). *Patterns of industrial democracy: A case study of modern factory administration*. New York, NY: Free Press.

Graham, Hugh Davis (1990). *The Civil Rights Era: Origins and Development of National Policy, 1960–1972*. New York: Oxford University Press.

Granovetter, Mark (1974). *Getting a Job: A Study of Contracts and Careers*. Chicago, IL: University of Chicago Press.

Guthrie, Douglas and Roth, Louise Marie (1999). Family-friendly policies in U.S. organizations: Institutional environments and maternity leave. *American Sociological Review*, 64(1): 41–63.

Hamner, W. Clay, Kim, Jay S., Baird, Lloyd, and Bigoness, William J. (1974). Race and sex as determinants of ratings by potential employers in a simulated work-sampling task. *Journal of Applied Psychology*, 59(6): 705–712.

Hegewisch, Ariane, Deitch, Cynthia H. and Murphy, Evelyn F. (2011). Ending sex and race discrimination in the workplace: Legal interventions that push the envelope. Washington, D.C.: Institute for Women's Policy Research.

Heilman, Madeline (1995). Sex stereotypes and their effects in the workplace: What we know and what we don't know. *Journal of Social Behavior and Personality,* 10(6): 3–26.

Hirsh, Elizabeth and Kmec, Julie A. (2009). Human resource structures: Reducing discrimination or raising rights awareness? *Industrial Relations: A Journal of Economy and Society,* 48(3): 512–532.

Hodson, Randy (1991a). Workplace behaviors: Good soldiers, smooth operators, and saboteurs. *Work and Occupations,* 18(3): 271–290.

Hodson, Randy (1991b). The active worker: Compliance and autonomy at the workplace. *Journal of Contemporary Ethnography,* 20(1): 47–78.

Hodson, Randy (1996). Dignity in the workplace under participative management: Alienation and Freedom Revisited. *American Sociological Review,* 61(5): 719–738.

Holzer, Harry J. and Neumark, David (2000). What does affirmative action do? *Industrial and Labor Relations Review,* 53(2): 240–271.

Ibarra, Herminia (1995). Race, opportunity and diversity of social circles in managerial networks. *Academy of Management Journal,* 38(3): 673–703.

Ito, Tiffany A., Chiao, Krystal W., Devine, Patricia G., Lorig, Tyler S., and Cacioppo, John T. (2006). The influence of facial feedback on race bias. *Psychological Science,* 17(3): 256–261.

Jacoby, Sanford (1984). The development of internal labor markets in American manufacturing firms. In P. Osterman (ed.), *Internal Labor Markets.* Cambridge, MA: MIT Press. pp. 23–69.

Johnson, Cathryn, Dowd, Timothy J. and Ridgeway, Cecilia L. (2006). Legitimacy as a social process. *Annual Review of Sociology,* 32(1): 53–78.

Judge, Timothy A., Thoresen, Carl. J., Bono, Joyce E., and Patton, Gregory K. (2001). The job satisfaction-job performance relationship: A qualitative and quantitative review. *Psychological Bulletin,* 127(3): 376–407.

Jung, Jiwook and Dobbin, Frank (2016). Agency theory as prophecy: How boards, analysts, and fund managers perform their roles. *Seattle University Law Review,* 39(2): 291–320.

Kaiser, Cheryl R., Major, Brenda, Ines, Jurcevic, Dover, Tessa L., Brady, Laura M. and Shapiro, Jenessa R. (2013). Presumed fair: Ironic effects of organizational diversity structures. *Journal of Personality and Social Psychology,* 104(3): 504–519.

Kalev, Alexandra and Dobbin, Frank (2006). Enforcement of civil rights law in private workplaces: The effects of compliance reviews and lawsuits over time. *Law and Social Inquiry,* 31(4): 855–879.

Kalev, Alexandra, Dobbin, Frank and Kelly, Erin (2006). Best practices or best guesses? Assessing the efficacy of corporate affirmative action and diversity policies. *American Sociological Review,* 71(4): 589–617.

Kamerman, Sheila B., Kahn, Alfred J. and Kingston, Paul (1983). *Maternity Policies and Working Women.* New York: Columbia University Press.

Kanter, Rosabeth Moss. (1977). *Men and Women of the Corporation.* New York: Basic Books.

Kelly, Erin A. (2003). The strange history of employer-sponsored childcare: Interested actors, uncertainty, and the transformation of law in organizational fields. *American Journal of Sociology,* 109(3): 606–649.

Kelly, Erin A. and Dobbin, Frank (1998). How affirmative action became diversity management. *American Behavioral Scientist,* 41(7): 960–984.

Kelly, Erin and Dobbin, Frank (1999). Civil rights law at work: Sex discrimination and the rise of maternity leave policies. *American Journal of Sociology,* 105(2): 455–492.

Kelly, Erin L., Moen, Phyllis and Tranby, Eric (2011). Changing workplaces to reduce work–family conflict: schedule control in a white-collar organization. *American Sociological Review,* 76(2): 265–290.

Kidder, Deborah L., Lankau, Melenie J., Chrobot-Mason, Donna, Mollica, Kelly A. and Friedman, Raymond A. (2004). Backlash toward diversity initiatives: Examining the impact of diversity program justification, personal and group outcomes. *International Journal of Conflict Management,* 15(1): 77–104.

Kochan, Thomas A., Katz, Harry C., and McKersie, Robert B. (1994). *The transformation of American industrial relations.* Ithaca, NY: ILR Press.

Konrad, Alison M. and Linnehan, Frank (1995). Formalized HRM structures – coordinating equal-employment opportunity or concealing organizational practices. *Academy of Management Journal,* 38(3): 787–820.

Kraiger, Kurt and Ford, J. Kevin (1985). A meta-analysis of ratee race effects in performance ratings. *Journal of Applied Psychology,* 70(1): 56–65.

Kruglanski, Arie W. and Freund, Tallie (1983). The freezing and unfreezing of lay-inferences: Effects on impressional primacy, ethnic stereotyping, and numeral anchoring. *Journal of Experimental Social Psychology,* 19(5): 448–468.

Lamont, Michèle (2000). *The dignity of working men: Morality and the boundaries of cass, race, and immigration.* Cambridge, MA: Harvard University Press.

Legault, Lisa, Gutsell, Jennifer N. and Inzlicht, Michael (2011). Ironic effects of antiprejudice messages: How motivational interventions can reduce (but also increase) prejudice. *Psychological Science*, 22: 1472–1477.

Lemm, Kristi and Banaji, Mahzarin R. (1999). Unconscious attitudes and beliefs about men and women. In U. Pasero and F. Braun (eds), *Perceiving and Performing Gender.* Opladen: Westdutscher Verlag. pp. 215–235.

Leonard, Jonathan S. (1989). Women and affirmative action. *The Journal of Economic Perspectives*, 3(1): 61–75.

Leonard, Jonathan S. (1990). The impact of affirmative action regulation and equal employment opportunity law on black employment. *Journal of Economic Perspectives*, 4(4): 47–63.

Lerner, Jennifer S. and Tetlock, Philip E. (1999). Accounting for the effects of accountability. *Psychological Bulletin,* 125(2): 255–275.

Lieberman, Robert C. (2002). Weak state, strong policy: Paradoxes of race policy in the United States, Great Britain, and France. *Studies in American Political Development*, 16(2): 138–161.

Mattison, E. G. (1965). Integrating the work force in Southern industry. In H. R. Northrup and R. L. Rowan (eds), *The Negro and Employment Opportunity: Problems and Practices.* Ann Arbor, MI: Bureau of Industrial Relations, Graduate School of Business Administration, University of Michigan. pp. 147–54.

McKay, Patrick F. and McDaniel, Michael A. (2006). A reexamination of black–white mean differences in work performance: More data, more moderators. *Journal of Applied Psychology*, 91(3): 538–554.

Meyer, John W. and Rowan, Brian (1977). Institutionalized organizations: Formal structure as myth and ceremony. *American Journal of Sociology*, 83(2): 340–363.

Miller, Joanne (1994). *Corporate Responses to Diversity.* Queens College, New York.

Mong, Sherry and Roscigno, Vincent J. (2010). African American men and the experience of employment discrimination. *Qualitative Sociology*, 33(1): 1–21.

Mori, Hideko and Mori, Kazuo (2013). An implicit assessment of the effect of artificial cheek raising: When your face smiles, the world looks nicer. *Perceptual and Motor Skills,* 116(2): 466–471.

Naff, Katherine C. and Kellough, J. Edward (2003). Ensuring employment equity: Are federal diversity programs making a difference? *International Journal of Public Administration*, 26(12): 1307–1336.

Nelson, Robert L. and Bridges, William P. (1999). *Legalizing Gender Inequality: Courts, Markets and Unequal Pay for Women in America.* New York, NY: Cambridge University Press.

Nelson, Thomas E., Acker, Michele and Melvin, Manis (1996). Irrepressible stereotypes. *Journal of Experimental Social Psychology*, 32(1): 13–38.

Neumark, David and Gardecki, Rosella (1996). *Women Helping Women? Role-Model and Mentoring Effects on Female Ph.D. Student in Economics.* Cambridge, MA: National Bureau of Economic Research.

Nonet, Philippe and Selznick, Philip (1978). *Law and Society in Transition: Toward Responsive Law.* New York: Octagon Books.

Oppler, Scott H., Campbell, John P., Pulakos, Elaine D. and Borman, Walter C. (1992). Three Approaches to the investigation of subgroup bias in performance measurement: Review, results, and conclusions. *Journal of Applied Psychology*, 77(2): 201–217.

Paluck, Elizabeth L. and Green, Donald P. (2009). Prejudice reduction: What works? A critical look at evidence from the field and the laboratory. *Annual Review of Psychology*, 60: 339–367.

Pernell, Kim, Jung, Jiwook and Dobbin, Frank (forthcoming). Doubling down on derivatives: Chief risk officers, CEOs, and fund managers. *American Sociological Review.*

Petersen, Trond, Saporta, Ishak and Seidelm, Marc David (1998). Offering a job: Meritocracy and social networks. *American Journal of Sociology*, 106: 763–816.

Pfeffer, Jeffrey and Sutton, Robert I. (2006). *Hard Facts, Dangerous Half-Truth and Total Nonsense: Profiting from Evidence-Based Management.* Cambridge, MA: Harvard Business School Press.

Plant, E. Ashby and Devine, Patricia G. (2001). Responses to other-imposed pro-Black pressure: Acceptance or backlash? *Journal of Experimental Social Psychology*, 37(6): 486–501.

Pulakos, Elaine D., White, Leonard A., Oppler, Scott H., and Borman, Walter C. (1989). Examination of race and sex effects on performance ratings. *Journal of Applied Psychology,* 74(5): 770–780.

Puma, John J. (1966). Improving Negro employment in Boston. *Industrial Management Review*, 8(1): 37–45.

Purcell, Theodore V. (1953). *The Worker Speaks His Mind on Union and Company*, Vol. 52. Cambridge, MA: Harvard University Press.

Reskin, Barbara F. (2003). Including mechanisms in our models of ascriptive inequality. *American Sociological Review*, 68(1): 1–21.

Reskin, Barbara F. and McBrier, Debra B. (2000). Why not ascription? Organizations' employment of male and female managers. *American Sociological Review*, 65(2): 210–233.

Reskin, Barbara F. and Roos, Patricia (1990). *Job Queues, Gender Queues: Explaining Women's*

Inroads into Male Occupations. Philadelphia, PA: Temple University Press.

Rivera, Lauren A. (2015). *Pedigree: How Elite Students Get Elite Jobs*. Princeton, NJ: Princeton University Press.

Roche, Gerard R. (1979). Much ado about mentors. *Harvard Business Review*, 57(1): 14–20.

Rodriguez, Robert (2007). *Latino Talent: Effective Strategies to Recruit, Retain and Develop Hispanic Professionals*. New York: Wiley.

Roos, Patricia and Manley, Joan E. (1996). Staffing personnel: Feminization and change in human resource management. *Sociological Focus*, 99(3): 245–261.

Roth, Philip L., Huffcutt, Allen I. and Bobko, Philip (2003). Ethnic group differences in measures of job performance: A new meta-analysis. *Journal of Applied Psychology*, 88(4): 694–706.

Roy, Donald (1952). Quota restriction and goldbricking in a machine shop. *American Journal of Sociology*, 57(5): 427–442.

Ruhm, Christopher J. and Teague, Jackqueline L. (1997). Parental leave policies in Europe and North America. In F. D. Blau and R. G. Ehrenberg (eds), *Gender and Family Issues in the Workplace*. New York: Russell Sage Foundation. pp. 133–156.

Rynes, Sara and Rosen, Benson (1995). A field survey of factors affecting the adoption and perceived success of diversity training. *Personnel Psychology*, 48(2): 247–270.

Schlanger, Margo and Kim, Pauline (2014). The Equal Employment Opportunity Commission and structural reform of the American workplace. *Washington University Law Review*, 91(6): 1519–1590.

Shaeffer, Ruth G. (1973). *Nondiscrimination in Employment: Changing Perspectives, 1963–1972*. New York: The Conference Board.

Shwed, Uri and Kalev, Alexandra (2014). Are referrals more productive or more likable? Social networks and the evaluation of merit. *American Behavioral Scientist,* 58: 288–308.

Sidanius, Jim, Devereux, Erik and Pratto, Felicia (2001). A comparison of symbolic racism theory and social dominance theory as explanations for racial policy attitudes. *Journal of Social Psychology*, 132(3): 377–395.

Silvia, Paul J. (2005). Deflecting reactance: The role of similarity in increasing compliance and reducing resistance. *Basic and Applied Social Psychology*, 27(3): 277–284.

Steeh, Charlotte and Krysan, Maria (1996). The polls – trends: Affirmative action and the public, 1970–1995. *Public Opinion Quarterly*, 60(1): 128–158.

Strang, David (2010). *Learning by Example: Imitation and Innovation at a Global Bank*. Princeton, NJ: Princeton University Press.

Strang, David and Meyer, John W. (1993). Institutional conditions for diffusion. *Theory and Society*, 22(4): 487–511.

Stryker, Robin (1996). Law sociology and public policy issues in equal employment opportunity. Paper presented at the Annual Meeting of the American Sociological Association.

Sturm, Susan (2001). Second generation employment discrimination: A structural approach. *Columbia Law Review*, 101(3): 459–568.

Tetlock, Philip E. (1985). Accountability: A social check on the fundamental attribution error. *Social Psychology Quarterly*, 48(3): 227–436.

Tetlock, Philip E. (1992). The impact of accountability on judgment and choice: Toward a social contingency model. In M. Zanna (ed.), *Advances in Experimental Social Psychology*. New York, NY: Academic Press. pp. 331–376.

Thomas, David A. (2001). The truth about mentoring minorities: Race matters. *Harvard Business Review*, April: 99–107.

Tsui, Anne S. and Gutek, Barbara A. (1984). A role set analysis of gender differences in performance, affective relationships, and career success of industrial middle managers. *Academy of Management Journal*, 27(3): 619–635.

Vernon-Gerstenfeld, Susan and Burke, Edmund (1985). Affirmative action in nine large companies: A field study. *Personnel*, 62(4): 54–60.

Yermack, David (1996). Higher market valuation of companies with a small board of directors. *Journal of Financial Economics*, 40(2): 185–211.

Zanna, Mark P. and Cooper, Joel (1974). Dissonance and the pill: An attribution approach to studying the arousal properties of dissonance. *Journal of Personality and Social Psychology*, 29(5): 703–709.

Zuckerman, Ezra W. (1999). The categorical imperative: Securities analysts and the illegitimacy discount. *American Journal of Sociology*, 104(5): 1398–1438.

PART VI

Reflections

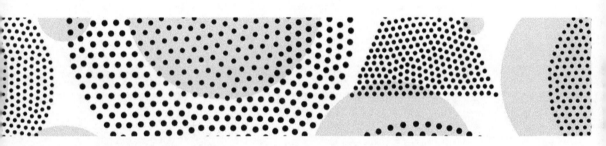

32

Reflections on Institutional Theories of Organizations

John W. Meyer

Contemporary institutional theorizing in the field of organizations dates back almost forty years. This particularly describes what are called new or neo-institutionalisms. These terms evoke contrasts with earlier theories of the embeddedness of organizations in social and cultural contexts, now retrospectively called the 'old institutionalism' (Hirsch & Lounsbury, 1997; Stinchcombe, 1997). They went through a period of inattention, so that when institutional thinking came back in force after the 1960s, it seemed quite new.

As they emerged in the 1970s, the ideas received much attention in the field, along with other lines of thought emphasizing the dependence of modern organizations on their environments. They continue to receive attention, and seem to retain substantial measures of vigor. One secondary aim, here, is to explain why. But I primarily review the status of the principal themes of institutional theory. I concentrate on sociological versions, which capture core ideas in their most dramatic form, rather than the limited versions emphasized in economics or political science.

Within sociological versions, I concentrate on phenomenological theories. These reflect my own interests, are continuing loci of research creativity, and contrast most sharply with other lines of social scientific theorizing about organizations. In practice, 'organizations' tends to be both a research field and a realist ideology about modern society: phenomenological thinking steps back from that commitment, and is useful in analyzing, for example, why so much formal organization exists in the modern world (Drori, Meyer, & Hwang, 2006; Bromley & Meyer, 2015).

BACKGROUND

Throughout the post-Enlightenment history of the social sciences, notions that human activity is highly embedded in institutional contexts were central. Individuals were seen as creatures of habit (Camic, 1986), groups as controlled by customs (famously, Bagehot's cake of custom or Spencer's folkways and mores), and societies as organized around culture.

The nature of the institutions and their controls over activity, in social scientific thinking, was never clear and consensual. Theories ranged from economic to political to religious, and variously emphasized cultural forms of control or organizational ones. Anything beyond the behavior of the people under study could be seen as representing a controlling institutionalized pattern (a clear definitional discussion is in Jepperson, 1991).

Over the long history of social scientific thinking through the mid-twentieth century, institutional theories grew and improved. Sophisticated syntheses like Parsons' were produced, with many variations on broad evolutionary schemes and typologies, as high Modernity progressed. But they came into dialectical conflict with another aspect of the same Modernity. As 'men' came to believe they understood the institutional bases of human activity, they also came to believe they could rise above, and control, them – no longer subject to, but playing the parts of, the now-dead gods. Embeddedness in culture and history was a property of the superstitious past, over which the Moderns had triumphed. So institutional thinking could survive in anthropology – about primitive societies (including earlier Western history) – but only tenuously in the social sciences of Modernity (Meyer, 1988).

In short, the old institutionalisms were driven into marginality by the rise of (often policy-oriented and scientistic – see Toulmin, 1990) conceptions of social life as made up of purposive, bounded, fairly rational and rather free actors. 'Society' was discovered, headed by the sovereign state as its central actor, putatively freed by the constitution of Westphalia. The human person as individual actor was discovered, unleashed by markets, democracy, property rights and religious freedom. Rationalized social life, made up of

bureaucracies essentially delegated from the state (as in Weber or Fayol) or of associations built up by individual actors (as in Barnard), was discovered and celebrated.

In the new schemes, built around notions of society as made up of empowered actors, older institutional theories tended to crumble. Studies of persons no longer attended to notions of habits (Camic, 1986), and concepts of culture and custom as driving forces receded. If the old institutions remained, they remained as dispositional properties of the actors involved – tastes and values of individuals, core values of states and societies.

The key concept in the new system was the notion of the 'actor' – variously, individual persons, nation-states and the organizations created by persons and states. Society was produced by these powerful entities. It was made up exclusively of actors, and even the rapidly disappearing peasants could be analyzed as individual actors. Social change was a product of such actors: thus the continuing use of an individualistic version of Weber's Protestant Ethic thesis as a proof text for proper social analysis (e.g., Coleman, 1986; Jepperson & Meyer, 2011). And all this had a normative cast – social institutions that restricted the choices of real social actors could be seen as inefficient at the least, and perhaps as destructive of progress.

The new models remain in force, and it is now conventional in social science publications to refer to 'actors' rather than people and groups (Hwang & Colyvas, 2011, 2013). But there have been doubts about models of society as made up mainly of interested actors. Too many studies of individual persons showed astounding levels of embedded nonactorhood in what were supposed to be political, economic and cultural choices. A whole literature on organization in actual social life showed the overwhelming importance of uncertainty in organizational (non)decisions (Cyert & March, 1992) and of the informal resolutions involved in practice (Dalton, 1959): formalistic or technicist analyses (e.g., Perrow, 1970;

Blau & Shoenherr, 1971) seemed much too limited. Notions of rationally organized sovereign nation-state action as driving development did not stand up against the realities of chaotic Third World nation-states, and the surrealities of the Cold War.

So, since the 1970s, in every social science field except anthropology (where older institutionalisms had never receded), 'new' institutionalist theorizing appeared, with models again envisioning people and groups as embedded in larger structures and cultures of one sort or another (see Jepperson, 2002a for a review). There have been many different varieties, but they all have had one main element in common. They all have come to terms with one or another version of the deeply institutionalized idea that society is made up of interested, purposive and often rational actors.

If the old institutionalisms had seen people and groups as rather naturally embedded in broad cultural and structural contexts, the new institutionalisms incorporate a tension in the conceptualized actor–environment relation. This is often seen as a stress between structure (i.e., the environment) and agency or actorhood (see e.g., Giddens, 1984; or Sewell, 1992), in replication of the debates in the old institutionalism about free will and determinism.

The new institutionalisms see the social environment as affecting the identities, behaviors and practices of people and groups now conceived or constructed as bounded, purposive and organized actors. Many different lines of thought are involved, varying in their conception of what an actor is, and what properties of which environments are relevant.

TYPES OF INSTITUTIONAL THEORY

Institutional theories generally see local actors – whether individuals, organizations or nation-states – as affected by institutions built up in much wider environments.

Individuals and organizations are affected by societal institutions, and nation-states by a world society. In this chapter, we focus on these lines of theory.

But it can be noted that some other lines of thought treat modern actors as affected by the institutionalization built into their own histories. Older ideas about habit, custom and culture are resurrected as theories of what is now called 'path dependence'. So individuals or organizations, faced with a new problem, use their accustomed older solutions whether or not these ever worked or can reasonably be expected to work (see the various essays by March and his colleagues, 1988).

In the present essay, we leave aside this line of theory, and concentrate on arguments locating institutionalized forces in wider environments than the history of the actor itself. These tend to fall on a broad continuum ranging from more realist theories to more phenomenological ones. After reviewing this range of arguments, we turn to focus more intensively on the phenomenological side of the spectrum, which is of special interest here, and the locus of the most distinctive advances – important in a field, often located in applied arenas, that tends to merge theory and realist ideology.

Realist Institutionalisms

Some institutionalist lines of thought, arising particularly in economics and political science, retain strong notions of society as made up of bounded, purposive, sovereign and rational actors. In economics, these might be individuals or organizations, operating in market-like environments. In political science, they might be sovereign nation-states operating in an almost anarchic environment. Institutionalism, in such schemes, involves the idea that some fundamental institutional principle must be in place before systems of such actors can effectively operate. The classic core principle required in economic versions is property rights (North & Thomas, 1973). In international relations theory it is the principle of nation-state sovereignty (Krasner, 1999).

Once the core principle is in place, systems of actors freed from further institutional influences are thought to function stably and effectively over time. Indeed, further institutional interventions in the market or international polity are thought, in extreme versions of these traditions, to be counter-productive disturbances of rationality. There is a tendency to see the situation as one of punctuated equilibrium. Collective history operates briefly, creating the crucial change, and then stable equilibria ensue. So there are accounts of the unique circumstances producing the construction of property rights in Western history. And there are discussions of the similarly unique circumstances producing the magic of Westphalia, thought to undergird the rise to world dominance of the Western nation-state system.

Extreme realist institutionalism retains strong assumptions about the capacities of actors, and very limited pictures of the institutional environment. The environment really contains only one narrow institutional rule – and in most versions it is a rule created by the actors themselves, whose existence and character are seen as entirely prior to the institutional regime.

Over time, realist institutionalism has tended to become a good deal less extreme (see, e.g., North, 1981). To property rights, the economists add a variety of other important institutions needed to make the modern system go (Jepperson & Meyer, 2011). A variety of institutions must reproduce and socialize the population, for instance, and a knowledge system is required to encourage and carry along technical improvements (Mokyr, 1992). And perhaps even some cultural supports for entrepreneurship are needed (Landes, 1998).

Similarly, realist political scientists add institutional elements necessary to make the world political system work: guarantees of agreements, and trust, for example. In political science realism, as well as in economics, however, the institutions thought to be required are also mainly thought to be products of the interests of the basic actors.

Compromises with Realism

Moving away from more extreme realist thinking, much modern social science is built up around more complex pictures of the institutional context, and a conception of the modern actor as rather more penetrable. The institutions have discursive dimensions, and also organizational ones. The key term describing institutionalized culture, here, is 'norm', especially common in political science (see, for examples, Katzenstein, 1996). The key notions of institutionalized organization, especially utilized in sociology, are 'relation' or 'network' (Granovetter, 1985).

A norm is a rule with some degree of binding authority over actors – for instance, in international relations, the principle that a state should not kill the diplomats representing other states; or the proscription of chemical weapons in war. In the most realist theories, a norm is created and supported by the actors involved. In less realist versions, norms may have been created by forces in the past, and may have binding power whether or not present actors support them. Thus, in a compromised realism, actors are partly creatures of the rules, not only creators of them.

Similarly, a network relation between actors is a simple form of organizational institutionalization. Such relations are thought to constrain actors, as well as provide opportunities for their activities. In the most realist versions, actors create their networks: in less realist models, the networks have prior histories and external determinants and thus generate considerable path dependence.

Sociological Institutionalism I: Social Organizational Versions

Moving further away from realist models, we come to some core ideas of modern sociological institutionalism (see DiMaggio & Powell, 1983; Powell & DiMaggio, 1991; Jepperson, 2002a; Hasse & Krücken, 2005; Scott, 2014). Here, actors are substantially controlled by institutional contexts which go far beyond a few norms or network structures. Further, these contexts are by no means simply constructions built up by the contemporary actors themselves, but are likely to have prior and exogenous historical origins.

Institutions, in these conceptions, are packages or programs of an expanded sort. 'Regimes' is a term employed in political science for the idea – organizational packages infused with cultural meaning (often from professions as epistemic communities). So one can refer to a neo-liberal regime in the contemporary world. Or an anti-trust program in earlier America (Fligstein, 1990). Sociologists capture this idea by referring to societal sectors, or social fields (Fligstein & McAdam, 2012). In research on organizations, the term 'logics' is increasingly employed (Thornton, Ocasio, & Lounsbury, 2012). Institutions, in all these conceptions, are complex and often coherent mixtures of cultural and organizational material.

Similarly, the institutions penetrate actors in multiple and complex ways, ranging from more realist formats to more phenomenological ones. DiMaggio and Powell (1983) provide a list that is much utilized (see Scott, 2014, for a related one). On the realist side, institutional structures affect actors through what they call 'coercive' processes, including nation-state legal actions. On the middle ground, they envision 'normative' controls of environments over actors, emphasizing the influence of professionalized standards. And then, moving to a more phenomenological perspective, they suppose that environments create patterns that actors adopt 'mimetically', reflecting taken-for-granted standards. At this point, actors are not really well-bounded entities any more, but may be built up of cultural and organizational materials from their environments.

Sociological Institutionalism II: Phenomenological Versions

A key turning point in the rise of the new institutionalism is the development of a perspective in which the actors of modern society are seen not simply as influenced by the wider environment, but as constructed in and by it (Jepperson, 2002a). Related ideas in political science are called 'constructivism'. Rationalized organizations as actors are creatures of rationalized environments (Meyer & Rowan, 1977; Zucker, 1977; Meyer & Scott, 1983). The individual as actor is a continually expanding construction of modernity (Meyer, 1986, following on a long discussion in the literature, including Berger, Berger, & Kellner, 1974). The nation-state as actor is a construction of a world polity (Thomas, Meyer, Ramirez, & Boli, 1987; Meyer, Boli, Thomas, & Ramirez, 1997).

The concept of 'actor' in this scheme is far removed from that envisioned in realist perspectives. The realists imagine that people are really bounded and purposive and sovereign actors, and that nation-states are too. And so are the organizations deriving from these. The sociological institutionalists, on the other hand, suppose that actorhood is a role or identity, as in a theatrical world (Frank & Meyer, 2002): individual actors, in this usage, have socially conferred rights and responsibilities, and socially conferred agency to represent these (and other) interests (Meyer & Jepperson, 2000). Actorhood, in this usage, is scripted by institutional structures; and the relation between actor and action is no longer a simple causal one – both elements have institutional scripts behind them, and their relation has strong elements of socially constructed tautology. The actor–action relation is a package, and as people and groups enter into particular forms of actorhood, the appropriate actions come along and are not best seen as choices and decisions. Institutional theories, thus, do not depend on particularly elaborate social psychological assumptions about people: almost any social psychological model is good enough to explain the effects that institutionalization has made socially obvious. Thus, when a group of modern people gather to assemble an organization, they do not do so from scratch. Everywhere, there are models put in place by law, ideology, culture and a variety of organizational constraints and opportunities. People are likely to install these in the organization they are building with little by way of thought or decision: exotic psychological assumptions are not required. There will be offices and departments that were unknown a few decades ago (CFO, or Chief Financial Officer; HR, or Human Relations Department). Few will spend time deciding to adopt these institutions, and thus perhaps the word 'mimetic' applies. But it is an imprecise term because the people adopting the new structures will often be able to articulate clearly the legitimating rationales for their actions, as if these were thought-out purposes. The purposes come along with the enterprise.

As an illustration at the individual level, any good student in a prestigious American university ought to be able, almost instantaneously, to write some paragraphs about 'why I decided to go to college'. But on inspection, it turns out that almost none of these students actually decided to go to college, as they had never contemplated any alternative. Going to college was taken for granted. Indeed, any student who had spent time deciding whether to go to college would be unlikely to have a record enabling admission to a prestigious one. Nevertheless, many researchers studying college attendance formulate their task as analyzing a 'decision'– a decision they and their subjects probably never made. A number of methodological errors follow, besetting the research tradition involved. Parallel errors characterize much research in the field of organizations: decision analyses of matters never in fact decided. Mistakes routinely follow from the established assumptions that human activity, more or less by definition, follows from choices.

Sociological institutionalism of the phenomenological sort is not only furthest from realism, but arises in some opposition to it.

Realist theory, it is argued, grossly understates the extreme cultural dependence of modern organizations. Thus, the institutionalists emphasize that much modern social rationalization has mythic functions encouraging the formation of organizations and their components. This sometimes leads to criticisms that institutionalism is only about 'symbols' rather than 'realities'. On the other hand, the realists, ignoring the dependence of modern organizational structure on the rapidly expanding myths of rationality, have no serious explanation for the rise – in every country, every social sector and almost every detailed social activity – of so much modern organization itself (Drori et al., 2006; Bromley & Meyer, 2015).

Phenomenological ideas are by no means incompatible with more realist ones – in most situations, both can make sense. Tensions arise because realist models tend to be exclusionary – in addition to analyses they are core modern ideologies, undergirding polity, economy, culture and society. They are normative models as well as cognitive ones, and thus alternative lines of thought are seen as in part normative violations. Closed-system realist models are often central to policy advice, and this function is limited and undercut by more open-system institutional theories (Coleman, 1993).

THE CAREER OF SOCIOLOGICAL INSTITUTIONALIST THEORY

The phenomenological perspectives of sociological institutionalism have prospered over the last three decades. Before discussing why this is so, we need to note why it should not have been so.

The Ideological Absorption of Institutional Ideas

Modern social science, following on modern ideology, celebrates a social world made up of strong actors, in the realist sense. Theory and ideology give great emphasis to notions of society as a product of such actors and their purposes. Methods of social research, and public data collection, build data on and around these units, and define proper analyses as focused on both their independence and their purposive action. Normative ideologies infusing both research and public life give preference to treatments that take individual persons (and organizations) as highly interested and agentic actors (Jepperson & Meyer, 2011).

More concretely, modern democratic political systems rest, for their legitimacy, on doctrines of free individual choice. If the individuals and their choices are constructions of the system itself, the legitimacy of democracy tends to disappear. Similarly, if choices of individuals and organizations in markets are in fact 'wired' consequences of the market system, the legitimacy of the free economy is undercut. The same points can be made about religious and cultural choices in the nominally free society. Thus, there are cultural tendencies in the modern actor-centered society to celebrate actors in a very realist sense: these tendencies are very strong ideological currents in the social sciences. Social science influence over policy tends to depend on them (Coleman, 1993).

Much organizational research goes on in schools of business, education and public policy. These schools are built on the notion that organizational leaders are decision-makers, and their main tasks are to train their students to be such decision-makers. They are in no position to emphasize that their students are, or should be, drifting non-decision-making followers of institutionalized currents. Scott (2007) defends realist institutional theory on precisely these grounds.

Thus, as new institutional forces are built up, the modern system itself tends to absorb them in expanded theories of actorhood and decision-making. Organizational members and research analysts tend over time to see the organizational elements newly adopted under institutional pressures as if they were functional, rational and reasonable organizational choices. This process is analyzed with care in studies of the developments, in American organizational life, around affirmative action pressures and requirements (see Dobbin & Sutton, 1998; Edelman, Uggen, & Erlanger, 1999; Dobbin, 2009). After the long wave of legalizing pressures on organizations, sets of schemes are produced – policies, offices and professions – responding to these pressures. Organizations incorporate packages of these. But after a time, it is all naturalized in the preferred models of rational actorhood. By now, any reasonable organizational manager would be able to explain why his or her organization has affirmative action policies – these policies are obviously the best way to ensure hiring the most able people. In exactly the same way, corporate social responsibility has become normalized – what were in the 1970s new normative ideas have become best practices, with the 'business case' for CSR (Pope, 2015; Tsutsui & Lim, 2015).

Given that the processes stressed by the phenomenological versions of institutional theory are constantly absorbed by evolving organizational systems, the question arises – what forces keep these lines of theory prospering? If the social world were moving toward a modern equilibrium, institutional theories would tend to be absorbed in a socially constructed realist ideology. Obviously, equilibrium is not what is going on.

The rapid social changes distinctive to the period since World War II have tended to create rapid cultural expansions of the sorts attended to by institutional theories. The period, in other words, creates both institutional theories and a globalizing social world which operates along the lines suggested by those theories.

Stateless Globalization

Recent world developments have created interdependencies transcending the organizational capacities of extant political systems to maintain control (classically, Wallerstein, 1974). Sweeping economic, political, social and cultural forms of (often conflictful) movement and integration extend far beyond the boundaries of controlling organizational structures. Forces for social control and stability, thus, emphasize both the authority and the responsibilities of the existing actors in national and world society. At the world level, meanings have piled up, rationalizing and expanding the powers and responsibilities of national states. Similarly, individualisms, stressing the rights, powers and capacities of individuals, have expanded enormously, supporting for example the long-term and dramatic expansion of education around the world (Ramirez and Boli, 1987; Meyer, Ramirez, & Soysal, 1992; Elliott, 2007, 2011, 2014). The whole process is analyzed in Tocqueville's discussion of social control in stateless America (1969 [1836]), and his emphasis on the resultant empowerment and control of the individual, including the rapid expansion of a great deal of mobilized and rationalized social organization. The term globalization now tends to refer to (a) economic interdependencies, and (b) very recent time periods. But for our purposes, the time frame is much longer, and the interdependencies involved more political, social, cultural and military than economic. The post-World War II period represented a dramatic upturn in the long history. The failure of social control in an interdependent world was dramatic and incontrovertible. Two devastating world wars (both between supra-state forces), a disastrous depression seen as rooted in nationalist provincialisms, the holocaust and sweeping destruction of social life, and the end of normal war given nuclear weaponry, all made it obvious that new forms of order and control were necessary. This was all enhanced by the Cold War conflict, and by the destruction of the older stabilizing colonial arrangements. An old world of conflicting nation-states was no longer remotely justifiable: war, for instance, lost meaning as a heroic achievement in interstate competition. But on the other hand nothing like a world state was plausible.

In the absence of much possibility for state-like world organization, with a cultural system organized around positive law, the world has produced an astonishing set of sociocultural movements building up a version of a world polity or society around notions of lawful nature, inherent rationality and the natural rights of humans (or, in general, natural law: Thomas et al., 1987; Meyer et al., 1997). These movements take the form of broad global wave-like developments, and a 'wave theory' like sociological institutionalism is appropriate for the massive changes involved.

Thus worldwide social change since World War II continually reinforces the more phenomenological versions of sociological institutional theory. I briefly note some of these massive social changes, and their wave-like diffusive character. All the changes involved refer to laws and rationalities and rights built into 'nature' rather than particular societies. They are built around rapidly expanding meaning systems and are formally structured in decentralized associational formats rather than around sovereign actorhood.

First, there is in place of positive law the dramatic expansion of science (Drori, Meyer, Ramirez, & Schofer, 2003). Science expands exponentially in terms of numbers of people and amounts of resources involved, and also in terms of the social authority it carries. It expands in terms of content coverage, as essentially all aspects of natural and social worlds come under scientific scrutiny. It expands spatially, finding a strong presence in essentially all the societies of the world. Science, as reality and even more as metaphor, provides a cognitive and normative base for all sorts of integrating world regulation – making the world more governable and organizable (Foucault, 1991; Drori & Meyer, 2006; Miller & Rose, 2008).

Beyond science, there is the enormous expansion of rationalizing social science – by far the most rapidly expanding fields in the life of the university in the last half of the twentieth century (Drori & Moon, 2006; Frank & Gabler, 2006). Theories expand rapidly and take the center stage in much policy-making around the world. In a world celebrating the equality of persons and societies, rationalistic social theories are seen as applicable everywhere: any country can develop, any person can be equipped with cultural capital, independent of time and place. And any organization, anywhere, can and should be a rational actor.

Second, in partial replacement for an older Modern celebration of the primordiality of the national state, there is the dramatic rise of a natural law emphasis on human rights. The standing of persons as citizens of national states is replaced by a greatly expanded set of doctrines of the person as an entitled and empowered member of the human race in a global society (e.g., Soysal, 1994; Elliott, 2007, 2011, 2014). More and more categories of humans are directly capacitated in this system – women, children, old people, handicapped people, gay and lesbian people, indigenous people, racial and ethnic minorities, and so on (for examples, see Ramirez, Soysal, & Shanahan, 1998; Berkovitch, 1999; Abu Sharkh, 2002; Frank et al., 2010). And the moral and legal principles involved rapidly take coverage (though commonly not practical effect) worldwide (Hathaway, 2002; Tsutsui & Wotipka, 2004; Cole, 2005, 2015; Hafner-Burton & Tsutsui, 2005; Cole & Ramirez, 2013).

The new human, in this expanding system, has greatly enhanced rights, and responsibilities – but also greatly expanded attributed capacities for economic, political, social and cultural action (Elliott, 2014; Bromley, Meyer, & Ramirez, 2011). These capacities support the extraordinary worldwide expansion in both mass and elite education in the world since World War II (Meyer et al., 1992; Schofer & Meyer, 2005).

The expanded model of empowered and entitled individuals, operating in a tamed and scientized natural and social environment,

generates – as in Tocqueville's America – the expanded modern picture of the human actor; and of the host of social organizations this actor creates. The world is now filled with human persons who assume the posture of empowered actor, and have the capacity to create and participate in collective organizations formed as social actors.

So organization and organizations blossom everywhere (Drori et al., 2006; Bromley & Meyer, 2015). The old nation-state, with its passive bureaucracies, is reformulated as a modern organization, filled with agencies that are to function as autonomous and accountable organizations (i.e., actors: Brunsson & Sahlin-Andersson, 2000). Old family firms are reconstructed as modern organizations with empowered managerial capabilities, and with work forces full of participatory modern individual actors. Traditional structures housing professionals – hospitals and schools, and legal and accounting partnerships – are reformulated as real agentic social actors, capable of the highly purposive pursuit of their own goals (Scott, Ruef, Mendel, & Caronna, 2000; Bromley & Meyer, 2014).

All of the institutionalizations of the new globalized (or 'knowledge', or 'postmodern') society noted above find a core basis in the dramatically expanded educational systems of the post-War world. The university, in particular, is the core home of the explosions of scientific analyses of nature, and rationalistic analyses of social life that try to tame the modern supra-national environment. And it is the core home where ordinary persons of an older world are transformed into knowledgeable and empowered carriers of 'human capital' for the new society (Frank & Meyer, 2007). If classic bureaucratic structures of the Modern society rested on populations equipped with mass education (Stinchcombe, 1965), the organizations of the Knowledge Society rest on university-installed knowledge and empowerment (Frank & Meyer, 2007). Worldwide, over 20 percent of a cohort of young persons is enrolled in university-level training (Schofer & Meyer, 2005).

Actors and Others

The post-War period has, thus, experienced dramatic expansion in cultural rationalization. On the one side there has been the exponential and global growth of the scientific and rationalistic analysis of natural and social environments. On the other lies a similar global growth in the powers attributed to the human beings who enter into society. In the center of all this, the result is the extraordinary modern growth in social actors. Passive old national-state bureaucracies turn into actors filled with plans and strategies. Persons everywhere shift from traditional (i.e., peasant) identities into modern schooled ones: as an indicator, persons turned actors are able to opine on all sorts of general questions – and survey research can now be done almost anywhere (Meyer & Jepperson, 2000).

But the question arises, who is doing all this cultural construction? Who or what supports the rationalization of the natural and social environments? Who props up all the new human rights and powers?

The world of actors – empowered beings with the rights to have goals and the capacities to be agents in pursuit of those goals – is also a world in which the same actors have the legitimated capacity to use their agency in pursuit of collective goods of all sorts. Indeed, the agency of actors is collectively legitimated and dependent. In this sense, a properly constructed actor is always partly an agent for one or another collectivity – in the modern system, often a fairly universal one – as well as an agent for his or her own needs and goals as actors (Meyer & Jepperson, 2000). Thus modern actors are partly above petty interest, and are agents for more general and universal goods. So the most rapidly expanding individual occupations, worldwide, are the nominally disinterested professions: they may partly serve particular interests, but they are in good part agents for the collective – more accurately for what used to be called God (Truth, and

the like). And the most rapidly expanding organizational structures in the world may, similarly, be the non-governmental and often non-profit organizations that serve as agents for various universal goods, often at the global level (Boli & Thomas, 1999; Bromley & Meyer, 2014). Even among the mundane profit-making organizations and occupations, agency with very constrained interested actorhood has been a great success: everywhere there are consulting firms, therapists, advisors, researchers and other creatures of a higher purity.

Thus actors themselves step out of their narrow actorhood, and take on the higher calling of agency for universal truths and the collective good. So we have successful nation-states offering themselves to their competitors as models of the proper conduct of business. And successful organizations are display their virtues, rather than concealing them from the competition. With modern survey research, we find individual persons entering into public life with disinterested analyses of what their President should do (Jepperson, 2002b).

If 'interested actor' is one core role in the modern system, we need a term for the roles of actors that adopt a legitimated posture of disinterest, and tell more interested actors how to be and what to do. I suggest the old Meadian concept of 'Other' (Meyer, 1999). The modern world is filled with these others. There are the representatives of the whales and other creatures, of the distant ecological future, and of the rights of humans in distant places and cultures (e.g., over issues like female genital cutting – see Boyle, 2002). There are the proponents of social rationality and critics of corruption anywhere in the world. Closer to home, there are the advisors and therapists, offering consultation to individuals and organizations on how to be more virtuous and effective actors.

This whole system offers explanatory opportunities calling for sociological institutional theories. The modern nominally realist interested actor is at every side surrounded by institutions with much cultural character and legitimacy – the sciences and professions constructing the rationalized environment of proper 'action', the legal and intellectual constructors of expanded human rights, and the 'Others' who create these arrangements. Of course, the actors themselves enhance their value by displaying their virtuous actorhood: This expanded actorhood is dependent on a host of sciences, legal and intellectual supports, and therapists and consultants. The modern individual actor tends to incorporate much of this material in the expanded 'self'. And the modern organizational actor certainly incorporates enormous amounts of this material – often as professionalized roles – within its formal structure (Bromley & Meyer, 2015).

From a narrowly instrumental point of view, all this otherhood can be quite expensive, as it is only partly present to facilitate effective action – it is to keep up appearances to all sorts of stakeholders, including a broad cultural environment and the self-esteem of the actor. Contemporary organizations adapt to multiple environments, and directly incorporate environmental elements on many fronts – often professionals. They often seem to devote more resources to these sorts of matters: it can be more expensive to be a proper actor than to act. Further, the tension between pressures to act and those to maintain the appearance of being an actor means that many inconsistencies and much conflict are being internalized in becoming an 'organized actor' (Krücken & Meier, 2006). Stresses of these sorts, in contemporary organizations, produce the evolution of rapidly expanding managerialism throughout the world (Bromley & Meyer, 2015), even – or perhaps especially – in what is called the 'non-profit' sector. A university that becomes an organization – a positive entity employing the pretensions of decision-making – requires much more management (Krücken & Meier, 2006; Bromley & Meyer, 2014).

THE STATUS OF THE CORE ARGUMENTS OF SOCIOLOGICAL INSTITUTIONALIST THEORY

Sociological institutional theory employs general phenomenological perspectives that often have many dimensions and can sometimes make up a broad vision of social life and of methods for studying it. Methodologically, a taste for qualitative and highly interpretive research is sometimes involved. Substantively, critical perspectives on the modern liberal society are often emphasized, sometimes from the conservative right, and on other occasions from the left. Sometimes, society itself is seen as entirely an interpreted construction, with other realities entering in only insofar as they enter social interpretive systems.

As it has developed, sociological institutional theory is tied to none of these broader philosophical perspectives. Methodologically, it has commonly been pursued with quite standard (often quantitative) procedures. Its ties to any normative perspective on modern society are weak: at the most, it carries an ironic distance from a naïve liberalism. There is no special tendency to deny the operation of many different theories (and variables) in the analysis of the modern system – sociological institutionalism emphasizes causal structures rooted in culture and interpretation, but is not given to denying other lines of causal process. Thus Barrett, Kurzman and Shanahan (2010) note that national population control policies tend to arise in countries with ties to modern demography, a typical institutional argument. But they are not surprised to find that national population control policies tend also to arise in countries with great population density. Institutional theory is not closely tied to broader philosophical concerns, but has rather developed as a set of very general sociological explanatory ideas.

To assess the status of sociological institutionalism, we review its four most important explanatory ideas. These ideas make up a simple causal chain accounting for modern organizational structures. First, expansive modern institutionalized models of states and societies are commonly generated, not only by interested actors, but by what above we called 'others' – collective participants like professions and social movements. Second, states and other organizations tend prominently to reflect institutionalized models, not simply the local resources and powers and interests that vary so greatly around the world. Third, because states and other organizations reflect highly standardized institutionalized models, but also variable local life in practice, a great deal of decoupling between more formal structures and practical adaptation is to be expected. Fourth, institutionalized models are likely to have strong diffusive or wave-like effects on the orientations and behavior of all sorts of participants in organizational life, whether or not they are incorporated in formal policies.

Cultural and Institutional Forces Affect the Development of Institutional Models

As a result of extensive research showing the impact of institutionalized models on organizations of all sorts, argumentation in macro-social research has shifted to the question of the origins of the models involved. For instance, we know that the worldwide emphasis on the rights of women has greatly impacted policy and practice everywhere (Bradley & Ramirez, 1996; Ramirez et al., 1998). So it becomes important to ask what produced the worldwide emphases involved.

Very extreme realists argue that institutions are produced by the mixture of power and interest in the actors of the system – the only entities they recognize as existing. This makes the institutions involved relatively minor in importance, since an adequate analysis can be obtained simply by understanding the extant structures of actor power and interest. A more moderate realism sees a 'sticky equilibrium' as involved – institutions are created by mixtures of actor power and interest, but may take on something of a life of their own afterwards. A still more moderate realism supposes that there are some mediators – some participants (possibly professionals, or other brokers) who help in the enterprise.

Beyond this point, realism may be combined with a more political or sociological view. Stinchcombe (2001) develops an argument along these lines, imagining that actors and perhaps some mediators struggle to work out general institutional rules that reflect local power and interest circumstances but also reflect functional requirements of the whole enterprise. In his work, he often thinks of institutional arrangements in complicated sectors like the construction industry. His arguments apply less clearly to the worldwide rise of gay and lesbian rights (Frank et al., 2010).

Given the success of institutionalist analyses in showing the impact of environmental models on the programs of organizational actors in the modern system, realism has been on the defensive. One position to which it has retreated is the stance that, while modern actors copy environmental models, these models themselves must have been put in place by hard-line forces of power and interest. Realism has, as noted above, strongly legitimated roots in the modern system, which rests on the assumption of very strong and agentic human actorhood. So attacks along the line that interested actors drive the creation of institutional models have been intensive (e.g., Hirsch, 1997; Hirsch & Lounsbury, 1997; Stinchcombe, 2001). And some institutionalists have taken positions that are almost apologetic in response (DiMaggio, 1988; Scott, 2007), apparently conceding that behind the facade of institutional structures inevitably lie real men of power.

Sociological institutionalists do not take issue with the argument that many institutionalized patterns directly reflect the power and interest of dominant organizations. But, especially under conditions of modern globalization, institutionalists observe dramatic effects that do not reflect the mechanics of power and interest. In global society, and also in other organizational arenas, many other phenomena operate – taking into account the dependence of modern expanded actors on institutionalized scripts operating in their environments.

Professionalized and scientized forces generate rules coming to terms with modern sciences and rationalities, and with modern notions of human rights and welfare. Despite powerful interests working in the opposite direction, for instance, environmental policies like the ozone layer agreements have taken on considerable force (Frank, Hironaka, & Schofer, 2000; Hironaka, 2014). Similarly, it is difficult to see power and interest – and easy to see professionalized forces – behind the worldwide movement to restrict female genital cutting (Boyle, 2002). Large-scale social movement structures and non-governmental organizations are obviously involved in the construction of many institutional systems. Thus many programs for organizational rationality, like the International Standards Organization, or various bodies stressing improved accounting arrangements, find their origins in forces removed from simple matters of power and interest (see the papers in Sahlin-Andersson & Engwall, 2002; Djelic & Quack, 2003; Djelic & Sahlin-Andersson, 2006; or Drori et al., 2006).

Constructions of institutional models may reflect successes and failures in organizational or international stratification systems, without necessarily reflecting the interests of the powerful bodies in that system. Because globalization involves the construction of myths of underlying world similarity, an extraordinary amount of diffusion goes on as a matter of fashion (Strang & Meyer, 1993).

So Japanese economic success of the 1980s produced a little wave of Japanified policies around the world, in no way reflecting the purposive power or interest of the Japanese national state. Similarly, there is much imitation of elite firms in any industry, whether or not the elite firms encourage, or gain from, this imitation.

When powerful or successful organizations in fact portray themselves as models for others, it is often unclear that they are acting in what is ordinarily conceived to be their interest. The American national state, for instance, likes to encourage others to do things the 'right' way – the American way – as a matter of encouraging virtue in the world. There is little evidence this aid activity benefits the interests of the American state.

Similarly, realists tend to see any diffusive influence of the stratification system as indicating the power and interest of the elites of that system. This is implausible. In global society, the world environment movement clearly reflects the values and orientations of American society. But the American national-state actor resists subscribing to this system, as do leading corporations. As another example, the world human rights movement clearly reflects American values: but the American national-state actor was reluctant to have a human rights declaration built into the United Nations; and continues to refuse to ratify various human rights treaties. In exactly the same way, massive worldwide efforts at all sorts of organizational reform and rationalization clearly reflect American ideologies of organization: but the American national state aggressively resists participation.

Exactly the same criticisms can be made of realist argument in other organizational arenas. Elite universities may be sources of much educational rationalist ideology, but are often organizationally primitive (e.g., Oxford, Harvard). The same is true of elite firms and agencies.

All in all, in the modern stateless but globalized world, institutionalist arguments explaining the dramatic rise of cultural models of expanded actorhood show every prospect of continued success. Only in a more stabilized world society would the process of social construction of actor motivations catch up, creating the proper appearance of an apparently realist world society.

Institutionalized Models Affect the Construction of Actors

The most conspicuous success of sociological institutional theory has been in the demonstration of powerful effects of institutional models on the construction and modification of actors. Thus nation-state structures reflect standard world models, despite the enormous resource and cultural variability of the world (Meyer et al., 1997; Schofer, Hironaka, Frank, & Longhofer, 2012). Schools similarly reflect both world and national social forms. So do firms and hospitals and organizations in essentially any other sector (Drori et al., 2006; Bromley & Meyer, 2015). Furthermore, extant actors change over time, reflecting changes in institutionalized models.

Now that effects of this sort are widely and routinely recognized in the field, discussion shifts to questions of mechanisms. Institutionalists, convincingly, show that organizational conformity to standard models is widespread and can occur in very routine ways through taken-for-granted understandings. They commonly show the effects of processes such as simple linkage between organizational settings and the wider environments carrying the institutions (Alasuutari, 2016; Longhofer & Schofer, 2010; Schofer & Longhofer 2011). Thus, at the nation-state level, world models are adopted more quickly in countries with many non-governmental organizational linkages to world society (Meyer et al., 1997; Schofer et al., 2012). Similarly, professional linkages facilitate the quick adoption of environmental policies (Frank et al., 2000, call

the professions 'receptor sites' for the local incorporation of wider rationalized models). At the organizational level, the adoption of fashionable personnel policies is enhanced by having professionalized personnel officers (Dobbin, 2009).

Processes of coercive power can be involved in such relationships. But the rapid social changes of globalization continue to generate waves of organizational change that cannot easily be conceived as reflecting straightforward coercive power and control. Wave-like processes are endemic in the modern system (Czarniawska & Sevón, 1996), and institutional theories gain much credibility from the obvious empirical situations involved.

Thus, with the global rise in conceptions of the nation-state as a development-oriented social actor, university enrollments shot up in every type of country (Schofer & Meyer, 2005). Coercive pressures were clearly not involved – indeed the centers of power in world society (e.g., the United States, the World Bank, or the major corporations) tended initially to be skeptical about the virtues of 'overeducation' for impoverished countries. Similarly, global standards of women's rights tended to produce national reactions quite apart from any coercive forces. In other areas – like environmental policy, or efforts to build international quality standards – where researchers try to discern coercive pressure, empirical analyses tend to be unconvincing.

Contested areas of interpretation, here, revolve around the impact of professional bodies and non-governmental organizations. The sorts of normative pressures produced by these forces can be given something of a realist interpretation. The problem is that the relevant professions and associations are amply represented inside actors, not only outside them. That is, modern national and organizational actors already incorporate in their own authority systems formal representatives of the wider world cultures dealing with the environment, organizational rationalization, human rights and so on (Bromley & Meyer, 2014, 2015). Modern organizations and nation-states appear to be eager to construct themselves as actors, thus incorporating, often wholesale, global standards (for nation-state examples, see Boli, 1987; McNeely, 1995).

In an expanding and globalizing world society, people and groups everywhere seem to be eager to be actors – this often takes precedence over other goals, and can produce assertions of actor identity far from any actual actor capability. People and organizations may put more effort into being actors than into acting. We can see this readily in the empirical studies of modern individuals in increasing numbers of countries. They produce opinions and judgments, routinely, in matters they know nothing about. A good American, it seems clear, would produce opinions about whether the United States should invade a country that does not exist. Good organizations have policies about things that never occur. National states promote world norms with which they have no capacity to conform. Agentic actorhood is now a central good (Meyer & Jepperson, 2000; Frank & Meyer, 2002).

Some of the intellectual tensions involved here – between a realistic institutionalism and an unrealistic realism – show up in a discussion by Mizruchi and Fein (1999). These researchers, committed to an older realist tradition in the study of organizations, seem puzzled by the extraordinary citation attention continuingly given to the classic paper by DiMaggio and Powell (1983). So they turn from their normal work as organizational researchers to become sociologists of science (it is often a dangerous business for social scientists to study their own fields), and to investigate the uses of the classic paper. They are disturbed by the fact that few references pick up on the more realist themes in the paper (coercive isomorphism, which can readily be subsumed by realists; and normative isomorphism, which a realist can re-shape into conformity). All the research emphasis goes to the famous 'mimetic isomorphism', which lies far from the realist track. The reason for this is obvious: any line of interpretation that can be given a realist spin, in modern social science, tends to be given that spin. So institutionalist arguments tend to survive best if they are furthest from realism. Oddly, Mizruchi himself later ends up employing mimetic isomorphism as an explanatory idea (Mizruchi, Stearns, & Marquis, 2006).

The Construction of Actors Is Often Loosely Coupled with Practical Activity

Sociological institutional theory, in part, arose from the observation that organizational policies and structures are often loosely coupled with practical activity (Meyer & Rowan, 1977; Alasuutari, 2016). Given this commonly recognized reality, the question arose – why are the structures and policies there? The question took force from the fact that conventional theories of organizational structure emphasize that, for functional and political reasons, structure is put in place to control activity.

The institutionalist answer is that actor structures, forms and policies reflect institutional prescriptions and models in the wider environment. Such institutional models make it possible to build great organizations in situations where little actual control is likely or possible – school systems, for instance; or in developing countries, national states.

This line of argument has had much empirical success in the cross-national study of nation-states. It is common, now, to discover that nation-states subscribe to human rights standards – but the subscribers are no more likely to implement these standards in practice than are the non-subscribers (Hathaway, 2002; Cole, 2005; Hafner-Burton & Tsutsui, 2005). Or if they do, the effects are very conditional and occur over time (Cole, 2015; Cole & Ramirez, 2013). The same finding holds for research on child labor rates (Abu Sharkh, 2002), and for research on the education of women (Bradley & Ramirez, 1996).

The line of argument has had dramatic empirical success in studies of organizations, too. Brunsson (1985, 1989) develops it as a contrast between policy talk and practical action. He sees a hypocritical inconsistency between the two as a central consequence and requirement for the rationalized society. Thus, inconsistency that to realists is a social problem is to Brunsson a stabilizing solution. In other work, the line of argument is extended to account for the high frequency of organizational reforms, and the lack of consequences of much reform (Brunsson, 2009). If reform is commonly a process of constructing improved actorhood, rather than improved action, the often noted 'failure of implementation' is to be expected. Given the enormously exaggerated models of the proper actor – individuals and organizations alike – characteristic of the modern globalized world, any respectable reform should have excellent prospects for disimplementation.

Despite its obvious uses, the concept of 'loose coupling' has been a considerable source of tension in the field (Bromley & Powell, 2012). This arises because realist thinking is quite central to modern ideology as well as to much social theory. From a realist point of view, decoupling between organizational rules and policies and programs and roles, on the one hand, and local practical action, on the other, is deeply problematic. Rules are created by powerful and interested actors, desiring to control action. They are put in place in particular organizations because the interests of powerful actors demanded it. They should normally be implemented in practice. Only limited realist theory can explain why not. (a) Perhaps the powerful actors creating rules want to deceive the world around them. But if they are so powerful, why would they need to do this? And if they do depend on impressions of others, why are these others

so easily deceived? (b) Perhaps particular actors subscribe formally to the rules intending to deceive the powerful forces behind these rules. But if so, why are the powerful forces so easily deceived? (c) Perhaps local participants simply cheat on the organized actor, suboptimally going their own way and violating the rules. If so, why are organized actors so little able to notice?

The extreme tension experienced by realist theorists over the 'loose coupling' notion can be illustrated by the treatment of a renowned initial essay on the subject. Before the rise of new institutional theories, March and his collaborators, working from the 'uncertainty' tradition, produced a precursor. Their essay was called 'A Garbage Can Model of Organizational Choice' (Cohen, March, & Olsen, 1972). Instead of working from rational decision models outward to incorporate more uncertainty, this essay started from the frame of decision-making under almost complete uncertainty. The authors illustrated their points with some quickly forgotten simulation models, but the impact of the paper – on a field that had grown a bit deadly – was as a strong fundamental theoretical image or metaphor. The paper is much cited for its grounding imagery rather than its specific analytic points.

Interestingly, thirty years later, several researchers committed to the extreme rational choice version of realism, found it necessary to mount a massive attack on this piece of poetry (Bendor, Moe, & Shotts, 2001). They proved that the illustrative simulation models (which had not in fact been taken very seriously) were inconsistent with the real arguments of the paper, and made dramatic assertions about this as indicating a fundamental failure of the scientific enterprise involved. (Again, the authors rested the importance of their paper on assertions about the nature of science itself – often a warning sign in the social sciences, e.g., p. 169: 'We evaluate the verbal theory and argue that it fails to create an adequate foundation for scientific progress.')

Institutionalized Models Impact Practices Independent of Organized Actor Adoption

In the modern system, institutionalized forces usually diffuse more as cultural waves than through point-to-point diffusion. Thus, standards arise in world discourse, promulgated by professional consensus and associational advocacy. The new emphasis might be, say, on the improved treatment of children with some specific handicaps. National states, of course, adopt appropriate policies with some probability, which might vary depending on their linkage to the world organizations and professions involved.

But of course organizations internal to that state are also immersed in responsible agentic actorhood organized by the global culture. So independent of national policy, schools and medical organizations and professional associations and even some business firms would be likely to notice the new models and incorporate aspects of them. This might depend on their own linkages to world society.

And independent of what policies and programs states and non-state organizations put in place, modern individuals too tend to be agentic actors immersed in wider society (including global society). So all sorts of local actors – parents, teachers, medical professionals, neighbors, relatives – have some probability of picking up the new world or national story lines, independent of the national state policies or of any organized actor at all.

Theories with limited conceptions of the embeddedness of actors in wider cultural arrangements, tend to have blind spots on such processes. For this reason, they – and thus much social scientific theory and ideology – have the greatest difficulty accounting for large-scale modern social change, because such change tends to flow through diffusive waves rather than down through an organized realist ladder of world to state to organization to individual effects. The global expansion of organization (and organization

theory) itself is an excellent example (Drori et al., 2006; Bromley & Meyer, 2015).

The social scientific failures in explaining large-scale change are stunning. The movement for racial and ethnic equality, the women's movement, the environment movement, the modern movements for organizational transparency, the breakdown of the Communist system, the movement for gay and lesbian rights – all these worldwide changes were poorly predicted, and are poorly explained, by social scientific thinking. Empirically, research on the diffusive impacts of world models on social practice independent of national-state action is convincing. The world models impact national policy, certainly: but they impact practice whether or not they impact policy. The world movement to constrain child labor seems to have very large effects on practice, whether or not countries subscribe to the appropriate prohibitions (Abu Sharkh, 2002). World movements for women's rights have dramatic effects increasing the educational enrollment of women, independent of any national policies (Bradley & Ramirez, 1996). Changed world models related to reproduction impact birth rates independent of national policy (Bongaarts & Watkins, 1996). The world environment movement impacts practice both through national policy and around it (Schofer & Hironaka, 2005; Hironaka, 2014). It is probably also true that the world human rights movements have impacted local practice independent of national policy subscriptions – the data on human rights practices over time are too weakly standardized to tell (Hafner-Burton & Tsutsui, 2005).

Similar studies at the organizational level of analysis show similar effects. Practices in the treatment of employees, for instance, drift along following world or national models in good part independent of formal policies (Drori et al., 2006). In the same way, the practices of teachers or doctors reflect shifting customs in good part independent of organizational policies (Coburn, 2004).

Most theories have little to say about such broader effects. So sweeping social changes occur, at the edges of social scientific notice. Modern society is organized around general and cultural models, as much as around hardwired organizational structures. And these models are increasingly worldwide in character (Meyer et al., 1997).

CONCLUSION

The rapid expansion of a stateless global society – in transactions and perceptions alike – has produced a great wave of cultural materials facilitating expanding organization at every level. Scientific and rationalistic professionals and associations generate highly rationalized and universalized pictures of natural and social environments calling for expanded rational actorhood of states, organizations and individuals. Legal and social scientific professionals generate greatly expanded conceptions of the rights and capabilities of all human persons, transcending national citizenship. Universities and other educational arrangements expand, worldwide, installing newly rationalized knowledge in newly empowered persons.

So models of organized actorhood expand, and penetrate every social sector and country (Bromley & Meyer, 2015). All sorts of older social forms – bureaucracies, family structures, traditional professional arrangements – are transformed into organizations. The process is driven by a cultural system that is a putative substitute for traditional state-like political arrangements – analyses that root the process in powerful interested actors miss out on important changes. The process spreads through the diffusion of models of actorhood. The changes transcend practicality, leaving great gaps between policy and practice essentially everywhere – almost any organization or national state can be seen as a failure, now. The changes diffuse at multiple levels – through central organizations and

through their professionalized memberships and populations.

Sociological institutional theory – especially its phenomenological version – captures the whole post-World War II enterprise very well, and for this reason has been successful. In a world less rapidly changing, the preferred models of modern ideology and social theory might have constructed realist explanations but change has been too rapid. Such theories and ideologies have not caught up with the explosion of human rights (e.g., gay and lesbian rights), of environmental doctrines and policies, of all sorts of social rationalization (e.g., a global standards movement), and the transformation of unlikely social structures into putatively rational organizations.

Much social theory, however, retains its theoretical/ideological preference for traditional realisms, leaving the great social changes of the modern period poorly explored. This leaves much intellectual space within which institutional theory can develop. In this context, the best strategy for institutional theory is to keep to its last, and to avoid attending to the clamor arising from realist ideological assumptions.

Thus, institutionalists sometimes are instructed to seek for the interested actors behind the new social models under construction, and to assume such actors exist by definition. It makes more sense to track the relevant professions and 'others' who are central – the authority of these people rests on their disinterestedness, not their interests. Most new models of organizational or national structure are developed with heavy influence from such sources. Naturally, successful models tend to be derived and edited from the most successful organizations – which could be called hegemonic if the term carried fewer connotations – but this does not mean that the interests of those organizations play a causal role.

Institutionalists are instructed to investigate the 'mechanisms' by which local structures conform to wider models taking seriously the pretenses of modern interested actorhood. Conformity to standard models may not involve much 'influence' or much decision-making. The relevant network linkages, for example, may simply involve elementary forms of information transmission.

Institutionalists are told to investigate the assumed true linkages that powerful interested actors put between policy and practice: it is wiser to imagine that developing the posture of the proper actor is a main goal of modern people and groups, transcending their needs to implement this posture in actions. In a world in which an enormous premium is placed on actorhood, entering into this identity is obviously central.

In some views, analyses of diffusion as wavelike are unscientific – the only correct approach is to assume each particle in such a wave is a properly rational and interested actor: following this advice would mean giving up on really trying to explain the dramatic social and organizational changes of our period. These changes occur much more through waves of conforming non-decision than through networks of fully formed and autonomous rationalized actors.

Note

1 Work on this paper was funded by a grant from the National Research Foundation (Korea) – NRF-2011-330-B00194.

REFERENCES

Abu Sharkh, M. (2002). History and results of labor standard initiatives. Unpublished doctoral dissertation, Free University of Berlin.

Alasuutari, P. (2016). *The synchronization of national policies: Ethnography of the global tribe of moderns*. Oxford: Routledge.

Barrett, D., Kurzman, C., & Shanahan, S. (2010). For export only: Diffusion professionals and population policy. *Social Forces, 88*(3), 1183–1207.

Bendor, J., Moe, T.M., & Shotts, K.W. (2001). Recycling the garbage can: An assessment of the research program. *American Political Science Review, 95*(1), 169–190.

Berger, P.L., Berger, B., & Kellner, H. (1974). *The homeless mind: Modernization and consciousness*. New York: Vintage Books.

Berkovitch, N. (1999). *From motherhood to citizenship*. Baltimore, MD: Johns Hopkins University Press.

Blau, P.M., & Schoenherr, R.A. (1971). *The structure of organizations*. New York: Basic Books.

Boli, J. (1987). World-polity sources of expanding state authority and organization, 1870–1970. In G. Thomas, J. Meyer, R. Francisco, & J. Boli (Eds.), *Institutional structure*. Beverly Hills, CA: Sage.

Boli, J., & Thomas, G. (1999). *Constructing world culture: International non-governmental organizations since 1875*. Stanford, CA: Stanford University Press.

Bongaarts, J., & Watkins, S.C. (1996). Social interactions and contemporary fertility transitions. *Population and Development Review, 22*(4), 639–682.

Boyle, E.H. (2002). *Female genital cutting: Cultural conflict in the global community*. Baltimore, MD: Johns Hopkins University Press.

Bradley, K., & Ramirez, F. (1996). World polity and gender parity: Women's share of higher education, 1965–1985. *Research in Sociology of Education and Socialization, 11*, 63–91.

Bromley, P., & Meyer, J.W. (2014). 'They are all organizations': The cultural roots of blurring between the nonprofit, business, and government sectors. *Administration & Society*, online ahead of print, 4 September. doi:10.1177/0095399714548268.

Bromley, P., & Meyer, J.W. (2015). *Hyper-organization: Global organizational expansion*. Oxford: Oxford University Press.

Bromley, P., Meyer, J.W., & Ramirez, F. O. (2011). Student-centeredness in social science textbooks, 1970–2008: A cross-national study. *Social Forces, 90*(2), 1–24.

Bromley, P., & Powell, W.W. (2012). From smoke and mirrors to walking the talk: Decoupling in the contemporary world. *Academy of Management Annals, 6*(1), 483–530.

Brunsson, N. (1985). *The irrational organization*. Chichester: Wiley.

Brunsson, N. (1989). *The organization of hypocrisy*. Chichester: Wiley.

Brunsson, N. (2009). *Reform as routine: Organizational change and stability in the modern world*. Oxford: Oxford University Press.

Brunsson, N., & Sahlin-Andersson, K. (2000). Constructing organizations: The case of public sector reform. *Organizational Studies, 21*, 721–746.

Camic, C. (1986). The matter of habit. *American Journal of Sociology, 91*, 1039–1087.

Coburn, C. (2004). Beyond decoupling: Rethinking the relationship between the institutional environment and the classroom. *Sociology of Education*, *77*(3), 211–244.

Cohen, M., March, J., & Olsen, J. (1972). A garbage can model of organizational choice. *Administrative Science Quarterly*, *17*(1), 1–25.

Cole, W. (2005). Sovereignty relinquished? Explaining commitment to the international human rights covenants, 1966–1999. *American Sociological Review*, *70*(3), 472–495.

Cole, W. (2015). Mind the gap: State capacity and the implementation of human rights treaties. *International Organization*, *69*(2), 405–441.

Cole, W., & Ramirez, F. (2013). Conditional decoupling: Assessing the impact of national human rights institutions, 1981 to 2004. *American Sociological Review*, *78*(4), 702–725.

Coleman, J.S. (1986). Social theory, social research, and a theory of action. *American Journal of Sociology*, *91*, 1309–1335.

Coleman, J.S. (1993). The rational reconstruction of society: 1992 presidential address. *American Sociological Review*, *58*(1), 1–15.

Cyert, R.M., & March, J.G. (1992). *A behavioral theory of the firm* (2nd ed.). Cambridge, MA.: Blackwell Business.

Czarniawska, B., & Sevón, G. (Eds.) (1996). *Translating organizational change*. Berlin: de Gruyter.

Dalton, M. (1959). *Men who manage*. New York: Wiley.

DiMaggio, P.J. (1988). Interest and agency in institutional theory. In L. Zucker (Ed.), *Institutional patterns and organizations*. Cambridge, MA: Ballinger.

DiMaggio, P.J., & Powell, W.W. (1983). The iron cage revisited: Institutional isomorphism and collective rationality in organizational fields. *American Sociological Review*, *48*(2), 147–160.

Djelic, M.L., & Quack, S. (2003). *Globalization and institutions*. Cheltenham: Edward Elgar.

Djelic, M.L., & Sahlin-Andersson, K. (Eds.) (2006). *Transnational governance*. Cambridge: Cambridge University Press.

Dobbin, F. (2009). *Inventing equal opportunity*. Princeton, NJ: Princeton University Press.

Dobbin, F., & Sutton, J.R. (1998). The strength of a weak state: The employment rights revolution and the rise of human resources management divisions. *American Journal of Sociology*, *104*, 441–476.

Drori, G.S., & Meyer, J.W. (2006). Scientization: Making a world safe for organizing. In M.L. Djelic & K. Sahlin-Andersson (eds.), *Transnational governance: Institutional dynamics of regulation* (pp. 31–52). Cambridge: Cambridge University Press.

Drori, G.S., Meyer, J.W., & Hwang, H. (Eds.) (2006). *Globalization and organization: World society and organizational change*. Oxford: Oxford University Press.

Drori, G.S., Meyer, J.W., Ramirez, F.O., & Schofer, E. (2003). *Science in the modern world polity*. Stanford, CA: Stanford University Press.

Drori, G.S., & Moon, H. (2006). The changing nature of tertiary education: Cross-national trends in disciplinary enrollment, 1965–1995. In D.P. Baker & A.W. Wiseman (Eds.), *The impact of comparative education research on institutional theory* (pp. 157–186). Oxford: Elsevier Science.

Edelman, L., Uggen, C., & Erlanger, H.S. (1999). The endogeneity of legal regulation: Relevance procedures as rational myth. *American Journal of Sociology*, *105*, 406–454.

Elliott, Michael (2007). Human rights and the triumph of the individual in world culture. *Cultural Sociology*, *1*(3), 353–363.

Elliott, Michael (2011). The institutional expansion of human rights, 1863–2003. *Journal of Peace Research*, *48*(4), 537–546.

Elliott, Michael (2014). The institutionalization of human rights and its discontents: A world cultural perspective. *Cultural Sociology*, *8*(4), 407–425.

Fligstein, N. (1990). *The transformation of corporate control*. Cambridge, MA: Harvard University Press.

Fligstein, N., & McAdam, D. (2012). *A theory of fields*. New York: Oxford.

Foucault, M. (1991). Governmentality. In G. Burchell, C. Gordon, & P. Miller (Eds.), *The Foucault effect: Studies in governmentality* (pp. 87–104). Chicago, IL: University of Chicago Press.

Frank, D.J., Bayless, J.C., & Boutcher, S.A. (2010). Worldwide trends in the criminal regulation of sex. *American Sociological Review*, *75*, 867–893.

Frank, D.J., & Gabler, J. (2006). *Reconstructing the university: Worldwide changes in academic emphases over the 20th century*. Stanford, CA: Stanford University Press.

Frank, D.J., Hironaka, A., & Schofer, E. (2000). The nation-state and the natural environment over the twentieth century. *American Sociological Review*, *65*(1), 96–116.

Frank, D.J., & Meyer, J.W. (2002). The contemporary identity explosion: Individualizing society in the post-war period. *Sociological Theory*, *20*(1), 86–105.

Frank, D.J., & Meyer, J.W. (2007). University expansion and the knowledge society. *Theory and Society*, *36*(4), 287–311.

Giddens, A. (1984). *The constitution of society*. Berkeley, CA: University of California Press.

Granovetter, M. (1985). Economic action and social structure: The problem of embeddedness. *American Journal of Sociology*, *91*(3), 481–510.

Hafner-Burton, E., & Tsutsui, K. (2005). Human rights in a globalizing world: The paradox of empty promises. *American Journal of Sociology, 110*(5), 1373–1411.

Hasse, R., & Kruecken, G. (2005). *Neo-Institutionalismus* (rev. ed.). Bielefeld: transcript Verlag.

Hathaway, O.A. (2002). Do human rights treaties make a difference? *Yale Law Journal, 111*, 1935–2042.

Hironaka, A. (2014). *Greening the globe: World society and environmental change*. New York: Cambridge University Press.

Hirsch, P.M. (1997). Sociology without social structure: Neoinstitutional theory meets brave new world. *American Journal of Sociology, 102*(6), 1702–1723.

Hirsch, P.M., & Lounsbury, M. (1997). Ending the family quarrel: Toward a reconciliation of 'old' and 'new' institutionalism. *American Behavioral Scientist, 40*(S), 406–418.

Hwang, H., & Colyvas, J.A. (2011). Problematizing actors and institutions in institutional work. *Journal of Management Inquiry, 20*(1), 62–66.

Hwang, H., & Colyvas, J. (2013). Actors, actors! actors? The proliferation of the actor and its consequences. Paper presented at European Group for Organization Studies Annual Meeting, 4 (July), Montreal, Canada.

Jepperson, R. (1991). Institutions, institutional effects, and institutionalism. In W.W. Powell & P.J. DiMaggio (Eds.), *The new institutionalism in organizational analysis* (pp. 143–163). Chicago, IL: University of Chicago Press.

Jepperson, R. (2002a). The development and application of sociological neo-institutionalism. In J. Berger & M. Zelditch, Jr (Eds.), *New directions in contemporary sociological theory* (pp. 229–266). Lanham, MD: Rowman and Littlefield.

Jepperson, R. (2002b). Political modernities: Disentangling two underlying dimensions of institutional differentiation. *Sociological Theory, 20*, 61–85.

Jepperson, R., & Meyer, J.W. (2011). Multiple levels of analysis and the limitations of methodological individualisms. *Sociological Theory, 29*(1), 54–73.

Katzenstein, P.J. (1996). *The culture of national security: Norms and identity in world politics*. New York: Columbia University Press.

Krasner, S.D. (1999). *Sovereignty: Organized hypocrisy*. Princeton, NJ: Princeton University Press.

Krücken, G., & Meier, F. (2006). Turning the university into an organizational actor. In G. Drori, J. Meyer, & H. Hwang (Eds.), *Globalization and organization: World society and organizational change* (pp. 241–257). Oxford: Oxford University Press.

Landes, D.S. (1998). *The wealth and poverty of nations*. New York: Norton.

Longhofer, W., & Schofer, E. (2010). National and global origins of environmental association. *American Sociological Review, 71*(4), 505–533.

March, J.G. (1988). *Decisions and organizations*. New York, NY: Blackwell.

McNeely, C.L. (1995). *Constructing the nation-state: International organization and prescriptive action*. Westport, CT: Greenwood Press.

Meyer, J.W. (1986). The self and the life course: Institutionalization and its effects. In A. Sorensen, F. Weinert, & L. Sherrod (Eds.), *Human development and the life course* (pp. 199–216). Hillsdale, NJ: Erlbaum.

Meyer, J.W. (1988). Society without culture: A nineteenth century legacy. In F. Ramirez (Ed.), *Rethinking the nineteenth century* (pp. 193–201). New York: Greenwood.

Meyer, J.W. (1999). The changing cultural content of the nation-state: A world society perspective. In G. Steinmetz (Ed.), *State/culture: State formation after the cultural turn* (pp. 123–143). New York: Cornell University Press.

Meyer, J.W., Boli, J., Thomas, G., & Ramirez, F. (1997). World society and the nation-state. *American Journal of Sociology, 103*(1), 144–181.

Meyer, J.W., & Jepperson, R. (2000). The 'actors' of modern society: The cultural construction of social agency. *Sociological Theory, 18*(1), 100–120.

Meyer, J.W., Ramirez, F., & Soysal, Y. (1992). World expansion of mass education, 1870–1970. *Sociology of Education, 65*(2), 128–149.

Meyer, J.W., & Rowan, B. (1977). Institutionalized organizations: Formal structure as myth and ceremony. *American Journal of Sociology, 83*(2), 340–363.

Meyer, J.W., & Scott, W.R. (1983). *Organizational environments: Ritual and rationality*. Beverly Hills, CA: Sage.

Miller, P., & Rose, N. (2008). *Governing the present*. Cambridge: Polity Press.

Mizruchi, M.S., & Fein, L.C. (1999). The social construction of organizational knowledge: A study of the uses of coercive, mimetic, and normative isomorphism. *Administrative Science Quarterly, 44*(4), 653–683.

Mizruchi, M.S., Stearns, L.B., & Marquis, C. (2006). The conditional nature of embeddedness. *American Sociological Review, 71*(2), 310–333.

Mokyr, J. (1992). *The lever of riches*. Oxford: Oxford University Press.

North, D.C. (1981). *Structure and change in economic history*. New York: Norton.

North, D.C., & Thomas, R.P. (1973). *The rise of the western world*. Cambridge: Cambridge University Press.

Perrow, C. (1970). *Organizational analysis: A sociological view*. Belmont, CA: Brooks/Cole.

Pope, S. (2015). Why firms participate in the global corporate social responsibility initiatives, 2000–2010. In K. Tsutsui and A. Lim (Eds.), *Corporate social responsibility in a globalizing world* (pp. 251–285). Cambridge: Cambridge University Press.

Powell, W.W., & DiMaggio, P.J. (Eds.) (1991). *The new institutionalism in organizational analysis*. Chicago, IL: University of Chicago Press.

Ramirez, F.O., & Boli, J. (1987). The political construction of mass schooling: European origins and worldwide institutionalization. *Sociology of Education, 60*(1), 2–17.

Ramirez, F.O., Soysal, Y., & Shanahan, S. (1998). The changing logic of political citizenship: Cross-national acquisition of women's suffrage. *American Sociological Review, 62*, 735–745.

Sahlin-Andersson, K., & Engwall, L. (Eds.) (2002). *The expansion of management knowledge*. Stanford, CA: Stanford University Press.

Schofer, E., & Hironaka, A. (2005). The effects of world society on environmental protection outcomes. *Social Forces, 84*(1), 25–47.

Schofer, E., Hironaka, A., Frank, D., & Longhofer, W. (2012). Sociological institutionalism and world society. In K. Nash, A. Scott, & E. Amenata (Eds.), *The new Blackwell companion to political sociology*. Oxford: Blackwell.

Schofer, E., & Longhofer, W. (2011). The structural sources of association. *American Journal of Sociology 117*(2), 539–585.

Schofer, E., & Meyer, J.W. (2005). The worldwide expansion of higher education in the twentieth century. *American Sociological Review, 70*, 898–920.

Scott, W.R. (2007). Approaching adulthood: The maturing of institutional theory. *Theory and Society, 37*(5) Special Issue, 427–442.

Scott, W.R. (2014). *Institutions and organizations* (4th ed.). Thousand Oaks, CA: Sage.

Scott, W.R., Ruef, M., Mendel, P., & Caronna, C. (2000). *Institutional change and healthcare organizations: From professional dominance to managed care*. Chicago, IL: University of Chicago Press.

Sewell, W.H., Jr (1992). A theory of structure: Duality, agency, and transformation. *American Journal of Sociology, 98*(1), 1–29.

Soysal, Y. (1994). *Limits of citizenship*. Chicago, IL: University of Chicago Press.

Stinchcombe, A.L. (1965). Social structure and organizations. In J. March (Ed.), *Handbook of Organizations* (pp. 142–193). Chicago, IL: Rand McNally.

Stinchcombe, A.L. (1997). On the virtues of the old institutionalism. *Annual Review of Sociology, 23*, 1–18.

Stinchcombe, A.L. (2001). *When formality works*. Chicago, IL: University of Chicago Press.

Strang, D., & Meyer, J.W. (1993). Institutional conditions for diffusion. *Theory and Society, 22*: 487–511.

Thomas, G., Meyer, J.W., Ramirez, F.O., & Boli, J. (1987). *Institutional Structure: Constituting state, society, and the individual*. Beverly Hills, CA: Sage.

Thornton, P.H., Ocasio, W., & Lounsbury, M. (2012). *The institutional logics perspective: A new approach to culture, structure, and process*. Oxford: Oxford University Press.

Tocqueville, A. de (1969 [1836]). *Democracy in America* (Ed. J.P. Maier, Trans. G. Lawrence). Garden City, NY: Anchor Books.

Toulmin, S. (1990). *Cosmopolis: The Hidden Agenda of Modernity*. New York: Free Press.

Tsutsui, K., & Min Wotipka, C. (2004). Global civil society and the international human rights movement. *Social Forces, 83*(2), 587–620.

Tsutsui, K., & Lim, A. (Eds.) (2015). *Corporate social responsibility in a globalizing world* (pp. 27–72). Cambridge: Cambridge University Press.

Wallerstein, I. (1974). *The modern world-system*, vol. I. New York: Academic Press.

Zucker, L.G. (1977). The role of institutionalization in cultural persistence. *American Journal of Sociology, 42*, 726–743.

33

Institutional Theory: Onward and Upward

W. Richard Scott

Institutional scholars are not intellectually shy. We are willing to take on the tough fundamental questions. Our subject is nothing more nor less than understanding the basis of social order. We address the processes by which social structures, incorporating both symbolic and behavioral elements, are established, become stable and undergo change over time. Institutional analysis takes place broadly throughout the social sciences, fueled by the efforts of anthropologists, economists, cognitive and social psychologists, political scientists and sociologists. Still, throughout the last century and a half, sociologists have been the most persistent pursuers of the puzzle of social order, and they have recently been joined by organization scholars in management schools.

In the subtitle of this chapter, 'onward' is intended to suggest that contemporary institutional theory is flourishing. There is substantial consensus on the ingredients or elements that together comprise these forms. Organizations have come to be one of the major types of social structures claiming the attention of institutional scholars and so we ask what is distinctive about an institutional approach to these forms. The adverb 'upward' signals my belief that some of the most interesting work currently underway relates to developments at the transnational level where we have recently witnessed a flurry of activities to construct new institutional forms as well as to develop scholarly frameworks to interpret and support these efforts. The latter sections of the chapter review these developments.

INSTITUTIONAL ELEMENTS

Although attention from sociologists has been relatively steady, the ways in which institutions are viewed and explained have varied substantially over time.[1] Early scholars wrestled with the relative importance of material and behavioral vs. cultural and symbolic factors. Leading classical European scholars exhibit, and were no doubt partly responsible for, this contestation. Marx (1972 [1844]) argued that materialist structures give rise to ideologies justifying their legitimacy – in effect, that behavioral systems determine symbolic systems. Durkheim (1949 [1893]) by contrast, insisted that normative/symbolic elements play an independent role in the structuring of social orders. Particularly in his later work (1961 [1912]), he stressed the importance of cognitive frames and belief systems – 'collective representations' – in undergirding the stability and constructing the meaning of social life. Weber (1968: 4 [1924]), for his part, stressed the importance of 'interpretation' – the symbolic processes that mediate between social actors and the materialist conditions they confront.

Grounded in these seminal beginnings, throughout the first half of the 20th century, sociologists pursued the ideas primarily at the societal level. Scholars such as Spencer (1876, 1896, 1910) and Sumner (1906) treated institutions as the specialized 'organs' of society that perform distinctive and interrelated functions. The norms and values defining appropriate behavior were observed to vary across political, economic, religious, and kinship sectors, as well as across societies, giving rise to diverse institutional complexes. Several generations of sociologists mined these topics productively (e.g., Davis, 1949) and provided the foundational frameworks unpinning most textbooks and handbooks of 20th century sociology. Parsons (1951) appropriated this work as the basis for his theoretical codification of the differentiation of societal sectors with his development of the 'pattern variables' (axes of value orientations, such as universalism/ particularism and ascription/achievement) as a guide to the analysis of social systems at all levels. Cultural anthropologists, such as Kroeber and Kluckhohn (1952) and Geertz (1973) contributed by defining cultures as semiotic systems crafted by collective action.

More recently, these same insights have more been recovered and reframed by contemporary scholars as competing institutional 'logics' (Friedland and Alford, 1991; Thornton et al., 2012).

Supplementing this work at the macro level, several generations of social psychologists examined the microfoundations of institutions. Cooley (1956 [1902]) and Mead (1934) pointed out that it was in the minds of social actors, in interaction with others, that connections between symbols and social actions were made. This line of research and theorizing was developed by later scholars, including Blumer (1969), Goffman (1974) and Weick (1969). Recent management scholars have reenergized these micro approaches with a new emphasis on 'institutional work'. Thus, Lawrence and Suddaby (2006: 219) apply a practice lens, calling attention to 'the awareness, skill and reflexivity of individual and collective actors ... as they work to create, maintain or disrupt institutions'.

The central pillars of 'neo-institutional theory' were crafted by Schutz (1967 [1932]) and Berger and Luckmann (1967). Unlike Parsons, who like most sociologists stressed the normative aspects of institutions, these scholars emphasized the centrality of shared cognitive conceptions – ideas, templates for organizing, and schema – in the establishment and preservation of social order. Important contributions to this line of thinking have also come from cognitive psychologists, including Kahneman, Slovic and Tversky (1982) and Shank and Abelson (1977).

The work of sociologists, social and cognitive psychologists, cultural anthropologists and management scholars has been complemented by parallel work in the field of political science and economics. From the turn of the 19th–20th century onward, political scientists have stressed the importance of legal and regulative frameworks as an unpinning of societal order. Early efforts by historical institutionalists, such as Burgess (1902) and Willoughby (1896), examined the development of constitutional frameworks undergirding the modern state. Later, institutional economists, including Commons (1924) and Williamson (1975), focused on the importance of transactions in economic exchanges and suggested that institutional frameworks such as rules and hierarchical systems were devised as a means to reduce transaction costs. Their efforts were joined by game theorists, including North (1990) and Greif (2006), who attempted to account for the development of stable markets. These ideas were appropriated by rational choice political scientists, including Moe (1984) and Weingast (1996), to examine the administrative frameworks devised to achieve and implement political agreements.

I have reviewed these and related ideas regarding the nature of institutional frameworks in more detail in *Institutions and Organizations*, a book now in its fourth edition (Scott, 2014), to conclude that there appear to be three types of elements used in the construction of institutions: *normative*, *cultural-cognitive* and *regulative*. These elements take priority in different arenas. The normative elements play a large role in the structuring of families, stratification systems, religious groups and associations – the types of units that have occupied much of the attention of sociologists. Anthropologists have focused on traditional societies, where the cultural-cognitive elements are prominent; and economists and political scientists have tended to concentrate on transactions between strangers in markets and adversaries in political systems, so that regulative elements loom large. Still, in all of these arenas, effective and robust institutional frameworks are likely to involve an admixture of all three elements. The elements are associated with diverse mechanisms that work in different ways and varied combinations. It is the task of the institutional analyst to unpack these complex systems to understand how and why they establish order or fail to do so.

THINKING INSTITUTIONALLY ABOUT ORGANIZATIONS

The focus of this volume is not on the general nature of institutions or all the varied forms and guises they assume, but rather the role they play in the world of organizations. It seems useful to pause a while to ponder more generally the question: What does it mean to think institutionally about organizations?[2] I propose three touchstones.

Recognition of the Importance of Founding Conditions

Origins are important moments for institutionalists. The conditions present at the time when a new entity emerges shape its nature and inflect its development. Stinchcombe (1965) applied this insight to account for differences in organization populations or forms that emerged at different times and places. The same arguments can be applied to the genesis of new ideas or areas of study.

Organizations, as specialized systems for managing complex work, did not become widespread in our social world until the emergence of the nation-state with its complex administrative structures in the 17th and 18th centuries and the advent of the industrial revolution with its agglomeration of productive forces in the 19th and 20th centuries. Early social theorists, from Marx, Weber, Durkheim to Veblen, thought seriously and deeply about these disruptive developments and the appearance of new forms, including bureaucracies and corporations.

American social scientists began to recognize organizations as important objects of study in the early 20th century. Unexpectedly, this work was pioneered by system engineers (Shenhov, 1995). Taylor (1911), the prophet of Scientific Management, together with others initiated studies to explore ways to improve the efficiency of technical production systems by redesigning tools and equipment. It was a natural follow-on for these researchers to extend their purview to the workforce and managers, seeking ways to rationalize production routines and the organization of work – the activities of individual workers as well as the division of labor and coordination systems. Their design proposals were widely adopted in manufacturing circles but led to reactive movements from workers and related work by social psychologists and sociologists during the 1930s and 1940s which emphasized the human and social aspects of work systems. Although stressing the importance of worker motivation and work group morale and, in some cases, the exploitation of labor (e.g., Bell, 1960), these Human Relations scholars primarily framed their arguments as a further means to improving efficiency.

In all of this work, while the settings were organizations, primary attention was given to individuals – workers or managers – or to work groups. A focus on organizations as the unit of analysis did not emerge until the late 1940s when, stimulated by the translation into English of Weber's (1946 [1906–1924]) seminal work on bureaucracy, Merton (Merton et al., 1952) encouraged a collection of sociologists, including Bendix (1956), Blau (1955), Gouldner (1954), Lipset, Trow and Coleman (1956) and Selznick (1949), to conduct a series of studies (many of them dissertations) empirically examining the structure and functioning of organizations.

These and related efforts culminated in the appearance of the first texts and treatises focusing on organizations *per se*. Books by March and Simon (1958), Etzioni (1961) and Blau and Scott (1962) provided conceptual frameworks, reviewed empirical research and set the agenda for a new field of academic study. The work was furthered by the launching in 1956 of a new journal devoted to the study of organizations, *Administrative Science Quarterly*, under the leadership of James Thompson. While Weber's work provided a significant stimulus, the approaches taken by American scholars were more

positivist, less historical and strongly influenced by the previous work of engineers and social scientists on work systems.

From the outset the proposed frameworks exhibited a markedly dualist structure. The rock on which our field was founded was a 'cleft rock', incorporating both technical and social features (Scott, 2004: 3). This dualism was institutionalized into the DNA of our field. A common narrative runs through our theory and research: organizations are viewed as working to reconcile the technical and the social, the rational and the natural, the formal and the informal. The dualism is enshrined in many of our concepts and approaches: social-technical systems, bounded rationality, embedded agency. We see the fateful role of origins and the path-dependent processes they set in motion.

Recognition of the Importance of Social Context

Intellectual context

Built out of American (mis-)interpretations of Weber (1946 [1906–1924])[3] and a collection of studies of production and administrative systems, early organization studies emphasized that organizations were different from other types of collectivities because of their efforts to embody rationality. Just as organization studies were getting underway, the fledgling field was invaded by the open systems intellectual revolution (e.g., Bertalanffy, 1956; Katz and Kahn, 1966) emphasizing the importance of the effects of environmental context on the structure and functioning of organizations. While this development literally opened up and transformed our understanding of organizations, for more than two decades organization scholars gave the lion's share of attention to the material environment. Attention was concentrated on the 'task' environment – stressing the nature of materials processed, the differentiation of tasks and departments to deal with more and less complex types of work, the resulting coordination mechanisms, dealing with make or buy decisions, staving off or developing alliances with competitors, and coping with the power and dependency consequences resulting from exchange relations. The primary theoretical perspectives governing macro organization scholarship (in which organizations are treated as the primary units of analysis) until well into the 1970s included contingency theory (e.g., Galbraith, 1973; Thompson, 1967); resource dependence (e.g., Pfeffer and Salancik, 1978); and transactions-cost economics (e.g., Williamson, 1975).

This theoretical hegemony of the materialists was challenged and rapidly broken by the application of neo-institutional perspectives to organizations. Applying the insights of Durkheim, Berger and Luckmann and others to organizations, Meyer and Rowan (1977) asserted that rather than following technological imperatives, executives and managers engaged in organization design were guided by cultural templates. Organization leaders were oriented more to legitimacy considerations than productivity concerns. Broadly shared beliefs regarding the 'proper' way to organize spread widely and rapidly in an increasingly globally connected world (Meyer et al., 2006), and were impressed on individual organizations through isomorphic and competitive processes.

Meyer and Rowan adopted the perspective that institutions are complexes of cultural rules. But not any or all cultural rules are supportive of organizations. Following Weber's and Berger's lead (Berger et al., 1973), they stressed the importance of rule and belief systems that are *rationalized* – formulated in ways that specify the design of rule-like procedures to be followed to obtain specific objectives. The most important creators and carriers of these rules systems in the modern era are the nation-state and the professions, which became ascendant in the 20th century (DiMaggio and Powell, 1983; Scott, 2008c). Post Meyer and Rowan, the dualism of the field was reconfigured to incorporate the

material and the symbolic. Rationality was grounded in myth and expressed in ritual (Meyer and Scott, 1983).

Over subsequent decades, neo-institutional views stressing cultural and cognitive elements were rejoined to other strands of institutional theory, including the more normative work of Parsons and Selznick as well as the more regulative emphasis of transactions-costs economists and rational choice political scientists. A largely unproductive 'family quarrel' between 'old' and 'new' institutionalists has largely been laid to rest (Hirsch and Lounsbury, 1997). For the last four decades, institutional theory has surged forward on this tri-partite confluence of elements, as we observe them to sometimes act in conflict, sometimes in concert. In my view, much of the vibrancy and appeal of the institutional approach lies in the variety of ideas it encompasses and the tensions these multiple strands of work generate.

Organizational context

The social structures within which activities and interactions take place importantly influence both the processes utilized and the outcomes achieved. If we apply this widely recognized truism to institutional work and institutional theory, we are quickly confronted with the fact that virtually all scholarly efforts to build and evaluate institutional theory have taken place within the confines of a university setting. It is surprising to me how little attention has been devoted to this fateful nexus.

Universities as a distinctive organization form first emerged over a thousand years ago, but the academic structure as we know it today was not set in place – institutionalized – until the end of the 19th century. By that time, a collection of academic disciplines had congealed and succeeded in imposing themselves on the structure of universities. As Clark (1983: 29) points out, in addition to being a network of varying enterprises, 'a national system of education is also a set of disciplines and professions'. Abbott underlines the centrality of the disciplines, arguing that the resilience of the academic disciplines within higher education rests in their 'dual institutionalization':

> On the one hand, the disciplines constitute the macrostructure of the labor market for faculty. Careers remain within discipline much more than within university. On the other hand, the system constitutes the microstructure of each individual university. All arts and sciences faculties contain more or less the same list of departments. (Abbott, 2001: 208–209)

In addition, universities comprise a variety of professional schools, which mobilize disciplines in the service of particular arenas of complex work (e.g., law, medicine, business).

As noted, organization studies began to emerge as a recognized area of inquiry in the 1950s, long after the basic framework of the university had been institutional. As a consequence, scholars with organization interests have been obliged to settle throughout the several departmental units and schools. Thus, we have, for example, organizational sociologists, organizational psychologists and organizational economists. And each of these disciplines tend to focus on a somewhat different aspect of organizations. For example, economists are likely to focus on the acquisition and allocation of scarce resources, matters of efficiency and productivity, and designing rules and hierarchies to reduce transaction costs. Psychologists are interested in variations in perceptions, cognition and motivation among participants. Political scientists are inclined to attend to power processes and decision-making systems. And sociologists will examine status structures, diversity issues and normative systems within organizations. Each ponders a different part of the elephant!

For their part, faculty in business schools largely limit their attention to business firms; political scientists in schools of public administration consider governmental agencies, political parties and regime structures;

law school scholars examine legal structures and law firms; medical school faculty study clinics, insurance programs and hospitals. Each examines a different beast in the menagerie. In short, the organization of the university has constrained us to abide by its structural vocabulary: differentiated by type of disciplinary approach and subject and by type of organization studied.

The consequence of this intellectual fragmentation is that scholars in one department or school working in isolation from each other cannot possibly comprehend the wide array of structures, processes and mechanisms that operate in the full range of organizations. In order to do so, we are compelled to disrupt and reconfigure the universities' institutional structures. We are forced to create specialized units and forums – centers, institutes, conferences, or workshops – to attempt to overcome the divisions imposed by our work settings. We must take what Jepperson (1991: 145) terms 'action' – the intentional collective mobilization of persons and behaviors. And in some times and places, these efforts become more stable ('institutionalized'). This helps to explain the fecundity of those few relatively stable collections of multiple, diverse organization scholars, such as those working, for example, in the University of Alberta's Department of Strategic Management and Organization, Carnegie Mellon's Graduate School of Industrial Administration, Copenhagen Business School's Department of Organization (IOA), the Max Planck Institute for the Study of Societies in Köln, the University of Michigan's Interdisciplinary Committee on Organizational Studies (ICOS), Stanford University's Center for Organization Research (SCOR) and the Scandinavian Consortium for Organizational Research (SCANCOR), the Swedish School of Economics' Stockholm Center for Organizational Research (SCORE), and the University of California, Irvine's Center for Organizations Research (COR).

Recognition of the Importance of Institutional Logics

Institutional approaches ushered in a recognition of the importance of symbolic elements in social life. Symbols are significant to the extent that they enable the development of common meaning systems (Mead, 1934). To explore the variety of values and norms around which social life is or has been organized, Friedland and Alford (1991) introduced the concept of 'institutional logics'. They focused on the societal level and, following the lead of earlier sociologists, as discussed above, stressed the ways in which varying logics define specialized societal sectors, such as the capitalist economy, the bureaucratic state, family kinship structures and the religious sphere, giving rise to distinctive patterns of cultural beliefs and material practices.

Thornton, Ocasio and Lounsbury (2012: 148) correctly point out that institutional logics reside at multiple levels within a social structure so that many cross-level effects occur. For example, although they do not use the term 'logics', Meyer and collaborators (Drori et al., 2006) have developed similar arguments at the world-system level to discuss the development and diffusion across societies of broadly defined rationalized structures and procedures. Like Friedland and Alford, Thornton and colleagues (2012) focus primary attention on the logics that differentiate among sectors or organizational fields within societies. These are clearly important for understanding how social arenas are differentiated and how activities and relations are structured within them.

Here, however, I want to call attention to institutional logics that penetrate into many types of organization fields. The types of logics I refer to each involve a complex of intellectual ideas produced and promulgated by social scientists. They function as 'meta-logics'. Intellectuals and other types of professionals have more influence on our social worlds than is often recognized as they help to shape the structure of organizations and organization fields (Scott, 2008c). I briefly give three examples.

The open systems revolution

This intellectual revolution was briefly described above. Beginning in the mid-1950s, a diffuse collection of scholars including von Bertalanffy (1956), Boulding (1956) and Ashby (1952), called attention to the commonalities that exist in the structure and functioning of all types of complex systems, from cells to solar systems, but also the substantial differences that separate the less from the most complex of these. Social systems operate at an extremely high level of complexity, as do other types of 'open' systems. An open system is one that is capable of self-maintenance based on a throughput of resources from its environment. These ideas rapidly transformed the fledgling field of organizations, causing scholars to revise and even transform their earlier conceptions (Katz and Kahn, 1966; Scott and Davis, 2007: ch. 4). Organizations were seen to be dependent for survival on managing the flows of information, energy and resources from their environment, principally from other organizations. Managers and executives were advised that their most critical tasks were not those of controlling and coordinating the activities of their employees, but rather managing relations with their suppliers, customers, competitors and regulators (e.g., Pfeffer and Salancik, 1978; Porter, 1980). Concepts like information flows, buffering the technical core, bridging, cybernetic models of control systems and loose coupling transformed the focus of organizational scholarship and, over time, the thinking of managers and the design of organizations.

The cognitive revolution

During the 1950s, another intellectual transformation was underway as psychologists began to rethink their rather mechanical models of stimulus–response behavioral theory to recognize that the organism (individual) mediates this interaction – interpreting the stimuli and formulating the response (Lewin, 1951). Among the most important topics addressed by this body of work are causal attribution – the ways in which individuals use information to determine the causes of social behavior – the types of errors that occur in making inferences from observations, the emergence of schemas to support interpretations, and the kinds of social heuristics employed to manage complex problems (Fiske, 2013; Kahneman et al., 1982; Nisbett and Ross, 1980; Shank and Abelson, 1977). As Markus and Zajonc (1985: 141) conclude, 'The idea of the human organism as an information processor became popular.'

This body of work was quickly absorbed into organizational research by a variety of scholars, with major implications for our theorizing. To select a single, highly influential example, consider the framework devised by Simon in his influential book *Administrative Behavior* (1997 [1945]) and extended in his work with March (March and Simon, 1958). In his examination of behavior by administrators in organizations, Simon focused primary attention on decisions and decision premises. Cohen (2007) points out how deftly Simon separated facts from values and means from ends, suggesting that as students of organizations we need not attempt to explain or attend to the values and ends, but take them as given. Although Simon's general approach was influenced by John Dewey and the pragmatist tradition, his choice to adopt a cognitive focus, leaving out emotional considerations or attention to the role of habit, 'marked the start of a long decline of these concepts in scholarly and journalistic interpretations of organizational action' (Cohen, 2007: 505). It was, indeed, the beginning of the enthronement of the cognitive lens into studies of decision-making and management. The hyper-version of this

perspective was built into the rational choice framework, which continues to dominate the work of organizational economists and, increasingly, the approach taken by political scientists to administrative systems. While there have been recent attempts to bring emotion back into our analysis of behavior (e.g., Voronov and Vince, 2012), there is little evidence that cognitive approaches have lost their grip.

The ascendance of neo-liberal logics

As early as the 1930s, alarmed by the rise of fascist and socialist regimes, a group of Austrian economists associated with Hayek (1944, 1948) espoused the value of a more competitive, less regulated economy and a less intrusive state. These broad ideas and concerns were adopted by a collection of economists at the University of Chicago and, under the leadership of Friedman (1962), codified into a portfolio of neoliberal ideas, arguments and policy proposals encouraging governments to reduce regulations and taxes on firms and to cut spending on programs these taxes supported, especially welfare spending (Campbell and Pedersen, 2001; Prasad, 2006). Embraced by conservative politicians and policy centers in the United States, these ideas spread quickly throughout Western societies. Their scope expanded to include the developing countries when they became the basis for policy and funding guidelines adopted by a variety of international multilateral financial institutions, such as the World Bank (Peet, 2009). Financial aid from these institutions was made conditional on the recipient country embracing neoliberal policies. These and related developments persuaded a number of political scientists that more attention needed to be devoted to the independent role of ideas, including worldviews, principled beliefs and causal beliefs, in the shaping of foreign policy (Goldstein and Keohane, 1993).

The neoliberal ideas were reconfigured to fuel a set of reform efforts directed at more delimited organization fields operating within specialized sectors of society. In the public sector, reformers promoted 'new management' changes in the administration of agencies intended to emphasize the importance of efficiency, market tests of performance, and the strengthening of managerial influence to curtail professional discretion (Christensen and Laegreid, 2001; Greenwood and Hinings, 1993). Soon thereafter, these same types of reforms were directed to non-profit organizations in a variety of arenas (Hwang and Powell, 2009). Even more broadly, over time this reform agenda has invaded one professionally dominated field after another – for example, accounting, architecture, education, medical care, publishing, and scientific research and training – challenging professional logics stressing decentralization and the delegation of discretion in favor of managerial centralization of decision-making and market-based templates of performance (e.g., Berman, 2012; Greenwood and Suddaby, 2006; Powell and Sandholtz, 2012; Scott et al., 2000; Thornton et al., 2005).

While all of these types of institutional structures, both societal- and field-level, have been subjected to strong and persistent pressures from neoliberal logics to change, pre-existing institutions have not been displaced. As Campbell (2004) has pointed out, too many would-be reformers and commentators put too much stock on regulatory changes: e.g., changes in rule systems and formal structures. He argues that rather than privileging the regulatory mechanisms, it is essential that we not ignore 'the mediating effects of the normative and cognitive aspects of institutions' (p. 130). While movements like neoliberalism are inherently cognitive in nature, they are carried by proponents who seek to impose their ideas by force of coercion – political, economic and legal. However, these efforts encounter pre-existing fields organized around divergent normative beliefs and cognitive frames. Whether at the societal levels (e.g., Hall and Soskice, 2001) or at the organization field level, existing systems are often surprisingly resistant to change efforts, and the resulting frameworks often represent a complex admixture of the new and pre-existing systems.

ORGANIZATION FIELDS AND THE TRANSNATIONAL ARENA

Organization Fields

The organization field has emerged as an extremely useful conceptual tool in guiding the work of scholars studying organizations. Early work in organization studies focused primary attention on individuals and groups within organizations, treating organizations as distinctive types of contexts. During the 1950s and early 1960s, scholars began to examine the organization itself as a unit of analysis, examining varying structural characteristics and configurations and differing modes of operation (e.g., Pugh et al., 1968). And, beginning with the ideas of Bourdieu (1971) and the related work of a number of researchers, including DiMaggio and Powell (1983), Hirsch (1985) and Scott and Meyer (1983), scholars converged around the ideas of focusing attention on a collection of interdependent organizations sharing broad cultural frames and a common relational system or network of interactions: the organization field. As I have noted: 'The concept of organization field celebrates and exploits the insight that "local social orders" constitute the building blocks of contemporary social systems' (Scott, 2014: 224). Fields call attention to the importance of the settings, fellow actors and distinctive dramatic plots around which much of our collective social life is organized.

This view of fields has been challenged by Fligstein and McAdam (2012), who argue that fields are primarily arenas of contestation and self-interested strategic action. While some early discussions of fields undoubtedly overstressed the amount of conformity and consensus, it is still helpful to point out that contention is difficult if not impossible when the players do not agree on what they are fighting about. More to the point, social movement theorists have quite usefully called for more attention to the marginal players and suppressed interests present in every complex field. However, the primary value of the field concept to the institutional theorist is to highlight the existence of *local social orders* – arenas within which social stability is produced and reproduced, actions are largely predictable and meanings are shared.

Still, as Friedland and Alford (1991) have pointed out, all organization fields are embedded in wider societal systems that host a variety of contradictory and competing logics for organizing (see also Thornton et al., 2012). These logics can be imported by actors into any delimited field, and provide the basis for tension and change. Also, as discussed in the previous section, meta-logics provide compelling symbolic frameworks that can invade and reconfigure multiple, diverse organizational fields.

Moreover, all organizations simultaneously operate in multiple fields and hence host multiple logics as well as alternative relational systems. For example, all organizations belong to a sectorally defined field containing a collection of forms engaged in similar or substitutable functions – e.g., newspapers, hospitals – together with their crucial exchange partners and support and governance system. Relations among similar organizations often involve competition or even conflict, but can become the basis for shared identities and for alliances around selected issues. At the same time, these same organizations participate in a geographically defined aerial or regional field whose members are structurally and functionally diverse, but because of shared locality, develop interdependencies, regularized relations and shared networks (Marquis et al., 2011). Such community systems are more likely to be based on common interests and give rise to collaborative structures. Unlike sectoral systems, community systems are based on symbiotic rather than commensalistic relations (Hawley, 1950: ch. 12). Regional economists argue that because of the economic advantages associated with agglomeration, regional studies are critical to understanding industrial systems. In particular, the emerging industries which often depend on high labor mobility and inter-firm partnerships, benefit from the proximate concentration of related firms (Benner, 2002; Saxenian, 1994). My colleagues and I (Scott, Kirst and associates, 2017), have been examining the connections and tensions that arise as colleges in the San Francisco Bay Area attempt to meet the demands of their support and control structures in higher education while at the same time attempting to satisfy the demands of firms and agencies utilizing their services in the region.

Transnational Fields

I have found it helpful to examine the contribution to field structure and dynamics of three kinds of interdependent components: *actors*, both individuals and collectives, and their relations; *institutional logics*; and field-level *governance structures* (see Scott et al., 2000: 170–175). To illustrate the value of this conceptual schema, I apply it to examine changes occurring in the transnational realm, arguably one of the most vibrant areas of institutional theorizing and research (Djelic and Quack, 2003, 2008).

For many decades – indeed, centuries – the global arena was structured around an enduring institutional framework: the Westphalian system, a set of international accords reached in 1648. This regime established the foundation for a world of nation-states defined as possessing sovereignty within their own borders (Krasner, 1993). An international focus attended to the types of relations, both adversarial and cooperative, that were devised and enforced by these nation-state actors. Beginning after World War II, political scientists observed basic changes in this framework as intermediate actors and relations began to emerge within and between nations, shifting analytic attention from an international to a transnational system, displacing a state-centric focus.

In the beginning these non-state relations were episodic, interpersonal and informal, but they have evolved in recent decades toward increasing formalization, structuration, codification and standardization (Djelic and Quack, 2003: 5; Whitley, 2003). The relations are anchored and enacted by a range of transnational actors, some old and many new. We focus on the organizational actors.

Types of actors

In recent decades, there has been a proliferation of actors in the international system, variously operating 'above, beside, and within the state' (Slaughter, 2002: 13), including:

The nation-state: Although no longer alone and unchallenged, the nation-state is still a formidable actor. With the rise of globalization, early observers predicted their demise or at least a serious weakening of their power. They remain important players, although now just one of several types of actors who exercise significant power. In addition to conventional nation-states, we also are experiencing the presence of a number of failed states, such as Syria, that are incapable of enforcing order within their own borders, and emergent states, such as ISIS, that are attempting to gain the status of a legitimate state.

Multinational corporations: Although headquartered in a specific country (often one that imposes the fewest demands and restrictions), multinational corporations are unlikely to be confined by this country's interests. They serve primarily their shareholders and produce for a global market through specialized facilities located around the world. Their increasing market share moves the world

economy from the 'shallow integration' manifested largely through the trade of goods and services characteristic of the first half of the 20th century to the 'deep integration' involving 'the production of goods and services in cross-border value-adding activities that redefine the kinds of production processes contained within national boundaries' (Gereffi, 2005: 163).

Institutional investors: Large investor organizations, including international insurance companies, investment trusts, pension funds and sovereign funds, are increasingly transnational in their operations. These market-driven ownership groups exert enormous influence on the politics and practices of corporations (see Davis, 2009).

International non-governmental organizations: Non-profit organizations have long operated in most democratic nation-states, but after World War II, their operations and organization have become transnational. Data reported by Smith (2005) indicates that their numbers grew more than 600 percent between 1973 and 2000. These non-governmental organizations (NGOs) are engaged in many contested arenas, especially human rights, environmental concerns, world peace, women's rights and global justice issues. They often link up into issue networks – transnational advocacy networks (Sikkink, 2002) – to pursue more complex and interconnected issues, such as childhood poverty.

Professional associations: Long engaged as powerful actors on the national scene, professional associations are now highly organized in the transnational arena. These associations often act as the 'conscience of the community', setting health and safety standards, proposing guidelines for 'best practice', and developing and promulgating technical processes and products (Brunsson et al., 2000). The standards they set are 'soft' in the sense that they are not backed by legal sanctions, but rather by 'expertise, science or similar authoritative knowledge' (Jacobsson and Sahlin-Andersson, 2006: 260; see also Drori and Meyer, 2006).

Religious communities: There was a time not so long ago when observers were widely predicting the triumph of secularism and the waning influence of religious groups. Rather than disappearing, the major religions have experienced a major rebirth, especially in their fundamentalist segments. Fundamentalism is a religiously based cognitive and affective orientation that resists change and the modernist movements championed by the mainstream (Antoun, 2001). All of the mainstream religious faiths – Christianity, Islam and Judaism – have developed more politicized factions, some engaged in insurgent activities and others organizing to influence the choice of political leaders and policies. All are active in the transnational arena.

Media and other information brokers: A growing number of media companies now operate at the transnational level, including CNN, Al Jazeera and Murdoch's media empire. Blumberg's financial information services play a vital intermediary role, and a specialized business press, including the *Financial Times* and the *Wall Street Journal*, collects and bundles fugitive and widely scattered information and publicizes events and practices to praise or to blame, to rate or to rank. International consulting companies, such as McKinsey and Boston Consulting, diffuse popular business policies, practices and modes of organizing.

My colleagues and I (Scott et al., 2011) have examined the complex ways in which various combinations of transnational actors – including national or provincial governments, companies, investors, multilateral agencies such as the World Bank, NGOs, professional engineering associations, and the media – come together around the construction of major infrastructure projects such as bridges, air ports and metropolitan rail projects. These actors enter into a transnational coalition but their projects are situated in a specific locality – an aerial field such as a community or region. Needless to say, the logics driving these two fields may not be well aligned so that conflict and failure are common.

Our world now hosts a disparate assortment of transnational actors operating in a wide range of specialized organization fields. Moreover, the actors identified are able to exercise influence based on their possession of varying types of capital. Some, such as nation-states and terrorist groups, possess coercive powers, whether legitimate or not. Others, such as investor groups, control financial resources. Corporations manage financial resources, but also exercise market

power. Groups like NGOs, professional associations and religious communities, exercise normative and cultural authority – and, sometimes, in the latter case, coercive power. Still others, such as the media and consulting companies, offer information and human capital.

Institutional Logics

As previously discussed, institutional logics not only provide the rationale and organizing principles around which specific specialized arenas of activity are structured, but also operate at broader levels, infiltrating settled organization fields with ideas and impetus for social change. We consider two influential logics active in the transnational realm: the idea of the rational actor and the related ideology of neoliberalism.

The rise of the rational actor

All of the new types of organizational actors that we have just enumerated are viewed as rationally structured collective actors. The nation-state has for many years attempted to connect the notion of an imagined society rooted in ethnic, religious or historical roots to that of a unified nation within the boundaries of a sovereign state (Anderson, 1991). (We are currently witnessing the result of what happens when these conceptions are mismatched, as in the states in the Middle East arbitrarily created by European fiat.) These actors for many centuries dominated the international sphere but, as discussed, have now been joined by new types of actors. Meyer and colleagues (Drori et al., 2006; Thomas et al., 1987) argue that this transformation has been possible because of the widespread adoption of a new cultural model constituting individuals and organizations and, as a special case of organizations, nation-states as rational actors. This model celebrates the centrality of individual persons, endowed with rights, duties, entitlements and powers, and of collective actors – organizations – that can bring together 'empowered and rational people' in 'a managed and rationalized structure to take purposive collective action on many fronts in a scientized environment' (Meyer et al., 2006: 40).

Common features attributed to contemporary organizations include: agency, legitimated goals, a technical structure to pursue its goals, procedures to manage its resources, and personnel with rights who participate, variably, in decision structures. This generalized model has diffused rapidly throughout world during the past century. As Parsons (1956: 225) observed a half century ago: 'the development of organizations is the principal mechanism by which, in a highly differentiated society, it is possible to "get things done", to achieve goals beyond the reach of the individual'. This mechanism now operates across as well as within societies. And, it is also being used by collectives such as ISIS who eschew the modernist eschatology but employ rationalized means to achieve their disruptive, terrorist ends.

The spread of neo-liberal ideologies

We have discussed above the penetration of neo-liberal logics into a diverse number of organization fields, but their effects at the transnational level has been even more pronounced. Neo-liberal views have not simply encouraged a significant reduction in the scale and scope of a country's government – lowering taxes and reducing welfare expenditures – but also induced them to curtail their attempts to regulate the behavior of the private sector. The widespread adoption of these logics has witnessed a wave of deregulation in most Western industrial societies since the 1970s. The logics remain surprisingly robust even after the financial turmoil associated with the deregulation of financial markets early in the first decade of this century.

Alternative Modes of Governance

Responding to the withdrawal of oversight of corporate behavior by the nation-state, many of the new types of actors in the transnational arena have attempted to fill this vacuum, but by wielding new types of weapons. The failure of governments has led to the emergence of new forms of governance. Lacking the legal and regulative authority held by nation states the new players, including NGOs, professional associations and information intermediaries, ground their control attempts in normative and cultural elements. The modes of influence that are evolving include rule-setting, in which standards are established to guide organizations, encouraging them to engage in self-regulation; monitoring, in which compliance is overseen by third parties; and agenda-setting, in which recommendations are promulgated so that reactions can be compared and employed to improve future role-setting (Jacobsson and Sahlin-Andersson, 2006).

Streeck and Schmitter (1985: 17) suggest that many of these kinds of control efforts are grounded in 'associational governance' involving the 'self-government of categories of social actors defined by a collective self-regarding interest that is at least partially compatible or identical with a collective good for the society as a whole'. They contrast this mode with that employed by either markets or nation-states. Of course, the associational mode has a strong affinity with network-types of control (see Powell, 1990). Empirical studies of systems employing self-regulation and monitoring include those by Bartley (2003), who examined the role of certification associations in the apparel and forest products industries; and by Sweet, Fligstein and Sandholz (2001), who studied the emergence of many cross-border associational networks of trade and professional groups attempting to set and enforce field-level standards within the European Union.

International NGOs are particularly effective in agenda-setting, in 'naming and shaming', and urging both private and public organizations to work toward achieving progress in areas as wide-ranging as protecting species diversity, slowing climate change, and safeguarding refugees and immigrants (Smith and Johnston, 2002). These private efforts sometimes give rise to governmental action in the form of new laws, policies and programs. Halliday and Carruthers (2007), for example, show how at the urging of NGOs, leading global institutions such as the World Bank and the International Monetary Fund crafted normative frameworks providing standards and guidelines that recursively interact with national law-making as countries work to standardize corporate bankruptcy requirements.

In sum, in a period of rapid globalizing efforts, the actions of nation-state actors are often joined if not replaced by those of a wide range of transnational organizations. As Djelic, Sahlin-Andersson and Quack point out, we are in an era of robust institution-building in the transnational arena, and the players, processes and mechanisms of control are different from those of earlier times. We are witnessing the genesis and structuration of new transnational fields with new modes of governance employed: soft power is supplementing if not replacing hard power. In an era when public actors are constrained by neo-liberal ideologies, private and public actors compete and collaborate in new ways.

These developments have not gone unnoticed by political scientists and international business scholars. After long domination by rational choice, contingency theory, resource-based and strategic management perspectives, both of these scholarly communities are increasingly employing institutional lenses and tools to better understand the ways in which our global world is changing (e.g., Henisz and Zelner, 2005; Peng et al., 2008).

CONCLUDING COMMENT

I feel privileged to have participated in two important intellectual projects: first, during the late 1950s and early 1960s, the establishment and development of organizations as a central topic of social science inquiry; and second, the rebirth of institutional theory during the 1970s as a dominant paradigm guiding the analysis of organizational behavior and organizational systems employed by multiple disciplines and applied at multiple levels of analysis. I have recounted my view of these developments in other forums (Scott, 2004, 2005). I have also described elsewhere my perspective on some of the important ways in which institutional theory has successfully evolved during the 1960s–1970s and onward from a somewhat awkward period of adolescence to a promising level of maturity (Scott, 1987, 2008a; see also, Scott, 2014: ch. 9).

One of the abiding strengths of contemporary institutional theory is its versatility in moving across various levels of analysis: from individual behavior, through sub-units, to organizations, to organizational fields, to societal systems and on to transnational and global arenas. The field of institutional theory was immeasurably informed and strengthened by Giddens' (1979) structuration theory, adopting his insight of the recursive interdependence of actors and structures. Actors are guided, constrained and supported by structures which they inhabit; structures are produced, reproduced and altered by the behavior of actors. In their work on the emergence of organizations, Padgett and Powell (2012: 2), as good network theorists, propose that 'In the short run, actors create relations; in the long run, relations create actors'; to which, as good institutional theorists, we would add, 'Also, in the short run, actors create meanings; in the long run, meanings create actors'.

I began this essay by claiming that institutional theory is about explaining the basis of social order. In a time when some of our most central institutional structures – political bodies, public agencies, financial institutions, corporations – are viewed by growing numbers as either corrupt, ineffective, or both, institutional theorists should be devoting more attention to examining what kinds of actions make them function better and what kinds undermine them. This line of investigation has been championed by Selznick (1992) and, as I have argued, more of us need to follow his lead (Scott, 2014: 273–274).

Notes

1 The first section of this chapter draws from Scott (2008b).
2 I am indebted to Kristian Kreiner for posing this question when he invited me in 2013 to participate in the celebration of the sixtieth anniversary of the founding of the Department of Organizations (IOA) at the Copenhagen School of Business.
3 Numerous commentators (including many Europeans) have noted the extent to which early attempts by American scholars to utilize Weber's work seriously misinterpreted his scholarship on bureaucracy. These interpretations were often based on the translation into English of a few of his essays and selected fragments of his vast writings (see, e.g., Collins, 1986; Thompson, 1980).

REFERENCES

Abbott, Andrew (2001). *Chaos of Disciplines*. Chicago, IL: University of Chicago Press.

Anderson, Benedict (1991). *Imagined Communities: Reflections on the Origin and Spread of Nationalism*, 2nd edn. London and New York: Verso.

Antoun, Richard T. (2001). *Understanding Fundamentalism: Christian, Islamic, and Jewish Movements*. Walnut Creek, CA: Alta Mira.

Ashby, W. Ross (1952). *Design for a Brain*. New York: John Wiley.

Bartley, Tim (2003). Certifying forests and factories: States, social movements, and the rise of private regulation in the apparel and forest products fields. *Politics & Society*, 31(3): 433–464.

Bell, Daniel (1960). Work and its discontents: The cult of efficiency in America. In Daniel Bell, *The End of Ideology*. Glencoe, IL: The Free Press. pp. 222–262.

Bendix, Reinhard (1956). *Work and Authority in Industry: Managerial Ideologies in the Course of Industrialization*. New York: John Wiley.

Benner, Chris (2002). *Work in the New Economy: Flexible Labor Markets in Silicon Valley*. Oxford: Blackwell.

Berger, Peter L., Berger, Brigitte and Kellner, Hansfried (1973). *The Homeless Mind: Modernization and Consciousness*. New York: Random House.

Berger, Peter L. and Luckmann, Thomas (1967). *The Social Construction of Reality*. New York: Anchor.

Berman, Elizabeth P. (2012). *Creating the Market University: How Academic Science Became an Economic Engine*. Princeton, NJ: Princeton University Press.

Bertalanffy, Ludwig von (1956). General systems theory. In Ludwig von Bertalanffy and Anatol Rapoport (eds), *General Systems: Yearbook of the Society for the Advance of General Systems Theory*, vol. 1. Ann Arbor, MI: The Society. pp. 1–16.

Blau, Peter M. (1955). *The Dynamics of Bureaucracy*. Chicago, IL: University of Chicago Press.

Blau, Peter M. and Scott, W. Richard (1962). *Formal Organizations: A Comparative Approach*. San Francisco, CA: Chandler.

Blumer, Herbert (1969). *Symbolic Interaction: Perspective and Method*. Englewood Cliffs, NJ: Prentice Hall.

Boulding, Kenneth E. (1956). General systems theory: The skeleton of science. *Management Science*, 2: 197–208.

Bourdieu, Pierre (1971). Systems of education and systems of thought. In M. K. D. Young (ed.), *Knowledge and Control: New Directions for the Sociology of Education*. London: Collier Macmillan. pp. 189–207.

Brunsson, Nils, Jacobsson, Bengt and Associates (2000). *A World of Standards*. Oxford: Oxford University Press.

Burgess, John William (1902). *Political Science and Comparative Constitutional Law*. Boston, MA: Ginn.

Campbell, John L. (2004). *Institutional Change and Globalization*. Princeton, NJ: Princeton University Press.

Campbell, John L. and Pedersen, Ove K. (eds) (2001). *The Rise of Neoliberalism and Institutional Analysis*. Princeton, NJ: Princeton University Press.

Christensen, Tom and Laegreid, Per (2001). *New Public Management: The Transformation of Ideas*. Aldershot, UK: Ashgate.

Clark, Burton R. (1983). *The Higher Education System: Academic Organization in Cross-National Perspective*. Berkeley, CA: University of California Press.

Cohen, Michael D. (2007). *Administrative Behavior:* Laying the foundations for Cyert and March. *Organization Science*, 18(3): 503–506.

Collins, Randall (1986). *Weberian Sociological Theory.* Cambridge: Cambridge University Press.

Commons, John R. (1924). *The Legal Foundations of Capitalism.* New York: Macmillan.

Cooley, Charles Horton (1956 [1902]). *Social Organization.* Glencoe, IL: The Free Press.

Davis, Gerald F. (2009). *Managed by the Markets.* Oxford: Oxford University Press.

Davis, Kingsley (1949). *Human Society.* New York: Macmillan.

DiMaggio, Paul J. and Powell, Walter W. (1983). The iron cage revisited: Institutional isomorphism and collective rationality in organizational fields. *American Sociological Review*, 48: 147–160.

Djelic, Marie-Laure and Quack, Sigrid (2003). Introduction: Governing globalization – Bringing institutions back in. In Marie-Laure Djelic and Sigrid Quack (eds), *Globalization and Institutions.* Cheltenham: Edward Elgar. pp. 1–14.

Djelic, Marie-Laure and Quack, Sigrid (2008). Institutions and transnationalization. In Royston Greenwood, Christine Oliver, Roy Suddaby and Kerstin Sahlin-Andersson (eds), *The SAGE Handbook of Organizational Institutionalism.* London: Sage. pp. 299–323.

Djelic, Marie-Laure, and Sahlin-Andersson, Kerstin (eds) 2006. *Transnational Governance: Institutional Dynamics of Regulation.* Cambridge: Cambridge University Press.

Drori, Gili S. and Meyer, John W. (2006). Global scientization: An environment for expanded organization. In Gili S. Drori, John W. Meyer and Hokyu Hwang (eds), *Globalization and Organization: World Society and Organization Change.* Oxford: Oxford University Press. pp. 50–68.

Drori, Gili S., Meyer, John W. and Hwang, Hokyu (eds) (2006). *Globalization and Organization: World Society and Organization Change.* Oxford: Oxford University Press.

Durkheim, Emile (1949 [1893]). *The Division of Labor in Society.* Glencoe, IL: The Free Press.

Durkheim, Emile (1961 [1912]). *The Elementary Forms of Religious Life.* New York: Collier Books.

Etzioni, Amitai (1961). *A Comparative Analysis of Complex Organizations.* New York: The Free Press.

Fiske, Susan T. (2013). *Social Cognition: From Brain to Culture*, 2nd edn. London: Sage.

Fligstein, Neil and McAdam, Doug (2012). *A Theory of Fields.* Oxford: Oxford University Press.

Friedland, Robert and Alford, Robert R. (1991). Bringing society back in: Symbols, practices, and institutional contradictions. In Walter W. Powell and Paul J. DiMaggio (eds), *The New Institutionalism in Organizational Analysis.* Chicago, IL: University of Chicago Press. pp. 232–263.

Friedman, Milton (1962). *Capitalism and Freedom.* Chicago, IL: University of Chicago Press.

Galbraith, Jay (1973). *Designing Complex Organizations.* Reading, MA: Addison–Wesley.

Geertz, Clifford (1973). *The Interpretation of Cultures.* New York: Basic Books.

Gereffi, Gary (2005). The global economy: Organization, governance, and development. In Neil J. Smelser and Richard Swedberg (eds), *The Handbook of Economic Sociology*, 2nd edn. Princeton, NJ: Princeton University Press; and New York: Russell Sage Foundation. pp. 160–182.

Giddens, Anthony (1979). *Central Problems in Social theory: Action, Structure, and Contradiction in Social Analysis.* Berkeley, CA: University of California Press.

Goffman, Erving (1974). *Frame Analysis.* Cambridge, MA: Harvard University Press.

Goldstein, Judith and Keohane, Robert O. (eds) (1993). *Ideas and Foreign Policy: Beliefs, Institutions and Political Change.* Ithaca, NY: Cornell University Press.

Gouldner, Alvin W. (1954). *Patterns of Industrial Bureaucracy.* Glencoe, IL: The Free Press.

Greenwood, Royston and Hinings, C. R. (1993). Understanding strategic change: The contribution of archetypes. *Academy of Management Journal*, 36: 1052–1081.

Greenwood, Royston and Suddaby, Roy (2006). Institutional entrepreneurship in mature fields: The Big Five accounting firms. *Academy of Management Journal*, 29: 27–48.

Greif, Avner (2006). *Institutions and the Path to the Modern Economy: Lessons from Medieval Trade.* Cambridge: Cambridge University Press.

Hall, Peter A. and Soskice, David (2001). *Varieties of Capitalism: The Institutional Foundations of Comparative Advantage.* Oxford: Oxford University Press.

Halliday, Terence C. and Carruthers, Bruce (2007). The recursity of law: Global norm making and national lawmaking in the globalization of corporate insolvency regimes. *American Journal of Sociology*, 112(4): 1135–1202.

Hawley, Amos (1950). *Human Ecology: A Theory of Community Structure.* New York: Ronald Press.

Hayek, Friedrich A. (1944). *The Road to Serfdom.* Chicago, IL: University of Chicago Press.

Hayek, Friedrich A. (1948). *Individualism and Economic Order.* Chicago, IL: University of Chicago Press.

Henisz, Witold J. and Zelner, B. A. (2005). Legitimacy, interest group pressures, and institutional change in emerging institutions: The case of foreign investors and home country governments. *Academy of Management Review*, 30(2): 361–382.

Hirsch, Paul M. (1985). The study of industries. In Sam B. Bacharach and S. M. Mitchell (eds), *Research in the Sociology of Organizations*, vol. 4. Greenwich, CT: JAI Press. pp. 271–309.

Hirsch, Paul M. and Lounsbury, Michael D. (1997). Ending the family quarrel: Toward a reconciliation of 'old' and 'new' institutionalism. *American Behavioral Scientist*, 40: 406–418.

Hwang, Hokyu and Powell, Walter W. (2009). The rationalization of charity: The influences of professionalism in the nonprofit sector. *Administrative Science Quarterly*, 54: 268–298.

Jacobsson, Bengt and Sahlin-Andersson, Kerstin (2006). In Marie-Laure Djelic and Kerstin Sahlin-Andersson (eds), *Transnational Governance: Institutional Dynamics of Regulation*. Cambridge: Cambridge University Press. pp. 247–265.

Jepperson, Ronald L. (1991). Institutions, institutional effects, and institutionalism. In Walter W. Powell and Paul J. DiMaggio (eds), *The New Institutionalism in Organizational Analysis*. Chicago, IL: University of Chicago Press. pp. 143–163.

Kahneman, Daniel, Slovic, P. and Tversky, Amos (eds) (1982). *Judgment under Uncertainty: Heuristics and Biases*. New York: Cambridge University Press.

Katz, Daniel and Kahn, Robert L. (1966). *The Social Psychology of Organizations*. New York; John Wiley & Sons.

Krasner, Steven D. (1993). Westphalia and all that. In Judith Goldstein and Robert Keohane (eds), *Ideas and Foreign Policy*. Ithaca, NY: Cornell University Press. pp. 235–264.

Kroeber, Alfred L. and Kluckhohn, Clyde (1952). Culture: A critical review of concepts and definitions. *Peabody Museum Papers 47*. Cambridge, MA: Harvard University Press.

Lawrence, Thomas B. and Suddaby, Roy (2006). Institutions and institutional work. In Steward R. Clegg, Cynthia Hardy, Thomas B. Lawrence and Walter R. Nord (eds), *The SAGE Handbook of Organization Studies*, 2nd edn. London: Sage. pp. 215–254.

Lewin, Kurt (1951). *Field Theory in Social Psychology*. New York: Harper.

Lipset, Seymour Martin, Trow, Martin A. and Coleman, James S. (1956). *Union Democracy*. Glencoe, IL: The Free Press.

March, James G. and Simon, Herbert A. (1958). *Organizations*. New York: Wiley.

Markus, Hazel and Zajonc, R. B. (1985). The cognitive perspective in social psychology. In Gardner Lindzey and Elliot Aronson (eds), *The Handbook of Social Psychology*, vol. 1, 3rd edn. New York: Random House. pp. 137–230.

Marquis, Christopher, Lounsbury, Michael and Greenwood, Royston (eds) (2011). *Communities and Organizations. Research in the Sociology of Organizations*, Volume 33. Bingley, UK: Emerald Group.

Marx, Karl (1972 [1844]). Economic and philosophical manuscripts of 1844: Selections. In Robert C. Tucker (ed.), *The Marx–Engels Reader*. New York: W. W. Norton. pp. 52–106.

Mead, George Herbert (1934). *Mind, Self, and Society*. Chicago, IL: University of Chicago Press.

Merton, Robert K., Gray, Alisa P., Hockey, Barbara and Selvin, Hanan C. (eds) (1952). *Reader in Bureaucracy*. Glencoe, IL: The Free Press.

Meyer, John W., Drori, Gili S. and Hwang Hokyu (2006). World society and the proliferation of formal organizations. In Gili S. Drori, John W. Meyer and Hokhu Hwang, *Globalization and Organizations: World Society and Organizational Change*. Oxford: Oxford University Press. pp. 23–49.

Meyer, John W. and Rowan, Brian (1977). Institutionalized organizations: Formal structure as myth and ceremony. *American Journal of Sociology*, 83(2): 340–363.

Meyer, John W. and Scott, W. Richard (1983). *Organizational Environments: Ritual and Rationality*. Newbury Park, CA: Sage.

Moe, Terry M. (1984). The new economics of organization. *American Journal of Political Science*, 28(November): 739–777.

Nisbett, R. E. and Ross, Lee (1980). *Human Inference: Strategies and Shortcomings of Social Judgment*. Englewood Cliffs, NJ: Prentice–Hall.

North, Douglass C. (1990). *Institutions, Institutional Change, and Economic Performance*. Cambridge: Cambridge University Press.

Padgett, John F. and Powell, Walter W. (2012). The problem of emergence. In John F. Padgett and Walter W. Powell, *The Emergence of Organizations and Markets*. Princeton, NJ: Princeton University Press. pp. 1–29.

Parsons, Talcott (1951). *The Social System*. Glencoe, IL: The Free Press.

Parsons, Talcott (1956). Suggestions for a sociological approach to the theory of organizations, II. *Administrative Science Quarterly*, 1: 225–239.

Peet, Richard (2009). *Unholy Trinity: The IMF, World Bank and WTO*, 2nd edn. London: Zed Books.

Peng, Mike W., Wang, Denis Y. L. and Jiang, Yi (2008). An institution-based view of international business strategy: a focus on emerging economies. *Journal of International Business Studies*, 35: 99–109.

Pfeffer, Jeffrey and Salancik, Gerald (1978). *The External Control of Organizations*. New York: Harper & Row.

Porter, Michael E. (1980). *Competitive Strategy: Techniques for Analyzing Industries and Competitors*. New York: The Free Press.

Powell, Walter W. (1990). Neither market nor hierarchy: Network forms of organization. In Barry M. Staw and L. L. Cummings (eds), *Research in Organizational Behavior*, Volume 12. Greenwich, CT: JAI Press. pp. 295–336.

Powell, Walter W. and Sandholtz, Kurt (2012). Chance, nécesssité et naiveté: Ingredients to create a new organizational form. In John F. Padgett and Walter W. Powell (eds), *The Emergence of Organizations and Markets*. Princeton, NJ: Princeton University Press. pp. 379–433.

Prasad, Monica (2006). *The Politics of Free Markets: The Rise of Neoliberal Economic Policies in Britain, France, Germany and the United States*. Chicago, IL: University of Chicago Press.

Pugh, D. S., Hickson, D. J., Hinings, C. R. and Turner, C. (1968). Dimensions of organization structure. *Administrative Science Quarterly*, 13: 65–91.

Saxenian, AnnaLee (1994). *Regional Advantage: Culture and Competition in Silicon Valley and Route 128*. Cambridge, MA: Harvard University Press.

Schutz, Alfred (1967 [1932]). *The Phenomenology of the Social World* (trans. George Walsh and Frederick Lehnert). Evanston, IL: Northwestern University Press.

Scott, W. Richard (1987). The adolescence of institutional theory. *Administrative Science Quarterly*, 32(4): 493–511.

Scott, W. Richard (2004). Reflections on a half-century of organizational sociology. *Annual Review of Sociology*, 30: 1–24.

Scott, W. Richard (2005). Institutional theory: Contributing to a theoretical research program. In Ken G. Smith and Michael A. Hitt (eds), *Great Minds in Management: The Process of Theory Development*. Oxford: Oxford University Press. pp. 460–484.

Scott, W. Richard (2008a). Approaching adulthood: The maturing of institutional theory. *Theory and Society*, 37: 427–442.

Scott, W. Richard (2008b). Institutional analysis in sociology. In William A. Darity, Jr (ed.), *International Encyclopedia of the Social Sciences*, vol. 7, 2nd edn. Detroit: Macmillan References. pp. 673–674.

Scott, W. Richard (2008c). Lords of the dance: Professionals as institutional agents. *Organization Studies*, 29(2): 219–238.

Scott, W. Richard (2014). *Institutions and Organizations: Ideas, Interests, and Identities*, 4th edn. Los Angeles, CA: Sage.

Scott, W. Richard and Davis, Gerald F. (2007). *Organizations and Organizing: Rational, Natural, and Open System Perspectives*. Upper Saddle River, NJ: Pearson/Prentice–Hall.

Scott, W. Richard, Kirst, Michael W. and Associates (2017). *Higher Education and Silicon Valley: Connected but Contested*. Baltimore: John Hopkins University Press.

Scott, W. Richard, Levitt, Raymond E. and Orr, Ryan J. (eds) (2011). *Global Projects: Institutional and Political Challenges*. Cambridge: Cambridge University Press.

Scott, W. Richard and Meyer, John W. (1983). The organization of societal sectors. In John W. Meyer and W. Richard Scott (eds), *Organizational Environments: Ritual and Rationality*. Newbury Park, CA: Sage. pp. 129–153.

Scott, W. Richard, Ruef, Martin, Mendel, Peter J. and Caronna, Carol A. (2000). *Institutional Change and Healthcare Organizations: From Professional Dominance to Managed Care*. Chicago, IL: University of Chicago Press.

Selznick, Philip (1949). *TVA and the Grass Roots*. Berkeley, CA: University of California Press.

Selznick, Philip (1992). *The Moral Commonwealth: Social Theory and the Promise of Community*. Berkeley, CA: University of California Press.

Shank, Roger C. and Abelson, Robert P. (1977). *Scripts, Plans, Goals, and Understanding: An Inquiry into Human Knowledge Structures*. Hillsdale, NJ: Lawrence Erlbaum Associates.

Shenhov, Yehouda (1995). From chaos to systems: The engineering foundations of organization theory, 1879–1832. *Administrative Science Quarterly*, 40: 557–585.

Sikkink, Kathryn (2002). Transnational advocacy networks and the social construction of legal rules. In Yves Dezalay and Bryant G. Garth (eds), *Global Prescriptions: The Production, Exportation, and Importation of a New Legal Orthodoxy*. Ann Arbor, MI: University of Michigan Press. p. 37.

Simon, Herbert A. (1997 [1945]). *Administrative Behavior: A Study of Decision-Making Processes in Administrative Organizations*, 4th edn. New York: The Free Press.

Slaughter, Anne-Marie (2002). Breaking out: The proliferation of actors in the international system. In Yves Dezalay and Bryant G. Garth (eds), *Global Prescriptions: The Production, Exportation, and Importation of a New Legal Orthodoxy*. Ann Arbor, MI: University of Michigan Press. pp. 12–36.

Smith, Jackie (2005). Globalization and transnational social movement organizations. In Gerald F. Davis, Doug McAdam, W. Richard Scott and Mayer N. Zald (eds), *Social Movements and Organization Theory*. Cambridge: Cambridge University Press. pp. 226–248.

Smith, Jackie and Johnston, Hank (eds) (2002). *Globalization and Resistance: Transnational Dimensions of Social Movements*. Lanham, MD: Rowman & Littlefield.

Spencer, Herbert (1876, 1896, 1910). *The Principles of Sociology*, vols 1–3. London: Appleton–Century–Crofts.

Stinchcombe, Arthur L. (1965). Social structure and organizations. In James G. March (ed.), *Handbook of Organizations*. Chicago, IL: Rand McNally. pp. 142–193.

Streeck, Wolfgang and Schmitter, Philippe C. (1985). Community, market, state – and associations? The prospective contribution of interest governance to social order. In Wolfgang Streeck and Philippe C. Schmitter (eds), *Private Interest Government: Beyond Market and State*. London: Sage. pp. 1–29.

Sumner, William Graham (1906). *Folkways*. Boston, MA: Ginn.

Sweet, Alec Stone, Fligstein, Neil and Sandholz, Wayne (eds) (2001). *The Institutionalization of Europe*. Oxford: Oxford University Press.

Taylor, Frederick Winslow (1911). *The Principles of Scientific Management*. New York: Harper.

Thomas, George M., Meyer, John W., Ramirez, Francisco O. and Boli, John (1987). *Institutional Structure: Constituting State, Society, and the Individual*. Newbury Park, CA: Sage.

Thompson, James D. (1967). *Organizations in Action*. New York: McGraw Hill.

Thompson, Kenneth (1980). The organizational society. In Graeme Salaman and Kenneth Thompson (eds), *Control and Ideology in Organizations*. Cambridge, MA: MIT Press. pp. 3–23.

Thornton, Patricia H., Jones, Candace and Kury, Kenneth (2005). Institutional logics and institutional change: Transformation in accounting, architecture, and publishing. In Candace Jones and Patricia H. Thornton (eds), *Transformation in Cultural Industries. Research in the Sociology of Organizations*, Volume 23. Greenwich, CT: JAI Press. pp. 125–170.

Thornton, Patricia H., Ocasio, William and Lounsbury, Michael (2012). *The Institutional Logics Perspective: A New Approach to Culture, Structure, and Process*. Oxford: Oxford University Press.

Voronov, Maxim and Vince, Russ (2012). Integrating emotions into the analysis of institutional work, *Academy of Management Review*, 37: 58–81.

Weber, Max (1946 [1906–1924]). *Max Weber: Essays in Sociology* (trans. and ed. Hand H. Gerth and C. Wright Mills). New York: Oxford University Press.

Weber, Max (1968 [1924]). *Economy and Society: An Interpretive Sociology*, vols 1–3 (ed. Guenther Roth and Claus Wittich). New York: Bedminister Press.

Weick, Karl (1969). *The Social Psychology of Organizing*. Reading, MA: Addison–Wesley.

Weingast, Barry R. (1996). Political institutions: Rational choice perspectives. In Robert Goodin and Hans-Dieter Klingemann (eds), *A New Handbook of Political Science*. New York: Oxford University Press. pp. 167–190.

Whitley, Richard (2003). Changing transnational institutions and the management of international business transactions. In Marie-Laure Djelic and Sigrid Quack (eds), *Globalization and Institutions: Redefining the Rules of the Economic Game*. Cheltenham: Edward Elgar. pp. 108–133.

Williamson, Oliver E. (1975). *Markets and Hierarchies: Analysis and Antitrust Implications*. New York: The Free Press.

Willoughby, Westel Woodbury (1896). *An Examination of the Nature of the State*. New York: Macmillan.

Index

Page references to Figures or Tables will be in *italics*, followed by the letters 'f' and 't', as appropriate, while references to Footnotes will be followed by the letter 'n' and note number.